The Oxford Guide to **Plays**

Michael Patterson is Emeritus Professor of Theatre at the School of English and Performance Studies, De Montfort University, Leicester, UK. His previous publications include *Strategies of Political Theatre* (2003), *German Theatre: A Bibliography* (1996), and *The First German Theatre* (1990). Three advisory editors assisted him in the compilation of this guide: Jean Chothia on American drama; Peter Holland on British drama; and J. Michael Walton on classical drama.

The Oxford Guide to **Plays**

Michael Patterson

OXFORD UNIVERSITY PRESS

OXFORD
UNIVERSITY PRESS

Great Clarendon Street, Oxford OX2 6DP

Oxford University Press is a department of the University of Oxford.
It furthers the University's objective of excellence in research, scholarship,
and education by publishing worldwide in

Oxford New York

Auckland Cape Town Dar es Salaam Hong Kong Karachi Kuala Lumpur
Madrid Melbourne Mexico City Nairobi New Delhi Shanghai Taipei Toronto

With offices in

Argentina Austria Brazil Chile Czech Republic France Greece
Guatemala Hungary Italy Japan South Korea Poland Portugal
Singapore Switzerland Thailand Turkey Ukraine Vietnam

Published in the United States
by Oxford University Press Inc., New York

First published in 2005 as *The Oxford Dictionary of Plays*
First published in paperback 2007

British Library Cataloguing in Publication Data

Data available

Library of Congress Cataloging in Publication Data

ISBN-13: 978-0-19-860418-1

1

Typeset by SPI Publisher Services, Pondicherry, India
Printed in Great Britain by
Clays, St. Ives, Bungay

To Alastair, Richard, and Juliet, their wives, husband, and children

Contents

Preface

This volume sets out to provide useful information and brief commentaries on the 1,000 most significant plays of world theatre.

The term 'play' is here defined as a dramatic text intended to be performed by live actors that may be staged on its own (thus a trilogy will count as three plays, even if they all appear under the same entry). It normally excludes stage adaptations of novels, films, television and radio plays, unless they have become particularly significant in their own right, the fame of the adaptation often exceeding that of the original (e.g. *The Bells, Lady Audley's Secret*). Texts that require music, like musicals and most operas, are excluded, but works that stand as plays, even if somewhat impoverished without music (like Brecht's *The Threepenny Opera* or melodramas) may be included.

In deciding what is 'significant', the author, with the guidance of expert advice, including especially that of Professors Peter Holland and J. Michael Walton and Dr Jean Chothia, has attempted to identify the 1,000 plays likely to be of most interest to the anglophone theatregoer, reader, and scholar. This naturally raises questions about the relative significance of a play's importance for the development of a dramatic genre, its popularity in the theatre both in the past and today, its literary merit, etc. While it is probable that a consensus might be arrived at for about two-thirds of the entries, the remaining choices will be much more contentious, and readers and reviewers may have fun complaining that one of their favourite plays is omitted. The author accepts complete responsibility for such disappointments.

Each entry contains the following information (where appropriate):

Title: ordered alphabetically, letter by letter (so **Heracles** comes before **He Who Gets Slapped**), except '**St**' is read as '**Saint**'. Where two plays have the same title, they are ordered chronologically (e.g. Sophocles' **Antigone** before Anouilh's)
(Foreign language or original title)

AT: *Alternative title(s)* – often variant translations

A: Author(s)

W: Date of Writing – given only where the date of composition preceded the first performance or publication by five years or more

Pf: Date and place of first performance. Where the premiere took place abroad, the first performance in the native language is normally also given

Pb: Date of first publication

Tr: Date of first published translation into English

G: Genre; number of acts (given as 'acts' even where the original calls them 'parts', 'episodes', etc) or scenes; original language (if not English); whether in prose or verse. After 1850 it is assumed, unless otherwise stated, that all English-language plays are in prose. The following designations of genre are used:

Auto sacramental	Spanish morality play written to accompany Corpus Christi Day processions
Ballad opera	A play linking episodes with songs
Burlesque	A play poking fun at contemporary theatrical practice
Com.	Comedy, a play intended to provoke laughter, with a happy ending
Commedia erudita	An Italian Renaissance genre, distinguished from *commedia dell'arte* by its literary elements
Documentary drama	A play based almost entirely on historical documents
Drama	Any play not categorized under one of the other terms
Fairy tale	A play containing unreal characters, situations, and magic
Farce	A comedy, the humour of which derives from improbable situations
Folk drama	A play featuring simple country people
Hist. drama	A play re-enacting historical events
Interlude	A play of edifying content intended to be performed during a banquet
Kabuki play	Traditional Japanese play, including more comedy and action than Nō plays
Kyōgen play	Traditional Japanese play, more farcical and improvised than kabuki
Masque	Court entertainment with allegorical content usually in a pastoral or mythical setting, using music, song, and dance
Monodrama	Play with only one performer
Melodrama	A play, intended to be accompanied by music, with a plot depending on exciting action and simple morality
Morality play	A play with universalized characters imparting a moral lesson
Musical drama	A play of which a significant element is musical, usually in the form of songs
Mystery plays	Medieval plays based on biblical narrative performed in cycles by amateurs
Nō play	Traditional Japanese masked play with music
Pastoral	A play in a bucolic setting, foregrounding the love of rural characters
Pol. com./drama	Political comedy or drama, written primarily to convey a political message

Romance	A play of epic time span with fantastical events including a love story
Romantic com.	Romantic comedy, a comedy where the love interest predominates
Scenario	dramatic outline for a performance without determining precisely characters' lines or moves
Satire	A play holding a specific target, familiar to the audience, up to ridicule
Satyr play	Play performed at the end of a cycle of Greek tragedies, characterized by the comedic antics of satyrs
Trag.	Tragedy, a serious play, ending with death or irrevocable loss suffered by the protagonist
Tragicom.	Tragicomedy, a play combining laughter or a happy ending with tragic elements
Zaju play	Classical Chinese play telling a simple story and accompanied by songs

S: Setting and time of action. Where a specific date cannot be given, the following terms are used:

indeterminate period
mythical past
medieval period (5th–15th centuries)
Renaissance period (15th–early 17th centuries)
Restoration period (1660–1714)

C: Composition of cast. 'Extras' are normally understood to be characters who are not named and have at most only a few lines to speak

Brief synopsis (sometimes omitting the sub-plot).
Brief commentary.

Play titles prefaced with an asterisk have individual entries elsewhere in the volume. Particularly where a famous play has been commented on widely elsewhere, the comments may well appear infuriatingly abrupt. The intention of this volume is to serve as a work of reference and offer pointers for further study; it does not lay claim to summarize the significance of a drama in a few words.

The volume concludes with two indexes:

1. an index of major characters, which may be used to identify in which plays they are to be found and to trace the occurrence of major historical and legendary characters in world drama.
2. an index of all playwrights (with dates) mentioned in the volume.

For those who like statistics – or 'Don't put your daughter on the stage, Mrs Worthington'

Discounting extras, choruses, and children, the average cast of the 1,000 plays listed here comprises 9.7 male characters and 3.8 female, i.e. a ratio of 2.6 : 1. Although the balance is more even with women playwrights, male performers are still slightly favoured, the averages being 5.5 male characters and 4.8 female, a ratio of 1.2 : 1. Only 6.5% of the 1,000 plays are by women, but this proportion increases in the latter half of the 20th century (14% from 1965 onwards, and 37% from 1975 onwards).

Acknowledgements

I wish to offer grateful acknowledgements to my three 'official' advisers, Jean Chothia, Peter Holland, J. Michael Walton, and also to those who have more informally assisted me in selecting plays for inclusion: Martin Banham, David Barnett, David Bradby, Mary Brewer, Michael Davies, Tony Lewis, Michael Mangan, Steve Nicholson, Jane Patterson-Prentice, John Peter, Robert Welch, and members of the American Society for Theatre Research mailing list, including Anne Bomar, James M. Brandon, Patrick Finelli, Ben Fisler, C. David Frankel, Franklin J. Hildy, Paul Iles, Daniel Larner, Dawn Lewcock, Benjamin R. Opipari, and Irina Rudakova. I also wish to thank J. Ellen Gainor for reminding me how little I know about world drama.

I also wish to acknowledge financial support from the Arts and Humanities Research Board and from the Faculty of Humanities of De Montfort University Leicester, generous hospitality from William de Marvell of the Euroversity, Oxford, and the valued help by Jean and Derek Bourgeois.

Select Bibliography

Anderson, Michael et al. (eds.), *A Handbook of Contemporary Drama* (London: Pitman, 1972).

Banham, Martin (ed.), *The Cambridge Guide to World Theatre* (Cambridge: Cambridge University Press, 1988).

Benson, Eugene, and Connolly, L. W. (eds.), *The Oxford Companion to Canadian Theatre* (Oxford: Oxford University Press, 1989).

Bordman, Gerald, *The Oxford Companion to the American Theatre* (2nd edn., Oxford: Oxford University Press, 1992).

Brown, John Russell (ed.), *The Oxford Illustrated History of Theatre* (Oxford: Oxford University Press, 1995).

Chambers, Colin, *The Continuum Companion to Twentieth Century Theatre* (London: Continuum, 2002).

Croft, Susan, *She Also Wrote Plays: An International Guide to Women Playwrights from the 10th to the 21st Century* (London: Faber and Faber, 2001).

Fletcher, Steve, and Jopling, Norman (eds.), *Harrap's Book of 1000 Plays* (London: Harrap, 1989).

Gassner, John, and Quinn, Edward (eds.), *The Reader's Encyclopaedia of World Drama* (New York: Crowell, 1969).

Hartnoll, Phyllis, and Found, Peter (eds.), *The Oxford Companion to the Theatre* (4th edn., Oxford: Oxford University Press, 1983).

Hawkins-Dady, Mark (ed.), *International Dictionary of Theatre*, 1. *Plays*; 2. *Playwrights* (Chicago: St James Press, 1992–4).

Holzknecht, Karl J., *Outlines of Tudor and Stuart Plays 1497–1642* (London: Methuen, 1947).

Kennedy, Dennis (ed.), *The Oxford Encyclopedia of Theatre and Performance* (Oxford: Oxford University Press, 2003).

Matlaw, Myron, *Modern World Drama: An Encyclopaedia* (New York: Dutton, 1972).

Melchinger, Siegfried, *The Concise Encyclopaedia of Modern Drama* (London: Vision, 1966).

Nicoll, Allardyce, *World Drama from Aeschlyus to the Present Day* (London: Harrap, 1949).

The Player's Library: The Catalogue of the Library of the British Drama League (London: Faber and Faber, 1950).

Taylor, John Russell (ed.), *The Penguin Dictionary of the Theatre* (rev. edn., Harmondsworth: Penguin, 1970).

Thompson, John Cargill, *An Introduction to Fifty British Plays 1660–1900* (London: Pan Books, 1979).
Thomson, Peter, and Salgādo, Gāmini, *The Everyman Companion to the Theatre* (London: Dent, 1985).
Warrack, John, and West, Ewan (eds.), *The Oxford Dictionary of Opera* (Oxford: Oxford University Press, 1996).
Welch, Robert (ed.), *The Oxford Companion to Irish Literature* (Oxford: Oxford University Press, 1996).
www.doollee.com (US website offering useful information on mainly contemporary plays and playwrights).

Family Tree of Main Characters in Shakespeare's History Plays

Names in square brackets do not appear in the plays

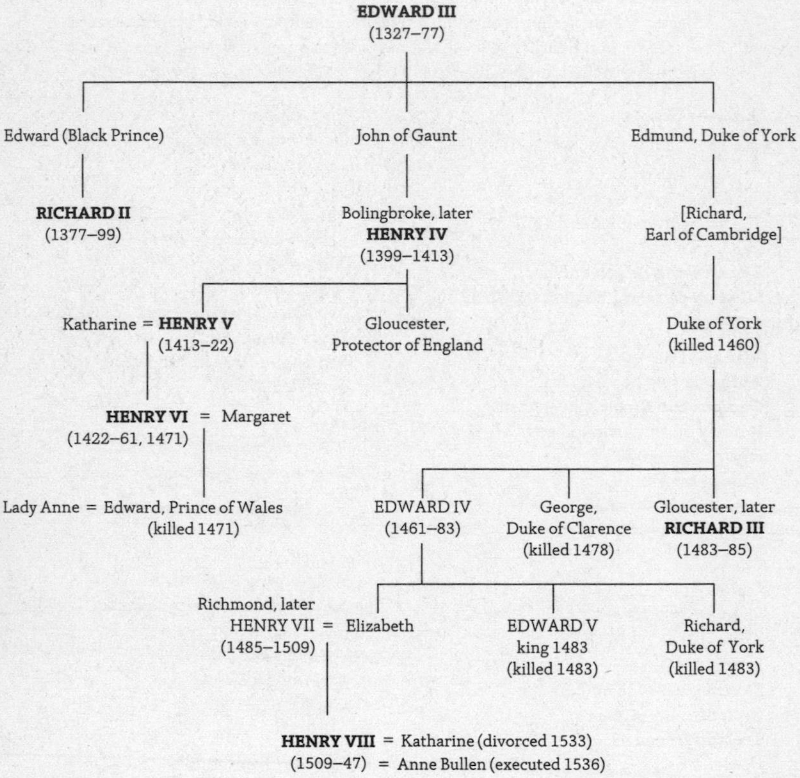

EDWARD III
(1327–77)

Children of Edward III:

- Edward (Black Prince)
  - **RICHARD II** (1377–99)
- John of Gaunt
  - Bolingbroke, later **HENRY IV** (1399–1413)
    - Katharine = **HENRY V** (1413–22)
      - **HENRY VI** (1422–61, 1471) = Margaret
        - Lady Anne = Edward, Prince of Wales (killed 1471)
    - Gloucester, Protector of England
- Edmund, Duke of York
  - [Richard, Earl of Cambridge]
    - Duke of York (killed 1460)
      - EDWARD IV (1461–83)
        - Richmond, later HENRY VII (1485–1509) = Elizabeth
          - **HENRY VIII** = Katharine (divorced 1533)
            (1509–47) = Anne Bullen (executed 1536)
        - EDWARD V king 1483 (killed 1483)
        - Richard, Duke of York (killed 1483)
      - George, Duke of Clarence (killed 1478)
      - Gloucester, later **RICHARD III** (1483–85)

Plays Selected for Entry

Ordered According to Country of Origin and Period

Note: Plays in bold type indicate longer entries. Plays are ordered chronologically within each section and subsection, except that all plays by a single author are listed together. Date is that of first known professional production or publication, whichever is the earlier. (W + date) indicates the date of writing, where this precedes the first production or publication by five years or more.

1. Ancient Greece

AESCHYLUS

Persians 472 BC
Seven Against Thebes 467 BC
Prometheus Bound c.466–459 BC
Suppliants c.463 BC
***The Oresteia* (*Agamemnon*; *Libation-Bearers*; *Eumenides*)** 458 BC

SOPHOCLES

Ajax c.441 BC
Antigone c.441 BC
Oedipus the King c.429–420 BC
Women of Trachis c.425 BC
Electra c.425–410 BC
Philoctetes 409 BC
Oedipus at Colonus 401 BC

EURIPIDES

Alcestis 438 BC
Medea 431 BC
Hippolytus 428 BC
Andromache c.425 BC
Hecuba c.424 BC
Electra c.422–416 BC
Cyclops c.420–406 BC
Trojan Women 415 BC
Heracles c.415 BC
Iphigeneia among the Taurians c.414–413 BC
Ion c.413 BC
Helen c.412 BC
Orestes 408 BC
Iphigeneia at Aulis 405 BC
Bacchae c.405 BC

ARISTOPHANES

Acharnians 425 BC
Knights 424 BC
Wasps 422 BC
Peace 421 BC
Clouds c.418 BC
Birds 414 BC
Lysistrata 411 BC
Women at the Thesmophoria 411 BC
Frogs 405 BC
Women in Assembly c.392 BC
Wealth 388 BC

MENANDER

The Bad-Tempered Man 316 BC
The Woman from Samos c.315–309 BC

2. Ancient Rome

PLAUTUS

Amphitryon 215–185 BC
The Brothers Menaechmus 215–185 BC
The Braggart Soldier c.205 BC
Pseudolus 191 BC
The Rope c.189 BC
Casina 185–184 BC

TERENCE

The Girl from Andros 166 BC
The Eunuch 161 BC
Phormio 161 BC
The Brothers 160 BC

SENECA

Oedipus (W AD 25–65)
Phaedra (W AD 25–65)
Thyestes (W AD 25–65)

3. Oriental Classics

? King Sūdraka
The Little Clay Cart (W ?5th c. AD)

Kālidāsa
Shakuntala (W ?5th c. AD)

Guan Hanqing
Injustice to Dou E 13th c.

Li Xingfu
The Chalk Circle c.1300

Zeami
Aoi-no-Ue (W 14th c.)

?Priest Genne-Hōin
Shopping for an Umbrella 17th c.

Chikamatsu Monzaemon
The Battles of Coxinga 1715

Namiki Gohei III
The Subscription List 1840

4. Medieval

Hrotsvitha
Paphnutius (W 10th c.)

Anonymous
The Play of Adam c.1140–74
The Chester Cycle of Mystery Plays 14th c.
The York Cycle of Mystery Plays (48 parts) 14th–15th c.
The Castle of Perseverance (W 1400–25)
Mankind c.1465–70
The N-Town Cycle of Mystery Plays 15th c.
The Towneley Cycle of Mystery Plays 15th–16th c.
Everyman c.1520 (W 15th c.)

5. Italian Renaissance

Ludovico Ariosto
The Strongbox 1508

Cardinal Bernardo Dovizi da Bibbiena
The Follies of Calandro 1513

Niccolò Machiavelli
The Mandrake c.1518–24

Pietro Aretino
The Stablemaster 1527

Ruzante
Conversation of Ruzante Returned from the Wars c.1529

Accademia degli Intronati di Siena
The Deceived 1532

Torquato Tasso
Aminta 1573

Giordano Bruno
The Candlestick 1582

Giovanni Battista Guarini
The Faithful Shepherd 1589

6. England and Scotland 1490–1642

Henry Medwall
Fulgens and Lucrece c.1497

John Heywood
The Play Called the Four P.P. c.1520

Sir David Lindsay
A Satire of the Three Estates 1540

Nicholas Udall
Ralph Roister Doister 1552

Thomas Norton and Thomas Sackville
Gorboduc 1561–2

Anonymous
Gammer Gurton's Needle 1562–3
Arden of Faversham 1592
A Yorkshire Tragedy c.1605–7

Thomas Kyd
The Spanish Tragedy c.1582–92

Christopher Marlowe
Tamburlaine the Great (*Parts 1 and 2*) c.1587
Doctor Faustus c.1588
The Jew of Malta c.1589
Edward II c.1592
The Massacre at Paris 1593

William Shakespeare
The Two Gentlemen of Verona 1587–9
Henry VI (*Parts 1, 2, and 3*) c.1589–92
The Comedy of Errors c.1591–4
The Taming of the Shrew c.1591–4
Romeo and Juliet c.1591–6
Titus Andronicus c.1592–4
Love's Labours Lost c.1594
Richard II c.1595

Richard III c.1595
Edward III c.1595
A Midsummer Night's Dream c.1596
King John c.1596–7
The Merchant of Venice c.1596–7
Henry IV (*Parts 1 and 2*) c.1596–8
The Merry Wives of Windsor c.1597
Much Ado about Nothing c.1598–9
Henry V c.1598–99
As You Like It c.1599
Julius Caesar 1599
Hamlet c.1599–1601
Twelfth Night c.1601–2
All's Well that Ends Well c.1602
Othello c.1602
Troilus and Cressida c.1602–3
Macbeth c.1602–6
Measure for Measure c.1603–4
King Lear c.1605–6
Antony and Cleopatra c.1606
Timon of Athens c.1607
Coriolanus c.1607–10
Pericles c.1608
Cymbeline c.1610
The Tempest c.1610–11
The Winter's Tale 1611

John Lyly
Endymion 1588

George Peele
The Old Wives' Tale c.1590

Robert Greene
Friar Bacon and Friar Bungay c.1590

Ben Jonson
Every Man in His Humour 1598
Volpone 1606
Epicene 1609
The Alchemist 1610
Bartholomew Fair 1614

Thomas Dekker
The Shoemaker's Holiday 1600

Thomas Heywood
A Woman Killed with Kindness 1603
The Fair Maid of the West (*Part 1*) c.1607

John Marston
The Malcontent (with John Webster) 1604

George Chapman
Bussy D'Ambois 1604

Thomas Middleton
A Mad World, My Masters c.1604–6
A Trick to Catch the Old One c.1604–6
The Revenger's Tragedy c.1606–7
A Chaste Maid in Cheapside 1613
Women Beware Women c.1625–7

George Chapman, Ben Jonson, and John Marston
Eastward Ho! 1605

Francis Beaumont
The Knight of the Burning Pestle c.1607

Cyril Tourneur
The Atheist's Tragedy c.1607–11

Francis Beaumont and John Fletcher
The Maid's Tragedy c.1608–11
Philaster c.1609–10

Thomas Dekker and Thomas Middleton
The Roaring Girl 1611

William Shakespeare and John Fletcher
Henry VIII c.1612
The Two Noble Kinsmen c.1613

John Webster
The White Devil 1612
The Duchess of Malfi c.1613

Thomas Dekker, John Ford, and William Rowley
The Witch of Edmonton 1621

Thomas Middleton and William Rowley
The Changeling 1622

Philip Massinger
A New Way to Pay Old Debts c.1625

John Ford
'Tis Pity She's a Whore c.1629–33

John Milton
Comus 1634

James Shirley
The Lady of Pleasure 1635

Richard Brome
A Jovial Crew 1641

7. Spanish Golden Age

Fernando de Rojas
Celestina 1499

Tirso de Molina
Don Gil of the Green Breeches c.1614–15
The Trickster of Seville 1625

Juan Ruiz de Alarcón y Mendoza
Suspect Truth 1619

Lope de Vega
Fuente Ovejuna 1619
Justice Without Revenge 1632

Pedro Calderón de la Barca
The Great Theatre of the World c.1633–5
Life Is a Dream 1635
The Mayor of Zalamea 1636

8. French Classical Theatre

Pierre Corneille
The Theatrical Illusion 1635
The Cid 1636

Molière
The School for Wives 1662
Tartuffe 1664
Don Juan 1665
The Misanthrope 1666
The Miser 1668
The Would-Be Gentleman 1670
The Hypochondriac 1673

Jean Racine
Andromache 1667
Britannicus 1669
Phaedra 1677

9. Restoration

George Villiers, 2nd Duke of Buckingham
The Rehearsal 1671 (W 1665)

John Dryden
Marriage à-la-Mode 1672
All for Love 1677

William Wycherley
The Country Wife 1675
The Plain Dealer 1676

George Etherege
The Man of Mode 1676

Aphra Behn
The Rover (*Part 1*) 1677

Thomas Otway
Venice Preserved 1682

John Vanbrugh
The Provoked Wife 1691–2
The Relapse 1696

William Congreve
The Double Dealer 1693
Love for Love 1695
The Way of the World 1700

George Farquhar
The Recruiting Officer 1706
The Beaux' Stratagem 1707

10. Eighteenth Century

10.1. Britain and Ireland

Joseph Addison
Cato 1713

Nicholas Rowe
Jane Shore c.1713

Susannah Centlivre
The Wonder! A Woman Keeps a Secret 1714

Richard Steele
The Conscious Lovers (with Colley Cibber) 1722

John Gay
The Beggar's Opera 1728

Henry Fielding
Tom Thumb 1730

George Lillo
The London Merchant 1731

John Home
Douglas 1756

David Garrick and George Colman the Elder
The Clandestine Marriage 1766

Richard Cumberland
The West Indian 1771

Oliver Goldsmith
__She Stoops to Conquer__ 1773

Richard Brinsley Sheridan
The Rivals 1775
__The School for Scandal__ 1777
The Critic 1779

Hannah Cowley
The Belle's Stratagem 1780

John O'Keeffe
Wild Oats 1791

Thomas Morton
Speed the Plough 1800

10.2. Continental Europe

Ludvig Holberg
The Political Tinker 1722

Pierre Carlet de Chamblain de Marivaux
The Double Inconstancy 1723
The Game of Love and Chance 1730

Voltaire
Zaïre 1732

Carlo Goldoni
The Servant of Two Masters c.1746
Mirandolina 1753

Carlo Gozzi
Turandot 1762

Gotthold Ephraim Lessing
Minna von Barnhelm 1767
Nathan the Wise 1779

Johann Wolfgang von Goethe
Götz von Berlichingen 1771
Faust *(Parts 1 and 2)* 1808; 1832 (W 1773–1831)

Jakob Michael Reinhold Lenz
The Tutor 1774

Pierre-Augustin Caron de Beaumarchais
The Barber of Seville 1775
The Marriage of Figaro 1783 (W 1778)

Friedrich Schiller
The Robbers 1781
Don Carlos 1787
Mary Stuart 1800
William Tell 1804

Denis Fonvizin
The Minor 1782

11. Romantic Period

Ludwig Tieck
Puss in Boots 1797

René-Charles Guilbert de Pixérécourt
Coelina 1800

Heinrich von Kleist
The Broken Jug 1808
The Prince of Homburg 1821 (W 1810)

Percy Bysshe Shelley
The Cenci 1819

Victor Hugo
Hernani 1830
Ruy Blas 1838

Aleksandr Pushkin
Boris Godunov 1831 (W 1825)

Alfred de Musset
Lorenzaccio 1834

Alfred de Vigny
Chatterton 1835

12. Realist Drama, Comedies, and Melodramas

12.1. Britain (including Irish-born authors writing for the English stage) 1825–1920

John Walker
The Factory Lad 1825

Anonymous
Maria Marten 1828

Douglas Jerrold
Black-Eyed Susan 1829

Edward Bulwer-Lytton
Money 1840

Dion Boucicault
London Assurance 1841
The Octoroon 1859

The Colleen Bawn 1860
The Shaughraun 1874

Mrs Henry Wood
East Lynne 1862

Colin Hazlewood
Lady Audley's Secret 1863

Tom Taylor
The Ticket-of-Leave Man 1863

T. W. Robertson
Caste 1867

Leopold Lewis
The Bells 1871

H. J. Byron
Our Boys 1875

W. S. Gilbert
Engaged 1877

Arthur Wing Pinero
The Magistrate 1885
The Second Mrs Tanqueray 1893
Trelawny of the 'Wells' 1898

Brandon Thomas
Charley's Aunt 1892

Oscar Wilde
Lady Windermere's Fan 1892
Salome 1893
A Woman of No Importance 1893
An Ideal Husband 1895
The Importance of Being Earnest 1895

George Bernard Shaw
Arms and the Man 1894
Candida 1897
The Devil's Disciple 1897
Mrs Warren's Profession 1898 (W 1893)
Caesar and Cleopatra 1901
Man and Superman 1903
Major Barbara 1905
Pygmalion 1913
Heartbreak House 1919
Back to Methuselah (*In the Beginning; The Gospel of the Brothers Barnabas; The Thing Happens; Tragedy of an Elderly Gentleman; As Far as Thought Can Reach*) 1921
Saint Joan 1923

Henry Arthur Jones
Mrs Dane's Defence 1900

J. M. Barrie
The Admirable Crichton 1902
Peter Pan 1904

Harley Granville Barker
The Voysey Inheritance 1905
The Madras House 1910

Elizabeth Robins
Votes for Women 1907

John Galsworthy
Strife 1909
Justice 1910

D. H. Lawrence
The Widowing of Mrs Holroyd 1914
A Collier's Friday Night 1934 (W c.1906–9)
The Daughter-in-Law 1936 (W 1911–12)

12.2. Realist Theatre, Comedies, and Melodramas, Continental Europe 1825–1920

Aleksandr Griboedov
Woe from Wit 1825

Georg Büchner
Danton's Death 1835
Woyzeck 1875 (W 1836–7)

Nikolai Gogol
The Government Inspector 1836

Eugène Scribe
The Glass of Water 1840

Johann Nestroy
On the Razzle 1842

Friedrich Hebbel
Mary Magdalene 1844

Eugène Labiche
An Italian Straw Hat (with Marc Michel) 1851

Alexandre Dumas *fils*
The Lady of the Camellias 1852

Ivan Turgenev
A Month in the Country 1855 (W 1848–50)

Aleksandr Ostrovsky
The Thunderstorm 1859
The Forest 1871

Émile Zola
Thérèse Raquin 1863

Henrik Ibsen
Brand 1866
Peer Gynt 1867
A Doll's House 1879
Ghosts 1881
An Enemy of the People 1882
The Wild Duck 1884
Rosmersholm 1886
The Lady from the Sea 1888
Hedda Gabler 1890
The Master Builder 1892
Little Eyolf 1894
John Gabriel Borkman 1896
When We Dead Awaken 1899

Bjørnstjerne Bjørnson
The Bankrupt 1874

Victorien Sardou
Let's Get a Divorce! 1880

Henry Becque
The Crows 1882 (W *c*.1872)

Leo Tolstoy
The Power of Darkness 1887

Anton Chekhov
Ivanov 1887
The Seagull 1896
Uncle Vanya 1897
The Three Sisters 1901
The Cherry Orchard 1904

Gerhart Hauptmann
Before Dawn 1889
The Weavers 1892

Arthur Schnitzler
Anatol (*Questioning Fate; Christmas Shopping; Episode; Memorial Stones; Farewell Supper; Agony; Anatol's Wedding*) 1892
La Ronde 1900

Edmond Rostand
Cyrano de Bergerac 1897

Gabriele D'Annunzio
Francesca da Rimini 1901

Eugène Brieux
Damaged Goods 1902

Maxim Gorky
The Lower Depths 1902
Summerfolk 1904

Georges Feydeau
A Flea in Her Ear 1907

F. T. Marinetti
Electric Dolls 1909

Peretz Hirshbein
The Haunted Inn 1912

13. Symbolism, Expressionism, and Non-Realistic Drama 1880–1920

August Strindberg
The Father 1887
Miss Julie 1888
The Stronger 1889
To Damascus (*Parts 1, 2, and 3*) 1900; 1904
The Dance of Death (*Parts 1 and 2*) 1901
A Dream Play 1902
The Ghost Sonata 1907

Frank Wedekind
Spring's Awakening 1891
The Lulu Plays (*Earth-Spirit; Pandora's Box*) 1895; 1902

Maurice Maeterlinck
Pelléas and Mélisande 1892
The Blue Bird 1908

Alfred Jarry
King Ubu 1896 (W 1888)

Stanisław Wyspiański
The Wedding 1901

Paul Claudel
Break of Noon 1906

Aleksandr Blok
The Puppet Show 1906

Oskar Kokoschka
Murderer, Hope of Womankind 1909

Ferenc Molnár
Liliom 1909
The Guardsman 1910

Carl Sternheim
The Underpants 1911

Reinhard Johannes sorge
The Beggar 1912

Walter Hasenclever
The Son 1914

Georg Kaiser
The Burghers of Calais 1914
From Morning to Midnight 1916
The Gas Trilogy (*The Coral; Gas I; Gas II*) 1917; 1918; 1920

Leonid Andreev
He Who Gets Slapped 1915

Guillaume Apollinaire
The Breasts of Tiresias 1917

Luigi Pirandello
Right You Are, If You Think So 1917
Six Characters in Search of an Author 1921
Henry IV 1922
Tonight We Improvise 1930

Solomon Anski
The Dybbuk 1918

Vladimir Mayakovsky
Mystery-Bouffe 1918
The Bedbug 1929
The Bathhouse 1930

Fernand Crommelynck
The Magnificent Cuckold 1920

Karel Čapek
RUR 1920
The Insect Comedy (with Josef Čapek) 1921

Ernst Toller
Masses and Men 1920
The Machine Wreckers 1922
Hoppla, We're Alive! 1927

14. America to 1944

Mercy Otis Warren
The Group 1775

Royall Tyler
The Contrast 1787

John Daly Burk
Bunker-Hill 1797

William Dunlap
André 1798

James Nelson Barker
The Indian Princess 1808

John Augustus Stone
Metamora 1829

James Kirke Paulding
The Lion of the West 1831

Robert Montgomery Bird
The Broker of Bogota 1834

W. H. Smith
The Drunkard 1844

Anna Cora Mowatt
Fashion 1845

Joseph Stevens Jones
The Silver Spoon 1852

George L. Aiken
Uncle Tom's Cabin 1852

Augustin Daly
Under the Gaslight 1867

Steele Mackaye
Paul Kauvar 1887

James A. Herne
Margaret Fleming 1890

Augustus Thomas
The Earl of Pawtucket 1903

Langdon Mitchell
The New York Idea 1906

WILLIAM VAUGHN MOODY
The Great Divide 1906

HENRY JAMES
The High Bid 1908

EDWARD SHELDON
Salvation Nell 1908

CLYDE FITCH
The City 1909

RACHEL CROTHERS
He and She 1911

SUSAN GLASPELL
Trifles 1916
The Verge 1921

EUGENE O'NEILL
The Emperor Jones 1920
Anna Christie 1921
The Hairy Ape 1922
Desire under the Elms 1924
Strange Interlude 1928
Mourning Becomes Electra (*Homecoming; The Hunted; The Haunted*) 1931
The Iceman Cometh 1946 (W 1939)
A Moon for the Misbegotten 1947
Long Day's Journey into Night 1956 (W 1940–1)

GILBERT EMERY
The Hero 1921

ANNE NICHOLS
Abie's Irish Rose 1922

ELMER RICE
The Adding Machine 1923
Street Scene 1929

MAXWELL ANDERSON AND LAURENCE STALLINGS
What Price Glory? 1924

SIDNEY HOWARD
They Knew What They Wanted 1924

JOHN HOWARD LAWSON
Processional 1925

PAUL GREEN
In Abraham's Bosom 1926

E. E. CUMMINGS
him 1927

BEN HECHT AND CHARLES MACARTHUR
The Front Page 1928

SOPHIE TREADWELL
Machinal 1928

MARC CONNELLY
The Green Pastures 1930

MOSS HART AND GEORGE S. KAUFMAN
Once in a Lifetime 1930

LILLIAN HELLMAN
The Children's Hour 1934
The Little Foxes 1939

LANGSTON HUGHES
Mulatto 1935

SIDNEY KINGSLEY
Dead End 1935

CLIFFORD ODETS
Waiting for Lefty 1935
Awake and Sing! 1935

ROBERT E. SHERWOOD
The Petrified Forest 1935

JOHN STEINBECK
Of Mice and Men 1937

THORNTON WILDER
Our Town 1938
The Skin of Our Teeth 1942

PHILIP BARRY
The Philadelphia Story 1939

WILLIAM SAROYAN
The Time of Your Life 1939

JOSEPH KESSELRING
Arsenic and Old Lace 1941

MARY CHASE
Harvey 1944

GERTRUDE STEIN
Doctor Faustus Lights the Lights 1949 (W 1938)

15. Canada and the Caribbean

JOHN COULTER
Riel 1950

Plays Selected for Entry

Marcel Dubé
Private Soldier 1958

George Ryga
The Ecstasy of Rita Joe 1967

Derek Walcott
Dream on Monkey Mountain 1967

Michel Tremblay
The Sisters-in-Law 1968

Antonine Maillet
The Slattern 1971

David French
Leaving Home 1972

James Reaney
The Donnellys (*Sticks and Stones; The St Nicholas Hotel; Handcuffs*) 1973; 1974; 1975

Michael Cook
Jacob's Wake 1975

Sharon Pollock
Blood Relations 1976

John Murrell
Waiting for the Parade 1977

John Gray
Billy Bishop Goes to War (with Eric Peterson) 1978

David Fennario
Balconville 1979

George F. Walker
Suburban Motel (*Problem Child; Criminal Genius; Risk Everything*) 1997

16. Australia and New Zealand

Louis Esson
The Drovers 1920

Ray Lawler
Summer of the Seventeenth Doll 1955

Bruce Mason
The Pohutukawa Tree 1957

James K. Baxter
The Wide Open Cage 1959

Patrick White
The Season at Sarsaparilla 1962

Alexander Buzo
The Front Room Boys 1969

David Williamson
The Removalists 1971

Dorothy Hewett
The Chapel Perilous 1971
The Man from Mukinupin 1979

Jack Hibberd
A Stretch of the Imagination 1972

Mervyn Thompson
O! Temperance! 1972

John Romeril
The Floating World 1974

Stephen Sewell
Traitors 1979

Greg McGee
Foreskin's Lament 1980

Louis Nowra
The Golden Age 1985

Jack Davis
No Sugar 1985

Michael Gow
Away 1986

Alma De Groen
The Rivers of China 1987

17. Africa, India, and Japan

Rabindranath Tagore
The Post Office 1913
Chandalika 1933

Kishida Kunio
The Two Daughters of Mr Sawa 1935

Wole Soyinka
The Lion and the Jewel 1959
The Road 1965
Madmen and Specialists 1970
Death and the King's Horsemen 1975

John Pepper Clark[-Bekederemo]
Song of a Goat 1961

Athol Fugard
The Blood Knot 1961
Sizwe Bansi Is Dead (with John Kani and Winston Ntshona) 1972
The Island (with John Kani and Winston Ntshona) 1973
Statements after an Arrest under the Immorality Act 1974

Ama Ata Aidoo
The Dilemma of a Ghost 1964

Mishima Yukio
Madame de Sade 1965

Ola Rotimi
The Gods Are Not to Blame 1968

Girish Karnad
Hayavadana 1971

Ngugi wa Thiong'o and Micere Githae Mugo
The Trial of Dedan Kimathi 1975

Efua T. Sutherland
The Marriage of Anansewa 1975

18. Ireland post-1880

Edward Martyn
The Heather Field 1899

W. B. Yeats
Cathleen ni Houlihan 1902
On Baile's Strand (with Lady Gregory) 1903
At the Hawk's Well 1916
Calvary 1921
The Words upon the Window-Pane 1930
The King of the Great Clock Tower 1934
Purgatory 1938
The Death of Cuchullain 1939

J. M. Synge
The Shadow of the Glen 1903
Riders to the Sea 1904
The Playboy of the Western World 1907
Deirdre of the Sorrows 1910

Lady Gregory
The Rising of the Moon 1904

Padraic Colum
The Land 1905

St John Ervine
John Ferguson 1915

Lennox Robinson
The Whiteheaded Boy 1916

James Joyce
Exiles 1918

Sean O'Casey
The Shadow of a Gunman 1923
Juno and the Paycock 1924
The Plough and the Stars 1926
The Silver Tassie 1928
Purple Dust 1940
Red Roses for Me 1942
Cock-a-Doodle Dandy 1949

T. C. Murray
Autumn Fire 1924

Denis Johnston
The Old Lady Says 'No!' 1929
The Moon in the Yellow River 1931

Paul Vincent Carroll
Shadow and Substance 1937

Brendan Behan
The Quare Fellow 1954
The Hostage (with Joan Littlewood) 1958

Tom Murphy
A Whistle in the Dark 1961
The Sanctuary Lamp 1975
The Gigli Concert 1983

Brian Friel
Philadelphia, Here I Come 1964
Lovers (*Winners; Losers*) 1967
Translations 1980
Dancing at Lughnasa 1990

John B. Keane
The Field 1965

Thomas Kilroy
The Death and Resurrection of Mr Roche 1968

Hugh Leonard
Da 1973

Stewart Parker
Spokesong 1978

Henry de Montherlant
The Queen Is Dead 1942

Jean-Paul Sartre
The Flies 1943
No Exit 1944
Dirty Hands 1948
The Condemned of Altona 1959

Albert Camus
Cross Purpose 1944
Caligula 1944

Jean Anouilh
Antigone 1944
Ring Round the Moon 1947
The Rehearsal 1950
The Waltz of the Toreadors 1952
The Lark 1953
Becket 1959

Jean Genet
The Maids 1947
Deathwatch 1949
The Balcony 1956
The Blacks 1958
The Screens 1961

Eugène Ionesco
The Bald Prima-Donna 1950
The Lesson 1951
The Chairs 1952
The Killer 1958
Rhinoceros 1959

Jean Tardieu
The Underground Lovers 1952

Samuel Beckett
Waiting for Godot 1952
Endgame 1957
Krapp's Last Tape 1958
Happy Days 1961
Play 1963
Come and Go 1966
Breath 1969
Not I 1972
Footfalls 1976
Rockaby 1981
Catastrophe 1982

Arthur Adamov
Professor Taranne 1953

Fernando Arrabal
The Automobile Graveyard 1958
The Architect and the Emperor of Assyria 1967

Boris Vian
The Empire Builders 1959

Armand Gatti
The Second Life of Tatenberg Camp 1962

Aimé Césaire
A Tempest 1969

Hélène Cixous
Portrait of Dora 1976

Marguerite Duras
Eden Cinema 1977
Musica Second Version 1985

Bernard-Marie Koltès
Struggle of the Dogs and the Black 1982
Quay West 1985

Jean-Claude Carrière
The Mahabharata 1985

Michel Vinaver
Portrait of a Woman 1986

Yasmina Reza
Art 1994

20.2. Italy, Spain, and Latin America

Ramón del Valle-Inclán
Bohemian Lights 1920

Federico García Lorca
Blood Wedding 1933
Yerma 1934
The House of Bernarda Alba 1945 (W 1936)

Ugo Betti
The Queen and the Rebels 1951

Antonio Buero-Vallejo
A Dreamer for the People 1958

Eduardo de Filippo
Saturday, Sunday, Monday 1959

Dario Fo
Mistero Buffo (*The Morality Play of the Blind Man and the Cripple; Death and*

the Fool; The Fool beneath the Cross Laying a Wager) 1969
Accidental Death of an Anarchist 1970
Can't Pay? Won't Pay! 1974
Female Parts (with Franca Rame) (*Waking Up; A Woman Alone; The Same Old Story*) 1977

GRISELDA GAMBARO
Information for Foreigners 1975

ARIEL DORFMAN
Death and the Maiden 1990

20.3. German-Language and Scandinavia

BERTOLT BRECHT
Baal 1922
Drums in the Night 1922
In the Jungle of Cities 1923
A Man's a Man 1926
The Threepenny Opera (with Elisabeth Hauptmann) 1928
The Measures Taken (with Slatan Dudow, Elisabeth Hauptmann, and others) 1930
The Mother 1932
St Joan of the Stockyards (with Elisabeth Hauptmann and others) 1932
Fear and Misery of the Third Reich (The Chalk Cross; The Jewish Wife; The Spy; Release; The Sermon on the Mount; Job Creation; Consulting the People) (with Margarete Steffin) 1938
Mother Courage and Her Children (with Margarete Steffin) 1941
The Good Person of Setzuan (with Ruth Berlau and Margarete Steffin) 1943
Life of Galileo (with Margarete Steffin) 1943
The Caucasian Chalk Circle (with Margarete Steffin) 1948
Mr Puntila and His Man Matti (with Hella Wuolijoki) 1948
Days of the Commune (with Margarete Steffin) 1956
The Resistible Rise of Arturo Ui (with Margarete Steffin) 1957
Schweyk in the Second World War 1957

CARL ZUCKMAYER
The Captain of Köpenick 1930
The Devil's General 1946

ÖDÖN VON HORVÁTH
Tales from the Vienna Woods 1931

PÄR LAGERKVIST
The Hangman 1934

FRIEDRICH DÜRRENMATT
The Visit 1956
The Physicists 1962

MAX FRISCH
The Fire Raisers 1958
Andorra 1961

ROLF HOCHHUTH
The Representative 1963
Soldiers: An Obituary for Geneva 1967

HEINAR KIPPHARDT
In the Matter of J. Robert Oppenheimer 1964

PETER WEISS
Marat/Sade 1964
The Investigation 1965

GÜNTER GRASS
The Plebeians Rehearse the Uprising 1966

PETER HANDKE
Offending the Audience 1966
Kaspar 1967
The Ride across Lake Constance 1971

TANKRED DORST
Toller 1968

RAINER WERNER FASSBINDER
Bremen Coffee 1971

FRANZ XAVER KROETZ
Stallerhof 1971

THOMAS BERNHARD
The Force of Habit 1974

HEINER MÜLLER
Hamletmachine 1977

BOTHO STRAUSS
The Tour Guide 1986

George Tabori
Mein Kampf 1987

20.4. Eastern Europe and Israel

Stanisław Ignacy Witkiewicz
The Madman and the Nun 1924

Sergei Tretyakov
Roar China! 1926

Mikhail Bulgakov
The Days of the Turbins 1926
A Cabal of Hypocrites 1936

Vsevolod Vishnevsky
Optimistic Tragedy 1933

Isaak Babel
Marya 1935

Evgeny Shvarts
The Dragon 1943

Witold Gombrowicz
The Wedding 1950

Sławomir Mrożek
Tango 1964

Václav Havel
The Memorandum 1965

Nikolai Erdman
The Suicide 1969 (W 1928–31)

Aleksandr Vampilov
Duck Hunting 1970

Joshua Sobol
Ghetto 1984

21. USA Post-1944

Tennessee Williams
The Glass Menagerie 1944
A Streetcar Named Desire 1947
Camino Real 1948
The Rose Tattoo 1950
Cat on a Hot Tin Roof 1955
Sweet Bird of Youth 1956
Orpheus Descending 1957
Suddenly Last Summer 1958
The Night of the Iguana 1959

Arthur Miller
All My Sons 1947
Death of a Salesman 1949
The Crucible 1953
A View from the Bridge 1955
After the Fall 1964
Incident at Vichy 1964
The Price 1968
Broken Glass 1994

William Inge
Come Back, Little Sheba 1950

John Van Druten
I Am a Camera 1951

Robert Anderson
Tea and Sympathy 1953

John Patrick
The Teahouse of the August Moon 1953

Paddy Chayefsky
The Tenth Man 1959

Jack Gelber
The Connection 1959

Lorraine Hansberry
A Raisin in the Sun 1959

Edward Albee
The Zoo Story 1959
The Death of Bessie Smith 1960
The American Dream 1961
Who's Afraid of Virginia Woolf 1962
Tiny Alice 1964
A Delicate Balance 1966
The Goat 2002

Adrienne Kennedy
Funnyhouse of a Negro 1962

James Baldwin
Blues for Mister Charlie 1964

Imamu Amiri Baraka (Le Roi Jones)
Dutchman 1964

Jean-Claude Van Itallie
America Hurrah (*Interview; TV; Motel*) 1965; 1966

Neil Simon
The Odd Couple 1965

Plaza Suite (*Visitor from Mamaroneck; Visitor from Hollywood; Visitor from Forest Hills*) 1968

Maria Irene Fornés
Promenade 1965
Fefu and Her Friends 1977
The Conduct of Life 1985

Alice Childress
Wedding Band 1966

Israel Horovitz
The Indian Wants the Bronx 1966

Luis Valdez
Los Vendidos (with El Teatro Campesino) 1967

Sam Shepard
La Turista 1967
Curse of the Starving Class 1976
Buried Child 1978
True West 1980
Fool for Love 1983
States of Shock 1991

Ed Bullins
Goin'a Buffalo 1968

Mart Crowley
The Boys in the Band 1968

Arthur Kopit
Indians 1968

Lonne Elder III
Ceremonies in Dark Old Men 1969

Charles Gordone
No Place to Be Somebody 1969

David W. Rabe
The Basic Training of Pavlo Hummel 1971

Ntozake Shange
for colored girls who have considered suicide | when the rainbow is enuf 1974

David Mamet
American Buffalo 1975
Glengarry Glen Ross 1983
Speed-the-Plow 1988
Oleanna 1992

Harvey Fierstein
Torch Song Trilogy (*The International Stud; Fugue in a Nursery; Widows and Children First!*) 1978; 1979

Beth Henley
Crimes of the Heart 1979

Mark Medoff
Children of a Lesser God 1979

Martin Sherman
Bent 1979

Charles Fuller
A Soldier's Story 1981

Romulus Linney
F. M. 1982

Marsha Norman
'Night, Mother 1983

August Wilson
Fences 1985
Joe Turner's Come and Gone 1986

Tina Howe
Coastal Disturbances 1986

David Henry Hwang
M. Butterfly 1986

Lanford Wilson
Burn This 1987

Wendy Wasserstein
The Heidi Chronicles 1988

The Wooster Group
Frank Dell's The Temptation of St Antony 1988

John Guare
Six Degrees of Separation 1990

Tony Kushner
Angels in America (***Millennium Approaches***; ***Perestroika***) 1991; 1992

Margaret Edson
W;t 1993

Suzan-Lori Parks
The America Play 1993

TERRENCE MCNALLY
Master Class 1995

RICHARD NELSON
Goodnight Children Everywhere 1997

RICHARD FOREMAN
Pearls for Pigs 1997

PAULA VOGEL
How I Learned to Drive 1997

DAVID AUBURN
Proof 2000

RICHARD GREENBERG
Take Me Out 2002

22. Britain Post-1956

JOHN OSBORNE
Look Back in Anger 1956
The Entertainer 1957
Luther 1961
Inadmissible Evidence 1964

SHELAGH DELANEY
A Taste of Honey 1958

JOHN MORTIMER
The Dock Brief 1958

WILLIS HALL
The Long and the Short and the Tall 1958

JOHN ARDEN
Live Like Pigs 1958
Serjeant Musgrave's Dance 1959
The Workhouse Donkey 1963
Armstrong's Last Goodnight 1964

HAROLD PINTER
The Birthday Party 1958
The Dumb Waiter 1959
The Caretaker 1960
The Lover 1963
The Homecoming 1965
Old Times 1971
No Man's Land 1975
Betrayal 1978
Mountain Language 1988

ARNOLD WESKER
Roots 1959
The Kitchen 1959
Chips with Everything 1962

ROBERT BOLT
A Man for All Seasons 1960

ANN JELLICOE
The Knack 1961

JOHN WHITING
The Devils 1961

JAMES SAUNDERS
Next Time I'll Sing to You 1962

CHARLES CHILTON AND THEATRE WORKSHOP UNDER JOAN LITTLEWOOD
Oh What a Lovely War 1963

BILL NAUGHTON
Alfie 1963

JOE ORTON
Entertaining Mr Sloane 1964
Loot 1965
The Erpingham Camp 1967
What the Butler Saw 1969

PETER SHAFFER
The Royal Hunt of the Sun 1964
Black Comedy 1965
Equus 1973
Amadeus 1979

FRANK MARCUS
The Killing of Sister George 1965

EDWARD BOND
Saved 1965
Early Morning 1968
Narrow Road to the Deep North 1968
Lear 1971
The Sea 1973
Bingo 1973
The Fool 1975

JOHN MCGRATH
Events while Guarding the Bofors Gun 1966
The Cheviot, the Stag and the Black, Black Oil 1973

TOM STOPPARD
Rosencrantz and Guildenstern Are Dead 1966

The Real Inspector Hound 1968
Jumpers 1972
Travesties 1974
The Real Thing 1982
Arcadia 1993
The Invention of Love 1997

Peter Nichols
A Day in the Death of Joe Egg 1967

Charles Wood
Dingo 1967

Alan Ayckbourn
Relatively Speaking 1967
Absurd Person Singular 1972
The Norman Conquests (*Table Manners; Living Together; Round and Round the Garden*) 1973
Joking Apart 1978
House and Garden (*House; Garden*) 1999

Peter Barnes
The Ruling Class 1968

Alan Bennett
Forty Years On 1968

Stanley Eveling
Dear Janet Rosenberg, Dear Mr Kooning 1969

Howard Brenton
Christie in Love 1969
Magnificence 1973
The Churchill Play 1974
Weapons of Happiness 1976
The Romans in Britain 1980

Christopher Hampton
The Philanthropist 1970

David Mercer
After Haggerty 1970

David Storey
Home 1970

Trevor Griffiths
Occupations 1970
Comedians 1975

Simon Gray
Butley 1971

David Rudkin
Ashes 1973

Margaretta D'Arcy and John Arden
The Non-Stop Connolly Show 1975

Howard Barker
Stripwell 1975
The Hang of the Gaol 1978
The Love of a Good Man 1978

Steven Berkoff
East 1975
Decadence 1981

David Hare
Fanshen 1975
Plenty 1978
Skylight 1995

Pam Gems
Dusa, Fish, Stas and Vi 1976

Caryl Churchill
Light Shining in Buckinghamshire 1976
Vinegar Tom 1976
Cloud Nine 1979
Top Girls 1982
Fen 1983
Serious Money 1987
Blue Heart (*Heart's Desire; Blue Kettle*) 1997
A Number 2002

Michael Frayn
Clouds 1976
Noises Off 1982
Copenhagen 1998
Democracy 2003

Barrie Keeffe
A Mad World, My Masters 1977

Mike Leigh
Abigail's Party 1977

Dennis Potter
Brimstone and Treacle 1977

David Edgar
The Jail Diary of Albie Sachs 1978
Mary Barnes 1978
Maydays 1983
Pentecost 1994

WILLY RUSSELL
Educating Rita 1980
Shirley Valentine 1986

RONALD HARWOOD
The Dresser 1980
Taking Sides 1995

RAY COONEY
Two into One 1981

JULIAN MITCHELL
Another Country 1981

C. P. TAYLOR
Good 1981

LIZ LOCHHEAD
Blood and Ice 1981

LOUISE PAGE
Salonika 1982

JOHN GODBER
Bouncers 1984
Up 'n' Under 1984

STEPHEN POLIAKOFF
Breaking the Silence 1984

JIM CARTWRIGHT
Road 1986

ANTHONY MINGHELLA
Made in Bangkok 1986

CHARLOTTE KEATLEY
My Mother Said I Never Should 1987

TIMBERLAKE WERTENBAKER
Our Country's Good 1988

SARAH KANE
Blasted 1995

MARK RAVENHILL
Shopping and Fucking 1996

MARTIN CRIMP
Attempts on Her Life 1997

PATRICK MARBER
Closer 1997

JOE PENHALL
Blue/Orange 2000

PETER GILL
The York Realist 2001

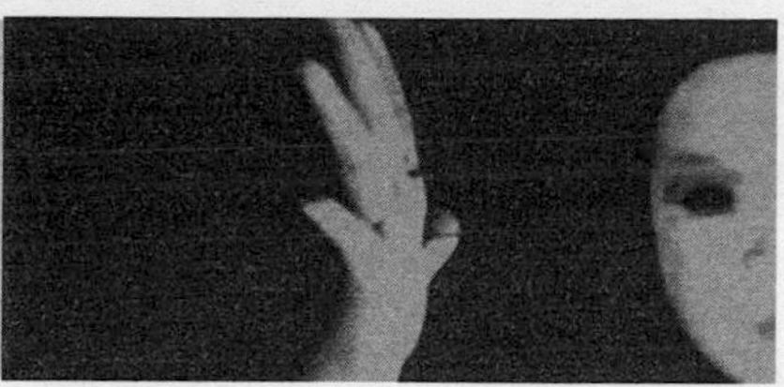

Abbiamo tutte la stessa storia. See FEMALE PARTS.

Abhijñānaśakuntala. See SHAKUNTALA.

Abie's Irish Rose

A: Anne Nichols Pf: New York, 1922 Pb: 1923
G: Com. in 3 acts S: New York, 1920s C: 6m, 3f

Abie Levy has married his 'Irish rose', Rose Mary Murphy. Since she is Catholic, he keeps this a secret from his father, Solomon, who hopes that Abie will find a Jewish wife and join the family business. Abie introduces Rose as his fiancée Rose Murpheski from a well-to-do Jewish family, and the delighted Solomon arranges a wedding. Believing the bride to come from California, he decorates the reception with oranges to help her feel at home, but this sectarian symbol horrifies her father Patrick, who assumes that she must be marrying a Protestant. When the fathers learn the truth, both insist that the couple must part, but Abie and Rose defy them both by marrying again in a Catholic church. A year later it is Christmas, and the two fathers secretly bring presents for the new grandchild, uncertain whether it is a boy or a girl. In fact, Rose has had twins, one named Solomon, the other Patrick. The two delighted fathers herald Christmas by becoming reconciled to each other and to their young family.

Abie's Irish Rose is a delightful and sentimental comedy, which proved very popular with American audiences in the inter-war years, though not in London – a famous example of the difficulties of transatlantic transfer. Beneath the somewhat predictable characterization, the stubbornness and gruffness of the older generation and the idealistic 'poor but happy' love of the young couple, Nichols spelt out a message of reconciliation across the ethnic divisions of American society.

Abigail's Party

A: Mike Leigh Pf: 1977, London Pb: 1979
G: Com. in 2 acts S: Laurence and Beverly's suburban home, 1970s C: 2m, 3f

Laurence is an estate agent, driven to work hard to fulfil the social aspirations of his airheaded wife Beverly. She has created a tasteless suburban home to which they have invited some new neighbours round for drinks, and is annoyed when Laurence has to go out on business. Tony, a computer operator and former footballer, and his wife Angela, a nurse, duly arrive, and Laurence leaves soon after. Eventually they are joined by another neighbour, Susan, a divorcee whose 15-year-old daughter is having a party and does not want her mother there. Laurence arrives back and his reports about Abigail's party 'hotting up' make Susan very anxious. As they get drunk, Beverly dances with pathetic sensuality, and Laurence leaps up to go with Tony to check on the party. Susan feels ill and has to be sick. Laurence returns without Tony, who has some fun with the teenagers before reappearing. Tensions mount. Beverly dances with Tony, Laurence with Angela and Susan. As Laurence gets more and more agitated about Beverly, he has a heart attack. An ambulance is called, but Laurence dies while Beverly prattles on mindlessly.

The most interesting aspect of Mike Leigh's plays is that he arrives at them almost entirely through improvisation. Actors are given the outlines of a role, and Leigh works with them individually, developing their character until they are ready to interact with the other characters in the piece. Out of these exchanges, a script then develops. While making for cringingly accurate characterization, there is a danger of giving character primacy over plot, and all too often, as here, one has an uncomfortable sense of the actors sneering at their characters.

Abschiedssouper. See ANATOL.

Absurd Person Singular

A: Alan Ayckbourn Pf: 1972, Scarborough Pb: 1974 G: Com. in 3 acts S: Three kitchens in neighbouring houses in an English town, 1970s C: 3m, 3f

House-proud Jane Hopcroft is cleaning her neat modern kitchen in preparation for a Christmas party, to which she and her husband Sidney have invited neighbours Ronald and Marion Brewster-Wright, a banker and his wife, and Geoffrey Jackson, an architect, whose marriage is less than happy, since he is a womanizer and his wife Eva is neurotic. While the party goes on in the living room, the hosts and guests wander in and out of the kitchen – except for Jane, who is mistakenly shut out in the garden in the pouring rain. The next Christmas, Geoffrey and Eva have invited guests to their untidy flat, where Eva, depressed, is still in her dressing gown. While Geoffrey welcomes the guests, Eva tries to jump from the fourth-floor window, and impale herself on a kitchen knife, then puts her head in the oven, but is interrupted by Jane, who volunteers to clean the stove. Eva attempts an overdose, a hanging with a clothes line, and finally an electrocution, but all fail. One year later, Marion's drinking has caught up with her and she stays in bed. When Geoffrey and Eva call, Marion gets up to join them for a drink. Annoyingly, Jane and Sidney, whose entrepreneurial schemes have all prospered, unexpectedly arrive and begin a dreadful game that involves dancing to an endless Scottish reel, hindered by various forfeits.

In his familiar territory of loathsome suburbanites, Ayckbourn creates hilarious situations, with pain at the core. The second Christmas, where Eva is trying to take her life, while everyone else ignores her, is paradoxically funnier because of her intense and silent suffering. Ayckbourn recognizes that comedy can be a very cruel affair.

Accidental Death of an Anarchist (*Morte accidentale di un anarchico*)

A: Dario Fo Pf: 1970, Milan Pb: 1970; rev. 1974 Tr: 1980 G: Satire in 2 acts; Italian prose S: Police headquarters, Milan, Jan. 1970 C: 5m, 1f

Inspector Bertozzo of the Milan police is interviewing the Maniac (or Fool), arrested for fraudulently claiming to be a psychiatrist. Left alone, the Maniac receives a phone call from Inspector Pissani who has just heard that an examining magistrate is coming to investigate the suspicious death of an anarchist, who 'fell' from a fourth-floor window in the building after being arrested for allegedly planting a bomb. The Maniac disguises himself as the magistrate and begins interrogating Pissani and his Superintendent, showing the absurdity of the official claim that the anarchist committed suicide. As the police argue amongst themselves about their contradictory evidence, the arrival of Maria Feletti, a journalist, is announced, and the Maniac is asked to pretend to be a forensic expert. Bertozzo arrives carrying a replica bomb and attempts to expose the Maniac, while the other police try to shut him up. The Maniac has recorded the police confessions on a hidden recorder and offers the evidence to Feletti. He handcuffs the police and sets the bomb to go off. Handing the handcuff keys to Feletti, the Maniac escapes, leaving her to decide whether to release the police. In one version, they are blown up. In another, she releases them and they handcuff her so that she will be killed.

The play is based on the suspicious death in police custody of Giuseppe Pinelli, an ineffectual anarchist, in December 1969. He had been arrested for allegedly planting a bomb, later shown to be the work of neo-Fascists. Fo uses farce, owing an obvious debt to *The *Government Inspector*, documentary material, and frequent updating to contemporary events, to expose the police cover-up and to show the links between the authorities and right-wing extremists in so-called democracies.

Acharnians (*Acharnēs*)

A: Aristophanes Pf: 425 BC, Athens Tr: 1816 G: Greek com. in verse S: Athenian Assembly, the farm of Dicaeopolis, and home of Lamachus, 5th c. BC C: 18m, 3f, extras, chorus (m)

The Peloponnesian War has lasted for nearly six years. The Athenian Dicaeopolis is weary of having his farm ruined each summer by the invading Spartan army, so he goes to the Assembly in Athens, demanding an end to the war. The Assembly however merely considers various ways of prolonging hostilities, so Dicaeopolis sends a messenger to Sparta to sue for a private peace treaty, and returns home to celebrate the Dionysia. Unfortunately, a chorus of old men from Acharnae, who are sworn to take revenge on the invaders, have learned of Dicaeopolis' personal peace plan. As he and his family prepare for the Dionysian ritual, they are stoned by the chorus of Acharnians. Eventually Dicaeopolis persuades the chorus to hear his case, and he goes to Euripides to borrow a costume in order to win over the angry Acharnians. In a parody of Euripidean tragedy, Dicaeopolis wins over half of the chorus. The other half then produce Lamachus, an Athenian general, to speak for them. Dicaeopolis defeats him in debate too, and begins to enjoy the benefits of his private peace initiative. In the final scene Lamachus returns wounded from battle, while Dicaeopolis celebrates a drunken banquet with the chorus.

This is the earliest extant play of Aristophanes and first comedy of world drama. The stage is used quite flexibly, first as the Assembly, then as Dicaeopolis' farm, finally as his farm and as the home of Lamachus. It seems that at least five speaking actors would have been needed to stage the opening scene in the Assembly, compared with the three speaking actors in tragedy. These elements, together with the many different incidents and a double-sized chorus, would have made this play seem a fairly lavish affair, the equivalent of our modern 'blockbuster musical'. In terms of content, *Acharnians* is a daring, anti-war piece, reminding the citizens of Athens, as they sink deeper into their pointless hostilities, of the benefits of peace. It is amazing that the Athenians tolerated such a play being staged in the midst of a bitter war. Moreover, it won first prize for Aristophanes.

Adam, Le Jeu d'. See PLAY OF ADAM, THE.

Adam, Le Mystère d'. See PLAY OF ADAM, THE.

Adam, The Play of. See PLAY OF ADAM, THE.

Adding Machine, The

A: Elmer Rice Pf: 1923, New York Pb: 1923 G: Drama in 7 scenes S: New York and heaven, 1920s C: 14m, 9f

Mr Zero lives a boringly suburban conventional life with his wife. At work, Zero fantasizes about his fellow clerk Daisy Diana Dorothea Devore. He also wonders whether his 25 years as a bookkeeper will be rewarded, when his boss tells him that he is to be sacked and replaced with a new adding machine. At a dinner party, where the guests chant their racist prejudices, Zero confesses to murdering his boss. At the trial, Zero's confused defence fails to impress the jury. He is found guilty and executed. In the graveyard, he encounters the puritanical Shrdlu, who murdered his mother. In heaven, Daisy, who committed suicide after Zero's execution, confesses her love for him, and they kiss and dance. Shrdlu is shocked to find immoral people like Swift and Rabelais in heaven, and Zero leaves in disgust. Contentedly operating a colossal adding machine, Zero is told that he must be reincarnated on earth, but that after many life cycles, Zero is now just 'a failure. A waste product.'

This internationally famous play stands as one of the boldest experiments in Expressionism in the American theatre: characters are devoid of individual psychology, much dialogue is unrealistic, and the protagonist passes through several 'stations'. The play's satirical depiction of the conformism and bigotry of white American lower middle-class society, with its disturbing tensions between subservience and violence, and between Puritanism and lust, remains both searching and funny.

Adelphi. See BROTHERS, THE.

Adelphoe. See BROTHERS, THE.

Admirable Crichton, The

AT: *Circumstances Alter Cases* **A:** J. M. Barrie **Pf:** 1902, London **Pb:** 1914 **G:** Com. in 4 acts **S:** Lord Loam's manor house and a desert island, early 20th c. **C:** 7m, 6f

In order to appear progressive, the Earl of Loam each month invites his family and staff to a tea hour where everyone is treated equally. The butler Crichton resists this undermining of traditional hierarchies and insists on his subservient role. During a world cruise the family become shipwrecked on a desert island. In this situation it is only Crichton who is able to cope, rapidly becoming the leader of the party. Honoured with the title 'Guv', he is now flattered by the attentions of Lord Loam's previously haughty daughters, Mary and Catherine. Crichton opts for Mary, and the whole family enjoy an idyllic existence on their island. When a ship appears, Mary, intending to marry Crichton, begs him to ignore it, but he knows that his brief spell as head of the family is over and arranges a rescue. Back at home, traditional roles are restored, but, aware that he is now an embarrassment to the family, Crichton decides to seek a new post. In the Definitive Edition the play ends with Lady Mary about to marry an aristocrat, but confessing that Crichton is 'the best man among us'.

It is a tradition of world drama at least as old as Plautus that servants are often more resourceful and inventive than their masters. This tradition is playfully exploited by Barrie (reinventing the original 'admirable Crichton', James Crichton, a 16th-century Scottish prodigy), while touching on serious issues of class. Significantly, Lord Loam's minimal gesture towards democracy is limited to one hour a month. Only when the family are uprooted from their social context by being stranded in the middle of the ocean can those of merit prove their superiority over those privileged by the accident of birth. Since the family, and especially the charming Lady Mary, remain reasonably likeable, Barrie's attitude was hardly revolutionary, but it was certainly subversive.

Advantages of Private Education, The. See TUTOR, THE.

Affairs of Anatol, The. See ANATOL.

After Haggerty

A: David Mercer **Pf:** 1970, London **Pb:** 1970 **G:** Pol. com. in 2 acts **S:** London, Budapest, Moscow, Havana, Prague, Chicago, New York, Long Island, and Yorkshire, 1956–70 **C:** 9m, 5f

Bernard Link, an overweight theatre critic of 45 with two failed marriages behind him, has leased a London flat belonging to Haggerty. Haggerty's aggressive separated wife Claire flies from New York to present Haggerty with his baby son Raskolnikov, only to find the alarmed Bernard in residence. She moves in with him. In flashback, we see Bernard the Marxist apologist in Budapest during the 1956 uprising, in Moscow, in Havana, and in Prague during the 1968 revolt. After each foreign visit, Bernard talks to his working-class father, a Yorkshire widower, whom we never see until he arrives one day at Bernard's flat because his own home is flooded. Haggerty, who moved to Paris, has mysteriously disappeared. Flashbacks show Claire talking to the unseen Haggerty in Chicago, during student riots in New York, and on Long Island. Bernard has a row with his father, and ends up putting a wreath round his neck. Two undertakers bring an empty coffin with a message that Haggerty was killed fighting as a guerrilla.

Mercer's clever play sets various political viewpoints against one another, while allowing the characters to operate as real people within a dysfunctionally constructed 'family'. Bernard is a nominal Marxist, but as a cynical theatre critic, is totally unproductive; Claire is a rich heiress who joins student protest as a fashion statement; Bernard's father is a genuine member of the proletariat, but his reactionary attitudes are deservedly commemorated with a wreath; only the unseen Haggerty commits himself fully to his revolutionary beliefs. What comes 'after Haggerty' is left to the audience to decide.

After the Fall

A: Arthur Miller **Pf:** 1964, New York **Pb:** 1964
G: Drama in 2 acts **S:** Three-level stage dominated by the blasted tower of a German concentration camp **C:** 8m, 7f, extras

Quentin, a lawyer in his forties, steps forward to begin a confessional to the audience, acting out scenes from his life, above all those involving the women he has known. He recalls how his late mother abused his father and lied to her son; how he helped a young star-struck divorcee; how he had difficulties coping with his first wife's need for independence. He is now half engaged to a German girl Holga, an archaeologist who is weighed down by her guilt about Nazi atrocities in the Second World War. He also summons up memories of his father, his brother, and friends, whose indictment by anti-Communist congressional committees drives one of them to suicide and recalls the oppression that led to concentration camps. His main focus for guilt is his second wife Maggie, an actress, singer, and sex symbol, lacking self-sufficiency ('all I am is love . . . and sex'). Maggie depended on Quentin and craved his love, but he urges her to take responsibility for her own life ('I am not the Savior and I am not the help'). Unable to do so, she commits suicide with an overdose. Now, 'after the fall', Quentin tries to seize life again and is greeted by Holga.

This is a strongly autobiographical piece, in which Miller thoughtfully and often guiltily dissects his life, especially the death of Marilyn Monroe ('Maggie') in 1962. While the play offers insight into Miller's past, his ability to relate his own life to the sources of guilt in the world at large lifts the piece above the merely voyeuristic.

Agamemnon. See ORESTEIA, THE.

Agonie. See ANATOL.

Agony. See ANATOL.

Ajax (*Aias*)

A: Sophocles **Pf:** *c.*441 BC, Athens **Tr:** 1714
G: Greek trag. in verse **S:** Before Ajax's tent and the seashore near Troy, during the Trojan War
C: 6m, 2f, extras, chorus (m)

When Achilles is killed in the war against Troy, his splendid armour is given to the wily Odysseus. Ajax, who believes himself much more deserving of this honour, becomes enraged and swears revenge on his fellow Greeks. Athene intervenes to make Ajax insane, so that while he believes he is killing Greek soldiers, he is in fact slaughtering sheep and cattle. When he recovers from his madness, his shame is so great that he takes his own life. Odysseus persuades the commanders Agamemnon and Menelaus to accord Ajax an honourable burial.

Ajax is possibly the earliest of Sophocles' tragedies, but written when he was already in his fifties. It is the only one of his plays in which there is visible divine intervention (if we except the appearance of Heracles in **Philoctetes*). It is also the only extant Greek tragedy which changes location (so making a nonsense of the neo-classical insistence on unity of place). Ajax leaves his tent to go to the seashore, leaving behind his wife Tecmessa, and remarkably without the accompanying chorus of seamen, to commit suicide alone. Although Ajax is the title figure, the main interest of the piece rests with Odysseus, who, though he was a rival to Ajax in the award of Achilles' armour, is finally moved to generosity of spirit. He boldly confronts his generals with his demand that, despite everything, Ajax should be honourably buried (a humane and pious insistence that Sophocles explored fully in his **Antigone*). In terms of its staging, it is likely that Athene would make her appearance above the action by means of a stage crane. This was the *mechane*, now familiar in the Latin phrase deus ex machina, although here significantly her intervention, while sparing Greek lives, by no means solves all the complications of the plot.

alcalde de Zalamea, El. See MAYOR OF ZALAMEA, THE.

Alcestis (*Alkestis*)

A: Euripides Pf: 438 BC, Athens Tr: 1759 G: Greek drama in verse S: Palace of King Admetus, mythical past C: 7m, 2f, extras, chorus (m/f)

In the Prologue Apollo reveals that Admetus, King of Pherae in Thessaly, will have to die unless he can find someone prepared to take his place in the underworld. No one is willing to make this sacrifice, not even his elderly parents, until his wife Alcestis offers her life for his. Already Thanatos, the God of Death, is approaching to claim her life, despite Apollo's pleas for her to be spared. The devoted Alcestis is resolved to perish, and having extracted from Admetus the promise that he will not remarry, she dies. Heracles now arrives and is treated as a welcome guest, unaware that the house is in deep mourning. Eventually, Heracles discovers the truth and is so shocked by Admetus' inappropriate behaviour that he resolves to win Alcestis back from Thanatos. He soon returns, supposedly leading in a captive slave, who, once Heracles is reassured that Admetus will henceforth love Alcestis as she deserves, is then revealed to the joyful Admetus as his wife returned from the dead.

This, the earliest extant play by Euripides, written when he was in his forties, formed the final part of a tetralogy, which earned him second prize in competition with Sophocles. *Alcestis* therefore occupies the place normally reserved for the satyr play. Certainly, it enjoys a happy ending, and the drunken feasting of Heracles is hardly the stuff of tragedy. On the other hand, the piece is distinguished by scenes of great tenderness, as, for example, the unmasking of the returning Alcestis. Characteristic for Euripides are the use of a prologue, the foregrounding of a female character, the relative unimportance of the chorus, and the resolving of the potential tragedy through the intervention of an immortal figure. Gluck composed an opera on the theme (1767). Robert Wilson staged a controversial production of *Alcestis* with the American Repertory Company in 1968.

Alchemist, The

A: Ben Jonson Pf: 1610, London Pb: 1612; rev. 1616 G: Com. in 5 acts; blank verse and prose S: House in Blackfriars, London, 1610 C: 10m, 2f, extras

Because of the threat of plague, a householder has left his home for the country, leaving his man Face in charge. Face has invited an alchemist Subtle and a prostitute Dol Common into the house, where they have formed a bargain to work together to exploit a series of gullible clients. They persuade a lawyer's clerk Dapper that he is allied to the Queen of Fairy. They promise advancement and good fortune to Drugger, a tobacconist. To Sir Epicure Mammon they undertake to reveal the secret of the philosopher's stone, which will turn base metal into gold. Despite the scepticism of his friend Surly, Sir Epicure dreams of untold riches, and is promised a meeting later that day with Dol Common, who pretends to be a learned noblewoman being treated for madness. The Puritan Ananias also comes in search of the philosopher's stone but is sent packing when he refuses to part with his money. Dapper returns to meet the Queen of Fairy, but has to be hustled into the privy, because Sir Epicure has suddenly arrived. Sir Epicure is led off to meet Dol, when Dame Pliant, a young widow, and her brother Kastril appear. A Spaniard – Surly in disguise – comes hoping for a meeting with Dol, and is introduced to Dame Pliant instead. Surly is so impressed with Dame Pliant that he casts off his disguise and woos her in earnest. Kastril, who has come to learn to quarrel, challenges Surly, and it is only through the timely arrival of the outraged Puritan Ananias that the 'idolatrous Spaniard' is driven from the house. Unexpectedly, Lovewit, the master of the house, returns. Eventually Face, once again the butler Jeremy, confesses; Subtle and Dol are sent on their way empty-handed; and Lovewit, by donning a Spanish costume, wins and marries Dame Pliant, and promises to repay the alchemist's angry clients only if they admit in writing how they have been cheated. Face invites the audience to future tricks – but as gullers or gulled?

Somewhat lighter in tone than **Volpone*, Jonson here again exposes to ridicule human greed and lust. We delight in the knavery of the three tricksters, and even develop some respect for the greedy Sir Epicure in his fantastical dreams of wealth, much of which he will devote to helping others as well as indulging his own sensual appetites. Significantly too, the virtuous and sensible Surly receives no reward; indeed he loses his potential bride through another trick. Coleridge regarded *The Alchemist* as one of three best-structured plays of all time. It is indeed remarkable how Jonson contrives a series of hilarious scenes, interruptions, and theatrical surprises (like the emergence of Dapper after several hours in the privy) without losing the coherence of the plot, as happens in **Every Man in His Humour*. *The Alchemist* is now the most frequently performed of Jonson's plays.

Alfie

A: Bill Naughton **Pf:** 1963, London **Pb:** 1963 **G:** Drama in 3 acts **S:** London, 1960s **C:** 9m, 9f

Alfie is a carefree, chirpy Cockney, whose main aim in life is to seduce as many women as he can, treating the audience to slick comments as he enters on to each new conquest. He has an affair with Siddie, a sophisticated and attractive married woman, who is attracted by Alfie's rough boyish charm. Less challenging is Gilda, a submissive girl who is easily available. Then there is Annie, whom he picks up in a motorway service station, and Ruby, a rich older woman. When Gilda becomes pregnant, Alfie, horrified at the thought of emotional commitment, is relieved when she marries her long-standing boyfriend Humphrey. But he becomes attached to the child and has to be sent away by Gilda. Unused to being rejected, he takes it out on Annie, who also leaves him. He takes the unprecedented step of proposing marriage to Ruby, and is dismayed when he discovers that she is unfaithful to him. Contracting tuberculosis, he is hospitalized and manages to seduce Lily, the wife of another patient. She becomes pregnant and elects to have an abortion. At last Alfie is deeply moved by this experience, and is just about to resign himself to a lonely life, when Siddie reappears.

Both on stage and in its film version with Michael Caine in the title role, this play became an influential reference point for the 'swinging sixties', the period when Britain emerged from post-war austerity and, assisted by the introduction of the contraceptive pill, decisively rejected Victorian morality. However, these new 'freedoms', Naughton implies, were not without their cost.

Alkestis. See ALCESTIS.

All Citizens Are Soldiers. See FUENTEOVEJUNA.

All for Love

AT: *The World Well Lost* **A.** John Dryden **Pf:** 1677, London **Pb:** 1678 **G:** Trag. in 5 acts; blank verse **S:** Alexandria, Egypt, 30 BC **C:** 6m, 4f, extras

Cleopatra's treacherous flight from battle has cost Antony the battle of Actium. His general Ventidius accuses Antony of throwing away his empire for love. Tricked into meeting Cleopatra, Antony becomes reconciled to her when she shows him that she has rejected an offer of peace from their enemy, Octavius. After winning a minor battle, Antony is confronted by his wife Octavia, who, like Ventidius, begs him to make peace with Octavius. Octavia then meets Cleopatra and accuses her of destroying Antony's life. Antony, roused to jealousy by Cleopatra's behaviour towards his closest friend Dollabella, banishes them, and is then told that Cleopatra has committed suicide. Facing military defeat and with his beloved queen supposedly dead, Antony falls on his sword. Cleopatra comes, and they are reconciled. A poisonous snake allows her to join him in death and so cheat Octavius of his prize.

Using the same material as in **Antony and Cleopatra* and claiming that he was writing 'in Shakespeare's style', Dryden has created a version that is clearly not as great as Shakespeare's but which offers its own special qualities. In place of Shakespeare's vast historical panorama, Dryden concentrates the action according to neo-classical rules, keeping to locations in Alexandria and beginning near the end of the story, so that the action seems to occupy a few days at most. This offers a much more concentrated experience than in Shakespeare. Cleopatra's character is different too: in Shakespeare Antony loves her because she possesses 'infinite variety'. Dryden's Queen is much more honourable, winning Antony over as much by argument as through her feminine wiles. Finally, Dryden exploits an opportunity not used by Shakespeare, to bring Cleopatra and Octavia together in a memorable if unhistorical meeting.

All Home, Bed, and Church. See FEMALE PARTS.

All in the Downs. See BLACK-EYED SUSAN.

All Is True. See HENRY VIII.

All My Sons

A: Arthur Miller **Pf:** 1947, New York **Pb:** 1947 **G:** Trag. in 3 acts **S:** Backyard of the Keller home on the outskirts of an American town, 1947 **C:** 5m, 4f, 1 child (m)

What starts out as a relaxed image of American life as neighbours congregate in Joe Keller's backyard on a summer's evening, soon begins to develop tensions. Ann Deever is coming from New York to visit Joe's 32-year-old son Chris. She was once engaged to Chris's brother Larry, a pilot who was lost in action in the Second World War, and Kate Keller, mother of Chris and Larry, refuses to believe that Larry is dead. Moreover, Ann is the daughter of Joe Keller's former business partner, now serving a jail sentence for equipping P-40 fighter planes with faulty engines, killing 21 pilots. Although it was Keller who instructed him to do so on the telephone, Keller denied his part in the crime, but Deever's son George has discovered the truth and comes to take Ann away from the Kellers. Despite everything, Ann still wants to marry Chris, and shows him a letter written by Larry before he went missing saying that he is going to kill himself because of his father's crime. Chris, horrified that his suspicions about his father are now confirmed, confronts Keller with the letter and demands that he give himself up to the authorities. Keller, realizing that the missing pilots 'were all my sons', goes indoors to shoot himself.

This was Miller's first Broadway success and is still widely performed. Its theme, a seemingly happy, prosperous family having to face guilt from the past, is like updated Ibsen, and the action is not free from melodramatic elements, not least in Keller's suicide and Chris's tearful response: 'Mother, I didn't mean to . . . '.

All's Well that Ends Well

A: William Shakespeare **Pf:** *c.*1602, London **Pb:** 1623 **G:** Romantic com. in 5 acts; blank verse and prose **S:** Roussillon, Paris, Florence, and Marseilles, medieval period **C:** 8m, 6f, extras

Count Bertram, with his companion Parolles, leaves his home in Roussillon for the King's court in Paris to the dismay of the lower born daughter of a physician, Helena, who loves Bertram. When the King falls ill, Helena brings a healing potion to the court in Paris and may choose a husband as a reward. When she chooses Bertram, he marries her but flees to the wars in Florence to avoid her, refusing to be with her unless she get the ring from his finger and become pregnant with his child. Distressed at having driven Bertram into exile, Helena undertakes a pilgrimage, which leads her to Florence and a chance encounter with her beloved. Pretending to be Diana, a girl Bertram hopes to seduce, Helena sleeps with Bertram and so fulfils his preposterous conditions. Despite Parolles's cowardly betrayal of his friend, Bertram returns to France, where Helena reveals herself to him. All ends reasonably happily, and even the unworthy Parolles is pardoned.

Based on one of Boccaccio's tales, *All's Well* is often regarded as a 'dark' comedy, since there are a number of disturbing elements in the plot. Bertram is one of the least likeable of Shakespeare's protagonists, and, while Helena shows admirable steadfastness of will, she achieves success through coincidence and manipulation rather than by the exercise of positive virtue. It may be that Shakespeare was exploring a new style of satirical comedy, involving elements like the 'bed-trick'. This genre yielded the much more thoughtful and well-crafted *Measure for Measure.

Alouette, L'. See LARK, THE.

Altona. See CONDEMNED OF ALTONA, THE.

Amadeus

A: Peter Shaffer Pf: 1979, London Pb: 1980; rev. 1981 G: Trag. in 2 acts S: Vienna, 1823, and 1781–91 C: 12m, 3f, extras

In old age, Antonio Salieri, Court Composer to the Austrian Emperor Joseph II, recalls his rivalry with the brilliant young composer Wolfgang Amadeus Mozart, in the last ten years of Mozart's life. He recreates scenes where Mozart's genius is acknowledged by the court and reveals his attempts to undermine this upstart 25-year-old, who is vulgar and often childish in behaviour. While Mozart's operas bring him popular acclaim, Salieri's jealousy of his talent develops into obsessive hatred, and he manages to further his own career at Mozart's expense; he tries to seduce his wife Constanze and, when Mozart's father dies in 1787, pretends to be his ghost in an effort to drive Mozart mad. Salieri's machinations are so successful that Mozart dies penniless and starving. Finally, Salieri, in the last hour of his life, writes a confession that he murdered Mozart, in the (successful) attempt to join vicariously in the celebration of Mozart's lasting fame, even if only as his killer.

Made into a very successful film, *Amadeus* tackles the difficult task of depicting a creative genius, without the play's becoming an empty eulogy. By contrasting the surprisingly naive and crude genius Amadeus ('the loved one') with a scheming rival of mediocre talent, Shaffer succeeds in showing a human side of Mozart within an intriguing detective story.

Amants du métro, Les. See UNDERGROUND LOVERS, THE.

America Hurrah (Interview; TV; Motel)

AT: (1) *Pavane;* (3) *America Hurrah*

A: Jean-Claude van Itallie Pf: (1 and 2) 1965, New York; (3) 1966, New York Pb: 1967 G: 3 satires in 1 act S: (1) Interview room, street, gymnasium, subway, hospital, etc., USA, 1960s; (2) Television viewing room, USA, 1960s; (3) Motel, USA, 1960s C: (1) 7m, 6f, extras, played by 8 actors; (2) 28m, 24f, played by 8 actors; (3) 1m, 2f

(1) *Interview.* Four applicants, a Housepainter, a Floorwasher, a Banker, and a Lady's Maid, are interviewed by four interviewers. They are asked trivial questions, and their answers are intercut with one another. The scene changes to a bustling street where the Floorwasher is lost, then to a gymnasium. A Telephone Operator falls sick, is operated on, and dies. The Banker, who has lost his job because of panic attacks, visits a psychiatrist, who responds with nothing but 'blah, blah, . . . *penis*, blah, blah, . . . *mother*'. The Housepainter confesses to a priest. A Politician utters platitudes and ignores the dying Telephone Operator. The play ends with interviewers and applicants forming the question: 'Can . . . you . . . help . . . me?' (2) *TV.* In a television studio, Hal and George, an older married man, are both trying to date their colleague Susan. Meanwhile, various television programmes are acted out, including commercials and images of dying Vietnamese: '*Ultimately, the control console itself will be taken over by television characters, so that the distinction between what is on television and what is occurring in the viewing room will be lost completely.*' As President Johnson speaks of fighting a war to maintain peace, Susan responds to a joke with a laughing fit, which stops only when Hal slaps her. While they celebrate Hal's birthday, more programmes and commercials are shown, including interviews with a rock band, an Evangelical preacher, and a decorated soldier from Vietnam who has left the army on conscientious grounds: 'We're committing mass murder.' Susan finally agrees to go out with Hal, but when George invites himself along, she says that she will stay at home and that the men can go out together. They all join in the canned laughter of a television situation-comedy. (3) *Motel.* An outsize doll, the Motel-keeper, proudly speaks of her up-to-date motel and welcomes two dolls, a

Man and a Woman. While the Motel-keeper sings the praises of her accommodation, the Man unpacks suitcases and throws clothes round the room, tears pages out of the Bible, and pulls down the curtains. The Woman flings objects from the bathroom, then enters and tears off her bra. Ignored by the Motel-keeper, the two doll-guests begin writing obscene graffiti and drawing images on the bedroom walls, and finally completely destroy the room. Still listing the merits of her motel, the Motel-keeper is finally torn apart to the deafening wails of a siren.

As written texts, these three short plays have little to commend them. Their absurdist quality harks back to Ionesco, and the satire is predictably banal compared with the contemporary work of Albee. Van Itallie's significance is that it is one of the earliest examples of improvisational work with actors, in this case with the Open Theatre of New York. The pieces exploit 'transformation', the actors' ability without changing set, costume, or props, to create entirely new locations and characters on a bare stage. A technique familiar in much oriental theatre, this freeing of the stage from the limitations of Western realism has become a recurrent feature of fringe theatre over the last 40 years and has allowed live performance to emulate the fluidity of the novel and the cinema.

American Buffalo

A: David Mamet **Pf:** 1975, Chicago **Pb:** 1977 **G:** Com. in 2 acts **S:** Don's shop in a Midwest town, 1970s **C:** 3m

Don Dubrow, the owner of a rundown 'resale shop' (i.e. junkshop), has two friends: Bob, a simple character who runs errands for Don, and Walter Cole ('Teach'), an individual of barely suppressed anger. Don is angry because he sold a buffalo-head nickel to a customer for $90 and now thinks it must be worth much more, so he plans to steal it back together with his whole coin collection, especially as Bob has reported that the customer has gone on holiday. When Teach learns that Bob is being sent to steal it, he insists that Bob is not up to the job, and that he ought to do it. Bob is told that the break-in has been postponed, and, when he is gone, Don and Teach plan the burglary for that night. Don now insists that they should invite Fletcher, a smart operator whom Don admires, in on the action. That night Bob arrives unexpectedly, wanting to sell a buffalo nickel that he has found. Teach comes, but there is no sign of Fletcher. Bob is sent away with $20 for his nickel. Teach becomes indignant that he is being made to wait for Fletcher, who, he claims, cheats at poker. To Don's dismay, Teach produces a revolver and plans to go off to do the job alone. Suddenly Bob reappears with the news that Fletcher has been mugged and is now in hospital. Don and Teach think he is lying and presume that Bob and Fletcher have stolen the collection themselves. Don hits Bob over the head. However, Bob was telling the truth about Fletcher, but now sheepishly admits that he bought his buffalo nickel for $50 to replace the one that Don sold. Teach is so outraged that he begins smashing up the shop. Bob then confesses that he lied about seeing the purchaser of the original nickel leaving his home. Teach goes to get a car to take Bob to hospital.

Eschewing the theatrical fireworks of Albee and Shepard, Mamet offers a searching analysis of American life by recreating with remarkable skill the earthy vernacular of ordinary Americans rather as Pinter did for Londoners. These characters are concerned with status, loyalty, fairness, and truth, while constantly undermining these concerns with the spiritual vacuity of their lives. The rough dialogue and shocking violence caused controversy when *American Buffalo*, one of Mamet's finest plays, was staged on Broadway in 1977 and at London's National Theatre in 1978, but it established the writer as a significant new force in American theatre.

American Dream, The

A: Edward Albee **Pf:** 1961, New York **Pb:** 1961 **G:** Satire in 1 act **S:** American living room, mid-20th c. **C:** 2m, 3f

Domineering Mommy tells henpecked Daddy about the hat she has bought. Grandma enters with a lot of boxes. Aware that Mommy would like to put her in a nursing home, Grandma reminds Daddy that she warned him against Mommy's grasping behaviour. Mrs Barker comes from the Bye-Bye Adoption Service and is invited to make herself comfortable; so she takes off her dress. Grandma explains to her that the 'bundle of joy' Mommy and Daddy adopted 20 years previously proved a disappointment to them. They blinded the baby, castrated it, chopped off its hands, and cut out its tongue. Finally, the child died. A beautiful Young Man now arrives. He tells how he has suffered all his life, ever since he was separated from his identical twin. Grandma leaves her obnoxious daughter, and Mommy and Daddy, delighted at the new if familiar child they have bought for adoption, drink to celebrate.

Using characters already presented in his short sketch *The Sandbox* (1960), this play contains echoes of Albee's own life (disappointing his rich adoptive parents instead of being the all-American boy they wanted), and of Ionesco's *The *Bald Prima-Donna* and Pinter's *The *Birthday Party*. Albee described the play as 'an examination of the American Scene, an attack on the substitution of artificial for real values in our society, a condemnation of complacency, cruelty, emasculation and vacuity'. Only Grandma, representative of a world now replaced by materialistic greed, shows some humanity.

America Play, The

A: Suzan-Lori Parks **Pf**: 1993, Dallas (workshop production); 1994, New York **Pb**: 1995 **G**: Hist. drama in 2 acts **S**: USA, 19th and 20th c. **C**: 3m, 2f, extras

In 'a great hole', a kind of theme park which is 'an exact replica of the Great Hole of History', the Founding Father, as Abraham Lincoln, delivers a long monologue. He tells of the Great Man (Lincoln) and the Lesser Known, a digger, who years after Lincoln's death makes money by displaying his remarkable likeness to the President. He re-enacts Lincoln's assassination by John Wilkes Booth by recreating the scene in Ford's Theatre, sitting in a rocking chair, and inviting the public to choose a pistol to shoot him with. Lucy, a widow, and her son Brazil, a digger (son of the Lesser Known?) listen to the echoes of the gunshot. Brazil's father dug the Great Hole of History, where he and Lucy saw American history re-enacted. Brief extracts are performed from *Our American Cousin*, the play Lincoln was watching when he was assassinated. In the Hall of Wonders Lucy and Brazil exhibit relics of America's past. Lincoln is shot again, and the nation mourns.

This young African-American playwright is often compared to Gertrude Stein and Adrienne Kennedy for her imaginative use of the theatre and for her language, with its quotations, repetitions, and ambiguities (what Parks has called 'rep' and 'rev', repetition and revision). *The America Play* interestingly does not make much of Abraham Lincoln's role in abolishing slavery. This is taken as read, but the repeated re-enactment of his assassination, with the role being played by a black actor, creates an image of oppression for which the nation must continue to mourn.

Aminta

AT: *Amyntas; The Countess of Pembroke's Ivychurch* A: Torquato Tasso **Pf**: 1573, Belvedere Island on the River Po **Pb**: 1581 **Tr**: 1591 **G**: Pastoral in 5 acts; Italian verse **S**: Timeless pastoral landscape **C**: 7m, 2f, chorus (m)

Aminta, a shepherd, has fallen in love with the disdainful Silvia, who is more interested in hunting than love and spurns Aminta, despite the urgings of her friend Dafne. Aminta's friend Tirsi advises him to seek out Silvia at the spring. Before he arrives, Silvia is surprised by a satyr, who strips her naked. Aminta chases him off, and Silvia flees in shame. Silvia's veil covered in blood is discovered near a pack of ravening wolves. Convinced that she is dead, Aminta prepares to plunge over a cliff. Silvia reappears and, seeing Aminta's lifeless body, regrets her treatment of him. Fortunately, he has been saved by a bush and has survived his fall. The play ends with their marriage.

Tasso, the court poet of Ferrara, is best known as a poet but wrote three plays, a comedy, a tragedy (*King Torrismondo* (1586), with echoes of **Oedipus the King*) and this pastoral play, the first and most famous example of the genre. There is no action in the piece, since all the events are reported. Everything depends on the exquisite lyrical verse, which tells of Aminta's love and despair, of the violent unfulfilled lust of the satyr, and of Silvia's change of heart, which she imagines to be too late. The pastoral play became widely imitated across Europe (e.g. Guarini's *The *Faithful Shepherd*, Milton's **Comus*, Goethe's *The Lover's Whim*, 1779). Pastoral elements are also in evidence in Shakespeare's **As You Like It*, and the mistaken belief that the beloved has died on finding a bloodstained cloth occurs in the Pyramus and Thisbe episode in *A *Midsummer Night's Dream*.

Amphitryon (*Amphitruo*)

A: Titus Maccius Plautus **Pf:** 215-185 BC, Rome **Tr:** 1694 **G:** Latin com. in verse **S:** Before the home of Amphitryon, Thebes, mythical past **C:** 5m, 2f, extras

In a prologue, Mercury reveals that his father Jupiter has fallen in love with Alcmena (Alcumena), whose husband Amphitryon (Amphitruo) is away in the wars as commander of the Theban army. In order to seduce the faithful Alcmena, Jupiter has assumed the form of Amphitryon and is at that very moment enjoying her body. Mercury has himself taken on the likeness of Amphitryon's servant Sosia. When the real Sosia arrives to announce that the victorious Amphitryon will return home shortly, he is thrown into confusion on encountering his mirror image (the disguised Mercury) and rushes off. Jupiter comes out of the house to bid a tender farewell to Alcmena, who is understandably confused and annoyed by the arrival moments later of the real Amphitryon, who cannot understand why his wife is behaving so oddly. When Alcmena tells him that he has only just left her, he flies into a rage, accusing her of being unfaithful and leaves in search of witnesses. Meanwhile Jupiter reappears, and, managing to reassure Alcmena, takes her inside the house. When Amphitryon returns, he is refused entry by Mercury, disguised as Sosia. Just as the wronged mortal is becoming desperate, he encounters his other self, and Jupiter reveals himself as a god. Despite the deceit and humiliation he has suffered, Amphitryon accepts that his wife has given birth to twins, his own son and one by Jupiter, the infant Hercules.

Based on an unknown Greek original, *Amphitryon* is characteristic of New Comedy (which differed from the Old Comedy of Aristophanes in its greater realism and concentration on domestic events) but is unique amongst extant New Comedy plays in that gods appear in the action. Although disguises and the resulting confusions are the stuff of comedy, there is a serious undertone to this piece, described in the prologue as a tragicomedy. Virtuous mortals are, as in tragedy, at the mercy of the amoral behaviour of the gods and are expected to accept this reprehensible divine behaviour. Perhaps it is this ambiguity which made the theme so popular in European drama, notably in the versions of Thomas Heywood (*The Silver Age*, *c.*1612), Jean Rotrou (*The Sosias*, 1638), Molière (1668), Dryden (1690), Kleist (1807), and Giraudoux (**Amphitryon 38*).

Amphitryon 38

A: Jean Giraudoux **Pf:** 1929, Paris **Pb:** 1929 **Tr:** 1938 **G:** Com. in prologue and 3 acts; French prose **S:** Amphitryon's palace, Thebes, mythical past **C:** 5m, 4f

Jupiter plots with his son Mercury how he may seduce Alcmena, who is devoted to her husband Amphitryon. Jupiter arranges for Amphitryon to go to war, and takes on the form of Amphitryon, so that he can gain access to his chaste wife. Although he impregnates Alcmena with Hercules, Jupiter's seduction is far from triumphant, since Alcmena's powerful personality treats him like her own husband, and he finds himself trapped in connubial bliss. Determined to take her as a god, Jupiter plans to return the following night, but Alcmena disdains Mercury's offer of sleeping with a god. Instead, she persuades Leda, Queen of Sparta, who had been seduced by Jupiter in the guise of a swan, to take her place in the conjugal bed. Both women assume that Jupiter will return as

Amphitryon, so when the real Amphitryon returns home, Alcmena happily gives him to Leda. When Amphitryon later discovers what has happened, he determines to fight Jupiter. Jupiter, whose anger over the substitution is assuaged by Alcmena's loyalty, agrees to help Amphitryon by making him forget what happened. In return, she agrees to pretend before the Theban populace that she had spent the previous night with a god, and the legend is born. Jupiter ascends aloft, leaving Alcmena unaware that she did indeed sleep with him.

Giraudoux reckoned that his witty retelling of the Amphitryon legend was the 38th version since Plautus' **Amphitryon*. Here the focus is less on the external complications of mistaken identities as on the effects the action has on both Jupiter and the mortals (echoing Kleist's treatment of 1807). The god is distinctly put out that he is forced to assume the role as well as the outer form of Amphitryon, and by introducing the character of Leda to the myth, Giraudoux explored questions of marital fidelity, which provide the old legend with new relevance.

Amyntas. See AMINTA.

Anarchy. See PAUL KAUVAR.

Anatol (Questioning Fate; Christmas Shopping; Episode; Memorial Stones; Farewell Supper; Agony; Anatol's Wedding)

AT: *The Affairs of Anatol* **A**: Arthur Schnitzler **Pf**: (1) 1896, Leipzig; (2) 1898, Vienna; (3) 1898, Leipzig; (4) 1916, Vienna; (5) 1893, Bad Ischl; (6–7) Berlin, 1901 **Pb**: 1892 **Tr**: 1911 **G**: 7 linked one-act dramas; German prose **S**: Vienna, 1890s **C**: 4m, 7f

(1) *Questioning Fate* or *The Crucial Question* (*Die Frage an das Schicksal*). Max envies Anatol's hypnotic power over women. So when Cora comes, Anatol hypnotizes her to discover whether she has been unfaithful to him. But he dare not question fate, preferring to live on with his illusions. (2) *Christmas Shopping* (*Weihnachtseinkäufe*). Out shopping for his mistress, Anatol meets Gabriele, a married woman whom he once tried to seduce. She helps him choose presents for his mistress and includes some flowers from herself with the message 'from a woman who could have loved as well as you but did not have the courage'. (3) *Episode*. Anatol visits Max with a parcel of mementoes, one labelled 'Episode'. This was a souvenir of his affair with Bianca, which lasted only two hours, but he boasts that she 'lay at his feet, thinking of nothing but him'. Bianca comes and cannot even remember Anatol, who leaves defeated. (4) *Memorial Stones* or *Milestones* or *Souvenirs* (*Denksteine*). On the day of his wedding to Emilie, Anatol discovers two precious stones which she has kept hidden. The ruby is a souvenir of her loss of virginity at 16 to a man she cannot even remember, the black diamond she has kept because it is worth a fortune. Disgusted, Anatol throws them in the fire and calls her a 'whore'. (5) *Farewell Supper* (*Abschiedssouper*). Anatol, dining with Max at the Hotel Sacher, nervously awaits the arrival of Annie, with whom he has resolved to end his affair. Annie infuriates him by announcing that she is finishing with Anatol, because she is going to marry a fellow dancer in her ballet troupe. Max comments that it proved after all quite easy to dump her. (6) *Agony* or *Dissolution* (*Agonie*). Anatol is having an affair with Elsa, a married woman. Neither is fulfilled by their relationship: he is often kept waiting to see her for a few hurried minutes, she cannot bring herself to leave her husband. Anatol tells Max that it is like a disease. (7) *Anatol's Wedding* (*Anatols Hochzeitsmorgen*). On the morning of his wedding Anatol is in bed with Ilona, a woman he had picked up at a Masquerade the night before. Even Max is shocked at his behaviour, and Anatol at first dare not reveal that he is off to his own wedding. When he finally admits it, Ilona angrily smashes his possessions, but Max reassures her that, once married, Anatol will keep her as his mistress.

This was the cycle of plays that established both Schnitzler's reputation as a playwright and his notoriety as a dangerously immoral influence. However, while Anatol's attitude to sexual morality, much of it based on Schnitzler's own life, is distinctly casual, his behaviour is not glamorized. Reinforced by

Max's cynical commentary, Anatol may be seen not so much as a predator but as a victim of his sexual appetite, and his many women, far from being victims of his philandering, usually manage to keep the upper hand. Harley Granville Barker's adaptation of 1911 helped *Anatol* to become one of the best known if not necessarily the best of Schnitzler's works for the stage.

Anatomist, The (*The Anatomist: A Lamentable Comedy of Knox, Burke, and Hare, and the West Port Murders*)

A: James Bridie Pf: 1930, Edinburgh Pb: 1931 G: Drama in 3 acts S: Edinburgh, 1828–9 C: 7m, 5f, extras

Dr Robert Knox is a leading Scottish anatomist who conducts important and innovative dissections of the human body. However, his reputation suffers through his association with Burke and Hare, two disreputable characters who supply him with corpses. His assistant Walter Anderson has a row with his fiancée Mary on this very matter, and Walter goes drinking in a tavern, where he is consoled by a cheap tart. Next day he is horrified to discover that Knox is dissecting the tart's corpse, and is further disturbed when it becomes clear that Knox is not interested in the provenance of the body. It is not long before it becomes common knowledge that Burke and Hare have not just robbed graves but have murdered to obtain bodies. Burke is arrested and hanged, and mobs converge on Knox's home. He flees to Mary's home, prepared to shoot on the crowd if need be. However, he is rescued by his students, and Knox coolly delivers his prepared lecture on the human heart.

Although Bridie does not probe the topic very deeply, *The Anatomist* is significant in being the first major play to debate a preoccupation of 20th-century drama, the social responsibility of the scientist (cf. Brecht's *Life of Galileo*, Dürrenmatt's *The *Physicists*, Frayn's **Copenhagen*). As Bridie said in his preface, the play shows 'the shifts to which men of science are driven when they are ahead of their times'. At the time of the premiere of *The Anatomist* there was someone else arguing the same Nietzschean belief that great men must not be limited by common morality: Adolf Hitler.

Andorra

A: Max Frisch W: 1946–61 Pf: 1961, Zurich Pb: 1962 Tr: 1962 G: Drama in 12 scenes; German prose S: Imaginary state of Andorra, mid-20th c. C: 9m, 3f, extras

Andri is a young Jewish boy whose life was saved when a benevolent schoolteacher brought him to Andorra to escape the Blacks' persecution of the Jews in the neighbouring state. He is now engaged to Barblin, the teacher's daughter, and finds employment as a carpenter's apprentice. The carpenter, believing that Andri should pursue a more 'Jewish' occupation, puts him in charge of sales. Abused and teased by everyone, including a Soldier, his fellow Apprentice, and the Doctor ('Never met a Jew yet who could take a joke'), Andri is told by the teacher that he cannot marry Barblin, because they are blood relatives. A Lady visitor (the Señora) from the Blacks turns out to be Andri's mother; his father had lied about his Jewishness to cover up the scandal. When the Lady is stoned to death by Andorrans, Andri is accused of her murder. Even though he now knows that he is not Jewish, Andri cannot shake off his 'Jewish' mannerisms. So when the Blacks invade and hold a 'Jew Inspection', Andri is singled out and led off to be executed. His father commits suicide, and Barblin goes mad. Between each scene, Andorrans take the witness stand and defend their actions.

This play, set in a semi-abstract world peopled by mainly anonymous characters, is one of the most powerful dramatic statements of the effect of stereotyping on individuals, felt particularly acutely in 1945, as the horrific consequences of the Nazis' branding of Jews as 'subhuman' came to light. The specious arguments used to justify the Andorrans' behaviour, while applying especially to Switzerland's refusal to get involved, are of universal relevance.

André

AT: *The Glory of Columbia: Her Yeomanry* A: William Dunlap **Pf**: 1798, New York **Pb**: 1798; rev. version 1817 **G**: Trag. in 5 acts; blank verse **S**: Tappan and environs, New York state, 1780 **C**: 9m, 2f, 2 children (1m, 1f), extras

Major John André, having plotted to betray the West Point garrison during the American War of Independence, is captured as a British spy and is condemned to death. A number of friends, including patriotic Americans, hold him in such high regard that they try to save him. In particular, Bland, whom André released from a British prison, speaks out on his behalf. Bland's mother, whose husband is being held as a hostage by the British, also pleads for clemency. Even the arrival from England of Honora, André's sweetheart, fails to change the decision of the military tribunal and their leader the General (George Washington). As he is led away to be hanged in the town of Tappan, André claims that he had acted in the best interests of America.

Predictably, given its controversial generosity towards a factually based enemy spy a mere fifteen years after the end of the War of Independence, *André* was not a success with the public. To make matters worse, the scene painter Charles Ciceri had not finished the sets in time for the premiere, and the actor playing Bland had not troubled to learn his lines. It was only when Dunlap turned the piece into a patriotic musical extravaganza, *The Glory of Columbia*, premiered in 1803, that he achieved success with the piece and helped to establish himself as the 'Father of the American stage'.

Andria. See GIRL FROM ANDROS, THE.

Andromache

A: Euripides **Pf**: *c.*425 BC, Athens? **Tr**: 1782 **G**: Greek trag. in verse **S**: Before the temple of Thetis in Thessaly, after the Trojan War **C**: 5m, 5f, extras, chorus (f)

A sequel to the story of **Trojan Women* (which was performed some ten years later). Andromache, widow of the Trojan hero Hector, is now the slave and concubine of Neoptolemus, son of Achilles. Neoptolemus is visiting the oracle at Delphi, so his young wife, Hermione, takes advantage of his absence to get rid of Andromache and her son. She plots with her father Menelaus to seize and kill her. Andromache is already bound with her little son clinging to her, when Peleus, Neoptolemus' grandfather, arrives just in time to save her and to take her under his protection. Because Hermione now lives in fear of Neoptolemus' anger when he returns, she begs the visiting Orestes to take her away with him. They depart, and news comes that Neoptolemus has been killed by the citizens of Delphi. Thetis, the sea nymph, with whom Peleus fathered Achilles, now orders that Neoptolemus shall be buried in Delphi and that Andromache shall be free to leave with her son.

Generally accounted one of Euripides' weaker plays, the action depends mainly on external incident rather than on the internal conflict which is such a strength of his major works. The main characters, Menelaus and Hermione, are also unsympathetically portrayed, perhaps reflecting the Greek hatred of Sparta (and we note that Menelaus also acquits himself badly in *Trojan Women*). Euripides' *Andromache* provided the basis for the psychologically compelling version by Racine.

Andromache (*Andromaque*)

AT: *The Distrest Mother* A: Jean Racine **Pf**: 1667, Paris **Pb**: 1668 **Tr**: 1675 **G**: Trag. in 5 acts; French alexandrines **S**: Pyrrhus' palace in Epirus, after the Trojan War **C**: 4m, 4f, extras

Although Pyrrhus is betrothed to Hermione, daughter of Helen of Troy and King Menelaus, he has fallen in love with the noble widow of Hector, Andromache, whom he has been given as one of the spoils of the Trojan War. Andromache however rejects his love, since she is devoted only to the memory of Hector and to her little son Astyanax. When Orestes, who desperately loves Hermione, arrives with an order from the Greek kings to surrender Astyanax to them in order to prevent him growing up to avenge his father's death, Pyrrhus seizes this as an opportunity to force Andromache into marriage. She complies in order to save her son, secretly planning to take her own life immediately after the wedding. The enraged and humiliated Hermione persuades Orestes to avenge her by taking Pyrrhus' life, but when Pyrrhus is mortally wounded, she is so disturbed at losing her beloved that she rejects Orestes and kills herself. Driven insane by guilt and by Hermione's treatment of him, Orestes is taken away by his companions, leaving Andromache and her son as the sole survivors.

It has been said that while Corneille depicted people as they ought to be, Racine showed them as they are. Here, in this chain of unrequited love, Racine explores the destructive force of passion, which leads to the curious paradox that the ostensibly weakest characters, Andromache and her son, for the time being at least, emerge unscathed from the events of the play. Racine's supreme achievement is to portray these conflicts, hesitations, and reversals within the strict limits of the neo-classical unities and through the medium of alexandrine verse, which establishes a powerful tension between the formality of the language and the power of the emotion it expresses.

And So Ad Infinitum. See INSECT COMEDY, THE.

Angels in America (Millennium Approaches; Perestroika)

A: Tony Kushner Pf: (1) 1991, New York; (2) 1992, New York Pb: (1) 1992; (2) 1994 G: (1) Drama in 3 acts; (2) Drama in 5 acts and an epilogue S: (1) New York, Salt Lake City, and Antarctica, 1985–6; (2) The Kremlin, Alphabetland in the Arctic, Antarctica, New York, and heaven, 1986, 1990 C: (1) 12m, 7f (2) 14m, 9f

(1) *Millennium Approaches.* Roy M. Cohn, a busy, blustering Jewish lawyer, offers his Mormon friend Joe Pitt a post in Washington. But when Joe asks his wife Harper, an agoraphobic, who likes talking to her imaginary travel agent friend, whether she would go to Washington, she refuses; she would rather have a baby. At his grandmother's funeral, Prior Walter reveals to his boyfriend Louis Ironson that he has AIDS. When Joe later comforts the tearful Louis, Louis propositions him. Prior appears in a valium-induced hallucination to Harper, and she later confronts Joe with being gay. Roy is told that he too has contracted AIDS, but he refuses to acknowledge that he is a homosexual. Prior is taken to hospital, and Louis consoles himself with sex with a stranger in Central Park. As Prior approaches death, he hears the voice of an angel. Roy and his Reaganite friend Martin Heller extol the virtues of the New Right and urge Joe to go to Washington, regardless of his wife's feelings. Roy is particularly keen to place Joe there, so that Joe can protect Roy from disbarment proceedings for embezzling a client. Joe encounters Louis again outside the Hall of Justice in Brooklyn, and goes off with him, 'Selfish and greedy and loveless and blind. Reagan's children.' In overlapping dialogue, Joe leaves his wife, and Louis leaves Prior. Prior is visited in hospital by his ancestors, one of whom died of the plague. Louis tells Prior's nurse, a black drag queen named Belize, that AIDS has exposed the limits of America's belief in human rights. Harper travels to Antarctica, Joe's mother leaves her home in Salt Lake City to be with him, and Joe refuses the job in Washington. Roy, who made sure that Ethel Rosenberg went to the electric chair as a traitor, is visited by her. As he lies in pain, she warns him: 'History is about to crack open. Millennium approaches.' Joe and Louis meet in the park and leave to go to bed together. The Angel crashes through Prior's ceiling to appear to him. (2) *Perestroika.* The world's oldest living Bolshevik complains that he has been left without any ideology. Louis seduces Joe in 'Alphabetland' in the Arctic. Harper's Antarctica morphs into Prospect Park, Brooklyn, where she is arrested for chewing down a pine tree like a beaver. Roy is admitted to hospital – not the easiest of patients. While Joe's mother encourages Harper to start living again, Joe begins having doubts about his love for Louis. Prior tells Belize about the visitation of the Angel, who foretold the 'Secret Catastrophe', preceded by a life that is 'completely unbearable'. Roy recognizes that 'Americans have no use for the sick'. Prior visits the Mormon Visitor Centre to learn about

angels, and watches as Louis discovers that Joe, part of the historical diorama, is a Mormon. Roy, angry with Joe for 'coming out', urges him to go back to his wife; Prior, failing to get Louis to come back to him, confronts Joe in his office; and Joe eventually returns to Harper. Joe's mother comforts Prior as his Angel approaches to take him off. Joe can no longer bear to be with Harper, but when he returns to Louis, they end up having a violent fight. Roy, now debarred as a lawyer, dies, watched by Ethel Rosenberg. Prior, after wrestling with the Angel, ascends into heaven. In heaven, a desolate and ruined city, Angels listen to news of the Chernobyl disaster, and Prior, discovering that God has abandoned the earth, urges the Angels to 'Sue the bastard for walking out.' As Prior finds his way back to earth, he sees Roy preparing God's defence in the impending lawsuit. Harper leaves Joe for good, and Prior refuses to let Louis come back to him. In an epilogue, Prior is still alive, and news comes of the collapse of totalitarianism in Eastern Europe.

Angels in America is one of the richest texts of recent American theatre, combining trenchant naturalistic dialogue with fantasy, political comment with humour, and an awareness of contemporary concerns with the appearance of historical figures, all in a style reminiscent of Caryl Churchill. The apocalyptic events of the spread of AIDS, the approach of the millennium, and the growing power of the Right are viewed with gentle cynicism by Kushner, the homosexual Jewish outsider. As Belize comments: 'The white cracker who wrote the National Anthem knew what he was doing. He set the word "free" to a note so high nobody can reach it.'

Anna Christie

AT: *Chris Christopherson; The Ole Devil*
A: Eugene O'Neill **Pf**: 1921, New York **Pb**: 1922
G: Drama in 4 acts **S**: New York saloon bar and a barge, *c.*1910 **C**: 8m, 2f, extras

To preserve his daughter Anna Christie from the rough ways of the sea, her father Chris Christopherson, a veteran seaman of Scandinavian origins, arranged for her to grow up on a farm in Minnesota. She has now written to announce her arrival in New York, and her delighted father tells the old prostitute with whom he shares his barge that she will have to move out. However, it soon becomes clear that Anna is not the pure young thing of her father's dreams. Corrupted by a male cousin, she has become a hard-drinking whore. At first she plays the innocent with her father, and on the barge with him does indeed feel cleaner and happier. They rescue some shipwrecked sailors, and one of them, an Irishman Mat Burke, falls in love with Anna. Her father, desperate that she might marry a sailor, fights with Burke. Anna, horrified that men are fighting over her yet again, reveals her past. Burke and Chris, dismayed at her confession, go ashore to drink. After two days her father returns, announcing that he has signed up on a ship. Burke, also the worse for wear, reappears, unable to forget Anna. When he is assured that she hated all the men she slept with and that he is the first man she loves, he asks her to marry him. However, he has signed up for the same ship as Chris, and both men will set off into the fog the following day.

After its failure in 1920 as *Chris Christopherson*, where Chris was the central character and Anna was pure, O'Neill rewrote the play twice. As *Anna Christie* it became immensely popular and provided Greta Garbo with her first screen role. The sentimental happy ending has been criticized, but O'Neill pointed out how uncertain Anna's and Burke's future is.

Another Country

A: Julian Mitchell **Pf**: 1981, London **Pb**: 1982
G: Drama in 2 acts **S**: Library, head of house's study, dormitory, and cricket field of English public school, early 1930s **C**: 10m

Seventeen-year-old Guy Bennett, a homosexual, and his friend Tommy Judd, a Marxist, rebel against the stifling discipline of Gascoigne House, despite the admonitions of their friend Donald Devenish. Prefect Menzies warns Bennett and Judd that a fellow prefect Fowler is waiting to catch them out, but they are both far cleverer than the bullying Fowler.

Martineau, a boy caught by a master in a homosexual act, hangs himself, and the prefects discuss how to minimize the damage to the school's reputation. Bennett attends his widowed mother's second wedding, and returns to school drunk, in love, and resolved to sleep his way to the top. After Martineau's suicide, Devenish's parents decide to remove him from the school, which leaves the unsuitable Judd to become a prefect. The school invites literary intellectual Vaughan Cunningham, Devenish's uncle, to give a talk to the school. Cunningham's bourgeois humanism disgusts Judd, while Bennett senses in the gay author a useful stepping stone. When Bennett is condemned to a beating for being badly turned out on the cadet parade, he threatens to reveal the names of all the boys, including prefects, he has had sex with. Devenish stays on to become a prefect, relieving Judd of potential compromise, and thwarting Fowler's bid to be Head of House.

Offering a thinly disguised portrait of the homosexual double agent Guy Burgess, Mitchell, best known as a novelist, uses, in a more realistic and serious vein than Alan Bennett in **Forty Years On*, the English public school as a metaphor of the British Establishment. Guy Bennett, with his moral anarchy, and Judd, with his revolutionary aspirations, represent two ways of asserting: 'there must be a better way to run things'.

Antigone

A: Sophocles Pf: *c.*441 BC, Athens Tr: 1729
G: Greek trag. in verse S: Thebes, mythical past
C: 4m, 3f, extras, chorus (m)

The sons of Oedipus, Eteocles and Polyneices, have killed each other in a battle over their inheritance. Since Eteocles died defending the city of Thebes, the new ruler Creon orders that he alone shall be accorded an honourable burial, while Polyneices' corpse is left to rot outside the walls of the city. Their mourning sisters Antigone and Ismene discuss this decree, Antigone resolving to defy Creon and bury Polyneices, while Ismene advises caution. Creon arrives with the chorus and justifies his decision. A guard comes with the news that Polyneices' body has been buried, and when he returns to the body, catches Antigone in the act of reburying her brother. Creon condemns her to death for disobeying the law, but she protests that she is obeying a higher law of religious observance and familial duty. Antigone is led away to be buried alive. Creon's son Haemon, who was to marry Antigone, threatens that he will commit suicide if she should die. When the prophet Tiresias warns Creon that his tyranny will be punished, Creon rushes off to free Antigone. He arrives to find that Antigone has already hanged herself, and the desperate Haemon threatens his father then plunges his sword into himself. When Creon's wife hears the news of the death of her son, she too commits suicide. Creon remains mourning and alone, the chorus hoping only that one may become wiser with age.

Antigone continues the curse of the house of Laius, which is depicted in **Oedipus the King*, and Aeschylus' **Seven Against Thebes* and finds its resolution in Sophocles' **Oedipus at Colonus*. It shares with many Greek tragedies the distinction of having a courageous woman as the central figure. While Antigone's defiant action would have been justified to an Athenian audience by the contemporary religious duty to bury the dead, one does not need to be a believer in Greek ritual to share her outrage at the inhumanity of Creon's decree. She chooses the path of righteousness, and, though meeting her death, is morally triumphant. By contrast, Creon's role is more complex and more interesting. Occupying the stage for most of the play, we see a man who attempts to act according to the law, and who is terribly punished for his incautious and inflexible decision. A typical Sophoclean figure, he is, like Oedipus, in no sense wicked, but must nevertheless undergo extreme suffering for his actions. Indeed, he is the truly tragic figure of the piece. The clash of two just viewpoints, of civil law versus religious law, of political expediency versus humanity, has encouraged later writers to revisit the theme, notably Hasenclever (1917), Anouilh, and Brecht (1948).

Antigone

A: Jean Anouilh **Pf:** 1944, Paris **Pb:** 1946 **Tr:** 1946 **G:** Trag. in 1 act; French prose **S:** Thebes, mythical past **C:** 8m, 3f

The plot of Anouilh's play is essentially the same as in Sophocles. The main differences are: (1) the anachronisms. The guards smoke cigarettes and play cards, Creon's wife knits, and there is mention of motor transport. (2) the tragic development. Whereas in Sophocles the characters behave as though they have free will, Anouilh makes it clear that each character is obliged to fulfil his or her given role – the tragedy is like a spring that inexorably unwinds. (3) Antigone, a childish figure, concerned about her pet dog, who buries Polyneices with a toy spade, acts not with reference to a higher law but 'for myself': 'what a person can do, a person ought to do'. (4) Creon is treated more sympathetically, a politician with a difficult task to fulfil, who at the end of the tragedy has to attend a meeting at five o'clock.

Anouilh's rewriting of Sophocles' **Antigone* is arguably the most successful modern theatrical treatment of ancient myth. Performed during the German occupation of Paris, its theme of authority in conflict with individual protest resonated powerfully with the public, and it enjoyed 645 consecutive performances. That the German authorities allowed it to be staged was no doubt largely due to the mythical topic, but is probably also a testimony to the somewhat nihilistic portrayal of Antigone, who in a world emptied of religious faith, appears a dangerously self-indulgent, self-dramatizing individual.

Antony and Cleopatra (*The Tragedie of Anthonie, and Cleopatra*)

A: William Shakespeare **Pf:** *c.*1606, London **Pb:** 1623 **G:** Trag. in 5 acts; blank verse and prose **S:** Egypt, Rome, Messina, Misenum, Syria, Athens, and Actium, *c.*40–30 BC **C:** 30m, 4f, extras

Mark Antony, one of the triumvirs ruling the Roman Empire after the defeat of Brutus (see JULIUS CAESAR) is captivated by the beautiful Queen Cleopatra of Egypt. News comes that Antony's wife has died and that the Roman Empire is threatened with enemies, and Antony is summoned to Rome to help defend it. To ease the tension between Antony and another triumvir, Octavius Caesar, Antony marries Octavius' sister Octavia. The triumvirs make peace with their main enemy Pompey. But conflict soon returns: Antony resents the power that Caesar is assuming, and Caesar is furious when Antony rejects Octavia to return to his beloved Cleopatra, making her queen over all the African lands. Confronting Caesar in a sea battle at Actium, Antony is defeated when Cleopatra's fleet suddenly takes flight. Caesar demands the surrender of Antony, in return for which he will spare Cleopatra. She is willing to accede to this offer, when Antony, raging at her cowardice, resolves to challenge Caesar once more, this time in personal combat. When this is rejected, the armies prepare for battle near Alexandria. At first Antony's forces prevail, but again he is betrayed by Cleopatra's troops. Defeated in battle and told by her servant that Cleopatra is dead, Antony falls on his sword. Cleopatra takes refuge in a monument, and the dying Antony is lifted up to her for a last farewell. Rather than face captivity in Rome, Cleopatra commits suicide with a snakebite. Caesar arranges for them to be buried together.

Based on Plutarch, *Antony and Cleopatra* is drawn on a very broad canvas, presenting scenes in different places of the Roman Empire and involving two major battles. But the major interest is the love between Antony and Cleopatra, amongst the greatest lovers of world theatre. Although it is clear that Cleopatra is selfish and manipulative and that Antony is a 'strumpet's fool' who throws away power and success, the audience celebrates with them the power of their love in contrast with the cold politics of Rome. Even though Antony's suicide is botched and Cleopatra's is deceitful, greatness and nobility emerge. Their relationship has been dramatized many times since, notably by Dryden in **All for Love.*

Aoi-no-Ue

A: Zeami **W:** late 14th c. **Tr:** 1921 **G:** Nō play in 2 acts, Japanese verse **S:** Palace of the Emperor Shujaku, 10th c. **C:** 3m, 2f, chorus (m)

Aoi-no-Ue, the Prime Minister's daughter, is married to Prince Genji, son of the Emperor. Genji has also been the lover of the Princess Rokujō, an older woman, widow of the Emperor's brother. One day at a festival there is a dispute over which of the women's carriages should have precedence, and their servants fight, Aoi's side eventually prevailing. At the start of the play, Aoi is now struck down by a mysterious illness. A courtier asks a witch to summon the spirit causing this sickness, and the living ghost of Rokujō appears. She bewails her situation and declares her hatred for Aoi, striking her on the head. She is then transformed into a demon. The courtier now summons the Little Saint of Yokawa, whose spiritual strength subdues the angry Rokujō and gets her to walk 'in Buddha's Way'.

One of the best known of the ancient Nō plays, it was written by one of its earliest and most famous exponents, who was also the author of critical writings about the genre. *Aoi-no-Ue* is an example of the *kyōjomono* or 'madwoman' plays, in which a jealous woman transforms herself into an avenging spirit. The elevated and austere style of Nō theatre, while barely accessible to Western audiences, has held a particular fascination for 20th-century European theatre (notably in the dramatic work of Yeats). The title character never appears, but is represented merely by a folded kimono; Rokujō's assault on her is effected by the masked actor striking the kimono with a fan; Rokujō's transformation into a demon takes place on stage, as masks are exchanged while she is semi-hidden by her cloak. Mishima Yukio's 1954 version is set in a modern hospital.

Arbeitsbeschaffung. See FEAR AND MISERY OF THE THIRD REICH.

Arcadia

A: Tom Stoppard **Pf:** 1993, London **Pb:** 1993 **G:** Drama in 2 acts **S:** Room in large country house in Derbyshire, 1809 and 1993 **C:** 8m, 4f

Lady Thomasina Coverly, a precocious 13-year-old, is being taught algebra by her tutor Septimus Hodge. Ezra Chater, an inferior poet, disturbs the lesson to challenge Septimus to a duel for seducing his wife, but is dissuaded by Septimus's flattery. Richard Noakes, a landscape gardener, is planning to turn the Capability Brown gardens at Sidley Park into a wild Gothic 'landskip', much to the dismay of Lady Croom and Captain Edward Brice. In the present day, the same room is now being used by the famous author Hannah Jarvis, who has come to research the early 19th-century custom of installing a hermit in the Gothic landscape. She meets Bernard Nightingale, who is visiting the house, believing that Chater was killed in a duel by Lord Byron. 1809: Septimus finally accepts Chater's challenge and will ask his friend Byron to act as second. 1993: Hannah discovers Thomasina's mathematics lesson book, which persuades her descendant Valentine Coverly, a mathematician, that Thomasina's thinking was a century ahead of its time. While Bernard is convinced of his theory about Byron, Hannah decides that the mad hermit was Septimus who devoted himself to working out Thomasina's mathematical discovery. 1809: Byron is discovered with Mrs Chater, and is sent from the house. Septimus wins over Lady Croom. 1993: the family dress up in Regency costume, and Valentine affirms the validity of Thomasina's equation. Just after learning that Thomasina was burnt to death the night before her 17th birthday, time shifts again, and Thomasina rushes in. Scenes from past and present run side by side: Bernard discovers that Byron did not kill Chater, Bernard and Chloe are found embracing, and Thomasina and Septimus dance their last dance together.

Generally regarded as Stoppard's finest play, *Arcadia* bears many of his characteristics: witty Wildean dialogue ('You must not be cleverer than your elders. It is not polite'); a spectacular use of the stage, the same room being seen almost 200 years apart until the two periods merge in the final scene; above all, a daringly playful and intriguing debate of ideas (it takes extraordinary skill to incorporate iterated algorithms and heat transference into an entertaining theatre-piece). Both periods stand before a new age: 18th-century enlightenment gives way to Gothic wildness; the end of the 20th century stands at the threshold of entirely new scientific insights: as Valentine says: 'It's the best possible time to be alive, when almost everything you thought you knew is wrong.' Meanwhile, Hannah and Bernard try to establish truth, but have to acknowledge: 'It can't prove to be true, it can only not prove to be false yet.'

Architect and the Emperor of Assyria, The (*L'Architecte et l'Empereur d'Assyrie*)

A: Fernando Arrabal Pf: 1967, Paris Pb: 1967 Tr: 1969 G: Drama in 2 acts; French prose S: A tropical island, mid-20th c. C: 2m

A primitive native of a tropical island, the 'Architect', who has built himself a neat dwelling, is disturbed by a tremendous crash. This announces the arrival from the sky of a gentleman, the sole survivor of an aeroplane crash, who asks the Architect for help. As the frightened savage utters inarticulate noises, the gentleman introduces himself as the 'Emperor of Assyria'. In order to acquaint the Architect with 'civilization', the Emperor gets him to act out roles with him: master and servant; priest and worshipper; sadist and masochist; mother and child; etc. All this, however, has the effect of reminding the Emperor of his own burden of guilt, so he asks the Architect to kill and eat him. The Architect duly does so, but he does not much enjoy eating the tough corpse, although he is relieved that it is not a Friday. Diving under the table to retrieve a bone, the savage re-emerges as the Emperor. The Emperor reappears as the Architect. The opening is repeated, with the new Emperor falling from the sky and the new Architect gibbering inarticulately.

The Spanish-French writer Arrabal often gave his absurdist theatre a violent twist, and in this, his best-known play, he depicts sadism and cannibalism. The remote setting allows Arrabal to question the values of contemporary civilization and to imply, in a manner reminiscent of Rousseau, that freedom from hierarchical structures might lead to the possibility of genuine structure (realized in the Architect's beautifully built hut).

Arden of Faversham (*The Lamentable and True Tragedie of M. Arden of Feversham in Kent*)

A: Anon. Pf: *c.*1592, London Pb: 1592 G: Trag. in 5 acts; blank verse S: Arden's home and various other locations near Faversham, Kent, 1551 C: 15m, 2f, extras

Arden, a wealthy landowner, admits his fears about the fidelity of his wife Alice, who has indeed fallen in love with their steward Mosbie (or Mosby). She promises both Michael, a servant, and Clark (or Clarke), a painter, that each can marry Mosbie's sister if either kills Arden. The first attempt at murder fails, when Arden refuses to drink a poisoned broth prepared by Alice. She now engages Greene, who bears a grudge about being dispossessed of land by Arden, to kill him too. Greene hires two villainous but incompetent killers, Black Will and Shakebag, whose three attempts on Arden's life fail hopelessly, in one case because Michael relents and locks all the doors against them. Finally, the conspirators succeed in stabbing Arden to death while he is playing backgammon at home, with Alice delivering the final blow. The body is carried outside, but the Mayor finds blood and the murder weapon in the house and footprints in the snow leading from the house to the body. The murderers of the household are all condemned to death, while the hired killers also meet violent ends.

Ascribed to Kyd and, even less probably to Shakespeare, *Arden of Faversham* was based on the murder of Thomas Ardern [*sic*] in 1551. It may therefore lay claim to being the first documentary drama of world theatre (although it may be argued that the mystery plays were documentary). It is also notable in that it creates a tragedy from the lives of ordinary people (conventionally the stuff of comedy), and so stands as an early example of a domestic tragedy. In its vigorous use of blank verse, free-ranging locations, disregard for the unity of time, and violent, even grotesque, action on stage, it – like *The *Spanish Tragedy* – anticipates the great tragedies of the Elizabethan and Jacobean stage, most obviously **Macbeth*, where guilty murderers are also haunted by images of blood. Lillo wrote a sanitized version, completed by John Hoadley in 1759.

Arise and Shine. See FEMALE PARTS.

Arms and the Man

A: George Bernard Shaw Pf: 1894, London Pb: 1898 G: Com. in 3 acts S: Bulgaria, 1885–6 C: 4m, 4f

Raina Petkoff is engaged to Sergius Saranoff, a Bulgarian officer, whose suicidal cavalry charge against the Serbs improbably succeeded, and who is now hailed as a hero. Bluntschli, an escaping Swiss mercenary serving with the Serbs, climbs into Raina's room at night and dismays her with his unheroic attitude: he even has chocolates in his cartridge-belt. However, she assists his escape. Sergius returns from the war and, after an overblown declaration of his love for Raina, begins to flirt outrageously with the maid Louka. When Bluntschli reappears to return the coat which he escaped in, Raina realizes that she loves him. On learning this, Sergius challenges Bluntschli to a duel. The challenge fails when Bluntschli suggests machine guns as duelling weapons. Raina will marry her 'chocolate soldier' Bluntschli, who has fortuitously just inherited a fortune from his father's hotel chain, and Sergius will console himself with Louka.

This notable anti-war comedy was the first play by Shaw to enjoy a professional production and is still popular across the world today. Although Shaw was satirizing 19th-century romantic comedy, we still laugh at the pricking of the bubble of romantic love and heroic sentiment, as we match the bombast of the 'hero' Sergius (a distant legatee of *The *Braggart Soldier*) against the honesty and pragmatism of the down-to-earth Bluntschli.

Armstrong's Last Goodnight

A: John Arden Pf: 1964, Glasgow Pb: 1965 G: Hist. drama in 3 acts; Scots dialect prose, with some verse and songs S: Royal palace, Armstrong's castle, and forest, Scotland, 1528–30 C: 30m, 7f

Sir David Lindsay (author of *A *Satire of the Three Estates*), James V of Scotland's Chief Herald, is attending a meeting in 1528 of Scots and English Commissioners 'to secure ane certain time of peace, prosperity, and bliss on ilk side of the Border'. One of the sticking points is the frequency of the borderers' cattle raids, especially those carried out by John Armstrong of Gilnockie. The Scots promise to get Gilnockie to obey the King's law, and Lindsay is charged with the task of winning him over. Gilnockie and fellow clansmen betray an old enemy, Johnstone of Wamphray, and bring about his death. Lindsay offers Gilnockie the title of warden of Eskdale if he will swear loyalty to James and refrain from further border raids. Lindsay, insisting that Gilnockie make his peace with Wamphray, is glad to hear that he is now 'in condition of peace'. Lindsay's mistress, arriving too late to join Lindsay, lodges with Gilnockie and is roughly seduced by him. The confirmation of Gilnockie's appointment is delayed by the opposition of Gilnockie's suzerain, Lord Maxwell. The impatient Gilnockie now demands Wamphray's lands. Lindsay has a vision of a free state ruled by the borderers like a Swiss canton. However, Gilnockie has led a raid into England, and Henry VIII threatens war in retaliation. Gilnockie is promised safe conduct to meet the King, but is treacherously seized and hanged.

In this well-constructed piece, Arden explores the relationship between honourable dealing and political expediency. Like the Pope being dressed in Brecht's **Life of Galileo*, Lindsay's honour disappears under his herald's tabard. Gilnockie is an anarchic, immoral rogue, reminiscent of Brecht's Azdak and cousin to Arden's Sailor Sawney and Butterthwaite. Only Lindsay's anachronistic vision of an autonomous border state hints at Arden's left-wing views.

Arsenic and Old Lace

AT: *Bodies in the Cellar* A: Joseph Kesselring Pf: 1941, New York Pb: 1942 G: Farce in 3 acts S: Brooklyn, 1940s C: 11m, 3f

Sisters Abby and Martha Brewster are sweet old spinsters, known for their charitable work, who murder lonely old men by inviting them home and giving them elderberry wine laced with arsenic. Fortunately, their brother Teddy imagines he is Teddy Roosevelt, who is digging the Panama Canal in their cellar and quite happily buries 11 bodies, 'the victims of yellow fever', down there. When nephew Mortimer, a theatre critic who is courting their neighbour Elaine Harper, finds a body in the window seat, he learns the truth about his aunts' activities. Jonathan, another nephew who is a hardened criminal, arrives with the sinister Dr Einstein. They need to dispose of a murder victim of their own and intend to set up the house as a plastic surgery clinic for criminals. Teddy's late-night bugling attracts the attention of the police, who arrest Jon and commit Teddy to a home. When Jon tries to tell the police of the bodies in the cellar, they assume he is mad too. Mortimer is relieved to learn that he was an adopted child and can marry Elaine without fear of congenital insanity. Abby and Martha decide to join Teddy in the home, but first, since the head of the home is lonely and unhappy, they give him a glass of their special elderberry wine.

Kesselring's only successful play ran for four years on Broadway and was made into a popular film in 1944, starring James Stewart. Originally, it seems that it was intended as a serious thriller, but the producers Howard Lindsay and Russel Crouse transformed it into a zany farce. It stands as one of the earliest examples of 'black' or grotesque comedy, which became so voguish in the 1960s and beyond.

Art

A: Yasmina Reza **Pf:** 1994, Paris **Pb:** 1994 **Tr:** 1996 **G:** Com. in 7 scenes, interspersed with monologues; French prose **S:** Serge's, Yvan's, and Marc's identical flats, Paris, 1990s **C:** 3m

Serge, a successful but divorced dermatologist, has just bought a painting, 'a white canvas with fine white diagonal scars', for 200,000 francs. His friend Marc, an aeronautical engineer with conventional tastes, is unimpressed with 'this shit'. Marc discusses this extravagant purchase with another friend Yvan, unsuccessful professionally but about to get married. Yvan goes to see the painting and expresses his admiration for it, although he later admits that he did not like it. The men are to meet to go out to dinner. Yvan arrives late, full of worries about his wedding. Tensions mount: Marc finds Serge pretentious; Serge considers Marc unimaginative; both are bored hearing about Yvan's wedding. As the three recognize that they have less and less in common, Yvan reveals that he spends 800 francs a week on therapy from an obvious charlatan. When Serge comments negatively on Marc's girlfriend, Marc flies at him but ends up hitting Yvan, who intervenes. As the three reach the point of crisis, Serge hands Marc a felt-tip pen and invites him to draw on his precious canvas – a demonstration that he values his friendship more than his painting. Serge and Marc later succeed in cleaning off Marc's graffiti. A catharsis has taken place.

By birth half Iranian, half Hungarian, Reza is one of France's major woman playwrights, and *Art* was immensely successful in Paris, London, and New York, a surprising achievement with such undramatic material. Reza traces the movements of loyalty and betrayal between the three 'bobos' (bohemian bourgeoisie) with subtlety, wit, and accuracy, while flattering the audience with an undemanding discussion of modernist art.

Arturo Ui. See RESISTIBLE RISE OF ARTURO UI, THE.

Ascent of F6, The

A: W. H. Auden and Christopher Isherwood **Pf:** 1937, London **Pb:** 1936; rev. 1937 **G:** Trag. in 2 acts; prose and some rhymed and blank verse **S:** Lake District and Colonial Office, England, and F6, a mountain in Asia **C:** 10m, 3f, chorus of 3 singers

Michael Forsyth ('M. F.') Ransom, a famous mountaineer, sits high up over the Lake District, reading Dante and feeling disillusioned. Interspersed with the main action, Mr and Mrs A. describe their humdrum lower middle-class lives as they listen to the news. Ransom's twin brother Sir James is anxious to annex F6, a mountain, reputedly haunted by a guardian demon, on the border between British Sudoland and the hostile Ostnian Sudoland. Ransom, who hates his brother, is unwilling to lead the expedition to conquer F6 but is persuaded by his mother to answer England's call. Preparing for the climb in a monastery on F6, Ransom has to reconcile differences in his party, especially between the steadily loyal Ian Shawcross and the flippant playboy David Gunn. The Abbot warns Ransom that he is using his prodigious powers of leadership in the vain hope of improving the world and urges him instead to seek abnegation of the will. Ransom ignores this advice, and one by one his men perish at the hands of the 'Demon': the young botanist Lamp is killed in an avalanche; Shawcross commits suicide when denied the chance for the final assault; Gunn dies in a blizzard. Ransom reaches the summit, but dies there, in his fevered imagination seeing his brother as the Demon, with whom he plays chess. Ransom's heroic achievement is cheapened by patriotic clichés of the Establishment.

This is a play of many themes and styles. It parodies the English Establishment, while celebrating the heroism of one of its agents; it urges revolt, while being cynical about the possibility of improving the world. It is an exciting adventure story and a philosophical meditation; it offers both prose parody and sinewy poetry.

As Far as Thought Can Reach. See BACK TO METHUSELAH.

Ashes

A: David Rudkin Pf: 1973, Hamburg; 1974, London Pb: 1978 G: Drama in 3 acts S: England (Warwickshire and Birmingham?), 1970s C: 4m, 4f

Colin Harding, a former writer, now a teacher in his early thirties from Northern Ireland, and his wife Anne, a former actress, now a teacher in her late twenties from Yorkshire, are trying hard to have a baby, but Colin initially has a low sperm count. Several medical tests and advice finally result in Anne becoming pregnant. At first all goes well, but she then begins to bleed and has to rest for weeks, waited on by the slightly incompetent Colin and tormented by the sympathy of a pregnant friend. Eventually, she is taken to hospital, where she miscarries and has her womb removed. They apply to adopt a child. Colin travels to Northern Ireland for the funeral of his uncle, who was blown apart by a Republican bomb, but is rejected by his relatives for living 'across the water'. Anne and Colin are refused permission to adopt; 'Their hopes for parenthood lie in ashes.'

Based on the experiences of his wife and himself, *Ashes* brings together the personal with the political in naturalistic scenes and elegantly lyrical monologues. Apart from the obvious irony of terrorists destroying life when others are desperate to create it, Colin allies the sterility of Northern Irish bigotry to the sterility of his marriage: 'the clan, from whose loins I come, had turned me out; to my own loins no child of tomorrow shall come.' Rudkin's reflections on terrorism seem particularly relevant to the suicide-bombers of the 21st century: 'If an undertribe can commit themselves to such atrocity, there must be some terrible misery they are trying to communicate.'

Assemblywomen, The. See WOMEN IN ASSEMBLY.

As You Like It

A: William Shakespeare Pf: *c.*1599, London Pb: 1623 G: Romantic com. in 5 acts; blank verse and prose S: Frederick's court and Forest of Arden, Renaissance period C: 17m, 4f, extras

Frederick has seized the lands of his brother the Duke, who now lives in exile in the Forest of Arden (or Ardennes?). Orlando, who has been dispossessed of his inheritance by his malevolent brother Oliver, overcomes Duke Frederick's wrestler and has to flee to the Forest. Rosalind, daughter of the banished Duke, who has fallen in love with Orlando, is also banished. Disguising herself as a man, she ventures into the Forest, accompanied by Frederick's daughter Celia and the clown Touchstone. Orlando joins the Duke's party, who are regularly entertained by Jaques's cynical remarks. Rosalind is delighted to discover that Orlando has pinned up verses declaring his love for her on the trees of the Forest. In her disguise as Ganymede, she instructs Orlando how to woo his beloved. Oliver enters the Forest in pursuit of Orlando, and when the latter rescues him from a lion, the brothers are reconciled. Finally, Rosalind reveals her true identity, and Hymen comes to preside over three weddings: Orlando to Rosalind, Oliver to Celia, and Touchstone to the peasant-girl Audrey. News comes that Frederick has been converted to a religious life, and the Duke, accompanied by his courtiers, except for the melancholy Jaques, returns to court to become ruler again.

Based on Thomas Lodge's pastoral novel, *Rosalynde* (1590), *As You Like It* is one of Shakespeare's finest and best-loved comedies, combining pastoral romance with comedy based on the true nature of loving. It reflects on the opposition between the merciless character of the court compared with uncomplicated life in the forest. Shakespeare subtly portrays this contrast, revealing honesty and generosity at court and discomfort and villainy in nature; after all, the courtiers – except for the cynical Jaques – are only too happy to abandon their 'idyll' to return to court. Most of the fun of the play is derived from Rosalind in disguise, playing with her unsuspecting lover. The male actor, dressed as a woman disguised as a man and pretending to be a woman, yields many levels of theatrical illusion and androgynous sexuality, something that has been explored by modern all-male revivals of the play by the National Theatre and Cheek by Jowl. In 1977 Peter Stein performed the play in a Berlin film studio after six years of careful research with his company.

At the Black Pig's Dyke

A: Vincent Woods **Pf:** 1992, Galway **Pb:** 1998 **G:** Drama in 2 acts, 2 prologues, and an epilogue; prose and rhymed verse **S:** Counties Leitrim and Fermanagh, Ireland, *c.*1940–70 **C:** 11m, 5f, 2 musicians

Mummers perform their traditional play: the First Hero from England, who has 'cut down the native scum', fights with the Second Hero, 'a Green Knight', but both are reconciled. The Mummers discover that men have shot Lizzie Boles and her daughter Sarah. Tom Fool and Miss Funny tell the story of Jack and Lizzie: Jack Boles, a Protestant, whose father was murdered in the Troubles, woos Lizzie Flynn, who works in their shop. The wedding of Tom Fool and Miss Funny is disrupted by the intervention of a Republican bigot Frank Beirne, who wants Lizzie for himself. Lizzie marries Jack and crosses the border to live with him in Fermanagh. Their daughter Sarah is born soon after. Jack is murdered by men with masks, and Frank Beirne gets his shop and asks Lizzie to marry him. Sarah marries Hugh Brolly, whose brother is killed by the British army. The Mummers come, but Hugh leaves, supposedly to work, but in fact 'risin' the black pig' with IRA men. When he learns that explosives he is to deliver are intended for the wedding of well-liked Protestant neighbours, he dumps the explosives and phones the police. Frank Beirne and fellow terrorists, played by the Mummers, catch Hugh and shoot him, then arrive at Lizzie's door.

In one of the most powerful plays written about the Northern Irish 'Troubles', Woods's use of Mummers and his poetic diction at once reinforce the awareness of the primeval ritual of revenge killings and at the same time distance the audience from the horror of the murders, avoiding sensationalist naturalism to concentrate on the underlying desperation of the conflict.

At the Bottom (of Life). See LOWER DEPTHS, THE.

At the Hawk's Well

AT: *Waters of Immortality* **A:** W. B. Yeats **Pf:** 1916, London **Pb:** 1917 **G:** Drama in 1 act; blank verse and irregular verse of 3- and 4-stressed lines **S:** A well, 1st c. AD **C:** 2m, 1f, 3 musicians

For 50 years an Old Man has waited for a well to flow whose waters grant immortality to any who drink from it. The well is guarded by a bird-like creature. When a Young Man (Cuchulain) comes, the Old Man tries to get him to leave claiming prior right to the water. Cuchulain insists on waiting, and the Guardian of the Well rises up and performs a hypnotic dance before him. The Old Man sleeps, Cuchulain rushes off in pursuit of the beautiful bird he imagines before him, and the waters of the well flow briefly. The Old Man is bitterly disappointed, but Cuchulain is now more interested in fighting Aoife's warriors and rushes into battle. The musicians sing of the pointlessness of waiting for a dream.

At the Hawk's Well incorporates elements of oriental performance with its musical commentary taken from Japanese Nō theatre and with its setting created by the unfolding of a cloth. Although seldom performed, this exquisite piece, the first of Yeats's *Four Plays for Dancers*, offers a memorable theatrical experience. In its simplicity and the symmetry of its characters, it may also be recognized as a forerunner of a much better known play about unfulfilled hopes, **Waiting for Godot*.

Atheist's Tragedy, The

AT: *The Honest Man's Revenge* **A:** Cyril Tourneur **Pf:** *c.*1607–11 **Pb:** 1611 **G:** Trag. in 5 acts; prose and blank verse **S:** France, Renaissance period **C:** 12m, 4f, extras

Lord D'Amville, for whom money is the only god, encourages his brother's son Charlemont to go to the wars, thus leaving the way clear for his sickly elder son Rousard to marry Charlemont's beloved, Castabella. A false report of Charlemont's death induces D'Amville's brother Lord Montferrers to make D'Amville his heir, whereupon D'Amville seizes an opportunity to murder him. The Ghost of his father appears to Charlemont, urging him to return home at once. D'Amville is saved from Charlemont's revenge by the intervention of his younger son Sebastian and by the restraining hand of the Ghost, who urges Charlemont to leave revenge to God. D'Amville rewards Sebastian with money, which the young man promptly uses to free Charlemont from prison. Since his elder son has failed to consummate his marriage, D'Amville resolves to seduce his daughter-in-law in order to continue his line. Abducting her to a graveyard, he is surprised by Charlemont, whom he believed to have been murdered by his servant, rising from the charnel house. In these macabre surroundings the young lovers are reunited. D'Amville's two sons die, the elder from sickness, the other killed by a jealous husband. Charlemont is tried and condemned to death for killing the servant sent to murder him, but D'Amville, wishing to carry out the execution, succeeds only in dashing out his own brains. Charlemont and Castabella are rich and free to marry.

The main interest of this play, of which only the main line of action is summarized above, is that, uncharacteristically for the amoral world of Jacobean tragedy, Charlemont remains a virtuous hero throughout and is duly rewarded by heaven. It may make for better morality, but for less successful theatre.

Attempts on Her Life

A: Martin Crimp **Pf:** 1997, London **Pb:** 1997 **G:** 17 scenarios **S:** Indeterminate locations in Britain, late 20th c. **C:** Any number of performers

In the course of 17 disjointed scenes, aspects of the life of Anne (Ann, Annie, Anny, Anya, Annushka) may be pieced together. It appears that she is 40, is trusting, travels widely, has appeared in films – perhaps as a porn star – and seeks fulfilment as a terrorist. She may have taken an overdose and be lying in a hospital bed. She may be married with two children and live with her husband in a rural commune and visit her mother-in-law. Perhaps she is an artist, offering her suicide notes as works of art. Perhaps she is stabbed to death, while a child looks on.

In *The Treatment* (1993) Crimp created the character of Ann, who is physically abused by her partner then harassed by film producers wanting to buy her story. Here, in a series of 'scenarios' linked only by enigmatic references to Anne, her personality is totally fragmented, reflected in the disjointed structure, in conflicting information, in the different variations of her name, and in the use of different languages. For lovers of postmodernist deconstruction, this offers an interesting challenge to an imaginative cast and a teasing puzzle to an audience.

aufhaltsame Aufstieg des Arturo Ui, Der.

See RESISTIBLE RISE OF ARTURO UI, THE.

August. See UNCLE VANYA.

Automobile Graveyard, The (*Le Cimetière des voitures*)

AT: *The Car Cemetery* **A:** Fernando Arrabal **Pf:** 1961, New York; 1966, Dijon **Pb:** 1958 **Tr:** 1960 **G:** Drama in 2 acts; French prose **S:** Automobile junkyard, mid-20th c. **C:** 5m, 2f, extras

Dila, a pretty 25-year-old woman, rings the bell for sleep in the automobile cemetery. Tiossido, a young sportsman, runs on, being coached by Lasca, a mature but tireless woman. The couple in Car 3 summon their valet Milos to order breakfast in bed. Milos forces Dila to visit all the occupants of the wrecked cars to kiss them goodnight. A knitting trumpeter, a clarinettist, and a dumb saxophonist come on and play. They contemplate becoming judges so that they can earn money killing people. The man in Car 2 orders Milos to bring him a woman, and Dila is forced to go. The trumpeter Emanou declares his love for Dila, and they make love, watched by the laughing car-dwellers, as they do every night. Dila is furious and now dominates Milos. She hurries off to save Emanou from the police, who seek him because he murders people who are bored. Tiossido and Lasca embrace, watched again by tittering onlookers. They book into Car 2 for the night. Dila manages to delay the police with her seductive charms. Tiossido and Lasca appear, dressed as police, and run off. Dila hands a chamber-pot from car to car. Lasca arrests Emanou, and the clarinettist claims his reward for betraying him. Emanou is whipped, and in Car 3 a newborn baby cries. Emanou, covered in blood, is wheeled in on a bicycle. Dila rings the bell for morning, and the same events begin to be repeated.

In this absurdist piece, convention and logic are undermined at every turn: Milos is violently jealous but is amused by Dila having sex with another man; Emanou is an innocent but kills people; the junkyard is horribly desolate but is waited on by a smart valet. Arrabal appears to imply that, in the decay of contemporary civilization, outer form is preserved in the place of substance.

Autres, Les. See NO EXIT.

Autumn Fire

A: T. C. Murray **Pf:** 1924, Dublin **Pb:** 1925 **G:** Drama in 3 acts **S:** Living room of Keegans' farmhouse and Mrs Desmond's cottage, rural Ireland, 1920s **C:** 5m, 3f

Nance Desmond, a pretty girl of 22, has come home to Tobarnabrosna from working in the town to stay with her elderly mother and to set up as a dressmaker. Ellen Keegan, a 27-year-old woman old before her time, upbraids Nance for her flighty manner, while Nance tells Ellen that she has a 'heart and mind half perished'. Owen, Ellen's widower father, a vigorous 50-year-old, flirts with Nance, and her brother Michael is also impressed with Nance's good looks. Six weeks later, Michael has fallen in love with Nance. However, Owen announces that he intends to marry her. Ellen believes Nance has schemed to win Owen's farm and predicts catastrophe for the family. Nine months later, Owen and Nance seem happily married, but Owen has become very ill and may die. Owen tells his elder brother Morgan that he wants to leave the farm to Nance. Morgan warns him not to, and is concerned that Nance and Michael have gone off to market together. By the time they finally return, Owen is consumed with jealousy and goes off to bed. Nance insists that Michael must go away, and he begs for a farewell kiss, which Owen observes. In fury, he drives Michael from the house, curses Nance for her treachery and Ellen for planting the seeds of jealousy in his mind, and finally sits alone: 'They've broken me . . . son – wife – daughter.'

This unadorned tale of an older man having his head turned by a younger woman and being made to suffer for his vanity is in the tradition of Abbey Theatre realism, but also contains within it tragic elements. The character of Nance is the most complex: sincerely devoted to Owen, she cannot resist the temptations of youth: 'I was drowned in a dream. I struggled like a bird in a net.'

Avare, L'. See MISER, THE.

Avariés, Les. See DAMAGED GOODS.

Aves. See BIRDS.

Awake and Sing!

AT: *I Got the Blues* A: Clifford Odets Pf: 1935, New York Pb: 1935 G: Pol. drama in 3 acts S: Bronx apartment, 1930s C: 7m, 2f

Bessie Berger is a Jewish matriarch who presides over her impoverished and unhappy family during the Depression. Her ineffectual husband Myron is a sententious windbag, her father Jacob is a Marxist dreamer, her cynical son Ralph lacks sense of direction, and her daughter Hennie loves an embittered war cripple, Moe Axelrod, but becomes pregnant by a stranger. Bessie makes Hennie marry a recent immigrant with reasonable prospects. One year later, the family are more miserable than ever: Ralph blames his mother for trapping Hennie in an unhappy marriage, and their poverty is felt more acutely owing to the visit of rich uncle Morty. Jacob makes Ralph the beneficiary of his life insurance policy and 'accidentally' falls from the roof. Regenerated by their grandfather's sacrifice, Hennie will elope with her true love Moe, and Ralph, rejecting his claim to the insurance money, will go out and fight for a new society.

This was the first success for the left-wing Group Theatre and Odets's best play. Reminiscent of O'Casey's **Juno and the Paycock*, it also looks forward to Wesker's early plays of Jewish family life, especially *Chicken Soup with Barley* (1958). Although firmly founded in strong characterization, the final message, taken from Isaiah 26:19, 'Awake and sing, ye that dwell in dust', is unambiguously political, an optimistic ending insisted on by the director Harold Clurman to replace the desolate ending of Odets's original, *I Got the Blues*.

Awakening of Spring, The. See SPRING'S AWAKENING.

Away

A: Michael Gow Pf: 1986, Sydney Pb: 1985 G: Drama in 5 acts S: Australian town, hotel, campsites, 1967–8 C: 5m, 5f, extras

Three families are going on vacation over the Christmas (summer) break: headmaster Roy, who has just directed his pupils in *A *Midsummer Night's Dream*, and his wife Coral, who suffers acute depression after they lost their son in Vietnam; Jim and his snobbish philistine wife Gwen with their rebellious daughter Meg, who played Titania; and Harry and Vic, who came to Australia eight years ago with their son Tom, who performed Puck and is in love with Meg. Roy and Coral have a tense holiday at a luxury Gold Coast Hotel in Queensland, and Coral becomes dangerously attracted to a young man on his honeymoon; Jim, Gwen, and Meg have a dismal Christmas on a campsite in their new caravan; Harry, Vic, and Tom have a good time camping with an old tent. When a storm destroys Jim and Gwen's caravan, by chance they meet Harry and Vic on their idyllic campsite. Coral has left Roy and found her way to the same spot. Harry reveals that his son Tom has cancer, and Tom tells Meg that he wants 'to do it once, just once', but she refuses. That evening at the campsite, there is a concert, at which Tom and Coral enact a version of *The Flying Dutchman*, with the hint that Tom has restored Coral to life. Roy appears, and he and Coral are reconciled in a silent scene. Back at school, Tom reads from **King Lear* how he will 'Unburden'd crawl toward death'.

In this well-observed and poignant portrayal of a more innocent age, Gow explores domestic relationships in an unspectacular but convincing way. Although the piece's naturalism seems better suited to television, the improbable coming together of the three couples in an idyllic location lifts the action almost on to the level of a dream.

b

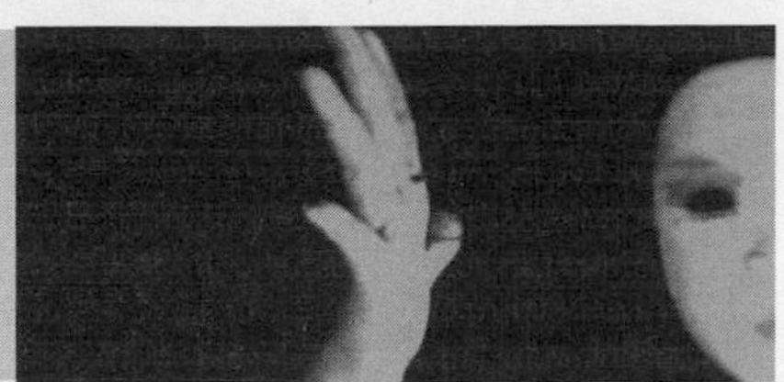

Baal

A: Bertolt Brecht **Pf:** 1923, Vienna **Pb:** 1922; rev. 1955 **Tr:** 1964 **G:** Drama in 22 scenes; German prose and songs **S:** Central Europe, 1920s **C:** 18m, 12f, extras

Baal is a dissolute wandering poet who plays his guitar and sings in bars and cheap clubs. His coarse ugly exterior and ambivalent sexuality do not prevent him from seducing a number of women, including the 17-year-old girlfriend of an admirer, the wife of his patron, and a girl he encounters in the street, who falls in love with him and is abandoned when she becomes pregnant. She commits suicide, but this hardly affects Baal, who continues to drink, sing his songs, and extol nature. His travelling companion Ekart, with whom Baal is in love, is appalled by Baal's ruthless behaviour. When Ekart flirts with a waitress, Baal becomes so jealous that he kills him. Fleeing from arrest, he finds himself alone in a hut in a rain-soaked forest. Appealing for help to some woodcutters, it is Baal's turn to be rejected. He will die alone.

This was Brecht's first play, written in 1918 as a conscious riposte to the idealization of the 'poet' in Expressionism (compare Sorge's *The *Beggar*). Baal was the Canaanite priapic god of fertility, condemned by Old Testament prophets, a suitable name for the gross and ugly sensualist whose charm and rebellious energy nevertheless exercise a dreadful fascination. Despite Baal's total lack of social concern, even the Marxist Brecht could not bring himself to repudiate him entirely.

Bacchae (*Bakchai*)

AT: *The Bacchic Women; Bacchants*
A: Euripides **Pf:** *c.*405 BC, Athens **Tr:** 1782 **G:** Greek trag. in verse **S:** Before the palace of Pentheus in Thebes, mythical past **C:** 7m, 1f, extras, chorus (f)

The god Dionysus returns in disguise to his birthplace, the city of Thebes. He is angry that the women of Thebes have denied that he is divine and so, with his chorus of Asian women, has driven them wild in Bacchic orgies. Pentheus, King of Thebes, is furious on his return to find his city in such uproar, especially when he discovers the priest Tiresias and his grandfather Cadmus have also joined with the Maenad women. Pentheus orders the destruction of Tiresias' shrine and the capture of Dionysus. Dionysus meekly accepts his arrest, but his women are miraculously freed from imprisonment. Pentheus confronts Dionysus and orders him to be incarcerated. Soon Dionysus too frees himself and then urges Pentheus to disguise himself as a woman in order to witness the Dionysian rites for himself. Pentheus enthusiastically accepts and goes off into the mountains to join the women. Once there, Dionysus denounces him as the man who mocked their sacred rites. The furious women dismember Pentheus, and his mother Agave, imagining she has slaughtered a lion-cub, triumphantly carries back his severed head to the city. Cadmus comes with the torn limbs of Pentheus, and Agave recognizes in horror what she has done. No longer disguised, Dionysus appears in order to justify his actions: Pentheus was judged because he neglected to worship a god. Complaining that the god's 'vengeance is too heavy', Cadmus and Agave must go into exile.

Although written right at the end of his life when in his seventies, *Bacchae* is one of the most powerful and accomplished of Euripides' plays. It won him a posthumous prize, his fifth, at the dramatic festival of the Great Dionysia. *Bacchae* is the only extant play to depict the god of tragedy, Dionysus, and elements like dressing in disguise, ecstatic dancing, and the confusion of reality and appearance were, appropriately, essential elements of the Greek theatre. In this regard, Pentheus may be seen as a forerunner of Plato with his stern condemnation of artists. This, however, does not explain the lasting power of the play. What we also find here, as in **Hippolytus*, is the misguided attempt by Pentheus to disregard his natural instincts, in Freudian terms to repress his sexuality. This can lead only to disaster. His comic enthusiasm about dressing as a woman betrays his true nature, and his refusal to accommodate Eastern mysticism and ecstasy in his Western demand for order produces a furious and destructive backlash. This has allowed later interpreters to view the play as the model of a fascist dictatorship, as in the Performance Group's *Dionysus in '69* (1969), or of the anarchy of drug culture, as in John Bowen's *The Disorderly Women* (1969). Caryl Churchill has also used the theme in a dance piece created with David Lan, *A Mouthful of Birds* (1986).

Back to Methuselah (In the Beginning; The Gospel of the Brothers Barnabas; The Thing Happens; Tragedy of an Elderly Gentleman; As Far as Thought Can Reach)

A: George Bernard Shaw **Pf**: 1922 **Pb**: 1921 G: Cycle of 5 dramas: (1) 3 acts, (2–3) 1 act, (4) 3 acts, (5) 1 act and an epilogue S: (1) The Garden of Eden and Mesopotamia, 4004–3700 BC; (2) Britain, 1920; (3) Britain, 2170; (4) Ireland, 3000; (5) Britain, 31920 C: (1) 2m, 2f; (2) 5m, 2f; (3) 4m, 2f; (4) 4m, 4f; (5) 7m, 5f, extras

(1) *In the Beginning*. Adam and Eve are alarmed when they encounter their first dead creature in the Garden of Eden. The wise Serpent explains that Lilith renewed life by tearing herself into two to create the first man and woman. While Eve remains optimistic, Adam is timid and unadventurous and opts to die after 1,000 years. The Serpent, to prevent life ending, teaches Eve how to procreate. Over three centuries later, one of Eve's descendants, Cain, has invented murder and warfare and tries to convert the toiling Adam to his way of life. While Eve is dismayed at the birth of violence, she recognizes that there are also thinkers and artists among her many descendants. (2) *The Gospel of the Brothers Barnabas*. In 1920 the brothers Conrad and Franklyn Barnabas have deduced that humankind will survive only if the normal lifespan is extended to 300 years, in order to gain sufficient maturity to avoid dreadful conflicts like the world war they have just endured. They interest two politicians in their idea, who want to adopt the slogan 'Back to Methuselah', but who are disillusioned when the brothers cannot supply a 'quick fix' elixir to guarantee longevity. The brothers patiently explain that only evolutionary forces can bring about the desired goal. (3) *The Thing Happens*. It is now 2170, and President Burge-Lubin, a descendant of the two politicians in Part 2, is ruling the British Empire successfully, mainly thanks to the efficient support of black African women and of the Chinese. He is alarmed to learn that the Archbishop of York is 283 years old but looks only 50. He has staged a number of mock drownings, knowing that he would be hated for his longevity. Barnabas's former parlourmaid, now the attractive Domestic Minister, has also willed for herself a long life, and the two agree to marry, in order to perpetuate the gene that will guarantee a decent lifespan. (4) *Tragedy of an Elderly Gentleman*. An Elderly Gentleman from Baghdad, now in AD 3000 the capital of the British Commonwealth since Britain is totally in the hands of the long-livers, has arrived in Ireland. He, with the Prime Minister and the Emperor of Turania, are taken by a young long-liver called Zoo to consult the oracle in Galway. The Emperor threatens to spoil the visit by his thoughtless behaviour towards the Oracle, and there is a discussion about the long-livers' plans to eradicate short-livers. The Oracle and Zoo put on a show for the visitors. When the Prime Minister seeks his own

political advantage, the Oracle simply tells him: 'Go home, poor fool.' She fulfils the embarrassed Elderly Gentleman's wish to stay in Ireland by striking him dead. (5) *As Far as Thought Can Reach*. By 31920 evolution has developed to the point where children hatch from eggs as 17-year-olds, have four years of carefree adolescence, and then become Ancients, who live on for many centuries without eating or sleeping. One of the youths, Pygmalion, sculpts statues of Ozymandias and of Cleopatra-Semiramis. These quarrel, rise up against Pygmalion and kill him, and must themselves be put to death, for Ancients have 'a direct sense of life' and no longer need art. In an epilogue, figures from Part 1 reappear: Cain is dismayed that there is no more war, but the Serpent and Lilith are well pleased with creation, Lilith especially because human beings 'are still not satisfied' and she looks forward expectantly to 'what lies beyond'.

Shaw's 90,000-word play cycle (a 'Metabiological Pentateuch') is a sprawling monster of dramatic invention. It contains philosophical and political comment, some sparklingly witty dialogue, some frankly tedious declamatory passages, and mythical characters that carry an air of reality about them. After the cataclysmic events of the First World War, many artists felt impelled to reassess where humankind was heading, and in his futuristic visions (which include video-conferencing), Shaw shows himself to be more optimistic than many (compare e.g. Kaiser's **Gas Trilogy*) in his anticipation of an ideal Platonic republic. As Shaw complained, only Wagner can get audiences to sit for several hours, so *Back to Methuselah* is hardly ever performed in its entirety (the premiere ran over three nights), but it is the closest, even if admittedly much inferior, that the English-speaking theatre gets to Goethe's **Faust*. Interestingly, both writers see as the best hope for humankind the fact that they are never wholly satisfied.

Bad-Tempered Man, The (*Dyskolos*)

AT: *The Malcontent; The Grouch; The Grumbler; The Man Who Didn't Like People; The Misanthrope; Feast of Pan; Old Cantankerous* A: Menander Pf: 316 BC, Athens Tr: 1960 G: Greek com. in verse S: Before a shrine between two farmsteads, Phyle in Attica, 4th c. BC C: 10m, 5f, extras

Cnemon, the 'bad-tempered man', lives alone on his farm with his daughter and an old female slave. He dislikes and distrusts everyone, and is estranged from his immediate neighbour, his stepson Gorgias. Pan causes a young man from town, Sostratos, to fall in love with Cnemon's lovely and virtuous daughter Myrrhine. Despite initial misgivings, Gorgias supports Sostratos in his wooing of Myrrhine. Sostratos' mother and sister now arrive, preparing to hold a banquet at the shrine, much to Cnemon's annoyance. When Cnemon falls down his well and has to be rescued by Sostratos and Gorgias, he undergoes a sudden change, regretting his former misanthropy and entrusting Myrrhine to the care of Gorgias. Gorgias arranges for Myrrhine to marry Sostratos, who in turn begs his father to allow Sostratos' sister to wed Gorgias. After some comic business, in which Cnemon shows something of his former surly self, the play ends with festivities to celebrate the joint betrothals.

The Bad-Tempered Man is the most complete surviving 'New Comedy' from ancient Greece, whose manuscript was not rediscovered until 1959. New Comedy differs from the Old Comedy of Aristophanes in its greater realism and concentration on domestic events. It also usually turns on what is now regarded as the staple of comedy, the progress towards a happy ending by lovers who, initially thwarted in their yearnings, are finally brought together. In form, the New Comedy abandoned the prominence of the chorus in favour of choral interludes. Here, it is significant that the title character does not make an appearance until Act 3. Like his distant descendant in Molière's **Misanthrope*, Cnemon is not wholly to be despised: he argues persuasively that, if everyone kept to themselves, as he does, then there would be no courts of law or wars. Such subtlety of characterization was one of the qualities praised by the ancients and led to Menander's serving as a model for Roman comedy.

Bakchai. See BACCHAE.

Balaganchik. See PUPPET SHOW, THE.

Balconville

A: David Fennario **Pf:** 1979, Montreal **Pb:** 1980 **G:** Drama in 2 acts; English and Canadian French **S:** Working-class tenement, Montreal, 1970s **C:** 5m, 4f

In the working-class area of Pointe-St-Charles, the inhabitants, who cannot afford to go on vacation, spend the hot summers on their balconies, where they can observe and be observed. The lives of three families are shown. The French-speaking Claude Paquette works in an unfulfilling job, but is devastated when he loses it in Act 2. He has an attractive daughter Diane, whom he enjoys fondling, and who is forced to give up her studies when her father becomes unemployed. The English-speaking Tom Williams idles away his time waiting for an unemployment insurance cheque and dreams about his former brief career as a minor rock star. The third family, also English-speaking, is held together by Irene Regan, a resourceful mother, coping with her feckless son Johnny, who dreams of escaping to New York to join a rock band, but who will inevitably end up working in a factory. Especially poignant is Johnny's failure, because of the language barrier, to get close to Diane. The women show themselves to be dependable, contrasted with their husbands and with the empty promises of a French Canadian politician Bolduc, who is seeking re-election. Finally, their tenement block is burnt down (possibly so that the landlord can collect on his insurance), and the families gather their possessions in a panic. The final question in both languages: 'What are we going to do?' Qu'est-ce qu'on va faire?' remains unanswered.

Balconville, which claimed to be the first bilingual play in Canada, represents Fennario's Marxist standpoint in an absorbingly naturalistic style reminiscent of Rice's **Street Scene*. There is even less action here, where Fennario depicts merely the effect of an industrialized and alienated society on the lives of the characters. The final 'What are we going to do?' refers not only to the destruction of their home but is a challenge to change the system.

Balcony, The (*Le Balcon*)

A: Jean Genet **Pf:** 1957, London; 1960, Paris **Pb:** 1956; rev. 1960, 1962 **Tr:** 1958 **G:** Drama in 9 scenes; French prose **S:** Brothel and café in a European city, mid-20th c. **C:** 17m, 7f

A Bishop hears the confession of a scantily clad young woman. He is interrupted by Irma, the Madame of a brothel: the 'bishop' is a client acting out his fantasy. Meanwhile there are riots on the streets outside. In another room, a beautiful young thief is whipped by the Executioner and makes the Judge lick her feet. Elsewhere, a General rides on his prostitute like a horse and acts out his death in battle. The Chief of Police, Irma's former lover, now impotent but still her protector, comes in search of a fantasy Chief of Police. The Executioner, Irma's present lover, announces the rebels' victory and is killed by a stray bullet. In a café, the revolutionary leader, a plumber, plans to make his beloved prostitute a symbol of the revolution. When the authorities collapse, the fantasists in the brothel are persuaded to act out their roles for real. Irma as Queen leads them out to be acclaimed by the crowds. The plumber's prostitute is shot dead, and the revolution is defeated. The clients begin to enjoy their new-found power. The Chief of Police comes to assert his authority, but gives way to the plumber, who assumes his identity, even to the extent of castrating himself. Irma dismisses the Bishop and the others and begins to give out new roles, reminding the audience that they too will be playing their own parts when they get home.

The shocking content of *The Balcony*, first directed by Peter Zadek in London, caused a furore, added to by Genet's pulling a gun on Zadek when he disapproved of Zadek's direction. The play offers a spectacularly theatrical exploration of the relationship between fantasy and reality and cynically analyses the way in which power is dependent on public reception, a theme to be developed by the Situationists two decades later.

Bald Prima-Donna, The (*La Cantatrice chauve*)

AT: *The Bald Soprano* A: Eugène Ionesco Pf: 1950, Paris Pb: 1954 Tr: 1958 G: Drama in 1 act; French prose S: Middle-class English home, late 1940s C: 3m, 3f

Mr and Mrs Smith are sitting after an evening meal, which she describes to him in stilted phrases. He finds fault with the newspaper for not giving the ages of the newly born. They then discuss Bobby Watson, who died two years previously but whose death was announced only recently, and all of whose family members are called Bobby Watson. The Smiths are joined by Mr and Mrs Martin, who feel they have met each other somewhere and then realize that they live together. The Maid however assures the audience that they are not who they think they are. The Fire Chief, the Maid's boyfriend, arrives in search of a fire. An exchange of absurd proverbs reaches a frenetic climax. The lights go out, and when they come on again, the Martins are sitting alone where the Smiths were and begin repeating exactly the same dialogue as at the beginning.

Ionesco's first play established the elements of his absurdist drama: inconsequential dialogue (much of it inspired by an English language course); stereotypical characters; surprising leaps in logic; and grotesquely excessive reactions to the trivial (e.g. embarrassment over the Fire Chief's mention of 'the bald prima-donna'). Underneath the playful theatrical treatment Ionesco expresses 'the tragedy of language' (that it is used to make social noises rather than to communicate) and the loss of humanity and individuality.

Banished Cavaliers, The. See ROVER, THE.

Bankrupt, The (*En Fallit*)

AT: *A Bankruptcy* A: Bjørnstjerne Bjørnson Pf: 1875, Stockholm Pb: 1874 Tr: 1914 G: Drama in 4 acts; Norwegian prose S: Tjaelde's home, Norway, 1870s C: 14m, 3f

Although the merchant Henning Tjaelde appears to be settled and wealthy and is preparing to invite guests to a lavish banquet, all is not well. He is actually on the verge of bankruptcy, a fact which he hides from his ailing wife and from his two grasping daughters, the haughty Valborg and her older sister Signe, who is engaged to a stupid army officer, Lieutenant Hamar. The banquet goes ahead, satirically parading the local worthies. His lawyer afterwards uncovers his ailing finances and persuades Tjaelde bravely to face up to the situation and to accept the shame of declaring himself bankrupt. Despite his wife's attempt to save him with her life savings, Tjaelde is stripped of his belongings, and angry creditors stone his house. Signe's fiancé abandons her, but Valborg undergoes a change of heart and supports her unhappy father. Three years later the family may be poorer, Tjaelde aged by worry, and his wife now confined to a wheelchair, but they are together and the bankruptcy is discharged. Tjaelde's secretary Sannaes, who has remained loyal throughout, is persuaded to stay on as the husband of Valborg.

Like Becque's *The *Crows*, *The Bankrupt* presents a damning picture of how bourgeois society treats its own when they fail. Even though the happy ending weakens the social critique, the huge success of Bjørnson's play across Europe was extremely influential in the development of social drama and encouraged Ibsen to turn from writing historical dramas to his better known domestic dramas like *A *Doll's House*.

Banya. See BATHHOUSE, THE.

Barber of Seville, The (*Le Barbier de Séville: ou La Précaution inutile*)

AT: *The Useless/Futile Precaution* A: Pierre-Augustin Caron de Beaumarchais Pf: 1775, Paris Pb: 1775 Tr: 1776 G: Com. in 4 acts; French prose S: Seville, Renaissance period C: 8m, 1f, extras

Figaro, former valet of Count Almaviva, finds that he can be of service to his sometime master. Almaviva has fallen in love with Rosine, a beautiful young heiress, who is kept locked up by her old guardian Dr Bartholo, who intends to marry her himself the next day. Now working as a barber, Figaro easily gains access to the household and introduces Almaviva disguised as a drunken soldier needing quarters. When this fails, Almaviva returns as a student of Rosine's music teacher, and they sing to each other of their love under Bartholo's nose. While the old man is away, Figaro uses the arrival of the notary who is to marry Bartholo to Rosine to marry Rosine to Almaviva. When Bartholo returns, he is furious at being cheated but is mollified when Almaviva happily forgoes the dowry.

As in Molière's **School for Wives*, the attempt by an old and possessive guardian to keep his ward in virtual imprisonment, is defeated by young love. The love is encouraged and helped to success by a roguish but loyal servant, who, in the tradition of Plautus and Terence, shows himself to be cleverer than his master. In addition to these comic models, Beaumarchais drew on the *commedia dell'arte* tradition (Bartholo derives from Pantalone, Figaro from Arlecchino). Despite all these obvious debts, Beaumarchais's skilful plotting and theatrical sense of fun make this comedy fresh and enjoyable in its own right. The operatic version by Rossini was premiered in 1816.

Barretts of Wimpole Street, The

A: Rudolph Besier **Pf:** 1930, London **Pb:** 1930
G: Drama in 5 acts **S:** Elizabeth Barrett's bed-sittingroom, Wimpole Street, London, 1845 **C:** 12m, 4f, 1 dog

Elizabeth Barrett is an invalid, her only regular companion her little dog Flush. Her youngest sister Henrietta warns her that their father is in a bad mood because of the impending visit of a female cousin who is getting married – something Barrett would not allow his daughters to do. Barrett forces Elizabeth to drink the foul-tasting porter that the doctor has prescribed. When the cousin arrives, Elizabeth confesses that she too has been asked for her hand by the handsome young poet Robert Browning. After his renewed declaration of love, she gets up and walks for the first time in years. Some months later, Elizabeth is so much better that she is planning a trip to Italy. However, her father cannot bear to let her go. When Browning begs her to marry him and leave for Italy together, Elizabeth pleads for time to spare her father unhappiness. When Barrett discovers that Henrietta has an admirer, he is so furious that he assaults her and makes her swear never to see him again. Elizabeth, recognizing that she must act decisively, secretly marries Browning and elopes with him. Barrett, who had tried to protect his children from the 'degradation and remorse' of love, is devastated. He orders Elizabeth's dog to be destroyed, but she has taken Flush with her.

The colossal popularity of Besier's one successful play, including an extensive tour to Allied troops in the Second World War, went far beyond the inherent merits of the piece. Based in part on the correspondence between Browning and Elizabeth, the play depicts a love story which succeeds against the will of her father. While this is normally the stuff of comedy, here the complex psychology of Barrett, tyrannical and possessive almost to the point of incest, creates a disturbing focus of interest.

Bartholomew Fair

A: Ben Jonson **Pf:** 1614, London **Pb:** 1631
G: Com. in 5 acts; prose **S:** Smithfield, London, early 17th c. **C:** 29m, 7f, extras

It is the day of Bartholomew Fair, and John Littlewit wants to go and have fun there but is afraid of his Puritan mother-in-law's disapproval. Conveniently, his pregnant wife is desperate for roast pork, and with the specious support of the arch-Puritan Zeal-of-the-Land Busy, the family is permitted to go to the fair. The fair is in full swing with booths and entertainment. Justice Adam Overdo is there in disguise, snooping around in the hope of uncovering crime, but only succeeds in being beaten as a pickpocket. The pickpocket's victim is a wealthy country lad Bartholomew Cokes, who soon loses his second purse and some of his clothing. Once again Overdo is accused and is taken to the stocks, where he suffers with Busy, who has caused a disturbance by preaching against the fair. Cokes's fiancée Grace Wellborn is so annoyed at Cokes's incompetence and extravagance that she welcomes the attentions of two other suitors Winwife and Quarlous, who devise means to ruin Cokes's impending marriage. When Quarlous discovers that Winwife has won Grace's favour, he accepts an offer from Littlewit's mother-in-law. Everybody gathers at a puppet show, which is denounced by Busy, and at which Overdo castigates everyone roundly until brought to a halt by the realization that a vomiting prostitute is his wife nursing a hangover. Nevertheless, he invites everyone back to his home for supper.

Ben Jonson's plays usually contain an ambiguous moral message: the wrongdoers must be punished, but their vitality and resourcefulness make them often more appealing than their less than innocent victims. This is the case here too, but with the essential difference that at the end everyone is forgiven by the badly used Overdo. With a plot that is almost incidental to the life, variety, and excitement of the annual summer fair, this could be accounted the first attempt at presenting a 'slice of life' on stage. Such is its continuing appeal that it provided the inspiration for Howard Brenton's *Epsom Downs* (1977).

Basic Training of Pavlo Hummel, The

A: David W. Rabe **Pf**: 1971, New York **Pb**: 1972 **G**: Drama in 2 acts **S**: Vietnam, Georgia and Pavlo's mother's home, USA, 1965–7 **C**: 18m, 4f, extras

The action of the play is given in flashback. As Pavlo Hummel, a US serviceman, dies from a grenade attack on a Vietnamese brothel, he relives his army career. Accompanied by his alter ego, a black sergeant named Ardell, Pavlo is trained in an army boot camp in Georgia, where he attempts to overcome his isolation from the other conscripts by telling tall stories about himself. He satisfactorily endures the rigours of basic training, and visits his dysfunctional family of mother and half-brother before being posted to Vietnam as a medic. After losing his virginity to a prostitute and having coped with the horror of observing an amputation, Pavlo volunteers for combat duty. Wounded three times, he is urged by Ardell to return home; instead, he is decorated with the Purple Heart and required to stay on in Vietnam. Back in the brothel, it emerges that the hand grenade was thrown not by the enemy, but by a fellow soldier in a fit of jealousy over Pavlo's prostitute Yen. Pavlo lying in his coffin is questioned by Ardell about his views on the war. He responds with the repeated word: 'Shit!', until Ardell finally closes the lid on him.

Written in the authentic language of soldiers, this play was the most successful of Rabe's *Vietnam* Trilogy, which also included *Sticks and Bones* (1969) and *The Orphan* (1973). Rabe had himself served in Vietnam and ended up disillusioned not only with the conflict but also with the lack of public understanding at home in the USA. The play was successfully revived on Broadway in 1977, with Al Pacino in the title role.

Bathhouse, The (*Banya*)

A: Vladimir Mayakovsky **Pf**: 1930, Leningrad **Pb**: 1930 **Tr**: 1963 **G**: Drama in 6 acts; Russian prose **S**: Soviet Russia, 1920s **C**: 16m, 3f, extras

A crazy inventor Chudakov has invented a time machine. He tries it out, causing a minor explosion, and receiving a letter from 1980, which announces the arrival of a figure from the future the following day. Chudakov and his friend go to a government office to announce the success of their invention. They push past petitioners with their petty complaints, only to be told that government plans will not at present accommodate their discovery, especially as this department is run by a bureaucrat Pobedonosikov, who is stupid, incompetent, and corrupt. The Director interrupts the play, and asks Pobedonosikov how it might be improved. Pobedonosikov is unimpressed with the portrayal of the official named Pobedonosikov in the previous scene, and suggests a crude agitprop performance, an allegory of the death of Capital and the victory of the Proletariat. As promised, the figure from the future arrives, the Phosphorescent Woman. She concludes that the successes of the Soviet Union are due to the hard work of the ordinary people and not to the interference of bureaucrats. The play ends with Pobedonosikov's plaintive appeal to the author: 'Do you mean that communism does not need me and the likes of me?'

While in *The *Bedbug* Mayakovsky has the obnoxious Prisypkin projected into a utopian future to reveal the inadequacies of the present, in *The Bathhouse* he brings a figure from the future to satirize bureaucracy and art in the new Soviet Russia. Indeed, given his scathing attack on officialdom, it is surprising that in 1935 Stalin declared him one of the great writers of the Revolution. Perhaps it was because Mayakovsky had saved further embarrassment by blowing out his brains in 1930. After the Leningrad premiere, the play was performed in Meyerhold's theatre in Moscow, though not directed by Meyerhold himself, where it flopped.

Bâtisseurs d'empire, Les. See EMPIRE BUILDERS, THE.

Battle of Angels. See ORPHEUS DESCENDING.

Battles of Coxinga, The (*Kokusenya Kassen*)

A: Chikamatsu Monzaemon Pf: 1715, Osaka Tr: 1961 G: Hist. drama for puppets in 5 acts (12 scenes); later kabuki play in 4 scenes; Japanese verse S: China and Japan, 17th c. C: 16m, 4f, extras

Watōnai (the Japanese name for the historical figure of Tei Seikō) is a young warrior who accompanies his Chinese father Tei Shiryū and his Japanese mother to China, in order to fight against the Tartar invaders from Manchuria and restore the Ming Dynasty. Tei Shiryū seeks help from his son-in-law Kanki, a Chinese general, who has however pledged loyalty to the new Tartar rulers and cannot break his oath for the sake of his wife's relatives. His wife nobly commits suicide in order to allow Kanki to act freely and in the interest of his nation. Kanki honours Watōnai with the name 'Kokusenya' (Coxinga), accorded to those who offer outstanding service to the Emperor. Watōnai with his father and Kanki fight a great battle and succeed in repelling the Tartar usurpers.

Originally written as a puppet play, *The Battles of Coxinga*, one of the popular historical dramas (*jidaimono*), proved the most popular of Chikamatsu's works and is generally accounted one of his best. When it was shortened and adapted for performance as a kabuki play, it provided a great opportunity for the larger-than-life style of acting (*aragato*) so beloved by kabuki audiences. The play offered patriotic fervour, noble self-sacrifice, and exotic Chinese locations, and ended with a spectacular battle scene. While Chikamatsu's domestic dramas now tend to be more accessible and popular, *The Battles of Coxinga* continues to be revived.

Beauty Queen of Leenane, The

A: Martin McDonagh Pf: 1996, Galway Pb: 1996 G: Trag. in 9 scenes S: Living room/kitchen of rural cottage, west of Ireland, and bedsit in England, 1990s C: 2m, 2f

Maureen Folan, a spinster in her forties, reluctantly cares for her chattering mother Mag, a widow in her seventies. At a neighbour's leaving party Maureen dances with Pato Dooley. Calling her 'the beauty queen of Leenane', Pato stays the night with her. Mag is horrified, especially when Maureen talks shamelessly of her night of passion (in fact, she has remained a virgin). Mag tries to drive Pato away by revealing Maureen had spent a month in a mental institution. Pato returns to England but writes to Maureen, asking her to come with him to America, where his uncle has offered him work. Ray, Pato's brother, is under strict instructions to hand the letter personally to Maureen, but he entrusts it to Mag, who reads it and burns it. On the night of Pato's leaving party before he goes – alone – to Boston, Maureen scalds Mag with boiling oil, and Mag blurts out the truth about the letter. Maureen dashes off to find Pato, and catches him at the station just in time. He says he will wait for her in Boston until she has solved the problem of her mother. Maureen strikes Mag dead with a poker, and persuades the coroner that Mag tripped on a stile. Ray tells Maureen that Pato was disappointed not to see her before he left (she had only imagined the leave-taking at the station), and is now engaged to another woman. Maureen passes on the message: 'The beauty queen of Leenane says goodbye,' and leaves the house.

This play was a brilliant debut for English-born McDonagh, a modern-day version of Synge, combining a remarkable ear for Galway speech, a masterful blending of comedy with violence, and an awareness of the alienation of the rural Irish, discontented with the narrowness of their home communities and their traditional obligations to parents, and mocked strangers in the countries to which they emigrate.

Beaux' Stratagem, The

A: George Farquhar **Pf**: 1707, London **Pb**: 1707 **G**: Com. in 5 acts **S**: An inn and Lady Bountiful's home, Lichfield, early 18th c. **C**: 11m, 5f, extras

Aimwell and Archer are gentlemen who have fallen on hard times and so decide to leave London and seek their fortunes in the country, travelling as a lord and his servant. They arrive at the inn of Boniface, who assumes that they are thieves and so plans to rob them. The two friends soon seek out a local heiress Dorinda, daughter to the munificent Lady Bountiful and sister-in-law to the frustrated Mrs Sullen. By pretending to fall ill, Aimwell gains access to the charitable Lady Bountiful and so meets Dorinda, while Archer woos Mrs Sullen. When thieves break into Lady Bountiful's house, Aimwell and Archer are on hand to apprehend them and so become heroes. Overcome by Dorinda's charms, Aimwell confesses his deception. She has discovered, however, that Aimwell's brother has just died and that he is indeed the Lord he pretends to be. Mrs Sullen and her boorish husband agree that they can no longer bear to live together and are granted an impromptu divorce, so that Archer is free to marry her.

As in *The *Recruiting Officer*, the setting is outside London and Farquhar again contrasts country virtues with urban corruption: the one society lady, Mrs Sullen, seems spoilt and affected, Dorinda is resourceful and dignified, and the trickery of Aimwell is swept aside by honourable impulse: 'O Archer, my Honesty, I fear, has ruin'd me.' The elderly Lady Bountiful, like the good-natured Justice Balance in *The Recruiting Officer*, is no longer the difficult, cantankerous representative of the older generation, but is an idealized figure, anticipating the sentimental drama later in the century. At a time when divorce required a special Act of Parliament, Farquhar's solution to the action is little short of revolutionary: divorce by mutual consent. Sadly, impoverished and ill with tuberculosis, Farquhar died shortly after the first performance of *The Beaux' Stratagem*.

Becket (*Becket, ou l'Honneur de Dieu*)

AT: *The Hono(u)r of God* A: Jean Anouilh **Pf**: 1959, Paris **Pb**: 1959 **Tr**: 1961 **G**: Trag. in 4 acts; French prose **S**: England and France, mid-12th c. **C**: 17m, 3f, extras

In Canterbury Cathedral, where Thomas Becket was martyred, Henry II is being scourged by four monks as a penance for the murder. In a flashback we see Henry appointing Becket as chancellor. They go hunting together, and Henry hands over a poor Saxon girl to Becket, calling in the debt by taking Becket's mistress, who stabs herself in his bed. Becket, concerned about his honour, ponders why he as a Saxon is serving a Norman king. In France, Henry decides to appoint Thomas archbishop, even though Thomas states that he will now owe his allegiance to God and that it will be the end of their friendship. Becket resigns the chancellorship and dedicates himself to the Church. Taking refuge in the French court after being tried on trumped-up charges, Becket fears that the Pope will betray him. The French King arranges for Henry and Becket to meet. Becket declares that he now serves only 'the honour of God', and Henry leaves sadly. When Becket returns to England, Henry demands that his barons rid him of this priest. The barons strike Becket down and are then transformed into the monks scourging Henry. Becket and Henry are acclaimed by the crowds, as Henry hypocritically sends out his barons to hunt down Becket's killers.

Although some of the material is similar to that of Eliot's **Murder in the Cathedral*, there are considerable differences. While Eliot focuses on the last days of Becket, Anouilh's play covers several decades; Eliot's Thomas is a holy figure dedicated to martyrdom; Anouilh's Thomas is seen growing from a sexy, worldly youth to become a committed priest. Above all, Anouilh explores the almost homoerotic relationship between Henry and Becket, and Henry's sense of loss when he loses Becket to God.

Bedbug, The (*Klop*)

A: Vladimir Mayakovsky **Pf:** 1929, Moscow **Pb:** 1929 **Tr:** 1960 **G:** Com. in 9 scenes; Russian prose **S:** Russia, 1929 and 1979 **C:** 12m, 3f, many extras

Ivan Prisypkin (= 'fried fish') is a worker with social aspirations. Having worked for the Revolution as a trade unionist, he now seeks to improve his status under the tutelage of a petit bourgeois, Oleg Barn. He rejects his working-class fiancée, driving her to attempt suicide, in order to marry a manicurist. At the wedding, Ivan, who has changed his name to Skripkin (= 'violin'), becomes involved in a brawl. A stove is overturned and the hall burns down. Undiscovered, Prisypkin is frozen solid in the firemen's water. He is thawed out 50 years later by the now worldwide Soviet authorities. A relic of an authentic proletarian, he, together with a bedbug that has survived with him, is viewed with curiosity, and then begins to disrupt normal life by reintroducing bad habits of the past, smoking, drinking, dancing, and love, which his former girlfriend now regards as inappropriate in the new order. The stinking Prisypkin, with his infectious bedbug, is finally caged in the zoo, from where he appeals to the audience to show him mercy.

With echoes of Molière's *The *Would-Be Gentleman*, *The Bedbug* can be seen as both a satire on the increasingly totalitarian restrictions of Soviet society (which got the play banned for some years) and an attack on the new breed of post-revolutionary proletarian who sought to become more bourgeois than the bourgeois. This ambiguity is part of the play's strength. The premiere was directed by Meyerhold with music by Shostakovich for a firemen's band.

Before Dawn (*Vor Sonnenaufgang*)

AT: *Before Daybreak; Before Sunrise* **A:** Gerhart Hauptmann **Pf:** 1889, Berlin **Pb:** 1889 **Tr:** 1909 **G:** Drama in 5 acts; German prose **S:** A village in Silesia, 1880s **C:** 10m, 9f

A young Socialist, Alfred Loth, comes to a mining district in Silesia to study the condition of the miners. He visits his old friend Hoffmann, a now unscrupulous engineer in charge of the mines. Hoffmann has married Martha, the daughter of Krause, a peasant grown rich from the coal on his land. Loth falls in love with her sister Helene, the only family member untainted by their suddenly acquired wealth. Helene reciprocates his love, seeing him as her only chance of escaping from her miserable existence. Old Krause is an alcoholic, and it turns out that Martha is an alcoholic too. Her first child died at the age of 3, and her next baby is stillborn, while her cousin, hearing her screams, jeers: 'Are you slaughtering a pig in there?' Hoffmann, fearing that Loth will stir up the underpaid miners, urges him to leave. Loth resists until the family doctor warns him that no offspring of Krause would be free from inherited degeneration and alcoholism. Believing that physical and mental health are essential 'before the dawn' of a new life, Loth leaves secretly. The desperate Helene commits suicide with a hunting knife.

This remarkable first play for a then unknown 27-year-old writer launched Hauptmann on a wave of controversy to become the leading figure of German naturalism. *Before Dawn* is innovative in its unflinching depiction of degraded lives, and also offers a new vision of the dramatic protagonist. In the past young idealists fail because of their unyielding idealism; here the unbending (and dangerously proto-Nazi) idealism of Loth is treated as priggish but commendable. He does not fail; the world fails him.

Beggar, The (*Der Bettler*)

A: Reinhard Johannes Sorge **Pf:** 1917, Berlin **Pb:** 1912 **Tr:** 1963 **G:** Drama in 5 acts; German prose **S:** A café, the Poet's home, and other locations, Berlin, 1900s **C:** 10m, 3f, extras

Rejecting conventional theatre, the Poet tells his friend that he seeks to dramatize his vision of 'glorious sublimity'. In a café, frequented by Newspaper-Readers, Critics, Prostitutes, and Airmen, the Poet refuses to compromise his art for the sake of his Patron. He finds himself quite alone, apart from a Young Girl, who, troubled by concern for her illegitimate child, follows him. At his home the Poet (now the Son) confronts his father, a mad engineer who is drawing futuristic plans for a technological utopia. When his pen runs out of ink, he smashes open the head of a small bird and dips the nib in its blood. The Poet, at his father's wish, poisons the drink with which he toasts the future, and both Father and Mother die. After working briefly as a journalist, the Poet once again refuses to alter his play to get it staged. The Girl becomes pregnant with the Poet's child, and gives up her illegitimate child. Poet and Girl embrace in expectation of the renewal of life, standing under a starry sky, as a hymn to the future is heard.

The Beggar, subtitled 'A Dramatic Mission', was the first truly Expressionist play to be published, with its universalized unnamed figures, its rejection of realism in setting, characterization, and dialogue, its destruction of the older generation, and its utopian vision. It was also the first Expressionist play to be staged in Berlin by Reinhardt. While virtually unplayable today, some scenes are memorable: the George Grosz-like café scene with its use of directional spotlights, or the portrayal of the mad scientist Father with his futuristic plans.

Beggar's Opera, The

A: John Gay **Pf:** 1728, London **Pb:** 1728
G: Ballad opera in 3 acts and an introduction; prose and songs S: London, early 18th c.
C: 14m, 12f, extras

The Beggar tells the Player that his opera is not 'unnatural, like those in vogue'. Peachum, who is both police spy and receiver of stolen goods, is dismayed to discover that his daughter Polly has married the notorious highwayman Macheath. He plans to deliver Macheath into the hands of the police, so that he will be executed, leaving Polly a rich widow. Polly warns Macheath, and they bid each other a fond farewell. Taking leave of his gang, Macheath is betrayed by whores and removed to Newgate Prison. Here he persuades the jailer's daughter Lucy Lockit, whom he has already made pregnant, that he will marry her if she helps him to escape. Peachum and the jailer Lockit join forces to recapture Macheath and succeed when he is tempted into a brothel. Facing execution, Macheath has to endure even worse: the anger and reproaches not only of Polly and Lucy but of another four 'wives', each nursing a baby. For Macheath death will be a welcome release, but the Player persuades the Beggar to provide a happy ending, and Macheath is reprieved.

Reputedly inspired by Swift's suggestion that Gay should write a 'Newgate pastoral, among the whores and thieves there', *The Beggar's Opera* proved a huge success both then and since. Accepted by John Rich to be performed at Covent Garden, it famously made 'Gay rich and Rich gay'. Its less successful sequel, *Polly*, was banned from performance but was read widely on its publication in 1929. The satire of Walpole's government (there is a clear reference to the First Minister's philandering in the characterization of Macheath) and of the contemporary fashion for 'unnatural' Italian opera (where every line was sung) may now be lost on a modern audience. However, the wider political observation, that the thieves and whores of Newgate 'have their vices in a degree as well as the rich', is still relevant. It was this insight, understood by the Marxist Brecht that crime and big business operate in concert, that led to his rewriting it as *The *Threepenny Opera*.

Belle Sauvage, La. See INDIAN PRINCESS, THE.

Belles-Sœurs, Les. See SISTERS-IN-LAW, THE.

Belle's Stratagem, The

A: Hannah Cowley **Pf:** 1780, London **Pb:** 1782
G: Com. in 5 acts; prose S: London, 1780
C: 15m, 6f, extras

Mr Hardy has arranged for his daughter Letitia to marry Doricourt, newly returned from the Continent. At their first meeting since childhood, Letitia is strongly attracted to Doricourt, but he is indifferent to her. She therefore plans a stratagem to win his love: she will play at being an ignorant country girl, while enchanting him at a masked ball with her wit and charm. Doricourt falls in love with the belle at the masquerade and so feigns madness to delay the dreaded wedding. Reluctantly, however, he finally agrees to marriage, partly from a sense of duty, partly because he is told that the woman at the ball is a kept mistress. After the wedding, Letitia visits him wearing her mask and reveals herself as his wife. In a sub-plot, Sir George Touchwood wants to preserve his naive wife from the corruption of London fashion. When their happiness is threatened by the interference of socialites, they agree to compromise by enjoying the delights of London – as a couple.

Borrowing the notion of feigning naivety from **She Stoops to Conquer*, Hannah Cowley otherwise creates an original and sparkling comedy in this, her best play. It is significant that Cowley, a neglected woman playwright, shows a woman who seeks love and not just a secure future, and who cynically recognizes that men are too easily swayed by external considerations in their choice of partner. Letitia Hardy was such a rewarding role that it was still being played by Ellen Terry 100 years later.

Bells, The

A: Leopold Lewis **Pf:** 1871, London **Pb:** 1871 **G:** Melodrama in 3 acts **S:** A village inn in Alsace, 24 and 26 Dec. 1833 **C:** 11m, 3f, extras

Mathias is the respected and prosperous burgomaster and owner of a village inn in Alsace. His daughter Annette is engaged to Christian, the honest but poor quartermaster of the gendarmes. As snow falls heavily on Christmas Eve, those drinking in the inn reminisce about a Polish Jew who was robbed and murdered 15 years previously in a snowstorm. Mathias is repeatedly haunted by the sound of the bells on the Jewish merchant's sledge, and when he has a vision of the murder victim, he collapses in terror. Two days later, he is recovered enough to urge Annette and Christian to marry that very day, since he hopes that by making him his son-in-law, Christian will never expose Mathias's crime. The wedding takes place, and Mathias leaves the revellers to sleep alone. He has a terrible dream, in which a Mesmerist forces him to confess the murder and he is condemned to be hanged. The following morning he staggers forward, clutching his throat, and falls dead.

Adapted from a French novel, *The Bells* is one of those plays important not for any literary merit but for its theatrical popularity. Although most people wrongly associate it with Quasimodo, the phrase 'The bells! The bells!' became immortalized through Henry Irving's highly charged performance, which he repeated over 800 times in the 1870s. In terms of the development of 19th-century melodrama, *The Bells* is innovative in that real sympathy is developed for the murderer despite the horror of his deed. The sophisticated devices of the Victorian stage are spectacularly exploited here to provide the flashback vision in the snowstorm and the dream of the court of law.

Bent

A: Martin Sherman **Pf:** 1979, London **Pb:** 1979 **G:** Drama in 2 acts **S:** Berlin, Cologne, a nearby forest, and Dachau concentration camp, 1934–7 **C:** 14m

Max and Rudy, two homosexuals in their thirties, live together in an apartment in Berlin in the early years of the Third Reich. Rudy is a dancer in a nightclub, where Max got drunk the previous evening and brought Wolf, a storm trooper, back to bed with him. This was also the night on which Ernst Röhm, protector of homosexuals, was arrested on Hitler's orders. Two Gestapo men come to the apartment and murder Wolf, while Max and Rudy escape. Greta, a transvestite friend, gives them money to get away. Two years later, they are hiding in the forest, while Max tries to get papers and tickets to flee to Holland. They are arrested and taken on a prison transport, where Max is forced to beat Rudy to death and to have sex with a dead girl to prove that he is not 'queer' but a Jew (a category that enjoys more privileges than homosexuals). In Dachau concentration camp, Max is helped by a fellow homosexual prisoner Horst. While moving rocks, they are able to converse and even fantasize about having sex together. Max helps Horst with medicine which he gets by offering sexual favours to the guards. Eventually, Horst is shot, and Max puts on Horst's jacket with its pink triangle, finally acknowledging that he is gay. He then deliberately executes himself on the perimeter fence.

Unlike many of his American contemporaries, Sherman dealt with socio-political issues in historical rather than in metaphorical terms. The influence of *Bent* was so great that in the 1980s gay activists adopted the pink triangle as an emblem.

Bergpredigt, Die. See FEAR AND MISERY OF THE THIRD REICH.

Best Garrotting Ever Done, The. See MAYOR OF ZALAMEA, THE.

Besuch der alten Dame, Der. See VISIT, THE.

Betrayal

A: Harold Pinter **Pf:** 1978, London **Pb:** 1978
G: Drama in 9 scenes **S:** London and a hotel in Venice, 1968–77 **C:** 3m, 1f

Jerry and Emma, who were once lovers but have not met for a couple of years, have a drink in a pub to catch up on each other's lives. Jerry is a literary agent married to Judith, a doctor. Emma runs an art gallery and is married to Robert, a publisher. However, she is leaving Robert after finding out that he had been having affairs with women for years. She has also confessed to Robert about her long-standing affair with Jerry. Earlier the same year, Robert tells Jerry that he thinks Emma is having an affair with an author that Jerry represents and Robert publishes. Two years earlier, Jerry and Emma agree that they must end their affair. A year previously, while Emma is putting a child to bed, Robert and Jerry converse amicably. Yet another year earlier, in 1973, on holiday in Venice Robert finds a letter for Emma and recognizes Jerry's writing. She confesses that she and Jerry are lovers. Unperturbed, Robert admits that he has always liked Jerry rather more than Emma. Earlier still, Jerry tells Emma that he is worried that his wife suspects him of having an affair. Later in 1973, Jerry and Robert meet over lunch. Back in 1971, it is near the start of the affair. Jerry says that his wife has an admirer, while Emma says that she is expecting Robert's baby. In 1968, Robert and Emma are giving a party. Jerry tells Emma that she is irresistibly beautiful and reminds Robert that he is his oldest friend.

Based on his affair with Joan Bakewell, Pinter here expresses his discomfiture on learning that his best friend knew for years that he had been sleeping with his wife. Playing the scenes in reverse order of time is therefore not just an intriguing dramatic device; it allows the audience to share the author's ignorance of his 'betrayal'.

Bettler, Der. See BEGGAR, THE.

Between Two Worlds. See DYBBUK, THE.

Biedermann and the Firebugs. See FIRE RAISERS, THE.

Biedermann und die Brandstifter. See FIRE RAISERS, THE.

Bill of Divorcement, A

A: Clemence Dane **Pf:** 1921, London **Pb:** 1921
G: Drama in 3 acts **S:** Margaret's home in the country, Christmas Day 1933 **C:** 5m, 4f

Margaret Fairfield married her husband Hilary during the First World War. Apparently as a result of shell shock, he was invalided and declared incurably insane. She now lives with her daughter Sydney and a pious maiden aunt Hester. She has at last divorced Hilary so that she is free to marry Gray Meredith, despite Hester's disapproval. Sydney is hoping to marry Kit, the son of the local clergyman. However, when his father learns that Margaret's husband is still alive, he not only refuses to marry her and Gray in his church but also withholds his consent to Kit's engagement to Sydney. Suddenly Hilary, escaped from his asylum, arrives and expects to be taken back. The family doctor is called and persuades Hilary that he must grant Margaret her freedom. However, he is so broken that

Margaret relents, prepared to sacrifice her own happiness. When Sydney learns that insanity runs in the family, she resolves that she can never marry and have children and turns Kit away. She convinces her mother to leave with Gray, promising to devote her life to caring for her father.

This play represents Dane's contribution to the debate about changes to the law of divorce, which would allow divorce from criminals, alcoholics, and the incurably insane. Set in the future after the new laws are in force, the play goes far beyond a mere thesis play to explore emotional dilemmas surrounding this theme. Mother and daughter are especially well drawn by this leading woman playwright, and the ending is both convincing and inspiring.

Billy Bishop Goes to War

A: John Gray with Eric Peterson **Pf:** 1978, Vancouver **Pb:** 1981 **G:** Drama in 2 acts; prose with songs **S:** Canada, England, and France, 1914–18; Canada, 1939 **C:** 2m, playing 17m, 2f

Billy Bishop tells the story of his involvement in the First World War. In 1914 he proves an unpromising recruit at the Royal Military College, Kingston, Ontario. In 1915 he is transferred to an army camp in England, volunteers for the Royal Flying Corps, and is sent as an observer to France. Helped by an influential lady aristocrat, Bishop is made a pilot, and returns to France in 1916. Eventually, despite his constant clumsiness, he becomes a flying ace, shooting down several German aircraft. Hailed as a war hero, he goes to Buckingham Palace to be decorated. In a flashback he re-enacts a daring raid on a German aerodrome. Finally, Bishop gives a rousing recruiting speech to young Canadians to go to war in 1939.

Based on the true story of a Canadian war ace, this play traces the career of an insignificant individual, whose sheer guts transform him into a daring war hero. All parts except the narrator/pianist are intended to be played by one actor. Despite the imprimatur of Mike Nichols, the play failed on Broadway, which was quite unsuited to the small-scale intimate revue format of the piece, with its gently ironical view of war, ending with the disheartening thought that in 1939 young men would again be sent to their deaths the other side of the world.

Bingo

A: Edward Bond **Pf:** 1973, Exeter **Pb:** 1974 **G:** Drama in 2 acts **S:** Garden and bedroom of Shakespeare's home; inn and countryside nearby, Warwickshire, 1615–16 **C:** 7m, 5f

The 51-year-old Shakespeare, living with his invalid wife and his daughter Judith, is visited in his garden by William Combe, a wealthy landowner. Combe is planning to enclose common land in the parish and to introduce sheep-farming, even though this will drive several families to destitution. Fearing local opposition, he guarantees the return on Shakespeare's land, provided the famous poet does not oppose the enclosures. Combe deals harshly with a young itinerant beggar-woman, ordering her to be whipped. Six months later, although Shakespeare would like to offer her shelter, the young woman is caught and hanged for burning down local farms. Shakespeare can no longer make sense of this violent world: 'You hear bears in the pit while my characters talk.' Shakespeare meets Ben Jonson in an inn and admits that he has nothing more to write about, while Jonson proudly recalls that he has experienced actual suffering, especially in prison. Young Puritan men organize opposition to Combe's enclosures. Shakespeare returns home drunk in the snow. He takes to his bed, but refuses to see his wife, succeeding in keeping her away by passing on his will, which pledges her 'her legal share. And the bed.' His old servant is killed in the confrontation between Combe's men and those opposing the enclosures. Shakespeare takes poison and dies.

Like Shaw before him, Bond is in awe of Shakespeare but determined to undermine the adulation of an uncritical public and the parasitic behaviour of academic critics. Here Shakespeare is shown to be a burnt-out writer, unwilling to be involved with the political upheavals around him, exemplifying what Bond calls 'the fascism of lazy men'. Although containing beautiful language, the play is devoid of onstage action, and is more contemplative than theatrical.

Birds (*Ornithes; Aves*)

A: Aristophanes Pf: 414 BC, Athens Tr: 1812 G: Greek com. in verse S: Cloudcuckooland, early 5th c. BC C: 21m, 1f, extras, chorus

Peisetaereus and Euelpides have had enough of warfare and corruption and go to seek advice from Tereus, who has turned into a hoopoe. After failing to find somewhere on earth where they can live in peace, the proposal is made that the chorus of Birds should build a new state in the skies, called Cloudcuckooland. The two protagonists grow wings, and the new city is built. A large number of different characters now arrive, some wishing to join the new state, others with a complaint, like Iris, who expresses the gods' annoyance that earthly sacrifices are no longer getting through to them. Prometheus comes to reveal that the gods are starving, so the birds can drive a hard bargain and insist on restoration of their ancient rights. Poseidon and Heracles appear as ambassadors of the gods and are eventually persuaded not only to give power back to the birds but also to hand over Basileia (Sovereignty) for Peisetaereus to marry.

Written after the fragile Peace of Nicias had failed and at a time when the Athenians were embarked on an ill-fated naval expedition against Sicily, *Birds*, despite its celebratory nature, is a bitter comment by Aristophanes. It seems that birds are more competent at creating an ideal state than humans and that birds can order the world more effectively than the gods. While the chorus of different birds was (and remains) a pretext for lavish costumes, it is remarkable that the 22 speaking parts in the play were probably performed by only three, possibly four, actors. Peter Brook used some elements of *Birds* in his *Conference of the Birds* (1976).

Birthday Party, The

A: Harold Pinter Pf: 1958, Cambridge, England Pb: 1959; rev. 1965 G: Drama in 3 acts S: Boarding house on the south coast of England, 1950s C: 4m, 2f

Petey Boles, a deckchair attendant, and his wife Meg run a seedy boarding house, which has only one lodger, Stanley Webber. Stanley, who cruelly teases Meg, claims that he was once a talented concert pianist whose career ended when he was 'carved up' by the nameless 'them'. Unexpectedly, two new guests arrive: Goldberg, a smooth-talking, expansive Jew, and his younger companion, a nervous Irishman, McCann. Stanley is disturbed by their arrival, and when Meg gives him a toy drum for his birthday to compensate for his lack of piano, he begins to bang it savagely. That evening, as they wait for the birthday party Meg has organized for Stanley, Goldberg and McCann begin to interrogate Stanley with increasingly absurd accusations. At the party, Goldberg flirts with a neighbour, Lulu. They then play Blind Man's Buff. Stanley is blindfolded, the lights go out, and when they come on again, he is discovered almost raping Lulu. The next morning, Petey is suspicious about the new lodgers, who tell him that they will look after Stanley, who has had a breakdown. Lulu is angry that Goldberg seduced her, but Meg, having seemingly forgotten everything, believes she was 'belle of the ball'. Goldberg and McCann take Stanley away with them.

The Birthday Party, Pinter's first full-length play, became after its unsuccessful premiere a classic of contemporary English theatre. It established the elements of 'Pinteresque' drama: dialogue and pauses which seemed to reproduce patterns of everyday speech but which were in fact carefully orchestrated rhetoric; comedy unexpectedly suffused with menace; above all, the unwillingness of people to communicate openly with one another. This led to the misplaced label of the 'absurd', but Pinter's characters are not incapable of communication; rather, they indulge in 'constant evasion'.

Bitter Oleander. See BLOOD WEDDING.

Black Comedy

A: Peter Shaffer Pf: 1965, Chichester Pb: 1967 G: Farce in 1 act S: London apartment, 1960s C: 5m, 3f

The play opens in complete darkness. We hear the young sculptor Brindsley Miller and his fiancée Carol Melkett preparing for the arrival of Carol's fiercely military father and, more importantly, of George Bamberger, a deaf millionaire who might be induced to buy one of Brindsley's artworks. In order to make a good impression on both his future father-in-law and Bamberger, Brindsley has helped himself to some of the precious antiques belonging to his absent neighbour Harold Gorringe. Suddenly the main fuse blows, and the stage is brilliantly lit. Miss Furnival from the flat upstairs is frightened by the dark and seeks shelter with Brindsley, while Carol manages to phone the Electricity Board. Colonel Melkett, Carol's father, arrives, exasperated by Brindsley's inefficiency. Harold returns unexpectedly, and the panic-stricken Brindsley tries to return his property. To make matters worse, Brindsley's former girlfriend, who is much sexier than Carol, arrives and causes havoc in the dark, eventually retiring to Brindsley's bed. A foreign-born electrician arrives to fix the fuse and is assumed to be Bamberger, and Brindsley shows off his sculptures, until the electrician reveals his identity and is put down the trapdoor to mend the fuse. When Bamberger arrives, he falls through the trapdoor and is half-electrocuted. At last the power is restored and the stage is plunged into darkness.

The idea behind *Black Comedy* is so effective and so simple that it is extraordinary that it has not been used before (the nearest approach is the mischief wrought by a supposedly invisible character like Ariel in *The *Tempest*). Reversing standard theatrical convention by here having a bright stage representing darkness, Shaffer exploits the traditional satisfaction of comedy that the audience sees more than the characters in the drama.

Black-Eyed Susan

AT: *All in the Downs* **A:** Douglas Jerrold **Pf:** 1829, London **Pb:** 1829 **G:** Melodrama in 3 acts; prose **S:** The town of Deal, Kent, and environs, and on board ship, 1820s **C:** 14m, 2f, extras

The beautiful young black-eyed Susan is married to William, who is away at sea. Her evil uncle Doggrass wants to evict her from her cottage, but the smuggler Hatchet pays her rent and pretends that William is drowned in the hope that he can win her for himself. When William returns unexpectedly, he exposes Hatchet's lies, and Hatchet is arrested for smuggling. Doggrass is accidentally drowned, and, since William soon hopes to be discharged from the navy, all bodes well for the young couple. However, William's Captain, Crosstree, gets drunk and tries to force himself on Susan. William, not recognizing the seducer, strikes him with his cutlass. He is court-martialled for wounding an officer and, despite the sympathy of the judges, is condemned to be hanged. Just in time, his discharge papers are produced and he is freed, since he was no longer a sailor when he defended his wife's honour.

Black-Eyed Susan was one of the first plays in English to enjoy a run of over 100 consecutive performances. It established a model for 19th-century melodrama, satisfying its audiences with its cliffhanger ending and its moral clarity: on the one hand the villainous Doggrass and Hatchet; on the other the noble William, the long-suffering Susan, and a number of minor characters, like the reformed bailiff Jacob Twig and the well-meaning if ineffectual Gnatbrain. Jerrold, himself a former midshipman, peppers the dialogue with nautical terms, offering the 1820s audience the additional frisson of feeling part of the glorious post-Trafalgar British navy.

Blacks, The (*Les Nègres*)

A: Jean Genet **Pf:** 1959, Paris **Pb:** 1958 **Tr:** 1960 **G:** Drama in 1 act; French prose **S:** Colonial Africa, 20th c. **C:** 8m, 5f

On an upper level, a court sits in judgement on those below. The members of the court, played by blacks wearing white masks, are: the Queen, her Valet, the Governor, the Judge, and the Missionary. On the lower level, four black couples in formal dress dance around a catafalque. Archibald, the master of ceremonies, steps forward and introduces the cast, who are, he explains, only actors. He reveals that the catafalque contains the body of a white woman they have murdered. Deodatus

Village, who loves the prostitute Stephanie Virtue, claims to have strangled the victim, a smelly old woman, who later turns out to be a young girl seduced by the blacks' superior virility. Diouf, the priest, is transformed into a woman, who gives birth to dolls mimicking the features of the members of the Court. A black is executed offstage, but, aware that their rule is at an end, the white Court members are murdered one by one, the Queen exclaiming as she dies: 'How well you hate!' They then stand to take their bow, before going off to hell. Archibald sums up: 'What lies behind this architecture of emptiness and words [?] We are what they want us to be.' Finally, there is a moment of tenderness between Village and Virtue.

This was at the time the most violently powerful dramatic treatment of racial tension. Significantly, Genet called it *Les Nègres*, deliberately using an offensive term to describe native Africans, and the main thrust of the drama is to show how they are stereotyped by whites and how the blacks can point up the absurdity of these stereotypes to make a mockery of racial prejudice.

Blasted

A: Sarah Kane **Pf:** 1995, London **Pb:** 1995; rev. 2000 **G:** Drama in 5 scenes **S:** Expensive hotel room in Leeds **C:** 2m, 1f

Ian Jones is an angry, racist, divorced 45-year-old journalist. He drinks heavily, has a diseased lung, carries a gun, and is clearly nervous. He has invited Cate, a former girlfriend of 21, prone to fainting fits, to spend the night with him in a hotel. She is reluctant to have sex with him, so he gets her to masturbate him. The following morning, Ian has obviously forced himself on Cate. Despite being angry with him, she fellates him while he talks of his work as an undercover government agent. Cate goes to the bathroom and makes her escape. A Soldier forces his way in, disarms Ian, urinates on the bed, and announces that it is 'Our town now'. The hotel is blasted by a mortar bomb. The soldier reveals that his girlfriend was raped and murdered in an atrocity. He rapes Ian, then sucks out his eyeballs and eats them. A while later, the Soldier has shot himself, and Cate returns holding a baby girl she has been given by a desperate woman in the town. Ian tries to shoot himself, but Cate has emptied the ammunition from the revolver. When she discovers that the baby has died, Ian comments: 'Lucky bastard'. Cate buries the baby under the floorboards and goes off to get food from the soldiers. Ian masturbates, tries to strangle himself, weeps, laughs, hugs the dead Soldier, digs out the baby's body, eats it, and lies down under the floor to die. Cate returns with food, bleeding from being raped, and feeds Ian in his hole.

This excessively bleak tale became notorious as the most extreme example of 'Inyerface' drama of the 1990s, all the more shocking because it was written by a woman (who, perhaps not altogether unpredictably, committed suicide four years later). In a world where there is 'No God. No Father Christmas. . . . No fucking nothing', any moment of tenderness, like that of Cate's burial of the baby, has a powerful redemptive force.

Blind Man and the Cripple, The. See MISTERO BUFFO.

Blithe Spirit

A: Noël Coward **Pf:** 1941, Manchester **Pb:** 1941 **G:** Farce in 3 acts **S:** Living room of the Condomines' house, Kent, *c.*1940 **C:** 2m, 5f

To gather material for his next novel, Charles Condomine has organized a seance at his home. The eccentric medium Madame Arcati arrives, and after fortifying herself with martinis and dinner, begins to summon her spirits. The sceptical Charles is astonished when his late wife Elvira, dead seven years, speaks to him, but she is not heard by anyone else present. After the seance, Elvira materializes to be seen only by Charles (and the audience) and begins to reproach him. When he tells her to shut up, his present wife Ruth imagines he is speaking to her and walks out in a huff. The following day Ruth is still angry, and the couple bicker over their marriage, especially Charles's drinking. When Elvira reappears, Ruth wonders whether Charles is going mad, but Charles proves Elvira's presence by inviting her to overturn furniture. When she smashes Ruth's favourite vase, Ruth fetches Madame Arcati to exorcize Elvira, but the spiritualist fails. A few days later it emerges that Elvira is trying to kill Charles to bring him over to her side. Ruth drives off again in search of Madame Arcati, unaware that Elvira has tampered with the brakes on Charles's car. A phone call informs Charles that Ruth has had a fatal accident. Faced now with two bickering, nagging spirit wives, Charles gets Madame Arcati finally to 'dematerialize' them both. He leaves on a long holiday, while the quarrelling wives start to smash up the house.

Although this is Coward's most popular and, some would say, best play, its misogyny now seems disturbing. Unfortunately, Elvira is anything but blithe, and her nagging and jealousy (together with Ruth's subsequent petty behaviour) turn Charles into a distressed male victim with whom the audience are invited to sympathize. The most impressive characterization is in fact that of Madame Arcati, memorably performed on screen by Margaret Rutherford.

Blood and Ice

AT: *Mary and the Monster* A: Liz Lochhead
Pf: 1981, Coventry Pb: 1985 G: Drama in 2 acts
S: Mary's nursery in London, and villa on Lake Geneva, 1816–24 C: 2m, 3f

Shelley and Mary have arrived with their infant son on Lake Geneva. Shelley's unconventional behaviour and their unmarried state have already shocked some English neighbours. Meanwhile, Mary's half-sister Claire Clairmont is adding to the scandal by having an adulterous affair with Lord Byron. Byron proposes a contest to see who can 'write the most terrifying tale'. Mary, as daughter of the freethinking Mary Wollstonecraft and William Godwin, is reluctant to waste her talent on a horror story. However, Byron is cynical about new ideas, especially in the light of the French Revolution. Three years later, Mary has lost her son but borne Shelley two more children and has published *Frankenstein*. Claire has been abandoned by Byron, who has taken their young daughter with him to be brought up by his latest mistress. Travelling to visit Byron in Venice, Mary's baby daughter falls ill and dies. Mary dismisses her maid Elise for becoming pregnant (possibly by Shelley?) – rights for women are seemingly confined to the wealthy. Mary is confronted by Byron, whose daughter has died. Mary's children have all died, although at her last childbirth Shelley saved her life by plunging her in a bath of ice to stop her bleeding. Shelley is drowned, Byron dies in Greece, but Mary pushes herself to continue writing.

This is the first play by Scottish poet Liz Lochhead, premiered as *Mary and the Monster* and twice revised. It juxtaposes the ideals of female emancipation, preached by Mary's mother, with the reality of the social situation of women and their biological vulnerability. Like Frankenstein's monster, the breaking of conventions has the potential for new life but can equally destroy.

Blood Knot, The

A: Athol Fugard Pf: 1961, Johannesburg
Pb: 1963; rev. 1987 G: Drama in 7 scenes
S: One-room shack in non-white settlement near Port Elizabeth, South Africa, *c.*1960 C: 2m

Zachariah works hard all day and comes home to be looked after by his fastidious brother Morris, who keeps house for him. Morris dreams of their setting up together on a small farm, but Zach is more immediately concerned that he has not had a woman since Morris moved in with him a year ago. Morris suggests a pen pal for Zach and composes a letter for his illiterate brother to send to Ethel, whose name they take from an advertisement in the newspaper. When a reply comes, Morris is horrified to discover that Ethel is white and is convinced that this 'game' will lead to disaster. When Ethel then writes that she will visit Zach, the brothers panic, fearing retribution from the whites. Zach suggests that Morris should meet her, because he is sufficiently light-skinned to pass for a white. Zach uses the money set aside for their farm to buy a smart suit for Morris to meet Ethel in. Morris tries on the clothes, and disconcerts Zach by beginning to behave like a white man. Morris is planning to leave, when a letter comes from Ethel saying that she is getting married. Relieved, the brothers play a game. Morris wears the suit, acts like a vicious white, and the brothers confront each other violently across the racial divide. Frightened by their own emotions, they remind each other that they are brothers, tied by a blood knot.

This was the play that established Fugard's reputation as the leading South African playwright, a reputation he exploited in 1963 to initiate a writers' boycott of South Africa. With gentle comedy, moving lyricism, and acute observation, he shows how apartheid reaches into the lives of ordinary people, inducing fear and viciousness.

Blood Relations

AT: *My Name Is Lisbeth* A: Sharon Pollock Pf: 1976, New Westminster, British Columbia Pb: 1981 G: Hist. drama in 2 acts S: Fall River, Massachusetts, 1902 and 1892 C: 3m, 4f

In 1892, 32-year-old Lizzie Borden was acquitted of murdering her father and stepmother with an axe. Ten years later, she is playing host to the Actress, who demands to know the truth about the murder. Lizzie responds by challenging the Actress to act her part in the events leading up to the death of her parents. Lizzie herself takes on the role of the Bordens' maid Bridget. The Actress experiences for herself what life as Lizzie was like under the tyrannical rule of her loveless father, stepmother, and the latter's evil brother. Prompted by 'Bridget', she considers the options of suicide or murder to escape from her living hell. As the Actress becomes more and more identified with her role, Lizzie/Bridget begins to understand that much of her own behaviour was prompted by her older sister Emma, who was also seeking release from her parents. At the end it is not clear whether Lizzie actually committed the murders. What is obvious is that she was capable of doing so and that she was subject to almost intolerable pressures.

Pollock, one of Canada's leading contemporary playwrights, bravely took on several controversial subjects (she also wrote a play about Jack the Ripper: *Saucy Jack* in 1993). Here she offers a feminist reading of the Lizzie Borden murders, immortalized in a nursery rhyme. Not only are the 19th-century social conditions which dictated the powerlessness of unmarried women seen as the source of Lizzie's violence; the contemporary audience are also implicated as they observe her role being created by the unnamed Actress, thus making Lizzie a figure shaped by the fantasy of the onlookers.

Blood Wedding (*Bodas de sangre*)

AT: *Bitter Oleander* A: Federico García Lorca Pf: 1933, Madrid Pb: 1933 Tr: 1939 G: Trag. in 3 acts; Spanish prose and verse S: Farmhouse in Andalusia, Spain, early 20th c. C: 8m, 11f, extras

A Mother, who has lost her husband and son in a bitter blood feud with the Félix family, is alarmed when she discovers that her other son is to marry a young woman who was once engaged to Leonardo Félix. Leonardo and the woman could not marry, because Leonardo was too poor; so he married his beloved's cousin. Mother and Groom visit the barren farm of the Bride's father and strike a deal over the marriage. Despite generous presents, the Bride is unhappy at the prospect of marriage to the Groom, and the hoofs of Leonardo's horse are heard outside. Some time later, it is the morning of the wedding. While the villagers sing gay songs, Leonardo visits the Bride and declares his undying love for her. Nevertheless, the wedding goes ahead, but the Bride becomes colder and colder towards the Groom and leaves the feast to rest. Hoofs are heard again: Leonardo has abducted the Bride and ridden off into the night with her. The Moon gives light to the lovers, and Death in the form of a Beggar-woman helps the Groom find them. The lovers embrace and go deeper into the woods. Screams are heard: Leonardo and the Groom have killed each other. Three women are left to mourn: the Mother, the Bride, and Leonardo's wife. The Mother demands that the Bride should die, but the Bride insists that she remained untouched. The three widows now look forward to a life of mourning.

García Lorca is accounted the major Spanish playwright of the 20th century, and *Blood Wedding* is his best-known play. Based on a true incident, Lorca's play could have become a trite sociological piece showing how peasants' cynical financial bargaining over marriage, by failing to regard powerful sexual impulses, could destroy lives. Openly acknowledging the influence of Synge's **Riders to the Sea*, Lorca goes beyond realistic debate to create a surreal poetic world, in which hoof-beats suggest Leonardo's passion, and the Moon and Death become active participants in the tragedy.

Bloomers, The. See UNDERPANTS, THE.

Blue-Apron Statesman, The. See POLITICAL TINKER, THE.

Blue Bird, The (*L'Oiseau bleu*)

A: Maurice Maeterlinck Pf: 1908, Moscow; 1911, Paris Pb: 1909 Tr: 1909 G: Fairy tale in 6 acts; French prose S: A woodcutter's cottage and various dream scenes, indeterminate period C: 38m, 48f, 30 children

Tyltyl and his sister Mytyl, woodcutter's children, are tucked into bed and begin to dream. An old fairy (Berylune) enters, seeking the Blue Bird to cure her sick daughter. She gives the children a magic diamond that will open their eyes to the fairy world. They see the souls of their dog and cat, of Milk, Fire, Water, Light, Bread, and Sugar, who accompany the children on their quest for the Blue Bird. From the Fairy's Palace the children enter the Land of Memory. Here they encounter the dead, including their grandparents, who have a blackbird that is blue. Taking it with them, its feathers disappointingly change to black. In the dark Night they capture 'blue birds of dreams', but these expire in the daylight. Escaping from an attack in the Forest, the children enter the Palace of Happiness (this episode was added later). Here they resist temptation and experience Joys, especially Maternal Love. Spending the night fearfully in a graveyard, the children are relieved at dawn to discover that it is a garden. In the Kingdom of the Future they encounter unborn children, including their own baby brother. The Blue Bird they find turns pink, and the children sadly take their leave of their companions. Waking the next day, the children are visited by their old neighbour, who resembles the Fairy. She asks Tyltyl for his pet dove. He discovers it is blue; the object of their quest has been in their home all the time. The neighbour's daughter is cured, but the Blue Bird flies away.

The wit and charm of *The Blue Bird* made it Maeterlinck's most popular piece, not least because of its allegorical message about the key to happiness being in preparedness to give (Tyltyl handing over his dove). Stanislavsky directed the premiere with great seriousness and lavish sets, and it has been made into films, a ballet, and a musical.

Blue Heart (Heart's Desire; Blue Kettle)

A: Caryl Churchill Pf: 1997, Bury St Edmunds Pb: 1997 G: 2 dramas, each in 1 act S: (1) Brian and Alice's kitchen; (2) Public places, Derek and Enid's flat, Vanes' house, geriatric ward, England, 1990s C: (1) 3m, 4f, extras; (2) 2m, 6f

(1) *Heart's Desire*. Brian and his wife Alice (about 60) are awaiting the return after many years of their 35-year-old daughter Susy from Australia. After a few moments of dialogue, the scene keeps 'rewinding' and beginning again, sometimes as an exact repetition, sometimes as a pared-down version, but usually progressing further into variant developments: they converse with Brian's sister Maisie; sometimes their alcoholic son (30) interrupts; another time a horde of children rush round the room. When the doorbell rings, two gunmen burst in and kill them all. Thereafter the doorbell heralds the arrival of: Susy herself; a young Australian woman; an official; a 10-foot-tall bird; nobody; Susy twice more. Finally, the play restarts and ends with the first line. (2) *Blue Kettle*. Derek (40), adopted as a baby, meets his real mother Mrs Plant (late fifties). He then meets his real mother Mrs Oliver (over 60). Talking to his partner Enid, it becomes clear that he is deceiving four different women into believing they gave him up for adoption. His next victim Mrs Vane (seventies) was married when her son was adopted. Mrs Oliver secretly

visits Derek at his home. Miss Clarence (80) was an Oxbridge don, when she had her son. Derek and Enid are invited to the Vanes' house, and Enid blurts out that Derek is not Mrs Vane's son, but she refuses to believe this. Derek visits his real mother in a geriatric ward. Enid is concerned that Derek is not making any money out of his confidence trick, and he suggests that they might blackmail his father, a journalist who made one or more of his 'mothers' pregnant. Mrs Plant and Mrs Oliver meet and realize that they are both supposedly Derek's biological mother. Derek tells a distraught Mrs Plant that he met her son in Indonesia, but that he died. Throughout the piece, the words 'blue' and 'kettle' are interspersed randomly in the dialogue, until in the final scene, both characters speak almost entirely in abbreviations ('bl', 'ket') and finally in letters (b, k, t, l).

Always playful, Churchill here comes close to reviving absurdist theatre. Both pieces deal with the return of a child to the parent, one genuine but superficial; the other false but moving. In *Heart's Desire* the tensions and trivial exchanges that characterize the common domestic experience of waiting for one's 'heart's desire' are reflected in constant repetition and break out into surreal events from frustration at the tedium. In *Blue Kettle* what could form the basis of a naturalistic piece is deconstructed by the insertion of 'blue' and 'kettle' in the dialogue. That characters' speeches still remain intelligible indicates the emptiness of communication, even in the acute emotional experience of encountering one's supposed son after some 40 years of separation.

Blue/Orange

A: Joe Penhall **Pf:** 2000, London **Pb:** 2000
G: Drama in 3 acts **S:** Consulting room of London psychiatric hospital, 1999 **C:** 3m

Christopher, an obstreperous black youth of 24, has been sectioned for 28 days for some unnamed delinquency and is now due for release. Dr Robert Smith, a senior consultant in his fifties, diagnoses Borderline Personality Disorder and wants him to be cared for in the community: 'maybe he's a *right* to be angry and paranoid and depressed and unstable'. The young Dr Bruce Flaherty, however, diagnoses Paranoid Schizophrenia, especially when Christopher thinks that oranges are blue and that he is the son of Idi Amin. That evening, Christopher tells Robert that he is now afraid to go home, because he is in fear of his life from police, skinheads, and people who know who his father is. Robert insists that he will be better off at home and that, if he stays in hospital, he will become institutionalized. Robert is particularly concerned that Bruce's diagnosis is 'ethnocentric' and does not take Christopher's racial background into account. The following morning, Bruce finds that he is being investigated for incompetence and a racist attitude (quoting Christopher, he had used the phrase 'uppity nigga'). Bruce pleads with Christopher and with Robert to withdraw the complaint, accuses Robert of exploiting Christopher's illness for his research, and loses his temper with Christopher. Christopher is sent home, Bruce attempts a reconciliation with Robert, but Robert sacks him.

Using skilfully observed dialogue, Penhall explores several themes: racial attitudes, mental illness, care in the community, and medical hierarchies. While the focus is principally on the question of colour (hence the title) and its relationship with a paranoia that may well be rooted in the real experiences of ethnic minorities, the play also subtly explores the changing personal relationships between the three men, the establishment of trust and its painful destruction.

Blue Room, The. See RONDE, LA.

Blues for Mister Charlie

A: James Baldwin **Pf:** 1964, New York **Pb:** 1964
G: Drama in 3 acts **S:** Small Southern town, early 1960s **C:** 15m, 6f, extras

The play opens with the racial killing of a black youth. The events that led up to the killing are presented as flashbacks in the subsequent trial. The victim is Richard Henry, the son of a black minister, Meridian Henry. Richard has recently returned to the South from New York, where he succumbed to drugs, and is now leading a non-violent civil rights movement (however, we see his father hiding Richard's gun under a Bible). Richard's militant attitude stirs up hatred between the 'Blacktown' and the 'Whitetown'. Lyle Britten, a white bigot who owns the local general store, is tried for Richard's murder. Richard's grandmother Mother Henry lies to protect Richard's reputation, and when Meridian speaks out for his son, he is branded a communist agitator. Only Parnell James, the liberal newspaper editor, is not caught up in the racial polarization in the community. He supports racial equality and has black friends. He also secretly loves Juanita, the beautiful black girl with whom Richard had intended to elope on the day of his murder. Caught between conflicting loyalties, James gives evidence that helps to acquit Richard's killer. At the end, the murder is re-enacted: Richard boasts of the sexual superiority of black men, as Britten indignantly fills him with bullets. Outraged at Britten's acquittal, the blacks prepare to march, and the whites get ready to prevent them.

Growing up in Harlem and aware of the humiliation to which African-Americans were subjected even in the 'liberal' North, Baldwin spoke out in his novels and plays about racial oppression. This play is based on the 1955 murder of Emmett Till in Mississippi. In cinematic scenes based on a fluid movement of time and place, Baldwin is at pains to show that Richard is himself flawed, and that stereotypes about racial superiority are not confined to the white community.

Bney Schney Olamot: Ha'Dibuk. See DYBBUK, THE.

Bodas de sangre. See BLOOD WEDDING.

Bödeln. See HANGMAN, THE.

Bodies in the Cellar. See ARSENIC AND OLD LACE.

Bohemian Lights (*Luces de bohemia*)

AT: *Lights of Bohemia* A: Ramón del Valle-Inclán Pf: 1963, Paris; 1971, Madrid Pb: 1920; rev. 1924 Tr: 1968 G: Tragicom. in 15 (originally 12) scenes; Spanish prose S: Various locations in Madrid, *c.*1917–20 C: 42m, 10f, extras

Max Estrella, a blind old writer, has been sacked by his newspaper, and has to resort to selling books to buy food for his wife and daughter. [Added in 1924 version: Max has an intellectual discussion with Don Latino, an unscrupulous publisher, in a bookshop.] Max holds court with down-and-outs in a tavern. Against a background of street riots, Max protests against the aestheticism of a group of modernist poets. He is arrested for disturbing the peace and responds wittily to the Inspector's questions. [1924 version: Max, by confronting the experiences of a fellow prisoner from Catalonia, recognizes how empty his own protests are.] The modernist poets protest at the newspaper office about Max's imprisonment. Max himself complains to the Minister of the Interior but is silenced by accepting money from the government. Disillusioned at being so easily bought, Max becomes sardonically self-deprecatory, first with his 'disciple' Rubén Darío, then with the prostitute Lunares. [1924 version: there is a confrontation between the army and workers, amongst them a woman holding a dead child.] Max believes that the only adequate response to the violence of the world about him is to represent it through the grotesque. Max dies, and the matter-of-fact talk of *Hamlet*-like gravediggers is contrasted with that of intellectual mourners. Don Latino has won with Max's lottery ticket, and will make money from an edition of his works. Max's desperate wife and daughter commit suicide. Mediocrity has triumphed.

Like Dürrenmatt over 30 years later, Valle-Inclán believed that the chaos of the 20th century must be depicted through the 'concave mirrors' of the grotesque; so he created his own genre of *esperpento*, 'an aesthetic criterion that distorts systematically'. *Bohemian Lights* with its wide theatrical range, anti-heroic protagonist, and effective blending of contemporary politics with personal tragedy, and comedy with suffering, made this the first major play of modern Spanish theatre.

Bonnes, Les. See MAIDS, THE.

Boris Godunov

AT: *The Drama of the Upheavals of the Muscovite State, of Tsar Boris, and of Grishka Otrepiev* A: Aleksandr Pushkin W: 1825 Pf: 1870, St Petersburg Pb: 1831 Tr: 1899 G: Trag. without scene divisions; Russian iambic pentameters and some prose S: Russia and Lithuania, 1598–1605 C: 23m, 5f, extras

Boris Godunov, friend of the late Tsar Ivan the Terrible and regent during the reign of his imbecile son Fyodor, has now, by ordering the murder of Dmitry, Ivan's youngest son and claimant to the throne, cleared his way to become tsar. Hoping to establish himself as a well-loved ruler hailed for bringing peace and prosperity to Russia, Tsar Godunov finds that he has to be as repressive as Ivan. A young monk Grigory (Grishka) Otrepiev, learning of Godunov's crime from an old monk, resolves to avenge Dmitry. He pretends to be Dmitry and, escaping to Lithuania, raises an army to march against Godunov. Eventually, after a number of setbacks Godunov is victorious. Plagued by his conscience, Godunov confesses his crime, collapses, and dies. Godunov's son Fyodor is named as his successor, but the 'false Dmitry' regroups his forces and succeeds in seizing power for himself. When the deaths of Fyodor together with his wife and daughter are announced, Grigory/Dmitry calls for public jubilation, but 'The people remain silent'.

Robert Frost said that poetry is what gets lost in translation, and this is apparently particularly true of *Boris Godunov*, the best play by Russia's greatest poet. Now best known to Western audiences in Mussorgsky's operatic version (1874), the play seems loosely structured and suffers from the lack of confrontation between its two protagonists. However, the quality of characterization, which has rightly been compared to Shakespeare, and the important role played by the common people, which caused the censor to ban its performance for almost half a century, make it a significant work.

Bouncers

A: John Godber W: 1977–84 Pf: Amateur: 1977, Edinburgh; professional: 1984, Hull Pb: 1987 G: Com. in 2 acts; prose and some 'rap' verse S: Disco in a provincial English town, 1980s C: 4m

Four bouncers of 'Mr Cinders' disco welcome the audience, then become female customers at the hairdresser's gossiping about clothes, then young men at the barber's talking about women. The lads go on a pub crawl, the girls sip their drinks in another pub. Making sexist and homophobic comments, the bouncers prepare for the night, and re-enact the time they had a fight with a drunken rugby team. Lucky Eric, 'the wise old owl of the bouncers', is concerned about the young girls who so easily give themselves to men at the disco: 'What else is there?' Girls come and dance, lads go to the toilets to urinate and vomit, the bouncers turn away people they do not like. The bored bouncers act out a pornographic film. The lads pick up girls with varying success. Eric is unhappy about the 'working class with no option left, exposing its weakness'. The lads get a taxi home, the bouncers clear up, and settle to watch a Michael Jackson video.

Bouncers stands chronologically between Berkoff's **East* and Cartwright's **Road* as a theatrical account of English working-class culture, focusing here on disco entertainment. Listening to working-class youths in the cinema shouting: 'Fast forward!', as they urged the film on to the next piece of action, Godber became aware that most theatre productions are tedious and intended for middle-class audiences. *Bouncers*, which depends 'as much on energy as it does on technique', is an impressively vigorous yet thoughtful piece of populist theatre. Godber has rewritten *Bouncers* many times (the Penguin version excludes the disco owner Marco, but names him in the cast list).

Bourgeois Gentilhomme, Le. See WOULD-BE GENTLEMAN, THE.

Bourgeois Gentleman, The. See WOULD-BE GENTLEMAN, THE.

Boys in the Band, The

A: Mart Crowley Pf: 1968, New York Pb: 1968 G: Com. in 2 acts S: New York apartment, 1960s C: 9m

Michael has invited five homosexual friends to a birthday party for Harold, an intelligent Jew of 32 with a liking for drugs. The guests are: Emory, a blatantly camp character; Hank and Larry, a homosexual couple, who came together after Hank left his wife and children; Donald, who, like Michael, is seeing a psychiatrist; and Bernard, a tall black. Harold's main present is a night with a handsome blond male prostitute, Cowboy. As everyone gets drunk, bitchy comments are made, the men addressing one another as 'she' and discussing gay icons like Judy Garland. Michael, who has stayed off alcohol for five weeks, now gets drunk and very abusive, especially towards the taciturn Cowboy. Matters are made worse by the unexpected arrival of Alan, a room-mate of Michael when they were at college together. Alan, who has quarrelled with his wife, has no idea that his friend – or any of the guests – are homosexuals, although he takes offence at the 'freakish' behaviour of Emory. As Alan begins to recognize the truth, Michael suggests that everyone should phone the person they most love, hoping that this will expose Alan's latent homosexuality. This fails, the party is ruined, and Michael's final words are: 'I don't understand any of it. I never did.'

Although of no great dramatic merit (Crowley wrote no other successful plays), *Boys in the Band* caused a stir on Off-Broadway, ensuring it 1,000 performances. Joe Cino (from 1960) and Charles Ludlam (from 1967) had staged gay plays in their clubs, but Crowley's play was the first opportunity for mainstream heterosexual audiences to witness overt homosexual interaction on stage, which unfortunately tended to reinforce a stereotype of frustrated bitchiness in the gay community.

Boy Who Would Not Grow Up, The. See PETER PAN.

Braggart Soldier, The (*Miles gloriosus*)

AT: *The Braggart Warrior; The Swaggering Soldier* A: Titus Maccius Plautus Pf: *c.*205 BC, Rome Tr: 1852 G: Latin com. in verse S: Before the home of Pyrgopolynices in Ephesus, 3rd c. BC C: 8m, 3f, extras

Pyrgopolynices is a boastful and lustful soldier who has abducted a young Athenian woman, Philocomasium, who is in love with a young gentleman called Pleusicles. By chance, Pleusicles' slave Palaestrio also finds himself in Pyrgopolynices' household, having been sold to him by pirates. Pleusicles is now living in a neighbouring house, and Palaestrio has contrived to break through the walls, so that the lovers can meet secretly. Unfortunately, another slave sees Philocomasium in the neighbouring house with Pleusicles; so she has to pretend that it was her twin sister he saw, requiring her to make sudden appearances via the secret passage. Palaestrio now persuades Pyrgopolynices that his neighbour's wife is in love with him, reinforcing the deceit by getting a courtesan to play the part. Losing interest in Philocomasium, Pyrgopolynices allows her to be taken away by a 'ship's captain' (in fact, Pleusicles in disguise) and pursues his affair with his supposed new conquest. On entering his neighbour's house, he is beaten for his adulterous behaviour and threatened with castration. Reduced to blubbering cowardice, he buys his way out of trouble and receives a contemptuous pardon.

Usually the character who blocks the lovers' path to happiness is a cantankerous older man, but here he is a vigorous and energetic younger figure, whose main vice is egotistical behaviour based on a claim to military prowess that is wholly undeserved. Based on a Greek original by an unknown playwright, *The Braggart Soldier* served as a model for a stock figure in European theatre, the bombastic soldier who is in fact a coward. He reappears in the figure of Thraso in Terence's *The *Eunuch*; Beolco's Ruzante; the Captain in *commedia dell'arte*, in Lodovico Dolce's *The Captain* (1545); in Udall's **Ralph Roister Doister*; in Shakespeare's Falstaff and Parolles; in Ben Jonson's Captain Bobadil (**Every Man in His Humour*); in Corneille's Matamore (*The *Theatrical Illusion*); and in Shaw's Sergius (**Arms and the Man*).

Brand

A: Henrik Ibsen **Pf:** 1866, Christiania; full version 1885, Stockholm **Pb:** 1866 **Tr:** 1906 **G:** Trag. in 5 acts; Norwegian rhymed verse **S:** Town on a Norwegian fjord, 1866 **C:** 11m, 4f, extras

Pastor Brand, uncompromisingly devoted to his beliefs and critical of his countrymen's tendency towards compromise, has come to the highlands of Norway. Meeting Einar, a friend from his youth, Brand's robust arguments and courage in crossing the fjord in a storm so impress Einar's fiancée Agnes that she goes with Brand. They live modestly, while Brand devotes himself to ministry in the little community. He demands that his mother give up all her wealth, and when she refuses, will not go to her when she is dying. He refuses to take his sickly son to a warmer climate, and when he dies, insists that Agnes give away all his clothes. She dies from grief. Now quite alone and still convinced of his rightness, Brand builds a new church but, dismayed by the congregation and their leaders, he throws away the key and challenges the populace to follow him into the mountains to found an ideal new community. They set off for the icy wastes but rush back to the town when news comes of a huge shoal of fish in the fjord. Resisting a last temptation by a dream figure of Agnes to accept compromise, he is led by the half-crazed gypsy child Gerd into an avalanche. As he dies, Brand hears the words: 'God is Love!'

Brand's fierce attacks on the complacency of his fellow Norwegians reflect much of Ibsen's thinking, especially after he was forced in 1864 into exile by his fellow countrymen. However, he also recognizes the dangers in the 'All or nothing' philosophy of Brand, which was based in part on an idealistic pastor whom Ibsen had known in his home town of Skien, and in part on the ideas of the Danish thinker Søren Kierkegaard, who, like Brand, rejected organized religion in favour of seeking truth within oneself.

Breaking the Silence

A: Stephen Poliakoff **Pf:** 1984, London **Pb:** 1984 **G:** Hist. drama in 2 acts **S:** A railway carriage, Russia, 1920–4 **C:** 5m, 2f

The once-rich Jewish family of the Pesiakoffs have, in the wake of the Bolshevik Revolution, had their mansion requisitioned by the army and are now obliged to live in a railway carriage on the outskirts of Moscow. The father Nikolai, appointed telephone examiner of the Northern Railway, is accompanied by his wife Eugenia, teenage son Sasha, and maidservant Polya. Nikolai's main interest is to explore ways of recording sound on to film, and he vainly insists that the new government should support his research. Nikolai goes off for an inspection, taking Sasha with him. A thousand miles up the line, Nikolai uses government money to buy scrap metal for his invention. That summer they are joined by the two women, who try to maintain pre-Revolution luxuries. Nikolai totally neglects his official duties, and Eugenia has to do his work for him, holding things together even during the civil war. Four years later, Eugenia is dressed like a peasant, and both she and Polya go out to work, while Sasha, now at school, is becoming critical of his father. Nikolai has at last succeeded in recording sound and requires only some lenses to make a talking film to prove it. On Lenin's death, the family are warned to leave the country at once, and Sasha smashes up the carriage, including the awaited lenses, in order to force his father to go. At the border, Nikolai is arrested, but is released when Eugenia pleads on his behalf. The family continues into exile.

Based on the experiences of Poliakoff's own family, *Breaking the Silence* carries a title with many meanings: Nikolai's invention, which will 'alter communications'; the revelation of the truth about the arbitrary exercise of power in post-Revolutionary Russia; and Eugenia's belated admission about her feelings for Nikolai.

Break of Noon (*Partage de midi*)

A: Paul Claudel **Pf:** 1948, Paris **Pb:** 1906; rev. 1948, 1949 **G:** Drama in 3 acts; unrhymed French verse **S:** Ship in the Indian ocean, a Hong Kong cemetery, and a temple in China, early 20th c. **C:** 3m, 1f

Travelling with her businessman husband by boat to China, the beautiful Ysé de Ciz encounters a Chinaman, Mesa, who is weakened by God's apparent deafness to his devotion. Bored by her husband De Ciz and her former lover Amalric, Ysé attempts to seduce Mesa. Landed in Hong Kong, Ysé's husband leaves on a business trip which leads to his death, and she and Mesa make passionate love in a cemetery. Finding no fulfilment with Mesa, even though she is bearing his child, she marries her former lover Amalric. Later, she and Amalric find themselves trapped in a Confucian temple during an uprising. They prepare to dynamite the building rather than be taken alive. Mesa comes through the enemy lines and in a long monologue to the silent Ysé declares his continuing love for her. Amalric knocks him out, steals his pass that will give them safe passage, and sets off with Ysé. She soon returns, however, to die in Mesa's arms.

Claudel, a devout Catholic, here explores, in a more subtle way than in his better known *The Tidings Brought to Mary* (1912), the search for reconciliation with the divine. In this hauntingly beautiful play, which Claudel rewrote for Jean-Louis Barrault's revival in 1948, Mesa (the name suggests 'half') becomes complete through his selfless devotion to love.

Breasts of Tiresias, The (*Les Mamelles de Tirésias*)

A: Guillaume Apollinaire **W:** 1903–17 **Pf:** 1917, Paris **Pb:** 1918 **Tr:** 1964 **G:** Drama in 2 acts and a prologue; French verse **S:** Marketplace, Zanzibar, early 20th c. **C:** 8m, 2f, extras

The Prologue expounds anti-naturalistic principles, that drama should offer not a 'slice of life, but life itself'. In a Zanzibar marketplace there are a 'speechless person who represents the people of Zanzibar', a megaphone, and a dancing kiosk. Thérèse, a figure with a blue face, rebels against her husband: opening her blouse, her breasts rise, fly up like balloons, and explode. She grows a beard and moustache and shouts into the megaphone: 'I feel as virile as the devil!' Thérèse has become Tiresias and forces her husband to exchange clothes. She plans to continue her new life in Paris, while female voices chant: 'Long live Tiresias | No more children, no more children!' Her husband is concerned about the need for children, but discovers a means of procreation, which produces 40,049 offspring in one day. He boasts of his success to reporters but soon finds that Zanzibar faces a food crisis. After a number of other surreal episodes, Tiresias returns to reassume the role of Thérèse. Releasing balloons and throwing balls at the audience, she asks them to feed the new population. The people of Zanzibar sing and dance.

Although Apollinaire claimed that his eccentric play dealt with the role of women and the risks of overpopulation, perhaps the main interest of the piece is that its subtitle *un drame surréaliste* was the first use of the term 'surrealism'. This movement of the 1920s and 1930s, which made more impact in painting than in the theatre, was explored by practitioners like Artaud and influenced plays like Wilder's *The *Skin of Our Teeth* and eventually the Theatre of the Absurd.

Breath

A: Samuel Beckett **Pf:** 1969, New York **Pb:** 1970 **G:** Scenario in 1 act **S:** Stage with litter, indeterminate period **C:** None

A faint light shines on a stage littered with rubbish. There is a faint cry and an inhalation of breath as the light increases. Finally, there is an exhalation as the light fades, followed by a cry.

This 35-second scenario is the most minimal piece of modern theatre and probably Beckett's most notorious. When Kenneth Tynan was planning his erotic revue *Oh! Calcutta!*, he asked for a contribution from Beckett, and this was the result. *Breath* (which Tynan livened up by placing some naked female bodies amongst the rubbish) is a stage realization of Pozzo's words in **Waiting for Godot*: 'They give birth astride of a grave, the light gleams an instant, then it's night once more.' Damien Hirst created a memorable television version, with an island of rubbish, much of it medical in origin, floating in space.

Bremen Coffee (*Bremer Freiheit*)

AT: *Bremen Freedom* **A:** Rainer Werner Fassbinder **Pf:** 1971, Bremen **Pb:** 1972 **Tr:** 1977 **G:** Drama in 1 act; German prose and songs **S:** Bremen, 1814–*c.*1820 **C:** 8m, 3f

Johann Miltenberger, owner of a saddle shop, brutally abuses his wife Geesche and drags her off to bed to rape her. After a blackout he is seen dying, while Geesche sings before the crucifix: 'World, farewell! of thee I'm tired.' She begins living with Michael Gottfried, who takes over the business. When her Mother reproaches her for living in sin, Geesche, determined to free her Mother from the miserable life she is leading, gives her coffee, and her Mother dies of 'intestinal inflammation'. Gottfried refuses to marry Geesche and begins to ill-treat her, so he too is given coffee, while she again sings her song before the crucifix. The priest marries Geesche to Gottfried on his deathbed. Her Father arrives with a cousin, who wants to marry Geesche and take over the business, which she is by now running very competently on her own. Father and cousin are served coffee, as is an importunate friend, who tries to call in a debt. Geesche's brother returns from the wars and demands to take over the business. He is given coffee, and Geesche sings her song. On learning that her friend Luisa is in a soulless marriage, she too is given coffee. Finally, a friend tells Geesche that he has had her sugar lumps analysed by the police, and Geesche prepares herself for execution by singing her song.

Bremen Coffee shares many characteristics with Büchner's **Woyzeck*: it is based on a historical murderer with whom the author has sympathy, the scenes are episodic, the dialogue sparse and punctuated by folk song. Fassbinder's play, however, attempts no psychological explanations, and the eight murders accumulate rapidly in Grand Guignol fashion, challenging the audience with Fassbinder's provocative belief that a short, intense life (like his own) is worth more than a life lived in an alienated, half-conscious state.

Brides of Garryowen, The. See COLLEEN BAWN, THE.

Brimstone and Treacle

A: Dennis Potter **Pf:** 1977, Sheffield **Pb:** 1978
G: Drama in 4 scenes **S:** Living room of suburban home in England, 1970s **C:** 2m, 2f

Grumpy Tom Bates, a middle-aged office-worker, tyrannizes his meek, house-proud wife Amy. Their daughter Pattie, once an attractive art college student, was brain-damaged in a car accident two years previously and can now only utter incoherent sounds. Their first visitor in ages, Martin Taylor, a dashing clean-cut young man, enters with the pretext of returning Bates's wallet to him. Claiming to have been secretly engaged to Pattie, he sings to her, soothes her, and speaks of his love. Martin invites himself to stay to look after Pattie, who, in her inarticulate way, seems desperately to protest. The next day Martin persuades Mrs Bates to go to the hairdresser, then has sex with Pattie. Mrs Bates returns home happily, and is curious about the smell of sulphur. She and Martin pray for Pattie's recovery. When Bates returns home that evening, he remains suspicious of Martin and argues with his wife. It becomes clear that Pattie had her car accident as a result of discovering her father having sex with her best friend. Encouraging his racist views, Martin ingratiates himself with Bates, sends the couple off to bed and begins molesting Pattie again. When she screams, he runs from the house, and the astonished parents discover that Pattie can speak again.

Best known for his television dramas, which mix naturalistic action with fantasy, Potter here follows the same formula by introducing into a dreary middle-class household a minor devil, who frequently exchanges meaningful looks with the audience. The irony that a demon exposes the emptiness of the Bates' marriage and brings about Pattie's cure is made problematic by seemingly condoning the rape of a mentally disabled character.

Britannicus

A: Jean Racine **Pf:** 1669, Paris **Pb:** 1670 **Tr:** 1714
G: Trag. in 5 acts; French alexandrines **S:** Rome, c.AD 56 **C:** 4m, 3f, extras

Nero, Emperor of Rome, having been a model ruler for three years, is weary both of being virtuous and of being dominated by his mother, Agrippina. By abducting a young noblewoman Junia, he strikes two blows: against his mother who protects the young woman, and against his half-brother Britannicus, who loves Junia. Britannicus is, like Nero, the son of Claudius, and being older, has prior claim to the throne but has been dispossessed by the machinations of Agrippina. Nero too falls in love with Junia, and forces her to reject Britannicus, secretly observing her as she does so. However, he later overhears her reassuring Britannicus that she does truly love him. Consumed with jealousy, Nero has Britannicus arrested. Nero is encouraged by his freed slave Narcissus, but opposed by his tutor and his mother, who reminds him of the sacrifices she made to put him on the throne: marrying her own uncle Claudius, then arranging his murder. Nero appears to relent and invites Britannicus to a banquet of reconciliation, but gives him poisoned wine to drink and watches impassively as he dies. Agrippina foretells Nero's future crimes, including matricide.

The title figure of *Britannicus* is merely a passive victim, and the focus is on 'the birth of a monster'. In order to sharpen Nero's moral conflict, he is shown to have reigned well for three years, whereas in history he murdered Britannicus within months of his accession. He is also motivated by genuine love for Junia, preventing his becoming a crude stage villain. As ever in Racine, powerful emotion is seen in productive tension with neo-classical decorum and the formality of the verse.

Broken Glass

A: Arthur Miller **Pf:** 1994, New York **Pb:** 1994 **G:** Drama in 11 scenes **S:** Brooklyn, New York, 1938 **C:** 3m, 3f

Phillip Gellburg, a Jewish New Yorker, works loyally and successfully for a firm of property developers, is proud of his son Jerome who has joined the army, and lives in comfortable circumstances with his wife Sylvia. When Sylvia reads of Nazi oppression of the Jews (the streets littered with broken glass from Jewish shops after *Kristallnacht*), she collapses, unable to walk. Their doctor Harry Hyman diagnoses 'hysterical paralysis', and Harry reminds Phillip that 'we get sick in twos and threes'. This leads to the gradual revelation of the state of Phillip and Sylvia's marriage. For 20 years, since shortly after the birth of Jerome, Phillip has been impotent. He is reluctant to discuss it, and even lies to Harry about having recently made love to Sylvia. Sylvia believes that his impotence stemmed from her desire to return to work after Jerome's birth, and Phillip's insistence that he would be the breadwinner for the family. Meanwhile, he confronts subtle anti-Semitism at work. His boss Mr Case refers to him as 'you people', and when a Jewish financier steals a march on a property that Case had hoped to buy, Phillip fears that Case suspects him of betraying secrets to a fellow Jew. With his job in trouble, and still unable to face the truth of his marriage, he has a heart attack. Sylvia comes to his bedside, and, just as she reassures him: 'There's nothing to blame,' he has another fatal attack, and she can suddenly stand.

With his usual acute insight, against the backdrop of Nazi persecution of the Jews, Miller here analyses a marriage, and debates the nature of identity. Sylvia is forced into her own kind of oppression by having reluctantly to assume the identity of a loyal Jewish housewife. Phillip, like Willy Loman before him, finds himself burdened with the identity of the clever and industrious Jew, and both collapse under the strain. Phillip can no longer bear to 'live so afraid', and is relieved to learn that there are Chinese Jews, thus shattering racial stereotypes. The somewhat melodramatic ending proceeds from genuine catharsis.

Broken Jug, The (*Der zerbrochene Krug*)

AT: *The Broken Pitcher* **A:** Heinrich von Kleist **Pf:** 1808, Weimar **Pb:** 1811 **Tr:** 1961 **G:** Com. in 13 scenes; German blank verse **S:** A courtroom in a Dutch village, late 18th c. **C:** 5m, 5f, extras

Adam, a village judge, is bandaging some cuts on his leg and has mysteriously lost his wig. He is alarmed to learn that a court official is on his way from the neighbouring town. The main case that Adam has to hear is brought by the voluble Frau Marthe against a peasant lad Ruprecht. She accuses him of having broken her jug, while secretly visiting her daughter Eve. It soon becomes clear that Adam has something to hide, especially when he enthusiastically encourages Ruprecht to accuse a fellow villager. However, the discovery of Adam's wig and Eve's denunciation of him confirms that it was the judge who forced his way into Eve and broke the jug when he left.

Acknowledged as one of the finest of the few classic German comedies, Kleist's play has serious undertones. The naming of the judge as Adam and the tempting young woman as Eve suggests that behind the levity of the trivial incidents of the play, Kleist is pointing to the irony that, since the Fall, man sits in judgement on his own guilt, just as Oedipus does in Sophocles' play. First directed by Goethe at the Court Theatre of Weimar, the play was received with hostility, one courtier even being placed under house arrest for hissing.

Broker of Bogota, The

A: Robert Montgomery Bird **Pf:** 1834, New York **Pb:** 1919 **G:** Trag. in 5 acts; blank verse and prose **S:** Bogota, New Granada (now Colombia), 1830s **C:** 9m, 2f, extras

Baptista Febro is an honourable citizen of Bogota, a moneylender devoted to his children. Unfortunately, his oldest son Ramon has got into bad company, and Baptista attempts to reform him by disinheriting him. On learning of this, the rich merchant Mendoza refuses to allow his daughter Juana to marry Ramon. Urged on by his immoral companion Antonio de Cabarero, Ramon takes his revenge on his father by stealing money from him and by then claiming that Febro himself staged the robbery. Febro is arrested and thrown into prison, where he learns that his daughter Leonor has eloped with Fernando, son of the Viceroy of New Granada. The pain caused by his children causes Febro more suffering than his unjust detention. Juana, learning of Ramon's treachery, angrily reproaches him, questioning whether she can love a man who has so cruelly betrayed his own father. Filled with remorse, Ramon commits suicide. Febro is declared innocent, but dies of a broken heart.

In some ways, this is a throwback to Jacobean tragedy (the exotic location – here in South America instead of Spain – the blank verse, and five-act structure). On the other hand, it is characteristic of the contemporary taste for bourgeois tragedy (the good old man who suffers unjustly, the lack of violent incident, and the penitence of the 'evil' character). Much of the play's contemporary popularity was due to the great tragedian Edwin Forrest's performance of the title role.

Brothers, The (*Adelphoe, Adelphi*)

A: Terence **Pf:** 160 BC, Rome **Tr:** 1598 **G:** Latin com. in verse **S:** Street in Athens, before the homes of Micio and Sostrata, 2nd c. BC **C:** 11m, 4f

Two brothers, Micio and Demea, have different lifestyles: Micio is an easygoing town-dweller, while Demea lives in the country and is much stricter. Micio, a bachelor, has adopted Aeschinus, one of Demea's sons, while Demea continues to bring up his other son, Ctesipho. Demea is horrified to learn that Aeschinus has stolen a music girl and blames Micio for his lax education. However, Aeschinus has actually stolen the girl for his brother, Ctesipho. Aeschinus himself has fallen in love with and seduced Pamphila, the daughter of a neighbouring widow Sostrata. Sostrata imagines that Aeschinus, by taking the music girl, is abandoning her daughter. Confronted by Micio, Aeschinus confesses everything to his uncle, who gives his blessing to his marriage to Pamphila and gets his brother Demea to recognise that he has been too strict. Accordingly, Ctesipho is granted permission to marry his courtesan, and Micio completes the happiness by marrying Sostrata.

The last of Terence's plays, *The Brothers* is generally accounted his greatest. Without resorting to any of the standard comic devices of disguise or sudden revelation of noble birth, Terence here contrives to create a strong piece of theatre. It combines intellectual interest (the relative merits of two educational methods), emotional involvement (generated by Aeschinus' apparent bad behaviour, when actually he is acting on behalf of his brother), and perceptive psychology in the depiction of the two sets of brothers. Plays which reveal the influence of *The Brothers* include George

Chapman's *All Fools* (*c.*1604), Beaumont and Fletcher's *The Scornful Lady* (*c.*1615), Molière's *The *School for Wives*, Shadwell's *The Squire of Alsatia* (1688), Steele's *The Tender Husband* (1705), Diderot's *The Father of the Family* (1758), Colman the Elder's *The Jealous Wife* (1761), Cumberland's *The Choleric Man* (1774), and Henry Fielding's *The Fathers* (1778).

Brothers Menaechmus, The (*Menaechmi*)

AT: *The Twin Brothers; The Twin Menaechmi; The Twins* A: Titus Maccius Plautus Pf: 215–185 BC, Rome Tr: 1595 G: Latin com. in verse S: Before the home of Menaechmus in Epidamnus, late 3rd–early 2nd c. BC C: 7m, 3f, extras

Identical twin brothers born in Syracuse were separated at the age of 7. One, Menaechmus, was adopted by a rich merchant and taken to Epidamnus. The other, Sosicles, remained in Syracuse and was renamed Menaechmus in honour of his missing brother. After an explanatory prologue, the play begins with Menaechmus I stealing his wife's dress to give to his mistress Erotium, and arranging a delicious meal with her. While he is gone, Menaechmus II appears in search of his long-lost brother. He is immediately mistaken for his brother. At first confused and then delighted, he accepts Erotium's invitation to dine with her. He emerges from his feast in possession of the dress and also a gold bracelet, which Erotium wishes to have altered. As he makes off with these expensive 'gifts', Menaechmus I returns to be confronted by his angry wife. Turning for solace to his mistress, he is now rebuffed by her, when he refuses to acknowledge that he has the dress and bracelet. Menaechmus II is now in turn subjected to an angry tirade by the wife, and gets rid of her only when he pretends to be obeying the commands of Apollo. Convinced he is mad, the wife's father goes to find a doctor, who now attempts to 'cure' Menaechmus I. When Menaechmus I is seized by slaves to carry him off to the doctor's house, he is rescued by the slave of Menaechmus II. The slave soon returns with his master. There is a recognition scene, and the confusions of the day's events are explained.

The plot confusions created by identical twins have been a recurrent theme of European comedy, most famously in Shakespeare's *The *Comedy of Errors*, which is based on Plautus' play, except that Shakespeare extends the situation by introducing twin servants, possibly modelled on Plautus' **Amphitryon*. Itself based on an unknown Greek original, *The Brothers Menaechmus* provided the theme for Trissino's *The Identical Twins* (1547), Hans Sachs's *Monechmo* (1548), Agnolo Firenzuola's *The Lucidos* (1549), Jean Rotrou's *The Menaechmae* (1636), Jean-François Regnard's *The Menaechmae* (1705), and Goldoni's *The Venetian Twins* (1748). Identical twins, sometimes impossibly brother and sister, also form an essential element of Juan del Encina's *The Deceived* (1496), Cardinal Bibbiena's *The *Follies of Calandro*, Accademi degli Intronati di Siena's *The *Deceived*, Niccolò Secchi's *The Cheats* (1549), Shakespeare's **Twelfth Night*, and Anouilh's **Ring Round the Moon*. The fame of Plautus' play as a model for later adaptations of the story may indeed obscure the fact that it is a very accomplished work in its own right. Although the ease with which both brothers descend to theft and to an abusive attitude towards both women may now seem distasteful, Plautus handles the complex plot with great deftness, making the play one of the great farces of world drama. Remembering too that Plautus' actors would have been masked, the mistaken identities of the play become even more plausible than in *The Comedy of Errors*.

Browning Version, The

A: Terence Rattigan Pf: 1948, London Pb: 1949 G: Drama in 1 act S: Living room of an apartment in an English public school, 1940s C: 5m, 2f

Andrew Crocker-Harris, a one-time brilliant classical scholar, now master of the Lower Fifth, is obliged by ill health to move to a lesser post. His fierce manner is loathed by his pupils (later he learns that he is known as 'the Himmler of the Lower Fifth'). He is also despised by his wife Millie, who is having an affair with a younger master Frank Hunter. The headmaster, who patronizes 'The Crock', tells him that he has no pension rights and asks him to give up his privileged spot at the farewell ceremony in favour of a younger and more popular colleague. Crocker-Harris bears all this in silence, but breaks down in grateful tears when a favourite pupil makes him a leaving gift of a copy of Robert Browning's version of *Agamemnon*. (see ORESTEIA, THE). Millie cruelly tells him that the pupil did this only to ensure good marks. Frank is so dismayed at her heartlessness that he breaks with her and, developing a new respect for the older master, reassures Crocker-Harris about his gift and is appalled when he learns that Millie has paraded her affairs in front of him. Discovering new strength and resolve, Crocker-Harris tells the headmaster that he will after all insist on his right to address the school at the leaving ceremony.

This long one-act play has offered a rewarding part to major actors both on stage and on screen, and in its deft and tight construction has become a classic of modern English theatre. Hints of Rattigan's homosexuality, which it was impossible at the time to be open about, emerge in the relationship between Crocker-Harris with his pupil and more particularly with Frank. But Rattigan's major achievement is to win the audience's sympathy for an initially not very likeable individual.

Büchse der Pandora, Die. See LULU PLAYS, THE.

Bunker-Hill

AT: *The Death of General Warren* **A:** John Daly Burk **Pf:** 1797, Boston **Pb:** 1797 **G:** Trag. in 5 acts; blank verse **S:** Boston and Bunker Hill, 1775 **C:** 8m, 2f, extras

The English are suffering heavy losses at the hands of the American rebels. Abercrombie, an English officer, has fallen in love with Elvira, the daughter of an American patriot. The American General Warren, elated at the rebels' victories, is invited to take command of the attack on Boston. He plans to seize Bunker Hill, which overlooks the city. Abercrombie's sense of duty forces him to fight against the rebels. He painfully renounces Elvira, swearing that he will never love another woman. She makes the same promise to him. A British officer offers Warren an amnesty if he will desert the rebel cause. Warren insists he must fight for freedom and defiantly refuses. The Battle of Bunker Hill takes place. At first the rebels are victorious, but finally Warren is shot, and the English gain the Hill but have endured crippling casualties. Elvira comes, driven insane by news of Abercrombie's death. Warren is carried on dying and proclaims the Republic of free men, as American soldiers carry standards: 'The Rights of Man', 'Liberty and Equality', etc.

Bunker-Hill is one of the most blatantly patriotic plays of the early American theatre. There is no depth of characterization, Warren's death has no sense of inevitability, and the only internal conflict between Abercrombie's love for Elvira and his duty as an officer is presented without subtlety. However, this once very popular piece offers opportunities for spectacular staging: more a pageant than a tragedy.

Burghers of Calais, The (*Die Bürger von Calais*)

AT: *The Citizens of Calais* **A:** Georg Kaiser **Pf:** 1917, Frankfurt **Pb:** 1914 **Tr:** 1971 **G:** Trag. in 3 acts; German prose **S:** Calais, 1347 **C:** 14m, 5f, extras

The French army has been defeated and their king killed. The English King will spare the port of Calais, only if six high-born citizens offer themselves in humility to be executed by the English monarch. In opposition to the French general Duguesclins who wants to fight the invaders, Eustache de Saint-Pierre persuades his fellow councillors to accept the ultimatum. Seven volunteer at once, so they draw lots to see which one will be spared. However, Eustache arranges for them all to draw a coloured ball – the accepted sign that they must offer themselves for death. It is then agreed that the last burgher to come to the marketplace the following morning will be free. The next day six citizens assemble, and Eustache is missing. Imagining he is a coward, the people go in search of him and find that he anticipated his self-sacrifice by committing suicide in the night. As his body is carried in, his ancient blind father proclaims the birth of the New Man. The English King has relented because his Queen gave birth to a son in the night. The King, sparing the city, enters the cathedral and pays homage to the nobility of Eustache.

Though not well known internationally, this is often in Germany accounted the most accomplished of Kaiser's plays. It was inspired by Rodin's 1895 sculpture of the Burghers. Written in monumental prose, with rolling cascades of language, the play offers an idealized image of self-sacrifice, the New Man who will save civilization from constant hostility – an optimistic vision for 1914, as Europe stood on the brink of war. Shaw's one-acter *The Six of Calais* of 1934 offers a predictably cynical view of the same episode.

Buried Child

A: Sam Shepard **Pf:** 1978, San Francisco **Pb:** 1979; rev. 1995 **G:** Drama in 3 acts **S:** Living area of farm, Illinois, 1970s **C:** 5m, 2f

Dodge, a sickly alcoholic in his seventies, bickers with his wife Halie, some 10 years his junior. Their oldest son Tilden, a simple-minded former athlete in his forties, has come home after some 'trouble' in New Mexico. He has a younger brother Bradley, who lost his leg in a chainsaw accident, but his mother mourns for her son Ansel, a soldier, whose death she blames on his Catholic bride. Dodge denies being Tilden's and Bradley's father, insisting that *his* child is buried in the back yard. Halie leaves for lunch with Father Dewis, and Tilden slips out when his father falls asleep. Bradley appears and begins cutting his sleeping father's hair. That night, Vince, Tilden's 22-year-old son, arrives with his tarty girlfriend from Los Angeles, Shelly. Vince has not seen Tilden for six years and is on his way to New Mexico, where he imagines his father to be still living. Neither Dodge nor the returning Tilden seems to recognize Vince. Dodge persuades Vince to go and buy him a bottle of whiskey. When he is gone, Tilden asks to touch and then hold Shelly's rabbit-fur coat. He then tells her about the baby that Dodge murdered and buried. Shelly becomes nervous, especially when Bradley enters and demands to put his fingers in her mouth. He drops the fur coat over Dodge's head and stares at Shelly. The following morning, Vince still has not returned with the whiskey, but Shelly appears to have settled in to the eccentric household. Halie brings in Father Dewis and is embarrassed to find Bradley asleep on the sofa beside his wooden leg. Shelly makes sure that attention is paid to her by demanding to know the secret about the buried child. Dodge says that the child was the product of Halie's adulterous affair and that he drowned it 'like the runt of a litter'. Vince arrives back very drunk, smashing empty bottles. He cuts a hole in the porch screen with a large knife and enters. Father Dewis and Halie hurriedly go upstairs to hide. Dodge wills the house to Vince, who refuses to leave with her when Shelly goes. Dewis goes, and Bradley crawls off after his wooden leg, which Vince cruelly threw out of the door. Dodge dies unnoticed, and Halie marvels at all the vegetables growing out back. Tilden appears, holding the decomposed corpse of a baby.

Buried Child earned Shepard the Pulitzer Prize and is arguably the most powerful of his many plays. While the events of the play can all be accepted on a realistic level, the eccentric characters and their repeated refusal to recognize each other or embrace their own past take the action into surrealist mode. There is also the pregnant symbol of the buried child, suggesting a sacrifice that has rendered the land fertile and also the potential for a fulfilled life which has been destroyed by Dodge and his sons, but which may be renewed with the arrival of young Vince.

Burlador de Sevilla, El. See TRICKSTER OF SEVILLE, THE.

Burn This

A: Lanford Wilson **Pf:** 1987, Los Angeles **Pb:** 1987 **G:** Romantic com. in 2 acts **S:** Manhattan apartment, 1980s **C:** 3m, 1f

Anna, a modern dancer and would-be choreographer, is devastated by the drowning of her gay flatmate Robbie, also a dancer. She is consoled by her boyfriend Burton, a successful screenwriter, and by her other flatmate Larry, a copywriter for advertisements. Pale, Robbie's older brother, comes to the apartment to collect his possessions and is cruelly insensitive towards Anna. Her suspicion that Pale's brash exterior merely hides his own grieving is confirmed when he breaks down in angry tears. Responding to 'the bird-with-the-broken-wing syndrome', she takes him to bed, but he is gone by the morning. Several months later, on New Year's Eve, Pale reappears drunk. Burton tries to throw him out, but Anna once again gives herself to Pale. She tries to overcome her passion for him by sending him away and by throwing herself into work, choreographing a new dance. Without Anna's knowledge, Larry invites Pale to the first showing of Anna's work. By means of Larry's note, which includes the question 'Why should love always be tragic?' and the instructions 'Burn this', Pale is also induced into meeting Anna alone in her apartment. At first reluctant to commit themselves, they confess their love for each other and burn the note, as instructed.

Conventionally, the young lovers of comedy are blocked by some outside force, frequently an inflexible older figure, but here the blocking is created entirely by the lovers themselves. Wilson deftly combines contemporary notions of liberation and its accompanying fear of submitting to commitment with the irresistible fact of a 'burning' passion, 'a juggernaut that knocks everything down in front of it'.

Bussy D'Ambois

A: George Chapman **Pf:** 1604, London **Pb:** 1607; rev. 1641 **G:** Trag. in 5 acts; blank verse **S:** Court of Henry III, Paris, *c.*1574–9 **C:** 17m, 7f, extras

Bussy D'Ambois, an adventurer, is introduced to the court of Henry III by Henry's brother, 'Monsieur', the Duc d'Alençon, who is himself a secret aspirant for the throne of France. Because of his arrogance and ambition, Bussy soon makes enemies at court, and three of these together with two of Bussy's friends lose their lives in a violent sword fight. Bussy, sole survivor of the quarrel, has his life spared by the intervention of Monsieur. Monsieur pays court to Tamyra, the virtuous wife of a count, but Bussy secretly loves her too. Bussy wins Tamyra's love, and Monsieur and the Duc de Guise plot to bring about Bussy's downfall. Monsieur taunts Tamyra's husband about her unfaithfulness, and the count tortures her by repeated stabbing to confess to her adulterous love and to write a letter inviting Bussy to come to her. Despite being warned by a ghost, Bussy hurries to his beloved where he is murdered by hired assassins. The dying Bussy urges Tamyra to be reconciled to her husband, but she swears that he shall never see her again.

This is generally acknowledged to be the most accomplished of the plays of Chapman, perhaps now best remembered for his translation of Homer. The implications of the plot, based on true events at the French court, remain ambiguous. On the one hand, there is the perennial tragic insight that those who overreach themselves will meet their downfall. On the other, Chapman seems to imply that Bussy is an admirable figure, whose colossal energy and steadfastness of purpose are thwarted by petty politicians. In a sequel of 1610, *The Revenge of Bussy D'Ambois*, Bussy's brother, Clermont, avenges Bussy's death.

Butley

A: Simon Gray **Pf:** 1971, London **Pb:** 1971 **G:** Drama in 2 acts **S:** Lecturer's study, college of London University, *c.*1970 **C:** 4m, 3f, extras

Ben Butley is a lazy, untidy, disorganized, but witty university lecturer in English, who has broken up with his wife Anne. He now lives with Joey, a former star pupil appointed assistant lecturer, who shares Ben's study. Joey is just back from a half-term break with his friend Reg, a publisher, and Ben is showing signs of jealousy. Anne is intending to marry another of Ben's pupils, a teacher called Tom, 'the most boring man in London'. Reg arrives in search of Joey and tells Ben that Joey is moving in with him. Ben is so rude about Reg's northern background that Reg eventually punches him. Joey moves out into a study vacated by a colleague who has resigned, in part from Ben's undermining of her position. Gardner, a student, comes for a tutorial, and, as with Joey, Ben begins to seduce him, getting him to read T. S. Eliot, but suddenly Ben, disillusioned and alone, sends him away: 'I'm too old to play with the likes of you.'

Canadian-born Simon Gray based *Butley* on his experiences teaching English at Queen Mary's College, London. Concentrated in one location and one day, *Butley* successfully creates a protagonist who is thoroughly irresponsible and unpleasant, but whose wit and delightfully maverick attitude to academic discipline wins the audience's sympathy with his ambivalent charm.

Bygmester Solness. See MASTER BUILDER, THE.

By the Bog of Cats

A: Marina Carr **Pf**: 1998, Dublin **Pb**: 1998
G: Trag. in 3 acts S: Irish Midlands, 1998 **C**: 8m, 5f, 1 child (f)

Hester Swane, a tough 40-year-old tinker-woman, is told by the Ghost Fancier that she will die that evening. She has been abandoned after 14 years with her 7-year-old daughter by Carthage Kilbride, who is marrying a woman of 20, Caroline Cassidy. Hester swears she will get Carthage back, even though he threatens her with eviction. The Catwoman, a weird blind old crone who eats mice, warns Hester to save herself and leave. Caroline comes in her wedding dress and tries to bribe Hester to go. Caroline fetches her father Xavier, a bullish farmer, who demands that Hester leave. She offers him money towards her house and insists that she will stay. At the Cassidys', the wedding feast is being prepared, when the ghost of Hester's half-brother appears. He had his throat cut at 18. As the wedding celebrations continue with hilarious speeches, Hester suddenly appears dressed as a bride. Hester begs to be allowed to stay in her home, but even this is denied her. Hester sets light to her house and to Carthage's cattle. Visited by her half-brother's ghost, Hester reveals that she murdered him out of jealousy. Xavier comes to threaten Hester with a gun, but is sent away by Carthage. Hester's daughter is thrilled that she can go on honeymoon with her father and Caroline. Hester decides to commit suicide, and when her daughter begs to be able to go with her, Hester cuts her throat. The Ghost Fancier arrives, and as the grieving Hester dances with him, her heart is cut out.

This play represents a remarkable achievement, combining the mythic force of its model, Euripides' **Medea* (eerie setting, ghosts, supernatural and strange characters) with psychological empathy (all the female figures, including Hester, are shown to be loving, and the men are blustering and weak not wicked). It is arguably the most powerful reworking of a Greek tragedy on the modern stage.

C

Cabal of Hypocrites, A (*Kabala sviatosh*)

AT: *Molière* A: Mikhail Bulgakov Pf: 1936, Moscow Pb: 1962 Tr: 1972 G: Drama in 4 acts; Russian prose S: Theatre, Molière's house, cathedral, and other locations in Paris, and royal palace in Versailles, 1660–73 C: 15m, 4f, extras

At the age of 38 Molière has just successfully performed the title role in his *Sganarelle* before King Louis XIV and been well rewarded. He resolves to reject Madeleine Béjart, his mistress of 20 years' standing, and marry her 19-year-old 'sister' Armande, not knowing that she is in fact her daughter. Several years later, two of Molière's sons have died in infancy, and the Church condemns him for **Tartuffe*, but the King approves the play for performance. Molière catches Armande making love to Moirron, his adopted son and the actor playing Don Juan, and throws him out of his house. Moirron denounces Molière before the League of the Holy Writ, testifying that he married his mistress's daughter. This is confirmed by Madeleine, who, dying and in fear of eternal torment, confesses to the villainous Archbishop Charron that Molière might be Armande's father. Charron tells Armande to leave Paris. Madeleine dies, Molière is deprived of the King's patronage, and the Marquis d'Orsigny who believes himself mocked in **Don Juan*, almost kills Molière in a duel. Moirron reappears vowing to protect Molière from his enemies. Some time later, Molière is performing in *The *Hypochondriac*, when the theatre is invaded by musketeers. Molière dies on stage killed by 'the king's disfavour and the evil work of the black League'.

In this epic adaptation of his novel, Bulgakov uses the life of Molière under Louis XIV as a coded message about the situation of the artist under Stalin (which prevented its publication until almost ten years after the dictator's death). With some reshaping of historical fact (e.g. Molière collapsed, but did not die on stage), Bulgakov traces the playwright's career from being favourite of the King to a man in danger of his life.

Caelina. See COELINA.

Caesar and Cleopatra

A: George Bernard Shaw W: 1898 Pf: 1906, Berlin, then New York Pb: 1901 G: Drama in 5 acts and a prologue S: Egypt, 48 BC C: 26m, 4f, extras

In a Prologue Ra cynically comments on Caesar and Cleopatra, asserting that human nature has not changed. In an Alternative Prologue we learn that Caesar is victorious in Egypt. Timidly encountering a strange 'old gentleman', Cleopatra is encouraged by him to assert her authority as rightful queen and then discovers that he is in fact Caesar. In Alexandria her young brother, the boy-king Ptolemy, is dependent on his Roman guardian Pothinus, who organizes resistance to Cleopatra's claim to the throne. In order to quell a revolt, Caesar occupies the lighthouse. Cleopatra is smuggled to him in a carpet. Later, with order re-established, Pothinus warns Caesar that Cleopatra is not to be trusted as queen. To Caesar's horror, Cleopatra secretly orders Pothinus' execution. This causes a new revolt to erupt, which Caesar once more suppresses.

Victorious over Ptolemy's troops, Caesar leaves for Rome, appointing a Roman general as governor and consoling Cleopatra with the promise of sending Mark Antony to her.

Shaw resented the universal adulation of Shakespeare, and set his *Caesar and Cleopatra* against **Antony and Cleopatra*, claiming that his characters were 'real' whereas Shakespeare's were 'love-obsessed'. While a comparison of the two plays shows how much more skilfully Shakespeare handled historical material, Shaw's play does introduce important political considerations, for example, the dangers of violence, for 'murder shall breed murder, always in the name of right and honour and peace'. Caesar, a 'naturally great' man, is the first example of a Shaw Superman, who, like Nietzsche's philosophical model, acts not according to a moral code but through superior insight.

Calandra, La. See FOLLIES OF CALANDRO, THE.

Caligula

A: Albert Camus W: 1938–44 Pf: 1945, Paris Pb: 1944 Tr: 1948 G: Trag. in 4 acts; French prose S: Imperial Roman palace, AD 38–41 C: 10m, 2f, extras

Caligula, desperate with grief over the death of his sister and lover Drusilla, is totally persuaded of the meaninglessness of existence and sets out to use his power as ruler of Rome to demonstrate that 'Men die; and they are not happy.' He first orders that all patricians will their fortunes to the state and are to be put to death as money is needed. Three years later, Caligula has become a feared and arbitrary tyrant. He orders famine for the masses and has many patricians murdered, some of them his friends. Cherea organizes opposition to him, not least because Caligula's beliefs lead only to despair. At dinner, Caligula jeers at a grieving patrician, whose son Caligula has murdered, and he debauches another patrician's wife. Despite Caligula having murdered his father, the young poet Scipio remains loyal to him. Grotesquely costumed as Venus, Caligula orders the people to worship him. Learning of the conspiracy, he summons Cherea, but forgives him and destroys the evidence against him. Scipio refuses to join the plot against Caligula and wins a contest in which poets write a poem about death. At last understanding that 'his freedom isn't the right one', Caligula despairingly murders his devoted mistress Caesonia and smashes his mirror. The conspirators rush in and stab him to death.

This is the first formulation on stage of what became known as the 'Absurd', the popular post-war belief that life is totally without meaning, exemplified by Camus's own essay *The Myth of Sisyphus*, 1942, and the central theme of Beckett's writing. This episodic and somewhat anachronistic version of Caligula's reign implies that a philosophy of despair may be logical, but that humanity needs its illusions to survive.

Calisto and Melibea. See CELESTINA.

Calvary

A: W. B. Yeats Pf: Not known Pb: 1921 G: Drama in 1 act; blank verse and irregular verse of 3- and 4-stressed lines S: The road to Calvary, AD 30 C: 6m, 3 musicians

On the way to his crucifixion, Christ encounters Lazarus, who reproaches him for denying him his death and bringing him back to life. He then meets Judas, who argues that, by betraying Jesus, he has at last proved that he has free will. Even if Christ's betrayal was preordained, Judas insists that he chose to be the betrayer. Three Roman soldiers, who will play dice for Christ's cloak, perform a dance for him as Christ hangs on the cross.

This brief poetic re-enactment of the Crucifixion forms the last of Yeats's *Four Plays for Dancers*, and as **At the Hawk's Well*, calls for masked performers in the manner of oriental theatre. As in **Oedipus the King*, a version of which Yeats had staged in 1926, there is opposition between predestination (represented by Christ) and chance (the Roman dice-players). Christ's philosophy is associated with suffering, while the Romans enjoy a jolly dance.

Camille. See LADY OF THE CAMELLIAS, THE.

Camino Real

AT: *Ten Blocks on the Camino Real*
A: Tennessee Williams Pf: 1953, New York

Pb: 1948; rev. 1953 G: Drama in 16 scenes and a prologue S: Latin American town, indeterminate period C: 21m, 7f, extras

Kilroy, the mythical American sailor of Second World War graffiti ('Kilroy was here'), finds himself trapped within the walls of an unnamed Latin American town. Here, on Camino Real (meaning both 'Royal Road' and 'Real Road'), 'Nothing wild or honest is tolerated', and all the legendary and fictional characters Kilroy encounters are victims of unfulfilled longing. Jacques [*sic*] Casanova knows he can never still his sexual yearnings. Lord Byron, who describes Shelley's cremation, is trapped in his fantasies of achieving heroism fighting for Greek independence. Esmeralda (from Victor Hugo's novel *The Hunchback of Notre Dame*) praises the world's misfits, and the hopes of Marguerite Gautier (see LADY OF THE CAMELLIAS, THE) must also remain unfulfilled. Kilroy is seized, and forced to act the clown to entertain hotel guests. However, he snatches his heart from students carrying out an autopsy. Since it is pure gold, Don Quixote, who has lost his companion Sancho Panza, now invites Kilroy to accompany him out of the town. The fountain, which had dried up, begins to flow again, and Don Quixote encourages Kilroy: 'The violets in the mountains have broken the rocks!'

In this curious Expressionist phantasmagoria, Williams confused and angered his critics by turning from the psychological studies of his early work to create this allegory of figures who cannot find the way out of their emotional impasse. Here, the symbolic elements already present in his realistic plays are writ large, and the desperate longings of Laura Whitfield and Blanche Dubois are seen embodied in legendary figures. It is the 'regular guy' Kilroy, forced like Williams to play the clown, who follows the Camino Real, the way to reality.

Candelaio, Il. See CANDLESTICK, THE.

Candida

A: George Bernard Shaw Pf: 1897, Aberdeen Pb: 1898; rev. 1930 G: Com. in 3 acts S: The Morells' home, London, 1894 C: 4m, 2f

Revd James Morell is a Christian Socialist, whose fiery denunciations of contemporary working conditions do not shrink from attacking his own father-in-law. His wife Candida returns from holiday in the company of a young poet Eugene Marchbanks. Marchbanks confesses to Morell that he loves Candida, and when Morell complacently dismisses Marchbank's claim on her, the poet, frightened as he is, denounces Morell's pomposity. Morell orders him out of the house, and Marchbanks accuses him of cowardice – that he dare not let Candida choose between them. Morell counters by inviting Marchbanks to stay alone with Candida that evening while he goes out to preach. When he returns to find Marchbanks worshipfully repeating Candida's name, Morell now insists that she must choose between them. He offers all the support of a Victorian husband, Marchbanks offers only his weakness. Candida says she will choose the weaker of the two, her husband. Chastened, Morell embraces his wife, and the poet has to go out, alone, into the night.

In some respects *Candida*, subtitled *A Mystery*, was written as a reversal of Ibsen's *A *Doll's House*. Here the 'doll' is not the wife but the molly-coddled husband, who believes himself the source of domestic strength, but is supported wholly by 'a castle of comfort and indulgence and love' provided by the wife. Candida (the name was invented by Shaw to reflect her candour) is one of the strongest women in 19th-century drama: not only does she understand that she is the source of Morell's strength but she makes the free choice to flirt outrageously and dangerously with an adoring 18-year-old, while remaining overtly faithful to her husband. Marchbanks, in whom Shaw perhaps dramatized his younger self, has the strength of acknowledging his own weakness.

Candlestick, The (*Il Candelaio*)

AT: *The Candle Bearer; The Candle-Maker*
A: Giordano Bruno Pf: Unknown, 1st recorded production 1968 Pb: 1582 Tr: 1964
G: *Commedia erudita* in 5 acts; Italian prose
S: A square in Naples, late 16th c. C: 15m, 4f

There are three focuses of the action: the first, Bonifacio, is an old lecher who is trying to seduce the courtesan Vittoria. He hires a magician to cast a spell on Vittoria, although the advice he is given by the portrait painter Giovan Bernardo is more useful: that he should give up 'candles' (i.e. small boys' penises) and concentrate more on 'thimbles' (i.e. sex with women). Bonifacio, believing that Vittoria is under the spell and is waiting to be loved by him, disguises himself as Giovan Bernardo, and goes to Vittoria's house, where he is in fact received by his own wife disguised as Vittoria. His lecherous plan is exposed, he is arrested by a bogus watch of opportunistic rogues, and is released only by offering bribes and by begging forgiveness of his wife and Giovan Bernardo, who becomes her lover. The second plot turns on the character of Bartolomeo, who is so obsessed with gold that he neglects his wife and is easily tricked by an unscrupulous alchemist. He too is arrested and stripped naked by the bogus watch. The final figure is Manfurio, a pedantic schoolmaster, who wearies everyone with his learning, is robbed, and is eventually beaten by the bogus watch, in part for sodomizing his pupils.

Giordano Bruno is best remembered as a sceptical philosopher, who was burnt at the stake in 1600 for his heretical views. *The Candlestick* is generally accounted the best Italian comedy of the second half of the 16th century and reflects Bruno's cynical views not only of superstition (Bonifacio and Bartholomeo being easily exploited by charlatans) but also of the greed and immorality of human society. This long and complex play is quite savage and obscene (the Italian title has an additional slang meaning of 'sodomite'), and only the two wives display any modicum of virtue. The pedant Manfurio is very similar to the Doctor of the *commedia dell'arte*, and Jonson's *The *Alchemist* clearly owes a debt to Bruno's play.

Cantatrice chauve, La. See BALD PRIMADONNA, THE.

Can't Pay? Won't Pay! (*Non si paga! Non si paga!*)

AT: *We Can't Pay? We Won't Pay!; We Won't Pay? We Won't Pay!* **A:** Dario Fo **Pf:** 1974, Milan **Pb:** 1974 **Tr:** 1978 **G:** Pol. com. in 2 acts; Italian prose **S:** Working-class suburb of Milan, 1970s **C:** 6m, 2f

Antonia and Margherita, two working-class housewives, stagger in with goods that they have stolen from the supermarket as part of a protest by local women against rising prices. Antonia is terrified that her husband Giovanni, a Communist factory-worker, will force her to return her booty. He notices Margherita's bulging coat and is told that she is pregnant. He is dismayed that some workers refused to pay for the overpriced food in the canteen and warns Antonia not to take part in the supermarket protest. When the police search the flat, Margherita pretends to be in labour and is carried to an ambulance. Margherita's husband Luigi is surprised to learn that he is about to become a father and goes off in search of her. When a lorry overturns in the street, Giovanni and Luigi, who have just learned that they are losing their jobs, steal sacks of sugar. An Inspector, checking on the two women who have now returned home, believes he has been blinded for his disbelief when their electricity is cut off, bangs his head in the dark, and passes out. The women confess to the men that they have been stealing, and the men admit to their theft. When he recovers, the Inspector is so relieved that he can see that he leaves happy.

In this fast-paced play, Fo employs traditional elements of farce to address political issues: the financial pressures of working-class life, unreasonable prices, the threat of unemployment, and unreformed and ignorant male views of women.

Captain, The. See STABLEMASTER, THE.

Captain of Köpenick, The (*Der Hauptmann von Köpenick*)

A: Carl Zuckmayer **Pf:** 1931, Berlin **Pb:** 1930 **Tr:** 1932 **G:** Com. in 3 acts; German prose **S:** Berlin and environs, 1910 **C:** 43m, 11f, 2 children (f)

Wilhelm Voigt is a 46-year-old cobbler in the working-class district of Köpenick in Berlin. Because he has been imprisoned for 15 years for a minor forgery, he is unable to obtain a residence permit and also has problems getting papers to allow him to leave Prussia. Observing how an army captain is treated with disrespect by the police because he is not wearing his uniform, Voigt becomes aware of the importance of military dress in a state like Prussia. After the death of a little child he read stories to, Voigt decides to be pushed around no longer and buys a captain's uniform from a second-hand clothes dealer. Suddenly, he is treated with respect. Aware of the power his uniform gives him, he goes to the town hall and has the mayor arrested and helps himself to municipal funds. After a drunken spree, he learns that there is a reward for the arrest of the 'Captain of Köpenick', and offers to give himself up in return for a passport. Ready to return to prison, he entertains the police with an account of his deception. Invited by the Chief of Police to don the uniform once more, Voigt looks at himself in the mirror and laughs until he cries.

The Captain of Köpenick was based on an actual case in Berlin in 1906. Although film adaptations and some English versions emphasize only the jolly romp of Voigt's impersonation of an officer (with the reassuring outcome that the Kaiser himself is amused by Voigt's antics), Zuckmayer's original play offers, beneath the comedy, a serious warning to the German nation, urgent enough in 1930, about the danger of allowing military hierarchies to determine the structure of society.

Car Cemetery, The. See AUTOMOBILE GRAVEYARD, THE.

Caretaker, The

A: Harold Pinter Pf: 1960, London Pb: 1960; rev. 1962 G: Drama in 3 acts S: Room in a London house, 1950s C: 3m

Mick, a man in his late twenties, is sitting alone in a room, heaped with junk. He quickly leaves when he hears people approaching. Aston, a man in his early thirties, enters, followed by an old tramp, Davies. Aston has rescued Davies from a fight in the street and now offers him a bed for the night. Davies, who is also known as Jenkins, claims that if he could get down to Sidcup, he could fetch his papers and sort out his life. The following morning Aston complains about the noises Davies was making in the night. Aston goes out, leaving Davies with a key. As Davies is looking around, Mick silently enters and grabs Davies, forcing him to the ground and withholding his trousers. Mick interrogates Davies, threatening to take him to the police for trespassing. Aston returns with Davies's bag, which Mick seizes, teasing Davies. When Mick leaves, Aston explains that Mick is his brother and that he's renovating the house for him. He offers Davies the job of caretaker, but Davies is uncertain. Later Davies enters the room, and is terrorized by a mysterious noise: Mick with a vacuum cleaner. Mick appears to take Davies into his confidence, expressing worries about his brother. When Mick also offers Davies the job of caretaker, Davies says that he must go to Sidcup for his papers. The next morning Aston tells him in a long speech how he used to have hallucinations and was forced to have electric shock therapy. This made him very ill, and he now avoids people. Two weeks later, Davies has settled into his new environment and has even begun complaining about how he is treated. Mick talks about his extravagant plans for the house. Aston brings Davies some shoes, and Davies reluctantly tries them: 'Maybe they'll get me down to Sidcup tomorrow.' That night, Davies is making his usual noises, and Aston wakes him. Davies, furious, turns on Aston: 'I never been inside a nuthouse!', and pulls a knife on him. Aston asks him to leave, but Davies triumphantly declares that he is to help Mick renovate the house. Davies goes, but returns with Mick that evening. Initially supportive, Mick turns on Davies, especially when Davies calls Aston 'nutty'. Aston returns, and the brothers exchange smiles. Mick leaves, and Davies pleads to the silent Aston to be allowed to stay. There is a long silence.

The Caretaker was Pinter's first successful play and has become a classic of contemporary theatre. It minutely observes the power relationships between Davies and the two brothers, the way he tries to ingratiate himself and to play them off against each other. In the low-key ending (Pinter had originally planned for the play to end with Davies's violent death), Davies has talked his way out of his chance of a settled life. Like the tramps in *Waiting for Godot*, he will continue to wait to 'get to Sidcup'; Pinter's image may not be as universal as Beckett's, but it is more immediately recognizable.

casa de Bernarda Alba, La. See HOUSE OF BERNARDA ALBA, THE.

Casina

A: Titus Maccius Plautus **Pf**: 185–184 BC, Rome **Tr**: 1852 **G**: Latin farce in verse **S**: Before the home of Lysidamus, 2nd c. BC **C**: 3m, 2f, extras

Lysidamus, an old lecher, is determined to spend a night with his wife's maid, Casina. In order to achieve this, he arranges for his slave Olympio to marry her. However, his plan is thwarted by another slave, Chalinus, who wants to marry Casina himself in order to further the interests of his master, the son of old Lysidamus. A lot will decide which of the slaves shall take Casina as his bride. To Lysidamus' great relief, Olympio wins the lottery. Lysidamus' ensuing excitement arouses his wife's suspicions, so she and Chalinus plot together to hinder Lysidamus. First, they put it about that Casina is mad, then Chalinus disguises himself as the bride, with hilarious and vulgar consequences. Lysidamus is shamed into confessing his lecherous desires to his wife and is forgiven, provided he undertakes to remain chaste henceforth. The prologue and epilogue indicate that Casina is in fact a nobly born foundling, whose identity will be revealed thus allowing her to marry Lysidamus' son, but none of this occurs in the action of the play.

Although it is one of the lesser known of Plautus' comedies, *Casina* is notable as one of the most lively and vulgar of his works, which led to its frequently being performed after the author's death. Indeed, it is possibly the piece which shows the closest link to the Latin farces that preceded the Roman New Comedy, which differed from the Old Comedy of Aristrophanes in its greater realism and concentration on domestic events. Based on a lost Greek original, *Cleroumenoe* of Diphilus, it provided a model for the recurring comic figure of the ridiculous old lecher, who is usually (though not here), outwitted by a younger lover: Pantalone in the *commedia dell'arte*, Morose in Jonson's **Epicene*, Falstaff in *The *Merry Wives of Windsor*, and several of the comic characters of Molière (e.g. Arnolphe in *The *School for Wives*).

Cassaria, La. See STRONGBOX, THE.

Caste

A: T. W. Robertson **Pf**: 1867, London **Pb**: 1868 **G**: Drama in 3 acts **S**: Eccles's house and D'Alroy's lodgings, London, 1860s **C**: 5m, 3f

Despite the warnings of his friend Hawtree about the importance of 'caste', the Honourable George D'Alroy woos and weds the beautiful dancer Esther Eccles, whose father is a drunkard. Her sister Polly becomes engaged to the honest plumber Sam Gerridge. George is posted with his regiment to India. When news comes of his death on active service, Esther takes up her dancing again in order to support her young son. She refuses to sell their child to her mother-in-law, the overbearing Marquise de St Maur, knowing that with the help of Polly and Sam, she will survive. George reappears, having escaped his captors, is delighted by Esther's resourcefulness, and is reconciled with his mother.

While *Caste* contains many of the stock figures of 18th-century plays, the innocent low-born heroine, the drunken father, the comically eccentric dowager, Robertson's naturalism and seriousness of purpose lend the play considerable weight. By confining the action to two familiar interior locations, there is, compared with a piece like *The *Colleen Bawn*, an authentic feel to the events of the play, which helped to consolidate the Victorian use of realistic box sets. In challenging fixed notions of class, Robertson is clearly progressive. However, one must accept Hawtree's point that such marriages may work in a play but are less successful in reality. How, for example, will Esther relate to Polly and Sam when she returns to her life of luxury? But then comedy always ends with a happy resolution, without feeling obliged to explore the consequences.

castigo sin venganza, El. See JUSTICE WITHOUT REVENGE.

Castle of Perseverance, The

A: Anon W: 1400–25 Pb: 1969 G: Morality play; Middle English verse S: Heaven and earth, especially the Castle of Perseverance C: 11m, 22f, extras

The World (Mundus), the Devil (Belyal), and Flesh (Caro) declare that they will destroy Mankind (Humanum Genus). The newborn Mankind turns from the Good Angel and is tempted by the Bad Angel to be taken by Pleasure (Voluptas) and Folly (Stulticia) to World, where he indulges in worldly pleasures and becomes acquainted with the Seven Deadly Sins. The Seven Virtues rescue Mankind and lead him to the Castle of Perseverance, where he is attacked on all sides by the Sins. Eventually Covetousness (Avaricia) succeeds in enticing Mankind out of the Castle by reminding him that he will need money in his old age. Once out of the Castle, the now ageing Mankind is waylaid by Death (Mors), and his soul is carried off by the Bad Angel. Mercy (Misericordia) now pleads for Mankind's soul before God, and God allows him to be fetched from hell to join him in heavenly splendour.

This is the first (almost) complete extant morality play in English. Like the more famous **Everyman*, it shows by way of abstract figures, how mankind can easily be led astray by earthly pleasures, must suffer for his sins, but may be redeemed by God's mercy. There is no record of its original production, but a sketch in the manuscript indicates that the audience would have been surrounded by five stages and that there would have been a central stage representing the Castle. Like the miracle plays therefore, one can assume a promenade performance with the audience moving with the action. Scenes, like those in which the Sins are repelled from the Castle by roses, symbolic of Christ's passion, would have been particularly spectacular. While the Seven Virtues, Seven Deadly Sins, and the 'Daughters of God' would seem to have feminine attributes, these roles would have all been played by men.

Catastrophe

A: Samuel Beckett Pf: 1982, Avignon Pb: 1984 Tr: 1984 G: Drama in 1 act; French prose S: Empty theatre, *c*.1980 C: 2m, 1f

A Director (D) and his Assistant (A) are discussing the Protagonist (P), a figure dressed in black wearing a wide-brimmed hat, standing motionless on a plinth on stage. D insists that the black gown should be removed, and P is revealed to be wearing dingy pyjamas. The hat is also removed, and he is made to clasp his hands. P submits to everything inertly but begins to shiver with the cold. D protests that he can see P's face, and A forces his head down. When D demands more nudity, A rolls up P's trouser legs and makes a note to whiten the flesh. Orders are now given to light only P's head. D is scornful of A's suggestion that P might show his face briefly: 'Where do you think we are? In Patagonia?' Delighted, D proclaims: 'There's our catastrophe.' The image is greeted with thunderous applause, but when P raises his head, the applause falters and dies.

Beckett insisted always that he was not a political writer (a significant contrast with the other major figure of 20th-century theatre, Bertolt Brecht). However, prompted by his concern over the imprisonment of Václav Havel, he dedicated this piece to the Czech dissident. Its implications of political manipulation and torture are tangentially presented as though in a theatre rehearsal. The simple gesture of defiantly raising his head, the only movement made by P, suggests the power of political defiance in the face of tyranny.

Cathleen ni Houlihan

AT: *Kathleen ni Houlihan* A: W. B. Yeats Pf: 1902, Dublin Pb: 1902 G: Drama in 1 act; prose and songs S: Cottage near Killala, Ireland, 1798 C: 3m, 3f, extras

Michael Gillane is preparing for his wedding the following day, when a strange old woman appears, mourning the loss of her four fields (the four provinces of Ireland). Inspiring Michael with her tales of those who have given their lives for her, she reveals that she is Cathleen ni Houlihan (the personification of Ireland). Cheers come from Killala harbour, signalling that French troops are landing, and Michael, despite the pleas of his bride, leaves to fight for freedom. Cathleen is no longer an old woman but 'a young girl' with 'the walk of a queen'.

By 1798 many of the uprisings by the United Irishmen against their British overlords had been brutally crushed. French Revolutionary troops tried to intervene, but after initial success, were heavily defeated. In this nationalist piece, which was on the opening bill of the Abbey Theatre, Yeats combines history with the mythical figure of Cathleen (played at its premiere by Maud Gonne), a figure he had already portrayed in *The Countess Cathleen* (1892). Later he was concerned about the effect his play had had on young Irishmen: 'Did that play of mine send out | Certain men the English shot?'

Cato

A: Joseph Addison **Pf:** 1713, London **Pb:** 1713 G: Trag. in 5 acts; blank verse S: The Governor's palace of Utica, North Africa, 47–46 BC C: 7m, 2f, extras

Caesar has defeated Pompey. Cato, dismayed by Caesar's tyranny, is isolated in the Phoenician town of Utica with a remnant of the Roman Senate. Juba, the Prince of the neighbouring Numidia, loves Cato's daughter Marcia and supports Cato. A treacherous Roman senator, Sempronius, also in love with Marcia, plans to betray the city to Caesar and claim Marcia as his prize. When offers of friendship come from Caesar, Cato rejects the hand of a tyrant and also refuses to flee to the comparative safety of Numidia. When Sempronius' mutiny fails, he plans to disguise himself as Juba, seize Marcia, and fly to Caesar. Juba kills him, and Marcia discovers the corpse, believing it to be her beloved Juba. When Cato's son Marcus dies fighting against forces loyal to Caesar, Cato, recognizing that he cannot survive, takes up Plato's treatise on the immortality of the soul and falls on his sword. With his dying breath he gives his blessing to the union between Juba and Marcia.

There is much that the modern reader finds problematic with Addison's heroic tragedy: the formality of his blank verse, the excessive nobility of Cato and the 'noble savage' Juba, and the crass ending. However, this was a highly political play: the Treaty of Utrecht, acknowledging Queen Anne as the rightful heir to the British throne, had just been signed with France, but Anne's illness and her lack of an heir still left Britain vulnerable, made worse by internal dissension between Whigs and Tories. Cato's model of self-sacrificing and courageous statesmanship offers a timeless Utopian example. It is refreshing too, at a time when so many tragedies derived from thwarted love, that love is here either the crude lust of Sempronius or, to honourable individuals, of secondary importance at a time of national crisis. Finally, by reminding us that tragedy does not reward the good but may end with their downfall, Addison offered here an alternative to the cliché morality of a play like Nahum Tate's rewriting of *King Lear* (1681).

Cat on a Hot Tin Roof

A: Tennessee Williams **Pf:** 1955, New York **Pb:** 1955; rev. 1975 **G:** Drama in 3 acts S: Bed-sittingroom in Big Daddy's home, Mississippi Delta, 1950s **C:** 7m, 3f, 4 children (2m, 2f)

Big Daddy Pollitt, a millionaire cotton-plantation owner, has reached his 65th birthday, and his two sons Gooper and Brick have come to celebrate it with their respective wives Mae and Margaret ('Maggie the Cat'). Only Big Daddy and his wife Big Mama are unaware that Big Daddy is dying of cancer. Gooper and Mae, who have five children, are anxious to secure the inheritance for themselves and sneer at Brick and Margaret's childless marriage. While Gooper is a successful lawyer, Brick is a former football hero and commentator, who has now taken to the bottle. Part of his decline is due to the fact that Margaret, suspicious of Brick's intimate relationship with his best friend Skipper, challenged Skipper, since dead, to prove he was heterosexual by sleeping with her. After that, their friendship disintegrated, Brick suffered a spinal injury, and both he and Skipper began drinking. Margaret now begs Brick to give her a child, but he admits that he cannot stand her. Big Daddy, a larger-than-life character, confronts Brick, his favourite son, about his drinking. Brick speaks of escaping from the world's mendacity, so Big Daddy attacks him for being unable to face the truth about his feelings for Skipper. Brick retorts that Big Daddy should face his own truth: that he is dying of cancer. When Big Mama learns the news, she urges Brick and Margaret to give Big Daddy a grandson to inherit the estate. Margaret, to the disbelief of her in-laws, declares that she is pregnant. She throws out Brick's crutch and liquor bottles and tells him that 'tonight we're going to make the lie true'. As Big Daddy's cries of pain are heard, Brick appears to yield to her insistent tenderness.

When Elia Kazan directed this play on Broadway, he urged Williams to make the ending more sentimental and less ambiguous: in the revised version, Margaret tells Big Daddy of her 'pregnancy', and Brick is more optimistic about the future of their marriage.

Caucasian Chalk Circle, The (*Der kaukasische Kreidekreis*)

A: Bertolt Brecht (with Margarete Steffin)
Pf: 1948, Northfield, Minnesota; 1954, Berlin
Pb: 1949 Tr: 1948 G: Pol. drama in 6 scenes and a prologue; German prose and some verse
S: USSR collective farm, 1946; and the imaginary province of Grusinia in Georgia, indeterminate period C: 39m, 11f, extras

Two groups of villagers meet to discuss who has the greater claim on a fertile valley, the goatherds who traditionally owned it or the fruit growers who are improving it with irrigation. The Singer stages a play to illustrate why the valley is to be awarded to the fruit growers. A tyrannous governor is overthrown by his nobles. In her panic to escape, the governor's wife abandons her baby son Michael. A palace maid, Grusche Vachnadze, who has just said farewell to her soldier boyfriend Simon, saves the baby and flees with it. In the mountains, she endures considerable hardships and only escapes pursuing soldiers by knocking one of them out and crossing a chasm on a rotting rope bridge. She arrives at her brother's house, but is forced to marry a dying peasant. In the middle of the wedding celebration, news comes that the war is over, and her husband leaps off his deathbed, fit and well. When Simon comes in search of Grusche, he sees Michael and leaves sadly. Soldiers arrive and seize Michael. Grusche follows them, determined to prove that she is his mother. The action rewinds to the night of the revolution, when Azdak, a drunken village scribe, unwittingly shelters the fleeing Grand Duke. He goes to the capital to denounce himself, and the soldiers, who have just executed the judge, are so amused by his antics that they appoint him the new judge. Azdak now tries a number of cases, accepting bribes but always deciding in favour of the dispossessed. Eventually, an old couple come before him, seeking a divorce. Azdak now has to judge the case of Michael, using the test of the chalk circle: both claimants are to take an arm each, and the one who pulls the child out of the circle will be declared the mother. Grusche soon stops pulling, crying out that she cannot hurt her son, and thereby proving that she is Michael's 'true' mother. The child is given to Grusche, the divorce petition is signed – 'unfortunately' divorcing Grusche from her husband – and Azdak urges her to flee with Simon and Michael, for the 'time that was almost just' is now over. The Singer concludes that, just as Grusche was the true mother, so too the valley must go to those who will care for it best.

This piece is the most mature example of Brecht's epic theatre, using many distancing devices, above all the commentary by the Singer, often speaking the thoughts of the characters. The Falstaffian Azdak is perhaps the most memorable character created by Brecht, and the moral of the tale, that human caring is more important than traditional rights of ownership, is both good Marxism and good sense.

Caught in the Act! See FLEA IN HER EAR, A.

Causes and Effects. See GLASS OF WATER, THE.

Celestina (*Comedia/Tragicomedia de Calisto y Melibea*)

AT: *Calisto and Melibea; The Spanish Bawd*
A: Fernando de Rojas **Pf:** 1909 (no known earlier performances) **Pb:** 1499 **Tr:** 1631
G: Drama in 16/21 acts; Spanish verse **S:** A city in Spain (Toledo?), early 16th c. **C:** 8m, 6f

The handsome young nobleman Calisto, pursuing his hawk, enters a garden where he encounters the beautiful but disdainful Melibea, and falls in love with her. Rejected by her, Calisto enlists the help of an old bawd, Celestina, to help him win his beloved. Posing as a pedlar, Celestina gains access to Melibea's house and persuades her that Calisto will die if Melibea will not see him. Taking pity on the young man, she agrees that Calisto may visit her under the cover of darkness. Celestina tries to cheat her servants of their share of the reward for bringing the lovers together, and is killed by them. That night Melibea succumbs to Calisto's passion, but, as he leaves by the ladder to her room, he falls and kills himself. Distraught, Melibea hurls herself from the tower of her house. In the revised 'tragicomedy' five further acts were inserted, in which the lovers enjoy a month of secret trysts, and Celestina's murder is avenged by her loyal prostitutes, before Calisto and Melibea fall to their deaths.

Because of its length and the leisurely way in which the action develops, *Celestina* has traditionally been regarded as a novel in dialogue rather than a play. However, abridged and adapted, as it has been on the Spanish stage since 1909, it has shown itself to be an enjoyably playable drama. The apparently simple moral message of vice being punished is undercut by the obvious innocence of Melibea and the seductive charm of the roguish old whore Celestina. It may be that Rojas, a converted Jew, is questioning the values of a nominally Christian society. *Celestina* was hugely influential on Renaissance drama across Europe, and traces of it can be detected in the unhappy fate of Romeo and Juliet.

Cenci, The

A: Percy Bysshe Shelley **Pf:** 1886, London **Pb:** 1819 **G:** Hist. drama in 5 acts; blank verse **S:** Interior locations in Rome, and a castle in the Apennines, 1599 **C:** 9m, 2f, extras

Count Francesco Cenci, a Roman nobleman, remains unpunished 'for capital crimes of the most enormous and unspeakable kind' by repeatedly paying large sums to Pope Clement VIII to buy his pardon. He invites Lucretia, his second wife, and Beatrice, his 16-year-old daughter, to join him in a feast. When he reveals that the feast is to celebrate the death of his two sons in Spain, Beatrice rebels against her unnatural father, demanding that leading churchmen and nobles protect her from his tyranny. Orsino, a duplicitous prelate who claims to love Beatrice, carries a petition to the Pope. Cenci remains untouched, and, when he rapes Beatrice, she realizes that the only way out is to kill her father. She plots with her stepmother and with her brother Giacomo to have Cenci murdered. When the crime is discovered, the three are condemned to be beheaded, and all pleas to the Pope fall on deaf ears. The play ends in the prison cell, their last hopes of clemency dashed.

Although based on historical fact, the violence and incest of *The Cenci*, which would have been de rigueur in Jacobean tragedy, prevented its reaching the stage for almost 70 years. Shelley's characteristic concern with tyranny and injustice is here cast in a fine dramatic poem rather than a piece for the theatre. Its main interest as a performance piece was the version staged by Artaud in Paris in 1935, one of the few actual productions achieved by this arch-experimenter. Artaud reduced Shelley's text to a shorter, though still remarkably wordy, four-act prose version (while Shelley's Beatrice cannot name his crime, Artaud's Beatrice simply states: 'Cenci, my father, has defiled me'). Artaud's focus, as ever, is on 'a whole language of gestures and signs . . . which . . . will blend together in a sort of violent manifestation of feeling'.

Ceremonies in Dark Old Men

A: Lonne Elder III **Pf:** 1969, New York **Pb:** 1969 **G:** Trag. in 2 acts **S:** Small barbershop, Harlem, 1960s **C:** 5m, 2f

Russell B. Parker is a 54-year-old African-American widower, with a daughter Adele and two sons Theopolis and Bobby. He notionally runs a barbershop below his apartment, but hardly ever has a customer, so Adele has to go out to work to feed the family ('who the hell ever told every black woman she was some kind of God damn saviour!'). Theopolis suggests that his confederate Blue Haven, a militant black leader and former killer, should sell bootleg whisky from the barbershop. Adele is furious at the men for their scheme and will have nothing to do with it. Theopolis asserts that there is no 'place where there are no old crippled vaudeville men', but Adele insists that 'you climb out of it!' Two months later, business is booming: the men, now wearing fine clothes (except for Theopolis who does most of the work), assemble for Blue to arrive. He comes with their money and quietly notes that Parker has been helping himself to the till. Blue wants to make Parker President of his 'Harlem De-Colonization Association' and to organize a demonstration in Harlem to boycott a white-owned store. In fact, it is the night-time raids of Blue's gang, in which Bobby is involved, that are getting the stores closed down. Bobby is killed by a nightwatchman, but Theopolis and Adele cannot bring themselves to tell their father, who now admits that in his barbershop he just 'acted out the ceremony of a game'.

A milestone in the development of African-American drama, this play, offering an authentic, often unflattering, but wholly sympathetic view of urban blacks, was premiered by the Negro Ensemble Company, and was one of the first plays to be written for an entirely black audience rather than trying to appeal to white theatregoers. The wastrel father, the long-suffering woman, and the background of political danger leading to the son's death are reminiscent of O'Casey's **Juno and the Paycock*.

Chaika. See SEAGULL, THE.

Chairs, The (*Les Chaises*)

A: Eugène Ionesco Pf: 1952, Paris Pb: 1954 Tr: 1958 G: Tragicom. in 1 act; French prose S: Room in a tower surrounded by water, indeterminate period C: 2m, 1f

A senile 'quartermaster-general' and his equally ancient wife Sémiramis are preparing a large room in a tower for many visitors, who are coming by water to hear the Old Man reveal his message to all humanity. The first arrival is a Lady, with whom they converse, but who is entirely invisible. As each new invisible visitor arrives, a chair is brought. Next is a Colonel, followed by a Photographer and his wife, a former sweetheart of the Old Man. While the Old Man reminisces about her, the Old Woman obscenely re-enacts some of the poses she adopted for the Photographer. The Old Woman talks about their son, while the Old Man regrets that they never had one. Eventually the room fills with invisible guests, and more and more chairs are placed in the room. A fanfare is heard, and the invisible Emperor arrives. Finally, the Orator enters, a real person dressed like a 19th-century artist. Convinced that their message will now be communicated and their life's work achieved, the Old Couple leap to their deaths from a window. However, when the Orator begins to speak, he is deaf-mute and can only mumble. He writes on a blackboard, eventually forming the word 'Adieu'. As he leaves, the voices of the invisible guests are heard.

In what was arguably his most accomplished play, Ionesco wrote 'a tragic farce', which in many ways anticipates Beckett's world: senile characters, an empty universe peopled by imaginary figures, and, above all, a world waiting for the message of deliverance that can never come (in the original production, the curtain fell during the mumbling of the Orator).

Chalk Circle, The (*Hui-Lan Ji*)

AT: *The Circle of Chalk* A: Li Xingfu (Li Ch'ien-fu, Li Hsing-tao) Pf: *c*.1300 Tr: 1929 G: Drama in 4 acts; Chinese prose and verse S: The home of Ma Chun-shing, and a court in Kaifeng, 11th c. C: 6m, 2f, extras

A 17-year-old nobly born girl, Hai-t'ang, is sold by her impoverished brother to become the secondary wife of the rich and kindly Ma Chun-shing. She bears him a son, Shoulang, and all is well. When the boy is 5 years old, however, the jealous first wife Ah-Siu poisons Ma Chun-shing with the help of her lover, and blames Hai-t'ang for the crime. Moreover, Ah-Siu now claims that Shoulang is her child. Hai-t'ang is arrested and, after being beaten until she confesses, is taken on a journey through a snowstorm to the court in Kaifeng. Here her brother pleads for her, and the wise judge Bao (or Pao) decides to test the truth of the accusations against her. He does this by having Shoulang placed in a circle drawn on the ground with chalk, and ordering the two wives to try to pull the boy out of the circle. Hai-t'ang soon stops pulling for fear of hurting her son, and thereby reveals herself as the true mother. Bao pardons her and punishes Ah-Siu.

The Chalk Circle is the best-known Chinese classic play in the West, a rich mixture of an intriguing plot, lyrical songs, farcical episodes, and larger-than-life characters. Through it all, the heroine Hai-t'ang moves, offering a model of Confucian patience and fortitude, to be rewarded finally by the just decision of a wise Mandarin. It became popular in the West, initially through the translation into German in 1923 by Klabund, which was performed many times and served as the source for Brecht's *The *Caucasian Chalk Circle*. The style of the play indeed now appears quite 'Brechtian', as characters enter and directly address the audience with information about themselves, sometimes in song. Similar ancient Chinese theatre also provided the inspiration for the popular *Lady Precious Stream* by S. I. Hsiung (1938).

Chalk Cross, The. See FEAR AND MISERY OF THE THIRD REICH.

Chalk Mark, The. See FEAR AND MISERY OF THE THIRD REICH.

Chandalika

A: Rabindranath Tagore Pf: 1933, Calcutta? Pb: 1933 Tr: 1938 G: Musical drama in 2 acts; Bengali prose and verse S: Indian village, 5th c. BC C: 1m, 2f

When Prakriti, a *Chandalika* (girl of the untouchable caste) falls in love with Buddha's celibate disciple Ananda, she pleads with her Mother to cast a spell over him. The spell succeeds in stirring Ananda's passions, but, when he comes to Prakriti's home to take her, she realizes that she had fallen in love with Buddha's pure disciple not the lustful monk who now approaches her. It was his 'light and radiance, shining purity, and heavenly glow' that caused her to adore him. So she now begs her Mother to reverse the spell, although it will cost her Mother her life. Filled with remorse, Prakriti is redeemed by her willingness to renounce her love, sacrificing her own pleasure for the sake of Ananda, who now chants his prayers to Buddha.

In his later plays, Tagore attempted to adapt traditional Indian drama to create lyrical texts that were partly sung by a chorus on stage. The original story is based on a Buddhist legend, in which Ananda succumbs to the Chandalika and prays to have the magic spell lifted by Buddha. Here, it is the outcast girl herself who brings about the redemption, offering a theatrical metaphor of the relationship between love and physical sex. During the 1930s the play was toured successfully across India and Sri Lanka.

Changeling, The

A: Thomas Middleton and William Rowley Pf: 1622, London Pb: 1653 G: Trag. in 5 acts; mainly blank verse, some prose S: The harbour, a castle, and a madhouse in Alicante, Spain; Renaissance period C: 11m, 3f, extras

Beatrice-Joanna has fallen in love with Alsemero, who has proposed to her. Since she has been promised to another and cannot disobey her father's wishes, she resolves to murder her fiancé, employing De Flores, a servant, whom she finds repulsive, to commit the murder on her behalf. When De Flores returns with the finger of the dead man, she is horrified that De Flores demands her virginity as his reward, thinking that was their bargain. Fearful of discovery by Alsemero, she substitutes her maid in her marriage bed. When the maid threatens the stratagem by staying in bed too long, De Flores disposes of her too. Eventually the guilt of Beatrice and De Flores is revealed, and he stabs her and then commits suicide. Alternating scene by scene is a comic sub-plot, in which the young Isabella is kept locked up in a madhouse by her jealous old husband. Two young suitors gain access to the asylum and to Isabella by feigning madness but fail to win the virtuous – and forgiving – wife.

It seems almost certain that Middleton wrote the main plot, based on a story, *God's Revenge Against Murder* by John Reynolds (1621), and Rowley the sub-plot. Now regarded as one of the best Jacobean tragedies, in both its characterization and language, *The Changeling* was totally neglected by the theatre during the 18th and 19th centuries. It is now quite frequently performed, notably by Peter Stein in Zurich in 1970. The major interest for modern audiences is – amidst the melodramatic and sometimes implausible events of the play – the relationship between Beatrice and De Flores. Although she detests him, it is clear that she is also powerfully attracted to him, a sexually charged liaison based on both repulsion and fascination. The madhouse scenes, modelled on the London asylum of Bedlam, are intended as comic, although modern audiences may find it harder to find mentally disturbed patients funny. Also characteristic of the theatrical style of the period are the robust depiction of onstage violence, the dumb show before Act 4, and the appearance of the victim's ghost.

Changes of Heart. See DOUBLE INCONSTANCY, THE.

chapeau de paille d'Italie, Un. See ITALIAN STRAW HAT, AN.

Chapel Perilous, The

AT: *The Perilous Adventures of Sally Banner*
A: Dorothy Hewett **Pf:** 1971, Perth **Pb:** 1972; rev. 1977 **G:** Musical drama in 2 acts; prose and verse **S:** Western Australia, 1930s–60s **C:** 6m, 5f (includes doubling), extras

Sally Banner is an intelligent, sensitive, and rebellious schoolgirl, who refuses to bow to the altar in the school chapel and defies authority by climbing the chapel tower. She explores her sexuality with her teenage lover Michael, then marries David, and has an affair with the Marxist Saul. Finding no fulfilment in her relationships with men, she turns to revolutionary politics but finds these as sterile. In her striving for independence, she writes profoundly felt poetry but alienates her family and lovers and tragically suffers the death of her child. A surreal trial takes place, in which all the characters she has caused to suffer return to accuse her, and she achieves a new insight into her own character. A rich celebrity in her middle age, she donates a stained-glass window of herself to her old school, and goes back to the chapel for its unveiling. She bows to the altar, but not so much as an act of submission but as a way of reclaiming her childhood and seeking harmony with herself and her contemporaries.

Hewett is one of the most acclaimed Australian playwrights, and this is regarded as her best play. It is a sprawling episodic piece, linked with song and dance, and moving in register from elegant lyricism to bawdy ballads. The central figure of Sally Banner shocked many audiences and critics with her frank sexuality and concerned others with her apparent submission to conformity at the end.

Charley's Aunt

A: Brandon Thomas **Pf:** 1892, London **Pb:** 1892 **G:** Farce in 3 acts **S:** St Oldes College and Spettigue's house, Oxford, 1892 **C:** 6m, 4f

Charley Wykeham is expecting a visit from his wealthy widowed aunt from Brazil, and he and his friend Jack Chesney plan to invite their respective girlfriends Amy and Kitty to lunch with the aunt, so that they have an opportunity to propose. They ask their friend Lord Fancourt Babberley ('Fanny-Babbs') to come along to keep the aunt occupied. Jack's father, Sir Francis Chesney, who is heavily in debt, arrives, and his son suggests that he might meet the aunt with a view to an advantageous marriage. A telegram comes from the aunt to say that her arrival is delayed. Fanny-Babbs just happens to be trying on a dress for an amateur theatrical role that he is to play, and is persuaded by Charley and Jack to impersonate the missing aunt. Mr Spettigue, guardian of Kitty and uncle to Amy, proposes to the 'aunt', who agrees on condition that he consents to the marriage of the two girls. Meanwhile, Donna Lucia, the real aunt, has arrived and has accepted a proposal of marriage from her 'old flame' Sir Francis. The long-suffering Fanny-Babbs is unmasked and successfully proposes to his beloved Ela, the now rich ward of Charley's aunt.

It would be a mistake to look for serious comic purpose in *Charley's Aunt*. It has a tightly woven plot, based on a series of coincidences and on the running joke of Fanny-Babbs's inept but nevertheless successful impersonation, a cross-dressing device not seen on the English stage since the Jacobeans. All the characters are likeable; even Spettigue is not wholly unsympathetic, and the play offers good honest fun. That this recipe succeeded is witnessed by the continuing popularity of the play, which initially ran for a record-breaking 1,466 performances and at one time was playing simultaneously in 48 theatres in 22 languages.

Chaste Maid in Cheapside, A (*A Chast Mayd in Cheape-Side*)

A: Thomas Middleton Pf: 1613, London Pb: 1630 G: Com. in 5 acts; blank verse with a little prose S: A shop, the street, a church, and a house, Cheapside, London, early 17th c. C: 28m, 19f

Moll Yellowhammer, daughter of a goldsmith in Cheapside, is wooed by two suitors: the lecherous Welsh nobleman Sir Walter Whorehound and by Touchwood Junior, whom Moll loves. Sir Walter is exercised by the need, before he marries, to dispose of his importunate mistress and his illegitimate children. Meanwhile, Sir Oliver Kix has to contend with his wife's complaints that he has not made her pregnant and is pleased to learn of a potion that will promote his virility. Touchwood and Moll almost succeed in getting married secretly, but her father intervenes at the last moment. Sir Oliver's wife is made pregnant by Touchwood's older brother, whose marriage is in financial trouble because they cannot stop having children, 'proving' the efficacy of the potion. Moll escapes once more from her father, but is recaptured. Touchwood fights a duel with Sir Walter and they wound each other. Sir Walter, fearing death, repents of his licentious behaviour. News comes of Touchwood's death, which apparently causes Moll to faint and die. The double funeral takes place, but suddenly the two lovers rise from their coffins and are married.

Apart from offering fascinating insights into life in early 17th-century London, the play is a fast-paced, intricate comedy, relying on the age-old formula of two young lovers overcoming the scheming of old men to come together at the end – here in the theatrically spectacular scene in which a funeral is transformed into a wedding. The dialogue is peppered with sexual innuendo, and scenes like the one where Sir Oliver is told to ride for several miles after taking the potion, so leaving his wife with the opportunist Touchwood Senior, still work very well in the theatre. Middleton, while satirizing the licentious and mercenary behaviour of his characters seems to enjoy it too much to condemn it. Edward Bond adapted the play for a production at the Royal Court Theatre in 1966.

Chatsky. See WOE FROM WIT.

Chatterton

A: Alfred de Vigny Pf: 1835, Paris Pb: 1835 Tr: 1847 G: Trag. in 3 acts; French prose S: John Bell's house, London, 1770 C: 5m, 1f

Chatterton, a 17-year-old poet from Bristol of considerable promise, has come to live in London, where he lodges with the self-made factory owner John Bell and his wife Kitty. Although Chatterton's withdrawn and sensitive nature makes it hard for him to befriend anyone, a fellow lodger, a Quaker, senses that all is not well with the young man, and Kitty develops a strong attraction for him. Since his writing has not produced anything approaching adequate financial support, Chatterton appeals to Lord Mayor Beckford for assistance. Beckford replies the same day by letter, offering him the post of footman. Insulted by this humiliating response, and despairing at the indifference of society towards his genius, Chatterton poisons himself in his garret.

Vigny wrote *Chatterton* partly in response to the colourful costume dramas like those of Victor Hugo. His play, written in prose, is based not on exotic events at the Spanish court, but on a historical episode from the previous century, which moreover, especially in the figure of the successful industrialist John Bell, seems to have an even more contemporary feel. In place of Hugo's predilection for incident and intrigue, the plot, which occupies the morning to evening of the same day, could hardly be simpler. Yet, by promoting an essentially self-indulgent young man as a maligned genius, Vigny expresses a Romantic ethos more powerful even than Hugo's. Indeed, during the highly successful first run, a young writer committed suicide.

Chayka. See SEAGULL, THE.

Cherry Orchard, The (*Vishnevy sad*)

A: Anton Chekhov Pf: 1904, Moscow Pb: 1904 Tr: 1908 G: Tragicom. in 4 acts; Russian prose S: Russian estate, 1900s C: 9m, 5f, extras

Madame Ranevskaya, born into the aristocracy but the widow of a simple lawyer, now finds herself in financial difficulties. She returns to her country estate from Paris with her daughter Anya. Because of her spendthrift behaviour, the heavily mortgaged estate will have to be auctioned by the bank to pay for outstanding interest. Lopakhin, who grew up as the son of a serf on the estate, is now a wealthy businessman and urges Ranevskaya to sell her famous old cherry orchard as plots of land for holiday homes. Ranevskaya is horrified at the idea and refuses, just as her brother Leonid Gaev will not consider taking employment with a regular income. The family desultorily debate various possibilities of financial salvation, including an attempt to get an old aunt to come to the rescue, but most of their energy is devoted to preparing for a ball. On the day of the ball the auction takes place, and Lopakhin buys the estate. Ranevskaya bursts into tears, takes the money her aunt has sent to cover the mortgage interest, and uses it to travel back to Paris. Her brother will take the offered job after all. The house is closed up, and the sound of an axe felling the first cherry tree is heard.

On the one hand, this last play by Chekhov is rightly described by the author as a comedy. Madame Ranevskaya and her family are laughable in the way that they continue to maintain their aristocratic attitudes to ownership and work in a world that is fast leaving them behind. On the other hand, Chekhov sees clearly how the world is changing, how capital now rules in place of privilege. While this to some extent anticipates the Bolshevik Revolution of 1917 when the aristocracy lost its last vestiges of power, it also suggests Chekhov's sadness at the loss of stability and beauty, symbolized by the cherry orchard. As Trevor Griffiths says, 'the play is objectively comic and subjectively painful'. The play is also remarkable, because, even more so than in Chekhov's other pieces, hardly anything happens in terms of dramatic action. Stasis rather than action becomes a possibility for modern theatre, to be most notably realized in **Waiting for Godot*. Originally premiered by Stanislavsky (who played Gaev) at the Moscow Art Theatre, *The Cherry Orchard* is, together with *The *Three Sisters*, one of the most performed Russian plays. Significant recent productions include Peter Brook's in Paris in 1981 and Peter Stein's in Berlin in 1989, and it has been translated by Frayn (1978) and adapted by Van Itallie (1977), Trevor Griffiths (1978), and Mamet (1985).

Chest, The. See STRONGBOX, THE.

Chester Cycle of Mystery Plays, The

A: Anon Pf: late 14th c., Chester Pb: 1925 G: Cycle of 25 mystery plays; Middle English verse S: Heaven and earth, from the Fall of Lucifer to the Last Judgement C: approx. 50m, 5f, many extras

The cycle stretches from before the Creation to the end of time, following roughly the same sequence of scenes as *The *York Cycle*. On the evidence of the five extant manuscripts of the complete cycle, *The Chester Cycle* probably comprised only 25 scenes, often contracting into one scene some of the 48 scenes of *The York Cycle*. Here also some incidents are omitted, e.g. from the Old Testament the crossing of the Red Sea, from the New

Testament the trials before Herod and Pilate, and from Catholic tradition the beatification of the Virgin Mary. Matter that is not found in *The York Cycle* includes the story of Lot, Christ's healing of the blind Chelidonius, Christ's confrontation with the Moneylenders, and scenes about the Antichrist.

Over three days the guilds of Chester performed different scenes on pageant wagons at different points in the city, often appropriate to their trade (e.g. 'The Waterleaders and Drawers of Dee' produced *Noah's Flood* and the Ironmongers, manufacturers of nails, were rather cynically given the task of staging *The Passion*). As at York, everyday medieval life is happily absorbed into biblical narrative and metaphysical events: so, at the end of *The Harrowing of Hell* a female taverner is obliged to wed a demon and suffer for eternity for watering down her ale. The last recorded performance was in 1575.

Cheviot, the Stag and the Black, Black Oil, The

A: John McGrath **Pf:** 1973; Edinburgh **Pb:** 1973; rev. 1975, 1981 **G:** Pol. drama in 1 act; prose and songs **S:** The Highlands of Scotland, 1813–1970s **C:** 7m, 2f (playing approx. 36 roles)

After a song telling of the love of the Scottish Highlands, a series of historical episodes reveal different phases of exploitation by the rich. The 'Clearances' in Sutherland from 1813: the absentee landlord arranges for the removal of the Highland crofters to make way for the Cheviot, a hardy breed of sheep; all resistance is brutally suppressed. Enforced emigration: Highland families are displaced to the British colonies, where they in turn oppress the native populations. A revolt initiated by the people of Skye, 1882: a small victory was achieved by remaining tenants who forced their landlords to treat them better. The Highlands become the playground of the nobility: emulating Queen Victoria at Balmoral, the rich and powerful come hunting the stag in the Highlands. This continues into the 20th century, with the Highlands becoming a holiday theme park. The discovery of oil, 1962: with the construction of oil rigs off the Scottish coast, the lives of the Highlanders are further disrupted, and in a grotesque conclusion the tourists now come to see the polluting oil refineries.

In 1971 McGrath co-founded the 7:84 Theatre Company, its named based on the statistic that a mere 7 per cent of the population of Britain owns 84 per cent of its capital wealth. Two years later, McGrath began touring Scotland with 7:84 (Scotland), and this piece is the best known of his many works for the company. Turning away from the naturalism of his earlier plays, he created a theatre 'which makes longer connections', using agitprop episodes within the framework of the traditional Scots ceilidh, offering an unsubtle but enjoyable history of Highlands oppression.

Child of Mystery, The. See COELINA.

Children of a Lesser God

A: Mark Medoff **Pf:** 1979, Las Cruces, New Mexico **Pb:** 1980 **G:** Drama in 2 acts **S:** American state school for the deaf, restaurant, James's home, etc., existing only 'in the mind of James', 1970s **C:** 3m, 4f

Franklin, the principal of a school for the deaf, gives James Leeds, one of his teachers, a particularly difficult case to deal with: Sarah Norman, deaf from birth, is now in her twenties, and stubbornly rejects all efforts to teach her to lip-read and to speak, although she signs very well. James is attracted to Sarah, and they meet for dinner and dance together. While James tries to get her to speak, Sarah insists that she is happier in her own deaf world, working as a maid. Despite the jealousy of other pupils and warnings by the Principal, they eventually marry. Sarah begins to live a 'normal' life, playing bridge with James, her mother, and Franklin, but she confesses that she feels 'caught between two worlds'. Sarah and James become involved in a campaign to employ more deaf teachers. Sarah is angry that a hearing lawyer is to speak on their behalf and decides that she will write the speech to the commission. Rehearsing her speech, she declares: 'All my life I have been the creation of other people.' James accuses her of seeing 'vanity and cowardice as pride', and of refusing to speak so that she can be different, and she does begin to use words. Chastened, she withdraws from giving her speech. Later, James is penitent about his outburst, and while Sarah for a while wishes to work things out on her own, they can look forward to a future together.

Whether for Oscars or for Tony Awards, the depiction of mental or physical disability is a great vote-winner. Unsurprisingly then, *Children of a Lesser God* won the 1980 Tony Award; though not just for its sympathy-inducing content, but also for the quality of its writing. It explores without sentimentality the vexed question whether the deaf should be encouraged to join with the hearing in trying to speak their language. On another level, it examines the central question of theatrical performance, the relationship between the image and the spoken word.

Children's Hour, The

A: Lillian Hellman **Pf:** 1934, New York **Pb:** 1934 **G:** Drama in 3 acts **S:** Boarding school and Mrs Tilford's home, New England, 1930s **C:** 2m, 12f

With stretched finances, Karen Wright and Martha Dobie run a girls' school. When they punish Mary, a difficult pupil, for lying, she pretends to have a heart attack. Martha tries to get her aunt Mrs Lily Mortar, who has a dubious influence on the girls, to go to Europe, and Lily angrily retaliates by accusing Martha of being jealous, because Karen is about to marry Mary's cousin, Dr Joe Cardin. Hearing of this accusation, Mary runs away from the school and tells her grandmother Mrs Tilford that Karen and Martha are lesbians. Horrified, Mrs Tilford informs the other parents, who begin to withdraw their daughters from the school. Joe manages to expose Mary's lies, but she first pleads confusion, then calls on another pupil, whom she blackmails into lying to support her story. Seven months later, the school has closed, and Karen and Martha have lost their libel case. Joe asks Karen to leave with him for Vienna, but she refuses when she realizes that he too had his doubts about her sexuality. Martha admits that perhaps she did love Karen, and, overwhelmed with guilt, goes next door and shoots herself. Mrs Tilford, now aware of Mary's lies, comes and tries to make amends, but it is too late.

The Children's Hour was the first play by Hellman, who was after O'Neill the most important American dramatist of the inter-war years. Controversial and often banned because of its open references to lesbianism, the main focus of the play is on the mechanisms of lying and gullibility. Karen's and Martha's lives are destroyed not so much by the mendacity of a disturbed young orphan but by the willingness of supposedly informed adults to join a conspiracy of suspicion, by which even the otherwise admirable Joe is corrupted. It is an irony that Hellman was later persecuted by the House Un-American Activities Committee.

Children Take Over. See VICTOR.

Chiltern Hundreds, The

A: William Douglas Home **Pf:** 1947, London **Pb:** 1949 **G:** Com. in 3 acts **S:** Sitting room of Lister Castle, 1945 **C:** 4m, 4f

Lord Tony Pym is waiting with his father, the Earl of Lister, his mother, and his feisty American girlfriend June, to learn whether he has won a seat in the 1945 General Election. As Labour unexpectedly sweeps to victory, he hears that he has been beaten by the rival Socialist candidate Cleghorn. Magnanimously, they invite Cleghorn to dinner, during which the new Prime Minister Clement Attlee phones Cleghorn to ask him, for tactical reasons, to take a peerage. Despite his egalitarian beliefs, Cleghorn is flattered into accepting, and a by-election is called. Tony, sensing the mood in the country, decides now to stand as the Labour candidate. June is so shocked by his lack of principle that she encourages the Earl of Lister's butler Beecham to stand against Tony as a Conservative. Tony in a huff consoles himself with the willing maid Bessie. Beecham is elected, but Cleghorn persuades him that he is far too professional to be a successful politician, a job better suited to amateurs. Beecham agrees to resign by applying for the stewardship of the Chiltern Hundreds, a centuries-old device for leaving Parliament. He also woos back Bessie, and Tony is reconciled with June. Everyone's station in life is restored, and they can look forward to another by-election.

Lacking biting satire and any serious political analysis, this was the first British play to deal with party politics, written by a Scots dramatist whose older brother was in 1963 to become prime minister. However, politics provides merely the backdrop to a portrayal of class, where, as in Barrie's *The *Admirable Crichton*, the butler is shown to be more able than his supposed superiors. Here too, despite this recognition, the comedy is resolved by everyone returning to their former positions in life.

Chips with Everything

A: Arnold Wesker **Pf:** 1962, London **Pb:** 1962
G: Pol. drama in 2 acts **S:** Royal Air Force base, *c.*1960 **C:** 20m

Pip Thompson is an idealist, who, when conscripted for National Service, insists that he wishes to be treated as one of the men and not trained to be an officer. His socialist views have been conditioned by observing the squalor of London's East End, typified by greasy cafés offering 'chips with everything'. In the midst of fierce discipline and mindless parade-ground drilling, Pip gradually wins over his fellow conscripts to his revolutionary thinking. When, at a Christmas party, the Wing Commander suggests that the men should sing a pop song, Pip gets his men to sing an old revolutionary folk song. The men still distrust Pip, but he wins them over when he leads a successful raid on some guarded stores. Because Pip refuses to join his class by becoming an officer, his fellow conscripts are made to suffer. Eventually, an officer persuades Pip that his motives are unworthy: 'Among your own people the competition was too great, but here, among lesser men . . . you could be king.' Pip relents, first by accepting an order to bayonet-charge a straw dummy, then by agreeing to become an officer. One of the recruits, who has been brutalized for having a smiley face, tries to escape, but is caught and beaten. When the men threaten to rebel, Pip, donning an officer's uniform, persuades them to fall into line. The play ends with the men drilling immaculately to the national anthem.

This play established Wesker as an international playwright. As in John McGrath's **Events while Guarding the Bofors Gun*, Wesker here examines the attempt and failure of a middle-class individual to become one of the proletariat, while (somewhat like Beatie in **Roots*) actually despising their 'chips with everything' mentality.

Choephori. see ORESTEIA, THE.

Chris Christopherson. See ANNA CHRISTIE.

Christie in Love

A: Howard Brenton **Pf:** 1969, London **Pb:** 1970
G: Drama in 1 act **S:** Garden of Christie's house, London, 1953 **C:** 3m

A tape announces the facts of Christie's life. Born in 1898, he was arrested and hanged in 1953 for the murder of six women, whose bodies were found buried in his garden and concealed in the house. Digging in a pile of newspapers, a Constable is unearthing corpses while reciting obscene limericks. His Inspector helps him carry off a body, warns him not to brood on the crimes, and speaks of the public's prurient interest. Christie rises out of the pile of newspapers. He is frightened and excited by women. The Inspector questions him about the murders. Christie masturbates, taunted by women's voices on the tape. The Inspector is disappointed that Christie is not demonic but merely a pathetic asthmatic. The Constable, using a doll, approaches Christie as a prostitute. Pretending to be a policeman, Christie takes her home and strangles her: 'I was in love with her.' The Constable refuses to believe it was love, and the Inspector says that society has 'got to keep love in bounds'. Together, they hang Christie.

In this provocative piece, Brenton challenges conventional notions of morality. The obscene rhymes of the Constable, the callousness of the Inspector, and the prurient interest of the public throw into question the accepted view of Christie as a monster. The danger with such moral relativism is that the brutalization of women, if not condoned, is rendered less objectionable.

Christmas Shopping. See ANATOL.

Churchill Play, The

A: Howard Brenton Pf: 1974, Nottingham Pb: 1974; rev. 1986 G: Drama in 4 acts S: Internment camp, England, 1984 C: 17m, 3f

Four servicemen guard the coffin containing the body of Winston Churchill at his lying in state in 1965. Suddenly Churchill rises out of his catafalque, and it is soon revealed that this is a rehearsal for a play at the Churchill Camp ten years hence in 1984. As an extension of the army's role in Northern Ireland, all political dissidents are now imprisoned in one of 28 internment camps, where they face punishment or death. The second half of the play shows the performance of the prisoners' play for the benefit of the visiting Parliamentary Commission. The play offers a retrospect of the Churchill years, rewriting the traditionally heroic view of Churchill and tracing the development towards ever greater oppression. When homes are bombed in the blitz, the workers warn: 'We can take it . . . But we just might give it back to you one day.' One of the detainees, Mike McCulloch, seizes a gun in preparation for a planned breakout from the camp. The escape fails, but it was pointless anyway, since there is no longer anywhere to run to.

Dismissed by many at the time as an alarmist prediction about the erosion of civil liberties, *The Churchill Play* (subtitled: *As It Will Be Performed in the Winter of 1984 by the Internees of Churchill Camp Somewhere in England*) was prompted by the introduction of internment in Northern Ireland in 1971 and by the treatment of striking miners in 1972/3. It can now be seen to offer an accurate vision of the future (British legislation enacted in the wake of the terrorist acts in New York on 11 September 2001 now allows for detention without trial and even without naming the alleged crime). Brenton debunks one of the most respected figures of British Parliament, and, in the use of a play-within-a-play introduces agitprop shocks into a realistic framework.

Cid, The (*Le Cid*)

AT: *El Cid* A: Pierre Corneille Pf: 1636, Paris Pb: 1637 Tr: 1637 G: Tragicom. in 5 acts; French alexandrines S: Royal palace in Seville, 11th c. C: 8m, 3f

Don Rodrigue loves the beautiful Chimène, who is also wooed by Don Sanche. Don Rodrigue's father Don Diègue is appointed tutor to the young royal prince, which leads to an angry confrontation with Don Gomès, Chimène's father. Since Don Diègue is too old to defend his own honour, Rodrigue is required to avenge the insult to his father and challenges Gomès to a duel. Despite arrogantly assuming that he will be victorious, Gomès is killed by Rodrigue. Honour now requires that Chimène demand from the King the head of the man she loves. At first, however, Rodrigue is sent out to lead the Spanish army against the Moorish invaders. Returning victorious, he is rewarded with the title of Cid. Despite Rodrigue being a national hero, Chimène's honour is still to be avenged, and she promises to marry whoever slays Rodrigue. Don Sanche, his rival, offers himself in a duel, and returns a while later, holding Rodrigue's sword. He explains to the swooning Chimène that he has been defeated but that Rodrigue spared his life, inviting Chimène to kill Rodrigue with her own hands. Feeling honour has been satisfied, the King orders Chimène to marry Rodrigue, but permits a delay of a year, while Rodrigue leaves again to fight the Moors.

One of the first major dramas of French neo-classicism, *The Cid* already displays the main characteristics of the period. Structurally, it is written in five acts in the 12-syllable lines of rhyming couplets, the alexandrine, and scrupulously observes the three unities of time, place, and action, supposedly derived from Aristotle. Indeed, the action-packed 24 hours of the plot have been maliciously described as 'Rodrigue's busy day'. Thematically, Corneille debates the conflict between love and honour: both Rodrigue and Chimène face impossible choices between their honourable love and their love of honour. Corneille still allows a happy outcome (highly suitable for a Hollywood treatment, as in the film version with Charlton Heston and Sophia Loren). Racine's later treatment of similar conflicts recognizes the destructive nature of love.

Cimetière des voitures, Le. See AUTOMOBILE GRAVEYARD, THE.

Circle, The

A: Somerset Maugham Pf: 1921, London Pb: 1921 G: Com. in 3 acts S: Champion-Cheneys' house, Dorset, 1920 C: 6m, 3f

Arnold Champion-Cheney MP, pleasant but a bit of a bore, still resents his mother for leaving his father and him 30 years previously. His wife Elizabeth persuades him to become reconciled with his mother Lady Catherine (Kitty) by inviting her and her lover Lord Hughie Porteous to a small party. Elizabeth has also invited Edward Luton, a businessman on leave from Malaya, and promptly falls in love with him. Unexpectedly, Arnold's father Lord Clive Champion-Cheney also arrives in time to greet the principal guests: Kitty, who turns out to be vain and empty-headed, plastered with make-up to disguise her advancing years, and Porteous, an irritable and unattractive individual. The older Champion-Cheney, aware that Elizabeth is attracted to Luton, suggests that she learn from the unhappy fate of Kitty. Indeed, Kitty asks to come back to her husband, but he enjoys his bachelor life too much. When Arnold learns that Elizabeth intends to run away with Luton, his father urges him to give her her freedom, because she will surely realize that she prefers the security of her marriage. Kitty and Porteous also warn the young lovers of the transience of love. While they all congratulate themselves on the skill with which they have prevented a scandal, Elizabeth and Luton leave happily together.

While better known as a novelist, Maugham wrote plays that continue to be successfully revived, thanks to their wit, interesting characters, and insights into human frailty. Elizabeth, despite all the warnings, may or may not be caught in 'the circle' of repeating Kitty's mistake. Although early audiences booed the immoral conclusion of the play, Elizabeth, not being as trivial as her mother-in-law, just may have found happiness.

Circle of Chalk, The. See CHALK CIRCLE, THE.

Circle of Love. See RONDE, LA.

Circumstances Alter Cases. See ADMIRABLE CRICHTON, THE.

Citizens of Calais, The. See BURGHERS OF CALAIS, THE.

Citizen Turned Gentleman, The. See WOULD-BE GENTLEMAN, THE.

City, The

A: Clyde Fitch Pf: 1909, New York Pb: 1915 G: Drama in 3 acts S: Middlebury, NY, and New York City, early 20th c. C: 7m, 5f

Without knowing it, George Frederick Hannock is the illegitimate son of a respected small-town businessman, George D. Rand. When he blackmails Rand with the threat of exposing some shady business deals, Rand dies of a stroke. The Rand family use this opportunity to move to New York. After some years, the eldest son George D. Rand Junior is immensely successful, about to be married to a rich heiress, Eleanor Vorhees, and standing for governor. He is anxious to promote an image of integrity, although, like his father, he has engaged in illicit activities. When he discovers that his sister Cicely has secretly married Hannock, he reveals to Hannock the truth of his parentage and demands that he annul the marriage. Distraught at finding he is married to his half-sister, Hannock shoots her and attempts suicide. Shocked into self-recognition, George confesses his misdemeanours, even though this will prevent his becoming governor and will jeopardize his impending marriage. However, his fiancée, impressed with his new-found honesty, stands by him.

Fitch was the first American playwright to develop an international reputation, and his many plays, several of them adaptations, were staged across Europe. Despite their melodramatic elements, plays like *The City*,

Fitch's last and arguably best play, and Sheldon's **Salvation Nell* were attempts to deal with current social problems, using the theatre for serious discussion rather than mere escapism and using realistic dialogue spoken by recognizably contemporary characters.

Clandestine Marriage, The

A: David Garrick and George Colman the Elder **Pf:** 1766, London **Pb:** 1766 **G:** Com. in 5 acts; prose **S:** London, mid-17th c. **C:** 9m, 6f

'The clandestine marriage' is that between Fanny, daughter of a rich merchant Sterling, and Lovewell, a decent young man of limited means. Fanny has to keep the marriage secret from her father, because he is hoping to improve the standing of his family by arranging for his daughters to marry above their station. One such suitor is Sir John Melvil, who is so struck by Fanny's beauty that he abandons his wooing of the eldest daughter in favour of Fanny. In desperation, Fanny turns for help to Sir John's uncle Lord Ogleby, who unfortunately imagines that he himself has chances with the lovely Fanny. In the last act, Sterling's house is in uproar, because it is thought that Sir John is locked in with Fanny. However, when the door is opened, Fanny emerges with Lovewell and reveals that they are married. Her father is furious, but is mollified when Lord Ogleby gives his blessing to the couple.

After the success of his *Jealous Wife* (1761), Colman collaborated – sadly for only this one occasion – with the great actor-manager and successful playwright David Garrick. Regarded as one of the finest comedies of the mid-18th century, this play is typical of its period. Well constructed, with lively dialogue, all the characters are good-natured and well intentioned. Though causing great problems, the intentions of Fanny and Lovewell are honourable. Sterling is no grasping mercenary father, Ogleby no mere lecherous aristocrat, as they might have been portrayed in Restoration comedy. Rather, the hope is that the comedy will deter 'young ladies' from committing a similar 'indiscretion' which has led to such 'uneasiness'.

Closer

A: Patrick Marber **Pf:** 1997, London **Pb:** 1997 **G:** Drama in 2 acts **S:** London, 1993–7 **C:** 2m, 2f

When Daniel Woolf's taxi knocks down Alice Ayres, they fall in love and begin living together. She gives up her job as an erotic dancer to become a waitress, and Dan stops writing newspaper obituaries to devote himself to writing a novel. When, a year and a half later, his novel is published, he is photographed by Anna and is powerfully attracted to her. Seeing her again a year later at an exhibition of her photographs, he begs her to be with him, but she is now attached to Larry, a doctor. Soon after, Anna begins an affair with Dan but marries Larry. A year later, Dan confesses his affair to Alice, and Anna tells Larry. Later Larry meets Alice in a table-dancing club, but she pretends not to know him. Anna meets Larry to get the divorce papers signed and has sex with him, which Dan finds hard to cope with. Larry and Alice become lovers, but Anna eventually goes back to Larry. Dan finds Alice, but his jealous questioning drives them apart. She is killed in New York. Larry and Anna split up. Dan, now head of obituaries, leaves for New York to identify the body.

Marber's award-winning play analyses with cruel but persuasively plausible insight the toing and froing between two couples. From these tangled relationships, the women prove to be the wiser and more sensible sex. As Larry admits: 'We're the old people, Dan; old men, shaking our fists over these women, like some ancient ritual.'

Cloud Nine

A: Caryl Churchill **Pf:** 1979, London **Pb:** 1979 **G:** Drama in 2 acts **S:** Clive's residence in Africa, Victorian period, and a London park, 1979 **C:** 7m, 8f

Clive is a British colonial administrator in Africa in Victorian times. With him live his wife Betty, his mother-in-law Maud, his two children Edward and Victoria, the governess Ellen, and his African servant Joshua. The native populace is rioting, and Mrs Saunders, a widow, comes to them to seek safety. Her arrival is soon followed by that of Harry Bagley, an explorer. Clive makes passionate advances to Mrs Saunders, Betty fancies Harry, who is, however, a homosexual who has sex with Joshua and the young Edward, and then mistakenly assumes Clive to be making advances towards him. Ellen, who reveals herself to be a lesbian, is forced into marriage with Harry. Act 1 ends with the wedding celebrations, the final tableau being of Clive giving a speech, while Joshua points a gun at him. Act 2 is set in a London park in 1979, with some of the characters from the first half reappearing, but only 25 years older. Betty has left Clive, Victoria is now married to Martin and has a son, and Edward lives with a promiscuous gay, Gerry. Victoria decides to leave Martin and begin a lesbian relationship with Lin, who has a young daughter, Cathy. When Gerry leaves him, Edward moves in with Lin and Victoria. After suggesting that she too might come and live with them, Betty begins a relationship with Gerry.

Caryl Churchill is one of the best living English-language playwrights, and *Cloud Nine* may be accounted one of her finest plays. Like **Fanshen*, the script was developed from improvisations with the Joint Stock Theatre Company, here on the theme of sexual politics ('cloud nine' being one woman's description of orgasm). The actors soon established a 'parallel between colonial and sexual oppression', showing how the British occupation of Africa in the 19th century and its post-colonial presence in Northern Ireland relate to the patriarchal values of society. To reinforce this, characters from Act 1 reappear only slightly aged in Act 2; furthermore, some characters are played by members of the opposite sex: in Act 1 Betty is played by a man in order to show how femininity is an artificial and imposed construct which can become the determining feature of behaviour. Act 1 is fun but fairly predictable in its condemnation of colonialism. Act 2, in which Betty is now played by a woman, initially seems to depict greater sexual freedom, but soon reveals new and subtler forms of oppression: as the *Sunday Times* drama critic John Peter wrote, being on Cloud Nine may feel good, but it is easy to get vertigo. Churchill here successfully unites the personal with the political, bringing together 'two preoccupations of mine – people's internal states of being and the external political structures which affect them, which make them insane'.

Clouds (*Nephelai; Nubes*)

A: Aristophanes W: *c.*418 BC Pf: 423 BC, Athens Tr: 1708 G: Greek com. in verse S: The household of Strepsiades near Athens, and Socrates' academy in Athens, 5th c. BC C: 11m, extras, chorus

The farmer Strepsiades is married to an aristocratic woman, whose expensive tastes have been inherited by their only son, Pheidippides. Consequently Strepsiades is now in debt, and, in order to evade his creditors, decides that Pheidippides should attend Socrates' academy, so that he may learn how to argue his way out of trouble. Pheidippides refuses to go back to school, so Strepsiades attends the academy himself. Socrates appears, floating serenely above the ground, and encourages Strepsiades to turn away from earthly things and worship the Clouds, who form the chorus. However, Strepsiades proves to be a very inferior pupil and is expelled. His son is sent to study in his place, and after watching a contest between Right, representing traditional values, and Wrong, representing modern sophistry, Pheidippides predictably elects to be educated by Wrong. Although this equips him to outwit his creditors, he ends up by striking his father and championing the new poets. Strepsiades is so dismayed that he sets fire to Socrates' school and drives him and his students away.

Imbued with conservative values and his love of Aeschylus, Aristophanes expresses his disdain for the clever philosophy of Socrates and the cynical viewpoint of his contemporary, Euripides. Aristophanes not only misrepresents Socrates' philosophy but also asserts that he is a charlatan and attacks him for his homosexual proclivities, naming leading figures of contemporary Athenian society as his lovers. Socrates was to blame Aristophanes for defaming him when Socrates was tried for impiety in 399 BC. The text of *Clouds* that we now have is a revised version, written some five years after its first performance.

Clouds

A: Michael Frayn **Pf**: 1976, London **Pb**: 1977 **G**: Com. in 2 acts **S**: Cuba, 1970s **C**: 4m, 1f

Three writers are sent to Cuba to research the country: Owen Shorter, a journalist working for an English colour magazine; moody Mara Hill, a novelist writing for a rival Sunday colour magazine; and Ed Budge, an ebullient American academic, who is a voluble supporter of Cuba's Communist revolution. They are all taken by their interpreter Angel and their driver Hilberto on a mind-numbing tour of a sugar mill, a cane-cutting brigade, a new town, a collective farm, and a fertilizer plant, accompanied by enthusiastic comments from Ed, acerbic observations from Owen, and silence from Mara. Mara begins to get close to Angel and questions him about his life, while Owen grows mildly jealous. At last Owen and Mara confess their love for each other, and Angel and Ed become somewhat disgruntled. Eventually, Owen and Mara have a row, and Angel springs to Mara's defence, hitting Owen. When Ed intervenes, there is a power cut and he mistakenly gets hit on the head in the darkness. Mara, weary of it all, falls into Hilberto's arms.

Set against a reasonably positive portrayal of Castro's Cuba, *Clouds* is a gentle, witty, and well-observed romantic comedy, which traces the tortuous relationships between Mara and her four travelling companions. The title *Clouds* suggests that, whatever the political system, like the uncontrollable clouds humans will fall in and out of love, creating formations that then disperse.

Coastal Disturbances

A: Tina Howe **Pf**: 1986, New York **Pb**: 1986 **G**: Romantic comedy in 2 acts **S**: Beach on north shore of Massachusetts, 1980s **C**: 3m, 4f, 2 children (1m, 1f)

On a beach there are: Leo, a handsome, impulsive lifeguard of 28, still smarting from a failed engagement; Holly Dancer, a somewhat depressive 24-year-old photographer from New York, who fancies Leo but seems to be going through some sort of crisis; pregnant Faith Bigelow (35) with her 7-year-old adopted daughter Miranda; her divorced friend Ariel Took (36) with her son Winston (8); and Dr Hamilton Adams, a retired eye surgeon, and his wife M.J., an amateur painter, trying with difficulty to sketch the scenery. Eventually, Leo confesses how attracted he is to Holly and makes to grab her, while she photographs him as he pursues her. When Miranda cuts her foot, and Leo gently but firmly attends to her, Holly is swept away with admiration, and confesses her love for Leo. They spend the night together on the beach and talk about their past lives. Suddenly, Andre Sor, a 49-year-old New York gallery owner and Holly's lover, appears, and she falls into his arms. A whale is washed ashore, and Leo explodes with anger because no one seems to care how it suffered. Leo pleads with Holly to recognize how superficial and exploitative Andre's love is for her, and she reluctantly gives Leo her address but leaves with Andre. The Hamiltons celebrate their anniversary, as Leo dreams of his next meeting with Holly.

In this gentle and convincing study of human relationships, which is one of the more conventional of Howe's works, there is little action and no particular 'message' to be read from the characters' behaviour. Fine art is central to many of her plays, and *Coastal Disturbances* is in some respects like an acted-out painting.

Cock-a-Doodle Dandy

A: Sean O'Casey **Pf**: 1949, Newcastle upon Tyne **Pb**: 1949 **G**: Drama in 3 acts **S**: Garden of a house in a small Irish town, 1940s **C**: 16m, 4f

On a hot summer's day, a Cock with deep black plumage dances through the garden. The elderly Michael Marthraun and Sailor Mahan enter and bemoan the disruptive influence of the attractive young Loreleen, Michael's daughter by his first wife. Michael wonders whether she is really his daughter or a being possessed by a bird, a belief kindled by an old charlatan Shanaar. The housemaid Marion bursts out of the house saying that the Cock is running wild indoors. The men hide in fear, while a 'Messenger' calmly takes the Cock off with him. As magic events threaten the complacent Catholic certainty of the township, the priest Father Domineer mobilizes the police to hunt down the Cock. Meanwhile, the three women (Loreleen, Michael's second wife, and Marion) appear, bathed in light and wearing bright clothes. They drink to the Cock, and eventually even the men join the drinking and dancing. Father Domineer arrives furious, and strikes dead a Lorry Driver who is 'livin' in sin'. The police and the army hunt the Cock, and Father Domineer exorcizes Michael's house. The Cock appears, shoots the men with harmless bullets, and farts so powerfully that their trousers are blown off. Loreleen is beaten and made to leave her home, accompanied by Michael's wife and Marion. The Cock is banished, and Michael finds himself quite alone.

Unfortunately O'Casey is remembered almost solely for his realistic Dublin trilogy, but this play, one of O'Casey's favourites, shows him able confidently to write a poetic fantasy. The Cock (a bird and also slang for a penis) represents the life force which the Irish Catholic Church did its best to suppress, a kind of Hibernian *Bacchae*. Significantly, it is the women who manage to break free, while most of the men remain timid and puritanical.

Cocktail Party, The

A: T. S. Eliot **Pf:** 1949, Edinburgh **Pb:** 1950 **G:** Com. in 3 acts; free verse **S:** Chamberlaynes' flat and Harcourt-Reilly's consulting room, London, 1940s **C:** 6m, 4f

Edward Chamberlayne, a middle-aged lawyer, is giving a cocktail party, at which there are: a voluble older woman Julia; Alex, who recounts amazing travellers' tales; Celia, an attractive young woman; Peter, a screenwriter; and a mysterious Unidentified Guest. Curiously, the hostess is missing, and when nearly all the guests have left, Edward confesses to the stranger that Lavinia has left him. The stranger promises to get her back on condition that Edward does not question her. Celia returns and hopes that, now Lavinia has gone, she and Edward can marry. But he refuses her, still hoping for Lavinia's return. The next afternoon Lavinia returns, and husband and wife indulge in mutual reproach. Some weeks later, the psychiatrist Sir Henry Harcourt-Reilly (the Unidentified Guest) gets Edward and Lavinia to discuss their marriage. Edward confesses to an affair with Celia, and she to one with Peter. They agree to make the best of their passionless marriage. Celia now comes and, rejecting the banality of married life, decides to tread a more difficult path. Two years later, the Chamberlaynes, now living in unexciting but happy companionship, are giving another cocktail party. Alex, home from an exotic island, reveals that Celia, who was working with a Christian nursing order, was crucified by natives. Terrible as it was, her death, according to Reilly, was 'triumphant'. But for the others, the party is about to begin.

Supposedly based on *Alcestis* and also owing something to the Orpheus and Eurydice legend, this was Eliot's greatest popular success. In it he attempted to debate spiritual concerns in the format of conventional drawing-room comedy, introducing a much lighter tone than in his earlier plays.

Cocu magnifique, Le. See MAGNIFICENT CUCKOLD, THE.

Coelina (*Coelina, ou L'Enfant du mystère*)

AT: *Caelina; The Child of Mystery; A Tale of Mystery* **A:** René-Charles Guilbert de Pixérécourt **Pf:** 1800 **Pb:** 1800; rev. 1841 **Tr:** 1802 **G:** Melodrama in 3 acts; French prose **S:** Dufour's house and garden, and a mountainside mill, France, late 18th c. **C:** 9m, 2f, extras

The heiress Coelina is in love with Stéphany, the son of her uncle and guardian M. Dufour, and hopes to marry him. However, another uncle Truguelin wants his son to marry her for her money. Dufour has offered hospitality to a dumb beggar Francisque, who had his tongue cut out by Truguelin eight years previously, so that Francisque could not reveal the secret of Coelina's birth. When Truguelin finds Francisque at Dufour's home, he plots to kill the beggar, but Coelina overhears his plan and saves him. During a party to celebrate Coelina's engagement to Stéphany, Truguelin sends word that Coelina is the illegitimate daughter of the old beggar Francisque and so cannot inherit the family wealth. Despite the protests of the young lovers, Dufour turns Coelina out of the house. Meanwhile, Truguelin has been denounced to the police by the doctor who treated Francisque's tongue. He is captured after a spectacular chase. It is revealed that Francisque had secretly married Coelina's mother. Her legitimacy proved, Coelina is now free to inherit her fortune and to marry Stéphany.

Pixérécourt is regarded as the father of 19th-century melodrama, and *Coelina* is one of his best. Although the dialogue is sententious, and the characters (the innocent young girl, the wicked uncle, the improbably uncommunicative old beggar) are stereotypical, the simple moral conflicts and the spectacular chase of the last act not only prepared the way for writers like Boucicault, but offer delightfully uncomplicated theatrical enjoyment.

Coffer, The. See STRONGBOX, THE.

Colleen Bawn, The.

AT: *The Brides of Garryowen* A: Dion Boucicault Pf: 1860, New York Pb: 1860 G: Melodrama in 5 acts S: Ireland, 1790s C: 9m, 6f, extras

Hardress Cregan is an impoverished Irish aristocrat who is secretly married to a beautiful peasant girl Eily O'Connor, the Colleen Bawn. Hardress's only hope of redeeming the mortgages on his widowed mother's estate is to marry the rich heiress Anne Chute. Hardress's friend Kyrle Daly is in love with Anne, but Anne doubts his love because she has been told that he secretly visits the Colleen Bawn. Meanwhile, Danny Mann, Hardress's foster-brother, offers to kill Eily, so that Hardress is free to marry Anne. Hardress angrily rejects the offer but agrees that if he should ever send Danny a glove, it will be a token to go ahead with the murder. Danny tricks Mrs Cregan into giving him one of Hardress's gloves and tries to drown Eily. She is saved by Myles-na-Coppaleen, a local poacher, who shelters her. Hardress is about to marry Anne, when soldiers arrive to arrest him for Eily's murder. Eily is brought in by Myles, and all is explained. Mrs Cregan gives her blessing to her son's marriage, and Anne, now aware of her mistake, agrees to marry Kyrle.

Based on a dime novel, *The Colleen Bawn* has all the ingredients of 19th-century melodrama. There is the impoverished widow who is threatened with foreclosure of her property by a villainous squireen; her son who is willing to commit bigamy with an unwanted spouse to save his mother; the innocent young woman who almost dies through no fault of her own; the loyal friend who remains silent rather than betray his friend; and the comical rogue Myles (played by Boucicault himself) who helps to put all to rights. In addition, there are the rural Irish locations, particularly attractive to an American audience, and the 'sensation' scene of the attempted drowning, all of which were created with realistic staging.

Collier's Friday Night, A

A: D. H. Lawrence W: *c.*1906–9 Pf: 1965, London Pb: 1934 G: Drama in 3 acts S: The Lamberts' house in a mining town (Eastwood?) near Derby, 1909 C: 4m, 5f

In the Lamberts' kitchen the mother is preparing supper for her husband on his return from working in the coal mine. Lambert comes in weary and covered in coal dust. He is surly and short-tempered and is soon rowing with his rebellious daughter Nellie. Their son Ernest returns from his day at the College in Derby. Men from Lambert's gang arrive at the house to share their wages for the week. After the men go off drinking, Nellie leaves with her friend, and Mrs Lambert goes out, asking Ernest to keep an eye on bread she is baking. Ernest's friend Maggie calls by, and he attempts to discuss poetry and art with her. Beatrice comes and utters sarcastic comments about Maggie. In the process the bread gets burned. Lambert comes home drunk and threatens first Mrs Lambert and then Ernest. When he goes off to bed, Mrs Lambert discovers the burnt bread, and mother and son share a moment of quiet intimacy.

Lawrence's declared aim in writing his plays, which never gained the recognition earned by his novels, was, under the influence of Synge, to write about the real problems of ordinary people. Embracing a style of gritty realism, which was subsequently much satirized, Lawrence creates an authentic setting and allows stage time almost to correspond with real time. Not very much happens, and the lack of dramatic drive perhaps helps to explain why Lawrence turned to narrative fiction. Indeed, the relationship of Ernest with his mother adumbrates the concerns of his novel *Sons and Lovers* (1913).

Combat de nègre et de chiens. See STRUGGLE OF THE DOGS AND THE BLACK.

Come and Go

A: Samuel Beckett **Pf:** 1966, Berlin; 1968, Dublin **Pb:** 1967 **G:** Drama in 1 act **S:** Indeterminate location and period **C:** 3f

Three women of indeterminate ages, wearing full-length coats and large-brimmed hats that shade their faces, sit in a row on a bench. When Vi leaves, Flo whispers to Ru a shocking secret about Vi. On Vi's return, Flo reminds them how they used to sit together as children, 'dreaming of love'. When Flo leaves, Ru imparts an alarming secret about Flo to Vi. Ru goes, and it is Vi's turn to whisper a secret about Ru in Flo's ear. Ru returns, and the women 'hold hands in the old way'. Flo says that she 'can feel the rings'.

This is one of the most minimalist stage plays Beckett wrote, with a playing time of only some five minutes, adding to his reputation for being obscure. In fact, in perfect symmetry and tight close-up, it tells the simple, poignant, and very accessible story of three women, whose childhood dreams of love end in the stultification of marriage.

Come Back, Little Sheba

A: William Inge **Pf:** 1950, New York **Pb:** 1950 **G:** Drama in 2 acts **S:** Delaneys' home in a Midwestern city, 1940s **C:** 8m, 3f

Doc Delaney and his childhood sweetheart wife Lola have been married for 20 years. They were forced to marry when Lola found that she was pregnant, and Doc had to give up his medical studies and become a chiropractor instead. Lola's baby soon died, and since then she has been childless and become a slattern, mourning her dead baby and pathetically calling for her long-lost puppy Sheba. Doc, similarly disillusioned, became an alcoholic, but has been abstinent for years now, begging Lola to forget the past and live in the present. They have as a lodger Marie Buckholder, an attractive young art student, whose neat appearance and trim body contrast with Lola's corpulent sloppiness. Lola encourages Marie's fiancé Turk, a javelin thrower, to spend the night with Marie. When Doc learns this, his suppressed desire for the seemingly virginal Marie drives him back to the bottle, and in a drunken fit he smashes up the home and chases Lola with a hatchet. Friends from Alcoholics Anonymous drag him off to hospital so that he can dry out. A week later Doc returns, and Lola tells him that she has dreamed that little Sheba is dead, and will not call her back any more.

Inge was one of the most successful American playwrights of the 1950s, and this is his best play, which, when performed with conviction, will easily win over audiences with its concoction of melodrama and popular psychology. It is like a sanitized version of Tennessee Williams, whose **Glass Menagerie* inspired Inge to write plays.

Comedians

A: Trevor Griffiths **Pf:** 1975, Nottingham **Pb:** 1976 **G:** Pol. drama in 3 acts **S:** Night school in Manchester, 1970s **C:** 13m

In a night school, a northern comedian Eddie Waters teaches a motley group of would-be comics how to perform stand-up comedy. Waters instructs his pupils in the need to perform acts that challenge rather than reinforce stereotypes. Unfortunately, Challenor, the talent scout who has come to judge their performances and so is able to launch their careers, believes that comedy should merely entertain. In Act 2 the would-be comedians go through their sets with more or less success, some belatedly changing their act to include sexist and racist jokes guaranteed to please Challenor. The performance culminates in a savage piece of performance art by the star pupil Gethin Price, in which he stabs a female dummy and makes it bleed. Those that followed Challenor's way of easy laughs get contracts, while the others have 'failed'. In a confrontation between Waters and Price, Waters reveals that he gave up being a comedian when at the end of the Second World War he entered a Nazi extermination camp and was confronted by the grotesque joke of a building designated as 'the Punishment Block'. Waters opposes his gentle humane comedy to the violent, revolutionary attitude underlying Price's approach.

As Griffiths wrote: '*Comedians* eschews political theory, professional ideologues and historically sourced discourse on political revolution . . . in favour of a more or less unmediated address on a range of particular contemporary issues including class, gender, race and society in modern Britain.' Using a realistic style where stage time equals real time, and employing a neat three-act structure, Griffiths offered one of the most accessible and enjoyable political plays of post-war British drama. After his experience in Germany, Waters rejects the use of the stereotype as a source of comedy: if one reduces women or foreign races to mere stereotypes, then it is that much easier to fail to recognize their humanity and to brutalize them. However, it is undeniable that the sexist and racist jokes of the 'successful' pupils provoke more laughter than the sinister performance by Price. In this way the audience are forced to reflect on and reconsider the value they place on 'entertainment'. Griffiths, however, does not seek to imply that Price has got it right. As Waters says: 'No compassion, no truth. You threw it all out, Gethin. Love, care, concern, call it what you like, you junked it over the side . . . It was ugly. It was drowning in hate. You can't change tomorrow into today on that basis.' Price responds by accusing Waters of having lost his capacity for anger: 'Truth was a fist you hit with. Now it's like . . . now it's like cowflop, a day old, hard until it's underfoot and then it's . . . green, soft. Shitten.' Defiantly he adds: 'I stand in no line. I refuse my consent.' Griffiths leaves us to choose between the 'cowflop' of Waters's humanity and the 'hate' of Price's revolution.

Come Dog, Come Night. See STRUGGLE OF THE DOGS AND THE BLACK.

Comedy of Calandro, The. See FOLLIES OF CALANDRO, THE.

Comedy of Errors, The

A: William Shakespeare Pf: *c.*1591–4, London Pb: 1623 G: Com. in 5 acts; blank verse and prose S: Ephesus, ancient Greece C: 11m, 5f, extras

Aegeon, a merchant from Syracuse, is under threat of death for daring to come ashore in the hostile city of Ephesus. He reveals to the Duke that he is seeking his lost son, a twin who was separated from his brother in a shipwreck. He is granted one day's stay of execution to allow him to find his missing son. Meanwhile, his other son Antipholus and his servant Dromio arrive in Ephesus from Syracuse and are immediately mistaken for their twin brothers, confusingly also named Antipholus and Dromio, who already live in Ephesus. Confusions arise with masters giving orders to the wrong Dromio, plans to escape back to Syracuse being revealed to the wrong Antipholus, and Antipholus of Syracuse falling in love with Luciana, the sister of Adriana, the ill-treated wife of the resident Antipholus. All ends happily with the two pairs of twins meeting, resolving all the complications, renewing vows of affection, and with old Aegeon finding his long-lost wife and his life being spared.

After *The *Taming of the Shrew*, this is the most successful and most frequently performed of Shakespeare's early comedies. Loosely based on Plautus' **Brothers Menaechmus*, the comic situation is taken a stage further by introducing identical twin companions, a characteristic Shakespearian device of reflecting the confusions of the higher born figures in the broader humour of the servants. Underlying the farcically improbable humour are darker elements: the threat of Aegeon's execution, and the arrest and suspected madness of Antipholus of Ephesus, anticipating the similar fate endured by Malvolio in **Twelfth Night*; above all, the frightening recognition that one's reason and senses cannot be trusted. *The Comedy of Errors* provided the source for *The Boys from Syracuse* (1938), a musical by Hart and Rodgers. Trevor Nunn successfully directed his own musical version of the piece at the RSC in 1976, with Judi Dench as Adriana.

Comic Mysteries. See MISTERO BUFFO.

Common Wheel, The. See SPOKESONG.

Comus (*A Mask Presented at Ludlow Castle*)

A: John Milton **Pf**: Ludlow Castle, Shropshire, 1634 **Pb**: 1637 **G**: Masque in 1 act; blank verse and songs **S**: Pastoral landscape, indeterminate period **C**: 4m, 2f, extras

The Attendant Spirit declares his duty to watch over the children of John Egerton, Earl of Bridgwater. Hearing footsteps, he moves aside, unseen, to watch the dance of Comus, son of Bacchus and Circe, and his retinue of riotous monsters. When the Lady approaches, the dance is broken off, and the monsters slip away. Imagining Comus to be a simple villager, she reveals to him that she has become separated from her brothers. He promises to lead her to them, and she follows him. The brothers come in search of their sister. The Elder Brother, who remains philosophical while the Younger Brother becomes ever more gloomy, are told by the Attendant Spirit, now disguised as Thyrsis their father's shepherd, that their sister has been abducted by Comus. The brothers discover their enchanted sister eloquently resisting Comus, but when they try to seize him, he escapes. Thyrsis summons Sabrina, the nymph of the nearby River Severn, to break the spell Comus has cast on the Lady. Finally, the children are presented to their parents, and the Attendant Spirit reminds the audience that Virtue alone is free and strong but that heaven would help her if she were ever to grow weak.

This masque, entitled *Comus* by its editors, is arguably the most memorable ever written, allowing its rich text to stand on its own as a play. Like the masque in *The *Tempest*, the piece is an admonition to chastity and a warning of the dangers threatening the young children of the Earl of Bridgwater: the Lady was played by Lady Alice Egerton, the Older Brother by Viscount Brackley, and the Younger Brother by Thomas Egerton, while the composer Henry Lawes performed the Attendant Spirit.

Condemned of Altona, The (*Les Séquestrés d'Altona*)

AT: *Loser Wins; Altona* **A**: Jean-Paul Sartre **Pf**: 1959, Paris **Pb**: 1960 **Tr**: 1960 **G**: Drama in 5 acts; French prose **S**: Von Gerlach's home, Altona, Hamburg, Germany, 1959 **C**: 7m, 3f

Von Gerlach, 'the Father', a prosperous German shipbuilder, dying of throat cancer, insists that his son Werner take over the family home and business. However, Werner's wife Johanna first wants to know about the older son Frantz, who since 1946 has confined himself to a windowless room upstairs. Frantz's story is told in flashbacks. When his father sold the Nazis some land for a concentration camp, the horrified Frantz sheltered a Polish rabbi, who was later seized and brutally murdered. While fighting on the Eastern Front Frantz tortured and executed some Russian peasants. Returning to a defeated and destroyed Germany, Frantz attacked an American officer who was attempting to rape his beloved sister Leni. Frantz now keeps to his room, cared for by Leni, with whom he has an incestuous relationship. Father sends Johanna to him to tell him of his imminent death and of his desire to see his favourite son. Frantz, on the verge of insanity, is defending himself before an imaginary 'Tribunal of Crabs', and is dismayed to learn that Germany, far from suffering in misery for its crimes, has become prosperous once more. Explaining to his father that his atrocity in Russia was the one time he acted freely, Frantz expiates his guilt by killing himself and his father in a car crash. Leni will now occupy Frantz's room, while Johanna and her husband leave for an uncertain future.

Not since Aeschylus' **Persians* has a playwright entered so successfully into the psyche of a defeated enemy. And as with

Aeschylus, the purpose is not merely to recreate history but to offer a warning, in Sartre's case about the Algerian War. Beyond this immediate political relevance, Sartre also explores the century's communal guilt about the atrocities it has witnessed.

Conduct of Life, The

A: Maria Irene Fornés **Pf:** 1985, New York **Pb:** 1986 **G:** Drama in 19 scenes **S:** Orlando's house and a warehouse, Latin American country, 1980s **C:** 2m, 3f

Orlando, an army officer, has a loveless marriage with the idealistic Leticia, who is 10 years his senior. He rapes Nena, a destitute girl of 12, in a warehouse. Since being promoted, Orlando is involved in political killings and torture. He continues his visits to Nena, whom he has imprisoned in the warehouse. When Leticia goes on a journey, Orlando brings Nena into his home. He faces an enquiry because a suspect died during an interrogation. Nena tells the servant Olimpia of her childhood: living in a box with her grandfather after her mother died, and being taken off the streets and eventually brought to Orlando. When Leticia returns, she becomes aware of Nena's presence in the house, and also knows that Orlando tortures his victims. Orlando, in front of Nena and Olimpia, accuses Leticia of having an affair. He brutally attacks her, and she shoots him. She puts the revolver in Nena's hand. Nena is 'in a state of terror and numb acceptance'.

With *Fefu and Her Friends,* Fornés turned from the anarchic writing of pieces like *Promenade* towards a more realistic mode, although there is still a dream-like, surreal quality to these minimal scenes, often containing little more than a single monologue. *The Conduct of Life* is a chilling account of political and gender oppression, including paedophilia. Orlando's self-defence of his treatment of Nena is disturbing: 'What I do to you is out of love.... It is a desire to destroy and see things destroyed and to see inside of them.'

Connection, The

A: Jack Gelber **Pf:** 1959, New York **Pb:** 1961 **G:** Drama in 2 acts **S:** Leach's room in an American city, 1950s **C:** 14m, 1f

Jim Dunn wants to make a documentary film based on a script called *The Connection,* written by his friend Jaybird. To provide authenticity, Jaybird has been living for four months with a group of heroin addicts who will perform in Jim's film. Two photographers and a four-piece jazz combo are also present. Now everyone is waiting around with Leach and his fellow junkies for the return of their supplier Cowboy with a fresh fix. Leach claims that he cannot get high any more and is only doing drugs for the business; Ernie was once a saxophonist who still imagines he can play his instrument; Sam is a likeable, uneducated black youth; and his friend Solly is something of a philosopher. They converse desultorily and the musicians play, while they continue to wait. At last Cowboy arrives, bringing with him Sister Salvation who has helped him dodge the police. She hopes to reform these young men, although she is not quite sure from what. One by one, the junkies go into the toilet (visible on stage) to inject themselves. Jaybird decides he must try to find the connection that binds these disparate people together and gives himself a fix. When Leach takes an overdose, the musicians leave, but Leach recovers from his coma. Jim feels that there is just not enough action or narrative in his film and wishes he had brought along some women. However, Jaybird now understands 'the connection'.

Hailed by the critic Kenneth Tynan as 'The most exciting new play that off-Broadway has produced since the war', *The Connection* introduced a new and disturbing realism to American theatre, laying the foundation for writers like Shepard and Mamet. Making few concessions to plot or coherent dialogue, Gelber offered instead brash live music and a shocking portrayal of heroin addicts first craving then injecting their chemical dream.

Conscious Lovers, The

A: Richard Steele (with Colley Cibber) **W:** 1713–22 **Pf:** 1722, London **Pb:** 1723 **G:** Com. in 5 acts; prose **S:** London, early 18th c. **C:** 8m, 5f, extras

Sir John Bevil has arranged that his son shall marry Lucinda, the daughter of a rich merchant, Mr Sealand. However, Young Bevil is in love with Indiana, an orphan whom he rescued from the clutches of an evil man. Not wishing to defy his father's wishes, he hopes that Sealand's daughter Lucinda will reject him, especially as his good friend Myrtle is in love with Lucinda. Lucinda's mother, Sealand's second wife, is at the same time trying to marry her daughter off to her boring and heartless cousin. Myrtle, imagining that Young Bevil is cheating him, challenges him to a duel. The two men are reconciled, and Myrtle then disguises himself as a rich uncle to get access to Lucinda. Sealand, concerned that Bevil, his prospective son-in-law, keeps Indiana as a mistress, visits her. Not only does Sealand discover how virtuous both Young Bevil and Indiana are, but also that she is his long-lost daughter, captured by pirates. The way is now open for Bevil to marry Indiana and for Myrtle to wed Lucinda, to everyone's satisfaction.

Based quite closely on the plot of Terence's *The *Girl from Andros,* Steele's play is nevertheless very much a product of the 18th century. The structure is determinedly neo-classical, packing the many events of the play into a single day, and develops by means of a series of duologues, only at the end improbably bringing all the characters together. Above all, a high moral tone is maintained throughout. Young Bevil is wholly obedient to his father's wishes, Indiana is selfless in her love for Bevil, the servants are intensely loyal, and where violence threatens, as in Myrtle's jealous rage, the exercise of reason saves both men from a pointless duel. This play played an important role in the contemporary theatre's defence against accusations of immorality, its moral probity unquestionable and its usefulness for the audience's education beyond reproach.

Consulting the People. See FEAR AND MISERY OF THE THIRD REICH.

Contrast, The

A: Royall Tyler Pf: 1787, New York Pb: 1790 G: Com. in 5 acts; prose S: New York, 1780s C: 5m, 4f

Mr Van Rough is hoping to marry his daughter Maria to Dimple, a foppish young man who yearns for pre-Independence days. Dimple, however, flirts openly with other young ladies, Letitia and Charlotte. Charlotte has a brother, Colonel Manly, who loves Maria. Although Manly fought honourably in the War of Independence, he is hesitant about pressing his suit with Maria. When Dimple gambles away his fortune, he abandons Maria in order to woo Letitia and Charlotte, both of whom he imagines to be much wealthier. Disappointed in Dimple, Van Rough gives his blessing to Maria's marriage to Manly. In a sub-plot, Dimple's supercilious manservant Jessamy has fun encouraging the naive but honest Jonathan into wooing the maidservant Jenny, but she has the sense to reject them both.

The Contrast is significant as the first comedy and play on a contemporary theme to be professionally produced in America. It was written in three weeks after the author had seen a production of *The *School for Scandal* and significantly gives its hero the same name as in Wycherley's *The *Plain Dealer.* Tyler's play also introduced the first native character of American theatre, the simple but honourable figure of the Yankee in the servant Jonathan. Though he may not be brainy and mistakes a play in the theatre for real life, he possesses a native wit that contrasts favourably with the arrogant cleverness of Jessamy.

Conversation of Ruzante Returned from the Wars (*Parlamento de Ruzante che iera vegnù de campo; Il Reduce*)

AT: *Ruzante Returns from the Wars* A: Ruzante Pf: *c.*1529, Padua Pb: 1551 Tr: 1958 G: Com. in 2 scenes; Italian prose S: A street in Venice, early 16th c. C: 3m, 1f

After an absence of four months, Ruzante, a Paduan, returns from the wars to look for his wife Gnua in Venice, where she is said to keep disreputable company. Ruzante, despite being filthy and emaciated from the wars, is confident that his wife will return to him and that he will be able to fight off any rivals. She, however, is disgusted by his appearance and disappointed that he has come home empty-handed. Gnua's protector arrives, wordlessly beats up Ruzante and takes Gnua off with him. The badly shaken

Ruzante swears that he was attacked by hundreds of assailants, pretends that he allowed himself to be defeated as a clever tactic, and then happily considers how funny it would have been to tie Gnua and her lover together and throw them in the canal.

Ruzante was the stage name adopted by Angelo Beolco in his role as actor, playwright, and organizer of festivities for the stone theatre of his patron, Alvise Cornaro of Padua. This short piece is generally accounted one of his best works. It does not have the complex plot of the *commedia erudita*, and the only action is provided by the thrashing of Ruzante. In this respect, Beolco's work anticipates the lively fun of the *commedia dell'arte*, and indeed Ruzante provides a link between the Braggart Soldier of Plautus and the Captain of the *commedia*. In addition to the knockabout humour, however, this piece also offers a distinctly moving confrontation between Ruzante, who has nothing to offer but his faithfulness, and his pragmatic wife, who now enjoys a better life with her Venetian protector.

Conversion of Thais the Harlot, The. See PAPHNUTIUS.

Conversion of Thais the Prostitute, The. See PAPHNUTIUS.

Copenhagen

A: Michael Frayn Pf: 1998, London Pb: 1998; rev. 2000 G: Drama in 2 acts S: The Afterlife, late 20th c., and Copenhagen, 1941 C: 2m, 1f

At the end of the 20th century, the Danish physicist Niels Bohr, his wife Margrethe, and German physicist Werner Heisenberg look back on their lives. They recall how Bohr and Heisenberg, 16 years his junior, became friends in Copenhagen in 1924, and how, despite disagreements, they collaborated in developing quantum mechanics, the uncertainty principle, and complementarity. They re-enact Heisenberg's wartime visit to Copenhagen in 1941, a mystery to later biographers and a source of tension since Denmark is occupied by German forces and Bohr is half-Jewish. While they try to stick to physics, they cannot avoid discussing politics ('sometimes painfully difficult to keep apart'). Taking a walk together, Heisenberg reveals to Bohr that it is possible to use nuclear fission to make weapons of mass destruction. The horrified Bohr has a row with Heisenberg, and they part on unfriendly terms. Heisenberg claims that his visit was an attempt to persuade Oppenheimer in America to put a stop to research into nuclear weapons, just as he hoped to in Germany. When Bohr points out that Heisenberg's project failed because he did not solve a simple equation, it is unclear whether he did so through neglect or as a clever move to deprive Hitler of the atom bomb. In the last analysis, it is seen that Heisenberg perhaps is more deserving of a place in heaven than Bohr, who after his escape in 1943, went to the USA and indirectly contributed to the deaths of thousands in Hiroshima.

It is remarkable that a play that is devoid of action and does not eschew the complexities of nuclear physics should have become a West End hit. By using Margrethe as a kind of chorus, a bridge between the audience and the central debate, and through an intelligent and skilful recreation of the facts, Frayn turns the scientists' meeting into an absorbing puzzle. It lends credence to Brecht's belief that audiences enjoy learning entertainingly.

Coral, The. See GAS TRILOGY, THE.

Corbeaux, Les. See CROWS, THE.

Coriolanus (*The Tragedie of Coriolanus*)

A: William Shakespeare Pf: *c.*1607–10, London Pb: 1623 G: Trag. in 5 acts; blank verse and prose S: Rome, Coriolani, and Antium, early 5th c. BC C: 16m, 4f, extras

Caius Marcius, although acknowledged as a brave soldier, is despised by the Roman mob for his arrogance. Against his will, the hungry populace is granted representation by tribunes. Marcius leads the Romans into war against the Volscians, single-handedly achieving victory despite being abandoned to his fate by the plebeians within the walls of Corioli. Honoured as Coriolanus, Marcius returns to Rome to become consul, but only if the common people support him. Thanks to his supercilious behaviour, they soon reject him, threatening to sentence him to death and finally banishing him from the city. In fury, Coriolanus goes to Antium to join with his old Volscian enemy Aufidius. Seeking vengeance, Coriolanus leads the Volscian army against Rome, until a visit from his mother Volumnia, together with his wife and son, persuades him to relent. Returning to Antium, Coriolanus is accused of treason and assassinated.

It is hard not to see in *Coriolanus* evidence of Shakespeare's lack of trust in the common people, a now unfashionable attack on democracy. But Coriolanus is not Shakespeare's mouthpiece; on the contrary, he depicts a great and noble character, who destroys himself and almost his own nation because of his unyielding arrogance. His 'crimes' may not be as heinous as Macbeth's, but in the context of his society, they are just as damaging. Small wonder that in 1951 Brecht was attracted to adapting the play, showing how force rather than reason keeps the mob subdued and how Coriolanus relents only when he sees the destructive effect of his own actions. This in turn provided Günter Grass with material for *The *Plebeians Rehearse the Uprising*, which depicts Brecht stolidly directing his *Coriolanus*, while real rebellion takes place on the Berlin streets outside.

Corn Is Green, The

A: Emlyn Williams Pf: 1938, London Pb: 1938 G: Drama in 3 acts S: Living room of Miss Moffat's home, remote Welsh village, late 19th c. C: 10m, 5f, extras

Miss Moffat, a 40-year-old spinster, comes to live in the small Welsh village of Glansarno with her cockney servant Mrs Watty and the latter's teenage daughter Bessie. When she discovers that the village children are offered no education and that the boys at 12 are forced to find employment in the mines, she decides to open a village school. When she is opposed by the local coal-mine owner, she almost gives up, but then reads the startling words of one of her pupils Morgan Evans: 'The mine is dark, where the corn is green.' Two years later, Miss Moffat's school, with the help of two assistants, is progressing well, and she intends to enter Morgan for a scholarship at Oxford. Mocked by Bessie, Morgan rebels at being 'the schoolmistress's little dog', but finally settles to his studies. As he is sitting his examination, Bessie announces that she is pregnant with Morgan's child. Seven months later, to the joy of the whole village, Morgan receives news that he has won the Oxford scholarship, but Bessie insists that he must marry her. Anxious that he should escape the confines of Welsh rural life and pass on his education to future generations, Miss Moffat adopts the baby, so that Morgan is free to go to university.

This play is based on Williams's own life and is an expression of gratitude to the teacher who liberated him from the narrow horizons of his working-class background in north Wales. Although Williams stands as Wales's first dramatist in the modern period, his relationship with his homeland is problematic: behind the rather shallowly optimistic outcome of the play, Morgan's success is achieved only through rejecting his own language and culture.

Così è (si vi pare). See RIGHT YOU ARE, IF YOU THINK SO.

Cottage on the Cliff, The. See EAST LYNNE.

Countess Julia/Julie. See MISS JULIE.

Countess of Pembroke's Ivychurch, The. See AMINTA.

Country Wife, The.

A: William Wycherley Pf: 1675, London Pb: 1675 G: Com. in 5 acts; prose S: Horner's lodgings, Pinchwife's house, and other locations in London, Restoration period C: 8m, 7f, extras

Horner has encouraged his doctor to let it be known that Horner is impotent, which is far from true but will allow him easy access to other men's wives. Although this plan looks as though it will succeed with Lady Fidget, the wife of the foolish Sir Jasper, Horner makes little progress with Pinchwife's wife, Margery. Pinchwife, who has brought Margery as an innocent from the country, is extremely jealous, even to the extent that he forces her to disguise herself as a boy when he takes her out shopping. Horner manages to kiss her, and the furious Pinchwife, threatening to mutilate Margery, forces her to write a dismissive letter to Horner. Instead she substitutes a love letter to him. Horner tricks Sir Jasper into guarding the door while he has sex with Jasper's wife. Pinchwife then accompanies Margery, masked and hooded, to Horner's lodgings. When Horner's lechery is exposed, he manages to persuade Pinchwife that, since he is impotent, no harm has been done.

Wycherley presents a very cynical view of life under Charles II. None of the main characters is admirable, although Horner's flamboyant and cunning pursuit of society women is a source of bawdy fun. In some ways reminiscent of Molière's *The *School for Wives*, here the girl kept in innocence soon learns the corrupting ways of London society and is as deceitful in the pursuit of sexual pleasure as the more experienced women of fashion. In contrast with Molière too, Horner does not meet his nemesis, but survives on the improbable and ultimately irrelevant lie that he is impotent, a device dating back to Terence's **Eunuch*. Garrick wrote a much less bawdy version, *The Country Girl* (1766).

Couples. See RONDE, LA.

Coventry Mystery Plays, The. See N-TOWN MYSTERY PLAYS, THE.

Crime passionel. See DIRTY HANDS.

Crimes of the Heart

A: Beth Henley **Pf:** 1979, Louisville **Pb:** 1982
G: Com. in 3 acts **S:** Kitchen of house in small town in Mississippi, 1970 **C:** 2m, 4f

On her 30th birthday, Lenora Josephine ('Lenny') MaGrath, a spinster looking after her elderly grandfather, awaits the return of her youngest sister Rebecca ('Babe', 24) from jail, where she has been taken after shooting her senator husband Zackery Botrelle in the stomach, because she 'just didn't like his looks'. The middle sister, the flirtatious Margaret ('Meg', 27), flies in from Hollywood, where she is unsuccessfully trying to become a singer. Their father left them, their mother committed suicide, hanging herself and her cat, Meg had a scandalous affair with the now married Doc Porter, and Babe's crime further blackens the MaGrath name. Babe, who had a lonely marriage, brutalized by her husband, reveals that she had an affair with a 15-year-old black boy, whom Zackery attacked for no reason. It was then that she shot him. Unfortunately, Zackery's sister had hired a private detective, who photographed Babe and her lover having sex. Babe's lawyer, however, intends to strike a deal with Zackery: he will withhold information about the Senator's shady dealings, if Zackery drops the charge against Babe. Meg spends a last happy night with Doc Porter. Zackery threatens to have Babe certified, and she makes futile efforts to kill herself. Grandfather is dying; so Lenny plucks up courage to get in touch with an old boyfriend. Finally, the three sisters happily eat birthday cake together.

This is Henley's most successful play, offering her usual blend of farce and seriousness. With obvious echoes of Chekhov's **Three Sisters*, it offers an insight into the frustrations and yearnings of modern women, relieved by female solidarity, which ultimately overcomes all 'crimes of the heart'.

Criminal Genius. See SUBURBAN MOTEL.

Critic, The

AT: *A Tragedy Rehearsed* **A:** Richard Brinsley Sheridan **Pf:** 1779, London **Pb:** 1781
G: Burlesque in 3 acts; prose and blank verse
S: Dangle's home and a theatre, London, late 18th c. **C:** 20m, 8f, extras

Mr Dangle is obsessed with the theatre and, to his wife's dismay, plays host to critics, actors, and playwrights. With his fellow critic Sneer, Dangle attacks the questionable literary abilities of their visitor Sir Fretful Plagiary, but they are induced by Mr Puff to go to see a rehearsal of his latest play. This is *The Spanish Armada*, in which, while England prepares for the Spanish invasion, Tilburina, daughter of the Governor of Tilbury Fort, has fallen in love with prisoner Don Whiskerandos, son of the admiral of the Armada. Puff and his two critics comment on the proceedings, and Puff is often exercised to explain that the cast have cut large chunks from his play. After a series of clichés and plagiarized lines, the 'tragedy' comes to a climax with a jealous Beefeater fencing with Whiskerandos and killing him. Tilburina is driven mad, and the play ends with a pageant of three actors attempting to represent the river Thames.

As with Buckingham's *The *Rehearsal*, much of the fun of this piece would have been better understood by an audience of the day, especially as the Armada would have been a particularly relevant topic in 1779, when Spain again declared war on England and sent its ships into the English Channel. However, there is still so much comedy derived from easily recognized theatrical conventions, like an implausible exposition or a pathetically staged pageant, that the play remains popular.

Cross Purpose (*Le Malentendu*)

AT: *The Misunderstanding* **A:** Albert Camus **Pf:** 1944, Paris **Pb:** 1944 **Tr:** 1948 **G:** Trag. in 3 acts; French prose **S:** Inn in central Czechoslovakia, 1930s **C:** 2m, 3f

A mother and her daughter Martha yearn to escape from their impoverished and miserable life in an isolated inn. Their chance of breaking free appears to come when a wealthy traveller stops at the inn. They are unaware that the stranger is in fact their son and brother, Jan, who has made his fortune after an absence of many years and is planning to surprise them with a sudden revelation. The two women murder him in the night in order to steal his money. Their dreams of wealth and freedom are dashed when the mother discovers her son's identity and commits suicide. When the son's wife Maria arrives in the morning, the daughter tells her that 'in the normal order of things no one is ever recognized', and she too kills herself. The distraught wife pleads for divine mercy and turns for help to the inn's old manservant, who simply answers: 'No!'

Based on an old folk tale, which Camus retold in *The Stranger*, *Cross Purpose* was, according to him, 'an attempt to create a modern tragedy'. It shares with **Oedipus the King* the terrible accident of the unrecognized identity of a son, but in Sophocles it forms part of a divine plan. In Camus, it is merely a cruel twist of blind fate in a world deaf to human suffering.

Crows, The (*Les Corbeaux*)

AT: *The Vultures; The Scavengers; The Ravens* **A:** Henry Becque **W:** *c.*1872–3 **Pf:** 1882, Paris **Pb:** 1882 **Tr:** 1912 **G:** Drama in 4 acts; French prose **S:** The Vignerons' homes, Paris, 1870s **C:** 12m, 6f

Vigneron, a hard-working manufacturer, is devoted to his wife, son, and three daughters. His sudden death from a stroke has terrible consequences. The son is sent to the army. The youngest daughter Blanche is engaged to a greedy widower, who abandons her when it is clear that the large dowry he was promised will not be forthcoming. Eventually, Blanche goes insane. The second daughter Judith is encouraged to take up a career in music by her music teacher, but is then cruelly rejected by him, and she considers turning to prostitution to survive. Vigneron's partner Teissier, ugly in looks and behaviour, claims that Vigneron died burdened by debt, and that only by selling their share of the factory can the family survive. Madame Vigneron refuses, but there seems no way out, especially when Marie, the eldest daughter, declines to become Teissier's mistress to save herself. Finally, forced to live in much-reduced circumstances by the 'crows' that have picked at their flesh, the Vignerons are offered some hope. Teissier now offers Marie his hand in marriage, and the Vignerons' lawyer will use this bargaining point to assure the family's financial future.

It took over five years for *The Crows* to reach the stage, since managers were disturbed both by its content (the merciless depiction of four vulnerable women hounded by seemingly respectable creditors until one of the daughters is sacrificed to the most unscrupulous) and its format (an epic structure like that of the novel rather than the preferred 'well-made play' which used a tight narrative to drive the complications of the plot towards a rapid resolution). Its premiere at the Comédie-Française, however, made Becque famous and assured him a place in the developing taste for naturalist drama. Ayckbourn adapted it in 1989.

Crucial Question, The. See ANATOL.

Crucible, The

A: Arthur Miller Pf: 1953, New York Pb: 1953; rev. 1954 G: Trag. in 4 acts S: Salem, Massachusetts, 1692 C: 10m, 10f, 1 child (f)

Salem's minister Revd Samuel Parris prays for his 10-year-old daughter Betty, who with other local girls had been dancing at night in the forest. Parris is concerned that, led by his black slave Tituba, the girls had 'trafficked with spirits'. At first, his beautiful niece Abigail Williams denies witchcraft. When Thomas Putnam and his wife declare that they have been bewitched, Abigail admits that Tituba and the Putnams' daughter Ruth conjured spirits, but she persuades the other girls to remain silent about Abigail's curse on John Proctor's wife. As Proctor's servant, she had had an affair with him, until his wife threw her out of the house, but she still longs for him. Rebecca Nurse, a respected grandmother, manages to soothe little Betty. A neighbouring minister Revd John Hale, an expert in witchcraft, interrogates Tituba and the girls. Under severe interrogation, Tituba confesses to witchcraft and names local women in league with the Devil. Abigail hysterically joins in, denouncing more women as witches. Betty sits up and joins in the denunciations. The marshal is summoned. A week later, the town court is trying witches. At their home, Proctor's wife Elizabeth urges him to report that Abigail had initially denied any witchcraft, since now even the gentle Rebecca Nurse is accused of being a witch. To Proctor's horror, Elizabeth is also arrested when a doll pierced by a needle is found in her home. He realizes that Abigail is plotting to have her condemned so that she can have Proctor to herself. Proctor gets his servant girl to admit that the doll was hers and goes before Deputy Governor Danforth to get Elizabeth released. When Abigail pretends to be bewitched, Proctor admits to his affair with her and declares 'it is a whore's vengeance'. However, Elizabeth when questioned denies the affair to protect Proctor's reputation. Proctor denounces the court and is arrested. Hale walks out in disgust. Although doubts increase when Betty steals her father's money and runs away with Abigail, Danforth insists that Proctor and the witches must be hanged. Proctor is offered life in exchange for a false confession, but he refuses, and goes bravely to his death.

This is arguably the best-known historical drama of the 20th century and secured Miller's reputation as one of America's leading playwrights. Although it clearly refers to the McCarthyite witch-hunt of Communists in the USA in the early 1950s, its concern with justice and the dignity of the individual at a time of hysterical suspicion transcends mere topicality. Proctor is, like Willy Loman, just an ordinary individual, but his moral courage, like that of Miller before the House Un-American Activities Committee, lifts him to heroic status. When the Wooster Group included a speeded-up version of *The Crucible* in *LSD* (*...Just the High Points...*) in 1983, Miller intervened to stop the deconstructive use of his material.

Curse of the Starving Class

A: Sam Shepard Pf: 1978, New York Pb: 1976 G: Drama in 3 acts S: Living area of a farm on outskirts of a town, California, 1970s C: 7m, 2f

Ella's husband Weston is a drunkard, who has lost his job and only comes home violent to sleep off his drinking bouts. Her son Wesley looks after the farm, while her daughter Emma, a teenager, dreams of escaping from her squalid home life. Ella plans to sell the farm and move with her children to Europe to start a new life, while Weston dreams of selling the farm and moving to Mexico. Ella stays out overnight with a lawyer Taylor while she prepares the sale of the farm. Meanwhile, Weston has already sold the farm to a nightclub owner Ellis for a price that barely covers Weston's heavy debts. A policeman comes to report that he has arrested Emma for damage she has caused to Ellis's nightclub. Ellis seizes back the sale money and runs off, pursued by Wesley. The next day, Weston is a changed man, intending to start a new life. Wesley comes back bleeding from his encounter with Ellis, and, reminding his father about the money he owes, urges him to escape to Mexico. Emma returns home briefly and leaves to embark on a life of crime. Two enforcers blow up Weston's car as a warning that he will have to settle his debts, and mother and son await their impending eviction.

With their dreams of beginning a new life elsewhere and the financial pressure to sell the farm to developers, Shepard's characters are like impoverished versions of those in Chekhov's *The *Cherry Orchard*. Despite being grittily naturalistic, *Curse of the Starving Class* contains bold theatrical elements, including a live lamb on stage, nakedness, and poetic monologues, especially the central image of the 'curse': an eagle that flies off with a cat, which defends itself so violently that both crash to the ground and die.

Cyclops (*Kyklops*)

A: Euripides Pf: *c.* 420–406 BC, Athens? Tr: 1782 G: Greek satyr play in verse S: Before the cave of Cyclops, after the Trojan War C: 3m, extras, chorus (m)

Silenus and his band of satyrs have been shipwrecked on the cliffs of Etna and are now enslaved by Polyphemus, the Cyclops. The satyrs dance on with a flock of sheep. At this point a Greek ship lands, from which disembark Odysseus and his companions. Bribing Silenus with wine, they slaughter some of the sheep, but before the feasting can begin, the hideous one-eyed Cyclops returns. Silenus pretends that the sheep were taken from him by force, and the Cyclops, disregarding the rules of hospitality, drives Odysseus and his men into his cave, where he intends to kill and eat them. Odysseus escapes and tells how, after the Cyclops had begun to devour his sailors, he has been plying the monster with wine. Once he is in a drunken stupor, Odysseus drives a red-hot stake into his solitary eye. As the Cyclops stumbles about blindly, Odysseus' men make their escape and set sail for home with the freed satyrs.

This is the only extant satyr play, conventionally the final piece added to the end of the performance of three serious plays. The satyr play, which always had a male chorus of dancers who leapt around wearing phalluses, offered a rough mixture of humour, violence, and frequently bawdiness, partly as a link to the origins of the drama in Dionysian ritual and partly as a relief from the tension created by the preceding tragedies. *Cyclops* is based on Book 11 of Homer's *Odyssey*, although here various details have been altered, presumably for ease of staging (all the violent action takes place offstage, the huge stone blocking the cave is not mentioned, and Odysseus' men do not resort to the device of hiding under the Cyclops' sheep in order to escape). Long dismissed as an unworthy product of Greek theatre, the predilection of our own age for black comedy makes a piece like *Cyclops* acceptably entertaining.

Cymbeline (*The Tragedie of Cymbeline*)

A: William Shakespeare Pf: *c.*1610, London Pb: 1623 G: Romance in 5 acts; blank verse and prose S: Ancient Britain and Rome C: 21m, 3f, extras

King Cymbeline banishes Posthumus, because he has secretly married Imogen, Cymbeline's daughter from his first marriage. Cymbeline's wife plots to marry Imogen to Cloten, her stupid son from her first marriage, in order to secure the throne. The exiled Posthumus arrives in Rome, where he enters into a wager with the villainous Iachimo, betting that the latter could never seduce Imogen. In Britain Iachimo fails to tempt Imogen, but pretends that he has won his bet. In despair over her supposed infidelity, Posthumus orders her death. But Imogen leaves the court, disguised as a boy, in search of Posthumus, closely followed by Cloten. In the mountains of Wales she encounters two sons of Cymbeline, who had been abducted many years before. One of these has an argument with Cloten and beheads him. When Imogen discovers the headless corpse, she imagines it to be that of her beloved Posthumus. War breaks out between Rome and Britain, in which Posthumus fights bravely and Cymbeline's sons free their father from captivity. Finally everyone comes together. Iachimo's treachery is revealed, Posthumus and Imogen are reconciled, the evil queen dies, and Cymbeline is reunited with his long-lost sons.

Based on a story in Boccaccio and containing elements from Holinshed (perhaps explaining the curious geography of the piece), *Cymbeline* is a convoluted and charming romance, which seems like a respite from the embittered character of **Timon of Athens*. Here nature, as in **As You Like It*, is regarded as a welcome escape from the court, and even the potentially grotesque violence of the scene in which Imogen discovers Cloten's headless body has its own gentle beauty.

Cyrano de Bergerac

A: Edmond Rostand **Pf**: 1897, Paris **Pb**: 1898 **Tr**: 1898 **G**: Romantic com. in 5 acts; French verse **S**: Paris and Arras, 1640 **C**: 42m, 15f, extras

Cyrano de Bergerac excels in both swordsmanship and wit, but suffers from having a very large nose. He is in love with his cousin Roxane, and so is disappointed when she confesses to him her love for the young and handsome Christian de Neuvillette. Since Christian's intelligence does not match his looks, Cyrano agrees to help him in his wooing. He writes a beautiful letter in Christian's name, and Cyrano prompts Christian from the shadows, while he speaks to Roxane on her balcony. To Cyrano's dismay, this is so successful that Christian is invited up to join Roxane, and they marry at once. The Comte de Guiche, who wanted Roxane for himself, orders his men, including Cyrano and Christian, into battle. While defending Arras against a Spanish siege, Cyrano continues to send to Roxane love letters supposedly from Christian. Christian knows that Roxane in fact loves not him but the writer of the letters and seeks his death in battle. Roxane retires to a convent to mourn her lost love. Mortally wounded by enemies, Cyrano visits her convent, and when he reads 'Christian's' last letter aloud to her, she at last recognizes the truth, but the dying Cyrano does not betray his secret.

One of the most popular plays of 19th-century France, *Cyrano de Bergerac* offers a counterblast to the tradition of the drawing-room comedy and to the harsh realism of the naturalist theatre by returning to a heroic past of derring-do and uncomplicated love. In addition to neo-Romantic nostalgia, the central role, based on a historical figure, combines action with intellect and impetuousness with sensitivity. It has been performed in film versions by Gérard Depardieu and Steve Martin.

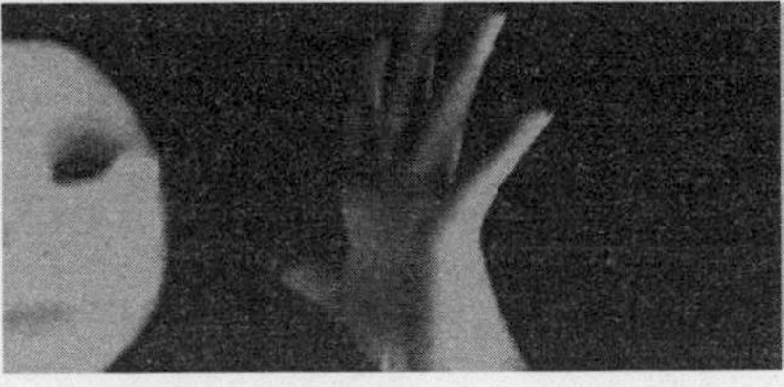

d

Da

A: Hugh Leonard Pf: 1973, Dublin Pb: 1973 G: Com. in 2 acts S: Kitchen and other locations, Dublin, 1968 C: 5m, 3f

Forty-year-old Charlie Tynan has returned to Dublin from London, because his foster-father ('Da'), a former gardener, has just died. As he goes through Da's papers, the old man appears to him. Charlie tries to drive him away, but they settle to reminiscing together. Charlie recalls how the Young Charlie got his first job as a filing clerk with Mr Drumm, and met and wooed Mary Tate. Throughout this, Charlie is half resentful at the way his foster-parents stifle his attempts at education and sophistication, and half admiring of their resilient earthiness. The 18-year-old young Charlie is dismayed to see what the older Charlie has turned into. Charlie gets married and works for Drumm for 13 years. Charlie leaves for London, now as a budding playwright, but the now widowed Da refuses to come with him, leaving Charlie guilty about his departure. Drumm surprises Charlie by handing him a large sum of money, which Da had saved up from the money Charlie had sent him from London. Charlie leaves for London again, with Da following behind.

Using a device similar to the two Gars in Friel's **Philadelphia, Here I Come!*, the two Charlies here confront each other over their relationship with Da in a semi-autobiographical piece, which is an amusing and moving tribute to Hugh Leonard's own foster-father.

Dachniky. See SUMMERFOLK.

Daisy, The. See LILIOM.

Dakghar. See POST OFFICE, THE.

Damaged Goods (*Les Avariés*)

A: Eugène Brieux Pf: 1902, Liège Pb: 1902 Tr: 1911 G: Drama in 3 acts; French prose S: Dupont's home, Paris, 1900s C: 5m, 6f

Georges Dupont is horrified to learn just before his wedding that his one youthful fling has infected him with syphilis. The doctor begs him to postpone his marriage for three years so that he may be fully cured without putting his innocent bride at risk. Dupont, the 'damaged goods', ignores the doctor's advice, marries, and has a child, who develops symptoms of syphilis. The wet nurse caring for the sick child soon learns what the problem is, and when Dupont's doting mother tries to prevent her leaving, she blurts out the truth. Dupont's wife collapses in horror and screams at Dupont not to touch her. Her father, a prominent politician, tries to get a statement from the doctor, so that his daughter may divorce Dupont. Instead the enlightened doctor lectures the politician (and the audience) on the need for better education about syphilis and its dangers, and urges that the matter should be debated in Parliament.

The first two acts of this 'thesis play' are melodramatic, and the ending with its lengthy discussion is frankly undramatic. However, it is the topic which is paramount and which made the play a sensation at the turn of the century. While Ibsen had in **Ghosts* two decades previously referred discreetly to syphilis, this was the first time that a playwright broke the 'gigantic conspiracy of silence' and openly debated the topic with the direct intention of legal reform. Though at first banned by the normally adventurous Théâtre Libre, the play was championed by Shaw and was eventually performed before the US Congress and the President.

Dame aux camélias, La. See LADY OF THE CAMELLIAS, THE.

Dance of Death, The, (Parts 1 and 2) (*Dödsdansen*)

A: August Strindberg **Pf:** 1905, Cologne; 1909, Stockholm **Pb:** 1901 **Tr:** 1912 **G:** (1) Drama in 2 acts; (2) Drama in 2 acts; Swedish prose
S: Island off the coast of Sweden, 1900s
C: (1) 3m, 3f; (2) 4m, 2f

Part 1. Edgar, Captain of an artillery fortress, lives in constant enmity with his wife Alice, a former actress. Their bitter isolation is relieved by a visit from Kurt, Alice's cousin and the new Quarantine Master, who senses the evil in their house. Edgar falls into catalepsy, then rushes out. Alice describes to Kurt her 25 years of unhappy marriage. When Edgar returns, Alice plays the piano and, dancing wildly, Edgar collapses again. Kurt tries to summon a doctor, but, alienated by the Captain's arrogance, they refuse to attend him. Even their servants are leaving. Kurt remains at Edgar's bedside all night. The next morning Alice reveals that Edgar had had an affair with Kurt's wife and taught her how to get custody of their children, but Kurt forgives him. Two days later the Captain has been in town, where he arranges for Kurt's son to be posted to his battery. Kurt is alarmed about the power Edgar will have over him. Moreover, Edgar has filed a petition for divorce, so that he may remarry. Alice begs Kurt for protection, especially as she claims that Edgar has already tried to drown her. She plans to have Edgar arrested for embezzlement, then begins to seduce Kurt. Crazed by his desire for her, he rushes at her and bites her throat. That evening Kurt admits his passion for her. Edgar confesses that he lied about Kurt's son and the divorce. Alice claims that Kurt has become her lover, and Edgar charges at him with his sabre. Hitting only furniture, he collapses again. Kurt has had enough and leaves. Husband and wife are temporarily reconciled, and she now regrets revealing Edgar's 'embezzlement'. However, there is no case against him, and Alice promises to stay with him. *Part 2.* The following summer Kurt's son Allan is in love with the Captain's daughter Judith, who tortures him by flirting with other men. Edgar, however, is trying to marry Judith off to the old Colonel. The Captain sets about destroying Kurt: he will lose his house, and Edgar is sending Allan to Lapland. Judith, now reciprocating Allan's love, swears to follow him anywhere and sends an impertinent telegram to the Colonel. When the Captain learns that his plans for Judith are frustrated, he has a final stroke. Alice jeers triumphantly over the dying Captain but then recalls that she once loved – and hated – him.

Originally to be entitled *The Vampire*, Strindberg's powerful dissection of a 'marriage of hell' (Swedenborg), relieved by the hope of young love in Part 2, is one of his most frequently performed works. Though essentially naturalistic, it contains many symbolic elements and flirts mischievously with farcical moments, like the repeated collapses and sudden recoveries of the Captain. It influenced Albee's **Who's Afraid of Virginia Woolf?* Dürrenmatt's *Play Strindberg* (1969) presented the piece as a boxing match between Edgar and Alice. Reinhardt staged both parts of *The Dance of Death* in Berlin in 1912, and Laurence Olivier and Geraldine McEwan performed in the National Theatre production of 1966.

Dancing at Lughnasa

A: Brian Friel **Pf:** 1990, Dublin **Pb:** 1990
G: Drama in 2 acts **S:** Kitchen and garden of the Mundy family, County Donegal, Ireland, 1936
C: 3m, 5f

Michael, the Narrator, reminisces about his childhood and especially the harvest-time Celtic Festival of Lughnasa, August 1936, when the five Mundy sisters bought a new wireless and their brother Father Jack returned after 25 years' working in a leper colony in Uganda. The five sisters are all spinsters and poor, because the oldest, Kate, a 40-year-old schoolteacher, is the only wage-earner, although Agnes and their simple sister Rose make a little money knitting gloves at home. Chris, the youngest and most attractive sister, is 7-year-old Michael's mother. Kate is outraged at stories of pagan dancing for Lughnasa, but when the wireless plays a sprightly jig, even she joins in the fun. Gerry Evans appears unexpectedly. He is Michael's father, an English travelling salesman who left Chris. He asks her to leave with him, but she knows his promises are empty. It becomes clear that Father Jack has been sent home because he became too involved in pagan African ritual. Gerry is leaving to fight in the Spanish Civil War. Rose's favourite rooster is killed, presumably as a blood sacrifice by Jack, and he ceremoniously exchanges hats with Gerry. When Agnes and Rose can no longer sell their gloves, because a new knitwear factory has opened, they disappear and end up destitute in London. Gerry is wounded in Spain, and Father Jack dies within a year.

While not his best play, the rural nostalgia of *Dancing at Lughnasa* made it Friel's most popular piece, being filmed, and playing in venues across the world, including New York, where one newspaper billed it as *Dancing at Lufthansa*. As in the reminiscence play Williams's *The *Glass Menagerie* (also set in 1936), Friel's drama, based on his own childhood experiences in Donegal, shows a world in transition. The healing rituals of the past are giving way to industrialization, warfare, and mass communication.

Dangerous Corner

A: J. B. Priestley **Pf:** 1932, London **Pb:** 1932 **G:** Drama in 3 acts **S:** Drawing room of the Caplans' country home, England, 1930s **C:** 3m, 4f

Robert Caplan, a publisher, and his wife Freda have held a dinner party for Freda's brother and his wife, Gordon and Betty Whitehouse, a novelist Maud Mockridge, the publishing firm's secretary Olwen Peel, and the cynical Charles Stanton. The company begins to discuss whether truth should be told in any circumstances. Betty argues that life has many 'dangerous corners' and that it may be wiser to 'let sleeping dogs lie'. Failing to find dance music on the radio, they pursue their discussion, and Robert is soon intent on uncovering the truth about his brother Martin's suicide. Martin supposedly committed suicide after being accused of stealing money. In fact, Stanton stole the money to spend on his mistress Betty, who felt ignored by her effete husband Gordon, who was in love with Martin. Martin, it turns out, was having an affair with Freda, while Robert adored Betty. Olwen, who is in love with Robert, reveals that Martin was accidentally shot when, crazed with drugs, he had tried to rape her, and the gun went off in the ensuing struggle. Robert is so shattered by these revelations that he goes upstairs and shoots himself. The play begins again with identical dialogue, but this time Gordon finds dance music on the radio, and the carefree couples begin dancing together.

This was the first of Priestley's 'time plays', written under the influence of Gurdjieff and Ouspensky, who argued that time is cyclical and that parallel time streams may proceed from the same moment. One does not need to subscribe to this philosophy, however, to find this a gripping piece of theatre, a kind of ethical striptease distantly reminiscent of **Oedipus the King*. That the whole tragedy might be avoided by something as trivial as finding music on the radio lends added poignancy, a still popular device as witnessed by the film *Sliding Doors* (1998).

Danton's Death (*Dantons Tod*)

A: Georg Büchner **W:** 1835 **Pf:** 1902, Berlin **Pb:** 1835 **Tr:** 1939 **G:** Drama in 4 acts; German prose **S:** Paris, 1794 **C:** 24m, 6f, extras

Danton, at one time a fiery leader of the French Revolution, now finds himself haunted by the deaths he has caused and so paralysed by lethargy that he will neither address the National Convention nor take any steps to save his own life. By contrast, the puritanical and ruthless Robespierre makes powerful speeches to the Jacobins and conspires to bring Danton to the guillotine. A meeting between the two men merely underlines their differences. Danton is brought to court, charged with betraying the Revolution. Although he defends himself eloquently, disturbances in the streets serve as a pretext to condemn Danton and his supporters. In prison he reflects on life and death, and he and his friends take leave of one another. His wife gets herself arrested, so that she will follow him into death.

Arguably the greatest historical drama of the 19th century, *Danton's Death* is very modern in conception, since the central figure is no active figure. Rather, he is world-weary, no longer willing to attempt to control what happens to him. This reflects not only Büchner's interest in the anti-hero but also his political belief that it is historical events that control individuals, who are merely 'froth on the wave'. Originally published as a text to be read, this episodic play with its 32 scenes and unaccustomed realism was thought until the 20th century to be unstageable.

Daughter-in-Law, The

AT: *My Son's Son* **A:** D. H. Lawrence **W:** 1911–12 **Pf:** 1936, London **Pb:** 1965 **G:** Drama in 4 acts; Nottinghamshire dialect **S:** Mrs Gascoigne's kitchen and Luther's new home, mining village near Eastwood, Nottingham, early 20th c. **C:** 3m, 3f

Joe Gascoigne admits to his mother that he broke his arm while fooling around at work and so will receive no accident pay. They are visited by Mrs Purdy, who demands money, since Mrs Gascoigne's other son Luther has made her daughter Bertha pregnant. This is particularly unwelcome news, since the colliers are about to strike, and moreover Luther has only recently married another girl, Minnie. That evening Joe and Mrs Purdy call on Luther. She demands money for her daughter but does not want to harm his marriage to Minnie. However, when Luther later returns home tipsy, the bickering develops into a row, and he blurts out the truth about Bertha. He does not feel Minnie's equal, since she has money of her own from her years in domestic service. Dismayed and angry, Minnie leaves him. Two weeks later, she returns to learn that the men are now out on strike. She tells Mrs Gascoigne that she has never allowed her sons to grow into real men. Minnie has spent her savings, so that Luther is now obliged to care for her and so gain self-respect. That night both men are missing, and shots are heard from the colliery. Luther returns injured but safe. They have fought the blacklegs and won. Luther and Minnie confess their love for each other.

Still in his mid-twenties, Lawrence was already developing his (unrecognized) talents as a dramatist. *The Daughter-in-Law* improves on *A *Collier's Friday Night* through the bold stroke of writing the dialogue in dialect and by allowing conflicts to develop and be resolved. The psychological insights Lawrence displays help to explain why Tennessee Williams held him in such high regard.

Day in the Death of Joe Egg, A

AT: *Funny Turns* **A:** Peter Nichols **Pf:** 1967, Glasgow **Pb:** 1967 **G:** Drama in 2 acts **S:** Living room of Bri and Sheila's home, England, 1960s **C:** 2m, 3f, 1 child (f)

Joe Egg is the affectionately mocking name given by her father Bri, a 33-year-old schoolteacher, to his 10-year-old daughter, who is totally paralysed from a damaged cerebral cortex. Despite obvious tensions in their marriage, Bri and his wife Sheila have learned to cope with living with a 'human wegetable', as Bri calls her in one of his 'turns' as a music-hall version of a German doctor. Indeed, despite the pain of the situation, their lives are made bearable by wit, humour, and fantasy games, and much of the dialogue is very funny. At the same time, Bri suspects Sheila of having an affair with a fellow amateur actor Freddie. Sheila is growing weary of Bri's self-pitying moods, which she believes are made worse by the indulgence of his mother Grace. Halfway through, in a dream sequence, little Joe Egg jumps up and skips, making her real-life condition all the more poignant. One evening after a rehearsal, Sheila brings home Freddie and his snobbish wife Pam, who offer well-meant but useless advice about little Joe. Bri is driven to such desperation that he pushes Joe out into the cold, hoping she will die of exposure. He relents, but goes out, while Sheila decides to put Joe into a home, so that they can build up their marriage again.

Rejected by the famous agent Peggy Ramsay as being quite unsuitable for the stage, this unlikely comedy based on Peter Nichols's experience with his own daughter became a huge success. The ending remains ambiguous: Will Bri come back? Can Sheila find a home where Joe is happy, since this has never worked before? Does joking about it provide a solution?

Days of the Commune (*Die Tage der Commune*)

A: Bertolt Brecht (with Margarete Steffin) W: 1948–9 **Pf:** 1956, Karl-Marx-Stadt (Chemnitz) **Pb:** 1957 **Tr:** 1971 **G:** Drama in 14 scenes; German prose **S:** Paris and Versailles, 1871 **C:** 42m, 12f, 2 children

The rise and fall of the Paris Commune, established in the aftermath of France's defeat in the Franco-Prussian War of 1870–1, is observed and debated by a motley group in and near a Montmartre café. A bourgeois complains that the war has destroyed opportunity for profit, while the workers and intellectuals are more concerned with oppression from their own authorities. When President Alphonse Thiers and his right-wing National Assembly at Versailles attempt to disarm the Paris National Guard, the Men in the Street resist. In March 1871 they take over the Hôtel de Ville, setting up a provisional government of Socialists and left-wing republicans. Inspired by the rhetoric of a new communal ideology ('*We* is much more than *you and I*!'), the Communards are weakened by their leaders' refusal to contemplate violence in the defence of their vulnerable democracy, urged by the young radical Raoul Rigault. Eventually in May, backed by the Prussian victor Otto von Bismarck, Versailles troops march on Paris. While the Men in the Street bravely die on the barricades, the bourgeoisie and aristocrats applaud from the walls of Versailles. They congratulate Thiers: 'You have restored Paris to its rightful master, France.' In Paris 20,000 are massacred.

This play, a critical response to Nordahl Grieg's *The Defeat* (1937), was the last to be (almost) completed by Brecht and performed posthumously as the first original production at the Berliner Ensemble. It traces the bold attempt to establish the first socialist government in history and argues that its demise was due to a dangerous reluctance to use violence to defend the revolution. Clearly, parallels were intended with the young German Democratic Republic, and the play's message could sadly justify oppression by the Communist regime.

Days of the Turbins, The (*Dni Turbinykh*)

AT: *The White Guard* A: Mikhail Bulgakov **Pf:** 1926, Moscow **Pb:** 1955 **Tr:** 1935 **G:** Hist. drama in 4 acts; Russian prose **S:** Kiev, winter 1918–19 **C:** 24m, 1f, extras

Kiev, capital of the Ukraine, is, before their defeat in the First World War, temporarily in the hands of the Germans, who have appointed Skoropadsky as Hetman (Commander-in-Chief). Colonel Aleksei Turbin and his younger brother Nikolai of the Russian White Guard have come to Kiev to defend the Hetman against the nationalist Cossacks in the east and against the Russian Red Army in the north. As the Germans withdraw, some of the White Guard leaders desert. Aleksei's sister Yeliena is treacherously abandoned by her husband, and the Hetman flees to Berlin. As the Cossacks enter Kiev, Aleksei finds himself isolated. Refusing to despair, the Turbins hold a party, at which Yeliena becomes engaged to an opera singer. Aleksei encourages his brigade of cadets to disband, but he and his brother fight bravely to cover the retreat of the Whites, Aleksei falling in battle and Nikolai being wounded. As the Red Army approaches singing 'The Internationale', Nikolai recognizes that it is with them that the future lies.

This stage adaptation by Bulgakov of his novel *The White Guard* of 1925 is the most significant dramatic treatment of the Russian civil war and one of the few that gave a sympathetic view of the White Army. Despite a successful premiere by Stanislavsky at the Moscow Art Theatre as the first new Russian play since 1917, the subject matter caused considerable controversy and led to frequent banning of the play. However Stalin, who had seen it 15 times, intervened, praising it as showing that the adversaries of the Revolution were 'intelligent and powerful'.

Dead End

A: Sidney Kingsley **Pf:** 1935, New York **Pb:** 1936 **G:** Drama in 3 acts **S:** Slum street, New York, 1930s **C:** 25m, 6f, 3 young boys

Tommy McGrath is the leader of a gang of six young lads, who live in a dead-end slum street ending at the East River. They play, dive into the polluted river, and sneer at rich passers-by heading for the adjacent luxury apartments. Gimpty Pete, an unemployed young architect crippled with rickets, continues to live in the slum but hopes to win the love of an attractive girl from the luxury apartments. Babyface Martin, a hardened gangster, returns to the slum to visit his mother and his former girlfriend, but his mother rejects him and his girlfriend is now a diseased prostitute. The dead-end kids challenge neighbouring rich kids to a game of poker, and cheat one of them out of his watch. When his father comes to retrieve his son's watch, Tommy stabs him in the wrist. Gimpty, desperate to gain enough money to impress his girlfriend, betrays Martin to the police, but the girl leaves him for another, knowing that the reward money will not last long. Martin is gunned down, and Tommy is betrayed by a frightened gang member. Tommy will be sent to a reform school, where he will learn only how to be a real gangster, and Gimpty comforts Tommy's sister Drina by offering the reward money to pay for Tommy's legal defence.

The naturalistic depiction of the contrast between the rich and the poor living side by side in New York made *Dead End* a huge success and led to a Congressional campaign of slum clearance. With a spectacularly realistic set by Norman Bel Geddes, the play ran for 684 performances. In 1937 it was made into a film, which made the 'dead-end kids' internationally famous and offered an early starring role to Humphrey Bogart as Babyface Martin.

Dead Fish. See DUSA, FISH, STAS AND VI.

Dear Janet Rosenberg, Dear Mr Kooning

A: Stanley Eveling **Pf:** 1969, Edinburgh **Pb:** 1971 **G:** Romantic com. in 2 acts **S:** Janet's room and Alec's room, Britain, *c*.1970 **C:** 1m, 1f

At the age of 19, Janet Rosenberg writes an appreciative letter to the 50-year-old novelist Alec Kooning, who replies warmly to her praise. When she writes again, he fantasizes about his youthful fan, but does not send the reply he wrote. Having heard nothing from him, she takes a near-fatal overdose, then asks whether he can help her find one of his out-of-print novels. She claims to receive copies of all his books and a large bunch of roses, but he denies sending them. He then fantasizes about meeting her and begs to be allowed to visit. She reluctantly agrees. He travels to see her, but meets only her mother (played by the same actress as Janet), who asks him to make love to her. He refuses and waits on alone in Janet's room. She appears to him, and they lie down on the bed together, but he cannot continue. He leaves, almost forgetting to put on his trousers. The correspondence continues, Alec veering from bouts of jealous melancholy to assertions that he is rejuvenated, Janet growing gradually weary of him. Eventually their exchanges become fused into 'a monologue for two', and Alec, facing the futility of his life and of his love for Janet, shoots himself. Finally, Janet/Mrs Rosenberg writes a letter thanking an admirer for his praise for her latest play, in which Janet and Alec meet and marry and enjoy an ironically happy ending.

In an ironic reference to his own play, Eveling speaks of 'the curious mixture of farce and misery which is the slight ripple left by the receding impulse of tragedy'. This comedy deftly portrays the interplay of reality and fantasy, Janet Rosenberg consciously assuming a younger, more glamorous identity, Alec Kooning also struggling with the question of who he really is.

Death and Resurrection of Mr Roche, The

A: Thomas Kilroy **Pf:** 1968, Dublin **Pb:** 1969 **G:** Com. in 2 acts **S:** Kelly's flat in Dublin, 1960s **C:** 6m

Death and the Fool

After a drinking session in a Dublin pub, six men repair to Kelly's flat to continue drinking and chatting. Only one of them is married: Seamus, a teacher, who after only two years of marriage is already weary of its 'sameness'. Their host Kelly is a 36-year-old civil servant, missing his home in the country where he grew up, but now resigned to being 'the success of my family'. The last to arrive is Mr Roche, an older man whose homosexual proclivities are a source of amusement to the others. For a joke, they lock him in the bathroom with Kevin, a student. Roche is unamused by the prank since he is claustrophobic, and when he complains, homophobic Kelly picks a quarrel with Roche. The men now force Roche into a basement recess, the 'holy hole', and leave him there for a few minutes. When they go to fetch him, Doc, a medical student, examines his inert body and pronounces him dead. Kelly persuades Doc and Kevin to take the body out and leave it on a bench. While they are away, Kelly confesses to his friend Seamus that he once had a brief homosexual affair with Mr Roche. Early the next morning, Doc, Kevin, and Roche reappear: the rain had revived Roche, just as the two students were about to abandon him in the park. Kelly is now afraid that Roche may blackmail him, but Roche claims to have forgotten everything.

Although public attention focused on the fact that this was the first Irish play openly to debate homosexuality, Mr Roche is primarily a catalyst to self-revelation for Kelly and Seamus. Both men are willing to collude in what appears to be homophobic manslaughter, but perhaps with Kelly's acknowledgement of his homosexuality and Seamus's looking for more in his marriage, the sterile lives of these men may be improved through the 'resurrection' and forgiveness of Mr Roche.

Death and the Fool. See MISTERO BUFFO.

Death and the King's Horsemen

A: Wole Soyinka Pf: 1976, Ife, Nigeria Pb: 1975 G: Trag. in 5 scenes; prose and verse S: Town of Oyo, western Nigeria, during the Second World War C: 9m, 3f, extras

Following Yoruba religious practice, Elesin Oba is about to commit ritual suicide in order to accompany his late chief, the Alafin of Oyo, on his journey to the spirit world. On the way to his death, Elesin, who is escorted by a group of praise-singers and drummers, encounters a beautiful young woman in the marketplace. Although she is engaged to the son of the market-woman Iyaloja, Iyaloja gives her blessing to Elesin's marriage to her before he dies. Meanwhile, the British District Officer Pilkings and his wife throw a fancy-dress ball to welcome the arrival of the Prince of Wales, and unwittingly commit sacrilege by dressing in *egungun* masquerade costumes, to be worn only when invoking the spirits of the dead. The ball is attended by Olunde, Elesin's eldest son, whom the Pilkings took from his native home to send to medical school in England. Far from being grateful, Olunde now feels alienated from his own community but equally not accepted by the white Europeans. At the ball he argues with Jane Pilkings about the colonial attitudes of the British. When Pilkings learns of the 'barbaric' ritual of Elesin's suicide, he orders the arrest of Elesin and the dispersal of the worshippers. However, the market-women, led by Iyaloja, hold back the soldiers long enough for Elesin and his bride to be wed. Elesin enters a trance, but does not die owing to 'a weight of longing on my earth-held limbs'. Elesin is arrested by the police, and Olunde confronts him angrily for reneging on his duty to the gods. Olunde offers himself instead for ritual sacrifice, and, when his corpse is carried in accompanied by a dirge from the worshippers, Elesin finally finds the strength to take his own life.

Death and the King's Horsemen, arguably the best play to emerge from West Africa, became the internationally most successful of Soyinka's plays and set him on the road to winning the Nobel Prize. While Western audiences tend to read the play as one about colonial intervention in native African tradition, Soyinka insists that this is merely a 'a catalytic incident'. Indeed, the timescale is confused: the incident on which the play is based occurred in 1946, the play is set in the Second World War, and yet there had been no

Prince of Wales since 1936. The focus of the piece is on the confrontation between the Western-educated Olunde, like Soyinka no longer truly a part of his own community and yet not accepted by the whites, who finds a path back to himself, to the spirits of the dead, and to his native soil by fatally embracing ancient ritual. It remains ambiguous, however, whether Olunde's sacrificial act will restore harmony.

Death and the Maiden (*La muerte y la doncella*)

A: Ariel Dorfman **Pf:** 1991, Santiago, Chile **Pb:** 1990 **Tr:** 1990 **G:** Pol. drama in 3 acts; Spanish prose **S:** Escobars' living room, Latin American country (Chile), *c.*1990 **C:** 2m, 1f

In a country where the former dictatorship has just been replaced with democracy, Gerardo Escobar (45) has been summoned to take part in a Commission investigating crimes by the former regime. Gerardo's wife Paulina (40), who was herself abducted, raped, and tortured 15 years previously, hopes he will discover the truth of her case. Roberto Miranda (50), a doctor, gives Gerardo a lift when his car has a puncture, and is invited to stay the night. Paulina, recognizing Roberto as her torturer, knocks him unconscious and ties him to a chair. She plays the music that Roberto always listened to while violating his detainees: Schubert's *Death and the Maiden Quartet*. She tells the horrified Roberto that they will try him in their own house. She declares that if Roberto confesses to his crimes, she will let him go. Roberto claims that he has nothing to confess, so Gerardo gets Paulina to tell him the details of what she suffered. He secretly passes on these details to Roberto, who duly confesses and signs. Paulina sends Gerardo off to fetch his car, and then threatens to shoot Roberto, because he is not truly repentant and only pretended to confess. He pleads with her to draw a line under the past, but she does not know why they 'are always the ones who have to make concessions'. They freeze, a mirror is lowered reflecting the audience, and a concert of Schubert begins, attended by Paulina, Gerardo, and Roberto (perhaps just 'an illusion in Paulina's head').

In this popular play by Chilean writer Dorfman about Pinochet's crimes, the desire for revenge and justice is opposed to the need for reconciliation. Despite the ambiguity of the ending, Dorfman seems to imply that the patient, unspectacular compromise of Gerardo is to be preferred to the radicalism of Paulina.

Death of a Salesman

A: Arthur Miller **Pf:** 1949, New York **Pb:** 1949 **G:** Trag. in 2 acts and a 'Requiem' **S:** Lomans' house and yard in Brooklyn, and other locations in New York and Boston, mid-20th c. **C:** 8m, 5f

Willy Loman is a travelling salesman in his early sixties, 'tired to the death' after a life of hard work. He tells his wife Linda how worried he is about their elder son Biff, 34 and unemployed. Biff is contrasted with his younger brother Happy, who has a steady job, his 'own apartment, a car, and plenty of women'. But Happy is not content, and the two brothers dream briefly of working on a ranch 'out West'. Willy drifts off into reminiscing about the past: we see Biff and Happy as young boys, and Willy boasting about his earnings, although Linda is having difficulty making ends meet. Willy's neighbour Charley offers Willy a job, but Willy drifts off into a dream about his Uncle Ben, an adventurer whom Willy admired and who has recently died. When Willy wanders off for a walk in his slippers, Linda tells her sons to respect him: 'I don't say he's a great man.... But he's a human being, and a terrible thing is happening to him. So attention must be paid.' Willy pretends to earn money as a salesman but is actually borrowing money. Worse still, he is preparing for suicide so that his family can get his life insurance money: Linda has found a length of rubber pipe by the gas pipe. Though Biff hates the city, he agrees to stay and help his parents and ask for a job from his former boss Bill Oliver. The following morning, Willy asks his boss Howard for an advance. Howard not only refuses; he even sacks Willy. Willy goes to Charley, again indignantly refuses the offer of a job, but borrows money from him. That evening Biff and Happy have invited their father out for dinner. Happy finds a woman for himself and his brother. Biff waited all day, only to discover that Bill Oliver could not even remember him. Dismayed, Biff stole his fountain pen and ran off. Willy arrives, and soon Willy and Biff are arguing again. A past episode that has haunted Willy throughout the play is now enacted: Biff comes to see Willy in his hotel room and discovers that he has got a woman with him. Biff and Happy abandon Willy to leave with their women. When they get home, they find their father in the dark planting seeds. Ben invites Willy to join him in death, and Willy drives off at high speed and kills himself. At his graveside Charley sums up his life: 'A salesman is . . . a man way out there in the blue, riding on a smile and shoeshine.'

Probably the best-known play to have come from the States and frequently revived, *Death of a Salesman* is arguably the closest any 20th-century playwright has come to writing a contemporary tragedy. Willy Loman ('low man'), 'a King Lear in mufti', as the critic John Gassner described him, is intended to demonstrate that even the most ordinary individual can be the focus of tragedy. When asked what Willy carried in his bags, Miller answered; 'Himself.' Having tried to sell himself as a salesman, all that is left is to sell his own death. In this 'mobile concurrency of past and present', which Miller originally thought of entitling *The Inside of His Head*, the writer skilfully blends naturalistic dialogue with dream-like reminiscence.

Death of Bessie Smith, The

A: Edward Albee **Pf:** 1960, Berlin; 1961, New York **Pb:** 1960 **G:** Drama in 8 scenes **S:** Hospital and other locations, Memphis, Tennessee, 1937 **C:** 5m, 2f

Two stories alternate. In one, Jack, the black driver and friend of the blues singer Bessie Smith, is stopping with her in Memphis on their way north to a big engagement in New York. He drinks, and they have a crash, but are refused admission to the ironically named Mercy Hospital, because they are black. In the other story, a Nurse at another hospital displays the racist attitudes that she has inherited from her irascible old Father. She reminds a black Orderly that his people have no right to aspire towards assimilation with the whites. She is willingly wooed by a young liberal-minded Intern, but recognizes that they cannot marry at this stage in his career and dominates him cruelly. The Intern dreams of achieving something more than treating the mayor's piles, perhaps of joining the Republicans in the Spanish Civil War. In the final scene, the stories converge: Jack pleads with the Intern to treat Bessie, while the Nurse tries to turn him away. The Intern goes out to Bessie but discovers that she has already died. The Nurse is furious over the Intern's behaviour and begins to 'sing and laugh at the same time', 'almost like keening'. The Intern slaps her hard.

It is tempting to see this as a play purely about race (especially as only the 'victims' Bessie and Jack have names). However, as Albee wrote: 'I am not concerned with politics . . . but I have a dislike of waste . . . stagnation.' As with the complacent middle-class figure in *The *Zoo Story*, Albee 'has a sense of urgency' about the failure of humanity to communicate and to recognize its own spirituality. By letting the 'Empress of the Blues' die so callously, white America shows it has lost its humanity.

Death of Cuchulain, The

A: W. B. Yeats **Pf:** 1945, Dublin **Pb:** 1939 **G:** Drama in 1 act; blank verse with a prose prologue **S:** Ireland, 1st c. AD **C:** 4m, 4f, 3 musicians

After a witty prologue by an Old Man (the author), Eithne Inguba, Cuchulain's young mistress, comes to him with a message from his wife Emer: that he must go out and fight an invading force under Queen Maeve. Eithne also carries a letter from Emer cautioning him to await reinforcements, and Eithne fears that Morrigu, the goddess of war, put the false message in her mouth. Although suspecting that Eithne wants to send him to his death, Cuchulain goes out to fight. Returning wounded, he binds himself to a stake. Aoife, former enemy and lover, comes, and they speak of the past. The Blind Man appears, hoping for a reward if he brings Cuchulain's head. As he is about to behead Cuchulain, the stage darkens, and Morrigu stands there holding Cuchulain's severed head. He has been slain by Maeve's lovers and sons, and Emer enters to perform a dance of mourning and anger. Street singers break into the solemn moment: they sing of the great heroes of the past and of Cuchulain, now nothing but a mediocre statue in the Dublin Post Office.

The Death of Cuchulain is, appropriately enough, Yeats's last play and is a reprise of many of the characters and themes of his Cuchulain cycle. Cuchulain did not die **On Baile's Strand*, in which the Blind Man and Aoife also feature, but was saved by Emer (whom we encounter in *The Only Jealousy of Emer* of 1919). Significantly, still in 1939 Yeats was treading his lonely symbolist path: a parallelogram represents the severed head, and there is a dance ('where there are no words there is less to spoil'). As Europe descended into chaos, Yeats mourned the passing of the great heroes of the past.

Death of General Warren, The. See BUNKER-HILL.

Deathwatch (*Haute Surveillance*)

A: Jean Genet **Pf**: 1949, Paris **Pb**: 1949; rev. 1965 **Tr**: 1954 **G**: Drama in 1 act; French prose **S**: Cell in a French prison, 1940s **C**: 4m

Three prisoners are confined in the same cell: Green Eyes, the most dominant, a murderer so dangerous that his feet are shackled; Lefranc, who is due to be released in a few days; and Maurice, the youngest, who is jealous of Lefranc's close relationship with Green Eyes. The men discuss Snowball, a magnificent black murderer on death row. Green Eyes, whose illiteracy has forced him to get Lefranc to write his letters, is afraid that Lefranc will now steal his girlfriend. When Green Eyes contemplates the guillotine and is concerned that his girl will find someone else, Maurice offers to kill her. Green Eyes insists that Lefranc and Maurice should draw lots to decide who should murder her. When she arrives at the prison to visit Green Eyes, he sends her away and says that the guard can have her. Lefranc, provoked by Maurice because he sneers at Lefranc's attempts to claim that his petty crimes make him a truly hard man, strangles Maurice. Lefranc now believes that he has become like Green Eyes, but Green Eyes rejects Lefranc's cowardly crime and calls the guards.

This was Genet's first play, though not produced until two years after *The *Maids*. With strong similarities to Sartre's **No Exit*, *Deathwatch*, based on Genet's own experiences in prison, explores particularly the agonizing struggle of two individuals trying to acquire the criminal glory enjoyed by Green Eyes and Snowball: 'It's not enough . . . to be shut up lifeless in a cell. We've got to kill each other off as well.' This mutual torture should be enacted 'as in a dream'.

Decadence

A: Steven Berkoff **Pf**: 1981, London **Pb**: 1981 **G**: Com. in 14 scenes; free verse, some rhymed **S**: Expensive homes, opera, and restaurant, England, *c*.1980 **C**: 2 performers, playing 2m, 2f

Upper-class Steve Forsyth visits his upmarket mistress Helen, but warns that his wife Sybil is having him followed by a private detective Les. Played by the same actors, Les reports to Sybil, who is lower class but rich from her father's hard work. She is having an affair with Les. Steve and Helen talk about their loveless childhoods and his homosexual experiences at public school. They leave to go to the theatre to see 'all those dishy soldiers in the raw with cocks a-flashing everywhere | . . . to shock us pink and crave for more' (almost certainly a reference to Brenton's **Romans in Britain*). Helen, riding on Steve's back, describes the excitement of fox-hunting; he expounds his racist views. They go to the opera and then eat until Steve is sick ('a wonderful night!'). Les, who has been plotting to murder Steve, decides not to bother, and Sybil throws him out, celebrating her independence. Steve and Helen luxuriate in their pampered lifestyle, but '*as the light fades they age in the results of their debauched lives*'.

From the working classes of **East*, Berkoff turns here to the English upper classes, 'so called by virtue of strangulated vowel tones rather than any real achievement'. While his intention is satirical, his envy seems almost as strong as his contempt.

Deceived, The (*Gl'ingannati*)

A: Accademia degli Intronati di Siena (?Lodovico Castelvetro) Pf: 1532, Siena Pb: 1538 Tr: 1964 G: *Commedia erudita* in 5 acts; Italian (Tuscan) prose S: A street in Modena, 1532 C: 12m, 5f

Having lost his fortune in the Sack of Rome of 1527, Virginio is now hoping to solve his money problems by giving his daughter Lelia in marriage to the wealthy and elderly Gherardo. Lelia is supposed to be in a convent, but has escaped, disguised as a man and calling herself Fabio. To be with the man she loves, Flamminio, Lelia has become his page and helps him to woo Gherardo's daughter, Isabella. Isabella, however, falls in love with Fabio/Lelia, and Lelia takes advantage of this to encourage Isabella to spurn Flamminio's love. Meanwhile Lelia's identical twin brother Fabrizio has come to Modena in search of Lelia. Virginio and Gherardo, having learned about Lelia's escape, assume that Fabrizio is Lelia in disguise, seize him, and shut him in Isabella's room. Isabella and her maid strip the bewildered youth, and are delighted to discover that he is in fact male. Fabrizio falls in love with Isabella. Meanwhile Flamminio flies into a jealous rage on learning of Isabella's love for his page and threatens to mutilate Lelia. When he discovers that she is a girl, he relents and asks to marry her, while Isabella will wed Fabrizio.

It is not known who wrote the piece performed by the Learned Society of the Intronati, at the '1531' Carnival in Siena. Clearly owing something to Bibbiena's *The *Follies of Calandro*, *The Deceived* indirectly provided the source of Shakespeare's **Twelfth Night*. In each of these pieces great fun is derived from the confusions arising out of the accident of cross-dressed identical twins. *The Deceived* is more than just the source for one of Shakespeare's great comedies, however. The cynical pragmatism of Lelia in exploiting Isabella's love for her and the bawdy undressing of the confused Fabrizio, together with its witty dialogue and satirically drawn characters like the Spanish braggart soldier, give this piece its individual stamp and justified its colossal popularity in the 16th century.

Deceiver of Seville, The. See TRICKSTER OF SEVILLE, THE.

Decision, The. See MEASURES TAKEN, THE.

Deep Blue Sea, The

A: Terence Rattigan Pf: 1952, London Pb: 1952 G: Drama in 3 acts S: London flat, *c.*1950 C: 5m, 3f

Hester Collyer lives separated from her husband, Judge Sir William Collyer, in quite basic accommodation in London. Her relationship with her younger live-in lover Freddie Page, an ex-RAF pilot, is very turbulent, and she is saved from suicide only by the intervention of a neighbour. She tried to kill herself, she explains, because the 'deep blue sea' looked more inviting than the 'devil'. Shaken by this and convinced too that there is no future for them together, Freddie plans to take a job abroad as a test pilot, even though he is now drinking heavily. Hester begs him to stay, but Freddie declares that he can no longer bear to make her unhappy: 'I'm not a sadist.' Sir William comes and asks Hester to come back to him, but she cannot face going back to the boredom of her marriage. About to put her head in the gas oven again, another neighbour, the struck-off doctor Miller, intervenes. Although he cannot promise her hope, he teaches her how she can live, as he has learned to do, without any hope but also 'without despair'. When Freddie unexpectedly calls to say goodbye, Hester has regained her equanimity and self-respect.

Generally accounted Rattigan's greatest play, this piece explores the emotional twists of an unhappy, almost obsessive relationship, but, as usual with Rattigan, offers a mildly optimistic conclusion (the 'deep blue sea' suggesting the uncharted future into which Hester finally launches herself). The depiction of Hester and Freddie's relationship may have been a coded portrayal of a homosexual affair, but this insight is not necessary to appreciate the qualities of this well-crafted and intense drama.

Deirdre of the Sorrows

A: J. M. Synge Pf: 1910, Dublin Pb: 1910
G: Trag. in 3 acts S: House on Slieve Fuadh, Ireland, before a tent in Alban (Scotland), and a tent below Emain Macha (Armagh), Ireland, 1st c. AD C: 8m, 3f

Conchubor, the ageing High King of Ulster, has raised Deirdre and now wishes to make her his queen. But Deirdre, who lives a simple life on the mountainside, does not wish to be queen or to marry an old man. Conchubor insists, saying that he will soon fetch her to his court. Dressed in the rich clothes that Conchubor has brought, Deirdre welcomes in three men caught in a storm. They are Naisi and his brothers, in whom Deirdre has already expressed an interest. Despite the prophecy that Deirdre of the Sorrows will bring about their downfall, Naisi elopes with her to Alban. Their seven-year idyll in Alban is broken by the arrival of Conchubor's friend Fergus, promising the brothers a safe return to Ulster. Despite fearing Conchubor's treachery, Deirdre and Naisi know that the prophecy must be fulfilled and set sail for Ireland. Beside a shabby tent erected to receive them, Deirdre and Naisi discover a freshly dug grave. Deirdre almost wins over Conchubor, but his men kill Naisi's brothers, and then Naisi too is slain. Fergus, outraged at Conchubor's treachery, attacks his capital, and Deirdre, knowing that she has caused this devastation and wishing never to grow old, takes her own life.

The legend of Deirdre is a favourite Irish legend dating from the 8th century and known to Synge through Lady Gregory's retelling of the story in *Cuchulain of Muirthemne* (1902). Yeats wrote a one-act version *Deirdre* (1906), focusing on Deirdre's last hours. This is the only one of Synge's six plays in a legendary setting, and he was still revising it when he died.

Delicate Balance, A

A: Edward Albee Pf: 1966, New York Pb: 1966
G: Drama in 3 acts S: Agnes and Tobias's suburban home in the USA, 1966 C: 2m, 4f

Agnes and Tobias are a comfortably settled retired couple living quietly in the suburbs of an American town. Agnes is so bored that she ponders the attraction of going mad. She accuses her laconic husband of having an affair with Claire, her alcoholic sister who lives with them. After a few drinks, Tobias tells how he had a cat killed because it would not love him. Suddenly they are joined by their best friends, an elderly couple Edna and Harry, who are too terrified to go home. Unable to explain the source of their fear, they ask to stay the night. Tensions arise between them all, which increase with the arrival of Agnes and Tobias's daughter Julia. She has just left her fourth husband and is very upset to discover that Edna and Harry have been given her room. Tobias tries to maintain the delicate balance between supporting his friends and helping his daughter. When his neighbours announce their intention of staying permanently, Tobias says: 'I don't want you here! . . . But by God . . . you stay!' They leave to face their unknown terror, and Tobias tries to justify his actions. Agnes comments: 'Well, they're safely gone . . . and we'll forget . . . quite soon.'

This play explores the territory of Albee's earlier *The *American Dream* in a less absurdist manner. The stylish suburban home with its stilted conversation is unable to offer a refuge to terrified friends (the fact that their fear is vague and nameless is more powerful than a specific event like a house-fire), for, as Claire observes: 'We're not a communal nation . . . ; giving, but not sharing, outgoing, but not friendly.'

Democracy

A: Michael Frayn Pf: 2003, London Pb: 2003
G: Hist. drama in 2 acts S: Bundestag, government offices, restaurants, bars, Guillaume's flat, Bonn, West Germany, and rural Norway, 1969–74 C: 10m

In 1969 Willy Brandt is called to become German chancellor, the first Social Democrat to hold the appointment for almost 40 years. Günter Guillaume, who defected from the German Democratic Republic 13 years previously, is plucked from relative obscurity to liaise between the trade unions and the new government. Guillaume, one of the few non-academics on the new staff, is working as an East German spy. As Brandt embarks on his policy of unfreezing the Cold War through a rapprochement with East Germany, his party leader Herbert Wehner expresses his misgivings: 'The more [democracy] you dare, the tighter the grip you have to keep on it.' Brandt, under threat from scheming within his own party and from left-wing extremists, narrowly survives a vote of confidence, then appoints Guillaume as his personal assistant during his election campaign. In 1972, Brandt signs a treaty with East Germany and makes gains in the elections. After the election, Brandt's government runs into difficulties and loses popularity. West German security suspects Guillaume of being a spy, and he is eventually unmasked. When Brandt is further threatened with sex scandals, he resigns. Guillaume spends six years in prison before being released on a prisoner exchange. The play ends with the sound of the Berlin Wall being demolished, and Guillaume reflects that 'I played my own small part in all this.'

With his usual intelligence and skill, Frayn takes a potentially rather dull political topic and transforms it into absorbing theatre. Brandt's own complex personality and his closeness to the man who was to cause his downfall provide a powerful personal interest, while Frayn also pursues an interesting debate into the nature of democracy. The East German Kretschmann, who acts as a kind of chorus commenting on Guillaume's career, dismisses the Federal Republic as 'The tower of Babel' and proudly predicts: 'we all speak with a single voice . . . we shall endure when this whole ramshackle structure finally comes tumbling down'. History was to prove him wrong.

Denksteine. See ANATOL.

Deputy, The. See REPRESENTATIVE, THE.

Design for Living

A: Noël Coward **Pf:** 1933, Cleveland, Ohio **Pb:** 1933 **G:** Com. in 3 acts **S:** Paris, London, and New York, 1930s **C:** 6m, 4f

Gilda is an interior decorator who has two lovers, the painter Otto Sylvus and the playwright Leo Mercuré. At first we see her with Otto, but when Leo comes back to her, Otto leaves in a fit of jealousy. When he returns, Gilda decides that she can take no more of the men's possessiveness and their jealous scenes, so she departs to New York to marry a conventional art dealer. The old friends and rivals Otto and Leo, united in their loss, decide two years later to pursue Gilda to America. When they turn up at her apartment, she is once again happy to share herself between her two lovers. Her infuriated husband stomps off, tripping over his canvases, while the threesome collapse in laughter.

Once again, as in **Hay Fever* and **Private Lives*, Coward seems to champion the volatile and supercilious behaviour of the bohemian artist over the tedium of conventional unadventurous lives. By giving his play a title that implied that this was the proper way to live, Coward attracted considerable opprobrium in the 1930s, but the uproarious laughter at the end may in fact conceal an emptiness in the three main characters' search for fulfilment.

Desire under the Elms

A: Eugene O'Neill **Pf:** 1924, New York **Pb:** 1924 **G:** Drama in 3 parts **S:** Farm in New England, 1850–1 **C:** 8m, 2f, extras

Twice-widowed 75-year-old Ephraim Cabot, a tough, proud Puritan, has transformed fields of stone into a fine farm, with a farmhouse dominated by two huge elms. When he leaves the farm in search of a new wife, his two elder sons seize the opportunity to escape the slavery of farm work and leave for California. Their younger half-brother Eben, who claims that, since Cabot stole the land off his mother, the farm is rightly his, pays them off with money stolen from Cabot's hiding place. Cabot returns with his new bride, attractive 35-year-old Abbie Putnam, who is delighted at her new home. Two months later, Cabot tells Abbie that she will inherit the farm if she gives him a son. One night she creeps to Eben to seduce him. He takes her passionately in his mother's parlour as an act of revenge against his hated father. The following spring, Abbie has given birth to a baby boy. When Eben learns that she will now inherit the farm, he feels he has been tricked into loving her. Even though she assures him of her love, he blames the baby for spoiling everything and prepares to leave. Desperate to hold on to him, she murders their child. Eben reports her to the sheriff, but then, reminded of his deep love for Abbie, insists to the sheriff that he was complicit in her guilt, and they leave for jail hand in hand.

O'Neill drew back from his experiments with Expressionism to create this powerful naturalist drama, although elements like the farm, the elms, and the 'purty' sunset in the West, all take on a symbolic function. The play, now recognized as one of his most powerful, had censorship difficulties in America and was banned until 1940 in Britain.

Deuxième Existence du camp de Tatenberg, La. See SECOND LIFE OF TATENBERG CAMP, THE.

Devils, The

A: John Whiting Pf: 1961, London Pb: 1961 G: Hist. drama in 3 acts S: Loudun and Paris, 1623–34 C: 19m, 5f, extras

Urbain Grandier is a handsome priest in the town of Loudun. He gives tuition in Latin to Philippe Trincant, the virginal but sensual daughter of a noted burgher. They become lovers and secretly marry. Meanwhile, the hunchbacked Prioress of the local Ursuline convent, Sister Jeanne, invites Grandier to become their spiritual adviser. When Grandier, feeling unworthy, rejects the invitation, Sister Jeanne begins to fantasize about him. Grandier has made enemies of fellow priests, of the town surgeon and chemist, and of the King's Special Commissioner by refusing to support a royal decree that the town walls should be demolished. When Father Mignon tells them of Sister Jeanne's 'visions', Grandier's enemies are handed a weapon to defeat him. When three priests attempt to exorcize Sister Jeanne, she is possessed by the devil Asmodeus, and other nuns claim to have been deflowered by the devil. When Philippe becomes pregnant, Grandier has to separate from her for fear of exposure. Although Henri de Condé, a member of the royal family, exposes the nuns' 'possession' as hysteria, Grandier's enemies are too powerfully ranged against him. He is shaved and horribly tortured but refuses to confess. He is carried, 'a ridiculous, hairless, shattered doll', first to the convent, where Sister Jeanne still yearns for him, then to be burned at the stake.

Based on Aldous Huxley's *The Devils of Loudun* (1952), this was the last full-length play written by Whiting and his most successful. With affinities to Miller's *The *Crucible*, the play, in tautly written scenes, unfolds an almost cinematic sequence of events, employing 'cross-cutting', e.g. between the trial of Grandier and Sister Jeanne in her convent. While Miller focuses on the political issues involved, Whiting explores more personal aspects, especially sexual enjoyment, which can be either degraded and perverse, or joyous and uplifting.

Devil's Disciple, The

A: George Bernard Shaw Pf: 1897, London Pb: 1901 G: Melodrama in 3 acts S: Websterbridge, New Hampshire, 1777 C: 18m, 6f, extras

It is 1777, and the British are having difficulty suppressing the American War of Independence. The pious and unsympathetic Annie Dudgeon is dismayed when her profligate son Dick returns to hear the reading of his late father's will. She is even unhappier when the arrogant lad, who defiantly calls himself the 'devil's disciple', is declared the sole beneficiary. Dick visits the local minister Anthony Anderson and is unexpectedly impressed by the churchman. When Anderson is called away, British soldiers come to arrest him, and Dick pretends to be Anderson and allows himself to be arrested. Returning home, Anderson takes Dick's coat and rides off. His pretty wife Judith visits Dick and, because of his bravery and her husband's cowardice, tells him that she loves him. Dick swears her to silence about his true identity, but when he is condemned to death by the military tribunal, she reveals that he is not Anderson. He must still hang, but as he stands on the gallows, Anderson, who has defeated a British force, rescues him. Anderson will now become a soldier, and Dick will join the Church, but promises Judith, reconciled to her husband, not to reveal her confession of love.

Shaw was a master at taking traditional structures and filling them with new content: despite purporting to despise the French well-made play with its tight plotting and neat resolution of complications, he exploited the form in many of his 'problem plays'; he used romantic comedy as in **Arms and the Man*; and in *The Devil's Disciple* he drew on melodrama. The innovation here was to introduce a refreshingly unheroic hero like Dick Dudgeon, who acts bravely not from any high moral code nor because he loves Judith, but simply on impulse. Thus Dick may be seen to be the progenitor of the many enigmatic figures of modern drama who act in extreme ways without their motivation being spelt out.

Devil's General, The (*Des Teufels General*)

A: Carl Zuckmayer **Pf**: 1946, Zurich **Pb**: 1946; rev. 1967 **Tr**: 1953 **G**: Drama in 3 acts; German prose **S**: Berlin, 1941 **C**: 20m, 5f

General Harras is an urbane, likeable flying ace in the German Air Force in the Second World War. At a party given for an airman on leave from the front, Harras admits that he is under suspicion from the Gestapo. Carelessly, he reproaches an industrialist for helping the Nazis to power, argues with a young pilot who believes in the Third Reich, and secretly offers help to some Jews. Only falling in love with a pretty young actress seems to slow his slide into self-destruction. He is arrested by the Gestapo and given ten days to find the saboteurs who are causing planes to crash. Together with his chief engineer Oderbruch, he sets about exposing them. To his dismay, he discovers that it is Oderbruch himself who is responsible for tampering with the aircraft engines. Recognizing that Oderbruch is right to undermine Hitler's war effort, Harras admits that he has been the 'Devil's general' for too long, and leaves to fly off in one of the defective planes. He dies in the air, and the Third Reich will claim him as a hero who gave his life for the Führer.

This was the first German post-war play to be written about the Nazis, and, despite a certain nervousness amongst the occupying Allies, was widely performed across Germany, granting Zuckmayer an inflated reputation as Germany's leading contemporary playwright. The play was reassuring to post-war Germany, portraying the good, self-sacrificing German, and demonizing Hitler as a mythical evil force in the background, thus avoiding the uncomfortable need to analyse how he came to power.

Diadia Vanya. See UNCLE VANYA.

Diccon of Bedlam. See GAMMER GURTON'S NEEDLE.

Dilemma of a Ghost, The

A: Ama Ata Aidoo **Pf**: 1964, Legon, Ghana **Pb**: 1965 **G**: Drama in 5 acts and a prelude; prose and free verse **S**: Courtyard of the Odumna Clan house, rural Ghana, 1960s **C**: 2m, 8f, 2 children (1m, 1f), 1 bird

The Wayside Bird tells of Ato Yawson, who has gone to the USA to study and is now returning to his ancestral home in Ghana. While at college, he meets and marries an African-American graduate Eulalie. His family are shocked that their oldest son has married a 'woman who has no tribe' and 'the daughter of slaves'. Eulalie is excited by being in Africa but fearful of being thought a witch. She would like to have children, but Ato urges her to wait. Ato dreams of a traditional song about a ghost who did not know in which direction to travel. His mother Esi Kom gives Eulalie some snails to cook, and she horrifies Esi by throwing them away. Esi complains to Ato that, after all the sacrifices made to pay for his education, he now shows no gratitude or respect towards the family. Ato blames Eulalie for his troubles. About a year after her arrival, Eulalie is the subject of malicious gossip, because she has borne no children and insists on spending money on household appliances. The relatives come with magic herbs to make Eulalie fertile, but Ato lacks the courage to admit they are using birth control. Eulalie smokes and drinks too much and finally has an angry confrontation with Ato, who slaps her. That evening, Ato explains to his mother about birth control, and she is sorry that her family has been made fools of. Eulalie arrives unhappily, and Esi gently leads her off, while Ato hears again the 'dilemma of the ghost'.

Together with Sutherland, Aidoo is one of Ghana's leading playwrights, and this is her best-known play. It deals, as does Soyinka's *Death and the King's Horsemen*, with the problematic relationship with traditional tribal customs experienced by Africans educated abroad, facing the dilemma of not knowing in which direction to travel. It is the generous warmth of the women, the tenderness of the mother towards her daughter-in-law, that may solve the dilemma.

Dingo

A: Charles Wood **Pf**: 1967, Bristol **Pb**: 1969
G: Drama in 3 acts **S**: North African desert, Second World War **C**: 12m

Dingo is a professional soldier fighting in the North African campaign alongside soldiers like Mogg, who has been called up. The screams of a soldier burning to death in his tank are heard, and thereafter his charred body is carried around like a dummy. A Navigating Officer loses his way. Rommel and a deserting British Officer have a gentlemanly chat: 'Such reunions we shall have.' A Comic, who has commented cynically on the war, becomes master of ceremonies at a concert held in the prison camp in which the second half of the play is set. While the concert, which includes a scene from *The *Importance of Being Earnest*, is in progress, officers, one of them dressed as a blonde chorus girl, attempt to escape. Finally, the camp is liberated, and Churchill (played by the Comic), whom we also see campaigning after the war, arrives to 'urinate on the West Wall of Hitler's Germany'. Tanky, in his repeated 'He killed me', ends the play accusingly.

Dingo, based on Wood's own experiences in the army, is a powerful anti-war play, protesting against 'All of it, from a small bit of it'. It contrasts the realities of war with sanitized images prepared for public consumption. Mixing realistic dialogue with violent images of warfare, it was written originally for the National Theatre but had to be withdrawn because of censorship problems.

Dirty Hands (*Les Mains sales*)

AT: *Crime passionel; Red Gloves* **A**: Jean-Paul Sartre **Pf**: 1948, Paris **Pb**: 1948 **Tr**: 1949
G: Drama in 7 scenes; French prose **S**: Illyria in the Balkans, 1943 and 1945 **C**: 11m, 2f

In the imaginary Balkan state of Illyria, Hugo Barine, a Communist Party activist, two years previously assassinated the Party leader Hoederer. After being released from prison, Hugo visits fellow party worker and former lover Olga Lorame. It is her task to judge whether he is 'salvageable' or whether he should be liquidated by Party gunmen. The assassination is re-enacted in flashback. When Hoederer proposes to form an alliance with the fascist Royalists and the bourgeois Liberals, Hugo is so incensed over the leader's betrayal of Socialist ideals that he becomes Hoederer's secretary in order to assassinate him. Hoederer is a man of great charm, and Hugo's wife Jessica begins to flirt with him. Hoederer escapes an assassination attempt when Olga throws a bomb into his house. When Hugo confronts Hoederer over collaborating with their enemies, Hoederer argues that practical politics must involve compromise, that it is impossible not to get one's 'hands dirty'. Jessica tells Hoederer of Hugo's plan, but Hoederer, convinced that Hugo would never kill him for a political ideal, invites him to continue working with him. As Hugo ponders this, he happens upon Hoederer kissing Jessica and shoots him. Back in the present, Hugo is still unsure of his real motive for the killing, and is horrified to learn that collaboration with the Royalists and Liberals is now official Party policy. In dismay, he kicks open the door and tells the waiting gunmen that he is 'unsalvageable'.

This was Sartre's most popular play, containing both political debate and theatrical suspense. Using a flashback technique, which had become so popular in the cinema, the audience knows that Hoederer will be shot, and so can concentrate on Hugo's motives. Both Hugo and Hoederer are well-drawn characters, the latter having a close affinity with Creon in Anouilh's **Antigone*.

Disbanded Officer, The. See MINNA VON BARNHELM.

Discharged. See FEAR AND MISERY OF THE THIRD REICH.

Dissolution. See ANATOL.

Distrest Mother, The. See ANDROMACHE (Racine).

Divorçons! See LET'S GET A DIVORCE!

Dni Turbinykh. See DAYS OF THE TURBINS, THE.

Dock Brief, The

A: John Mortimer **Pf**: 1958, London **Pb**: 1958 **G**: Com. in 1 act **S**: Cell below the courts, England, 1950s **C**: 2m

Wilfred Morgenhall is a washed-up lawyer whose dream has come true: he has lived all his life waiting to be called as the 'dock brief', a barrister appointed by the court to represent a defendant. His client Fowle is a bird-fancier charged with the murder of his wife. Clearly he has a better grasp of the law than Morgenhall and instructs him about the defence, most of which will rest on the intolerable nagging of his wife. Morgenhall dreams of his brilliant court performance, but in the event is unable to utter a single word, because 'a tremendous exhaustion overcame him'. However, his client is acquitted on the grounds that his defence was so incompetent that he did not receive a fair trial. Morgenhall is devastated, but his client reassures him that the brilliance of his 'dumb tactics' saved him. The two men leave whistling and dancing, with the now buoyant Morgenhall promising to be his new friend's legal adviser.

Mortimer, himself a lawyer, repeatedly wrote comedies 'on the side of the lonely, the neglected, the unsuccessful'. Originally performed on radio, *Dock Brief* depicts the paradoxical triumph of a failed lawyer, and in the gently amusing comedy, it is easy to overlook, as Mortimer does, that an unrepentant murderer goes free.

Doctor Faustus (*The tragicall history of the horrible life and Death of Doctor Ffaustus*)

A: Christopher Marlowe (and others) **Pf**: *c.*1588, London **Pb**: 1604 ('A' text), 1616 ('B' text) **G**: Trag. in 1 act; blank verse and prose **S**: Wertenberg (= Wittenberg), Germany, and other locations in Europe, early 16th c. **C**: 30m, 2f, extras

The learned Doctor Faustus, dissatisfied with his academic learning, decides to devote himself to the study of magic. He summons up the evil spirit Mephistophilis, insisting that he appear in the form of a Franciscan friar. Faust offers a pact to Mephistophilis, that if the latter serve him for 24 years, the devil may have his soul when he dies. After a comic scene in which Wagner, Faust's servant, and a Clown summon two devils, Mephistophilis returns from Lucifer agreeing to the pact. This is duly signed in Faust's blood. Mephistophilis answers Faust's metaphysical and astronomical questions and gives him a book containing the secrets of the universe. Although Faust begins to have doubts about the pact and is repeatedly urged by his Good Angel to repent, he finds he cannot turn back from his impending damnation. Lucifer appears to entertain Faust with the Seven Deadly Sins. Mephistophilis takes Faust to the Pope's court in Rome, where Faust has fun stealing the Pope's food and causing general alarm. After another comic scene in which two lads meddle with magic, Faust visits the Emperor of Constantinople and fulfils his wish to see Alexander the Great and his paramour resurrected. After another comic interlude with a horse dealer, Faust entertains the Duke of Vanholt. After warnings from an Old Man, Faust now demands to see Helen of Troy, 'the face that launched a thousand ships'. At last the hour of Faust's death approaches, and, as the clock strikes, he succumbs to terror at the thought of his eternal damnation. He is dragged off to hell by Devils, and Chorus comments on the dangers of attempting 'To practise more than heavenly power permits'.

The 1616 B text is generally a more reliable text than the much shorter 1604 A text, but contains added scenes (which may or may not be Marlowe's), like Faustus at the Pope's court and an expansion of the horse-dealer episode. *Doctor Faustus* is arguably the greatest tragedy in the English language before Shakespeare, and contains some of Marlowe's finest verse. It presents an image of Renaissance man, whose desire to know everything is presented as a threat to individual salvation and to the traditional order. It is however no accident that the Faust legend sites him at Wittenberg, the birthplace of Lutheran Protestantism. Thus the implications of the piece are ambiguous: like the Evil Angel we cannot help but champion Faust's energy and commitment to explore the limits of human knowledge; but like the Good Angel we fear where this might lead. Because the same fears about the outcome of scientific probing, especially in nuclear physics and biogenetics, have become particularly acute in our own age, Marlowe's play remains intensely topical. The legend was dramatized most famously by Goethe in his monumental **Faust*.

Doctor Faustus Lights the Lights

A: Gertrude Stein W: 1938 Pf: 1951, New York Pb: 1949 G: Drama in 3 acts; prose and verse S: Faustus's house and environs, indeterminate period C: 3m, 3f, 2 children (m and f), 1 dog, chorus

Doctor Faustus rejects Mephisto, not caring whether the devil has his soul, because there is no soul. The electric lights burn more brightly. Faustus tries to rid himself of a boy and a dog, which keeps saying 'Thank you', and then encounters the composite figure of Marguerite Ida and Helena Annabel, who 'is not ready yet to sing about day-light and night light, moonlight and star-light electric light and twilight she is not she is not but she will be'. When she is stung by a viper, she seeks help from Doctor Faustus. Because Faustus sold his soul, he eventually cures her: 'See how she lights, | the candle lights.' A man 'from over the seas' comes to woo her. Faustus resolves to go to hell by getting the viper to kill the boy and the dog. Rejuvenated, Faustus demands that Marguerite Ida and Helena Annabel accompany him to hell, but she sinks into the safety of the arms of the man from over the seas.

In 77 rarely staged plays written between 1913 and 1946 Gertrude Stein attempted to apply to playwriting the elements of deconstruction and shifting identity familiar from modernist painting. More a prose poem than a text for performance, this rewriting of the Faustus legend introduces a virginal composite character derived from Margarete and Helen of Troy, who, Eve-like, comes to knowledge through a snakebite (penetration by a phallus?) but rises above Faustus's invitation to descend into hell with him. For some irritating, for others fascinating, Stein's revolutionary explorations have had an undeniable influence on theatrical experimenters like Julian Beck, Robert Wilson, and Richard Foreman.

Doctor Last in His Chariot. See HYPOCHONDRIAC, THE.

Dödsdansen. See DANCE OF DEATH, THE.

Doll's House, A (*Et dukkehjem*)

AT: *Nora* A: Henrik Ibsen Pf: 1879, Copenhagen Pb: 1879 Tr: 1880 G: Drama in 3 acts; Norwegian prose S: Middle-class home in Norway, Christmas, 1870s. C: 4m, 4f, 3 children

At first sight the marriage of Torvald Helmer and Nora seems happy: he has just been appointed manager of his bank, and the seemingly light-headed Nora, indulged by him, buys little luxuries for Christmas. When an old friend Christine Linde visits her, Nora reveals that none of this would have been possible, had she not found the money to pay for a year abroad when Helmer was very ill. Unfortunately, in order to borrow the money off a disreputable individual, Krogstad, she forged her father's signature. She has been paying back the loan, but Krogstad now demands more. Helmer intends to dismiss him from the bank, and Krogstad threatens to expose Nora's forgery if she cannot persuade Helmer to keep him. All her efforts to save Krogstad are in vain, and when she considers confessing all to an old family friend Dr Rank, he reveals that he is dying and is in love with Nora. While Nora prepares for a fancy-dress party, Krogstad's letter arrives and sits menacingly in the letter box in the hall. Nora resolves to confess her crime to Helmer, hoping that he will protect her. Her wild dancing at the party excites Helmer, but the mood changes when Helmer finds Dr Rank's card announcing his impending death, together with Krogstad's threatening letter. Furious at Nora's dishonesty, Helmer considers only how he can avoid any scandal and declares Nora unfit to be a wife and mother. Thanks to Christine's influence, Krogstad relents and returns Nora's forgery. Helmer is relieved and imagines that the marriage can continue as before. But Nora, her eyes opened by his selfishness, insists on the first serious talk that they have had in eight years of marriage. Even after seeing her children, she resolves to leave Helmer in order to become an independent woman, with the vague hope that they can one day have a marriage of equals.

This is the best known of Ibsen's plays and an excellent example of the way in which he exploited the domestic setting and tight plotting of the well-made play of the French theatre in order to debate important social issues. The 'doll's house' in which Nora finds herself trapped was a powerful proto-feminist image and was so disturbing for audiences of the day that Henry Arthur Jones and Henry Herman wrote a widely performed version, *Breaking the Butterfly* (1884), which ends happily with the heroine staying after seeing her children. Despite his obvious sympathy for the wife treated like a doll, Ibsen also portrays Nora's selfishness, complacency, and secretiveness, so that the conflict between wife and husband is far more subtle than good versus evil.

Dom Juan. See DON JUAN.

Don Carlos (*Don Karlos, Infant von Spanien*)

A: Friedrich Schiller W: 1782–7 Pf: 1787, Hamburg Pb: 1787 Tr: 1798 G: Trag. in 5 acts; German blank verse S: Madrid, mainly at the court of Philip II, and Aranjuez, 1568 C: 17m, 6f, extras

The Marquis of Posa returns to Spain to find his friend Don Carlos, heir to the Spanish throne, no longer the young idealist committed to bringing freedom to Spanish possessions. Carlos is in love with his mother-in-law, Queen Elizabeth. The Queen rejects his advances, urging him to prepare himself one day to rule Spain. Betrayed by the Princess of Eboli, who loves Carlos, the King's suspicions are aroused, especially when Don Carlos asks to be put in charge of the Spanish army in its expedition to pacify the Netherlands. Trusted by the King, Posa is able to denounce Eboli's slander and secretly plans to take Carlos, by force if necessary, to Brussels to lead a revolt against Spanish oppression. Learning of his imminent capture, Carlos believes himself betrayed by Posa, and once again confesses everything to Eboli. Posa, aware that Eboli will reveal all to the King, sacrifices himself by pretending to love the Queen himself. He is executed, but leaves a message with the Queen, urging Carlos to continue the fight for freedom. Carlos, discovered in the Queen's company, is handed over to the Inquisition as adulterer and traitor.

One of the longest plays in German, *Don Carlos* represents a transition from Schiller's *Sturm und Drang* writing to the historical tragedies of his maturity. The first German historical drama to be written in blank verse, Schiller had to 'translate' it into prose for the unskilled actors at its premiere. Despite the title, the focus of the tragedy is the invented character of Posa, the dangerous idealist, whose noble attempts to confront Philip's realpolitik end only in disaster for himself and his friend. Verdi wrote an operatic version in 1867.

Don Gil of the Green Breeches (*Don Gil de las calzas verdes*)

A: Tirso de Molina Pf: *c.*1614–15, Madrid Pb: 1635 Tr: 1991 G: Com. in 3 acts; Spanish verse S: Madrid, late 16th c. C: 14m, 3f, musicians

Don Martin abandons Donna Juana to go to Madrid, assumes the identity of Don Gil, and begins to woo the rich Ines. Juana follows him, dressed as a man wearing green breeches. When she discovers where the faithless Martin intends to court Ines, Juana appears early at their tryst claiming to be Don Gil and charms Ines so much that she falls in love with 'him'. When Ines's father and Martin arrive, Ines wishes to have nothing to do with this new Don Gil and desires only the one in green breeches.

Martin cannot imagine who his rival might be, especially as he is fed the false information that Juana has gone into a convent to bear their baby and died soon after. Plagued by his guilty conscience, Martin fears that the rival Don Gil may be an avenging spirit. By now Ines's friend, Donna Clara, has also fallen in love with Don Gil of the green breeches, and one of her admirers, Don Juan, is consumed by jealousy. Eventually four Don Gils in green breeches appear under Ines's balcony, Juana, Martin, Clara, and Don Juan, and it takes some time for the resulting complications to be resolved. Finally, Don Gil's green breeches are laid to rest with holy candles.

This 'cloak and dagger' comedy is one of the best crafted of Molina's many plays, predictably offering excellent operatic material, as in Walter Braunfels's version of 1924. It is written in a punchy unrhymed verse, with short lines of between seven and nine syllables. This infuses the piece with a driving energy, which sweeps the audience along, helping them to ignore the outrageous improbabilities of the plot.

Don Juan (*Dom Juan, ou Le Festin de pierre*)

AT: *The Statue at the Feast/ at the Banquet; The Stone Guest; The Libertine* **A:** Molière **Pf:** 1665, Paris **Pb:** 1683 **Tr:** 1665 **G:** Trag. in 5 acts; French alexandrines **S:** Sicily, mid-17th c. **C:** 13m, 4f, extras

Don Juan, having abducted Dona Elvira from a convent and seduced her with promises of marriage, has now abandoned her. Sganarelle, Don Juan's servant, warns Dona Elvira's squire Gusman of his master's immorality. When Elvira arrives, Don Juan claims that his sense of morality will not allow him to enter into marriage with her. While travelling to his next intended sexual conquest, his boat capsizes and he is rescued by a peasant, whose fiancée he is about to seduce when he has to flee from armed men. Don Juan and Sganarelle hide in disguise in a forest, where Don Juan courageously rescues a nobleman from robbers. When he turns out to be Elvira's brother Don Carlos, the latter repays Don Juan by abandoning his pursuit. In the tomb of the Commander, whom he killed, Don Juan encounters the old man's statue and jokingly invites him to dine with him. Returning to his lodgings, Don Juan remains impervious to pleas by his father and Dona Elvira to reform. At last, however, Don Juan tells his father he has repented. In fact, as he confides to Sganarelle, he has discovered that a religious front is the best cover for licentiousness. The statue appears and leads Don Juan into hell as punishment for his misdeeds. Sganarelle is dismayed that he will not now get his wages.

Based on Molina's *The *Trickster of Seville*, Molière's version is extraordinary in that it does not have the cohesion of Molina's version (let alone observing the neo-classical unities): the good are not rewarded as in Molina (Elvira returns to her convent, Don Juan's father is duped), the scenes are episodic, characters are introduced without preparation (the relationship to the Commander is not explained). Perhaps most innovatory in this spectacular version, complete with shipwreck and hellfire, is the way theatrical spectacle and implied morality are cynically commented on by Sganarelle, who was played by Molière himself.

Don Karlos, Infant von Spanien. See DON CARLOS.

donna è mobile, La. See ELECTRIC DOLLS.

donna sola, Una. See FEMALE PARTS.

Donnellys, The (Sticks and Stones; The St Nicholas Hotel – Wm. Donnelly Prop.; Handcuffs)

A: James Reaney **Pf:** (1) 1973, Toronto; (2) 1974, Toronto; (3) 1975, Toronto **Pb:** (1) 1974; (2) 1976; (3) 1977 **G:** Trilogy of hist. drama, each in 3 acts **S:** Ontario, (1) 1844–67; (2) 1873–9; (3) 1880 **C:** 7m, 4f, extras (played by 11 actors)

(1) *Sticks and Stones*. In 1844 Donnelly and his wife emigrate from Ireland and come to live in the Biddulph Township near London, Ontario, an area full of sectarian tension between Catholics and Protestants. They raise seven sons and one daughter, and the family becomes notorious in the district, instigating murder and arson, and suffering themselves as victims of violence. The father is sentenced to seven years for murder, their barn is burnt down and their water pump destroyed, but they refuse to be driven out. (2) *The St Nicholas Hotel – Wm. Donnelly Prop*. It is now 1873, and Will Donnelly, owner of the hotel, reminisces about the deaths of his two brothers in the 1870s. The Donnellys have now set up a stagecoach line, which is opposed with tollgates, and eventually this leads to the murder of Michael Donnelly. Another brother dies of tuberculosis, and yet another is sentenced to two years in prison for assault. Throughout, a Chorus 'in a drifting voice' refers to other events from 1875, the 1880s, 1891, and 1925. (3) *Handcuffs*. The events of the final part of the trilogy are seen in flashback from the early 1970s. In the graveyard of St Patrick's, Biddulph, which has become a tourist attraction, a trial is re-enacted. It returns us to 1880, the year when a 'Vigilante Committee' murdered the two parents, two sons, and a cousin, Bridget. James Carroll, the leader of the vigilantes, was acquitted in a local court, and no one was convicted of the murders.

This is one of the major plays of Canadian theatre, a vast historical panorama which embraces events and attitudes not only in the 19th century but also in post-war Canada, and which employs a large variety of theatrical devices: shifting time-frames, the supernatural, song and dance. The Donnellys are like Canadian versions of Ned Kelly's gang: thoroughly disreputable, but curiously likeable and gaining sympathy through their unjust treatment by the local community.

Double Dealer, The (*The Double-Dealer*)

A: William Congreve **Pf**: 1693, London **Pb**: 1694 **G**: Com. in 5 acts; prose **S**: Lord Touchwood's house, London, 1690s **C**: 7m, 4f, extras

Mellefont, a dashing young wit, is about to wed Cynthia, the daughter of Sir Paul Plyant. The only problem is that his uncle's wife Lady Touchwood is also in love with him and is determined to prevent the marriage. She is ably supported by her lover Maskwell, a 'double dealer', who pretends to be Mellefont's friend. The two villains manage to manipulate the other characters so successfully that the marriage seems doomed. However, Maskwell overplays his hand and tries to win Cynthia for himself. Lady Touchwood, outraged that he has been a double dealer to her as well, quarrels with Maskwell. Their altercation is overheard by Cynthia and Lord Touchwood, and the villains are unmasked, so that Mellefont can now marry his beloved Cynthia. In one sub-plot, Mellefont's friend Careless easily seduces Lady Plyant, who demands almost total sexual abstinence from her modest husband. In another sub-plot, Lady Froth, who fancies herself as a poet, has an affair with a conceited fop Brisk, although her husband is too complacent to recognize her infidelity.

Despite its well-crafted dramatic focus, observing the unities of time and place, this proved the least popular of Congreve's four comedies, probably because he broke with convention by allowing the villains of the piece to be cleverer (and very nearly more successful) than the honest lovers. Indeed, he had to defend the piece against the accusation that 'the Hero of the Play . . . is a Gull, and made a Fool'. Free of such scruples, contemporary directors have revived the play with some success.

Double Inconstancy, The (*La Double Inconstance*)

AT: *Double Infidelity; Infidelities; Changes of Heart* **A**: Pierre Carlet de Chamblain de Marivaux **Pf**: 1723, Paris **Pb**: 1724 **Tr**: 1901 **G**: Romantic com. in 3 acts; French prose **S**: The Prince's palace, indeterminate period **C**: 4m, 3f, extras

While out hunting, the Prince has met and fallen in love with a simple country maiden Silvia. However, she loves Arlequin and, although brought to court and offered status and wealth, rejects the Prince's advances. The courtiers try to fulfil the Prince's wishes: the servant Trivelin's promises of riches fail to impress the simple country lad Arlequin, who sees no merit in having two homes and many servants. He refuses to yield Silvia to the Prince, and the beautiful Lisette tries unsuccessfully to seduce him. Despite Arlequin's swearing eternal love to Silvia, he is obviously affected by Flaminia, who pretends to be mourning her dead lover. Disguising himself as an officer, the Prince woos Silvia, and Flaminia begins to push home her advantage with Arlequin. Despite their hesitation in becoming unfaithful to each other, Arlequin begins to love Flaminia and Silvia her 'officer', who finally reveals himself as the Prince.

Marivaux's gentle comedies do not depend on external action but on the subtle processes of love and the movements of the heart. Suspended in a timeless sphere (even if Arlequin's scepticism about wealth has a contemporary satirical edge), his characters, even the servants, are stylishly elegant and all speak charming dialogue, which was subsequently pilloried as *marivaudage*. A play like *The Double Inconstancy* may now be revisited not just as a nostalgic voyage into a prelapsarian idyll but also as a gently humorous insight into romantic love.

Dou E yuan. See INJUSTICE TO DOU E.

Douglas

A: John Home **Pf**: 1756, Edinburgh; rev. version 1757 London, **Pb**: 1757 **G**: Trag. in 5 acts; blank verse **S**: Lord Randolph's castle and nearby woods, medieval period **C**: 4m, 2f, extras

Lady Randolph still mourns the death of her first husband Lord Douglas and of her infant son, but is now married to Lord Randolph (in the first version she is Lady Barnard, wooed by Randolph). Randolph's son Glenalvon is in love with his stepmother and plots to kill Randolph, but his murderous hirelings' attempt is thwarted by a passing stranger, Norval, who turns out to be Lady Randolph's lost son. Suspecting that Norval is Lady Randolph's lover, Lord Randolph conspires with his son to murder this apparently arrogant upstart. In an offstage encounter in the woods, Glenalvon is killed and Norval mortally wounded. He dies in the arms of his mother, who then commits suicide. Now aware of his tragic error, Randolph goes off to repel a Danish invasion.

The hugely successful premiere of *Douglas* was famously greeted with a shout: 'Whaur's yer Willy Shakespeare noo?', and the play remained popular well into the 19th century. Although neo-classical in style (all the violence takes place off stage, and the action lasts only one day), the melodramatic nature of the plot and the Gothic setting in a medieval castle and Scots woodland made it a favourite with the Romantics and beyond.

Down and Out. See LOWER DEPTHS, THE.

Dragon, The (*Drakon*)

A: Evgeny Shvarts **Pf**: 1943, Leningrad **Pb**: 1960 **Tr**: 1963 **G**: Satirical fairy tale in 3 acts; Russian prose **S**: A mythical city, indeterminate period **C**: 19m, 6f, extras

For 400 years a Dragon who can assume different human shapes has ruled over the city. Everyone has adjusted to the Dragon's rule and even his victims accept the need for him to devour a virgin annually. The smooth running of the city is upset by the arrival of the brave knight Lancelot, who regularly campaigns for people's rights and moreover falls in love with Elsa, this year's virgin sacrifice. Despite efforts by the local populace to prevent him, Lancelot, aided by a Cat who provides him with weapons and a helmet of invisibility, prepares to do battle with the Dragon. Elsa falls in love with Lancelot and refuses the Dragon's order to murder the knight. After a sky battle during which the townspeople are given misleading reports, the Dragon is defeated. However, Lancelot is badly wounded and disappears. A year later, the Burgomaster, who takes credit for defeating the Dragon, now rules the city as tyrannically as the Dragon had done. Just as the Burgomaster is about to force Elsa into an unwanted marriage, Lancelot returns and throws the Burgomaster and his son Henry into prison, releasing those that had been incarcerated, demanding: 'Why did you submit and go to prison? There are so many of you!' Lancelot, taking Elsa's hand, now realizes that he must stay in order to continue killing dragons.

The Dragon ran for only three or four nights before being banned by the authorities in 1943. Its reference to the replacement of the tyrannical Tsar by the even more tyrannical Stalin was all too obvious, although Shvarts insisted that he was not anti-Communist but opposed to any political system that threatened personal liberty. When his plays were published in 1960, two years after his death, they soon became internationally famous.

Dreamer for the People, A (*Un soñador para un pueblo*)

A: Antonio Buero-Vallejo **Pf:** 1958, Madrid **Pb:** 1959; rev. 1989 **Tr:** 1994 **G:** Hist. drama in 2 acts; Spanish prose **S:** Street, Esquilache's home, and royal palace, Madrid, 1766 **C:** 22m, 5f

Carlos III has given the Italian-born Don Leopoldo de Gregorio, Marquis of Esquilache, two ministries to oversee reforms, especially those concerned with improving life in 18th-century Spain: public hygiene and street lighting in Madrid. Against a background of general discontent, Carlos and Esquilache, decide to ban the wearing of long capes and wide-brimmed hats. This is a measure not just to reject traditional attire, but because these garments were worn by those committing criminal acts, hiding their faces and concealing weapons. Attempts to enforce the new ruling are unsuccessful: there are calls for an uprising against Esquilache, and when soldiers attempt to arrest two men provocatively parading in the forbidden dress, the soldiers are attacked by the mob. While Esquilache, who has fallen in love with the beautiful Fernandita, asks the King to allow him to separate from his wife, the crowd march on the palace, demanding Esquilache's head. Because there are uprisings all over Spain and the King fears all-out civil war, Esquilache advises that he should give way to the rebels, 'allowing the people to dress according to custom', and banish Esquilache. Esquilache takes leave of Fernandita: he has now lost everything, but the dreams of this idealist will live on to benefit the people.

Buero-Vallejo, considered Spain's greatest playwright of the second half of the 20th century, here, in the guise of recreating an episode in Spanish history, debates concerns affecting Spain under Franco: the relationship between tradition and reform, and the alternative of violently suppressing discontent or making concessions to restore harmony. For Esquilache there is also the hard choice between personal power and the nation's welfare.

Dream on Monkey Mountain

A: Derek Walcott **Pf:** 1967, Toronto **Pb:** 1970 **G:** Drama in 2 acts; prose, verse, and songs, with some English and French patois **S:** Jail on St Lucia, 1960s **C:** 8m, 2f, extras, chorus, and drummers

Makak, a black charcoal-burner, has been imprisoned for his own safety, after getting drunk and smashing things in the local market. In jail he has a vision of a white Goddess, who urges him to return to Africa. Unhappy about the way the mulatto warder Corporal Lestrade approves of 'white man's law', Makak despises himself for being black and longs to lead his people back to Africa, where, in his dreams, he will become a fearless warrior. Even Lestrade will join his exodus, while various hangers-on pretend to lend Makak his support while trying to undermine and rob him. Amazingly, he receives a floral tribute from the Ku Klux Klan. Finally, he beheads the white apparition. Waking from his drunken dream, he finds he has overcome his obsession with whiteness and calls himself by his real name, Felix Hobain. Reconciled to life on his Caribbean Island, Makak resolves to return to his home on Monkey Mountain and looks forward to a new life.

Walcott is the leading Caribbean dramatist, and this is his best-known play. In it the playwright, himself of mixed race, urges his fellow countrymen neither to imitate the whites nor to get trapped in dreams of returning to Africa. Instead, he encourages his audience to embrace the multiracial, multicultural character of Caribbean society and celebrate its richness, which is reflected in the mixture of languages and theatrical styles, including song and dance.

Dream Play, A (*Ett drömspel*)

AT: *The Dream Play* **A:** August Strindberg **Pf:** 1907, Stockholm **Pb:** 1902 **Tr:** 1912 **G:** Drama without act or scene divisions; Swedish prose and some verse **S:** Indeterminate locations in Europe, 1900s **C:** 26m, 15f, extras

Indra invites his daughter to descend to earth to discover the source of humankind's misery. She approaches a castle growing on manure, topped by a flower bud. Here she frees the imprisoned Officer. After visiting his parents, he stands at the stage door of the opera, waiting, as he has done for seven years, for his bride to emerge. Indra's Daughter becomes the Stage-Door Keeper, so that she can learn about human unhappiness. When the Officer, now aged from his constant waiting, is forbidden from opening an intriguing door, he goes to the Advocate (or Lawyer) to seek an injunction. The Advocate, contaminated from years of dealing with other people's crimes, is denied a doctor's degree. Feeling sorry for him, Indra's Daughter marries him. The Daughter, now named Agnes, is unhappy with the squalor and bickering of her marriage and leaves the Advocate and their baby son. She travels with the rejuvenated Officer to the seashore, arriving in Foulstrand rather than the intended Fairhaven. The resident Quarantine Master fumigates an Old Dandy and a Coquette (the bride for whom the Officer had been waiting) and an ineffectual Poet. Two optimistic young lovers are soon disappointed by their foul surroundings. The Officer finds himself back at school, being disciplined by a fearsome Schoolmaster. The Daughter returns to her Advocate husband, and together they visit a beautiful beach, but she learns from Coal-Carriers that there is suffering here too. The Advocate tells her that people who try to improve their lot end in prison or the madhouse. Visiting Fingal's Cave with the Poet, Indra's Daughter sees how the sea has taken the lives of many, wonders if she has dreamt everything, and reads the Poet's verse describing human misery. Back at the opera house, Indra's Daughter commands that the mysterious door should at last be opened: 'People feel that the riddle of existence is hidden there.' When, after much learned disputation, the door is opened, there is nothing. After being threatened with a flogging, Indra's Daughter bids a painful farewell to the Advocate. Returning to the rising castle, where flowers have begun to bloom, she takes her leave of the Poet. Characters return briefly, and Indra's Daughter promises to speak of their unhappiness when she returns to her father. The castle burns, and the bud on the roof bursts open into a giant chrysanthemum.

Reflecting aspects of Strindberg's own life, especially his disappointment over his third marriage to the actress Harriet Bosse, this extraordinary play stands as one of the most influential works of modern drama. The 'Author's Note' is a manifesto of modernism: 'this dream play . . . [imitates] the inconsequent yet transparently logical shape of a dream. Everything can happen, everything is possible and probable. Time and place do not exist. . . . The characters split, double, multiply, evaporate, condense, disperse, assemble. But one consciousness rules over them all, that of the dreamer.' Ingmar Bergman memorably staged a shortened version on an almost bare stage in 1970.

Dreigroschenoper, Die. See THREEPENNY OPERA, THE.

Dresser, The

A: Ronald Harwood **Pf:** 1980, Manchester **Pb:** 1980 **G:** Tragicom. in 2 acts **S:** Dressing room and backstage of a provincial theatre, England, 1942 **C:** 8m, 3f

Norman, for 16 years Sir's loyal dresser, has had to take the elderly actor to hospital, because he discovered him ranting and throwing away his clothes in the market just after an air raid. Now he is worried because Sir is due to perform King Lear that night. Just as his common-law wife ('Her Ladyship') and the stage manager Madge are about to cancel the performance, Sir walks in, still weeping but determined to go on. Coaxed by the patient

Norman, Sir makes himself up for the performance, which suffers from a lack of good actors, since many have been called up into the army, and one has been arrested for homosexuality. An air raid begins, but the performance of **King Lear* begins. After a delayed start, Sir gets into his stride, but is furious that the storm is not loud enough. He triumphantly concludes the play, but is exhausted when he gets back to his dressing room. As Norman gets him ready to go home, Sir quietly dies, and Norman, bitter with grief and frightened about his own future, comments: 'Wasn't much of a death scene. Unremarkable and ever so short.'

Harwood's fond recreation of one of a dying breed of actor-managers draws parallels between Sir and Lear: both are men whose lives are transformed by being dispossessed of their former power; both find themselves cast adrift in a scene of desolation, the war and the blasted heath. 'Under threat from the powers of darkness', Sir tenaciously serves 'the greatest poet-dramatist who has ever lived': 'each word I speak will be a shield against your savagery.'

drömspel, Ett. See DREAM PLAY, A.

Drovers, The

A: Louis Esson **Pf:** 1920, Melbourne **Pb:** 1923 **G:** Drama in 1 act **S:** Droving camp, Barklay Tableland, Australia, *c.*1920 **C:** 6m, 1 child (m)

It is early morning in the camp for the men driving cattle across the great plains.
A Jackeroo, a novice from the city, foolishly shoots at a dingo, causing the cattle to stampede. Briglow Bill is knocked from his horse and badly injured. Some painkiller is found, but he is too ill to continue. Boss Alec McKay, who has worked with Briglow for years, tells him that they must press on and leave Briglow behind, which Briglow accepts with serenity. Jackeroo protests, but, with a man short, he must go to help the others. The aboriginal boy Pidgeon is told to stay behind to watch over Briglow, and chants as Briglow dies.

While Australian theatre was performing almost exclusively foreign imports, Esson from 1910 onwards wrote authentic Australian drama, usually set amongst the poor and often in the bush. In *The Drovers* he depicts the rough male camaraderie of the cattle men and the tough decisions that have to be faced. Briglow unsentimentally assents to being abandoned by his mates, because death has 'to come sooner or later'. Through this acceptance, he becomes close to the soul of Australia, and the Aborigine will organize a 'big-fellow corroboree alonga you'.

Drums in the Night (*Trommeln in der Nacht*)

A: Bertolt Brecht **Pf:** 1922; Munich **Pb:** 1922; rev. 1955 **Tr:** 1966 **G:** Drama in 5 acts; German prose **S:** Berlin, 1919 **C:** 13m, 6f

Anna Balicke has been engaged to a soldier, who has not been heard of for four years. Persuaded by her smug middle-class parents, and since she is now pregnant by him, she agrees to marry a repulsive war-profiteer, who has been courting her. During the celebrations for the engagement in the Piccadilly Bar, Andreas Kragler, Anna's former fiancé, suddenly appears. A prisoner of war from North Africa, he is now smelly, dishevelled, and emaciated. Kragler argues with Anna's parents and new fiancé, and Anna sends him away. She soon relents however and follows him out on to the streets. Kragler, now drunk, has found himself actively involved in the left-wing Spartacist uprising. When Anna confesses her love to him and admits that she is pregnant, Kragler abandons the revolution to take her to bed. Warning the audience not to be won over by this 'romantic' ending, Kragler tears down the stage moon to show that it is all just 'theatre'.

The later Brecht with his Marxist views found his first play **Baal* and this, his first play to be staged and winner of the Kleist Prize, somewhat uncomfortable in their refusal to adopt a political or moral stance. However, he never repudiated them, and one can see in Baal and Andreas Kragler materialist protagonists, ready to dismiss the hypocrisy of the bourgeoisie, whose energy and cynicism would provide an admirable foundation for radical revolution. The final tearing down of the scenery also points forward to Brecht's concept of *Verfremdung* ('distanciation').

Drunkard, The

AT: *The Fallen Saved* **A:** W. H. Smith **Pf:** 1844, Boston **Pb:** 1844 **G:** Melodrama in 5 acts; prose **S:** American countryside, rural cottage, and New York, 1840s **C:** 13m, 6f, extras

Even though he has acted on behalf of the Middleton family for many years, the villainous Lawyer Cribbs holds a grudge against them. When old Mr Middleton dies, he seizes his chance. He persuades Middleton's young son Edward that the family is financially stretched, and urges him to evict two of his tenants, a poor mother and her daughter Mary. However, Edward falls in love with Mary, and they marry. Cribbs now works on Edward's liking for alcohol. Losing his self-respect and apparently impecunious, Edward runs away to Five Points in New York, an area frequented by down-and-outs, and has an attack of delirium tremens. Cribbs tries to make Edward take up forgery, but Edward resists this final descent into crime. Edward's foster-brother William and a wealthy philanthropist Arden Rencelaw find him as he is about to kill himself and cure him of his addiction, reuniting him with his wife and little daughter. Finally, Cribbs's villainy is unmasked: he had hidden Edward's grandfather's will, under which Edward is in fact a wealthy man.

Though of little merit as a piece of drama, this piece is notable, not only for the virtuoso acting demanded in the delirium tremens scene and for its immense contemporary popularity, but because it provides one of the earliest modern examples of theatre performed for the social message it contained, recalling the *propaganda fides* of the Middle Ages and the Baroque period and anticipating the political theatre of the 20th century. Initially at least, *The Drunkard* was presented in conjunction with temperance crusades. Later it became a commercial success, notably in a 1933 revival in Los Angeles, where, played for laughs, it set an American record for a 'straight' play of 7,510 performances over 20 years.

Duchess of Malfi, The

A: John Webster **Pf:** *c.* 1613, London **Pb:** 1623 **G:** Trag. in 5 acts; blank verse and some prose **S:** Malfi (= Amalfi), Rome, Loretto, the countryside near Ancona, and Milan, 1504–13 **C:** 21m, 4f, extras

The malevolent brothers of the Duchess of Malfi, Ferdinand and the Cardinal, are anxious to prevent their widowed sister from remarrying. To this end they place the unscrupulous Bosola as a spy at her court. The Duchess has fallen in love with Antonio Bologna, her steward, and they marry secretly. Bosola later discovers that the Duchess is pregnant, and when her son is born, he informs the Duchess's brothers. Eventually she bears a further two children, and in order to avert suspicion from Antonio, she has him sent from the court 'in disgrace', in fact arranging for him and their son to settle in Ancona, where she will join them. Unfortunately, she reveals her plan to Bosola, who places her under arrest. Her brother Ferdinand, who had already confronted her over her shameful behaviour, now comes to her, bearing a dead hand supposedly cut from the corpse of Antonio. He torments her with a display of waxworks of Antonio and their children appearing as if they were dead, and prevents her sleeping by releasing dancing and singing madmen. Executioners then strangle the Duchess, her lady-in-waiting, and her two younger children. Ferdinand and Bosola immediately begin to repent their crime. Ferdinand is struck down with lycanthropia, which causes him to behave like a wolf, and Bosola resolves to save Antonio's life. Antonio, ignorant of his wife's death, travels to Milan to seek reconciliation with the Duchess's brothers, despite being warned by her voice from the grave. Bosola, fearing that he will be murdered by the Cardinal, kills Antonio by mistake. Finding the Cardinal, Bosola fights with him and Ferdinand, and all three are mortally wounded. Only the young son of Antonio and the Duchess survives to renew the dynasty.

Based on a true story, this is one of the best known and goriest of Jacobean tragedies, with its onstage killings of no less than nine individuals, its horrific moments of dead hands and macabre wax figures, and its disturbing scene of released lunatics. The violence and the pace of action, reinforced by sinewy language, may obscure Webster's strong characterization. Indeed, there is little internal psychological conflict in the play, and the sudden repentance of Ferdinand and Bosola is not analysed in depth. However, Bosola is a subtle villain, who inspires trust, and Antonio, in his stubborn pursuit of his own goals, is a less than perfect hero. At the centre of the action is the Duchess herself, instinctively choosing the right path, and displaying considerable courage at the extremes of suffering.

Duck Hunting (*Utinaya okhota*)

A: Aleksandr Vampilov **Pf**: 1976, Riga, Latvia **Pb**: 1970 **Tr**: 1980 **G**: Drama in 3 acts; Russian prose **S**: Zilov's apartment and other imagined locations, Russia, 1960s **C**: 6m, 3f, 1 child (m)

While Zilov is waiting to go for his annual duck-hunting holiday with his friend Dima, a waiter, a funeral wreath is delivered, dedicated to Zilov from his friends. This shocking practical joke precipitates a series of flashbacks of his misspent life. He re-enacts the beginnings of married life, the deterioration of his marriage, his worsening alcoholism, his cruel treatment of his mistress, his encounter with and seduction of the innocent 18-year-old Irina, and fraud committed at work. His wife Galina becomes pregnant, but, uncertain that Zilov wants a child, has an abortion. He is so dismayed by this that he attacks her verbally and physically. She locks the door to prevent his getting at her, and Zilov, through the closed door, confesses his guilt and promises to make a fresh start – unaware that his wife has gone out and left him. When the fraud is discovered, Zilov almost loses his job. His father dies, but Zilov misses the funeral to be with Irina. His wife leaves him for good, as eventually does Irina. Back in the present, at a party to celebrate the start of the duck shooting, Zilov is so insulting to his friends that they plan to send him the wreath. When the wreath arrives, he sees himself for what he is – a living corpse – and attempts suicide but fails. He lies sobbing on his bed, but it is not clear whether he is laughing or crying. Eventually, he telephones Dima to say that he will join the duck shoot after all.

Vampilov is the most important Russian playwright of the second half of the 20th century, but has suffered from being thought of merely as a latter-day Chekhov. There are indeed strong similarities with Chekhov: the sense of wasted lives, the mixture of the comic and tragic, the understated emotional conflicts. But Vampilov has a strong contemporary voice that deserves to be better heard in the West.

dukkehjem, Et. See DOLL'S HOUSE, A.

Dumb Waiter, The

A: Harold Pinter **Pf**: 1959, Frankfurt am Main; 1960, London **Pb**: 1960 **G**: Com. in 1 act **S**: Basement somewhere in England, 1950s. **C**: 2m

Two men, Ben and Gus, who appears the more dominant, are lying on beds in a basement room conversing desultorily, discussing items from the newspaper and arguing about making the tea. They talk about their 'upcoming assignment' and wonder when they will be informed of the details. An envelope is slid under the door, but it does not contain any instructions. Fetching a revolver from under his pillow, Gus opens the door, but there is no one there. Suddenly there is a clatter behind the serving hatch in the middle of the back wall: it is a 'dumb waiter', a service lift to the upper floors. In the dumb waiter is an order for a cooked two-course meal with tea. Increasingly exotic orders arrive, so Gus and Ben send up what they can in an attempt to satisfy whoever is sending down the orders: crisps, biscuits, and an Eccles cake. Gus discovers a speaking tube and apologizes that they could not fulfil the orders and for the fact that what they sent was not good enough. They now plan the killing for which they have been summoned. Responding to a whistle from the speaking tube, Ben listens to further instructions and is asked to prepare for the arrival of the victim, while Gus goes off to get a glass of water. Ben calls for Gus, who staggers into the room, stripped of his jacket and revolver. Ben raises his revolver, and they stare at each other in silence.

In this short and very funny piece, Pinter continued his skill at blending comedy with menace. Here, two figures like Goldberg and McCann from *The *Birthday Party* become more and more desperate to appease the authority controlling them from above until one is obliged to exterminate the other. While theatrical metaphors of religion and rigid hierarchies suggest themselves, one must be reminded of Pinter's statement that he wouldn't recognize a symbol if he saw one.

Dusa, Fish, Stas and Vi

AT: *Dead Fish* A: Pam Gems Pf: Edinburgh, 1976 Pb: 1977 G: Trag. in 2 acts S: Bed-sittingroom, British city, 1970s C: 4f

Dusa Gilpin, in her late twenties, mother of two small children, has separated from her husband and comes to stay with Fish, only to discover that Vi (Violet), a teenage anorexic, has moved into the flat Fish shares with Stas. Stas (Anastasia) is a physiotherapist working with brain-damaged children, who, in order to get enough money to study for a Ph.D. in Marine Biology, works as a glamorous call girl in the evenings. Fish, from a well-to-do background but now a socialist, has broken up with her boyfriend Alan. While an ambulance is fetched for the now very weak Vi, and Dusa negotiates with her husband over the return of her children, Alan phones to say that he has just married his new woman, who threatened suicide if they could not be together. Discovering that her husband has taken the children to South America, Dusa has a hysterical attack. Fish spends the night spying on Alan making love to his woman. Some time later, Alan, who still sees Fish, is to be a father. Dusa, learning that her children are being sent home, goes to the airport with Stas and Vi to fetch them. When they return, they find Fish, on her birthday, has committed suicide.

Pam Gems was one of the new wave of women playwrights, who, despite the miserable history of women gaining access to the theatre, now became successful with a wide range of plays on women's issues. With great honesty, which drew criticism from some feminists for its negative portrayal, this piece showed how, despite the new sense of empowerment enjoyed by women, they remained vulnerable in contemporary society, summed up by the final words of Fish's suicide note: 'What are we to do?'

Dutchman

A: Imamu Amiri Baraka (LeRoi Jones) Pf: 1964, New York Pb: 1964 G: Drama in 1 act S: Subway carriage, New York, 1960s C: 3m, 1f, extras

On a hot summer's day, Clay, a young black college graduate, is riding the subway to a friend's party. Lula, an attractive white woman, sits down beside him, saying that she came to find him after seeing him through the window at the last station. She begins to flirt with him, surprising him by making accurate guesses about his aspirational lifestyle. Prompted by her, he asks her to the party, and she promises 'fun in the dark house' afterwards at her apartment. As the carriage fills with passengers, Lula becomes more and more uncontrolled, finally swaying sensuously and demanding that Clay dance with her and 'rub bellies on the train'. When he refuses, she jeers at him, calling him 'Uncle Tom' for assuming white respectability. Throwing aside a white drunk, he flings Lula back on to her seat, and in a violent outburst admits that his middle-class behaviour is just a thin veneer over his 'pumping black heart'. As Clay prepares to leave the train, Lula stabs him twice, then orders the other passengers to throw his body off the train. Another black youth gets on at the next stop. Lula eyes him up, just as a black Conductor enters and greets the young man with: 'Hey, brother!'

This short play, which launched the playwright's career, is completely naturalistic, stage time corresponding to real time, and is conceived in almost cinematic terms, moving from close-ups to long shots (indeed, the piece was successfully filmed). Baraka's later work tended to be either agitprop stylized pieces or grand pageants with music and dance. In

Dutchman (the name recalling the Flying Dutchman who, like Clay, is now nowhere at home), the true feelings of the young black are unmasked by the provocative Lula. In all his differing styles, Baraka explored and even celebrated racial hatred, in stark contrast with the message of reconciliation in Baldwin's **Blues for Mister Charlie*, premiered in the same year.

Dyadya Vanya. See UNCLE VANYA.

Dybbuk, The (*Tsvishn Tsvey Veltn: Der Dibuk*)

AT: *Between Two Worlds: the Dybbuk; Bney Schney Olamot: Ha'Dibuk* **A:** Solomon Anski **Pf:** 1920, Warsaw **Pb:** 1918 **Tr:** 1925 **G:** Drama in 4 acts; Russian (1914), Yiddish (*c.*1916) prose and some verse **S:** Brinnitz, Poland, and Miropolye, Russia, early 20th c. **C:** 23m, 7f, 3 children, extras

Reb Sender has a beautiful daughter Leah, but will let her marry only someone rich. A young student Khonnon (or Channon) has fallen in love with her, but his fasting and prayers are in vain, since Sender has found her a husband. As the engagement celebration begins, Khonnon is found dead. Three months later Leah goes to the cemetery to invite the soul of her mother and other souls to her wedding. When she returns, she speaks with the voice of a man, rejecting her bridegroom and denouncing her father as a murderer. She has been possessed by a 'dybbuk', a dead person inhabiting the body of a living being. Sender takes Leah to a wise Russian Rabbi Azrielke (or Asrael). The Rabbi dreams of Khonnon's father, and before he attempts to exorcize the dybbuk, insists on examining Sender further. The spirit of Khonnon's dead father claims that Sender had promised to marry his daughter to Khonnon, but that Sender's greed had kept this pledge secret. Even though Sender did not know Khonnon was his friend's son, he made no effort to check. As a penance he is required to give half his wealth to the poor. With difficulty the dybbuk is then exorcized. Leah is restored to normality, but, before her wedding can take place, she joins Khonnon in the other world.

Originally written in Russian for Stanislavsky but banned by the censor, *The Dybbuk* became the best-known Yiddish drama, largely through the worldwide tour of the Habima Theatre of Moscow, directed by Vakhtangov, 1920–5 (although this version was in Hebrew). In this 'dramatic legend' Anski expresses his faith in divine justice.

Dyccon of Bedlam. See GAMMER GURTON'S NEEDLE.

Dyscolos. See BAD-TEMPERED MAN, THE.

Dyskolos. See BAD-TEMPERED MAN, THE.

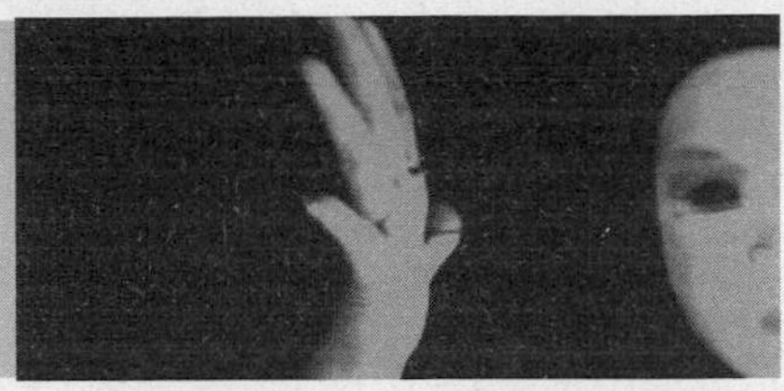

Earl of Pawtucket, The

A: Augustus Thomas **Pf:** 1903, New York **Pb:** 1903 **G:** Com. in 3 acts **S:** Pawtucket, Rhode Island, 1900s **C:** 6m, 2f

Lord Cardington has run away to America from England to avoid a summons from the House of Lords and to see how well he can survive without his title. He assumes the identity of a certain Putnam, an American he had befriended in England. He begins to woo Harriet Fordyce, unaware that she is the former Mrs Putnam. A further complication develops when, because Putnam was the last person seen together with Lord Cardington before his mysterious disappearance, Putnam is suspected of his murder. The fake Putnam now finds himself pursued by the police. In a further comic twist, he is also hounded by lawyers demanding alimony from the very woman he is intending to marry. Eventually, all the complications are resolved, and his lordship settles down to a happy future as an American commoner and husband to an amused Harriet.

Augustus Thomas, author of some 36 original plays, is noted for the American themes of most of his plays, many of them set in the Civil War. Here, underneath the plot complications of conventional comedy, Thomas explores the contrast between the world of privilege and constraint represented by the English class system and the freedom offered by the New World, significantly located in Pawtucket, home of the first water-driven cotton mill and cradle of the American industrial revolution.

Early Morning

A: Edward Bond **Pf:** 1968, London **Pb:** 1968 **G:** Drama in 21 scenes **S:** Windsor Castle and Great Park, Slough, Beachy Head, and heaven, mid-19th c. **C:** 12m, 3f, extras

Disraeli and Prince Albert are plotting a military coup against Queen Victoria. George, the Prince of Wales, who is the Siamese twin of Arthur, is to marry Florence Nightingale. Len is tried by Victoria for eating a man who pushed in a cinema queue. Victoria rapes Florence. In the bungled coup, Victoria poisons and strangles Albert, and George gets shot. A lynch mob, led by Gladstone, prepare to hang Len for letting Victoria escape. Victoria and her sons are lined up before a firing squad, but are let go when Gladstone drops dead. George shoots himself dead. As the civil war continues, Albert carries the corpse of his brother with him. Victoria, enjoying her lesbian relationship with Florence, has regained control. Everyone now meets in heaven, where Victoria puts Arthur on trial and Len shares a human leg with the others. Arthur, who is desperate to die properly, is spoiling heaven for everyone else. Victoria and Albert resolve to eat Arthur, but Florence tries to conceal his head from them. This gets eaten too, and Arthur is laid to rest in a coffin, from which he rises in the air. Victoria declares that in heaven 'There's only peace and happiness, law and order.'

This nightmare vision of a world in which respected rulers and historical icons are revealed to be violent, amoral, and lustful, was banned *in toto* by the Lord Chamberlain. It offered trenchant political analysis coupled with poetic statement, violent imagery with outrageous humour, fantastic invention with a historical perspective. The cannibalism that so shocked audiences is merely a metaphor for the behaviour of the capitalist who devours his own kind.

Earth-Spirit. See LULU PLAYS, THE.

East

A: Steven Berkoff **Pf**: 1975, Edinburgh **Pb**: 1977 **G**: Drama in 19 scenes; prose and some free verse **S**: East End of London, 1970s **C**: 3m, 2f

Mike and Les are firm mates since they fought with razors over Mike's fiancée, Sylv. Sylv's Mum and Dad are a bored, deprived couple. Nostalgically, Dad recalls the 1938 Cable Street riots when Oswald Mosley led his Nazi Blackshirts through the East End. Mike seduces Sylv, Sylv dreams of being a man, and the family and Mike go on holiday to Southend. Les has sex with a 14-year-old and is sent to prison for rape. Les represents a motorbike and Mike rides off on it, flying 'like a king'. Dad sentimentally reminisces about old times, and Mum soliloquizes about masturbating a young stranger in the cinema, only to discover when the lights come on that it is Mike. They all dance at the Lyceum, and Mike delivers his 'Cunt Speech', describing his sexual conquests at the ballroom. Finally, Mike and Sylv plan for the future, rejecting the empty lives of her parents: 'we will not end our days like this'.

Berkoff claimed *East* to proceed from 'a desire to turn a welter of undirected passion and frustration into a positive form'. In episodic scenes, many of them mimed, and in language which combines Cockney slang with pseudo-Shakespearian lyricism, Berkoff depicts the vitality, humour, sexiness, and violence of East End youth, contrasted with the empty lives of their elders, and implies the vague hope that the energy of the young will find a way out for themselves. At the very least, Berkoff has lent articulacy to those heretofore neglected by the theatre: 'Now you know our names.'

East Lynne

AT: *The Marriage Bells, or The Cottage on the Cliff* A: Mrs Henry Wood (adapted by Clifton W. Tayleure) **Pf**: 1862, New York; 1864, London **Pb**: As novel 1861; many subsequent adaptations from 1862 **G**: Melodrama in 5 acts **S**: Archibald Carlyle's home and environs, England, and Isabel's room in France, mid-19th c. **C**: 8m, 5f

Lady Isabel marries Archibald Carlyle, a country solicitor, more from liking and respect than from love, and comes to live in East Lynne. Several years pass. Isabel, now a mother, is fiercely jealous of her husband's friendship with the pretty Barbara Hare, a jealousy intensified by the gossip of her servants and by the treacherous Sir Francis Levison, who has designs on Isabel. She discovers Archibald meeting secretly with Barbara, who seeks help for her brother Richard, falsely accused of murder. In desperation she runs off with Levison to France, has a child by him, and is abandoned. Barbara marries Archibald and reveals that it was Levison who committed the murder of which her brother is accused. Lady Isabel returns to East Lynne, disguised as Madame Vine the governess, just in time to hold her son William as he dies. Levison is arrested and found guilty. Isabel, dying of grief, is forgiven by Archibald as she expires.

East Lynne is the best-known Victorian melodrama. It contains the familiar line after young William's death (in this adaptation: 'my child is dead! And never knew that I was his mother'), and it developed such a reputation amongst touring companies that 'Next week *East Lynne*' became a stock phrase for a standard repertoire. In 1879, when three different London theatres were performing adaptations of *East Lynne*, *A *Doll's House* was premiered, another play in which a woman leaves her husband and children. But while the penitent Isabel confirmed Victorian values, Nora challenged them – to the outrage of contemporary audiences.

Eastward Ho!

A: George Chapman, Ben Jonson, and John Marston **Pf**: 1605, London **Pb**: 1605 **G**: Com. in 5 acts; blank verse and prose **S**: London, 16th c. **C**: 19m, 8f, extras

William Touchstone, goldsmith, has two daughters, Gertrude and Mildred, one vain, the other modest, and two apprentices, Quicksilver and Golding, one lazy and spendthrift, the other industrious and sober. While Gertrude is to marry a nobleman, Sir Petronel Flash, Touchstone arranges for Golding to marry Mildred. Aided by Quicksilver, Sir Petronel cheats his new bride out of her dowry, but they are both shipwrecked while trying to escape 'eastward' to Virginia. They are arrested and brought before Golding, who is now a magistrate. Golding takes pity on the repentant adventurers but can only persuade Touchstone by forcing Touchstone to go to prison to see Quicksilver's and Petronel's conversion for himself. Petronel and Gertrude are reconciled, Quicksilver is forgiven, and all ends happily.

At first sight this comedy seems based on conventional morality, that vice will be punished and virtue rewarded. But in this picture of bustling London life a little more emerges. The priggish young Golding develops into a wise and compassionate judge, and the knavery of Sir Petronel, Quicksilver, and their associates offers such opportunity for fun at the expense of the somewhat tedious Touchstone and his vain daughter that it is hard to condemn them – or indeed believe totally in the sincerity of their repentance.

Ecclesiazusae. See WOMEN IN ASSEMBLY.

École des femmes, L'. See SCHOOL FOR WIVES, THE.

Ecstasy of Rita Joe, The

A: George Ryga Pf: 1967, Vancouver Pb: 1970 G: Pol. drama in 3 acts; prose and songs S: Western Canada, *c.*1950–67 C: 15m, 3f

Framed by sentimental ballads sung by a white folk singer and by a court trial, for which Rita Joe is given eight hours to find character witnesses to defend her on a charge of prostitution, the action develops through a series of flashbacks, as Rita, a Native Canadian, tries to piece her life together. We see her childhood on a reservation: she picks berries and plays lacrosse, her father David Joe refuses to sell her to a white man whose own child has died, and she acts protectively like a substitute mother towards her younger sister. She moves to the city, where the pavements make her feet hurt, and gets a job in a tyre store, where she is sexually harassed. She experiences love in the uncongenial surroundings of a graveyard. She sees an Indian mother giving away her children in order to survive. Rita is repeatedly arrested for vagrancy, shoplifting, drunkenness, assault, and prostitution, and receives no help from her patronizing white Teacher, from an unsympathetic white Priest, or from social services, in the form of Mr Homer of the Indian Centre. There seems to be no way out offered either by the traditional values of her father or by the radicalism of her Native Canadian lover Jaimie Paul. Finally, a gang of rapists violate her and murder both her and Jaimie Paul.

Based on newspaper accounts of the death of Native Canadian girls in Vancouver, this play was one of the most important in the nascent Canadian theatre. Performed in Vancouver, Ottawa, the USA, and Britain, it was also the first major dramatic work to draw attention to the situation of many Native Canadians in a supposedly liberal and tolerant society.

Eden Cinema (*L'Éden Cinéma*)

A: Marguerite Duras Pf: 1977, Paris Pb: 1977 Tr: 1988 G: Drama in 2 acts S: Bungalow and surrounding country, Upper Cambodia, Central Hotel, Saigon, 1931 C: 3m, 2f

The Mother bought a concession in French Indochina with money saved from working at the Eden Cinema, but because she didn't pay any bribes, the land was useless. It was regularly flooded by the sea, even when sea walls were built, and she and her two children, Suzanne and Joseph, and their loyal servant 'the Corporal' were reduced to poverty. They go to the local port of Réam, where they meet the millionaire Mr Jo, who is attracted to Suzanne. Suzanne insists on marriage before she will accede to Mr Jo's pleadings for sex. However, Mr Jo knows that his father wants him to marry a rich heiress, and so promises Suzanne a diamond ring worth 20,000 piastres if she will spend three days with him in Saigon. The Mother is already planning to use the money to rebuild the sea walls. Suzanne, more in love with her brother Joseph than with Mr Jo, refuses the ring and tells him to leave, but he gives her the diamond anyway. Mother and children travel to Saigon to sell the diamond. When she is offered no more than 11,000 piastres for the diamond, the Mother becomes obsessed, and offers Suzanne for sale. Joseph goes off and meets a rich married white woman and sells the diamond to her. The family returns home. The woman comes for Joseph, Suzanne gives herself to a local peasant, and the Mother dies. Suzanne and Joseph leave the plain for good: 'All of us were always strangers in your country.'

Based on her own youth in Indochina, Duras here recounts an absorbing tale of a family struggling to survive in an alien environment. The unreal images projected in the Eden Cinema and the sea walls built in a vain attempt to shut out the Pacific are potent metaphors of colonialism. Duras's tale is told mainly by narration, undramatic but haunting.

Educating Rita

A: Willy Russell **Pf:** 1980, London **Pb:** 1981 **G:** Com. in 2 acts **S:** Tutor's room in northern English university (Liverpool), 1970s **C:** 1m, 1f

Frank, failed poet and unenthusiastic university lecturer in English, is earning some extra income by tutoring on an Open University (OU) course. His wife has left him, he is now living with a younger woman, and he cheers his desolate existence with copious amounts of alcohol. His first OU pupil is Rita White, a 26-year-old alert and voluble hairdresser, who has determined to improve her life by taking a degree. Slowly he teaches her formal education in which judgements have to be 'purely objective'. Rita's husband becomes unhappy with her new enthusiasm, and when he discovers that she is on the pill, burns her books and eventually forces her to choose between her degree and her marriage. Rita becomes even more committed to her course. That autumn Rita has been to summer school, where she excelled. She has moved into a flat with a stylish new friend, works in a bistro, and plans a holiday with fellow students at Christmas. Frank is alarmed to see her slipping from his influence and begins to drink more heavily. Finally, the university authorities send him off to Australia. Rita comes to say goodbye; she now knows that education is not everything, but at least she now has a choice.

This witty and moving two-hander, made into a successful film with Julie Walters and Michael Caine in 1983, offers an analysis of formal education, and optimistically shows a woman succeeding in surmounting her deprived background to be able to make choices – an encouraging message that has successfully transferred to many cultures in the so-called Third World where women are demanding equal access to education.

Edward II (*The Troublesome Raigne and Lamentable Death of Edward the Second, King of England*)

A: Christopher Marlowe **Pf:** *c.*1592, London **Pb:** 1594 **G:** Trag. in 1 act; blank verse **S:** Paris, Edward's court, and different locations in England, 1307–30 **C:** 27m, 2f, extras

Gaveston, exiled in Paris, is summoned back to England by Edward II, now that he has succeeded to the throne. Despite the opposition of the barons led by Mortimer the elder and his nephew, Mortimer the younger, together with Warwick and Lancaster, Edward heaps honours on Gaveston. He orders Gaveston's enemy, the Bishop of Coventry, to be locked in the Tower. His love for Gaveston also causes him to neglect his Queen, Isabella. Eventually, Edward is forced to banish his favourite, but Isabella, in an attempt to win back her husband's love, entreats Young Mortimer to pardon Gaveston. Mortimer and the barons agree, hoping that this 'creeping ant' will cause the downfall of Edward. Edward arranges for Gaveston to marry his niece. On Gaveston's return to England, Mortimer stabs Gaveston before the King in an act of open defiance. When Edward refuses to ransom Old Mortimer from his capture by the Scots, the barons rise in rebellion and seize the fleeing Gaveston. Despite Edward's efforts to save him, Gaveston is treacherously murdered by beheading. Edward now adopts Spencer as his new favourite, and with the help of his family defeats the nobles. Warwick and Lancaster are beheaded. Young Mortimer escapes to the

French court to join Isabella and her son Edward, and becomes the Queen's lover. As Isabella gathers an army against her husband, Edward and Spencer attempt to flee, but are captured. Edward, regretting the turmoil his love for Gaveston brought to his realm, is forced to resign in favour of his son, Edward III. Mortimer becomes Protector and, after repeatedly humiliating Edward II, orders his murder by being crushed to death. The Young Edward avenges his father's death by beheading Mortimer and imprisoning his mother.

Probably Marlowe's last play, *Edward II* is an epic piece, dealing with the events of over 20 years of English history, without any attempt to structure the plot into acts. But it is much more than just a chronicle play. Although packed with incident, Marlowe explores the motivation and inner life not only of Edward but also of some of the other major figures like Gaveston, Isabella, and Mortimer. Even if this is not achieved with the depth attained by Shakespeare, it was a significant step towards character drama. Partly because Edward is an 'anti-hero' in his weakness and irresolution, partly because the play powerfully depicts homosexual love, it has been frequently revived in the last century, most notably in Brecht's version of 1924. It was memorably filmed by Derek Jarman in 1991.

Edward III (*The Raigne of King Edward the third*)

A: William Shakespeare (and others?)
Pf: *c.*1595, London Pb: 1596 G: Hist. drama in 5 acts; blank verse S: Westminster Palace, Roxborough [= Roxburgh] Castle, and locations in France, including Crécy, Calais, and Poitiers, 1337–56 C: 32m, 3f, extras

Edward III, persuaded of his right to the French throne, rejects King John of France's demand for fealty. Before engaging in conflict with the French, Edward has to deal with the rebellious Scots, who have captured the Countess of Salisbury. When he frees her, he falls in love with her. She says that she will submit to the King only if he has his Queen and her husband Salisbury murdered. Edward agrees, but the Countess was only testing him, and now insists that he abandon his suit. Turning his attention to the French wars, Edward commands a successful assault on the French navy. At Crécy, together with his son 'the Black Prince', Edward confronts and defeats King John. Despite his defeat, King John remains optimistic, because of a prophecy that he will succeed in reaching London. Edward besieges Calais, while his son fights the French at Poitiers. In mortal danger, the Black Prince fights on and wins a resounding victory, taking King John and the Dauphin prisoner. Meanwhile, Edward is prepared to spare Calais, only if six leading burghers sacrifice their lives. However, his Queen persuades him to show mercy. When King John learns that he will be brought to London as a prisoner, he now understands the prophecy. The Black Prince warns future nations never to challenge England's power.

The episodic nature of this play, only recently accepted into the Shakespeare canon, suggests a chronicle play rather than a well-structured historical drama (even though it contracts the history of the period from the declaration of war in 1337, 13 years before John ascended the throne, to the Battle of Poitiers in 1356). It foreshadows several elements of **Henry V*: conflict with France, the King's achieving maturity and seriousness of purpose, the balance between the exercise of power and that of mercy, and above all, the jingoistic celebration of English victories. Edward's treatment of Calais forms the subject of Kaiser's *The *Burghers of Calais*.

Eirēnē. See PEACE.

Ekklēsiazousai. See WOMEN IN ASSEMBLY.

Elckerlijc. See EVERYMAN.

Electra (*Elektra*)

A: Euripides Pf: *c.*422–416 BC, Athens Tr: 1782 G: Greek trag. in verse S: Before a peasant's cottage near Mycenae, some years after the Trojan War C: 7m, 2f, chorus (f)

In a prologue the Peasant reveals that Agamemnon's daughter Electra has been forced into marriage with him but that he respects her and has never come to her bed.

Accompanied by Pylades, Orestes arrives at his birthplace, from which he was taken as a child after his mother's brutal murder of Agamemnon, his father. The reluctant Orestes has a duty to avenge the death of his father by killing his mother Clytemnestra. Orestes speaks to Electra without revealing that he is her brother and is dismayed at the way she is treated. The kind Peasant invites the strangers into his cottage. The Old Man who saved Orestes comes to Electra and reveals that someone has sacrificed a ewe on Agamemnon's tomb. As Orestes steps out of the cottage, the Old Man recognizes him by a scar on his forehead, and Orestes and Electra are reconciled. Orestes arranges to be invited by Aegisthus, his mother's lover, to share in a religious ceremony and uses the opportunity to kill him. By pretending to have given birth to a son, Electra tempts Clytemnestra to visit her. Despite Orestes' misgivings and Clytemnestra's insistence that she killed Agamemnon merely to avenge the sacrifice of their daughter Iphigeneia, Clytemnestra is murdered. Orestes and Electra are overwhelmed with guilt. The gods Castor and Polydeuces appear and order Electra to marry Pylades and foretell that Orestes will be absolved by the Athenian court but will have to do penance for many years.

This version by Euripides differs from Aeschylus and Sophocles in two major respects: the poor rural setting and the portrayal of the psychological anguish endured by Electra and Orestes both before and after the killing of Clytemnestra. Thus, in place of the almost ritualistic enactment of revenge in the other two Greek tragedians, we see here a much more realistic portrayal of events. The ill-treated virgin Electra seems almost more disapproving of her mother's licentiousness than of her murdering Agamemnon, and Orestes' indecisiveness before killing his mother is like the wavering purpose of Hamlet.

Electra (*Elektra*)

A: Sophocles Pf: *c*.425–410 BC, Athens? Tr: 1649 G: Greek trag. in verse S: Before the Palace of Mycenae, some years after the Trojan War C: 4m, 3f, chorus (f)

Accompanied by his tutor and by his friend Pylades, Orestes arrives at his birthplace, from which he was taken as a child after his mother's brutal murder of his father Agamemnon. Orestes is determined to avenge the death of his father by killing his mother Clytemnestra. In order to gain access to the house, his tutor pretends to be bringing news of Orestes' death. Clytemnestra is overjoyed to be free of the fear of vengeance, but the news is devastating for Orestes' sister Electra, who has been awaiting Orestes' arrival for many years. Electra now determines to carry out the deed of revenge herself, despite the admonitions of her sister Chrysothemis. Moved by Electra's suffering, Orestes reveals his identity, and there is a touching reunion. Soon, however, Electra spurs Orestes on to commit the deed of vengeance. He murders his mother in the palace. Aegisthus her lover comes triumphantly to view the supposed corpse of Orestes, only to discover that it is that of Clytemnestra. He too is led into the palace to his death.

The story of Orestes and Electra avenging their father's death is the only one treated in the extant tragedies of all three major tragedians, in Aeschylus' *The *Libation-Bearers*, here by Sophocles, and in Euripides' **Electra*. Sophocles and Euripides must have both known Aeschylus' version, but, since the dating is uncertain, it is not clear which of the later versions was written first. Sophocles focuses on the predicament of Electra. In Aeschylus Orestes finds himself at the centre of a cosmic dilemma: in order to obey the will of the god Apollo, he must incur the guilt of matricide. In Sophocles, he commits the deed, and that is that; there is no suggestion that he will be pursued by the Furies. The complexity arises in the figure of Electra, who suffers powerlessly, yearning for the return of her brother, only to have her hopes dashed by the false news of Orestes' death. Sophocles' portrayal of her commitment to the violent death of her mother is shocking and tragic in a young woman, yet she shares what Goethe called one of the tenderest moments of world literature, in the reunion with her brother. Hofmannsthal's intense rewriting of *Electra* (1903) is now best known as an opera by Richard Strauss, and modern-dress adaptations were written by Benito Pérez Galdós (1900) and by O'Neill in **Mourning Becomes Electra*. Giraudoux wrote a version in 1937.

Electric Dolls (*La donna è mobile; Elettricità (sessuale); Fantocci elettrici*)

AT: *Poupées électriques; Electric Puppets*
A: F. T. Marinetti **Pf**: 1909, Paris (as *Poupées électriques*); 1926, Turin (as *La donna è mobile*) **Pb**: 1909 in French; 1926 in Italian **Tr**: None known **G**: Drama in 3 acts; French prose **S**: A seaside resort in the south of France, 1900s **C**: 7m, 6f, 2 robots (1m, 1f), extras

Count Paul de Rozières, a young naval officer on shore leave, flirts with women in a dance hall, much to the distress of his cousin Juliette, who loves him passionately, and to the annoyance of his rich American friend John Wilson, to whose wife Mary Paul is also paying court. Juliette and Paul have a tender leave-taking, but her mother reminds her that Paul, who is penniless, will have to marry a rich heiress. Juliette grows hysterical and throws herself into the sea. A year later at the Wilsons' home, two lifelike electric puppets invented by John sit at table, while John pretends to seduce Mary as a little girl. He horrifies her by pretending to be Paul, and Mary accuses him of treating her like one of his robots. To appease her, John flings the two robots in the sea, but fishermen think he is trying to murder two people, until the dummies are recovered. Paul returns, asking to see Mary. John persuades her that they should leave that very night, then kisses her violently and almost strangles her: 'a little more and the mechanism will be broken'. When John leaves for the rendezvous with Paul, Paul appears and declares his passion for Mary. They embrace as John returns. John hands her a revolver, and she shoots herself, hoping that when she is dead, John will love her as much as he does Juliette.

This is the one play written by Marinetti, famous for his championing of Futurism, whose manifesto declared: 'Literature until now has celebrated intellectual immobility, ecstasy and sleep. We want to exalt aggressive movement, feverish insomnia, . . . the perilous leap, the slap in the face, and the punch of a fist.' Curiously though, this is a conventionally structured psychological drama, its main interest (over a decade before Čapek's **RUR*), is the relating of human emotions to the behaviour of machines.

Emperor, The. See HENRY IV (Pirandello).

Emperor Jones, The

A: Eugene O'Neill **Pf**: 1920, New York **Pb**: 1921 **G**: Drama in 8 scenes **S**: West Indian island, 1920 **C**: 7m, 1f, extras

Brutus Jones, a larger-than-life black American, has by emulating the whites' grasping behaviour become emperor of a West Indian island. Now, after two years' reign, he faces a revolt from the natives. He is well prepared, with food hidden in the jungle and a stolen fortune on Martinique, where he intends to escape to. He has also persuaded the gullible natives that he can be killed only by a silver bullet. Setting off into the jungle, accompanied by the ceaseless drumming of his pursuers' tom-toms, he soon gets lost, fails to find his food, and is haunted by visions. He first shoots at 'little formless fears' then at the vision of Jeff, a fellow porter he once killed, then at the ghost of a prison guard he murdered. Suddenly he finds himself at a slave market, and although he shoots the imaginary Auctioneer and Planter, he is led away amongst naked slaves. Finally, at an altar, a witch doctor indicates that he should offer himself as a sacrifice. Jones uses his last bullet on a huge crocodile which is about to devour him. The natives, having melted down coins to make silver bullets, wait for Jones to emerge from the jungle. As he does so, he is shot dead.

Following closely on O'Neill's first success with *Beyond the Horizon* (1920), *The Emperor Jones* was not only the first play to offer a leading role to a black actor in a mainly white company; it also showed what an individual voice O'Neill already possessed. The exotic location, familiar to O'Neill from his sea voyages, the blending of the realistic framework with expressionistic visions in the jungle, the relentless drumming (stipulated to begin at heart rate and gradually accelerate), all combined to make this play stand out from the conventionally realistic fare of contemporary American theatre and can still work powerfully in performance.

Empire Builders, The (*Les Bâtisseurs d'empire*)

A: Boris Vian Pf: 1959, Paris Pb: 1959 Tr: 1967 G: Drama in 3 acts; French prose S: An apartment building, France, mid-20th c. C: 3m, 3f

A family comprising Father, Mother, their daughter Zénobie, and their maid Cruche, have been forced, like their Neighbour, to vacate the apartment below because of the threat emanating from a mysterious Noise and from the *Schmürz*, a bleeding creature swathed in bandages. They refuse to investigate the source of the Noise, and only Zénobie treats the *Schmürz* with any kindness. The others attempt to defeat it by brutally attacking it, only each time to flee to a new apartment higher up in the building, relentlessly pursued by the Noise and the *Schmürz*. As they do so, their possessions become fewer and fewer. Eventually, the maid has left them, and the Neighbour's son has died. When Zénobie crosses the landing to the Neighbour, she finds his door sealed, and on returning to her parents, discovers their door locked. She is abandoned as her parents escape to the attic apartment, where the Mother meets her end. Alone at the top of the building, the Father dons his army uniform and persuades himself that he is still intact by checking all his body parts. As the sounds of the Noise and a knocking at the door grow louder, he retreats to the balcony, where an ambiguous stage direction leaves it unclear whether he drops to the floor or falls out of the window. Finally, '*And perhaps the door opens, and perhaps schmürzes enter, vague outlines in the dark.*'

The Empire Builders is an absurdist piece similar to those of fellow Pataphysician Ionesco, but has not lasted so well, perhaps because the physical presence of the *Schmürz* lends too much definition to the indefinable menace to bourgeois complacency, achieved more persuasively by the undefined Noise.

En attendant Godot. See WAITING FOR GODOT.

Endgame (*Fin de partie*)

A: Samuel Beckett Pf: 1957, London Pb: 1957 Tr: 1958 G: Drama in 1 act; French prose S: Room in indeterminate location, the future C: 3m, 1f

In a bare room with one door and two high windows, a figure sits draped with a dust sheet, behind whom stand two dustbins. A stiff-legged servant Clov moves around, finally removing the sheet to reveal Hamm. Clov begins with: 'Finished, it's finished, nearly finished.' Although Hamm, blind and confined to a wheelchair, is at Clov's mercy, Clov serves him grudgingly. When asked why Clov doesn't kill him, Clov replies that he does not know the combination of the larder. When Hamm asks for things (including later painkillers and coffins), Clov tells him that there are none left. Out of one of the dustbins arises a pale face, that of Nagg, demanding his 'pap' – but 'there's no more pap'. Nagg is Hamm's father. After a bicycle accident in which they lost their legs, Nagg and Hamm's mother Nell have been confined to the dustbins. Even Nagg's story of the tailor fails to amuse Nell now. To pass the time, Hamm gets Clov to push him round the room, then to look out of the windows to tell him what he sees, but all is grey outside. Hamm feels a flea, and is terrified that evolution may begin all over again. Clov brings Hamm a toy dog as a companion. Hamm delivers a long rhetorical story, which suggests that Clov is his son. Clov looks out once again and is horrified to see a small boy outside. He is going out to murder this 'potential procreator', but Hamm dissuades him, since the boy will die or come to them. Clov agrees to leave Hamm and dresses to depart, but while Hamm delivers his 'final soliloquy', Clov remains motionless at the door.

Endgame has been variously interpreted. The title and phrases like 'Me to play' refer to chess; the bare stage, with its two high windows, suggests the inside of a skull; Hamm, sounding like the colloquialism for a poor actor, and his mentions of 'asides' and 'soliloquies' point to the theatrical experience of repeating the same role again and again; the isolation, greyness, and the unavailability of goods suggest the remains of life after a nuclear holocaust. As ever, amongst these mystifying clues, Beckett succeeds in creating a beautifully written, tense drama in which almost nothing happens, a drama that offers a relentlessly bleak image of the end of humanity. At least in **Waiting for Godot* there was some hope of redemption, even if illusory. Here there is none.

Endymion (*Endimion, The Man in the Moone*)

A: John Lyly **Pf:** 1588, London **Pb:** 1591 **G:** Com. in 5 acts; prose **S:** A fantasy court, in the mythical past **C:** 16m, 7f, extras

Like his mythical namesake's love for the moon, Endymion secretly loves the chaste and distant Cynthia. His friend Eumenides loves Semele, Cynthia's lady-in-waiting, whose wit and sarcasm cause her to be forced to be silent for a year. Tellus, a lady at the court, is so jealous of Endymion's love for Cynthia that she arranges for a witch to cast a spell on Endymion and make him sleep for 20 years. Eumenides is granted one wish at a magic well, and, after much soul-searching, decides in favour of his suffering friend rather than seeking the fulfilment of his love for Semele. Endymion is released from his spell by Cynthia's kiss, Eumenides wins Semele, and Semele is freed from her enforced silence – to point out that Eumenides' generous act of male friendship has resulted in losing Endymion to Cynthia. A sub-plot of low comedy involves roguish pages and nubile servant-girls, Sir Tophas extravagantly wooing a witch, and two philosophers seeking wisdom at court.

Lyly is perhaps now best remembered for his *Euphues, the Anatomy of Wit* (1578), a prose narrative, written in a highly ornate, elaborate style, which was also to distinguish his writing for the stage. No longer appealing to modern taste, a play like *Endymion* is still worthy of note. First, despite its mythical setting, it offers a revealing image of the romantic intrigues of the Elizabethan court. Cynthia is a flattering portrayal of Elizabeth herself, and there are obvious references to the Earl of Leicester (Endymion) and Mary Queen of Scots (Tellus). Secondly, Lyly, unlike many of his contemporaries, wrote in an elegant, almost rarefied style (the low comedy is kept well apart from the main action), which reminds one of the Italian pastoral. His influence on Shakespeare (in plays like *A *Midsummer Night's Dream*) is regarded as decisive. *Endymion* was performed at court by boy actors.

Enemy: Time, The. See SWEET BIRD OF YOUTH.

Enemy of the People, An (*En folkefiende*)

AT: *A Public Enemy* **A:** Henrik Ibsen **Pf:** 1883, Christiania **Pb:** 1882 **Tr:** 1888 **G:** Drama in 5 acts; Norwegian prose **S:** Norwegian spa town, 1880s **C:** 9m, 2f, extras

Dr Thomas Stockmann has helped to transform his home town into a successful spa, made prosperous by an annual influx of visitors. However, he discovers that the spa waters are contaminated and insists that the baths will have to be closed while the problem is solved. His brother Peter Stockmann, the mayor, points out the cost to the town, and the citizens turn against the doctor. His brother intervenes to prevent an exposure appearing in the press, and Stockmann finds it impossible to hire a hall for a public meeting. At a meeting in the home of Captain Horster, one of his few supporters, Stockmann denounces the authorities not just for the cover-up of the contamination but for their general corruption and complacency. The enraged populace attack his house. His daughter Petra loses her job as teacher, he is no longer the spa doctor. When it is learned that his father-in-law has bought shares in the spa very cheaply, Stockmann is suspected of having manipulated everything for financial gain. Unrepentant, he continues his campaign for the truth, declaring that 'the strongest man is he who stands alone'.

This is one of the most overtly political of Ibsen's plays and, no doubt inflamed by the controversy surrounding **Ghosts*, reflects his cynicism about democratic processes in which the blinkered majority act only out of self-interest. However, he is also harsh in his depiction of Stockmann, a dangerous idealist who destroys his home and family rather than seek any form of compromise.

Engaged

A: W. S. Gilbert **Pf**: 1877, London **Pb**: 1877
G: Farce in 3 acts S: Cottage garden near Gretna on the Scots–English border and Symperson's house in London, mid-19th c.
C: 5m, 5f

Maggie, a simple Scots lass, loves the roguish Angus, who boosts his income by derailing trains and exploiting delayed passengers. Two passengers arrive, Belvawney and his fiancée Belinda Treherne, who is on the run to escape marrying Major McGillicuddy. Belvawney has an income of £1,000 a year, so long as his close friend Cheviot Hill, who proposes to every woman he meets, never marries. If Cheviot marries or dies, his uncle Symperson will get the money. Cheviot and Symperson now come from the train. Symperson is keen that Cheviot should marry his daughter Minnie, but Cheviot proposes to Maggie and then to Belinda. McGillicuddy bursts in to claim his bride, and Cheviot, to protect Belinda, pretends to be her husband. Unbeknown to Cheviot, under Scots law this declaration constitutes a wedding ceremony. Three months later Cheviot is planning to marry Minnie, but Belvawney, fearful of losing his income, declares that he will be committing bigamy because of his Scottish 'wedding'. Symperson, horrified that he will not get his money, encourages Cheviot to commit suicide. Cheviot is saved by the news that Maggie's cottage was on the English side of the border. Learning that Minnie is interested only in his money, Cheviot turns again to Belinda. When it is discovered that the garden itself where the marriage declaration was made, lay in Scotland, Belinda happily accepts him as her husband, and Belvawney must console himself with Minnie.

Although far better known as Arthur Sullivan's librettist, Gilbert wrote a number of 'straight' plays, of which *Engaged* is the finest. Its immaculate plotting and its satire of both rural melodrama and middle-class romance suggest a combination of Boucicault and Wilde.

Enrico IV. See HENRY IV (Pirandello).

Entertainer, The

A: John Osborne **Pf**: 1957, London **Pb**: 1957
G: Drama in 13 scenes; prose and songs
S: English seaside resort, 1956 C: 5m, 2f

Domestic scenes of the Rice household alternate with Archie Rice's stage act. Archie is a second-rate music-hall comedian and singer, attempting to keep this traditional entertainment alive, despite telling unfunny jokes, singing maudlin songs, and facing the threat of the mass media. He lives in the shadow of his father Billy's success as a music-hall star, is bored with his marriage to the dowdy Phoebe, ten years his senior, and has an uneasy relationship with his son Frank and daughter Jean. His other son Mick is sent to fight at Suez and is killed just before he is expected home. Archie's response is to sing the blues. When Archie plans to leave Phoebe to marry a 20-year-old woman whose family might be induced to put up money for his touring show, his father Billy ruins his plans by revealing to her parents that Archie is already married. Soon after, Billy dies. Archie's daughter Jean decides that she does not want to marry the stuffy lawyer Graham Dodd and breaks off the engagement. Finally, in a desperate attempt to 'improve' his show, Archie introduces nude tableaux and makes sexist jokes, ending with the song: 'Why should I care?'

After *Look Back in Anger*, this was Osborne's most popular play. While Archie Rice is neither angry nor young like Jimmy Porter, both plays portray the decline into the confusions of post-war Britain from past certainties, here represented by the metaphor of the enjoyable fun of traditional music hall. Significantly, Mick loses his life at Suez, the last attempt by Britain to operate as an independent world power. The music-hall format allows for a highly theatrical episodic presentation, exploited by Laurence Olivier in the main role both on stage and screen.

Entertaining Mr Sloane

A: Joe Orton Pf: 1964, London Pb: 1964
G: Com. in 3 acts S: Living room, England, 1960s C: 3m, 1f

Sloane, a rootless handsome 19-year-old, is offered a home by an older woman, Kath, in her house built on a rubbish dump. After looking round, Sloane and she engage in innuendo-filled conversation, as they gradually seduce each other. With a characteristic mixture of predatory sexuality, maternal protectiveness, and English middle-class morality, Kath tells him: 'I'll be your mamma. I need to be loved. Gently. Oh! I shall be so ashamed in the morning.' Her brother Ed appears and offers Sloane a job as chauffeur. Ed, a homosexual, tries to seduce Sloane as well, but Sloane tantalizes him by pretending to be a virgin. Sloane begins to dominate Kath and Ed by playing them off against each other. However, Ed's puritanical father Kemp recognizes Sloane as the killer of his former boss, a photographer specializing in pornographic images. In order to silence Kemp, Sloane murders him too. Ed and the now pregnant Kath gain the upper hand: they blackmail Sloane into agreeing to be their lover for six months at a time each.

This, Orton's first full-length play, has similarities with Pinter's *The *Caretaker*: an outsider coming into a home, attempting to manipulate the two occupants but ending up the victim. The major differences are in Orton's language, 'a combination of elegance and crudity', dialogue that generates 'a sort of seismic disturbance', and in the shocking juxtaposition of comic wit with violent action and immoral behaviour. In the process, Orton unmasks the hypocrisies of contemporary British society in a disturbingly cruel manner. As the critic John Bull astutely observes: 'We are invited to enjoy the games but never to feel sympathy for the players.'

Entlassene, Der. See FEAR AND MISERY OF THE THIRD REICH.

Epicene

AT: *Epicoene; The Silent Woman* A: Ben Jonson Pf: 1609, London Pb: 1616 G: Com. in 5 acts; prose S: London, early 17th c. C: 11m, 6f, extras

Morose, a rich bachelor, so hates noise that he is seeking a silent wife. He is pleased to learn that Epicene, who lives nearby, hardly speaks. Morose has disinherited his nephew, Sir Dauphine Eugenie, and, in fact, it is Sir Dauphine who has planted Epicene in order to trap his uncle. When Morose meets Epicene, he is so delighted with this silent woman that he marries her immediately. However, once married, Epicene hardly stops talking and invites wits, admirers, and hangers-on for a rowdy wedding feast at Morose's home. Morose tries to escape the row and then attempts to drive the revellers from his house. Finally he pleads for a divorce. When his nephew agrees to arrange this for him, Morose agrees to pay him handsomely and to restore him as his heir. Sir Dauphine then reveals that Epicene is in fact a boy, so providing unquestionable grounds for divorce.

By establishing Morose as an unsympathetic, mean, and obsessive individual, Jonson draws on the tradition of the absurd old man of Roman comedy and of the *commedia dell'arte* and pre-dates the extreme characters of Molière. This makes *Epicene* a lighter, less complex play than Jonson's other great comedies, where we cannot help having a sneaking admiration for the villains. Here we are treated to the fun of a kind of **Taming of the Shrew* in reverse, the silent woman who becomes a harridan, and, as in **Twelfth Night*, the spoiler of social gaiety receiving his just deserts. The play was originally performed by the boys of the Children of the Queen's Revels.

Episode. See ANATOL.

Equites. See KNIGHTS.

Equus

A: Peter Shaffer Pf: 1973, London Pb: 1973
G: Drama in 2 acts S: Psychiatrist's office, and horse stables, southern England, 1970s C: 5m, 4f, 6 horses

The events of the play are narrated by Dr Martin Dysart, a middle-aged psychiatrist, who is confronted with a youth, Alan Strang, brought to him because he has blinded six horses. Dysart probes Alan's home background: a father, who is a secret voyeur, and a mother, who is a religious fanatic. As a child Alan adored, even worshipped horses, but his unhappy childhood and a disastrous attempt at a love affair with a stable lass drive his obsession with horses towards his terrible act of mutilation. Dysart uses his psychiatric skills to restore Alan to sanity, but then regrets that, by getting him to conform to conventional codes of behaviour, he has removed Alan's capacity for worship and has destroyed the myth Alan had created.

Equus is a profoundly immoral play, far more worthy of censorship than sexual display. Prompted by the true story of a boy who mutilated horses, Shaffer's play implies that being mentally unbalanced is somehow a special state, more noble and insightful than that enjoyed by rational individuals. Admittedly, Alan's parents are sad people, whom one would not wish to emulate, but to exalt the unhinged behaviour of Alan is an insult to those suffering the torments of mental illness. None of this might matter much, but for the fact that the play is gripping and theatrical, and has proved to be very popular.

Erdgeist. See LULU PLAYS, THE.

Ermittlung, Die. See INVESTIGATION, THE.

Erpingham Camp, The

A: Joe Orton **Pf:** 1967, London **Pb:** 1967 **G:** Farce in 11 scenes **S:** English holiday camp, 1960s **C:** 6m, 3f, extras

Erpingham runs his eponymous holiday camp, with its chalets, communal dining, and so-called entertainment, on military lines. His guests are like internees who are forced to 'enjoy themselves' in the way Erpingham dictates. Redcoat Riley is a disappointment to Erpingham, because he is inefficient and clearly does not consult his manual closely enough. It is therefore with some reluctance that Erpingham gives Riley the job of Entertainments Officer when the old one dies. Indeed, Riley's 'entertainment' goes horribly wrong: called out from the audience of campers, Eileen, who keeps on pointing out that she is pregnant, is insulted and struck by Riley. Her partner Kenny leaps to her defence and knocks Riley to the floor. In retaliation for insubordination towards one of his staff, Erpingham locks away the campers' food and prevents them entering their chalets. Despite the reservations of some of the more timid campers, Kenny leads a revolt against Erpingham, heading a march on the stores. In the ensuing mêlée, Kenny beats up Erpingham, who crashes through the rotten floor, killing a number of dancers beneath. The Padre, notorious for his unwelcome visits to young girls' chalets, holds an impromptu funeral service for Erpingham, at which Riley gives the oration for his late lamented boss.

Originally written for television, this is the only large cast play by Orton. In a rewriting of Euripides' **Bacchae*, the forces of repression are destroyed by the celebratory anarchism of the campers. However, the revolt does not stem from a philosophy of liberation, but rather from moral outrage, not least because their womenfolk have been insulted. Erpingham camp will endure and continue to attract acquiescent British holidaymakers.

Eumenides. See ORESTEIA, THE.

Eunuch, The (*Eunuchus*)

A: Terence **Pf:** 161 BC, Rome **Tr** 1598 **G:** Latin com. in verse **S:** A street in Athens, before the homes of Phaedria and Thais, 2nd c. BC **C:** 13m, 5f, extras

A young man, Phaedria, is in love with Thais, an Athenian courtesan. However, she is also being wooed by a braggart soldier, Thraso, who makes Thais a gift of a young girl, Pamphila. Not to be outdone, Phaedria resolves to give Thais a present of a eunuch. When Phaedria's younger brother Chaerea sees Pamphila being brought to Thais' home, he resolves to disguise himself as the promised eunuch to gain access to her. A young gentleman, Chremes, now appears. He has been summoned by Thais, who eventually reveals that he is Pamphila's sister and that the jealous Thraso intends to carry her off by force. Thraso's assault on Thais' house is repelled, and Chaearea, discovering that

Pamphila is a freeborn lady, asks for her hand in marriage. Phaedria is now persuaded to share Thais with Thraso, and so the play ends happily for everyone.

Based on a no longer extant play of the same name by Menander, with two characters borrowed from Menander's *Kolax*, this proved to be the most popular of Terence's plays in ancient Rome, winning him the highest fee ever paid for a comedy. In addition to the characteristically tightly woven plot, Terence here engages in a great deal of fun in a farcical manner that might more readily be associated with Plautus, derived mainly from the stock figure of the ineffectual braggart soldier, Thraso. The figure of Thais reappears in Hrotsvitha's **Paphnutius*, and *The Eunuch* provided a source for Ariosto's *The Pretenders* (1509) and for the first English prose comedy, George Gascoigne's *The Supposes* (1566), which in turn provided the sub-plot of Bianca and her suitors in Shakespeare's *The *Taming of the Shrew*. Other versions include Charles Sedley's *Bellamira, or the Mistress* (1687), Thomas Cooke's *The Eunuch, or the Darby Captain* (1736), Edmund Ball's *The Beautiful Armenia* (1778), and the figure of the Braggart Soldier recurs in the plays named under Plautus' play of that name.

Events while Guarding the Bofors Gun

A: John McGrath **Pf:** 1966, London **Pb:** 1966
G: Drama in 2 acts **S:** Gun-park in British Zone, Germany, 1954 **C:** 11m

Lance-Bombardier Terry Evans is at 18 'a nice boy, trying hard to be liked, but not really succeeding', in charge of six tough older gunners during his National Service. Their task is to guard an obsolete Bofors gun. Amongst the men, there are two particularly hard cases: Featherstone, 'a rough Cockney . . . and a large poxy man', and O'Rourke, 'an Irish bandit with a terrifying death-wish'. While the men joke obscenely and aggressively, Evans announces that he is returning home the next day for an Officer Selection Board. Rather weakly, Evans allows Featherstone and O'Rourke to go to the Navy, Army, and Air Force Institutes (NAAFI) for cigarettes shortly before they are to do their turn of guard duty. O'Rourke gets drunk and smashes up the NAAFI, but Evans is too irresolute to put him on a charge. Sergeant Walker orders the guard out to find most of them missing. Still covering for his absent men, Evans lies to Walker. Flynn, the oldest gunner, then insists that Evans must choose between supporting army discipline and becoming a rebel himself; he cannot sit on the fence any longer in a feeble attempt to be popular. Eventually, Featherstone drags O'Rourke back to the guard hut, and they are sent out on sentry duty. Finally, O'Rourke falls on his bayonet, and Evans is desperate when he realizes that he now has no chance of going home.

Based on his own experiences during National Service, McGrath here explores the futile discipline and hierarchical structures of the British army, which can stand as a metaphor for any similar organization (as in Wesker's **Chips with Everything*). The focus is on Evans, attempting to be one of the men but failing miserably. Naturalistic in style, apart from O'Rourke's direct address to the audience, this is a better structured and more carefully written piece than some of his later agitprop work for the 7:84 Theatre Company.

Everyman

A: Anon **W:** ? late 15th c. **Pb:** *c.*1520
G: Morality play in verse **S:** Heaven and earth
C: 17 (m and f)

God sends out Death to bring Everyman to account. Being quite unprepared for death and judgement, Everyman pleads with Death to spare him until the following day, but Death is unrelenting and will soon return. Despite promising unconditional friendship, Fellowship refuses to accompany Everyman to his death. Kindred and Cousin similarly refuse, and Everyman can find no support in Goods, which, it transpires, he does not own but were merely lent to him while on earth. Since he has so neglected Good Deeds, they cannot help him, but introduce him to Knowledge, who promises to escort Everyman on his journey to death. Everyman is led by Knowledge to Confession, and he repents of his selfish, sinful ways. Encouraged by the now revived Good Deeds, together with Beauty, Strength, Discretion, and Five Wits, Everyman gives away his worldly possessions and goes to receive the holy sacrament. As he approaches his grave, all but Knowledge and Good Deeds forsake him, and only Good Deeds goes with him to his death. Redeemed by God's mercy through Jesus Christ and his Church, Everyman is welcomed by an Angel into heaven. Finally, a Doctor sums up the moral of the story.

It is now generally accepted that *Everyman* is a translation of the Dutch play *Elckerlijc*, the earliest manuscript of which dates from 1495. Unlike *The *Castle of Perseverance*, *Everyman* does not cover the whole span of a man's life but shows him on the day of his death, unprepared to meet God and answer to his judgement – a powerful piece of Church propaganda. What makes the play still popular is the lively depiction of allegorical figures, which made William Poel's revival of 1901 so memorable and induced Hugo von Hofmannsthal to create his colourful *Jedermann* (*Everyman*, 1911), which has been regularly performed as the centrepiece of the Salzburg Festival since 1920.

Every Man in His Humour

A: Ben Jonson **Pf**: 1598, London **Pb**: 1601; rev. version 1616 **G**: Com. in 5 acts; prose and blank verse **S**: London (Florence in 1st version), late 16th c. **C**: 14m, 3f, extras

Young Edward Knowell (Lorenzo in the first version) is a quiet, studious scholar, whose only perceived weakness is a liking for poetry. He is sent a letter by Wellbred, a friend, inviting him to meet in the Windmill Tavern. Edward's father reads the letter and fears his son is getting into bad company. Wellbred's brother-in-law, the puritanical Kitely, is concerned about the welfare of his young wife and sister, and indeed Knowell has fallen in love with Bridget, Kitely's sister. Humour is derived from intrigues and counter-intrigues, involving Knowell's servant Brainworm, his cousin, and a bombastic associate, Captain Bobadill, amongst others. Knowell's father fails to catch his son in his presumed debauchery. Eventually writs are served by Knowell's servant in disguise, and finally an old judge has to sort out all the entanglements. When he learns of Knowell's elopement with Bridget, he forgives the young lovers, and all ends happily.

This play was Jonson's first success and already established characteristic elements of his comedies: a delightfully complex plot, a recognizably contemporary setting, robust and inventive dialogue, and strongly drawn but not unsubtle characters. These are on the one hand, as implied here in the title, prey to their own humours, blood, phlegm, yellow bile (melancholy), and black bile (anger), according to Elizabethan medicine. On the other hand, they are endearing tricksters, especially the figure of Brainworm, reminiscent of the mischievous servant of Roman comedy. Above all, it is the young and witty who profit from and thrive in the new urban world of Jonson's London.

Exiles

A: James Joyce **Pf**: 1919, Munich **Pb**: 1918 **G**: Drama in 3 acts **S**: Living rooms of Richard's and Robert's homes, Dublin suburbs, 1912 **C**: 3m, 3f, 1 child (m)

With the promise of a professorship, Richard Rowan, a moderately successful writer, returns to Ireland from 'exile' with his naive, earthy common-law wife Bertha and their 8-year-old son, Archie. They are visited by Robert Hand, a journalist, and his former fiancée Beatrice Justice, now Archie's music teacher. Beatrice is strongly attracted to Richard, while Robert lusts after Bertha, kisses her, and invites her to his cottage that night. Later, Bertha confesses this to Richard, who insists that she must be free to decide for herself. That evening Richard visits Robert to tell him that he knows about the affair and even welcomes it, longing 'to be dishonoured for ever in love and lust'. Robert offers a duel, but Richard rejects such romanticism. Bertha arrives at Robert's cottage and is unnerved to discover Richard there, who again refuses to tell her what to do. Robert persuades her that sleeping with him will assuage Richard's own guilt. The next morning,

Bertha returns home and is reassured by Beatrice's innocence and unhappy longing. She confesses that she is intellectually far below Richard. When Richard returns from a walk, Bertha tells him that nothing happened with Robert, which Robert then confirms, but Richard cherishes his doubt. Bertha tells Richard that she still longs for her lover: him.

This semi-autobiographical piece (Richard, a Stephen Daedalus figure, clearly represents the tortured Joyce, and Bertha, a prototype of Molly Bloom, Joyce's wife Nora), was considered too obscene by Shaw to be performed at the Stage Society. It is actually a highly moral play, in which 'exiles' from conventional morality have to work out their own rules of conduct. The pity is that Joyce, who displayed in the Night Town sequence in *Ulysses* his remarkable talent for visual drama, should, in his one major piece for the stage, remain within the confines of naturalism.

Exorcism, The. See WHO'S AFRAID OF VIRGINIA WOOLF.

Factory Lad, The

A: John Walker Pf: 1832, London Pb: 1825 G: Melodrama in 2 acts S: The homes of a factory worker and a factory owner, outside a factory, an inn, a courtroom, and surrounding countryside, England, 1830s C: 11m, 3f, extras

In the face of industrial competition, Squire Westwood feels obliged to introduce steam looms into his factory and to dismiss his loyal workers. Their appeals for mercy fall on deaf ears. They join forces with the poacher and outcast Will Rushton, whose wife died from starvation as a result of the Poor Laws, and together they take revenge on Westwood by setting fire to his factory and his home. The factory lad, George Allen, escapes arrest thanks to the daredevil bravery of Rushton, but eventually all end in court together. The corrupt Justice, named Bias, commits them to the local assizes, which will almost certainly sentence them to death. When Allen's wife's pleas to Westwood for mercy are spurned, Rushton produces a pistol and shoots him dead.

This is a remarkable melodrama, written by a writer about whom nothing but the name is known. In place of the usual theme of wicked landlord, threatened woman, and falsely accused hero, *The Factory Lad* deals with events of recent history, the Luddite uprising of 1811–16, and portrays a genuine political confrontation. While the dialogue is undeniably wooden and the plot dependent on moments of exciting action and overblown emotion, Walker brings his characters to life quite convincingly and allows even the villain Westwood reasonable justification for his unyielding attitude. This is the first play to deal with industrial conflict, a theme that was to re-emerge later in Hauptmann's *The *Weavers* and Galsworthy's **Strife*.

Fadren. See FATHER, THE.

Fairground Booth, The. See PUPPET SHOW, THE.

Fair Maid of the West, The (Part 1)

AT: *A Girl Worth Gold* A: Thomas Heywood Pf: *c.*1607 Pb: 1631 G: Romantic com. in 5 acts; blank verse and prose S: Plymouth and Fowey, England; Fayal in the Azores, Morocco, and at sea, 1597 C: 21m, 2f, extras

Bess Bridges, barmaid of the Castle Inn in Plymouth, is the toast of the town. She loves only Spencer, who is about to sail to the Azores to plunder Spanish wealth. Spencer is involved in a tavern brawl and, defending Bess's honour, kills a quarrelsome customer. Now forced to fly the country, he gives Bess the Windmill Tavern at Fowey. Here Bess is once again a great success. Her beloved Spencer, however, is mortally wounded in Fayal and sends his friend Goodlack to seek out Bess and bestow on her his wealth, provided she has remained virtuous. Goodlack reports to the faithful Bess that Spencer has died in the Azores, and she buys and equips a ship to fetch back his body, taking charge as captain. On arrival in the Azores she finds the Spanish back in charge and wages war on them, believing that they have desecrated her lover's body. Spencer has however survived his wound and has been captured by some Spaniards. Bess takes their ship, but when Spencer appears amongst the prisoners, she thinks he is a ghost. Putting in to

Morocco to take on water, Bess is courted by the King of Fez. She dispenses justice, is reunited with Spencer, and they marry. The King throws a sumptuous wedding banquet for the happy couple.

Heywood discovered a popular mix of ingredients for this piece: confident patriotism, an honourable hero, and a strong female adventurer with obvious echoes of Elizabeth I. Part 2, written in the wake of the success of Part 1 and generally accounted a much weaker play, sees the couple suffering under the King of Fez, enduring shipwreck and separation, until after many more adventures they are reunited in Florence.

Faithful Shepherd, The (*Il pastor fido*)

A: Giovanni Battista Guarini Pf: 1595, Crema Pb: 1589 Tr: 1602 G: Pastoral in 5 acts; Italian verse S: A timeless pastoral landscape in Arcadia C: 15m, 3f, chorus (m and f)

Silvio so loves hunting that he has little interest in Amarilli, to whom he is engaged, nor in Dorinda, who loves him passionately. Amarilli loves and is loved by Mirtillo, but he is pursued by the rapacious Corisca. Learning of Amarilli's love for Mirtillo, Corisca betrays the pair, and Amarilli is condemned to death for her faithlessness. Mirtillo, 'the faithful shepherd', offers to take her place in death, but tragedy is averted for both, when it is revealed that Amarilli is engaged to the shepherd Silvio (in fact Mirtillo) and not to the hunter Silvio. Meanwhile Silvio the hunter has wounded Dorinda, mistaking her for a wolf, and repents by offering to marry her. The chorus prepares to celebrate the weddings.

Guarini's play stands alongside Tasso's **Aminta* as one of the best-known and most frequently translated pastoral plays. Though not as highly regarded as *Aminta*, it contains a much more complex plot, comédy and sensuality, and its integration of a musical chorus anticipates the development of Italian opera towards the end of the century. The main importance of *The Faithful Shepherd* is that it may be accounted the first tragicomedy, a play which is on the verge of a tragic outcome, but which ends happily. John Fletcher's *The Faithful Shepherdess* (1609) is indebted to Guarini.

Fallen Saved, The. See DRUNKARD, THE.

Fallit, En. See BANKRUPT, THE.

Family Reunion, The

A: T. S. Eliot Pf: 1939, London Pb: 1939 G: Drama in 2 acts; free verse S: Drawing room and library of the Monchenseys' home, north of England, 1930s C: 7m, 5f, chorus (f)

Amy, Dowager Lady Monchensey, a widow, presides over the family home of Wishwood, and has kept the estate unchanged for many years. With her to celebrate her birthday are her three younger sisters and her two brothers-in-law, who are awaiting the return after eight years of Amy's eldest son Harry. He has been travelling abroad, where his wife drowned a year previously, a death unmourned by the unforgiving Amy. Harry arrives, pursued by visions of the avenging Eumenides. He is racked with guilt over the death of his wife, although, when questioned, his manservant assures the family it was an accident. Alone with a relative Mary, Harry reminisces about their youth at Wishwood together, and is horrified to see the Eumenides in the window embrasure. The family doctor Warburton reveals to Harry that his mother is dying, but Harry seems more concerned to find out about his dead father. News comes that both Harry's brothers have been delayed by car crashes. Amy's youngest sister Agatha reveals to Harry that she was in love with his father and prevented him from murdering his mother, so that Harry could be born. Harry, feeling he must expiate his father's guilt, decides he must leave again, as he has his 'course to pursue'. Amy dies, and the play is brought to a choral close.

Loosely based on the Orestes legend, Eliot here tried to combine drawing-room drama with mythic guilt and retribution. As he himself admitted, the Eumenides were never acceptable in this setting, appearing, in his own words, 'like a rugger-scrum'. The play's strength lies in the strange atmosphere of the old house of Wishwood, and its dangerous invitation to remain in stasis, both emotionally and in social terms, an invitation which Harry does well to resist.

Fanshen

A: David Hare **Pf**: 1975, Sheffield **Pb**: 1976 **G**: Pol. drama in 2 acts **S**: Village of Long Bow, China, 1945–9 **C**: 7m, 2f, performing numerous roles

In a Chinese village after the defeat of the Kuomintang, the peasants undertake the arduous process of *fanshen*, a total restructuring of their society. The first task is to hold a public meeting, the first for 20 years, and overcome their timidity in order to denounce former collaborators with the Japanese, resulting in their execution. A visiting Communist Party Secretary Liu establishes a Peasants' Association, which has the difficult task of overseeing the redistribution of the landlords' property and of assessing the needs of the community. Decisions are reversed, open criticism is invited, a bandit is re-educated, Communist ideology is propagated: 'Without the party the village is a bowl of loose sand.' The official policy of Agrarian Land Reform is now replaced with a new policy promoting collective farming. While *fanshen* promises a better future for the formerly oppressed peasants, there is still much to be done to ensure that the revolution is successful.

Fanshen was remarkable in two respects: it was the first significant play to be created by a writer working on a script with actors, here the Joint Stock Company improvising on a historical work by William Hinton; and it was one of the few political plays to depict a positive model of socialist revolution rather than document the injustices of capitalism. In the process, Hare does not idealize the Communist revolution in China: it is acknowledged to be inconsistent and sometimes inhumane, even if ultimately it offers the fairest system. The audience is confronted with a choice. As Hare wrote, the audience is not 'there to find out what this man on the stage thinks . . . They're there to find out what *they* think.'

Fantocci elettrici. See ELECTRIC DOLLS.

Farce. See PUPPET SHOW, THE.

Farewell Supper. See ANATOL.

Farmyard. See STALLERHOF.

Fashion

AT: *Life in New York* **A**: Anna Cora Mowatt **Pf**: 1845, New York **Pb**: 1850 **G**: Com. in 5 acts; prose **S**: The Tiffany residence and Counting House, New York, 1840s **C**: 8m, 5f

The parvenu Mrs Tiffany is determined to achieve social status. She employs many servants and attempts, without much success, to learn French. Naturally, none of the eligible young men paying court to her daughter Seraphina is good enough for Mrs Tiffany, until Count Jolimaitre appears on the scene. Though unappealing to Seraphina, Jolimaitre has the advantage of being titled. However, Adam Trueman, a solid American and an old friend of Mr Tiffany, questions Mrs Tiffany's values. Even more seriously, Snobson the clerk, who has uncovered some shady dealings by Tiffany, attempts to blackmail him into giving him his daughter. Trueman's long-lost granddaughter helps expose Jolimaitre as an old French chef Gustave Treadmill, and Snobson is accused of forgery. Trueman then persuades Tiffany to take his wife and daughter to the country, so that they can learn 'economy, true independence, and home virtues, instead of foreign follies'.

Though somewhat derivative (there are strong similarities with Paulding's *The *Lion of the West*, and the figure of the snobbish parvenu is an echo of Molière's *The *Would-Be Gentleman*), this is accounted the best comedy of 19th-century American theatre. Once again, as with Tyler's Jonathan (*The *Contrast*) and Paulding's Wildfire, it is the honest country-born American who cuts through urban and 'foreign' manipulation. It is notable too that, although the play ends with several marriages, the young heroine must first learn some true values before she finds a partner.

Father, The (*Fadren*)

A: August Strindberg **Pf**: 1887, Copenhagen; 1888, Stockholm **Pb**: 1887 **Tr**: 1889 **G**: Trag. in

3 acts; Swedish prose **S:** Middle-class home in Sweden, 1880s **C:** 5m, 3f

The Captain recognizes the difficulty of disciplining a cavalryman suspected of seducing the kitchen maid, since it is impossible to prove paternity. The Captain insists on his right to send his daughter Bertha to live in the town, where she may become a teacher and free herself from this female-dominated home. His wife Laura is bitterly opposed to this plan, and resolves to defeat her husband. She tells a newly arrived Doctor that the Captain is losing his mind, and then hints to her husband that Bertha is not his own child. She admits that she has intercepted his mail to prevent his further scientific work and produces a letter in which he speaks of the fear of losing his sanity. Driven into a rage, he flings a lighted paraffin lamp at her – seemingly proving his unbalanced mind. In despair, the Captain mocks the Doctor and his brother-in-law the Pastor for having wives that deceive them. He then threatens to shoot both Bertha and himself. Soothed by his old Nurse, he is slipped into a straitjacket. Cursing women, he dies of an apoplectic fit. Laura reclaims Bertha as her own.

The Father was the first major play by Strindberg to be performed and soon earned him an international reputation. Though naturalist in style and in a realistic setting, the generalized nature of the principal characters (referred to in the text as Captain, Doctor, Pastor – significantly, only Laura and Bertha are named) and the intense emotional conflicts point forward to Strindberg's Symbolist writings. Based on Strindberg's disastrous first marriage, the play continues to fascinate for its dissection of sexual conflict.

Faust (Parts 1 and 2)

A: Johann Wolfgang von Goethe **W:** (1) 1773–1808; (2) 1800–31 **Pf:** (1) 1819, Berlin (private perf.); 1829, Braunschweig (public perf.); (2) 1854, Hamburg; (1 and 2) 1876, Weimar **Pb:** 1790 (as fragment); (1) 1808; (2) 1832 **Tr:** 1833 **G:** (1) Trag. in 25 scenes and 2 prologues; (2) Drama in 5 acts; German verse, mainly blank verse and 'Knittelvers' (doggerel of 3–4-stress rhymed lines) **S:** Heaven, Germany, and ancient Greece, 16th c. and mythical past **C:** (1) 18m, 4f, 4 choruses, many extras; (2) 55m, 25f, 12 choruses, many extras

Part 1. God is persuaded that, despite Faust's errant ways, Faust is worthy of salvation. So he strikes a bargain with Mephistopheles: if he can persuade Faust to abandon striving and seek rest, Mephistopheles may claim his soul. Faust is so weary of academic learning that he dabbles in magic. Rejected by the Earth-Spirit, he contemplates suicide but is called back to life by Easter bells. He takes a walk, during which he encounters a beautiful young virgin, Margarete (Gretchen), and then a black poodle, which he takes back to his study. The dog transforms into Mephistopheles, who signs a pact with Faust: if Faust should ever rest from striving, he will lose his soul. At first, Mephistopheles tries to delight Faust with japes and drunken gatherings. Faust's only desire, however, is to renew his acquaintance with the modest Gretchen. Mephistopheles organizes the rejuvenation of Faust and helps him seduce the young virgin. She becomes pregnant and disgraced, while Faust cavorts with witches at Walpurgis Night. Gretchen murders her child and is sentenced to death. Faust visits her in prison, but is dragged away by Mephistopheles. *Part 2.* Faust sleeps and awakes refreshed, his enthusiasm for life renewed. At the Emperor's court he solves the financial problems of the Empire by issuing paper money and then participates in a colourful court masque. Summoning Helen of Troy with some difficulty, he delights the men of the court, but she disappears when Faust tries to seize her. Mephistopheles returns to Faust's study and has a debate with a homunculus created by Faust's former pupil. Homunculus persuades Mephistopheles to take Faust to a classical Walpurgis Night. While Mephistopheles engages with classical monsters and Homunculus gains life through the four elements, Faust meets Helen again, seduces her, and they give birth to a beautiful son, Euphorion. Euphorion flies up so high that he falls dead at his parents' feet. Euphorion takes Helen with him back to the dead, leaving Faust alone with Mephistopheles. They help the ageing Emperor win a battle, and Faust is rewarded with a stretch of coastal land, which he plans to win from the sea. Though blinded by the allegorical figure of Care, Faust is so delighted by his new endeavour that he utters the fatal words that this moment should last for ever. He dies, and Mephistopheles is confident of having won his wager. However, female saints with Gretchen intervene to save him: 'The Eternal-Womanly draws us upwards.' Faust is taken up into heaven.

Goethe is the major literary figure in the German language, and *Faust* is his most significant work, with which he was engaged throughout his life. Over 2,500 commentaries have been written on this one play. It encompasses bourgeois tragedy, philosophical speculation, literary, economic, political, scientific, and alchemical debate, and explores the nature of goodness and evil. Characteristically, Goethe avoids a tragic outcome for Faust: despite his association with evil and his often callous behaviour, his ceaseless striving guarantees him salvation. Sadly, this viewpoint could all too easily be perverted to justify the excesses of the Nazi regime. By contrast, Brecht was sufficiently attracted to the material to write his own adaptation of the first version (the *Urfaust*) in 1952. Sometimes regarded as more a dramatic poem than a work for the theatre, *Faust* has, despite its discursive and rambling structure, often been successfully staged (Reinhardt, 1909 and 1911; Gustaf Gründgens in the 1930s and 1940s; Peter Stein in 2000). Even more than Marlowe's **Doctor Faustus*, Goethe's version spawned a huge number of versions, most notably Grabbe's *Don Juan and Faust* (1829), Berlioz's dramatic legend *The Damnation of Faust* (1846), Boucicault's *Faust and Margaret* (1854), Gounod's opera *Faust* (1859), and Thomas Mann's novel *Doctor Faustus* (1947).

Faustus. See DOCTOR FAUSTUS.

Fear and Misery of the Third Reich (The Chalk Cross; The Jewish Wife; The Spy; Release; The Sermon on the Mount; Job Creation; Consulting the People) (*Furcht und Elend des III. Reiches*)

AT: *The Private Life of the Master Race; 99%; Germany: A Tale of Horror* A: Bertolt Brecht (with Margarete Steffin) Pf: 1938, Paris Pb: 1945 Tr: 1944 G: 7 [of 27] linked one-act dramas; German prose and verse choruses S: Germany, 1933–8 C: (3) 3m, 2f; (8) 1m, 1f; (9) 1m, 2f, child (m); (15) 2m, 1f; (22) 3m, 1f; (23) 1m, 2f; (27) 2m, 1f.

(3) *The Chalk Cross* or *The Chalk Mark* (*Das Kreidekreuz*). In the kitchen of a gentleman's house, an SA Man flirts with the young maidservant. A worker, the cook's brother, drops by, and he begins to tease the SA Man. The SA Man shows how dissenters are arrested: provoking the worker into criticizing the Nazis, he jokingly plants a chalk cross on the worker's back. Alone together, the maidservant questions the SA man about money missing from their joint account, and he responds harshly. She now wonders whether she has a chalk cross on her back. (8) *The Jewish Wife* (*Die jüdische Frau*). Judith Keith, a Jewess married to a surgeon, is preparing to leave Germany in 1935, as the Nazi attacks on the Jews become more virulent. She phones her friends to wish them goodbye, then rehearses what she will say to her 'Aryan' husband. She goes over recent developments: the inhumanity of the Nazis, his being ostracized at the hospital, and the way he too has changed towards her. She hopes he will not lie to her and pretend that her absence will be only temporary. Her husband comes home and, finding her packing, agrees that it is best that she should leave: 'After all it's only for two or three weeks.' (9) *The Spy* or *The Informer* (*Der Spitzel*). After Sunday family lunch, the Man, a teacher, complains about the state of affairs under the Nazis. Suddenly he and his wife notice that their young son, who is in the Hitler Youth, has slipped out. Terrified that he has gone to denounce them, they begin to panic and prepare for arrest, the Man pinning on his Iron Cross and considering hanging a picture of Hitler more prominently. The door opens, and their son returns munching chocolate. The parents are still uncertain whether he merely

went to buy sweets. (15) *Release* or *Discharged* (*Der Entlassene*). A worker, who has just been released from a concentration camp, visits an old comrade and his wife in their kitchen in Berlin. There is considerable awkwardness between them all, especially when the Released Man's hand shows evidence of torture. The men find it impossible to be open with each other, which the Released Man accepts. (22) *The Sermon on the Mount* (*Die Bergpredigt*). A fisherman is dying in his Lübeck kitchen in 1937. Despairing over the misery of his life, he asks the Pastor whether the future will be better. He grows angry over the way Hitler is preparing for war, denying fishermen motors for their boats. He insists that the Pastor should tell his son, who is in the SA, that 'blessed are the peacemakers'. The frightened Pastor responds by quoting: 'Render unto Caesar the things which are Caesar's.' (23) *Job Creation* or *Providing Jobs* (*Arbeits-beschaffung*). A worker, who has just got a job in an aircraft factory, comes home to find his wife in mourning over the death of her brother, a pilot supposedly killed on a night exercise. Their gossipy neighbour suspects that he died in the Spanish Civil War and then attacks the husband for making bombers. The husband points out that everything that is manufactured is now intended for the war effort, and insists that his wife take off her mourning clothes. The wife angrily rebels, saying that she would rather be put in a concentration camp. He pleads with her: 'It doesn't help.' She answers: 'What does help then? Do something that does!' (27) *Consulting the People* or *Plebiscite* (*Volksbefragung*). On the day of Germany's *Anschluss* with Austria in 1938, three socialist workers listen to the cheering Viennese crowds on their radio. They discuss whether there is any point responding to Hitler's referendum over unification with Austria, especially as they have just lost the comrade Karl who composed their leaflets. The two men despair over their powerlessness against the might of the Nazis, but the woman reads out Karl's last defiant message to his son before his execution. Their resolve strengthened, the workers will issue a referendum leaflet containing just one word: 'NO!'

When Brecht, as one of the first playwrights to do so, addressed the barbarism of Nazi rule, he abandoned the distancing techniques he had been exploring in order to write a series of short entirely naturalistic scenes (even if the characters still appear as 'The Man', 'The Woman', etc.), of which the most important are described above. Significantly, Brecht did not attempt to dramatize the Nazis themselves (apart from one or two small-fry SA men and camp guards) and only obliquely depicted the oppression of Jews and dissidents. The focus is on the lives of ordinary Germans, remarkably well observed for someone living in exile in Denmark: the breakdown in trust between individuals, even within the same family, the sense of powerlessness before the overwhelming might of the Nazis, and the difficulty of maintaining integrity and moral courage in these conditions. Although Brecht welcomed attempts to stage the piece in America to support the campaign against Nazi Germany, it was not performed (unsuccessfully) until after the end of the European war in 1945 under the unfortunate title of *The Private Life of the Master Race*.

Feast of Pan. See BAD-TEMPERED MAN, THE.

Fefu and Her Friends

A: Maria Irene Fornés Pf: 1977, New York Pb: 1980 G: Drama in 3 acts S: Living room, lawn, study, bedroom, kitchen, country house in New England, 1935 C: 8f

Fefu has an eccentric marriage with Philip ('They drive each other crazy'). She shoots at him frequently, although she always hopes that the gun is loaded only with blanks. Her friends, Cindy and Christina, are mildly alarmed by her behaviour. Fefu wishes she were a man, for 'Women are restless with each other'. Julia arrives. She has been confined to a wheelchair since she collapsed a year ago beside a deer that was shot, although she herself was not injured. It seems that she had formerly been tortured, and the gunshot by recalling her trauma induced her paralysis. Emma, Paula, Sue, and Cecilia arrive to prepare for some kind of performance. Act 2 consists of four scenes, each watched by a quarter of the audience, who then move on to the next scene, repeated by the performers. *On the lawn*: Fefu and Emma enjoy each other's company in the garden; *In the study*: Cindy tells Christina her dream; *In the bedroom*: Julia, alone, recalls being interrogated – Sue brings her some soup; *In the kitchen*: Sue prepares Julia's soup, while Paula speaks of the transitory nature of love affairs. They are joined by Cecilia, and Fefu invites everyone for croquet. In Act 3, the women rehearse their fund-raising presentation, Emma making a powerful appeal for the Environment. Julia gets out of her wheelchair to fetch sugar, and Fefu challenges her to 'fight' her illness. Fefu shoots a rabbit, and Julia drops to the ground bleeding.

Containing some of the anarchic quality of **Promenade*, as in the Act 3 water fight, Fornés's most frequently performed play *Fefu and Her Friends* represented a new departure for her by creating realistic, often inconsequential dialogue in a domestic setting. Julia's experiences adumbrate the later political concerns of Fornés, seen for example in *The *Conduct of Life*. The simultaneous playing of four scenes in different locations looks forward to Ayckbourn's similar technique in **House and Garden*.

Female Parts (Waking Up; A Woman Alone; The Same Old Story) (*Venticinque monologhi per una donna*)

AT: *Tutto casa, letto e chiesa (All Home, Bed, and Church)* A: Dario Fo and Franca Rame Pf: 1977, Milan Pb: 1978 Tr: 1981 G: 3 [of 25] monodramas in 1 act; Italian prose S: (1 and 2) Apartments in an Italian tenement building, 1970s; (3) Apartment, doctor's surgery, hospital, 1970s C: 1f in each

(1) *Waking Up* or *Arise and Shine* (*Il risveglio*). It is 6.30 a.m., and the woman has overslept. While her husband Luigi sleeps on, she leaps out of bed, changes the baby's nappy ready for the nursery, panics about the loss of her door-key, and has to change the nappy again. She complains that, while she has a full-time job in the factory, she also has to do all the housework and child care. Luigi, who was spoilt by his mother, is penitent and has said that he will change. As she is about to rush out, she suddenly realizes it is Sunday. Joyously, she goes back to bed. (2) *A Woman Alone* (*Una donna sola*). Maria, in her thirties, dressed in a flimsy negligée, is ironing and chatting to a neighbour opposite. Her jealous husband locks her in their apartment when he goes to work and phones to check on her, while she does the housework and looks after her baby and her invalid brother-in-law. She threatens to shoot a peeping Tom opposite. She tells of a young student with whom she had an affair, which is why her husband now keeps her locked up. Her lover comes and gets his hand stuck in the door after unpicking the lock, the brother-in-law is intent on molesting her, the baby cries, and she gets a phone call from a father claiming her husband has made his daughter pregnant. Driven to distraction, she almost shoots herself. Instead, she pushes the baby outside, shoots at the peeping Tom, and aims the gun at the door, ready for her husband's return. (3) *The Same Old Story* (*Abbiamo tutte la stessa storia*). A woman is being made love to inexpertly by a left-wing activist. Pregnant, she goes to the doctor, but refuses an abortion when she learns how much it will cost. Passing rapidly through the stages of pregnancy, she complains that men never have to give birth. She is disappointed when she gives birth to a baby girl, but gets into the routine of caring for her. She tells her daughter a lengthy story of a girl with a doll, who grows up to marry an electronic engineer and settles to a tedious life. Eventually the doll gets stuck up the engineer's rear, causing him to explode. At last she is free, and when she begins to tell other women the bizarre tale, they reply: 'It's the same old story for us all!'

Franca Rame developed these scenes with her husband Dario Fo, who then scripted them. Depending on the lively comic tradition of the *commedia dell'arte*, the pieces do not contain any great subtlety, but are amusing populist pieces of theatre, requiring minimal scenery. Although the stance is uncompromisingly feminist, the plays do not offer crude propaganda: there is an understanding of

Luigi's situation in *Waking Up* and, tellingly, the woman in *The Same Old Story* is initially sorry that her child is not male.

Fen

A: Caryl Churchill Pf: 1983, Colchester Pb: 1983 G: Drama in 21 scenes S: A village in the Fens, 1980s C: 6m, 16f

A Japanese businessman welcomes the audience to the fen, the 'most expensive earth in England', owned by a multinational corporation. Women pick potatoes, and Val leaves early: she is fed up with her marriage and plans to run away with Frank, who has left his wife. He invites her to stay with him, and she says goodbye to her daughters. Angela is cruel to her stepdaughter Becky. Val's daughters and Becky viciously tease old Nell. Val's mother May reproaches Val for leaving her daughters. Frank's boss is persuaded to sell his land to a City corporation, then sees the Ghost of a 19th-century woman working in his field. Val is torn between love for her children and for Frank, and eventually moves back home. At a Baptist meeting, Margaret describes how unhappiness drove her to drink; but religion is no comfort to Val, and she goes back to Frank. Frank takes an overdose, but recovers. Val begs him to kill her. He hits her with an axe and puts her body in the wardrobe. Val enters and speaks of the ghosts she has seen, Becky and Angela appear, and Nell walks past on stilts. May, who wanted to be a singer but never sang, breaks into song.

Fen, 'containing more direct quotes of things people said to us than any other I've written', was the product of doing workshops and collecting material with the Joint Stock Theatre Company in the Fens. This semi-documentary piece with its dream-like ending depicts the deprivation of a typical village, where the old rural community no longer exists but does not yet enjoy the conveniences of modern living.

Fences

A: August Wilson Pf: 1985, New Haven, Connecticut Pb: 1986 G: Drama in 2 acts S: Yard of the Maxsons' home, US city, 1957, 1965 C: 5m, 1f, 1 child (f)

Troy Maxson, a 53-year-old black garbage collector, arrives home from work with his friend Bono. Troy has been complaining that only white men are allowed to drive the trucks, while the blacks have to deal with the rubbish. Troy has a son Lyons (34) by his first marriage, a charming wastrel, and is now married to Rose (43), with whom he has one son Cory, who works in a local store and is a keen footballer. Troy's brother Gabriel suffered a head injury in the Second World War and now believes that he is the Archangel Gabriel. Cory has been selected for a football team and will be able to go to college, but Troy objects, saying that blacks can never prosper in sport. Troy recalls how at 14 he left his family to travel up north, only to find himself without a job or a home. He was shot trying to rob a man and was jailed for 15 years. Now he has been made a driver – even though he does not have a licence. Troy refuses to let Cory sign with the team and confesses to Rose that he has made his mistress Alberta pregnant. In the ensuing quarrel, Troy is about to hit Rose, when Cory intervenes. Six months later, news comes that Alberta has died in childbirth, and Troy resolves to build a fence round his yard to keep death out. Rose adopts Alberta's baby but freezes Troy out. Troy fights with Cory and sends him away. Seven years later, Lyons, paroled from prison; Cory, now a corporal in the Marines; and Gabriel vainly trying to blow his trumpet, arrive to attend Troy's funeral.

Troy is a semi-tragic figure with echoes of King Lear. Living beyond his time and maintaining outmoded patriarchal values, he is sensitive neither to the real needs of his family nor to the wider changes taking place in society. As Rose reminds him: 'The world's changing around you and you can't even see it.' Thus in this second play by poet turned playwright, Wilson creates not only a family drama but documents the growing power of African-Americans.

Ferrex and Porrex, The Tragedy of. See GORBODUC.

Field, The

A: John B. Keane Pf: 1965, Dublin Pb: 1966 G: Trag. in 3 acts S: Bar and lane, south-west Ireland, 1960s C: 10m, 3f

Maggie Butler comes to Mick Flanagan's bar in the small village of Carraigthomond. asking him to auction her field for her. The field is let for grazing to Thady ('Bull') McCabe, a local farmer, who will be keen to buy the field since it borders his land. Bull hopes to get the land cheap, since he paid rent on it for five years and tended the field. He will not allow any locals to bid against him and intends to frighten off any outsiders; so he bribes Mick to accept his bid. The next day, a stranger arrives in the bar: William Dee from Galway, newly returned from England, is looking for some land to use as a site from which to sell concrete blocks. The auction is held, and William outbids Bull, but the reserve price is not met. Mick undertakes to sell the field by private treaty. Bull gathers his clan together that night and they decide to frighten away the stranger. Bull and Tadhg lie in wait for William and give him a beating which kills him. Five weeks later, the community will not reveal the truth behind William's death, despite a moving sermon from the Bishop in which he denounces 'the unappeasable hunger for land' and threatens to place the whole village under interdict. Still the authorities fail to get anyone to testify against Bull, and when Bull is challenged direct, he points out how the law favours the rich and educated, while there's no law for the poor: 'if there's no grass, there's the end of me and mine'.

Despite the monstrosity of Bull's crime, Keane, himself a publican in County Kerry, has sympathy with a community that resists the intrusion of outsiders and the concreting over of their land. *The Field* was made into a successful film in 1991, with Richard Harris as Bull.

Figaro's Marriage. See MARRIAGE OF FIGARO, THE.

Fin de partie. See ENDGAME.

Fire Raisers, The (*Biedermann und die Brandstifter*)

AT: *Biedermann and the Firebugs* A: Max Frisch **Pf**: 1958, Zurich **Pb**: 1958 **Tr**: 1962 G: Drama in 6 scenes, prelude, and epilogue; German prose **S**: Middle-class home in Central Europe, late 1940s, and hell C: 5m, 3f, chorus (m)

Gottlieb Biedermann (the name suggests a solid middle-class citizen), a hair-tonic manufacturer, is visited one evening by a homeless wrestler, Joseph Schmitz. Despite his fears about arsonists in the area, Biedermann is inveigled into offering Schmitz shelter for the night. The Chorus of firemen report that all is quiet. The following day, Biedermann is alarmed to discover that his wife has taken in Schmitz's friend Willi Eisenring, who lost his job as waiter when his establishment burnt down. When Biedermann discovers his two unwanted guests rolling in barrels of petrol, he threatens to throw them out. He is interrupted by a policeman, informing him that an employee that he unfairly sacked has committed suicide. Telling the policeman that the barrels contain only hair-tonic, Biedermann finds himself implicated in Schmitz and Eisenring's plan. In order to appease the two, Biedermann invites them to dinner. Turning to the audience, he voices his suspicions but asks what they would have done – and when. At the end of the dinner, as a sign of trust, the arsonists ask Biedermann for matches. The whole district bursts into flames, and the chorus of firemen bewail the calamity. In the Epilogue, hell is presided over by Satan (Eisenring). Biedermann tries to defend his actions, and when the Chorus sing of the fine new city that has been built, he assumes that he and his wife are saved.

Although often assumed to be an allegory about the rise of Nazism, the immediate inspiration for *The Fire Raisers* was the Communist takeover of Czechoslovakia in 1948. The exploration of the way in which the complacent middle classes can be manipulated is relevant to many situations. Although essentially realistic, the parody Chorus and direct address to the audience lend the piece added theatricality.

Flea in Her Ear, A (*La Puce à l'oreille*)

AT: *Caught in the Act!* A: Georges Feydeau **Pf**: 1907, Paris **Pb**: 1909 **Tr**: 1966 G: Farce in 3 acts; French prose **S**: The Chandebises' drawing room, Paris, and a hotel in the suburbs, 1900s C: 10m, 5f, extras

Victor Emmanuel Chandebise manages the Paris office of an international insurance company. His wife Raymonde has a 'flea in her ear' because she is convinced that he is unfaithful. She engages her friend Lucienne to expose him by writing him a love letter inviting him to an assignation at a hotel. Chandebise, who is suffering from impotence, can only imagine that the letter is intended for his better-looking friend Tournel, and sends him off to the hotel. When Lucienne's violently jealous Latin American husband recognizes her handwriting, Chandebise rushes off to stop Tournel from going. Raymonde duly appears at the hotel to be welcomed by the astonished Tournel, who is in love with her. Eventually all the characters arrive at the hotel, which becomes the scene of complete mayhem: because they look identical, the hotel porter is mistaken for Chandebise, a revolving bed makes people instantaneously appear and disappear, Chandebise's nephew Camille loses the plate that corrects his cleft palate and becomes unintelligible, and a lecherous Englishman tries to seduce any woman who comes near him. The following day at home, Raymonde and Lucienne wait terrified for their husbands' return, and are further confused when the hotel porter arrives, whom they still imagine to be Chandebise. Eventually all is explained, and Chandebise promises to squash the flea in his beloved wife's ear that very night.

This is one of the best known of Feydeau's more than 50 'boulevard farces', especially to English-speaking audiences through John Mortimer's sparkling translation (1966). Feydeau's manipulation of the plot is fast-paced and hilarious, the mad confusions of the hotel scenes ranking as some of the funniest in world theatre. Beneath the farce lies a tender love story of a wife who mistakes her husband's impotence for infidelity and unknowingly helps him towards recovery.

Flies, The (*Les Mouches*)

A: Jean-Paul Sartre Pf: 1943, Paris Pb: 1943 Tr: 1946 G: Drama in 3 acts; French prose S: Argos, mythical past C: 6m, 6f, chorus (f), extras

Orestes in disguise returns with his Tutor to his birthplace of Argos. The town is swarming with flies, drawn there after the murder of Orestes' father Agamemnon 15 years earlier. The whole town offers penance to a blood-smeared statue of Zeus, seeking absolution from their communal crime in allowing their victorious king to be brutally killed by his wife Clytemnestra and her lover Aegisthus. Encouraged by Zeus, who is disguised as a traveller, Orestes is on the point of leaving, when he witnesses the degradation suffered by his sister Electra and decides to remain for the annual 'Dead Men's Day'. This ceremony of self-flagellation is interrupted by Electra, who, deriding the superstitious rites, dances joyfully in a white dress. When Electra almost wins over the crowd, Zeus has to intervene to force the worshippers into abjection once more. Resolving to act as a free individual, Orestes reveals himself to his sister and agrees to exact vengeance on his father's murderers. Despite Zeus' warning, Aegisthus hardly resists Orestes' attack. Orestes then slaughters his mother in a neighbouring room. Surrounded by the avenging Furies, Orestes and Electra seek shelter at Apollo's shrine. Rejecting Zeus' demands for penance, Orestes declares his freedom to act as he believes right. Electra however succumbs to the admonitions of Zeus. Orestes urges the people to take control of their lives as he has done, refuses the throne, and followed by the Furies and the flies, departs into the light.

The most important, albeit somewhat overwritten, modern treatment of *The *Oresteia*, *The Flies* is on one level a political piece, justifying Sartre's involvement in the French Resistance, fighting against the oppression of the German occupation. It is also a statement of Sartre's existentialist belief that the individual can find meaning only within his or her own self: 'once freedom lights its beacon in a man's heart, the gods are powerless against him'.

Floating World, The

A: John Romeril **Pf**: 1974, Melbourne **Pb**: 1975 **G**: Drama in 20 scenes **S**: A cruise ship to Japan and Yokohama, 1975 **C**: 6m, 1f

Les and Irene Harding, a middle-aged working-class Australian couple, are on a cut-price cruise from Australia to Japan. While Irene chatters, flirts, and generally enjoys herself on board, her husband sinks into a sullen mood and begins to drink heavily. His depression is occasioned by memories of the time he spent in a Japanese prisoner-of-war camp in Burma in the Second World War. Soon his depression verges on insanity: he thinks a Malaysian waiter is a Japanese officer, believes the man he shares a cabin with is a dying comrade who reproaches him for agreeing to visit Japan, the land of the enemy, and imagines that a sympathetic retired Royal Navy officer is a British officer in the camp lording it over the 'colonials'. Things get so bad that on arrival in Yokohama, Harding attacks some Japanese and has to be restrained in a straitjacket. As he sinks further into madness, he describes with great clarity how he managed to recover from beriberi and get 'well again'.

In this play Romeril helps to explain the prevailing xenophobia of Australians, especially of the working-class male. As the critic Christian Moe writes: 'Romeril effectively presents the paradox of the crude, brazen Australian, which is illusion, as opposed to the vulnerable insecure man behind the mask, which is reality.' The levels of illusion and reality are theatrically presented by moving from scenes of comic realism to the expressionistic fantasies of Harding's disturbed mind.

F. M.

AT: *Gardens of Eden* **A**: Romulus Linney **Pf**: 1982, Philadelphia **Pb**: 1984 **G**: Drama in 1 act **S**: Classroom of small southern college near Birmingham, Alabama, 1981 **C**: 1m, 3f

Celebrated novelist Constance Lindell, an attractive woman in her thirties, is teaching a creative fiction course, for which, owing to a dreadful tutor the previous year, only three students have enrolled: May Ford (forties), mother of three, gushingly admiring of Constance's writing; Suzanne Lachette, a pretty young divorcee; and Buford Bullough, a wild-looking young man who presents as a hick. Constance invites the students to read aloud from their work. May, who likes writing about the beauty of nature, begs Suzanne to go first. Suzanne reads from her novel *Scaulded Dogs*, which is a poorly written feminist diatribe against her husband. Buford then reads from his novel, enigmatically entitled *F. M.* Despite his inarticulacy when speaking, his writing is brilliant: 'hit's different when ah write. I reckon that's why ah do it.' Constance is enthralled by his story of a young man's incestuous relationship with his mother. May and Suzanne are horrified by this 'downright repulsive' pornography, and, when Constance divines that *F. M.* stands for 'Fucking Mother', they storm out, intent on reporting Constance to the college authorities. Constance asks Buford to read on and takes his hand.

The critic Martin Gottfried described Linney as 'one of the best kept secrets of the American theatre, a playwright of true literacy'. Like Buford, Linney came from a simple Appalachian background and no doubt shocked many people with the candour of his writing. This play is a tribute to the artist who is prepared to sacrifice the approval of the conventional May and the radical Suzanne in order to portray the truth.

folkefiende, En. See ENEMY OF THE PEOPLE, AN.

Folle de Chaillot, La. See MADWOMAN OF CHAILLOT, THE.

Folle Journée, La. See MARRIAGE OF FIGARO, THE.

Follies of a Day, The. See MARRIAGE OF FIGARO, THE.

Follies of Calandro, The (*La Calandra*)

AT: *The Comedy of Calandro* **A**: Cardinal Bernardo Dovizi da Bibbiena **Pf**: 1513, Urbino **Pb**: 1523 **Tr**: 1964 **G**: *Commedia erudita* in 5 acts; Italian (Tuscan and Roman dialect) prose **S**: A square in Rome, early 16th c. **C**: 6m, 5f, extras

A young man, Lidio, has come to Rome in search of his long-lost identical twin sister, Santilla. Here he has fallen in love with Fulvia, the wife of the elderly Calandro. So that Lidio can meet Fulvia, he puts on women's clothes and calls himself Santilla. Calandro promptly falls in love with his wife's new young friend. His servant, Fessenio, persuades Calandro to be concealed in a trunk in order to gain access to Santilla. His adventure is ended by Fulvia, who having gone to find Lidio, discovers Calandro at Santilla's house. Meanwhile Santilla, who has been living disguised as a boy called Lidio, is to marry the daughter of her protector. Because it is at first believed that a magician has turned Lidio into a woman, brother and sister have difficulty recognizing each other. However, a reconciliation is at last effected, Santilla saves her brother from being caught with Fulvia, and Lidio agrees to take Santilla's place in the arranged marriage, while Santilla is to marry Fulvia's son.

Based on Plautus' **Casina*, the humiliation of a ridiculous old lecher is given full comic scope in Bibbiena's play, a more sophisticated version of the coming *commedia dell'arte* scenarios, in which Pantalone's similar behaviour appears equally grotesque. The theme of the identical twins, derived from Plautus' *The *Brothers Menaechmus*, is given a new twist here by the use of cross-dressing, an idea exploited in *The *Deceived* and by Shakespeare in **Twelfth Night*. To his classical models, Bibbiena added his own acute observation of contemporary Italian life. Indeed, when the play was staged before the stage-struck Pope Leo X in 1514, the setting was provided by elaborate perspective scenery depicting contemporary Rome, one of the first examples of the use of perspective scenery in the history of theatre.

Fool, The

A: Edward Bond **Pf:** 1975, London **Pb:** 1976 **G:** Drama in 8 scenes **S:** East Anglia and London, 1815–*c.*1845 **C:** 37m, 7f

The poet John Clare is one of the mummers performing their play at Christmas for Lord Milton and his guests. The Parson urges the mummers to 'work for the common good' and accept a cut in wages. Clare fondles his fiancée Patty but then goes into the house with the kitchen-maid Mary. Milton starts to drain the fens and clear the woodland. Mary is sacked, and Clare proposes to her. The local men begin to loot from the rich. The Parson is stripped naked in the woods, but freed by the arrival of Milton's men, who shoot one of the poor. Clare escapes, but visits his friends, who are sentenced to death. All but Darkie, the ringleader, are reprieved and will be transported. Clare, now married to Patty, gains fame as a poet and is brought to London, where he is lionized and meets Charles and Mary Lamb. Clare is warned not to write subversive or erotic poetry. Five years later, Patty is urging Clare to get a proper job as a labourer, since his publisher tells Clare that there is no market for his poetry. Fearing for his sanity, Milton and the Parson remove Clare forcibly to an asylum. Four years later Clare escapes and finds Mary, who barely remembers him. He imagines he sees the dead Darkie. Some while later Clare is back in the asylum with Mary Lamb and 'Napoleon'. Milton visits him with Patty, but Clare has been rendered inarticulate.

Subtitled 'Scenes of Bread and Love', *The Fool* expresses Bond's affinity with Clare, a fellow poet from a working-class background. Set against contemporary political upheavals, Clare is shown being manipulated and finally silenced by the Establishment.

Fool beneath the Cross Laying a Wager, The.

See MISTERO BUFFO.

Fool for Love

A: Sam Shepard **Pf:** 1983, San Francisco **Pb:** 1983 **G:** Drama in 1 act **S:** Motel room on edge of Mojave Desert, 1980s **C:** 3m, 1f

The Old Man sits in his rocking chair, reminiscing about and commenting on the passionate love–hate 15-year-old relationship between Eddie and May. It is revealed with much self-justification by the Old Man that they are both his children, though by different women, and that he unsuccessfully tried for years to keep them apart. Eddie returns with his horses from touring the Western USA with his rodeo show to meet May in a motel room. She is consumed with jealousy, because of his supposed affair with a Countess. The Countess, herself jealous, fires shots at May's cabin, while

May taunts Eddie with the announcement that she has a date with Martin. Martin arrives to find Eddie and May drunk on tequila. Eddie tries to cool Martin's interest in May by revealing that she is his incestuous lover. May now tells how her mother committed suicide because her father abandoned them, when after years of searching, they at last tracked him down. The Countess returns, sets fire to Eddie's pickup truck and horse trailer and lets his horses loose. When Eddie rushes out to assess the damage, May imagines he has left with the Countess, packs a bag, and leaves in pursuit of him. The Old Man rocks on alone in his chair.

Just as Austin and Lee in **True West* hate and love each other at the same time, so here half-sister and half-brother almost destroy each other, yet May still goes after Eddie at the end. According to the stage directions, the Old Man 'exists only in the minds of May and Eddie', and once again Shepard explores the way in which children become like their parents (cf. Wesley and Weston in **Curse of the Starving Class* and Vince and Dodge in **Buried Child*).

Footfalls

A: Samuel Beckett **Pf:** 1976, London **Pb:** 1976 **G:** Drama in 1 act **S:** Narrow strip downstage, indeterminate period **C:** 2f

May is pacing, as ever, with great regularity to and fro along her strip. She calls her mother, whose voice only is heard from the dark upstage. May asks solicitously whether her mother needs anything, injection, bedpan, etc., but to everything the mother says it is too soon. May tells her mother she is 90, while May is dismayed to be reminded that she is still only 40. The mother tells how May from her childhood never left the house but just paced to and fro listening to her footfalls. May reveals that she sometimes went to the church to pace up and down. She then tells the story of Mrs Winter, who believed she saw something strange during evensong, but her daughter Amy saw nothing, since, to Mrs Winter's disbelief, Amy claims she was not there. May wonders if she will ever cease 'revolving it all.'

In this brief and powerfully atmospheric piece, Beckett rehearses a favourite topic, the curse of being born and the desire to leave life as soon as is possible. Meanwhile, there is no escape from the drudgery of ceaseless pacing.

Fopling Flutter, Sir. See MAN OF MODE, THE.

Force of Habit, The (*Die Macht der Gewohnheit*)

A: Thomas Bernhard **Pf:** 1974, Salzburg **Pb:** 1974 **Tr:** 1976 **G:** Drama in 3 scenes; German free verse **S:** Garibaldi's caravan, 1970s **C:** 4m, 1f

In order to escape from the drab repetition of his life as circus ringmaster and from the soulless 'asphalt-covered sites' of venues like Augsburg, Garibaldi has for the last 22 years been rehearsing Schubert's *Trout Quintet*. He is accompanied reluctantly by the Juggler, who dreams of working in France, by his Granddaughter, a tightrope artist who does not feel well, by a depressed Clown, and by a melancholy Lion-Tamer, Garibaldi's nephew, whose arm is in a bandage. During a circus performance the five come and go in Garibaldi's caravan: the Lion-Tamer is angry at the way Garibaldi exercises his power over them all and recalls how Garibaldi's daughter died, exhausted, when she fell from the tightrope. Eventually, they are ready to rehearse and await the arrival of the Lion-Tamer, while the Clown's hat keeps falling off. The Lion-Tamer arrives drunk, thumps the piano a bit, and has to be carried out. Resignedly, Garibaldi abandons the rehearsal, repeats yet again: 'Augsburg tomorrow', and turns on the radio, which plays the start of the *Trout Quintet*.

The Austrian Thomas Bernhard is one of the most often performed contemporary German-language playwrights. His poetic language, repetitions, and focus on situation rather than on plot development remind one of Beckett, especially **Waiting for Godot*. Here, however, 'Augsburg tomorrow' is not some promise of future redemption, but rather yet another stage in Garibaldi's dreary existence (for which the Mayor of Augsburg threatened to sue Bernhard). The only escape and dignity lie in

Garibaldi's hope: 'If we succeeded just once | ... in completing | the *Trout Quintet* | one single time perfect music.'

for colored girls who have considered suicide | when the rainbow is enuf

A: Ntozake Shange **Pf**: 1974, Berkeley, California **Pb**: 1976; rev. 1977 **G**: Drama in 1 act; free verse **S**: Indeterminate US location, 1970s **C**: 7f

The 'lady in brown' invites the six others: 'somebody | anybody | sing a black girl's song'. In poetry and dance they tell their stories: the 'lady in yellow' describes how she lost her virginity after a graduation dance; the 'lady in red' talks of unrequited love; the 'lady in orange' loves to dance; the 'lady in blue' has been raped; the 'lady in purple' represents Sechita, a sexy 'goddess of love'; the 'lady in brown' is inspired by the Haitian freed slave and revolutionary leader Toussaint Louverture. The 'lady in red' consoles herself with casual sex, while the 'lady in blue' is now unable to enjoy normal relationships. All of the women declare that their love is too special 'to have thrown back on my face'. The 'lady in green' (Ntozake) seeks her own identity. The 'lady in red' (Crystal) relates how a Vietnam veteran, Beau Willie Brown, made her pregnant twice and beat her terribly. He begs to marry her, and when she refuses, he throws their two children to their deaths from the fifth floor. She considers suicide, but: 'i found god in myself | & i loved her', words that are repeated by all the women.

The experiences of 'colored girls' (African-American and distinguished by their coloured costumes) are narrated as a 'choreopoem', poetic monologues punctuated by music and dance. In addition to the powerful verse, the piece is impressive for its complete lack of bitterness for the terrible suffering endured by these women. Shange, the most influential black woman playwright, does not portray women as defeated victims but as survivors who 'are movin to the ends of their own rainbows'.

Foreskin's Lament

A: Greg McGee **Pf**: 1980, Auckland **Pb**: 1981 **G**: Tragicom. in 2 acts; prose and some verse **S**: Rugby changing room and verandah outside Larry's house, *c.*1980 **C**: 7m, 2f

Urged on by the coach Tupper, a rugby team are practising for a big match on Saturday. Ken the captain, who has recently had concussion, falls to the ground and is carried off. Their manager Larry, a local businessman, massages Ken gently, and is made fun of by the players when they come from training. Foreskin (Seymour), who is a university student, reassures Larry. Larry invites everyone back after the big game to see the New Zealand–South Africa rugby match, but Foreskin refuses to watch an apartheid-selected team in action. Tupper encourages his men to play dirty on Saturday, but Foreskin objects strongly, then asks Tupper not to make Ken play. At Larry's party after the game, Ken is lying in a coma in hospital, and Foreskin remains detached from the general merriment. Clean (Lindsay), a thuggish and now very drunk policeman, pesters Moira, but backs off when he discovers that she is a lawyer. Foreskin warns Moira that New Zealand is run by people like Clean, whatever high-flown ideas the intellectuals may have. Tupper tries to persuade Moira to settle down with Foreskin, so that he will become a steadier, more dependable member of the team. Foreskin reveals that he saw Clean kick Ken in the head. When Tupper hears this, he fights with Clean. Larry intervenes and is knocked unconscious. Foreskin smashes the television screen and addresses the audience: Ken has died, and, breaking into verse, Foreskin laments the state of his nation.

Using rugby as a lively and powerful metaphor for the unfeeling nature of New Zealand society ('a junkyard for obsolete mentalities'), McGee wrote one of the most important plays of antipodean theatre. Its onstage nakedness, references to Larry's homosexuality, and provocative subject matter made it extremely controversial.

Forest, The (*Les*)

A: Aleksandr Ostrovsky **Pf**: 1871, St Petersburg **Pb**: 1871 **Tr**: 1926 **G**: Com. in 5 acts; Russian prose **S**: The Gurmyzhskaya estate, Russia, mid-19th c. **C**: 5m, 2f, extras

Raisa Gurmyzhskaya, a rich 50-year-old widow and owner of a large estate, is in love with the young, handsome but stupid Alexey Bulanov. To prevent gossip, she would like him to marry her ward, the pretty young Aksyusha. Aksyusha loves Pyotr, the son of the timber merchant Vosmibratov, who wants his son to marry a girl with a large dowry. Rather than leave her wealth to her one close relative, a nephew whom she hardly knows, Gurmyzhskaya is selling parts of her forest to the grasping Vosmibratov. Now the nephew Gennadius arrives unannounced at the estate. He is a travelling actor who plays tragic roles, and is accompanied by a colleague, Arkadius, who plays comic parts. Not wishing his aunt to know of his lowly calling, Gennadius 'the Tragedian' pretends to be the servant of 'the Comedian', leading to a number of comic misunderstandings. Moved by Aksyusha's plight, and even saving her from suicide, Gennadius suggests that she should run away with him to the theatre. She cannot bear to part from Pyotr, so Gennadius demands his inheritance from his aunt, gives it to Pyotr as her dowry, and the two can now marry. Gurmyzhskaya will marry Alexey, and the Tragedian and Comedian set off again.

This is the most popular of Ostrovsky's 47 plays, not least because of the opportunities offered by the roles of the Tragedian and the Comedian, who play out their characteristics to the full. Beneath the gentle humour there is however some social concern about the power which a silly old widow may wield, especially in the selling off of rural estates, a theme which Chekhov would explore in *The *Cherry Orchard*.

Forty Years On

A: Alan Bennett **Pf:** 1968, London **Pb:** 1969 **G:** Com. in 2 acts; prose and songs **S:** Assembly hall of English public school, 1968, and a historical review 1900–45 **C:** 5m, 2f, 20 schoolboys

The Headmaster gives a speech of farewell, concerned that he is handing over to Franklin, a liberal successor. Preparations are made to stage the school play, *Speak for England, Arthur*. This begins in the basement of Claridge's hotel, London, at the outbreak of the Second World War, where Hugh, a Conservative MP, his wife Moggie, and son Christopher are sheltering. The time shifts back to 1900, to the end of Victoria's reign, discussed in Wildean pastiche, then to Lawrence of Arabia travelling to Mesopotamia in 1909. In 1940, Christopher gets left behind during the Dunkerque evacuation. 1913: Lady Sybilline Quarrell agrees to an assignation with Bertrand Russell. 1914: young men are swept up into the First World War. In the interval, the Headmaster complains to Franklin about the content of the play, which continues with mourning the fallen in 1918. Time-switch to the London Blitz, then back to 1922 and the founding of the Bloomsbury Group. In the 1940s, Christopher is a German prisoner of war. Franklin now shocks the Headmaster by enacting a class on sex education. 1936: the Abdication of Edward VIII. Neville Chamberlain is put on trial in the court of history for appeasing Hitler. The school play ends with victory in 1945, but the Headmaster laments the post-war loss 'of honour, of patriotism, chivalry and duty', 'great words' that 'came to be cancelled out' because social justice was neglected.

By means of an episodic, funny, and frequently interrupted school play, Bennett's first work for the stage offers a 20th-century retrospect that combines nostalgic regret with a recognition of the errors made by British public figures. While offering a lively experience to a predominantly young cast, there is sometimes too much clever talk in place of stage action.

Four P's, The. See PLAY CALLED THE FOUR P.P., THE.

Fox, The. See VOLPONE.

Frage an das Schicksal, Die. See ANATOL.

Francesca da Rimini

A: Gabriele D'Annunzio **Pf:** Rome, 1901 **Pb:** 1902 **Tr:** 1902 **G:** Trag. in 5 acts; Italian blank verse **S:** Ravenna and Rimini, 13th c. **C:** 3m, 1f

In the hope of putting an end to the long feud between two warring families, Francesca of Ravenna is to marry Giovanni (Gianciotto) of Rimini, unaware that he is an ugly cripple. Gianciotto's handsome brother Paolo is sent to fetch Francesca, and she and her women assume that he is the intended bridegroom. When she later discovers her mistake, she blames Paolo for misleading her. The feuding has begun again, and Paolo's youngest brother Malatestino is brought in with his eye gouged out. When Paolo enters the battle, Francesca declares that whether he survives will be a test of the judgement of God. Paolo returns safely, and Francesca gives him her love, feeling little guilt about her adultery. When Francesca rejects the advances of Malatestino, he betrays her secret to Gianciotto. Gianciotto surprises Paolo and Francesca together and stabs them to death.

Based on the lovers in the fifth canto of Hell in Dante's *Divine Comedy*, this was the most successful of D'Annunzio's 16 romantic and lyrical plays. Its premiere was inauspicious: written as a vehicle for Eleanora Duse and directed by the inexperienced D'Annunzio, it ran for six hours and the battle scenes filled the theatre with smoke. In a shortened version, its spectacular staging guaranteed its popularity, but it belonged to the 19th rather than the 20th century. Indeed the same story, dramatized by George Henry Boker in 1855, was to become a staple of the American repertory. D'Annunzio's version was made into an opera by Riccardo Zandonai in 1914.

Frank Dell's The Temptation of St Antony

A: The Wooster Group **Pf**: 1988, New York **Pb**: 1996 **G**: Scenario in 7 scenes **S**: Hotel room in Washington, DC, 1980s, and the desert, 3rd c. AD **C**: 5m, 4f

In a hotel room with Dieter, J.J., and Sue, Frank Dell runs a tape, which discusses love, philosophy, sex, etc., and talks to Cubby on the phone. Phyllis and Onna dance, and the Queen of Sheba appears and withdraws. There is a meditation on death, taken from Geraldine Cummins's *The Road to Immortality* (1932), and St Antony experiences ecstasy at the richness of Nature. 'Onna and Phyllis practice some verbal routines', and persuade the German chambermaid Eva and the French bartender Jacques to join in. There is a further meditation on death and another phone call to Cubby. Onna, Phyllis, and Jacques perform an odd magic show, ending with St Antony driving away the demons and awaiting the dawn. Phyllis and Onna pack up to leave, but there's something wrong with Frank.

The Wooster Group, formed from elements of Richard Schechner's Performance Group, create multilayered, multi-media performances, improvising around literary and found texts, deconstructing them so much in the process that they ultimately lurk hidden like objects in an abstract painting (indeed, their juxtaposition of Arthur Miller's *The *Crucible* with drug-taking in their *LSD* (*...Just the High Points*) of 1983 led them into copyright dispute). Here Flaubert's *La Tentation de Saint Antoine* (1874), based on the 3rd-century Egyptian ascetic, provides an imaginative source, hardly perceptible in their provocative, almost impenetrable, and highly charged performance, directed, as ever, by Elizabeth LeCompte.

Fremdenführerin, Die. See TOUR GUIDE, THE.

Friar Bacon and Friar Bungay (*The Honorable Historie of Frier Bacon, and Frier Bongay*)

A: Robert Greene **Pf**: *c.*1590, London **Pb**: 1594
G: Com. in 5 acts; blank verse and prose
S: Edward's court and University of Oxford, 13th c. **C**: 28m, 4f, extras

Edward, Prince of Wales, has fallen in love with the gamekeeper's daughter, Margaret. He sends his friend Lacy to woo the girl on his behalf, while the Prince goes to Oxford to seek the help of Friar Bacon, who is reputed to have magical powers. Bacon invokes the Devil, who promises that a brass head that the Friar has made will utter prophecies. He then reveals to Edward in a magic glass that Lacy and Margaret have fallen in love and that Friar Bungay is to marry them. Edward rides off in rage to confront the lovers, at first threatens to force Lacy to marry another woman, but ends by giving his blessing to their marriage. At last the brass head speaks, but, thanks to his stupid servant, Bacon sleeps through it. When his magic leads to bloodshed, Bacon repudiates his dark arts. He finally predicts a golden future for England under Edward and his new bride, Elinor (Eleanor) of Castile.

Curiously titled, since Bungay has a very minor role, Greene's play unites in a charming comedy the love story of the nobly born characters with the humour of Friar Bacon and his servant. In addition there is the opposition between the political life of the court, represented by Edward, and the unsullied rural life, revealed through Margaret's character; and again between the worlds of innocence and university learning, which is misused by Bacon in his magic experiments. In this respect, Bacon is a close if comic companion to Marlowe's Faustus, although uncertainty about dates prevents us ascribing influences one way or the other. What is clear is that Greene manages to lend artistic unity to disparate themes in a way that would benefit Shakespeare.

Frogs (*Batrachoi; Ranae*)

A: Aristophanes Pf: 405 BC, Athens Tr: 1785 G: Greek com. in verse S: The outskirts of Athens and the underworld, early 5th c. BC C: 10m, 3f, extras, 2 choruses

Dionysus, the god of tragedy, is on his way to the underworld in search of Euripides, who has only recently died. He has disguised himself ineffectually as Heracles in an attempt to ward off danger. Undeterred by fearful warnings from the real Heracles, he reaches the lake bordering the underworld and is ferried across by Charon, while engaging in a verbal exchange with a chorus of frogs. In the underworld he first encounters a chorus of initiates. Then, arriving at the door of the palace of Pluto, the god of the underworld, Dionysus alternately forces his slave to wear the Heracles disguise and then assumes it himself, culminating in their being beaten in an attempt to discover which is the genuine immortal. When it is discovered that Dionysus has arrived in the underworld, Pluto asks him to judge a contest between the newly arrived Euripides and the great Aeschylus to establish which is the weightier tragedian. After a prolonged contest, Aeschylus is found to offer sounder political advice, and Pluto generously allows him to return with Dionysus to the world of the living.

Frogs was performed just months before the collapse of the Athenian state caused by their final defeat at the hands of Sparta, and represents Aristophanes' last-ditch attempt to remind his fellow Athenians of their noble spiritual heritage. It was so successful that it is the only ancient Greek play known to have been granted a repeat performance by public acclaim. Sadly, its theatrical success, as so often in the history of drama, seems to have had little effect on the politicians. *Frogs* is also notable because it contains the first discussion of theatrical quality, some three-quarters of a century before Aristotle's *Poetics*, offering invaluable insights into the staging and reception of Greek tragedy.

Fröken Julie. See MISS JULIE.

From Morning to Midnight (*Von morgens bis mitternachts*)

A: Georg Kaiser W: 1912 Pf: 1917, Munich Pb: 1916 G: Drama in 2 acts (7 scenes); German prose S: A small town and a large city, Germany, *c.*1912 C: 22m, 12f, extras

The Cashier is silently and mechanically working in a provincial bank, when a suspiciously elegant lady is refused the facility to cash a cheque. He steals a large amount of cash from the till and rushes to the lady's hotel. He declares that he has stolen the money for her and pleads with her to run away with him. A respectable woman, she rejects his ludicrous advances. Deciding that there is no turning back, he returns home to reassure himself that he must put his bourgeois existence behind him. This break in his routine kills his mother and drives his wife to despair. Arriving in the big city, the Cashier goes to the bicycle races, where he induces ecstasy in the crowd by offering ever greater amounts of prize money. The arrival of the monarch subdues the spectators, and, disappointed, the Cashier goes to a nightclub. Disgusted by most of the women, he finds a mysterious beauty, who refuses to dance. When he discovers that she has a wooden leg, he leaves for a Salvation Army Hall, where the Cashier joins those confessing their sins. Recognizing that money can bring no happiness, he flings his cash into the congregation, who fight wildly over the banknotes and run from the hall. Only a Salvation Army girl remains behind. The Cashier, finally disillusioned when he discovers that she has stayed only to collect the reward money on his head, shoots himself, crying 'Ecce homo!' as he dies against a cross.

One of the best-known German Expressionist plays, this piece shows the nameless protagonist passing through seven episodes or 'stations' to arrive at the recognition that money is meaningless. Typically for Kaiser, the focus is on the suffering individual, but here there is no hope of redemption.

From the Life of Insects. See INSECT COMEDY, THE.

Front Page, The

A: Ben Hecht and Charles MacArthur **Pf:** 1928, New York **Pb:** 1928 **G:** Drama in 3 acts **S:** Press room of Criminal Courts, Chicago, 1920s **C:** 19m, 5f

A group of cynical journalists await the hanging of Earl Williams, a 'Bolshevik' who has murdered a black policeman. For the unscrupulous Mayor and bungling Sheriff, the execution is crucial in securing the African-American and law-and-order vote in the impending election. Hildy Johnson, a crime reporter for 15 years, arrives in the press room to say goodbye, since he is marrying, moving to New York, and taking a job in advertising. When news comes that Williams has escaped, the reporters rush off, leaving Hildy alone. Williams appears through the window, and Hildy hides him in a large folding desk. On the verge of scooping the best story of his life, Hildy callously delays his wedding, and phones his boss, the hard-bitten editor Walter Burns. When the police arrive back, Hildy and Burns are arrested for harbouring a criminal, but are released when it becomes clear that the Mayor and Sheriff Hartman have been trying to conceal Williams's reprieve. Hildy and his long-suffering fiancée Peggy finally leave, and Burns gives Hildy his gold watch as a present. Burns then telegraphs the police in Indiana, insisting that they arrest Hildy for stealing his watch.

The world of modern journalism, with its 'dramatically' breaking news stories and sceptical view of society and politics, has provided dramatists with interesting material (e.g. Wesker's *The Journalists* (1975); Hare and Brenton's *Pravda* (1985)), and *The Front Page* stands as the first major play set in a press room. It allows the writers opportunities for not only a robust and lively comedy but also for a sharply satirical view of the insensitive and misogynistic world of newspapermen and of corrupt and bungling local government, anticipating the similarly farcical but thought-provoking Dario Fo's **Accidental Death of an Anarchist*. Of the three film versions, Howard Hawks's *His Girl Friday* (1940), with Hildy as a woman, was the most successful.

Front Room Boys, The

A: Alexander Buzo **Pf:** 1969, Sydney **Pb:** 1970 **G:** Com. in 12 scenes **S:** An office, 1960s **C:** 7m, 2f

Each scene takes place in a different month of the year, beginning with January. The front room clerks welcome newcomer Vittorio Gasconi and a new secretary Sundra Gerstad. The back room boys, of whom we see only the young executive Hendo, are planning cutbacks. In the stifling heat of February, the boys discuss 'upper-crust snobs', and Vittorio throws out of the window a picture of the Duke of Edinburgh, which lands on Hendo's head. When smoke pours out of the boardroom, the boys think there is a fire. Hendo appears, smoking a huge cigar, and is drenched by a bucket of water. While Jacko takes Sundra out to lunch, the boys throw paper and water at a street demonstration against the bosses. The demonstrators call them 'suckers'. Jacko, now in love with Sundra, begs her to get a divorce. An annual office revue features terrible jokes, Vittorio playing Hendo getting abuse and objects hurled at him, and an oriental sequence in which Sundra looks stunningly beautiful and another secretary does a striptease. A month later, Sundra is now going out with Gibbo. They celebrate the arrival of spring by dancing around scattering a bunch of flowers, then rehearse a ceremony of unveiling a plaque listing the firm's directors, which ends with each of them kissing Hendo's shoes. At the Christmas party, some promotions are announced, but Jacko is to be sacked. Furious, he tries to get into the back room to attack Hendo, but the front room staff, hailing Hendo as 'a good bloke', tie him up and abandon him.

Described by Buzo as 'a gag-style comedy', this play lurches from the tedious naturalism of office life to anarchic humour to absurdist moments and to agitprop satire. The front room boys are willing slaves: 'My old man . . . was a union man, the fool. But not me, boy. I got here by the sweat of my brow.' But the political point tends to get swamped by the madcap comedy.

Fruen fra havet. See LADY FROM THE SEA, THE.

Frühlings Erwachen. See SPRING'S AWAKENING.

Fuente Ovejuna (*Fuenteovejuna*)

AT: *All Citizens Are Soldiers; The Sheep Well*
A: Lope de Vega Pf: Early 17th c. Pb: 1619
Tr: 1936 G: Drama in 3 acts; Spanish verse
S: The town of Fuente Ovejuna and surrounding countryside, Spain, 1476 C: 16m, 4f, extras

King Ferdinand has granted authority over the town of Fuente Ovejuna to the nobleman Fernán Gómez de Guzmán. Guzmán is a brutal tyrant, who importunes Laurencia, a young virgin. When he finds her in the woods, he attempts to rape her and is fought off by Frondoso, the son of a rich farmer. Despite having formerly rejected him, Laurencia is now so impressed by Frondoso's bravery that she agrees to marry him. However, the ceremony is rudely interrupted by Guzmán, who immediately throws the lovers into captivity and has her father beaten. Outraged by this tyrannical behaviour and incited by Laurencia, who manages to free herself, the townspeople storm Guzmán's castle, where he is about to torture Frondoso to death. Guzmán is killed by the mob, and the populace now await judgement from King Ferdinand. It is agreed that everyone must share responsibility for this act of rebellion, and all attempts by the judge to establish who killed Guzmán are answered by: 'Fuente Ovejuna did it.' The King orders the people to be exonerated.

Though often appropriated, especially by directors in Soviet Russia, as a model of pre-Communist revolution, it must be acknowledged that the people of Fuente Ovejuna are spared only by the goodwill of the absolute monarch. Although the play is ground-breaking by placing at its centre the collective protagonist of the townspeople and by acknowledging that peasants may possess a greater sense of justice than the nobility, harmony is finally restored by reconciling the monarchy with the people not through any suggestion of continuing revolution against authority.

Fugue in a Nursery. See TORCH SONG TRILOGY.

Fulgens and Lucrece (*A godely interlude of Fulgens Cenatoure of Rome. Lucres his doughter. Gayus flaminius. and Publius Cornelius. of the disputacyon of noblenes*)

A: Henry Medwall Pf: *c.*1497, London?
Pb: *c.*1512 G: Interlude in 2 parts; verse
S: Ancient Rome C: 5m, 2f, extras

Fulgens, senator of Rome, invites his daughter Lucrece (or Lucres) to choose between two suitors, the reprobate Publius Cornelius and the noble and virtuous Gaius Flaminius. Cornelius is a patrician, while Flaminius comes from much humbler origins. Nevertheless, Lucrece declares that she will marry the more honourable of the two, and after the two suitors have pleaded their case before Fulgens, Lucrece reveals to the audience that she will opt for Flaminius. This serious theme is mirrored by a comic sub-plot, in which two members of the audience, A and B, join the cast to become the incompetent servants of the two suitors. They spend most of their time desperately wooing Lucrece's maid, only to find themselves both rejected when it is revealed that she is already engaged.

This piece is notable as being the first secular play in English. It was performed as an interlude in two parts, the first during a banquet, the second later in the evening at supper. The guests were not simply entertained by the comic sub-plot, which contains a number of contests, including a mock-joust between the two servants trussed up like chickens. They were also edified by the debate on the nature of nobility, based on a Latin tract, Montemagno's *Concerning True Nobility* (*c*.1428). Lucrece's decision to favour the man who has nobility of spirit rather than nobility of birth documents the growing importance of the 'new men' at the court of Henry VII who had achieved power through industry and innate 'nobility' rather than through the accident of birth. Despite its importance both in terms of its sociological significance and of the development of English drama, the play remained lost until it came to light in a London saleroom in 1919.

Funnyhouse of a Negro

A: Adrienne Kennedy **Pf**: 1962, New York **Pb**: 1969 **G**: Drama in 1 act **S**: New York apartment, indeterminate time **C**: 3m, 5f

A mumbling sleepwalker, her face hidden, carries a bald head across the stage. The curtain opens on Sarah's New York apartment. She is a pale-skinned African-American, concerned about her frizzy hair, which she is gradually losing. Her mother was pale-skinned, and spent hours combing her hair. She refused to allow Sarah's missionary father to 'touch her in their wedding bed and called him black'. Sarah is the product of her father's rape of her mother, who dies, her hair falling out. In a series of dream-like sequences, Sarah identifies with different selves: Queen Victoria (symbol of Western dominance?), the Duchess of Hapsburg (perhaps the obsolescence of her tribe, a once powerful family), a hunchbacked Jesus Christ (suffering allied with the imposition of a foreign culture on African peoples), and Patrice Lumumba (African freedom fighter who had been killed a year previously allegedly with the connivance of the United Nations General Secretary). Eventually, her selves murder her father, but 'he keeps coming back forever'. She then hangs herself, and Funnyman Raymond and a Funnylady (Sarah's landlady) discuss her story, concluding that she was out of touch with reality.

In this atmospheric piece for which she received an Obie Award, African-American Kennedy, who had just returned from a lengthy visit to Ghana, explores aspects of her own life as a black woman educated amongst whites, who finds herself mentally split between her African inheritance and her situation as a middle-class American intellectual.

Furcht und Elend des III. Reiches. See FEAR AND MISERY OF THE THIRD REICH.

Furies, The. See ORESTEIA, THE.

Futile Precaution, The. See THE BARBER OF SEVILLE, THE.

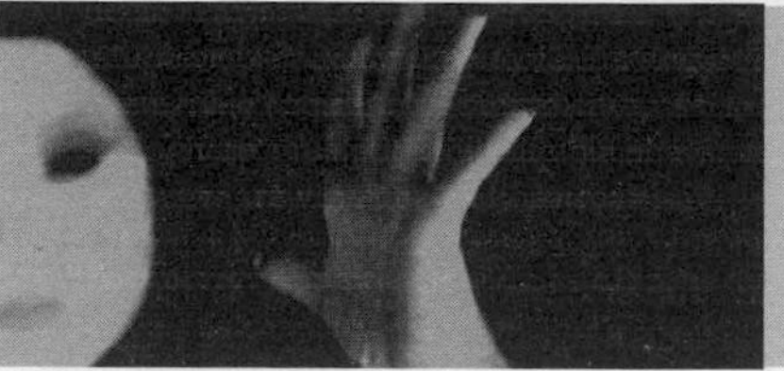

g

Galileo. See LIFE OF GALILEO.

Game of Love and Chance, The (*Le Jeu de l'amour et du hasard*)

AT: *Love in Livery; Successful Strategies*
A: Pierre Carlet de Chamblain de Marivaux
Pf: 1730, Paris **Pb:** 1730 **Tr:** 1901 **G:** Romantic com. in 3 acts; French prose **S:** Paris, early 17th c. **C:** 4m, 2f, extras

Kindly Monsieur Orgon wishes his daughter Silvia to marry Dorante, but she is fearful of marriage. She agrees to receive her suitor, provided that she can change places with her maid Lisette to give her a chance to observe his behaviour. Orgon learns that Dorante has similarly swapped roles with his valet Arlequin. Silvia finds herself soon enchanted by the 'manservant' and dismissive of her supposed suitor, since Arlequin exploits the situation to behave in an affected and high-handed manner. Meanwhile Lisette is alarmed to discover that her mistress's 'suitor' has fallen in love with her. Eventually Dorante reveals his true identity to Silvia and begs her to marry him. Despite being reminded by her of the supposed difference in their class, Dorante's love for the 'maidservant' remains unshaken. Convinced now that she has found a husband she can trust, Silvia too reveals her identity. Arlequin is only too pleased to make a match with Lisette.

Before Marivaux, well-born ladies in French comedy had tended to be little more than pawns in a game beyond their control (only their servants showed ingenuity and spirit in manipulating events). The play began with their being in love, and it was external hindrances (a difficult father, an insuperable class distinction) that had to be overcome before they could enjoy their love. Here the father is gentle, and willing to join in the game of his daughter, and, ironically, class is the one thing that is not a problem. It is Silvia's distrust and vanity that have to be overcome before she finds love, and Marivaux paints a subtle and persuasive portrait of this process.

Gammer Gurton's Needle (*A Ryght Pithy, Pleasaunt and merrie Comedie: Intytuled Gammer gurtons Nedle*)

AT: *Dyccon/Diccon of Bedlam* **A:** Anon. (probably William Stevenson) **Pf:** pre-1575, Cambridge **Pb:** 1562–3 **G:** Com. in 5 acts; rhyming verse **S:** Before the homes of Gammer Gurton and Dame Chat in an English village, mid-16th c. **C:** 6m, 4f, extras

While mending the breeches of Hodge, her servant, Gammer Gurton has lost her precious needle. Consternation reigns at this loss, and everyone in the household joins in the search. Diccon the Bedlam, a wandering fool, pretends that the needle has been stolen by Dame Chat, a gossip. Diccon then angers Dame Chat by telling her that Gammer Gurton has accused her of stealing her cock. When Gammer arrives at Dame Chat's to demand her needle back, misunderstandings ensue, ending with Chat soundly beating Gammer and Hodge. In her pursuit of justice, Gammer sends for Doctor Rat, the curate. Diccon helpfully shows Rat where he can hide in Chat's house. Chat, believing that Hodge has entered her house to steal her chickens mistakenly beats the unfortunate Rat. Finally, Bailey, the clerk, discovers that Diccon has been behind all the misunderstandings, and, when Hodge is slapped on the backside, his cry of pain reveals that the needle is still in his breeches.

Ralph Roister Doister and *Gammer Gurton's Needle* represent the two earliest extant comedies of English theatre, although there were comic episodes in the earlier mystery plays. Like Udall's play, *Gammer Gurton* derives much from Roman comedy: the five-act structure, the setting before two neighbouring houses, the interfering servant figure (here a wandering fool). But Diccon, like Merrygreek, owes a great deal to the Vice character of the English morality play, and in other respects there is an even stronger native English quality than in *Ralph Roister Doister*. This is due not only to the authentic Tudor characters but above all to their robust colloquial language.

Garden. See HOUSE AND GARDEN.

Garden City. See SUDDENLY LAST SUMMER.

Gardens of Eden. See F. M.

garrote más bien dado, El. See MAYOR OF ZALAMEA, THE.

Gas Trilogy, The (The Coral; Gas I; Gas II)
A: Georg Kaiser **Pf**: (1) 1917, Munich and Frankfurt; (2) 1918, Frankfurt and Düsseldorf; (3) 1920, Brünn (Brno) **Pb**: (1) 1917; (2) 1918; (3) 1920 **Tr**: (1) 1963; (2) 1925; (3) 1963
G: Trilogy of three dramas: (1) 5 acts, (2) 5 acts, and (3) 3 acts; German prose **S**: (1) Margarine factory and at sea, early 20th c.; (2) A gas factory, mid-20th c.; (3) The same gas factory, late 20th c. **C**: (1) 19m, 3f, extras; (2) 15m, 4f, extras; (3) 15m, extras

(1) *The Coral* (*Die Koralle*). The Billionaire (or Millionaire) is the autocratic boss of a margarine factory, intent on acquiring as much wealth as possible in order to create a distance between himself and his unhappy poverty-stricken childhood. He makes regular gifts to the poor to salve his conscience, but, so that he can avoid contact with the downtrodden, gets his secretary to hand out alms. The Secretary is the secret double of the Billionaire, distinguishable only by the coral he wears on his watch chain. The Billionaire's son rebels against his father and becomes a stoker on a ship. When his father on his luxury yacht encounters him at sea, the Son's behaviour inspires his sister, and they both turn against their father, a rejection intensified when the Billionaire shows no charity after a factory disaster. The Billionaire, believing that his dream of creating a capitalist bulwark against chaos has been shattered by his children's attitude, discovers that his Secretary had a happy prosperous childhood. He kills his Secretary and assumes his identity by transferring the coral to his own watch chain. Arrested for murder, the Billionaire eventually eagerly embraces the Secretary's identity. He is visited by a Socialist, who had appeared earlier but, thanks to the Billionaire's exhortations, is now a successful capitalist. The Son congratulates the presumed Secretary for ridding the world of a tyrant, and the priest fails to impress the Billionaire with religion. Clutching his coral, the Billionaire goes resolutely to his execution. (2) *Gas I*. Many years have passed, and the Billionaire's Son now manages a gas factory, in which the workers all share in the profits. The Engineer reports that despite having an infallible formula, the gas will explode. The factory is devastated, and the Billionaire's Son determines that, rather than rebuild the factory, he will spare his workers from the drudgery of their repetitive tasks and free them from their machines. He proposes to divide the factory plot into smallholdings, so that the workers can live from the land. He tries to win his son-in-law to his cause, but this young soldier, having made debts from gambling, cannot free himself from the military code of honour and shoots himself. World capitalists, Men in Black, gather and demand the restitution of gas manufacture. At a mass meeting of the workers the Billionaire's Son pleads for the workers to abandon the factory and to live the simple life of a smallholder. However, they are won over by the arguments of the Engineer, who sneers at this rustic idyll and urges them to rebuild the factory. The

workers storm back to the factory entrance, but their way is barred by the military, whom the Billionaire's Son has summoned. A Commissioner arrives and insists that the factory be reopened, since gas is needed for an impending war. The gates are opened, the workers pour in, and the Billionaire's Son finds himself alone with his vision of the New Man. His widowed daughter declares that she will give birth to him. (3) *Gas II.* The Billionaire's great-grandson is now a mere Billionaire Worker in the factory. The war is in full swing, and the Figures in Blue find that they are threatened with defeat, since the gas supply is failing. The Billionaire Worker explains that the workers no longer wish to produce gas, at last fulfilling his grandfather's dream of freedom from the machine. When the Figures in Yellow invade, the Chief Engineer urges the Blues to use poison gas to defeat the enemy. Despite the opposition of the Billionaire Worker, the gas is released, leading to universal annihilation.

The Gas Trilogy, by a writer known as 'der Denkspieler' (the playful thinker), is the most significant dramatic product of German Expressionism. Its unnamed characters, lack of concern with individual psychology, concentration on wider ideological issues, powerful scenes stretching the resources of the theatre to the limit, and a chiliastic vision, all proclaim the authentically Expressionist piece. Kaiser's drama had a strong influence on Brecht, and *Gas I* inspired Fritz Lang's memorable silent film *Metropolis* (1926). Although, as with virtually all science fiction, much of the action now seems dated, its concerns with ecology and global annihilation remain of considerable relevance.

Gengangere. See GHOSTS.

George Barnwell. See LONDON MERCHANT, THE.

Germany: A Tale of Horror. See FEAR AND MISERY OF THE THIRD REICH.

Geschichten aus dem Wiener Wald. See TALES FROM THE VIENNA WOODS.

gestiefelte Kater, Der. See PUSS IN BOOTS.

Ghetto

A: Joshua Sobol **Pf:** 1984, Haifa, Israel **Pb:** 1984 **Tr:** 1986 **G:** Drama in 21 scenes; Hebrew prose and songs **S:** Vilna Ghetto, Eastern Poland, 1941–3; Tel Aviv, 1983 **C:** 15m, 4f, extras

In 1983, Srulik, a former ventriloquist, reminisces about the Vilna Ghetto. As deportees arrive in the Ghetto, Kittel, a Nazi officer, orders that these talented Jews should stage shows in their own theatre. Despite being reminded by the librarian Kruk of the tastelessness of performing where 50,000 Jews were recently massacred, Gens, the chief of the Jewish police, welcomes the theatre as a way of saving some Jews. Weiskopf, an entrepreneur, gives employment to 150 Jews, mending and cleaning German uniforms. The actors rehearse a scene, in which they debate whether it is right to withhold their limited medical supplies from the more seriously sick. Meanwhile, Gens agonizes over choosing whom to condemn to the death transports. Dr Paul, a German scholar working on Jewish history, warns Kruk about the dangers of Zionist nationalism. Gens presides over the hanging of three Jewish black-marketeers. At an orgiastic cabaret, Kittel gives Gens the task of selecting 2,000 Jews for deportation from a neighbouring ghetto. Gens haggles the number down to 600. Weiskopf is killed for hoarding black-market goods. The actors stage their final performance: Nazi uniforms being harangued by a Jew-hating Hitler uniform. Kittel then guns down them and Gens, but Srulik survives.

Sobol's play, which is based on Herman Kruk's diaries of the Vilna Ghetto, goes beyond documentary in both its imaginative staging and its warnings to the Jewish public of today. As Dr Paul warns: 'you'll . . . leave Zion, leave Palestine to the likes of Gens who'll grab it with both brutish hands'. Courageously, while depicting the horrors of Nazi genocide, Sobol's play also contains a message to those who survived.

Ghosts (*Gengangere*)

A: Henrik Ibsen **Pf:** 1882, Chicago; 1883, Helsingborg **Pb:** 1881 **Tr:** 1888 **G:** Trag. in 3 acts; Norwegian prose **S:** Mrs Alving's estate, western Norway, 1880s **C:** 3m, 2f

Mrs Alving has built an orphanage in honour of her husband, who died 10 years previously. She reveals to her old friend Pastor Manders the truth about her marriage: Captain Alving was a dissolute reprobate who made her life a misery. She reproaches Manders for insisting that she return to her husband, when she had come to the Pastor seeking help. Now her artist son Osvald has returned home from Paris and begins to flirt with the maid Regina, the daughter of Alving and a former maidservant. To Mrs Alving it is as though the ghosts of the past have returned. She tells Osvald and Regina that they are related, and Regina goes off to work as a hostess in a disreputable seamen's home which her husband is opening. The uninsured orphanage burns to the ground, and Osvald, already unwell, now begins to suffer from brain disease caused by syphilis inherited from his father.

This is the darkest of Ibsen's plays and was widely attacked for its frank treatment of a taboo subject. The underlying irony of the play is that the colour and gaiety of Osvald's life as an artist in Paris, his attraction to Regina, even his father's supposedly dissolute life, appear so much more congenial than the grey starkness of Norway and the unyielding moral rectitude of Manders. That this life should be so horribly punished with a creeping brain disease is the tragedy of the play and may be once again well understood by a generation witnessing the transference of the HIV virus to children.

Ghost Sonata, The (*Spöksonaten*)

AT: *The Spook Sonata* A: August Strindberg Pf: 1908, Stockholm Pb: 1907 Tr: 1916 G: Drama in 3 scenes; Swedish prose S: Fashionable house and the street outside, 1900s C: 7m, 8f, extras

The Student (Arkenholz), weary after spending much of the night rescuing people from a collapsed house, meets a sinister Old Man (Jacob Hummel). The Old Man asks the Student to attend a concert, so that he may meet the Colonel and his daughter (the Young Lady). The Colonel lives in the house with his wife, a Mummy; the Dark Lady (or Lady in Black), daughter of the Caretaker's Wife by the Dead Man (the late Consul who lived upstairs); and the Fiancée, formerly engaged to Hummel. When he sees the Colonel's Daughter, the Student falls in love with her and agrees to woo her on Hummel's behalf. Some evenings later Hummel arrives in the Colonel's apartment. The Mummy emerges from the cupboard where she has sat for 20 years. Hummel, who was once her lover and is in reality the Young Lady's father, intends to make the Student his heir and marry him to the Young Lady. The young couple talk in the hyacinth room, while at a 'ghost supper' Hummel is exposed as a murderer and fraudster and hangs himself in the Mummy's cupboard. A few days later in the hyacinth room the Cook tells the young couple that she is draining the strength from the family. The Young Lady rejects the Student's offer of marriage, fearing the drudgery that it will bring, and he now realizes that the house is rotten and that she is infected with its poison. The Young Lady collapses dying, and the Student sings the 'Song of the Sun' from the *Elder Edda*: 'Man reaps as he sows.'

The best of his 'Chamber Plays', *The Ghost Sonata*, despite its complex symbolism, exerts a powerful fascination in the theatre. While concentrating the action on to the tiny stage of the Intimate Theatre in Stockholm, a whole world of strange universalized figures and evocative images are offered. The musical structure and limbo-like existence recur in the plays of Samuel Beckett.

Giall, An. See HOSTAGE, THE.

Gigli Concert, The

A: Tom Murphy Pf: 1983, Dublin Pb: 1988; rev. 1991, 1994 G: Drama in 8 scenes S: J. P. W. King's office and living quarters, Ireland, 1980s C: 2m, 1f

J. P. W. King ('JPW') is a 46-year-old slovenly English therapist, promoting himself as a 'dynamatologist', who is separated from his wife. He is visited by an Irish Man, a builder and developer, who refuses to give his name and is prone to outbursts of violent temper and to believing that he is the great tenor Beniamino Gigli. JPW feels out of his depth, but the Irish Man insists that he wants to be treated by him. JPW mulls it over with his middle-aged promiscuous girlfriend Mona. The Irish Man comes for a third session bringing a record player and plays an aria sung by Gigli as Mephistopheles. JPW talks of his longing for a married woman (his wife?), while the Irish Man, still imagining himself as Gigli, speaks of his rejection by an Italian woman. The next day, the Irish Man arrives in desperation: his wife has left him, taking their son. JPW promises that he will soon be able to sing like Gigli. The next day, the Irish Man announces that his wife has returned, and he dismisses JPW as a charlatan. Mona reveals that she has terminal cancer and declares her love for JPW. Alone, JPW is listening to Gigli when the Irish Man arrives. He is fully 'cured' and thanks JPW for his treatment and urges JPW to go back to England. JPW sings Gigli's aria and leaves his office.

A complex and multilayered play, Murphy's arguably finest piece deals with the 'mess' of existence and how the solution derives from 'the rising darkness of our despair' by creating fulfilling fantasies. By expressing themselves through Gigli's passionate music, first the Irish Man then JPW transform themselves.

Girl from Andros, The (*Andria*)

AT: *The Lady/Woman from Andros* A: Terence Pf: 166 BC, Rome Tr: *c.*1520 G: Latin com. in verse S: A street in Athens, before the houses of Simo and Glycerium, 2nd c. BC C: 9m, 3f

An Athenian gentleman, Simo, has arranged for his son Pamphilus to marry his neighbour's daughter. However, Pamphilus has already fallen in love with a foreign girl from Andros, Glycerium (who never appears in the play). Even though Simo learns that Glycerium is expecting Pamphilus' child, he insists on the arranged marriage going ahead in order to test the sincerity of his son's feelings. Davus, a slave, advises Pamphilus to agree to his father's plan, causing complications with Pamphilus' friend, who is in love with the neighbour's daughter. Pamphilus is on the point of marrying the wrong girl, when the wedding is cancelled because Glycerium has given birth to Pamphilus' child. It is now discovered that Glycerium is after all another long-lost daughter of the neighbour, so that she is free to marry Pamphilus, and Pamphilus' friend can marry his beloved.

Based on a no longer extant play of the same name by Menander, *The Girl from Andros* is the earliest of Terence's six comedies. Despite turning on the standard plot element of the long-lost child whose identity is improbably revealed at the end, the play has some quite sophisticated touches: the irony that Pamphilus, though unwilling to marry his neighbour's daughter, in fact ends up doing so; the scheme recommended by his slave that almost plunges him into misfortune; and the parallel plot, added to Menander's play by Terence, of the friend who wishes to wed the spurned bride. The play provided source material for the anonymously written *The Buggbears* (1564), Richard Steele's *The *Conscious Lovers*, Daniel Bellamy's *The Perjured Devotee* (1739), and Edward Moore's *The Foundling* (1748).

Girl from Samos, The. See THE WOMAN FROM SAMOS, THE.

Girl Worth Gold, A. See FAIR MAID OF THE WEST, THE.

Glass Menagerie, The

A: Tennessee Williams Pf: 1944, Chicago Pb: 1945; rev. 1970 G: Drama in 2 acts S: Tenement apartment, St Louis, 1944 and 1930s C: 2m, 2f

The action is presented as a reminiscence of his home life some 10 years previously by Tom Wingfield, now a merchant seaman in the Second World War. His mother Amanda, whose husband deserted her years ago, keeps house for Tom and his gawky and crippled 24-year-old sister Laura. Amanda, who dreams of an imagined past when she was wooed by a rich plantation owner, is furious when she discovers that Laura has dropped out of secretarial school. Instead of trying to find a husband, Laura spends much of her free time tending her menagerie of glass animals. After a row with his domineering mother, in which some glass animals get broken, Tom agrees to see whether in the warehouse where he works he cannot find a suitable boy to bring home for Laura. Amanda dresses in girlish fashion to receive the 'gentleman caller' Jim O'Connor. Laura is horrified to discover that he is the high-school boy on whom she once had a crush, but they share a certain intimacy and even dance together and kiss, causing a glass unicorn's horn to get broken off. When Jim tells Laura that he is already engaged, her hopes are dashed. Unable to bear any more pressure from life at home, Tom goes to sea, but cannot forget his unfortunate sister.

This was the first successful play by Williams, even though his first had been staged in 1930. It is a bitter-sweet recollection of his own youth and, while the scenes of dialogue are to be acted naturalistically, Williams makes use of narrator's commentary, mimed action, cutaway sets, atmospheric music, lighting, and the symbolism of the fragile glass animals, reflecting the theme of illusion and reality in the dreams and aspirations of the family.

Glass of Water, The (*Le Verre d'eau, ou Les Effets et les causes*)

AT: *Causes and Effects* A: Eugène Scribe Pf: 1840, Paris Pb: 1840 Tr: 1850 G: Hist. drama in 5 acts; French prose S: St James's Palace, London, 1710 C: 4m, 3f

Although the Duke of Marlborough has won several impressive victories in the War of the Spanish Succession, Viscount Bolingbroke, a Tory, is attempting to end hostilities in Europe. He is bitterly opposed by the Duchess of Marlborough, the Whig Sarah Churchill, a childhood friend and now adviser of Queen Anne. The Duchess wants the war to continue so that her husband can reap yet more glory. All Bolingbroke's attempts to win the Queen to his point of view are successfully countered by the Duchess, until he discovers that both women have fallen in love with a young guardsman Samuel Masham. The Duchess secretly arranges for him to be given a commission, and Anne surreptitiously sees to it that Masham's fiancée Abigail is made a lady-in-waiting. In the midst of intrigue and jealousy, Bolingbroke cunningly plots the downfall of his rival the Duchess. At a court party Anne's request for a glass of water reveals to the astonished Duchess that her rival in love is the Queen herself. She is so shocked that she insults Anne, who rejects her as her confidante, replacing her with Abigail, who is married off to Masham to protect the Queen's reputation. Soon the French ambassadors are admitted to the Queen, and peace negotiations can begin. A trivial cause (the glass of water) can have an effect on international conflict.

Scribe is always associated with the term the 'well-made play', and this drama is one of his best. It does not offer historical accuracy or subtle characterization, but one cannot but be impressed by the skilful construction and manipulation of the complicated plot with its unassailable message that the smallest of incidents can have world-changing consequences.

Glengarry Glen Ross

A: David Mamet Pf: 1983, London Pb: 1984 G: Drama in 2 acts S: Chinese restaurant and real estate office, Chicago, 1980s C: 7m

Shelly Levene sells real estate for a Chicago firm specializing in the sale of Florida scrubland, which is dignified by names like 'Glengarry' and 'Glen Ross'. Levene's sales have fallen off badly, especially when compared with those of a younger man Richard Roma, in line to win a Cadillac. Despite pleading with and trying to bribe his boss John Williamson, Levene now faces the sack. Another disgruntled salesman Dave Moss persuades his colleague George Aaronow into stealing the firm's list of contracts to sell to a competitor. When the burglary is discovered, Williamson calls in the police. He has to placate Roma, angry that the contracts proving his recent sales have gone missing, and is surprised when Levene comes to him, having pulled off a major deal. When Detective Baylen interviews the salesmen, it becomes clear that Moss and Aaronow had nothing to do with the burglary. But when Levene lets slip information that can only have come from one of the stolen documents, he immediately becomes the chief suspect. Indeed, his big deal, whose success has given him a new lease of life ('I got my *balls* back'), was achieved only by using one of the stolen contracts.

Just as Pinter, to whom this play is dedicated, moved from lower-class vernacular to recreate middle-class idiom, so here Mamet turns from the no-hopers of **American Buffalo* to Chicago businessmen, whose ethic is summed up by Levene's 'a man's his job'. As the critic Dennis Carroll said, this play, arguably Mamet's most powerful although now overshadowed by the film version (1992), 'became the *Death of a Salesman* of the 1980s'.

Glory of Columbia, The. See ANDRÉ.

Goat, The

AT: *Who Is Sylvia?* A: Edward Albee Pf: 2002, New York Pb: 2003 G: Drama in 3 acts S: New York apartment, *c.*2000 C: 3m, 1f

Martin, a successful prizewinning 50-year-old architect, liberal, witty, and humane, is happily married to Stevie, his intellectual equal. When his lifelong friend Ross comes to set up a television interview, Martin confesses that, beside Stevie, he has another love: Sylvia, with whom he has been having an affair for six months. When it transpires that Sylvia is a goat, Ross feels obliged to inform Stevie by letter. She and their gay son Billy angrily confront Martin, who tries to defend himself by declaring the beauty of his love for Sylvia. Billy storms out, and the desperate Stevie begins smashing up their apartment, before she too leaves. Martin and Billy are reconciled, and their love almost slips into homosexual incestuous lovemaking. When Ross arrives, Martin is furious that he betrayed his confidence. He had been to a therapy group, but everyone there was so sad, whereas Martin found fulfilment in his love of a goat; Ross was the only person left he felt he could tell his secret to. Stevie exacts a terrible and bloody revenge by slaughtering Sylvia and dragging her carcass into the apartment: 'Are you surprised? What did you expect me to do?'

In a world where all kinds of sexual freedom are now openly discussed in the theatre, Albee pushed the Broadway audience to the limits of its tolerance by offering a positive depiction of bestiality (although one assumes that they take Titania's affair with a donkey in their stride). However, Martin's obsessive love never seems sordid to him but is full of tenderness. In this play, subtitled 'Notes Towards a Definition of Tragedy', the choice of goat as a love object and ultimately sacrificial animal contains mythic and tragic resonance: there is a sense of inevitability in Stevie's revenge, and a feeling of catharsis when the innocent beast is sacrificed creating the potential for renewal.

Gods Are Not to Blame, The

A: Ola Rotimi Pf: 1968, Ife Pb: 1971 G: Trag. in 3 acts; prose and verse S: Yoruba kingdom, Nigeria, indeterminate period C: 13m, 3f, 4 children, extras

In this reworking of **Oedipus the King*, the action is transposed to Africa. Right at the start of the play, the Priest of Ifa predicts that the newborn son of King Adetusa and his Queen Ojuola will 'kill his own father and then marry his own mother!' The baby's feet are tied with a string of cowries and sacrificed to the gods. Now years later, the child Odewale is King and married to Ojuola. An old man Alaka, half clown, half philosopher, who combines the characters of the Messenger and the Shepherd of Sophocles' play, comes to tell Odewale that his 'parents' have died. However, Alaka also lets slip that they were not Odewale's real parents. Shamed by the suggestion that he is illegitimate, Odewale brutally forces Alaka to reveal the truth: that Alaka found him in the bush and brought him to the neighbouring Ijekun chief to be fostered. The terrible revelation that the Priest of Ifa's prophecy has been fulfilled leads to the suicide of Ojuola and blinding of Odewale.

Rotimi was one of the clutch of prominent Nigerian playwrights who emerged in West Africa in the 1960s, the most notable being Soyinka. Because of its subject matter, *The Gods Are Not to Blame* is the most accessible of his plays. Rotimi's main intervention is to dispense with the gradual revelation of the truth of Sophocles' original: here, the prophecy is known at the outset, and the disclosing of the past by one wonderfully eccentric character helps to drive the play with greater speed towards its terrible conclusion. The prior knowledge of the prophecy, as the title implies, means that the complacent mortals were given fair warning; they cannot blame the gods, just as, Rotimi implies, the future of Nigeria too is in the hands of its people.

Goetz von Berlichingen. See GÖTZ VON BERLICHINGEN.

Goin'a Buffalo

A: Ed Bullins **Pf**: 1968, New York **Pb**: 1969 **G**: Drama in 3 acts **S**: Curt's apartment and strip club, Los Angeles, early 1960s **C**: 10m, 2f, extras

Curt and Rich, two blacks in their twenties, are playing chess and being served beers by Curt's attractive, long-suffering wife Pandora, when they are visited by Art Garrison, a quiet thoughtful young black, who saved Curt's life in the county jail during a riot between white and black prisoners. Curt is planning a job which will pay for them all to go to Buffalo and begin a new life, and Art is persuaded to join them. Pandora and her white friend Mamma Too Tight, who has to feed her drug habit, leave to go to work as hookers in a local club. At the club, Art and Mamma get close, and Mamma's pimp Shaky comes and threatens her. Deeny, the club owner, then arrives from a meeting with the union and announces that he is closing the club. When he refuses to pay any wages, a fight breaks out, in which Curt is injured and Shaky knocked unconscious. Curt, Pandora, Mamma, and Art escape just as the police arrive. Three days later, Curt plans to raise bail for Shaky, who has been jailed for possession, by selling Shaky's heroin. Then they will all leave for Buffalo. Art, who has secretly fallen in love with Pandora, betrays Curt's heroin deal to the police, and then leaves town with Pandora – to go to Buffalo.

Although Bullins has been a militant black activist, becoming minister of culture with the Black Panthers, *Goin'a Buffalo* does not contain an obvious political message; it is 'theatre of reality' from which we may derive our own insights into the lives of some unspectacular African-Americans. Like Chekhov's three sisters yearning for Moscow, the characters dream of escape to Buffalo, but we know that life for blacks will be little different there: 'It's cats like you and your boss who make us all the time have to act like thugs, pimps and leeches to just make it out here in the world.'

Golden Age, The

A: Louis Nowra **Pf**: 1985, Melbourne **Pb**: 1985; rev. 1988 **G**: Drama in 2 acts; English with some patois **S**: Hobart, Collingwood, and south-west forests, Tasmania, and Berlin, 1939–45 **C**: 12m, 7f

Peter Archer, a geologist and son of a Hobart doctor, sets out with his working-class friend Francis Morris, an engineer, to explore the wilderness of the south-west forests of Tasmania. They come across a tribe of curious individuals, descendants of 19th-century escaped convicts and failed colonists, left behind by modern civilization and speaking an odd patois of archaic British dialects and swearwords. Although their matriarch Ayre tries to explain, Peter and Francis remain bemused and rather frightened by these strange creatures. Francis begins to be attracted to the savage young Betsheb. When Ayre realizes that her tribe will die out, she asks to be brought to Hobart, where they become the objects of humane but supercilious curiosity. An MP insists that they must be hidden away in an asylum; otherwise their primitive behaviour will add weight to Nazi propaganda. Francis joins the army and is posted to Europe, taking leave of Betsheb, whom he now loves. Ayre dies, leaving Betsheb and her autistic son Stef as the only survivors. When Stef too dies, Betsheb becomes demented, and Peter's father feels so guilty about his role in destroying the tribe that he slits his throat. In the ruins of Berlin in 1945, Francis calmly kills a Nazi. He returns to Tasmania and, despite appeals by Peter, goes into the wilderness with Betsheb.

In this rich play, based on historical fact, Nowra, without sentimentalizing the primitives ('Golden Age' is ironic), explores the alienation of post-colonial society: 'Their culture is more authentic than ours. We Australians have assumed the garb of a hand-me-down culture, but at our heart is a desert.' So-called civilization, which produced Nazi death camps and Allied bombing of civilians, offers a poor alternative to living in the wilderness.

Good

A: C. P. Taylor **Pf:** 1981, London **Pb:** 1982 **G:** Trag. in 2 acts; prose with songs and recitative **S:** Hamburg, Berlin, Frankfurt, etc., 1933–40 **C:** 9m, 3f, musicians, extras

Dr John Halder is a lecturer in German literature at Frankfurt University. Married with two children to a concert pianist, Helen, who never cooks or cleans, he eventually leaves her for a student Anne. His best friend is a Jewish psychiatrist Maurice Gluckstein, who becomes an ever-greater embarrassment to Halder, as anti-Semitism sweeps the country. Halder has a mother suffering from senile dementia, and his novel supporting euthanasia comes to the attention of the Nazi leadership. He is invited to advise on the use of euthanasia in cases of severe mental disability. Persuaded that he might be able to ensure that any programme remains humane, he accepts and even joins the SS. Halder becomes more and more drawn into Nazi excesses: disposing of mental patients, book-burning, lecturing on the pernicious Jewish influence on literature, eventually participating in the horrors of the *Kristallnacht*. Eichmann now orders Halder to oversee the transportation of Jews to labour camps, and then, to cope with overcrowding, to establish at Auschwitz a camp where those who are unfit can be disposed of 'humanely'. Throughout, in his head, Halder hears songs and music (played by a live band), even Hitler playing a Jewish folk song on a fiddle. Arriving at Auschwitz, he discovers the band is real.

Taylor tries to understand how an essentially 'good' man could become embroiled in events that led to the worst deliberate genocide of human history, and by so doing offers a metaphor for the rapid decline of a civilized country into barbarism. Believing that he can ensure humaneness in the execution of Nazi policy, Halder slides from a not unreasonable belief in euthanasia to becoming a war criminal.

Goodnight Children Everywhere

A: Richard Nelson **Pf:** 1997, Stratford-upon-Avon **Pb:** 1997 **G:** Drama in 8 scenes **S:** Large flat, Clapham, south London, spring 1945 **C:** 3m, 4f

In the last months of the Second World War, Peter, now 17, who had been sent away five years previously to Canada, returns to his sisters in London: Vi (19), a would-be actress; Ann (20), pregnant and married to Mike (fifties), a doctor; and Betty (21), a nurse who works for Mike. Their parents are dead, and they all mother Peter, wondering at how he has grown. Vi and Ann had been evacuated to Wales. A song played on the radio, 'Goodnight Children Everywhere', makes Peter and Ann sad, as they think of their mother killed by a bomb and their father killed in action in France. When Peter has a bath, Ann masturbates him and makes him come. That evening, another doctor, Hugh, comes to see if Peter would like to work for him. He brings with him his daughter Rose, who is studying to be a teacher. Mike tells Peter that Ann confessed her odd behaviour to him, and he says he understands. Hugh invites Betty out for a meal. Ann suggests sex with Peter, and they make love the following day. Vi gets a part she has auditioned for by sleeping with the director. Betty goes off with Hugh but soon returns, having decided that he repelled her. Some months later, Mike and Ann call with their new baby to show it off, and Ann discovers Rose emerging from Peter's bedroom.

Peter's return to his family is warm, shocking, and unpredictable. It is as though he has found himself in Chekhov's **Three Sisters* after they have abandoned conventional morality and now pursue without inhibition their desires and aspirations, limited by the war and by their emotional and economic vulnerability.

Good Person of Setzuan, The (*Der gute Mensch von Sezuan*)

AT: *The Good Woman of Setzuan/Schezwan/Sezuan/Sichuan* **A:** Bertolt Brecht (with Ruth Berlau and Margarete Steffin) **Pf:** 1943, Zurich **Pb:** 1953; rev. 1958 **Tr:** 1948 **G:** Pol. drama in 10 scenes, prologue, 9 interludes, and epilogue;

German prose, verse, and songs S: Sichuan Province, China, mid-20th c. C: 17m, 8f, extras

When three gods descend to earth in search of 'a good person', only Shen Te, a prostitute, offers them hospitality. She finds it hard to obey their exhortation to be good, since 'everything is so expensive'; so the gods reward her with a sum of money, with which she opens a small tobacco shop. She is soon exploited by the poor and homeless, who come to live in her shop. As her business starts to collapse, Shen Te invents a hard-hearted cousin Shui Ta (Shen Te masked), who drives the parasites away. Shen Te stops a young unemployed airman, Yang Sun, from hanging himself. In love with Sun, she is disappointed, when reappearing as Shui Ta, to be told by Sun that he is interested in Shen Te only for her money. Nevertheless, she still plans to marry him, but is rejected by Sun, when not enough money is forthcoming. Happy to find that she is pregnant, Shen Te has to resort to bringing back Shui Ta to safeguard her child's future. Shui Ta manages the tobacco shop so successfully that he provides employment for many and grows rich. Since Shen Te has gone missing, Shui Ta is put on trial for her murder and appears before three judges, the three gods. Revealing herself as Shen Te, she pleads with the gods: 'To be good to others | As well as to myself was impossible.' Unable to answer her cry of despair, the gods reascend to their cloud, praising 'the good person of Setzuan'.

In this play Brecht addresses the perennial problem, originally debated in Shaw's **Major Barbara*, that 'goodness' is not enough to ensure social prosperity. Brecht's implication is that the capitalist structure must be replaced with a society that will allow people to be good and not suffer for it, but the play itself nowhere makes such a suggestion. The failure of the gods to help Shen Te in her dilemma is the closest Brecht comes to tragic insight.

Good Woman, A. See LADY WINDERMERE'S FAN.

Gorboduc (*The Tragidie of Ferrex and Porrex*)

A: Thomas Norton and Thomas Sackville Pf: 1561–2, London Pb: 1565 G: Trag. in 5 acts with dumbshows and choruses; blank verse S: Ancient Britain C: 15m, 2f, chorus (4m)

While still King of Britain, Gorboduc divides his realm between his two sons, Ferrex and Porrex. Urged on by the flattery of young parasites at court, the brothers turn against each other, and Porrex kills his elder brother. Videna, the Queen, is so outraged by this that she kills Porrex. Incensed by this act, the people rise in rebellion and slay Gorboduc and his Queen. The nobles now wreak terrible revenge on the rebels, and because there is no heir to the throne, fall to civil war and lay waste the country for a further 50 years.

Regarded as the earliest extant 'regular' (i.e. five-act) tragedy, *Gorboduc* has echoes of the sibling conflicts of Greek myth (Eteocles and Polyneices, Thyestes and Atreus), but was based on the chronicles of Geoffrey of Monmouth. Geoffrey also described the consequences of Lear dividing his kingdom, which Shakespeare was to dramatize some 40 years later. This theme and the dangers inherent in having no legitimate heir would have been of particular interest to the audience, whose Queen, Elizabeth I, remained childless. While in some respects following the model of ancient classical drama – the five acts, the use of a chorus to comment on the action, all violent action taking place offstage and being merely reported – the authors also introduced important innovations – the dumbshows prefacing each act, the disregard for the unities of time and place, and the first extant use of blank verse, the wonderfully flexible unrhymed iambic pentameter, which was to be so successfully exploited by Shakespeare. An 'academic tragedy', it was written by two politicians and performed by students at the Inns of Court, not by professionals.

Gore ot uma. See WOE FROM WIT.

Gospel of the Brothers Barnabas, The. See BACK TO METHUSELAH.

Götz von Berlichingen (*Geschichte Gottfriedens von Berlichingen mit der eisernen Hand*)

AT: *Ironhand* A: Johann Wolfgang von Goethe **Pf**: 1774, Berlin **Pb**: 1771; rev. 1773 **Tr**: 1799 **G**: Drama in 5 acts; German prose **S**: Germany, early 16th c. **C**: 24m, 4f, many extras

Götz von Berlichingen, a noble knight with an iron hand, is hated by the rich and powerful and loved by the oppressed and poor. His behaviour invokes the enmity of the Bishop of Bamberg, whose follower Weislingen is captured by Götz. Weislingen is persuaded to join forces with Götz and becomes engaged to his sister. However, Weislingen is tempted back to the Bishop's court, not least by the charms of Adelheid von Walldorf, whom he marries. When Götz robs some Nuremberg merchants to give to the poor, the Emperor outlaws Götz. At first Götz easily repels attempts to capture him, but, when a truce is declared, he leaves his castle. He is treacherously seized by the imperial forces but freed by a loyal follower. He seems a broken man, until the leaders of the Peasants' Revolt enlist his support. He breaks with them, however, when they become excessively violent, but is nevertheless arrested. Adelheid, weary of Weislingen, poisons him and is condemned to death. Götz dies in prison, his last words being 'Freedom! Freedom!'

Based on Götz's memoirs, published in 1731, Goethe's play reflected the eagerness with which *Sturm und Drang* (Storm and Stress) writers rejected the neo-classical formality of French drama in favour of the freedoms of Shakespeare. The result is a sprawling epic packed with exciting incident, which was to inspire a whole genre of *Ritterdramen* (knight dramas) throughout the Romantic period. In celebrating this national figure, the young Goethe embraced apparent contradictions. The despising of the refinements of court life and championing a plain German life-style pointed to conservatism. The defiance of authority (including – to the delight of generations of German schoolchildren – the famous utterance 'lick my arse!'), also stood as a revolutionary challenge to a corrupt age.

Government Inspector, The (*Revizor*)

AT: *The Inspector; The Inspector General* **A**: Nikolai Gogol **Pf**: 1836, St Petersburg **Pb**: 1836; rev. 1841, 1842 **Tr**: 1892 **G**: Com. in 5 acts; Russian prose **S**: Small Russian provincial town, 1830s **C**: 20m, 5f, extras

The Police Chief of a small Russian provincial town censors all the local mail and so discovers that a Government Inspector is on his way to review the workings of the local government. Given the level of corruption in the town, its elders are thrown into panic by the impending inspection. When news comes that a well-dressed young man is staying at the local inn where he is refusing to pay his bills, everyone assumes that the Inspector has arrived incognito. The Police Chief immediately invites the bemused Khlestakov to his own home, and even attempts to manipulate him into a liaison with his daughter. Khlestakov imagines that this treatment is due to his superior manners from St Petersburg. He happily accepts the many bribes brought to him by the townsfolk. His faithful servant Osip realizes that Khlestakov ought to quit while he still can. Narrowly missing an affair with both the Police Chief's wife and daughter, Khlestakov travels off, laden with gifts. A letter from Khlestakov to a friend is intercepted, and his identity finally revealed to the dismay of all. At that moment the arrival of the real Government Inspector is announced.

This is the most frequently performed Russian play. Although set unmistakably in provincial Russia in the early 19th century, the comedy deriving from the mistaken identity of Khlestakov and from the depiction of small-town corruption has resonance wherever local officials fill themselves with self-importance. It is a theme, for example, explored by John Arden in *The *Workhouse Donkey*.

gran teatro del mundo, El. See GREAT THEATRE OF THE WORLD, THE.

Great Divide, The

AT: *The Sabine Women* **A**: William Vaughn Moody **Pf**: 1906, Chicago **Pb**: 1909 **G**: Drama in 3 acts **S**: A cabin in the Arizona desert, a home in the Cordilleras Mountains, and a house in Milford Corners, Massachusetts, early 20th c. **C**: 10m, 3f, 1 child (m)

With her brother Philip and his wife Polly, 19-year-old Ruth Jordan has left New England to live simply in the Arizona desert in order to establish a cactus-fibre industry. Refusing the hand of a young doctor, she dreams of a grander relationship – with 'a sublime abstraction – of the West'. Her yearning is cruelly realized. Three drunks threaten to rape her. She bargains with one of them, Stephen Ghent: if he saves her, she will marry him. He bribes one companion and shoots the other. About a year later, Ghent is a prosperous partner in a gold mine. Despite immaculate behaviour towards her, he is met by unforgiving coldness from Ruth. Refusing financial support, she earns her keep selling home-made baskets and rugs. Paying Ghent back the bribe for preventing the rape, she claims to have bought freedom for herself and her baby son, and leaves with her brother, who has tracked her down. Some months later in Massachusetts, Ruth is unhappy and sick. Her family face financial ruin, because the cactus-fibre project was sold when she disappeared. When Ghent offers to buy back the cactus-fibre enterprise for the family, Ruth reveals the truth of their first meeting. Ghent speaks of the Great Divide: between their puritan existence and his own free life beyond the Rockies. Ruth, recognizing that he has become a better man through her, relents and joyfully agrees to return to the West with him.

That *The Great Divide* was thought by many at the time to be the greatest American play ever written, suggests that, all too often, size rather than quality appears to matter. The bombastic language and melodramatic action do not reveal greatness. However, the play does offer a model exploration of the 'divide' in American consciousness between urban sophistication and the robustly assertive 'romance of the West', which made cowboy films so attractive, and is arguably still a force in American foreign policy.

Great Theatre of the World, The (*El gran teatro del mundo*)

AT: *The Great World-Theatre; The Great Stage of the World* **A:** Pedro Calderón de la Barca **Pf:** *c.*1633–5, Madrid **Pb:** 1655 **Tr:** 1856 **G:** *Auto sacramental* in 1 act; Spanish verse **S:** The World, indeterminate period **C:** 8m, 2f

The Author (God) calls upon World to provide the setting for the lives of the figures he calls forth: the Rich Man, the Worker, the Poor Man, the King, Beauty, and Discretion. The World provides a prologue, describing the progress of time from the earliest beginnings to the salvation offered by Christ. The figures summoned by the Author are told that they must follow their respective roles in life, playing out their parts without rehearsal, and must choose between good and evil. The Author watches from his throne, as a globe opens with a stage for the characters to live out their lives. The Prompter, the Law of Grace, admonishes and encourages them with the repeated phrase: 'Do good, for God is God.' As the characters approach death, and their globe closes, they must return their costumes to World, so that the King is once more reduced to the level of the Poor Man. The globe opens once more to reveal the sacrament of the Eucharist, to which initially only Discretion and Poor Man are admitted, although the King is eventually rewarded after a spell in purgatory.

Calderón was the supreme master of the *auto sacramental*, the performative accompaniment to the Corpus Christi day processions. As well as teaching a moral lesson, the *auto sacramental* was a rallying point for the Catholic faith, now threatened by the Reformation, and for its alliance with the Spanish Crown and the theatre. From the point of view of theatre history, the play offers an allegory, not dissimilar from **Everyman*, but now staged with spectacular stage effects and here implying that 'all the world's a stage'. Hofmannsthal adapted the original for the Salzburg Festival in 1892, where it was staged by Max Reinhardt.

Green Pastures, The

A: Marc Connelly **Pf:** 1930, New York **Pb:** 1930 **G:** Folk drama in 2 acts of 10 and 8 scenes **S:** Black church in Louisiana, early 20th c., heaven and earth, from the Creation to 8th c. BC **C:** 43m, 14f, extras

A black Sunday school preacher Mr Deshee describes heaven to the children, which then appears on stage: God, a tall black man, and his angels eat fried fish and smoke cigars. Then God creates the universe. The Fall from the Garden of Eden follows, and then Cain's murder of Abel. God 'don' like de way things is goin' atall', so he decides to visit earth and, amidst all the sinning, encounters Noah as the one pious being. God initiates the Flood, making sure that Noah and his wife survive in the ark. He begins all over again, saying, 'I only hope it's goin' to work out all right.' The cleaning women in God's office complain about the trouble that humans cause God. Making the Jews his chosen people, he appears before Moses and instructs him to lead his people out of bondage. After Moses has freed his people from Egypt, Joshua eventually takes them to the Promised Land. However, God is so disgusted with their ensuing debauchery (even the High Priest is strutting his stuff in a Babylonian nightclub), that he agrees once more to return to earth. Impressed by the faith of Hezdrel, God realizes that even he must suffer and prepares to die on the cross for humankind.

Based on Roark Bradford's stories *Ol' Man Adam an' His Chillun*, this Pulitzer Prizewinner was a ground-breaking attempt to reinterpret Bible stories in the context of black American culture, a race that, like the Israelites, had not long been freed from slavery. That it was undertaken so successfully by a white Catholic writer is remarkable, but this has also meant that it now tends to be dismissed as patronizing.

Grouch, The. See BAD-TEMPERED MAN, THE.

Group, The

A: Mercy Otis Warren **Pf**: No known professional production **Pb**: 1775 **G**: Drama in 2 acts; blank verse **S**: Massachusetts in the American colonies, 1770s **C**: 16m, 1f

A group of men, loyal to George III and Britain, have gathered together to discuss the threat posed by the American colonials who are striving for independence. They are a motley und unattractive collection, motivated by different considerations, and include figures of the law (Chief Justice Hazelrod and Judge Meagre), soldiers (General Sylla, Brigadier Hateall), foppish aristocracy (Sir Sparrow Spendall), and hangers-on (Dupe). Significantly, Hateall is also a wife-beater. They implore Sylla to repress with force the aspirations of the rebels, but he is moved by his sense of humanity and justice, acknowledging their right to live in freedom. In a short epilogue, a lady pleads that no more men should have to die in the cause of freedom.

Warren was the wife of one of the leaders of the American War of Independence, James Warren, president of the Provisional Congress of Massachusetts, and also a close friend of John and Gabriel Adams. Written a year before the Declaration of Independence, *The Group* is one of the earliest play texts dealing with contemporary America (the first professionally produced play by a native author, Thomas Godfrey's *The Prince of Parthia* (1767) was on a classical subject). Virtually devoid of dramatic action, Warren's satirical piece was acted by amateurs but was read widely.

Groza. See THUNDERSTORM, THE.

Grumbler, The. See BAD-TEMPERED MAN, THE.

Guardsman, The (*A testör*)

AT: *Where Ignorance Is Bliss* A: Ferenc Molnár **Pf**: 1910 **Pb**: 1910 **Tr**: 1910 **G**: Com. in 3 acts; Hungarian prose **S**: Vienna, 1900s **C**: 3m, 4f

The six-month-old marriage between Nandor, an actor, and his actress wife Ilona is already showing strains. He questions her jealously, she insists on playing Chopin, which the husband thinks hints at the melancholy of autumn, while it is still in fact only May. The husband resolves to test her fidelity by courting her disguised as an Austrian guardsman. He first passes beneath her window and is then invited into the house. Later at the opera the wife admits to the Guardsman that she still loves her husband but continues to welcome her 'lover's' advances. The husband, who has pretended to have been away on a journey, returns unexpectedly, finding his wife on the point of meeting the Guardsman. Screened by his costume trunk, he dons the Guardsman's uniform and steps out to reveal his true identity. However, the wife is unsurprised: she had seen through his disguise and is unimpressed with his ability as an actor, but says that she would like to continue with this game.

Although Molnár's *Liliom* is better known, indeed the most internationally successful Hungarian play, *The Guardsman* is a more polished piece. Its probing examination of a marriage is both witty and moving, and, like Schnitzler, Molnár masterfully portrays the ambiguities and tensions of a marriage where the wife is able to assert her individuality. The game played by wife and husband would find its echo in Pinter's *The *Lover*.

Guid Sisters, The. See SISTERS-IN-LAW, THE.

Guilty. See THÉRÈSE RAQUIN.

gute Mensch von Sezuan, Der. See GOOD PERSON OF SETZUAN, THE.

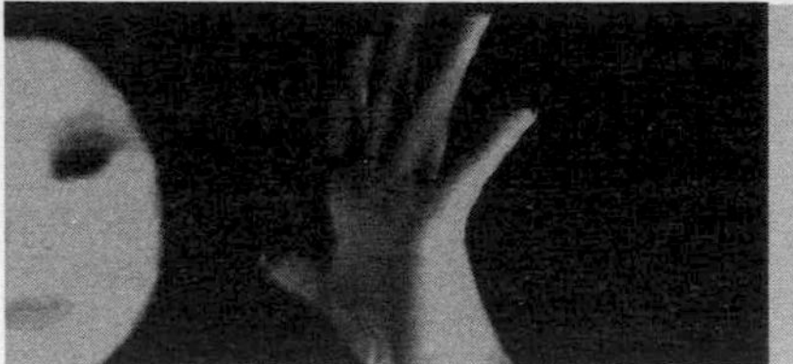

h

Hairy Ape, The

A: Eugene O'Neill **Pf**: 1922, New York **Pb**: 1922 **G**: Drama in 8 scenes **S**: Boiler room of a liner, New York street, prison, and zoo, 1920s **C**: 7m, 2f, extras

In the crew's cramped living quarters on a transatlantic liner, Yank considers himself superior to his fellow stokers, rejecting the Marxist-Christian beliefs of Long and the nostalgia for 'the good old days' of Paddy. His complacency is shattered by Mildred Douglas, a rich heiress travelling with her aunt. Having an interest in social work, she inspects the boiler room and faints in alarm at seeing Yank, who appears to her as a 'hairy ape'. Swearing revenge, he takes Long to Fifth Avenue, where he harangues a crowd of New York socialites leaving church. He is arrested and sent to prison where he learns of the IWW (the left-wing International Workers of the World). He is eager to help the cause by blowing up the Douglas Steel Works, but is thrown out as 'a brainless ape'. Visiting the zoo, he greets a gorilla as a kindred spirit. He forces his way into the cage, tries to embrace the gorilla, and is crushed to death. The gorilla leaves Yank dying in the cage, while the zoo monkeys chatter. As the stage direction comments: '*perhaps the Hairy Ape at last belongs*'.

In this extraordinary parable for our times, O'Neill in a series of Expressionistic 'stations' explores the alienation of the individual in a world of technology and capital. Having lost the animal's harmony with nature, humankind has failed to find a spiritual harmony with the world. 'Man', writes O'Neill, is now engaged in a struggle 'with himself, his own past, his attempt "to belong"'. Peter Stein directed the play spectacularly in 1987.

Hamlet (*The Tragicall Historie of Hamlet, Prince of Denmarke*)

A: William Shakespeare **Pf**: *c.*1599–1601, London **Pb**: 1603 (1st quarto), 1604 (2nd quarto), 1623 **G**: Trag. in 5 acts; blank verse and prose **S**: Elsinore and environs, Denmark, 10th c. **C**: 26m, 2f, extras

On learning of the death of his father, the King of Denmark, Hamlet returns to Elsinore from Germany, where he has been studying, only to discover that his uncle Claudius is already on the throne and has married Hamlet's mother Gertrude. The ghost of Hamlet's father reveals that he was murdered by Claudius. Distraught at this heinous crime and at his mother's infidelity, Hamlet swears revenge. He repulses Ophelia, whom he had been wooing, and behaves with suspicion towards all except his old friend Horatio. When travelling players come to the court, he arranges for them to re-enact the murder of his father. Claudius, overwhelmed by guilt, storms out of the play and goes to pray, offering Hamlet an easy target for his revenge. But Hamlet cannot bring himself to kill Claudius while he is praying for forgiveness. Instead Hamlet confronts his mother in her bedroom. Hearing a movement from Ophelia's father Polonius, who is secretly eavesdropping, Hamlet runs him through with a sword. Claudius arranges for Hamlet's deportation to England with orders that he should be executed there. However, Hamlet escapes and returns to Denmark. Meanwhile Ophelia has lost her sanity and has drowned herself. In pain at her death, Hamlet leaps into her grave to confront Ophelia's brother Laertes. It is resolved that they shall fight a duel. Claudius plots with Laertes to poison his foil and to prepare a poisoned chalice to make certain of Hamlet's death. In the duel Hamlet is hit with the poisoned foil, Laertes is also fatally wounded, Gertrude drinks from the poisoned cup, and Hamlet, learning of Claudius's plot, stabs Claudius and forces him to drink the poison. On to this scene of death comes the victorious Norwegian Fortinbras, who will assume rule in Denmark.

Probably both the most famous, most-quoted play and the one containing the most sought-after title role of world theatre, *Hamlet* was based on a story in the *Historia Danica* by Saxo Grammaticus and on a lost *Hamlet* play of 1589, probably by Kyd. The long and complex action, about which T. S. Eliot observed that 'there is too much plot for the play', contains political intrigue, exciting physical action, humour, and a fascinating psychological study of the protagonist. Some interpreters of the role, faced with the task of playing a hero whose major feature paradoxically is that he finds it hard to be 'heroic' and carry out the revenge that he has been ordered to commit, have emphasized Hamlet's melancholia. Post-Freud, as in Olivier's famous portrayal (seen in his 1948 film version), Hamlet's character was interpreted in the light of the 'Oedipus complex'. A more recent view is to regard Hamlet as a young intellectual, whose eyes have been opened to progressive thought, struggling with the atavistic codes of the Danish court, just as Shakespeare and his more enlightened contemporaries found themselves on the cusp between medieval superstition and Renaissance enlightenment. Each age has come to its own understanding of this complex play, and there have been many attempts to refashion the original, including a comic treatment in a working-class Jewish setting, *The Hamlet of Stepney Green* (1958) by Bernard Kops. Two of the most inventive treatments of recent years have been Stoppard's **Rosencrantz and Guildenstern Are Dead* and Müller's **Hamletmachine*.

Hamletmachine (*Hamletmaschine*)

A: Heiner Müller **Pf:** 1979, Paris; 1979, Essen **Pb:** 1977 **Tr:** 1984 **G:** Drama in 1 act (5 scenes); German and some English prose and verse **S:** Indeterminate place and period **C:** 1m, 1f, extras

(1) *Family Scrapbook*. Hamlet recalls his father's funeral procession, which he stopped so that he could cut off chunks of his father's flesh to distribute for the mourners to eat, while his mother and uncle had sex on the coffin. He greets Horatio, and confesses his love–hate for his mother: 'A mother's womb is not a one-way street.' (2) *The Europe of Women*. Ophelia rejects her suicide and rebels against male oppression. (3) *Scherzo*. In the university of the dead, Claudius and Ophelia emerge from a coffin. Hamlet dresses in Ophelia's clothes, poses as a whore, and dances with Horatio. (4) *Pest in Buda/Battle for Greenland*. Hamlet has given up his role. He envisages a violent popular revolt which is crushed: 'the hope has not been fulfilled'. All that remains is the 'nausea' of television. Marx, Lenin, and Mao preach revolution, but Hamlet splits open their heads with an axe. (5) While two men wrap white gauze round Ophelia in a wheelchair, she rejects 'the happiness of submission' and threatens vengeance: 'When she walks through your bedrooms carrying butcher knives you'll know the truth.'

This postmodernist treatment of **Hamlet* was the distillation of a 200-page play, which East German Müller wrote about a young man rebelling against Communist oppression. The present text, what Müller called 'the shrunken head of the Hamlet tragedy', is barely penetrable, its themes of political unrest, neurotic obsessions, and female emancipation being communicated in obliquely powerful poetic language and strikingly surreal theatrical images. Robert Wilson staged *Hamletmachine* in 1986.

Handcuffs. See THE DONNELLYS, THE.

Hands Around. See RONDE, LA.

Hangman, The (*Bödeln*)

A: Pär Lagerkvist **Pf:** 1934, Bergen and Stockholm **Pb:** 1946 **Tr:** 1966 **G:** Drama in 1 act;

Swedish prose S: Medieval tavern and 20th c. nightclub C: 12m, 4f, extras

In a medieval tavern, where the guests drink raucously and the tales they tell are often acted out, the gigantic Hangman sits silently and alone, wearing a blood-red robe. A carpenter tells how the Hangman saved a doomed boy, and all agree that the Hangman is 'good sometimes, too': he always asks the victim's pardon before executing them. The story is also told of the Hangman's marriage to a girl he could not bear to hang. However, his bride strangled their child, and he had to hang her after all. Suddenly the tavern is transformed into a modern nightclub, with smartly dressed customers eating, drinking and dancing to jazz, played by a group of black musicians. Excited by the presence of the Hangman, the guests salute him with 'Heil!', wonder about his sexual prowess, and agree that his violence helps to keep order. They throw out some importunate beggars, except a radiant woman beggar who seats herself beside the Hangman. The customers curse at the black musicians, hitting and shooting some so that they will play faster, and then dance in a frenzy of sex and violence. At last the Hangman speaks. He tells his listeners that he has done what they have asked of him, destroying humanity (represented by the woman beside him) and even took the life of Christ. The woman tries to comfort him, saying that she will wait for him, but he goes out to continue his duties.

This Expressionistic warning about the dangers of Fascism was the most successful and controversial Scandinavian play of the inter-war years. While immensely theatrical, its symbolism now seems rather heavy-handed.

Hang of the Gaol, The

A: Howard Barker **Pf**: 1978, London **Pb**: 1982 G: Pol. com. in 2 acts S: Burnt-out shell of Middenhurst Gaol, the moors, and the Coopers' drawing room, 1970s C: 9m, 3f

The historic Middenhurst Gaol has burned down to the distress of the Governor, Colonel Cooper. Two gay fire inspectors and Home Secretary Stagg arrive to inspect the damage. Three ministry officials, Scottish ex-Communist George Jardine, the long-suffering Elizabeth Matheson, whom Jardine desires, and junior civil servant Barry Ponting, conduct an inquiry into the fire. The self-effacing Ponting surprises himself by bullying one of the prison officers into admitting that there was a discipline problem after Cooper had introduced reforms. Cooper, a former officer responsible for suppressing rebels in the Colonies, is now distraught to find himself blamed. Although an eccentric and highly intelligent killer called Turk willingly claims to have started the fire, his attempt at arson failed. The evidence begins to point to Cooper, the failed idealist, as the arsonist, but the session is interrupted when Cooper's wife Jane enters, bleeding from a head wound inflicted by Turk. Stagg, concerned to avoid a scandal before an impending election, persuades Jardine in exchange for a knighthood to blame Turk for the fire and exonerate Cooper.

Barker's savagely comic genius uses the metaphor of a burnt-out jail for contemporary Britain, which he regards as being in a similar state of collapse. The socialist Stagg manages to corrupt the vicious but principled Jardine with his pragmatism: 'the party-system' gives most people 'the impression it is freedom.... We did not choose the system, but we have got to get the hang of it.' Jardine's falsified report about the fire shows that he has got 'the hang of the gaol'.

Happy Days

A: Samuel Beckett **Pf**: 1961, New York **Pb**: 1961 G: Drama in 2 acts S: A mound of sand, the future C: 1m, 1f

Winnie, a buxom blonde of about 50, is sleeping, buried in a mound up to her breasts. When a bell rings, she happily sets about starting her daily routine. Chattering gaily, she pulls objects out of her handbag, including a revolver, brushes her teeth and hair, drinks medicine, and tosses the bottle away. This lands on her husband Willie, who appears from behind the mound. He starts to read items out of an old newspaper and then studies a pornographic postcard, which Winnie insists on seeing and then throws away in disgust.

Willie retreats into a hole to escape from the 'hellish heat', and Winnie erects her parasol, which soon bursts into flames. She reminisces about the past, including a meeting with a couple named Shower or Cooker. Declaring this to have been another happy day, Winnie settles herself for sleep. When she is next woken by the bell, she is buried up to her neck. Although she cannot even move her head, she continues to chatter away gaily. Willie suddenly appears, 'dressed to kill' in morning coat and top hat. Winnie is delighted, as he crawls towards her (and towards the revolver). The bell rings, and they stare at each other as the curtain falls.

As in **Endgame*, it appears that we are in some post-nuclear holocaust future, in which there is constant blazing light, and days are marked by the ringing of a bell. The difference is that, while Hamm and Clov suffer from their awareness of the end of human civilization, Winnie remains buoyantly optimistic about her dreadful existence, which makes the play both funnier and more poignant.

Harvey

AT: *The Pooka* **A**: Mary Chase **Pf**: 1944, New York **Pb**: 1950 **G**: Com. in 3 acts **S**: Dowd's mansion and Chumley's Rest asylum, USA, 1940s **C**: 6m, 6f

Veta Louise Simmons, an empty-headed socialite, lives with her daughter Myrtle Mae, a plain, supercilious woman, in their brother's home. Although their brother Elwood P. Dowd is wise and good-natured, he is a social embarrassment, because his constant drinking has led him to believe that he is accompanied everywhere by Harvey, an invisible giant white rabbit. When Elwood upsets the rich and well-connected Mrs Ethel Chauvenet by introducing Harvey to her, Myrtle decides it is time to lock her uncle away. However, when they arrive at the asylum, it is Myrtle who is assumed to be insane. The confusion is settled, although the matter becomes complicated when the head doctor starts to believe in Harvey too. When Veta is told by a taxi driver how insufferable patients become after they have been cured in the home, she relents, preferring her kindly brother as he is. Elwood is allowed to return home, bringing Harvey with him.

Often treated as merely escapist, this hugely successful comedy, which has been filmed and often revived, contains a serious theme. Its original title *The Pooka*, a Celtic word for a spirit in animal form, points to Chase's belief that human nature is impoverished without the enjoyment of harmless fantasies. That the part of Elwood was played by the recovering alcoholic Frank Fay added to the poignancy of the premiere.

Haunted, The. See MOURNING BECOMES ELECTRA.

Haunted Inn, The (*Di Puste Kretshme*)

AT: *The Idle Inn* **A**: Pere(t)z Hirs(c)hbein **Pf**: 1912, New York **Pb**: 1914 **Tr**: No pub. translation known **G**: Romantic com. in 4 acts; Yiddish prose **S**: Russian farmhouse and environs, *c.*1910 **C**: 3m, 1f, extras

Meta is the daughter of a provincial horse trader, who has arranged for her to marry an unattractive individual, although she is in love with her tearaway cousin Itsik. Her father's wedding gift is an abandoned inn, which is supposed to be haunted. At the wedding, Itsik and Meta run away together, and the distraught father assumes that some passing merchants who have joined the wedding feast are in fact phantoms who have spirited Meta away. When Itsik and Meta fall out with each other, she returns home to her father. Following her, Itsik discovers that her superstitious father has set fire to the inn to rid it of its evil spirits and prevent further abductions. In the conflagration, both the inn and the father's house are burnt to the ground, and Meta, now despairing over the loss of Itsik, threatens to throw herself in the flames. Itsik pulls her back and carries her off, declaring that he will never let her go.

Born in Russia, Hirshbein was prominent in developing Yiddish theatre, touring his own group through Russia 1908–10, until Tsarist oppression drove him into exile. In New York he made a major contribution to providing theatre for the growing Jewish immigrant community, and *The Haunted Inn* inaugurated Reicher's Jewish Art Theatre in New York in

1919, being later transferred in an English version to Broadway. This comedy is a loving and sentimental recreation of Hirshbein's homeland, where superstition is rife but the young peasants are vigorous and healthy.

Hauptmann von Köpenick, Der. See CAPTAIN OF KÖPENICK, THE.

Haute Surveillance. See DEATHWATCH.

Hayavadana

A: Girish Karnad **Pf**: 1972, Madras **Pb**: 1971 **Tr**: 1972 **G**: Drama in 2 acts; Kannada prose and songs **S**: City of Dharmapura, mythical past **C**: 4m, 2f, 1 child, 2 dolls, chorus, musicians

Before the main play can get under way, Bhagavata the narrator is interrupted by Hayavadana, a man born with a horse's head, who has tried everywhere to become a complete being. Bhagavata sends him to seek help from the priestess Kali. The story begins: the clever poet Devadatta is close friends with the powerful athlete Kapila. Devadatta confesses to his friend that he has fallen in love with a beautiful young girl named Padmini and sends his friend to seek her out. Kapila is overwhelmed by her beauty. Devadatta and Padmini marry, but she also grows close to Kapila. All three go on a journey, and when Devadatta becomes aware how much Padmini is attracted to Kapila's physique, he cuts off his head. Kapila promptly decapitates himself to follow his friend. Kali allows Padmini to replace their heads and restore them to life, but in her confusion Padmini transposes the two heads. At first, it seems as though Padmini has created the perfect husband. However, gradually Devadatta both loses the strength in his body and stops writing poetry, and two dolls parody Devadatta and Padmini's declining marriage. Kapila's new body grows strong again but is haunted by his friend's memories of embracing Padmini. Finally, the two friends decide matters by fighting a duel in which both die. Padmini commits *satī* (suttee). Hayavadana returns from his pilgrimage, content with being a complete horse.

Framed by the title figure's story, *Hayavadana* was derived from an ancient Sanskrit story and from Thomas Mann's retelling of it. Though potentially tragic, the events are performed with great wit and a sense of the absurd, and reflect an amusing scepticism about the importance of identity, urging instead an acceptance of each individual in his or her own right.

Hay Fever

A: Noël Coward **Pf**: 1925, London **Pb**: 1925 **G**: Com. in 3 acts **S**: The Blisses' home on the Thames, 1920s **C**: 4m, 5f

David Bliss, a writer of best-selling romantic novels, lives in an elegant country house in Cookham with his ex-actress wife Judith, his 19-year-old daughter Sorel, and his artist son David. Unknown to the others, each has invited a guest to the house for the weekend. The guests duly arrive to find themselves initially ignored then treated with scant attention. David is busy finishing his latest novel, Judith is preoccupied with thoughts of making a comeback in her great success *Love's Whirlwind*, and Clara the housekeeper grumbles about the extra work the arrival of the guests has occasioned. Sorel has invited Richard Greatham, a rather stiff older diplomat; David's guest is an empty-headed adoring flapper Jackie Coryton. Young Sandy Tyrell comes to worship Judith, and Mrs Myra Arundel, a predatory older woman, has designs on Simon. After dinner the family humiliate their guests with a witty word game and then begin to play at romantic entanglements, often quoting from *Love's Whirlwind*. In the process, Judith appears to be ending her marriage so that she can elope with Richard, while David apparently forms a liaison with Myra. Meanwhile, Sorel and Sandy begin kissing, and Simon declares that he will marry Jackie. The following morning, after a dreadful breakfast, the guests make their getaway, while the Blisses settle down to hear David's last chapter.

Coward's first major comic success still entertains audiences today. Its delightfully eccentric family that gives their guests such a confusing and distressing time may live in an English country house, but the theme is as old as Roman comedy: self-seeking and rather silly people, attracted by the Blisses' fame and sexual attraction, get their just rewards when they find themselves hopelessly out of their depth.

He and She

AT: *The Herfords* A: Rachel Crothers Pf: 1911, Poughkeepsie, NY Pb: 1917; rev. 1925 G: Drama in 3 acts S: The Herfords' home, USA, *c*.1910 C: 3m, 5f

Ann and Tom Herford are both sculptors, who have been married for 17 years. Separately, they enter a competition for a frieze design, and despite Tom regarding himself as the better artist, Ann wins the $100,000 prize, while Tom comes second. At first, Tom seems delighted at his wife's success but soon begins to question aggressively how she will be able to attend to her household duties if she is to fulfil this commission. Their teenage daughter Millicent arrives unexpectedly from her boarding school to announce that she is engaged to the school chauffeur. She had fallen in love with him when her mother's engagement in artistic activities forced her to spend her vacations at school. Fearing the break-up of her marriage and determined to devote herself more to her daughter to dissuade her from her proposed marriage, Ann reluctantly gives up the commission in favour of Tom. In a parallel plot, Tom's assistant Keith renounces the love of an ambitious woman in favour of Tom's domesticated sister Daisy.

Crothers was not only the most successful woman playwright of early 20th-century America, but distinguished herself also as one of the few female theatre directors of the period. The problems facing a gifted career woman were therefore familiar to her, and, although some critics thought that *He and She* implied that a woman's place was in the home, Ann Herford's sacrifice, while hardly militant, is shown to be highly problematic.

Heartbreak House

A: George Bernard Shaw W: 1913–19 Pf: 1920, New York Pb: 1919 G: Drama in 3 acts S: Shotover's home, England, the future C: 6m, 4f

Captain Shotover, an eccentric 88-year-old inventor, lives in the country with his daughter Hesione Hushabye and her family. Various visitors arrive: the young Ellie Dunn, destined to marry a rich industrialist, 'Boss' Mangan, only because he helped her inept idealistic father Mazzini Dunn; Lady Ariadne Utterword, Hesione's sister, and her weak husband Randall. Hesione's feckless husband Hector flirts with both Ellie and Lady Utterword. When Mangan falls in love with Hesione, he tells Ellie that she need not marry him, since he actually ruined rather than helped her father. However, she looks forward to a life of financial security, even though Shotover warns her against seeking material comforts. A burglar is caught and persuades everyone to contribute to a collection to finance his reform. Ellie is now completely in Shotover's spell and would gladly marry him but for his Caribbean wife. When an air raid begins, everyone awaits the onslaught with excitement. A bomb falls, but it kills only Mangan and the burglar, who were sheltering in Shotover's store of dynamite.

Claiming that his play was written in 'the Russian manner', Shaw wrote the most enigmatic of his plays in a realistic setting, imitating some of the elements of Chekhov: the gathering of an idle community in a country house, where they talk, flirt, eat, fall in and out of love, and make vague pronouncements about their future. The only genuinely engaged individual is Shotover, to some extent based on Shaw himself, who may appear mad but who recognizes that humanity will need to navigate carefully if it is to avoid apocalyptic destruction from aerial warfare.

Heart's Desire. See BLUE HEART.

Heather Field, The

A: Edward Martyn Pf: 1899, Dublin Pb: 1899 G: Trag. in 3 acts S: Tyrrell's house, west coast of Ireland, 1890 C: 6m, 2f, 1 child (m)

Carden Tyrrell, a west of Ireland landlord, is an idealist who wants to transform a heather field on his estate into productive land. His beautiful wife Grace, whom he now regrets marrying, is alarmed at the expense and effort Tyrrell is devoting to his obsessive task. As he plunges the estate deeper into debt, Tyrrell confesses to his younger brother Miles, a law student, that he sometimes finds it difficult to distinguish between domestic reality and his dream, and tells his wife that the 'simple barren prose' of her mind is driving him mad. Grace summons two doctors on the pretext that her son Kit is ill, and seeks support from her neighbours, Lord and Lady Shrule. Tyrrell refuses to be dissuaded from his project and tells the doctors that, when he is out in the field, he hears 'past ecstasies of sound'. The doctors are about to certify Tyrrell, but he is saved by the intervention of his friend Barry Ussher, who begs Grace to win her husband over with gentleness. Miles arrives with news that Tyrrell's debts are being called in and that he will lose the estate. Clinging still to the hope of the transformed heather field, he is driven to despair when his son brings home from there a bunch of heather buds: 'The wild heath has broken out again in the heather field.' His mind unhinged, Tyrrell has visions of beauty at last.

Strongly influenced by Ibsen (Tyrrell's final madness is reminiscent of **Ghosts*), this play has neither the depth of characterization nor the skilful dialogue of the Norwegian playwright. It is, however, significant as being the first major play of the Irish literary revival and was highly praised by Yeats, who with Martyn and George Moore went on to found the Abbey Theatre.

Hecuba (*Hekabe*)

AT: *Hecabe* **A:** Euripides **Pf:** *c.*424 BC, Athens? **Tr:** 1728 **G:** Greek trag. in verse **S:** Before Agamemnon's tent on the Thracian shore, after the Trojan War **C:** 5m, 3f, extras, chorus (f)

Hecuba, former Queen of Troy, is now the slave of Odysseus. The Greeks are waiting to set sail for home, when the ghost of their slain hero Achilles demands the sacrifice of Hecuba's daughter. Hecuba reminds Odysseus that she once saved his life, when he came as a spy to Troy. Odysseus promises to spare Hecuba her own life, but is bound by duty to sacrifice her daughter, who goes bravely to her death. As Hecuba is preparing to bury her daughter, servants carry in the body of her youngest son, Polydorus, treacherously murdered by Polymestor, King of Thrace. Hecuba begs Agamemnon to fetch Polymestor to the Trojan women's camp. The unsuspecting Polymestor pretends that Polydorus is alive and well, and the furious Hecuba and her women tear out Polymestor's eyes and murder his two sons. Agamemnon is called on to judge whether Hecuba's act was justified, and because Polymestor the barbarian had offended against the laws of hospitality by killing the guest entrusted to him, he must stand condemned. The blind Polymestor in revenge foretells the death of Hecuba at sea, and the murder of Cassandra in Greece. Agamemnon prepares joyfully to sail for home, while Hecuba buries her two dead children.

Like **Andromache*, *Hecuba* falls into two distinct halves: first the sacrifice of Hecuba's daughter, then the revenge taken on Polymestor. The long *agon* or dispute, in which Hecuba and Polymestor argue the justice of their behaviour, would have challenged Euripides' audience, already embroiled in the Peloponnesian War for some seven years, to reflect on the effects of war and the cyclical nature of revenge, as they were forced to do again in Euripides' **Trojan Women*. Agamemnon's optimistic departure for home, where he was to be murdered himself, was perhaps an ironic comment on the misplaced optimism of Athens in its struggle with Sparta. A translation by Frank McGuinness was successfully performed in London in 2004.

Hedda Gabler

A: Henrik Ibsen **Pf:** 1891, Munich **Pb:** 1890 **Tr:** 1891 **G:** Trag. in 4 acts; Norwegian prose **S:** Tesman's home, Norway, 1880s **C:** 3m, 4f

Hedda Gabler has married the boring academic Jørgen Tesman. After a long honeymoon the now pregnant Hedda looks forward to a life of tedium, relieved only by visits from a family friend, Judge Brack. Another surprise visitor is Ejlert Løvborg, with whom she was formerly very close. Through the efforts of Hedda's friend Thea Elvsted, the dissolute Løvborg has become a reformed character and has written an amazing thesis, which will secure the professorship sought by Tesman. When invited out to a male gathering, Løvborg refuses, until challenged by Hedda to celebrate his new-found strength. However, he succumbs to alcohol and in his drunken state loses his manuscript. When it is found, Hedda deliberately burns it, burning his and Thea's 'child'. She gives the desperate Løvborg one of her father's pistols, so that he will commit a beautiful suicide. He shoots himself in the stomach, and there is the threat of a scandal when Hedda's pistol is found. Judge Brack is prepared to conceal the evidence if Hedda will offer him sexual favours. While Tesman and Thea try to reconstruct the thesis from Løvborg's notes, Hedda shoots herself.

In contrast with most of Ibsen's women characters, who tend to be long-suffering and more capable than his men, he here creates one of the most destructive female characters since Lady Macbeth. Hedda, who continues to use her maiden name and whose decision to marry Tesman is never satisfactorily explained, thrills to her power over Løvborg, urging him to a beautiful death, but succeeding only in creating an act that is 'ludicrous and despicable'. Her own death is unexpected; it would be perhaps a more tragic outcome if she had to live on with Tesman.

Hegge Plays, The. See N-TOWN CYCLE OF MYSTERY PLAYS, THE.

Heidi Chronicles, The

A: Wendy Wasserstein Pf: 1988, Seattle (workshop production); 1988, New York Pb: 1990 G: Com. in 2 acts S: New York, 1977–89; Chicago, 1965, 1974; Manchester, New Hampshire, 1968; Ann Arbor, Michigan, 1970 C: 7m, 12f

1989: Heidi Holland lectures on neglected women painters at Columbia University, New York. 1965: Heidi meets clever and charming Peter Padrone at a high-school dance. 1968: Heidi comes to New Hampshire to canvass on behalf of Eugene McCarthy and is seduced by charismatic but arrogant Scoop Rosenbaum. 1970: Heidi attends a feminist group in Ann Arbor and admits that she is in the thrall of Scoop while recognizing that Peter can offer her more. 1974: Heidi pickets the Chicago Art Institute for exhibiting so few women artists. Peter, now an intern at a Chicago hospital, reveals that he is gay. 1977: Scoop, a lawyer about to start a magazine, marries Lisa, an ugly, boring, but devoted girl, and admits that he could not marry Heidi, because she wants 'Self-fulfillment. Self-determination. Self-exaggeration'. 1980: Reagan has been elected president, John Lennon has been shot, and the women gather for a baby-shower for Lisa, whose husband Scoop is having an affair. 1982: Heidi, Peter, and Scoop are interviewed on television, and Heidi is hardly allowed to speak. 1984: Heidi and her old schoolfriend Susan compare notes about being a modern woman. Heidi is asked to write a sitcom about single women, 'unhappy, unfulfilled, frightened of growing old alone'. Heidi refuses. 1986: Heidi recognizes that she feels no solidarity with other women: 'I feel stranded.' 1987: Heidi says goodbye to Peter before moving to Minnesota. 1989: Heidi adopts a Panamanian baby and returns to New York.

Winner of both the Pulitzer Prize and the Tony Award, *The Heidi Chronicles* offers an amusing and episodic account of the development of feminist beliefs in one woman's life. It honestly acknowledges setbacks and disillusionment, but finally shows Heidi able to 'fulfil her potential' by adopting an unwanted child and by successfully promoting the work of women artists.

heilige Johanna der Schlachthöfe, Die. See ST JOAN OF THE STOCKYARDS.

Hekabe. See HECUBA.

Helen (*Helene; Helena*)

A: Euripides Pf: *c.*412 BC, Athens? Tr: 1782 G: Greek drama in verse S: Before the palace of the King of Egypt, after the Trojan War C: 7m, 3f, extras, chorus (f)

Helen reveals that her adulterous reputation is undeserved. She is living chastely in Egypt, where she was transported while a 'phantom Helen' was abducted by Paris to Troy. She longs to see her husband Menelaus again, but learns that he has been shipwrecked on his way home from Troy. The Chorus persuades Helen to test the truth of the rumour of Menelaus' death by consulting the oracle. No sooner has Helen been assured that her husband is still alive, than he arrives at the palace. However, as he is in rags, the Portress refuses him entrance, since no Greek may approach 'Zeus' daughter Helen'. Menelaus wonders how Helen can be both the woman he has just left in a cave by the seashore and also live in this royal palace. When Helen and Menelaus eventually meet, she refuses to believe that this ragged man is her husband, while he, after all the suffering at Troy, cannot accept that Helen now stands before him, an innocent victim. Finally, there is a joyful reconciliation, and the phantom Helen disappears. Helen and Menelaus then engage the help of the prophetess to make good their escape. Castor and Polydeuces appear to speed them on their way.

Although *Helen* is a light-hearted and rather fantastic drama, with typical comic confusion of identities and a happy ending, it contains much more serious elements. To recognize how easily the gods can mislead mortals with regard to appearance and reality is a frightening insight. In particular, the Greeks have fought at Troy for ten bitter years, only to win back a phantom. In this sense, *Helen* stands as a warning to the Athenians of the danger of prosecuting the Peloponnesian War in pursuit of illusory advantage. The story was used by Hofmannsthal in *The Egyptian Helen* (1928), scored as an opera by Richard Strauss, but here Menelaus believes the Trojan Helen to be a phantom only because he has drunk a potion of lotus juice.

Henry IV (*Enrico IV*)

AT: *The Emperor* **A:** Luigi Pirandello **Pf:** 1922, Milan **Pb:** 1922 **Tr:** 1922 **G:** Trag. in 3 acts; Italian prose **S:** Villa in Umbria, 1920s **C:** 11m, 2f

What appears to be the throne room of Henry IV, the 11th-century Holy Roman Emperor, is in fact a private asylum for a nobleman. Many years previously he had taken part in a pageant, riding beside Matilda Spina, whom he loved. He was costumed as Henry IV and she as the historical Matilda, friend to Henry's arch-enemy Pope Gregory VII. The nobleman was thrown from his horse, hit his head, and, on recovering consciousness, believed he really was Henry IV. Matilda now visits him, accompanied by her lover Baron Belcredi, her daughter Frida with her fiancé, and a self-regarding Doctor, who hopes to cure 'Henry'. Henry IV appears, treating his visitors as historical figures, identifying Belcredi as a clerical enemy, and pleading with Matilda to intercede for him to the Pope. Henry then unmasks himself as sane to his servants, saying that he chooses to live in the permanence of historical time rather than in the flux of the present. The Doctor wants to give Henry a shock that will restore his sanity: Frida stands costumed as her mother in the place where a portrait of Matilda has been hanging. When she speaks to Henry, he momentarily believes that he is insane then admits to his visitors that he lives on in the asylum by choice. He reveals that Belcredi startled his horse deliberately and castigates Matilda for not yielding to his love. Seizing Frida in his arms, he claims the young woman that he lost. When Belcredi intervenes, Henry kills him with his sword. Now there can be no way back; the nobleman is sentenced to life in his historical role.

As with **Six Characters in Search of an Author* Pirandello explores the relationship between appearance and reality, the mask and the face, permanence and flux. Even when supposedly mad, Henry's distracted mutterings are coded messages to Matilda, revealing his love and his anguish at the presence of Belcredi. Thus, the play contains both challenging philosophy and psychological exploration, presented in a gripping theatrical format. A version of *Henry IV* by Tom Stoppard was performed in London in 2004.

Henry IV (Parts 1 and 2) (*The History of Henrie the Fourth; The Second Part of Henrie the Fourth*)

A: William Shakespeare **Pf:** (1) *c.*1596–7, London; (2) *c.*1597–8, London **Pb:** (1) 1598; (2) 1600 **G:** Hist. dramas, each in 5 acts; blank verse and prose **S:** England and Wales, 1401–13 **C:** (1) 19m, 3f, extras; (2) 38m, 4f, extras

Part 1. Despite Henry's hopes for stability in his kingdom, England is threatened on all sides. The Welshman Owen Glendower has defeated an English army. Henry 'Hotspur' Percy has repelled a Scottish invasion, but now joins forces with the Welsh and with his father, the Earl of Northumberland, to rise up against Henry. Henry has domestic concerns too: his son, Prince Hal, spends most of his time in the company of an old reprobate, Sir John Falstaff, and even gets involved in criminal activities with him. However, at the Battle of Shrewsbury between Henry and the rebels, Hal kills Hotspur in face-to-face combat. The rebels are defeated, but peace has not been achieved. *Part 2.* The remaining rebels in the north seek to parley with the royal forces, led by Prince John. They agree to disperse their army with the promise that their grievances will be redressed, but are then seized and executed. Meanwhile in London, Henry is dying. He has learned of the death of Glendower, and now of the defeat of the northern rebels. He and Hal are finally fully reconciled. Meanwhile, Falstaff, who has been recruiting men in the country, learns of Henry's death and rushes back to London to claim favours from Prince Hal. However, the newly crowned Henry V publicly rejects Falstaff.

Henry IV, mainly based on Holinshed's *Chronicles*, is on one level a chronicle play, picking its way dexterously through a tumultuous period of British history, always with the underlying recognition that Henry IV is a usurper and therefore can hardly hope that his nation can live in peace. On another level, the play traces the growth of Hal from irresponsible playboy to become the most heroic figure of Shakespeare's history plays in **Henry V*. To depict this, Shakespeare created one of the greatest comic figures of all time: Falstaff, based on the *miles gloriosus* character, is so much larger than life that, although strictly only an element of the sub-plot, he threatens to dominate the whole piece, and his rejection by Hal can too easily be seen as betrayal by a young prig than as an essential stage in the assumption of kingship.

Henry V (*The Chronicle History of Henry the fift*)

A: William Shakespeare **Pf:** *c.*1598–9, London **Pb:** 1623 ('bad' 1st quarto, 1600) **G:** Hist. drama in 5 acts; blank verse and prose **S:** England and France, 1413–20 **C:** 38m, 4f, extras

The young Henry V makes a legally founded claim to the throne of France. When the French respond with an impertinent gift of tennis balls, Henry resolves to invade France. Before embarking, he arrests three traitors and has them executed. The English army, both common men and officers, and the French court are seen preparing for battle. After gallantly taking Harfleur, Henry's vastly outnumbered forces march towards a confrontation with the French at Agincourt. On the eve of battle, Henry, disguised as a common soldier, goes amongst his troops. The bloody battle is fought, and the English triumph. To seal his victory and the right to the throne when the French king dies, Henry woos and wins the French princess Katharine.

The main thrust of *Henry V* is a patriotic celebration of the valour and determination of the British (not only English, but also Scots, Welsh, and Irish soldiers are portrayed with affection) under the leadership of 'the mirror of all Christian kings'. This heroic portrayal characterized Laurence Olivier's film treatment of 1944, which served as a rallying cry to the beleaguered British in the Second World War. However, Shakespeare is not presenting an uncomplicated historical pageant: on the eve of Agincourt, Henry is revealed to be full of self-doubt, and his slaughter of the French prisoners is a possibly necessary but nevertheless brutal act. While celebrating the glorious victory, Shakespeare also recognizes the ugliness of warfare. The Chorus's apology for attempting to present a massive battle 'Within this wooden O' may suggest that Shakespeare was chafing at the limitations of Elizabethan staging; or he may have been ironically celebrating the power of the human imagination.

Henry VI (Parts 1, 2, and 3) (*The First part of King Henry the Sixt; The First part of the Contention betwixt the two famous houses*

of Yorke and Lancaster; The true Tragedie of Richard Duke of Yorke, and the death of good King Henrie the Sixt)

A: William Shakespeare **Pf:** *c.*1589–92, London **Pb:** 1623 (Parts 2 and 3 as 'bad' 1st quartos, 1594–5) **G:** Hist. dramas, each in 5 acts; blank verse, some prose in Part 2 **S:** England and France, 1422–71 **C:** (1) 31m, 3f, extras; (2) 40m, 4f, extras; (3) 36m, 3f, extras

Part 1. England is weakened by the squabbling of the English nobles, and the conquests of the recently deceased Henry V are lost in France. The young King Henry VI, a Lancastrian, tries in vain to reconcile the hostile parties. Meanwhile, in France, Joan la Pucelle (Joan of Arc) leads the French to victory, and is defeated only when the English army at last unites. Margaret of Anjou is captured and is taken to become the English queen. *Part 2.* Henry marries Margaret, but the generous dowry of French lands angers his uncle Gloucester, eventually leading to his arrest and death in prison. Richard, Duke of York incites Jack Cade to lead a people's rebellion against Henry, but the fickle mob turns on their leader, and the revolt fails. Instead, York leads his own forces against Henry, who is defeated at the Battle of St Albans, the first of the Wars of the Roses. *Part 3.* Since York is in control of Parliament, Henry attempts to bribe him to win his support, but Queen Margaret leads a victorious army against York near Wakefield. York is put to death, but Margaret's triumph is short-lived. York's ally, Warwick, leads a counter-attack near Towton, defeating the Lancastrians. Edward, the son of York, is proclaimed king, and his brothers made dukes of Gloucester and Clarence. Henry is swept back to power for a brief period, but, largely thanks to Richard Gloucester, Edward is restored to the throne after the Battle of Tewkesbury, and Richard murders Henry in the Tower of London. The trilogy ends with Edward on the throne, his new wife at his side, and Richard muttering of his own ambition to be king.

Henry VI is amongst the earliest of Shakespeare's works, certainly his first serious drama, and possibly not exclusively his own work. No one before him had attempted to dramatize history on this scale. He documents the tortuous and violent progress of the Wars of the Roses, leading to the less episodic and more focused work of **Richard III.* It is perhaps the sense of being unable to escape the savage twists of history in *Henry VI* that makes the arrival of Henry Richmond so welcome at the end of *Richard III* – a king neither weak like Henry nor evil like Richard. The trilogy (with *Richard III*) was played over three evenings by the RSC as *The Wars of the Roses* (1963), an adaptation by John Barton that has also been successfully performed abroad.

Henry VIII (*The Life of King Henry the Eight*)

AT: *All Is True* **A:** William Shakespeare and John Fletcher **Pf:** *c.*1612, London **Pb:** 1623 **G:** Hist. drama in 5 acts; blank verse and some prose **S:** London, Westminster, and Kimbolton, 1520–36 **C:** 35m, 4f, extras

Cardinal Wolsey, who is the most powerful man at the court of Henry VIII, orders the arrest of the supposed traitor, the Duke of Buckingham. He is tried, found guilty, and sent to his death. Wolsey now uses his influence to persuade the King to divorce his wife Katharine, in preparation for a marriage with a French princess. Archbishop Cranmer is sent to Rome to negotiate the divorce. Henry's fancy has been caught by the young Anne Bullen (Boleyn). They marry in private. Wolsey now falls into disfavour by complaining to the Pope about Henry's liaison with Anne and by accumulating colossal wealth. Wolsey is stripped of office and dies. Katharine, approaching her own death, forgives Wolsey. Cranmer is tried by the Catholic hierarchy but is exonerated by Henry. The play ends with the birth of Anne's daughter, the future Elizabeth I.

Critical opinion is divided over *Henry VIII.* It is often dismissed as a historical pageant, an occasional piece written in collaboration with Fletcher, concentrating several events over sixteen years of Henry's reign into weeks. Seen like this, *Henry VIII* breaks the pattern of Shakespeare's last plays by reverting to the long abandoned history plays of his youth. Others regard the play more highly, detecting in its action the powerful forces of history, and nostalgia for a world of absolute monarchy and Roman Catholic religious certainties, which contrasts with the confusions of the early 17th century.

Hepta epi Thēbas. See SEVEN AGAINST THEBES.

Heracles (*Herakles*)

AT: *The Madness of Heracles/Hercules (Furens)* A: Euripides **Pf:** *c.*415 BC, Athens? **Tr:** 1782 **G:** Greek trag. in verse **S:** Before the palace at Thebes, in the mythical past **C:** 6m, 2f, extras, chorus (m)

Amphitryon, the father of Heracles, fears that his son has died on his mission to fetch Cerberus from the underworld. This will allow Lycus, the King of Thebes, to take advantage of Heracles' demise to kill Heracles' wife and children, and Amphitryon himself. Lycus comes to justify his intended action: having killed Heracles' father-in-law Creon to seize the Theban throne, he does not want Heracles' sons to grow up and avenge their grandfather's murder. Unable to win mercy from the ruthless Lycus, Amphitryon and Heracles' wife Megara prepare themselves and the three boys for death. Heracles returns just in time to save them from the knife and to kill Lycus in the palace. Sent by the goddess Hera, Madness now makes Heracles insane. Soon after, a messenger reveals that, after killing Lycus, Heracles turned on his own sons and wife and slaughtered them all in a terrible bloodbath. Only Amphitryon survives to mourn the dead and despair over Heracles' insanity. Soon, however, Heracles awakes from his madness and is horrified to discover what he has done. Theseus, whom Heracles had saved from the underworld, persuades Heracles not to commit suicide, but to come with him to Athens to begin his penance.

Heracles has traditionally been regarded as one of Euripides' less powerful tragedies, because the action derives not so much from internal conflict as from external factors: the unrelieved wickedness of Lycus, and the violence of Heracles as the result of divine intervention. The play however offers an audience one of the most spectacular tableaux in Greek theatre: the *skene* opened to reveal the corpses of Megara and her sons soaked in blood and Heracles bound to a pillar. It is also one of the most sceptical of Euripides' tragedies, in which Heracles dismisses tales of the gods' adultery as 'poets' lamentable myths'. The only secure foundation for human existence appears to lie in friendship, as exemplified by Theseus' generous attitude towards Heracles. The story was retold by Seneca in his *Hercules Furens* (1st c. AD).

Herfords, The. See HE AND SHE.

Hernani

A: Victor Hugo **Pf:** 1830, Paris **Pb:** 1830 **Tr:** 1830 **G:** Trag. in 5 acts; French alexandrines **S:** Madrid and Aix-la-Chapelle (Aachen), 1519 **C:** 21m, 3f, extras

Hernani, his father murdered and dispossessed of his lands, has become a bandit leader, in love with the beautiful Doña Sol, who is due to marry her elderly guardian Ruy Gomez. She is also being courted by Don Carlos (Charles I of Spain). Hernani, although sworn to vengeance against the King, is sufficiently moved by Carlos's willingness to help him escape from Ruy Gomez that he spares the King's life. However, when he is later captured by Gomez, Gomez refuses to hand over Hernani, who begs to be allowed time to avenge himself on the King and swears that he will then surrender himself to death at Gomez's hands. In Aix-la-Chapelle Carlos is crowned Charles V, Holy Roman Emperor, and in his hour of triumph, pardons all his enemies, reinstating Hernani as Duke of Aragon and giving him Doña Sol's hand in marriage. Hernani and Doña Sol marry, but Gomez appears at the wedding demanding that Hernani fulfil his promise. He does so by stabbing himself and his bride. The despairing Ruy Gomez takes his own life.

In *Hernani* the 28-year-old Victor Hugo was trying to break free from the constraints of French neo-classicism. He removed the action from the rarefied atmosphere of a palace antechamber and sought to imbue his piece with historical colour, even setting Act 4 improbably in Charlemagne's tomb. When

Hernani came on stage and shook raindrops from his cloak, this injection of reality into the hermetically sealed world of French tragedy provoked a riot in the theatre. This powerful if melodramatic story of doomed lovers set a pattern for Romantic tragedy and was exploited by Verdi in his opera *Ernani* (1844).

Hero, The

A: Gilbert Emery **Pf**: 1921, New York **Pb**: *c.*1921 **G**: Drama in 3 acts **S**: The Lanes' home, New York, 1919 **C**: 3m, 3f

Throughout the First World War, Andrew Lane has worked hard as an insurance salesman to support his family, his wife, his son, his widowed mother, and a young Belgian girl, who escaped from the German occupation to come to America. His brother Oswald has been wounded in action in France and now returns home as a much-decorated war hero. This is a surprise to the family, because Oswald had always been the black sheep of the family. Despite his heroic status, he turns out to be as immoral as ever. He very soon seduces the Belgian refugee and then steals church funds. However, as he is running away, he stops to rescue some boys from a fire and is burned to death. Andrew concludes that his brother was a true hero after all.

This play and **What Price Glory?* were the two best American plays to emerge from the Great War. However, the ambivalent character of Oswald, which questioned the model of the clean-living US war hero, was clearly too challenging for audiences watching it less than three years after the end of hostilities: the play ran for only 80 performances and Emery's name is now almost forgotten.

Herr Puntila and His Servant Matti. See MR PUNTILA AND HIS MAN MATTI.

Herr Puntila und sein Knecht Matti. See MR PUNTILA AND HIS MAN MATTI.

He Who Gets Slapped (*Tot, kto poluchaet poshchechiny*)

AT: *The Painted Laugh* **A**: Leonid Andreev **Pf**: 1915, Moscow **Pb**: 1916 **Tr**: 1921 **G**: Drama in 4 acts; Russian prose **S**: The ante-room of a circus in a French city, early 20th c. **C**: 14m, 5f, extras

'Papa' Louis Briquet manages a circus, whose star is the beautiful bareback rider Consuela. Consuela's father Mancini threatens to take her from the circus if Briquet does not lend him money. A strange middle-aged intellectual comes and asks to join the circus. He is engaged as a clown and is known only as 'He who gets slapped'. Overhearing Briquet's common-law wife Zinida plead for the love of Bezano, a young equestrian, Consuela's fellow performer, 'He' longs to love too. When a fat baron wants Consuela for himself, Mancini offers to sell her in marriage. Hypnotizing Consuela, 'He' warns her that marriage to the Baron will kill her and that 'He' loves her. 'He' then confronts a Gentleman, whom he addresses as 'Prince', a writer who has stolen 'He's' ideas and his wife but 'He' says he will remain in the circus. Consuela gives a final performance before marrying the Baron. 'He' is so desperate to prevent the wedding that he gives Consuela poison then drinks some himself. 'He' reassures her that she will now live eternally. The grieving Baron shoots himself, and 'He' says that they will fight for Consuela's love in heaven.

This is the best known and most intriguing of Andreev's 28 plays composed between 1905 and 1916. Written in a bold Expressionist manner, this 'dramatic presentation' opposes the doubts and ponderings of the nameless intellectual ('He') to the vigorous life force of the circus folk. 'He's' loving is neither crudely successful like the lustful Baron nor as romantically beautiful as the yearning of the lion-tamer; his is inept and leads only to death. The morose Andreev, who himself attempted suicide three times, knew that 'He' deserves to get slapped.

He Will Go on a Spree. See ON THE RAZZLE.

High Bid, The

A: Henry James **Pf**: 1908, Edinburgh **Pb**: 1949 **G**: Com. in 3 acts **S**: Hall of an English country house, 1900s **C**: 4m, 2f, extras

Prodmore is a vulgar, expansive, well-to-do businessman, who invites his daughter Cora and Captain Clement Yule to join him at a large country house in rural England, looked after by an elderly servant. Yule has recently inherited this elegant pile, but the property is heavily mortgaged to Prodmore, who wants to use this as a lever to get Yule to wed Cora. Yule arrives, and as a man of socialist principles, is only too happy to allow the outraged Prodmore to keep the ancestral home. Prodmore urges Yule to use his family name to stand as Conservative candidate for the local constituency, settle down, and marry his daughter. Mrs Gracedew, an attractive American widow who appreciates art and architecture, visits the house, then shows round some sightseers, expounding its merits. She persuades Yule to accept Prodmore's offer, but Cora is determined to reject Yule in favour of Hall Pegg, with whom she is in love. Mrs Gracedew then urges Prodmore to let his daughter marry Pegg, and when he refuses, buys the house off him. Yule, relieved to be freed of his 'High Bid', asks Mrs Gracedew to become his wife.

After the failure of his *Guy Domville* in 1895, Henry James devoted himself mainly to the novel. However, prompted by Johnston Forbes-Robertson, who played Yule, with his wife Gertrude Elliott playing Gracedew, James expanded his one-act play *Summersoft* (written 1895) into *The High Bid*, which became his most popular comedy. It is a literary piece, proceeding by set pieces of duologue, betraying especially in its lengthy stage directions the novelist's interest in visual detail.

Hiketides. See SUPPLIANTS.

him

A: E. E. Cummings **Pf:** 1928, New York **Pb:** 1927 **G:** Drama in 3 acts **S:** Various surreal locations, 1920s **C:** 50m, 25f, extras

A painting, with two heads pushed through, depicts a Doctor anaesthetizing a woman. Three old women called Weird knit and gossip in rocking chairs in front of the painting. Him and his girlfriend Me discuss his latest play. He has doubts about this play and about Me's love for him. At his request, Him shows Me scenes from a popular vaudeville play that he has also written. Many of these feature the Doctor in various guises and include three fat drunks who prefer to play tennis rather than be seduced by a virgin; a soapbox orator selling 'radium' to cure people of 'cinderella'; a black song-and-dance routine interrupted by the Society for the Contraception of Vice; Mussolini surrounded by camp homosexuals presiding over the burning of Rome; a spoof private detective sequence. Finally, all the characters appear in a freak show, with the Doctor acting as barker. The high point is the announcement of the birth of a child to 'Princess Anankay', who is revealed to be Me. Back in their room, Me looks out into the audience and tells Him that there are people there pretending that Him and Me are real.

Best known as an avant-garde poet, *him* is Cummings's most successful play. Its surrealist elements, innovatory at the time of writing, may now appear dated. But the richness of the colourful phantasmagoria of the vaudeville scenes can still delight in performance.

Hindle Wakes

A: Stanley Houghton **Pf:** 1912, Manchester **Pb:** 1912 **G:** Drama in 3 acts **S:** Hawthorns' and Jeffcotes' homes, Hindle, near Manchester, 1900s **C:** 4m, 5f

Fanny Hawthorn, a working-class girl, has gone off during the 'wakes' (the annual holiday) from the fictitious Lancashire mill town of Hindle and has had a weekend fling with Alan Jeffcote, the good-looking but feckless son of the mill owner. When her horrified parents find out, they insist that the pair must marry, and Mr Hawthorn visits Mr Jeffcote Senior to demand this. Jeffcote reluctantly agrees, even though his wife and son Alan, who is engaged to Beatrice Farrar, the beautiful daughter of the Mayor, are strongly opposed to marriage with a mill girl. The honourable Jeffcote is adamant, threatening to disinherit Alan if he disobeys, and, when Beatrice also tells Alan that he must marry Fanny, he at last acquiesces. But no one has yet sought Fanny's opinion on the subject. It turns out that Fanny regards their weekend as a bit of fun and has no intention of marrying the feeble Alan. Her outraged mother bans her from home, but this suits Fanny too: as an emancipated young woman she is quite ready to stand on her own. The relieved Alan will seek out Beatrice to see if she will still have him.

Yet again we have here a play, like **Our Boys* and *The *Admirable Crichton,* where the lack of deviousness and basic common sense of a working-class figure is contrasted with the flaccid and cowardly behaviour of a supposedly social superior. What is innovative here is not only the authentic setting, with its use of Lancashire dialect, but also that it is a young woman who displays independence of spirit and scorns conventional morality, producing a working-class variant of Nora in *A *Doll's House.*

Hippes. See KNIGHTS.

Hippolytus (*Hippolytos*)

A: Euripides **Pf:** 428 BC, Athens **Tr:** 1782
G: Greek trag. in verse **S:** Before the palace of Theseus at Troezen, in the mythical past **C:** 4m, 4f, 2 choruses (m and f)

In the Prologue, Aphrodite, the goddess of love, denounces Hippolytus for his chaste behaviour and his renunciation of her in favour of Artemis, goddess of chastity and hunting. Aphrodite will punish him for his neglect of *eros* by arranging for his stepmother Phaedra to fall in love with him. The goddess will then reveal the truth to Phaedra's husband, King Theseus, so that he will curse his son Hippolytus. Hippolytus enters with his chorus of huntsmen, as ever refusing to honour the 'gods worshipped by night'. Phaedra, weakened by her hidden passion for her stepson, finally reveals the truth to her Nurse and the chorus of women. The well-meaning Nurse tells Hippolytus of Phaedra's love. He refuses to believe her and curses all women. Phaedra, having lost all hope, withdraws to die, leaving behind a suicide note, accusing Hippolytus of having raped her. Despite his son's denials, Theseus in his desperate grief banishes Hippolytus, calling on Poseidon to punish him. A sea monster rushes up the beach to destroy Hippolytus, and his mangled body is brought on stage, just in time for Theseus, who has been told the truth by Artemis, to be reconciled with his dying son.

The ancient Greeks believed in theomachy, that their gods could be at war with one another. Here we see how Aphrodite is jealous of the devotion paid to Artemis by Hippolytus, and determines to make him suffer for it. However, this does not mean that the mortals are mere puppets: Hippolytus is undeniably priggish and dangerously neglectful of the sexual side of his nature; it is not Aphrodite but the well-intentioned nurse who initiates the tragedy by revealing Phaedra's love; it may be part of Aphrodite's plan, but it is Theseus whose anger causes his son to die. Mortals carry out what the gods have laid down for them. Sophocles' earlier innovation of the third actor is especially effective here, as the silent Phaedra is witness to Hippolytus' angry denunciation of the Nurse and indeed all women. The theme was to form the basis of Seneca's **Phaedra,* of the finest of Racine's tragedies, **Phaedra,* and of Rameau's opera *Hipploytе et Aricie* (1733), and was revisited by Sarah Kane in 1996.

Hippolytus (Seneca). See PHAEDRA.

Hobson's Choice

A: Harold Brighouse **Pf:** 1915, New York
Pb: 1916 **G:** Com. in 4 acts **S:** Hobson's and Mossop's Boot Shops, Salford, England, 1880
C: 7m, 5f

Henry Horatio Hobson is a widower who runs a successful boot shop in Salford. He bullies his three daughters, Alice, Vicky, and Maggie, who work in his shop, and is particularly unkind to the eldest, the 30-year-old Maggie, dismissing her as 'an old maid'. However, Maggie persuades Hobson's self-effacing chief bootmaker Willie Mossop to marry her, and when Hobson objects, he and Maggie leave to set up their own business. Hobson drowns his troubles on a drunken binge, during which he falls down a corn merchant's cellar, causing an amount of damage. Willie grows in confidence, as his and Maggie's business prospers, while Hobson's starts to go into decline. He also faces a lawsuit for trespass and damage on the corn merchant's property. Maggie manages to agree an out-of-court settlement and even arranges for her sisters to marry the corn merchant's son and the solicitor representing him. When Hobson's health begins to suffer from his heavy drinking, Alice and Vicky refuse to return home to nurse him. Maggie says she will, provided Willie agrees. He insists that he become partner in Hobson's enterprise and that their two firms should merge. Hobson, facing the unhappy choice between giving in or being uncared for, finally agrees, and the happiness of Willie and Maggie's marriage and their future prosperity seem assured.

'Hobson's choice' was a familiar phrase indicating that there really was no choice at all. Much of the development of this play depends on tracing Willie Mossop's growth to confident manhood with the support of the resourceful Maggie, which results in Hobson being obliged to accept his new situation. The huge popularity of the play was a result of the authentic working-class setting and dialogue, making the play a kind of plebeian **King Lear*.

Hodoshe Span, Die. See ISLAND, THE.

Hoei Lan Kia. See CHALK CIRCLE, THE.

Hofmeister, Der. See TUTOR, THE.

Home

A: David Storey **Pf**: 1970, London **Pb**: 1970 **G**: Drama in 2 acts **S**: Terrace of a residential home, England, 1960s **C**: 3m, 2f

Two elegantly dressed middle-aged gentlemen, Harry and Jack, meet on a terrace and talk in desultory fashion. They discuss Jack's recent illness, their schooldays, the weather, the sea, the Vale of Evesham, moustaches, the army, families, arthritis, etc., and Jack performs some card tricks. They leave for a walk before lunch. The atmosphere changes when two middle-aged women, Kathleen and Marjorie, enter. They swear, exchange rude jokes, and are unembarrassedly of a lower class than the two gentlemen. The men return and converse in a slightly odd manner with the women, then accompany them to the dining hall. After lunch, Alfred, who is a simple younger man, tests his strength by lifting the metal table and chairs on the terrace. As Kathleen and Harry now converse, it becomes apparent that they are confined to a mental institution. The women penetrate the evasive clichés of the men: Kathleen admits she attacked the milkman, and reminds Alfred that he painted obscenities in the town centre; Jack imagines he will soon be out, but Marjorie knows better. The men end the play gently weeping.

There is virtually no plot in the conventional sense, and the piece depends for its effect on the skill and precise observation of its dialogue. With its elliptical utterances and evasions, it is reminiscent of Pinter, but more naturalistic. Its premiere, directed by Lindsay Anderson, with John Gielgud as Harry and Ralph Richardson as Jack, was a success both in London and New York.

Homecoming (O'Neill). See MOURNING BECOMES ELECTRA.

Homecoming, The

A: Harold Pinter **Pf**: 1965, London **Pb**: 1965; rev. 1968 **G**: Drama in 2 acts **S**: House in north London, early 1960s **C**: 5m, 1f

Max, a 70-year-old retired butcher and widower, lives in a house with his fastidious younger brother Sam, a chauffeur, and his two sons, Lenny, a pimp, and Joey, a demolition man and would-be boxer. Max, who enjoys reminiscing about the past, dominates the household, which is characterized by bickering and arguments. That night, Teddy, Max's oldest son, arrives unexpectedly with his English wife Ruth. Teddy is professor of philosophy at a university in America, where he lives with Ruth and their three sons. He now wants to introduce the somewhat apprehensive Ruth to his family. Everyone is asleep, and Ruth goes out for a night-time stroll. Lenny comes down and the brothers exchange awkward greetings, before Teddy goes up to bed. Ruth arrives back, and Lenny tries to intimidate Ruth with lengthy stories about his violent treatment of women. Ruth says she will 'take' him; Lenny asks if this is some kind of proposal, but Ruth silently goes to bed. The next morning Max is horrified that Teddy has brought 'a smelly scrubber' into the house. When Teddy explains that Ruth is his wife and mother of Max's grandchildren, Max relents and embraces

Teddy. After a lunch cooked by Max, Lenny tries to engage Teddy in a conversation on philosophy, and Ruth seductively describes her former career as 'a model for the body'. Teddy decides it is time to leave, but Ruth begins to dance with and kiss Lenny, then cuddles Joey. Teddy waits patiently and unmoved while Ruth and Joey go to bed together. Lenny is furious to discover that Teddy has eaten a cheese roll that he had prepared. Joey appears, frustrated because he 'didn't get all the way'. Max is concerned about Joey, but Sam is outraged. Max suggests that Ruth might stay and look after the house. Lenny proposes that she earn her keep as a prostitute, with Teddy recommending her to American visitors. Teddy's only concern is that she would age very quickly. Ruth coolly negotiates a deal for herself, when Sam staggers forward and blurts out that one of Max's best friends had Max's wife in the back of Sam's car. Teddy politely takes his leave, and Ruth sits in Max's chair surrounded by her men. Max crawls towards her, insisting: 'I'm not an old man.'

Pinter's finest play shows him at the height of his ability to manipulate language and pauses, giving the impression of everyday speech but actually marshalling clichés, slang, repetitions, and ellipses with the skill of a musical composer. The play is shocking, mainly because of the lack of involvement displayed by Teddy rather than the conventional dramatic experience of extreme emotion. Ruth is attracted to the rough, grubby, amoral atmosphere of the family home rather than their 'clean' home in America. In the event, it proves to be Ruth's 'homecoming'.

Honest Man's Revenge, The. See ATHEIST'S TRAGEDY, THE.

Honneur de Dieu, L'. See BECKET.

Honour of God, The. See BECKET.

Hoppla, We're Alive! (*Hoppla, wir leben!*)

AT: *Hoppla, Such Is Life!; Hoopla!* A: Ernst Toller Pf: 1927, Hamburg Pb: 1927 Tr: 1928 G: Trag. in 5 acts and a prologue; German prose S: Prison, 1919, and ministerial offices, lodgings, hotel, courtroom, prison, etc., Berlin, 1927 C: 45m, 6f, extras

In the Prologue set in 1919, the reprieve of six revolutionaries in the condemned cell proves too much for one of their number, Karl Thomas, and he goes insane. Another prisoner Kilman is unconditionally pardoned. In 1927 Thomas, discharged from the mental asylum, seeks help from Kilman, only to discover to his disappointment that Kilman has become a Social Democrat minister, courted by financiers and nationalist aristocracy. Thomas now lives with one of the original prisoners, the progressive Eva Berg, who urges him to join the Party in the fight for true socialism. Thomas takes a job as a hotel waiter, planning to assassinate Kilman. Before Thomas can succeed, however, a nationalist student shoots the Minister. Thomas fires after the student, and is arrested by the police holding a smoking gun. After a psychiatric examination, Thomas is sent back to prison. News comes that Kilman's assassin has been arrested, but it is too late: unable to bear the thought of further imprisonment and destroyed by the failure of the revolution, Thomas has hanged himself.

This is the first major play of the 20th century to explore the failure of socialism, to set political ideals against political reality, as Toller was forced to do on his release from prison after his involvement in attempting to establish a soviet republic in Bavaria. At a time of growing prosperity in Germany it was a timely and unfashionable warning. It is also one of the first plays to portray a persuasive socialist feminist in the (admittedly peripheral) character of Eva Berg. Piscator opened his 'Piscator-Bühne' in Berlin with this play, staged on a spectacular constructivist set, and using a revised ending, as described above.

Horse Eats Hat. See ITALIAN STRAW HAT, AN.

Hose, Die. See UNDERPANTS, THE.

Hostage, The (*An Giall*)

A: Brendan Behan (with Joan Littlewood) Pf: 1958, Dublin Pb: 1981 Tr: 1958; rev. 1962 G: Drama in 3 acts; Irish prose and songs S: Dublin brothel, late 1950s C: 8m, 5f, extras

A Dublin brothel, owned by Monsewer, English-born but now a committed Irish republican, is run by an old IRA comrade, Pat, with the help of an older whore Meg Dillon. The place is full of odd characters from the lower depths of Dublin society: a gospel-singing social worker, two homosexuals, a couple of prostitutes, and a maidservant from the country Teresa. An IRA man is due to be hanged for terrorist activity, and fellow Volunteers kidnap a British soldier Leslie in the North and hide him as a hostage in the brothel. Far from being frightened, Leslie joins in the fun and sings a song. Teresa falls in love with Leslie, and Miss Gilchrist tries cheering him up by reading him a newspaper article about the royal family. After Leslie and Teresa have jumped into bed together, he discovers a report in the paper about his predicament and begins to be concerned. The inhabitants of the brothel also worry that the likeable Leslie will be executed by the IRA. In a sudden police raid Leslie is shot and killed. As Teresa weeps over his body, Leslie sits up and sings 'The bells of hell go ting-a-ling-a-ling'.

Originally performed in Gaelic as a realistic piece, Joan Littlewood's Theatre Workshop transformed the script into a light-hearted romp with song and dance, which was so successful that it transferred to London's West End. Here it was lapped up by middle-class audiences, who could giggle at quaint Irish politics, quaint Irish queers, and quaint Irish folk, without suffering any of the discomfiture experienced in Behan's one other completed play *The *Quare Fellow*.

House and Garden (House; Garden)

A: Alan Ayckbourn Pf: 1999, Scarborough Pb: 2000 G: Two linked coms., each in 2 acts S: (1) Living room of English country house; (2) Garden of same, 1990s C: 7m, 7f, extras

(1) *House*. Trish Platt, an attractive woman in her forties, has invited a French film star Lucille Cadeau to open their village fête. Trish treats her husband Teddy as though he were invisible because of his affair with a married neighbour Joanna Mace. Teddy seeks the advice of their doctor Giles Mace, who has no idea that his wife and Teddy are seeing each other. Teddy, who manages a large printing firm, is thinking of following his father into politics and standing as MP. He has invited the celebrated novelist Gavin Ryng-Mayne, a friend of the prime minister, to lunch, and does not want Trish's moods to spoil things. Joanna reveals her affair to Giles, who seeks support from Trish. Trish tells Giles that her own marriage has been dead for many years. Gavin arrives and offers Teddy the constituency candidacy, hoping that he will be able to head up a committee investigating immoral behaviour amongst MPs. Trish, Giles, Joanna, and Sally all ignore Teddy. Lucille finally arrives, and everyone, including the Platts' daughter Sally, chatters away in French to her, while Teddy feels more and more excluded. After lunch, Gavin charms Sally, and Lucille and Teddy get drunk together. The fête is called off because of a downpour. Gavin and Sally continue to flirt, until Gavin tells her of his sexual fantasy, driving Sally from the room. Jake confronts Gavin for upsetting Sally. Teddy and Lucille stagger in from the rain, soaked through and missing items of clothing. Gavin leaves, withdrawing the offer of putting Teddy's name forward as party candidate. Trish announces that she is leaving Teddy. Jake finally succeeds in telling Sally that he loves her. Sally bursts into tears. (2) *Garden*. The events of this part run exactly contemporaneously with those of the first. At the bottom of the garden Joanna secretly meets Teddy, who has come to tell her that he wishes to end their affair. Trish comes into the garden to cut some roses and finds the distraught Joanna wanting to confess. Trish is very abrupt with her, and insists that she must tell Giles. Joanna confesses her affair to Giles, who goes off in distress. Barry and his wife Lindy begin to erect tents and enclosures for the fête. Jake sympathizes with his father over his mother's affair, but Giles is very forgiving and looks forward to his Morris dancing. Barry and Linda find Joanna hiding in the bushes and are worried because she is to supervise the maypole dance. They communicate their concerns to Giles. Joanna has become

convinced that Giles has been substituted by a dangerous clone called Harold and then fears that Jake too has been 'replaced'. Despite the downpour, Lucille and Teddy play hoop-la and paddle in the fountain. Although they cannot comprehend a word each other is saying, they reach a genuine understanding, and disappear into the tent together, which collapses on them. Joanna suddenly appears and begins attacking Teddy violently, while Lucille attempts to defend him. Lindy begs a lift off Gavin, in order to get away from Barry. Lucille is taken off to her clinic where she is to dry out, and Teddy is left on his own.

Ayckbourn parades his usual sequence of desperate marital relationships, including a total mental breakdown by Joanna, which nevertheless remains funny. The particular twist of these two plays is that they are meant to be played simultaneously in two neighbouring venues, with the actors and their characters moving from play to play, in a manner employed by Fornés in Act 2 of **Fefu and Her Friends*, and which is an extension of the parallel action explored in Ayckbourn's **Norman Conquests*.

House of Bernarda Alba, The (*La casa de Bernarda Alba*)

A: Federico García Lorca **W:** 1936 **Pf:** 1945, Buenos Aires **Pb:** 1945 **Tr:** 1947 **G:** Trag. in 3 acts; Spanish prose **S:** Spanish farm, early 20th c. **C:** 10f, extras

Bernarda Alba's second husband has just died, and she orders her five daughters to lock up the house and observe eight years of mourning. During this time, they are to see no men, and 'not a breath of air will get in this house from the street'. The youngest daughter, 20-year-old Adela, rebels unsuccessfully against her tyrannical mother. But despite the old servant's warnings, Bernarda insists that none of her daughters need husbands. Only the oldest daughter of 39, from Bernarda's first marriage, who has inherited her father's money, is allowed to be wooed by a handsome young man, who is never seen. The previous night, having spoken to his intended through a grille, the fiancé then went to Adela's window and talked to her passionately until dawn. A hunchback daughter, jealous of her older sister's impending marriage and of Adela's success with the fiancé, steals his picture. The frustrations of these three daughters surface in the ensuing fight. The other two daughters, one stupid, the other cynically resigned to her fate, seem unaffected by Bernarda's tyranny. When a village woman is discovered to have murdered her illegitimate baby, Bernarda urges that hot coals should be put 'in the place where she has sinned'. A stallion, kicking at the stable from sexual frustration, is released by Bernarda. Adela creeps back in after meeting her lover and is denounced by her hunchback sister. Far from wilting under Bernarda's angry reproaches, Adela breaks Bernarda's cane and declares that she belongs to her lover. Furious, Bernarda rushes out with a gun. A shot is fired, and the hunchback triumphantly tells Adela that her lover is dead. Adela goes out and hangs herself, although in fact her lover has escaped. Bernarda suppresses her grief and orders that Adela be buried as a virgin.

The last of his 'rural trilogy', this play was completed shortly before Lorca's death. It is arguably his finest, and a reminder of the terrible loss to theatre caused by his execution by Fascists at the age of 38. Although Lorca intended the piece to be 'a photographic document', his writing, though not as surreal as in **Blood Wedding*, is nevertheless full of symbolic undertones. The restless stallion and the image of the enclosed house in the summer heat powerfully suggest suppressed passion that boils over to bring about tragedy. It may well be that Lorca, as a homosexual, experienced similar desperation as he tried to hide and suppress his emotions in a society which condemned such yearnings.

How I Learned to Drive

A: Paula Vogel **Pf:** 1997, New York **Pb:** 1998 **G:** Drama without act or scene divisions **S:** Suburban Maryland, 1963–1990s **C:** 2m, 3f

(The action is interrupted with advice about driving and admonitions from Li'l Bit's mother, and all parts except her and Peck are played by a 'Greek Chorus' of one man and a woman.) Li'l

Bit grows up with her mother, grandparents, and Aunt Mary and Uncle Peck, an attractive man in his forties originally from South Carolina. When the family joke about the big bosom she is developing, only Peck shows her kindness. In flashbacks, we see her at school, already at 13 attracting attention with her full breasts. Peck photographs her young body. When she is 15, Peck begins to teach her how to drive, while she flirts with him. He takes her out for dinner. When she goes to boarding school, he sends her love letters and gifts. As soon as she reaches her 18th birthday, they meet in a hotel room, but Li'l Bit says that they must not meet any more. Soon she is thrown out of school for drunkenness, and takes to driving around the roads at night. Within five years, Peck drinks himself to death. At 27, Li'l Bit sleeps with a man but thinks only of Peck. In a final flashback to the age of 11, she recalls how traumatized she was when Peck fondled her breasts, while he allowed her to drive.

In this Pulitzer Prize- and Obie-winning play, Vogel ventures into the problematic area of paedophilia, boldly allowing Peck to be a very positive character, who gently initiates Li'l Bit into learning to drive and learning to love. Only in the final flashback do we understand how Peck has actually damaged Li'l Bit's life: 'That day was the last day I lived in my body. I retreated above the neck, and I've lived inside the "fire" in my head ever since.'

Hui-Lan Ji. See CHALK CIRCLE, THE.

Huis Clos. See NO EXIT.

Human Voice, The (*La Voix humaine*)
A: Jean Cocteau Pf: 1930, Paris Pb: 1930
Tr: 1951 G: Monodrama in 1 act; French prose
S: Young woman's bedroom, Paris, *c.*1930 C: 1f

The curtain goes up on what appears to be the corpse of a woman. However, she gets up and is just leaving the room when the phone goes. It is late evening. The caller is her lover, a lawyer, who after they have been together for five years has left her for another woman. She describes her day shopping, having dinner with a friend, and pretends to be coping well with their separation. She arranges for him to collect his love letters to her, although she would like to hand them over personally. She also asks him to take away the dog they bought together. At one point, his voice fades: 'It's like being dead. You can hear but you can't make yourself heard.' When they are cut off, she phones his home, but reaches only his manservant. When her ex-lover rings back, her brave front has gone, and she admits with tears that she has not left her apartment because she has been waiting for him to phone. She took an overdose of sleeping pills the night before but phoned her friend who brought a doctor. She begs him to stay on the line: 'This wire, it's the last thing that still connects me to us.' She fears that he may be with his new woman. He appears to hang up, and she becomes almost hysterical. He phones back and she soon lets him go, uttering her love for him, as she winds the flex tight round her neck, and the receiver drops from her hand.

In this painful analysis of a woman coping with being abandoned by a treacherous lover, Cocteau describes 'the solitude to which we are condemned by a universe where tears continually triumph over laughter', and in which 'the telephone is sometimes more dangerous than a revolver'. This mini-tragedy was made into an opera by Poulenc in 1959.

Hunted, The. See MOURNING BECOMES ELECTRA.

Hypochondriac, The (*Le Malade imaginaire*)
AT: *Doctor Last in His Chariot; The Imaginary Invalid; The Would-Be Invalid* A: Molière
Pf: 1673, Paris Pb: 1674 Tr: 1769 G: Com. in 3 acts in French alexandrines; with prologue, entr'actes, and finale of song and dance
S: Argan's home, Paris, 17th c. C: 8m, 4f, dancers and singers

Argan is a hypochondriac, whose obsession with his health is willingly exploited by his doctor and his apothecary. His second wife, Béline, while pretending to be sympathetic about his 'illnesses', is only after his money, and wants to see her two stepdaughters confined in a convent. Argan would like his elder daughter Angélique conveniently to marry a doctor, but she is already in love with Cléante, who comes to the house disguised as a music teacher. Béralde, Argan's sensible brother, having failed to persuade Argan to let his daughter marry the man of her choice, plays a trick on Argan. He gets the feisty maid Toinette to disguise herself as a doctor, who recommends to Argan the amputation of an arm and the removal of an eye. Returning as herself, Toinette then convinces Argan to pretend that he is dead. Learning of her husband's 'demise', Béline is overjoyed, while Angélique is grief-stricken, so Argan throws out his wife and agrees that Angélique may marry Cléante, provided he becomes a doctor. Béralde, however, persuades Argan to take up medicine himself.

In Molière's last play he explores one of his favourite themes, the person who makes himself ridiculous by taking what might be a sensible concern to absurd extremes. At the same time, Molière can make a barbed attack on the lack of scruples of the medical profession. It is the typically moderate and shrewd figure of the *raisonneur* in the form of Argan's brother, who helps to restore Argan to health and so permits the coming together of the lovers and the happy end required by comedy. That Béralde is helped in his plan by the lower-class figure of the maid Toinette draws on the Roman comedic tradition of servants who are wiser than their masters, and looks forward to a pre-Revolutionary figure like Figaro in Beaumarchais's plays. In one of theatre history's greatest moments of irony, Molière collapsed while playing the role of Argan during the fourth performance of the play and died the following evening.

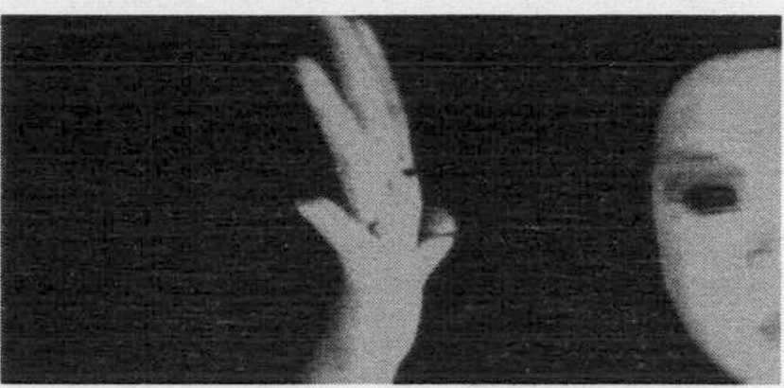

I Am a Camera

A: John Van Druten **Pf**: 1951, New York **Pb**: 1952 **G**: Drama in 3 acts **S**: Fräulein Schneider's flat, Berlin, *c*.1930 **C**: 3m, 4f

Christopher Isherwood is a young English writer who has come to Berlin and rented a room from Fräulein Schneider. He wishes to note as objectively as possible his impressions of the city and especially its political upheavals with street battles between Fascists and Communists: 'I am a camera, with its shutter open, quite passive.' He meets and falls in love with fellow lodger Sally Bowles, a flamboyant English singer at a local nightclub, even though she openly admits that she has just had an abortion. Each pretends not to be possessive about the other: Christopher agrees not to probe her past and stifles his jealousy when she becomes pregnant by another man. However, the growing Nazi threat moves him so deeply that he has to give up his pose of objectivity. He decides he must leave Berlin ('The camera's taken all its pictures, and now it's going away to develop them'). He fails to persuade the apolitical and amoral Sally to come with him, but she promises to send him postcards.

London-born Van Druten left Britain for the USA in the 1930s after problems with the British censor. Based on Christopher Isherwood's *Goodbye to Berlin* (1939), *I Am a Camera* is one of the best-known works by this prolific and successful playwright, not least because of its transposition into the musical *Cabaret* (1966). The play offers an interesting insight into a writer's need for commitment at a time of political upheaval, an aspect that is hardly explored in *Cabaret*.

Iceman Cometh, The

A: Eugene O'Neill **W**: 1939 **Pf**: 1946, New York **Pb**: 1946 **G**: Trag. in 4 acts **S**: Rooming house in New York, 1912 **C**: 16m, 3f

Harry Hope's saloon is filled with down-and-outs, who habitually sit drinking while dreaming of the past and future. Apart from Harry himself, who has not gone outdoors for 20 years, there are: Larry Slade, a cynical anarchist, the philosopher of the group, who believes that their pipe dreams are all that keep them going; Joe Mott, an African-American, who once owned a gambling house; Hugo Kalmar, former newspaper editor; Rocky Pioggi, a pimp; two army officers, who fought on opposing sides in the Boer War; Jimmy Cameron, a correspondent who covered that war; a graduate of Harvard Law School; a former circus con man; and a former police lieutenant. Don Parritt arrives with the news that his mother, Larry's former mistress, has been arrested for political activities, but Larry does not want to know. Three prostitutes, Pearl, Maggie, and Cora, arrive, insisting as ever that they are 'tarts' not 'whores', followed by the day barman Chuck Morello. All await the arrival of Hickey (Theodore Hickman), a travelling salesman, who can be guaranteed to lay on a party for everyone and will regale them with stories about his wife and the iceman (the tradesman who brought ice to houses in the days before refrigerators). Hickey's arrival is a disappointment, however: he has undergone a conversion, and while promising that the party will go ahead, he urges everyone to abandon their pipe dreams and do something with their lives. The party is not the usual success, since

Hickey has been busying himself urging people to face the truth. Parritt admits that he betrayed his mother, and old friendships collapse under the strain. Hickey reveals that his change of heart has been occasioned by his wife's death. By next morning, Hickey's 'Reform Wave' is going strong: Hope, Jimmy, the Boer War officers, and the Harvard lawyer, all set off in search of jobs, and Chuck and Cora decide to marry and move to a farm. When Hope is back within minutes, terrified of the world outside, Hickey predicts that they will soon all return. When Larry suggests that Hickey drove his wife to suicide, Hickey admits that he killed her. By midnight, with everyone back in the bar, Hickey reveals in a long confession that his wife's constant love and forgiveness had driven him to kill her, because he was unable to live with the guilt. As the police come to arrest him, Hickey claims that he was insane when he committed the murder. Nearly everyone now believes they were merely humouring Hickey, except for Parritt, whose betrayal of his mother drives him to suicide, and Larry, who now contemplates death with equanimity.

With echoes of Christ's words, 'The bridegroom cometh', *The Iceman Cometh* is arguably the most complex and profound American drama of all time. Reminiscent of Gorky's *The *Lower Depths*, it also anticipates Beckett's **Waiting for Godot* in presenting a play almost devoid of action, in which the characters are waiting in vain for some ill-defined source of renewal and salvation.

Ideal Husband, An

A: Oscar Wilde Pf: 1895, London Pb: 1899
G: Drama in 4 acts S: Sir Robert's and Lord Goring's homes, London, 1895 C: 9m, 6f

Sir Robert Chiltern seems to be an ideal husband, a rich and successful politician and devoted spouse. However, Mrs Cheveley threatens to expose Sir Robert, whose whole career is founded on the former sale of a Cabinet secret to a financier. When Mrs Cheveley tells Lady Chiltern of her husband's dishonesty, Lady Chiltern writes to seek help from a good friend, Lord Goring. Goring discovers Mrs Cheveley in possession of a stolen brooch, and uses the threat of calling the police to force her to hand over the letter incriminating Sir Robert. Mrs Cheveley now tries to destroy Sir Robert's marriage by sending him the note Lady Chiltern sent to Goring. This fails too, and Sir Robert is even offered promotion. Although his wife at first feels that he should confess everything, she is persuaded that this will gain nothing and tears up Sir Robert's letter of resignation. Finally, Goring is to marry Sir Robert's sister Mabel.

Although this play has a conventional happy ending, even including a marriage, the preparation for which has been a very peripheral element of the plot, it hardly offers a satisfying dramatic resolution. Instead of injustice being exposed, Wilde's cynicism allows the somewhat less than 'ideal' husband to continue his successful career with impunity. Only the loyal friend and devoted wife provide positive models of behaviour, but they can maintain the moral high ground only because they are not required to be involved in political life.

Idle Inn, The. See HAUNTED INN, THE.

If a Claw is Caught the (Whole) Bird is Lost. See POWER OF DARKNESS, THE.

I Got the Blues. See AWAKE AND SING!

Illusion, The. See THEATRICAL ILLUSION, THE.

Illusion comique, L'. See THEATRICAL ILLUSION, THE.

Imaginary Invalid, The. See HYPOCHONDRIAC, THE.

Im Dickicht der Städte. See IN THE JUNGLE OF CITIES.

Importance of Being Earnest, The

A: Oscar Wilde Pf: 1895, London Pb: 1899
G: Com. in 3 (originally 4) acts S: Algernon's residence in London and Jack Worthing's house in the country, 1890s C: 5m, 4f

John ('Jack') Worthing leads a double life: in the country he is a respected JP, in charge of a young ward, Cecily. In London, where he is visiting his friend Algernon Moncrieff, he calls himself Ernest, a fictitious brother whom the sober Jack has to help out of various scrapes. Algernon's cousin Gwendolen Fairfax accepts a proposal of marriage from Jack, because she has always wanted to marry someone called Ernest. However, her mother, the fearsome Lady Bracknell, on learning that Jack is an orphan who was found in a handbag, refuses her permission. Algernon arrives at Jack's house in the country, pretending to be Jack's wicked brother Ernest. Cecily immediately agrees to marry him, since she too has always wanted to marry someone called Ernest. Jack returns in mourning for his dead brother Ernest, only to find that he is alive, well, and engaged to Cecily. When Gwendolen arrives in pursuit of Jack, she and Cecily get very heated on learning that they are both engaged to Ernest. Confronted by their angry fiancées, Jack and Algernon own up to their deception and immediately agree to be christened Ernest. Lady Bracknell, following her eloping daughter, agrees to Algernon's marrying Cecily, but Jack refuses his permission, if he cannot marry Gwendolen. The impasse is resolved by the discovery that Jack was mistakenly abandoned by Cecily's governess, Miss Prism, and is Algy's long-lost elder brother, who, mercifully, was christened Ernest John. Both marriages may now go ahead.

One of the most enduringly popular comedies in the English language, the success of *The Importance of Being Earnest* is due to a number of factors. First, there is the clever plotting, a parody of contemporary melodrama, allowing of a number of hilarious situations, e.g. Jack's arrival in deep mourning for the brother who has appeared on his doorstep, or the sudden reversal from lasting friendship between Cecily and Gwendolen to sworn enmity on discovering that they are supposedly both engaged to the same person. Secondly, there are the unforgettable characters, above all the formidable Lady Bracknell, a much sought-after role by older actresses, but also smaller roles like the delightful Miss Prism or Canon Chasuble. Thirdly, there is the gentle satire of contemporary manners, seen especially clearly in the opposition between Gwendolen's sophistication and Cecily's unadorned forthrightness. Finally and above all, Wilde's gift for witty repartee means that whole scenes can carry the audience along without much concern for the probability of the events or characterization, rather in the manner of the slick one-liners of much contemporary television comedy.

In Abraham's Bosom

A: Paul Green **Pf:** 1926, New York **Pb:** 1927
G: Trag. in 7 scenes **S:** North Carolina, 1885–1906 **C:** 10m, 2f

Abraham ('Abe') is the illegitimate son of mixed race of Colonel McCranie, a Southern gentleman. Concerned to help the African-American workers in the Colonel's turpentine woods, he asks his father for a schoolhouse. The Colonel's legitimate white son objects to Abe's forwardness and strikes him. Abe hits him back and is punished by the Colonel with a beating. Three years later Abe is married and has a son. His father, impressed by Abe's initiative, deeds him his house and land and even builds the schoolhouse. Eventually, most of Abe's pupils drop out of school. Fifteen years later Abe's school is long closed, and his arrogance has forced the family to move to town where his wife takes in washing. Their son grows up a guitar-playing wastrel, and Abe loses his job for answering back to his white employers. Undaunted, three years later Abe delivers a speech, demanding the building of a new school for his 'fellow Negroes', but he is chased off by the crowds. His white half-brother criticizes him for neglecting his crops. Furious, Abe murders him. Returning home, Abe warns his family to run away, but his wife stays with him, as he goes out to be shot by the lynch mob.

Paul Green, the first and arguably the best American folk dramatist, never made concessions to the tastes of a predominantly white theatregoing audience and wrote in an authentic Carolina dialect. In the course of the sprawling action of a play like this, there is some predictable criticism of white notions of superiority and violence, but Green also shows that Abe is failed too by those he is trying to help. Abe himself is a complex character, whose dreams of heroic leadership undermine his admirable social concern. The play benefits from its song and dance and from moments of comedy, provided mainly by Abe's aunt Muh Mack.

Inadmissible Evidence

A: John Osborne **Pf**: 1964, London **Pb**: 1965 **G**: Drama in 2 acts **S**: Solicitor's office, London, 1960s **C**: 3m, 5f

In a dream sequence, 39-year-old Bill Maitland, practising as a solicitor for 25 years, finds himself on trial for having depended 'almost entirely on other people's efforts'. The dream dissolves: the Judge is revealed as Hudson, the Managing Clerk, who now works for Bill. Bill arrives in his office, deals offensively with his secretary Shirley, who gives her notice, and patronizingly with the amiable Hudson. Instead of working, Bill is more interested in discussing his many affairs, particularly his present liaison with Liz, which is not going well. In a series of telephone calls, which may or not be part of his dream, Bill tries to calm Liz, and then his wife Anna, after she walked in on him about to have sex with his secretary Joy. When clients come with divorce petitions, Bill behaves as though he were called on to defend his own behaviour. His daughter comes, and Bill condemns himself in a long monologue addressed to her. Finally, he is abandoned by Hudson and even Joy, and eventually by Liz. Bill phones his wife, but decides that he will just sit and wait for the inevitable reckoning.

The contraceptive pill and a general relaxation of public morality in the post-war period created a sexual freedom explored by many playwrights. Here, as in **Alfie*, a severe moral tone is adopted, and it is clear that Bill's philandering and cavalier attitude to the law will be paid for by guilt, recrimination, and loneliness. In terms of presentation, Osborne moved away from his early naturalism to a style where dream and reality intermingle, and different characters appear identical.

In Camera. See NO EXIT.

Incident at Vichy

A: Arthur Miller **Pf**: 1964, New York **Pb**: 1965 **G**: Drama in 1 act **S**: Place of detention, Vichy, France, 1942 **C**: 21m

Six men and a boy have been taken off the streets by the police in Vichy, capital of unoccupied France in the Second World War. They are Marchand, a self-important businessman; Lebeau, a painter; Bayard, an electrician; Monceau, an actor; a Gypsy; a Waiter; and a boy of 15. None of them knows why they have been arrested. Three more detainees are brought in by the police: an old Jew, the indignant Doctor Leduc, who insists that he is a captain in the French army, and the Austrian aristocrat Prince von Berg. The men begin to discuss the deportation of the Jews which has begun in Vichy France. As they are interrogated one by one by a Professor of 'racial anthropology', the detainees begin to suspect each other of being Jewish and exchange stories about extermination camps in Poland. As they become more aware of their plight, they consider trying to overpower the guard, but as Leduc recognizes, the authorities 'rely on our own logic to immobilize ourselves'. Leduc confronts the German army Major about his complicity in this racist action, but admits his own moral weakness: he would abandon the others if he were set free. Von Berg is given a pass when his credentials are checked, but, partly to assuage his own guilt, he nobly gives it to Leduc, so that he can escape.

This well-wrought long one-acter recognizes not only that racism is found the world over, but also that the victims, in this case the Jews, were often partly complicit in their own oppression.

Indian Princess, The

AT: *La Belle Sauvage* **A**: James Nelson Barker **Pf**: 1808, Philadelphia **Pb**: 1808 **G**: Melodrama in 3 acts; blank verse **S**: Jamestown and its hinterland, 1607–*c*.1614 **C**: 12m, 5f

In April 1607 a group of English colonists land to establish a settlement at Jamestown in Virginia. While some sing sentimentally of the loves they have left behind, one attempts to ravish another settler's wife. Captain John Smith leads an expedition into the interior and is captured by Indians. Lieutenant John Rolfe and some companions set out in search of their leader and eventually reach the Indian encampment. Pocahontas, the daughter of the Chief Powhatan, has saved the life of Smith. Her brother Nataguas joins Smith and his company to learn the ways of the white man he admires. Pocahontas was to have married Miami, the prince of a neighbouring tribe, but falls in love with Rolfe. Persuaded by Miami, Powhatan invites the English to a banquet, where they will be slaughtered. Pocahontas rushes in to warn them in time. Miami kills himself. Powhatan, his treachery forgiven, agrees to the marriage of Rolfe and Pocahontas.

Although Barker's later play about Puritan excesses, *Superstition, or The Fanatic Father* (1824) is arguably a more accomplished piece, *The Indian Princess* is significant in being the first 'Indian play' of the New World and also the first to be transferred to London, where it was performed at the Drury Lane Theatre in 1820. The gentle lyricism, especially of the love relationship between Pocahontas and Rolfe, was reinforced by its musical accompaniment, composed by John Bray.

Indians

A: Arthur Kopit **Pf**: 1968, London **Pb**: 1969 **G**: Hist. drama in 13 scenes **S**: Wild West Show and US government building, 1886 **C**: 36m, 4f, extras

Scenes alternate between Buffalo Bill Cody's Wild West Show and the hearings of an Indian Commission. The Wild West Show scenes promote an apolitical championing of the frontier spirit and celebrate the heroic myths of the white settlers who make the land their own. This is contrasted with the debate in the Indian Commission, where the whites cannot understand why the Indians keep breaking their treaties, and the Native Americans cannot comprehend why these treaties are based on the possession of territory, since owning land is a totally alien concept. When Colonel Forsythe excuses a massacre of Indians with the words: 'Of course innocent people have been killed. In war they always are,' this is a verbatim quotation from General Westmoreland with reference to the Vietnam War 80 years later. Twice we also hear Chief Joseph in 1877 capitulating before the inflexible might of the government: 'I am tired of fighting. . . . My heart is sick and sad! From where the sun now stands, I will fight no more, forever.'

After his early absurdist pieces, Kopit here turned to a more serious political investigation of the white settlers' treatment of Native Americans, initially as their protectors and then killing and exploiting them. While the acknowledgement of America's past guilt is now commonplace, Kopit's play (significantly premiered in London and not very successful in the States) was one of the first major pieces to confront the issue and to relate it to continuing genocide in South-East Asia.

Indian Wants the Bronx, The

A: Israel Horovitz **Pf**: 1966, Waterford, Connecticut **Pb**: 1968 **G**: Drama in 1 act **S**: Bus stop, New York, 1960s **C**: 3m

Gupta, an 'East' Indian in his early fifties, is waiting for a bus. Two loud-mouthed delinquents in their early twenties, Joey (of Jewish descent) and Murph (of Irish descent), arrive and tease Gupta, imagining that he is Turkish. Gupta is frightened and alone in the big city: he speaks only Hindi, and shows the lads the address of his son in the Bronx. The youths continue to play around with a high level of aggression, then do a 'war dance' in the street. They play hide-and-seek, which involves Joey spinning Murphy until he is sick, then violently forcing Gupta into a hiding place. Gupta becomes so frightened that he hits Joey, who then gives him a beating. Murphy, returning from vomiting, offers to phone Gupta's son. When he gets through, however, he claims to have found an elephant wandering the streets. Gupta is desperate to speak to his son, but Murphy pushes him aside, then cuts the cord of the hand-piece. Joey goes off distraught. Murphy cuts the Indian's hand, leaving him crying, alone, in despair.

With obvious affinities to Albee's **Zoo Story* and to the contemporaneous baby-stoning scene in Bond's **Saved*, this simple piece of naturalistic action encapsulates the latent violence of urban youth, not evil but bored, swaggering but insecure. The teasing of the outsider, here significantly by two people themselves from immigrant backgrounds, escalates to violence, although Horovitz creates an even greater sense of despair by leaving the victim alive and alone than by staging his death.

Infant, The. See MINOR, THE.

Infernal Machine, The (*La Machine infernale*)

A: Jean Cocteau **Pf:** 1934, Paris **Pb:** 1934 **Tr:** 1936 **G:** Trag. in 4 acts; French prose **S:** Thebes, mythical past **C:** 12m, 5f

A Voice tells the story of Oedipus, 'one of the most perfect machines devised by the infernal gods for the mathematical destruction of a mortal'. Jocasta and Tiresias, walking on the ramparts of Thebes, are warned of impending tragedy by the ghost of Laius but cannot see or hear him. When Oedipus appears, the Sphinx, an attractive young woman allied with the Egyptian god of the dead Anubis, falls in love with Oedipus and reveals her secret; he callously abducts her. Oedipus marries Jocasta, happy to find an older woman, but is alarmed when he looks into Tiresias' eyes. Jocasta notices his pierced feet but remains silent. Seventeen years later Oedipus learns the truth. Jocasta hangs herself, and Oedipus blinds himself with her brooch. The dead Jocasta appears and, with her daughter Antigone, leads Oedipus away. Tiresias prevents Creon from stopping them, since they now belong 'to the people, poets, and unspoiled souls', but Creon speaks of their 'dishonour and shame'.

Cocteau's rewriting of the Oedipus myth, based on his own earlier version of *Oedipus the King* of 1928, is one of the most important of the score of significant versions written since Sophocles (see CHARACTER INDEX, p. 495). Adopting a Senecan view of the tragedy (Oedipus as the innocent victim of malignant fate), Cocteau presents a grotesquely desolate view of the world. While Sophocles traces the gradual revelation of truth, Cocteau, particularly in Act 3 in Jocasta's bedroom, takes us behind closed doors into a nightmare experience, at once banal and terrifying.

Information for Foreigners (*Información para extranajeros*)

A: Griselda Gambaro **Pf:** No Argentinian production (premiered 1978 in Spain) **Pb:** 1975 (in Italian trans.); 1987 (in Spanish) **Tr:** 1989 **G:** Drama in 20 scenes; Spanish prose and some free verse **S:** Spacious residential house, Argentina, 1971 **C:** *c.*50m, 15f, children

A Guide or Guides lead the spectators from room to room in a house. A Girl drenched in cold water is observed by a Man (is he an interrogator?). A Coordinator shows how learning can be accelerated by administering increasingly severe electric shocks for wrong answers. When the Pupil associates prison with nation, the strength of the resulting shock kills him. A Father and Mother discuss the cases of two 'disappeared', a lawyer and his client. Another man is set upon by thugs. A Mother and Father are arrested in front of their children. Sacks are prepared for them, but the children are let go: 'We don't have any small sacks.' A lawyer resists kidnap. When angry neighbours call the police, it turns out that the kidnappers are police themselves. A man from the audience steps forward and murders a Girl by suffocating her. Her distraught Husband and Mother come looking for her. A married couple are kidnapped. She loses a shoe, and the police order a doorman to clean up the blood. Police interrupt a performance of **Othello*. A children's game erupts into violence. Guards dress prisoners handcuffed to the wall in women's underwear and jewellery. A man is attacked, while Prostitutes sing and dance.

The 'information for foreigners', read out by the Guides, comprises a number of news items about political kidnappings, torture, and assault in Argentina (which is why the play remains unperformed in her homeland). Gambaro is nevertheless the most internationally performed Latin American playwright, who explores innovative styles, here a promenade performance round a house, the audience experiencing something of the disorientation of those wrenched from their normal existence, as each room reveals a moment of oppression, like a series of mini-dramas.

Informer, The. See FEAR AND MISERY OF THE THIRD REICH.

ingannati, Gl'. See DECEIVED, THE.

Injustice to Dou E (*Dou E yuan*)

AT: *Snow in Midsummer; The Injustice Done to Tou O; Tou O Was Wronged* **A:** Guan Hanqing **Pf:** 13th c., China **Tr:** 1958 **G:** *Zaju* play in 4 acts; prose and song **S:** The town of Chuchow in China during the Yuan dynasty, 13th c. **C:** 8m, 2f, extras.

A poor scholar, Dou Tien-Chang, owes money to Mrs Tsai, a widow. In order to settle his debt, he gives his only daughter, later named Dou E (Tou E, Tou Ngo), to marry Mrs Tsai's son. The son dies shortly after the wedding, so Dou E, at the age of 20, is also widowed. Angered that Dou E rejects his advances, Donkey Chang plots to kill Mrs Tsai. By mistake, however, he poisons his own father and then accuses Dou E of the murder. Although she refuses to confess when she is beaten, Dou E falsely admits to the crime when Mrs Tsai is threatened with a beating. As Dou E is led to her execution, she prophesies that there will be snow in midsummer at the outrage of her death. She is beheaded, and snow falls. At last her father returns, now a high official. Prompted by the ghost of his daughter, he reviews the case, uncovers the injustice, and orders the execution of Donkey and the beating of the Court Prefect.

This is probably the best-known example of the *zaju* style of drama ('variety drama'), popular in the second half of the 13th century and for most of the 14th in China, and Guan Hanqing was its greatest exponent. *Zaju* plays usually tell a simple story, containing quite a degree of repetition, and so seem quite childlike to Western readers. One of the main features is the use of songs, sung by a single singer irrespective of the character, which comment poetically on the action. *Injustice to Dou E* is one of the popular courtroom dramas (cf. *The *Chalk Circle*) which reflect the injustice of Mongolian rule during the Yuan dynasty.

Inn Keeper, The. See MIRANDOLINA.

Insect Comedy, The (*Ze života hmyzů*)

AT: *The Insect Play; (From) the Life of (the) Insects; The World We Live In; And So Ad Infinitum* **A:** Karel and Josef Čapek **Pf:** 1922, Brno **Pb:** 1921 **Tr:** 1923 **G:** Com. in 3 acts, prologue, and epilogue; Czech prose and verse **S:** Parts of a forest, indeterminate period **C:** 21m, 5f, extras

Prologue and (1) *The Butterflies*. A drunken Tramp falls asleep and dreams of butterflies. Felix, a butterfly-poet, is still a virgin though he is chased by females. Iris, failing to seduce him, flirts with the Tramp, who chases her off. Iris's new lover is eaten by a bird, which she finds highly amusing. Still reciting love poetry, Felix flies off. (2) *The Marauders*. While a chrysalis struggles into life, promising that 'something great is at hand', two beetles roll on a ball of dung, which is stolen by another beetle. Mr and Mrs Cricket are gleeful about the fate of another cricket caught by a fly, but they too are also seized by the fly and impaled on a thorn. The Tramp is shocked at the war going on 'between blades of grass' and witnesses a parasite happily eating the wriggling crickets. (3) *The Ants*. As the chrysalis struggles to be born, an ant colony proclaims that since they all work for the welfare of their state, they are masters of the earth. When a colony of yellow ants invades, there is a bloody war. The triumphant yellow leader declares himself ruler of the world but is crushed underfoot by the Tramp. Epilogue: *Life and Death*. At last the chrysalis bursts forth as a moth but dies almost immediately. The Tramp dies, as a woman takes her baby to baptism. In an alternate ending the Tramp awakes from his dream and, relieved, joyfully accepts the offer of a job.

In this cynical allegory the Čapek brothers present an entertaining view of Europe in the aftermath of the First World War: the effete and irresponsible butterfly-intellectuals, the capitalist beetles and greedy flies and crickets, and the totalitarian ants and their self-important leader. The positive aspect is that the Tramp belatedly (in the original version at least) learns the meaning of existence, and that life goes on (the newborn child is to be baptized).

Inspector, The. See GOVERNMENT INSPECTOR, THE.

Inspector Calls, An

A: J. B. Priestley Pf: 1946, Manchester Pb: 1947 G: Drama in 3 acts S: Dining room of the Birlings' home, English Midlands, 1912 C: 4m, 3f

Arthur Birling, a prosperous north of England factory owner, has two reasons to celebrate: his daughter Sheila is engaged to the eligible Gerald Croft, and Arthur is to be awarded a knighthood for services to industry. As the Birlings and Gerald dine, congratulating themselves on their achievements, they are visited by police inspector Goole. Goole is investigating the suicide of a destitute young girl. At first the family members deny any involvement with her, but it is gradually revealed that they all contributed to her death: Arthur Birling refused to raise her pitifully inadequate wages and then sacked her for going on strike; Sheila's intolerant attitude had her dismissed from her subsequent job as a shop assistant; Gerald had an affair with her then abandoned her; Eric Birling, in turn, left her when he discovered she was pregnant; Mrs Birling's charity committee refused to help her, because she was deemed to be immoral and undeserving. When the Inspector leaves, Birling, terrified of the impending scandal, phones the police and learns that there is no such person as Inspector Goole. Relieved, the family agree it must have been a tasteless hoax, when a telephone call informs them that a young woman has committed suicide and that an inspector is on his way.

With obvious echoes of *The *Government Inspector*, events here take a much more serious turn: Priestley the socialist uncovers, as in **Dangerous Corner*, just below the surface of the respectable and moneyed middle classes the lies and heartlessness which lead in both plays to the death of an offstage figure who returns to accuse them. Priestley's pushing the boundaries of conventional drawing-room realism was realized spectacularly by Stephen Daldry in an expressionistic staging at the National Theatre in 1992.

Inspector General, The. See GOVERNMENT INSPECTOR, THE.

Intelligence Comes to Grief. See WOE FROM WIT.

International Stud, The. See TORCH SONG TRILOGY.

Interview. See AMERICA HURRAH.

In the Beginning. See BACK TO METHUSELAH.

In the Jungle of Cities (*Im Dickicht der Städte*)

A: Bertolt Brecht Pf: 1923, Munich Pb: 1927 Tr: 1961 G: Drama in 11 scenes; German prose S: Chicago, 1912–15 C: 13m, 3f

Shlink, a Malayan timber merchant, picks a quarrel with Garga, an inoffensive, idealistic, but stubborn librarian. Despite being poor, Garga refuses to sell Shlink his opinion about an unimportant book. Abandoning his girl Jane Larry to one of Shlink's henchmen, Garga throws away most of his clothes, and runs off. The battle lines are now drawn. Visiting Shlink in his office, Garga is dismayed to discover that his sister Marie has fallen in love with Shlink. In order to balance the unequal conflict, Shlink makes over his timber enterprise and his home to Garga, who immediately commits fraud in Shlink's name. Rejected by Shlink, Marie, together with Jane, turns to prostitution. Mainly to spite each other, Garga marries Jane, and Shlink sleeps with Marie. When Garga's fraud is exposed, he opts to go to prison in Shlink's place, but also prepares a document denouncing Shlink for raping his sister and for molesting his wife. Three years later, Garga is released from prison, and Shlink has regained control of his business. Producing his document, Garga awaits the lynching of Shlink by a racist mob. At a last meeting between the two antagonists, Shlink confesses that he loves

Garga but concedes that no one can ever escape from isolation in the 'jungle' of existence. Garga claims victory in their fight, and, just before the lynch mob arrives, Shlink dies. Garga sells the timber business, intending to move to New York.

This is the most complex and enigmatic of Brecht's plays, suggesting the obscurely modernist direction he might have taken, had he not through Marxism become persuaded of the need for social relevance in his playwriting. In this desolate image of contemporary capitalist 'dog-eat-dog' society, Brecht offers no insight into the sources of the two men's quarrel, but, as in a boxing match, urges the audience simply to 'concentrate on the finish'.

In the Matter of J. Robert Oppenheimer (*In der Sache J. Robert Oppenheimer*)

A: Heinar Kipphardt **Pf:** 1964, Berlin and Munich **Pb:** 1964; rev. 1978 **Tr:** 1967
G: Documentary drama in 2 acts; German prose
S: Tribunal, USA, 1954 **C:** 14m

The action is devoted entirely to hearings called to establish whether J. Robert Oppenheimer should have his security clearance renewed. Oppenheimer, whose team created the atom bomb dropped on Hiroshima, is now, in the post-war period, dragging his heels over the development of the hydrogen bomb. The first part deals with his association with left-wing sympathizers during the construction of the atom bomb, including his relationship with his communist ex-fiancée. Oppenheimer insists that members of his team were chosen for their expertise not for their political views. In the second part, the emphasis is on the present, and Oppenheimer openly admits that he has concerns about the use to which a new bomb might be put. He rejects Edward Teller's argument that the USA must take a lead in this area, before other, less scrupulous nations develop the H-bomb. He also dismisses Hans Bethe's argument that no single scientist would carry responsibility for further discoveries. Belatedly aware of the social responsibility of the scientist, Oppenheimer asserts: 'we scientists have never had such importance and never been so powerless.' His McCarthy-ite interrogators, of whom he says: 'There are people who are prepared to defend freedom until there is no more of it left,' predictably refuse his security clearance.

Hochhuth's success with *The *Representative* sparked off a plethora of documentary dramas in West Germany, and this play by Kipphardt, staged by 22 more theatres after its joint Berlin and Munich premiere, succeeded better than most by concentrating, like Weiss's *The *Investigation,* on one clearly defined topic. Kipphardt here discusses the social responsibility of the scientist, central to so many contemporary plays, from Brecht's **Life of Galileo*, through Zuckmayer's *The Cold Light* (1955) and Dürrenmatt's *The *Physicists*, to Michael Frayn's **Copenhagen*.

In the Shadow of the Glen. See SHADOW OF THE GLEN, THE.

In Time o' Strife

A: Joe Corrie **Pf:** 1928, Scottish tour **Pb:** 1928
G: Drama in 3 acts; Scots dialect **S:** Kitchen of the Smiths' home, Carhill, Scotland, 1926
C: 5m, 5f

Jock Smith is a miner on strike with the rest of his men, while his wife, two daughters, and a son manage as best they can, living in primitive conditions without enough to eat. When the Parish Council offers no more support, the strikers consider accepting defeat, but cousin Kate urges them to fight on. When Jock's wife Jean returns home, exhausted from her attempts to get food on credit, Jock resolves to go back to work rather than let his family starve, until the thought of being labelled a 'blackleg' stops him. Jean pawns her wedding ring to provide food. Wull Baxter, who is engaged to Jock's older daughter Jenny, goes back to work and is banned from the house. Jock has a win on the horses, but his bookie is arrested before Jock can get his money. When Wull returns from work, he provokes a riot that is bloodily suppressed by the police. The strike leader, Kate's boyfriend, is sentenced to three years in prison. Tam Pettigrew, Kate's father, gets drunk to console himself for his wife's death from malnutrition. Wull tries unsuccessfully to get Jenny to emigrate to Canada with him. The miners are forced back to work, but Jean knows that they'll 'win through yet'.

In the early 20th century there was a vigorous naturalistic school of vernacular writing, closer to continental models like *The *Lower Depths* than to the mainstream English theatre set in drawing rooms and peopled by middle-class characters. O'Casey in Ireland, D. H. Lawrence in Nottingham, and this play by Corrie from Scotland showed how powerful faithfully recorded working-class conflict could be on stage. Set at the time of the General Strike, *In Time o' Strife*, premiered by the Bowhill Players formed from a group of miners, was successfully revived by the 7:84 Theatre Company in 1982, when Margaret Thatcher was squaring up for the 1984 miners' strike.

Invention of Love, The

A: Tom Stoppard **Pf**: 1997, London **Pb**: 1997 **G**: Drama in 2 acts **S**: The Underworld, 1936; Oxford, 1877–80; Worcestershire 1881 and 1897; London, 1882–97 **C**: 21m, 1f, extras

The poet and classical scholar A. E. Housman has died and is being ferried across the Styx by Charon. The scene transforms to his arrival at Oxford at the age of 18, where he meets Moses John Jackson, a science scholar. At Oxford, indulging in witty and learned discourse are also John Ruskin, Walter Pater, Benjamin Jowett, and the young Oscar Wilde. Housman reflects on Catullus' invention of the love poem, but Pater is reprimanded for cultivating the homosexual friendship of an undergraduate, who is sent down. The dead Housman (AEH) discusses textual criticism with his younger self, who admits that he also writes poetry. In the 1880s Housman and Jackson are living together and working in London. At a men's club, politicians and journalists discuss the press and the successful campaign to raise the age of sexual consent to 16. Housman watches Jackson win a race, while a colleague divines that Housman is in love with Jackson. Housman believes that his lengthy research into Propertius' elegiac love poems establishes his 'humanness', because it is 'useless knowledge for its own sake'. Housman confesses his love for Jackson, but they agree to live apart. By 1897 Housman has written poems to Jackson, and published his successful *A Shropshire Lad*. AEH meets a disillusioned Oscar Wilde after his prison sentence for homosexuality.

In this exploration of Housman's career as both classical scholar and poet, Stoppard displays his considerable erudition, while at the same time interestingly juxtaposing, in the manner of his **Travesties*, famous characters from the past. The play turns on the 'invention of love', first in the poetry of the ancients then in the more recent acknowledgement of 'the love that dare not speak its name'. Like Propertius, his classical forebear, Housman writes love elegies for a love that never was.

Investigation, The (*Die Ermittlung*)

A: Peter Weiss **Pf**: 1965, Berlin, 15 other German theatres, and 'reading' in London **Pb**: 1965 **Tr**: 1966 **G**: Documentary drama in 11 scenes; German verse **S**: Courtroom, Frankfurt-am-Main, 1964 **C**: 28m, 2f

In 11 'cantos', the proceedings of the 1964 investigation into the atrocities committed at the Auschwitz Nazi extermination camp in Poland are re-enacted. A judge, prosecutor, and defence counsel cross-examine nine witnesses and 18 defendants over the killing of some four million people at the camp. The anonymous witnesses describe the camp: the rail heads, the gas chambers, the crematoria, the beatings and the medical experiments, concluding that 'what they did | could not have been carried out | without the support of millions of others'. Grotesque details are given, e.g. that in the 'sanatorium' an aspirin was hung on a thread. Those with a temperature were allowed one lick, those with fever two. The accused, who are all named, deny their guilt, claiming that they were merely following orders. They sometimes applaud each other and laugh at the testimony of the witnesses.

This was the first attempt by a German writer to address squarely the most shameful episode of Germany's – and Europe's – recent past, the Holocaust. Significantly, Weiss abandoned the wild theatricality of his successful *Marat/Sade to present the material in as cool and objective a form as possible. Using only court transcripts, together with notes he himself made at the trial, Weiss showed how almost wholly authentic documentary drama could create absorbing theatre. Its simultaneous opening at 16 theatres across West and East Germany gave its staging something of the function of a national act of penance.

Invitation au château, L'. See RING ROUND THE MOON.

Ion

A: Euripides Pf: *c*.413 BC, Athens? Tr: 1782 G: Greek drama in verse S: Before the Temple of Apollo at Delphi, in the mythical past C: 5m, 3f, extras, chorus (f)

Hermes tells how the childless Creusa and Xuthus are coming to seek help from the oracle at Delphi, unaware that Creusa already has a son who resides there. The son, Ion, had been fathered by Apollo and abandoned as a baby in the temple precincts. Creusa arrives at the temple and tells Ion of her lost child. Ion doubts whether Apollo's oracle will be willing to betray Apollo's secret, but she and Xuthus enter the temple in search of the truth. The oracle declares that Xuthus' child will be the first person he meets on leaving the temple. Encountering Ion, he joyfully greets him as his son. Ion accepts the word of Apollo but is still anxious to find out who his mother is. When Creusa learns that Xuthus has found a son and that she will have to accept his illegitimate offspring into her house, she plots to poison Ion. The plot is discovered, and Creusa is condemned to death. As Ion comes to exact revenge, the Priestess of Apollo brings the cradle in which Ion was found as a baby. When Creusa recognizes the cradle, mother and son are reconciled. Athene appears to command Ion to return with his mother and stepfather to Athens, where Ion shall henceforth rule.

The reconciliation of a long-lost foundling with his mother, which takes such a tragic twist in *Oedipus the King,* is here given its first treatment with a happy outcome, and was to become a popular theme, not only of Greek New Comedy, but also of comedies throughout the ages. The averting of tragedy is achieved here not, as so often in Euripides, by divine intervention, but by producing a stage property, the cradle in which Ion was abandoned. Though not one of Euripides' greatest plays, Ion has an impressively intricate plot, which veers between potential tragedy and joyous revelation.

Iphigeneia among the Taurians (*Iphigeneia he en Taurois; Iphigeneia Taurica*)

AT: *Iphigeneia in/on Tauris* A: Euripides Pf: *c*.414–413 BC, Athens Tr: 1759 G: Greek drama in verse S: Before the Temple of Artemis in Tauris, some years after the Trojan War C: 5m, 2f, extras, chorus (f)

Iphigeneia is priestess to the goddess Artemis, who brought her to Tauris after saving her from the sacrificial altar in Aulis. Her brother Orestes and his friend Pylades come to Tauris in search of a statue of Artemis, which they have been commanded by Apollo to bring back to Greece to cleanse Orestes of the guilt of his matricide. It is Iphigeneia's duty as priestess to sacrifice any strangers that land in Tauris. Eventually, however, she and Orestes recognize each other, and there is a touching reconciliation between brother and sister. When Thoas, the King of Tauris, comes to hasten the sacrifice, Iphigeneia pretends that the statue of Artemis must first be cleansed in the sea. She leads off a procession, carrying the statue, taking with her Orestes and Pylades. In this way they make good their escape. Thoas resolves to fetch them back, but the goddess Athene intervenes and orders Thoas to let the Greeks go.

There was no shame in tricking a barbarian with Greek cunning, as Iphigeneia does successfully with Thoas. By the time Goethe came to write his version in 1787, Iphigeneia has to rely on Thoas' generous nature to let her and her brother go. The most impressive feature of Euripides' play is the beautifully managed revelation of the identity of the two siblings. Once he has found his sister, one feels that Orestes' healing can at last begin. Thus, while the leading authority on Greek theatre H. D. F. Kitto argues that a Euripidean tragicomedy like *Iphigeneia among the Taurians* offers 'entertainment divorced from tragic reality and serious themes', there is sufficient potential tragedy in the play to engage an audience at the deepest level. The story was used by Gluck in his opera (1779).

Iphigeneia at Aulis (*Iphigeneia he en Aulidi; Iphigeneia Aulidensis*)

A: Euripides **Pf:** 405 BC, Macedon **Tr:** *c.*1555 **G:** Greek drama in verse **S:** The Greek camp at Aulis, shortly before the Trojan War **C:** 5m, 2f, extras, chorus (f)

The Greek fleet, waiting to sail for Troy, is becalmed in Aulis. The priest Calchas has told Agamemnon that, in order to gain favourable winds, he will have to sacrifice his daughter, Iphigeneia. Pretending that he wishes to marry her to Achilles, Agamemnon sends for her and her mother Clytemnestra. A second message telling them not to come is intercepted by Menelaus, anxious to get the expedition under way so that he can fetch home his errant wife Helen. When Clytemnestra and Iphigeneia arrive with the young Orestes, they soon discover that they have been tricked into coming. Despite their pleas, the reluctant Agamemnon feels it his duty to the Greek army to go ahead with the sacrifice. Only the heroic Achilles promises to defend Iphigeneia. However, the whole army, led by Odysseus, insist on proceeding with the sacrifice. With great dignity and courage, Iphigeneia now willingly goes to her death, but is saved by the goddess Artemis, who at the last moment substitutes a deer as the sacrificial victim and removes Iphigeneia to the island of Tauris.

This play, which was performed after Euripides' death and was almost certainly finished by another hand, is a melodramatic piece, with its main strength being the portrayal of the noble Iphigeneia. She is one of the most admirable of Euripides' female creations, even though Aristotle felt that her sudden willingness to embrace her sacrifice displayed inconsistent characterization. Notable too is the portrayal of Agamemnon, whose psychologically convincing uncertainty is like the vacillation of Orestes in Euripides' **Electra*, and perhaps throws doubt on the wisdom of the Greek expedition against Troy. The story was used by Seneca (1st c. AD), Racine (1674), Gerhart Hauptmann (1943), and by Gluck in his opera (1774).

Ironhand. See GÖTZ VON BERLICHINGEN.

Island, The

AT: *Die Hodoshe Span* **A:** Athol Fugard, with John Kani and Winston Ntshona **Pf:** 1973, Cape Town **Pb:** 1974 **G:** Drama in 1 act **S:** Robben Island prison, *c.*1970 **C:** 2m

John and Winston have been sentenced to 10 years' imprisonment on Robben Island for burning their passbooks. The (unseen) sadistic guard Hodoshe (= 'carrion-fly') subjects them to humiliating punishments and beatings. John reminds Winston that he must prepare for his role as Antigone in a prison concert in six days' time and talks the rather slow-witted Winston through the plot of Sophocles' **Antigone* and her trial for burying her brother Polyneices, a traitor to the state. John then pretends to phone his friend Scott in Port Elizabeth: sending love to Winston's wife, and to his own, their mood suddenly becomes subdued. Five days later, Winston tries on his costume, false breasts and a wig made of rope. John collapses in hysterical laughter, and Winston grows angry and almost refuses to do the role. John is called away to be told that his sentence has been reduced and that he will be free in three months' time. At first both men are jubilant, but then John feels guilty and Winston resentful: 'Your freedom stinks, John, and it's driving me mad.' At the concert, John as Creon condemns Winston as Antigone to be immured on 'the Island'. 'Antigone' takes her leave: 'I go now to my living death, because I honoured those things to which honour belongs.'

One of the simplest and finest products of anti-apartheid theatre, *The Island* draws on Greek tragedy to suggest that there is a higher law of humanity than the law of the state. The play moves flawlessly from comedy to high seriousness, creating thought-provoking entertainment.

Italian Straw Hat, An (*Un chapeau de paille d'Italie*)

AT: *A Leghorn Hat; Horse Eats Hat; The Italian Straw Hat* **A:** Eugène Labiche (with Marc Michel) **Pf:** 1851, Paris **Pb:** 1851 **Tr:** 1917 **G:** Farce in 3 acts; French prose **S:** Paris, 1850s **C:** 11m, 6f, extras

Fadinard, a young gentleman due to be married that very day, is kept from his wedding by the hysterical Anais Beauperthuis, a young married woman. Fadinard's horse has chewed a straw hat which Anais had hung in a tree while she had a secret meeting with her lover. Now she dare not return hatless to her jealous husband and insists that Fadinard replace it. The wedding party, including the bride's domineering father and her deaf uncle, arrive at Fadinard's home, and he sets off with them in search of a hat, while they imagine they are going to the wedding. The quest leads him to the shop of a milliner, who turns out to be a jilted lover, which the guests think is the city hall, and to a society hostess, who mistakes Fadinard for an Italian opera singer, and everyone sits down to the 'wedding breakfast'. Fadinard marries his bride in the street, and the trail leads eventually to someone who bought an identical hat. Unfortunately, this is Beauperthuis himself, to whom Fadinard explains the reason for his search. Just as Beauperthuis is about to confront his wife, Fadinard finds an identical hat amongst the wedding presents, which saves Anais from disgrace.

One of the best known of the 174 plays by Labiche, the greatest comic playwright of 19th-century France, this has all the classic elements of farce: a recognizably normal individual who gets caught in an extraordinary situation, here the conflicting demands of getting married and finding a hat, and pursues this with relentless logic. The improbabilities of the plot are helped along by the disabilities of the elderly guests, notably deafness and short-sightedness. This may not seem 'politically correct', but the joke is much more at the expense of those who fail to understand than on the disabled themselves.

It Is So! If You Think So. See RIGHT YOU ARE, IF YOU THINK SO.

Ivanov

A: Anton Chekhov **Pf:** 1887, Moscow **Pb:** 1888 **Tr:** 1912 **G:** Drama in 4 acts; Russian prose **S:** Ivanov's estate and Lebedev's home, central Russia, 1880s **C:** 11m, 5f, extras

Nikolai Ivanov, a 35-year-old government official, feels 'paralysed. Half dead or something.' His debts are mounting, he is exhausted, and he feels guilty about his adoring Jewish wife Anna, who defied her family to change her name and religion to marry Ivanov. She is now dying of tuberculosis, and Ivanov no longer loves her. Refusing to spend the evening with her, he goes to visit his friend Paul Lebedev, where Lebedev's 20-year-old daughter Sasha has been defending Ivanov against local gossips. Alone together, Sasha declares her love for Ivanov, and begs him to elope with her. As they embrace passionately, Anna enters. Ivanov is consumed with guilt and self-recrimination, intensified by Anna's accusations that he married her for her money and is now pursuing Sasha to get out of his debts to Lebedev. Furious, he calls her 'a Jewish bitch' and reveals the secret that she is dying. A year later, Anna is dead, and Ivanov is that day getting married to Sasha. However, Ivanov cannot bear to inflict his 'moaning and groaning' on the lovely young Sasha and calls off the wedding. His young friend Dr Lvov, who secretly loved Anna, publicly denounces Ivanov. Ivanov takes his gun and shoots himself.

In his first performed full-length play, which he revised at least seven times, Chekhov mocks the rural landowning class, especially their anti-Semitism, and shows what an empty, idle, self-pitying life Ivanov leads, 'playing at Hamlet'. Chekhov had not yet succeeded in creating his own special theatrical style: *Ivanov* abounds in stock characters and melodramatic incidents, and the protagonist's many monologues, which increased with each rewriting, slow the action. Nevertheless, *Ivanov* is a work of humour and insight, foreshadowing his four major plays.

Jacob's Wake

A: Michael Cook Pf: 1975, Lennoxville, Quebec Province Pb: 1975 G: Trag. in 2 acts; Newfoundland dialect S: The Blackburns' home on the Newfoundland coast, 1970s C: 4m, 2f

Skipper Blackburn is lying upstairs in bed, as he has done for the last 30 years since his elder son Jacob died. He is waited on by his long-suffering daughter-in-law Rosie. His surviving children are Mary, a prim teacher, and Winston, Rosie's husband, a good-for-nothing who lives off his illegal still and welfare payments. Rosie and Winston's three sons come home for Easter: Alonzo, Brad with his wife Mary, and Wayne, all of them with guilty secrets, although Wayne is a member of the provincial legislature. In less than 24 hours, the action unfolds and the past is revealed. Alonzo forges his father's signature, so that Skipper will be removed to an institution, but his fraud is exposed. Brad, facing his guilt over the death of a girl he made pregnant, leaves the house to die in a storm. It transpires that Jacob lost his life when his father ordered him out on to the ice to hunt seals, just as a storm was brewing. Skipper now imagines that Winston is Jacob. As another storm gathers momentum, Skipper is dying. His ghost appears in full Master's uniform as the storm reaches its height. Ordering the women below decks, he assumes command of his ship during a seal hunt. Suddenly, the whole house is engulfed by a huge wave which drowns everyone.

With echoes of Ibsen and O'Neill, Michael Cook's bleak image of a family living in Jacob's 'wake' (both the trail he has left behind, and the celebration of his death) has been staged internationally. The Blackburns represent the decline in the traditional values of their Newfoundland fishing community: although Skipper is a crazy old man, he stands for something more solid than the mendacity and callousness of the younger generation.

Jail Diary of Albie Sachs, The

A: David Edgar Pf: 1978, London Pb: 1978 G: Drama in 2 acts S: Cells in Cape Town prisons, seaside, and Albie's office, 1963–6 C: 18m

Albie Sachs, a 29-year-old lawyer who has dared to speak out against the arbitrary exercise of law under apartheid, is confined to a concrete cell and given only the Bible to read. He refuses to answer questions from the Special Branch Officers, especially when they assert that he has been to sabotage school. Albie finds ways of overcoming the boredom of being in solitary confinement. At the end of the 90-day period during which suspects can legally be detained, he is released and immediately rearrested. While being no militant, he understands the need for armed struggle. He strikes up a relationship with Synman, the Station Commander, who talks of the oppression that the Afrikaners suffered under British rule. After 138 days in detention, Albie's mind starts to deteriorate. He is persuaded that any information he might have is now useless, and that the authorities simply want to break his resistance. He is about to answer questions, when he learns that the Sergeant once cruelly murdered a black servant and was sentenced to just two years' prison. Albie is eventually released then arrested two years later. This time, tortured by sleep deprivation, he confesses. He is finally released and leaves for England.

Adapted from Sachs's *Jail Diary*, this episodic piece with lengthy monologues is probably the most successful anti-apartheid play by a non-South African. At a time when so-called democracies, in the wake of 9/11, detain terrorist suspects without trial or legal representation, the piece is perhaps due for revival.

Jane Shore (*The Tragedy of Jane Shore*)

A: Nicholas Rowe **Pf**: 1714, London **Pb**: *c.*1713 **G**: Trag. in 5 acts; blank verse **S**: London, 1483 **C**: 6m, 2f, extras

Richard, Duke of Gloucester, is preparing to seize the throne. Hastings intercedes on behalf of Jane Shore, the former King's mistress, now destitute. Richard rightly suspects that Hastings wants to have Jane for himself. Jane's husband appears, disguised as Dumont, and is taken on as her servant. Encountering Hastings attempting to rape Jane, Dumont fights with him but spares his life. A jealous friend Alicia, who is in love with Hastings, tells Richard that Jane is plotting with Hastings against him. When Jane refuses to support Richard's claim to the throne, Richard denounces her and Hastings. Jane is condemned to die miserably on the streets, while Hastings is to be executed. Alicia goes mad with guilt. Dumont finds Jane starving in the street, and she dies in his arms. Dumont is arrested for offering her support, against Richard's decree.

As in Dryden's rewriting of **Antony and Cleopatra* in **All for Love*, Rowe here offers not so much a watered-down version of **Richard III* as a much more concentrated view of one episode taken from Shakespeare's history. Unlike Dryden, we now find ourselves in a domestic world, in which means of financial support become more important than the leading of armies, the perfidy of friends more significant than the betrayal of rulers. By introducing a more accessible and democratic view of tragedy and by giving prominence to the more subtle and passive character of the female hero, Rowe begins to undermine notions of conventional tragedy: 'No princes here lost royalty bemoan, But you shall meet with sorrows like your own.'

Jeu d'Adam, Le. See PLAY OF ADAM, THE.

Jeu de l'amour et du hasard, Le. See GAME OF LOVE AND CHANCE, THE.

Jewish Wife, The. See FEAR AND MISERY OF THE THIRD REICH.

Jew of Malta, The (*The Famous Tragedy of the Rich Jew of Malta*)

A: Christopher Marlowe (with other author/s?) **Pf**: *c.*1589, London **Pb**: 1633 **G**: Com. in 5 acts; blank verse **S**: Barabas's house and other locations on Malta, 16th c. **C**: 16m, 5f, extras

The play is introduced by Machiavel(li). The Governor of Malta is under pressure by the Turks to pay tribute money. He therefore orders that half the wealth of the Jews should be seized. When a rich Jew, Barabas, protests, all his possessions are confiscated, and his home is turned into a nunnery. Seeking revenge, Barabas orders his daughter Abigail to become engaged to the Governor's son, Lodowick, and also to her beloved, Mathias. Playing on their mutual jealousy, Barabas gets his rascally servant to deliver forged challenges to the two fiancés. In the ensuing duel both young men are killed. The grieving Abigail becomes a nun, and her father is so angry that he decides to poison her, succeeding in killing all the nuns in the convent. On her deathbed Abigail reveals the truth to her confessor, who tries to convert Barabas and gain his wealth for his order. Barabas strangles the Friar and blames his murder on another friar, who is hanged. Barabas's servant reveals Barabas's misdeeds to his mistress, who reports them to the Governor. Barabas opens the gates of the city to the besieging Turks, temporarily becomes governor, but dies by falling into a boiling cauldron intended for the invaders. The Turks are defeated and the Governor triumphs.

Although the play is based on the failed siege of Malta by the Ottomans in 1565, most of the action derives from grotesque and violent incident, generated primarily by the evil figure of the Jew Barabas, originally played with huge success by Edward Alleyn. The play indulges in distasteful stereotyping of a Jew who gets his just deserts, and shows the Christian conquering of the heathen Turks, which no doubt accounted for its great contemporary popularity. On the other hand, the Christians are not idealized. Barabas is wronged, and the Christians are devious, grasping, and hypocritical.

Job Creation. See FEAR AND MISERY OF THE THIRD REICH.

Joe Turner's Come and Gone

A: August Wilson **Pf**: 1986, New Haven, Connecticut **Pb**: 1988 **G**: Com. in 2 acts **S**: Boarding house in Pittsburgh, 1911 **C**: 5m, 4f, 2 children (1m, 1f)

Seth Holly, a northern black in his early fifties, owns a boarding house and makes pots and pans. Other residents of the boarding house are: Jeremy Furlow, a road-worker and guitar player; Bynum Walker, who grows herbs and is a bit of a mystic; and the newly arrived Herald Loomis and his 11-year-old daughter Zonia. Herald has come looking for his wife Martha. Mattie Campbell comes to ask Bynum's help in getting her man back, who had left her after the death of their two babies. Bynum cannot bring her man back but promises her a new one. Immediately, Jeremy asks her to come with him to a concert where he is playing that night. Rutherford Selig, a 'People Finder', will try to locate Martha for Loomis. Jeremy wins a prize at the concert, and Mattie agrees to move in with him. An attractive woman Molly Cunningham rents a room in the boarding house. That night they have a wild African dance, interrupted by Loomis, who leaps around speaking in tongues. Jeremy is sacked for refusing to give up some of his wages to a white bully. Jeremy flirts with Molly, and she agrees to be his woman. Bynum realizes that Loomis had been captured for Joe Turner's chain gang and was torn from his family for seven years. Selig finds Martha, and mother and daughter are reunited. When Martha will not take him back, Loomis cuts his chest and at last feels free, 'cleansed and given breath'.

This is one of the finest of poet August Wilson's plays. Like an African-American version of Gorky's **Lower Depths* (Bynum having strong similarities with Luka), the lives of poor blacks are explored, together with the effects of continuing racial oppression.

John Ferguson

A: St John Ervine **Pf**: 1915, Dublin **Pb**: 1915 **G**: Trag. in 4 acts **S**: Rural Ireland, 1885 **C**: 8m, 2f

Old John Ferguson, an invalided Ulster farmer, is deeply religious, finding consolation in the Bible when his life seems in ruins. Because his son Andrew is not managing the farm very well, a bullying neighbour Henry Witherow is threatening to foreclose their mortgage. There are two hopes: a cheque from Ferguson's brother in America; or Ferguson's daughter Hannah will have to marry the well-to-do local grocer James Caesar. She agrees to go out with him, but recognizes that she could not bear to marry such a repulsive individual. While Caesar furiously demands of the family that Hannah should marry him, Hannah runs in distressed, announcing that Witherow has raped her. Caesar strides off, planning to exact revenge. Despite Fergusons's admonitions about Christian forgiveness, Hannah's brother Andrew, aware that Caesar is too cowardly to do anything, leaves with his gun. The following morning Witherow has been shot, and, despite protesting his innocence, Caesar is arrested for his murder. Hannah responds by being kind to him for the first time. The cheque arrives from America, but too late: 'One man's dead and another's in jail because uncle forgot the mail day.' Finally, Andrew admits that he killed Witherow, and despite his mother's urging him to run away, gives himself up and faces hanging.

St John Ervine, who managed the Abbey Theatre 1915–16, directed *John Ferguson*, probably his finest play, while he was there. As a Northern Irish Protestant, Ervine was keen to extend the Abbey repertoire beyond its limited repertoire. He sacked the whole company and resigned over the Easter Rising. *John Ferguson* has undeniably melodramatic moments, but its image of unmoving Presbyterian faith remains powerful.

John Gabriel Borkman

A: Henrik Ibsen Pf: 1897, Helsinki; 1897, Oslo Pb: 1896 Tr: 1907 G: Drama in 4 acts; Norwegian prose S: The Rentheim estate outside Oslo, 1890s C: 3m, 5f

Although John Gabriel Borkman loved Ella Rentheim, he expediently married her twin sister Gunhild. Imprisoned for fraudulent business dealings, he was released eight years ago. He and his wife came to live with Ella on her estate, where she had been bringing up the Borkmans' son Erhart. Mrs Borkman now dreams that Erhart will live to redeem her husband's name, but Ella wants to control his future. Borkman, confined to an upstairs room, quarrels with Vilhelm Foldal, a worn-looking clerk, whom he normally tolerates because Foldal flatters his illusions of greatness. Ella visits Borkman and tells him that his decision to marry her sister murdered their souls. Since she is soon to die, she wants to adopt Erhart and leave him all her wealth. Mrs Borkman bursts in furious about this proposal, addressing her husband for the first time in eight years. Unrepentant about seeking wealth and power, Borkman asks Erhart's help to begin again, while Ella begs him to stay with her until she dies. Erhart rejects them all and their suffocating lives, preferring to leave with Fanny Wilton, a strong-willed divorcee. For the first time Borkman leaves the house, going out into the snowy night followed by Ella. He speaks of the riches he sought to harvest from the mountain ores. He collapses and dies in the cold, and the sisters are joined in their grief.

In this, his second-last play, Ibsen shows himself a master of his craft. He blends contemporary capitalist endeavour with a primitive relationship with the earth and its treasures. He combines naturalistic dialogue and settings with a deep sense of the unreal. He allows comic moments to stand next to moments of high emotion, and he creates a play depicting the wasted life of the elderly juxtaposed to the hope of a better and freer life for the young.

Joker of Seville, The. See TRICKSTER OF SEVILLE, THE.

Joking Apart

A: Alan Ayckbourn Pf: 1978, Scarborough Pb: 1979 G: Com. in 2 acts S: English garden, 1966–78 C: 4m, 7f (4 roles to be played by same actress)

Richard Clarke and Anthea, a divorcee with two children, are a charming and successful couple in their twenties. They have invited people to their bonfire party: their new neighbours, Revd Hugh and Louise Emerson, their old friend Brian with his latest girlfriend Melody, and Sven and Olive Holmenson. Sven, a rather self-important Finn, is Richard's business colleague in a firm of importers of Scandinavian household goods, and Brian works for them. Melody is unhappy, because Brian is still in love with Anthea. Four years later, Brian is visiting with a new girlfriend Mandy (played by the same actress as Melody). Sven is worried because Richard keeps making unilateral decisions in their firm, although they always work out well. Sven warns the other guests that Richard and Anthea are dangerous, because 'they have to take people over'. On Boxing Day four years later, everyone is gathered again, Brian having brought Mo this time. Sven envies Richard for his flair in business, and Hugh confesses to having fallen in love with Anthea. A further four years on, and Richard and Anthea are organizing a party for their daughter Debbie's birthday. Sven is now suffering from a heart condition and is depressed by Richard's continuing brilliance. Hugh is miserable, his wife is on drugs. Brian dyes his hair and hopes that Debbie may pay him some attention – but in vain.

The common comparison of Ayckbourn with Chekhov is particularly apposite here. Characters come and go, but virtually nothing happens. The interest lies in the way that the attractive and happy partnership of Anthea and Richard, a model of the success of bungling English pragmatism, sucks on the happiness of all their friends like a leech. But as Richard says to Sven: 'I don't quite see what I'm supposed to do.'

Journey's End

A: R. C. Sherriff **Pf:** 1928, London **Pb:** 1929 **G:** Drama in 3 acts **S:** British dugout before Saint-Quentin, France, May 1918 **C:** 11m

Lieutenant Osborne, an elderly former schoolmaster, welcomes young Second Lieutenant James Raleigh to their company, deployed in the trenches in the First World War. However, Osborne warns him that the company commander Captain Stanhope, whom Raleigh had hero-worshipped at school, is a changed man after three years at the front. Stanhope has been able to survive the horrors of war only by drinking heavily. Now Stanhope is angry that Raleigh has joined his company, not least because he fears that Raleigh will write to his sister, Stanhope's fiancée, and reveal that Stanhope 'reek[s] of whisky all day'. Amidst the soldiers' banter and awareness of the futility of the war, orders come that Osborne, Raleigh, and ten men are to be sent on a mission to capture a German soldier for interrogation. Raleigh succeeds in bringing in a prisoner, but it has cost the lives of Osborne and six men. While the other officers celebrate the success of the mission, Raleigh mourns the death of Osborne. Aware of his implied reproach, Stanhope insists that this is the only way hardened soldiers can cope. The next dawn, Raleigh is shot in a German attack. He dies in Stanhope's arms, and Stanhope, reconciled to his old schoolfriend, goes out to face the enemy.

This was the most important British drama to emerge from the First World War. By contrast with the American **What Price Glory?*, Sherriff's play appears class-ridden and somewhat dated. Anderson and Stalling's brash rough soldiers consoling themselves with sex are here replaced with mainly public-school products surviving on whisky and champagne, all the action occurring in the officers' dugout with ordinary soldiers kept to the background. Nevertheless, the play succeeds well in communicating the tensions and horrors of life in the trenches, and was successfully revived in the West End in 2003.

Jovial Crew, A

AT: *The Merry Beggars* **A:** Richard Brome **Pf:** 1641, London **Pb:** 1652 **G:** Com. in 5 acts; prose and blank verse **S:** Mapledown, Kent, and the environs, at an indeterminate (late medieval?) period **C:** 22m, 4f, extras

Squire Oldrents, a charitable old gentleman, is made unhappy by a prophecy that his daughters will become beggars. He is also worried that his steward Springlove may return to his life as a vagabond. Indeed, in spring, when the beggars who have been sheltered by Oldrents over the winter take to the road again, not only are they joined by Springlove but also by Oldrents's two daughters and their sweethearts. Life as a beggar is not as romantic and free as the young people had dreamed. An eloping couple who join the beggars fall out of love with each other, and Springlove wins the girl for himself. Returning to Oldrents, all are forgiven for running away. Springlove is discovered to be Oldrents's illegitimate son, and the three couples prepare for marriage.

Brome served as an apprentice to Ben Jonson, but retains none of the mordant satire of the older writer. Indeed, Pepys described this light-hearted comedy as 'the most innocent play' that he had ever seen. Ironically, but perhaps predictably, in the year before the Puritan closing of the theatres, this comedy is pervaded by nostalgia for an earlier time, when it was possible to play at being a jolly beggar and suffer nothing worse than an uncomfortable night and an empty belly and to be saved by the beneficence of a country squire. A musical version of 1731 achieved great success.

jüdische Frau, Die. See FEAR AND MISERY OF THE THIRD REICH.

Julius Caesar (*The Tragedie of Julius Caesar*)

A: William Shakespeare **Pf:** 1599, London **Pb:** 1623 **G:** Trag. in 5 acts; blank verse and prose **S:** Rome, Sardis, and near Philippi, 45–42 BC **C:** 33m, 2f, extras

Flushed with his success in the foreign wars, Caesar returns to Rome, cheered by the crowds and virtually assuming the role of dictator.

A group of idealistic conspirators, led by Cassius and Brutus, Caesar's friend, decide that Caesar must be assassinated. Despite warnings from a soothsayer and his wife, Caesar goes to the Senate, where he is stabbed to death. Mark Antony persuades the conspirators to let him give Caesar's funeral oration and succeeds in turning the mob against Cassius and Brutus. Caesar's nephew Octavius returns to Rome and forms a triumvirate with Antony and Lepidus. Cassius and Brutus, after quarrelling, march towards Philippi to meet the Roman army. Troubled by his conscience and visited by Caesar's ghost, Brutus faces defeat. Cassius brings about his own death, and Brutus commits suicide. The victorious triumvirate have avenged Caesar's death but acknowledge Brutus' greatness.

Based on Roman history as recounted by Plutarch, *Julius Caesar* remains a highly relevant political drama. Although the title figure is dead by the beginning of Act 3, his spirit dominates the second half of the play. By contrast, Brutus presents a modern anti-hero, full of self-doubt while acting from the highest motives. Thus we are presented with the choice between strong dictatorial rule and the democracy favoured by the conspirators. Significantly, neither the conspirators nor, eventually as we shall see in **Antony and Cleopatra*, the new triumvirate, succeed. The Duke of Saxe-Meiningen staged *Julius Caesar* with ground-breaking realism in the 1870s, a production which subsequently influenced both Stanislavsky and Antoine. In 1937 in New York, Orson Welles set his notorious production of the play in Nazi Germany.

Jumpers

A: Tom Stoppard **Pf:** 1972, London **Pb:** 1972; rev. 1973, 1986 **G:** Com. in 2 acts and a coda **S:** Study, bedroom, and hall of George's apartment, *c.*1970 **C:** 12m, 2f

Dorothy (Dotty) Moore, a beautiful prematurely retired musical-comedy actress, lives with her husband George, a Professor of Moral Philosophy. She gives a surreal party, at which George's po-faced Secretary strips, Dotty fails to sing about the moon, and a group of acrobats ('Jumpers') perform incompetently. The Jumpers form a pyramid, and one of their number is shot. The following morning, Dotty calls distractedly for help, while George prepares a paper on the existence of God. To illustrate Zeno's paradox, he fires off arrows and intends to use his tortoise and hare as an empirical test of the truth of Aesop's fable. However, the hare has gone missing. Inspector Bones, an ardent fan of Dotty, comes to investigate the murder of the acrobat. Dotty is visited by the Vice-Chancellor Sir Archibald Jumper, a philosophical relativist and psychiatrist, who is 'helping' Dotty through a breakdown occasioned by the landing of men on the moon, which has ruined her romantic songs. Archie is also chief gymnast, and probably the murderer of the dead Jumper, who turns out to be another philosopher and a potential rival for Dotty's affections. George is distraught when he discovers that his arrow has impaled his pet hare, and he then steps fatally on his tortoise. Sobbing, he finds himself in a dream symposium, in which public figures behave anarchically, with the Archbishop of Canterbury questioning the existence of God, and where George delivers a confused version of his paper.

Stoppard once stated that 'plays are events rather than texts', and this is borne out by the wildly varied and theatrical quality of *Jumpers*, which spectacularly combines philosophical argument, musical comedy, witty dialogue, and farcically improbable situation. The play can be read as a profound commentary on the nature of evidence (both criminal and philosophical), or it may be enjoyed merely as a piece of brilliant trivia.

Juno and the Paycock

A: Sean O'Casey **Pf:** 1924, Dublin **Pb:** 1925 **G:** Tragicom. in 3 acts **S:** Dublin tenement living room, 1922 **C:** 14m, 5f

Despite the 'peacock', her drunken and idle husband 'Captain' Jack Boyle, his wife Juno struggles to keep the family going. Her son Johnny, who was wounded in the nationalist struggle against the English, cannot work and lives in terror during the mounting civil war between republican factions. Her pretty daughter Mary is on strike for 'a principle'. When Juno tells Boyle of a job, he pleads leg cramps and settles down to a cup of tea with his fawning companion Joxer Daly. They are surprised by Juno's return. She has met an English schoolteacher Charles Bentham, who tells them that the family may expect to inherit a fortune from a distant relative. Boyle dismisses the wastrel Joxer and looks forward to a new life of wealth and sobriety. Two days later the Boyles give a party amidst the vulgar decorations bought from loans that Boyle has borrowed in anticipation of his inheritance. Joxer is back in favour, and Bentham makes overtures to Mary. Johnny's terror about the shooting of a neighbour whose funeral passes down the stairs, spoils the jollity briefly, but they soon resume their drinking and songs. Eventually all but Johnny leave for the funeral. A young man summons Johnny to a meeting later that evening. Two months later Mary has been abandoned by Bentham, and she discovers that she is pregnant. Boyle is outraged and wants his daughter thrown out of the house. Creditors demand repayment of their loans, and it becomes clear that Boyle may never get his promised inheritance. Two 'Irregulars' (IRA members who have not disbanded) come to take away Johnny to make him pay for his neighbour's death. Boyle goes off drinking with Joxer, and bailiffs arrive to take away all their possessions. News of Johnny's death comes, and Juno laments his passing. She leaves with Mary, promising that at least her baby will have two mothers. The drunken Boyle and Joxer stagger in, reeling around in search of the missing furniture, and Boyle comments that the whole world is in 'a terrible state of chassis' (chaos).

This is the most frequently performed of O'Casey's plays and offers rewarding opportunities for actors. The events of the play could hardly be more devastating and are worthy of melodrama. But O'Casey's theatrical genius lifts the play well above melodrama through its courageous and perfectly judged balance between tragedy and comedy. Probably based on O'Casey's own mother, Juno is a tragic but not self-pitying figure, whose speech, using the simplest language, sometimes rises to lyrical heights. Boyle and Joxer are a comic duo, whose Falstaffian antics constantly relieve the tension. The masterstroke is to bring the two elements together at the end, so that the two drunks stagger around comically on a tragically empty stage, challenging each audience member to choose between laughter and tears.

Justice

A: John Galsworthy. **Pf:** 1910, London **Pb:** 1910 **G:** Trag. in 4 acts **S:** A lawyer's office, a law court, and a prison, 1900s **C:** 17m, 1f, extras

William Falder is a diligent and honest clerk in the legal firm of the How Brothers. His record is impeccable until he becomes involved with Ruth Honeywill, a young mother and the victim of a violent husband. Desperate to help her, he forges a cheque, and his crime is soon discovered. Although his office manager Cokeson tries to save him, and despite a very able legal defence, William is sent to prison. Spending three years in solitary confinement and refused any outside visits, William suffers a breakdown. When, a shadow of his former self, he is finally released after two years, he seeks employment with his former boss. The latter will only give William his job back if William promises to abandon the fallen woman Ruth. He refuses, and, driven by his need to get a job, he forges a reference. When this forgery too is discovered, William cannot face the prospect of prison again and commits suicide by throwing himself down stone steps.

Clearly this piece with its ironic title owes much to Tom Taylor's *The *Ticket-of-Leave Man*, although in the earlier play the hero was totally innocent of his 'crime'. By having his hero commit forgery twice, Galsworthy introduces welcome complexity into the theme of the released prisoner. We recognize that William acts foolishly; yet he maintains our sympathy, because we see that he acts from the highest motives. His fate is tragic, because there is no honourable way out for him, whereas Taylor's melodrama could provide a conveniently happy end. The impact of the play in 1910 was so great that it led Home Secretary Winston Churchill to reform the penal code.

Justice Without Revenge (*El castigo sin venganza*)

AT: *Lost in a Mirror* **A:** Lope de Vega **Pf:** 1632, Madrid **Pb:** 1634 **Tr:** 1961 **G:** Trag. in 3 acts; Spanish verse **S:** Ferrara, Italy, and its environs, 15th c. **C:** 10m, 4f, extras

When Federico, bastard son of the Duke of Ferrara, learns that his father is to marry, he is pleased that this may spell an end to his father's licentious behaviour at court, but, on the other hand, fears that he shall no longer be heir. Federico aids his father's intended bride, Cassandra, on her way to Ferrara, and they fall in love with each other. The Duke plans for Federico to marry his cousin, Aurora, but Federico spurns her. When the Duke is called away from court, Cassandra gives herself to Federico. Returning to court, the Duke is told of his son's adultery with his stepmother, an allegation which Federico's professed desire to marry Aurora, fails to counter. Cassandra's horror at learning that Federico seeks Aurora's hand in marriage incites the Duke to greater jealousy. His honour affronted, he seizes Cassandra and binds her, hooded, to a chair. He then insists that Federico kill this hooded 'traitor'. When Federico obeys, his father denounces him, and Federico is killed by Cassandra's cousin.

Based on a true incident, this is one of the finest of Lope de Vega's extraordinary output of some 300 to 400 plays. It is an elegantly structured play with a violent climax worthy of Jacobean tragedy (here performed offstage in an inner room, revealed by pulling back a curtain – not unlike the *ekkuklema* of Greek theatre). Central to the play is the concern for honour, which, though recognized as the 'cruel enemy of mankind', nevertheless demands punishment of those who cause dishonour, even though it may cause greater pain than would forgiveness. In this way 'honour' is an unreal game, but it may here offer the only bastion against the chaos of natural desire.

Jux will er sich machen, Einen. See ON THE RAZZLE.

Kabala sviatosh. See CABAL OF HYPOCRITES, A.

Kanjinchō. See SUBSCRIPTION LIST, THE.

Kaspar

A: Peter Handke Pf: 1968, Frankfurt-am-Main Pb: 1967 Tr: 1969 G: Drama in 1 act (65 scenes); German prose and free verse S: Bare stage, indeterminate period C: 6m, 3 voices (m or f)

Kaspar, an innocent, clown-like figure, stumbles around on the stage, trying to come to terms with his environment. At first he is unable to speak, but then manages to repeat the one sentence he knows: 'I want to become someone like somebody else was once.' He is bombarded by the voices of three invisible speakers, who gradually destroy Kaspar's sentence, and he begins the slow process of learning language. With more linguistic control, he gains more confidence; for now that he can name things, he can establish order: 'Every sentence helps you along.' This confidence grows as he is joined by other Kaspars, until he pronounces all the rules of social propriety. But this is followed by disintegration, as he declares, 'Every sentence | is for the birds,' and asserts that language is inadequate as a means of expression. Finally, his words no longer make sense, and as the curtain jerks shut, he utters his last sentence: 'I am only I by chance' (inexplicably, the standard English translation closes with Othello's demented 'Goats and monkeys').

This 'speech-torture' play is based on the historical figure of Kaspar Hauser, who claimed, when found wandering the streets of Nuremberg in 1828, that he had spent the first 16 years of his life confined to a chicken coop. Initially he was able to speak only one sentence. After the controversial **Offending the Audience*, which consisted almost entirely of words, Handke here wrote a piece in which the protagonist must first learn to speak. In the process, his innocence is destroyed, his perception distorted, and language is seen as an instrument of oppression.

Kathleen ni Houlihan. See CATHLEEN NI HOULIHAN.

kaukasische Kreidekreis, Der. See CAUCASIAN CHALK CIRCLE, THE.

Kentuckian, The. See LION OF THE WEST, THE.

Key West. See QUAY WEST.

Killer, The (*Tueur sans gages*)

A: Eugène Ionesco Pf: 1959, Paris Pb: 1958 Tr: 1960 G: Drama in 3 acts; French prose S: Paris, mid-20th c. C: 15m, 3f, extras

Bérenger, an ordinary French citizen, is hugely impressed by a 'radiant city within a city', proudly shown to him by the Architect, who says that it never rains there. The only drawback is that there is a remorseless killer on the loose in the area. The Architect's secretary Dany, with whom Bérenger promptly falls in love, becomes the Killer's next victim. Resolving to do something, Bérenger returns to his apartment to discover that his invalid friend has a briefcase containing the Killer's plans for mass extermination. Bérenger persuades his friend that they must go to the police, but the friend leaves the briefcase behind. In the street, a mass meeting is being addressed by a female demagogue proclaiming totalitarian ideas. A drunken heckler is beaten to the ground. Discovering the missing briefcase, Bérenger looks at those in the crowd, but fails to find the right one. When two burly policemen refuse to help him, Bérenger heads for the police station. On his way there, as it grows dark, Bérenger encounters the Killer, a misshapen one-eyed dwarf. Bérenger tries to reason with him, urging him to give up his murders. When the Killer merely chuckles at him, Bérenger draws two pistols, but is powerless to shoot. Still chuckling, the Killer approaches Bérenger with a knife.

In a more coherently satirical mode than in his early absurdist pieces, Ionesco here explores the general complicity of contemporary society, not only the blind eye turned towards dictators like Hitler (the contents of the friend's briefcase could represent *Mein Kampf*), but also in the post-war willingness to accept 'progress' (here the new city) without questioning its human cost.

Killing of Sister George, The

A: Frank Marcus **Pf:** 1965, Bristol **Pb:** 1965 **G:** Drama in 3 acts **S:** June's living room, London, 1960s **C:** 4f

Sister George, played by the actress June Buckridge, is the district nurse character in a popular BBC radio serial *Applehurst*. Something of a national figure, Sister George rides her bicycle down country lanes singing hymns and is loved by everyone for her goodness. Unfortunately, June's private life does not match that of Sister George: she is a heavy drinker and is constantly having rows with her lesbian partner Alice (Childie) McNaught, a spoilt and childish woman. Matters come to a head when June is involved in a drunken incident in a taxi with some nuns. Mercy Croft, a BBC executive and June's immediate boss, visits her to warn her that she must do more to maintain her public image. Just as June and Childie are about to go to a fancy-dress party as Laurel and Hardy, Mercy returns with the news that the decision has been reached to kill off Sister George in a road accident in two weeks' time. This will rid the show of the now awkward June and boost ratings considerably. At the same time, Mercy promises to find a job for Childie. June listens to her death on the radio and is further humiliated when Mercy offers her a part in a new series as a cow. The strain proves too much for June and Childie's relationship, but Mercy is more than willing to provide comfort to Childie.

German-born Frank Marcus broke ground with this play in two main ways: it deals openly with lesbian relationships, and it is the first play to explore the phenomenon of the nationally acclaimed soap-opera figure, now a staple of British tabloids. Both on stage and on screen, Sister George in Beryl Reid's performance became a moving image of an ageing woman rejected by society, a kind of female **Death of a Salesman*.

King Henry IV. See HENRY IV (PARTS 1 AND 2).

King Henry V. See HENRY V.

King Henry VI. See HENRY VI (PARTS 1, 2, AND 3).

King Henry VIII. See HENRY VIII.

King John (*The Life and Death of King John*)

A: William Shakespeare **Pf:** *c.*1596–7, London **Pb:** 1623 **G:** Hist. drama in 5 acts; blank verse **S:** England and France, *c.*1200–16. **C:** 18m, 4f, extras

King John's claim to the throne is challenged by his young nephew, Arthur, a claim that is backed by the French King Philip. Supported by the ebullient bastard Philip Faulconbridge, John invades France, and succeeds in capturing Prince Arthur. John's new ally Hubert cannot bring himself to obey John's orders to murder Arthur, but when Arthur tries to escape, the boy falls to his death from the ramparts. At first excommunicated by the Pope, then reconciled with him once more, John has to repel an invasion of England by the Dauphin, who now lays claim to the English crown. Deserted by his nobles, and falling ill, John withdraws to an abbey, where he is poisoned by the monks and dies. With peace restored between the French and English by papal intervention, John's son becomes King Henry III.

This is generally regarded as the least successful of Shakespeare's history plays. The plot is convoluted, and characters appear and disappear as historical events dictate. The ruthless John does not acquire tragic stature, becoming instead a comic hero of an extraordinarily radical kind. Even though its conflicts are not satisfactorily resolved at the end, the play contains some powerful scenes and some memorable characters, notably the passion of Constance, Arthur's mother, and the cynical and admirable figure of the Bastard Faulconbridge, a model for the unpretentious bravery of Shakespeare's Henry V.

King Lear (*True Chronicle Historie of the life and death of King Lear and his three Daughters*)

A: William Shakespeare Pf: *c.*1605–6, London Pb: 1608 (1st quarto), 1619 (2nd quarto), 1623 G: Trag. in 5 acts; blank verse and prose S: Ancient Britain C: 19m, 3f, extras

King Lear decides to abdicate, dividing his kingdom between his three daughters. First, he invites them to tell him how much they love him. His two eldest daughters, Goneril and Regan, respond with words of flattery, and are duly rewarded. However, his youngest and favourite daughter, Cordelia, finds it impossible to utter words of love. Lear flies into a rage, banishing her and giving her third of the kingdom to her two sisters. When Kent tries to intervene, he too is sent into exile. Cordelia departs with her suitor the King of France, and Kent leaves the court, only to return in disguise to continue serving the King. Lear prepares to stay with his knights at Goneril's home. Meanwhile, Gloucester is deceived by his bastard son Edmund into thinking that his legitimate son Edgar has been plotting against his life. Edgar is hounded from the court. Quarrelling with Goneril over the riotous behaviour of his knights, Lear sets off to stay with Regan. Forewarned, Regan removes herself to Gloucester's home. Here, despairing over their ingratitude, Lear is thrust out into a storm, where he at last recognizes the worthlessness of material things and encounters Edgar, who is now roaming as a naked beggar. Gloucester arranges for Lear to be brought to Dover where he may meet Cordelia, who is returning with a French army. Gloucester is terribly punished for his loyalty: his eyes are put out by Regan and her husband. Gloucester is led towards Dover by Edgar, where he encounters Lear, who has lost his reason. Under the gentle care of Cordelia, Lear regains his wits, but only in time for them both to be captured, when their forces are defeated by Edmund leading Goneril's and Regan's armies. Edmund is killed in single combat by Edgar, and Goneril and Regan, who had both been wooed by Edmund, die, one by suicide, the other by poison. On Edmund's orders Cordelia has been hanged, and Lear dies of grief, leaving Kent and Edgar to restore order in the land.

Arguably Shakespeare's greatest tragedy, *King Lear* is painted on a broader canvas than the more personal tragedy of *Hamlet*. While the flawed character of an irascible and petty old man who achieves tragic status is a fascinating study, it is the elemental power of scenes like the storm-tossed heath and the blinding of Gloucester that live on in the imagination. Each production tends to emphasize either the mythical or the historical dimension of the play, and the cynical words of the great designer and director Edward Gordon Craig that no performance of Shakespeare can yield all that is in the text, may be truest here. Despite being performed by leading actors of the day, like Burbage, Garrick, Olivier, and Paul Scofield (in Peter Brook's bleak version, 1962) the play has therefore never had quite the glamorous stage history of *Hamlet*. There have been significant adaptations of *King Lear*, notably Nahum Tate's version with a happy ending (1681) and Bond's radical rewriting, **Lear*.

King Oedipus. See OEDIPUS THE KING.

King of the Great Clock Tower, The

A: W. B. Yeats Pf: 1934, Dublin Pb: 1938 G: Drama in 1 act; blank verse and 3- and 4-stressed lines S: The King's palace, in the mythical past C: 4m, 1f

The King of the Great Clock Tower complains yet again about the silence of the mysterious woman who came to him a year previously and whom he made his queen. A stroller comes to his court and demands to see the beautiful Queen, declaring that she will dance for him, that he will sing for her, and that she will kiss his mouth. Infuriated by his insolence, the King has the man beheaded. When the Captain of the Guard returns with the head, the Queen begins to sing and dance. The severed head sings too, the Queen kisses its lips, and the King is about to strike her down with his sword, when he relents and kneels before her.

With obvious echoes of **Salome*, this curious theatrical gem reflects in mythological terms the despair felt by Yeats when his 'spiritual bride' Maud Gonne married the boorish soldier John MacBride. It seemed as though only this man of action could release her physical passion (although the marriage was short-lived), and, like the King, Yeats had to resign himself to this fact. Ninette de Valois, to whom the play is dedicated, performed the Queen in a mask. In a second version, *A Full Moon in March* (1935), Yeats dispenses with the King, and the Stroller becomes a swineherd.

King Richard II. See RICHARD II.

King Richard III. See RICHARD III.

King Ubu (*Ubu Roi*)

AT: *Ubu Rex; King Turd* A: Alfred Jarry W: 1888 Pf: 1896, Paris Pb: 1896 Tr: 1951 G: Farce in 5 acts; French prose S: Poland, Russia, Ukraine, Lithuania, Livonia, and at sea, indeterminate period C: 18m, 2f, extras (including 'the entire Russian and Polish armies')

'Shrit!' shouts Pa Ubu, as his wife urges him to murder King Wenceslas of Poland and seize the throne for himself. At a banquet Ubu poisons several of his guests with a toilet brush, then enlists Captain Bordure's support in his plot against the King. Wenceslas summons Ubu, who fears that his treachery has been discovered, but the King ennobles him further. Ubu and Bordure murder the King and his two older sons at the royal parade the following day. The youngest, Bougrelas, fighting bravely, escapes with his mother into the mountains. She dies, but the souls of his ancestors give Bougrelas a sword with which to avenge his parents. Urged by Ma Ubu, King Ubu buys popularity by distributing food and putting up prize money for a race. Ubu consolidates his royal power by 'debraining' the nobility and seizing their wealth. He then rids the kingdom of judges and tax-collectors and personally goes off to gather swingeing taxes from the grumbling peasants. When Bordure is cheated of his promised reward and rebels, Ubu has him locked up. Bordure escapes to Russia and obtains the Tsar's help in opposing Ubu. Ubu marches off to meet the impending Russian invasion. While Ma Ubu hunts for treasure in the vaults of Warsaw cathedral, Bougrelas takes the city, and Ma Ubu only just escapes. Meanwhile in the Ukraine, Ubu kills Bordure in battle and almost captures the Tsar, but is then forced to run away. Hiding in a cave in Lithuania, Ubu is attacked by a bear but is saved by two of his men. Boasting of his bravery, he falls asleep and has terrible dreams. Ma Ubu, on the run from Poland, arrives in the cave and admits to trying to steal the treasure. Ubu hurls the dead bear at her and begins to torture her, when Bougrelas and his troops arrive. Fighting his way out, Ubu and his wife get on board ship and dream of the countries they will visit but already miss Poland.

Written by Jarry at the age of 15 as an attack on an authoritarian physics teacher, *Ubu Roi* was premiered by Lugné-Poe and became a rallying point for iconoclastic modernism. With obvious echoes of **Macbeth*, the piece, beginning with one of the most famous opening words in world theatre ('Merdre!'), is a joyously anarchic and amoral voyage through murder, oppression, and gross vulgarity. Jarry wrote sequels: *Ubu Cuckolded*, written in 1891, and *Ubu Enchained*, published in 1900, but the joke, once told, could not easily be repeated. That *King Ubu* has been turned into an excellent cartoon film says much about the nature of the piece. Small wonder that Yeats on seeing the premiere wrote: 'After this the savage god!'

Kitchen, The

A: Arnold Wesker Pf: 1959, London Pb: 1959; rev. 1961 G: Drama in 2 acts S: Kitchen of a London restaurant, 1950s C: 18m, 12f

The action follows a day in the kitchen of the Tivoli, a busy London restaurant, owned by Mr Marango. The play begins with the night porter lighting the ovens, while staff from different backgrounds (German, French, Cypriot, Italian, Jewish, Irish, and English) get ready for the day's work. They argue, flirt, and joke together. One of the cooks Peter, a German, is having an affair with one of the waitresses Monique, but she is uncertain about leaving her husband. We then see the cooks preparing meals, and, as the first guests arrive for lunch, waitresses appearing from the unseen dining room with orders. The tempo and heat increase, until there is a frenzy of activity in the kitchen. Eventually there is a lull: the pace slackens, and the staff can relax for a while. A tramp cadging food provokes an argument, and an exhausted pregnant waitress has to be taken to hospital. Provoked by a trivial quarrel with a waitress, Peter vents all his pent-up frustration, smashing crockery and slashing his hands. Mr Marango, who considers himself a good employer, wonders why his staff would want to sabotage his establishment.

This play is remarkable in taking the realism of post-war British theatre towards almost total naturalism. Ideally to be played without an interval (although Wesker 'recognizes the wish of theatre bars to make some money'), the author, who had himself worked as a pastry-cook, reproduces the frenetic activity of a typical restaurant kitchen with lifelike detail and without one's interest in the action ever flagging. *The Kitchen* may be regarded as a forerunner of television 'fly-on-the-wall' documentaries.

Klop. See BEDBUG, THE.

Knack, The

A: Ann Jellicoe Pf: 1961, Cambridge, England Pb: 1962; rev. 1964 G: Com. in 3 acts S: Rented house in Tottenham, London, *c.*1960 C: 3m, 1f

Tom, Colin, and Tolen, three young men who have rented a house in north London, are now inexpertly attempting to decorate it. Tolen, a flashy motorcycle-riding individual, is head of the pecking order, so does not help with the work, but impresses the others with boasting about his 'knack' for sexual conquests. Tom, a voluble schoolteacher, has persuaded Colin, the lowest in the pecking order, in whose name the house is rented, to help him decorate Tom's room, which now contains nothing but a ladder, a couple of chairs, and a bed. When Nancy Jones, a young new arrival in London, knocks on the window to ask for directions to the YWCA, Tolen invites her in, and then tries to demonstrate his knack in seduction for the benefit of the others. In the event, Nancy feels so terrorized by Tolen's advances that she falls into a faint. When she recovers, she accuses the men of having raped her. Tolen dismisses this as a sexual fantasy, which Tom objects to, but both men are visibly frightened of the potential consequences. However, Colin sees this as his opportunity to prove that 'he is a man' and so confesses to raping her. Tolen, eager to show Colin's claim to be false and to give Nancy what he believes she is craving for, begins to force himself on her. Colin leaps to her defence, and Nancy goes to Colin.

The Knack was ground-breaking in offering for the first time a woman's analysis of sexual games. Jellicoe brilliantly and amusingly uncovers the pathetic manoeuvrings of young males (what would now be called 'laddism'), the homoerotic element underlying this bravado, and the inept way in which they attempt to develop the 'knack'. Today, however, it is unthinkable that a woman writer would depict a woman making a false claim of rape and then submitting to Colin's newly discovered machismo.

Knight of the Burning Pestle, The

A: Francis Beaumont Pf: *c.*1607, London Pb: 1613 G: Com. in 5 acts with an induction; blank and rhymed verse and prose S: London, Waltham, Moldavia, and their environs, at an indeterminate (medieval?) period C: 23m, 5f, extras

The audience are gathered to see *The London Merchant*, but the start of the play is delayed while the Grocer insists that his apprentice, Rafe, should appear in a heroic role. The play begins with Venturewell, the London merchant, insisting that his daughter Luce should marry Master Humphrey rather than the man she loves, his apprentice Jasper. Meanwhile Rafe declares that he will carry out noble deeds as the Knight of the Burning Pestle. Unfortunately, his first attempt results in terrifying Jasper's mother in Waltham Forest. Jasper finds her abandoned valuables and, encountering Humphrey with Luce, chases his rival away. The Grocer insists that Rafe and Jasper should meet in a fight, but the bold Knight fails miserably and retires to a nearby inn. Jasper decides to test Luce's love by threatening her with his sword, but his dangerous game is interrupted by Venturewell and Humphrey, who carry Luce away to safety, before Jasper can explain. After defeating the giant Barbaroso, alias Nick the barber, Rafe continues his heroic exploits in Moldavia, where he spurns the princess. Jasper now pretends to have died and asks for his body to be brought to Luce. Discovering that Luce still loves him, Jasper appears to Venturewell as a ghost and persuades him to send Humphrey packing and to give his blessing to his marriage to Luce. Finally, Rafe dies a mock-heroic death with an arrow through his head.

This, the first genuine play-within-a-play that allows audience figures to comment on and interfere with the action, was intended as a gentle satire of the crude taste of the contemporary London burghers for heroic adventure. Today the play still works well in the theatre, offering great opportunities for comedy and inventive interplay between the 'actors' and their 'audience'.

Knights (*Hippēs; Equites*)

A: Aristophanes Pf: 424 BC, Athens Tr: 1820 G: Greek com. in verse S: The household of Demos in Athens, 5th c. BC C: 5m, extras, chorus (m)

In the home of Demos all is not well: the slaves are tyrannized by the master's favourite, a 'Paphlagonian', a coarse and deceitful slave. Two of the slaves discover an oracle that foretells that the Paphlagonian will be overthrown by a sausage-seller. At that very moment a Sausage-Seller arrives, and the slaves inform him that he is destined to rule over Athens. Reluctant to confront the Paphlagonian, the Sausage-Seller is however emboldened by the arrival of a chorus of eager Knights. The Paphlagonian goes off to the Council to denounce the Sausage-Seller's conspiracy to overthrow him. We soon learn that the Paphlagonian has been outwitted. In desperation, the Paphlagonian calls Demos out of his house to choose between them, and in a lengthy contest is once again defeated, most notably when the Sausage-Seller offers him a box with nothing in it, while the Paphlagonian reveals a box containing tasty morsels. Demos recognizes now how the Paphlagonian slave has cheated him and stolen from him. Rejuvenated, Demos resumes power in his own household, banishes the Paphlagonian, and undertakes to behave more responsibly in the future.

In the second of Aristophanes' extant comedies, he delivers a bold and thinly disguised attack on the Athenian demagogue and general Cleon. The transparent allegory of the piece shows Demos' (= 'the people's') house in chaos because of the deceitfulness and bullying of Cleon. His overthrow by an ordinary passer-by, supported by the aristocratic officers of the Athenian cavalry, heralds a new age for Athens, with the people in control once more. It is said that Aristophanes himself was the only person brave enough to perform the role of the dictator; it is certain at least that he produced the play himself. While the play may seem inextricably linked with Athenian politics, and some of its references are undeniably obscure, its picture of a self-serving tyrant remains disturbingly relevant.

Kokusenya Kassen. See BATTLES OF COXINGA, THE.

Koralle, Die. See GAS TRILOGY, THE.

Krapp's Last Tape
A: Samuel Beckett **Pf:** 1958, London **Pb:** 1958
G: Monodrama in 1 act **S:** Krapp's study, *c.*1990
C: 1m

Krapp, a 'wearyish old man' of 69 in shabby clothes, eats a banana, slips on the discarded skin, eats another, then shuffles off into the darkness, where he is heard having a drink. He returns with a ledger which lists events in his past life. Selecting the tape made on his 39th birthday, he places it on his recorder and begins to listen. The first mention of a former girlfriend causes him to switch off the machine and have another drink. He listens to the description of his mother's death, but when he gets to the section where he has seen 'the light at last', he grows impatient and fast-forwards until he reaches the part where he is lying with a girl in a punt, telling her that they must end their relationship. Krapp broods, goes for another drink, then records his 'last tape'. He sneers at the young man who threw away his 'chance of happiness' for the sake of his 'homework', only 17 copies of which have been sold in the last year. Finding 'nothing to say, not a squeak', Krapp wrenches the tape from the machine, and as he listens again to the scene on the lake, he stares vacantly out into the darkness.

This was the first published play of Beckett's to be written in English and is his most accessible. Uncharacteristically, it suggests that Krapp might have found happiness if he had valued the love of a woman higher than his determination to be a writer. For Beckett, this is an almost sentimental implication and a rueful comment on his own troubled relationships with women. Beckett brilliantly uses a tape recorder (still a novelty in the 1950s) to allow a character to confront his former self.

Kreidekreuz, Das. See FEAR AND MISERY OF THE THIRD REICH.

Kyklops. See CYCLOPS.

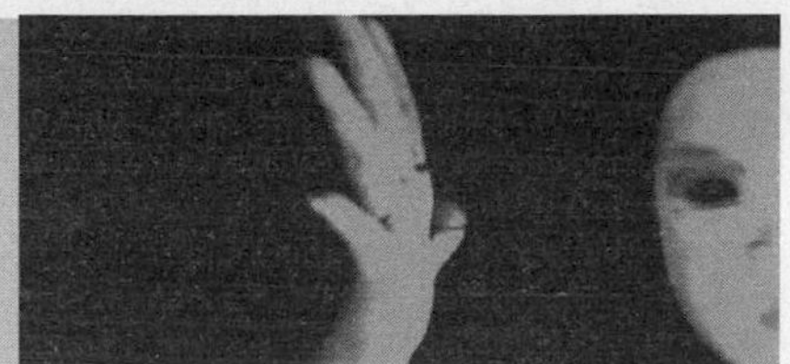

Ladies' Day. See WOMEN AT THE THESMOPHORIA.

Lady Audley's Secret

A: Colin Hazlewood Pf: 1863, London Pb: 1863 G: Drama in 2 acts S: Audley House and its grounds, and the Castle Inn, 1863 C: 4m, 3f, extras

The 24-year-old Lady Audley, formerly the governess to Sir Michael Audley, is now happily married to her elderly employer. Her 'secret' is that some years previously she married George Talboys, who went off to India to make his fortune. When she heard nothing from him, she pretended to die so that she could begin a new existence. Her present prosperity is jeopardized by the return of her husband George, the friend of Sir Michael's nephew Robert. When George threatens to denounce her as a bigamist, she hits him over the head and throws him down a well. A drunken lout Luke Marks witnesses the crime and blackmails her. Robert has also developed his own suspicions about Lady Audley; so when Robert and Luke begin drinking together at the Castle Inn, Lady Audley locks them in and sets fire to the building. Robert manages to save them, and the badly burned Luke denounces Lady Audley with his dying words. George now appears (his life had been saved by Luke), and Lady Audley goes mad and dies.

Hazlewood's version of Mary Elizabeth Braddon's novel *Lady Audley's Secret* of 1862 was one of several adaptations for the stage, the most popular being that by George Roberts in 1863, but which was never published. While lacking any particular literary merit, it is a well-constructed piece, building the tension well towards its spectacular denouement. The upper-class ambience also reflects the fact that polite society were now becoming patrons of melodrama.

Lady from the Sea, The (*Fruen fra havet*)

AT: *The Mermaid* A: Henrik Ibsen Pf: 1889, Christiania and Weimar Pb: 1888 Tr: 1891 G: Drama in 5 acts; Norwegian prose S: Dr Wangel's house and garden in, and a prominence near, a town on a northern Norwegian fjord, 1880s C: 5m, 3f, extras

Ellida feels so bound to the sea that she swims in it daily and is known locally as 'the lady from the sea'. She loves her widowed husband Dr Wangel, but does not relate well to her two stepdaughters Bolette and Hilde, and feels stifled in the small town. Her fascination with the sea is now explained: ten years previously she fell under the spell of a strange seaman and entered into a symbolic betrothal with him. Guilty of murder, he had to flee, but now returns, demanding Ellida as his wife. Wangel sends him away, but he says he will return so that Ellida may come to him 'of her own free will'. Bolette agrees to marry the elderly schoolmaster, so that she can 'have a chance to live'. The Stranger comes to claim Ellida, and Wangel bravely gives her her freedom. At once the Stranger's hold over her is broken, and she exercises her freedom to stay with Wangel.

*A *Doll's House* and **Hedda Gabler* offer pessimistic views of marriages in which the wife feels stifled, but here Ibsen suggests that, if both partners are free to relate as equals, there can be a happy outcome. The exploration of Ellida's obsession with the sea and with the unnamed Stranger from the sea is not only an interesting psychological study; the story assumes mythic elements, recalling northern legends of mermaids who come to land but can never settle away from their native element. It indicates how Ibsen, even within a realistic context, was beginning to turn towards a more symbolic drama, as in *The *Master Builder*, in which Hilde Wangel reappears.

Lady Julia/Julie. See MISS JULIE.

Lady of Pleasure, The

A: James Shirley **Pf:** 1635, London **Pb:** 1637 G: Com. in 5 acts; blank verse **S:** The Strand, London, 1630s. **C:** 10m, 6f, extras

Sir Thomas Bornwell has been persuaded by his wife Aretina to sell his country estates and set up home in London. Here Aretina seems intent on spending her husband's fortune on fashion, flirtation, and gaming. Bornwell decides that he will also abandon thrift and pursue a beautiful young widow, Celestina, in the hope of shocking his wife into sensible behaviour. Far from reforming, however, Aretina induces her sober nephew Frederick to live extravagantly and plots to undermine Celestina's position in society. Celestina rises above the taunts of Aretina's sycophants, and is rescued from them by Bornwell. Aretina employs the services of an old bawd, Madam Decoy, to abduct young Master Alexander Kickshaw and have him brought to a secret assignation, where he enjoys Aretina in the dark. Celestina and the Lord, who has rejected the offer of an affair with Aretina, declare their mutual love. Aretina and Bornwell now claim to outdo each other in extravagance. Celestina refuses to become the Lord's mistress, and he repents his lasciviousness. Aretina too is finally persuaded to give up her extravagant ways and is relieved to learn that Bornwell has merely pretended to gamble away his fortune.

One of the mot popular playwrights of Charles I's reign, Shirley combines wit with lyricism, and ribald behaviour with a high moral tone. Anticipating Restoration comedies, *The Lady of Pleasure* is written not for the broad public of the Jacobean playhouses but for a refined gentry. However, unlike the Restoration, Shirley, who had taken holy orders, ends his play with (not very clearly motivated) repentance.

Lady of the Camellias, The (*La Dame aux camélias*)

AT: *Camille* A: Alexandre Dumas *fils* **Pf:** 1852, Paris **Pb:** 1852 **Tr:** 1930 **G:** Trag. in 5 acts; French prose **S:** Paris and a house in the country, 1840s **C:** 14m, 6f, extras

Marguerite Gautier, witty, generous, and flirtatious, whose favourite flower is the camellia, receives a wide variety of friends in her salon. Despite having had many lovers, she has never committed herself to one man. But the young Armand Duval, whose shyness conflicts with his passion, wins her love, and they begin a life of bliss in a house in the country. However, Armand's father, whose daughter's impending marriage might be endangered by Armand's liaison with a fallen woman, pleads with Marguerite to give up Armand. She agrees, and, in order to drive Armand away, pretends to take up with one of her former lovers. The desperate Armand publicly humiliates her. Marguerite succumbs to consumption. Just as Armand's father relents, and the two lovers are reconciled, Marguerite dies in Armand's arms.

Based on Dumas's own novel of 1848, which reflects an episode in his life, this play has been staged worldwide, not least because of the highly charged central role, performed by actresses like Sara Bernhardt and Eleanora Duse, and on film by Greta Garbo. Although obviously shot through with sentimentality (fully exploited in Verdi's operatic treatment in *La traviata* of 1853), *The Lady of the Camellias* is well constructed and contains serious elements of social criticism, especially about the role of women, elements which were to resurface in the plays of Ibsen and the **Lulu Plays* of Wedekind. Pam Gems rewrote it with an even stronger feminist slant in *Camille* (1984).

Lady's Not for Burning, The

A: Christopher Fry **Pf:** 1948, London **Pb:** 1949; rev. 1950, 1958 **G:** Com. in 3 acts; blank verse **S:** English market town, *c.*1450 **C:** 8m, 3f, extras

Mayor Tyson is beset with problems: his nephews are fighting over the same bride; a strange character Thomas Mendip insists that he is tired of life and wants to be hanged; and a rich young woman Jennet Jourdemayne seeks protection from the Mayor because the mob accuse her of being a witch who turned a missing rag and bone merchant into a dog. The Mayor decides that Jennet is indeed a witch, in thrall to Mendip, the devil. The town's Justice Tappercoom fails to find any evidence to convict the pair, so the Mayor eavesdrops outside their cell. When Jennet, who has fallen in love with Mendip, says that she would follow him to hell, the Mayor orders her burning the following day—not least because her property will fall to the town. First, however, the Justice orders that Mendip should be made to go to the wedding feast, so that he will abandon his desire for judicial suicide, and he insists on taking Jennet. At the party the two nephews abandon the bride for Jennet, and one offers to save her if she will give herself to him. The jilted bride goes off with the town clerk, the rag and bone merchant appears, thus freeing Jennet, and Mendip leaves with her.

Greatly admired at the time for its wit and verbal dexterity, Fry's play was hailed as a potential source of renewal for poetic drama and a return to the theatrical achievements of the Elizabethan age. While one cannot with hindsight accord it such significance, it stands nevertheless as an interesting attempt to break out of the conventional drawing-room setting to present striking individuals from the past, a territory that would be explored more successfully in John Arden's poetic prose.

Lady Windermere's Fan

AT: *(A Play About) a Good Woman* A: Oscar Wilde **Pf:** 1892, London **Pb:** 1893 **G:** Drama in 4 acts **S:** Lord Windermere's House and Lord Darlington's rooms, London, 1892 **C:** 7m, 9f

Lady Windermere is 21 today, and her seemingly devoted husband has given her a fan for her birthday. She reproaches Lord Darlington for courting her, but is dismayed to learn that her husband is known to be associating with a Mrs Erlynne, to whom he gives regular sums of money. Worse still, Windermere insists that Mrs Erlynne should attend the birthday party. Lady Windermere, humiliated by her presence, leaves the party to go to Darlington's rooms, leaving her husband a note. It is now revealed that Mrs Erlynne is Lady Windermere's mother. She left her husband and daughter to run away with a lover who then abandoned her. She threatens to reveal herself to Lady Windermere, if Windermere does not finance her return to society. Finding Lady Windermere's note, her mother rushes to Darlington's rooms to prevent a repetition of her own mistake. Hiding her from the men coming from the party, Mrs Erlynne persuades her daughter to return home and say nothing about her attempt at unfaithfulness. When Lady Windermere's new fan is discovered, Mrs Erlynne comes out of hiding, pretending that she took it by mistake. The next morning Windermere, sneering at Mrs Erlynne's presence in Darlington's rooms, no longer feels threatened by her, and she promises never to reveal her identity to her daughter. She prepares to go abroad with her elderly suitor.

In this, Wilde's first London success, he treats a favourite Victorian theme, that of the 'fallen woman'. Even more than in *The *Second Mrs Tanqueray* and **Mrs Dane's Defence*, Wilde is sympathetic towards her situation (she is the 'Good Woman' of the subtitle and original title). Despite its wit and realistic contemporary setting, the piece has not yet wholly removed itself from conventional sentimentality to carry the mark of Wilde's brilliantly cynical observation of society.

Land, The

A: Padraic Colum **Pf:** 1905, Dublin **Pb:** 1916 **G:** Drama in 3 acts **S:** Cosgar's farm, Irish Midlands, 1905 **C:** 4m, 2f, extras

The Wyndham Land Act of 1903 provided for the break-up of the old estates, allowing tenant farmers to buy their land over a 68-year period. Murtagh Cosgar is an enterprising farmer who has taken advantage of the Act and so disapproves of his son Matt's love for Ellen Douras, a teacher whose father, unwilling to purchase his farm, has remained a 'peasant', even though he had been jailed for his efforts in the land agitation. Ellen's brother, the simple-minded Cornelius, is in love with Murtagh's daughter Sally. Matt finally persuades his father that he should marry for love not to acquire land. But Ellen herself rejects Matt, choosing freedom in preference to land. Matt emigrates to America, hoping that he may later unite there with Ellen, leaving the farm to be inherited by Sally's intended, the cloddish Cornelius.

The Land was the Abbey Theatre's first popular success and shared with Synge a realistic depiction of life in rural Ireland. While for Colum the play celebrated 'the redemption of the soil of Ireland' from its ownership by Anglo-Irish landlords, it also depicted a generation of young Irish who for the first time could choose emigration rather than be forced into it, and who valued personal fulfilment above the conservative pressure to get married, settle down, and acquire land. It anticipates similar conflicts, between conservative desire to own land and more progressive ideas, in John B. Keane's *The *Field*.

Landscape with Figures. See STREET SCENE.

Lark, The (*L'Alouette*)

A: Jean Anouilh **Pf**: 1953, Paris **Pb**: 1953
Tr: 1955 **G**: Drama in 2 acts; French prose
S: Rouen, France, 1431 **C**: 17m, 3f

Joan of Arc ('the lark') has been captured and brought to trial, but her judge Bishop Cauchon insists that scenes from her past should be re-enacted: her departure from her humble life in Domrémy, her persuading Beaudricourt to provide her with a horse and escort, her convincing the Dauphin to be brave and fight the English by putting her in command of the army. The Earl of Warwick is less impressed, believing that Joan merely provided a rallying symbol for people to go out and get killed. At last, the trial gets under way. Joan glorifies the contradictory nature of humanity, which is both heroic and cruel. The Inquisitor perceives this celebration of 'natural man' to be a serious threat to the authority of the Church. Cauchon persuades Joan to recant, but she feels stifled and shamed in prison. She withdraws her recantation, and is brought to the stake. Before she can be burned, Beaudricourt intervenes to insist that Joan should be seen in her moment of glory – the coronation of Charles as king of France. The play ends on a heroic tableau of 'a lark in the free sky'.

Strongly influenced by Shaw's **Saint Joan*, Anouilh's version follows the incidents of Shaw's play, mostly in flashback on a bare stage. The focus of Anouilh's treatment is on the trial and the threat Joan's belief in humanity offers to the Catholic faith. Both Christopher Fry's and Lillian Hellman's versions for the English and American stages tended to lessen the importance of this theological debate.

Last of the Wampanoags, The. See METAMORA.

Lear

A: Edward Bond **Pf**: 1971, London **Pb**: 1972
G: Pol. drama in 3 acts **S**: England, indeterminate period **C**: 48m, 5f, extras

Lear is a tyrannical king of England who has built a huge wall to keep out his enemies, the Duke of Cornwall and the Duke of North. His daughters Bodice and Fontanelle rebel against Lear's despotism, marry the two Dukes, and lead armies against him. Warrington, Lear's aide, is captured and is horribly tortured by Fontanelle and Bodice, who drives knitting-needles into his eardrums. Lear, defeated, dishevelled, and mad, seeks refuge with a Gravedigger's Boy. Soldiers arrive, kill the Boy, and rape his wife Cordelia. Lear is captured, judged to be mad, imprisoned, and has his eyes removed in a surgical operation. Cordelia leads the fight against Bodice and Fontanelle, proving to be as ruthless as her opponents. Lear, freed once more, rejects both the totalitarian methods of Cordelia and the temptations offered by the Ghost of the Gravedigger's Boy to live his life in peaceful isolation. Instead, he returns to the Wall, makes a brave gesture by beginning to dismantle it and is shot. As the Workers are led off, '*One of them looks back.*'

Bond, unhappy with the 'idea of total resignation' which he believed Shakespeare's

*King Lear to propound, decided 'to rewrite it so that we now have to use the play for ourselves, for our society, for our time, for our problems'. Using an epic structure, forcefully minimalist language, and his notorious 'aggro-effects' like the blinding of Lear, Bond created a contemporary masterpiece, in which the Wall stands as a symbol of oppression justified in the name of national defence (a clear reference to the nuclear deterrent on which post-war world powers depended). After Lear's tyrannical rule is replaced first by his daughters then by the Stalinist figure of Cordelia, he is faced with the choice between withdrawing from political life, embracing the violent rule and maintenance of the wall by Cordelia, or making a powerful non-violent political gesture by inviting death as he begins to dismantle the wall. It is a small but not futile gesture, and at least one worker 'looks back'. It is a myth for our age, expressing what Bond has called 'pessimistic optimism'.

Leaving Home

A: David French **Pf:** 1972, Toronto **Pb:** 1972
G: Drama in 2 acts **S:** Working-class house in Toronto, late 1950s **C:** 4m, 3f

Bill Mercer is about to get married to Kathy Jackson, who is pregnant. His brother Ben, just graduated from high school, and their mother Mary await the arrival of Jacob Mercer, the father, to go to the rehearsal for the wedding. Ben plans to leave home too to live with Bill and Kathy. Jacob comes home in a jolly mood, but he is upset, as the son of an Orangeman, that Bill is becoming a Catholic to marry Kathy. Kathy arrives looking pale, and tells Bill that she has lost the baby. Kathy's mother Minnie, tipsy and coarse, and her boyfriend Harold now join the party, and embarrass Kathy. When Bill suggests to Kathy that they now call off the wedding, since they no longer have to marry, Kathy flirts outrageously with Harold. When Kathy reveals to everyone that she has lost her baby, Mary wants to cancel the marriage, but Minnie insists it should go ahead. After a flare-up, calm is restored, and Bill and Kathy become reconciled and they leave for the rehearsal. When Jacob learns that Ben is leaving home too, he becomes so angry that he even tears up Ben's graduation diploma. Mary reveals that Ben worked to save the family when Jacob had been laid off from work. Jacob begs Ben to stay, but Ben goes, leaving Mary and Jacob alone together, as she gently explains why she chose to marry him.

French's play is a well-observed unspectacular piece about family life, most of which is unspecific to Canada. Jacob provides the focus of interest, a well-intentioned but clumsy individual, both warm-hearted and intolerant, both generous and selfish. Though the children leave home, the ending is mildly optimistic.

Leben des Galilei. See LIFE OF GALILEO.

Leçon, La. See LESSON, THE.

Leghorn Hat, A. See ITALIAN STRAW HAT, AN.

Les. See FOREST, THE.

Lesson, The (*La Leçon*)

A: Eugène Ionesco **Pf:** 1951, Paris **Pb:** 1954
Tr: 1958 **G:** Drama in 1 act; French prose **S:** The Professor's study, mid-20th c. **C:** 1m, 2f

A timid Professor welcomes a confident young Pupil to his home. Her parents want her to prepare for the 'total doctorate', and the Professor, delighted that she knows the capital of France and can do simple addition, is confident that she will achieve her goal. However, when he moves on to subtraction, she is quite unable to take one amount from another. Although she can multiply extraordinarily large numbers, she fails utterly at division. Despite the warnings of his Maid, the Professor now turns to Philology. While the Pupil succumbs to debilitating toothache, the Professor grows ever more assured, launching into a tirade to the effect that words mean the same in all languages. Finally, to prove his point, he takes a knife, called 'knife' in every language, and in a mounting ritual frenzy stabs his Pupil orgasmically with it. Suddenly distraught, he calls the Maid, who chastises him for having killed 39 pupils already that day. However, she will arrange for another coffin and gives the Professor a swastika armband to ensure that no one questions his behaviour. The bell rings, and the next pupil is admitted.

In this deftly constructed one-acter, Ionesco continues his absurdist theme, suggesting the meaningless of all language: 'only words that are charged with significance, heavy with meaning, dive downwards and always succumb in the end'. This meaninglessness is reinforced by the grotesquely violent outcome, sanctioned by dangerously insane politics, and the cyclical nature of the action, allowing no escape.

Let's Get a Divorce! (*Divorçons!*)

AT: *Let Us Be Divorced!* A: Victorien Sardou (with Émile de Najac) Pf: 1880, Paris Pb: 1883 Tr: 1881 G: Com. in 3 acts; French prose S: Prunelles' salon and a restaurant, 1870s C: 6m, 5f, extras

Cyprienne is disappointed in her marriage with Monsieur des Prunelles, and has fallen in love with her cousin Adhémar de Gratignan. If Parliament passes the new law allowing divorce, Cyprienne says that she will seek a divorce at once. She explains her disappointment in marriage: for her husband, who has sown his wild oats, it is a matter of settling down; for the wife, with no adventures to look back on, she seeks excitement in marriage. When a telegram arrives, purporting to bring the news that divorce is now legal, Prunelles immediately agrees to a divorce. Cyprienne confesses everything and reveals that she has never actually had sex with Adhémar. No longer having to hide her love for Adhémar, she suddenly finds him very boring. When her husband declares that he will leave her to Adhémar, she follows him to a restaurant, driven by 'posthumous jealousy'. Here the couple become reconciled, and Adhémar, failing even to recognize his lover's foot tantalizingly displayed from a private room, has to admit that he has lost Cyprienne to her husband.

Condemned by Bernard Shaw as 'Sardoodledum', the tradition of the French well-made play, in which a carefully crafted plot neatly solves the complications arising out of the action, is exploited interestingly here by Sardou. Admittedly, in the 100 or so plays he wrote, often with collaborators, there are many that depend on mechanical plots and contrived theatrical effects. Here, however, the nature of middle-class marriage is examined with some insight, and the play offers an interesting variation on the traditional plot in which lovers succeed in duping a tedious husband. Once it lacks deception and intrigue, Cyprienne's affair becomes less exciting than her marriage.

Libation-Bearers, The. See ORESTEIA, THE.

Libertine, The. See DON JUAN.

Life among the Lowly. See UNCLE TOM'S CABIN.

Life and Love in These Times. See UNDER THE GASLIGHT.

Life in Louisiana. See OCTOROON, THE.

Life in New York. See FASHION.

Life Is a Dream (*La vida es sueño*)

AT: *Life's a Dream; Such Stuff as Dreams Are Made of* A: Pedro Calderón de la Barca Pf: 1635, Madrid Pb: 1636 Tr: 1865 G: Drama in 3 acts; Spanish verse S: The court of Poland, a nearby fortress, and the open country, *c.*15th c. C: 8m, 2f, extras

Basilio, King of Poland, has confined his son Segismundo to a tower, because he caused the death of his mother in childbirth and omens foretold that he would grow up to become a tyrant and overthrow his father. However, urged by his courtiers, the King relents and abandons his plan to make Duke Astolfo his heir by releasing Segismundo and offering him the opportunity to rule the kingdom. Meanwhile, Astolfo's life is under threat from his spurned mistress Rosaura. Segismundo is drugged and brought to the palace, where he is overwhelmed by the sudden splendour and respectful treatment by those around him. He behaves so violently, even threatening the King because of the treatment he endured, that Basilio returns him to the tower. Shortly after awakening in prison, Segismundo is freed by the angry populace, and he leads an armed revolt against the King. However, when he succeeds in defeating his father, he is so wary that he might again awake to find himself in prison that he forgives Basilio, and promises to be a wise ruler. Rosaura is to wed Astolfo, and Segismundo will marry Astolfo's former fiancée Estrella.

The Spanish word *sueño* means 'sleep' as well as 'dream', suggesting that life is a complete illusion, and so provides the philosophical basis for the 17th century's preoccupation with appearance and reality. Calderón explores the theme masterfully through the process of redemptive self-discovery in Segismundo and in the restoration of Rosaura's honour in the sub-plot. The play is also distinguished by long and powerful speeches, vigorous stichomythic exchanges, strikingly contrasted locations, and injections of good comic writing. Hugo von Hofmannsthal adapted the original in *The Tower* (1925).

Life Machine, The. See MACHINAL.

Life of Galileo (*Leben des Galilei*)

AT: *Galileo* **A:** Bertolt Brecht (with Margarete Steffin) **Pf:** 1943, Zurich **Pb:** 1955; rev. 1957 **Tr:** 1953 **G:** Hist. drama in 15 scenes; German prose with 1 song **S:** Padua, Venice, Florence, Rome, 1609–37 **C:** 42m, 10f, extras

Galileo scrapes a living, teaching students in Padua. When he learns of a new Dutch invention, the telescope, he sells the idea to the Venetian senate and then uses the new instrument to prove the Copernican system: that the earth revolves around the sun. Although warned of the dangers of disseminating his views, Galileo places his faith in human reason. He even leaves the liberal regime of Venice to earn a higher salary at the court of Florence, where he meets with opposition from reactionary academics. Galileo continues to work on in the city even when it is affected by the plague. In Rome, the papal astronomer confirms Galileo's findings, but the Church forbids him to publish them. A Little Monk begs Galileo not to rob the poor of the stability of their faith, but is won over by Galileo's appeal to truth. Eight years later, a new pope, a scientist, is enthroned, and this encourages Galileo to resume his research. As his ideas become known, even the common people celebrate the new age that has begun to question established authority. In 1633 Galileo is summoned to Rome, and the Grand Inquisitor persuades the Pope, as he is being robed, that Galileo must be silenced. Galileo recants when he sees the torture instruments, and his loyal pupil Andrea cries out: 'Unhappy the land that has no heroes!' Galileo replies: 'Unhappy the land that has need of heroes.' Forced to live under house arrest, Galileo, though half blind, secretly continues his work. When Andrea visits him, Galileo, aware that he has betrayed his belief in truth and his responsibility as a scientist, gives him the manuscript of the *Discorsi*, which Andrea smuggles across the Italian border to be published in the Netherlands.

Undoubtedly the best 20th-century play about a historical figure, *Life of Galileo*, like all Brecht's great plays, contains ambiguities and caused the author much heart-searching. Galileo himself is full of contradictions: a sensualist who loves intellectual activity, a coward who bravely defies the plague, and an unrelenting seeker after truth who perpetrates fraud and subterfuge. Especially after the explosion of the atom bomb, Brecht began to question whether he had been too indulgent towards Galileo, and he added a lengthy speech in the penultimate scene warning of the dangers of scientists abdicating their social responsibilities. Although essentially realistic, the play offers many opportunities for 'gestic' acting (action clarified by the visual element, as in Scene 12, where the Pope's individual beliefs disappear under his robes of office). The American premiere in 1947, co-directed by Brecht, boasted Charles Laughton in the title role.

Life of (the) Insects, The. See INSECT COMEDY, THE.

Light Shining in Buckinghamshire

A: Caryl Churchill **Pf:** 1976, Edinburgh **Pb:** 1978 **G:** Hist. drama in 2 acts **S:** Putney and various rural locations, England, 1640s **C:** 19m, 5f, extras

In a series of set pieces, aspects of life during the Civil War are shown: a vicar regrets the war; a beggar is given no charity by the Justices of the Peace; men are recruited to fight against the King's forces with promises of salvation, and Briggs joins up; Hoskins, a female vagrant preacher, interrupts a sermon, which declares that only a few are to be saved. Hoskins is beaten by the congregation and is taken home by a working man Claxton, to whom Hoskins preaches free love. Women loot a house, and Briggs recalls a battle. In 1647, with Charles I defeated, the Putney debates take place: while some press for democracy and the Levellers demand an end to all private property, Cromwell and his followers insist on a strong parliament and ownership of property. As Cromwell prevails, the Levellers see the opportunity radically to change society slip away. Diggers who attempt to cultivate common land are persecuted. Briggs and others are dismayed at the repression of Ireland by Cromwell's army, former English rebels become landlords, and the Levellers are finally crushed. In a fantastical Ranters' prayer meeting, Claxton, Hoskins, Briggs, and others dream of the second coming of Christ to bring the utopia they yearn for.

In her first historical drama, its title taken from a Digger pamphlet, Churchill used documents from the English Civil War to show how the aspirations of common people were betrayed. As Briggs says: 'people . . . can't take hold of their own lives, like us till we had this chance, and we're losing it now'. Churchill comments: 'Though nobody now expects Christ to make heaven on earth, their voices are surprisingly close to us.'

Lights of Bohemia. See BOHEMIAN LIGHTS.

Liliom

AT: *The Daisy* A: Ferenc Molnár Pf: 1909, Budapest Pb: 1909 Tr: 1921 G: Drama in 7 scenes and a prologue; Hungarian prose S: Budapest and 'the Beyond', early 20th c. C: 17m, 9f, extras

When Liliom (Andreas Zavocki), a swaggering fairground barker, fondles a naive servant girl Julie Zeller, he is sacked by the jealous carousel-owner. Although warned about Liliom by the police, Julie decides to stay with him. They marry and live with Julie's aunt. Though now out of work, Liliom continues to swagger about and even beats the ever patient Julie. Reluctantly, Liliom falls in with a friend's plan to steal money from a factory cashier, but the robbery goes wrong, and Liliom stabs himself rather than go to prison. Dying, he is carried back to Julie. Everyone assures her she is well rid of him, but she still loves him. Two men lead Liliom to the 'Beyond'. He is sentenced by a celestial court to burn for 16 years to purge him of his pride. Allowed to return to earth for one day, he appears at Julie's house as a beggar. Invited in, he tells their daughter Lujza (Louise) that her father was a bully who hit her loving mother. Julie defends Liliom's memory and tells the old tramp to leave. When Liliom is rejected by his daughter, he slaps her hand, but she feels nothing. As Liliom is led away, Louise asks why the slap did not hurt. Her mother answers: 'someone may beat you . . . and not hurt you at all'.

Allegedly based on an incident when Molnár had slapped his daughter, this internationally successful play suggests that, as with Solveig and Peer Gynt, love can overcome everything, from social prejudice to unprovoked violence. The play moves from the naturalism of the first five scenes to the surreal depiction of the hereafter. In 1945 Rodgers and Hammerstein used the material for the musical *Carousel*.

Lille Eyolf. See LITTLE EYOLF.

Lion and the Jewel, The

A: Wole Soyinka Pf: 1959, Ibadan, Nigeria Pb: 1963 G: Com. in 3 acts S: Nigerian village, 1950s C: 2m, 2f, extras

The young village schoolmaster Lakunle, an inept intellectual who has learned modern ways, is wooing Sidi, the 'jewel' of the village, an attractive and self-confident young woman. His modern thinking will not allow him to buy her with the traditional bride price, and he repels her by adopting a Western style of loving: she complains that his kissing consists of 'strange unhealthy mouthing' and the 'licking of my lips with yours'. Sidi's beauty is such that she is photographed for a national magazine, which makes her even more vain and unapproachable than before. Angered by her fame, and wanting her now for himself, Baroka, the village headman ('the lion') tries to seduce her, but she rejects him. However, when his senior wife Sadiku assures Sidi that the old chief is impotent, Sidi agrees to go to him, in order to tease him about his lack of virility. To her surprise, the old lion lacks nothing, and the next day she admits that she will now be marrying without bride money after all. Pushing the disappointed schoolmaster aside, she invites the village maidens to sing 'of children sired of the lion stock'.

This was the second play by Soyinka, which consolidated his international fame through a production at the Royal Court in London in 1963 (*The Invention* had been staged there in 1959). Like many African intellectuals, he had an ambiguous attitude towards the gradual decline of tribal power in the 20th century, and this gentle comedy makes a plea that some of the old values be retained in the Nigerian drive for modernization.

Lion of the West, The

AT: *The Kentuckian; A Trip to New York; A Trip to Washington* A: James Kirke Paulding Pf: 1831, New York Pb: 1954 G: Farce in 2 (originally 4) acts; prose S: Freeman's house and City Hotel, New York, 1830s C: 6m, 5f, extras

Mrs Freeman, wife of a New York merchant, is delighted when her daughter Caroline is courted by Lord Granby, although Caroline has a much worthier suitor in the honourable English visitor Mr Percival. Another visitor to New York is Mrs Freeman's nephew Colonel Nimrod Wildfire, 'the Lion of the West', a rough backwoodsman from Kentucky, who alarms a snobbish visitor to America, Mrs Wollope. At Freeman's party that evening, Mrs Wollope, who has been amazed that civilization extends to America, is surprised to discover that 'Lord Granby' is her own brother, Mr Jenkins. Wildfire falls in love with Mrs Wollope, and she pleads with her brother to get rid of this wild Kentuckian. As Lord Granby, he challenges Wildfire to a duel, but plans to kidnap Caroline and run away before he has to fight. By mistake, Mrs Wollope is seized by Jenkins's henchmen and only saved by Wildfire's timely intervention. Jenkins is exposed as a fraud, Mrs Wollope returns haughtily to England, and Freeman gives his blessing to Caroline's marriage to Percival.

This play (the version given here is the 1833 revision undertaken with William Bayle Bernard) won Paulding first prize in a competition to write 'an original comedy whereof an American should be the leading character'. Its popularity rested on the uprightness and virility of Percival and Wildfire compared with the deception and cowardice of Jenkins and the snobbishness of Mrs Wollope. Although Paulding denied that Wildfire was based on Davy Crockett (like Wildfire a Congressman), this rough Kentuckian became a national hero, and his buckskin clothes, western dialect, and rough manners were widely imitated.

Little Clay Cart, The (*Mrcchakatikā; Mrichchhakatikā*)

AT: *The Toy Cart* A: ? King Sūdraka W: ? 5th c. AD Tr: 1905 G: Drama in 10 acts and a prologue; Sanskrit prose and verse S: City in northern India (Ujjayini), 3rd c. AD C: 21m, 7f, extras

Chārudatta, an impoverished and pious Brahmin, is loved by Vasantasenā, a courtesan, who is pursued by the oafish but evil prince Sansthānaka. Fleeing to Chārudatta's house, Vasantasenā leaves jewels with him for safekeeping. A burglar steals the jewels, and when the theft is discovered Chārudatta's wife nobly gives away her necklace to replace the loss. The burglar Sharvilaka has stolen the jewels in order to buy the freedom of Vasantasenā's maid and is alarmed to discover that he is now returning the jewels to their owner. He therefore pretends to be a servant of Chārudatta bringing back the jewels. Soon after, another servant comes, claiming that Chārudatta has gambled away Vasantasenā's jewels and offering the necklace in its place. Vasantasena now journeys to Chārudatta through a storm, returns the jewels to him, they embrace, and she becomes his slave.

Vasantasenā offers to return the necklace to Chārudatta's wife, but when the latter gracefully declines, Vasantasenā fills with jewellery a little clay cart, a toy belonging to Chārudatta's son. A bullock cart is prepared to take Vasantasenā to a tryst with Chārudatta, and Aryaka, an exiled prince fleeing from persecution, leaps into it to escape. Brought to Chārudatta, the latter offers to protect Aryaka. By mistake Vasantasenā travels in another bullock cart which brings her to the evil Sansthānaka. When she rejects his advances, he strangles her and leaves her for dead. On Sansthānaka's testimony, Chārudatta is convicted of the murder, and just as he is to be executed, is saved by the reappearance of Vasantasenā, who revived from the strangling. Chārudatta is freed, Sansthānaka's evil is exposed, and news comes that Aryaka has been restored to the throne.

Shakuntala and *The Little Clay Cart* are the two great classics of Sanskrit drama, the former based on legends depicting heroes and gods (*nataka*), the latter an invented story in a primarily domestic setting (*prakarana*). It is a very long play, including incidental passages of poetic description and comic action, and containing characters familiar the world over: the noble and patient hero (Chārudatta), the foolish and vicious tyrant (Sansthānaka), the devoted lover (Vasantasenā), a parasite, a fool, a burglar with good intentions, comic policemen – even the executioners are allowed a few laughs. While this classic Sanskrit drama does not portray the powerful interior conflicts of Western tragedy, it is immensely rich and theatrical.

Little Eyolf (*Lille Eyolf*)

A: Henrik Ibsen **Pf**: 1895, Berlin; Christiania **Pb**: 1894 **Tr**: 1907 **G**: Drama in 3 acts; Norwegian prose **S**: Allmers' Estate near a fjord, Norway, late 19th c. **C**: 2m, 3f, 1 child (m)

Alfred Allmers, a 36-year-old landowner and writer, lives on a large estate with his wife Rita and their 9-year-old crippled son Eyolf. Allmers has just returned from a trip to the mountains, a break from his 'life's work' on a book about 'human responsibility'. He is welcomed home by Rita and his younger sister Asta. Allmers has decided to give up writing and devote himself to Little Eyolf. Rita is jealous of his love for Asta and Eyolf, wanting to have Allmers entirely for herself. A passing Rat Wife, who had offered to rid the estate of any vermin, is followed by Eyolf, who drowns in the fjord. Overcome by remorse, Allmers and Rita reproach each other: in a moment of sexual passion they had neglected their infant son, who had rolled off a table and injured himself. Now, Allmers insists, they must seek 'resurrection' through atonement. He would like to leave with Asta, because her love never changes, but discovers that she is only a half-sister. Pointing out that their relationship is also subject to change, Asta leads Allmers back to Rita and leaves with her dependable suitor, the engineer Borghejm. When Allmers threatens to leave Rita, she decides to atone by offering a home to the homeless waifs of the fjord. Allmers agrees to stay and help her.

Henry James wrote of *Little Eyolf*: 'He simplifies too much and too suddenly.' Though initially more popular in its day than *Hedda Gabler*, it is now regarded as one of Ibsen's weaker plays: the structure is formulaic, the Rat Wife too obvious a symbol, and the happy ending unconvincing. However, it maintains other strengths characteristic of Ibsen: the gloomy Nordic setting, the probing analysis of extreme emotions, and the question of responsibility for one's past.

Little Foxes, The

A: Lillian Hellman **Pf**: 1939, New York **Pb**: 1939 **G**: Drama in 3 acts **S**: The living room of the Giddens' home in the south, spring 1900 **C**: 6m, 4f

Ben and Oscar Hubbard and their sister Regina gloat over the deal they have struck with a Chicago businessman to build a cotton mill, which will guarantee them all wealth. Regina's husband Horace Giddens is away, recuperating from a heart ailment in Baltimore, so Regina's third share of the investment is still outstanding. She negotiates an improved deal for herself, in part by offering to marry her daughter Alexandra to Oscar's son Leo. Leo's mother Birdie secretly warns Alexandra not to end up in a miserable marriage like her own. Leo, who works in Horace's bank, reveals to his father that he has found $88,000 worth of negotiable bonds in Horace's safe-box. When Horace returns home and refuses to contribute to the scheme, Leo is sent to steal the bonds, and Ben tells Regina that her investment is no longer needed. Furious, she argues viciously with Horace, urging him to die. When Horace discovers the theft, he cynically resolves to leave the bonds to Regina in his will, bequeathing the rest of his money to his daughter. Regina's angry reaction provokes a heart attack, and she ignores his pleas to fetch his medicine. Once he is dead, Regina blackmails her brothers into giving her a 75 per cent share of future profits. Ben is impressed with her spirit of enterprise: 'people like you and me . . . will own this country some day'. But Alexandra now wishes to part from her mother.

Generally accounted Hellman's best play, *The Little Foxes* is a reference to the Song of Solomon, where 'the little foxes . . . spoil the vines', just as predatory capitalists destroy the environment and the lives of their African-American workers. Thus, underneath a taut, intense depiction of family greed and manipulation, a picture of a nation in thrall to money emerges. Regina was played forcefully by Tallulah Bankhead at its premiere and by Bette Davis in Hellman's 1941 film version.

Live Like Pigs

A: John Arden Pf: 1958, London Pb: 1961
G: Drama in 17 scenes; prose and songs
S: Council estate in northern English industrial town, 1950s C: 6m, 7f, 1 child (f), extras

The Sawneys, a family of travelling people, are unwillingly being resettled from their derelict tramcar into a home on a council estate. They comprise Sailor, the 70-year-old patriarch; his woman, Big Rachel, a tough woman about 40; Rosie, a 22-year-old single mother of Sally and baby Geordie; and Rachel's son Col, a belligerent teenager. Their neighbour Mrs Jackson comes to welcome them, but is chased away with abuse. Mrs Jackson's daughter Doreen befriends Col, and Mr Jackson is dangerously attracted to Rachel. Blackmouth, Sally and Geordie's father, suddenly arrives to impose himself on the Sawneys, bringing with him the dotty Old Croaker and her manipulative teenage daughter Daffodil. Jackson goes to bed with Rachel, but cannot cope with her passion. Blackmouth finds Col in bed with Daffodil and threatens him with a knife, but is driven from the house by Col. Doreen claims that Col sexually assaulted her. An Official from the Housing Department warns the Sawneys that they will be evicted if they do not look after their house better. Mrs Jackson learns of her husband's infidelity and shuts him out of the house. The women of the estate set upon Col and claw wildly at him. Pursuing him home, they hurl bricks through the windows. After a night of siege, the police arrive and search for stolen goods. Col and Daffodil run away, Sailor is injured, Rachel sets off on the road, and the Official comes to evict them all.

In this boisterous play with its parade of colourful characters, vital language, and old ballads, Arden contrasts the Sawneys, 'direct descendants of the "sturdy beggars" of the 16th century', with the strait-laced Jacksons, epitome of the English bourgeoisie. While obviously thrilling to the full-blooded anarchy of the Sawneys, Arden insisted that he could not approve of them 'outright'.

Living Together. See NORMAN CONQUESTS, THE.

locanderia, La. See MIRANDOLINA.

London Assurance

A: Dion Boucicault Pf: 1841, London Pb: 1841
G: Com. in 5 acts; prose S: Sir Harcourt's house, London, and Oak Hall, Gloucestershire, 1830s C: 10m, 3f

Charles Courtly is a spendthrift about to be arrested for debt but has managed to convince his father Sir Harcourt that he is a sober young man. Sir Harcourt, despite being 63, has arranged a financially beneficial marriage with a friend's niece Grace Harkaway, who is only 18. Sir Harcourt travels to Harkaway's home, Oak Hall in Gloucestershire, for the wedding. Charles disguises himself in order to elude his creditors and also arrives at Oak Hall. Here Charles falls in love with Grace, while his father is taken with Grace's cousin Lady Gay Spanker. Unrecognized by his father, the disguised Charles woos Grace, then reappears as himself, a trick which Grace quickly and willingly sees through. Sir Harcourt, planning to elope with Lady Gay, is challenged to a duel by her husband. They are easily disarmed, and the shamefaced Sir Harcourt resigns his claim to Grace. When bailiffs come to arrest Charles for debt, he confesses everything.

Written when Boucicault was only 18, it is no surprise that the plot of *London Assurance* possesses elements of 18th-century comedy: the improbable disguise used to woo the loved one, the foolish elderly suitor, and the failed duel. However, Boucicault's play introduces a new note in the intelligence, seriousness, and plain common sense of the heroine Grace Harkaway. Faced with the choice between poverty and a husband 45 years her senior, she is not only resigned but is relieved that she will not have to pretend to love him, as would be expected with a young husband. Much of the success of the first performance was due to one of the first uses of a box set and real furniture by the Vestris–Mathews management at Covent Garden.

London Merchant, The (*The London Merchant: or, The History of George Barnwell*)

AT: *George Barnwell* **A:** George Lillo **Pf:** 1731, London **Pb:** 1731 **G:** Trag. in 5 acts; prose **S:** Thorowgood's and Millwood's homes, a prison, London, and a walk near a country house, 1630s **C:** 5m, 3f, extras

George Barnwell is clerk to the decent London merchant Thorowgood, whose daughter Maria is secretly in love with Barnwell. However, Barnwell is infatuated with Millwood, who, having suffered at the hands of men, has abandoned all virtue. Claiming that Barnwell's seduction of her has left her destitute, she first encourages Barnwell to steal money from Thorowgood, a crime that Maria covers up. She then urges him to murder his rich uncle, who dies blessing his nephew. Fearful that Barnwell's repentance will lead him to confess, Millwood hands him over to the law. Millwood's maid reveals all to Thorowgood, who denounces Millwood as an accessory to murder. Both Barnwell and Millwood go to the gallows, he repentant and at peace, she defiant and frightened.

Based on an old ballad, *The London Merchant* revives the domestic tragedy of **Arden of Faversham* and *A *Yorkshire Tragedy*, once again pursuing the democratization of drama encountered in **Jane Shore* and *The *Beggar's Opera*. There is a strong moral thread in Lillo's plays: the merchant is an idealized good old man, and Barnwell, though led astray by passion, redeems himself by repenting his sins. For our more cynical age, however, the character of Millwood, driven by the abuse of men to evil scheming in a way reminiscent of Lady Macbeth, provides the focus for the tragic interest. Lillo's play directly influenced Lessing and helped to initiate a Europe-wide taste for 'bourgeois tragedy'.

Long and the Short and the Tall, The

A: Willis Hall **Pf:** 1958, Nottingham **Pb:** 1959 **G:** Drama in 2 acts **S:** Hut in the Malayan jungle, Second World War **C:** 8m

Seven British soldiers have taken refuge in a primitive hut in the Malayan jungle during the Second World War. They have got separated from their unit and have lost radio contact with their base. During the night they are surprised by a Japanese soldier, who wanders into the hut to have a quiet smoke. They take him prisoner, but realize that they must be much closer to the Japanese lines than they thought. A patrol discovers that the Japanese are advancing around them, so they decide to retreat swiftly and silently. The question is what they should do with their prisoner. At first they intend to bring him back to base for interrogation, but realizing that he might put them in danger, the leader of the patrol Sergeant Mitcham, supported by Corporal Johnstone, decide to kill their prisoner in cold blood. Lance Corporal MacLeish protests against this brutal decision but changes his mind when the soldier is found to have a British cigarette case containing British cigarettes, obviously looted from the bodies of fellow combatants. Only Private Bamforth, an extrovert Cockney who anyway resents Mitcham's heavy discipline, now seeks to protect the unfortunate Japanese soldier. As Mitcham and Johnstone are about to force Bamforth to disarm, Private Whitaker, who has been guarding the prisoner, accidentally shoots him, thus alerting the surrounding Japanese forces.

While the British and American cinema kept on replaying the Second World War, and a number of major plays had been written after the First World War, post-war theatre seemed hesitant to choose the Second World War as a setting. Perhaps the scale was too vast, and significantly one of the few important war plays, *The Long and the Short and the Tall* by Willis Hall, later better known for his radio, television, and film scripts, focuses on one isolated setting and on a clear moral dilemma, for which the War forms a backdrop rather than being an essential component of the drama.

Long Day's Journey into Night

A: Eugene O'Neill **W**: 1940–1 **Pf**: 1956, Stockholm; 1956, New York **Pb**: 1956 **G**: Drama in 4 acts **S**: Summer home in Connecticut, August 1912 **C**: 3m, 2f

James Tyrone, a famous 65-year-old actor, has made a fortune repeating his most successful role across America. He is now on summer holiday with his wife Mary and his two sons Jamie and Edmund. Mary is 54, of a nervous disposition, and has recently been released from hospital. Jamie, 33, who has never succeeded at anything, is a cynic who is too fond of his drink. Edmund, 23, is sensitive and intelligent, and is racked by a disturbing cough. Jamie attacks his father's meanness in taking Edmund to cheap quacks, when what Tyrone pretends is a cold might in fact be consumption. Jamie also believes his mother to be taking dope again, the addiction which caused her hospitalization. Edmund too warns his mother about a relapse, but she denies taking drugs. However, she hates their cheap summer home and cannot forget the past, so says that it would serve them all right if she were to return to her addiction. Before lunch, Tyrone has a drink with his sons. Mary, left alone, has clearly taken drugs. She blames Tyrone for giving Edmund a drink, since this hastened her consumptive father's death. She is horrified at voicing her fear that Edmund has consumption, momentarily admits that she has returned to her addiction but then denies it once more. After lunch, the doctor, having diagnosed Edmund's consumption, asks him to come to see him. Mary, insisting on being driven to the drugstore, reveals that it was the morphine given her for the pains of Edmund's childbirth that began her addiction. Back from the drugstore, Mary recounts her past to the maid: how she had wanted to be a nun or a concert pianist but how she met and fell in love with Tyrone. Tyrone and Edmund return from the doctor, but Mary does not even ask about the diagnosis. It is midnight and the fog is closing in. Edmund returns home drunk, and he and his father play cards and talk. Edmund is dismayed that his father wants to save money by sending him to a state sanatorium. Tyrone justifies his meanness by referring to his impoverished youth, and confesses that he has ruined his artistic career by repeating one box-office success. Jamie comes home very drunk and tells his brother that, though he loves Edmund, he also hates him, and is trying to dissipate him with drink. Piano playing is heard, and then Mary appears in a drug-induced trance clutching her wedding-dress. She does not even hear Edmund's despairing cry that he has consumption, but recalls that, after meeting Tyrone, she 'was so happy for a time'.

Often regarded as the greatest American play, this long naturalistic piece is a relentless exploration of O'Neill's own life, and the sensitive nature of the content delayed performance until three years after the author's death. A remarkable achievement, it concentrates into one day the depiction of four tortured lives, their loves and hates, their dreams and their despair.

Look Back in Anger

A: John Osborne **Pf**: 1956, London **Pb**: 1957
G: Drama in 3 acts **S**: Jimmy Porter's living room in a flat, English Midlands, 1950s
C: 3m, 2f

On a typical English Sunday, Jimmy Porter and his friend Cliff Lewis read newspapers and converse desultorily, while Jimmy's wife Alison is ironing. Jimmy, owner of a sweet-stall, sneers at Alison's upper-class family and fulminates against the British Establishment: 'Nobody thinks, nobody cares. No beliefs, no convictions and no enthusiasm.' In a mock-fight with Cliff, Jimmy knocks over the ironing board, and Alison's arm gets burnt. Jimmy goes out, while Cliff comforts Alison, who reveals that she is pregnant but afraid to tell Jimmy. When Jimmy returns, they make up by playing their favourite game of bears and squirrels. This is interrupted by a phone call from Helena Charles, an actress friend of Alison. When Alison invites her to stay, Jimmy is so furious that he viciously hopes for something that would wake her out of her 'beauty sleep', perhaps that she could experience the death of her own child. Two weeks later, Helena is staying on, because Alison is unwell. Jimmy is deliberately offensive towards both women, especially when Alison agrees to go to church with Helena. When Jimmy learns that his friend's mother is dying, he asks Alison to accompany him to London. She refuses; instead, prompted by Helena, she gets her father, a retired colonel, to come and take her away. When Jimmy returns from London, distraught at his friend's mother's death, Helena is alone in the flat. After an angry confrontation, she seduces him. On a Sunday several months later, Jimmy and Cliff are reading the papers while Helena stands ironing and bears the brunt of Jimmy's invective. Alison arrives unexpectedly, and while Jimmy goes to Cliff's room angrily to play his trumpet, Alison reveals that she has lost her baby. Helena leaves Jimmy, and Alison hopes that her suffering is what he wanted: 'I'm in the mud at last! I'm grovelling! I'm crawling!' Jimmy embraces her, and they go back to their game of bears and squirrels.

Look Back in Anger became the most famous British play of the decade, was the seminal text of the so-called 'Angry Young Men', and, as the first 'kitchen-sink drama', was regarded as a turning point in post-war theatre. The play is conventional in structure, and while Jimmy's tirades contain brilliant verbal fireworks, some of the writing, especially in the Alison–Helena scenes, is weak. What was recognized as a breakthrough was that, in a tawdry lower middle-class setting, a young post-war British generation found its voice in its denunciation of traditional values and bourgeois conformism. With the subsequent raising of gender consciousness, Jimmy, far from appearing as a spokesman for the young, now appears as an objectionable and thuggish male.

Loot

A: Joe Orton **Pf**: 1965, Cambridge **Pb**: 1967
G: Farce in 2 acts **S**: Living room, England, 1960s **C**: 5m, 1f

Hal McLeavy exploits the fact that his friend Dennis drives a hearse for an undertaker: together they rob the bank next to the funeral parlour and have an ideal getaway vehicle. Hal's mother has just died, and is lying embalmed at home in her coffin. Fay, the nurse who was attending her, is a sexy young thing, already widow to seven deceased husbands. She now has designs on Hal's father, Mr McLeavy, but Dennis seduces her by offering her marriage and (allegedly) greater financial security. Inspector Truscott of Scotland Yard, on the trail of Hal and Dennis, comes to the house, but since he does not have a warrant, poses as a Water Board official. Hal and Dennis, in a panic to hide the loot, remove Hal's mother from her coffin, lock her in a cupboard, and stash their money in the coffin. When Truscott discovers Mrs McLeavy's corpse, the lads pretend that it is a dummy which Fay uses for dressmaking. To buy Fay's silence, they have to promise her a third share of the stolen cash, which is now on its way to the cemetery. Truscott now deduces that Fay poisoned Mrs McLeavy, but, unfortunately for him, the evidence in the form of her internal organs preserved in a casket is destroyed when the hearse has a crash.

Truscott nevertheless manages to discover what has happened to the loot and has to be cut in for a quarter-share. When Mr McLeavy finds out what is going on, he threatens to expose them all, so Truscott has him arrested for the robbery, and the others agree to testify against him. Fay accepts Dennis's proposal of marriage.

Winner of both the *Evening Standard* and *Plays and Players* awards for the best play of 1966, *Loot* was Orton's most popular drama. As in **Entertaining Mr Sloane*, *Loot* is set in a shabby English lower middle-class environment, with its self-seeking manipulation, hypocritical posturing, sexual tensions, and corrupt police. Lest this should become weighed down with social criticism, Orton creates a 'black farce', in which the conventional hiding of a body becomes particularly grotesque, since it is that of the mother of one of the leading characters. Some critics were repelled by Orton's cynicism, others revelled in it as a window into the carefree immorality of the 'swinging sixties'; the most perceptive recognized that, in the best Jonsonian tradition, Orton was a bitter moralist, who had personally suffered from the twisted values of British morality, which confronted him daily as a homosexual and which led to his imprisonment for six months for defacing books from a public library.

Lorenzaccio

A: Alfred de Musset **Pf**: 1896, Paris **Pb**: 1834 **Tr**: 1907 **G**: Drama in 5 acts; French prose **S**: Florence and Venice, 1537 **C**: 22m, 4f, extras

Alessandro de' Medici, Duke of Florence, a despotic libertine, is aided in his amorous exploits by his cousin, the unsmiling Lorenzo de' Medici. When the Duke tires of his present mistress, Lorenzo helps to ensnare his own aunt. The Strozzi family plot against the Duke, since they are appalled at the behaviour of the Duke and his followers, especially towards their daughter Louisa. Eventually it becomes clear that Lorenzo has befriended the Duke with the intention of assassinating him, even though he is unconvinced that this will make any real difference. Louisa Strozzi is poisoned, and her brothers swear vengeance. When Filippo, the head of the Strozzi family, refuses to join the conspiracy, Lorenzo acts alone and assassinates Alessandro. Lorenzo goes into hiding in Venice, while Cosimo de' Medici is named as the new Duke. Knowing that to emerge from hiding means almost certain death, Lorenzo, weary of life, goes out on to the Rialto.

Lorenzaccio is untypical of French theatre, which helps to explain why it took over 60 years to reach the stage, when it was premiered in a shortened version with Sarah Bernhardt in the title role. Written in prose in a multiplicity of short scenes, it introduces characters as much to provide historical colouring as for their significance in the action. This makes the play in some ways closer to Shakespeare than to French neo-classical theatre. Its most modern element is the unheroic nature of Lorenzo; he is no Romantic assassin but someone who feels obliged to attack tyranny even though he acknowledges that this will achieve nothing. His tragedy is not so much his demise but his recognition that he wore 'vice like a garment, but that it is now stuck to [his] skin'.

Losers. See LOVERS.

Loser Wins. See CONDEMNED OF ALTONA, THE.

Lost in a Mirror. See JUSTICE WITHOUT REVENGE.

Love for Love

A: William Congreve **Pf**: 1695, London **Pb**: 1695 **G**: Com. in 5 acts; prose **S**: Valentine's lodgings and Foresight's home, London, Restoration period **C**: 9m, 6f, extras

Valentine has run up heavy debts through his profligate lifestyle and his unsuccessful pursuit of a rich young heiress, Angelica. His dismayed father Sir Sampson Legend offers to pay off his debts, provided Valentine signs away his inheritance to his brother Ben, who is due home from seafaring. Angelica's uncle Foresight, a superstitious old fool, has arranged with Sir Sampson for his daughter Miss Prue, a simple country lass, to marry Ben, but they take an instant dislike to each other. In order to avoid signing away his inheritance, Valentine feigns madness. Displeased now with both sons, Sir Sampson proposes marriage to Angelica with the intention of producing a new heir. When Valentine finally agrees to sign away his fortune, since life without Angelica would be meaningless anyway, Angelica relents: she seizes the papers disinheriting Valentine, tears them up, and agrees to marry Valentine.

The main strength of this play lies not in the fairly predictable plot, with its reformed rake and its happy ending guaranteeing prosperity for the lovers, but in the boldness of its comic characterization. The fearful Foresight (reminiscent of the gulls in *The *Alchemist*), the simpleton Miss Prue (similar to Margery in *The *Country Wife*), the bluff sea dog Ben, and the lustful old Sir Sampson all offer opportunities for hilarious comic acting, and the play has remained popular as a consequence.

Love in Livery. See GAME OF LOVE AND CHANCE, THE.

Love Lies a-Bleeding. See PHILASTER.

Love of a Good Man, The

A: Howard Barker **Pf**: 1978, Sheffield **Pb**: 1980
G: Drama in 3 acts **S**: Battlefield subsequently war cemetery, Passchendaele, Belgium, 1920
C: 11m, 2f

Two years after the end of the First World War, soldiers are still burying the dead in the mud of Passchendaele (scene of a disastrous British offensive in 1917). The site is visited by Edward, Prince of Wales, and by Hacker, an undertaker who will make money creating a war cemetery for the fallen. Mrs Toynbee, an attractive widow, comes with her daughter Lalage in search of her son Billy, who is 'missing, presumed dead'. Hacker claims to have found his remains, and his mother kisses the headless body farewell, although the corpse is in fact that of a German soldier provided by an unscrupulous soldier Riddle. Colonel Hard recruits amongst the gravediggers for the Black and Tans to 'hold the Empire together' in Ireland. Lalage, who favours the new socialism where everyone is treated equally, threatens to denounce to the police her mother's plan to smuggle Billy's body home. The Prince of Wales opens the new cemetery and is tricked by Hacker into choosing Billy's supposed corpse to be the Unknown Warrior. Mrs Toynbee holds a seance, the mentally disturbed War Graves Commissioner Bride shoots himself, and the Prince of Wales declares his love for Mrs Toynbee. The cemetery completed, everyone returns to England – or Ireland.

The grotesque humour of this powerful satire of the Establishment is reminiscent of Bond's **Early Morning*. It shows how the 'love of a good man' for his country can be exploited in the defence of Empire that led to the slaughter of millions in the First World War and will continue the killing in Ireland. Hacker sums it up memorably: 'You people . . . yer gobs are clamped so tight on the tits of privilege, yer can't stop sucking even when the dugs are dry.'

Lover, The

A: Harold Pinter **Pf**: 1963, London **Pb**: 1963
G: Com. in 1 act **S**: A middle-class home near Windsor, 1960s **C**: 2m, 1f

Richard, leaving for work, asks his wife Sarah whether her lover is coming that day. She replies that she will be seeing him at home that afternoon. That evening, Richard chats about Sarah's lover and is surprised to see her wearing very high-heeled shoes. Richard then admits that he regularly sees a prostitute. The following afternoon, Sarah has prepared herself for her lover, wearing a tight low-cut dress and her high heels. She greets her lover as Max, and Richard enters. He gets out some bongo drums, and they play a sensuous game, tapping out a rhythm with entangled fingers. They play more games: Max/Richard pretending to accost Sarah in the park, then rescuing her. They disappear under the table and have sex. Later, Max/Richard alarms Sarah by saying that they will have to stop their game, because their children will soon be home from boarding school. That evening Richard returns 'from work' and insists that Sarah should not receive her lover any more and that he has 'paid off' his whore. Sarah becomes desperate that their game must end, and Richard 'finds' the bongo. Tapping it, he starts to confuse Sarah by assuming the role of Max. She enters into the new game and offers to change her clothes for him. He calls her: 'You lovely whore!'

First shown on television, *The Lover*, with its middle-class setting and sophisticated humour, is not typical of Pinter's early work. However, Pinter is able to explore his favourite themes of game-playing and reality, which here become dangerously confused.

Lovers (Winners; Losers)

A: Brian Friel **Pf:** 1967, Dublin **Pb:** 1968 **G:** (1) Trag. in 2 scenes; (2) Com. in 1 act **S:** (1) Hill overlooking an Irish town, 1966; (2) Working-class home, Ireland, 1960s **C:** (1) 2m, 2f; (2) 1m, 3f

(1) *Winners*. A Man and a Woman ('Commentators') introduce Mag and Joe, two 17-year-old schoolchildren, who are to get married in three weeks' time, because Mag is pregnant. On a warm summer Saturday, they meet on top of the hill overlooking their home town in order to revise for their imminent examinations. While Joe attempts to study, Mag prattles on happily about the flat they are going to occupy, about her father, a dentist, and about their awaited child. Mag ponders whether they will end up loveless like their own parents, and Joe, losing patience at last, says that he was trapped into marrying her and that he intends to become a maths teacher and lead his own life. While Mag weeps, the Commentators reveal that later that day they were drowned in the local lough. As Mag sleeps, Joe reveals how much he loves her. Reconciled, they run off happily down the hill. No one can explain how their boat capsized on such a calm day. (2) *Losers*. Andy is so bored by his marriage to Hanna that he sits in the back yard pretending to look through binoculars. In flashback we see the two courting. Andy Tracey is a 50-year-old joiner, and Hanna Wilson a spinster in her late forties who works in a shirt-factory and lives with her widowed mother, a pious woman. Mrs Wilson's frequent summoning of her daughter with a hand-bell makes courting difficult; so the couple pretend to recite poetry while kissing and cuddling. They marry and live with the dreadful Mrs Wilson. An equally pious old neighbour Cissy regularly joins Hanna's mother in prayer to St Philomena, and Andy is so overjoyed when one day the Vatican pronounces that Philomena is no longer a saint, that he comes home drunk and wrestles with Hanna and Cissy over the Saint's statue. After this brief rebellious outburst, he sinks back into the tedium of his marriage.

In these two linked pieces Friel combines accurate realism with detached narration in *Winners*, which juxtaposes the fun of the young couple with their impending tragedy, and with direct address to the audience in *Losers*, which invites us to see his unhappy marriage from Andy's point of view. Ironically, it is the young whose deaths mean that their dreams will never be destroyed by the harshness of reality who are the winners, whereas the older couple who end up married are the losers. In the midst of the comedy, Friel's assessment is gloomy.

Love's Labour's Lost (*A Pleasant Conceited Comedie called Loues labors lost*)

A: William Shakespeare **Pf:** *c*.1594, London **Pb:** 1598 **G:** Romantic com. in 5 acts; blank verse and prose **S:** The King of Navarre's Park, Renaissance period **C:** 13m, 5f, extras

The King of Navarre and three of his lords resolve to devote themselves to academic study, requiring them to avoid the company of women for three years. Their resolve is immediately threatened by the arrival of the Princess of France. Despite refusing her admittance to his court, the inevitable happens when they meet in the King's park: he falls in love with the Princess, and his lords secretly woo her ladies-in-waiting. When the truth is revealed, they agree to abandon their vow of chastity and to visit the women disguised as Russians. Being forewarned of this plan, the Princess and her entourage mask themselves, so that each man pays court to the wrong partner. The women reproach them for their faithlessness, and together they watch a ridiculous masque performed by the curate, the schoolmaster, and a fantastical Spaniard. News comes of the death of the Princess's father. She and her ladies must mourn for a year and charge their suitors to be faithful and do good works, so that they may claim their loves after 'a twelvemonth and a day'.

Long believed to be Shakespeare's first play, *Love's Labour's Lost* reflects his immaturity. He is intoxicated with language, from the saccharine verse of the lovers to the overblown pomposity of Holofernes, the schoolmaster. The plot is schematic, with the neat pairing off of lords and ladies. The use of disguises and the parodied heroic masque, which adumbrates the 'rude mechanicals' of *A *Midsummer Night's Dream,* are a source of easy humour. But already Shakespeare's genius shows through in the subtle variations of attitude and language in the lovers, in his gently cynical treatment of the male sex, and in the play's refusal to end; for who knows what will happen in a year and a day's time: 'That's too long for a play.'

Lower Depths, The (*Na dne*)

AT: *A Night's Lodging; Submerged; At the Bottom (of Life); Down and Out* **A**: Maxim Gorky **Pf**: 1902, Moscow **Pb**: 1903 **Tr**: 1905 **G**: Drama in 4 acts; Russian prose **S**: A lodging house in a Volga town, 1900s **C**: 12m, 5f

The basement of Mikhail Kostyliov's lodging house is full of down-and-outs. The thief Vasily Pepel is having an affair with Kostyliov's wife Vasilisa but now turns his attention to her younger sister Natasha. There are also a brutal locksmith Kleshch and his ailing wife; a Baron; an embittered cap-maker; a failed and now drunken Actor; a dumpling-seller wooed by a corrupt policeman; a cobbler; a card-sharp named Satin; two porters; and Nastya, a prostitute who dreams of genuine romance. This motley crew is joined by a 60-year-old pilgrim Luka, who brings comfort to these unhappy and destitute beings. He consoles Kleshch's dying wife with promises of peace after death and tells the Actor of a free clinic that will cure alcoholics. Vasilisa encourages Pepel to murder her husband, but Luka arrives in time to prevent him, urging Pepel to leave with Natasha. Vasilisa retaliates by scalding her sister's feet and causing a fight between Pepel and Kostyliov. Pepel accidentally kills Kostyliov and is to be tried for murder. Luka leaves during the brawl, and while the others discuss him over drinks and cards, the Actor, disappointed that Luka never gave him the address of the clinic, quietly goes into the yard and hangs himself.

The Lower Depths is one of the major texts of naturalist theatre. In Lukács's terms, it does not 'narrate' but 'describes'. The description is of a group, skilfully individualized by Gorky, living at the bottom of society, whose only comfort comes from their dreams, fed by the gentle but ultimately mendacious Luka. There is little plot and no central figure. The death of the Actor does not proceed from necessity as in conventional tragedy but is arbitrary and meaningless, provoking Satin's response: 'he spoiled our song – the fool!'

Loyal Brother, The. See REVENGER'S TRAGEDY, THE.

Luces de bohemia. See BOHEMIAN LIGHTS.

Ludus Coventriae. See N-TOWN CYCLE OF MYSTERY PLAYS, THE.

Lulu Plays, The (Earth-Spirit; Pandora's Box)

A: Frank Wedekind **Pf**: (1) 1898, Leipzig; (2) 1904, Nuremberg **Pb**: (1) 1895; (2) 1902; rev. 1904, 1906, 1911 **Tr**: 1914 **G**: Dramas of 4 acts and 3 acts, each with verse prologue, otherwise German prose with some French and English **S**: (1) Artists' studio, theatre dressing room, drawing rooms, Germany; (2) Germany, Paris, and London, 1890s **C**: (1) 11m, 2f, extras; (2) 12m, 6f, extras

(1): *Earth-Spirit* (*Erdgeist*). In the prologue, an animal-tamer introduces the fascinating and dangerous Lulu. Lulu is married to an elderly doctor Goll, who takes her to have her portrait painted by the artist Schwarz. When Goll discovers that Lulu and Schwarz have become lovers, he dies of a stroke. She marries Schwarz but continues to receive other men, including a depraved old man Schigolch, whom she pretends is her father. She begins an affair with the worldly wise newspaper editor Dr Schön, and refuses to let him go when he becomes engaged to a wealthy young society girl. When Schwarz learns about her infidelity, he cuts his throat. Lulu now becomes a famous dancer, starring in a ballet written by Schön's son Alwa. Courted by the rich and famous, she still wants Schön for herself and finally succeeds in driving away his fiancée. Once married to Schön, she takes a series of lovers, the Countess Geschwitz, Schigolch, an acrobat Rodrigo Quast, a student Hugenberg, Alwa, and even her servants. Confronting her, Schön gives her a pistol to shoot either herself or him. She kills him, 'the only man I ever loved!', and is arrested by the police. (2) *Pandora's Box* (*Die Büchse der Pandora*). In the Prologue, characters in a bookshop defend literature against the charge of immorality. After Lulu has spent a year in prison, Countess Geschwitz effects her escape, having become a prison nurse and having infected herself and Lulu with cholera. Rodrigo had planned to take Lulu to London and tame her with a whip, but is disgusted by her invalid state. She is still able, however, to seduce Alwa on the couch where his father bled to death. They go to Paris, where they marry. A pimp threatens to betray her to the police unless she agrees to be sold to work in an Egyptian brothel. When Rodrigo also threatens to blackmail her, she begs Schigolch to kill him. She manages to persuade her lesbian lover Countess Geschwitz to go with Rodrigo. The police arrive to arrest her, and she and Alwa flee to London with Schigolch. Here she works as their prostitute. An African client whom she brings back to their sordid attic becomes aware that Alwa is hiding in the next room and kills him. Schigolch removes the corpse and goes off drinking. Countess Geschwitz, who has loyally followed Lulu, attempts suicide but fails. Finally, Lulu brings in her last customer Jack the Ripper, who stabs Geschwitz and cuts up Lulu, while the dying Geschwitz looks on.

Seldom has the power of sexual fascination been so intensely explored as in the *Lulu Plays,* which, thanks to constant rewriting, now exist in different versions. Unsurprisingly, their publication guaranteed Wedekind's reputation as a pornographer. In fact, the piece is highly moral. The men who enslave themselves to Lulu's erotic charms are shown to suffer in their abasement, and Lulu herself is punished horribly by a male-dominated bourgeois society for the intensity of her natural drives. Only the Countess Geschwitz reveals herself capable of true love but must also succumb. The grotesque characters living on the edge of existence, the primacy of dramatic situation over individual psychology, the clipped dialogue, all point forward to Expressionism. In 1929 G. W. Pabst used the material for a silent film starring Louise Brooks.

Luther

A: John Osborne **Pf:** 1961, Nottingham **Pb:** 1961 **G:** Hist. drama in 3 acts **S:** Erfurt; Juterbög [=Jüterbog], Wittenberg, Augsburg, and Worms, Germany, and Magliana [=Magliano], Italy, 1506–30 **C:** 13m, 1f, extras

Martin Luther, witnessed by his father, a prosperous merchant, is received into the Augustinian Order in Erfurt. His father is sceptical about the vision which called his son to be a monk, but, despite chronic constipation, Luther performs menial tasks and flagellates himself. Only when alone does he reveal doubts about his vocation. While the notorious Dominican monk Johann Tetzel hawks indulgences to the gullible faithful, Luther furiously criticizes this commercialism and superstition, and, despite his growing reputation as a scholar, has to be reprimanded by his superiors. Luther responds by becoming even more rebellious, preaching against indulgences and in 1517 nailing his 95 theses to the church door in Wittenberg. When he refuses to retract these, he is excommunicated by Pope Leo X. Scornfully, Luther burns the Pope's decree and denounces him as Satan's lackey. Luther, summoned to the Diet of Worms in 1521, refuses to recant: 'Here I stand: God help me; I can do no more.' In 1525, after the peasants' revolt at Bundschuh and its brutal suppression, Luther is blamed for stirring unrest. However, he insists that he is only bringing the word of God to the common people, an achievement praised even by the vicar-general of the Augustinians. At the end,

Luther is seen living in domestic harmony with his wife and children in a vacated cloister in Wittenberg.

Although Osborne's *Luther* has some elements in common with Brecht's historical plays, especially its epic construction in a series of short scenes in different locations and its undramatic ending, there is little political analysis. Osborne instead relates Luther's rebellion to his historically documented constipation, which makes him an anal compulsive out of joint with the world.

Lysistrata (*Lysistratē*)

AT: *Revolt of the Women* A: Aristophanes Pf: 411 BC, Athens Tr: 1878 G: Greek com. in verse S: Before the Acropolis in Athens, early 5th c. BC C: 10m, 13f, extras, chorus (m), chorus (f)

Lysistrata (= 'disbander of armies'), an Athenian woman, persuades the wives of Athens and other warring states to withhold their sexual favours from their husbands and lovers until they give up their senseless war. They join forces with the chorus of old women who have already taken over the Acropolis. A chorus of old men attempt to smoke the women out of the Acropolis, but they and the police are repelled by the women. It is proving difficult for the women to maintain their resolve, but one of them, Myrrhine, acquits herself well, exciting her husband to a sexual frenzy only to abandon him and return to the women. A Spartan herald arrives, somewhat hindered by his permanent erection, to announce that the women's revolt has been successful in the enemy camp too. At the prospect of peace, the opposing choruses of old men and old women are reconciled. When the Spartan and Athenian negotiators then meet, Lysistrata is able to call forth Reconciliation, a lovely young woman, who brings the two warring sides together. Lysistrata reminds them of their common heritage, and peace is rapidly restored. The play ends with general feasting, a dance, and the final recognition that Athene, the goddess of wisdom, is worshipped in both Athens and Sparta.

By 411 BC the Peloponnesian War against Sparta was – apart from a brief cessation in hostilities after 421 BC – dragging on into its twentieth year. The expedition against Sicily had been a dismal failure, Athens' allies were deserting her, the city was almost bankrupt. Aristophanes now wrote a play with a truly radical solution, as extreme to the male Athenian mind as building an ideal state in the sky (see BIRDS): let the women take charge. Not only do the Athenian women withhold their sexual favours (which is what is best remembered about the play), but they occupy the Acropolis, taking over the treasury and therefore the economic means to prosecute the war. It is notable that *Lysistrata* is the only extant play by Aristophanes that bears the name of an individual, and this is the first European comedy with a female lead. Lysistrata has something of the toughness exhibited by the great tragic heroines of Sophocles and Euripides, even if some of the other wives are shown to be weak and shallow. She succeeds where the politicians and generals have failed. She not only brings about a genuine peace, but also paves the way for reconciliation, reminding the Athenians how much common heritage they share with the Spartans. It would have been the equivalent of staging a play in London in the First World War, reminding the English that the hated Kaiser Wilhelm II was the grandson of Queen Victoria. Inevitably, it is the bawdy element of the play which has made it Aristophanes' best known, and it has been adapted again and again to offer a light-hearted appeal for men to abandon their violent conflicts.

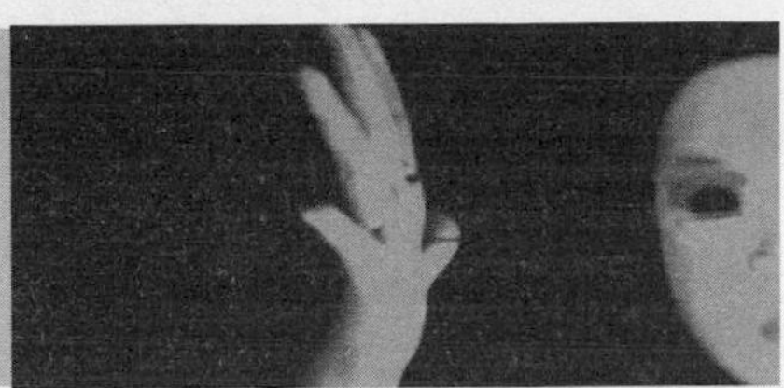

Macbeth (*The Tragedie of Macbeth*)

A: William Shakespeare Pf: *c.*1602–6, London Pb: 1623 G: Trag. in 5 acts; blank verse and prose S: Scotland and England, 1040–57 C: 21m, 8f, extras

The Scottish king Duncan grants Macbeth the title Thane of Cawdor in honour of his bravery in helping to repel a foreign invasion. Macbeth learns of this new title from three witches who meet him and his companion Banquo after the battle. The witches also foretell that Macbeth shall become king and that Banquo's sons shall be kings. When Lady Macbeth hears of this prophecy, she urges her husband to murder Duncan while he is sleeping at their castle. Macbeth carries out the deed, and blame falls on Duncan's sons, who flee from Scotland. Macbeth is elected king, but, unable to trust Banquo, orders his death. Banquo is murdered, but his son escapes. Macbeth gives a banquet, which is disrupted by the appearance of Banquo's ghost. Consulting the witches again, Macbeth learns that he cannot be defeated by any man born of woman. On learning that Macduff has fled to England, Macbeth orders the murder of his wife and children. Macduff joins with Duncan's son and heir Malcolm to lead an army against Macbeth. As Macbeth prepares to defend himself, Lady Macbeth, overcome by the guilt of Duncan's murder, takes her own life. Finally, Macbeth confronts Macduff in battle. Because Macduff was 'from his mother's womb untimely ripped' and so not born of woman, he defeats the tyrant Macbeth. Malcolm will become king.

Based on Holinshed's *Chronicles, Macbeth* is the shortest and most intense of Shakespeare's tragedies with no sub-plot and developing over weeks rather than years. The study of an essentially brave and noble character, who turns more and more to evil to gain his ends, engages us much more deeply than the superficially similar fate of Richard III. This is achieved partly by the way Macbeth is manipulated by the witches, who predict but do not determine the future, and, above all by his wife, who challenges his manhood to drive him to murder. Indeed, the role of Lady Macbeth is the most powerful female role in Shakespeare. The play is traditionally associated with bad luck, partly because of its invocation of evil, partly because its brevity, relatively small cast, and popular appeal have made it the last resort of a dying theatrical company. The most notable adaptation was Verdi's opera (1847).

Machinal

AT: *The Life Machine* A: Sophie Treadwell Pf: 1928, New York Pb: 1929 G: Drama in 9 scenes S: New York and a seaside hotel, 1920s C: 17m, 10f, extras

The Young Woman, a stenographer, endures a miserable and oppressive life, both at home and at work. So when her unattractive and boring boss asks to marry her, she accepts. However, life with her Husband offers no joy: the honeymoon is a hideous experience, and she hates her baby when it is born. In a speakeasy, she meets the Young Man, an outlaw on the run. She falls in love with him, and her affair with him is 'all she ever knew of Heaven'. When her Husband refuses to let her go, she murders him, is tried and sentenced to death. When told her head must be shaved, she resists for the first time in her life. Rejecting remorse, she goes steadfastly to the electric chair.

Based on the real-life murder trial of Ruth Snyder, the first woman to be executed in the electric chair just eight months before the play's premiere, *Machinal* is a powerful Expressionist treatment of a woman whose crime appears almost justified. The clamour of contemporary technology, the routines of urban life, and, above all, the oppression of her gender, drive her to make her futile bid for freedom and fulfilment. The Young Man was played at its premiere by Hal K. Dawson (known later as Clark Gable). Because of its early feminist implications, *Machinal* has been successfully revived in recent years.

Machine infernale, La. See INFERNAL MACHINE, THE.

Machine Wreckers, The (*Die Maschinenstürmer*)

A: Ernst Toller **Pf:** 1922, Berlin **Pb:** 1922 **Tr:** 1923 **G:** Drama in 5 acts and a prologue; German prose and verse **S:** The House of Lords and Nottingham, 1812–16 **C:** 26m, 7f, 5 children, extras

Despite Lord Byron's support for the weavers, a bill is passed in Parliament making destruction of machinery a capital offence. In Nottingham misery reigns, as women and children work for a pittance at the new steam looms, while the male weavers starve. When Jimmy Cobbett, an idealistic rebel, becomes leader of the discontented men, his brother Henry, fearing for his job as foreman, plots with the treacherous weaver John Wible to get rid of Jimmy. Jimmy tries to persuade the mill owner Ure to employ his machines for the benefit of all, but Ure hides behind a Darwinian concept of survival. Wible incites the men to destroy the machines. When Jimmy tries to hold them back, he is beaten to death. The weavers defiantly march off to be arrested, while only an old weaver is left to mourn Jimmy's passing.

Owing much to Hauptmann's *The *Weavers*, Toller's play on the Luddites goes beyond the familiar depiction of misery and starvation of the weavers. He suggests instead that there should be a positive response to the introduction of machinery, which can 'lift the Scriptural curse of toil', if only employed for the good of all. The play was given a spectacular premiere in Reinhardt's 'Theatre of Five Thousand' in Berlin, with a functional steam loom, the realism of which however militated against the poetic Expressionism of the piece.

Macht der Gewohnheit, Die. See FORCE OF HABIT, THE.

Madame de Sade (*Sado Kōshaku Fujin*)

A: Mishima Yukio **Pf:** 1965, Tokyo **Pb:** 1965 **Tr:** 1968 **G:** Drama in 3 acts; Japanese prose **S:** Madame de Montreuil's house, 1772, 1778, 1790 **C:** 6f

When Alphonse Marquis de Sade is imprisoned for administering aphrodisiacs to, and whipping and sodomizing, four prostitutes, his mother-in-law Madame de Montreuil attempts to free him, for the sake of her daughter Renée and for the family name. She summons two influential women, Comtesse de Saint-Fond, herself a libertine, and the saintly Baronesse de Simian, to intercede on Alphonse's behalf. Renée surprises everyone, including her sister Anne, by declaring her unswerving loyalty to Alphonse. In 1778 Alphonse is freed from prison, and his record is wiped clean. Saint-Fond describes how she took part in a black mass where her naked body was used as an altar, and declares that she can now identify with the extreme sexual longings of the Marquis de Sade: 'Alphonse is obsessed with seeing, I with being seen.' Renée admits that she allowed Alphonse to beat her until she bled, revealing her utter devotion to her husband: 'Alphonse is myself!' Twelve years later, in the wake of the French Revolution, Alphonse is once again about to be freed from jail, where he was regularly visited by Renée. Saint-Fond, disguised as a Marseilles prostitute, is accidentally trampled to death by a revolutionary mob, and even Simian admits she was excited by Alphonse's exploits. Alphonse has given word that he will help his aristocratic friends in the revolutionary purges. Renée declares her undying love and respect for

Alphonse, but when he comes to the door, she refuses to see him.

Mishima's novels, his unfashionable embracing of traditional Japanese values, and his spectacular suicide, are all better known than his plays, but he was responsible for a large and significant dramatic output. *Madame de Sade*, the best known of his plays, was staged by Ingmar Bergman in 1989, and reflects Mishima's familiar theme of enlightenment through extreme experience. The puzzle which drew him to the topic, why Renée after a lifetime's devotion refuses to see Alphonse when he is freed, remains an enigma.

Mad Day's Work, A. See MARRIAGE OF FIGARO, THE.

Made in Bangkok

A: Anthony Minghella Pf: 1986, London Pb: 1986 G: Drama in 2 acts S: Airport, hotel, factory, massage parlour, Bangkok, and launch tied up at Ayuthya, 1980s C: 7m, 9f

A group of English travellers arrive in Bangkok: friends Adrian and Gary; a married couple Stephen and Frances Bitter; and Edward Gover, a dentist on his way to work with Vietnamese refugees in Hong Kong. Adrian and Gary have come to buy cheap clothing, and Gary is hoping for some cheap sex. They visit a clothes factory, and tensions appear in Stephen and Frances's marriage. Everyone meets in the hotel bar, and Frances gets angry about Adrian and Gary visiting a sex show. Stephen is secretly envious, Edward comments negatively on the political aspect, and Adrian and Frances grow close. While Gary takes Stephen secretly to a massage parlour, Frances and Adrian become lovers. Adrian and Frances arrange to have dinner together, and Gary and Stephen pay for three prostitutes to come to their room. Stephen and Frances have a row, which ends with Stephen hitting her. Edward steps down from his high moral stance to pay for sex with a male hotel worker, and accidentally sets off the hotel's fire alarms. Adrian realizes that Stephen and Gary have abandoned their call girls in the 'fire', and rushes to rescue them. The following morning, little is said. Adrian and Gary, having completed their deal in Thailand, are flying home, while the others are going on to Hong Kong, but 'Nothing can stay the same now can it.'

Now best known as a film director (especially for *The English Patient*, 1996), Minghella has written several successful plays, this being the first to be premiered in London. Against a backdrop of sexual and economic exploitation of the Third World, each English visitor to Bangkok reveals both moral corruption and emotional vulnerability.

Madman and the Nun, The (*Wariat i zakonnica*)

AT: *There Is Nothing Bad Which Could Not Turn into Something Worse* A: Stanisław Ignacy Witkiewicz W: 1923 Pf: 1924, Toruń Pb: 1925 Tr: 1968 G: Drama in 3 acts; Polish prose S: Cell in a lunatic asylum, 1920s C: 6m, 2f

Alexander Walpurg, a handsome but dishevelled 29-year-old poet, is a patient in a lunatic asylum, diagnosed with *dementia praecox* 'stemming from a forgotten incident in his past'. Sister Anna, a beautiful 22-year-old nun, is assigned to him to bring this to light. Anna entered a convent after her fiancé shot himself, while Walpurg tormented his lover to death. The two are instantly attracted to each other, and, after Anna has released Walpurg from his straitjacket, they become lovers. The following morning, Walpurg feels a changed man, ready to begin a new life with Anna and to start writing poetry again. Two doctors visit him: the psychiatrist Dr Grün is overjoyed at Walpurg's progress, while the brain-surgeon Dr Bidello so enrages Walpurg that he stabs him to death with a pencil. Grün imagines that he has now 'resolved his complex', but Anna is horrified. That evening, Anna comes to Walpurg again, and they are surprised in a passionate embrace by Grün and the Mother Superior. Grün orders that Walpurg be tied up, but Walpurg hangs himself from his window frame. Shortly afterwards, Walpurg enters, immaculately dressed, followed by Bidello, carrying a new dress for Anna, who leaves with them. Grün, his assistants, and the Mother Superior find themselves locked in the cell. They begin to fight like madmen.

What begins as a psychological and realist drama suddenly launches into unreality with the arrival of the two people we have witnessed die on stage. At the end, Grün wails: 'I don't know what the hell is going on here!' The audience are similarly mystified as Witkiewicz kicks away rationality, making us share the Mother Superior's insight: 'I cannot tell any more who is mad.'

Madmen and Specialists

A: Wole Soyinka **Pf:** 1970, Waterford, Connecticut **Pb:** 1971 **G:** Drama in 2 acts **S:** Dr Bero's surgery and the space before it, Nigeria, 1969 **C:** 7m, 3f

Four eccentric beggars, crippled in the recent civil war between the breakaway state of Biafra and the Nigerian government, are posted outside Dr Bero's surgery. They are guarding someone, who turns out to be Bero's father. Bero, who switched from being a medical specialist to become an army intelligence officer, arrives back from the conflict. Welcomed home by his sister and the Priest, Bero reveals that he has become a cannibal. His father, so outraged by the inhumanity of the war, had served up human flesh to the officers, and they, Bero included, developed a liking for it. Bero now keeps the Old Man, his father, safely under guard in his surgery. While pretending to protect his 'mad' father, Bero is actually hoping to learn from him the secrets of the cult of 'As', so that he can use them to evil ends. When the Old Man refuses to divulge the secrets of his harsh religion and threatens to attack the Cripple who dared to question his cult, Bero shoots him dead. Two Earth Mothers, who have been watching over the action, destroy their store of herbs, so that they will not fall into Bero's hands.

This play was written as a response to the Nigerian civil war (1967–70), which had led to Soyinka's imprisonment when he protested against the brutal suppression of the Biafran population. By showing the way Bero, a decent country doctor, can be perverted to become an evil cannibalistic figure, Soyinka has written a powerful and often enigmatic African sequel to Brecht's *A *Man's a Man.*

Madras House, The

A: Harley Granville Barker **Pf:** 1910, London **Pb:** 1911; rev. 1925 **G:** Com. in 4 acts **S:** The Huxtables' and Madras's homes and business offices, London, 1900s **C:** 8m, 17f

Henry Huxtable, recovering from an illness, is preparing to sell the drapery business that he co-owns and manages with his nephew Philip Madras, who wishes to leave the trade so that he can become a reformer. Huxtable is unhappy to learn that Philip's father is returning from abroad to be involved in the negotiations for the sale. Madras Senior is in ill odour with Huxtable, because he left his wife, Huxtable's sister, 30 years previously. We also meet Huxtable's six daughters, who are at a loss how to fill their time meaningfully. The next day at the office, Philip has to adjudicate a crisis amongst his employees: an unrepentant member of staff has become pregnant and a fellow employee is falsely accused of being the father. While mannequins vacuously parade past them, the directors negotiate the sale of the firm. Philip's father Constantine Madras is repulsed by the hypocritical views of the American purchaser, who regards fashion as a means to emancipate women, and proclaims instead the virtues of Islam. In the final act, Constantine and his wife fail to effect a reconciliation, and it is revealed that it was Constantine who made the young employee pregnant. Philip and his wife quarrel and recognize that their life is empty. Philip will attempt to make amends by going into politics, and the play ends with a kiss.

While there is a narrative of sorts, the play is really a series of scenes exploring the emptiness and questionable moral codes of contemporary society. The place of women is especially examined: they are either dressed like dolls or exploited like slaves. Barker skilfully blends naturalism with satire, creating a piece which, with its many rewarding female roles, deserves to be performed more frequently.

Madwoman of Chaillot, The (*La Folle de Chaillot*)

A: Jean Giraudoux **Pf:** 1945, Paris **Pb:** 1945 **Tr:** 1949 **G:** Com. in 2 acts; French prose

S: A café and a cellar in the Chaillot Quarter of Paris, spring 1945 C: 27m, 12f

Financiers meet in a café to discuss their latest moneymaking venture. Oil has been discovered beneath the streets of Paris, and they are preparing to wreck the city in order to exploit this hidden wealth. They are constantly distracted by the colourful poor people of the quarter and especially by a madwoman, who claims to be the Countess Aurelia. A Young Man is brought in half-drowned. He had been given the task of laying explosives to frighten the authorities into giving permission to drill for oil, but in desperation threw himself in the river. He falls in love with the waitress Irma. The Madwoman encourages him to enjoy life again and protects him by hitting his boss over the head with a soda siphon. The Madwoman, resolving to rid the world of these corrupt capitalists, sends out notes, claiming that there is oil in the cellar of her house. Summoning madwomen from other Parisian quarters, she holds a mock trial, in which the capitalists are condemned. Eventually, financiers, oil-prospectors, politicians, and newspaper men arrive, and are shown a tunnel where they will find oil. They rush to descend, and the Madwoman closes the trap so that they cannot escape. Suddenly the world is transformed, and, encouraged by the Madwoman, the Young Man kisses Irma.

Giraudoux's best-known play, performed posthumously at a premiere attended by Charles de Gaulle, is a joyful, sentimental celebration of the common people of Paris. Although it offers no serious political analysis, it was an achievement for Giraudoux in the last year of his life to be looking beyond the immediate concerns of German occupation to post-war issues of capitalist exploitation and the environment.

Mad World, My Masters, A

A: Thomas Middleton Pf: 1604–6, London Pb: 1608 G: Com. in 5 acts; prose and some blank verse (some rhymed) S: London, *c.*1600 C: 13m, 3f, extras

Spendthrift Richard Follywit, impatient to inherit from the rich and generous Sir Bounteous Progress (variously described as his uncle and as his grandfather), tricks Sir Bounteous. Disguised as Lord Owemuch, he enjoys Sir Bounteous's hospitality and robs him; he then poses as his uncle's courtesan Gullman and steals from him again. Follywit falls in love with a 'modest virgin' (in fact, the courtesan Gullman) and marries her. In a parallel plot, a country gentleman Master Penitent Brothel uses Gullman to help him to the bed of Mistress Harebrain, who is jealously guarded by her husband. Penitent, harassed by the devil in the form of Mistress Harebrain, repents and goes with the Harebrains to a banquet given by Sir Bounteous. At the banquet, Follywit disguises himself as a player and uses his role to steal again from Sir Bounteous, but is apprehended by a Constable. Follywit escapes by pretending that the Constable is part of their play, but, returning without disguise, is betrayed by a watch ringing in his pocket. When Follywit pleads with Sir Bounteous that he has become honest because he has married 'a gentlewoman and a virgin', Sir Bounteous is so delighted that Follywit has been gulled by his courtesan that he forgives him. Follywit's bride promises to reform.

Although designated a 'city comedy', the action of Middleton's play could be set virtually anywhere, and indeed its central theme of the trickster ending up being tricked himself could have been written by Plautus. The bawdy comments and situations must have sounded especially scandalous in the mouths of the boy actors of St Paul's.

Mad World, My Masters, A

A: Barrie Keeffe Pf: 1977, London Pb: 1977 G: Pol. com. in 2 acts S: London, 1977 C: 8m, 4f

In an updating of Middleton's play for the Queen's Silver Jubilee, Keeffe offers a snapshot of London some 370 years later. An insurance scam goes wrong and leads to the death of the claimant, Harry Sprightly. Horace Claughton, a wealthy financier making preparations for the Jubilee, refuses to pay compensation to Sprightly's mother, so Grandma Sprightly gets her grandson Bill to burgle Claughton's home, and Grandma, Bill, Fox, and their accomplices plot to have their revenge on Claughton. Vi, Grandma's granddaughter, does a striptease as the newscaster Angela Rippon, and Claughton seduces her in her dressing room. He is photographed by newshound Fox but promptly saved by Superintendent Sayers, who, disguised as a woman, inspires Claughton to passion. Claughton is induced to come to Buckingham Palace mews to receive his hoped-for knighthood. He is told to wear a Mother Goose costume and to donate £20,000 to the royal coffers. Vi, disguised as the Queen, collects the £20,000, and when the real Queen appears, Claughton is led off to the Tower. Grandma comes to triumph over Claughton and is shot dead by him. Sayers covers up her murder: 'She tried to take on the upper class | Now the worms are gnawing at her arse.'

Apart from the title, Keeffe's play has little to do with Middleton: true, disguises proliferate, and the rich man is tricked into parting with his money, but Claughton is a one-dimensional capitalist villain, whereas Middleton's Sir Bounteous is a worthy old benefactor. The main interest of Keeffe's play is as a social document: like the contemporary punk-rock band, the Sex Pistols, it offered a fast-moving, outrageously irreverent and bawdy response to the Silver Jubilee.

Magistrate, The

A: Arthur Wing Pinero **Pf:** 1885, London **Pb:** 1892 **G:** Farce in 3 acts **S:** Posket's home, a supper room, and a Magistrate's room, London, 1890s **C:** 13m, 3f

Cis Farringdon is a remarkable 14-year-old: he flirts, drinks, and gambles. In fact, he is 19, but his mother Agatha lied about her age when she married her second husband, the amiable Mr Posket, magistrate of the Mulberry Street Police Court. Encouraged by Cis, Posket and Cis go off on a binge to a smart hotel, unaware that Mrs Posket has also gone there secretly. She is meeting Cis's godfather Captain Lukyn, who has just returned from Bengal, in order to persuade him not to reveal the truth about her age. In a police raid for after hours' drinking, everyone but Cis and Posket are arrested, and the next day the dishevelled Posket finds himself passing sentence on his own wife. His fellow magistrate quashes the sentence, and the penitent Agatha admits her real age. When the coat that Posket left at the hotel is found, he too may have to come before the law. Cis, however, will marry his piano teacher, the lovely Beatie, and, thanks to a large financial bribe from his stepfather, will emigrate to Canada.

With *The Magistrate* Pinero not only had an instant success (it ran for 363 performances), but it also was the first in a line of well-plotted and funny farces, influenced by French models, but set in a convincingly English setting. The main focus and source of fun is the title character Posket, a decent man, who is tempted by a supposed 14-year-old, suffers indignities in escaping from the police, passes a severe sentence on a woman defendant only to find out that she is his wife, and then faces criminal charges himself.

Magnanimous Cuckold, The. See MAGNIFICENT CUCKOLD, THE.

Magnificence

A: Howard Brenton **Pf:** 1973, London **Pb:** 1973 **G:** Pol. drama in 8 scenes **S:** Bare room, street, and living room, London, 1970s; college garden and river, Cambridge, 1970s **C:** 9m, 2f

Three young men, Will, Jed, and Cliff, and two young women, Mary and Veronica, break into an unoccupied building to squat there. While Will suggests using vaguely anarchic slogans like 'Seize the weapons of happiness', the more hard-headed Veronica insists that they must draw attention to the homeless in London. An Old Man suddenly appears from a pile of newspapers in the corner. Slaughter the Bailiff breaks in to evict the squatters. In the ensuing mêlée, Mary, who is pregnant, gets kicked, and she loses her baby. Jed, Mary's husband, is imprisoned and comes out seeking revenge. Babs, an ex-Cabinet minister, visits his former lover, Cambridge don and Conservative politician Alice, and the two men go punting together on the river, where Babs, already terminally ill, dies. Jed is furious with Will's gestural politics and imagines he sees Lenin urging him to anger against capitalism. Jed and

Will acquire some gelignite and decide to blow up Alice. The gelignite fails, and Alice bravely confronts Jed, even inviting him for a drink. Suddenly, the explosive ignites, and over the corpses of Alice and Jed, Cliff comments on the 'waste' of Jed's anger.

Brenton, who famously spoke of tossing 'petrol bombs through the proscenium arch', here reflects the Situationists' angry desire to 'disrupt the spectacle'. At the same time, by generating some sympathy for the elderly Conservative politician Alice and by showing the futility, first of the squatters' protest then of the political assassination, the play challenges the audience to consider more effective means of channelling the justified anger of the young. In an age of suicide-bombers, this drama still seems relevant.

Magnificent Cuckold, The (*Le Cocu magnifique*)

AT: *The Magnanimous Cuckold* A: Fernand Crommelynck Pf: 1920, Paris Pb: 1921 Tr: 1966 G: Farce in 3 acts; French prose S: Belgian village, early 20th c. C: 8m, 4f, extras

The beautiful young Stella is deeply in love with her husband Bruno, the village scribe, despite being importuned by other admirers. Bruno is fiercely jealous and strikes his cousin Pétrus, simply because he detected a glimmer of lust in his eye. Confronting Stella, Bruno is at first reassured and blames his silent secretary for inciting him to jealousy. When Stella weeps, Bruno again fears she must love another. Three months later Bruno is obsessed with Stella's infidelity. He orders his secretary to entrap her and makes Stella wear a black cloak and a hideous paper mask. Becoming sick with worry, he seeks relief in certain knowledge and commands Stella to sleep with Pétrus. To the amusement of the villagers, even Stella's enforced adultery does not satisfy Bruno, because he is convinced that she was trying to trick him. Bruno now invites all the men of the village to have their way with Stella. Even he seduces her in disguise. Realizing too late that he could have had her for himself, he has to abandon Stella to the outraged village women, who carry her off. She is saved by a cowhand. Her love for Bruno has been killed, and she leaves happily with her rescuer. Bruno is convinced that this is another of Stella's tricks.

The Magnificent Cuckold may seem yet another French farce in the tradition of Feydeau and Labiche, and this is how Lugné-Poe directed it at its premiere. However, the overblown language, the absurdly extreme behaviour of Bruno, and the grotesquerie of the action (Stella masked, Bruno dishevelled, the mute secretary, the Breughel-like villagers) all make this a piece which goes decisively beyond realism. Indeed, it became internationally famous through Meyerhold's 1922 modernist production as *The Magnanimous Cuckold*.

Mahabharata, The (*Le Mahabharata*)

A: Jean-Claude Carrière Pf: 1985, Avignon Pb: 1985 Tr: 1987 G: Drama in 3 parts; French prose S: India, in the mythic past C: 30 performers playing 16 main characters (13m, 3f) and many minor characters

(1) *The Game of Dice*. Vyasa dictates to a Boy 'the poetical history of mankind'. Because the king's son Bhishma takes a vow of chastity, the succession passes through the king's stepson Vyasa, father of Dhritarashtra the Blind and of Pandu the Pale. Gandhari, King Dhritarashtra's wife, bears him 100 sons, the Kauravas. Pandu's wife Kunti gives birth to the five Pandavas, and much of the story turns on the enmity between these two families. Because Kunti orders that the Pandava brothers must share everything, they all marry the beautiful Draupadi. The Kauravas are envious of the success and happiness of the Pandavas and challenge the oldest brother Yudhishthira to a game of dice. He loses everything, Draupadi is humiliated, and the Pandavas, vowing revenge, are forced into exile in the forest for 12 years. (2) *Exile in the Forest*. Not content with imposing exile on their cousins, the Kauravas hunt for the Pandavas in the forest. In the 13th year the Pandavas hide at the court of King Vitara, but Arjuna, son of Kunti and Indra king of gods, is recognized on a cattle raid. Both sides prepare for war, and the god Krishna offers to drive Arjuna's chariot. (3) *The War*.

A devastating war takes place, many of the heroes are killed, their children are all murdered, millions are slain, even Krishna dies. The Pandavas' victory costs far too dear, and all but Yudhishthira subsequently perish in the mountains. In 'the last illusion' he mounts to heaven to find the Kauravas in bliss and the Pandavas suffering in torment.

The world's greatest epic poem (15 times the length of the Bible) was adapted for a nine-hour performance under the imaginative direction of Peter Brook and was toured widely and made into a film. While Brook has been criticized for 'cultural piracy' of a religious text, others have welcomed the access it offers to the richness of Indian legend.

Maids, The (*Les Bonnes*)

A: Jean Genet **Pf:** 1947, Paris **Pb:** 1948; rev. 1954, 1958 **Tr:** 1954 **G:** Drama in 1 act; French prose **S:** Bedroom in a Paris apartment, *c.*1947 **C:** 3f

A lady gives orders to her servant Claire to prepare her clothes. The servant is by turns obsequious and dominating, while the lady sneers cruelly at Claire's ugliness and at her infatuation for the milkman. The lady says that she has denounced her lover, a criminal, to the police. Suddenly an alarm clock goes off, and the two women huddle together fearfully. The servant is in fact Solange, and the 'Madame' turns out to be her younger sister Claire. They are the two maids of Madame, a young high-class kept woman. These two ugly, shabby spinsters console themselves by playing the role of mistress and servant when Madame is away. But now they have to tidy things up quickly before Madame's return. As they are doing so, Monsieur, Madame's lover, phones to say that he has been released from custody. Unwilling to continue in their miserable servitude and afraid that Claire will be identified as the person informing on Monsieur, they plan to poison Madame. Madame returns, kind to her servants, but self-dramatizing and thoughtless. On learning that Monsieur is free, she sends Solange for a taxi. Claire unsuccessfully tries to get Madame to drink the poisoned tea, and Madame rushes off to meet her lover. Their plan failed, with seemingly no escape from their miserable existence, Claire once more assumes the role of mistress and abuses the cringing Solange. When Claire feels ill, Solange takes her to the kitchen, then returns, declaring that she has strangled Madame and fantasizes about her spectacular forthcoming public execution. Claire silently returns and, in the role of mistress, orders Solange to pour her some poisoned tea. As Claire dies on Madame's bed, Solange ecstatically cries that they are now 'beautiful, joyous, drunk, and free!'

Based on an actual murder case, Genet created possibly the most shocking exploration on stage of perverse sexuality up to the mid-20th century (only Wedekind's **Lulu Plays* come close). The sadomasochistic homoerotic relationship between the two downtrodden maids (in French having the ironically ambiguous designation of *les bonnes*, 'the good women') is intensified if Genet's recommendation is followed that they should be played by men. Genet, himself abandoned by his parents and living a criminal existence until sentenced to life imprisonment for recurrent theft in 1948, here pleads that attention be paid to 'the ranks of the despised'.

Maid's Tragedy, The

A: Francis Beaumont and John Fletcher **Pf:** *c.*1608–11, London **Pb:** 1619 **G:** Trag. in 5 acts; blank verse **S:** Rhodes, in the ancient world **C:** 15m, 7f, extras

Under orders from the King of Rhodes, Amintor rejects his promised bride Aspatia in order to wed Evadne, the sister of his best friend Melantius. After the wedding and a court masque, Evadne confesses that she and the King are lovers, and that the marriage to Amintor is merely a device to conceal their liaison. Amintor reports this to Melantius, who vows revenge on the King for dishonouring his sister. Confronting Evadne, Melantius extracts from her both a confession of guilt and a promise to kill the King. Melantius and his followers seize the fort, while Evadne stabs the King in his lustful bed. Aspatia disguises herself as her brother returned from the wars, and challenges Amintor to a duel, in which she is mortally wounded. Evadne, rejected by Amintor and recognizing the horror of her deed, stabs herself. Aspatia, revealing her identity, dies in Aminor's arms. In despair Amintor stabs himself.

It is now hard to imagine that for over a century plays by Beaumont and Fletcher were far more frequently performed than those of Shakespeare. But it is undoubtedly true that, while they do not in fact offer any deep tragic insight, the vigorous scenes of confrontation and the sudden reversals of the action play well in the theatre. What is less easy to accept is the series of suicides and deaths at the end of the action. Pieces like this, which essentially offer entertainment rather than enlightenment, work better, as in **Philaster*, with a happy ending.

Mains sales, Les. See DIRTY HANDS.

Major Barbara

A: George Bernard Shaw Pf: 1905, London Pb: 1907; rev. 1930 G: Drama in 3 acts S: Lady Britomart's home and a Salvation Army shelter, London, and a munitions factory, Middlesex, 1906 C: 10m, 6f

Lady Britomart has been separated for 20 years from her husband, the wealthy munitions manufacturer Andrew Undershaft. She invites him to her house, because she needs money to support her son Stephen and her two daughters Barbara and Sarah. Sarah is marrying a fool, who will inherit money only later. Undershaft arrives, and to the annoyance of Lady Britomart and her son, charms everyone. He takes a particular liking to Barbara, who has joined the Salvation Army and is engaged to a Professor of Greek Adolphus Cusins. Undershaft agrees to visit Major Barbara's Salvation Army shelter if she will come to his munitions factory. At the shelter Undershaft and Cusins, who has become a Salvationist to be near Barbara, get on well together. When a whisky distiller makes a generous donation and Undershaft agrees to match it, Barbara is horrified that the Army takes money earned from 'drunkenness and murder' and resigns on the spot. Undershaft and Cusins go off to a thanksgiving meeting, which produces several conversions. Barbara now visits the 'factory of death' and is amazed at the way in which it provides for its workers. It preserves them from the 'worst of crimes', poverty, and allows them to live happy and prosperous lives in a way that the Salvation Army can only dream of with its ineffectual charity. When it becomes clear that Cusins qualifies as a foundling who alone may, according to a curious tradition, inherit the Undershaft empire, he decides to commit himself to working in the factory. While her brother Stephen, who 'knows nothing and thinks he knows everything', is eminently suited to a career in politics, Barbara will now preach to the well-fed workers, agrees to marry Cusins, and intends to live in Undershaft's model town.

This is both one of the most popular and one of the subtlest of Shaw's plays. There is no socialist didacticism here: on the contrary, Shaw confronts his audience with the dilemma that well-intentioned charitable work achieves little, while money that is dependent on the arms trade creates a virtual social paradise on earth. The real army proves a greater benefactor than the Salvation Army. It is the same dilemma posed by Brecht in *The *Good Person of Setzuan*. Neither writer, clearly, wished to champion exploitative capitalism over social conscience, but both make it clear that charitable works are not enough, indeed that they may simply make poverty endurable. In this sense *Major Barbara*, which could be read as an affirmation of a right-wing viewpoint, is a profoundly revolutionary play, implying that only a radical restructuring of society will yield a permanent amelioration of working conditions. Whether this restructuring can be left to a 'superman' figure like Undershaft or should come from a collective response to injustice, Shaw declines to discuss.

Malade imaginaire, Le. See HYPOCHONDRIAC, THE.

Malcontent, The. See BAD-TEMPERED MAN, THE.

Malcontent, The

A: John Marston (with John Webster) Pf: 1604, London Pb: 1604 G: Tragicom. in 5 acts with an induction; prose and blank verse **S:** The court of Genoa, Italy, late 16th c. **C:** 19m, 5f, extras

In the Induction, two spectators, who are eventually escorted off the stage, engage in banter with the actors and are warned not to read too much into the story about to be performed. The rightful Duke of Genoa, Altofronto, has been deposed by his brother Pietro. Altofronto returns to court disguised as a 'malcontent', a sarcastic jester named Malevole. The cunning courtier Mendoza, the power behind the throne, commits adultery with Pietro's wife Aurelia, daughter of the Duke of Florence, but manages to shift the blame on to a rival, who is exposed. Pietro is so grateful that he names Mendoza his heir. Mendoza then plots to take Pietro's life, but Malevole reveals his treachery. Malevole then reports that Pietro has committed suicide over his wife's infidelity, and Mendoza declares himself duke. Aurelia is so overcome with remorse that she withdraws from the court, and Pietro, moved by his wife's repentance, pledges to strive to return the throne to his brother. Mendoza orders a masque, at which the brothers, disguised as masquers, are reconciled with their wives and Mendoza is forced to beg for his life, a request scornfully granted by Altofronto.

With echoes of **Hamlet* (the malcontent at a corrupt court), **Measure for Measure* (a duke returned to court in disguise) and pre-dating *The *Tempest* (an Italian duke deposed by treachery), the complex plot of *The Malcontent* offers much that is original and theatrically effective. There is good satirical comedy, especially in Malevole's caustic commentary on court life, and surprising twists in the plot, many of which contain the potential for a typically Jacobean onstage bloodbath, but which do not yield a single death.

Malentendu, Le. See CROSS PURPOSE.

Mamelles de Tirésias, Les. See BREASTS OF TIRESIAS, THE.

Man and Superman

A: George Bernard Shaw **Pf:** 1905, London; complete text 1915, Edinburgh **Pb:** 1903 **G:** Com. in 4 acts **S:** England and Spain, 1900s, and hell **C:** 18m, 7f

On the death of her father, Ann Whitefield is given as guardian two very different men: Roebuck Ramsden, a respectable man of about 60, and Jack Tanner, a rich radical in his thirties, whom Ramsden considers an anarchist. Although wooed by Octavius (Tavy) Robinson, a sensitive poet, Ann has fallen for Tanner. In order to escape Ann's designs on him, Tanner flees to Spain with his chauffeur Straker. Captured by brigands, Tanner has a dream, 'Don Juan in Hell': Don Juan (Tanner) greets Doña Ana (Ann), indignant that she is in hell, and Ana's father the Statue (Ramsden). There follow lengthy debates, mainly between Don Juan and the Devil, about the 'Life Force'. Bored with hell, Don Juan decides to pursue the Life Force in heaven and is followed there by Ana. They awake to find that Ann has followed Tanner to Spain. Rejecting Octavius, she insists that she will win Tanner for herself. At first Tanner stubbornly resists but eventually succumbs to the inevitable Life Force, surrendering his freedom for a life of domesticity.

Described by Shaw as 'a comedy and a philosophy', *Man and Superman* can be enjoyed as a comedy in which the girl gets her man, or, especially through the 'Don Juan in Hell' scenes (which, as at the London premiere, are often omitted in performance), as a philosophical debate which informs the comic outcome. The comedy sparkles with wit and presents well-drawn characters, even in the sub-plot involving Ann's sister. The philosophical debates, though protracted for modern theatrical taste, are lively and thought-provoking in their discussion of the Life Force, derived from the thinking of Nietzsche and Bergson.

Man and the Masses. See MASSES AND MEN.

Mandragola, La. See MANDRAKE, THE.

Mandrake, The (*La Mandragola*)

A: Niccolò Machiavelli **Pb:** *c.*1518–24 **Pf:** *c.* 1520, Florence **Tr:** 1927 **G:** *Commedia*

erudita in 5 acts; Italian (Tuscan) prose S: A square in Florence, early 16th c. C: 5m, 2f

The young and handsome Callimaco has fallen in love with Lucrezia, the virtuous and beautiful wife of the elderly lawyer Nicia. Since the marriage has failed to produce any children, Nicia arrogantly believes Lucrezia to be sterile and so welcomes to his house Callimaco disguised as a doctor. Callimaco proposes as a cure to administer a mandrake potion, which will however have the unfortunate effect of causing the death of the first man to have sex with Lucrezia. To avoid this fate, Nicia agrees to seize a passer-by and shut him up in the room with Lucrezia overnight. Lucrezia is persuaded by her mother and her priest to agree to the plan, and Callimaco, in another disguise, arranges to be the kidnapped passer-by. After a night of passion with this young lover, Nicia can now look forward to an heir, and Lucrezia happily sets her scruples aside and agrees to continue the affair.

Best known for *The Prince*, Machiavelli was also the author of three comedies, which reflect the same cynical pragmatism as his political writing. *The Mandrake* is generally accounted the finest comedy of the Italian Renaissance. It is more tightly plotted than many contemporary comedies, and its depiction of character is outstanding, not only in the major characters but also in the satirical portrayal of figures like the disreputable priest Fra Timoteo and the devious parasite Ligurio. It is also extraordinary in that Lucrezia is as much a victim of the plot as Nicia, which may yield an ambiguous response to the comic situation. It was successfully revived at the National Theatre, London, in 1984.

Man Equals Man. See MAN'S A MAN, A.

Man for All Seasons, A

A: Robert Bolt Pf: 1960, London Pb: 1960 G: Hist. drama in 2 acts S: Various locations in London and environs, 1526–35 C: 11m, 3f

The Common Man as narrator introduces the play and comments throughout. Sir Thomas More is an incorruptible and generous Privy Councillor with a wife Alice and a daughter Margaret. Cardinal Wolsey tries to persuade More that the young King Henry VIII, still in his thirties, should reject his present wife Catherine of Aragon, who is as 'barren as brick', so that he can remarry and have a male heir. When Wolsey dies in disgrace in 1530, More is appointed Lord Chancellor. Wolsey's former secretary, the devious Thomas Cromwell, urges More to support the King's application for an annulment, and the Spanish ambassador calls on him to resist it. More is finally visited by Henry himself, who, failing to win More's support, resigns himself to ordering More to remain silent on the matter. However, when Henry, unable to persuade the Pope to annul his marriage to Catherine, severs the connection with Rome and declares himself head of the Church, More resigns, but is careful not to denounce Henry's actions. This is not enough for Henry, who seeks More's declared approval of his marriage to Anne Boleyn and acknowledgement that her children are legitimate heirs to the throne. Cromwell and Cranmer help to devise trumped-up charges against More, who is condemned to death. He bids farewell to his family and is beheaded.

The title is curious, for More distinguishes himself by his unchanging faith and integrity, refusing to alter with the prevailing political 'season'. Although Bolt referred to Brecht and states that this, like all centuries, is 'the Century of the Common Man', the play focuses on dramaturgically conventional machinations of those in power. At this level, Bolt has written a well-researched and compelling piece of theatre.

Man from Mukinupin, The

A: Dorothy Hewett Pf: 1979, Perth, Australia Pb: 1980 G: Musical drama in 2 acts S: Mukinupin, Western Australia, 1912–20 C: 7m, 7f (includes doubling)

In the town of Mukinupin, members of the community have *Doppelgänger* (performed by the same actors), who emerge at night as dangerous and evil counterparts to the seemingly respectable citizens. It is at night that the god-fearing lay preacher Eek Perkins, urged on by the Mukinupin wives, leads the massacre of a tribe of Aborigines in the creek-bed. The young Jack Tuesday leaves with his brother Harry to fight in the Great War, imagining that Polly Perkins, the storekeeper's daughter, has refused to marry him. When he returns from the war older and wiser, he successfully woos her, saving her from marriage to an elderly travelling salesman Cecil Brunner. When Jack marries Polly, their wedding is paralleled by a pagan marriage between Harry, now an alcoholic, and Polly's half-sister, an aboriginal girl called Touch of the Tar. The manager of a visiting theatre company performing a dreadful production of **Othello* is impressed with Jack's theatrical talent, and he and Polly leave to join a musical comedy troupe.

This is one of the most performed Australian plays, offering a rich theatrical experience with song, dance, humour, and powerful incident. Hewett's concerns with the environment and with the substratum of Australian society with its history of violent suppression of the native culture of the Aborigines, have clearly found resonance with contemporary Australian audiences.

Man-Hater, The. See MISANTHROPE, THE.

Man Is Man. See MAN'S A MAN, A.

Mankind

A: Anon. Pf: *c.*1465–70, East Anglia Pb: 1897 G: Morality play in verse S: A plot of ground, medieval period C: 7 (m and f)

While Mercy preaches the way of salvation, Mischief, eventually joined by three other vices New Guise, Nowadays, and Nought, interrupts and makes fun of her homily. Mankind appears. He is an agricultural labourer, who is admonished by Mercy to be productive, but he is distracted from his work by the vices, who try to persuade him to be lazy and self-indulgent. He beats them off with his spade. Mischief heals their wounds, and they all conspire to invoke the devil Titivillus, who puts a stop to Mankind's labours by sliding a board under the soil to prevent him digging. When Mankind then kneels to pray, Titivillus arranges for him to have to relieve himself and so abandon his prayers. Disheartened, he falls asleep and is then easily led astray by the vices. Guilty and desperate, he is about to commit suicide, when Mercy appears and rescues him from sin.

Although containing much the same moral lesson as **Everyman*, *Mankind* offers a much more robust and lively theatrical experience. It contains broad humour, music, dance, a lewd song, and audience participation, not only in the singing of the song but also in collecting money to bribe the devil to appear. It was probably performed in Lent, since it preaches abstinence and industry (it is notable that the vices, apart from Mischief, are not so much wicked as fashionable wastrels). Given its simple staging requirements and small cast, *Mankind* may have been toured by professionals to inn-yards and big houses.

Mann ist Mann. See MAN'S A MAN, A.

Man of Mode, The

AT: *Sir Fopling Flutter* A: George Etherege Pf: 1676, London Pb: 1676 G: Com. in 5 acts; prose S: Various locations in London, Restoration period C: 13m, 9f, extras

Dorimant is attracted to a beautiful young heiress, Harriet. Old Bellair intends his son to marry Harriet, but Young Bellair is in love with Emilia. Dorimant plans to rid himself of his mistress Loveit and uses Belinda's devotion to him to attempt to break with her. Dorimant disguises himself to gain access to Harriet, but he still remains sexually entangled with both Loveit and Belinda. Young Bellair secretly weds Emilia, and, since Harriet is now freed from the marriage plans of Old Bellair and her mother, Dorimant is given leave to pay court to Harriet. Throughout, the foppish Sir Fopling Flutter is used to provoke spurious jealousy or act as the butt of jokes.

Dorimant, the 'man of mode', is a typically amoral Restoration figure, who succeeds through his wit and charm. Unlike Wycherley, whose observations on contemporary society were bitterly sarcastic, Etherege allows us to enjoy the success of this sexy rogue, especially when the game of wooing Harriet becomes serious, 'a settled ague' in place of his 'irregular fits' of philandering. Significantly, Etherege does not reward him with the conventional comedic outcome of marriage, for he must yet prove himself worthy of Harriet.

Man's a Man, A (*Mann ist Mann*)

AT: *Man Is Man; Man Equals Man* A: Bertolt Brecht Pf: 1926, Darmstadt Pb: 1927; rev. 1957 Tr: 1961 G: Com. in 11 scenes; German prose with songs S: India, 1925 C: 8m, 2f, extras

Galy Gay is a simple Irish porter, who goes out one day to buy a fish. A British machine-gun squad mounting a raid on a pagoda loses one of its men, Jeraiah Jip, and the soldiers, terrified of the anger of their sergeant Charles Fairchild ('Bloody Five'), persuade Galy Gay to take Jip's place at roll-call. When the wily priest of the pagoda refuses to release the captured soldier, the men have to transform the mild Galy Gay into a brutal killer. He is persuaded to pretend not to know his wife when she comes looking for him, and he helps to prepare for departure by dismantling Widow Begbick's mobile canteen, while she sings that although 'a man's a man', one can dismantle him and reassemble him like a car. In order to fully ensnare Galy Gay, the soldiers induce him to auction a mock elephant, then charge him with illegally disposing of government property. He is subjected to a mock court martial and a mock execution and is even obliged to deliver the funeral oration over his coffin. Now Galy Gay is 'dead', his transformation into a fighting machine is complete. Meanwhile, made randy by the rain, Bloody Five, ridiculously attired, arrives to sleep with Begbick's three daughters, but is so ashamed the next day that he shoots off his genitals. Galy Gay single-handedly destroys a Tibetan fortress and prepares for further vicious conflict.

Planned as early as 1918, *Man Equals Man* represents a turning point in Brecht's career. Here for the first time, the impulses towards his *Verfremdungseffekt* ('distanciation'), seen at the end of **Drums in the Night*, become integrated into the action: direct address to the audience, songs 'separated from the rest', simple white lighting, half-curtain, etc. Brecht's political ideology is still ambivalent: Galy Gay's misfortune is to lose his identity and become a brutal tool of imperialism, but his only alternative is to hold on to his individualism, which, for the Marxist, is bourgeois and reactionary.

Man Who Didn't Like People, The. See BAD-TEMPERED MAN, THE.

Marat/Sade (*Die Verfolgung und Ermordung Jean-Paul Marats, dargestellt durch die Schauspielgruppe des Hospizes zu Charenton unter Anleitung des Herrn de Sade*)

AT: *The Persecution and Assassination of Jean-Paul Marat as Performed by the Inmates of the Asylum of Charenton under the Direction of the Marquis de Sade* A: Peter Weiss Pf: 1964, Berlin Pb: 1964 Tr: 1965 G: Hist. drama in 2 acts; German verse and songs S: Bathhouse of the Charenton Asylum, France, 1808 C: 15m, 7f, extras

The Director of the Charenton Asylum welcomes his audience of Parisian bourgeoisie to the play being presented by one of the inmates, the Marquis de Sade. The Herald introduces the main characters: Jean-Paul Marat, leader of the French Revolution, whose skin condition forces him to spend much of his life in the bath, played by a paranoiac; the idealistic Charlotte Corday, played by a narcoleptic; and her lover Duperret, played by an erotomaniac. It is 1793, and the Revolution has still not brought the promised prosperity to the poor. A rebellious priest, Jacques Roux, incites the patients to revolt and has to be violently suppressed. Corday, persuaded that Marat must be killed to end the bloodbath of the Terror, comes to his door but is reminded by Sade that she has to come three times before gaining admittance. After a re-enactment of guillotinings, Sade and Marat conduct a debate, Marat still believing that change can be achieved only through political revolution, Sade insisting that meaning can only be found within the individual. He emphasizes this by getting Corday to whip him, while he talks about the Revolution, which has led only to a dull uniformity. Despite Duperret's efforts to detain her, Corday goes to Marat a second time, again being turned away. Marat in a delirium sees his parents, schoolmaster, Voltaire, and Lavoisier, all of whom cruelly denounce him. After the interval, Marat addresses the National Assembly, and the Director protests at Marat's attacks on authority. Corday visits Marat a third time, and just as she is poised to stab him, the Herald interrupts to recount the course of the Revolution: how Napoleon has come to power and led the French into one war after another. Corday delivers her final blow, and the patients continue to chant and march on, while Roux tries to stop them. The patients lose all control, while Sade laughs triumphantly, and they have to be suppressed violently.

This stunningly theatrical and complex play is arguably the best play in German since Brecht. On one level it deals with historical fact: Marat's death in the bath, immortalized in David's picture, and Sade's theatricals at Charenton. On another, it opposes the revolutionary ideals of Marat to the cynical individualism of Sade. On yet another, it confronts a contemporary audience with their own complacency about supposed progress. In terms of presentation, it contains many of the elements of Brecht's epic theatre (episodic scenes, awareness that we are watching a play) with Artaudian 'theatre of cruelty' (scenes of violence, deafening music, anarchy that threatens to spill out into the audience). While the Berlin premiere was quite Brechtian, focusing on the philosophical debate, Peter Brook's spectacular 1964 production placed the emphasis on the mental asylum setting.

Marescalco, Il. See STABLEMASTER, THE.

Margaret Fleming

A: James A. Herne **Pf**: 1890, Lynn, Massachusetts; rev. version 1891, Boston **Pb**: 1890 **G**: Melodrama in 4 acts **S**: Canton, Massachusetts, 1890 **C**: 1m, 3f, extras

Philip Fleming is ostensibly a good husband to his wife Margaret and a good father to their 1-year-old daughter. However, one of his adulterous affairs comes to haunt him. He has fathered the child of his nursemaid's sister, who, when she learns that she is dying, asks to see Margaret. Margaret arrives at the poor woman's cottage to find her already dead, and her angry sister Maria reveals the secret of Philip's adultery. Despite her own distress, Margaret cannot bring herself to abandon the crying baby, and begins to nurse it. Fleming enters on this scene, and, overcome with guilt, flees. Margaret begins to lose her sight as a result of glaucoma, intensified by her mental suffering. She adopts the baby. Fleming comes back to her, and begs for forgiveness.

Despite its melodramatic plot (the revised version is given here) and its moralistic theme, Herne's play represented a significant development in American realist theatre, which he championed in his 1897 essay 'Art for Truth's Sake in the Drama'. The play's willingness to address a social problem of marital infidelity by husbands, to which normally a blind eye was turned, led to its being rejected by mainstream theatres. However, William Dean Howells, who hailed Herne as the greatest living American dramatist, helped it to success, with Herne's wife Katharine Corcoran playing the title role.

Mariage de Figaro, Le. See MARRIAGE OF FIGARO, THE.

Maria Magdalene. See MARY MAGDALENE.

Maria Marten

AT: *Murder in the Red Barn; The Murder of Maria Marten* A: Anon. **Pf**: 1828, Mile End?; earliest recorded production 1840, London **Pb**: 1928 **G**: Melodrama in 2 acts; prose **S**: Polstead, Suffolk, and environs, Corder's London home, and a condemned cell, 1827–8 **C**: 5m, 9f, extras

Maria Marten is a poor but pretty country girl in Suffolk. Since she dreams of a better life than drudgery on the farm, she is delighted when the gypsy Crazy Nell foretells that she will be wooed by a rich gentleman. In fact, Nell is plotting revenge on the local squire's son William Corder, who had seduced and then abandoned Nell's sister. When Nell tells Corder that Maria is in love with him, her plan is complete. Corder meets Maria on her way to the country fair, seduces her, and, when she becomes pregnant, abandons her. Afraid that his father may learn the truth, Corder poisons the baby and murders both Maria and Nell. Before she dies, however, Nell is able to name Corder as her killer. The crime might still have remained undiscovered, but Maria's mother's dreams prompt Maria's father to search in the Corders' Red Barn. When Maria's body is discovered, the police are called. The police officer, who is Nell's brother, arrests Corder, who is eventually hanged for his triple murder.

Maria Marten was perhaps the most sensational, and therefore one of the most popular, 19th-century melodramas. Based on a true story (although heavily distorted), it was adapted many times for the stage. Now hard to take seriously with its stereotypical characterization and extraordinary coincidences, it continued the domestic murder tradition of **Arden of Faversham* and *A *Yorkshire Tragedy*, and elements of the story re-emerge in the sophisticated narrative of Thomas Hardy's novel *Tess of the D'Urbervilles* (1891).

Maria Stuart. See MARY STUART.

Mariya. See MARYA.

Marriage, The. See WEDDING, THE (Gombrowicz).

Marriage à-la-Mode

A: John Dryden **Pf**: 1672, London **Pb**: 1673
G: Com. in 5 acts; verse and prose **S**: Sicily, indeterminate period **C**: 7m, 7f

Polydamas has seized the throne of Sicily in a successful revolt, and is now intent on finding the whereabouts of his long-lost only child. He commands a young fisherman Leonidas to marry the beautiful and virtuous Amalthea, the daughter of the man who helped him to power, but Leonidas refuses, wishing to remain faithful to his peasant sweetheart Palmyra. Furious at Leonidas' refusal, Polydamas orders the execution of Palmyra, only to discover that she is his missing child. Polydamas now requires Palmyra to marry Argaleon, Amalthea's wicked brother. When it is discovered that Leonidas is the son of the deposed king, Palmyra orders his execution. As he is led to his death, the desperate Palmyra, torn between her love for him and for her father, faints away. However, Amalthea comes to the rescue, leading a successful popular revolt, which overthrows Polydamas in favour of the rightful heir. The new King Leonidas marries Palmyra and pardons her father. In a comic sub-plot, Rhodophil and Doralice, bored by their marriage, attempt to seduce the engaged couple Melantha and Palamede, but, their plans constantly thwarted, both men agree 'not to invade each other's property' and are instrumental in restoring Leonidas to the throne.

Together with his delightful reworking of **Amphitryon* in 1690, this is Dryden's most successful comedy, based on a story by Madeleine de Scudéry. The conventional heroic plot is balanced by the Restoration comedy of manners of the sub-plot, which not so much undercuts the main action as reinforces it, for in both, fidelity and virtue eventually triumph, even if the most honourable character, Amalthea, remains unrewarded.

Marriage Bells, The. See EAST LYNNE.

Marriage of Anansewa, The

A: Efua T. Sutherland **Pf**: 1980, Ghana **Pb**: 1975
G: Romantic com. in 4 acts **S**: Ghana, mid-20th c. **C**: 6m, 7f, extras

Ananse is an old rogue who wants to make as much money as possible by marrying off his daughter Anansewa. He promises her to four chiefs at the same time: the Chief of the Mines, Togbe Klu IV, the Chief of Sapa, and Chief-Who-Is-Chief. Anansewa receives gifts from all four chiefs, who are unaware of their rivals. Ananse suddenly finds himself facing a catastrophe when the chiefs all decide to come and offer the 'head-drink' which will place the seal on their marriage. To get out of his difficulties, Ananse persuades Anansewa to pretend to die, and announces her sad death to the chiefs. They respond by sending messengers who tell how the chiefs would have cared for Anansewa. The Chief of the Mines declares that she could have brought up his children; the Chief of Sapa had hoped that she would replace his 'bitchy, ugly' wife; Togbe Klu's messengers announce that their Chief would have been happy to exploit Anansewa's secretarial skills in his business, and having recently been converted to Christianity will not follow the old custom of sending a funeral gift. Finally, the Chief-Who-Is-Chief lets it be known that he is devastated since he regarded himself as already married to Anansewa and that he will therefore bear the whole cost of the funeral. Touched by his kindness and generosity, Ananse 'miraculously' brings his daughter back to life, and she prepares to marry her one honourable suitor.

With obvious similarities with the casket scene in *The *Merchant of Venice*, and drawing on the traditional lovable rogue in the character of Ananse, Ghana's leading playwright has here created a delightful romantic comedy of considerable wit and charm, using the Property Man as a kind of Brechtian chorus.

Marriage of Figaro, The (*La Folle Journée, ou, Le Mariage de Figaro*)

AT: *Figaro's Marriage; The Follies of a Day; A Mad Day's Work* **A:** Pierre-Augustin Caron de Beaumarchais **W:** 1778 **Pf:** 1783, Gennevilliers (private perf.); 1784, Paris (public perf.) **Pb:** 1785 **Tr:** 1785 **G:** Com. in 5 acts; French prose **S:** The Castle of Aguas-Frescas, near Seville, Spain, mid-18th c. **C:** 13m, 5f, extras

Count Almaviva, now Governor of Andalucia, wishes to invoke his feudal right to sleep with Suzanne, the bride of his servant Figaro. Figaro is trying to extricate himself from a long-standing promise to wed the Count's housekeeper, Marceline. Invoking the help of the Countess, who is angry at her husband's philandering, Figaro plans to outwit both his master and Marceline. Almaviva is consumed with jealousy over his wife's supposed love of Chérubin, and sends the young page to join the army. However, Almaviva is outwitted in his plan to seduce Suzanne: she changes clothes with her mistress, and Almaviva finds that his night-time wooing is directed at his wife. Shamed into marital fidelity, Almaviva withdraws from his pursuit of Suzanne, and Figaro, having discovered that he is Marceline's long-lost son, is free to marry his beloved.

Now best known in its operatic version by Mozart (1786), this sequel to *The *Barber of Seville* remains one of the best comedies of the 18th century. Apart from the hilarious intrigues, disguises, and the way in which characters are hidden and revealed with the dexterity of one shuffling a pack of cards, the play contained revolutionary dynamite. 'For this play not to be a danger, the Bastille would have to be torn down first,' declared Louis XVI with prophetic insight. Figaro's famous monologue, in which he points out that those in power 'took the trouble of being born and nothing more', was greeted with thunderous applause by the Parisian audiences, giving rise to Napoleon's description of the piece as 'the Revolution in action'.

Marya

AT: *Mariya* **A:** Isaak Babel **Pf:** 1964, Italy **Pb:** 1935 **Tr:** 1966 **G:** Drama in 8 scenes; Russian prose **S:** Petrograd (Leningrad), 1920 **C:** 17m, 8f

The action focuses on two households, that of a Jewish speculator Isaak Markovich Dymshits, and that of a former Tsarist army officer General Mukovnin. Dymshits's business is suffering, because the crippled soldiers he employs to smuggle in his black market goods are having difficulty entering the besieged city during the civil war. He is also frustrated, because the General's flirtatious daughter Lyudmilla seems to welcome his advances but will not give herself to him. When a former lover of Lyudmilla is shot in a fight, she is accused of the crime. At the same time the General receives a letter from his older daughter Marya, who writes of the progress of the Revolution and says that she will not be coming home. This double blow affects the old man so deeply that he has a heart attack and dies. The Mukovnin apartment is taken over by a working-class couple, and everyone now looks forward to a better future.

Based on his own experiences during the civil war, *Marya* was published but never performed during Babel's lifetime, probably because of his sympathetic portrayal of 'negative' and 'reactionary' characters.

Intended as the first part of a trilogy, the play reflects the difficulties the older generation experience in adapting to the new Bolshevik order.

Mary and the Monster. See BLOOD AND ICE.

Mary Barnes

A: David Edgar Pf: 1978, Birmingham Pb: 1979 G: Drama in 3 acts S: Living room and bedroom of large old house, east London, 1965–*c.*1972 C: 8m, 5f

Dr Douglas Walker (30) has, together with fellow psychiatrists Brenda (33), Hugo (in his late thirties), and Zimmerman (in his twenties), set up a commune, to which they will invite mental patients for humane and gentle therapy. The first is Mary Barnes (42), who has a history of mental illness and imagines that she is a nurse. They are joined by American psychiatrist Eddie (25) with his new girlfriend Beth. When Mary refuses to eat, Eddie, fearing that she may have to be returned to hospital, wins her over with games. Beth is jealous of the attention he pays to her. Locals smash windows in the house, protesting about having 'nutters' in the area. Zimmerman leaves, a new patient Laurence joins the group, and tensions become apparent within the 'Community'. Mary appears naked, covered in her own faeces, and Eddie cleans her. When Eddie has to go away for three weeks, Mary pines for him and refuses to eat again. Three years later, Angie, a disturbed rich girl of 20, comes to the house, where Mary is now well enough to help her. Some time later, Angie is restored to health, but slips back into madness when her mother comes to take her away. Mary has an exhibition of paintings, which proves a great success. Mary's brother, whose drugs for mental illness make him 'like wax, a robot', comes to stay, leaves, but returns. Some years later, everyone has had to leave, because the lease ran out; Angie returns but, having endured conventional treatment, can now remember nothing about her stay.

In the wake of R. D. Laing's theories, several plays and films appeared extolling the virtue of living through madness rather than 'curing' it with drugs, shock therapy, and surgery. Edgar wrote this episodic adaptation of a true story, based on the book *Mary Barnes* by Mary Barnes and Joseph Berke.

Mary Magdalene (*Maria Magdalene*)

A: Friedrich Hebbel Pf: 1846, Leipzig Pb: 1844 Tr: 1914 G: Trag. in 3 acts; German prose S: Medium-sized German town, 1830s C: 7m, 2f, 2 children (1m, 1f)

The master-carpenter Anton has two children, Klara and Karl. Klara has lost her virginity to an unscrupulous young man, Leonhard, and the two find themselves facing marriage without any love between them. Karl is arrested on suspicion of stealing jewellery, and the shock kills his mother. Leonhard uses this shameful development as an excuse to break off his engagement to Klara. Anton makes his daughter swear that she will never bring shame on the house, and says that he will cut his throat if she 'loses her honour'. The Secretary, a former beloved of Klara, offers her his hand in marriage, but leaves when she tells him that she is no longer a virgin. In desperation she begs Leonhard to marry her, but he is furthering his ambition by wooing the mayor's hunchbacked niece. Karl is acquitted of his alleged crime, and the Secretary kills Leonhard in a duel but is himself mortally wounded. Klara commits suicide by throwing herself into a well, and it is left to the dying Secretary to point out that all their troubles stemmed from the unyielding attitude of Anton.

Although most of his plays are historical tragedies, Hebbel here takes up the tradition of the bourgeois tragedy in order to show that 'in the most limited circles a devastating tragedy is possible'. Ibsen was surprised at his success in Germany, when they had 'their own Hebbel', and clearly he was influenced by the realism of this tragedy. In the 20th century *Mary Magdalene* (the title presumably a reminder that Christ forgave penitent sinners) was Hebbel's most frequently performed play.

Mary Stuart (*Maria Stuart*)

A: Friedrich Schiller Pf: 1800, Weimar Pb: 1801 Tr: 1801 G: Trag. in 5 acts; German blank verse S: The Castle of Fotheringhay and the Palace of Westminster, 1587 C: 15m, 4f, extras

Mary Stuart, the deposed Queen of Scotland, who came to England to seek the help of her cousin Queen Elizabeth of England, has been imprisoned for several years in the castle at Fotheringhay. Here she remains a dangerous inspiration to a number of disaffected Catholic noblemen, who conspire against the Protestant Elizabeth. One such is the young Mortimer, who, dazzled by Mary's beauty, plans to free her from her prison. He seeks the help of the Earl of Leicester, confidant of Elizabeth, but also former suitor of Mary. Urged by her cynical adviser Lord Burleigh to execute Mary, Elizabeth seeks instead to involve Mortimer in a secret plot to murder her rival. Rejecting Mortimer's dangerous plot to free Mary, Leicester instead arranges for the two Queens to meet. Despite Mary's humble pleas for mercy, Elizabeth treats her with scorn, and Mary retaliates by denouncing Elizabeth as illegitimate. Elizabeth sweeps off in fury, and when she is nearly assassinated on her homeward journey, Mary's fate is sealed. Elizabeth signs Mary's death warrant and gives it to Davison with ambiguous instructions. Burleigh seizes it from him and hurries to Fotheringhay, where Mary's execution is prepared. Leicester, in order to avoid suspicion falling on him, agrees to witness her death. Mary faces death with serenity, having been absolved from her past sins. Elizabeth's throne is now secure, and she blames Davison and Burleigh for Mary's death. News comes that the unhappy Leicester has left for France, and Elizabeth sits entirely alone in her palace.

Loosely based on historical fact (in fact the Queens never met), this is acknowledged to be the greatest historical tragedy in German. Although ostensibly the tragedy of Mary, the truly tragic figure is Elizabeth. While Mary rises to a state of serenity, detached from the uncertainties and yearnings of life, Elizabeth is forced to commit judicial murder by the political pressures she lives under and ends utterly isolated on her throne, condemned to live on in the real world of politics. Schiller once again demonstrates how the idealist figures of Karl Moor, Posa, and here Mortimer, once they become involved in political life, find their well-intentioned actions contaminated and invariably destructive. On the other hand, by witnessing the serenity of Mary's death, Schiller intended that the audience would prepare themselves for their own deaths, what he called 'the inoculation of inevitable fate'.

Maschinenstürmer, Die. See MACHINE WRECKERS, THE.

Mask/Masque Presented at Ludlow Castle, A. See COMUS.

Massacre at Paris, The

A: Christopher Marlowe (and others?) **Pf:** 1593, London **Pb:** 1594 **G:** Trag. in 1 act; blank verse **S:** Paris, 1572–89 **C:** 28m, 6f, extras

Secretly supported by Catherine de'Medici, the Queen Mother, the Duke of Guise plots the destruction of all Protestants in France. He tries to poison the new 'heretic' Queen of Navarre, but by mistake it is the Old Queen who dies. The High Admiral is wounded in the street, then murdered on Guise's orders. Orders are then given by the King for the massacre of the Huguenots to commence under Guise's direction. A series of short scenes follows, depicting the slaughter of St Bartholomew's Night. Overcome by a sudden sickness, the King dies, and his brother Henry accedes to the throne. Resenting the growing power of Guise, Henry arranges for him to be murdered. A Catholic faction reacts by sending a priest to stab Henry with a poisoned knife. As he dies, Henry renounces the evils of Catholicism, and Navarre succeeds him, promising to avenge his death.

The Massacre of St Bartholomew's Night of 1572, in which some 10,000 Protestants were butchered in France, and which gave the word 'massacre' to the language, was still two decades later regarded by Protestant England as a warning of the treachery and violence of the Catholic faith, a terrible reminder of the five years' persecution of Protestants under 'Bloody' Queen Mary I (1553–8). Here the main responsibility for the massacre lies with Guise rather than, as traditionally, with Catherine de'Medici. There is no internal debate or soul-searching in the main character, and the play, not one of Marlowe's strongest, depends primarily on the episodic enactment of violent incidents.

Masses and Men (*Masse-Mensch*)

AT: *Masses and Man, Man and the Masses*
A: Ernst Toller **Pf**: 1920, Nuremberg **Pb**: 1921
Tr: 1923 G: Drama in 7 scenes; unrhymed German verse S: Indeterminate town, 1918–19 C: 5m, 1f, many extras

In the back room of a pub, a workers' council agree to strike. The Woman (Sonja Irene L.) offers to lead them, despite the protests of her husband, a government official. In a dream sequence at the stock exchange top-hatted bankers speculate on the progress of the war, then perform a fantastic dance. At a mass meeting the workers threaten the destruction of machines, and Sonja urges them to protest peacefully. However, the violent and ruthless Nameless One carries the masses behind him. In a dream Sonja tries to protect her husband from death by order of the Masses. While Sonja continues to urge the workers to love even those who are oppressing them, the army defeats the workers, breaks up the meeting, and arrests Sonja. In a dream dead workers blame Sonja's pacifism for their deaths. In prison Sonja is visited by her husband, a priest, and the Nameless One. The last has come to free her, but when she learns that this means that a guard must be killed, she refuses and is taken to her execution.

Together with Georg Kaiser, Toller was the leading dramatist of German Expressionism, although his idealistic socialism contrasted strongly with Kaiser's right-wing views. In this play, allegedly written in two days while in prison for political agitation, Toller champions belief in the brotherhood of all men over political expediency. Such idealism prompted Brecht to dismiss Toller's writing as 'Poetic newspaper. Flat visions. Abstracted man.'

Massnahme, Die. See MEASURES TAKEN, THE.

Master Builder, The (*Bygmester Solness*)

A: Henrik Ibsen **Pf**: 1893, Trondheim **Pb**: 1892
Tr: 1893 G: Trag. in 3 acts; Norwegian prose
S: Solness's home, Norway, late 19th c. C: 4m, 3f, extras

From humble beginnings, Halvard Solness has worked his way up to become a master builder, now even giving employment to his former boss, the architect Brøvik, whose son Ragnar and niece Kaja also work for Solness. His material success is undermined, however, by personal tragedy: his two young children died in a fire, and his wife now mourns them lifelessly. The unexpected arrival of the 22-year-old Hilde Wangel changes everything. Ten years previously she had ecstatically witnessed Solness climbing to the top of a church tower he had just built, and has come now to demand fulfilment of the promise he made to her then: to take her off as a princess to his troll kingdom. She encourages him to approve the young Ragnar's drawings and inspires him to dream of fantastic castles in the air. Finally, she urges him to climb and place a wreath on the top of the tower he has recently built. Suffering from vertigo, he falls to his death. Hilde is nevertheless ecstatic once more: her Master Builder reached the top before he fell.

At the age of 61 Ibsen began a relationship with a young woman from Vienna Emilie Burdach, and there is some truth in Maeterlinck's description of *The Master Builder* as 'an allegorical autobiography'. However, its themes go far beyond a depiction of Ibsen's own life. The confrontation of the typically desiccated existence of provincial Norway with the life and energy of the youthful Hilde Wangel reflects concerns that preoccupied Ibsen in many of his plays. Hilde is a more benevolent Hedda Gabler, pushing people to – and beyond – their limits.

Master Class

A: Terrence McNally **Pf**: 1995, Philadelphia
Pb: 1995 G: Drama in 2 acts S: Stage, Juilliard School, New York, 1972 C: 3m, 3f

Maria Callas, approaching 50, with an internationally successful career behind her, has retired from singing and is teaching opera to young students. By turns imperious, charming, arrogant, amusing, bitchy, and vain, she speaks of her past and instructs a soprano, Sophie De Palma, in Amina's aria from Bellini's *La sonnambula*. In a flashback she recalls the words of Aristotle Onassis: 'You give me class. I give you my wealth.' She then relives her greatest moment at La Scala, when the director Visconti brought the houselights up on her final aria as Amina to reveal the audience of *glitterati* in the stalls. Her second student is a soprano called Sharon Graham, who wishes to sing the Letter Scene from Verdi's *Macbeth*. When Maria criticizes her gown, Sharon disappears from the stage. Her place is taken by a tenor, Tony Candolino, who sings Cavaradossi's aria from Puccini's *Tosca*. He has a beautiful voice but little imagination. Sharon returns from being sick in the toilets. When she shows Sharon how to sing the aria, Maria's ageing voice is now 'a voice in ruins'. There is a flashback to Maria's debut performance at La Scala as Lady Macbeth in 1952. Maria advises Sharon to sing simpler roles, and Sharon accuses Maria of being envious of anyone younger. Maria's final advice to her students is to 'sing properly and honestly'.

Maria Callas was the most charismatic singer of the 20th century, and this play demands a central performance which can recapture the size of Callas's personality. The poignancy of her 'voice in ruins' is not quite accurate: after teaching opera, Callas undertook another international tour, and while her voice was not all it had been, she still enthused her audiences.

Matchmaker, The. See ON THE RAZZLE.

Maydays

A: David Edgar **Pf**: 1983, London **Pb**: 1983; rev. 1984 **G**: Pol. drama in 3 acts **S**: England, Hungary, USA, and USSR, 1945–early 1980s **C**: 24m, 8f, extras

On May Day 1945, as Nazi Germany faces defeat, Jeremy Crowther speaks to the crowds of the triumph of international socialism. Budapest, 1956: a Soviet lieutenant Pavel Lermontov, sent to repress the Hungarian uprising, lets a dissident Hungarian student go free. 1962: Jeremy now teaching at a public school, recognizes that 'there's all the difference in the world, between liberty and liberation'. 1967: one of Jeremy's pupils Martin Glass takes part in an anti-Vietnam demonstration in the USA. In the student revolts of 1968, Martin finds himself unable to commit to any of the warring socialist splinter groups, and Jeremy finds that his university office is occupied by a sit-in. Lermontov, working as a translator, is arrested as a Soviet dissident. May Day 1970: Nixon announces the US invasion of Cambodia. 1972: Jeremy is alarmed at Martin's new-found dogmatism and ruthless revolutionary stance. Two years later, Martin is sacked from his party. May Day 1975: Communists celebrate victory in Saigon. 1978: Lermontov defects to the West and, when he finds himself being exploited to support right-wing views in England, rejects the award offered by the Committee in Defence of Liberty. Early 1980s: while Martin helps to invade a US airforce base, Soviet dissidents meet in secret.

Premiered shortly after Margaret Thatcher was returned for a second term in office, *Maydays* is an epic elegy for socialism, cleverly combining 'May Days', the workers' celebration, with 'mayday', the international distress call. Edgar contrasts the seriousness of political struggle in Eastern Europe with the pathetic infighting of socialist groups in the West, both of which, as Edgar feared, contributed to the eventual triumph of capitalism.

Mayor of Zalamea, The (*El alcalde de Zalamea; El garrote más bien dado*)

AT: *The Best Garrotting Ever Done* **A**: Pedro Calderón de la Barca **Pf**: 1636, Madrid? **Pb**: 1651 **Tr**: 1959 **G**: Drama in 3 acts; Spanish verse **S**: The town of Zalamea, Spain, and its environs, near the Portuguese border, 1580 **C**: 10m, 3f, extras

The Spanish army, on its way to conquer Portugal, is billeted in the border town of Zalamea. A captain, Don Alvaro de Ataide, is quartered with a rich peasant, Pedro Crespo. The Captain tricks his way into the bedroom of Crespo's daughter Isabel, but the Commander-in-Chief intervenes and orders Don Alvaro to live elsewhere. This inflames Don Alvaro's passion further: he kidnaps Isabel and rapes her, abandoning her in the woods. Crespo, who has been wounded attempting to protect his daughter, rejects the possibility of killing his daughter to protect the family's honour. Instead, appointed mayor, he arrests the Captain rather than trust to a military tribunal. When the Captain arrogantly refuses to marry Isabel, Crespo sentences him to death. The Captain is garrotted. The King pardons Crespo and appoints him mayor in perpetuity. Isabel has entered a convent, becoming 'the bride of One who cares nothing for differences in social origin'.

Supposedly based on an actual incident, the play shares this and other characteristics with Lope de Vega's *Fuente Ovejuna*, above all the recognition that common people can act more honourably than their supposed superiors, and the avoidance of a tragic outcome by the benevolent intervention of the monarch. What distinguishes Calderón's play is the psychological realism with which Crespo is portrayed. Audiences can identify with his dilemma in needing to restore his family's honour, while showing love and concern for his daughter.

M. Butterfly

A: David Henry Hwang **Pf**: 1988, New York **Pb**: 1986 **G**: Trag. in 3 acts **S**: Aix-en-Provence, 1947; Beijing, 1960–6; Paris, 1968–70, 1986 **C**: 8m, 8f

René Gallimard, in his prison cell in 1986, looks back at the events that ended his marriage and diplomatic career. He remembers his adolescent youth and his search for the ideal woman. In 1960, he was posted with his wife Helga to the French embassy in Beijing, where at a reception he meets the beautiful and sensitive performer Song Liling singing an aria from Puccini's *Madame Butterfly*, expressing the Western view of the ultimate devotion of the oriental woman. After meeting her again at the Chinese Opera, Gallimard and Song become lovers. Her modesty will not allow him to see her naked, but she teaches him the ancient ways of making love. He is promoted to vice-consul and charged with gathering information for the Americans. Gallimard assures the Ambassador that the Chinese will accept a US invasion of North Vietnam: 'Orientals will always submit to a greater force.' Meanwhile Song passes on military secrets to Comrade Chin, and when she pretends to be pregnant, asks Chin to provide a baby. In 1966, Mao's Cultural Revolution begins, the Chinese Opera is closed, and Gallimard is sent back to Paris for his wrong prognosis about Vietnam. His marriage has collapsed and his career is on hold, when Song appears in Paris. He takes a job as courier for sensitive documents and is arrested with Song for spying. At the trial, it emerges that Song is a man (hence *M*[*onsieur*]. Butterfly), and the court cannot believe that Gallimard lived with him for years without knowing. Gallimard, feeling betrayed by Song, creates his 'feminine ideal' by committing suicide to the music of Puccini.

Based on a true story, Hwang's play embraces the improbability that Gallimard did not know that his ideal woman was male by suggesting that 'only a man knows how a woman is supposed to act'. In fact, male fantasy and Western arrogance combine to project an image of self-effacing devotion, which Gallimard can achieve only through his final pathetic masquerade.

Measure for Measure

A: William Shakespeare **Pf**: *c*.1603–4, London **Pb**: 1623 **G**: Drama in 5 acts; blank verse and prose **S**: Vienna, Renaissance period **C**: 17m, 5f, extras

Vincentio, the Duke of Vienna, is alarmed at the immorality in his state, and resolves to reintroduce an ancient law that punishes sexual misdemeanours with death. However, he leaves the implementation of this law to Angelo, while he conceals himself in a monastery. The first victim of the law is Claudio, who has made his bride pregnant. Claudio's sister, Isabella, who is about to become a nun, pleads with Angelo for Claudio's life. Angelo, lusting after Isabella, offers to spare Claudio if she will sleep with him. Isabella indignantly refuses, even when Claudio begs her to agree. The disguised Vincentio now intervenes, advising Isabella to accede to Angelo's demands, but in fact arranging for a former mistress of Angelo to take Isabella's place. Despite apparently achieving his desire, Angelo treacherously insists on Claudio's execution. Once again, the Duke intervenes, exposing Angelo as a hypocrite but sparing his life when he agrees to marry his mistress. Claudio marries his bride, and the Duke declares that he will wed Isabella, even though her wishes remain unknown.

Based on a 1578 play by George Whetstone, this is a curiously problematic drama. In many ways, it has all the elements of a Renaissance comedy: especially the night-time assignation with a substitute lover and the happy ending with a triple wedding in prospect. However, the issues debated by Shakespeare are so serious and – for Claudio at least – life-threatening, that it would be impossible to describe the piece as a comedy. The ending is also very ambiguous: Isabella, who had intended to take a vow of chastity, now finds that the Duke intends to sweep her off to the altar. Wagner used the play as the basis for his opera *Forbidden Love* (1836), and, because of its exploration of sexual politics, the play has received many performances in recent years.

Measures Taken, The (*Die Massnahme*)

AT: *The Decision* A: Bertolt Brecht (with Slatan Dudow, Elisabeth Hauptmann, and others) Pf: 1930, Berlin Pb: 1931 Tr: 1957 G: Pol. drama in 8 scenes; German prose with songs S: China, 1920s C: 4m or f playing 12m, chorus

Three agitators are called on to explain to a Communist Party tribunal (the Control Chorus) why they executed a comrade during their mission to infiltrate Communism into China. They demonstrate the errors he committed. The Young Comrade, seeing coolies suffering from terrible conditions as they pull a boat up the river, steps forward and gives them assistance, alleviating their discontent and so delaying the revolution. By intervening when a worker is arrested, he endangers the success of a strike. Unable to negotiate amiably with an exploitative capitalist, he ruins the team's chances of using him to further their aims. By attempting to spark off a premature revolution, he endangers the whole mission by revealing the identity of the agitators. Fleeing from the authorities, it is agreed – by the Comrade as well – that he must die and be thrown in a lime pit to obliterate his identity. The Control Chorus approves of the measures taken.

It would be reassuring to imagine that this brutally Stalinist *Lehrstück* ('teaching play') was intended by Brecht to debate the extreme behaviour that a desirable revolution requires. But there is no debate; it is accepted that there is only one way of dealing with the Young Comrade (Why? How will his death help the others to escape?). More important than its unpleasant political content, *The Measures Taken*, according to Brecht, pointed to the future of theatre: at the premiere, with music by Hanns Eisler, there was no audience, the 3,000 workers present forming the Control Chorus, in an anticipation of Augusto Boal's concept of the 'spect-actor'.

Medea

A: Euripides Pf: 431 BC, Athens Tr: 1782 G: Greek trag. in verse S: The palace of the King of Corinth, in the mythical past C: 5m, 3f, extras, chorus (f)

The prologue by the Nurse tells how Medea, a foreigner from Colchis, who deceived her father and killed her brother to help Jason win the Golden Fleece, now finds herself betrayed by him: Jason has determined to abandon her in order to marry the daughter of the King of Corinth. Worse still, Medea will be forced to leave Corinth, never to see Jason or her children again. Medea resolves to kill the King and his daughter, and, in order to cause Jason the greatest possible suffering, she will also murder their two young sons. Jason appears and tries to justify his decision by claiming that it is the only way their children can be protected. Medea pretends to agree and sends a wedding garment to Jason's bride. The garment is, however, poisoned and brings about the death of both the princess and her father. After a deep inner struggle, Medea finally stabs her two sons to death. She avoids Jason's vengeance by being carried off in a chariot provided by Helios, the Sun God. She will seek sanctuary, promised by Aegeus, King of Athens.

The horror of Orestes' matricide is exceeded here by the terrible image of a mother murdering her own children, which was a sensational addition by Euripides to the original legend of the Golden Fleece. It is therefore unsurprising that it was placed last of the three tragedies competing in that year's festival. The intensity of Medea's passion, our revulsion at her crime, and, at the same time, Euripides' willingness to help the audience understand why she acts in the way she does has, however, made Medea one of the most powerful tragic creations ever. Schiller recognized that, as with Macbeth, an audience suspends its moral judgement in the face of the passionate energy of Medea, who, despite her cruelty, effectively behaves with more integrity than the weak and equivocating Jason. Compared with the more public and political interest of the tragedies of Aeschylus and Sophocles, this is a domestic, almost psychological study of a woman *in extremis* – so much so that the chorus are here much more detached from the action than is normally the case. So powerful is this figure of female revenge that she has been recreated in many theatrical adaptations: by Seneca (1st c. AD), Corneille (1635), Hans Henny Jahnn (1926), Anouilh (1937), Dario Fo and Franca Rame (1981), and by Marina Carr, **By the Bog of Cats*. The opera by Cherubini (1797) is but one of 53 operatic versions.

Meet My Father. See RELATIVELY SPEAKING.

Mein Kampf

A: George Tabori **Pf**: 1987, Vienna **Pb**: 1987 in German; 1996 in English **G**: Hist. drama in 5 acts; English prose **S**: Flop-house in Vienna, early 20th c. **C**: 4m, 2f, extras

Two Jews, bookseller Shlomo Herzl and unemployed cook Lobkowitz, who imagines he is God, converse about Herzl's projected book *Mein Kampf*. Hitler comes to Vienna to take the entrance exam at the Academy of Fine Art. The following morning, Hitler dresses in a panic, and Herzl trims his moustache and combs his hair. Hitler returns drunk that evening, rejected by the Academy for which he blames the Jews. The next day, Herzl receives a visit from young Gretchen, an aristocratic orphan. She gives him a present of a hen, and cuts his toenails. Hitler returns delirious, but is comforted by Gretchen and Herzl, who recommends that he should go into politics. The next day Frau Death seeks Hitler not as a corpse, but as 'a mass murderer, an exterminating angel, a natural talent'. Some time later, Hitler has gone into politics 'to save the world', seven Tyrolean leather freaks are painting the walls brown, Gretchen has become a Hitler Girl, and Hitler and his friend Heinrich Himmlisch demand to see Herzl's *Mein Kampf*. When he refuses to betray its content, Himmlisch grabs Herzl's pet hen, strangles it, and begins to cook it 'in blood sauce'. As the Nazis dance, Frau Death arrives and leads Hitler away. He promises that he will not disappoint her.

Prefaced by the poet Hölderlin's words that 'only the desperate' resort to 'playing and jesting', Tabori's play is, like his *Cannibals* of 1968, a remarkably funny piece about the Holocaust. Based on Hitler's embittered experiences as a penniless would-be artist in Vienna, 1910–12, and with obvious references to the Zionist Theodor Herzl and the Nazi Heinrich Himmler, *Mein Kampf* ranges from revue-like repartee to surreal images. Tabori's admirable stoicism, humour, and humanity in coming to terms with the personal tragedy of losing his father in Auschwitz, can inspire us to confront one of the major atrocities of the 20th century.

Memorandum, The (*Vyrozumění*)

A: Václav Havel **Pf**: 1965, Prague **Pb**: 1965 **Tr**: 1965 **G**: Pol. com. in 12 scenes; Czech prose **S**: Czech office building, 1960s **C**: 12m, 3f

Gross, the Managing Director of a large firm, is disturbed to receive a memorandum written in 'Pytdepe', a new bureaucratic language which is to be imposed on all businesses. When he orders his deputy Balas to put a stop to the introduction of this incomprehensible language, he learns that he is already too late. A large number of Pytdepe experts are already installed in the building, forcing the accounts department down to the cellar. Gross now sets out to find out the meaning of his Pytdepe memo. He visits the Pytdepe classroom and translation section. As he becomes more and more demoralized, he breaks down and confesses to a minor breach of regulations which Balas had induced him to commit. He resigns in favour of Balas, but Balas, recognizing that it is in fact the second in command who wields the true power, restores Gross to the Managing Directorship. As Pytdepe proves too difficult for the employees to learn, Balas puts pressure on the disgraced Gross to introduce a new language, 'Chorukor'.

In this satirical comedy, Havel depicts a broad range of typical office life (not confined to the Communist Czechoslovakia on which it is based): the empty routines, the complacency of those with a little power over others, the time-wasting as office workers chat, smoke cigars, and wander off to the toilets. What to Western audiences might seem an amusing parody, was for the Czechs a disturbing analysis of a society where claims to open up channels of communication (represented here by the introduction of Pytdepe) in fact led to greater oppression – witnessed in the banning four years later of all Havel's work.

Memorial Stones. See ANATOL.

Menaechmi. See BROTHERS MENAECHMUS, THE.

Men Should Weep

A: Ena Lamont Stewart Pf: 1947, Glasgow Pb: 1983 G: Drama in 3 acts; Glaswegian dialect S: Kitchen in Morrisons' home, east end of Glasgow, winter 1930s C: 4m, 9f, 2 children (1m, 1f)

Because her socialist husband John Morrison is out of work, his wife Maggie has to go out to work as a charwoman to support her family. When she comes home, she has to catch up with the housework, because such chores would be beneath the husband's dignity. One young son has tuberculosis, and another, married to a grasping wife, is constantly trying to borrow money from Maggie. Her daughter Jenny decides to become a wealthy man's mistress, raising the question whether her behaviour is any more immoral than entering into an unsuitable marriage. Encouraged by her tough sister Lily, Maggie accepts money from Jenny (dismissed by her father as 'whore's winnins') and dreams of a new home away from the slums.

Stewart was the major woman Scottish playwright of the first half of the 20th century. Often writing in Scots vernacular, she declared war on the middle-class taste for drawing-room comedies, in a 'red-hot revolt against cocktail time, glamorous gowns and underworked, about-to-be-deceived husbands'. This moving but funny piece suggests that 'men should weep' over the conditions women are forced to work in, but also that, if men could only abandon their concern with masculinity and weep themselves, the world might be a better place. Originally written for Glasgow Unity Theatre, *Men Should Weep* was successfully revived by John McGrath's 7:84 company in 1982, allowing Stewart to take her place as a neglected pioneer of socialist feminist playwriting.

Merchant Gentleman, The. See WOULD-BE GENTLEMAN, THE.

Merchant of Venice, The (*The most excellent Historie of the Merchant of Venice*)

A: William Shakespeare Pf: *c.*1596–7, London Pb: 1600 G: Com. in 5 acts; blank verse and prose S: Venice, and Portia's house in Belmont, Renaissance period C: 16m, 3f, extras

Bassanio asks his friend Antonio to finance his wooing of the rich heiress Portia. Antonio is obliged to borrow money from the Jew Shylock, who agrees to lend him the requested amount, provided Antonio pledges to give him a pound of flesh if the debt is not repaid. Meanwhile Portia is plagued by unwelcome suitors, who have to choose one of three caskets in order to win her hand in marriage. To her delight, Bassanio chooses the right casket, and their happiness seems assured, when news comes that Antonio's ships have been wrecked, and that he will have to go to court to settle his bond with Shylock. Portia disguises herself as a young doctor of law and acts as judge at the trial. When Shylock rejects her plea for mercy, she awards the pound of flesh to him. However, she then insists that Shylock must cut precisely one pound of flesh and not spill any blood. Faced with an impossible task, Shylock relents, but is forced to give up his estates and become a Christian. Portia and Bassanio return to Belmont to celebrate their wedding together with Shylock's daughter Jessica, who has eloped with Lorenzo, and with Nerissa, Portia's servant, who is to marry Gratiano.

Although Shakespeare generates sympathy for Shylock by showing how ill-treated he is by the Venice gentry, not least when they agree to twist the word of the law to force him to abandon his faith and live in penury, Shylock is nevertheless a villain. He is merciless in demanding his pound of flesh, and, when his daughter elopes, his main concern is with the money and jewels she has stolen. It may fairly be asked whether such stereotyping is acceptable after the Nazi Holocaust. Some contemporary directors have tended to play down Shylock's Jewishness; others have emphasized the unpleasant character of Shylock, confronting the audience with their own racism, as Peter Zadek did controversially in 1972 in West Germany. Arnold Wesker wrote a memorable adaptation, *The Merchant* (1977).

Merchant of Yonkers, The. See ON THE RAZZLE.

Mermaid, The. See LADY FROM THE SEA, THE.

Merry Beggars, The. See JOVIAL CREW, A.

Merry-Go-Round. See RONDE, LA.

Merry Wives of Windsor, The (*A Most pleasaunt and excellent conceited Comedie, of Syr John Falstaffe, and the merrie Wiues of Windsor*)

A: William Shakespeare Pf: *c.*1597, London Pb: 1623 ('bad' 1st quarto, 1601) G: Com. in 5 acts; prose with a little blank verse S: Various locations in and near Windsor, late 16th c. C: 16m, 4f, extras

Attracted as much by their money as by their charms, Falstaff woos two married women in Windsor, Mistress Ford and Mistress Page. Sending them identical letters, which the two women compare, they resolve to make assignations with him in order to humiliate him. When Ford learns of Falstaff's attempted adultery with his wife, he visits him in disguise, pretending to seek a liaison with Mistress Ford himself. Thus learning about the secret meeting, Ford attempts to apprehend Falstaff, but the knight escapes in a laundry basket and is later dumped in the Thames. Eventually, Falstaff's antics are exposed. Meanwhile, a young gentleman Fenton has secretly married Mistress Page's daughter, and the play ends in revelry.

Allegedly written to satisfy Queen Elizabeth's demand to see Falstaff in love, the play is weakly constructed and has no memorable characters (Falstaff here is a pale shadow of the Falstaff of **Henry IV*). Despite this, *The Merry Wives of Windsor* offers the opportunity for some riotous knockabout humour, and so it has remained popular: it has formed the basis of three successful operas, Verdi's *Falstaff* (1893), Nicolai's *Die lustigen Weiber von Windsor* (1849), and Vaughan Williams's *Sir John in Love* (1929). It is also notable in being the only Shakespeare play set in the England of the day and for being almost entirely in prose.

Mesyats v derevne. See MONTH IN THE COUNTRY, A.

Metamora

AT: *The Last of the Wampanoags* A: John Augustus Stone Pf: 1829, New York Pb: 1943 G: Melodrama in 5 acts; prose S: Indian encampment, council chamber, and settlers' homes, America, late 17th c. C: 13m, 2f, 1 boy, extras

Mordaunt welcomes his daughter Oceana, arrived from England to marry Lord Fitzarnold. She has been rescued from a panther by an imposing 'Indian', Metamora, Chief of the Wampanoags. Metamora declares he wishes to be a friend to the white man, but will not let his people be enslaved to them. Walter, a noble-minded orphan, loves Oceana and hopes that she will not marry Fitzarnold. A council is held, where Metamora is fraudulently accused of treachery. Metamora escapes, and in the scuffle, Mordaunt is wounded. While Fitzarnold tries to force Oceana into a wedding ceremony, Metamora returns with his braves, burning boats and attacking Mordaunt's house. Oceana saves her father and falls into Walter's arms. Walter is captured by the Wampanoags, and Metamora's wife is held by the whites. The whites offer an exchange and treacherously capture Metamora. Oceana, mourning the death of her father and the loss of Walter, is saved from Fitzarnold's rape by the intervention of Metamora, who has escaped. The settlers mount an armed attack on the Indian camp and are victorious. Oceana and Walter are freed. Metamora stabs his wife to preserve her from slavery and then bravely faces the guns, cursing the white man as he dies.

In 1828 the great tragedian Edwin Forrest offered a $500 prize for a play whose hero was a Native American. *Metamora* won, and the role of the Chief remained one of Forrest's favourites throughout his career. Popularity of the play continued into the 1880s. Packed with melodramatic incident and characters, and written in flowery language, its main asset is the impressive figure of Metamora.

Middle-Class Gentleman, The. See WOULD-BE GENTLEMAN, THE.

Midsummer Night's Dream, A (*A Midsommer nights dreame*)

A: William Shakespeare Pf: *c.* 1596, London Pb: 1600 G: Romantic com. in 5 acts; blank verse and prose S: Athens and a nearby wood, in the mythical past C: 13m, 8f, extras

Theseus, King of Athens, is about to marry Hippolyta, the Queen of the Amazons. Egeus complains to Theseus that his daughter Hermia refuses to wed Demetrius, since she loves Lysander. Standing under threat of death for disobeying her father, Hermia plans to elope with Lysander. Meanwhile six artisans decide to rehearse a play to be presented at court. Oberon, King of the Fairies, is in dispute with Titania, his Queen, and resolves to punish her. He orders his fairy Puck to pour a potion into the eyes of the sleeping Titania, so that she falls in love with the first living thing she sees. One of the artisans, Bottom the Weaver, is transformed into an ass, and it is he who becomes the astonished object of Titania's affection. By now Hermia and Lysander have got lost in the woods. Hermia is pursued by the jealous Demetrius, who is followed by Helena, who loves Demetrius. Puck has fun pouring the love potion into Demetrius' eyes, so that he falls in love with Helena, thus removing the obstacle to the marriage of Hermia and Lysander. Bottom is restored to normality, and Titania and Oberon are reconciled. The artisans present their 'very tragical mirth' of Pyramus and Thisbe, are suitably rewarded, and the couples go off to celebrate their nuptials.

Although largely played out in a magical fairyland setting and full of joyful comedy, much of which is based on the recognition of the arbitrary nature of 'falling in love', the play is shot through with disturbing contradictions. The royal wedding results from Theseus subduing his bride in brutal conquest. The world of nature is in turmoil, because of discord in the fairy kingdom, and Oberon punishes his wife by giving her a 'rape drug' so that she commits an act of bestiality with a donkey. Even the farcical play presented by the Athenian workmen is undercut by the courtiers' supercilious sneering. Mendelssohn wrote somewhat saccharine incidental music to the play in 1826. Max Reinhardt made theatre history by first using a revolving stage as an integral element of his production in Berlin in 1905. In 1935 he filmed the play in Hollywood, and in 1970 Peter Brook transformed British Shakespearian production with his radical approach to the text.

Miles gloriosus, See BRAGGART SOLDIER, THE.

Milestones. See ANATOL.

Millennium Approaches. See ANGELS IN AMERICA.

Mine Hostess. See MIRANDOLINA.

Minna von Barnhelm (*Minna von Barnhelm, oder Das Soldatenglück*)

AT: *The Soldier's Fortune; The Disbanded Officer; The School for Honour* A: Gotthold

Ephraim Lessing **W**: 1760–3 **Pf**: 1767, Hamburg **Pb**: 1767 **Tr**: 1786 **G**: Com. in 5 acts; German prose **S**: The entrance hall and neighbouring room in an inn, Berlin, 1763 **C**: 7m, 3f

Major von Tellheim, an officer in the Prussian army, has fought bravely in the Seven Years War but now finds himself dishonourably discharged and impoverished. Feeling himself unworthy, he breaks off his engagement with Minna von Barnhelm, his fiancée from the former enemy state of Saxony. He now lives in an inn in Berlin. The landlord insists that Tellheim must vacate his room to make way for a well-to-do lady, who turns out to be none other than Minna, come in search of her fiancé. Tellheim refuses to allow her to marry a poor and disgraced soldier, so Minna now pretends that she has herself been disinherited and is living in poverty, which brings about a change of heart in Tellheim. Fortunately, the arrival of Minna's uncle and a message from the King that Tellheim has been reinstated and his fortune restored allow the couple to look forward to a future together.

Considered the first German comedy, and still one of the best, *Minna von Barnhelm* shows Lessing, the so-called 'father of German theatre', turning from the tragic mode of his *Miss Sara Sampson* and the seriousness of **Nathan the Wise*. *Minna* goes beyond conventional comedy in placing the source of the action not in the external discovery of the identity of Tellheim and Minna, but in Tellheim's exaggerated sense of honour and his gradual inner reform to becoming less self-centred and more loving. In his gently comic depiction of Prussian stubbornness and Saxon charm, Lessing also hoped to heal some of the wounds of the Seven Years War. Howard Barker adapted it in 1994.

Minor, The (*Nedorosl*)

AT: *The Young Hopeful; The Infant* **A**: Denis Fonvizin **Pf**: 1782, St Petersburg **Pb**: 1783 **Tr**: 1933 **G**: Com. in 5 acts; Russian prose **S**: Prostakov's country estate, Russia, 1780s **C**: 12m, 3f

The 'minor' is the lazy, spoilt 16-year-old Mitrofan, whose father Prostakov is tyrannized by his grasping and boorish wife. On their estate are their ward Sophia and an aristocrat Pravdin, who has been secretly sent to follow up reports that Madam Prostakova has been ill-treating her serfs. Prostakova, who has illegally seized Sophia's estate, is hoping to marry her to Prostakova's brother, who is however only interested in his pigs. When news comes that Sophia's rich uncle is on his way, Prostakova decides that Sophia would be a good catch for her son. However, Sophia falls in love with a new arrival Milon, a handsome army officer. When her uncle refuses to approve Sophia's marriage to either Prostakova's brother or her son, Prostakova attempts to kidnap Sophia but is prevented by Milon. Pravdin reveals his identity and orders that Prostakova should be held to account for her treatment of the serfs. Her power gone, Milon and Sophia are free to marry.

This is the only 18th-century Russian play still regularly performed in Russia today. Owing an obvious debt to Holberg, the play is a typical neo-classical comedy: the action takes place in one location and in just over 24 hours, and there is very tight plotting. What brings the piece to life, however, is the range of strong characters, all bearing symbolic names, which would provide comic types for generations of Russian dramatists.

Mirandolina (*La locandiera*)

AT: *Mistress of the Inn; Mine Hostess; The Inn Keeper* **A**: Carlo Goldoni **Pf**: 1753, Venice **Pb**: 1753 **Tr**: 1922 **G**: Com. in 3 acts; Italian prose **S**: Mirandolina's inn, Florence, mid-18th c. **C**: 5m, 3f

Mirandolina, a clever, beautiful, and charming landlady, is wooed by two of her guests, a poor Marquis and a rich Count, while her servant Fabrizio has also fallen prey to her charms. It was her late father's wish that she should marry Fabrizio. Offered status by the Marquis and lavish presents by the Count, she devotes herself to running the inn, until she turns her attention to the Baron of Ripafratta. He is a confessed woman-hater, who ignores the attentions of two actresses purporting to be aristocrats, and so represents a challenge to

Mirandolina. With feminine wiles she wins the heart of the Baron, then forces him publicly to deny his feelings for her and declares that she will marry Fabrizio. The Baron storms off, and Mirandolina reflects that as a married woman she will now have to abandon her flirtatious behaviour.

In attempting to reform the Italian theatre, Goldoni abandoned the improvisation, predictability, and knockabout farce of the *commedia dell'arte* and replaced it with plays whose main interest lies in character relationships. In Mirandolina he created one of the most vibrant figures of Italian theatre, a woman who overcomes her humble background to enchant a trio of aristocrats with her charm and intelligence. Surprisingly, however, she does not use this to improve her social standing but merely to teach these men a lesson. She gives her heart and hand to the honest commoner Fabrizio.

Misanthrope, The (Menander). See BAD-TEMPERED MAN, THE.

Misanthrope, The (*Le Misanthrope*)

AT: *The Man-Hater* A: Molière Pf: 1666, Paris Pb: 1667 Tr: 1762 G: Com. in 5 acts; French alexandrines S: Célimène's home, Paris, 17th c. C: 8m, 3f

Alceste is totally committed to honesty and despises the hypocritical manners of his contemporaries. For example, he tells the poet Oronte precisely what he thinks of his poor verse, which determines Oronte to try to win Alceste's beloved Célimène from him. When Oronte and Alceste discover that Célimène has been dishonestly playing off one suitor against another, Oronte abandons her, while Alceste perversely continues steadfast in his devotion to her. News comes that, despite the justice of his cause, Alceste has lost a lawsuit. Characteristically, he refuses to appeal against the judgement, in order to prove yet again how corrupt the world is. Since he is obliged to leave Paris, he asks Célimène to come with him as his wife. She is willing to marry him, but only if they can remain in Paris society. Refused too by Célimène's cousin, Alceste prepares to depart angrily for the country, while his reasonable friend hopes to persuade him to stay.

The Misanthrope is the most complex of Molière's comedies, because here, although the main character behaves in an extreme fashion, his behaviour is not as reprehensible as that seen in *The *Hypochondriac* or *The *Miser*. Indeed, to a modern audience, as to Rousseau, Alceste seems a sympathetic figure when compared with the flatterers and hypocrites of contemporary Parisian society. However, the audience of Molière's day would have recognized that, while Alceste's devotion to the truth may be praiseworthy, his obsession with being outspoken and his willingness to adopt the role of victim is every bit as extreme as Argan's obsession with his health or Harpagon's with money. Thus, while Molière, who had just endured the banning of his **Tartuffe* and **Don Juan*, joyfully satirized the superficiality of Parisian society, Alceste is no hero. Indeed, he is more than likely to return to Célimène's salon, since part of the joke is that this hater of humankind needs people around him to provide an audience for his embittered diatribes.

Miser, The (*L'Avare*)

A: Molière Pf: 1668, Paris Pb: 1669 Tr: 1672 G: Com. in 5 acts; French alexandrines S: Harpagon's home, Paris, 17th c. C: 9m, 6f

Harpagon, a widower, is a rich old miser with two children. His son Cléante is in love with Mariane, a poor neighbour. His daughter Élise is in love with Valère, who has managed to gain employment as Harpagon's steward. Exploiting the poverty of Mariane's mother, Harpagon forces her to offer her beautiful young daughter in marriage. Cléante's servant loyally intervenes on his master's behalf, and with his girlfriend steals Harpagon's gold, which will be returned only if he abandons his lustful pursuit of Mariane. By an extraordinary coincidence it turns out that Mariane and Valère are brother and sister, the lost children of Harpagon's neighbour and friend Anselme, who is in fact a wealthy Italian count. At the end everyone is joyous: the Count reunited with his family, the lovers free to wed, and Harpagon in possession of his gold once more.

Loosely based on Plautus' *The Pot of Gold*, this comedy differs from most of Molière's in that the ending does not bring about the defeat or cure of the blocking figure, Harpagon. He remains a miser and in possession of his wealth. Indeed, Harpagon is not a typical obsessive figure, in that, although his first love is his gold, he also wishes to marry a young woman, which conflicts with his miserliness (there is no suggestion that marriage might bring him more money, since he is taking a penniless bride). It is only the improbable discovery of the birth of Mariane and her brother that saves a situation, in which lives might otherwise be destroyed by Harpagon's avarice.

Misery of Having a Mind, The. See WOE FROM WIT.

Misfortune of Being Clever, The. See WOE FROM WIT.

Miss Julie (*Fröken Julie*)

AT: *Lady/Countess Julie/Julia* A: August Strindberg Pf: 1889, Copenhagen Pb: 1888 Tr: 1912 G: Trag. in 1 act; Swedish prose S: The kitchen of a count's home, Scandinavia, Midsummer's Eve, 1880s C: 1m, 2f, extras

The Count's valet Jean gossips with his fiancée, the kitchen maid Kristin, about the Count's daughter Miss Julie. Having recently broken off her engagement, she is now behaving wildly at the servants' dance in the barn. She drags Jean off for another dance with him. They return to the kitchen, and, when Kristin falls asleep eventually retiring to bed, Julie flirts outrageously with Jean, who confesses that he used to yearn for her. The dancers approach the kitchen, and Jean hides with Julie in his room. When the dancers retire, it is clear that Jean and Julie have had sex, and his subservient attitude changes. He demands that she run away with him and that they open a hotel in Switzerland together. Though full of remorse, she obeys Jean and steals her father's money. Only when Jean insists that she cannot take her little bird with her and kills it, does she lose self-control, declaring her hatred of all men. Emerging from her room, Kristin is disgusted at their behaviour, haughtily refuses their invitation to leave with them, and goes to church. Unexpectedly, the Count summons Jean to clean his boots, and he becomes the dutiful servant once more. Julie begs him to order her to kill herself. He gives her a razor, and she goes out to commit suicide.

Miss Julie (*Fröken* implies higher status than that contained in 'Miss', hence the alternative titles of *Lady* or *Countess Julie*) is the best known of Strindberg's plays. It stands as a model of naturalist drama, set in one realistic location, and with stage time coinciding with real time. In his Introduction to the play, Strindberg insisted on the need for theatre to create rounded characters speaking everyday language in place of conventional stock types uttering neatly polished phrases. He urged his performers to imitate real life by daring to turn their backs on the audience and to make up their faces naturally. For us the main interest of the piece is now in the sexual tension between Jean and Julie, and in the way in which their respective status changes. Although coloured by Strindberg's fear of the growing power of women and his view that destructive man-haters like Julie are commonplace, the play still offers an intense experience in performance.

Mistakes of a Night, The. See SHE STOOPS TO CONQUER.

Misteriya-Buff. See MYSTERY-BOUFFE.

Mistero Buffo (The Morality Play of the Blind Man and the Cripple; Death and the Fool; The Fool beneath the Cross Laying a Wager)

AT: *Comic Mysteries* A: Dario Fo Pf: 1969, Milan Pb: 1970 Tr: 1988 G: 13 linked one-act monologues and dramas; Italian prose and some verse S: Various locations, 1st c. AD and medieval period C: (4) 2m; (10) 4m, 2f; (12) 6m

(1) The Actor, using slides, introduces the tradition of *mistero buffo* (comic mystery plays). There follow (2) *The Flagellant's Laude* and (3) *The Slaughter of the Innocents*. (4) *The*

Morality Play of the Blind Man and the Cripple. A blind man and a cripple are appealing for alms. Becoming aware of each other, the cripple mounts the blind man's back, so that they can both get about more easily. They see Jesus being scourged and then forced to carry his cross. As the procession passes by, both beggars are cured. The blind man is jubilant, but the cripple realizes that he must now suffer: 'I'll have to go and work for an employer, sweating blood in order to eat.' (5–9) *The Marriage at Cana; The Birth of the Jongleur; The Birth of the Villeyn; The Resurrection of Lazarus; Boniface VIII.* (10) *Death and the Fool.* In a tavern Matazone the Fool is winning at cards, when a group of people sit down to dine in the next room: it is Christ with the 12 apostles. Death enters, a pale young woman, and the Fool's fellow players flee. The Fool welcomes her and praises her beauty. She reveals that she has come for Christ, who knows of his fate. The fool concludes that Christ, who still loves those that will betray him, must be crazier than him. (11) *Mary Hears of the Sentence Imposed on her Son.* (12) *The Fool Beneath the Cross Laying a Wager.* Jesus is nailed to the cross, and the Fool joins the Crucifiers gambling with dice and tarot. When he wins, he offers to hand back all his gains if the Crucifiers will give him Jesus in exchange. He suggests that they replace Jesus with the corpse of Judas hanging from a nearby tree, and even offers to give them the 30 pieces of silver that the Fool found nearby. However, when the Fool goes to take Jesus from the cross, Jesus refuses, because he must die to redeem mankind. The Fool warns him how his sacrifice will be exploited by the rich and powerful, but Jesus remains determined. The Fool once again concludes that the Son of Man is mad, and that he was sane only when he drove the moneychangers from the temple. (13) *The Passion: Mary at the Cross.*

Assuming the role of the *giullare* ('jester' or *jongleur*), Fo performed this series of short pieces with tremendous vitality and physical energy ('The *jongleur* was a figure who came from the people, and who from the people drew anger and transmitted it through the medium of the grotesque'). These monologues and playlets, of which three are summarized above, serve to humanize the figure of Christ while propagating a socialist message regarded as too gentle by Fo's more militant comrades.

Mistress of the Inn. See MIRANDOLINA.

Misunderstanding, The. See CROSS PURPOSE.

Molière. See CABAL OF HYPOCRITES, A.

Moll Cutpurse. See ROARING GIRL, THE.

Money

A: Edward Bulwer-Lytton **Pf:** 1840, London **Pb:** 1840 **G:** Com. in 5 acts; prose **S:** Sir John Vesey's house, Evelyn's house, and a gentlemen's club, London, 1830s **C:** 18m, 3f, extras

Alfred Evelyn is a poor, hard-working, intelligent young man, factotum to a distant relative, the mercenary Sir John Vesey. When Evelyn asks for £10 for his mother's old nurse, Sir John and his friends refuse to help. Only Clara Douglas, another poor orphaned relative living in Sir John's house, secretly sends money to the nurse. When Evelyn proposes to Clara, she refuses, unable to contemplate a life of poverty with him. Evelyn inherits a huge fortune, and suddenly everyone becomes his friend. Sir John urges his daughter Georgina to forget her intended, the young dandy Sir Frederick Blount, and to entrap Evelyn. When Evelyn is told that the secret gift to his nurse came from Georgina, he becomes engaged to her. He still loves Clara, but Clara finds now that 'his wealth, even more than poverty, separates [them] for ever'. Secretly he provides for Clara. Suspicious of Georgina's motives, Evelyn pretends to have gambled away his fortune. She goes back to Blount, and Clara admits that she not only sent the £10 to the nurse but even secretly provided for Evelyn when he was seemingly destitute. Evelyn's fortune is intact, and he and Clara can now marry happily.

Bulwer-Lytton was one of the few English playwrights of the early 19th century to possess both dramatic and literary merit, and *Money* is his best play. The plotting is intricate, scenes with several characters on stage are skilfully managed, and the theme of the play is striking. While most romantic comedies solve their problems by providing the hero with a fortune, *Money* starts with the acquisition of wealth and develops the action from there.

Monologhi per una donna, See FEMALE PARTS.

Month in the Country, A (*Mesyats v derevne*)

A: Ivan Turgenev W: 1848–50 Pf: 1872, Moscow Pb: 1855 Tr: 1924 G: Com. in 5 acts; Russian prose S: The Islaev estate, Russia, 1840s C: 6m, 2f, extras

The beautiful 29-year-old Natalia is married to a rich landowner Arkadi Islaev, seven years her senior. She is bored by life on their estate and so welcomes the attentions of Mikhailo Rakitin without letting their relationship develop into a romance. The arrival of the handsome 21-year-old student Aleksei Belyaev as tutor to her son suddenly breaks the boredom. Natalia falls in love with Aleksei, while Aleksei is attracted to Vera (Verotshka), the 17-year-old foster-daughter of the Islaevs. In order to rid herself of her rival, Natalia suggests that Verotshka should marry a rich old neighbour. Rakitin struggles with his love for Natalia, she wrestles with hers for Aleksei, and the two young people grow closer, while Natalia's husband begins to develop his own suspicions. Rakitin therefore feels obliged to leave the estate and persuades Aleksei to come with him. Verotshka, to escape from her foster-mother, accepts the neighbour's offer of marriage, and after this 'month in the country', Natalia must resign herself again to boredom.

Not performed until 22 years after its composition, *A Month in the Country* is a delicate, closely observed comedy of love, which owes a debt to French models like Marivaux, but displaying more realistic psychology. Turgenev brings together his love of Western literature with the authentic depiction of Russian society, anticipating by half a century Chekhov's classic comedies of Russian rural life, in which the boredom of summer visitors is cruelly and amusingly portrayed. It has been adapted by Emlyn Williams (1943) and Friel (1992).

Moon for the Misbegotten, A

A: Eugene O'Neill W: 1943 Pf: 1947, Columbus, Ohio Pb: 1952 G: Drama in 4 acts S: Dilapidated farmhouse in Connecticut, September 1923 C: 4m, 1f

Josie and her father Phil Hogan are tenants of a farm owned by James Tyrone Jr. Josie is a heavily built 28-year-old Irishwoman, noted for her promiscuity, who has designs on Tyrone, their dissipated landlord. Her father suggests that she should secure their tenancy by seducing Tyrone when he is drunk and there is a full moon, but she fears he prefers 'Broadway tarts' to 'an ugly cow' like herself. Tyrone comes, and he and Hogan exchange friendly insults, and together they all make fun of a millionaire neighbour who complains about their pigs coming on to his land. Tyrone has fallen in love with Josie, but is so full of self-loathing that he finds it hard to approach her. Josie now admits that her stories of promiscuity were invented to compensate for her unattractiveness, and that she is a virgin. She pulls him to her room, but he turns on her with cruel cynicism. Soothing him, she listens to his confession: how grief over his mother's death had driven him back to drink. She lulls him to sleep under the full moon. At dawn, he wakes grateful for the beauty of the night and the sense of absolution he now feels. He leaves her tenderly, knowing he will soon die. Hogan returns, admitting that he had hoped to have Tyrone as a son-in-law, and daughter and father resume their customary banter.

This last play by O'Neill is to some extent a sequel to **Long Day's Journey into Night*, but here the tone is gentler, funnier, and more optimistic. Significantly, such redemption as is possible in this world comes not from religion but from the love of a big-hearted woman, a goddess in the guise of a crude Irish farmhand.

Moon in the Yellow River, The

A: Denis Johnston Pf: 1931, Dublin Pb: 1932 G: Drama in 3 acts S: An old fort on the Liffey Estuary, Ireland, 1927 C: 7m, 3f

Dobelle, a distinguished but disillusioned railway engineer, lives in an old fort near the sea with his daughter Blanaid, whom he rejects because she was the cause of her mother's death in childbirth. The fort also houses the workshop of two eccentric inventors who are working on an improved gun. A German engineer Tausch comes to oversee the installation of a new power plant in the estuary. Local rebel elements strongly oppose the desecration of their country with this new technology. When their leader Blake arrives with some men to blow up the power station, Tausch summons assistance. Blake is shot in cold blood, and Tausch is horrified, believing that they could have settled their differences. Dobelle believes otherwise, saying that Blake and his kind will always want to keep the reflection of the moon in the river. The two inventors carelessly throw away one of their shells believing it to be a dud, and it blows up the power station. The only good to come of it all is that Dobelle is reconciled with his daughter.

Johnston's second and best-known play, which was performed at the Abbey Theatre, shows that he could write interestingly in realistic as well as in Expressionist mode, although admittedly the strange setting and odd characters lend a slightly surreal air to the action. As in *The *Old Lady Says 'No!'*, Johnston criticizes contemporary Ireland, both the government's high-handed attitude to local sensitivities (as evidenced in the Free State's Shannon Scheme of 1925) and the hot-headed response of romantic rebels.

Morality Play of the Blind Man and the Cripple, The. See MISTERO BUFFO.

Mörder, Hoffnung der Frauen. See MURDERER, HOPE OF WOMANKIND.

Morte accidentale di un anarchico. See ACCIDENTAL DEATH OF AN ANARCHIST.

Motel. See AMERICA HURRAH.

Mother, The (*Die Mutter*)

A: Bertolt Brecht **Pf**: 1932, Berlin **Pb**: 1932; rev. 1938 **Tr**: 1965 **G**: Pol. drama in 15 scenes; German prose with songs **S**: Russia, 1905–17 **C**: 18m, 7f, extras

Pelagea Vlassova is so poor that she can afford to give only watery soup to her son Pavel. She asks the audience what a poor widow can do, especially as Pavel's wages have been cut by the Suchlinov works. When Pavel invites revolutionary workers back to their apartment, Vlassova is very worried. The Tsarist police raid the house, leaving it in a mess. In order to protect Pavel, Vlassova offers to distribute revolutionary pamphlets and so finds herself being drawn into political involvement. When she witnesses the brutal suppression of a peaceful demonstration, she becomes fully committed to the socialist cause. Pavel is arrested and sent to Siberia, and she becomes an active revolutionary, learns to read, and helps striking workers. When Pavel escapes from Siberia, mother and son feel closer than ever before. Even when Pavel is arrested and shot, she does not waver in her commitment, rejecting the hypocritical sympathy of her neighbours. Vlassova, as an old woman, carries the red flag in the 1917 anti-war demonstration that will lead to the Bolshevik Revolution.

Loosely based on a novel by Gorky, Brecht traced here the development of an ordinary working-class woman into full revolutionary consciousness. Employing many of his 'distancing' techniques, including direct address to the audience and songs set to Hanns Eisler's music, Brecht was attempting to inspire his contemporaries to resist Fascism, despite the obvious setbacks that the socialist cause was suffering.

Mother Courage and Her Children (*Mutter Courage und ihre Kinder*)

A: Bertolt Brecht (with Margarete Steffin) **Pf**: 1941, Zurich **Pb**: 1949; rev. 1950 **Tr**: 1941 **G**: Pol. drama in 12 scenes; German prose with songs **S**: Sweden, Poland, and Germany, 1624–36 **C**: 19m, 6f, extras

Anna Fierling ('Mother Courage') follows the Swedish armies in the Thirty Years War with her mobile canteen, accompanied by her children from three different fathers, Eilif, Swiss Cheese, and the mute Kattrin. Although Courage depends on war for her livelihood, she tries to keep her children out of it. However, one by one they are taken by the conflict. Eilif becomes a soldier and is decorated for risking his life appropriating some peasants' cattle. Later, in a brief lull of peace, he repeats the same exploit and is shot for looting. Swiss Cheese tries to save the regimental cash box when captured by the enemy, and faces execution. Yvette, a tarty camp-follower, has seduced an ancient colonel, and offers to buy Swiss Cheese's freedom in exchange for Mother Courage's canteen. Mother Courage haggles so long over the price that Swiss Cheese is shot before a deal can be struck. Soldiers bring in his corpse, but the grieving mother must pretend not to know him in order to save herself and Kattrin. Kattrin, already made dumb by a soldier's brutality when still a child, is attacked by soldiers and her face scarred. A Cook, who has been wooing Courage, to the annoyance of a cowardly Protestant Chaplain, now joins her on her march. He offers to marry her and settle down, but Courage refuses when it becomes clear that he will not take Kattrin with them. While Courage is in Halle buying fresh supplies, Kattrin learns of a surprise night attack on the town planned by Catholic troops. Horrified at the thought of the innocent townspeople who will die in the onslaught, Kattrin 'finds her voice' by bravely drumming a loud warning. The soldiers shoot her to silence her, and Courage arrives back to find herself quite alone. She pays for Kattrin's burial, hitches herself to her cart, and trudges off after the departing troops.

Initially inspired by concern at how neutral countries were profiteering from the war, *Mother Courage*, arguably Brecht's greatest play, contains a much wider message: that to depend on capitalism and the conflicts it engenders not only leads to disaster but to a coarsening of humanity. While it is essential that some empathy is generated by the action (it is impossible to remain unmoved by the bravery of the drumming Kattrin), there is also the danger that an audience can become uncritically involved in Mother Courage's progress, as happened at the New York premiere. Apart from the device of stating the content of each scene so as to focus attention on the process rather than the outcome, the use of songs, and the epic structure of 'each scene standing for itself', the play adopts a fairly realistic style. Only in the masterful playing of an actress like Helene Weigel, notably her famous 'silent scream' on seeing the body of Swiss Cheese, is the balance between empathy and critical evaluation maintained.

Mouches, Les. See FLIES, THE.

Mountain Language

A: Harold Pinter Pf: 1988, London Pb: 1988 G: Pol. drama in 1 act S: Prison camp of unspecified nation, late 20th c. C: 6m, 2f

Two women have been waiting for eight hours in the snow outside a military prison camp holding 'enemies of the state': the Young Woman Sarah Johnson to see her husband; the Elderly Woman to see her son. The latter has had her hand bitten by a guard dog, but the Officer refuses to register a complaint, because the women cannot name the dog. They are warned that they must not speak the Mountain Language but only 'the language of the capital'. The Mother tries to speak with her son, but is warned by the Guard not to use her native tongue. When the Prisoner dares to point out that he has a wife and three children, the Guard summons the Sergeant to come and deal with the 'joker'. The Young Woman sees her husband covered in a hood and being manhandled. The Sergeant assures her that if she has sex with the interrogator, 'everything will be all right'. The Mother still sits with her son, who has been very badly beaten. The Guard announces that, under new rules, they may use their mountain language, but the Mother is so traumatized that she can no longer speak. The desperate Prisoner sinks to the floor, groaning inarticulately. The Sergeant enters, furious: 'You go out of your way to give them a helping hand and they fuck it up.'

Mistakenly regarded as being totally non-political, Pinter proved critics wrong with plays like *One for the Road* (1984) and *Mountain Language*. There is still no specificity about place or political context, and the dialogue bears the stamp of Pinter's rhetoric of the everyday. Here the stamping out of mountain language (bearing echoes of Latin American countries, where the native peoples are subject to Spanish-speaking landlords) in favour of the language of the 'capital' (a word with a double meaning), stands as a metaphor for the repression of dissidents everywhere.

Mourning Becomes Electra (Homecoming; The Hunted; The Haunted)

A: Eugene O'Neill **Pf:** 1931, New York **Pb:** 1932 **G:** (1) Trag. in 4 acts; (2) Trag. in 5 acts; (3) Trag. in 4 acts **S:** Mannons' home in New England and a clipper ship, 1865–6 **C:** (1) 5m, 5f; (2) 7m, 5f; (3) 7m, 2f

(1) *Homecoming*. The rumoured end of the American Civil War means that General Ezra Mannon and his son Orin will be returning home. In their absence, his striking foreign-born wife Christine has taken a lover, Adam Brant, a sea captain who is supposedly courting the Mannons' daughter Lavinia. Lavinia discovers that Brant is Mannon's nephew, whose lowborn wife Mannon let starve to death after his brother had died. She suspects Brant of taking revenge on her father by seducing her mother. When Lavinia confronts her mother, Christine accuses Lavinia of sexual jealousy. Christine and Brant plot to poison Mannon, so that they are free to marry. When Mannon returns, he takes Christine to bed, to Lavinia's dismay. By morning, Christine has taunted him with declarations of hatred and a confession of adultery into having a heart attack. She substitutes poison for his medicine, and Lavinia arrives in time to learn the truth from her dying father. (2) *The Hunted*. Two days later Orin returns and is welcomed by his mother. She warns him that Lavinia will try to turn him against his mother, but Lavinia succeeds in persuading Orin of the truth of their father's death. Christine flees to Brant's ship, and the two guilty lovers prepare to leave to seek their happiness. Orin and Lavinia, hidden on deck, overhear their plans, and Orin shoots Brant, after his mother has left. The following night Orin cruelly tells his mother that he has killed her lover. Lavinia is prepared to spare Christine, but Christine shoots herself in despair. Lavinia accepts her suicide as justice. (3) *The Haunted*. A year later Lavinia and Orin return from a long trip. He is obsessed with guilt, while she, having shaken off the past, is prepared at last to accept Peter Niles's offer of marriage. Orin writes down a chronicle of the family's crimes, and then suggests to Lavinia that they should become lovers, so that they can damn themselves totally. She goads him to suicide. He agrees that, since he drove his mother to suicide, this would be justice. He shoots himself in his father's library, while Lavinia clings to Peter. Three days later Lavinia begs Peter to have sex with her, to wash away the guilt and pain of the past. She begs him: 'Want me! Take me, Adam!' Horrified at her slip of the tongue, she recognizes that Adam Brant and the dead will always come between her and happiness. Ordering the windows to be boarded up, she enters the Mannon home, to live alone with the dead and never to leave again.

This monumental attempt to retell the Atridean myth, as enacted in Aeschylus' **Oresteia*, is one of the best known of O'Neill's plays, but is flawed. Comparisons with the original are inevitable, and without the mythic faith underlying the ancient Greek trilogy, and above all its cosmic resolution in the transformation of the Erinyes into the Eumenides, this modern version seems melodramatic. Individual neurosis, though admittedly compelling in performance, is no substitute for genuine tragic conflict.

Mousetrap, The

A: Agatha Christie **Pf:** 1952, London **Pb:** 1954 **G:** Drama in 2 acts **S:** Monkswell Manor guesthouse, *c*.1950 **C:** 5m, 3f

Giles and Mollie Ralston have recently opened Monkswell Manor as a country guesthouse, and are about to receive their first guests in a heavy snowstorm. First to arrive is a mature lady, the fussy Mrs Boyle. Then come: amiable Major Metcalf; Christopher Wren, a delicate and sensitive young man; a somewhat manly woman Miss Casewell; and finally, the rather sinister Mr Paravicini. By next morning they are totally cut off by the snow. The local police phone to say that Detective Sergeant Trotter is making his way out to them on urgent business. Trotter duly arrives on skis and reveals that he is investigating a murder. Some years previously, three local children were sent to be fostered by a farming couple called the Stannings, who abused them so seriously that one of the children died. Stanning was sent to prison, where he died. Now Mrs Stanning has been murdered in London. The guests wonder what they have to do with this matter, when suddenly Mrs Boyle is found murdered, and it turns out that she was the magistrate who issued the court order for the children to be fostered. There appear to be six possible suspects left, but this may not be the whole story . . .

Christie adopted a dependable formula for country house mysteries in both her novels and plays: a well-to-do, isolated locale, with a line-up of potential suspects, each with a possible reason for murder. The horror of the crime becomes submerged in the intellectual fun of spotting the perpetrator, and is therefore arguably a profoundly immoral exercise. However, one cannot deny Christie's popularity with amateurs and some regional theatres, nor the remarkable fact that *The Mousetrap* has played for an unbroken record run for over half a century, now as established a London tourist attraction as the Changing of the Guard.

Mrcchakatikā. See LITTLE CLAY CART, THE.

Mrichchhakatikā. See LITTLE CLAY CART, THE.

Mr Puntila and His Man Matti (*Herr Puntila und sein Knecht Matti*)

AT: *Herr Puntila and His Servant Matti; Puntila and Matti, His Hired Hand* **A:** Bertolt Brecht (with Hella Wuolijoki) **Pf:** 1948, Zurich **Pb:** 1950 **Tr:** 1977 **G:** Com. in 12 scenes; German prose and songs **S:** Finland, 1930s **C:** 14m, 7f, extras

Puntila, a Finnish landowner, is sociable and entertaining when drunk but mean-spirited and carping when sober. After three days of drinking, he becomes good friends with his loyal chauffeur Matti Altonen. He invites four village girls to come and live as his wives on his estate, seeks farmhands in the local town, and insists that his daughter Eva should break off her engagement with a diplomat and marry his 'good friend' Matti instead. Unfortunately, the expansive drunken Puntila turns into the mean sober Puntila: he abuses his servants, throws out the village girls, and now demands that Eva marry her stuffy diplomat. However, Eva has by now become attracted to Matti, and when Puntila is suitably drunk again, the diplomat, offended by Matti's behaviour towards his fiancée, is sent packing by Puntila. Matti tests Eva to see whether she will make a suitable working man's wife, but, because of her privileged background, she fails. As Puntila drinks more heavily, Matti constructs a 'mountain' out of furniture in Puntila's library and helps his master scale the summit. Knowing how Puntila will be when he sobers up the next day, Matti takes his leave, knowing that 'oil and water don't mix'.

Based on Hella Wuolijoki's play *The Sawdust Princess* (1940), Brecht's play offers a comic parallel to *Mother Courage* (a warning that it is impossible to derive benefit from the rich capitalist without coming to harm), and to *The Caucasian Chalk Circle* (the drunken Puntila being like the gloriously anarchic Azdak).

Mrs Dane's Defence

A: Henry Arthur Jones **Pf:** 1900, London **Pb:** 1900 **G:** Drama in 4 acts **S:** Lady Eastney's and Sir Philip Carteret's houses, Sunningwater, near London, *c.*1900 **C:** 8m, 4f

James Risby tells his gossipy aunt Mrs Bulsom-Porter that he has recognized 28-year-old Mrs Dane, a newcomer to the area, as Miss Hindemarsh, who was at the centre of a scandal five years previously in Vienna. Hindemarsh was a governess who had an affair with her employer, driving his wife to suicide and him to madness. Although Risby now admits he made a mistake, Mrs Bulsom-Porter's slander isolates Mrs Dane from the community. Lionel (Lal) Carteret has fallen in love with Mrs Dane, so his adoptive father Sir Daniel, an experienced lawyer, mounts Mrs Dane's defence. He wishes to force Bulsom-Porter to retract her story and clear Mrs Dane's name, so that she is free to marry Lionel. However, his skilful questioning reveals that she is indeed Hindemarsh, mother of an illegitimate child, who has lied in order to be able to re-enter society. Her real defence is that, in the harsh world of Victorian morality, she had no other way of beginning a new life. Sir Daniel is sufficiently sympathetic towards her to hush up her story, but, knowing that Lionel will never again be able to trust her, he sends his son away to forget her.

Very much in the tradition of the well-made play, a genre whose main strength lies in its tight plotting, *Mrs Dane's Defence* is a well-constructed piece that keeps the audience in suspense about the outcome and possesses a strong third act, in which the truth is gradually winkled out of Mrs Dane. Despite the obvious social criticism regarding the difficult role of the 'fallen woman' in contemporary society, this is no proto-feminist piece. It is made quite clear that Mrs Dane/Judith Hindemarsh knew that she was doing wrong and that her past can now never allow her to be a respectable wife.

Mrs Warren's Profession

A: George Bernard Shaw **W**: 1893 **Pf**: 1902 (private performance); 1925 (public), London **Pb**: 1898 **G**: Drama in 4 acts **S**: Haslemere, Surrey, and London, 1890s **C**: 4m, 2f

Vivie Warren is a strong-minded young woman, who has excelled at Cambridge and now wishes to have a career in law. She is wooed by the local Rector's son Frank Gardner, and has also attracted the attentions of a rich old roué Sir George Crofts. On a visit her mother Mrs Warren reveals that her wealth and the funds that have provided Vivie's education and lifestyle have all come from the profits of running brothels on the European continent. Vivie rejects the advances of Sir George, who has profited from her mother's 'profession' and who now retaliates by declaring that Vivie is Revd Gardner's daughter and so Frank's half-sister. Vivie flees to her law offices in London, where Frank agrees to treat her as his sister, and where, despite Mrs Warren's pleadings, Vivie rejects her mother and begins a life of independence.

Because of censorship by the Lord Chamberlain, public performance of this play was delayed by over three decades. Shaw's purpose in tackling as sensitive a subject as prostitution was not just to shock the Victorian public, but to argue that women could only with the greatest difficulty achieve success in society without resorting to prostituting themselves, either as harlots – or as wives (as such it was intended as a corrective to Pinero's *The *Second Mrs Tanqueray*). He also suggested, as Brecht does in *The *Threepenny Opera*, that illegal activities like prostitution merely reflect the acceptable exploitation of society by capitalism. But Shaw is not writing a political tract: the final confrontation between mother and daughter, whose priggishness prevents her becoming a tiresomely idealized figure, has considerable emotional power, which has assured the play continuing popularity.

Much Ado about Nothing (*Much adoe about Nothing*)

A: William Shakespeare **Pf**: *c.* 1598–99, London **Pb**: 1600 **G**: Com. in 5 acts; prose and some blank verse **S**: Messina, Renaissance period **C**: 14m, 4f, extras

Don Pedro, Prince of Arragon, helps Claudio woo Hero, daughter of the Governor of Messina. Don Pedro's villainous bastard brother Don John tries to prevent the match by faking an assignation with Hero, casting doubt on her chastity. Claudio confronts Hero at the wedding. She falls in a faint, and is later reported dead. Meanwhile, two courtiers, Beatrice and Benedick, who claim to despise each other, are manoeuvred by their friends into discovering their love for each other. Finally, the repentant Claudio weds Hero, who has been 'restored to life', and Benedick weds Beatrice, while news comes of the capture of Don John.

Because of the delight of what is essentially the sub-plot between Beatrice and Benedick, and with the hilarious interventions of the malapropistic Constable Dogberry, the main plot can easily become swamped in production.

Indeed, Berlioz's 1862 opera is entitled *Béatrice et Bénédict*. Compared with the romantic and chivalric behaviour of Claudio and Hero, based on an Italian source, the sparring of these lovers seems very modern. The wrongly accused woman, who appears to have died and so makes her accuser suffer regret, reappears with greater force in the figure of Hermione in *The *Winter's Tale*.

muerte y la doncella, La. See DEATH AND THE MAIDEN.

Mulatto

A: Langston Hughes **Pf:** 1935 **Pb:** 1963 **G:** Trag. in 2 acts **S:** The Big House, plantation in Georgia, 1930s **C:** 9m, 2f, 1 child (m)

Colonel Thomas Norwood, a rich plantation owner, has fathered several children with his long-suffering black housekeeper Cora Lewis. Two of his 'mulatto' children, Sallie and Robert, impress their father sufficiently for him to send them to be educated in the freer atmosphere of the north. When Sallie returns home, she is seduced by the Colonel's evil overseer Talbot. Robert is much less compliant than Sallie and now feels himself the equal of his white compatriots. However, when he demands of his father that he be treated as a white, the Colonel, furious at his son's perceived impudence, threatens to shoot him. Robert strangles his father, and, in order to avoid falling into the hands of a lynch mob, commits suicide.

Mulatto is notable as the first full-length play by an African-American writer to be performed on Broadway, where it ran for 373 performances, while it was banned in other cities because of its controversial depiction of so-called miscegenation. Sadly, despite its worthy intentions, this play by 'the Poet Laureate of Harlem' reinforces the stereotype of the primitive half-caste, who, like Abe in Green's **In Abraham's Bosom*, resorts to violence when pushed to his limits.

Murderer, Hope of Womankind (*Mörder, Hoffnung der Frauen*)

AT: *Murderer, Hope of Women/Women's Hope* **A:** Oskar Kokoschka **Pf:** 1909, Vienna **Pb:** 1910; rev. 1913, 1917 **Tr:** 1963 **G:** Drama in 1 act; German prose **S:** Battlefield with tower and cage, in the mythical past **C:** 1m, 1f, 2 choruses (m and f)

The Man, a warrior in ancient times, has defeated the Woman and her band of Amazonians. To seal his victory, he attempts to brand her with his sign, but she breaks free and wounds him in the side with a knife. He is taken to the tower and imprisoned in a cage, while his warriors mate with the women in an orgiastic frenzy. The Woman taunts him, pressing her body to the bars of the cage. When she releases him to couple with him, he treats her like a mother figure, seeking peace with her. She is frightened, because this appeal to her maternity saps her strength. She collapses, and the Man strides away, killing all in his path. In the 1917 version, a flame tears the tower open from top to bottom.

This curious piece has regularly been identified as one of the forerunners of Expressionism, although in fact its mythical setting and elemental conflicts belong more to neo-Romanticism. The violent confrontation between the sexes echoes the work of Strindberg, but is here taken from a domestic context to a universal plane, between the male principle of Eros (Love) and the female Thanatos (Death). The piece is intensely theatrical: it is unintelligible without the stage directions, and the dialogue is mere word-music that amplifies the visual elements. It thus fulfilled the great designer and director Craig's demand for a play that was 'incomplete anywhere except on the boards of a theatre'. Hindemith wrote an operatic version in 1921.

Murder in the Cathedral

A: T. S. Eliot **Pf:** 1935, Canterbury **Pb:** 1935 **G:** Drama in 2 acts and an interlude; free verse and prose **S:** Archbishop's Hall and Cathedral, Canterbury, Dec. 1170 **C:** 13m, chorus (f), extras

On 2 December 1170 Archbishop Thomas Becket is returning from seven years of exile in France after quarrelling with his former friend Henry II. The Chorus of Canterbury women have been drawn towards the Cathedral by some premonition of disaster. A messenger announcing the triumphant approach of Thomas warns three priests that Thomas is still not reconciled to his King. The Chorus, fearing the upheaval Thomas's return may bring, prays that he may return to France. Thomas arrives and predicts his own demise: 'End will be simple, sudden, God-given.' Thomas is visited by Four Tempters, who offer increasingly subtle rewards. The First urges him to return to the gaiety of his youth when he would carouse happily with Henry, but Thomas tells him he comes 20 years too late. The Second invites him to become Lord Chancellor again and wield political power, but Thomas insists it is more important to wield spiritual power. The Third Tempter suggests that Thomas should lead a revolt of the barons, but Thomas will not sink to treason. The Fourth Tempter offers the greatest reward: the glory of martyrdom. Reflecting that 'The last temptation is the greatest treason: | To do the right deed for the wrong reason,' Thomas prayerfully awaits his fate. In the Interlude Thomas holds his Christmas Day sermon, in which he exhorts his congregation to remember Christian martyrs, predicting that they may soon have a new one. On 29 December the Christmas festival is drawing to a close, when four Knights appear. Declaring their loyalty to the King, they denounce Thomas for his treachery and demand that he return to France. To all accusations Thomas replies that he is bound only by the law of Christ's Church and will now not abandon his flock. The Knights withdraw to dine. Terrified, the Chorus and Priests urge Thomas to fly and then bar the doors of the Cathedral, but Thomas insists that they should be thrown open. Witnessed by the Chorus, the Knights enter and murder Thomas. Immediately the four Knights step forward and justify their actions. The Priest and Chorus mourn Thomas but celebrate his martyrdom.

Eliot's best-known play and a classic of 20th-century British theatre is theatrically static, the only action being the killing of Thomas, and contains little conventional dramatic tension, since it is made obvious from the outset that Thomas is doomed. It employs the antiquated device of a chorus; the largely unnamed characters are not explored psychologically; and there are long passages of monologue. Yet the play still makes considerable impact. This is largely due to the ritualistic quality of the play, especially when, as at its premiere, it is performed by candlelight in a sacred building, and Eliot's verse with its sinewy clarity lends power to an experience that a mere plot summary can only hint at.

Murder in the Red Barn, The. See MARIA MARTEN.

Murder of Maria Marten, The. See MARIA MARTEN.

Musica Second Version (*La Musica deuxième*)

AT: *La Musica* A: Marguerite Duras Pf: 1985, Paris Pb: 1985 Tr: 1992 G: Drama in 1 act; French prose S: Entrance lounge of luxury hotel, northern France, *c.*1985 C: 1m, 1f

Two years after separating, 'She' (Anne-Marie Nollet, née Roche) and 'He' (Michel Nollet) meet in a hotel where they lived for the first three months of their marriage. He telephones reassuringly to his present partner, pretending to her that Anne-Marie is staying at another hotel. He is a moderately successful architect working in Paris; she now lives in Lübeck and is soon going to remarry and move to the States. They begin to analyse the agony of their failed marriage, sifting through their memories, and he learns for the first time that she attempted suicide when he asked for a divorce. She tells him too how she began her affair with her present partner when she went to Paris and visited a nightclub. She stayed on in Paris, and Michel bought a revolver to kill her with when she stepped off the train, but he relented. The actors pause, and the second version of *Musica* starts. Michel's mistress phones, and this time he tells her the truth. He begs Anne-Marie not to go to America, fearing he may never see her again and speaking of his continuing love for her, but she has lost hope of rediscovering their passion. She leaves the hotel, and goes out into the night.

This is a reprise of *La Musica* of 1965. Like the love between Anne-Marie and Michel, the play continued to haunt Duras, until she felt obliged to rewrite it. Like Cocteau's **Human Voice*, this is a disturbingly authentic account of the end of a relationship, here a love that was hell at the time, but from which there seems to be no escape. Memory ambushes rather than illuminates the former lovers: 'Don't you think it's strange that we remember so little?'

Mutter, Die. See MOTHER, THE.

Mutter Courage und ihre Kinder. See MOTHER COURAGE AND HER CHILDREN.

My Mother Said I Never Should
A: Charlotte Keatley **Pf:** 1987, Manchester **Pb:** 1988 **G:** Drama in 3 acts **S:** Manchester, Oldham, and London, 1940–87 **C:** 4f
The play focuses on four generations of mothers and daughters: Doris Partington, born 1900; Margaret Bradley; born 1931; Jackie Metcalfe, born 1952; Rosie Metcalfe, born 1971. Repeatedly, the four women play together as girls, each in their contemporary costume. 1940: Doris (40) and her daughter Margaret (9) prepare for an air raid. 1961: Jackie (9) visits her grandmother Doris (61). 1969: Jackie (17) rebels against her mother Margaret (38). 1961: Margaret (30) has a miscarriage. 1971: Jackie (19) has an illegitimate baby Rosie, and her mother Margaret (40) takes her away to bring her up as her own. 1951: Margaret (20) tells Doris (51) that she is going to marry an American Air Force pilot, live in London, and have a career. Jackie (27) goes to Margaret's for Rosie's eighth birthday. Rosie believes Jackie is her elder sister. 1982: Doris's husband has died, and the four generations of women clear up the family home with all its memories. 1987: Margaret (56) tells Doris (87) that her husband has left her. Rosie (15) and Jackie (34) return from holiday, and Rosie tells Margaret that she wants to live with Jackie. Margaret dies of stomach cancer, Rosie, on discovering that Jackie is her mother, is angry with her, and goes to live with Doris. Rosie celebrates her 16th birthday with Doris. 1923: Doris excitedly tells her mother that she is engaged.

In this intricately constructed piece, which makes great demands on the four actresses, Keatley offers a keenly observed and non-judgemental narrative of women in the 20th century, summed up by Doris: 'You expected too much. So did I. And Jackie expects even more.' The growing assertiveness of women is documented, applauded, but also recognized as being problematic.

My Name Is Lisbeth. See BLOOD RELATIONS.

My Son's Son. See DAUGHTER-IN-LAW, THE.

Mystère d'Adam, Le. See PLAY OF ADAM, THE.

Mystery-Bouffe (*Misteriya-Buff*)
A: Vladimir Mayakovsky **Pf:** 1918, Petrograd **Pb:** 1921 **Tr:** 1933 **G:** Drama in 6 acts, prologue, and epilogue; Russian prose, verse, and songs **S:** The Ark, hell, paradise, Land of Fragments, Promised Land, 20th c. **C:** 55m, 4f, extras
The Unclean, seven pairs of grimy workers, enter from the audience and tear down the front curtain, proclaiming: 'The land, swollen with blood, has given birth to us!' At the North Pole an international group of survivors speak of the new flood of the Bolshevik Revolution which has engulfed the world. However, Western politicians, the Clean, have commandeered an ark built by the Unclean. On the ark the Unclean are brutally oppressed, first by a tsar and then by a 'democratic' government of the Cleans – which is merely a 'tsar with a hundred mouths'. The Unclean throw them overboard and follow the Man of the Future towards an earthly paradise, which they will build for themselves. In hell the Unclean tell Beelzebub and his fellow devils that earthly torments are far worse than anything hell can offer. In paradise the Unclean condemn those who are venerated but who had unproductive lives, e.g. Rousseau and Tolstoy. God is so outraged that he threatens to destroy the Unclean, but they appropriate his thunderbolts to produce electricity. Entering the gate to the Promised Land, the Unclean are fed by Storegoods, brought to them by Hammer

and Sickle. The machines apologize for the harm they did the Unclean, explaining that they were exploited by the fat men but that they will now serve the workers. In a final triumphant chorus, workers, machines, and tools sing of the joyful revolution.

Combining in its title the allegorical medieval mystery play and the fun and theatricality of comic opera, *Mystery-Bouffe* was the first significant dramatic product of the 1917 Russian Revolution. Staged by Meyerhold in 1918 and in a revised form in 1921, it celebrated with spectacular pageant and charming if misplaced optimism the achievements and hopes of the young Soviet Union.

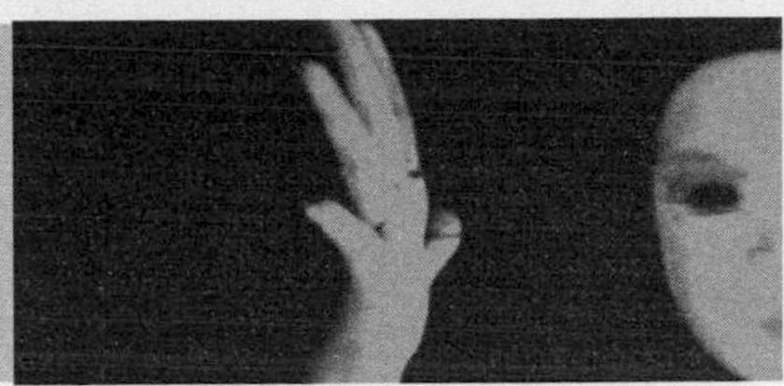

Na dne. See LOWER DEPTHS, THE.

Narrow Road to the Deep North

A: Edward Bond Pf: 1968, Coventry Pb: 1968 G: Drama in 2 acts S: Japan, late 17th–19th c. C: 16m, 4f

Basho, the great poet, journeying to the north of Japan to seek enlightenment, sees a baby abandoned by the riverside. Basho returns 30 years later to find a city where there was once only a village. It is ruled over by a cruel tyrant Shogo. Two years later, Basho is arrested and brought before Shogo, who orders him to bring up the child of the emperor he deposed. Basho, dismayed at Shogo's cruelty, conducts the tyrant's prime minister to a leader 'five times more ruthless than Shogo'. This is the Commodore, a British colonialist, who with his evangelical sister Georgina will invade the south and depose Shogo, with promises of restoring the infant Emperor to the throne. Shogo escapes, disguised as a priest. Georgina reorganizes the city and renders the populace submissive by converting them to Christianity. Shogo mounts a counter-attack, and unable to identify the young Emperor, kills all five children under Basho's protection, driving Georgina insane. The Commodore, using gunboats, regains control, and Shogo, who is revealed as the abandoned baby by the riverside, is brutally executed for his atrocity.

Subtitled 'a comedy', this minimalist almost cartoon-like version of 17th-century Japan combined with 19th-century British colonialism examines the interplay of power politics. The European concern with justice and order, coupled with missionary zeal, all supported by a ruthless army, are seen to be as oppressive and objectionable as the crude violence of the peasant-born tyrant. Bond rewrote the play in 1978 as *The Bundle*, transposing the action to modern Asia, and it could now usefully be employed as a commentary on the 2003 invasion of Iraq.

Når vi døde vågner. See WHEN WE DEAD AWAKEN.

Nathan the Wise (*Nathan der Weise*)

A: Gotthold Ephraim Lessing Pf: 1783, Berlin Pb: 1779 Tr: 1868 G: Drama in 5 acts; German blank verse S: Nathan's house, a town square, the Sultan's palace, monastery, and Sittah's harem, Jerusalem, *c.*1190 C: 7m, 3f, extras

Nathan, a rich and virtuous Jewish merchant, adopted a Christian orphan Recha, after his seven sons had been murdered by the Crusaders. Recha, unaware that she is adopted, is saved from a fire by the bravery of a young German Knight Templar, who has been captured by the Saracens. All attempts by the old Jew to reward the Templar by inviting him to his house are spurned, until a chance encounter moves the Templar to a more tolerant attitude. Meanwhile the Sultan Saladin, who had recaptured Jerusalem from the Christians, discusses his financial problems with his clever sister Sittah and decides to seek help from Nathan the Wise. Saladin asks Nathan which of the three religions, Christianity, Judaism, and Islam, is the true faith. Nathan answers with a parable: a valuable ring had been passed down from father to son, until one day it was to be bequeathed by a father who loved his three sons equally. He therefore had two more identical rings made, so that no son could ever know which was the original. Saladin's caravan arrives, and he is able to repay his debt to Nathan. By a series of astonishing revelations it is revealed that Recha is the Templar's sister and that the Templar is the long-lost nephew of Saladin. The play ends in general rejoicing, with members of the three faiths embracing.

This 'dramatic poem' was the first play in German to be written in Shakespearian blank verse, establishing a precedent for the verse dramas of Goethe, Schiller, and Kleist. Predictably banned during the Nazi period, this plea for religious tolerance, though clearly a product of the century of Enlightenment, still carries a powerful message in a world where bigotry derived from religious extremism continues to cause so much suffering.

Nedorosl. See MINOR, THE.

Nègres, Les. See BLACKS, THE.

Nephelai. See CLOUDS.

New Way to Pay Old Debts, A.

A: Philip Massinger **Pf:** *c.*1625, London **Pb:** 1633 **G:** Com. in 5 acts; blank verse and some prose **S:** Nottinghamshire, 1621 **C:** 15m, 5f, extras

Frank Wellborn is penniless through loose living and because his miserly uncle Sir Giles Overreach has cheated him out of his estates. His best friend Tom Allworth serves a noble soldier Lord Lovell, and is in love with Margaret, the young daughter of Sir Giles. Tom's mother Lady Allworth, a widow, agrees to pretend that she is being courted by Wellborn. When news of this gets back to Sir Giles, the old man hopes to get his hands on Widow Allworth's supposed wealth and encourages his nephew in his courtship, even making him a gift of £1,000. Meanwhile, Sir Giles hopes to marry Margaret to Lord Lovell, who is however interested only in promoting young Allworth's interests. By insisting on Margaret's getting married, Sir Giles mistakenly arranges for the secret wedding of his daughter to Tom Allworth. Lord Lovell is to marry Widow Allworth, and the documents proving his ownership of Wellborn's estates have disintegrated. All this drives Sir Giles mad, and he is taken off to Bedlam. Wellborn seeks a commission with Lord Lovell to fight for king and country.

Based in part on Middleton's *A *Trick to Catch the Old One* and in part on a historical Sir Giles who fled abroad in 1621 to avoid a trial for extortion, Massinger's play is a much more moral piece than Middleton's. The pretended object of the young debtor's wooing is here a virtuous widow not a courtesan, and it is much clearer here that Sir Giles deserves the harsh outcome that he endures. Massinger's play was hugely popular, being performed at least as often as Shakespeare's comedies, and attracting Garrick, Kemble, both Keans, Henry Irving, and others to the larger-than-life role of Sir Giles Overreach.

New York Idea, The

A: Langdon Mitchell **Pf:** 1906, New York **Pb:** 1906 **G:** Romantic com. in 4 acts **S:** New York, 1900s **C:** 9m, 6f

The dashing John Karslake and his pretty wife Cynthia are imbued with the 'New York idea' that marriage and divorce are matters not to be taken too seriously. Consequently, they have become divorced and now seek new partners. Cynthia becomes engaged to a pompous, conservative judge Philip Phillimore, while Karslake starts to develop an interest in the judge's divorced wife Vida, who is something of a maneater. Just before her wedding, however, Cynthia has second thoughts about marrying the boring judge. She fears that Karslake may marry Vida and rushes off to see him. To her great relief, the ex-wife has married an English ladies' man, and both she and Karslake realize how much they still love each other. Fortunately, their divorce is disallowed on a technicality, and they settle down happily to marriage together once more.

This was the most popular American comedy of its period and achieved international success. Its gently romantic plot offers persuasive insights into the competing attractions of marital congeniality and exciting new conquests, somewhat reminiscent of Shaw's **Candida.* As its title implies, it also offers a satirical view of New York high society, with its disregard for solid middle-class values. In 1916 Max Reinhardt directed it in Berlin as *Jonathans Tochter* (*Jonathan's Daughter*).

Next Time I'll Sing to You

A: James Saunders **Pf**: 1962, London **Pb**: 1963
G: Drama in 2 acts **S**: A theatre, *c.*1960 **C**: 4m, 1f

Meff, a casual joker, and Dust, more serious and pedantic, have arrived for the rehearsal of a philosophical play, but the director Rudge is late. They are joined by Lizzie, who claims that she is standing in for her identical twin sister, also called Lizzie. Rudge eventually arrives and plays a game of 'verbal cricket', while Lizzie wonders what she is doing amongst these eccentrics. When the Hermit arrives, the rehearsal can begin. The play is based on the life of Alexander James Mason, the Hermit of Great Canfield, Essex, who spent the last 36 years of his life alone in a hut almost without human contact. The Hermit wants to know more about his character, but Rudge's point is that his mind is unknowable. The Hermit insists that at least his story should be told with understanding. As the Hermit identifies more and more with his role, he turns Mason into a latter-day St Francis of Assisi, even though Mason had a pathetic long-distance relationship with Fanny Bell, an exploitative young girl many years his junior. Rudge denies that the Hermit's existence had any meaning: 'Its name is grief and it signifies – nothing.' The Hermit sobs himself into total silence.

Based on Raleigh Trevelyan's *A Hermit Disclosed*, this was James Saunders's most significant play. However, nothing dates so quickly as the avant-garde of yesteryear. Considered at the time to be audaciously metatheatrical (the critic Kenneth Tynan dubbed it 'Actors in search of a character'), it now seems wordy and self-conscious. Nevertheless, some of the dialogue is beautifully written, and its search for elusive identity remains of interest.

'Night, Mother

A: Marsha Norman **Pf**: 1983, NewYork **Pb**: 1983
G: Drama in 1 act **S**: Living room and kitchen of a house in the country, 1983 **C**: 2f

Jessie Cates is about 40 years old. She has a brother Dawson, who is married with children, but Jessie does not like her fastidious sister-in-law. Jessie has been married herself but is now separated from her husband Cecil. Their son Ricky never gets in touch and has had two prison sentences for robbery. Without knowing it, Jessie had inherited her father's epilepsy and suffered from minor seizures, until one day she fell while riding a horse, an activity she had taken up to please Cecil. The fall made her fits much more serious, and she became quite ill. After breaking up with Cecil, Jessie was encouraged to come and live with her mother. The action of the play takes place on the last evening of Jessie's life. In between organizing the household to carry on without her, Jessie calmly announces to her mother that she intends to commit suicide in a few hours. Mama pleads with her, reminds her that her medicine now has the epilepsy under control, tempts her with promises of future happiness, and says that she cannot manage without her. Serene in the face of death, Jessie remains resolute, goes to her bedroom after wishing ''Night, mother', locks her door, and shoots herself.

Winner of the Pulitzer Prize, *'Night, Mother* explores with gentle insight the relationship between mother and daughter. This is accomplished with convincing dialogue and no action apart from the pistol shot at the end. The play also investigates attitudes to death: on the one hand, Mama's natural terror of dying; on the other, the calm choice by Jessie, when, paradoxically she is at last in control of her life again, to go through the doorway to her death.

Night of the Iguana, The

A: Tennessee Williams **Pf**: 1959, Spoleto, Italy; 1961, New York **Pb**: 1962 **G**: Drama in 3 acts
S: Seaside hotel in Mexico, 1940 **C**: 8m, 6f

T. Lawrence Shannon is a 35-year-old former Episcopalian minister, defrocked for blasphemy and sexual misdemeanours, who now works as a tour guide. He arrives with a busload of Baptist women schoolteachers at a rundown hotel overlooking a beach, which is run by a sexy widow, Maxine Faulk. The ladies are displeased with Shannon for showing them the seamier side of Mexican life and for seducing Charlotte, one of the girls in the party. At the hotel there is a German family, overjoyed at Hitler's conquests in Europe, and a curious couple, a 97-year-old poet Jonathan (Nonno) Coffin and his spinster granddaughter Hannah Jelkes, a watercolourist. When one of the Baptist ladies gets Shannon fired, he goes berserk and has to be restrained by Maxine, who ties him into a hammock the way Mexicans tether iguanas to a tree to fatten them for eating. In a night-long talk, Hannah reveals to him her unfulfilled yearnings, and Shannon tells her of his loss of faith and utter disillusionment with life. The jealous Maxine comes to take Shannon off for a swim in the moonlight, and he agrees to stay with her in her hotel. Hannah's longings remain unfulfilled, and Nonno writes his last poem and dies.

After exploring sexual perversion and violence in many of his plays, this, Williams's last commercial success, is by comparison gentle and reflective in mood. It explores again the terrible isolation in which human beings (even the superficially jolly Baptist teachers) live, but his play, Williams asserts, shows 'how to live beyond despair and still live'.

Night's Lodging, A. See LOWER DEPTHS, THE.

99%. See FEAR AND MISERY OF THE THIRD REICH.

No Exit (*Huis Clos; Les Autres*)

AT: *In Camera; Vicious Circle* A: Jean-Paul Sartre Pf: 1944, Paris Pb: 1944 Tr: 1946 G: Drama in 1 act; French prose S: Room in hell, 1940s C: 2m, 2f

A servant ushers three people into the faded plush of what appears to be a hotel room. All three have recently died: Joseph Garcin, a South American pacifist journalist, who has been executed; Inès (or Inez) Serrano, a lesbian post-office assistant who has been gassed; and Estelle Rigault, who has died of pneumonia. Inès realizes that they have been locked together in this room with no exit and constant lighting, so that they will torture each other, a kind of self-service hell. They are tormented by glimpses of life on earth, and despite the pain of recalling the past, each confesses to his or her guilt: Garcin recalls how he made his loving wife serve him and his mistress coffee in bed. Inès seduced her cousin's wife; distraught, he was run over by a tram, and the wife gassed Inès and herself. Estelle had a daughter by her younger lover, and drove him to suicide when she murdered the infant. Estelle attempts to seduce Garcin, while Inès sneers at her pathetic passion. Garcin, who deserted the army, is haunted by his fear of being thought a coward, and pleads with Estelle to believe in his heroism. Her willingness to do so leaves him dissatisfied, because he knows that she is only trying to please him. In his desperation, Garcin suprisingly manages to open the door. Estelle urges him to throw Inès out, but he has to persuade Inès of his heroism, and claims that he died before he could accomplish his deeds. Inès remains unimpressed, and, when Estelle begins to make love to Garcin, Inès jeers: 'lovely scene: coward Garcin holding baby-killer Estelle in his manly arms!' Garcin, casting Estelle aside, now recognizes the true nature of hell: 'Hell is – other people!' Frustrated, Estelle tries to stab Inès with a paper knife, but fails, since she is dead already. They all laugh hysterically, and prepare to spend eternity torturing one another.

No Exit is Sartre's best-known play and one of the most-performed modern French plays. The philosophical dimension of the work now seems less important than it once did. The famous phrase: 'Hell is – other people' is at best unverifiable, at worst patently untrue. Moreover, post-Vietnam, Garcin's desertion of the army does not necessarily seem the shameful act that it must have been to an audience in occupied Paris. Nevertheless, the play survives well because of its nightmarishly claustrophobic setting and its relentless exploration of memory, jealousy, and desire. There is 'no exit' for these people, because, even when the door is open, they cannot contemplate the responsibility of being free. It is small wonder that Harold Pinter acknowledged his debt to this play.

Noises Off

A: Michael Frayn Pf: 1982, London Pb: 1982 G: Farce in 3 acts S: Stage set of an English country home in three different theatres, *c.*1980 **C:** 7m, 3f

'Mrs Clackett', 'a housekeeper of character', answers a telephone enquiry about the house. She breaks off: she is a famous but ageing actress Dotty Otley, rehearsing a play *Nothing On* that opens the following day under the direction of Lloyd Dallas. Estate agent 'Roger' enters with the attractive young 'Vicki' for a quick seduction and is surprised to find 'Mrs Clackett' at home. 'Philip' and 'Flavia Brent', the owners, arrive back home unexpectedly, and there is some delay to the rehearsal while doors are fixed, and an elderly alcoholic in the cast Selsdon Mowbray goes missing. Farcical complications in *Nothing On* ensue: 'Philip' loses his trousers, and a 'Burglar', played by Selsdon, turns out to be 'Vicki's' father. Tempers get frayed as the rehearsal continues into the early hours of the morning, especially as Lloyd is having an affair with both Brooke ('Vicki') and Poppy, the long-suffering Assistant Stage Manager. A month later, the play is on tour, seen now from backstage. Two of the actors are having a jealous row, and Lloyd arrives from London to calm Brooke, who is suffering from 'nervous exhaustion'. As the play is performed, a desperate mimed farce is played out by the actors backstage, culminating in Poppy's announcement that she is pregnant with Lloyd's child. At the final venue, the backstage dramas have spilt over into the play itself, with 'Mrs Clackett' and 'Flavia' continuing a row onstage. The performance develops into surreal chaos, ending with the wedding of Lloyd and Poppy.

This may well be the cleverest farce of the 20th century, written to the well-tried formula of misunderstandings, characters who narrowly avoid meeting, and disappearing props. A new level is added by the tensions that develop between the actors, so that theatre and real life become hilariously but disturbingly entangled.

No Man's Land

A: Harold Pinter **Pf:** 1975, London **Pb:** 1975 **G:** Drama in 2 acts **S:** Hirst's home, north London, 1970s **C:** 4m

Hirst and Spooner, two men in their sixties who have met in a pub, are drinking and conversing in a large room in Hirst's 'well but sparely furnished' home near Hampstead Heath. They exchange reminiscences, drunkenly and unenthusiastically rehearsing their moderate success as writers, and discussing their mothers, wives, and friends. Spooner even suggests that he may have seduced Hirst's wife. Eventually, Hirst is so drunk that he collapses on the floor and is led out by Briggs, one of his servants. Foster, a somewhat younger servant who at first claims to be Hirst's son, seems to resent Spooner's presence, switches off the lights, and locks the door, leaving Spooner alone in the dark. The next morning, Spooner is still alone in the room. Hirst reappears and behaves as though he has known Spooner for many years and denies that Spooner had an affair with his wife, although he, Hirst, may have seduced Spooner's wife. Finally, the conversation of the two men and the servants slows to a standstill, and Hirst, picking up on a comment by Hirst the previous evening, says: 'You are in no man's land. Which never changes, never grows older, but which remains forever, icy and silent.' Hirst answers: 'I'll drink to that.' The lights fade to darkness.

This play with virtually no action contemplates old age and the virtual death that precedes it with a bleakness reminiscent of Beckett. However, the recognizable domestic setting, the status games between the men, and the way in which memory is invoked and mistrusted is typical of Pinter. The premiere benefited from having Ralph Richardson playing Hirst and John Gielgud performing Spooner.

Non si paga! Non si paga! See CAN'T PAY? WON'T PAY!.

Non-Stop Connolly Show, The

A: Margaretta D'Arcy and John Arden **Pf:** 1975, Dublin **Pb:** 1977 **G:** Hist. drama in 6 parts (15 acts); prose and verse (mainly rhymed) **S:** Edinburgh, Ireland, and USA, 1868–1916 **C:** 3m, plus numerous smaller parts and extras

played at the premiere by 13m, 9f, several children
(1) *Boyhood 1868–1889.* James Connolly, born among the Irish in Edinburgh, can find no work, so joins the army and is sent to Ireland. He discovers Irish nationalism and international socialism. (2) *Apprenticeship 1889–1896.* Connolly, in Edinburgh once more, and married, seeks political office as a socialist and fails to find it; he seeks to earn a living and fails likewise. (3) *Professional 1896–1903.* In Dublin Connolly founds the Irish Socialist Republican Party. He disrupts the Royal Jubilee and leads his party in militant opposition to the Boer War. He clashes with the British Labour Party, members of the Socialist International, and with his own party. (4) *The New World 1903–1910.* Connolly emigrates to the USA, joins the Socialist Labor Party led by Daniel De Leon, but is frustrated by its doctrinaire sectarianism. He forms the Irish Socialist Federation among immigrants to the USA and becomes Organizer of the IWW (Industrial Workers of the World). Struggling against the odds in New York, he returns to Ireland. (5) *The Great Lockout 1910–1914.* There he meets James Larkin, who sends him to Belfast to organize the new Irish Transport Workers' Union. When Dublin employers impose the 'Great Lockout', Larkin, aided by Connolly, responds with a general strike. Without support from the British trade-union leadership, the strike collapses. The Irish Citizen Army and the Irish National Volunteers are formed. (6) *World War and the Rising 1914–1916.* Connolly sees international socialism collapse in the face of the outbreak of the First World War. He brings the Irish Citizen Army into the Easter Rising of 1916, is forced to surrender, and is executed.

In his Preface to *The *Workhouse Donkey* Arden spoke of his hopes for a 'casual or "prom-concert"' theatre, which would last all day. In this agitprop cycle, which runs for over 12 hours, he realized his dream. Written from an unashamedly Marxist viewpoint, D'Arcy and Arden portray the life of Connolly, 'the first working-class leader to enter the world conflict in the cause of Socialism', concentrating especially on the opposition between his revolutionary ideas and the reformist tendencies of contemporary Labour leaders.

No Place to Be Somebody

A: Charles Gordone **Pf:** 1969, New York **Pb:** 1969 **G:** Trag. in 3 acts; prose, verse, and songs **S:** Johnny's Bar, New York City, 1960s **C:** 11m, 5f

Johnny's Bar is starting up for the day, and his staff arrive: Shanty, a young white would-be drummer; Melvin, a young black would-be dancer; and three hostesses, Dee, Johnny's white girlfriend, Cora, Shanty's black girlfriend, and Evie. Gabe, a young black writer and actor, comes in and performs a black militant poem. Mary Lou, a white civil rights protester, comes in for a drink, and Johnny tells her to stay away from black politics. Sweets Crane, an elderly black who was 'like a father' to Johnny, is released from jail. Sweets steals off Gabe and off a small-time Mafia crook, then reveals that he is dying and is leaving all his considerable property to Johnny. Cora buys a drum kit for Shanty, but his playing is unimpressive. Johnny starts seeing Mary Lou, whose father is a judge; Johnny hopes that she can find information from her father that may stop a mafioso Pete Zerroni from forcing Johnny to close his bar. Dee, feeling rejected, blacks her face, then slashes her wrists and dies. Mary steals information from her father, which Johnny is in fact going to use to blackmail Zerroni, so that he can set up his own black mafia. Judge Bolton, who is in Zerroni's pay, comes to retrieve the stolen information, and in a shoot-out, Sweets gets killed. When Johnny insists that he will continue to fight the war against the whites, Gabe is provoked into killing him.

This first black play to win a Pulitzer Prize attempts to take on too many issues: the bar setting and unfulfilled dreams, like a reprise of O'Neill's *The *Iceman Cometh*; a B-movie theme about the corruption of the Mafia; questions raised about the relationships between blacks and whites and the legitimacy of using illegal methods in the liberation struggle; several emotional relationships; and the celebration of the delightfully unreformed character of Sweets.

Nora. See DOLL'S HOUSE, A.

Norman Conquests, The (Table Manners; Living Together; Round and Round the Garden)

A: Alan Ayckbourn Pf: 1973, Scarborough Pb: 1975 G: Trilogy of coms.; 2 acts each S: Dining room, sitting room, and garden of a rural Victorian English house, 1970s C: 3m, 3f

(1) *Table Manners*. On a Saturday evening in July, Sarah has come with her husband Reg, an estate agent, to his mother's home to give Reg's sister Annie a weekend off from caring for their (unseen) cantankerous invalid mother. It is assumed that Annie will go off with Tom, a vet who woos her lackadaisically. Norman, Annie's brother-in-law, a scruffy assistant-librarian who dreams of sexual conquests, also arrives. Sarah soon learns that Norman, having had sex with Annie the previous Christmas, now intends to take her away for a dirty weekend to East Grinstead (because Hastings is fully booked). Sarah is so morally indignant (and secretly jealous) that Annie agrees to stay on, while Norman gets drunk to console himself. The following morning, Ruth, Norman's wife and Annie's elder sister, arrives, having been summoned by Sarah, and finds the idea of Norman's abortive affair hilarious. That evening, Sarah insists that they should all sit down for Sunday dinner in a civilized manner. Norman looks grotesque in his late father-in-law's clothes, and an absurd scene of false manners ensues. The following morning, Norman suggests taking Sarah away to Bournemouth, but also promises Annie that they will one day get to East Grinstead.

(2) *Living Together*. The same events that occur in the dining room in *Table Manners* are re-enacted, but this time by characters in the sitting room. It is Saturday evening, slightly later than at the start of the trilogy: Reg, Sarah, and Norman have arrived at the house. Norman is supposedly due to go to a librarians' conference but claims it has been cancelled. Sarah confronts Norman over his plans to have a dirty weekend with Annie. Annie apologizes to Norman for backing off, and Tom tries to find out from Norman where he's going wrong in his courtship of Annie. Norman gets drunk on home-made wine and falls asleep on the floor. After dinner, Reg insists that they play a dreadful game that he has invented. Norman awakes and tries drunkenly to phone his wife Ruth. On Sunday evening, Ruth expresses her regrets about coming to the house. Norman sneaks an embrace with Annie but is discovered by Sarah. As the two squabble over Norman, Ruth enters and insists that Norman come to bed with her. Instead, he takes her on the hearthrug. The following morning, Norman begs Ruth to take the day off work. Sarah and Annie are shocked at Ruth's sleeping with Norman. Sarah tells Reg that she would like to get away to Bournemouth for a weekend.

(3) *Round and Round the Garden*. The same events are re-enacted by characters in the garden. It is Saturday evening before any of the guests have arrived. Tom has come to say goodbye to Annie. Norman arrives unexpectedly early, and Annie begs him to wait for her in the village until after Reg and Sarah have settled in. Unfortunately, Reg and Sarah arrive before Norman can get away. Sarah announces that Annie will not be going away after all. On Saturday evening, after his drunken phone call to Ruth, Norman is helped into the garden to sober up. He and Sarah end up kissing passionately. When Sarah goes, Annie comes to apologize again about the ruined weekend and invites Norman to her room. On Sunday morning after breakfast, Sarah cannot believe how indifferent Ruth is. Ruth attempts to provoke Tom into some display of emotion, which leads to a jealous row between Tom and Annie. On Monday morning, there is a frosty leave-taking, and Norman contrives to smash his car into Reg's, so that no one can leave. Ruth suspects him of doing it deliberately in order to prolong his 'conquests', but all three women turn their backs on him, as he shouts: 'I only wanted to make you happy.'

Ayckbourn is frequently compared to Chekhov, who offers the same tolerant amusement at the foibles of humanity. As Ayckbourn wrote in his Preface to *The Norman*

Conquests: 'the more fond of people I become, the more amusing I tend to find them'. In this deft interweaving of the same events viewed from different locations, Ayckbourn looks deeply into the clumsy way in which we relate to each other, exemplified by the ambiguous figure of Norman, well meaning but inept.

No Sugar

A: Jack Davis **Pf**: 1985, Perth, Australia **Pb**: 1986 **G**: Drama in 4 acts; English and Nyoongarah (Aboriginal) **S**: Northam, Perth, and Moore River Reserve, Western Australia, 1929–34 **C**: 12m, 8f

Everyone in Northam in Western Australia is feeling the effects of the Depression, including the cheery, rough Munday family, Aborigines confined to their reserve. Auber Octavius Neville, Chief Protector of Aborigines, is having difficulty finding a suitable location for a new reserve. Jimmy Munday and his brother-in-law Sam are found in possession of alcohol and are locked up. Three years later, Neville removes all the Aborigines from Northam to another reserve at Moore River, falsely claiming that they have skin disease. Moore River is run by a lecherous Superintendent, who threatens the happiness of the young lovers Joe and Mary, who decide to run away. Joe fights off the man sent to recapture them, and they arrive at the reserve in Northam, which is now burned to the ground. They are taken into custody by the Northam police, while Neville addresses the Historical Society on the mistreatment of Aborigines in the past. Mary, now pregnant, is brought back to Moore River, where she is beaten by Neal. On Australia Day 1934, Neville is given an official reception, which is undermined by an angry tirade by Jimmy, who collapses and dies. Mary gives birth to a boy, and Joe returns. They are allowed to leave on condition that they do not return to Northam. They pack up and leave for Northam.

Davis is the major Aboriginal playwright, who here documents the resilience and defiance of native Australians during the oppressive so-called 'Protection' laws of the 1930s. The title refers not only to the lack of luxuries enjoyed by the Aborigines, but also to their anger ('sugar catches more flies than vinegar', but they are in no mood to offer sweetness). After success in Perth and Vancouver (where a similar play on Native Canadians, Ryga's *The *Ecstasy of Rita Joe*, had been premiered), *No Sugar* was seen in London in 1988.

Not I

A: Samuel Beckett **Pf**: 1972, New York **Pb**: 1973 **G**: Monodrama in 1 act **S**: Darkened bare stage, indeterminate period **C**: 1m, 1f

At the back of a darkened stage, only a Mouth is visible. Downstage stands the Auditor, cloaked in black, who listens intently to the Mouth and three times raises his arms in a gesture of compassion. Even before and after the curtain, the Mouth is heard speaking. When the curtain rises, a flood of disjointed phrases become audible. In essence, the Mouth describes how she was born and lived an uneventful life. Perhaps because of some trauma, she is unable to speak. She is perhaps simple-minded. She finds herself in court at one point. Then at the age of 60 or 70, her mind starts to work differently (has she died?), and from being virtually mute, she is now unable to stop the ceaseless flow of words.

Beckett was constantly pushing towards more and more abstraction in the theatre, a difficult task when faced with flesh-and-blood actors. In **Happy Days* and **Play*, he reduced the performer to a motionless head. Here he goes one stage further and offers only the mouth in this brief torrent of words.

N-Town Cycle of Mystery Plays, The

AT: *Ludus Coventriae; The Coventry Mystery Plays; The Hegge Plays* **A**: Anon. **Pf**: Late 15th c., various English towns, including Lincoln **Pb**: 1922 **G**: Cycle of 40 mystery plays; Middle English (East Anglian dialect) verse **S**: Heaven and earth, from the Fall of Lucifer to the Last Judgement **C**: approx. 50m, 5f, many extras

Based on the one manuscript, there are approximately 40 plays, which closely follow the sequence of events in *The *York Cycle*. Major omissions, however, are any plays dealing with the Israelites in Egypt, while additions are *The Tree of Jesse* and those uniquely dealing with the early life of Mary, including her conception and betrothal.

Long thought to be a cycle of mystery plays staged in the city of Coventry or possibly Lincoln, this manuscript is now regarded as being a collection of plays to be performed, probably on stationary platforms, in different locations in the Midlands. *N-Town* is derived from the banns, which did not specify the town, but simply referred to 'N.town', requiring the name of the venue to be inserted, while Hegge refers to the first known owner of the manuscript. In tone these plays keep emphasizing the redemptive and merciful quality of God and contain little of the robust humour of the three major cycles (**York, *Chester, *Towneley). So, for example, instead of the usual wrangling between Noah and his wife, she is here shown to be as pious as he.*

Nubes. See CLOUDS.

Number, A.

A: Caryl Churchill **Pf**: 2002, London **Pb**: 2002
G: Drama in 5 scenes **S**: Salter's home, *c.*2000
C: 2m, playing 4m

Salter, in his early sixties, is talking to his son Bernard (B2), 35. He is horrified to learn that his son has been cloned a number of times, and threatens to sue the hospital doctors responsible for damaging Bernard's uniqueness, weakening his identity. However, Bernard is concerned that he is perhaps not the original. Salter admits that when his wife and 4-year-old son died in a car crash, he wanted to replace his son. Salter explains to the original Bernard (B1), who is 40, that he had him cloned but had no idea so many would be created. B2 has met B1, and now tells Salter that he is 'a nutter'. Salter admits that his wife threw herself under a train when his son was 2, and he later sent him to be cloned. B2 fears B1 may kill him. Salter asks B1 how he murdered B2. Salter meets Michael Black, 35, a perfect clone of Bernard. He is a mathematics teacher, married with three children. Michael seems quite relaxed about being a clone, but Salter mourns the death of his two Bernards (the original has committed suicide). Michael points out that all humans share 99 per cent of the same genes, and admits that he likes his life.

A Number is arguably the most important play to date of the new millennium. In a series of skilfully written duologues, Churchill grasps the nettle of the scientific possibility that human beings may be cloned, and. by doing so, debates the nature of identity. In Michael's optimistic conclusion that he is happy to be 30 per cent genetically the same as a lettuce, Churchill puts into perspective the contemporary obsession with individuality.

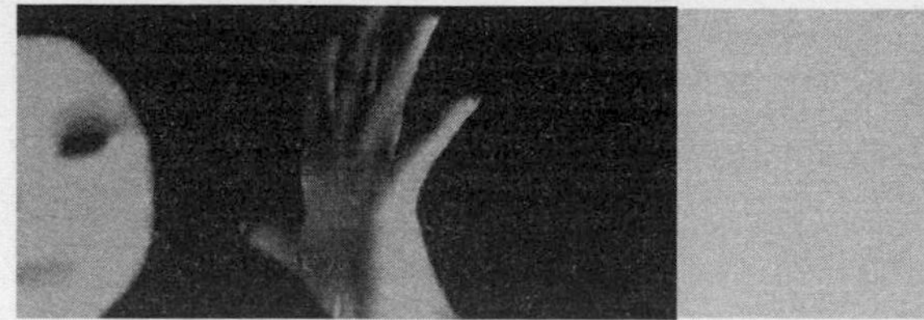

O

O! Temperance

A: Mervyn Thompson **Pf:** 1972, Christchurch, New Zealand **Pb:** 1984 **G:** Hist. drama in 2 acts; prose with songs **S:** Meeting hall, New Zealand, 1919 **C:** 10m, 4f, many extras

At a meeting on the eve of the 1919 licensing poll, temperance workers campaign for prohibition of alcohol and re-enact episodes from the history of the Temperance Movement. A Witness tells how he succumbed to drink and lost his health, security, and happiness. Observing how a drinking companion turned from his wife and dying child, the Witness is reformed and now lives joyously with the abandoned wife. Reviewing the corruption of alcohol in colonizing New Zealand, its effect on Maori and workers is described, alcoholism becoming the new country's worst social evil. The Temperance Movement, with a strong women's presence, grows during the 1880s and 1890s. The women gain the vote, and a bill controlling the sale of alcohol is passed in 1893. Where total prohibition is introduced, there is 'a wonderful difference'. Elsewhere, the police are corrupt in their enforcement of the licensing laws. Tommy Taylor becomes the voice of temperance in Parliament, but dies unexpectedly in 1911; 45,000 people line the streets for his funeral. Despite the government insisting on a 60% majority to introduce prohibition, the necessary votes are achieved in the 1919 poll. However, after strenuous campaigning amongst New Zealand troops abroad, the decision is reversed. Today, despite an estimated annual cost to the nation of $500 million from excessive alcohol consumption, the Temperance Movement is barely remembered.

Thompson, one of New Zealand's most successful contemporary playwrights and directors, documents an almost forgotten aspect of New Zealand history. At the same time, *O! Temperance* is a vigorously entertaining show based on revivalist meetings, full of fervour and sentimentality, but also throwing down a challenge to the audience.

Observe the Sons of Ulster Marching towards the Somme

A: Frank McGuinness **Pf:** 1985, Dublin **Pb:** 1986 **G:** Hist. drama in 4 acts **S:** Ulster, *c.*1980 and *c.*1915; the Somme battlefield, 1916 **C:** 9m

Kenneth Pyper, an Ulster veteran of the First World War, reminisces about the War and compares it to contemporary violence in Ulster: 'Why we let ourselves be led to extermination? In the end, we were not led, we led ourselves.' Eight Ulster volunteers assemble in a barracks on a training camp: they are all determined to fight for Ulster and turn on Crawford, when he is suspected of being Catholic. Pyper, a mad, rebellious character, deliberately cuts his hand and holds it up as the Red Hand of Ulster. On leave from the War, the eight men pair off: two row out to an island together; two pray in a Protestant church; one challenges his partner to cross a rope-bridge; two Belfast men, who missed the Orange parade, now march to 'The Field'. The groups then intermingle as though in a dream, and Pyper, a former sculptor, especially becomes aware of the burden of tradition weighing on them all: 'my hands . . . were not mine but the hands of my ancestors, interfering'. Waiting in a trench for the Battle of the Somme to begin, the men re-enact the Battle of the Boyne, and, disturbingly, King James 'wins'. Donning orange sashes, the men go into battle. Only Pyper survives.

It is remarkable that a Southern Irish Catholic should write arguably the finest play to celebrate the bravery of Northern Irish Protestants. McGuinness's play tellingly relates the devastation of the First World War to contemporary events in Ireland, and the piece was revived by the Abbey Theatre in 1994 as a contribution to the Peace Process. Even outside its immediate political context, the play's potent language and effective time-shifts deservedly made it the winner of many awards.

Occupations

A: Trevor Griffiths **Pf:** 1970, Manchester **Pb:** 1972 **G:** Pol. drama in 7 scenes **S:** Hotel room and factory, Turin, 1920 **C:** 6m, 2f

In the early days of Communism, Kabak is sent from Moscow in response to the workers' occupation of the Fiat motor-car factories in Turin, led by the activist Antonio Gramsci. He has in his care an unreformed Russian émigrée, Angelica, who is addicted to cocaine and is dying. Gramsci is a popular leader, encouraging proletarian revolution in a way that is coloured by dangerously optimistic idealism. Kabak is the steely emissary from the Comintern sent to place a proto-Stalinist check on the workers' subversion. To Gramsci, Kabak's intervention seems like betrayal; to Kabak, his firmness is essential to prevent the workers sliding into dangerous anarchy and thus delaying the hoped-for national revolution, which has to be worked for in a painstakingly disciplined fashion. Kabak therefore reaches an agreement with Valetta, the factory-owner, and the workers' strike collapses. Kabak leaves for Moscow, abandoning Angelica.

Griffiths's first full-length play for the stage was written 'as a sort of Jacobinical response' to the failure of the 1968 student revolt in France. Griffiths recognized that capitalism was not generally perceived as 'an irreducible, inescapable ugliness', and that romantic gestures of revolt would not suffice to dislodge it. While emotionally it is easier to empathize with the dashing Gramsci, intellectually one has to recognize that Kabak's insistence on discipline is a necessary prerequisite for revolution. As with Dorst's **Toller*, the audience must consider whether such harsh discipline is worth the cost.

Octoroon, The

AT: *Life in Louisiana* **A:** Dion Boucicault **Pf:** 1859, New York **Pb:** 1859 **G:** Melodrama in 5 acts **S:** Terrebonne plantation and Mississippi wharf, Louisana, 1850s **C:** 11m, 8f, extras

George Peyton is hoping to inherit the Terrebonne plantation from his aunt Mrs Peyton, although the extravagance of her late husband forced him to mortgage half to a villainous overseer, Jacob M'Closky, and to entrust the other half to the honest but incompetent Salem Scudder. Dora Sunnyside, a wealthy heiress, loves George, but he is attracted to the beautiful octoroon Zoe. On learning that Mrs Peyton is hoping to receive money owing to her, M'Closky murders Paul, the slave carrying the hoped-for banker's draft, and steals it. So the estate has to be auctioned, and Mrs Peyton begs George to marry Dora and save the property, but he cannot deny his feelings for Zoe. Zoe, however, is declared legally to be a slave and therefore must be auctioned with the estate. Dora's father buys the estate, but M'Closkey outbids everyone for Zoe, after whom he lusts. An Indian is almost lynched for Paul's murder, but a photographic plate is discovered which proves M'Closky's guilt. He is arrested, but makes his escape by setting a river boat on fire. He is recaptured, and news of his guilt is brought to Terrebonne, but too late, since Zoe has taken poison and dies in George's arms.

Staged just two years before the outbreak of the American Civil War, this melodrama is notable for its anti-slavery message. Boucicault based the central story on Mayne Reid's novel *The Quadroon*, but makes the race laws even more absurd by showing the regal Zoe to be an outcast for possessing a mere eighth of 'foreign' blood. In a telling denunciation, the honest Scudder describes the lynch mob as 'a circle of hearts, white with revenge and hate.... It is such scenes as these that bring disgrace upon our Western life.' The piece is also notable for being the first to use photographic evidence to prove guilt.

Odd Couple, The

A: Neil Simon **Pf:** 1965 **Pb:** 1966 **G:** Com. in 3 acts **S:** Oscar Madison's Manhattan apartment, 1960s **C:** 6m, 2f

Oscar Madison is a sports writer, an easygoing slovenly divorcee, who is having problems with his ex-wife over alimony payments, and who regularly hosts poker games in his apartment. Felix Ungar is late for the game, and when he eventually arrives, is distraught because his wife has thrown him out. Oscar offers to share his apartment with Felix – an arrangement that is less than satisfactory, because, although Felix cooks and cleans, his obsessive tidiness gets on Oscar's nerves. When they invite Gwendoline and Cecily Pigeon, two Englishwomen from the apartment above, to dinner, Oscar arrives late, and the sisters are annoyingly attracted by the unhappiness of the 'sensitive' Felix. Oscar tells Felix to leave, and then fears that he may commit suicide. However, Felix happily moves in with the Pigeons. Thanks to Felix's good management, Oscar is now able to pay off his alimony, and the friends meet as usual for their game of poker – but Oscar warns them not to flick ash on the floor.

Arguably the most popular of Neil Simon's many comedies, *The Odd Couple* has been performed all over the world and made into a television series and a successful film (with Walter Matthau, who created the stage role, as Oscar, and Jack Lemmon as Felix). The strength of the piece derives from the skilfully drawn characters, not just the contrasting protagonists, but also the other four friends, each with an individual quirk. In 1985, Simon rewrote it for a female cast, with the sisters from upstairs becoming Latin American brothers.

Oedipus

A: Lucius Annaeus Seneca **W:** AD 25–65 **Tr:** 1563 **G:** Latin trag. in 5 acts; verse **S:** The palace at Thebes, in the mythical past **C:** 6m, 2f., chorus (m)

The city of Thebes is devastated by the plague, and its king, Oedipus, himself has a sense of foreboding, since he is fated to kill his father and marry his mother. Creon arrives with a message from the oracle at Delphi that the killer of the former king, Laius, must be brought to justice. The seer Tiresias performs a sacrifice of a bull and a heifer in order to learn more, and then decides to summon Laius' ghost to give testimony. Creon reports that Laius' ghost has accused Oedipus of his murder. Oedipus accuses Creon of engineering a conspiracy to overthrow him and has him arrested. A messenger arrives to tell Oedipus that his supposed father has died. Since Oedipus is reluctant to return to his mother for fear of incest, the messenger reveals that Oedipus was a foundling and not her child. A shepherd confirms his story and identifies the real mother of the foundling as Oedipus' wife Jocasta. Horrified to learn the truth, Oedipus decides that suicide would be too easy an option and tears his eyes out of their sockets with his bare hands. Jocasta plunges a sword into her polluted womb, and Oedipus stumbles off blindly, calling on the Fates, Disease, and Pain to be his guides.

Although based on Sophocles' play written some 500 years previously, and retelling the same story, Seneca's tragedy has a quite different character. Instead of the mounting dramatic tension of the Greek original, Seneca's piece is more like a dramatic poem – indeed, it is quite possible that Seneca's plays were never performed in ancient Rome but merely offered as recitals. Here Oedipus lacks the blithe confidence of the Sophoclean hero, already declaring at the start that 'Fate is preparing . . . some blow for me'. The choral interludes offer linguistic embellishment rather than commenting on the action. Seneca's achievement lies less in the dramatic structure than in his powerful use of language, which was to be very influential on Renaissance dramatists and helped to engender the violent excesses of many Elizabethan and Jacobean plays, most notably Shakespeare's **Titus Andronicus*. In philosophical terms, Seneca reproduces none of the moral dilemma of

Sophocles (a virtuous man who commits evil in the very act of trying to avoid it). In Seneca, all is fated, there can be no escape. The only nobility rests in the fact that man can outdo the gods in their suffering. By causing his mother's death, Oedipus endures even more than Apollo has foretold. With a huge golden phallus as its centrepiece, Peter Brook directed a memorable production of *Oedipus* in a version by Ted Hughes in 1968.

Oedipus at Colonus (*Oidipous epi Kolonoi; Oedipus Coloneus*)

A: Sophocles Pf: 401 BC, Athens Tr: 1729 G: Greek drama in verse S: Countryside near Colonus, in the mythical past C: 6m, 2f, extras, chorus (m)

Ever since the terrible discovery of his guilt that he killed his father and married his mother, the blind Oedipus has been wandering in exile, guided by his faithful daughter Antigone. At last he comes to a grove of the Eumenides, and here learns to his delight that he is near Colonus, where an oracle has foretold that he will at last find rest. However, Creon arrives from Thebes, demanding that Oedipus should return, as a prophecy has warned that there will be no peace in the city if Oedipus is not buried there. Oedipus refuses to return, and Creon's attempts to take him by force are thwarted by Theseus, the Athenian king, who has promised to protect Oedipus. Polyneices, Oedipus' son, now arrives, begging forgiveness from his father and seeking Oedipus' help in recapturing the city of Thebes. Once again Oedipus remains adamant. The moment of his death approaches, and, accompanied by Theseus, he leaves, gently to meet his end.

Oedipus at Colonus was Sophocles' last play, performed after his death, and is untypical of his work in that the plot consists of a series of episodes rather than in concentrated action. It could also hardly be described as tragic in any conventional sense, since Oedipus' progress in the play is from pathetic old man, ridden with guilt, to a figure of power, courted by his former enemies, and an enlightened being who joyfully embraces his mystical death. The theme was explored by T. S. Eliot in *The Elder Statesman* (1958) and in a musical version in Lee Breuer's *Gospel at Colonus* (1983).

Oedipus the King (*Oidipous tyrannos; Oedipus tyrannus*)

AT: *King Oedipus; Oedipus Rex* A: Sophocles Pf: *c.*429–420 BC, Athens Tr: 1715 G: Greek trag. in verse S: The city of Thebes, in the mythical past C: 7m, 2f, extras, chorus (m)

Because the city of Thebes is suffering from a plague, its king Oedipus has sent Creon to consult the oracle of Apollo at Delphi. The oracle declares that the plague will be lifted only when the city rids itself of an unclean person, the killer of the former king Laius. Oedipus strenuously attempts to identify the criminal. While his queen Jocasta begs him not to dig too deep into the past, Oedipus reveals that the same oracle had prophesied to him that he would murder his father and marry his mother. However, he feels safe in the knowledge that he abandoned his parents in Corinth, so as to avoid fulfilling the prophecy. On his way to Thebes he had killed an old man and now fears that this man might indeed be Laius. Far worse is to follow: news comes that his 'father' has died in Corinth, but that Oedipus was adopted as a foundling. He had been set out on a mountain to die, in an attempt by Laius to thwart a similar prophecy. When it is finally revealed that Oedipus murdered his own father and has been living in incest with his mother Jocasta, she hangs herself. Oedipus stabs out his eyes and prepares to go into exile once more.

One of the most important plays of world theatre, Sophocles' *Oedipus*, greatly admired by Aristotle, is full of tragic irony and is a model of analytic plot structure, in which the past is gradually revealed with cataclysmic effect in the present. It is often mistakenly assumed that Oedipus is a totally innocent victim, a plaything of the gods. However, in his retelling of this well-known myth, Sophocles carefully motivates Oedipus' original visit to the oracle by reference to a drunk who tells Oedipus that he is adopted. With his parentage in doubt, Oedipus acts foolishly by running away and trying to prevent the oracle being fulfilled. Moreover, he has never asked about the fate of the former king, his wife's former husband. He, Jocasta, and the Thebans have been living a lie – and the plague is the result. Indeed, because of a prophecy to Laius that his son would kill him, Oedipus as a baby is mutilated and put out to die. It is impossible to flout the oracle: the will of the gods is inexorable, but Laius and Oedipus help to bring it about, through a hubristic lack of piety. That Oedipus is so terribly punished is unfair, but Sophocles knew that the world does not operate according to human notions of justice. As the classical scholar Gilbert Murray said, the Greek hero is like a man who drinks untreated water during a typhoid outbreak. He is not wicked, merely foolish, but is nevertheless terribly punished. While preserving the traditional form of Greek tragedy, Sophocles' innovation of a third speaking character is especially effective here. As Oedipus probes for the truth from the Messenger, his wife/mother Jocasta tries to prevent him from hurtling towards his doom, thus increasing the tension of the scene. *Oedipus* has provided the source for many later versions, notably by Seneca, Tasso (*King Torrismondo*, 1586), Dryden (1678), Voltaire (1718), Hofmannsthal (1910), Yeats (1926), Cocteau (*The *Infernal Machine*), Berkoff (*Greek*, 1980), Anouilh (1986), and was used by Sigmund Freud in his formulation of the 'Oedipus complex'.

Offending the Audience (*Publikumsbeschimpfung*)

AT: *Tongue-Lashing* **A:** Peter Handke **Pf:** 1966, Frankfurt/Main **Pb:** 1966 **Tr:** 1968 **G:** Drama in 1 act; German prose **S:** Bare stage, 1966 **C:** 4m or f

The audience is ushered into the theatre with even more formality than usual, and those whose clothing is too casual are to be refused admittance. When the curtain rises, the stage is empty but for four speakers, who, after initially ignoring the audience, begin to address them directly. At first, the speakers destroy any illusions the audience might have about the nature of the piece. They then make statements about the relationship of the audience to the stage: they even congratulate the spectators on being so lifelike, such good performers. In the final section they intersperse insults among the compliments, rising to a crescendo of abuse. Finally, thanking the audience for being 'perfect', the curtain falls only to rise again immediately while boisterous taped applause is fed into the auditorium.

Never in the history of the theatre had a play, and a first play at that, so totally rejected all the normal expectations of a drama, making **Waiting for Godot* seem conventional by comparison. The young Austrian Handke here offers a 'speech play' without plot, characters, scenery, or even actors, 'a prologue to future theatre visits' that challenges the 'thoughtless thinking' of the public. The surprise of the piece, like that of a practical joke, can occur only once, and depends on the formality of conventional theatregoing and on received notions about drama. In a village hall or in a postmodernist context, what once seemed explosive now looks like a wet squib.

Of Mice and Men

A: John Steinbeck **Pf:** 1937, New York **Pb:** 1937 **G:** Trag. in 3 acts **S:** Farm in the Salinas Valley, California, 1930s **C:** 9m, 1f

Lennie Small is a strongly built, simple-minded itinerant farm worker who arrives at the Boss's farm in the company of his protective friend George Milton. Lennie is repeatedly getting into trouble, because, although he always tries to be gentle, his massive strength and clumsiness frighten people. Right now he and Gerorge are on the run, because Lennie's stroking a woman's dress was misinterpreted as attempted rape. Lennie and George dream of having their own farm, where Lennie could tend the animals, which he loves with touching tenderness. When his tart of a wife flirts with Lennie, the Boss's vicious son Curley attacks him, and retires with his hand crushed. The wife visits Lennie in his barn, where he is hiding a puppy that he has accidentally squeezed to death, and he begins to caress her.

She objects to his 'mussing up her hair', and, in his desperate desire to placate her, Lennie accidentally kills her. George manages to divert the lynch mob assembled to take their revenge, calms Lennie with talk of their dream farm, and mercifully shoots him.

Not since Büchner's **Woyzeck* had a play offered such a sympathetic portrayal of a simple-minded protagonist. Based on his novel of the same name, Steinbeck presents an image of the Depression, with its rootless migrant workers, dreaming of amassing enough money to settle down. In Lennie's case, such an environment might contain his homicidal clumsiness, but the audience's certainty of impending disaster creates a dramatic tension based on the awareness that tragedy will strike long before their dream can be realized.

Oh What a Lovely War

A: Charles Chilton and Theatre Workshop under Joan Littlewood **Pf:** 1963, London **Pb:** 1965 **G:** Hist. drama in 2 acts; prose and songs **S:** Pierrot show portraying events in Europe, 1914–18 **C:** 11m, 4f

The Pierrots introduce themselves with songs and jokes, and the Master of Ceremonies announces 'the ever-popular War Game'. Using news panels, slides, and contemporary songs, the history of the First World War is told. 1914: Britain, France, and Germany prepare for war. Archduke Ferdinand is shot, and the nations use this as a pretext to rush into war. Troops are mobilized, and Belgium is invaded. Recruits are drilled, and French, British, and Belgian generals talk at cross-purposes. The first wounded are brought home, while a sentimental song is sung. During the first Christmas, British and German troops leave their trenches to fraternize. 1915: general conscription is introduced. On a shoot in Scotland international arms manufacturers boast about their profits, while men die in the trenches. 1916: at an elegant party in London, the smart set, amongst them Sir Douglas Haig, indulge in political infighting. As Haig delivers a patriotic speech, the news panel records the loss of half a million men at Verdun. Some Irish soldiers push forward so far that they are shelled by their own artillery. Mrs Pankhurst pleads for peace. Suicidal attacks are launched on the German lines. 1917: still stalemate, as the battlefields become a sea of mud. 1918: the warring nations all look forward to victory, and the soldiers advance, baa-ing like sheep.

In this collectively devised piece, Joan Littlewood with her left-wing Theatre Workshop members created one of the most powerful commentaries on the First World War. By juxtaposing popular song with the horrors of war, the empty optimism of the leaders with mass slaughter, and the profits made by the Establishment with the realities of trench warfare, the piece does not offer a balanced view (no mention of the colossal contribution by capitalist USA, for example) but provides satirical entertainment of the highest order.

Oidipous epi Kolonoi. See OEDIPUS AT COLONUS.

Oidipous tyrannos. See OEDIPUS THE KING.

Oiseau bleu, L'. See BLUE BIRD, THE.

Old Cantankerous. See BAD-TEMPERED MAN, THE.

Old Lady Says 'No!', The

AT: *Shadowdance* **A:** Denis Johnston **Pf:** 1929, Dublin **Pb:** 1932 **G:** Drama in 2 parts with choral interludes; prose with some verse and songs **S:** Dublin, 1803, and 1920s **C:** 10m, 10f

A Speaker representing Robert Emmet on the night of his failed rebellion of 1803 gives stirring speeches about Irish nationalism and delays his escape while he bids farewell to his fiancée. He is arrested by English soldiers, in the course of which the Speaker is wounded in the head. A doctor is called from the audience to attend to him. The Speaker begins to dream of mustering his men, who whisper jumbled phrases in rhythm. He then meets the 18th-century nationalist politician Henry Grattan, interspersed with scenes from 1920s Dublin: passers-by fussing over trivialities, Cathleen ni Houlihan reduced to selling flowers, a republican political meeting, a guided tour to the scene of Emmet's arrest. The second part opens in a drawing room, where a number of modern Irish notables are gathered. The

Speaker/Emmet joins the party and is dismayed by their hypocrisy and materialism. After a dance by Shadows 'coming to dance at a wake', the Speaker/Emmet gives a final rousing speech and falls asleep as the Doctor covers him with a blanket.

Influenced by Kaufman and Connelly's *Beggar on Horseback* (1924) and Josef Čapek's *The Land of Many Names* (1923), this was one of the earliest ventures by Irish theatre into Expressionism. This first play by Denis Johnston was considered stylistically too adventurous by Lady Gregory at the Abbey Theatre. This may explain the title, although it can equally be understood as disapproval of contemporary Ireland by the mythical figure of Cathleen ni Houlihan. With bold staging and some updating of its political references, the play need not be as dated as it may at first appear.

Old Times

A: Harold Pinter **Pf:** 1971, London **Pb:** 1971 **G:** Drama in 2 acts **S:** Rural home, England, 1960s **C:** 1m, 2f

Kate lives in the country with her husband Deeley, whose work as a film-maker occasionally takes him from home. They are awaiting the arrival of Anna, who is married to a wealthy husband and who shared a flat with Kate when they were both secretaries in London. In fact, Anna is on stage from the start, and abruptly enters the conversation after her 'arrival'. Deeley is threatened by Kate's relationship with Anna, and is further thrown off equilibrium by being strongly attracted to Anna. Kate reminisces about visits to the cinema and parties they attended. Sexual tension is increased when Anna describes how she witnessed Kate enduring an inept seduction in their flat. When Kate returns from a bath in a white bathrobe, Deeley and Anna compete with each other over the best way to dry her. Deeley now gives a totally different account of the seduction described by Anna. Kate remains silent, refusing to authenticate either version. Deeley counters by describing a meeting with Anna years previously, when he tried to look up her skirt. Deeley eventually begins to weep as he struggles to maintain his hold over Kate, while Kate intimates that she has never belonged to him or Anna.

This is the first full-length play by Pinter in which the action is clearly unreal, established by Anna's silent presence on stage at the start. She is perhaps always – or only – in the minds of the married couple; the play certainly has the atmosphere of a dream. The play explores memory, its inaccuracies, its inventions, and the way it permeates the present.

Old Wives' Tale, The

AT: *The Old Wife's Tale* **A:** George Peele **Pf:** *c.*1590, London **Pb:** 1595 **G:** Com. in 1 act; prose and verse **S:** Woods, a cottage, and imaginary locations in a fantastic past **C:** 17m, 6f, extras

Three men, lost in the woods, are given shelter for the night. Old Madge entertains them with stories that are acted out before them: the story of the princess Delia, abducted by the sorcerer Sacrapant, who is being sought by her two brothers. They in turn are told the story of Erestus, who is regularly transformed into a bear, and of Lampriscus, who suffers from his two daughters, one beautiful but evil-tempered, the other incredibly ugly. The boastful Huanebango appears, intent on outdoing Sacrapant, and so hoping to win the love of Delia. Delia is given the spell of forgetfulness, and so fails to recognize her brothers, who are struck by lightning. Eventually, everyone gets their just deserts. Eumenides, a wandering knight, pays for the burial of a poor man, and is rewarded with wealth and the hand of the fair Delia. Sacrapant is overcome, Erestus is freed from his spell, and Lampriscus' two daughters get husbands: the beautiful but spiteful one having to marry the now deaf Huanebango. So Madge's tale ends, and she invites her guests to breakfast.

This light and rambling comedy might be more properly called 'The Old Wife's Tales', because there is one narrator and several folk tales, which form a loosely structured piece. The main interest is in the variety of colourful characters, each with his or her own story to tell. It is also interesting to observe the play-within-a-play, a device to be frequently emulated (as in Shakespeare's *The *Taming of the Shrew*) and the metatheatrical device of an onstage audience commenting on the action (as in *The *Knight of the Burning Pestle*).

Oleanna

A: David Mamet Pf: 1992, New York Pb: 1992 G: Drama in 3 acts S: College professor's room, USA, 1990s C: 1m, 1f

John, a college professor who has been promised tenure, agrees to discuss a failed paper with Carol, one of his students. After phoning his wife about the purchase of their new house, he tries to explain to Carol where she has gone wrong. She is eager but not very bright, he tries to help but is inarticulate. She apologizes for not understanding; he apologizes for not making himself understood. Because he is guilty about the nature of higher education, John suggests that they do a deal: they will 'start over' the class, and she will get an 'A', because he likes her, and puts a reassuring arm round her shoulder. Carol registers a formal complaint against him, denying him approval of his tenure, accusing him of sexism, of embracing her, and of offering her better grades in exchange for regular meetings. Aware that she is using language fed to her by her 'Group', he pleads with her to communicate her true feelings. As she tries to leave, in desperation he restrains her, and she shouts for help. At their final meeting, John is now suspended from his post and has lost the new house. Still begging Carol to explain what he has done wrong, she offers to get her Group to treat him more favourably if he agrees to ban books of which they disapprove. Furious, he tells her to get out, then learns from a phone call that she has filed an accusation of attempted rape against him. Finally losing all control, he knocks her to the floor and calls her 'a little cunt'. 'That's right,' she replies.

This controversial play is the most searing examination in contemporary theatre of 'political correctness'. Ironically, it is John's well-meaning but clumsy efforts to undermine the elitist division between tutor and student that embroils him in the difficulties engineered by the Stalinist feminists of the 'Group'. Carol herself moves from inarticulacy via platitudes to her own insights into gender conflict.

Ole Devil, The. See ANNA CHRISTIE.

On Baile's Strand

A: W. B. Yeats (with Lady Gregory) Pf: 1904, Dublin Pb: 1903; rev. 1906 G: Drama in 1 act; blank verse, prose, and songs S: Great hall at Dundealgan (Dundalk), Ireland, 1st c. AD C: 5m, extras

The Fool and the Blind Man reveal that the High King Conchubar is coming to exact an oath of allegiance from Cuchulain, the great warrior and King of Muirthemne, and that the Scottish warrior queen Aoife has sent her son to kill Cuchulain. Despite initial resistance, Cuchulain, recognizing that at the age of 40 he can no longer live 'like a bird's flight', swears loyalty to Conchubar. Aoife's son presents himself and challenges Cuchulain. Cuchulain refuses to fight, but is ordered to do so by Conchubar. Cuchulain defeats the young stranger but then learns that he was his own son. Crazed with grief, Cuchulain, imagining he is attacking Conchubar, dashes into the sea, and drowns fighting the waves. The Fool and the Blind Man exploit the distraction to steal food.

This was the first of Yeats's Cuchulain plays, which retell stories from the Ulster cycle of legends, which Lady Gregory had drawn together as *Cuchulain of Muirthemne* (1902). The plot is clear and simple, and there is no attempt to enter into the psychology of the characters, owing a debt to symbolist and oriental theatre and rejecting the contemporary vogue for naturalism. The result is a hauntingly beautiful piece, undercut by the antics of the grotesque masked pair of clowns, the Fool and the Blind Man.

Once in a Lifetime

A: Moss Hart and George S. Kaufman Pf: 1930, New York Pb: 1930 G: Com. in 3 acts S: New York, a Pullman car, and Los Angeles, 1927 C: 23m, 15f

Because the vaudeville act of Jerry Hyland, his fiancée May Daniele, and their somewhat dim-witted friend George Lewis is failing, the three decide to leave New York to seek their fortune in the expanding film industry in Los Angeles. The cinema business is in chaos, wasting money, devoid of any artistic policy, and now facing the crisis of the new 'talkies' with actors unused to speaking. The three wholly unqualified new arrivals set up a school of elocution and persuade movie mogul Herman Glogauer to employ them. Jerry becomes so obsessed with Hollywood that May leaves him to return to New York. Despite his incompetence and impudence, George Lewis is made production supervisor. His bungling efforts, including the casting of the utterly untalented girl he fancies in the lead role, are responsible for a dreadful film, which is an immediate critical success. He appeals for May and Jerry, who has pursued her, to return. May and Jerry will marry, while George looks forward to further successes in his new career.

Predictably, at a time when live theatre feared its survival was threatened by the 'movies', a play satirizing the commercialism and philistinism of Hollywood and its sycophantic critics was bound to be a success. However, its endearing trio of central characters and their success, achieved despite rather than because of their efforts, can still delight audiences today.

On the Razzle (*Einen Jux will er sich machen*)

AT: *He Will Go on a Spree; The Merchant of Yonkers; The Matchmaker* **A:** Johann Nestroy **Pf:** 1842, Vienna **Pb:** 1844 **Tr:** 1939 **G:** Farce with songs in 4 acts; German prose **S:** Vienna, and Zangler's home in a neighbouring town, early 19th c. **C:** 14m, 7f

Weinberl, assistant to a grocer, is put in charge of the shop while Zangler his employer is away. However, impelled to undertake a big adventure, he and the apprentice Christopherl set off for Vienna. Seeing Zangler, they seek refuge in the salon of the fashionable Madame Knorr. In order to explain his presence here, Weinberl pretends to be the new husband of the rich widow Frau von Fischer. She then arrives, but is so intrigued by Weinberl's effrontery that she does not betray him. There follows a series of farcical situations, during which Weinberl gets mistaken for the fiancé of Zangler's niece. On returning home, Weinberl manages to foil a burglary and so redeems himself in the eyes of his employer. He wins the love of his young widow, and Zangler's niece is free to marry when her fiancé inherits a fortune.

Based on *A Day Well Spent* by a contemporary librettist John Oxenford, this is Nestroy's most popular play and is a fine example of the Viennese farces of the first half of the 19th century. As theatre director and actor (Nestroy played the role of Weinberl), Nestroy was prolific in writing and producing satirical comedies about Viennese life. Since many of the references are to contemporary Vienna, most translations tend to be adaptations. Thornton Wilder adapted the piece as *The Merchant of Yonkers* (1939) and again as *The Matchmaker* (1954), leading to the musical *Hello, Dolly!* (1964), and Tom Stoppard wrote a version *On the Razzle* (1981).

On the Run. See SHADOW OF A GUNMAN.

Optimistic Tragedy (*Optimisticheskaya tragediya*)

A: Vsevolod Vishnevsky **Pf:** 1933, Kiev **Pb:** 1933 **Tr:** 1937 **G:** Hist. drama in 3 acts; Russian prose **S:** Naval cruiser, Baltic port, and battlefield, Russia, 1918 **C:** 15m, 2f, extras

In the upheavals following the Bolshevik Revolution, anarchists have taken over a naval ship of the Russian Baltic Fleet. They are shabby, demoralized, bored, and frustrated; easy prey to sex and liquor; and ready to organize themselves in a democratic but arbitrary manner. When an old woman accuses a sailor of stealing her purse, he is summarily executed. Suddenly she finds her purse, so she must die too. In order to restore order, the Party sends a female Commissar to take control of the ship. She soon establishes her authority: when a sailor attempts to rape her, she shoots him on the spot. After initial resentment, especially by the anarchist leader, the sailors gradually submit themselves to the new order. When it seems impossible to reform the anarchist leader, the Commissar has him shot.

Another deserts, but one, Aleksei, willingly joins the Bolsheviks. Marching for almost 4,000 miles to engage with the White Army in the Ukraine, the 'First Red Army Regiment', including their brave Commissar, are defeated on the battlefield. This is the tragedy, but there is room for optimism, because the Second Red Navy Regiment is on its way to the southern front and will ultimately defeat the counter-revolution.

This forms a parallel piece to *The *Days of the Turbins*, tracing the formation of one element of the Red Army from its unpromising anarchist beginnings to a disciplined fighting force. While not as subtle a piece as Bulgakov's, *Optimistic Tragedy* addresses important issues regarding the limits of individual freedom. Peter Stein's 1972 production contributed to the debate surrounding anarchist groups like Baader-Meinhof.

Ordo Representationis Ade. See PLAY OF ADAM, THE.

Oresteia, The (Agamemnon; Libation-Bearers; Eumenides)

A: Aeschylus Pf: 458 BC, Athens Tr: 1777
G: Greek trag; trilogy in verse S: Mycenae, Delphi, and Athens after the Trojan War C: 4m, 4f, extras, and 3 choruses (1m, 2f)

(1) *Agamemnon*. After ten years, the Trojan War has at last ended, and the palace of Mycenae prepares to welcome home their victorious king Agamemnon. His wife Clytemnestra, who has entered into an adulterous relationship with Aegisthus, plots to kill her husband. She dissembles pleasure at his return, even when she finds he has brought home as a trophy of war the young seer Cassandra, priestess of Apollo. Cassandra foretells the terrible end that awaits her and Agamemnon. After entering the palace, Agamemnon and she are brutally murdered. Clytemnestra is jubilant and claims that she has merely exercised justice in avenging the death of her daughter Iphigeneia, whom Agamemnon had sacrificed to gain favourable winds for the fleet sailing to Troy. To the dismay of the Chorus, Aegisthus declares himself king. (2) *Libation-Bearers* (*Choephori*). Agamemnon's son Orestes, who was taken from the palace when a child, now returns to avenge his father's death. He observes his sister Electra and her servants, who have been ordered to bear libations to Agamemnon's grave, since the murdered Agamemnon's restless spirit has been haunting Clytemnestra in her dreams. Orestes reveals himself to Electra, and together they plot the murder of Aegisthus and Clytemnestra. Orestes pretends to be a messenger bringing news of his own death. Aegisthus is fetched to share in this 'good news', and is killed by Orestes as he enters the palace. Despite his mother's pleadings, Orestes then kills her, but soon has to flee in madness, as he senses gathering round him the avenging spirits of the Erinyes, who are outraged at his matricide. (3) *Eumenides* (or *The Furies*). Orestes seeks refuge in the oracle at Delphi, where the god Apollo promises to protect him. Orestes is sent before the Areopagus, the court of Athens, presided over by the goddess Athene. The Erinyes (or Furies), incited by Clytemnestra's ghost, pursue Orestes to the court. The judges divide evenly, but Athena gives the casting vote in favour of Orestes, accepting Apollo's argument that a son is a closer relation to his father than to his mother, since her womb merely provides nurture for the father's seed. Athene also transforms the avenging Erinyes into the gentle Eumenides. The trilogy ends in universal rejoicing.

The Oresteia is the only surviving trilogy of Greek tragedy and is the source of the best-known cycle of Greek mythology: the curse of the Atrides, which works itself through successive generations. The story was used by Sophocles, Euripides, Seneca, Racine, Goethe, Eugene O'Neill, Gerhart Hauptmann, and T. S. Eliot, to name but a few. In Aeschylus, justice (*dike*) is invoked to justify Clytemnestra's murder of her husband, as it is to justify Orestes' killing of his own mother. The cycle of avenging past crimes can be broken only through divine intervention. The spurious biology which informs Athene's judgement is now understood to be an assertion of the patriarchy of the state of Athens as a rejection of primitive matriarchy, which was perceived as a threat to the fledgling democracy. As the classical scholar Richard Beacham says, *The Oresteia* is 'a triumph of hope over despair, reason over superstition, and justice over brutality'. It is also one of the first dramas which employs dialogue in the way that we now regard as virtually essential to theatre. In Aeschylus' earlier works most of the action develops through poetic recitals between a character and the chorus; they have the static feel of dramatic poems. Here some of the most effective scenes, as between Orestes and Clytemnestra, depend on two characters in conflict, creating a genre that is more recognizably 'dramatic'. Furthermore, the trilogy made use of the recently invented *skene*, the building at the rear of the orchestra, which could be opened to reveal a deliberately repeated image, the horrific tableaux of the murders of Agamemnon and Clytemnestra.

Orestes

A: Euripides **Pf:** 408 BC, Athens **Tr:** 1780
G: Greek drama in verse **S:** Before the palace at Mycenae, some years after the Trojan War
C: 7m, 3f, extras, chorus (f)

Orestes, having avenged the death of his father Agamemnon by murdering his mother, has descended into madness and feels himself pursued by the avenging Furies. He sinks into sleep and is tended by his sister Electra. Menelaus, Agamemnon's brother, arrives, questions Orestes, and promises to support him. Orestes and Electra are taken before the Argive tribunal to be arraigned for matricide. Treacherously, Menelaus withdraws his support, and brother and sister are condemned. Spurred on by Orestes' friend Pylades, Orestes plots to take revenge on Menelaus and engineer their escape by murdering Helen, his wife, and kidnapping his daughter Hermione. The plans are foiled by Helen being wafted up into the heavens and by the appearance of the god Apollo. Apollo orders that Orestes shall be released and taken for trial in Athens, that Electra and Pylades shall marry, that Orestes shall be betrothed to Hermione, and that Menelaus should return to Sparta to allow Orestes to return to take his father's throne after he has been cleansed of his crime.

Predictably, Euripides' version of the Orestes story differs strongly from that of the deeply religious Aeschylus. Here the concentration is on the emotional breakdown of Orestes and his attempt before the tribunal to justify his matricide in terms of political expedience rather than by reference to divine law. Euripides' portrayal of a young man willing to commit further acts of extreme violence implies that perhaps it was not just a divine command that drove Orestes to murder his mother. Of the many extreme figures in Greek drama, Orestes, as seen in this play, might be regarded as the most pathological.
Significantly, this was the most popular tragedy of the ancient world, enjoying many revivals.

Ornithes. See BIRDS.

Orpheus (*Orphée*)

A: Jean Cocteau **Pf:** 1926, Paris **Pb:** 1927
Tr: 1933 **G:** Drama in 13 scenes; French prose
S: A room in Thrace, and heaven, mythical past
C: 6m, 2f, 1 horse

Eurydice is jealous of Orpheus' affection for his horse, which dictates poetry to Orpheus by tapping its hoof. Orpheus is submitting the latest poem to Thrace's annual poetry contest. Arguing over his neglect of Eurydice, Orpheus smashes a mirror. The glazier Heurtebise comes to fix it, and gives Eurydice poison to rid her of the horse. By mistake, Eurydice poisons herself, and Death, a beautiful young woman, comes to take her through the mirror to the underworld. Orpheus is distraught, but Heurtebise helps him through the mirror. Orpheus is allowed to bring back Eurydice on condition that he does not look at her. During a quarrel he looks at her, perhaps deliberately, and she is returned to the other side. Orpheus now learns that the horse has tricked him: his poem 'Madame Eurydice reviendra des enfers' contains the obscene acrostic 'Merde' ('shit'), and he is declared a fraud. The Bacchantes are coming to tear him apart, but he gladly goes to meet death so that he can be reunited with Eurydice. His severed head is tossed on to the stage, and Eurydice comes to accompany his invisible body to the underworld. When the police arrive, Eurydice comes for Heurtebise too, and all questions have to be answered by the severed head. The final scene is in heaven, where Orpheus, Eurydice, and Heurtebise are living in harmony.

In the wake of Apollinaire's *The *Breasts of Tiresias* (1917), it became voguish to reinterpret classical myth with anachronisms and a refreshingly iconoclastic wit (cf. Anouilh's **Antigone* and Sartre's *The *Flies*). Cocteau's version of the Orpheus legend is full of theatrical surprises (Heurtebise suspended in mid-air, Death borrowing a watch from the audience, one scene repeated word for word, a talking head, etc.). Below the surrealist fun, Cocteau explores a strained relationship with the ambiguous presence of the friend Heurtebise.

Orpheus Descending

AT: *Battle of Angels* A: Tennessee Williams Pf: 1940, Boston (as *Battle of Angels*); rev. 1957, New York (as *Orpheus Descending*) Pb: 1945; rev. 1958, 1976 G: Drama in 3 acts S: Dry goods store, small Southern town, *c.*1940 C: 10m, 9f

The Orpheus figure is a 30-year-old blues guitarist Val Xavier, who 'descends' penniless on a small Southern town and is taken in by Lady Torrance, the proprietress of a local store, whose elderly husband Jabe is dying of cancer. While Val offers Lady release from her loveless marriage, other women show interest in the handsome newcomer, including the town's richest and most promiscuous woman, now married to Lady's former lover, David Cutrere, who jilted Lady. When Vee Talbot, the neurotic sex-starved wife of the Sheriff, is treated with kindness by Val, the Sheriff accuses him of adultery and orders him to leave the town or face a lynch mob. Lady discovers that her husband Jabe had been one of those who had murdered her father for serving blacks in his wine garden, and is delighted to discover that she is carrying Val's baby. When Jabe threatens Val with a gun, Lady interposes herself and gets shot. Jabe accuses Val of the murder, and Val is led away to his death by the mob.

Although Williams's favourite play, this work never achieved success, neither on stage nor as a film (*The Fugitive Kind*, 1960). In its original version *Battle of Angels,* Williams's first professional production in 1940, it was booed off the stage. Its characteristic format of the younger man whose youth is slipping away, and the dominant, sex-hungry older woman, parades the same kind of intriguing characters familiar from **Sweet Bird of Youth*.

Othello (*The Tragoedy of Othello, The Moore of Venice*)

A: William Shakespeare Pf: *c.*1602, London Pb: 1622 G: Trag. in 5 acts; blank verse and prose S: Venice and Cyprus, late 16th c. C: 10m, 3f, extras

Iago, who is angry that Cassio has been promoted above him, determines to destroy his general, the Moor Othello. First, he incites Rodrigo to denounce Othello for having stolen away Desdemona. But Othello reveals before the Venetian Senate how honourable his love for Desdemona is and that they have married in secret. Othello is now charged with defending Cyprus from a Turkish invasion, and sets sail at once. Arriving victorious in Cyprus to be greeted by Desdemona, Othello soon falls prey to jealousy, subtly encouraged by the treacherous Iago. First, Desdemona pleads on Cassio's behalf for him to be spared from being disciplined for drunken behaviour, then Iago arranges for Cassio to find a precious handkerchief that Othello had given to Desdemona, finally he arranges for Othello to overhear Cassio jesting about his whore, while Othello imagines he is mocking Desdemona. Othello, driven to the limits of jealous despair, strangles Desdemona in her bed. When the truth is revealed, he takes his own life.

While some modern critics regard *Othello* as a play about racial tension, in fact little reference is made to Othello's race; he is a Moor (a Mediterranean African) rather than the kind of primitive negro with flaring nostrils and rolling gait which Laurence Olivier created in his 1964 performance. Nevertheless, Othello is an outsider, whose lack of sophistication lays him open to Iago's scheming. Because he so easily dismisses the possibility of jealousy, he all the more easily falls victim to it. *Othello* is also notable for the very concentrated action, which, once in Cyprus, occupies only a matter of hours. Indeed, Desdemona would hardly have had time to commit adultery. Not only is this hardly perceived by an audience, it in fact makes Othello's jealousy even more poignant and misguided. The theme was used by Voltaire in his tragedy **Zaïre*, decorously replacing the handkerchief with a satin cushion, and in Verdi's opera *Otello* (1887).

Our Boys

A: H. J. Byron **Pf:** 1875, London **Pb:** 1880 **G:** Com. in 3 acts **S:** Country houses in Hertfordshire and lodgings in London, 1870s **C:** 6m, 4f

On a European tour Talbot Champneys befriends the son of a retired dairy manufacturer, Charles Middlewick. His father, the snobbish Sir Geoffry Champneys, 'a county magnate', thus finds himself compelled to join with the ebullient Perkyn Middlewick to greet their respective sons. When the sons arrive, it becomes clear that Charles, who has benefited from a good education, is charming and well spoken; by contrast, Talbot is a spoilt young man, whose indolence has left him an aristocratic oaf. Also come to greet the two young men are Talbot's intended bride, the heiress Violet Melrose, and her impoverished cousin Mary Melrose. To the dismay and confusion of the fathers, Violet falls in love with Charles, and Mary with Talbot. At first the fathers banish their sons into poverty, but, when they begin to miss them, they relent, and the families are happily reunited.

Although the play is somewhat formulaic in its over-neat opposition of the aristocrat and the meritocrat, seen in both fathers and sons, the play, which originally ran for a record-breaking four years (1,362 performances) at the Vaudeville Theatre in London, remains a heart-warming experience in the theatre. As a social document, it stands as one of a whole series of Victorian plays, beginning with Bulwer-Lytton's **Money* and ending with Barrie's *The *Admirable Crichton*, that reflected the triumph of industry and intelligence over aristocratic privilege.

Our Country's Good

A: Timberlake Wertenbaker **Pf:** 1988, London **Pb:** 1988 **G:** Drama in 2 acts **S:** Convict ship and settlement, Australia, 1787–9 **C:** 17m, 5f

In 1787 the first convicts are shipped to Australia, guarded by naval officers who rule the colony with military discipline. Despite the humane attitude of Governor Arthur Phillip, convicts are flogged for insubordination, and three are hanged for theft. Midshipman Harry Brewer is haunted by Handy Baker, a marine whom he hanged for stealing and who was his rival in love for Duckling, a young convict. Second Lieutenant Ralph Clark proposes to stage Farquhar's *The *Recruiting Officer*, to celebrate the King's birthday in 1789 and to humanize the convicts. His plan is opposed by more conventionally minded officers, but Governor Phillip, wishing to 'help create a new society in this colony', gives his blessing to the project. Many of his cast are illiterate, none has experience of acting, and there is tension between the participants, especially when they are joined by the hangman Ketch Freeman. Problems mount, when 'Melinda', played by convict Liz Morden, narrowly avoids hanging for allegedly helping prisoners to escape, and Harry Brewer finally collapses and dies. Ralph becomes close to convict Mary Brenham, and purportedly rehearsing his role of Plume, declares his love for her as the character Silvia. Ralph rejects as too political a prologue written by a convict: 'We left our country for our country's good.' At last, the play is performed to resounding success, the first to be staged on Australian soil. Throughout, an Aborigine observes the curious white arrivals and concludes that they are not from the Dreamtime.

Based on Thomas Kinneally's novel *The Playmaker* (1987), itself based on historical fact, Wertenbaker's best-known play celebrates the redemptive power of theatre and explores the ethics of punishment and redemption in the creation of a new society.

Our Town

A: Thornton Wilder **Pf:** 1938, Princeton, New Jersey **Pb:** 1938 **G:** Drama in 3 acts **S:** Grover's Corners, New Hampshire, 1899–1913 **C:** 17m, 7f, extras

The Stage Manager introduces the small township of Grover's Corners in 1901, in particular Dr Gibbs, the town doctor, and his family, and Mr Webb, editor of the local newspaper, and his wife and children. Professor Willard and Mr Webb provide more information about the town and answer questions from the audience. After an insight into daily life, we move forward four years, when Dr Gibbs's son George and Mr Webb's daughter Emily are getting married. We then arrive in 1913, and Emily has died in childbirth. She joins the dead in the cemetery, but asks to revisit the living. She comes back to her home in 1899, but returns to the dead, recognizing that the living have too little awareness of the beauty of life and that it is with the dead that she now belongs.

This 'attempt to find a value above all price for the smallest events in our daily life' is Wilder's best-known play and one of the most popular American dramas of the 20th century, not just for its loving and somewhat sentimental recreation of America before the advent of motorized transport, but also for its staging without props or scenery. Fulminating against the empty realism of 19th-century theatre, Wilder experimented with a bare stage and taking the action out of the proscenium arch into the audience. While this suggests Pirandello's influence, Wilder never referred to him, claiming his theatrical ancestry from Shakespeare. Wilder, in his turn, in the graveyard scene may have suggested the central image of Beckett's **Play*.

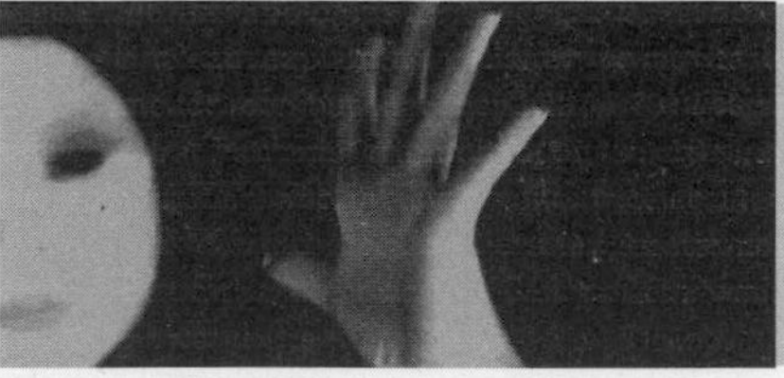

p

Painted Laugh, The. See HE WHO GETS SLAPPED.

Pair of Drawers, A. See UNDERPANTS, THE.

Pandora's Box. See LULU PLAYS, THE.

Pantagleize

A: Michel de Ghelderode **Pf:** 1930, Saint-Trond, Belgium **Pb:** 1934 **Tr:** 1960 **G:** Pol. com. in 3 acts and epilogue; Flemish prose **S:** A European city, in an indeterminate period between two wars **C:** 12m, 1f, extras

Pantagleize is by his own admission a complete nonentity who writes for a fashion magazine. On his 40th birthday he decides to greet people with 'What a lovely day!' – unaware that this is the signal for the planned uprising of the Liberals to begin. Observed by a plain-clothes policeman, revolutionaries are gathered in a café, where Pantagleize goes to take coffee. Greeting everyone with his chosen phrase, Pantagleize sparks off the revolution and is hailed as their leader. One revolutionary, a Jewess, knocks out the policeman, embraces Pantagleize, and declares that he has saved humanity. Falling in love with her, he follows her instructions to raid the state bank and seize the Conservatives' treasure. Unaware that she has been killed by the policeman, Pantagleize succeeds in his daring raid, because he tells the militia and their cowardly commander 'to go to hell' – again unaware that this is the official password. At a banquet given by the revolutionaries in his honour, the rebels are killed off one by one by the waiters. The remaining revolutionaries are brought to trial, and Pantagleize is condemned to death, despite his counsel's argument that he was the victim of coincidences. As he dies before the firing squad, Pantagleize still manages to utter: 'What a lovely day!'

As society became more complex and bureaucracy invaded people's lives more and more, many writers celebrated the resourcefulness and resilience of the little man in the face of authority (cf. novels by H. G. Wells, Heinrich Mann, and Jaroslav Hašek, and plays like Brecht's **Schweyk in the Second World War*). Usually, such characters survive, but though Pantagleize dies, he retains his cheerful optimism to the end, a prototype for Beckett's Winnie in **Happy Days*.

Paphnutius

AT: *The Conversion of Thais the Prostitute/the Harlot* **A:** Hrotsvitha of Gandersheim (Hroswitha, Roswitha) **W:** 10th c. **Pb:** 1501 **Tr:** 1923 **G:** Drama in 13 scenes; Latin prose **S:** A hermitage, a brothel, and a convent, ancient (but Christian) Greece **C:** 3m, 2f, extras

After a lengthy theological discourse with his disciples about cosmic harmony and the conflict between the flesh and the spirit, the pious hermit Paphnutius resolves to save the soul of a famous prostitute, Thais. Disguising himself as a potential lover, Paphnutius is welcomed by Thais, who reveals herself to be concerned about her sins and so is readily converted by the old man to a new life of chastity. Witnessed by her lovers, Thais commits all her ill-gotten wealth to the flames, and then leaves with Paphnutius. He brings her to a convent, where she is to do penance by being incarcerated in a tiny cell. Despite her concerns about being overwhelmed by her own faeces, Thais agrees to this mortification. After three years Paphnutius learns of a fellow hermit's vision that a 'celestial couch' is prepared for Thais in heaven. Paphnutius therefore releases her, and fifteen days later she dies, redeemed by God's grace and raised up to paradise.

Hrotsvitha, a German noblewoman living in a community of nuns, claims to have written religious plays in order to counteract the frivolous and often salacious plays of Terence. She is notable for being the first woman playwright and indeed for being the first significant dramatist in the post-Roman era. Her six extant plays are all episodic in structure and deal with religious themes of sacrifice and martyrdom, based on Latin and Greek legends of the early Church. It is now fashionable to detect a strongly ironical element in her work. The absurdity of the old ascetic hermit disguising himself as a prostitute's lover (an episode worthy of Terence), and the shocking but very realistic concern of Thais about her toilet arrangements do indeed suggest that Hrotsvitha's focus was not solely on spiritual matters. Massenet's opera *Thais* (1894) was indirectly based on *Paphnutius*.

Paravents, Les. See SCREENS, THE.

Parlamento de Ruzante che iera vegnù de campo. See CONVERSATION OF RUZANTE RETURNED FROM THE WARS.

Parliament of Women, The. See WOMEN IN ASSEMBLY.

Partage de midi. See BREAK OF NOON.

Pastor Fido, Il. See FAITHFUL SHEPHERD, THE.

Paul Kauvar

AT: *Anarchy* A: Steele MacKaye Pf: 1887, New York Pb: Not known G: Melodrama in 5 acts S: Paris, 1794 C: 8m, 2f, extras

Paul Kauvar, a leader of the French Revolution, is so dismayed by the Reign of Terror initiated by Robespierre that he offers refuge to worthy aristocrats. He provides asylum, under false names, for the Duc de Beaumont and his daughter Diane, whom he secretly marries. When the villainous Gouroc, formerly the Marquis de Vaux, discovers Paul's secret, he denounces the Duc and blames Paul for the betrayal. In order to demonstrate his innocence, Paul is prepared to take the Duc's place at the guillotine, but they both manage to escape. Ironically, Paul is now captured by royalist forces. When threatened by Revolutionaries, Paul assumes the identity of the royalist general and allows him to escape. Once gain, Paul faces death at the guillotine. He is just bidding a last farewell to his young wife Diane, when news comes that Robespierre has fallen prey to his own Terror and that Paul is able to go free.

Steele MacKaye was an extraordinary individual, justly famed for his many innovations in American theatre: he founded the first American school of acting, and introduced overhead lighting and movable stages that allowed fast scene changes. Despite acknowledging the naturalistic influence of François Delsarte, whom he encountered in Paris, MacKaye's plays did not succeed in breaking free from 19th-century melodrama, still favouring unsubtle characterization, exciting incident, and a happy ending. *Paul Kauvar*, however, by placing humanity above political loyalty, provided a potent comment on the execution of the Chicago anarchists in 1887 and contained some exciting crowd scenes.

Pavane. See AMERICA HURRAH.

Peace (*Eirēnē; Pax*)

A: Aristophanes Pf: 421 BC, Athens Tr: 1840 G: Greek com. in verse S: Mount Olympus and a farm near Athens, 5th c. BC C: 15m, 5f, extras, chorus (m)

Trygaeus, an Attic farmer, is weary of the war and so resolves to fly up to Mount Olympus on a dung-beetle to plead with the gods to create peace. Hermes comes to the door of heaven and explains that the gods have moved further away from the turmoil on earth, leaving War in charge. War has cast Peace into a deep cave. When Trygaeus calls on his fellow Greeks to release Peace, Hermes intervenes to warn that Zeus will strike dead anyone attempting to open the cave. Trygaeus flatters and cajoles

Hermes into letting them release Peace, and she is freed, with her two beautiful maidservants. Trygaeus resolves to marry one of the maidens and returns to earth with her. Unwelcome guests, especially those dealing in arms, are sent away, and a happy wedding takes place.

Performed a year after the death of Cleon, and with hopes of an end to the Peloponnesian War in sight, *Peace* is a much gentler play than the earlier ones that survive from Aristophanes. The fun of flying up to Olympus, using the comic actor's standard phallus as a joystick, the thrill of outwitting Hermes, and the optimistic conclusion of the release of Peace and the joyful wedding, all stand in contrast to the often bitter satire which characterizes much of Aristophanes' other work. A version of the play by the East German writer Volker Braun was staged in 1979 as a parable of Communist Utopia.

Pearls for Pigs

A: Richard Foreman **Pf**: 1997, Hartford, Connecticut **Pb**: 2001 **G**: Drama in 1 act; prose and some free verse **S**: Large panelled room containing proscenium, indeterminate period (possibly *c.*1900) **C**: 7m, 1f

The Maestro, attended by four Large Male Dwarfs, encounters Pierrot and Colombine and declares that he hates the actors in the play and wonders whether to begin improvising. He cancels the play and promptly has sex with Colombine, asking the audience how he can be stopped from doing that. He slits Colombine's throat and forces her into a coffin. Pierrot stabs the Maestro, but it is all just theatre. The Maestro, costumed by the dwarfs in a white dress and feather headdress, speaks of the stage as his 'private kingdom' which has no effect on the world outside. The Doctor appears, wearing a frogman suit and flippers (the aqua therapy took longer than expected), prepared to cure the Maestro's anger. The Doctor decides that he cannot help him, but soon reappears dressed for golf and carrying a platter with a severed head. The Maestro recognizes that reality does not exist: 'mere fictions projected on a network of underlying nonexisting atomic nothings'. The Doctor and the Maestro debate this at length, and Colombine brings on a dummy of the Maestro. The Maestro promises to save everyone from 'mind attack' and is guillotined. Finally, his dummy appears astride a black horse.

Possessing even less narrative coherence than *The *Breasts of Tiresias* or one of Gertrude Stein's plays, Foreman's piece is a characteristic theatrical firework, full of physical action and dance, crazy moments, blatant sex, fantastic characters, outrageous costumes, and philosophical comment. Through the swirling mist of the stage happening one glimpses a tantalizing meditation on the nature of reality and theatre and on the role of the audience, referred to in the provocative title as 'pigs'.

Peer Gynt

A: Henrik Ibsen **Pf**: 1876, Christiania **Pb**: 1867 **Tr**: 1892 **G**: Drama in 5 acts; Norwegian verse **S**: Gubrandsdal and mountains in Norway, the Moroccan coast, the Sahara Desert, a madhouse in Cairo, the North Sea, mid-19th c. **C**: 24m, 14f, extras

When the 20-year-old Peer Gynt learns that Ingrid, a rich young local girl who is attracted to him, is about to get married, Peer rushes off and abducts her from the wedding. He soon tires of her, his head full of thoughts of the lovely Solveig, whom he has just met. He is led into the Troll kingdom, where he feels at home amongst their coarse sensuality, until they threaten to slit his eyeballs. Church bells dispel the vision. After wrestling with the Boyg, an unseen monster, Peer begins to build a hut on the mountainside. Here Solveig seeks him out, and the two begin an idyllic existence together. Soon, however, one of the troll women comes with a deformed child, declaring it to be Peer's son. Feeling unworthy of Solveig, Peer leaves her, while she promises to wait for him. Returning home, he finds his mother dying, and comforts her with a story. Years later, Peer is a rich and unscrupulous merchant entertaining guests on the Moroccan coast. The guests hijack his yacht, but Peer, asking help from the heavens, watches as his ship bursts into flames.

Dressing in Arabian garb, he is mistaken for the Prophet and is entertained by the beautiful dusky Anitra. She runs away, stealing his wealth. Peer begins to inspect the antiquities of Egypt. He is taken to a madhouse in Cairo, where he is crowned 'the Emperor Self'. Now an old man, Peer is returning by sea to Norway when there is a shipwreck. Peer saves himself by forcing the ship's cook to drown, and, though terrified by a 'Strange Passenger', arrives safely on land. No one in his home village recognizes him, and setting out to find Solveig, he encounters the Button-Moulder, who will melt down Peer to make a new person, since Peer has never established a real identity. Determined to prove that he is in fact someone, Peer is allowed to travel on, but even the Thin Man, a devil figure, does not consider him a proper sinner. At last willing to stand account for all he has done, Peer attempts to confess all to Solveig. But she, overjoyed at his return, wishes only to speak of her love. She takes his head in her lap and sings him a lullaby, defending him from the evils of the world, even the insistent demands of the Button-Moulder.

Although originally intended as a dramatic poem, *Peer Gynt* has proved a difficult but spectacular piece for performance. Written as a mirror image to Brand's refusal to compromise, Peer is a man unwilling to commit himself to anything. His egoism, whether in his dealings with women or in his capitalist enterprises, is essentially the same as the Cairo madmen who see the world only in terms of their own personal vision. By finally confronting his past, and, as in Goethe's **Faust*, through the selfless love of a devoted woman, Peer can be redeemed. In depicting the journey of one individual through several stages of his life and by introducing symbolic characters like the Button-Moulder, Ibsen prepared the way for the philosophical plays of Strindberg and the Expressionists. Peter Stein directed the play in two parts in 1971, using six actors to play Peer.

Pelléas and Mélisande (*Pelléas et Mélisande*)

A: Maurice Maeterlinck **Pf:** 1893, Paris **Pb:** 1892 **Tr:** 1896 **G:** Fairy tale in 5 acts; French prose **S:** Castle and environs, medieval period **C:** 6m, 2f, extras

While out hunting, Prince Golaud encounters a beautiful girl, Mélisande, weeping by a spring. Her crown lies at the bottom of the spring, but she will not allow Golaud to retrieve it. Golaud marries Mélisande and they come to his grandfather King Arkel's palace in Allemonde, where they are welcomed, especially by Pelléas, Golaud's half-brother, who shares an affinity with Golaud's child-wife. Together at the Fountain of the Blind, Mélisande drops her wedding ring into its depths, which arouses Golaud's suspicions. When Mélisande combs her hair at a tower window, she leans out to greet Pelléas and he luxuriates in the long tresses that envelop him. Golaud's jealousy pushes him almost to kill Pelléas in the vaults of the castle, to interrogate his son from his first marriage about the young couple, and to use physical violence on Mélisande. When Pelléas meets Mélisande to take his leave of her, they at last declare their love and embrace. Golaud leaps from the shadows, runs Pelléas through with his sword, and pursues Mélisande into the forest. They are later found, both injured, Mélisande having given birth to a baby daughter. Brought back to the castle, she dies, proclaiming her innocence to Golaud, her head turned towards her child, the hope for the future.

This is Maeterlinck's most important work and a key text of Symbolist drama. The lyrical quality of the language, the evocative settings, and the enigmatic characters all contribute to create a play of highly charged atmosphere, whether in the erotic cascade of Mélisande's hair that pours down over Pelléas, or in the sinister journey through the castle vaults. Debussy wrote an operatic version in 1902, in which Mélisande dies before answering Golaud's question about the innocence of her love for Pelléas.

Pentecost

A: David Edgar **Pf:** Stratford-upon-Avon, 1994 **Pb:** 1995 **G:** Drama in 2 acts; mainly English, also some Russian, Bulgarian, Turkish, Azeri, prose **S:** Church in unnamed south-east European country, 1990s **C:** 18m, 12f, extras

In an abandoned Romanesque church, which has been used as prison, warehouse, and museum, the art curator Gabriella Pecs has discovered a unique 13th-century fresco. She shows her find to Oliver Davenport, a British art historian, and they persuade the Minister of Culture to authorize restoration work. Professor Leo Katz of Cornell University flies in, and a former dissident Anna Jedlikova, now a magistrate, is called upon to rule on the ownership and fate of the fresco. Leo persuades 'the court' that the fresco is probably a 14th-century copy, and that the restorers will remove it for an international tour and perhaps never return it. A gang of armed international asylum seekers enter the church and seize Gabriella, Oliver, and Leo as hostages. When the church is surrounded by police, the refugees threaten to murder the hostages, and an Orthodox priest is sent in to negotiate. He brings insulin for the diabetic Oliver, secretly concealing a radio transmitter. Leo, now claiming that the fresco is a major art treasure, suggests that the refugees use it as a bargaining tool. A Catholic priest brings assurances that some hostage-takers will be resettled, but that the rest will be deported. A Palestinian woman refuses this offer, and prepares to torch the fresco. Commandos break in through the fresco, and Oliver and three refugees are shot dead.

In arguably David Edgar's most accomplished play, he once again displays his talent for dramatizing contemporary political concerns, here those of countries in south-east Europe after the fall of Communism, the desperate plight of international refugees, and the international heritage business. The fresco, which may have been a totally innovative work by a Muslim or merely an inferior copy, stands as a metaphor for new countries choosing between establishing their own national identity or merely imitating the West. Stewart Parker also wrote a *Pentecost* (1987) about four Belfast people during the Ulster Workers' Strike of 1974.

Perestroika. See ANGELS IN AMERICA.

Pericles (*The Late, And much admired Play, Called Pericles, Prince of Tyre*)

A: William Shakespeare (with George Wilkins?) Pf: *c.*1608, London Pb: 1609 G: Romance in 5 acts; blank verse and prose S: Antioch, Tyre, Tarsus, Pentapolis, on board ship, Ephesus, and Mitylene, indeterminate period in the ancient world C: 15m, 7f, extras

Pericles, Prince of Tyre, wishing to marry the daughter of the King of Antioch, must first solve a riddle. In succeeding, Pericles learns that the King has had incest with his daughter. Knowledge of this secret may cause Antioch to go to war against Tyre, so Pericles leaves his homeland. He is shipwrecked and lands at Pentapolis, where he wins the hand of Thaisa. Heading back to Tyre, he is once again caught in a storm. Thaisa, who has just given birth to a daughter, dies, and is buried at sea. Pericles leaves his daughter Marina with the Governor of Tarsus and returns to Tyre. The Governor's wife, growing jealous of Marina's beauty, orders her murder, but Marina is captured by pirates and sold to a brothel on the island of Mitylene. She is so virtuous that the clients of the brothel refuse to take her virginity. One day Pericles lands on Mitylene and is reunited with his daughter. Prompted by a dream, Pericles goes to the temple of Diana in Ephesus, where he discovers his lost wife Thaisa, who has after all survived.

Based on a poem by the 14th-century John Gower, who appears as a narrator in Shakespeare's play, *Pericles* is the earliest of Shakespeare's four romances, and is of contentious authenticity. The play did not appear in the 1623 Folio, and the writing in the first two acts is markedly weaker than the rest, either the result of a poorly reconstructed script or because they were written by a less able collaborator, possibly George Wilkins. The action describes a less than ideal hero, a man prepared to quit his kingdom and to abandon his daughter, who is ultimately redeemed by that same daughter and his faithful wife.

Perilous Adventures of Sally Banner, The. See CHAPEL PERILOUS, THE.

Persecution and Assassination of Jean-Paul Marat as Performed by the Inmates of the Asylum of Charenton under the Direction of the Marquis de Sade, The. See MARAT/SADE.

Persians (*Persai; Persae*)

A: Aeschylus Pf: 472 BC, Athens Tr: 1777 G: Greek trag. in verse S: The Persian royal palace at Susa, 480 BC C: 3m, 1f, chorus (m)

The chorus of old men sings of the massive army that the Persian King Xerxes is leading against the Greeks to avenge the shame of his defeat at Marathon. They and Xerxes' mother Atossa, wait anxiously for news from the battle. A messenger arrives with the terrible news that the Persian army has been destroyed by the Greeks. Amidst the general mourning, the ghost of the last king Darius appears. He foretells the destruction of the last remnants of the Persian army. Xerxes now returns, and the play ends with his lamentation and self-reproach.

Persians is the earliest extant Greek tragedy and the only one to be based on a historical rather than a mythical incident: the victory of the Greeks at the sea battle of Salamis in 480 BC, in which Aeschylus himself took part. It formed the central piece of a trilogy, possibly following one about the Battle of Marathon (in 490 BC) and preceding one that celebrated the Athenian victory. As it stands, we have a remarkable piece that, far from being a jingoistic celebration of the most decisive victory in Greek history, focuses on the suffering of the vanquished. At the same time, it reflects the Greek tragic view that *hubris* (pride), as displayed by the great Xerxes, is followed by *nemesis* (retribution). It offers a warning to the Athenians that they should not themselves now become hubristic, for fear of the consequences. *Persians* also employed dramatic devices that were to become well used by subsequent writers: the messenger's report and the ghostly apparition.

Peter Pan

AT: *The Boy Who Would Not Grow Up* A: J. M. Barrie. Pf: 1904, London Pb: 1928 G: Com. in 5 acts S: The Darling household, London, and Never Land, 1900s C: 16m, 9f, a dog, extras

When Wendy, John, and Michael are put to bed each night by their mother Mrs Darling and their nanny Nana the dog, their mother always tells them a bedtime story. Listening to these stories is Peter Pan, the boy who never grew up, who returns to Never Land to repeat the stories to the Lost Boys, who were lost when they fell out of their prams. Despite the interference of the jealous fairy Tinker Bell, Wendy and Peter become friends. Peter teaches the children to fly, and they all depart to Never Land, where Wendy becomes mother to the Lost Boys and where they have all sorts of adventures, including confrontations with the evil Captain Hook and his pirates. Eventually Peter Pan defeats Hook in a swordfight, and Hook is swallowed by a crocodile. The Darling children return to their relieved parents, bringing with them the Lost Boys who are reunited with their families. But Peter stays in Never Land, where he will never age.

Just as in *The *Admirable Crichton* Barrie transplants an English family on to a desert island to create a temporary respite from conventional society, here he creates a fabulous Never Land in which Peter Pan and the Lost Boys are removed from the flux of time to remain as children. Despite the excitements and pleasures of Never Land, however, the Darling children and the Lost Boys return to rejoin real life. So, although the play is regularly performed as a Christmas pantomime, an uncomplicated entertainment for children, it touches on serious issues of escape from reality.

Petrified Forest, The

A: Robert E. Sherwood Pf: 1935, New York Pb: 1935 G: Drama in 2 acts S: Diner in the Arizona desert, autumn 1934 C: 18m, 3f

Jason Maple runs a service station and lunch room in the Arizona desert but would like to move to Los Angeles. His daughter Gabrielle (Gabby) dreams of going to France, her mother's home. A disillusioned writer Alan Squier comes to the diner, and Gabby and he establish a close rapport, to the dismay of the pump attendant Boze Hertzlinger. Squier is offered a lift by a rich couple, but they all soon return as hostages of Duke Mantee, a gangster on the run, who is waiting with his gang for his girl. Squier is impressed with Mantee, considering him to be 'the last great apostle of rugged individualism', and suggests that they should both be buried in the nearby petrified forest like the once living trees there. Weary of life, Squier makes out his life insurance to Gabby and asks Mantee to shoot him. When the police arrive, tipped off by Mantee's girl, there is a shoot-out, and Mantee, true to his word, shoots Squier. As Squier dies in Gabby's arms, Duke Mantee makes his escape.

In the dark days of the Depression, the lonely world-weary poet and the rebellious man of action encapsulated much of the frustration and desperation of contemporary American society. That the two roles were performed by Leslie Howard and Humphrey Bogart, to be reprised in the film version of 1936, also helped it to success, although the critic Joseph Krutch's description of it as 'a melodramatic farce-with-a-moral' now seems a fair evaluation.

Pewterer a Politician, The. See POLITICAL TINKER, THE.

Pewterer Who Would Be Politician, The. See POLITICAL TINKER, THE.

Phaedra

AT: *Hippolytus* A: Lucius Annaeus Seneca W: AD 25–65 Tr: 1566 G: Latin trag. in 5 acts; verse S: The palace of Theseus in Athens, in the mythical past C: 3m, 2f, chorus (m), extras

While Theseus, King of Athens, is away on an adventure, his wife confesses to her Nurse that she lusts after her stepson, the chaste hunter Hippolytus. Despite the warnings of the Nurse, Phaedra seeks to end her life if she cannot have Hippolytus. He firmly repels the advances of Phaedra, declaring that he hates all women. He is on the point of killing Phaedra with his sword, when he relents, deciding she will suffer more if she lives on. The Nurse plots revenge, and, when Theseus returns, the Nurse and Phaedra accuse Hippolytus of raping Phaedra at sword-point, producing Hippolytus' sword as evidence. In a fit of rage Theseus calls on the God of the Sea to destroy his son, and a messenger comes to describe Hippolytus' violent end. Phaedra is distraught at Hippolytus' death and, having confessed to lying about the rape, commits suicide to join her stepson in Hades. Theseus is left alone to piece together the mangled remnants of his son's corpse.

Based closely on Euripides' **Hippolytus*, Seneca's version distinguishes itself in several respects. The tragic events are unleashed not by a jealous goddess but by blind passion ('We know no love that is not bound to sin'). Phaedra (who has now assumed the title role) herself declares her passion to Hippolytus, and the Nurse, no longer well meaning, becomes the engineer of the disaster. The final scene, in which Theseus tries to piece together the macabre jigsaw of his son's body, adumbrates the excesses of some Jacobean tragedy and borders on the grotesquely comic. Seneca's play is nevertheless a powerfully poetic exploration of passionate love.

Phaedra (*Phèdre*)

A: Jean Racine Pf: 1677, Paris Pb: 1677 Tr: 1756 G: Trag. in 5 acts; French alexandrines S: Theseus' palace in Troezen, in the mythical past C: 3m, 5f, extras

Phaedra is in thrall to Venus, the goddess of love, and is consumed by passion for her stepson Hippolytus. Yet again her adventuring husband Theseus has left her alone in the palace with Hippolytus, and, when news of Theseus' death comes, Phaedra is persuaded by her nurse and confidante to confess her love to Hippolytus. However, Hippolytus, who loves the Athenian princess Aricia, is horrified at his stepmother's declaration and cruelly rejects her. When Theseus unexpectedly returns, Phaedra, fearing that Hippolytus will denounce her, accuses him of having attempted to rape her. Theseus is so furious that he calls on the god Neptune to punish Hippolytus. Phaedra is about to relent and tell the truth, when she learns of Hipploytus' love for Aricia, and her jealousy prevents her from speaking. Neptune sends a huge tidal wave to destroy Hippolytus. Phaedra at last confesses the truth and poisons herself. Theseus is left to grieve over the deaths of his son and wife and to offer protection to Aricia.

Based on Euripides' **Hippolytus* and Seneca's **Phaedra*, Racine's play is the most accomplished of French classical tragedies. In the ancient Greek version Hippolytus' priggish chastity has affronted Aphrodite, the goddess of love, and so must be punished. Here, as in Seneca, he is an innocent victim of Phaedra's passion. In Racine, Hippolytus shows himself not only capable of love for Aricia, but offers her unselfish protection and pursues her claims to the throne of Athens. It is Phaedra, now the title figure, who is in the grip of uncontrolled passion, and, while she blames Venus, her situation derives from her own psychology not from some external divinity. At the start only Phaedra knows of her guilty secret. Imagining herself on the point of death, she tells her nurse, who then, because it seems that Theseus is dead, urges her to reveal her secret to Hippolytus. Twice Phaedra is misled by false evidence to speak. Twice she remains silent when she could have saved Hippolytus by telling the truth. There is no clearly defined divine pattern, as in Euripides: Phaedra's passion gradually seeps out like a stain of blood, bringing about destruction. Racine may be referring to the Jansenist philosophy of predetermination, or simply recording how a single passion can cause such suffering. Perhaps as a result of staring into this abyss of seemingly inescapable pain, Racine wrote nothing more for the stage other than a light musical piece and two biblical tragedies performed over a decade later at a girls' school.

Philadelphia, Here I Come!

A: Brian Friel **Pf**: 1964, Dublin **Pb**: 1965
G: Com. in 3 acts **S**: Gar's home, imaginary town of Ballybeg, County Donegal, Ireland, 1950s **C**: 11m, 3f

Twenty-five-year-old Gareth ('Gar') O'Donnell works in his widowed father's grocery and is frustrated by his father's taciturn coldness and the constrictions of his home town, dominated by the Church. He is now excited at the prospect of freedom, because a childless aunt, Lizzy Sweeney, has invited him to join her in Philadelphia. On the eve of his departure, his two personae, 'Public Gar' and 'Private Gar', reminisce about his life, mixing happiness at the prospect of a new life with nostalgia for the old. While Private Gar passes cynical comments, Public Gar re-enacts moments from his past: his unhappy relationship with his father, S. B. O'Donnell, whose inability to communicate hides love for his son; his affection for the housekeeper Madge, a mother-substitute; the disappointment when Kate Doogan, the girl he loved, is forced by her parents to turn down Gar's offer of marriage. He joyfully recalls too his aunt's offer of a prosperous living in the States, while being repelled by the hollow materialism she represents. In the early hours of the morning, Gar and his father spend their last moments together, still unable to communicate but silently sharing happy memories from Gar's childhood.

This play established Friel's reputation as a major Irish playwright and has become one of his most popular both on stage and as a film. It was one of the first plays to introduce a wider audience to small-town life in rural Ireland, which Friel views with a mixture of fondness and apprehension. While understanding the pressures on the young to emigrate, he also shows his concern over the kind of materialistic world to which they are escaping.

Philadelphia Story, The.

A: Philip Barry **Pf**: 1939, New York **Pb**: 1939
G: Com. in 3 acts **S**: Mansion outside Philadelphia, June 1939 **C**: 8m, 7f

Tracy Lord, a wealthy and beautiful divorcee, is about to remarry. Her fiancé George Kitteredge, although he began as a coal miner, is now an insufferable rich snob, but seems an improvement on her first husband C. K. Dexter Haven, whom she divorced for 'cruelty and drunkenness'. *Destiny* magazine is invited to cover the wedding to divert the society columns from her father's scandalous affair with a dancer in New York. Tracy becomes infatuated with their reporter Macaulay (Mike) Connor, a liberal and sensitive writer. Her ex-husband

Dexter and her father arrive uninvited for the wedding and sting Tracy with their searching comments about her priggish attitude, her father declaring her 'a perennial spinster, however many marriages'. In defiance, she gets drunk and swims naked in the pool with Mike, who is too honourable to take advantage of her. When confronted the next morning by her stuffy fiancé, she recognizes the hollowness of her forthcoming marriage. Having learnt new tolerance and understanding, she resolves that the marriage should go ahead – with ex-husband Dexter as her groom.

In the guise of his most popular comedy, Barry explored the tensions in American society between (usually new-found) wealth and wider humane understanding (a seam that is still being mined, as in James Cameron's film *The Titanic*). The play, which has echoes of Coward's **Private Lives*, was written mainly as a vehicle for Katharine Hepburn, who reprised the role in a film version with Cary Grant and James Stewart. It formed the basis for the musical *High Society* (1956).

Philanthropist, The

A: Christopher Hampton **Pf:** 1970, London **Pb:** 1970 **G:** Com. in 6 scenes **S:** Philip's college room, traditional English university, 1970s **C:** 4m, 3f

John has read his new play to Philip, a lecturer in Philology, and Donald, a fellow tutor in English. The critical remarks of the latter particularly upset John. John's play ends with a suicide, and to demonstrate its effectiveness, he puts a revolver in his mouth and accidentally blows his head off. A few days later, Philip is giving a dinner party, to which he has invited Donald, his fiancée Celia, Braham Head, a fashionable novelist, and two young women Elizabeth and Amarinta. Donald reports that the Prime Minister and his cabinet have been assassinated by a mad right-wing army officer. Donald questions Philip's decision to marry Celia, and suggests that he should choose Elizabeth. After the dinner party, Braham offers Celia a lift home, Donald leaves with Liz, and Amarinta stays behind and seduces Philip. The next morning, Celia discovers Amarinta in Philip's room and leaves, saying that she will never see him again. Amarinta expresses disappointment with Philip's performance and is offended by his refusal to try again. Celia returns, tells Philip that she spent the night with Braham, and parts from Philip, unable to envisage a marriage with someone who is so unassertive. That evening, Philip has decided to ask Liz to marry him, but then learns that Donald and Liz have fallen in love. He points a gun at himself, pulls the trigger – and lights a cigarette.

The Philanthropist is a witty response to Molière's *The *Misanthrope* (with the same constellation of characters, Celia even echoing the name of Célimène). Both Argan and Philip are emotional incompetents, but Philip attempts to be nice to everybody, which merely alienates them. His good nature and his detachment from the violent political events happening in the real world make him as eccentric and as destructive as his classical forebear.

Philaster (*Phylaster Or, Love lyes a Bleeding*)

AT: *Love Lies a-Bleeding* **A:** Francis Beaumont and John Fletcher **Pf:** *c.*1609–10 **Pb:** 1620 **G:** Tragicom. in 5 acts; blank verse and prose **S:** The court of Sicily and neighbouring woods, indeterminate period **C:** 11m, 5f, extras

Philaster is the popular heir to the throne of Sicily, but has been deprived of his crown by the usurping King of neighbouring Calabria. Worse still, Philaster loves the King's daughter Arethusa and is loved by her, but her father has determined that she is to wed a boastful Spaniard, Pharamond. Pharamond tells Philaster that Arethusa has had sex with Philaster's favourite page Bellario. Despite Bellario's denials, Philaster believes the lie. When the court goes hunting, Philaster discovers Arethusa fainting in Bellario's arms and, driven by jealousy, wounds them both. Overcome with remorse, Philaster confesses the deed and is condemned to death. In prison, Arethusa forgives him and marries him. When the people rise up in support of Philaster, the King is forced to accept the marriage. Once again Arethusa is accused of having slept with Bellario, whereupon Bellario reveals 'himself' to be a woman, who disguised herself as a man in order to serve her beloved Philaster. The King abdicates in Philaster's favour, and all ends happily.

Using a number of themes from Elizabethan comedies, like the girl disguised as a boy to serve her beloved master (**Twelfth Night*) and false reports of infidelity, *Philaster* contrives (as does **Cymbeline*) to turn these elements into a potentially tragic outcome (as in **Othello*). It is only the generosity of spirit of the noble characters, especially of Arethusa and Bellario, that saves the play from becoming a tragedy. By contrast, the tyrannical King (possibly a warning to James I about the limits of royal power) and the hated Spanish figure of Pharamond appear weak. Implausibly idealistic as the play might be, it plays well on the stage and was very popular in the 17th century.

Philoctetes (*Philoktetes*)

A: Sophocles Pf: 409 BC, Athens Tr: 1725
G: Greek drama in verse S: Before a cave on the Island of Lemnos, during the Trojan War
C: 5m, chorus (m)

On the way to Troy, the heroic Greek archer Philoctetes is bitten in the foot by a snake. The festering wound stinks so strongly that the Greeks abandon him on the Isle of Lemnos and continue to the war without him. Having now received a prophecy that Troy will never be defeated without Philoctetes' bow and arrows, Odysseus and Neoptolemus, son of Achilles, return to the island, hoping to induce Philoctetes to come to Troy with them. Knowing that Philoctetes will refuse to lend support to those who so mercilessly abandoned him nine years previously, Odysseus resorts to cunning. He uses Neoptolemus to win over Philoctetes with promises of bringing him to his homeland, and the suffering Philoctetes trustingly hands over his weapons. Before Odysseus can, however, celebrate the success of the expedition, Neoptolemus regrets this deception and gives back the bow and arrows. Indeed, he is so willing to help the desperate Philoctetes that he now promises to accompany him home to Greece, thus endangering the whole Greek army at Troy. With no apparent possibility of a satisfactory resolution, Heracles appears, ordering all three Greeks to Troy, where Philoctetes will be healed and become a great hero.

This version of the Philoctetes myth is the only one to have survived of those known to have been written by all three Greek tragedians. Sophocles' version explores themes of trust and deception, of expediency and humanity. For all his despicable behaviour (quite unlike the noble depiction of him in **Ajax*), Odysseus is acting in the best interests of the Greeks as a whole. Though praiseworthy, Neoptolemus' humanity would cost many noble lives, and he is vindicated only by the intervention of an immortal. One of Sophocles' last plays, written when he was in his eighties, it appears to reveal, especially in this use of the deus ex machina, the influence of Euripides, who was by now regularly outdoing Sophocles in the competitive drama festivals of Athens. The theme was used in one of the earliest pieces of Heiner Müller in 1968 and by Seamus Heaney in *The Cure at Troy* (1990).

Phoenix Too Frequent, A

A: Christopher Fry Pf: 1946, London Pb: 1946
G: Com. in 1 act; blank verse S: Tomb near Ephesus, ancient Greece C: 1m, 2f

A beautiful young Greek widow Dynamene, mourning the death of her husband Virilius, has been fasting by his tomb for two days with her servant Doto. Doto still yearns for men, but Dynamene is committed only to the memory of her husband. Weeping pitifully, she falls asleep. A handsome young soldier Tegeus, guarding the corpses of six hanged men, approaches the tomb, and shares his wine with Doto, who rapidly becomes tipsy and amorous. Waking, Dynamene drinks wine too and soon she and Tegeus have fallen in love with each other. Dynamene is convinced that her husband would approve and sends Doto away. Before they can consummate their love, Tegeus checks on his corpses and discovers that one has been stolen. Since this means certain death for him,

Dynamene graciously offers the body of her husband to replace the missing corpse.

Based on a story from Petronius' *Satyricon*, this short comedy offers an entertaining conflict between duty to the dead and the obligation to live life to the full. So the grotesque act of handing over her husband's corpse is justified by Dynamene: 'And now we can give his death | The power of life.' The classical setting and use of blank verse point backwards rather than forwards, and Fry's playwriting, while it enjoyed some popularity, now seems dated.

Phormio

A: Terence Pf: 161 BC, Rome Tr: 1598 G: Latin com. in verse S: A street in Athens, before the homes of Phaedria and Antipho, 2nd C. BC C: 11m, 2f, extras

Two cousins Phaedria and Antipho have fallen in love, the former with a courtesan whom he cannot afford, the latter with an impoverished orphan, Phanium, who is in fact his uncle's daughter, the product of a bigamous relationship in Lemnos. Phormio, a helpful parasite, helps Antipho by invoking an Athenian law which stipulates that a close relative must marry an orphan (having no idea that Antipho is indeed Phanium's nearest relative). When their fathers return, they are outraged at Antipho's marriage and pay Phormio to have it dissolved. Instead Phormio hands over the cash to Phaedria, allowing him to buy his courtesan. Finally, Phaedria's father is shamed into compliance by having his bigamy exposed and Phanium revealed as his daughter.

Based on a no longer extant Greek original, *Phormio* is arguably the most sophisticated of Roman comedies, thanks to its intricate plot, comic ironies, parallel situations (in which the two cousins are envious of each other, both believing the other to be more fortunate in love), and, above all, to the character of Phormio. While Plautus' slaves (as in Plautus' **Pseudolus*) are often scheming rogues, Phormio, while naturally self-serving, is clever enough to use the law to his own ends and appears as the righter of wrongs. He provided the prototype for Molière's *The Rogueries of Scapin* (1671), in turn imitated by Thomas Otway (*The Cheats of Scapin*, 1677), Edward Ravenscroft (*Scaramouch as Philosopher*, 1677), and Colman the Elder (*The Man of Business*, 1774).

Phylaster. See PHILASTER.

Physicists, The (*Die Physiker*)

A: Friedrich Dürrenmatt Pf: 1962, Zurich Pb: 1962 Tr: 1963 G: Drama in 2 acts; German prose S: Private mental sanatorium, *c.*1960 C: 16m, 4f

Police are investigating the murder of a nurse by one of the sanatorium patients, who believes himself to be Einstein. A patient calling himself Sir Isaac Newton has also recently strangled a nurse, but he insists that he is not mad, because he is merely pretending to be Newton; in fact, he claims, he is the real Einstein. A third mad physicist, Johann Wilhelm Möbius, believes himself ruled by King Solomon. He is visited by his embarrassed family, but refuses to recognize them. When a nurse tells Möbius that she does not think him mad and believes in his genius, he strangles her tearfully. Once again, the police are powerless to arrest a madman: 'Justice is on holiday.' 'Newton' now reveals that he is in fact a Western scientist who has been sent to spy on Möbius. 'Einstein' explains that he too has simulated madness, in order to win Möbius's discoveries for the East. All have had to kill the nurses who guessed their secret. Newton and Einstein attempt to persuade Möbius to leave with them, the Westerner promising freedom to develop his ideas regardless of where they will lead, the Soviet apologist promising him political power to manipulate the use of his ideas. Möbius refuses, saying that his discoveries must be kept secret, for exploiting them will destroy the world. All three agree to remain incarcerated in their asylum. However, the sanatorium's director Dr Zahnd, who is truly mad, has copied all Möbius's findings. Armed with these, King Solomon will help Zahnd to gain control of the world.

As in Brecht's **Life of Galileo*, Dürrenmatt here debates the social responsibility of the scientist. In contrast with Brecht's essentially realistic and historical setting, however, Dürrenmatt concentrates the action into one room and one day, schematically playing with his three figures to reach a deeply pessimistic conclusion: 'What was once thought can never be unthought.'

Plain Dealer, The

A: William Wycherley **Pf**: 1676, London **Pb**: 1677 **G**: Com. in 5 acts; prose **S**: Private lodgings, Westminster Hall, and The Cock in Bow Street, London, Restoration period **C**: 7m, 5f, extras

Captain Manly, a misanthropic 'plain dealer', returns from fighting at sea, where a shipwreck has incurred heavy losses for him. He placed a large sum of money in the care of his fiancée Olivia, but she and her friends mock at the plain-spoken sea dog and she has secretly married Manly's best friend Vernish. Fidelia, who is in love with Manly, disguised herself as a boy to be near Manly at sea, and is now employed as an intermediary to win back Olivia. Olivia falls in love with Fidelia and arranges to meet with 'him'. Manly goes instead and exposes Olivia's treachery. Discovering Fidelia's true identity, not only as a woman but as a rich heiress, Manly prepares to reward her loyalty by marrying her. In a sub-plot, Manly's lieutenant Freeman, who is much more cunning than his superior, gets the better of the avaricious and litigious Widow Blackacre, Olivia's cousin.

The central figure may owe something to Molière's **Misanthrope*, and the story of the servant who is sent to woo a reluctant beloved echoes **Twelfth Night*, even naming the scornful mistress Olivia. However, the biting satire of Restoration superficiality is very much Wycherley's own, and is more reminiscent of Jonson than of Molière or Shakespeare. Wycherley had himself been a soldier and spent most of his life in debt, so his attacks on contemporary society were founded on bitter experience. Significantly, Freeman, who adapts to the corruption of society, succeeds in his enterprise, while Manly's honesty may lead to an improbable fairy-tale ending but not to the satisfaction of avenging himself on those that have tricked him.

Play

A: Samuel Beckett **Pf**: 1963, Ulm, Germany; 1964, London **Pb**: 1964 **G**: Drama in 1 act (repeated) **S**: Three urns in the afterlife **C**: 1m, 2f

The heads of W1 (Woman 1), W2 (Woman 2), and M (Man) are seen protruding from three identical grey urns. Each speaks only when a spotlight is on him or her. In rapid toneless voices, they relive an unhappy love triangle. W1 is married to M, who is having an affair with W2, a well-to-do woman in Kent. Although she has no proof, W1 is convinced of M's infidelity and insists that he give up his mistress. W1 visits W2, demanding that she leave her husband alone. M confesses to W1, and they are reconciled. W1 goes to have a gloat over her rival, and W2 is furious at M for betraying their secret. M leaves W1, and W1, stricken, goes to W2's house to find it 'bolted and barred'. It would seem that W1 is killed in a car crash on her way home. Meanwhile, M has stopped coming to W2, and she burns all his things and leaves home. Now in death, the three speculate on the situation of the others, and M says: 'I know now, all that was just . . . play.' The whole piece is then repeated almost identically.

In *Play* Beckett pushed his abstract theatre further than it had gone before. Based partly on his own difficult relationships with Peggy Guggenheim and his wife Suzanne, Beckett envisages the torment of hell as being caught in an endless cycle of repetition of a sordid sexual game, from which M hoped to have escaped but which, prompted by the unrelenting interrogation of the spotlight, he will have to relive to eternity.

Playboy of Seville, The. See TRICKSTER OF SEVILLE, THE.

Playboy of the Western World, The

A: J. M. Synge **Pf**: 1907, Dublin **Pb**: 1907 **G**: Com. in 3 acts **S**: A shebeen near a village on the coast of Mayo, Ireland, 1900s **C**: 7m, 5f, extras

Pegeen Mike (Margaret Flaherty) lives with her father Michael James in a rough country public-house. She is engaged to a local farmer Shawn Keogh, but he is so afraid of the priest's disapproval that he flees rather than stay with her alone. A tired young man Christy Mahon arrives. Eventually Christy confesses that he is on the run from the police because he has murdered his father. He becomes the centre of attention, and Michael James offers him a job as potboy, since he is clearly a brave young fellow. Pegeen becomes attracted to the stranger and repels the advances of Shawn's cousin the Widow Quin, who takes a fancy to Christy as well. By the following morning Christy's fame has spread: the village girls dance attendance on him until they are chased away by Pegeen. Shawn Keogh and Widow Quin come and attempt to bribe him to leave. All is going well for him until suddenly Christy's father, wounded but decidedly not dead, appears, and Christy has to buy Widow Quin's silence with the promise of money when he becomes owner of the shebeen. Christy distinguishes himself at the village sports, becoming 'the champion Playboy of the Western World'. Widow Quin tries to persuade everyone that Mahon is a lunatic. Michael James, concerned about his daughter's infatuation with a stranger, insists that she marry Shawn that very day. When Christy challenges Shawn for her hand, Shawn runs away in terror, and Michael James gives his blessing to Christy. Mahon reappears and begins to beat Christy. Christy picks up a spade and runs at his father. There is a yell outside and Christy returns, saying that he has finally killed his father. Everyone reacts with horror and seizes hold of Christy to take him to the police. Mahon staggers in again, frees Christy, and they leave together. Christy is no longer afraid of his father, and Pegeen is left to mourn the loss of her Playboy.

Not only is *The Playboy* arguably the best Irish comedy, it also formed a milestone on Ireland's halting journey towards a national theatre. When it was premiered on 26 January 1907, riots broke out at the recently founded Abbey Theatre. Nationalist elements in the middle-class audience were outraged that the rural Irish should be portrayed as violent, fickle, and willing to glamorize patricide. The riots were repeated by Irish Americans in New York, Boston, and Philadelphia on the Abbey tour 1911–12. Synge's comic but profound point is that, as could be seen later in the success of Noraid (Irish Northern Aid Committee), people may delight in the idea of violence but be horrified by violence itself, for 'there's a great gap between a gallous [gallows's] story, and a dirty deed'. There is also an Oedipal motif in the way the nonentity Christy grows into manhood through the symbolic slaying of his father.

Play Called the Four P.P., The (*The Playe called the foure P.P.: a newe and a very mery interlude of a palmer, a pardoner, a pothecary, a pedler*)

A: John Heywood **Pf:** *c.*1520 **Pb:** *c.*1543
G: Interlude in rhyming couplets **S:** England, medieval period **C:** 4m

The four P's argue their cases in turn: The Palmer (a pilgrim who has visited the Holy Land) boasts of all the shrines he has seen. The Pardoner (a man licensed to sell papal indulgences) questions the value of these pilgrimages, when the Palmer could have found redemption merely by buying a pardon. The Pothecary (apothecary or pharmacist) points out that nobody dies in a state of grace without help from him. The Pedlar questions the need for the other three, whereas he keeps women happy by selling them trifles. The Pedlar now challenges the other three to a contest in lying. The Pardoner boasts about his absurd relics and the Pothecary about his fatuous cures, but the Palmer tops them both by claiming that on all his travels he never saw a woman who lost her temper.

Like **Fulgens and Lucrece*, this interlude, intended as an entertainment during a banquet, represents a link between the medieval morality play and the robust secular drama of the Elizabethan period. Although there is neither action nor plot development, the confrontation between the four characters is enlivened with wit, bawdy comments, and wordplay. The stereotype of the angry woman, supposedly never encountered by the lying

Palmer, was to be explored more interestingly by Shakespeare in *The *Taming of the Shrew*.

Play of Adam, The (*Le Jeu d'Adam; Le Mystère d'Adam; Ordo Representationis Ade*)

A: Anon. Pf: *c*.1140–74, France Pb: 1918 Tr: 1928 G: Mystery play in three parts, mainly medieval (Anglo-Norman) French and some Latin verse S: Paradise, hell, and earth, the biblical past C: 10m, 1f, extras

The three parts deal with Adam and Eve in the Garden of Eden, the slaying of Abel by his brother Cain, and a procession of Old Testament prophets. It begins with a reading of the first chapter of Genesis, with responses by the choir taken from the Septuagesima liturgy. There follows the acting out of the Fall, with Adam and Eve finally being driven towards hell, the first murder, and concludes with a series of prophecies by Abraham, Moses, Isaiah, and King Nebuchadnezzar of the Redeemer who will cleanse humankind of their sins and offer salvation to the world.

This is the first biblical piece to have been written in the vernacular (French) rather than in Latin and performed outdoors and not in a church. It was also acted not sung, unlike the 11th-century *Sponsus*, and so stands as the first of the popular mystery plays that dominated medieval theatre in Europe. While there are many long didactic speeches, some of the text relates more closely to the experience of the contemporary audience. In the telling of the story of the banishment from Eden one notes the realism of the personal confrontations: God (here called the Figura) warning Adam, Eve being cleverly tempted by Satan, Adam resisting temptation but then being taunted by his wife until he finally gives way and brings about the Fall of humankind. While over 150 French mystery plays survive, English speakers will be more familiar with cycles such as **York*, and **Chester*.

Plaza Suite (Visitor from Mamaroneck; Visitor from Hollywood; Visitor from Forest Hills)

A: Neil Simon Pf: 1968, New York Pb: 1969 G: 3 linked 1-act dramas S: Plaza Hotel, New York, 1960s C: (1) 3m, 2f; (2) 2m, 1f; (3) 2m, 2f

(1) *Visitor from Mamaroneck*. Because their suburban house is being painted, Sam and Karen Nash make the seemingly romantic gesture of taking the same suite at the Plaza Hotel they had for their honeymoon 24 years previously. But Karen discovers that it is the wrong date, the wrong room, and then that Sam is having an affair with his secretary. She is left to drink champagne alone when he goes out to be with his mistress. (2) *Visitor from Hollywood*. Jesse Kiplinger is a successful movie producer, in New York on business. He calls up Muriel Tate, a former high school sweetheart, and she comes to his room. They talk of their own lives, of his three divorces and of her humdrum life as a mother of three in the suburbs. By following his career, she has experienced some vicarious excitement. Finally, they go to bed together. (3) *Visitor from Forest Hills*. Roy and Norma Hubley face a crisis: their daughter Mimsey, minutes before her wedding, has locked herself in the bathroom and refuses to come out. She has had second thoughts about the marriage, because she does not want to end up like her bickering parents. In desperation, Roy tries breaking down the bathroom door and even climbing on to the ledge outside to get in the window. Eventually the bridegroom Borden Eisley arrives and takes charge of the situation. He speaks just two words, and the bride emerges radiant, ready for her wedding. The two words were: 'Cool it.'

These three short plays, which can be performed separately or as an exercise in virtuosity by the same actors performing the roles of man and wife/lover in each piece, offer a fine example of Simon's gently probing depiction of contemporary American marriage. In each there are failed dreams: the hopeless attempt by Karen and Sam to revive the romance of their honeymoon; the admission by Jesse and Muriel that their lives have been loveless; and the frantic, bickering behaviour of the Hubleys. Only Borden's calm authoritative manner seems to hold out promise for the future.

Plebeians Rehearse the Uprising, The (*Die Plebejer proben den Aufstand*)

A: Günter Grass **Pf**: 1966, Berlin **Pb**: 1966 **Tr**: 1967 **G**: Pol. drama in 4 acts; German prose and blank verse **S**: Theatre in East Germany, 17 June 1953 **C**: 24m, 2f

The 'Boss' (i.e. Bertolt Brecht) is preparing for a rehearsal of his own version of Shakespeare's **Coriolanus*, in which he will show the Plebeians to be 'class-conscious enemies' of the aristocratic hero, represented by a life-size puppet. During the rehearsal, news comes of workers' uprisings against the State's excessive demands for increased productivity. Some workers then appear in the theatre and demand that the Boss support their cause. He refuses to commit himself. Quoting Lenin, that 'revolt, like war, is an art', the 'Boss' recognizes the senselessness of the workers' uprising, which is an outburst of frustration and not a coherent political action, but he still cannot side with the rulers against them. Instead, he involves the workers in the *Coriolanus* rehearsals, recording on tape their comments. Half-jokingly, workers threaten to hang the Boss and his dramaturg, but these two, using Menenius' story of the body politic, manage to talk themselves free. An injured worker is brought in, and news comes that the uprising is being brutally suppressed. Finally, the Boss issues an ambiguous statement, mildly criticizing but ultimately supporting the government ('pussyfooting' as 'Volumnia' remarks). Everyone knows that only the last part of his statement will be made public, but the Boss's theatre will be safe. He withdraws into artistic isolation: 'Guilty myself, I accuse you.'

Grass, better known as a novelist, here wrote a searching examination of the role of the artist at a time of social upheaval, focusing on Brecht's ambiguous response to the 1953 uprisings in the German Democratic Republic. The play, by creating the rather improbable situation of workers getting involved in a theatre rehearsal while their fellows are marching in the streets outside, also explores the Situationists' recognition of the theatricality of political demonstrations.

Plebiscite. See FEAR AND MISERY OF THE THIRD REICH.

Plenty

A: David Hare **Pf**: 1978, London **Pb**: 1978 **G**: Pol. drama in 12 scenes **S**: London, 1947, 1950s, and 1961–2; Blackpool, 1962; St Benoît, near Poitiers, France, 1943–4; and Brussels, 1947 **C**: 9m, 5f

1962: Susan Brock, née Traherne, is leaving her husband Raymond. 1943: Susan, working in Special Operations in occupied France encounters 'Code Name' Lazar, a fellow agent dropped by parachute. 1947: Susan meets Raymond, who works in the diplomatic service in Brussels. He visits her at weekends in London, where she works in a boring secretarial post and lives with artistic Alice. 1951: Susan, keen to have a child, asks Mick, a spiv, if he will oblige. 1952: Susan, now an advertising copywriter, is still not pregnant. She persuades Mick to leave by firing a revolver at him. 1956: Susan, now married to Raymond and living in luxury, entertains guests, including Raymond's former boss, who admits that Britain's Suez expedition is based on a lie. Susan, under strain, shocks the guests by incoherently talking of political sham and her mental illness. 1961: Susan and Raymond return from his posting in Iran to attend his boss's funeral. Susan gives money for drugs to an attractive teenager, confesses her attraction to Alice, and decides to stay in London. 1962: Susan is concerned that her behaviour has damaged her husband's career. Raymond leaves the diplomatic service, and Susan has a breakdown, tearing up dresses and throwing away their possessions. In a seedy hotel in Blackpool she meets up with Lazar, who is now married and living in the suburbs. He leaves her drugged on her bed, and the scene transforms to France in 1944, where Susan insists: 'We will improve our world.'

Plenty shows the ideals for which people fought in the Second World War betrayed by the 'plenty' and self-indulgence of post-war Britain. Susan is not idealized, for her behaviour is equally self-indulgent. However, as Hare says, 'people go clinically mad if what they believe bears no relation to how they live'. The piece was made into a successful film with Meryl Streep in 1985.

Plot Discovered, A. See VENICE PRESERVED.

Plough and the Stars, The

A: Sean O'Casey **Pf:** 1926, Dublin **Pb:** 1926; rev. 1952 **G:** Trag. in 4 acts **S:** Living rooms of the Clitheroes and of Bessie Burgess in a tenement house, the street outside, and a public house, Dublin, 1915–16 **C:** 10m, 6f

Against the background of mounting resistance to British rule in Ireland, we meet the inhabitants of an old Georgian tenement house in a Dublin street: Jack Clitheroe, a bricklayer, and his pretty wife Nora; his uncle Peter, a labourer who fancies himself in an antiquated uniform; his cousin, The Covey, a fitter with aggressively left-wing views; Bessie Burgess, a loyalist fruit-vendor; Fluther Good, a commonsensical carpenter; and Mrs Gogan, a charwoman with a consumptive daughter. At last Jack and Nora are alone together, but their romantic interlude is broken by news that Jack has been made a commandant in the Irish Citizen Army, which is preparing to rise up against the British. Nora is distressed as Jack marches off with his men. In a nearby pub, the drinkers comment on events while a noisy meeting of nationalist rebels takes place outside: the prostitutes complain that business is bad, Uncle Peter is inspired by the rhetoric, and The Covey argues for a Marxist revolution. Fluther leaves with a prostitute, while Jack Clitheroe is heard marshalling his men. Half a year later, and the 1916 Easter Rising is in full swing. Outside the tenement house the inhabitants are discussing the crisis, when Fluther carries in Nora. She is now pregnant and had gone through the battle lines in search of Jack, when she collapsed. Bessie denounces the Rising, while The Covey insists it is the wrong fight. Bessie and Mrs Gogan seize the opportunity to do some looting with an old pram. Clitheroe rushes in unhurt, and, despite Nora's desperate pleas, he returns to the battle. Half crazed, Nora goes into labour, and Bessie bravely goes off in search of a doctor. A few days later, everyone is hiding in Bessie's attic room. Nora has lost the baby and is now completely deranged. The men nervously play cards, when news comes that Clitheroe has been killed. British soldiers come and take the men away. Nora stands by the window, and her life is saved by Bessie who, pushing her away, gets shot herself. She dies singing a hymn. The British are victorious, and the soldiers return to make themselves a cup of tea and have a song.

This final part of O'Casey's Dublin trilogy (with *The *Shadow of a Gunman* and **Juno and the Paycock*) is chronologically the earliest, dealing with the Easter Rising. While it seemed just acceptable that O'Casey should mock elements of Irish nationalism in the two earlier plays, the Easter Rising, ill-conceived as it was, had become a sacred event in republican thinking. O'Casey's sober assessment, together with the depiction of prostitutes on stage, led, as with *The *Playboy of the Western World*, to rioting in the theatre, and caused Yeats to denounce the Abbey audience once again. O'Casey considered this his best play, because the comic element did not dominate as much as in *Juno*, thus allowing the political commentary to emerge with greater clarity. We may disagree.

Ploutus. See WEALTH.

Plutus. See WEALTH.

Poet and the Women, The. See WOMEN AT THE THESMOPHORIA.

Pohutukawa Tree, The

A: Bruce Mason **Pf:** 1957, Wellington, New Zealand **Pb:** 1960; rev. 1985 **G:** Trag. in 3 acts **S:** New Zealand, 1950s **C:** 7m, 6f

Aroha Mataira, a Maori matriarch, lives in a house dominated by a large pohutukawa tree, planted by her grandfather so that its red blossoms would commemorate the blood spilt in a great battle against the British. Aroha has been converted to the strict Protestantism of the colonialists, so that she is no longer fully a part of the tribe whose ancestral land she lives on; nor, as a Maori in the 1950s, can she hope to be integrated with the local *pakeha* (European) community. Problems mount for her: her rebellious daughter Queenie has an affair with a feckless white barman Roy McDowell and becomes pregnant; her son Johnny gets drunk and desecrates the local church; pressure is brought to bear by her minister to sell her land, which she guards for her ancestors, so that it can be used as an orchard. European values and Christian teaching urge her to give way to the encroachment of the dull, philistine, alien *pakeha* community, but her ancient warrior blood stirs her to defiance: 'God made this land for us. It cannot be sliced.' Finally, she finds the way out of her dilemma by taking her own life.

Mason stands as the first New Zealand writer to be primarily a playwright in a country at a time when the one professional theatre company, the New Zealand Players, who premiered *The Pohutukawa Tree*, collapsed for lack of funding in 1960. This play (the first New Zealand play to appear on the school syllabus) distinguishes itself also by offering the first major role to a Maori actress and analyses with great sympathy, if not always with total authenticity, the situation of the Maori in their relationship with European settlers.

Political Tinker, The (*Den politiske kandestøber*)

AT: *The Blue-Apron Statesman; The Pewterer (Who Would Be) a Politician* **A:** Ludvig Holberg **Pf:** 1722, Copenhagen **Pb:** 1723 **Tr:** 1885 **G:** Com. in 5 acts; Danish prose **S:** Von Bremen's home and environs, Hamburg, early 18th c. **C:** 10m, 4f, extras

Hermann von Bremen, a respectable pewterer in Hamburg, decides to take up politics. He abandons his trade to devote himself to reading political books without understanding. He rejects the wheelwright Anton as a fitting suitor for his daughter Engelke, seeking instead a son-in-law who has studied politics. Every day he hosts a meeting of Hamburg tradesmen, the 'Collegium Politicum', who debate the state of the German nation. Two young men decide to cure him of his passion for politics by disguising themselves as officials and offering him the post of mayor. At first, he and his wife are thrilled at this elevation, but, as 'official' papers mount around him, he is driven to such desperation that he even contemplates suicide. He is so relieved to learn that the whole thing has been a joke that he abandons his political ambitions and gives his blessing to his daughter's marriage to Anton.

By ridiculing the vices of an extreme comic type, the first native Danish comedy clearly owes much to Molière. But Holberg injects into the French model an authentic northern European setting, and by establishing a testing situation for his comic figures, creates a comedy which raises significant social questions. Indeed, the satirical elements of the play almost led to its banning. However, the immediate popularity of the piece (many of the first-night audience were forced to remain in the yard outside the theatre) launched both a native Danish theatre and the playwriting career of Holberg, who wrote a further 25 comedies in the following five years.

Pooka, The. See HARVEY.

Portrait d'une femme. See PORTRAIT OF A WOMAN.

Portrait of a Woman (*Portrait d'une femme*)

A: Michel Vinaver **Pf:** 1985, Lyons (public reading); 1988, Paris **Pb:** 1986 **Tr:** 1989 **G:** Drama without act divisions; French prose and free verse **S:** Paris courtroom, Paris apartment, Lille, Dunkirk, Ulm, 1944, 1950–3 **C:** 12m, 5f (to be performed by 8m, 3f)

When Sophie Auzanneau discovers that the man she loves, fellow medical student Xavier Bergeret, has become engaged to another woman, she lies in wait for him, shoots him three times, then tries to gas herself. She is put on trial for murder. In a series of intercut flashbacks we see Sophie and Xavier's early courtship, his meeting with Sophie's parents, Xavier's relationship with his fiancée, and Sophie's purchase of a gun. After Xavier falls desperately in love with Sophie, Sophie has an affair with one of the medical tutors and refuses to marry Xavier. She goes to Vienna and has an affair with a French engineer. In a further flashback to the war, Sophie is seen at 17 having an affair with a German doctor in the army of occupation. In 1950, she visits him in Ulm, now acknowledging her love for Xavier, and is confused about where she is heading. When Xavier rejects her, Sophie threatens to poison herself (just as later in prison she tries to commit suicide by cutting a vein). Finally, Sophie is given a life sentence.

Vinaver is the major dramatist of the *théâtre du quotidien* ('theatre of the everyday'), and *Portrait of a Woman* is based on an actual murder case, that of Pauline Dubuisson, convicted in 1951 of murdering her lover. Vinaver does not use the elements of Sophie's past (the deaths of her brothers in the war, her exploitation by an older German officer, her parents' lack of warmth) to justify her crime. Rather, he shows in a collage of voices from present and past, many taken verbatim from court reports, that no one, perhaps not even Sophie herself, understands this murderess who is represented only in a 'portrait'.

Portrait of Dora (*Portrait de Dora*)

A: Hélène Cixous **Pf**: 1976, Paris **Pb**: 1976; rev. 1986 **Tr**: 2004 **G**: Drama in 1 act; French prose **S**: Vienna, 1899–1900 **C**: 3m, 2f, voice (m or f)

At the age of 12, Dora has coughing spells and is unable to speak. Her father Mr B seeks the help of Sigmund Freud, who analyses her for some years. Dora reveals that a friend Mr K, whose wife has become very close to Mr B, tried to seduce Dora by a mountain lake, but Mr B wonders whether this is merely a hysterical fantasy. Dora speaks of cutting the throat of a man who abused her (a dream?). She imagines Mrs K to be the Madonna and herself the Infant Jesus. Obsessed with Mrs K, Dora contemplates suicide. Mr K wants to take away the key to the jewellery box he gave Dora (Freudian images of phallus and vulva). Dora tells how she used to wake up with a man beside her bed (her father? Mr K? her imagination?). The 18-year-old Dora takes Freud to the lake where she claims to have been molested. Dora gives up her course of analysis. When she sees Mr K run over by a carriage, a burden is lifted from her.

Cixous has been one of the most prominent women writers in the move to develop a feminine aesthetic of drama. In place of plot, action, and climax, all of which can be dismissed as essentially male in their preoccupations, Cixous here offers a play for voices which, eschewing linearity and overt structure, recounts dreams, moments, insights, and ambiguities based on one of Freud's most famous case studies. In his attempt to probe the 'hysteria' of his young female patient, Freud's rational questioning fails to penetrate the true nature of Dora.

Post Office, The (*Dakghar*)

A: Rabindranath Tagore **Pf**: 1913, Dublin; 1917, India **Pb**: 1912 **Tr**: 1914 **G**: Drama in 2 acts; Bengali prose **S**: Indian village, early 20th c. **C**: 8m, 2 children (1m, 1f)

The young boy Amal has fallen sick, and, since autumn is approaching, the doctor advises Amal's guardian to keep him to his room. Amal's only contact with the outside world is through his window. From here he watches village life, talks to passers-by, gives his toys to some boys so that he may see them playing from his window, and is promised by the flower-seller's daughter Sudha that she will bring him some flowers. From the watchman, he learns that the big building with the flag is His Majesty's new Post Office, and, the watchman suggests, the King himself may send Amal a letter. The village headman hands Amal a blank sheet of paper, which he claims to be a letter from His Majesty. Amal dreams of being a royal postman himself, delivering the King's messages to small boys. While he awaits a visit from the King, another doctor comes and orders doors and windows to be opened, so that the stars may shine in. As Amal slowly falls asleep, perhaps to die, Sudha keeps her promise, and brings him some flowers.

In the year he gained the Nobel Prize for Literature, this short lyrical play added to Tagore's international fame, being seen in Dublin (thanks to Yeats), Paris, and Berlin before being performed in his native India. In addition to offering a charming and mercifully unsentimental tale, the play has also been regarded as a metaphor of the artist, looking out on but never wholly engaging in life, and beyond that, the whole human experience of the soul with its yearning and flights of imagination being trapped in the limitations of the body.

Poupées électriques. See ELECTRIC DOLLS.

Power of Darkness, The (*Vlast tmy, ili 'Kogotok uvayaz, vsey ptichke propast'*)

AT: *If a Claw is Caught the (Whole) Bird is Lost* A: Leo Tolstoy **Pf:** 1888, Paris; 1895, St Petersburg **Pb:** 1887 **Tr:** 1905 **G:** Drama in 5 acts; Russian prose **S:** Russian village, end 19th c. **C:** 11m, 11f, extras

Anisya, a vain and attractive 32-year-old, is married to the peasant Pyotr, a sickly widower 10 years her senior. She begins an affair with the 23-year-old farm hand Nikita. Nikita's mother realizes this when his parents come to fetch him home to fulfil his promise to marry a local girl Marina; so she gives Anisya a sleeping potion to give to her husband. The potion kills the husband, and Nikita and Anisya marry. However, Nikita goes with Akulina, Pyotr's daughter from his first marriage, to the nearby town, spending cash stolen from Pyotr, and begins an affair with the simple girl. When she becomes pregnant, the baby is murdered so as not to endanger her chances of making a good match. When she eventually finds a husband, Nikita encounters at Akulina's wedding the rejected Marina, now happily married. This meeting drives him to the brink of suicide, but persuaded back to the wedding party by his mother and wife, he confesses everything before the astonished guests.

Although actively committed to reforming the lot of Russian peasants, Tolstoy had no sentimentality about their lives. In a way that was uncomfortable for the authorities (the play was not licensed for performance in Russia until 1895), Tolstoy here exposes their financially and sexually acquisitive nature, portraying them as both selfish and as victims. Nineteenth-century realism once again allows the action of a play to span several years, and this epic structure and harsh depiction of simple peasants made the play very popular amongst the naturalists, influencing writers like Gerhart Hauptmann.

Price, The

A: Arthur Miller **Pf:** 1968, New York **Pb:** 1968 **G:** Drama in 2 acts **S:** Attic of Manhattan brownstone about to be demolished, 1960s **C:** 3m, 1f

Police Sergeant Victor Franz and his wife Esther wait in the apartment of Victor's late father for the arrival of a dealer who will offer them a price for all his old furniture and ornaments. Victor joined the police when he had to drop out of college to support his father in the hard days of the Depression. Nearing retirement, he is extremely resentful of his brother Walter, who became a famous surgeon while contributing only a few dollars a month to his father's upkeep. At last the elderly dealer arrives. He is Gregory Solomon, an 89-year-old Jew in failing health but with a warm sense of humour. After checking on the items for sale, he finally offers $1,100, which Victor uncertainly accepts. At this moment, Walter, whom Victor has not seen for 16 years, enters. The brothers confront each other, Victor complaining that he sacrificed his life while Walter was able to go on to be a success. However, Walter reveals that he has had a breakdown and is now divorced; moreover, Victor's sacrifice was an illusion, because their father kept a secret horde of his own money. Insisting that their home life was a sham, Walter says: 'What was unbearable is not that it fell apart, it was that there was never anything here.' Finally, Solomon is left alone to complete the inventory. He puts on a 'laughing record' and begins to laugh 'with tears in his eyes'.

In this wholly realistic piece, Miller explores some of his recurrent themes of guilt, resentment, and of the search for success in a materialistic society. All four characters, in different ways, have had to pay the price for a life without love and honesty.

Prince of Homburg, The (*Prinz Friedrich von Homburg*)

A: Heinrich von Kleist **W:** 1810 **Pf:** 1821, Vienna **Pb:** 1821 **Tr:** 1875 **G:** Drama in 5 acts; German blank verse **S:** The battlefield of

Fehrbellin and environs, 1675 **C:** 13m, 2f, extras

The Prince of Homburg is general of the cavalry in the army of Friedrich Wilhelm, the Elector of Brandenburg, who is preparing to confront the Swedish forces at Fehrbellin. Homburg, in a somnambulistic state, dreams of glory and of the love of the Elector's niece Princess Natalie. When the orders are given out, he hardly pays attention, so that in the ensuing battle he attacks before the command is given. Although he achieves a resounding victory, he is placed under arrest for disobedience. At first he is terrified of the impending death sentence and pleads with Natalie to intervene on his behalf. However, when the Elector offers to free him if Homburg is able to protest his innocence, Homburg agrees that he must die. He asks only that the Elector does not make peace with the Swedes but pushes home his victory. Blindfolded, Homburg is led out for his 'execution', only to be given the hand of Natalie and to be hailed by the army as the victor of Fehrbellin.

This is an extremely problematic play. On the one hand, it would seem to glorify Prussian military discipline – and the Nazis happily appropriated it for this purpose. On the other, the play so powerfully reflects on the insubstantiality of real experience that the play can equally be seen to question the Prussian ethic. Tellingly, when the Prince is led out to his mock execution and then has his blindfold removed amidst the adulation of his comrades, he asks: 'Is this a dream?' He is answered: 'A dream, what else?' This latter reading of the play was embraced in Peter Stein's memorable production in Berlin in 1972, significantly subtitled *Kleist's Dream of Prince Homburg.* That Kleist shot himself less than a year after writing the play also suggests disillusionment rather than nationalistic commitment.

Private Life of the Master Race, The. See FEAR AND MISERY OF THE THIRD REICH.

Private Lives

A: Noël Coward **Pf:** 1930, Edinburgh **Pb:** 1930 **G:** Com. in 3 acts **S:** Balcony of a hotel on the French Riviera and living room in a Paris apartment, *c.*1930 **C:** 2m, 3f

Elyot Chase is honeymooning with his new bride Sybil, a pretty but not very bright young blonde. He keeps reminiscing about his ex-wife Amanda, whom he divorced five years previously. When they withdraw into their hotel room, Amanda steps on to the adjoining balcony. By pure chance, she is honeymooning there with her new husband Victor Prynne, a tediously conventional individual, who complains that she keeps talking about her marriage to Elyot. When Elyot and Amanda discover that they are honeymooning in the same hotel, they unsuccessfully try to persuade their respective partners to leave for Paris. Left alone together, they reminisce about old times, embrace, and decide to go to Paris themselves. In Paris they discuss their private lives since they parted, which ends in a furious row. As they fight rolling around on the floor, Sybil and Victor enter. The following morning, Elyot refuses to fight with Victor, insisting that he has no interest in getting together with Amanda, 'a vile tempered wicked woman'. When the two couples have breakfast together, a vicious row erupts between Sybil and Victor. Quietly, Elyot and Amanda pick up their suitcases and leave arm in arm.

Coward's most popular and sophisticated play, subtitled 'An Intimate Comedy', begins with a preposterous coincidence, but, once this is accepted, it offers an amusing and insightful commentary on romantic relationships. It acknowledges the disturbing fact that sexual attraction and marital harmony seldom go together. Elyot and Amanda's relationship is doomed ('like two violent acids bubbling about in a nasty little matrimonial bottle'), but it seems preferable to the boredom of living with their new spouses.

Private Soldier (*Un simple soldat*)

A: Marcel Dubé **Pf:** 1958, Montreal **Pb:** 1958; rev. 1967 **Tr:** None known **G:** Drama in 2 acts; French prose **S:** Canada and Korea, 1945–52 **C:** 3m, 3f, extras

Joseph Latour returns to his father's home at the end of the Second World War. He had joined the army after he became a disaffected teenager and dropped out of school. His father Édouard lives in Montreal with Joseph's half-sister Fleurette and with his latest wife Bertha and her two children Marguerite and Armand. Joseph, unable to tolerate unreasonable authority, drifts from job to job, which takes him all over Canada. When he returns once more to his father's home, he causes Édouard so much hurt and disappointment that the old man dies. Joseph leaves and joins the army again, ending in Korea, where he is killed.

In this play, originally written for television, Dubé, one of Canada's leading francophone playwrights, spoke for a whole generation of young Canadians. Especially as a French Canadian, he expressed the alienation of returning soldiers who had given so much for a British Empire that meant little to them. Now, at home, the sense of frustration persists. Like a Canadian James Dean, Joseph fights the system, reflected in the Asbestos strike, the nuclear threat, and the crisis over conscription, without himself having any clear sense of direction. The '*simple*' of the title is ironic: Joseph is a deeply complex character and is the focus of some powerfully emotional scenes.

Problem Child. See SUBURBAN MOTEL.

Processional

A: John Howard Lawson **Pf:** 1925, New York **Pb:** 1925 **G:** Pol. drama in 4 acts **S:** Outskirts of a West Virginia mining town, 1920s **C:** 17m, 3f, 8 extras

On 4 July, striking jazz-playing coal miners pass Isaac Cohen's store, and his flighty daughter Sadie dances with a city slicker. When a Man in a Silk Hat attempts to deliver a patriotic speech, his hat is shot off. In jail, miner Dynamite Jim Flimmins plans his escape. A depressed 'Negro' is trying to break into jail, and helps Jim's escape by carrying him off in a coffin. Emerging from his hiding place, Jim kills one of the soldiers sent to break the strike. Shocked at what he has done, Jim hides in his mother's basement. When the Sheriff searches the house, Jim's mother admits that she has slept with soldiers for money. Jim is furious at his mother's promiscuity, and resolves to go out and kill again. As the miners fight the soldiers and the Ku Klux Klan, Jim escapes once more and rushes into Sadie's welcoming arms. Eventually he is captured and blinded by the Ku Klux Klan. Sadie has become pregnant with Jim's child, and is threatened by the Ku Klux Klan (two of whose members are her father and the Negro). Finally, the Man in the Silk Hat announces a pardon for the miners and an agreement to their demands (which will never be implemented). The Sheriff marries Sadie to Jim, and all join in a final procession.

Lawson was one of the first overtly political playwrights in America, and in 1947 was imprisoned by the House Un-American Activities Committee. *Processional* was his best-known play, an Expressionist mix of disjointed scenes, jazz music, and some staccato and chanted dialogue, joined together by the improbable story of the anti-hero Dynamite Jim. The stereotyped characters of the Jew and the 'Negro' date the play and do little to further its political message.

Prodigious Snob, The. See WOULD-BE GENTLEMAN, THE.

Professor Taranne (*Le Professeur Taranne*)

A: Arthur Adamov **Pf:** 1953, Lyons **Pb:** 1953 **Tr:** 1962 **G:** Drama in 2 scenes **S:** Police station and hotel, France, 1950s **C:** 9m, 5f

A middle-aged man has been arrested by the police for indecent exposure. He protests his innocence, insisting that he is the famous Professor Taranne who has recently been lecturing in Belgium. However, he is unable to prove his identity, and the one woman who recognizes him thinks he is Taranne's colleague, Professor Ménard. Later in his hotel, the police charge Taranne with a further offence, of littering his beach cabin. The nightmare worsens, when he finds himself unable to read the notes for his lectures, which are in an almost blank notebook. He receives a chart from the liner he is to board, indicating where he should sit at the captain's table, and a letter from the Belgian university where he gave his lectures, which will finally establish that he is Taranne. However, the letter accuses him of plagiarizing his lecture from Ménard.

When he hangs up the seating chart, it is blank. Slowly he begins to undress.

This short absurdist piece, considered by Adamov to be his finest, was based on a dream. In it, Adamov expresses the repeated 20th-century concern with individual identity and a Kafkaesque feeling of undefined guilt.

Promenade

A: Maria Irene Fornés Pf: 1965, New York Pb: 1971 G: Drama in 2 acts; prose and songs S: Prison cell, banqueting hall, street, park, battlefield, and dining room, indeterminate 20th-c. period C: 13m, 6f (6 male roles played by 2 actors)

Prisoners 105 and 106 dig their way out of their cell and make their way to a banquet, where rich guests flirt in song and abuse the Servant. A girl appears from the cake, and the three women guests strip naked. The incompetent Jailer comes in search of his prisoners but is thrown out by the Servant. Prisoners 105 and 106 steal from all the guests, leave with the Servant, and rob an Injured Man, hurt in a car crash, of his possessions. They give their prison jackets to the Injured Man and Driver, whom the Jailer promptly arrests. Prisoners 105 and 106 dress the Servant with the stolen jewellery and lace, put her in their bag, and carry her off. On the battlefield, soldiers swathed in bandages are visited by the Mayor, and a bizarre garden party ensues, with all the characters from the earlier scenes reappearing, while the Jailer tries unsuccessfully to apprehend the thieves. At the Mayor's subsequent party, the Mother, who has been searching throughout for her lost children, mimes stabbing herself to the delight of the Mayor, who orders the arrest of all his guests for keeping him up late. Everyone is crammed into the cell, and they begin to escape through the hole, leaving only 105 and 106 and the Mother. She identifies them as her children who went off but did not 'find evil'; then she too leaves.

This was the first major success by Cuban-born Fornés, recipient of more Obie Awards than anyone except Sam Shepard. Her surreal poetic style is reminiscent of Wilder (but is not as innovative), of Gertrude Stein (but her language is not as haunting), and of Albee (but her social comment is not as acute).

Prometheus Bound (*Prometheus desmotes; Prometheus vinctus*)

A: Aeschylus? Pf: *c.*466–459 BC Tr: 1777 G: Greek trag. in verse S: A rocky gorge in the mountains, in the mythical past C: 6m, 1f, chorus (f)

Cratos and Bia drag on the bound Prometheus, in order to assist Hephaestus, the gods' blacksmith, to forge Prometheus' chains to a rock. Prometheus is to be punished terribly for disobeying Zeus and bringing fire to the human race. Remaining silent until he is alone, the Titan Prometheus unleashes a monologue of anger and defiance: he bewails the fact that, although he is himself a god, he must suffer divine injustice. The chorus of the daughters of the sea god Oceanus attempt to console him. But Prometheus is unrelenting in his angry denunciation of the gods, even when Oceanus himself arrives to urge him to be moderate. Prometheus insists that he will give himself up to suffering and so cause Zeus more anguish. Io, the daughter of the King of Argos, comes: she too is a victim of the anger of the gods and has been struck with madness. Finally Hermes appears to threaten Prometheus with more severe punishments if he does not stop his tirade. The latter responds with even more vehement outbursts, and so amidst thunder and lightning is cast down into the depths of Tartarus.

It is not certain that Aeschylus wrote *Prometheus Bound*, but it is convenient to continue to attribute the piece to him. It was probably the second part of a trilogy (the third would have shown Prometheus unbound). In creating the potent image of someone prepared to defy the gods and to embrace his punishment in the same defiant spirit, Aeschylus (or another) established the model for the tragic hero, and one that was to become particularly popular with the Romantics. Other cultures have always celebrated their victorious heroes. The tragic view of life, initiated by the Greeks and adopted by the Western world, celebrates figures who, though destined to defeat, inspire us with their individualism and courage. Thus, while tragic figures must succumb to their fate (how could it be otherwise?), tragedy, by celebrating their courageous spirit, is not an urge to conform, but rather a celebration of what makes them uniquely human. *Prometheus Bound* is also notable for its spectacular effects, especially the final descent of Prometheus into the underworld, probably achieved with a trapdoor (the *ekkukleme*). Hence Aristotle cited it as a prime example of *opsis*, theatre as spectacle.

Proof

A: David Auburn **Pf:** 2000, New York **Pb:** 2001 **G:** Drama in 2 acts **S:** Back porch of a house in Chicago, *c.*1996–2000 **C:** 2m, 2f

Robert, once a brilliant mathematician, became mentally sick in his twenties. When his wife died, he was cared for by his daughter Catherine, who was forced to give up her studies. On her 25th birthday, a week after Robert's death, she still imagines that he is alive, which adds to her worry that she may inherit his mental instability. Hal, an eager 28-year-old research assistant, is working on Robert's notebooks, even though Catherine insists they are full of gibberish. Boringly practical older sister Claire, a currency analyst, arrives for the funeral; she is concerned about Catherine and suggests she should come and live with her in New York. At a post-funeral party, Catherine and Hal kiss and go to bed together. Claire, before she leaves, tells Catherine that she intends selling the family home. Hal finds a proof relating to prime numbers which will revolutionize mathematics. Catherine claims that she wrote it. Flashback to four years previously during a lucid period in Robert's life: Catherine tells him that she has a place at university to study maths and meets Hal for the first time. Returning to the present, Claire and Hal find it almost impossible to believe that the proof could have been written by Catherine. Flashback to three and a half years ago: Catherine returns home from university to discover that Robert has lost his sanity again. Finally, in the present, Hal tells Catherine that the proof checks out and contains so much recent thinking that he is now convinced that it was written by her. Catherine begins to talk through the proof with Hal.

As with many first plays, Auburn attempts to deal with a plethora of issues: the relationship between sanity and genius; the fear of inherited mental illness; the clash between sisters with very different characters; above all, how hard it is for innovative women to gain recognition (an echo of Stoppard's **Arcadia*). That Auburn can keep so many balls in the air and introduce some effective theatrical surprises, suggests that he is a writer of considerable potential. The role of Catherine was played at the London premiere by Gwyneth Paltrow.

Proper Gent, The. See WOULD-BE GENTLEMAN, THE.

Providing Jobs. See FEAR AND MISERY OF THE THIRD REICH.

Provoked Wife, The (*The Provok'd Wife*)

A: John Vanbrugh **W:** 1691–2 **Pf:** 1697, London **Pb:** 1697 **G:** Com. in 5 acts; prose **S:** London, Restoration period **C:** 10m, 6f, extras

Lady Brute, 'the provoked wife', is married to an ill-tempered drunkard Sir John. She is being courted by Constant, whose friend Heartfree, despite being a professed woman-hater, has fallen in love with Belinda, Lady Brute's niece. The two women arrange to meet their suitors in Spring Garden. Meanwhile on a drunken escapade, Sir John, wearing woman's clothes, is arrested by the watch. (In the original version he was dressed as a bishop.) Lady Brute's meeting with Constant is disrupted by Lady Fanciful, who is a rival for his affections. Certain that her husband will be away from home, the four lovers retire to Lady Brute's residence. Sir John returns unexpectedly, and Constant and Heartfree have to hide. Lady Fanciful disguises herself in a last attempt to win Heartfree, pretending to Belinda that she is married to him. Sir John, convinced that he is being cuckolded, confronts Constant, who proposes a duel. Sir John backs off, Lady Fanciful is exposed, Heartfree will marry

Belinda, and possibly the provoked wife will find solace with Constant.

Vanbrugh claimed that he wrote the first draft of the play in the Bastille, where he was imprisoned as a spy. Apart from the wonderfully rumbustious role of Sir John, the particular interest of the play is that, within the framework of a conventional comedy, the serious issue is raised of how to cope with a loveless marriage when there is no possibility of divorce. Lady Brute has still not committed adultery by the end of the play, and Vanbrugh does not provide any happy ending for her. Despite this reticence, he was strongly castigated for immorality by Jeremy Collier in 1698. Vanbrugh defended himself by pointing out that people like the Brutes existed in real life, but it may be that Collier's attacks on the play encouraged him to devote himself more decisively to architecture.

Pseudolus

AT: *The Trickster* A: Titus Maccius Plautus Pf: 191 BC, Rome Tr: 1827 G: Latin com. in verse S: Before the homes of Simo and Ballio in Athens, 2nd c. BC C: 10m, 1f, extras

Calidorus confesses to his slave Pseudolus that he is in love with a girl Phoenicium, who is about to be sold to a Macedonian soldier. The purchase price is 2,000 drachmas, and Pseudolus undertakes to find this amount for his master. The pimp Ballio comes out of his house, cruelly herding his women, among them Phoenicium. Despite having promised Phoenicium to Calidorus, Ballio insists that he will sell her to the Macedonian. Pseudolus warns Calidorus' father Simo that the old man will be giving him 2,000 drachmas before the day is out. Pseudolus now arranges for a fellow slave to disguise himself as the Macedonian's emissary, and Phoenicium is handed over. Ballio is so pleased to have concluded the transaction that he bets 2,000 drachmas with Simo that his son will never get Phoenicium. When the genuine emissary arrives, Ballio is obliged to pay back the purchase money to him and, recognizing that he has been tricked by Pseudolus, is also obliged to settle his bet with Simo. Simo pays the 2,000 drachmas to Pseudolus, who agrees to share it with him so that they can celebrate Simo's son's success.

Based on an unknown Greek original, *Pseudolus* establishes a recurrent theme of European comedy, the cunning and inventiveness of the servant who can outwit his master. It is a common feature of the *commedia dell'arte*, occurs in Molière (e.g. *The Rogueries of Scapin*, 1671) and in Beaumarchais (e.g. *The *Marriage of Figaro*). Here Plautus handles a complex (if not wholly consistent) plot with his usual deftness. It is a longer play than most of his, giving him time to develop character more fully, especially that of the obnoxious Ballio, who, in the best comic tradition, gets his deserved comeuppance.

Public Enemy, A. See ENEMY OF THE PEOPLE, AN.

Publikumsbeschimpfung. See OFFENDING THE AUDIENCE.

Puce à l'oreille, La. See A FLEA IN HER EAR, A.

Puntila and Matti, His Hired Hand. See MR PUNTILA AND HIS MAN MATTI.

Puppet Show, The (*Balaganchik*)

AT: *The Fairground Booth; Farce* A: Aleksandr Blok Pf: 1906, St Petersburg Pb: 1906 Tr: 1950 G: Drama in 1 act; Russian prose and verse S: A room, early 20th c. C: 4m, 1f, extras

The silent and beautiful Columbine is wooed by a sad Pierrot and a lively Harlequin. Pierrot, who believes that he is to marry Columbine, is warned by a group of fashionable mystics that she is the bringer of death. A writer comes to complain that his realistic work is being misinterpreted. At a masked ball three couples declare their love for each other. A clown bleeds, wounded by a cardboard sword. Harlequin, leading a torchlight procession, attempts to reach the countryside by smashing his way through the paper set. Death appears, and Pierrot realizes it is Columbine. When the author appears to reunite the lovers, the scenery and all the characters but Pierrot disappear. Left alone, he plays a sad tune on his pipe.

The Puppet Show, Blok's first play, was based on a poem of the same name, and its poetic and symbolic elements persist in the stage version, presented with great wit and charm and, importantly, with a deconstructive satirical edge. The original production by Meyerhold, who played Pierrot and whose ideas are now incorporated into published versions of the text, transformed the play into a theatrical feast. Thus, even if the allegory of Columbine, representing both the death of the old Tsarist regime and hope for the new order, is no longer relevant to a modern audience, this elegant one-acter can still operate its charm.

Purgatory

A: W. B. Yeats **Pf**: 1938, Dublin **Pb**: 1939 **G**: Drama in 1 act; mainly 4-stressed lines **S**: Before a ruined house, early 20th c. **C**: 2m

An Old Man and his young son wandering the roads stop before a ruined house. The Old Man says that the souls in purgatory revisit the places of their past and relive their transgressions. He tells how his mother who lived in the great house married the groom, who squandered all her wealth and eventually burned down the house. She died giving birth to the Old Man and now must again and again live through the agony of conceiving her son with her drunken husband in the now ruined house. The Boy, demanding his share of his father's money, tries to wrest it from him, pointing out that the Old Man had killed his father. The house lights up once more, and the Old Man, desperate to release his mother's soul, stabs his son, so that the pollution cannot be passed on. But hoof-beats are heard, and the re-enactment begins again. The sacrifice of the Boy has been in vain.

Composed with 'extraordinary theatrical skill' (T. S. Eliot), this short and savage piece can work powerfully on stage, provided the vision of the past is not staged too literally, which would steer the action close to melodrama. It works as an intense poetic recital of a cursed family with obvious echoes of the Atrideans (see e.g. ORESTEIA, THE). But for the Old Man there are no Eumenides, only the plea that God will 'Appease | The misery of the living and the remorse of the dead', a plea that had considerable relevance to the political situation in Europe of the late 1930s.

Purple Dust

A: Sean O'Casey **W**: 1937–40 **Pf**: 1945, Liverpool **Pb**: 1940; rev. 1951, 1960 **G**: Com. in 3 acts **S**: Chamber in a 16th-c. mansion in rural Ireland, 1930s **C**: 12m, 3f

Cyril Poges and Basil Stoke, two English businessmen, buy an old Irish mansion, where they intend to live off the land with their mistresses, who originally come from the area. To the amusement of the workmen called in to refurbish the rotting building, the newcomers perform what they imagine to be a country dance. Basil's mistress Avril flirts outrageously with O'Killigain the foreman. While the Englishmen try to get the house in order and immerse themselves in its past, locals arrive trying to sell them animals. Basil goes out riding and immediately falls. The ceiling is broken through by a workman installing a light. The next day the Englishmen have slept badly and regret having settled large annuities on their mistresses, thus making them independent. A huge garden roller crashes through a wall, and Basil shoots a cow believing it to be a bull. An antique desk is smashed by incompetent workmen, and eventually the constant rain leads to flooding. Poges's mistress has ridden off with her Irish lover, and as the floodwaters begin to immerse the building, O'Killigain rows Avril to safety.

This play offers an enjoyably satirical view of English urban characters trying to accommodate to the ways of rural Ireland, and, as so often with O'Casey, opposes the life force of the native Irish to the absurd and desiccated attitude of their supposed betters. Regrettably, the plot consists of little more than an accumulation of incidents, rather in the manner of a television situation comedy.

Puss in Boots (*Der gestiefelte Kater*)

A: Ludwig Tieck **Pf**: 1844, Berlin **Pb**: 1797 **Tr**: 1914 **G**: Fairy tale in 3 acts, with interludes, prologue, and epilogue; German prose **S**: Royal court and environs, indeterminate period **C**: 35m, 2f, animals, extras

Members of the audience complain about the play, but the Author pleads for a fair hearing. The youngest of three sons, Gottlieb, inherits only a tomcat Hinze, who, to Gottlieb's surprise, can not only speak but also promises to win his master fame and fortune. Equipped with new boots, Hinze sets out for the royal palace, where the Princess has rejected all her suitors. Hinze catches a rabbit, which he gives to the King as a present from the 'Count of Carabas'. When at a banquet the rabbit is brought burned to the King, he rages tragically, causing the audience to erupt in fury. The Author calms everyone by staging a dance with animals. The learned Leander and the royal Fool Hanswurst hold a debate about the merits of Tieck's *Puss in Boots*, including the depiction of the audience. When the 'Count of Carabas' sends the King two partridges, the King takes his daughter to visit his benefactor. As the King's carriage approaches, Gottlieb jumps in the water, pretending his clothes are stolen, which the King replaces with his own. Hinze rushes ahead to the palace of the neighbouring Tyrant, who can become any animal he chooses. Persuading him to turn into a mouse, Hinze kills him. Gottlieb, after passing through fire and water, is now fit to rule and to wed the Princess. The apologetic Author hoped that his audience would become like children to enjoy his play.

This is a classic example of 'Romantic irony', the yearning to return to the innocent perceptions of childhood and the simultaneous recognition that this is impossible. The result is a witty and complex retelling of a favourite fairy tale, peppered with contemporary references, including the fire and water of Mozart's *Magic Flute*. Metatheatrical elements (the audience discussing the play, the actors and Author pleading to be allowed to finish, the debate about the merits of the piece) all anticipate Brecht's *Verfremdungseffekt* and pieces like Handke's **Offending the Audience* by well over a century.

Puste Kretshme, Di. See HAUNTED INN, THE.

Pygmalion

A: George Bernard Shaw **Pf:** 1913, Vienna; 1914, London **Pb:** 1913 (in German); 1914 (in English); rev. 1941 **G:** Com. in 5 acts **S:** London, 1912 **C:** 6m, 5f, extras

While sheltering from the rain, Henry Higgins, a brilliant professor of phonetics, encounters a Cockney flower girl Eliza Doolittle, and sneers at the way she distorts the English language. The following day she comes to ask him to give her speech lessons so that she can become a lady in a flower shop. His friend Colonel Pickering bets with him that he cannot train her to pass muster at the ambassador's party six months later. Eliza's first test comes after a few months at a party given by Higgins's mother. Her enunciation is perfect, but her vocabulary is startling. She shocks everyone by using the word 'bloody', but Freddy Eynsford-Hill is enchanted with her. The ambassador's party passes very successfully, and Higgins glows with satisfaction. The experiment over, Eliza is furious that Higgins has lost interest in her, and storms out. Next day at his mother's house, Eliza declares that she will marry Freddy, although Higgins complacently believes that she will come back to him.

Although Shaw's play has now been overshadowed by the saccharine musical version by Lerner and Loewe, *My Fair Lady* (1956), his play, immediately popular from its German-language premiere, still works well today. While it can be seen as a very male piece of manipulation of a vulnerable woman, Higgins, though unquestionably clever, is shown to be smug and thoughtless, and the main thrust of the play is to reveal the hollowness of social convention. That the 'squashed cabbage leaf' Eliza can, with the help of soap, clothes, and phonetics, rise to become accepted so easily is a comic indictment of the judgement of fashionable London society.

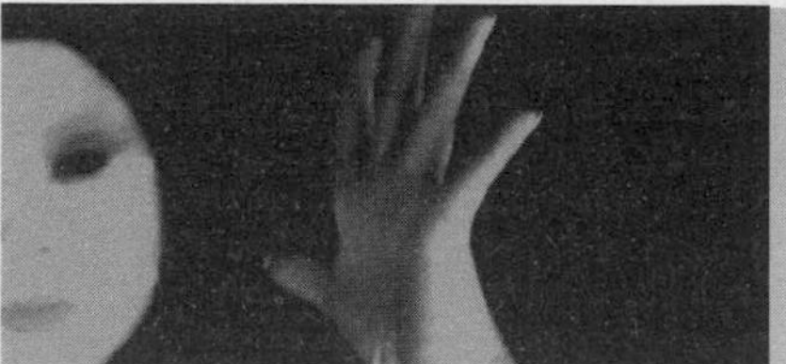

q

Quai ouest. See QUAY WEST.

Quare Fellow, The

AT: *The Twisting of Another Rope* **A**: Brendan Behan **Pf**: 1954, Dublin **Pb**: 1956 **G**: Drama in 3 acts **S**: Corridor and yard of a Dublin prison, 1950s **C**: 22m

Prisoners discuss the fate of two fellow inmates: one, who killed his wife, has been reprieved, while another, the 'Quare (= "queer") Fellow', who savagely murdered his brother with a meat chopper, is to be hanged. The reprieved murderer is depressed at the thought of life imprisonment and later tries to hang himself, but the old prisoner Dunlavin assures him that it is better than hanging, which he describes with relish. An examiner from the Justice Department perfunctorily checks on the welfare of the prisoners. That evening the prisoners exercise in the yard where the grave has been dug for the Quare Fellow's body. Regan, a kindly old warder, briefs a young warder on the execution, and the hangman arrives. The following morning the hanging takes place offstage, and the prisoners emit 'ferocious howling'. A body is carried in by the warders, but it is not that of the Quare Fellow but of the young warder, who fainted as the man was hanged. Regan tosses the hanged man's letters into the grave, and the prisoners scramble for them, intending to sell them to the Sunday papers.

Two years before Osborne's **Look Back in Anger* caused a stir in the British theatre by representing a world outside the gentility of middle-class drawing rooms, Behan had mounted this powerful naturalistic attack on state institutions, although it became widely known only through Joan Littlewood's 1956 production with the Theatre Workshop. Based on Behan's own experiences of prison in England and Ireland, the piece combines humour with dramatic focus (the events take place within 24 hours, and the central figure of the Quare Fellow is never seen).

Quay West (*Quai ouest*)

AT: *Key West; Western Dock* **A**: Bernard-Marie Koltès **Pf**: 1985, Paris **Pb**: 1985 **Tr**: Not known **G**: Drama without act divisions; French prose with some Spanish **S**: Deserted jetty on a river, indeterminate location, indeterminate 20th-c. period **C**: 5m, 3f

Maurice Koch has got Monique to drive him at night to the deserted spot on the river where he secretly intends to commit suicide by drowning. He orders her to drive home leaving him there. She reluctantly watches him go into a disused hangar, where Charles helps him on his way. On the jetty, Koch explains that he wishes to kill himself to escape from the scandal of embezzling money. He puts stones in his pockets to weigh himself down. Fak arrives with Claire, intent on seducing her in the hangar. Monique, hearing Koch throw himself into the water, seeks help from Claire. Charles rescues Koch and carries him ashore. Claire reproaches her elder brother Charles for attempting to leave without telling his family; Charles threatens to beat her for going with Fak. Day dawns. Charles's mother Cécile pleads with him to stay with her in the country of filth and not to return to the land 'where the streets are so clean'. Monique cannot leave, because the car has been immobilized. Koch begs to be taken home, but all four tyres on his car have been slashed. Cécile supports Koch, and they leave together. Rodolfo, Charles's Spanish father, comes, and is rejected by Charles. Rodolfo gives a Kalashnikov to Abad, a silent black man. At night everyone comes together in the hangar. Koch is shot on the jetty, and Fak throws his body in the river. Fak fires at Charles.

In vain does one seek for a coherent plot or for characters' motivation in this piece. The scenes of the play, set in a *film noir* location, written in a heightened poetic style, and often consisting of long monologues, are like images from a nightmare, a nightmare in which the figures are trapped beside the sludge-filled river as surely as the dead in Sartre's **No Exit*.

Queen after Death. See QUEEN IS DEAD, THE.

Queen and the Rebels, The (*La regina e gli insorti*)

A: Ugo Betti **Pf:** 1951, Rome **Pb:** 1951 **Tr:** 1956 **G:** Drama in 4 acts; Italian prose **S:** Town hall in an Italian mountain village, mid-20th c. **C:** 7 m, 3f, 1 child (m), extras

Rebel forces searching for Queen Elisabetta, who is trying to escape to safety, have stopped a bus, forcing the passengers to disembark. The military interpreter who interrogates them recognizes the prostitute Argia as his former mistress but now wants nothing to do with her. Argia realizes that a peasant woman is the Queen and denounces her to the rebel chief Commissar Amos. When the Queen tells Argia of the ordeals she has endured, Argia takes pity on her and helps her to escape, and is then suspected by Amos of being the Queen herself. She explains that her superior manner is her response to a life of humiliation. The summoned interpreter refuses to recognize her, and the peasant woman, the real Queen, commits suicide. With no one to identify her, Argia is condemned to death. Amos, threatening her with torture, offers her her life in exchange for an admission of guilt and a list of her accomplices. However, Argia has grown fully into the role of the Queen and haughtily refuses to contemplate any deals. Only when the Queen's young son is brought and threatened, does she relent, but can no longer remember the names that the Queen gave her. She goes out serenely to meet her death.

Regarded in Italy as one of their greatest 20th-century playwrights, Betti is not well known internationally, although this play did become popular. It is one of his few plays on a political theme, although its main interest is in the nature of identity, which everybody can create for themselves. As Argia says: 'I am as I should always have wished to be . . . Palaces have nothing to do with it.'

Queen Is Dead, The (*La Reine morte, ou Comment on tue les femmes*)

AT: *Queen after Death* A: Henry de Montherlant **Pf:** 1942, Paris **Pb:** 1942 **Tr:** 1951 G: Hist. drama in 3 acts; French prose S: Portugal, Renaissance period C: 14m, 5f

To consolidate an important alliance, Prince Don Pedro of Portugal is to marry Donna Bianca, Infanta of Navarre. However, he has already secretly married his beloved Donna Ines de Castro, who is pregnant by him. Angry over the Prince's devotion to her rival, the Infanta complains to King Ferrante, who assures her that his son's infatuation will soon pass. The King then tries to get Don Pedro to marry the Infanta and keep Ines as his mistress. While Don Pedro dithers over revealing the truth to his father, Ines tells the King about their marriage. Ferrante throws his son into prison, and asks Ines to persuade him to have their marriage annulled and to wed the Infanta. Fearing for Ines's life, the Infanta urges her to escape to Spain with her, but, to the Infanta's amazement, Ines cannot tear herself away from Don Pedro. The Pope refuses an annulment, and the despairing Ferrante finds himself compelled to have Ines executed, even though he has grown to like and admire her. The revelation that Ines is pregnant only hardens his resolve, and while assuring her of her safety, he orders her execution. When she is murdered, Ferrante collapses and dies. The Prince is released from prison and confirmed as King, and Ines's body is brought and mourned over as the dead Queen.

Although Montherlant's wordy historical tragedies were criticized for looking backwards rather than forwards, there are elements of interest in this, his best play. The characterization of the vacillating Prince contains echoes of Hamlet, and Ferrante is a complex figure, caught between humanity and realpolitik. Moreover, the strength and integrity of the two women form an admirably progressive balance to the weakness and cruelty of the men.

Questa sera si recita a soggetto. See TONIGHT WE IMPROVISE.

Questioning Fate. See ANATOL.

Quite Early One Morning. See UNDER MILK WOOD.

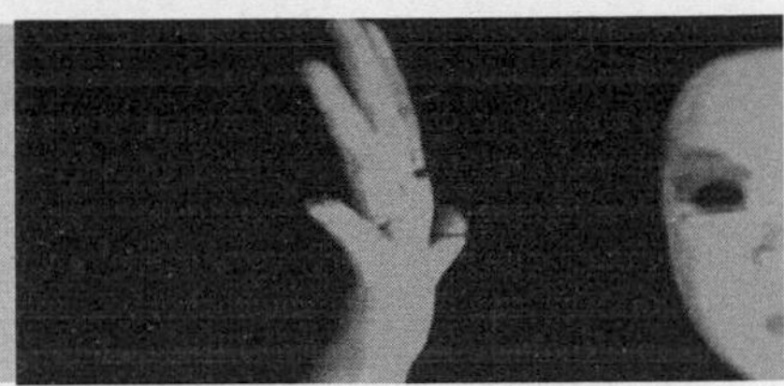

Raisin in the Sun, A

A: Lorraine Hansberry **Pf:** 1959, New York **Pb:** 1959 **G:** Drama in 3 acts **S:** Youngers' living room, Chicago, late 1940s–50s **C:** 7m, 3f, 1 child (m)

Lena Younger ('Mama') lives in cramped conditions in a poor area of Chicago with her family: her daughter Beneatha, a would-be medical student; her son Walter Lee, a chauffeur with aspirations to making his fortune; and his wife Ruth and son Travis. Mama is determined to use the $10,000 life insurance from her late husband as down payment on a house in a good neighbourhood. Walter, however, would like to invest money in a liquor store. Mama rejects what she sees as his gambling with the money. She is also worried about Beneatha, who shows no interest in a rich suitor, preferring to go out with a visiting Nigerian student. When Ruth discovers that she is pregnant, there is even greater pressure to move out of their 'rat-trap'. Mama puts a deposit on a house in a white neighbourhood, but reveals to the disconsolate Walter that she has kept back enough money for him to buy his liquor store. Lindner, a potential neighbour of the Youngers, calls to tell them that they are not wanted in a white area and offers a financial incentive to sell back their new house. Walter tells him to get out. When Walter learns that his business partner has absconded with his money, and the family face financial ruin again, he decides to accept Lindner's offer. When Lindner comes, however, Walter realizes that he could never look his son in the eyes again and sends Linder away once more. The moving men begin packing for the new home.

The title derives from a Langston Hughes poem: 'What happens to a dream deferred? |Does it dry up| Like a raisin in the sun?' In this, the first play on Broadway by a black woman writer, the Younger family refuse to defer their dream, despite financial problems (similar to the failure of the inheritance in O'Casey's **Juno and the Paycock*), and despite threats from the white community. By growing into proud defiance, Walter 'finally come into his manhood today'.

Ralph Roister Doister

A: Nicholas Udall **Pf:** 1552, Windsor **Pb:** 1566–7 **G:** Com. in 5 acts; rhymed verse **S:** Before the house of Dame Custance, mid-16th c. **C:** 10m, 4f, extras

Ralph Roister Doister, a bombastic and stupid individual, wishes to woo a virtuous widow Dame Christian Custance. Despite holding Doister in contempt, his parasitic friend Merrygreek promises to help him. However, Dame Custance is betrothed to a wealthy merchant and firmly rejects Doister's advances. Bolstered by Merrygreek's flattery, Doister plans to storm Dame Custance's house and force her to his will. Merrygreek, who has already undermined Doister's courtship, warns Custance, and together with the maidservants they repel the cowardly Doister, giving him a sound thrashing. Custance's fiancé returns from a journey, and, once persuaded that his beloved is innocent, initiates the wedding celebration, in which all, even Doister, take part. The play ends with a song in praise of Queen Mary.

The first comedy in English, *Ralph Roister Doister* combines Latin models (Terence's *The* **Eunuch* and **Phormio*) with witty observation of contemporary life. The title figure is clearly based on the 'braggart soldier' figure originally derived from Plautus, while Merrygreek is reminiscent of the Roman parasite, at the same time owing something to the traditional Vice of the English morality play. The comedy was written for performance by children, probably the boys Udall taught at Westminster School, and would have been performed in a great hall. It contains so much good comedy, ranging from a clever misreading of a love letter because of poor punctuation to the broad slapstick of Doister being beaten with kitchen utensils, that it has been frequently revived with success.

Ranae. See FROGS.

Räuber, Die. See ROBBERS, THE.

Ravens, The. See CROWS, THE.

Real Inspector Hound, The

A: Tom Stoppard **Pf:** 1968, London **Pb:** 1968 **G:** Com. in 1 act **S:** Stage set of country-house living room, with auditorium behind, 1960s **C:** 5m, 3f

Moon and Birdboot, two theatre critics, settle to watch a murder mystery. Ambitious young Moon is unhappy, because he remains his newspaper's second-string critic, junior to someone for whom he has no respect, while middle-aged unattractive Birdboot wonders whether he can win an actress's favours by flattering her with a good review. The play begins, using every cliché in the book: dependable housekeeper Mrs Char, a good-looking young couple in their twenties Simon and Felicity, the aristocratic Lady Cynthia Muldoon, the sinister cripple Magnus, all isolated by rising fog. The critics comment on the action, and when, at the start of Act 2, the telephone rings on stage, Moon impatiently gets up to answer it. The call is for Birdboot, and soon the two critics find themselves embroiled in the action of the play. Moon is murdered, and the identity of the real Inspector Hound is finally revealed.

This very funny play parodies traditional English murder mystery plays like *The* **Mousetrap*. By introducing critics into the action, Stoppard draws on the metatheatrical game played by Tieck in **Puss in Boots*, so that reality and events on stage become hopelessly intermingled, generating not only humour but an uneasy sense of shifting levels of reality.

Real Thing, The

A: Tom Stoppard **Pf:** 1982, London **Pb:** 1982; rev. 1983, 1984 **G:** Com. in 2 acts **S:** Various interiors in London, *c.*1980 **C:** 4m, 3f

Max discovers that his wife Charlotte has been unfaithful, but this is revealed to be a scene from Henry's latest play, *House of Cards*. In fact, Max's real-life wife Annie is having an affair with Henry, who is married to Charlotte. Henry, a successful writer of 40, shortly to appear on *Desert Island Discs*, leaves Charlotte to set up home with Annie, 10 years his junior. Two years later, Annie is involved with an AWOL Scots soldier Brodie, who agrees to join her on an anti-nuclear demonstration. In an attempt to impress Annie, he sets fire to a wreath on the Cenotaph and is jailed. She asks Henry to rewrite Brodie's autobiographical television play, but it is so poorly written that he refuses. Henry now discovers that Annie has had a fling with a 22-year-old actor Billy (while performing the title role in **Tis Pity She's a Whore*). Despite everything, Henry and Annie decide that they have discovered 'the real thing' and remain together, while Henry begins work on Brodie's play.

This play represented a new departure for Stoppard: for the first time he abandoned both obvious theatricality (apart from the trick of revealing the opening scene to be from a play) and clever intellectual pyrotechnics to concentrate on the portrayal of human emotion. Uncharacteristically 'shedding inhibitions about self-revelation', Stoppard here considers the nature of true love, whether it is to be found in passion, commitment, generosity of spirit, or whether 'the real thing' exists nowhere outside the fiction of theatre.

Recruiting Officer, The

A: George Farquhar **Pf**: 1706, London **Pb**: 1706 **G**: Com. in 5 acts; prose **S**: Shrewsbury, early 18th c. **C**: 18m, 6f, extras

Captain Plume and Sergeant Kite are in Shrewsbury recruiting for the army, often using devious means. Despite Plume's being a serial seducer and father of several illegitimate children, he is now seriously in love with Silvia, daughter of Balance, a local justice. Plume's friend Worthy is in love with Silvia's cousin Melinda, a lady of fortune, who is also being wooed by a rival recruiting officer, the bombastic Captain Brazen. When the death of her brother makes Silvia the sole heir to Balance's fortune, her father makes her swear that she will not dispose of herself without his consent. Plume pays court to Rose, a simple country wench, who is taken off him by the young Jack Wilful, in fact Silvia in disguise. Rose's brother complains to Justice Brazen, who unwittingly orders his disguised daughter to enlist with Plume and go with him, thus allowing them to marry without her breaking her promise. Worthy eventually wins the hand of Melinda, and Brazen is appeased when Plume resigns his commission and hands over all his recruits to Brazen.

Despite conventionally being regarded as a Restoration dramatist, one sees how Farquhar's writing has moved on from that of his predecessors. Most notably, rather than the traditional setting of London society, we find ourselves in the provinces, and Melinda's affectations, which would be the norm in the capital, here appear ridiculous. Plume may be a philanderer, but his behaviour is not tainted with that sense of moral corruption anatomized by a writer like Wycherley. The women too, Silvia and even the simple Rose, possess an unaccustomed dignity. Thanks to its uncharacteristically political exploration of the contemporary practice of 'pressing' men into the army, *The Recruiting Officer* was adapted by Brecht as *Trumpets and Drums* (1956), influenced Arden's **Serjeant Musgrave's Dance*, and is central to Wertenbaker's **Our Country's Good*.

Red Gloves. See DIRTY HANDS.

Red Roses for Me

A: Sean O'Casey **Pf**: 1943, Dublin **Pb**: 1942; rev. 1951, 1965 **G**: Drama in 4 acts; prose and some rhyming verse **S**: The Breydons' home, a street, and Protestant church grounds, Dublin, *c.*1913 **C**: 16m, 5f

Ayamonn Breydon, who lives with his mother in a poor area of Dublin, is a young railway-yard worker. As well as leading a strike for a shilling raise, he loves the arts and is seen rehearsing **Richard III*. He is visited by his sweetheart Sheila Moorneen, who braves her Catholic parents' objections to her loving a Protestant, but begs Ayamonn to spend less time on the strike. After several other visitors, news comes that the strike will go ahead, despite Revd Clinton's warnings about the likely response by the authorities. When Sheila begs Ayamonn to abandon the strike, he angrily rejects her. At a public meeting Ayamonn offers the poor a vision of a golden future and dances ecstatically with Finnoola, a poor young neighbour. The strike meeting is broken up by the police, and Ayamonn gets shot. He is honoured as a martyr, and Sheila lays red roses on his body, recognizing that 'Maybe he saw the shilling in th' shape of a new world.'

Unashamedly proclaiming a socialist utopia, *Red Roses for Me* is loosely based on O'Casey's own life and on that of the great Irish trade unionist Jim Larkin, especially at the time of the Dublin Lock-Out of Larkinite transport workers in 1913. As nationalism began to dominate Irish politics, Larkin emigrated to the United States, and O'Casey emigrated to literature. This play is as much an elegy as an expression of hope.

reduce, Il. See CONVERSATION OF RUZANTE RETURNED FROM THE WARS.

regina e gli insorti, La. See QUEEN AND THE REBELS, THE.

Rehearsal, The

A: George Villiers, 2nd Duke of Buckingham, and others **W**: 1665 **Pf**: 1671, London **Pb**: 1672; rev. 1675 **G**: Burlesque in 5 acts; prose and rhyming couplets **S**: Drury Lane Theatre, London and Brentford, Restoration period **C**: 26m, 7f

The author Bayes invites two gentlemen to attend the rehearsal of his latest play, *The Two Kings of Brentford*. After some difficulty getting started, a series of scenes follow in which the conventions of heroic tragedy are satirized: the Physician, having plotted inaudibly with the Gentleman Usher, now overthrows the government, and a civil war fought by eight men takes place. After more scenes making fun of specific contemporary dramas, Prince Volscius falls in love with a young maiden and then soliloquizes to his boots. Lardella, beloved of the two usurpers, is brought in dead, but before they can commit suicide from grief, she is found to be alive. Volscius and another Prince quarrel because they do not love the same woman. Another civil war takes place, this time with only one man on each side. Weary of this tedious display, the two gentlemen leave the rehearsal, the actors have also had enough, and Bayes angrily withdraws his play.

While the play-within-a-play was already a well-known dramatic device (e.g. *The *Knight of the Burning Pestle*, *The *Taming of the Shrew*), and the mechanicals are seen preparing their play in *A *Midsummer Night's Dream*, *The Rehearsal* is the first play in English to take us backstage in the theatre to observe a rehearsal. It gave birth to a line of plays in this setting (e.g. Anouilh's *The *Rehearsal*, Wertenbaker's **Our Country's Good*, and Frayn's **Noises Off*). Many of the contemporary references, including the mockery of Dryden and Davenant in the figure of Bayes, are lost on a modern audience. But there is still enough fun, absurdity, and amusing comment on dramatic conventions (as in the way standard exposition is handled by characters telling each other what they must already know), for the play to provoke laughter on the stage today.

Rehearsal, The (*La Répétition, ou L'Amour puni*)

A: Jean Anouilh **Pf:** 1950, Paris **Pb:** 1950 **Tr:** 1958 **G:** Romantic com. in 5 acts; French prose **S:** A salon and an attic room in an 18th-c. chateau, France, *c.*1950 **C:** 5m, 3f

The Count ('Tiger'), a man who realizes that 'futility must be taken quite seriously', has inherited a chateau, on condition that he stays one month every year and provides a home for 12 orphans. In order to make this sojourn bearable, he and his wife Éliane decide to stage Marivaux's *The *Double Inconstancy*, and are already wearing their 18th-century costumes. To play the other parts, he has invited his long-suffering mistress Hortense, his friend the womanizer Héro, his wife's airhead lover Villebosse, his wife's lawyer Damiens, and Damiens' god-daughter, the simple and poor Lucile, who is to play Marivaux's heroine, the innocent Silvia. While rehearsing the role of the Prince, the Count declares his love for Lucile. Damiens, concerned about the Count's intentions towards Lucile, asks to marry her, but she rejects him. When the Count offers to share with Lucile the little money he still possesses so that she can be independent, she falls in love with him. The Countess pretends that a ring has been stolen, in the hope that being suspected of the theft will drive Lucile away. When that fails, she asks Héro to seduce her. With consummate cynicism, and by warning Lucile against 'sentimentalists' like the Count, Héro succeeds. Lucile leaves for good, and Héro is so disgusted with himself that he seeks suicide by getting Villebosse to challenge him to a duel.

In one of his wittiest, cleverest, and darkest comedies, Anouilh exploits the traditional theme of the bored aristocrat who finds love with the simple peasant girl (as in Marivaux's play) but allows 18th-century elegance and romanticism to be undercut by 20th-century common sense and cynicism.

Reigen. See RONDE, LA.

Reine morte, La. See QUEEN IS DEAD, THE.

Relapse, The

AT: *Virtue in Danger* **A:** John Vanbrugh **Pf:** 1696, London **Pb:** 1696 **G:** Com. in 5 acts; prose and some blank verse **S:** London and the country, Restoration period **C:** 16m, 4f, extras

Loveless, a reformed rake, and his wife Amanda have been married for six months. They arrive in London from the country, convinced that they can resist the temptations of the capital. Meanwhile Young Fashion, who is penniless, tries to borrow money off his brother Lord Foppington. When the latter refuses him, Fashion plots to marry the rich heiress destined for his brother. Loveless falls for the charms of his wife's cousin Berinthia, who is encouraged by Mr Worthy, who himself is hoping to seduce Amanda. Fashion seeks out his heiress in the country and gains access to her by pretending to be his rich brother. They marry secretly. Even when Amanda learns that her husband has had a relapse and been unfaithful to her, she resists the advances of Worthy. At a bridal masque organized to celebrate Lord Foppington's wedding, it is revealed that his bride is already married to his brother, a discovery which Foppington accepts with good grace.

Written in under six weeks by someone who became better known as an architect, *The Relapse* was based on Cibber's *Love's Last Shift* (1676). The earlier play showed Amanda tricking her unfaithful husband back into the marriage bed and bringing about his reformation. Here Loveless is a supposedly reformed character who cannot however resist the charms of Berinthia. Once again the true heroine is Amanda, who by resisting Worthy, and indeed bringing about his reformation, shows herself to be a woman of virtue and sets a precedent for the moral tone of subsequent 18th-century comedy.

Relatively Speaking

AT: *Meet My Father* **A:** Alan Ayckbourn **Pf:** 1967, London **Pb:** 1968 **G:** Com. in 2 acts **S:** London bedsit, and patio of house in the country, 1960s **C:** 2m, 2f

Alerted by mysterious phone calls, gifts of flowers, chocolates in the drawer, and men's slippers under the bed, Greg, who has known Ginny for a month, now suspects her of having an affair. She claims she is going to visit her parents, but refuses to take Greg with her. Greg proposes to her, but she asks for time to decide. Greg leaps into a taxi, armed with the address of Ginny's destination, and heads for the country. Philip and Sheila have a somewhat strained marriage, and when Sheila seems to be trying to get Philip out of the house, he suspects that she has a lover. When Greg arrives unexpectedly, Philip's fears are confirmed, especially when Greg says that he hopes to marry 'her' soon. Ginny arrives, intending to break off her affair with Philip; horrified to find Greg there, she quickly introduces Philip as her father. When Greg talks of Ginny's affair with a married man, Sheila realizes that he must be referring to Philip, who was once Ginny's boss. Philip almost blackmails Ginny into coming on a business trip with him, but Sheila forces him to turn this into a honeymoon for Ginny and Greg. Greg leaves, still imagining he has spent the day with his bride's parents.

Originally premiered in Scarborough in 1965 as *Meet My Father*, *Relatively Speaking* was written 'to make people laugh when their seaside summer holidays were spoiled by the rain'. Transferring to London as his first major success, this deftly constructed play characteristically probes beneath the laughter to expose the pain, boredom, and deception in Philip and Sheila's marriage. Sadly too, the young couple are 'quite wrong for each other of course'.

Release. See FEAR AND MISERY OF THE THIRD REICH.

Removalists, The

A: David Williamson **Pf:** 1971, Melbourne **Pb:** 1972 **G:** Play in 2 acts **S:** Police station and the Carters' flat, Melbourne, 1970s **C:** 4m, 2f

Sergeant Dan Simmonds is an old-time cynical policeman in his fifties who seeks only a quiet life, so when the keen young Constable Ross joins his station, Simmonds quickly cuts him down to size. Kate Le Page, the wife of a dentist, comes with her younger sister Fiona to register a complaint of wife-battering by Fiona's working-class husband Kenny Carter, and Simmonds seizes the opportunity to examine her bruised thighs with great care. Kate has already arranged for Fiona to leave Kenny, and Simmonds, hoping to get to know Kate better, volunteers his and Ross's help with the removalists (i.e. furniture removers) the following evening. The next day, all Fiona's attempts to get her husband Kenny to go out to the pub fail, so he is present when Kate, the removalist, and the two policeman arrive at his flat and begin removing furniture. When Kenny becomes abusive, Simmonds handcuffs him to the door. After the women and the workman have left, Ross, who has been an unwilling participant in this venture, becomes so incensed with Kenny's insults and the deprecating remarks of his boss that he finally lashes out at Kenny and kills him. Simmonds and Ross agree to pretend that they were acting in self-defence and begin hitting each other to create 'evidence' that Kenny had been violent.

Through pieces like this and *Don's Party*, Williamson has become Australia's most popular and successful playwright, charting with cool detachment the macho culture of the Australian male. *The Removalists* is a tragedy of human idealism: all Ross's good intentions to work for a better world are swallowed up in a culture of violence and abuse. Men are 'the removalists', emptying their lives of gentleness, love, and understanding for fear of being thought unmanly.

Répétition, La. See REHEARSAL, THE (Anouilh).

Representative, The (*Der Stellvertreter*)

AT: *The Deputy* A: Rolf Hochhuth Pf: 1963, Berlin Pb: 1963 Tr: 1963 G: Hist. drama in 5 acts; German verse S: Berlin, Rome, and Auschwitz, 1942–4 C: 36m, 4f, 2 children (1m, 1f)

In Berlin in 1942, Father Riccardo Fontana and a humane SS officer Kurt Gerstein plead with the Papal Nuncio to get the Pope to denounce the Nazi's slaughter of the Jews. In Rome, Riccardo begs his wealthy father Count Fontana to use his influence with the Pope to intercede on behalf of the Jews, but the Count supports the Pope's neutrality. As persecution of the Jews reaches Rome and the Pope still fails to speak out, Riccardo says that he will join the Jewish transports to the death camps. When the Pope appears at last, he is busy discussing Church finances with Count Fontana. Angrily confronting the Pope, Riccardo is told that Hitler is preserving Europe from Communism and that the Church cannot be sacrificed for the sake of the Jews. Issuing a totally ineffectual proclamation, the Pope prays for the suffering of the persecuted. Riccardo pins on a yellow star and is taken to Auschwitz, where he encounters and tries to kill the evil Doctor. He is shot and burned alive, while the gas chambers continue to operate.

This proved probably the most controversial play in the history of theatre, immediately generating over 12 books and sparking debate and even rioting across the world. Accompanied by 65 pages of historical documentation, Hochhuth sets out a very plausible case for attacking the guilty silence of the Catholic Church, which did not even excommunicate Hitler. Unfortunately, the plot is melodramatic, focused on individuals, and is expressed in pedestrian verse. The evil Doctor becomes an almost mythical figure, and the real causes of Fascism and the support it generated are obscured by moral outrage about the Pope – what Armand Gatti called 'the worst kind of bourgeois hypocrisy'.

Resistible Rise of Arturo Ui, The (*Der aufhaltsame Aufstieg des Arturo Ui*)

A: Bertolt Brecht (with Margarete Steffin) W: 1941 Pf: 1958, Stuttgart Pb: 1957 Tr: 1976 G: Pol. drama in 17 scenes, prologue, and epilogue; German hexameter verse S: Chicago and Cicero, 1929–38 C: 28m, 2f, extras

Arturo Ui is a small-time gangster who decides to take over control of the greengrocery protection racket in Chicago. First he wins the support of a hitherto decent politician Dogsborough. A projected text reminds us that this was how Hitler won President Hindenburg to his cause. Ui's hoodlums set fire to the warehouse, a crime for which the unfortunate Fish is condemned in a farcical trial (= the Reichstag fire in 1933, and the subsequent trial of the mentally deficient Dutchman Van der Lübbe). Ui then murders his rival Ernesto Roma (= Ernst Röhm, head of the SA, who threatened Hitler's hold on power). Finally, by gunning down Ignatius Dullfeet, Ui succeeds in taking over the market in neighbouring Cicero as well (= the assassination of the

Austrian Chancellor Dollfuss and the Nazi annexation of Austria in 1938). An epilogue warns us that the womb that bore Hitler is still fertile.

A farcical portrayal of the rise to power of Hitler using the figures of Hollywood gangster movies was a brilliantly conceived and much-imitated way of portraying how a ridiculous individual can manipulate and bully his way to power. According with Dürrenmatt's view that the only thing that tyrants fear is mockery, this play was nevertheless too controversial to reach the stage until almost two decades after it was written. While closely based on Hitler, this 'historical farce' finds resonance in many political contexts, urging audiences to recognize that moves towards the right are 'resistible'.

Revenger's Tragedy, The

AT: *The Loyal Brother* A: Thomas Middleton Pf: *c*.1606–7, London Pb: 1607 G: Trag. in 5 acts; blank verse S: A dukedom in Italy, Renaissance period C: 13m, 3f, extras

Because she rejected his advances, the Duke has poisoned the beloved of Vindice, who now swears revenge. He sees his chance when the Duke's son Lussurioso seeks a go-between to win a woman at court for his pleasure. Disguised as Piato, Lussurioso's pander, Vindice tries to bribe his own sister Castiza to become Lussurioso's lover. She chastely refuses, and Vindice hinders Lussurioso's pursuit of Castiza by revealing that the Duchess, Lussurioso's stepmother, is having an affair with his bastard half-brother Spurio. Outraged at her behaviour, Lussurioso rushes to denounce her, but is imprisoned by the Duke under the impression that Lussurioso's anger is directed towards him. His half-brothers try to have Lussurioso executed, but the Duke has already released him from prison, and their younger brother, a rapist, is executed by mistake. The Duke now engages the services of Vindice, disguised again as Piato the pander, to take him to a lady in the dark. Helped by his brother Hippolito, Vindice takes the skull of his murdered mistress, poisons her mouth, dresses her in rich clothing, and urges the Duke to kiss her. Succumbing to the poison, the Duke is stamped on and forced to watch his wife and son Spurio making love. Lussurioso now engages Vindice and Hippolito to track down the treacherous Piato and bring him to justice. The brothers dress the body of the Duke in Piato's disguise, so that it looks as though Piato has murdered the Duke and fled. Lussurioso now declares himself duke, but is assassinated by Vindice and Hippolito with the support of disaffected noblemen. The evil half-brothers are killed in the ensuing quarrel, and Vindice and Hippolito, betraying themselves by boasting, are led away to their execution. The dukedom is put into the hands of the virtuous Antonio, whose wife had been brutally raped by the Duke's youngest son.

Following in the tradition of *The *Spanish Tragedy* and **Hamlet*, this is the most powerful of the Jacobean revenge tragedies – so much so that it is hard to believe that it was written by Tourneur, to whom it was later ascribed after its anonymous publication. Most critics now believe that the author was Middleton, and it certainly echoes some of the more grotesque elements of *The *Changeling*. Here we are confronted with a wholly amoral world. Although Vindice may have some justification for his desire for revenge, his methods are extremely dubious: he tries to corrupt his own sister, he stages a horribly violent death for the Duke, and is damned because he is so proud of his violent retribution that he cannot help boasting about it. The strength of the play lies in the impact of so many violent incidents, piling relentlessly on top of one another, sometimes generating a satisfying irony, as when the youngest brother is executed by mistake, always with a dreadful fascination of the corruption and destruction of the innocent through evil. T. S. Eliot called the play 'an intense and unique and horrible vision of life'.

Revizor. See GOVERNMENT INSPECTOR, THE.

Revolt of the Women. See LYSISTRATA.

Rhinoceros (*Rhinocéros*)

A: Eugène Ionesco Pf: 1959, Paris Pb: 1959 Tr: 1960 G: Drama in 3 acts; French prose

S: Small provincial French town, mid-20th c. C: 11m, 6f, extras
Bérenger, a scruffy Chaplinesque figure, meets his fastidious friend Jean in a café. While Bérenger drinks to escape from the tedium of his daily routine, a rhinoceros suddenly thunders past in the street. The following day at work, Bérenger and Daisy, a fellow worker whom he fancies, discuss the damage wrought by the rhinoceros, but the boss insists that work must go on as normal. A woman arrives late at work, pursued by her husband who is transformed into a rhinoceros. The wife leaps on his back and rides off. When Bérenger visits Jean, he discovers that Jean too is turning into a rhinoceros, and that the town is filling with these destructive pachyderms. As all the citizens endure this transformation, soon only Bérenger and Daisy are left as humans. They declare their love for each other but soon end up bickering like an old married couple. Seduced by the gentle lowing of the rhinoceros outside, Daisy leaves to join them. Becoming increasingly embarrassed about his human features, Bérenger contemplates becoming a rhinoceros himself but finally resolves that 'as the last man left', he is 'staying that way until the end'.

Rhinoceros, Ionesco's commercially most successful play, was understood internationally to be an allegory about the rise of Nazism, although its implications extend far beyond this. In the scruffy figure of Bérenger, Ionesco portrays an individual courageously holding on to his humanity in the face of conformism – a conformism which can have many other sources than extreme political movements.

Richard II (*The Tragedie of King Richard the second*)

A: William Shakespeare **Pf:** *c.* 1595, London **Pb:** 1597 (1st quarto); 1623 (1st folio) **G:** Hist. drama in 5 acts; blank verse **S:** England and Wales, 1397–1400 **C:** 23m, 4f, extras

Henry Bolingbroke has accused the Duke of Norfolk of treason, and to decide the matter, Richard orders that they settle their quarrel in a trial by combat. At the last minute, however, Richard stops the contest and orders both lords into exile. Richard is upbraided by Bolingroke's father, John of Gaunt, for being a spendthrift and for surrounding himself with sycophantic courtiers. When Gaunt dies, Richard seizes his lands. While Richard is suppressing a rebellion in Ireland, Bolingbroke, supported by a number of disaffected noblemen, returns to England to head a rebellion and succeeds in forcing Richard to abdicate in his favour, so becoming Henry IV. Richard is murdered in prison by a zealous nobleman. Henry, denying any complicity in the deed, plans a pilgrimage to the Holy Land to expiate the crime.

Based primarily on Holinshed's *Chronicles*, *Richard II* forms the first part of Shakespeare's second tetralogy of historical plays (followed by **Henry IV* and **Henry V*). *Richard II* is remarkable in that, unlike his earlier chronicle plays (**Henry VI*, **Richard III*, **King John*), it is tightly constructed and presents the first of Shakespeare's genuinely tragic heroes taken from history. Richard is a weak individual but nevertheless blessed with the divine right to rule; so the audience is disturbed by the way in which he is treated while having to acknowledge, as in Marlowe's **Edward II*, performed a few years earlier, that he has brought his fate upon himself. Meanwhile, the usurper Bolingbroke, far from leading England into a promised era of stability, will have to confront new uprisings in his realm.

Richard III (*The Tragedy of King Richard the third*)

A: William Shakespeare **Pf:** *c.* 1595, London **Pb:** 1597 (1st quarto); 1623 (1st folio) **G:** Hist. drama in 5 acts; blank verse and prose **S:** England, 1471–85 **C:** 33m, 5f, extras

Edward IV is the new king, and England is celebrating an unfamiliar period of peace. For the misshapen warrior Richard Gloucester, the inactivity of peace is burdensome. He resolves to cause mischief in the new kingdom, and begins by arranging for his brother Clarence to be taken to prison, where he is murdered. Richard also successfully woos Anne, the young widow of Henry VI's son, whom Richard and his brothers killed. When Edward dies, Richard, supported by the faithful Buckingham, eliminates his rivals, and becomes regent to the two young princes, Edward V and his brother. As imagined threats to the state mount, the manipulated populace beg Richard to become king. Once on the throne, he orders the murder of the two princes in the Tower, abandons his former supporters, and rejects his wife Anne. Eventually he has to face invading forces led by Henry Richmond. After being haunted by his victims, Richard leads his troops at the Battle of Bosworth, is defeated and killed. Henry will usher in a new age of peace. The Wars of the Roses are at last over.

Despite being one of Shakespeare's earliest works, and still containing elements of the medieval morality play, *Richard III* in its portrayal of a ruthless, ugly, evil figure held a fascination for Shakespeare's and for succeeding generations. It is Tudor propaganda and poor history, but excellent theatre. Richard Burbage played the role several times, Colley Cibber's version was frequently performed in the 18th and 19th centuries, and it remains popular in the modern repertoire, memorably in Laurence Olivier's performance, immortalized in his film version of 1955. It has been adapted many times, e.g. by Anouilh (1964) and by David Edgar in *Dick Deterred* (1974).

Ride across Lake Constance, The (*Der Ritt über den Bodensee*)

A: Peter Handke **Pf**: 1971, Berlin **Pb**: 1971 **Tr**: 1973 **G**: Drama in 1 act; German prose **S**: Elegant room with large staircase at rear, indeterminate period **C**: 3m, 6f

Emil Jannings is dozing in a chair, while a woman vacuum-cleans the room and removes dust covers. He is joined by Heinrich George, and the two converse cryptically. Down the staircase comes the beautiful Elisabeth Bergner, followed by Erich von Stroheim and Henny Porten. Jannings and George miscount the steps as Porten and von Stroheim descend, and they stumble. Bergner glides down and takes tea. Von Stroheim treats Porten like a doll. George coughs, and Jannings kicks him. Porten falls forward as though kicked. Porten buys a whip from George. Bergner and Porten dance. They all conduct disconnected semi-philosophical discussions, interrupted by songs, slapstick routines, guitar playing, etc. Alice and Ellen Kessler arrive, apparently entering the play by accident. They first duplicate each other's moves, then undo what the other has done. Finally, the cleaning woman returns with a destructive doll. Everyone sits motionless, as the stage darkens.

The title refers to a legendary horseman who, without knowing it, rides across the frozen Lake Constance. When he learns what he risked, he dies of fright – not from any real cause but as a result of his mental processes. This is reflected in Handke's play: people in a dream, people in a film, living at one remove from reality, isolated from one another, constantly misinterpreting one another's signals, both verbal and gestural. Even their identity is arbitrary: named for German stars of the 1920s, Handke requires that 'the characters should bear the names of the actors playing the roles'. In his rejection of conventional characterization and narrative, and in his meticulous choreography and deconstructed dialogue, Handke anticipates postmodernist experimentation.

Riders to the Sea

A: J. M. Synge **Pf**: 1904, Dublin **Pb**: 1905 **G**: Trag. in 1 act **S**: Cottage on an island off the west of Ireland, 1900s **C**: 1m, 3f, extras

Nora brings her sister a bundle of clothes taken off a drowned man in Donegal, and they wonder whether they belong to their brother Michael missing at sea. They hide the bundle from their mother Maurya. Maurya is suffering a terrible premonition and begs her youngest son Bartley not to cross the sea in a storm to a horse fair on the mainland. Alone again, the sisters unwrap the bundle and find that Michael, like his father, grandfather, and four brothers before him, has been taken by the sea. Maurya has had a vision of eight riders to the sea, all her men including Bartley, heading to their deaths. Her last son Bartley is carried in. He was thrown from his horse and drowned in the waves. The women begin their keening, while Maurya reflects that the sea can now harm her no more.

Arguably the most powerful one-act play in English, *Riders to the Sea* was based on Synge's experiences on the Aran Islands, which he visited several times 1898–1902. Tragedy is created from the simplest means. Fate is seen in the power of the sea, which provides the islanders with their livelihood but easily destroys them, and as with all true tragedy, there is a sense of release and resolution in Maurya's final recognition that, despite her terrible losses, she is now free from the terror she has had to endure. Brecht adapted the same theme in the setting of the Spanish Civil War in *The Rifles of Señora Carrar* (1937).

Riel

A: John Coulter **Pf:** 1950, Toronto **Pb:** 1962 **G:** Hist. drama in 2 acts **S:** Northwest Territories, 1869–85 **C:** 36m, 3f, extras

Louis Riel inherits his father's role as leader of the Métis, a group of mixed race of Native American and French. In their name he resists the incorporation of the Northwest Territories into the British Dominion of Canada and the encroachment of English-speaking settlers in what is today Manitoba. Riel does not strive to set up an independent state but insists on acknowledgement of the rights of the Métis to their land. When Riel's provincial government orders the execution of the Ontario Orangeman Thomas Scott, the British use this as a pretext to occupy the territory. In 1869 there is a Métis uprising, the Red River Rebellion, which the British violently suppress. Riel escapes to Montana in the USA, where he settles down, marries, and raises a family. In 1885 the Métis beg him to return to lead another uprising against the British. Once again, he is unsuccessful, and this time the British are determined not to let him get away. Riel is tricked into meeting with the British leader with the offer of a peaceful settlement. He is seized, tried, and hanged in Regina, Saskatchewan.

Coulter, originally from Ireland, became the first major playwright of Canadian theatre, and *Riel* has been called 'the first Canadian play of genuine stature'. Streamlining historical events (the period when Riel sat in the House of Commons in Ottawa is passed over), and showing Riel to be a complex and not wholly positive character, Coulter created a fine historical drama, which was not granted a major production until 1975. To aid amateur groups keen to perform the piece, he rewrote it in a shortened version as *The Crime of Louis Riel* (Pf 1966; Pb 1976), and also wrote a documentary *The Trial of Louis Riel* (Pf 1967; Pb 1968), which is performed annually in Regina.

Right You Are, If You Think So (*Così è (si vi pare)*)

AT: *Right You Are (If You Think You Are); It is So! If You Think So* **A:** Luigi Pirandello **Pf:** 1917, Milan **Pb:** 1918 **Tr:** 1922 **G:** Drama in 3 acts; Italian prose **S:** Provincial Italian town, 1916 **C:** 9m, 7f

The arrival in town of Signor Ponza with his mother-in-law Signora Frola sets tongues wagging. While she moves into an expensive town apartment, he lives with his wife on the outskirts in a tenement house. Signora Frola visits them daily, but is never allowed to enter their apartment and communicates with her daughter by passing up messages in a basket. Ponza explains that her daughter died four years previously, but that his mother-in-law was unable to accept this, so he hides his second wife from her. Signora Frola then claims that Ponza is mad, believing that his wife died and that her daughter is his second wife. Unable to find any relevant documents, the town busybodies arrange a confrontation between the two. It becomes clear that Ponza is indeed insane, until, after Signora Frola has left, he reveals that he only played mad to humour her. Despite protests by Ponza and Signora Frola, the Prefect decides to interrogate Ponza's mysterious wife. The wife speaks of a 'hidden misfortune' and says that she is both Signora Frola's daughter and Ponza's second wife: 'I am she whom you believe me to be.' The rational Laudisi, who throughout has critically observed the townspeople's nosiness, laughs derisively.

This play, written in six days, marked a turning point from Pirandello's early realism to writing pieces that explore the relationship between appearance and reality and proclaims the relativity of truth. It is one of the first major open-ended dramas of the 20th century, which, rather than offering a neat conclusion, leaves the audience with more questions than answers.

Ring Round the Moon (*L'Invitation au château*)

A: Jean Anouilh **Pf**: 1947, Paris **Pb**: 1948 **Tr**: 1950 **G**: Romantic com. in 3 acts; French prose **S**: Winter garden of a French chateau, *c.*1947 **C**: 8m, 6f

Frédéric is infatuated with his fiancée, the rich heiress Diana Messerschmann, but she treats him cruelly. His identical twin brother Horace (Hugo), whom Diana secretly loves, is as hard and carefree as Frédéric is gentle and melancholy. Horace hires a beautiful young ballet dancer Isabelle to appear at the forthcoming ball given by Mme Desmermortes, dowager aunt of Horace and Frédéric, in order to jolt Frédéric out of his misguided devotion. At the ball Frédéric is indeed attracted to the graceful and innocent Isabelle, and she responds to his sad demeanour, but remains secretly in love with Horace. Diana haughtily confronts Isabelle and tears her ball dress, leading to the girls fighting. Diana's father Messerschmann tries to buy off Isabelle, but she refuses to take his money. Defeated by her integrity, Messerschmann tears up his banknotes and goes off to dispose of his millions. The following dawn, Isabelle jumps into the lake but is rescued by Horace. Mme Desmermortes persuades Isabelle that she will be happy with Frédéric, who has broken off his engagement to Diana. Now that Diana is no longer rich, Horace agrees to marry her. With the couples happily paired off, news comes that Messerschmann is now richer than ever.

In the best of his *pièces brillantes* (sparkling plays), Anouilh plays skilfully with standard elements of comedy: identical twin brothers played by the same actor (ultimately derived from *The *Brothers Menaechmus*), a rich dowager aunt who sorts out the complications of the plot, a fantastically rich man whose efforts to become poor only make him richer, and the Cinderella-like figure of Isabelle who meets her Prince Charming at the ball. Christopher Fry's witty translation (in which Horace becomes Hugo) was directed by Peter Brook in 1950.

Rising of the Moon, The

A: Lady Gregory **Pf**: 1907, Dublin **Pb**: 1904 **G**: Com. in 1 act; prose and songs **S**: Quayside of an Irish seaport, 1900s **C**: 4m

A Sergeant in the Royal Irish Constabulary and two of his men are on the lookout for a man wanted for crimes against the British authorities. A ballad singer helps the Sergeant while singing songs, including 'Shawn O'Farrell', the rebel who gathers his fighters 'at the Rising of the Moon'. Discarding his disguise, the 'ballad singer' reveals himself as the wanted man and persuades the Sergeant to forgo the £100 reward and let him go rather than betray a fellow Irishman.

Lady Gregory, best known for her part in founding the Abbey Theatre with W. B. Yeats and J. M. Synge in 1904, also wrote many plays, of which this is the best known. Capturing well the rhythms of Irish speech, the two men are sketched in skilfully, the roguish outlaw and the big-hearted Sergeant, whose love of his country outweighs his desire for personal gain.

Risk Everything. See SUBURBAN MOTEL.

risveglio, Il. See FEMALE PARTS.

Ritt über den Bodensee, Der. See RIDE ACROSS LAKE CONSTANCE, THE.

Rivals, The

A: Richard Brinsley Sheridan **Pf**: 1775, London **Pb**: 1775 **G**: Com. in 5 acts; prose **S**: Bath, 1770s **C**: 9m, 5f, extras

Captain Jack Absolute is the son of the wealthy Sir Anthony Absolute. He has come to Bath, pretending to be mere Ensign Beverley, knowing that this will offer him more success in his wooing of Lydia Languish, a young beauty devoted to sentimental novels. However, he finds himself encountering opposition, not only from Lydia's shrewish aunt Mrs Malaprop but also from the fiery old Sir Lucius O'Trigger and the country bumpkin Bob Acres. When Jack's father arranges for him to marry Lydia, Lydia imagines at first that Ensign Beverley has tricked the old man into believing that he is his son. Challenged to a duel by both Acres and Sir Lucius, Jack goes out to meet his rivals. Acres relents as soon as he discovers that Captain Absolute is in fact his friend Jack, and Sir Lucius, discovering that the letters he supposedly received from Lydia came from her aunt, also willingly withdraws. Jack is now free to marry Lydia, who is reconciled to his unromantic wealth.

Not only did Mrs Malaprop with her talent for confusing the meaning of words add a new term to the English language, but *The Rivals* also remains one of the finest British comedies in its own right. Significantly, while in *The *Beaux' Stratagem*, the hero has to pretend to be of higher birth than he is, Jack Absolute in the latter half of the century must 'stoop to conquer'. In establishing opposition between the old way (the arranged marriage agreed by Sir Anthony and Mrs Malaprop) and the new way (love of the individual, however poor), Sheridan continues the 18th-century trend towards the romanticization of love.

Rivers of China, The

A: Alma de Groen **Pf:** 1987, Sydney **Pb:** 1988
G: Drama in 2 acts **S:** Gurdjieff's Institute, Fontainebleau, France, 1922–3, and hospital, Sydney, 1987 **C:** 7m, 6f (performed by 4m, 3f)

In 1922 Katherine Mansfield, the writer, tells her husband John ('Jack') Middleton Murry that she is going to seek a cure for her tuberculosis by visiting Gurdjieff's Institute for the Harmonious Development of Man in Fontainebleau. Russian mystic Gurdjieff, telling Katherine that she has been asleep and does not know who she is, subjects her to a rigorous regime designed to bring her back into harmony with her self and her body. In 1987, Wayne, a hospital cleaner, becomes interested in a male patient who has woken from plastic surgery convinced that he is Katherine Mansfield. Wayne is surprised to learn that there have been male poets. It seems that, after being 'silenced for centuries', women have taken their revenge by criminalizing male creativity. If necessary, women can now use the Medusa look, which avenges earlier male exploitation of women by inducing paralysis. While Katherine's physical condition deteriorates, the hospital patient, unable to get any Shakespeare, begs Wayne to bring him writing materials. Katherine loses faith in Gurdjieff, convinced that he is an old lecher who despises women. When Wayne discovers the patient is dying of TB, Dr Rahel, who created him, offers Wayne the choice between letting the Man live an ordinary life or die having written like Katherine Mansfield. Wayne says that he should be allowed to die.

De Groen's finest play contains two major themes: a futuristic vision in which the suppression of women's creativity by men is reversed, so that men's history is blanked out; and the choice faced by many creative people, that they may lose their artistic talent if they are rendered psychologically normal. The interweaving of the two time periods offers a fascinating framework for these explorations.

Road

A: Jim Cartwright **Pf:** 1986, London **Pb:** 1986
G: Drama in 2 acts, with pre-show and interval
S: Road in a small Lancashire town, 1980s
C: 17m, 13f

In the Pre-Show, the theatre bar is converted to a pub, and actors represent drinkers. Then boozy wideboy Scullery takes the audience on a tour of the 'Road' (its sign has fallen down, and the rest of the name has been forgotten). In the living rooms of different families and on the road outside we see: Louise arguing with her Brother; Brenda nagging at her daughter Carol, who goes out drinking with Louise; Eddie and Brink going out together; Dor and Lane, two tarty women, on their way to the pub; Molly, a dotty old woman, getting ready to go out; the 'Professor', a seedy individual, claiming to be researching the Road; Skin-Lad, violent and mad. When Scullery tries to enter a derelict house, Bald drives him away; Jerry lives in his RAF past; Joey is depressed after losing his job, and Clare comforts him with sex, but they both end up feeling desperate. In the Interval there is a disco in the auditorium and a pub in the bar. After the pubs close, most of the characters, some seen for the first time, are drunk, and many eat a chip supper. Carol, Louise, Brink, and Eddie have a party, where they finally all join in a chorus: 'Somehow a somehow a somehow – might escape!'

Road, much beloved of amateur groups for its wide range of roles and opportunities for improvisation around the text, presents a series of loosely arranged vignettes of one evening in a deprived Lancashire town. Its lyrical use of slang, blatantly sexual behaviour, and constant threat of violence, suggests a northern version of Berkoff's *East*.

Road, The

A: Wole Soyinka **Pf:** 1965, London **Pb:** 1965 **G:** Drama in 2 acts **S:** The Professor's store by a roadside, Nigeria, 1960s **C:** 8m, extras

The Professor is a likeable scoundrel. He was expelled for embezzlement from the church in which he was a lay reader, and now makes a living forging driving licences and selling spare parts of cars that he has caused to crash on 'the road' by removing traffic signs. His store, where he holds religious services, provides a meeting place for layabouts, crooks, lorry drivers, and corrupt police. Some of their stories are revealed in flashbacks, especially that of Kotonu, a lorry driver, who knocked down an *egungun* masquerader. Resourcefully, Kotonu loaded the body into his lorry, took the man's mask, and danced in the festival until he could escape at daybreak. Kotonu has now brought the wounded masquerader Murano to the Professor, and the Professor gives him a job as his servant, even though Murano is now unable to speak. At a religious service that evening, Murano dons his mask and becomes possessed. This sparks off a fight, in which the crooks' leader Say Tokyo Kid stabs the Professor, and is then killed by Murano. The Professor's dying words are: 'Breathe like the road, be even like the road itself . . . '.

To appreciate *The Road* fully, it would be necessary to have a proper understanding of Yoruba belief. And yet it raises issues to which Western audiences can relate. In the opposition between the rational arguments and lack of integrity of the Professor and the religious ritual of the mute *egungun* masquerader Murano, Soyinka explores the confrontation between human reason and religious ecstasy, which is at least as old as *Bacchae* (which Soyinka adapted in 1973). Ultimately, it is the quest, 'the road', that matters.

Road to Damascus, The. See TO DAMASCUS.

Roar China! (*Rychi Kitai!*)

A: Sergei Tretyakov **Pf:** 1926, Moscow **Pb:** 1926 **Tr:** 1931 **G:** Drama in 9 scenes; Russian prose **S:** Wharf by the Yangtze and on gunboat *Chinon*, 1924 **C:** 22m, 8f, extras

An American trader Ashlay demands that the Chinese foreman gets his coolies to work harder and threatens paying less. A Journalist buys a girl off a procuress, and tourists take pictures. When Ashlay sacks the workmen and cynically flings a handful of coins amongst them, a riot breaks out, which has to be suppressed by the police. On the English gunboat, Ashlay negotiates a deal with a French businessman. When Ashlay tries to return to shore, the boatman Chee refuses to take him, but is tricked into being brought alongside. Reprimanding Chee, Ashlay strikes him in the face, then misses his footing, falls in the water, and drowns. Chee flees as the police arrive. The Captain demands reparation for Ashlay's death: a lavish funeral, financial compensation to his relatives, and the execution of two boatmen; otherwise he will bombard the town. The English stop the Daieen's (Mayor's) telegram being sent to Peking and reject all pleas for mercy. The Chinese cabin-boy hangs himself in protest. Two boatmen are picked out and executed by strangling. The angry Chinese know that one day they will drive the imperialists from their country, and indeed the gunboat is summoned to meet a force of revolutionaries in Shanghai.

This is a piece of uncompromising Soviet propaganda, which was premiered at Meyerhold's theatre in Moscow. It does not attempt to explore the psychology of the characters but reproduces a recent historical incident, naturalistically recreating the bustling wharf and the genteel life aboard the gunboat. *Roar China!* was performed internationally, in New York, London, by Reinhardt in Berlin, and eventually, after the Communist takeover in 1949, in Shanghai. Brecht referred to Tretyakov as 'my teacher'.

Roaring Girl, The

AT: *Moll Cutpurse* **A**: Thomas Dekker and Thomas Middleton **Pf**: 1611, London **Pb**: 1611 **G**: Com. in 5 acts; prose and blank verse **S**: London, 1611 **C**: 30m, 5f

Sebastian Wengrave wishes to marry Mary Fitzallard, but his father, Sir Alexander, is opposed to the match. So Sebastian pretends to woo Moll Cutpurse, a notoriously dissolute character, in the hope that his father will be so alarmed that he agrees to the marriage to Mary. While others are pursuing a number of illicit love affairs, Moll, dressed as a man, defeats one of the lechers in a duel, and after quarrelling with Trapdoor, hires him as a servant, unaware that he is also in the pay of Sebastian's father. All attempts by Trapdoor to ensnare Moll in a crime fail, and Sir Alexander is horrified to imagine that his son might marry Moll. His worst fears appear confirmed when Sebastian arrives home with a veiled woman, who turns out to be Moll. But Mary is soon revealed as his true bride, now welcomed by Sir Alexander, and Moll declares that she would never marry anyway.

In a reasonably authentic London setting, but with highly stylized rogues and lechers, Middleton, here in collaboration with Dekker, once again explores the cunning of the young in outwitting the old, a theme stretching back to the fooling of the *senex* (old man) in Roman comedy. At the centre of the action and sometimes distracting from the main thrust of the plot, stands the Roaring Girl herself, a highly idealized representation of the unscrupulous historical Moll Cutpurse (*c.*1584–1660), arguably the first truly independent woman in world theatre.

Robbers, The (*Die Räuber*)

A: Friedrich Schiller **W**: 1777–80 **Pf**: 1782, Mannheim **Pb**: 1781 **Tr**: 1792 **G**: Drama in 5 acts; German prose **S**: Germany, mainly the castle of Count von Moor, and the Bohemian Woods, mid-18th c. **C**: 14m, 1f, extras

Through the machinations of his evil brother Franz, the noble Karl Moor is disinherited. Franz tries unsuccessfully to seduce Karl's fiancée Amalia. Driven to desperation by the rejection of his father, and in rebellion against the corrupt and flaccid society he lives in, Karl and his friends form a band of robbers. While one faction led by the ruthless Spiegelberg becomes totally anarchic, even attacking a convent and raping the nuns, the main band led by Karl robs from the rich to give to the poor. Franz tries to kill his father by bringing a false report of Karl's death. The old man faints as though dead, and Franz becomes count. Amalia is forced to defend her honour with a knife. After several battles against government forces, Karl arrives at his home in disguise. Here he discovers his father incarcerated in a tower. Karl frees him, but the shock of their reconciliation kills the old man. Following the demands of the robbers, Karl stabs Amalia, who is happy to die at his hands. As the castle is attacked and set on fire, Franz commits suicide, and Karl, acknowledging the error of his ways, disbands the robbers and surrenders himself to a poor man who will collect a large reward for his capture.

This theatrical firework of the 20-year-old Schiller is full of overblown writing and melodramatic incident (including the distasteful murder of Amalia). But, together with **Götz von Berlichingen*, it helped to transform the future of European theatre, providing a model of Romantic drama: an episodic structure, the staging of exciting incidents pushing the capabilities of theatre to its limits, intensely memorable characters (the evil and deformed Franz, reminiscent of Edmund in **King Lear*, and the more complex Karl, at once thoughtful and impulsive), and, above all, a shout of defiance against a corrupt world. Popular from its stormy premiere, *The Robbers* is a staple of the German repertory, most famously being staged by Piscator in 1926.

Rockaby

A: Samuel Beckett **Pf**: 1981, Buffalo, New York State **Pb**: 1982 **G**: Monodrama in 1 act
S: Rocking chair on bare stage, indeterminate period **C**: 1f

A prematurely old woman W, with unkempt grey hair, wearing a black evening gown and headdress, rocks in her rocking chair, speaking short, often repeated phrases in time with her recorded voice. She knew it was 'time she stopped', so she ceased going to and fro and sat in her chair by the window looking out at other windows. All the blinds were down in the other windows (the occupants were dead?), but her blind remained up. Then one day she went 'down the steep stair', lowered her blind, and settled to rocking in her chair as her mother had done before death overtook her.

Beckett was obsessed with his mother, the person who gave him the unwanted gift of life, and whose possessive love haunted much of his adult life. Here, as in **Footfalls*, Beckett meditates on the desolation, isolation, and repetition of life (especially for the widowed or unmarried woman), as one waits for death. The mesmerizing effect of the short beautifully phrased lines as W rocks, is suddenly shattered with the verbal violence of the ending: 'stop her eyes | fuck life | stop her eyes | rock her off | rock her off.'

Rogue of Seville, The. See TRICKSTER OF SEVILLE, THE.

Romans in Britain, The

A: Howard Brenton **Pf**: 1980, London **Pb**: 1980 **G**: Hist. drama in 2 acts **S**: River Thames, 54 BC; Britain, AD 515; Northern Ireland, AD 1980
C: 49m, 9f, 3 children (1m, 2f)

Envoys come to a Celtic village on the Thames to warn them of the advance of the Roman army. But the villagers are too concerned with hounding two Irish criminals on the run and with past quarrels with neighbouring tribes to get their young men to defend the land. Three off-duty Roman soldiers murder two young Celts and attempt homosexual rape with Marban, a young Druid priest. Roman troops burn the village and murder the Mother, its chief. Julius Caesar, leader of the invasion, is displeased with the ruthlessness of his army. Marban commits suicide, and one of the escaping Irishmen is killed by a slave. Suddenly it is 1980: Roman forces in British army uniforms arrive and shoot the Slave. Thomas Chichester, an undercover British soldier, is conducting a secret operation near the Northern Irish border. The time reverts to AD 515: Celts are brought news of the Saxon invasion. When Cai, a veteran fighter, refuses to acknowledge the danger, his daughters kill him. 1980: Chichester, full of self-doubt about the British presence in Ireland, reveals his identity to his intended IRA victim. Just before he is shot, he denounces all forms of imperialism. 515: a cook turned poet invents the legend of the Celtic King Arthur.

Although the play became best known for the absurd legal action that was brought against the director Michael Bogdanov 'for procuring an act of gross indecency' in the scene of attempted homosexual rape, it stands as one of the finest of many political pieces dealing with Britain's relationship with Ireland. By depicting the Roman and Saxon invasions of Britain, Brenton was able to show that the audience was once on the receiving end of the kind of imperialism which Brenton saw in the British presence in Northern Ireland. Significantly, no Protestant voice is heard in the 1980 scenes, so that the republican Irish can be portrayed simply as victims.

Romeo and Juliet (*An excellent conceited Tragedie of Romeo and Iuliet*)

A: William Shakespeare **Pf**: *c.*1591–6, London **Pb**: 1597 ('bad' 1st quarto); 1599 ('good' 2nd quarto) **G**: Trag. in 5 acts; blank verse and prose **S**: Verona and one scene in Mantua, Renaissance period **C**: 24m, 4f, extras

The Montagues and Capulets, two of the leading families of Verona, are sworn enemies. A sword fight between members of the two houses is stopped by Prince Escalus, who threatens the direst consequences for anyone who continues the feud. Meanwhile, Romeo, the son of the Montagues, remains untouched by all this hostility; he can think only of his unrequited love for Rosalinde. His companions,

Benvolio and Mercutio, try to interest him in other beauties by urging him to gatecrash the party being given by the Capulets. The masked friends arrive at the ball, are confronted by the hot-headed Tybalt, but remain long enough for Romeo to fall desperately in love with Juliet, and she with him, although she is betrothed to be married to the lord Paris. Immediately after the ball, Romeo observes Juliet on her balcony expressing her love for him. They resolve to get married at once, and Romeo seeks out Friar Laurence, who weds them, hoping that this might at last lead to the reconciliation of the two warring houses. However, tragedy intervenes: Mercutio and Tybalt begin to duel, and Romeo, in trying to intervene, succeeds only in causing Mercutio to be killed. In despair and fury over the death of his friend, Romeo kills Tybalt. Escalus imposes the threatened sentence on Romeo, who is banished from Verona. He secretly visits Juliet at night and they consummate their love before he has to flee to Mantua. Capulet now insists that Juliet should marry Paris. She seeks help from Friar Laurence, who prepares her a sleeping potion, which will give her the semblance of death. On her planned wedding day, then, it seems that she is dead, and her body is laid to rest in the family tomb. Romeo, hearing the news of her 'death', rushes to her side, kills the mourning Paris, and, after a last embrace with his beloved, swallows poison. At last Juliet awakes, discovers Romeo dead beside her and swallows the last drops of remaining poison. Prince Escalus and the parents arrive, Friar Laurence explains all, and in their communal grief the Montagues and Capulets are reconciled.

Based on Arthur Brooke's poem of 1562, *Tragicall Historye of Romeus and Iuliet*, Shakespeare's *Romeo and Juliet* is one of his earliest tragedies, and one of his most concentrated. There are virtually no sub-plots, and nearly all the action takes place within one city, and within two days. Indeed, without the magnificent quality of Shakespeare's verse, which generates such intense feelings of love and loss, the compression of so many violent events and twists of fate into so short a time span would seem hopelessly melodramatic.

Romeo and Juliet has repeatedly served as a model for the doomed love of members of opposing houses, e.g. in Peter Ustinov's Cold War comedy *Romanoff and Juliet* (1956), in the New York gangland musical *West Side Story* (1957), and in the modern-dress film version of Shakespeare's play by Baz Luhrmann (1996). There have been many musical treatments: a dramatic symphony by Berlioz (1839), an opera by Gounod (1867), a symphonic poem by Tchaikovsky (1869), and a ballet by Prokofiev (1938). Frederick Delius's opera, *A Village Romeo and Juliet* (1907), is based on a short story by Swiss writer Gottfried Keller.

Ronde, La (*Reigen*)

AT: *Hands Around; Couples; Circle of Love; Merry-Go-Round; The Round Dance; The Blue Room* **A**: Arthur Schnitzler **Pf**: 1903, Munich (part); 1920, Berlin (full version) **Pb**: 1900 (private); 1903 (public) **Tr**: 1920 **G**: Com. in 10 linked scenes; German prose **S**: Vienna and environs, 1890s **C**: 5m, 5f

(1) A prostitute persuades a soldier in a hurry to take her there and then on the banks of the Danube, but curses him when he refuses to tip her. (2) The same soldier seduces a housemaid at the Prater amusement park but then abandons her to go off to dance. (3) The housemaid is interrupted while writing to her lover by the summons of a young gentleman, who proceeds to seduce her. After he leaves, she steals one of his cigars. (4) The gentleman has succeeded in getting a young married woman into bed in his specially rented love nest, but cannot achieve an erection. He blames his impotence on the fact that he loves her too much, and talks of lovers who spend nights together just weeping with happiness. Eventually they make love, and the young wife comments that it was better than weeping. (5) The young wife is warned by her complacent husband to avoid the company of 'loose women'. When they have made love, the husband smugly recalls their honeymoon five years previously. (6) The husband seduces a 'sweet young thing' in a private room in a restaurant but fears that he might have picked up a venereal disease through this casual encounter. (7) The sweet young thing goes to

bed with a conceited young poet, whose main concern is whether this enchanting but simple creature will appreciate his new play. (8) The poet succumbs to the advances of an actress, whose lover has just left her, and makes love to her in a country inn. (9) The next day in her bedroom the actress seduces a visiting count, despite his reservations about sex in the early morning. (10) The count wakes up to find himself in a brothel lying beside the prostitute of the first play. She tells him that he was so drunk the previous night that before they could have sex, he fell fast asleep beside her.

In this witty and colourful series of episodes Schnitzler makes no attempt to develop strong plots or anything but the briefest of characterizations of his nameless figures. Instead he offers vignettes of sexual behaviour of *fin de siècle* Vienna at the time Freud was developing his theories there. *La Ronde* was predictably banned for public performance because of its shocking content, and even Max Reinhardt's production in Berlin a couple of decades later met with great hostility. It still exerts a fascination for the public, especially with contemporary awareness of the merry-go-round of genital infection. The cycle enjoyed a recent revival in London as *The Blue Room* (adapted by David Hare, 1999), with Nicole Kidman playing all the female roles.

Rookery Nook

A: Ben Travers **Pf:** 1926, Southsea **Pb:** 1930 **G:** Farce in 3 acts **S:** English seaside cottage, Somerset, 1920s **C:** 5m, 6f

The formidable Gertrude Twine has rented a charming country cottage, Rookery Nook, as a holiday home for her sister Clara, freshly married to Gerald Popkiss, but they have been delayed by the illness of Gertrude and Clara's mother. Gerald's cousin Clive, 'a sport in his 30s', offers to wait in the cottage until Clara and Gerald arrive. Gerald arrives, but Clara has been further delayed. On the point of retiring, Gerald is surprised by the arrival of Rhoda, a pretty young woman dressed only in her pyjamas, who is running away from her bullying German stepfather Putz. Nobly, Gerald allows her to stay in one of the bedrooms, and he and Clive are then obliged desperately to try to hide the runaway girl from being discovered, not only from Gertrude but also from inquisitive neighbours. Finally, Rhoda manages to acquire some clothes and is dressed just in time for Clara's arrival. Gerald nevertheless succeeds only with difficulty in persuading Clara of his innocence. They end in each other's arms, as do Rhoda and Clive.

Rookery Nook, based on his novel, was one of the popular nine 'Aldwych farces' that Travers wrote for the Aldwych Theatre in London from 1925 to 1933. Following in the tradition of French farces like Feydeau's *A *Flea in her Ear*, Travers writes about a put-upon man, who finds himself in a compromising situation and is unjustly suspected of adultery. Being English, Travers's 'compromising situations' never involve anything approaching immorality, usually, as here, depending only on the accident of a young woman wearing few clothes. His plays are still widely performed by amateur groups and enjoyed professional revivals in London in the late 1970s.

Roots

A: Arnold Wesker **Pf:** London, 1959 **Pb:** 1959 **G:** Pol. drama in 3 acts **S:** Rural homes, Norfolk, England, 1950s **C:** 5m, 4f

Beatie Bryant, who has been living in London with her boyfriend Ronnie Kahn for three years, comes home to visit her family in Norfolk. In Act 1, she tells her sister and brother-in-law, a farm mechanic, how much she has learned from Ronnie and denounces the empty lives of her family. Stan Mann, a neighbour, jokingly says he'll take her if Ronnie doesn't hurry up and marry her. In Acts 2 and 3, Beatie stays with her mother and father, also a farm labourer. Again she tells her mother how intellectually deprived the family is, and is dismayed by her father's resigned attitude when he is threatened with the sack. News comes of Stan Mann's death. A high tea is prepared for Ronnie's arrival, and the family, including Beatie's brother and sister-in-law, gather to meet Ronnie, the socialist intellectual. Instead, a letter comes from Ronnie, breaking off the relationship with Beatie. Angry and disappointed, she feels that she now has no roots, neither at home nor in the town. In this recognition, she discovers a newfound articulacy: 'I'm talking... I'm not quoting no more.'

In the wake of *Look Back in Anger*, British theatre relinquished its polite conversations in middle-class drawing rooms in favour of so-called 'kitchen sink' drama. *Roots*, the central and best part of the 'Wesker Trilogy' (which includes *Chicken Soup with Barley* and *I'm Talking about Jerusalem*), was one of the most significant contributions to this new wave of realism, using a rural working-class setting and naturalistic dialogue. However, the poor are not sentimentalized; rather, to Beatie's frustration, they lead empty, passive lives. Beatie herself is not idealized: she tries to impose progressive ideas borrowed from her treacherous boyfriend, without attempting to understand her family. Only when she begins to speak with her own voice at the end, is there a sense that genuine political education might be possible.

Rope, The (*Rudens*)

A: Titus Maccius Plautus Pf: *c.*189 BC, Rome Tr: 1694 G: Latin com. in verse S: Before the home of Daemones near Cyrene on the African coast, 2nd c. BC C: 8m, 3f, extras

Daemones is an ageing gentleman from Athens whose daughter was kidnapped in infancy. Having given away his fortune through generosity, he lives in humble circumstances near Cyrene on the African coast. His daughter, now called Palaestra, has been brought by her pimp to Cyrene, where a young Athenian Plesidippus has fallen in love with her. While attempting to sail to Sicily, the pimp and his slaves are shipwrecked by a storm invoked by the divine Arcturus, and Palaestra is washed ashore at Daemones' home. She and her maid take refuge in the neighbouring temple of Venus, where her pimp attempts to seize her, but she is defended by Daemones and Plesiddipus, who takes the pimp off for trial. When a trunk tied with rope is fished from the sea, evidence is found in it of Palaestra's childhood, so father and daughter are reunited, and she is now free to marry Plesiddipus.

The Rope is the lightest and most joyful of Plautus' comedies. The one villain, the pimp, is quickly disposed of (with the help of divine intervention); for the rest there is a rural setting, the reuniting of father and lost daughter, and the fulfilment of young love. Above all, we see how nobility of mind is rewarded (this time without the help of scheming slaves), especially when Daemones, insisting that the trunk be returned to its rightful owner, is richly repaid by discovering his lost daughter. Plautus' play provided the source material for Lodovico Dolce's *The Ruffian* (1560), and Thomas Heywood's *The Captives* (1624), and elements of it are found in Shakespeare's *The *Tempest* and in his later romances. Plautus' *The Rope* has nothing to do with Eugene O'Neill's one-act play *The Rope* (1918), nor Patrick Hamilton's murder-story *Rope* (1929), made into a tense film by Alfred Hitchcock.

Rosencrantz and Guildenstern Are Dead

A: Tom Stoppard Pf: 1966, Edinburgh Pb: 1967; rev. 1968 G: Com. in 3 acts; prose and blank verse S: Court of Elsinore and a ship at sea, Elizabethan period C: 14m, 2f

Rosencrantz and Guildenstern pass the time tossing coins and playing word games, while they await their entrance. They are not sure why they have been summoned; they are not even certain which is Rosencrantz and which Guildenstern. A Player arrives with his troupe and performs *The Murder of Gonzago*, in which two lords with an uncanny resemblance to Rosencrantz and Guildenstern are killed. The two recognize some hidden meaning: 'Operating on two levels, are we?! How clever!' Attempting to manipulate Hamlet as instructed, they find that he gets the better of them. On board ship bound for England, they open Claudius's letter to the English king demanding Hamlet's execution, but remain unaware that Hamlet substitutes his own letter condemning them to death. Attacked by pirates, the Danes return to dry land, where Rosencrantz and Guildenstern learn of their ordained death: 'To be told so little . . . to such an end – and still – finally – to be denied an explanation.' Dazed and weary, they approach their deaths in the final scene of *Hamlet*.

Of the many reinterpretations of *Hamlet* (see CHARACTER INDEX, p. 481) this is undoubtedly one of the cleverest. The minor roles of Rosencrantz and Guildenstern are foregrounded, while the main characters appear irrelevant and obsessed with their own concerns. Stoppard's first successful play has been understood both as an absurdist comment on the human situation and as a critique of theatre, especially in its most famous manifestation, which, like society, prescribes roles from which it is very difficult to break free.

Rose Tattoo, The

A: Tennessee Williams **Pf**: 1950, Chicago **Pb**: 1951 **G**: Com. in 3 acts **S**: Cottage on Gulf coast between New Orleans and Mobile, 1947–50 **C**: 9m, 13f, 2 children (1m, 1f)

Serafina delle Rose, a seamstress of Sicilian descent, is, together with her 12-year-old daughter Rosa, excitedly awaiting the return of her husband Rosario, who drives a truck and is involved in drug running. Serafina has good news: she is pregnant again (his rose tattoo imprinted itself on her breast when they made love). News comes that he has been shot dead, and she has a miscarriage. Three years later, Serafina has become an untidy slut. Rosa tried cutting her wrists after Serafina prevented her from seeing Jack Hunter, a new boyfriend she met at a dance, but is allowed out for her high school graduation. When Serafina learns that her husband had an affair with a blonde blackjack dealer, she makes Jack swear to 'respect the innocence' of her daughter. Serafina meets Alvaro, a young simple-minded truck-driver, and feels her prayers are answered: 'A clown of a face . . . with my husband's body!' That evening, Serafina dresses beautifully to welcome Alvaro. He has had his chest tattooed with a rose. In the early hours when Rosa comes home still a virgin, she screams at finding a strange man in the house. Serafina, rushing to her aid, smashes the urn containing her husband's ashes. Rosa leaves to take Jack to a hotel room, and Serafina feels the imprint of a rose on her breast once more.

This is one of the few comedies written by Tennessee Williams, using the theme, at least as old as **Twelfth Night*, of passion that overcomes self-indulgent grief. Significantly, he set this in the life-affirming community of American Sicilians in the southern sun.

Rosmersholm

A: Henrik Ibsen **Pf**: 1887, Bergen **Pb**: 1886 **Tr**: 1891 **G**: Trag. in 4 acts; Norwegian prose **S**: Rosmersholm Estate, western Norway, 1880s **C**: 4m, 2f

Johannes Rosmer, a former pastor, was widowed about one year previously when his wife Beata drowned in the millpond. He has lost his Christian faith, and now believes in a utopia where all humankind will be free. He lives on his estate with his young housekeeper Rebekka West, and regards their friendship as a model of 'spiritual marriage'. His former wife's brother Rector Kroll accuses Rosmer of having driven Beata to suicide, and Johannes, now believing that she took her life so that he would be free to marry Rebekka, proposes to the young woman. At first jubilant, Rebekka then rejects his proposal and confesses to the two men that it was she that drove Beata to her death. As she prepares to leave, Rebekka tells Rosmer of her former passion for him, which has now become a pure spiritual love. To cleanse them of their guilt and in order to preserve the purity of their love, they agree to a mutual suicide in the millpond that took Beata's life.

Like **Oedipus the King*, *Rosmersholm* has an analytic structure, in which nearly all the action derives from revelations about the past. While it offers Ibsen opportunities to reflect profoundly on the nature of love and of individual belief, it creates difficulties as a tragic piece. While in Sophocles the outcome is inevitable, in a realistic play like this the exposure of the past opens up many possibilities, so that Rosmer's and Rebekka's suicide pact may appear at best misguided, at worst melodramatic.

Round and Round the Garden. See NORMAN CONQUESTS, THE

Round Dance, The. See RONDE, LA.

Rover The (Part 1)

AT: *The Banished Cavaliers* A: Aphra Behn Pf: 1677, London Pb: 1677 G: Com. in 5 acts; prose and some verse S: Naples, 1650s C: 12m, 7f, extras

It is carnival time in Naples. Two Spanish sisters, Hellena and Florinda, plan to have fun in disguise, Hellena because she is obliged to become a nun, Florinda because she is threatened with marriage to a rich old gentleman. They soon begin flirting, Hellena with Willmore the Rover, Florinda with Belvile, an English colonel. Florinda's brother Don Pedro hopes that she will marry his friend Don Antonio, but Antonio is too taken up with the attractions of a famous courtesan Angellica. However, Angellica is won over by the charms of the Rover Willmore. When Willmore goes to visit Angellica, he fights with Antonio and wounds him. Belvile intervenes to part them, Willmore leaves, and Belvile is arrested for attacking Antonio. Antonio asks Belvile to take his place in a duel against Don Pedro, who is outraged by Antonio's love of Angellica. Belvile, begged by Florinda not to harm her brother, abandons the duel and so confirms his love for her. Despite further misunderstandings, helped by a multiplicity of disguises, Belvile marries Florinda, and Willmore, though threatened with a pistol by Angellica, weds Hellena.

Based on Thomas Killigrew's *Thomaso* (published 1664), *The Rover* has an untidy plot and depends for much of the action on conventional devices like disguise and characters unintentionally causing misunderstandings. But its great strength does not lie alone in the fact that Aphra Behn was the first woman to be a professional playwright, but also in the sheer exuberance of the action reflecting the high spirits of the Restoration. With honest bawdy in the depiction of the exploitative nature of men in their sexual relationships, in contrast with Hellena's vigorous dignity, *The Rover* offers incident-packed entertainment. It was successfully revived at the RSC in 1986. Part 2 (1681) shows another courtesan winning the widower Willmore.

Royal Hunt of the Sun, The

A: Peter Shaffer Pf: 1964, Chichester Pb: 1964 G: Hist. drama in 2 acts S: Spain and Peru, 1529–33 C: 21m, 2f

The events of the play are narrated by Martin Ruiz, formerly the page of Francisco Pizarro. Pizarro, a veteran Spanish soldier in his fifties, intent on the conquest of Peru, recruits Spanish soldiers with promises of the vast golden treasures possessed by the Incas, although the Church claims that their mission is to bring Christianity to the 'savages'. After enduring harsh jungle conditions and climbing snow-peaked mountains, his tiny force of less than 200 men eventually enter Cajamarca, the city where the Inca, the Emperor Atahuallpa, is residing. Although Pizarro is vastly outnumbered by Inca forces, Atahuallpa is convinced that Pizarro's courage must mean that he is the white god of Inca legends. The unarmed Inca troops are slaughtered in a bloodbath, and Atahuallpa allows himself to be captured. The two men develop an affinity, and Pizarro begins to believe in Atahuallpa's divinity: 'I've gone god-hunting and caught one.' Pizarro promises to free Atahuallpa if the Incas fill a huge room with gold, booty for the Spaniards to take home. The room is duly filled, but Pizarro is reluctant to free Atahuallpa, because the Emperor has sworn reprisals on all the Spanish except Pizarro. Pizarro believes his dilemma solved when Atahuallpa assures Pizarro that if he dies, his relation, the Sun, will resurrect him the next day, thus proving his divinity. Atahuallpa is garrotted, and Pizarro waits tensely for the sunrise. When Atahuallpa remains dead, Pizarro feels cheated and sinks into sullen disillusionment.

This spectacular piece, with its exciting action and epic sweep, addresses several issues: on a political level, there is the clash between the brutality of the conquistadors and the gentle trust of the Incas; on a spiritual level, there is the conflict between the weary orthodoxy of European religion and the nature-based spirituality of the New World. In the event, neither faith offers Pizarro an answer, and he recognizes that humankind is bound 'to live without hope of after'.

Rudens. See ROPE, THE.

Ruling Class, The

A: Peter Barnes **Pf**: 1968, Nottingham **Pb**: 1969 **G**: Com. in 2 acts; with prologue and epilogue **S**: Gurney Manor and other locations, England, 1960s **C**: 17m, 5f

When the 13th Earl of Gurney accidentally hangs himself, his remaining son Jack inherits the earldom. Unfortunately, Jack is barking mad: he believes he is God, and is happy to spend time hanging from a cross. When he declares that all men are equal, his horrified uncle Charles declares: 'he's not only *mad*, he's *Bolshie*!' The family's only hope is for Jack to have a son, who could then take over the title. Jack announces that he is already married – to Marguerite Gautier, the Lady of the Camellias. Charlie arranges for his mistress Grace Shelley to appear as Gautier and marry Jack. Nine months later, while Grace is giving birth to a baby boy, Jack is overcome by a Scots madman who also thinks he is God. Confronting an 8-foot beast, Jack is restored to sanity. Jack fights against the remains of his mental illness, but the family summon the Master in Lunacy in order to have him committed. When Jack fulminates against 'chaos, anarchy, homosexuality and worse', the Master is fully persuaded of Jack's sanity. From being the God of Love, Jack now believes he is Jack the Ripper. When Charles's wife seduces him, he slits her open with a knife, but Tucker, the old family retainer, is exposed as a Communist and arrested for the murder. Jack speaks in the House of Lords, and his rousing speech, asserting that 'The strong MUST manipulate the weak', is cheered to the rafters. As Grace embraces the triumphant Jack, he reaches for his knife . . .

Barnes's funny and vituperative dark comedy attacks the British Establishment, suggesting an unholy alliance between religion, politics, and law, and is based on the not wholly implausible premiss that preaching a gospel of love is regarded as madness, while messages of hatred and intolerance are treated as sane. Jack the Ripper is more acceptable than God.

RUR

AT: *R.U.R. (Rossum's Universal Robots)*
A: Karel Čapek **Pf**: 1921, Prague **Pb**: 1920 **Tr**: 1923 **G**: Drama in 3 acts and a prologue; Czech prose **S**: A remote island, in the future **C**: 9m, 4f, extras

Helena Glory, the daughter of the company president, visits one of his factories on a remote island. The manager Harry Domin explains that the success of the undertaking is due to the robots invented by a scientist called Rossum and speaks of a future in which humans will be free of all drudgery. Helena, surprised at how lifelike the robots are, confuses humans and robots. Domin proposes to her and she accepts. Ten years later the robots have become so threatening that Domin gives her a gunboat as an anniversary present. Helena, discovering that the robots are killing all humans, destroys the formula for creating robots, but it is too late. The robots exterminate everyone but the old engineer Alquist. He continues to serve the robots, but they become increasingly desperate when they realize that they are unable to procreate. However, a male and female robot enter, and Alquist recognizes that they have developed human feelings and are in love with each other. Addressing them as Adam and Eve, Alquist is reassured that 'Life will not perish'.

From Georg Kaiser's **Gas Trilogy* to Stanley Kubrick's film *2001: A Space Odyssey* the idea that machines may rebel and overcome humans was a major preoccupation of the 20th century. The colossal international success of *RUR* is due largely to this concern: the characters are not developed; the action tends towards the melodramatic (the last chance is to negotiate by offering the robots the formula – but Helena has destroyed it); the ending is saccharine. Yet a play that added the word 'robot' to the languages of the world can still exert a curious fascination.

Rutherford and Son

A: Githa Sowerby **Pf**: 1912, London **Pb**: 1912 **G**: Drama in 3 acts **S**: John Rutherford's home, northern England, early 20th c. C: 4m, 4f

The autocratic John Rutherford, boss of a metalworks on bleak moorland in northern England, lives with his curmudgeonly sister Ann, his desiccated daughter Janet, and his ineffectual son Richard, who is in the Church. His older son John has reluctantly returned home with his wife Mary and their baby son, and the young family endure a miserable winter in the cheerless household. Young John Rutherford has, with the help of a workman Martin, invented a new manufacturing process which would revive the fortunes of Rutherford's factory. When he offers to sell the patent to his father, Rutherford is outraged that his son should try to profit from something he should use to benefit the family business and persuades Martin to hand over the secret formula. Learning that Janet has been seeing Martin, Rutherford is so furious that his daughter is consorting with a worker that he throws her out of the house. Martin is sacked, and still fearing Rutherford, can no longer love Janet. She leaves in distress. John, discovering that Rutherford has his formula, steals money from him, and sets out to make a new life, promising to send for Mary. Mary offers Rutherford a deal: if she is allowed to bring up her son in his house, she will let Rutherford take him over as the next boss of the factory and so preserve the family business. Rutherford, abandoned by his own children, feels obliged to agree.

In the 20th century at last, women, who had scored notable successes in the novel, now began to write in large numbers for the stage, and Githa Sowerby was one of the pioneers. While the scenes between father (based on Sowerby's own patriarchal parent) and son are powerful, her writing is most telling in the terrible disappointment endured by Janet when Martin can no longer love her.

Ruy Blas

A: Victor Hugo **Pf:** 1838, Paris **Pb:** 1838 **Tr:** 1860 **G:** Trag. in 5 acts; French alexandrines **S:** Madrid, 1690s **C:** 13m, 4f, extras

Ruy Blas, valet of the unscrupulous Don Salluste, loves the beautiful German Queen, wife of the cruel and weak Carlos (Charles II of Spain). Don Salluste wishes to avenge himself on the Queen, because she banished him for refusing to marry the lady-in-waiting he seduced. He orders Ruy Blas to impersonate his cousin, the absent nobleman Don César, in order to win the Queen's heart and so bring about her downfall. With his new identity the noble-minded valet at last has the opportunity to approach the Queen he loves and to become an exemplary courtier, who reproaches the self-seeking behaviour of many of the royal counsellors. The real Don César now returns to court, and Ruy Blas, glowing from a declaration of love by the Queen, has to choose between bringing about her disgrace or losing her by revealing his identity. To save her honour, he kills Don Salluste and then takes poison. Dying, he learns that she loves him even as a valet.

Ruy Blas is the most accomplished of Hugo's plays, offering linguistic richness and variety of incident, from Don César's farcical return down a chimney to the violent acts of the last scene. The highly charged atmosphere of the play lends credence to the author Charles Nodier's observation that 'Romantic drama is nothing but melodrama ennobled by verse', but it is melodrama of the highest order and far surpasses anything that the British stage could offer in the same period. Because of its 'subversive' depiction of a commoner denouncing the nation's leaders, the play was banned during the Second Empire (1852–71).

Ruzante Returns from the Wars. See CONVERSATION OF RUZANTE RETURNED FROM THE WARS.

Rychi Kitai! See ROAR CHINA!

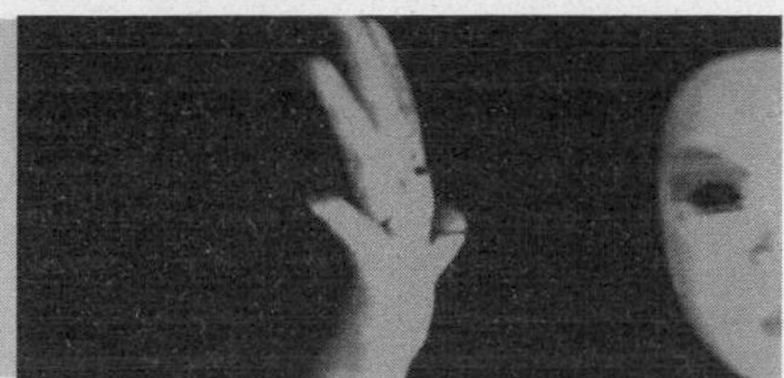

Sabato, domenico e lunedì. See SATURDAY, SUNDAY, MONDAY.

Sabine Women, The. See GREAT DIVIDE, THE.

Sado Kōshaku Fujin. See MADAME DE SADE.

Sagouine, La. See SLATTERN, THE.

Saint Joan

A: George Bernard Shaw Pf: 1923, New York Pb: 1924 G: Hist. drama in 6 scenes and an epilogue S: Vaucouleurs, Chinon, near Orléans, Rheims, and Rouen, France, 1429–31, and 1456 C: 22m, 2f, extras

Joan, 'the Maid of Lorraine', persuades her local squire that her voices require him to provide her with horses and armed support to cross territory occupied by the English, so that she may visit the Dauphin. Despite being young and feeble, the Dauphin is immediately recognized by Joan amongst a group of courtiers. Together with Dunois, the 'Bastard of Orléans', Joan drives the English from Orléans. Alarmed by her success, the English, represented by the Earl of Warwick, strike an unlikely alliance with the French Church authorities, represented by Cauchon, Bishop of Beauvais. The Dauphin is crowned Charles VII in Rheims cathedral, but, when Joan insists on driving the English from Paris, the French leaders withdraw their support. Joan is captured by the English and brought before Cauchon. After a lengthy trial for heresy, Joan condemns herself by insisting that she must follow her own judgement and not that of the Church. She is burnt at the stake, but her heart will not burn. In the Epilogue 25 years later she appears in a dream to Charles VII. When other players in her life arrive, they are astonished to learn that she will be canonized in 1920. However, they do not want her back, and Joan wonders how long it will be before the earth is ready to receive its saints.

Saint Joan is one of the most popular history plays of the 20th century, not least thanks to its rewarding title role. Characteristically, Shaw attempted to remove the romantic aura surrounding Joan of Arc and to present her as a simple, stubborn woman, endowed with admirable energy and determination. She is an embodiment of the Shavian life force, in opposition not only to the English but also to the orthodoxy of her own Church.

St Joan of the Stockyards (*Die heilige Johanna der Schlachthöfe*)

A: Bertolt Brecht (with Elisabeth Hauptmann and others) Pf: 1959, Hamburg Pb: 1932 Tr: 1956 G: Drama in 11 scenes; German prose and verse choruses S: Chicago stockyards, stock exchange, etc., *c.* 1930 C: 11m, 3f, choruses (m and f), extras

Joan Dark, a lieutenant in the Salvation Army (here called the 'Black Strawhats'), 'descends to the depths' in order to bring God to 'dehumanised humanity'. Her main target is Pierpoint Mauler, a ruthless capitalist who has closed his meatpacking factory, causing poverty and misery amongst the workers. Moved by Joan's appeal, he donates money to the Strawhats, but insists that she sees for herself that the poor are so evil and lazy that they are not worth helping. She recognizes however that their degradation and selfishness are caused by poverty. She therefore persuades Mauler to buy unwanted meat and livestock, which, as well as helping the poor, eventually makes Mauler even richer. Other speculators now offer money to the mission, if Joan will use her influence on Mauler to release the livestock. Joan indignantly refuses this bribe, but it is accepted by the head of the mission Snyder. Since Mauler refuses to reopen his slaughterhouses, Joan joins a strike in the snow, but leaves when the Communists threaten violence. With the support of the Strawhats, Mauler negotiates a favourable settlement with the strikers, condemning the workers to continued poverty. Joan, dying of pneumonia, denounces God, the class system, and the path of non-violence. But her words are drowned out as she is canonized as the saviour of the workers and the meat industry.

This Marxist retelling of the St Joan story, based on Elisabeth Hauptmann's *Happy End* (1929), shows someone, who like the Young Comrade in *The *Measures Taken*, acting from the noblest social motives, paradoxically helps the capitalists to greater power. The implication is that only violent revolution will change society, something, which apart from a radio broadcast in 1932, prevented its being performed for almost three decades.

St Nicholas Hotel, The. See DONNELLYS, THE.

Sakuntalā. See SHAKUNTALA.

Salome (*Salomé*)

A: Oscar Wilde Pf: 1896, Paris Pb: 1893
Tr: 1894 G: Trag. in 1 act; French prose S: The Palace of Herod Antipas, Judea, early 1st C. AD
C: 11m, 2f, extras

Jokanaan (John the Baptist) has been incarcerated by Herod Antipas, because the prophet denounces the King's unlawful marriage to Herodias, widow of his brother. While a feast is being given in the palace, Herodias's daughter, Salome, approaches Jokanaan and expresses her yearning for him. Delighting in his repulsiveness, she demands to kiss his mouth. Cursing her, Jokanaan returns to his prison. Herod, Herodias, and the guests come from the banquet, and, to his wife's annoyance, Herod pays special attention to Salome. He then asks her to dance for him, promising her anything she wishes if she will oblige him. She dances the dance of the seven veils, and then demands as reward the head of Jokanaan on a silver charger. Despite Herod's desperate attempts to offer her riches and jewellery, she remains adamant. The severed head of Jokanaan is brought, and at last Salome kisses his mouth. Herod, terrified and disgusted, orders her death, and Salome is crushed beneath the soldiers' shields.

Although based on Matthew 14 and Mark 6, some elements of Wilde's plot were so imaginatively introduced that they now form the accepted version of the Salome story. Neither Salome's love for John the Baptist, nor the seven veils, nor Salome's death, are recorded in the Bible. Wilde's version is a shocking and pathological representation of a young woman (something Hofmannsthal would imitate in his *Electra* of 1903), overlaid with *fin de siècle* decadence and deliciously ornate language. Invoking an old law about representing biblical characters on stage, the English censor banned the play until 1905. The operatic version by Richard Strauss was premiered in Dresden the same year.

Salonika

A: Louise Page Pf: 1982, London Pb: 1983
G: Drama in 3 acts S: Beach near Salonika, Greece, *c.* 1980 C: 3m, 2f

Eighty-four-year-old Charlotte has come on holiday with her daughter Enid, a retired draper's shop owner in her sixties. They are visiting the grave of Charlotte's husband Benjamin (Ben), who was killed at Salonika in the First World War. While they settle to enjoy the sun, gently bickering with each other, Ben rises from the sand and speaks first to Charlotte then to his daughter, who dances for him. Charlotte's friend Leonard unexpectedly arrives, because he is missing her. To Enid's dismay, Leonard and Charlotte decide to get married. On the same beach is a young Englishman Peter, who spends his time sunning himself and sleeping with tourists, and survives by selling his blood and semen. While the women go looking for Ben's grave, Leonard reprimands Peter for his way of life. Leonard had fought in the Second World War and returned home to find his wife and daughter gone. Ben appears again and reveals that he was not killed in action but drowned himself in terror. That evening, Leonard and Charlotte discuss the practicalities of living together, and Charlotte is worried about Enid's future. Enid, leaving her mother and Leonard alone in the hotel, visits Peter on the beach. They become close, and she offers him money to sleep with her. Peter tells Enid of her father's unheroic death. He dies of a heart attack, and Enid gently washes his naked body. Charlotte comes to her. She cannot sleep because Leonard snores; now she doesn't know what to do.

Page set out in *Salonika* 'to write a play about old age', but gradually recognized that this could be seen best in the context of stories and memories from the past (Ben) and in relation to the values of the younger generation (Peter). The false values of those fighting in a disastrous war and the self-indulgent values of the young are juxtaposed without moralizing. Enid, freed of her mother and of the weight of her father's memory, now sees new possibilities: 'Look at the stars.'

Salvation Nell

A: Edward Sheldon **Pf:** 1908, Providence, Rhode Island **Pb:** 1967 **G:** Drama in 3 acts **S:** A bar, a tenement apartment, a street corner, New York, early 20th c. **C:** 27m, 20f, extras

Nell Sanders works long hours as a cleaner in a bar in order to support her lover Jim Platt, a charming but indolent individual, by whom she becomes pregnant. He repays her by constant abuse. Because of his drunkenness, he loses his job and gets into a fight with another drinker who has been pestering Nell, beats and kicks him, finally killing him. Jim is arrested and Nell is sacked from her job. Nell rejects the temptation to become a prostitute and joins the Salvation Army. Eight years later, she is a leading light in the Army and has become close to one of the majors who loves her. Her happiness is shattered by the return of Jim from prison, who meets his child and demands that Nell return to him. When she learns that Jim and his gang are about to commit a robbery, she tries to dissuade him, and begins to call the police but cannot go through with it. Jim beats her, and she collapses. He runs away, fearful of having to return to prison. The Major declares his love for Nell, but she admits to still loving Jim. Jim returns, but Nell says that they can be together only when he admits God to his life. On the point of leaving once more, he overhears Nell addressing the Salvation Army congregation. Moved by her words, he asks for time to reform, and they look forward to a changed existence together.

Salvation Nell by the 22-year-old Sheldon was his first and arguably greatest success, hailed at the time, despite its melodramatic plot, as a play exploring social problems in the manner of Gorky's **Lower Depths*. Interestingly, the Salvation Army becomes an image of living faith in major international plays of the period (e.g. Shaw's **Major Barbara*, Kaiser's **From Morning to Midnight*, Brecht's **St Joan of the Stockyards*).

Same Old Story, The. See FEMALE PARTS.

Samia. See WOMAN FROM SAMOS, THE.

Samian Woman, The. See WOMAN FROM SAMOS, THE.

Samoubiytsa. See SUICIDE, THE.

Sanctuary Lamp, The

A: Tom Murphy **Pf:** 1975, Dublin **Pb:** 1976; rev. 1984 **G:** Drama in 2 acts **S:** A city church, 1970s **C:** 3m, 1f

Harry Stone was the strong man in a circus, where his wife Olga was a contortionist. When she went off with Francisco the juggler, Harry left his wife and beloved daughter and became a homeless tramp. While sheltering in a church he meets Monsignor the priest, who offers him the job of clerk, and Harry happily sets about his duties while conversing with Jesus's presence in the sanctuary lamp. He discovers Maudie, a waif-like teenager running away from her cruel grandparents, who are fostering her because she was abandoned by her parents. The two settle down for the night in the church. While Harry goes to buy fish and chips,

Francisco unexpectedly appears. Francisco drinks altar wine and reveals that he is now without Olga. Maudie tells how her illegitimate baby son died soon after birth. When Harry returns, there is obvious tension between him and the younger Francisco, which erupts into Harry punching him to the ground. Francisco jeers at Harry for being Jewish, although Harry defends religious belief against Francisco's cynical remarks. Francisco reveals that they used to perform in people's living rooms, with Olga doing a striptease and Harry fighting with a dwarf. At their last gig, without Harry, amongst a set of intellectuals, they are thrown out when Olga has sex with one of the guests, and two days later, she takes a fatal overdose. Maudie decides to return to her grandparents, and Harry and Francisco agree to leave together.

The Sanctuary Lamp caused considerable controversy and was denounced by the Catholic clergy for the anticlerical sentiments uttered by Francisco. In fact, it is a deeply moral and curiously life-affirming play, in which Harry's final cliché utterance 'Y'know!' sets a seal of approval on Francisco's belief that Jesus, 'Man, total man', will welcome 'all those rakish, dissolute, fornicating goats' while dismissing the priests 'weaving their theological cobwebs'.

Satire of the Three Estates, A (*Ane Satyre of the Thrie Estaits*)

A: Sir David Lindsay (or Lyndsay) **Pf:** 1540, Linlithgow **Pb:** 1602 **G:** Morality play in 2 parts; verse in Scots dialect **S:** Scotland, 16th c. **C:** 27m, 9f

A learned doctor Diligence delivers a sermon on Christian doctrine. The main character then appears King Humanity (*rex humanitas*), who is at first led astray by Sensuality and the Vices. He even consigns Charity and Verity to the stocks. The Poor Man, emerging from the audience, establishes an alliance with John the Commonweal to demand reform, and Diligence reappears to announce that the King will seek to improve his realm. In the second part the three Estates are summoned: Spirituality (the Church), Temporality (the aristocracy), and Burgesses (merchants). All three are subjected to scathing criticism, which Temporality and Burgesses accept, but which is rejected by Spirituality, who acknowledges no authority but the Pope. John the Commonweal presses his case more strongly, and there are a number of comic scenes illustrating the excesses of the clergy. Temporality and Burgesses agree to join forces to put an end to the Church's misuse of its power and wealth. In an epilogue Folly denounces all men, including the king, declaring them all to be fools.

This is the only surviving play of a Scottish theatrical tradition of mystery and morality plays that was probably as vigorous as that in England. It is a lively and forceful piece, which was premiered before James V of Scotland, who was moved by the performance to exhort the Scots clergy 'to reforme their facions and maners of lyving'. The piece has enjoyed a number of modern revivals, especially in Scotland.

Saturday, Sunday, Monday (*Sabato, domenico e lunedì*)

A: Eduardo de Filippo **Pf:** 1959, Rome **Pb:** 1960 **Tr:** 1974 **G:** Com. in 3 acts; Italian (Neapolitan dialect) prose **S:** Priores' house, Naples, 1950s **C:** 11m, 6f

On a Saturday, Rosa Priore is preparing *ragù* for Sunday lunch with her maid. She is married to Peppino, the owner of a successful men's clothing shop in Naples, and, after 30 years, their marriage is showing the strain. Two of her three children live at home and are also causing her concern: her son Rocco would like to open his own shop, but his father resists this; her daughter Giulianella has the opportunity to work in television, but her boyfriend will not let her. At the major ritual of a Neapolitan Sunday lunch, the family members are joined by the family of the third son, who lives away from home, by Rosa's elderly and eccentric father Antonio, by Peppino's dotty sister Meme and her son, and by various neighbours. Instead of being a jolly communal occasion, it is an opportunity for the hostility that has been smouldering to erupt into fierce rows, especially when Peppino accuses Rosa of having an affair with a neighbour. On the Monday, however, Rosa is able to persuade Peppino that she still loves only him, and other conflicts are resolved – at least, until the following Sunday.

Thanks largely to Franco Zeffirelli's superb production of *Saturday, Sunday, Monday* at the Old Vic in 1973, starring Laurence Olivier and Joan Plowright as the Priores, this became the internationally best-known of De Filippo's colossal output, although he was known and loved in Italy from the 1930s. Himself an actor (from the age of 4), director, and theatre manager, De Filippo creates well-crafted pieces for the theatre, offering rewarding roles to strong actors.

Saved

A: Edward Bond **Pf**: 1965, London **Pb**: 1966 **G**: Drama in 13 scenes **S**: Living room and bedroom in Harry's house, a park, police cell, and café, south London, 1960s **C**: 7m, 3f

Len, a 21-year-old youth, and Pam, a slightly older woman he has just met, make love in the living room of her parents' home. Len moves in with Pam and discovers that her parents Harry and Mary have hardly spoken since their son was killed by a bomb in the park. Pam starts a relationship with Fred, a handsome blond 21-year-old, and has a baby with him, but Len refuses to leave because, unlike Pam, he is devoted to the child. Fred does not come to see Pam, even when she's ill, and takes no interest in the baby. When Pam wheels the baby in a pram through the park, she encounters Fred fishing and leaves the baby for him to look after. The local lads, who have already boasted about acts of violence, start shoving the pram, then punching the baby, and finally stoning it. Pam returns and wheels the pram off, unaware that her baby is dead. Fred is sentenced for manslaughter, and, when he comes out of prison, Pam hopes he will live with her, but is cruelly rejected by him. During a marital row – Harry had seen Len sewing Mary's stockings while she was wearing them – Mary hits Harry over the head with a teapot. When Pam and Len return, Harry threatens Len, and a chair gets smashed. Pam begs Len to leave, but Harry persuades him to stay. In a final silent scene, Len repairs the broken chair.

Unfortunately, the controversy surrounding the baby-stoning scene made *Saved* such a cause célèbre in the battle against British censorship that the merits of Bond's second play were obscured: its disturbing analysis of working-class Britain, no longer materially but culturally and emotionally deprived, and the accuracy of the language, staccato, semi-articulate communication, recorded by a writer who took pride that, unlike most of his contemporaries, he had never been subjected to higher education.

Sawa-shi no futari musume. See TWO DAUGHTERS OF MR SAWA, THE.

Scavengers, The. See CROWS, THE.

School for Honour, The. See MINNA VON BARNHELM.

School for Scandal, The

A: Richard Brinsley Sheridan **Pf**: 1777, London **Pb**: 1780; 'good' text 1799 **G**: Com. in 5 acts; prose **S**: Lady Sneerwell's, Sir Peter Teazle's, Charles Surface's, and Joseph Surface's homes, London, 1770s **C**: 12m, 4f, extras

Although herself the victim of gossip, Lady Sneerwell plots with the hypocritical and sanctimonious Joseph Surface to discredit his extravagant but likeable brother Charles, so that Joseph can marry the rich heiress Maria, who loves Charles. To get closer to Maria, Joseph pays court to the pretty young Lady Teazle, wife to the elderly Sir Peter and Maria's guardian. Lady Teazle visits Joseph in his rooms, and when her husband arrives, she hides behind a screen. She overhears how Sir Peter has arranged to make a generous settlement on her. Charles suddenly arrives, and Sir Peter hides in a closet. The Teazles overhear Charles declaring his love for Maria. Sir Peter is relieved, for he had suspected Charles of wishing to seduce his wife. When Lady Teazle is suddenly discovered, she rejects Joseph's lecherous advances and is eventually reconciled to Sir Peter. Meanwhile Sir Oliver Surface, a rich uncle, has arrived in London from India and tests the worth of his two nephews. Although Charles is selling off the family portraits, he refuses to part with that of his Uncle Oliver. When a deserving old relative seeks money, Charles parts with some of the proceeds from the sale of the pictures, while Joseph blames his miserly uncle for being unable to make a contribution himself. Joseph's duplicity is revealed, and Charles, whose actions have endeared him to his uncle, will marry Maria.

The School for Scandal was first staged in an attempt to save the Drury Lane Theatre, which had declined under Sheridan's first year of management. It proved an instant success, and is now recognized as the best English comedy of the 18th century. On the one hand, it manipulates the characters with great theatrical skill: the scene in which the Teazles are forced to hide works unfailingly in the theatre, as does the scene in which Charles sells off the portraits but doggedly refuses to part with his Uncle Oliver's picture. On the other hand, it offers a bitingly satirical comedy of manners, exposing London society's delight in malicious gossip. Although names like Sneerwell, Snake, and Backbite hardly point to subtle characterization, Sheridan's figures are not mere stereotypes. The conventional relationship of the Teazles, the old husband who has brought a pretty young wife from the country to London, develops in an unexpected way with their joyful reconciliation. Such optimism, coupled with the essentially good and generous nature of Charles, lifts the play above the cynicism of earlier Restoration comedy to provide a truly celebratory experience.

School for Wives, The (*L'École des femmes*)

A: Molière Pf: 1662, Paris Pb: 1663 Tr: 1926 G: Com. in 5 acts; French alexandrines S: A town square, 17th c. C: 6m, 2f

Arnolphe, a middle-aged Parisian gentleman, is so dismayed by the loose living of contemporary women and the way they betray their husbands that he determines to bring up his young ward Agnès in a state of total innocence. He thereby hopes to guarantee for himself a virtuous wife. However, he discovers that Horace, the son of an old friend, has fallen in love with Agnès. Horace tells Arnolphe of his plans to steal Agnès away from her old guardian, not realizing that this is Arnolphe himself. Arnolphe is at first able to thwart Horace's plans, but Agnès shows her resourcefulness by eloping with Horace. Arnolphe's jealous resolution to kill Horace is averted by the arrival of Horace's father, who forces his son to an arranged marriage – to none other than Agnès herself.

This is accounted the first great comedy by Molière. Its subtlety derives from the ambiguous nature of Arnolphe. Like all Molière's comic figures he is obsessed with one idea, in this case the need to keep his future wife in a state of ignorance. On the other hand, Arnolphe's desire for a virtuous wife, contrasted with the decadent behaviour of many contemporary women, is understandable. As a suitor over twice the age of his prospective bride, he appears inevitably comic – an act of supreme self-irony by Molière, who at the age of 40 had just married the 19-year-old Armande Béjart. Moreover, as a jealous lover who can keep his beloved only by virtual enslavement, Arnolphe shows himself to be despicable. Thus, while Arnolphe's cynicism about contemporary society, like that of Alceste in *The *Misanthrope*, may win him some sympathy, the audience nevertheless delights in his failed enterprise. Modern audiences can take particular pleasure in the way that a young woman rises above her cruel treatment to display considerable emotional maturity.

Schweyk in the Second World War (*Schweik im zweiten Weltkrieg*)

A: Bertolt Brecht W: 1941–4 Pf: 1957, Warsaw Pb: 1957 Tr: 1976 G: Com. in 8 scenes, prologue, interludes, and epilogue; German prose and songs S: Prague and the Russian front, 1942–3 C: 12m, 3f

Schweyk is a patriotic Czech who deals in dogs in occupied Prague. He spends much of his time in a bar run by an attractive widow, where, feigning simple-minded obedience to authority, he entertains his patriotic comrades by making fools of the German officers who drop by.

Whatever scrape he gets into, he manages eventually to talk his way out of it, whether it is arrest by the Gestapo, enforced labour with a 'Voluntary' German Labour Service, or detention in a military prison. Despite all his attempts to scheme his way out of it, Schweyk is called up for military service and is sent to fight on the Russian front. Managing to avoid joining his unit, he finds a stray dog near Stalingrad and assures it that 'the war won't last for ever, any more than the peace'. He then encounters Hitler, who is lost in the snow and is looking for the way back to Germany. Schweyk tells him to go to hell, and his fellow patriots sing a rousing song about the Moldau (the River Vltava, on which Prague stands, and which feeds Czech waters into the German Elbe). In interludes, Hitler is reassured by his cronies that he is loved by the Little Man.

In 1928 Brecht collaborated with others in adapting Jaroslav Hašek's novel *The Good Soldier Schweik* (1920–3) for Piscator's production. Here he updates to the Second World War the adventures of the cunning little Czech, a role originally intended for Peter Lorre.

Screens, The (*Les Paravents*)

A: Jean Genet Pf: 1961, Berlin; 1966, Paris Pb: 1961; rev. 1976 Tr: 1963 G: Drama in 17 scenes; French prose S: Algeria, 1954–61 C: 76m, 21f, extras

Saïd is an Arab so poor that he can afford only Leila, a wife so ugly that her face has to be covered by a hood. He visits the whorehouse, while she expresses her longings to a pair of trousers. To escape the drudgery of working for his colonial boss and the mockery of his fellow workers over his ugly wife, Saïd plans to go to mainland France. He steals money and is arrested. Appearing before an eccentric Cadi, Saïd fails to persuade the judge that he should be imprisoned. Leila too is caught stealing from other houses. Saïd's fellow workers complain to their bosses about him, but the colonialists regard all Arabs as untrustworthy. Arab rebels set fire to a colonialist's orange grove. A coarse Lieutenant in the Foreign Legion prepares to suppress the revolt, and a Dutch colonialist plants man traps round his property. An Arab woman is shot by the Dutchman's son, and, from the dead, she curses the colonialists. Saïd's mother, helping a legionnaire with his water-bottle, strangles him. Under the eyes of the dead, the Lieutenant is killed. Saïd is shot for betraying Arab soldiers, and Leila dies of hunger and cold. Saïd is not admitted to the ranks of the dead, but lives on 'in a song'.

A cast list of some 100 characters and a playing time of several hours makes *The Screens* a notable contribution to modern theatre. Its staging, using masks and movable screens, some of them painted by actors on stage, creates an innovative style of presentation. Its grotesque depiction of both French colonial oppression and Arab resistance delayed its performance in France and caused violent audience reaction thereafter.

Sea, The

A: Edward Bond Pf: 1973, London Pb: 1973 G: Com. in 8 scenes S: Beach, draper's shop, Mrs Rafi's house, and a cliff-top, east coast of England, 1907 C: 7m, 7f, extras

On a wild stormy night, Willy Carson swims ashore after a shipwreck, desperate because his friend Colin has drowned after their boat overturned. The local draper Hatch refuses to help Willy, convinced that he is an alien who has murdered Colin and is now preparing to take over the town. The next day Willy seeks the help of Evens, an eccentric old seaman, to discover where Colin's body will be washed up. Hatch warns them both that he is on to them. While Rose mourns the loss of her fiancé Colin, Mrs Rafi and local ladies comically rehearse a play about Orpheus and Eurydice. Hatch and his coastguard cronies meet to prepare for the threat from 'space travellers', and Mrs Rafi refuses to deal with Hatch, since he denied help to a drowning man. When she will not pay for cloth she had ordered, Hatch starts slashing it in a frenzy then cuts Mrs Rafi with his shears. Willy and Rose discover Colin's body on the beach. Hatch, imagining it to be Willy, stabs the corpse with his knife. Colin's cliff-top funeral becomes a farce thanks to Mrs Rafi's eccentric behaviour, fainting gentlewomen, and the arrival of the raving Hatch, who is overpowered when he sees Willy still alive. Willy and Rose agree to go away together.

Within a decade, Bond had proved the wide range of his playwriting: from the naturalistic violence of *Saved, to Brechtian parable play in *Narrow Road to the Deep North, to a rewrite of Shakespeare in *Lear, and now The Sea, the closest he came to writing a comedy of manners (Mrs Rafi is like an East Anglian Lady Bracknell). Hatch is paranoid, because 'People are cruel and boring and obsessed'. It is up to the young Willy to go out and free people from their terror.

Seagull, The (*Chayka*)

A: Anton Chekhov **Pf:** 1896, St Petersburg **Pb:** 1896 **Tr:** 1912 **G:** Drama in 4 acts, Russian prose **S:** Sorin's estate in rural Russia, late 19th c. **C:** 7m, 7f

Konstantin (Kostya) Treplev and his mother, the famous actress Irina Arkadina, are staying on his uncle Sorin's estate. She is having an affair with Boris Trigorin, a celebrated novelist. Treplev decides to stage one of his Symbolist plays with Nina Zaryechnaya, the neighbour's daughter whom he loves, in the central role. Just as he feared, his mother has no understanding for 'new forms', and in a temper he ends the performance. The next day Treplev tries to impress Nina by presenting her with a seagull he has shot. Trigorin comes and flirts with the starstruck Nina, saying he will write a story about a young girl who is arbitrarily destroyed like the seagull. Treplev is so desperate that he tries to shoot himself but only wounds himself in the head. Arkadina and Trigorin are leaving, so Trigorin, with whom Nina is now in love, arranges to meet her in Moscow. Two years later Arkadina returns to nurse her sick brother. Treplev has had some success with his writing but despairs over his lack of purpose. Nina appears suddenly. She was made pregnant by Trigorin, her child died, and she was rejected by both Trigorin and her father. Distractedly calling herself 'the seagull', she claims to have found some contentment as a jobbing actress. Despite Treplev's protestations of love, she leaves, and Treplev destroys his manuscripts and shoots himself.

The premiere of *The Seagull* was a failure, but it enjoyed a great success at the new Moscow Art Theatre (MAT) two years later, establishing the significance of both Chekhov and Stanislavsky, who played Trigorin. This understated drama stretching over two years, which Chekhov called a 'comedy' because it gently ridiculed the empty lives of his characters, needed the depth of characterization and truthful behaviour that only the MAT actors were capable of producing. *The Seagull* has attracted many playwrights to adapt it, including McGrath (1961), Jellicoe (1964), Van Itallie (1973), French (1977), Murrell (1980), Kilroy (1981), Frayn (1986), and Stoppard (1997).

Season at Sarsaparilla, The

A: Patrick White **Pf:** 1962, Adelaide **Pb:** 1965 **G:** Drama in 2 acts **S:** Kitchens and yards of 3 middle-class families, suburbs of Sydney, 1960s **C:** 9m, 5f, 2 children (f)

Three families are beginning their day in Sarsaparilla: business executive Clive Pogson and his fastidious wife Girlie, with their daughter Judy, a keen violinist, and their second precocious daughter Pippy; Harry Knott, trading in men's wear, and his pregnant wife Mavis, with her brother Roy, a teacher with pretensions to becoming a writer; and the Boyles, which the others look down on, because Nola is jolly and blowsy, and her husband Ernie is a sanitary man. Judy and Roy, who are close, suffer from the philistinism of their families. Housework is carried out, and the day passes. Visitors call by after work: Ron, who also fancies Judy; Julia, a beautiful model, with her 'sugar-daddy' Erbage; and Masson, an old mate of Ernie's, who stays the night and seduces Nola, watched by Pippy. Ernie, deducing what has happened, punches Masson, and Masson leaves. Mavis goes into labour, and the ambulance comes for her. Judy declares her love for Roy, but when he responds coolly, she goes off happily with Ron. Erbage tells Roy that Julia has deliberately killed herself in a car crash, and begs him not to expose their relationship. Nola and Ernie are reconciled, and the Knotts have a baby boy. Roy decides to leave but knows that he will come back.

With echoes of Rice's **Street Scene*, this play offers an affectionate but unsentimental view of Australian suburban life. Much of the action is purely naturalistic, but this is expanded with almost ritual enactments of daily routines and lyrical commentary, especially by the would-be writer Roy. In the background, there are dogs in heat, and the suburbanites of Sarsaparilla, in their unending cycle of birth and death, of passion and remorse, can be seen to have their own 'season'.

Second Life of Tatenberg Camp, The (*La Deuxième Existence du camp de Tatenberg*)

A: Armand Gatti **Pf**: 1962, Lyons **Pb**: 1962 **Tr**: 2000 **G**: Pol. drama in 2 acts; French prose **S**: Fairground at Grein, Prater in Vienna, 1960s, Tatenberg Camp, 1950s **C**: 6m, 2f, 3 puppets (m), extras

Scenes alternate between a fairground, in which Hildegard Frölick (29) presents puppets which summon memories of the past, and flashbacks to the concentration camp of Tatenberg, where some former inmates still live: Abel Antokokoletz (60), Cracovian Jew, probably a collaborator, now employed by Frau Frölick; Ilya Moïssevitch (45), Baltic Jew; Gregori Kravchenko (30), a Ukrainian boxer; and Manuel Rodriguez (52), a Spanish Republican. We also encounter Solange Valette (39), French mother of deported twin sons that disappeared, and Guinguin Valette (15), her crippled son working Frau Frölick's musical robot. Appearing as puppets are Frau Frölick's corporal husband, a Captain, and a private in the German army, all three shot as deserters in Russia. Images of Tatenberg Camp are recreated: the dummy station; the gas chambers; the ways in which prisoners exploited each other. Ordinary Germans suffer too: Frau Frölick cannot understand war: 'The voice of the wind is blowing too far above them.' Mme Valette seeks her missing sons, is led on by false information, and settles to live at Tatenberg with Rodriguez. When Guinguin goes missing, she commits suicide, 'the first to die in the imaginary life of the camp'. Moïssevitch avenges the death of the Jews by shooting the German soldier-puppets, Antokokoletz, Rodriguez, and Guinguin. He plans to create a wonderful circus with Frau Frölick, but the ghosts of the past carry him away beyond her reach.

Declaring that 'It is not easy to survive on a scale as vast as yours', Gatti, himself deported to a labour camp at the age of 17, recognized that naturalism could never encompass the enormity of the Holocaust. In a series of fantastical stage images, 'a carnival of compassion', he explores the memories of survivors, both of the fictional Tatenberg Camp (based on Mauthausen) and of a war widow. The effect is that of Brecht on lysergic acid.

Second Mrs Tanqueray, The

A: Arthur Wing Pinero **Pf**: 1893, London **Pb**: 1895 **G**: Drama in 4 acts **S**: Tanqueray's rooms in London and his house in Surrey, 1890s **C**: 7m, 4f

To his friends' surprise, Aubrey Tanqueray, a respectable widower of 42, is to marry Paula, a 27-year-old woman with a 'past'. She hands him a sealed letter describing her past adventures, but he burns it, wishing to start afresh with her. Aubrey's daughter Ellean, abandoning her plan to become a nun, comes to live with them. Some months later, it is clear that the marriage is not going well. The Tanquerays are cut by society, and Ellean is standoffish. Aubrey agrees that a neighbour should take Ellean with her on a trip to Paris, and later admits to Paula that this was a way of removing his daughter from her bad influence. Ellean returns from Paris, aglow because she has fallen in love with a young officer Captain Hugh Ardale. To Paula's horror she recognizes in him a former lover, and begs him to leave. Hugh returns to Paris, while Paula confesses the truth to Aubrey. When Ellean learns why she can no longer marry Hugh, she denounces Paula. The miserable Paula offers to give Aubrey his freedom, goes to her room, and commits suicide.

This is perhaps the most thought-provoking of Pinero's many plays and created a considerable stir when it was first performed (indeed many leading actresses refused to play the 'scandalous' role of Paula, until the then-unknown Mrs Patrick Campbell took the part). Pinero challenges the severity of Victorian morality, especially in his denunciation of the sexual freedom enjoyed by men while women had to suffer the consequences. But the play also debates the relationship of past and present in a way that does not depend on the mores of the time.

Sei personaggi in cerca d'autore. See SIX CHARACTERS IN SEARCH OF AN AUTHOR.

Self-Made Gentleman, The. See WOULD-BE GENTLEMAN, THE.

Septem contra Thebas. See SEVEN AGAINST THEBES.

Séquestrés d'Altona, Les. See CONDEMNED OF ALTONA, THE.

Serious Money

A: Caryl Churchill **Pf:** 1987, London **Pb:** 1987 **G:** Satire in 2 acts; free verse, mostly rhymed, and some prose **S:** London, 1692; London and New York, 1980s **C:** 17m, 7f, extras

After a scene of stock dealing from Thomas Shadwell's 1692 comedy *The Volunteers, or The Stockjobbers*, 1980s' stockbrokers trade and meet later in a champagne bar: Scilla Todd, her brother Jake, and the yobbish Grimes. It is a world where at least two dozen brokers earn over £1 million a year, people retire, rich, in their thirties, and banks make more money from share-dealing than from traditional banking. Jake commits suicide, apparently because of an impending government investigation, but Scilla fears he may have been murdered to shut him up. In flashback, one of Jake's contacts Billy Corman, ruthless corporate raider, plans a hostile takeover of a firm called Albion. Jake recommends to Marylou Baines in New York that she should buy Albion shares. Jacinta Condor from Peru, despairing of the hopeless economic situation of Latin America, invests in Corman's takeover but betrays him by reselling her stake. An African conman persuades Corman to part with £2 million. The Conservative government puts pressure on Corman to abandon his deal, so as to avoid scandal. When they are re-elected, he gets a peerage. Perhaps the government ordered the killing of Jake, perhaps he committed suicide after all. Scilla gives up her search for his murderer and becomes Marylou's assistant. 'Five more glorious years' of Conservative government will make sure that the City remains 'pissed and promiscuous, the money's ridiculous'.

Churchill's scathing onslaught on post-Thatcher Britain and the 'get-rich quick' dealers who flourished in the 1980s and 1990s was surprisingly popular both in Britain and the USA with audiences drawn from the moneyed classes that the play was attacking. Churchill points out that capitalist greed is nothing new: 'We're only doing just the same | All you bastards always done.... Just as clever, just as vile.'

Serjeant Musgrave's Dance

A: John Arden **Pf:** 1959, London **Pb:** 1960 **G:** Pol. drama in 3 acts **S:** Northern English mining town, 1879 **C:** 13m, 2f

Serjeant Musgrave arrives with three soldiers, Sparky, Attercliffe, and Hurst, in a northern mining town, apparently recruiting for the army. The town is in unrest, with striking miners rebelling against the forces of law and order: the Parson, the Constable, and the Mayor, who is also the mineowner. The miners are concerned that the soldiers have come to break the strike, while the Establishment figures welcome the recruiters, hoping that they will 'get rid o' the troublemakers'. The soldiers lodge at an inn, and Sparky reveals that they have taken part in an atrocity in the colonies. The recruiting meeting will be an opportunity for them to tell the English citizens what is being done in their name. In the night, Sparky is killed in a brawl over Annie, a local girl who offers warmth and compassion to the soldiers. At the 'recruiting' meeting, Musgrave dances and chants as the skeleton of a youth formerly from the town is hauled aloft. Manning a Gatling gun, Musgrave then threatens to kill 25 of the townspeople as a reprisal for the atrocity. The dragoons arrive and restore order violently, killing Hurst, and everyone joins in a celebratory dance. At the end, only Musgrave and Attercliffe remain in prison awaiting execution.

Now regarded as one of the finest plays of British post-war theatre, *Serjeant Musgrave's Dance* was initially unsuccessful. Influenced by Brecht and by medieval and Elizabethan theatre, Arden, 'pleading for the revival of Poetic Drama', dispensed with individual psychology in favour of a historical setting, colourful action, and songs, and created an artificial dialogue characterized by short sentences, archaic-sounding constructions, and potent monosyllables. The effect is that of a dramatized ballad, reinforced by the use of repetition, pseudo-biblical images, dialect turns of phrase, and primary colours (one reason Arden gave for setting the play in the 19th century was to be able to introduce redcoats). The play advocates the 'very hard doctrine' of 'complete pacifism': based on an actual atrocity by British soldiers while Arden was on National Service in Cyprus, Musgrave sets out to right a wrong. However, he is a dangerous idealist, whose 'logic' that five times as many English civilians must be killed to avenge the atrocity, is patently misguided. As Attercliffe says, 'You can't cure the pox by further whoring.' The only mild hope is that the seed they have planted might 'start an orchard'.

Sermon on the Mount, The See FEAR AND MISERY OF THE THIRD REICH.

Servant of Two Masters, The (*Il servitore di due padroni*)

A: Carlo Goldoni **Pf:** *c.*1746, Estate dell'Anno, Italy **Pb:** 1753 **Tr:** 1928 **G:** Com. in 3 acts; Italian prose **S:** Venice, 18th c. **C:** 10m, 3f, extras

Pantalone, a Venetian merchant, intended to marry his daughter Clarice to a suitor from Turin Federigo Rasponi. When word comes that he has been killed in a duel, Clarice is free to marry her beloved Silvio. However, Federigo (actually his sister Beatrice in disguise) arrives to claim his bride. In fact, Beatrice has come to Venice in search of her lover Florindo. Beatrice's resourceful and cheeky servant Truffoldino also gets Florindo to employ him, and for the rest of the action tries to keep Beatrice and Florindo apart, so that they will not discover that he is servant of two masters. When the truth is revealed, Florindo and Beatrice are so happy that Truffoldino is forgiven. Silvio is free to marry Clarice, and Truffaldino will wed Clarice's maid Smeraldina.

As Goldoni gradually introduced reforms to the Italian theatre, he drew on but moved beyond the improvised scenarios of the *commedia dell'arte*. Here stock *commedia* characters appear (Pantalone as Clarice's and Dottore as Silvio's father), and the part of Truffaldino was played by Giovanni Antonio Sacchi, famed for his role as Arlecchino. Indeed, much of the text, which underwent several revisions, was due to the comic improvisations of Sacchi. The result is a delightful comedy, which exploits much of the fun of traditional *commedia,* but in which the characterization of the independently minded Beatrice and the ingenuity of her servant lend an unprecedented depth to the action.

Seven Against Thebes (*Hepta epi Thēbas; Septem contra Thebas*)

A: Aeschylus **Pf:** 467 BC, Athens **Tr:** 1777 **G:** Greek trag. in verse **S:** Thebes, in mythical times **C:** 3m, 2f, extras, chorus (f)

The sons of Oedipus, in dispute over their inheritance, are at war. Eteocles is preparing to defend Thebes against attack by his brother Polyneices with his six supporters and their armies. Each of the seven invading heroes is allocated a gate of Thebes to attack, and Eteocles, admonishing the terrified chorus of women not to panic but to pray for victory, names a Theban warrior to defend each of the gates. He himself takes on the task of defending the gate to be attacked by his brother. Despite the pleas of the chorus not to go, Eteocles leaves. The chorus sing of the continuing curse of Laius and Oedipus, which can now lead only to fratricide. News comes that the invaders have been repelled, that Thebes is safe, but that Eteocles and Polyneices have killed each other.

Amidst the general lamentation of the women, a herald appears to announce that only Eteocles is to be accorded an honourable burial. Antigone, the sister of the two dead brothers, declares that she will oppose this decree and is followed offstage by one half of the chorus.

Seven Against Thebes is the second oldest surviving Greek tragedy and shares the static quality of the earlier piece, *The *Persians*. The action depends on anticipation and narration, with the major event of the battle being experienced only through the messenger's report. Indeed, the main dramatic development, the decision that Polyneices' body should remain unburied and Antigone's declaration of opposition to this (to be explored in Sophocles' **Antigone*), may have been a later addition by actors to Aeschylus' text. In rejecting the pleas of the women not to engage in combat with his own brother, Eteocles does the very thing that will fulfil the curse of the house of Laius, which had destroyed his father Oedipus and will eventually claim the life of Antigone. Here for the first time the paradox underlying most Greek tragedy is shown: the hero wilfully chooses what is laid down for him and so becomes deserving of his fate.

Shadow and Substance

A: Paul Vincent Carroll **Pf**: 1937, Dublin **Pb**: 1937 **G**: Drama in 4 acts **S**: Parochial house, Ardmahone, County Louth, 1930s **C**: 6m, 4f

The Very Reverend Thomas Canon Skerritt, an intellectual priest of Irish-Spanish ancestry, lives unhappily amongst the small-minded populace of a town in the south of Ireland. His one consolation is his 20-year-old housekeeper Brigid, who has visions of her namesake St Brigid, and aspires to become a nun. The Canon's 'dumpling' niece Thomasina seeks his help in becoming a teacher, and the next day a spinster makes the same request on behalf of her brainless nephew Francis O'Connor. Two curates, whom Skerritt earlier humiliated, head a delegation wishing to take action against an anonymous book criticizing the Irish Catholic Church's domination of education, but Skerritt, having some sympathy with its views, prevents them. When Skerritt discovers that the book has been written by Dermot O'Flingsley, the local teacher, he confronts him, has a row, removes him from his post, gives his job to the 'spineless imbecile' nephew, and arranges for Thomasina to marry Francis. A mob arrives, intent on attacking O'Flingsley for his anticlerical book. Attempting to protect him, Brigid is struck down by a stone and dies. Skerritt, prepared now to believe in her visions, tries to befriend O'Flingsley, but the latter leaves to 'work this out' on his own.

The Catholic-driven Censorship of Publications Act of 1929 had lead to a dearth of good contemporary plays about Ireland. Carroll, by using considerable wit, and by exploring the complexities of faith and clerical practice rather than attacking them, managed to get past the censor and win over audiences at home and abroad. The hilariously drawn local characters and the Canon's sardonic comments help to lighten the polemic against the Church's domination of education, which caused Carroll himself to leave his native Dundalk to teach in Glasgow.

Shadowdance. See OLD LADY SAYS 'NO!', THE.

Shadow of a Gunman, The

AT: *On the Run* **A**: Sean O'Casey **Pf**: 1923, Dublin **Pb**: 1925 **G**: Trag. in 2 acts **S**: A tenement house in Dublin, 1920 **C**: 8m, 3f

In a Dublin tenement house during the war between the English authorities and the Irish Republican Army, Donal Davoren, a would-be poet, shares a room with Seumas Shields, an indolent pedlar. Maguire, a fellow pedlar, calls to leave a bag in their room. The landlord, having heard a rumour that Davoren is an IRA gunman on the run, gives the two young men their notice to quit. Davoren is flattered to think that he is mistaken for a brave fighter, especially when the attractive young Minnie Powell is attracted to his heroism. Other tenement dwellers come to pay court to Davoren, who basks in this glory until he learns that Maguire has been killed in an ambush. That night shots are heard outside, and soon the Black and Tans (English auxiliaries) surround the house. The terrified

Seumas and Davoren discover that Maguire's bag contains explosives. Minnie bravely takes it up to her room. She is arrested and gets shot when the Black and Tan lorry is ambushed. Seumas reassures himself that he was not to blame, and Davoren assumes the mantle of the suffering poet.

This was the first play by O'Casey, at the age of 43, to meet with success, and, together with his other Dublin plays, made him the darling of the Abbey Theatre. Its blending of comedy and terror and its brilliant depiction of contemporary Dublin at once elevated him to being one of Ireland's major playwrights. His satirical but understanding depiction of the sentimentality, self-dramatization, and fake heroism of the Irish provides urban echoes of *The *Playboy of the Western World* and would remain a recurrent element in his work.

Shadow of the Glen, The

AT: *In the Shadow of the Glen* A: J. M. Synge Pf: 1903, Dublin Pb: 1904 G: Com. in 1 act S: Isolated cottage in Wicklow, Ireland, 1900s C: 3m, 1f

Nora Burke is preparing the wake for her recently departed cantankerous elderly husband, when a tramp comes to her door and is invited in. Hearing that a young farmer she knows is on the road below, Nora goes out to meet him. Suddenly the 'dead' husband Dan rises up and, concealing a stick in his bed, urges the tramp to pretend he is asleep. Nora returns with the farmer Michael Dara, and the tramp pretends to sleep. Nora and Michael plan their wedding once Dan is buried and she has inherited his money. Dan leaps up, and Michael tries to escape. Dan orders Nora out of his house, and the tramp promises her a life of freedom on the roads. Dan forgives Michael and they settle down for a drink together.

This, the first of Synge's plays, contains most of the elements of his later work: the simple story in a rural setting taken from a known folk story; the lyrical peasant speech, consisting of a delightful combination of English vocabulary with Irish sentence structures; and a thoroughly unsentimental view of Irish peasants, devious and shallow, but big-hearted.

Shakuntala (*Abhijñānaśakuntala*)

AT: *Sakuntalā; The Lost/ Recovered/ Fatal Ring* A: Kālidāsa W: ? 5th c. AD Tr: 1761 G: Drama in 7 acts and a prologue; Sanskrit verse and prose S: A hermitage in the Himalayas, King Dushyanta's palace in Hastinapura, and a sacred grove, in the mythical past C: 16m, 14f, extras

After a formal prologue, with introduction and song, the action starts. While hunting a gazelle, King Dushyanta enters a hermitage in the mountains, where he encounters Shakuntala and falls in love at once. She too falls in love with the stranger, at first unaware that he is the King. They are betrothed, but Dushyanta must return to the city. Because her love has caused her to neglect her religious duties, Shakuntala is cursed by an angry sage. At first she is condemned to be forgotten by her husband; then the punishment is relaxed to allow Dushyanta to be reminded of her by the ring that he gave her. When she hears nothing from him, Shakuntala, who has by now discovered that she is pregnant, sets off for the city. There Dushyanta refuses to recognize her, since she has lost the ring while bathing. A priest at court cares for her until she has given birth to her child, and she is given sanctuary in a sacred grove. Meanwhile a fisherman arrives at court with a ring that he has found in the belly of a fish. Seeing his ring again, Dushyanta remembers his bride and recalls with horror his rejection of her. He is then summoned by the god Indra to fight against demons. After successfully winning the battle, he finds himself in a sacred grove, where he is reconciled with Shakuntala and encounters his son. The reunited family returns joyfully to Dushyanta's palace.

Shakuntala, based on a story from the Mahabharata, represents the high point of ancient Indian drama. The themes of purity of love and patient acceptance of the will of the gods are characteristic of the genre. It is significant that Dushyanta should be plagued by guilt when he sees the ring, even though he could not have acted otherwise. In this respect the play, despite its comic conclusion, has elements of tragedy, familiar from the guilt felt by Oedipus, even though he too acted in ignorance.

Shaughraun, The

A: Dion Boucicault Pf: 1874, New York Pb: *c*.1883 G: Melodrama in 3 acts S: Various homesteads, coastal locations, Ballragget House, and the barracks, west of Ireland, mid-19th c. C: 12m, 6f, extras

Robert Ffolliott, sentenced to be deported to Australia for Fenian activities, returns secretly to the rural community of Suil-a-Beg, where live his fiancée Arte O'Neal and his sister Claire. The two young women are tyrannized by Kinchela, the unscrupulous trustee of their family estate. Their only support comes from Father Dolan and, unexpectedly, from an honourable English officer Captain Molineux, who has taken a shine to Claire. Robert's escape has been assisted by the cunning and resourceful Conn the Shaughraun (storyteller and fiddler), but Robert is soon arrested at Father Dolan's house by Molineux. Kinchela, who hopes to have Arte for himself, sees a way of disposing of Robert. He encourages him to escape, but will post a guard to make sure that he is shot dead. Once again with Conn's help, Robert escapes unhurt from prison. Two shots are required to signal that a ship lying offshore should come to pick up Robert. Conn, by pretending to be Robert, gets fired at and falls. Robert swims out towards the rescuing ship, summoned by the shots. All ends happily: Robert learns that all Fenian prisoners have been pardoned, Conn, after enjoying his own wake, reveals himself very much alive, Kinchela gets his comeuppance, and the two young couples look forward to married bliss.

This is the best crafted of Boucicault's many melodramas, and as in *The *Colleen Bawn*, offers an idealized view of Irish rural life, establishing a pattern to be followed by a number of Irish playwrights. Apart from the evil Kinchela and some turncoats, everyone is honest and noble. Even the English officer, though the butt of gentle satire, shows himself to be honourable. *The Shaughraun*, with which Boucicault toured in the role of Conn, was a huge success in both Europe and America and has been successfully revived since.

Sheep Well, The. See FUENTE OVEJUNA.

She Stoops to Conquer

AT: *The Mistakes of a Night* A: Oliver Goldsmith Pf: 1773, London Pb: 1773 G: Com. in 5 acts; prose S: An old-fashioned house in the country and a nearby inn C: 7m, 4f, extras

Old Mr Hardcastle, a country gentleman, has two children, Kate from his first marriage and a stepson Tony Lumpkin, the boorish son of his second wife, the domineering Mrs Hardcastle. Hardcastle has arranged for his daughter to marry Young Marlow, while Mrs Hardcastle wants Tony to marry Constance, Kate's cousin, so as to keep Constance's jewels in the family. Constance, however, loves Hastings, the best friend of Marlow. Constance tells Kate that Marlow is very modest with women of quality, but that he has 'a very different character among creatures of another stamp'. At a local inn Marlow and Hastings are tricked by Tony into believing that the Hardcastle residence is also an inn but that the 'landlord' has pretensions beyond his station. Arriving at Hardcastle's home, Marlow and Hastings treat the astonished Hardcastle with curt behaviour. Constance encounters Hastings and agrees with him to leave Marlow believing in his mistake, for otherwise his embarrassment would force him to leave at once. When Marlow meets Kate for the first time, he is so shy that he cannot even look at her. Hardcastle and daughter therefore have very different opinions of her intended husband. Kate, learning who Marlow is, now, dressed simply, flirts with the suddenly emboldened Marlow, who takes her for a servant. When Marlow's servants get drunk on the 'landlord's' wine, Hardcastle has had enough and orders Marlow and Hastings to leave. Having learnt of Constance's plan to elope with Hastings, Mrs Hardcastle orders Tony to prepare a carriage to convey her and Constance to an aunt. Tony drives his mother round in circles, finally depositing her in a horse-pond. Marlow's father has arrived, and the mistake is explained. Enlightened by Kate's explanation, Hardcastle gives his blessing to her marriage to Marlow, and the now chastened Mrs Hardcastle agrees to let Constance marry Hastings.

This play is one of very few that Goldsmith wrote. It is one of the best comedies in English and helped to rescue comedy from the sentimentality into which it was sinking, thus making possible the masterpieces of Sheridan. What was refreshing about *She Stoops to Conquer* and why it is still popular on the stage, is the naturalness of the characters. The basic 'mistake' of the plot may seem far-fetched (although Goldsmith claimed it was based on a true incident), and the neo-classical concern with unity of time packs a lot of incident into one night, but Goldsmith's characters can be performed and identified with ease of familiarity in any age.

Shirley Valentine

A: Willy Russell **Pf:** 1986, Liverpool **Pb:** 1988
G: Monodrama in 2 acts **S:** Kitchen of Shirley's house, Liverpool, and Greek seaside village, 1980s **C:** 1f

Shirley Bradshaw, née Valentine, is a lonely 42-year-old housewife, whose son and daughter have left home, and who lives in a loveless marriage with her husband Joe. While she prepares an evening meal of egg and chips (although Joe is expecting mince), she converses with the wall of her kitchen. Her best friend Jane, a feminist divorcee, has bought her a ticket to join her for two weeks' holiday in Greece, but she knows that Joe will not allow her to go. Three weeks later, Shirley is about to leave for Greece. She has resolved to go without telling him, after Joe threw the egg and chips all over her. Five weeks later, in Greece, Shirley now chats with a rock. Jane had already met a man on the plane, and Shirley has to suffer the ordeal of being alone with unbearable English tourists in her hotel. Escaping from her fellow countrymen, she meets a local taverna owner, Costas, and they become lovers. At the airport, she wonders why 'there is all this unused life?', and suddenly decides she is never going home. She returns to Costas, who is embarrassed to be caught seducing another tourist. But Shirley merely asks to work in his taverna, where she cooks egg and chips for nervous tourists. Joe is coming out to fetch her, but she knows he will no longer recognize her, because she is 'Shirley Valentine again'.

As in **Educating Rita*, Russell is aware of the missed potential in most people's lives, and shows one woman who is prepared to 'find some life'. Made into a popular film in 1989, it is an impossibly optimistic piece (how will Shirley survive in the winter?), but Shirley's Liverpudlian wit and common sense deflect such concerns.

Shoemaker's Holiday, The (*The Shomakers Holiday or The Gentle Craft*)

A: Thomas Dekker **Pf:** 1600, London **Pb:** 1600
G: Com. in 5 acts; prose and blank verse
S: London, indeterminate (late medieval?) period **C:** 17m, 4f, extras

Lacy is in love with Rose, the daughter of the Lord Mayor of London. Lacy's uncle the Earl of Lincoln is opposed to his marrying a commoner and arranges for Lacy to be sent to the wars in France. Lacy, however, soon returns, disguised as a practitioner of the 'gentle craft', i.e. as a shoemaker, in order to continue wooing Rose, who is meanwhile being pursued by a gentleman Hammon. Simon Eyre, a 'mad shoemaker', becomes Lord Mayor by devious means and marries Lacy to Rose, while another shoemaker Ralph, returning from the wars, discovers Hammon now trying to abduct his wife. Hammon is forced to yield his prize, and the King arrives to pardon Lacy and give his blessing to Lacy's marriage to Rose.

The Shoemaker's Holiday suffers from a rambling structure and implausible incidents (it is not clear, for example, why the King should be so ready to pardon Lacy's desertion in France). However, the play is full of lively characters and vibrant language, and it works well in production, as was shown in the Mercury Theatre production by Orson Welles in the late 1930s and at the National Theatre in 1981. The play is significant in that it shows the growing power of the merchant class, who are willing to challenge the nobility and gain royal approval in so doing. There may be an inconsistency between Eyre's insistence on honest labour and his own means of achieving power, but this is easily overlooked in the boisterous fun of the action.

Shopping and Fucking

A: Mark Ravenhill **Pf**: 1996, London **Pb**: 1996 **G**: Drama in 14 scenes **S**: A flat, interview room, bedsit, pub, hospital, and department store, London, 1990s **C**: 4m, 1f

Robbie and Lulu are lovers of Mark, who leaves to seek treatment for his drug addiction. Lulu, an actress, is interviewed by the sinister Brian for a television job in advertising, and is given Ecstasy tablets to sell. Mark reappears, but is reluctant to commit to Robbie again. Mark, in search of impersonal sex, pays to lick 14-year-old Gary's anus, but is alarmed that he is bleeding. Robbie goes to sell his Ecstasy tablets but gets so high himself that he gives them away and then gets beaten up. Gary reveals to Mark that he was abused by his stepfather and invites Mark to stay. Brian gives Robbie and Lulu one week to find £3,000 for the missing Ecstasy tablets. They begin to offer phone sex to get the money. Mark introduces Gary to Robbie, who is violently jealous. Gary is willing to pay Robbie for finding the kind of powerful father figure that Gary is looking for. Robbie plays the role of dominant master, has sex with him, but draws the line at penetrating him with a knife, which Gary begs for: 'I thought you were for real. Pretending, isn't it. Just a story.' Robbie and Lulu give Brian his money. Insisting that 'money is civilization', Brian hands the money back. Robbie and Lulu share their food with Mark in a final scene of togetherness.

In the desolate world portrayed by 'Inyerface' theatre of the 1990s, Ravenhill's play at least allows words like 'love' to continue to possess some residual meaning. The main hope of redemption in an empty universe is to establish connections by making stories: 'Big stories' about God or socialism 'all died, or the world . . . forgot them, so now we're all making up our own stories', 'stories so that we can get by'.

Shopping for an Umbrella (*Suehirogari*)

A: Priest Genne-Hōin ? **Pf**: early 17th c., Japan **G**: *Kyōgen* play in Japanese prose **S**: The Master's home and a street in Kyoto, medieval period **C**: 3m, musicians

The servant Tarōkaja is sent by his master to Kyoto, the ancient capital of Japan, to buy some fans for a New Year's party. Unfortunately, Tarōkaja is unfamiliar with the special name for these fans, *suehirogari*, and arrives in the city, uncertain what it is that he is meant to buy. Taking advantage of his ignorance, a clever market-trader sells him an old umbrella, assuring Tarōkaja that it is a *suehirogari* and instructing him how to reply to his master if the latter questions him. Returning home, Tarōkaja finds his master furious at his mistake and is unimpressed with the carefully rehearsed answers that Tarōkaja has learned. Tarōkaja is thrown out of the house, but he begins to sing and dance with such gusto that his master relents and joins in the fun.

Deriving from a popular oral tradition, *kyōgen* plays portrayed brief, farcical incidents, with witty dialogue, stock characters, and slapstick. They correspond in many respects to the European *commedia dell'arte*, although *kyōgen* lasted for much longer. Only after many years of being performed were the first *kyōgen* plays published (an anthology of 203 plays appeared in 1638), and this one is a fairly typical example of the genre. Tarōkaja is a stock servant figure (with similarities to the *commedia* Arlecchino), who traditionally wore a medieval costume of a kimono with broad checks, baggy trousers, and yellow socks. The *kyōgen* plays were conventionally performed in a programme with the much more elevated Nō drama, rather as the ancient Greeks combined tragedy with satyr plays.

Silent Woman, The. See EPICENE.

Silver Spoon, The

A: Joseph Stevens Jones **Pf**: 1852, Boston **Pb**: *c.*1852 **G**: Com. in 4 acts **S**: The Austin residence, Boston, 1850s **C**: 5m, 2f, extras

Jefferson S. Batkins, a simple and honest countryman from Cranberry Center, has come to Boston to take up his post in the General Assembly of Massachusetts, to represent the interests of his farming community and oppose the big city cliques, which he refers to as 'klinks'. He stays with Ezra Austin, nephew to Hannah Partridge, whom Batkins had wooed unsuccessfully some years previously. Another visitor is the young Glandon King, who has returned from Europe for the reading of his father's will and falls in love with Austin's daughter Sarah. The will leaves only a silver spoon to Glandon, since he has already been given everything he ever wanted in life, and bequeaths the rest of King's fortune to founding a college. A disreputable lawyer Simon Feedle tries to break the will and at the same time claim that his law clerk Tom Pinfeather is legitimate heir to the money. Feedle's plan is exposed, and a later will is discovered, which stipulates that, if Glandon makes no effort to break the first will, he may inherit everything. Glandon can now marry Sarah, and Hannah at last agrees to wed Batkins.

It was not so much the conventional plot about an inheritance that is at first denied then granted, that made this the most popular of 19th-century Boston comedies. Rather, it was the figure of Batkins, who in the best American tradition, may be naive and poorly educated (his attempts at rehearsing a speech for the assembly are a source of much humour), but is honest and plain-speaking. As in Paulding's *The *Lion of the West*, a sophisticated urban audience delighted in these token figures of rural American rectitude.

Silver Tassie, The

A: Sean O'Casey **Pf**: 1929, London **Pb**: 1928 **G**: Tragicom. in 4 acts; prose and some verse **S**: Heegan's home, hospital, and a football club, Ireland, and a war zone, France, First World War **C**: 20m, 5f

As an Irish contingent are about to depart for war in France, Mrs Heegan waits anxiously for her son Harry. His father Sylvester's chat with a friend Simon is interrupted by the pious admonitions of Susie Monican, frustrated over her unrequited love for Harry. Harry loves the vivacious Jessie Taite, who is one of those who now enter celebrating Harry's prowess on the Gaelic football field. He drinks from the silver cup (the 'tassie'), and with his mates, the cheeky Barney Bagnal and the aggressive Teddy Foran, head off for their ship. Amidst the ruins of a French monastery a group of dispirited soldiers chant about the horrors of war, while Barney stands tied to a gun-wheel, and casualties are carried past. They are ordered to the guns. Some time later Sylvester, Simon, Harry, now crippled in a wheelchair, and Teddy, now blinded, are all patients in an Irish hospital where Susie is a nurse. Susie flirts with a surgeon, and Jessie shows interest in Barney, who has been awarded the VC for saving Harry's life. Several weeks later everyone is at a dance given by Harry's old football club. Barney and Jessie are watched by the embittered Harry, as they dance and have fun. Harry insists on drinking from the silver tassie, gets into a fight with Barney, and smashes the cup. Teddy, understanding his misery, wheels him home.

The Silver Tassie is one of the greatest anti-war plays ever written, and Yeats's misjudgement in rejecting it for the Abbey and O'Casey's consequent self-imposed exile in England are now legendary. It is a difficult play, combining Expressionist elements with naturalism and comedy (Sylvester and Simon answering a telephone creates a classic comic scene). The key is to recognize that, understandably, O'Casey could not describe the horrors of war realistically and had to adopt a more poetic style. This lyrical Expressionism is not confined to Act 2, as commonly asserted; it permeates the other acts whenever the War impinges on the comfortable lives of distant civilians.

simple soldat, Un. See PRIVATE SOLDIER.

Sisters-in-Law, The (*Les Belles-Sœurs*)

AT: *The Guid Sisters* A: Michel Tremblay **Pf**: 1968, Montreal **Pb**: 1968 **Tr**: 1974 **G**: Com. in 2 acts; Canadian French prose **S**: Kitchen in a working-class area of Montreal, 1965 **C**: 15f

Germaine Lauzon has won a million free gift stamps in a competition and can now realize her dream of entirely refurnishing her home. However, there are three large crates of stamps and a crate of booklets, and it will be an immense task to stick them all in. So she holds a party, at which all her female guests (sisters-in-law and neighbours) can help with this Herculean labour. During the gathering, the lives of the different women are revealed, their unhappiness, their aspirations, and their fear of stepping beyond the narrow limits of their existence. There is the snob, the young innocent, the do-gooder, etc. Finally, as tensions mount, the helping women begin stealing Germaine's precious stamps. Fights break out, stamps fly in every direction, women rush from the room clutching their horde of stamps. Germaine collapses in despair, but, as she hears 'O Canada' being sung offstage, she gets up and stands to attention, as more stamps drift down from above.

Turning his back on the predominantly realistic mode of Canadian theatre, Tremblay, influenced by the absurdist theatre of Metropolitan France, wrote this delightfully satirical analysis of French Canadian society, its pretensions and its timidity. While poking gentle fun at the carefully delineated 15 women, Tremblay offers an affectionate portrayal of their lives. By writing his play in *joual* (French Canadian dialect), Tremblay helped to make it a legitimate literary tool.

Six Characters in Search of an Author (*Sei personaggi in cerca d'autore*)

A: Luigi Pirandello **Pf:** 1921, Rome **Pb:** 1921; rev. 1925 **Tr:** 1922 **G:** Drama without acts (but 2 'interruptions'); Italian prose **S:** Stage of an Italian repertory company, 1920s **C:** 10m, 7f, 2 children (1m, 1f), extras

An irascible Producer and his company of actors gradually assemble on stage to begin rehearsing Pirandello's *Rules of the Game*, which the actors find ridiculous. Suddenly from the auditorium appear six 'Characters' (Father, Mother, Stepdaughter, Son, Boy, and Little Girl). Their author created them but failed to put them in a work of art; so they are now searching for an author to complete the process. The initially sceptical actors gradually become intrigued by their story: the Father tells how he married the Mother, with whom he had a Son. Sensing his wife's unhappiness, he sent his Son to be brought up in the country and made her go and live with his secretary, with whom she had three further children, the Stepdaughter, the Boy, and the Girl. When the family moved away, the Father lost contact with his wife and stepchildren. Returning after the secretary's death, the Mother worked as a seamstress for Madame Pace, who also kept a brothel. To everyone's horror, a new client received by the Stepdaughter is recognized as the Father. The Father takes the family back into his home, creating tensions, especially with his now adult Son. The Producer is sufficiently intrigued to invite the Characters into his office to plan the play. Returning, he sets the scene for the focal confrontation at Madame Pace's, while Father and Stepdaughter complain about inaccuracies. Madame Pace arrives mysteriously, conjured by the scene, but, being real, speaks inaudibly. Father and Stepdaughter act out the scene, which is then reproduced by the actors, with critical comments from the Characters, who complain that the actors are not real enough. After another break, the Father insists that the Characters are more real than the performers, because the former enjoy an 'immutable reality'. They now perform a scene in a garden with a fountain. Protesting that the actors are unable to capture the essence of the Characters' truth, the Son describes the final tragedy: unsupervised by the Mother, who is focused on the Son, the Little Girl drowns in the fountain, and her brother shoots himself. The actors discover that he is dead, but no one can distinguish any more between pretence and reality. The Producer cancels the rehearsal, the actors leave, but the theatre is still haunted by the Characters.

The best known of Pirandello's plays, it still stands, despite its occasional wordiness, as one of drama's most original and profound meditations on the nature of the theatrical process. In fact, the Characters have already found the author that created them; what they now require is realization through performance. The irony is that, especially at the mercy of superficial actors (the contemporary equivalent would be the television studio of a soap opera), such a 'realization' is unattainable.

Six Degrees of Separation

A: John Guare Pf: 1990, New York Pb: 1990 G: Drama in 1 act S: East Side, New York, *c*.1990 C: 14m, 4f

John Flanders ('Flan') Kittredge (44), an attractive New York art dealer, and his wife Louisa ('Ouisa'), about to go to dinner with a South African friend, are surprised by the arrival of Paul, a young black, who has just been mugged in Central Park. Paul claims to be a fellow student of their children at Harvard and to be the son of Sidney Poitier. The Kittredges awake to find that Paul has brought a hustler into their apartment; they are disgusted, and throw Paul and the hustler out. They meet friends who have had exactly the same experience. All efforts to contact Sidney Poitier fail, and, since nothing was stolen, the police are not interested. A Dr Fine has also been taken in by the charming Paul, and the Kittredges discover that Poitier never had a son. Tess, the Kittredge's daughter, establishes that a homosexual high-school classmate had an affair with Paul and told him details of the families. Paul, a poor black hustler, resolved to infiltrate the best homes in New York. Ouisa reflects that there are at most only six degrees of separation between us and everybody else on this planet. Paul cons a young couple from Utah and sleeps with the man, who commits suicide. Now in serious trouble, Paul phones Ouisa and begs her to treat him as her son. Ouisa tells him to give himself up, and promises to help him. Before they can get to him, the police arrest him, and, since Ouisa does not know his real identity, the authorities are unable to trace him. But Flan is convinced he will find them again.

John Guare, writer of a number of award-winning dramas, to some extent reprising the theme of Shaw's **Pygmalion*, in this his most popular play offers an amusing, fluid, and perceptive analysis of the cultured rich of New York, the emptiness of their lives and their guilt, and reminds us that there are hardly any degrees of separation between them and the poorest people on the planet.

Sizwe Bansi Is Dead

AT: *Sizwe Banzi Is Dead* A: Athol Fugard, with John Kani and Winston Ntshona Pf: 1972, Cape Town Pb: 1974 G: Drama in 1 act S: Photographic studio and other locations, Port Elizabeth, *c*.1970 C: 3m

Styles, having grown weary of working on the assembly line at the Ford factory, opens his own photographic studio in a black township. Styles tells the audience how he helps people to live out their dreams and gets them to smile, despite all their hardships. Sizwe Bansi, pretending to be Robert Zwelinzima, comes to him for a photograph to send to his wife, whom he has left behind in the barren Ciskei, while he illegally seeks work in Port Elizabeth. After his arrival, he was discovered and given orders to leave at once. He is helped by Buntu, who allows him to stay with him and takes him out on the town. They discover a corpse, but Buntu will not allow Sizwe to call the police. The dead man's passbook shows him to be Robert Zwelinzima and contains a work-seeker's permit. Buntu has the bright idea of taking his passbook, 'killing off' Sizwe Bansi, and giving him a new identity. Sizwe can then get a job at a local factory. At first reluctant to give up his name, Sizwe agrees to become Robert: 'Shit on names . . . if in exchange you can get a bit of bread.' Sizwe is afraid he may be found out in the end, for, after all, 'Our skin is trouble.'

With humour and lively theatricality Fugard the playwright and actors Kani and Ntshona address the serious problem of the dignity and identity of the blacks under an apartheid regime. Sizwe can maintain hope only by acting inhumanely towards a dead stranger: 'What's happening in this world, good people? Who cares for who in this world?' It is a question that is relevant wherever people are oppressed.

Skin of Our Teeth, The

A: Thornton Wilder Pf: 1942, New Haven, Connecticut Pb: 1942 G: Drama in 3 acts S: The Antrobus home in Excelsior and the waterfront, Atlantic City, New Jersey, indeterminate period C: 23m, 11f, 1 dinosaur, 1 mammoth

George Antrobus, a pillar of the suburban community, has invented the wheel and the alphabet. He lives with his wife, daughter, and son, formerly named Cain (he killed his brother), now called Henry. They also have a maid Sabina, an actress who hates this play she has been cast in and has to be persuaded to carry on playing the role of a servant. The ice age threatens to destroy civilization, which is at first welcomed by Antrobus, but eventually he is persuaded to light a fire to save humanity, piling on to it chairs from the auditorium. Antrobus is elected president of the Order of Mammals, Subdivision Humans, and has to attend a convention in Atlantic City, where Mrs Antrobus reveals that they are celebrating their 600,000th wedding anniversary. Antrobus awards Sabina first prize in a bathing beauty contest and is about to elope with her when the Deluge threatens to engulf them, and everyone climbs aboard the ark. The final act takes place after a great war, in which Henry has become a general on the enemy side. He comes to kill his father, and their confrontation becomes so vehement that it has to be interrupted by Sabina. The actors apologize, and Antrobus seeks the 'most important thing of all. The desire to begin again.' It seems that this will be granted him, but, Sabina tells us, 'The end of the play isn't written yet.'

Admitting a debt to Joyce's *Finnegan's Wake*, this is a sprawling piece of absurdist theatre, defying traditional expectations of coherence and theatrical illusion. As the Second World War raged on, Wilder seems to express the optimistic belief that yet again humanity would survive by 'the skin of our teeth'. Yet, given his depiction of the complacent attitude of suburban America in the face of disaster, this outcome is by no means certain.

Skull in Connemara, A

A: Martin McDonagh **Pf:** 1997, Galway **Pb:** 1997 **G:** Com. in 4 acts **S:** Mick Dowd's cottage and a cemetery, rural Galway, 1990s **C:** 3m,1f

Mick Dowd, a widower in his fifties, is asked by the parish priest to exhume bodies from the cemetery to create more space for fresh burials. Mick is disturbed that he will have to raise the body of his wife Oona, who died seven years previously in a car crash. While Mick digs Oona's grave in the cemetery, assisted by the young and rather simple Mairtin Hanlon, the guard (policeman) Thomas, Mairtin's older brother, hints that Mick's wife might have been killed before Mick drunkenly drove her into a wall. Mick is horrified to discover that Oona's body is no longer in its coffin. Back at Mick's cottage, Mick and Mairtin, now drunk on poteen, smash the skulls and bones with hammers before they get dumped in the lake. Mairtin lets slip that he saw the locket on Oona's neck, something he can only have known if he was involved in stealing her corpse. Mick gets the incapable Mairtin to drive them to the lake and soon returns home drenched in blood. Thomas appears holding Oona's skull, which displays a hammer blow to the head, and insists that Mick write his confession. Mick agrees, but confesses only to the murder of Mairtin. Suddenly Mairtin appears, very much alive, and reveals that Thomas dug up Oona's body and hit her skull with a hammer to 'prove' that she was murdered. Mick burns his confession and swears that he never raised a finger to Oona.

This dark comedy has obvious echoes of Synge, especially of *The *Playboy of the Western World*, with the unexpected return of the 'murdered' man and subsequent reconciliation between 'murderer' and victim. After the hilarity of the comic violence, the final image of Mick kissing Oona's skull is quite moving.

Skylight

A: David Hare **Pf:** 1995, London **Pb:** 1995 **G:** Drama in 2 acts **S:** London flat, 1990s **C:** 2m, 1f

Kyra Hollis, a 30-year-old teacher at a rough school in the East End of London, lives in a shabby flat in north-west London. She has a surprise visit from 18-year-old Edward Sergeant, with whose family until a few years previously Kyra was very close. Edward's mother died of cancer a year ago, and he now seeks Kyra's help to save his father Tom, a 50-year-old successful hotelier and restaurateur, from his misery. Unexpectedly, Tom calls round. He speaks of his wife Alice's illness, how she lay there, looking at birds through the skylight. They recall how Kyra on arriving in London had applied for a job as waitress in one of Tom's restaurants, how Alice had invited her to run the place, how Kyra fell in love with Tom, leading to a six-year affair, which ended when Alice found out. Tom admits that he has not been in touch for three years because he has been plagued by guilt but has missed Kyra terribly. Their confessions lead to a passionate embrace, and Kyra invites Tom to stay the night. Buoyant after their sex, Tom is planning a new future for Kyra and him, intending to take her away from her cold and ugly flat, but Kyra is committed to her work as a teacher and refuses to consider leaving her shabby surroundings. Tom condemns her idealism: 'Loving the people's an easy project for you. Loving a person . . . now that's something different.' Recognizing the gulf between them, they part for ever. The following morning Edward arrives with a luxurious breakfast for Kyra.

In this analytic drama, which devotes much time to revisiting the past, there is almost no external action: everything is focused on the relationship between Tom and Kyra, which reflects the gulf between two elements in post-Thatcher Britain: those who believe they are contributing through 'the creation of wealth' and those who by setting themselves possibly only 'one private target' hope to change the world for the better.

Slattern, The (*La Sagouine*)

A: Antonine Maillet **Pf:** 1971, New Brunswick **Pb:** 1971 **Tr:** 1979 **G:** Monodrama in 16 scenes; Acadian (Canadian French) prose **S:** A room on the east coast of Canada, 1972 **C:** 1f

'The Slattern' is a 72-year-old woman with a mop and a bucket, who reminisces in a long monologue about her life. She describes a life of poverty: how she married an oyster fisherman who scraped a living from the sea. When state benefits dried up, and the seashore could no longer provide enough to eat, the Slattern earned money cleaning houses for those with a little money. And when it became difficult even to earn a few cents from this drudgery, she went on the streets to get enough to feed herself and her children. As a result, she is treated with contempt, elbowed aside at the Christmas festivities, banned by the priest from taking part in a bingo game organized by the Church for the relief of the poor. Despite everything, she is proud to be able to express herself in the vigorous tongue of her ancestors. She does not bemoan her lot, knowing that a poor woman like her can do little to change things. All she hopes for now is a peaceful end to her life.

Maillet has become the spokesperson for Acadia, the east coast area around New Brunswick, whose culture and language developed separately from Quebec. Maillet offers an inspiring vision of life at the bottom, despite the deprivations she has suffered, 'without retouching her wrinkles, her chapped hands, or her language'. As the author Jacques Cellard writes: 'Mother, wife, slave, prostitute; . . . stranger in her own country, proletarian without homeland: the Slattern is all these things. She HAS nothing. She IS.'

Ślub. See WEDDING, THE (Gombrowicz).

Snow in Midsummer. See INJUSTICE TO DOU E.

Sohn, Der. See SON, THE.

Soldatenglück, Das. See MINNA VON BARNHELM.

Soldiers (*Soldaten: Nekrolog auf Genf*)

A: Rolf Hochhuth **Pf:** 1967, Berlin **Pb:** 1967 **Tr:** 1968 **G:** Hist. drama in 3 acts, prologue, and epilogue; German verse and 'rhythmic prose' **S:** Coventry, battleship, London bedroom, garden at Chequers, 1943 and 1964 **C:** 12m

In Coventry cathedral in 1964, a theatre director Dorland, guilty about his abuse of the Geneva Convention by bombing German civilians, rehearses his play about Churchill: On the North Sea in 1943, Churchill and his friend Wladysław Sikorski, head of the Polish government-in-exile, discuss the future of Poland, and Churchill recognizes that Sikorski may damage Britain's relationship with the USSR. In London, he arranges for Sikorski to be killed in a plane crash off Gibraltar. While trying to justify the terror bombing of German cities to the Bishop of Chichester, Churchill is informed of Sikorksi's death. Visibly shaken,

Churchill comforts himself with the thought that 'Soldiers must die, | but by their death – they nourish | the nation that gave them birth.' Back in 1964, the director receives a telegram stating that his play is banned in England.

Subtitled 'An Obituary for Geneva', this play was banned at the National Theatre and, as with *The *Representative*, unleashed a storm of controversy, especially in Britain. Once again, the accompanying historical apparatus is more impressive than Hochhuth's rather wooden characterization and flaccid verse. There is no denying, however, that he possessed an astounding ability to provoke debate.

Soldier's Fortune, The. See MINNA VON BARNHELM.

Soldier's Story, A

A: Charles Fuller Pf: 1981, New York Pb: 1981 G: Drama in 2 acts S: Fort Neal, Louisiana, 1943–4 C: 12m

Sergeant Waters, a 'light brown-skinned man', is shot dead by an unseen man. Five black enlisted men are carefully searched for weapons by their corporal, since their officer Captain Charles Taylor is concerned that they may avenge Waters's death, which the men blame on the Ku Klux Klan. Captain Davenport, exceptional in being a black officer, is charged with investigating the murder. Taylor, a racist, fears that any investigation conducted by a 'Negro' is doomed to failure. Davenport begins to question the men, and episodes with Waters are re-enacted. Waters, from the North, is determined that after the war, he will send his children 'to some big white college', to challenge the white man 'in his arena'. Taylor reveals that two white officers had a fight with Waters on the night he died but other officers, including the Colonel, have provided an alibi for them. Meanwhile, it turns out that the previous year a Southern black, C. J. Memphis, wrongly accused by Waters of killing a man, hit the Sergeant, was placed under arrest, and hanged himself. Davenport discovers that Private Peterson, finding Waters drunk, decided to avenge C. J.'s death and shot him. Taylor grudgingly congratulates Davenport on his detective work, and Davenport assures the white officer that he will get used to 'Negroes being in charge'.

This Pulitzer Prizewinning play works on several levels: it is a good detective story; it describes the frustration of African-American soldiers at initially not being allowed to fight in the Second World War; and it explores tension between whites and blacks and – with great honesty – between blacks from the Northern States and those from the South.

Son, The (*Der Sohn*)

A: Walter Hasenclever Pf: 1916, Prague Pb: 1914 Tr: None known G: Drama in 5 acts; German prose and some verse S: Middle-class home, meeting hall, and hotel room in a German town, early 20th c. C: 8m, 2f

Despite believing in his own genius, the 20-year-old Son has again failed his examinations, and is confined to his room by his tyrannical father. Lyrically yearning for fulfilment away from this arid learning, he contemplates but rejects suicide. Encouraged by his Friend, he woos his young Governess. His Father, unmoved by his Son's filial devotion and furious that he reads literature rather than study for his exams, will arrange for the Son to go into business. The Son is called from despair by his Friend magically appearing and inviting him to escape through the window. At midnight, an assembly of young men gathers to discuss the 'possibility of a new religion'. Backstage, they argue over who is to address the meeting, and the Son steps through the curtain to speak. Baring his chest to reveal the scars from his Father's beatings, the Son calls for a revolt against Fathers and is received with ecstatic jubilation. Exploiting his freedom, the Son meets a prostitute in a hotel room. The Friend, to provoke a final confrontation, tells the Father of his Son's whereabouts and hands the Son a loaded revolver. The Son is arrested by the police, and the Friend, his task complete, commits suicide. In a final meeting with his Father, the Son produces the revolver, and the mere shock kills his Father. The Son and the Governess declare their love and celebrate their newly won freedom.

Although now rarely staged, *The Son* is significant in being the first truly Expressionist play to be performed (a year before Sorge's *The *Beggar*). It replaced psychological interest in character (indicated by their lack of names) with an elemental conflict between the generations: as it transpired, an accurate allegory of the eventual overthrow of the Kaiser to be replaced by a young (nominally) socialist government, without a shot being fired.

soñador para un pueblo, Un. See DREAMER FOR THE PEOPLE, A.

Song of a Goat

A: John Pepper Clark[-Bekederemo] **Pf:** 1961, Ibadan, Nigeria **Pb:** 1961 **G:** Trag. in 4 acts; free verse **S:** Coastal village, Nigeria, indeterminate period **C:** 3m, 2f, 1 child (m), chorus

Zifa, fisherman and part-time ship pilot on one of the Niger estuaries, has conceived one son with his wife Ebiere, but though her womb is still 'open and warm as a room', she has since remained barren. The half-possessed aunt Orukorere, who woefully comments throughout, blames Zifa for coming from another tribe and so bringing a curse on the family. Encouraged by the village Masseur, Ebiere gives herself to Zifa's younger brother Tonye. When Zifa learns of Ebiere's infidelity, he ritually slaughters a goat, which would normally legitimize the adultery. But he forces Tonye to ram the goat's head into an earthenware pot, shattering the vessel – a powerful visual symbol of Tonye assaulting Ebiere's womb. Stricken by guilt, Tonye hangs himself, Zifa walks into the sea to drown, and Ebiere prepares to give birth to her child.

Although the title hints at the origin of the Greek word 'tragedy' (= 'goat-song'), Clark insists that the source of this intense drama is an Ijaw tale. The sequel, *The Masquerade* (1964), is a more gentle play about Ebiere and Tonye's child. The premiere of *Song of a Goat*, directed by Soyinka, caused a considerable stir when a live goat was killed on stage. Essentially, though, the play's poetic diction and elemental conflict might remind Western audiences of Yeats's sparsely written plays.

Souvenirs. See ANATOL.

Spanish Bawd, The. See CELESTINA.

Spanish Tragedy, The

A: Thomas Kyd **Pf:** *c.*1582–92, London **Pb:** *c.* 1592 (1602 with anon. additions) **G:** Trag. in 4 acts; blank verse **S:** The Spanish and Portuguese courts, Renaissance period **C:** 35m, 6f, extras

The Ghost of Andrea, a Spanish nobleman who died fighting against the Portuguese, seeks revenge on Don Balthazar, the Viceroy of Portugal's son. The Spanish are victorious, and Balthazar is captured by Horatio, son of Hieronimo, Marshal of Spain, and by Lorenzo, the King of Spain's nephew. While in captivity, Balthazar falls in love with Bellimperia, Lorenzo's sister, who once loved Andrea but now loves Horatio. Lorenzo is keen to marry his sister to Balthazar, a match that would seal the new peace between Spain and Portugal. On learning that Bellimperia loves Horatio, Lorenzo plots with Balthazar to murder him. Surprising the lovers in an arbour, they hang up Horatio and stab him. Bellimperia's cries summon Hieronimo, and he finds his son hanging dead. He and his wife swear revenge. A letter from Bellimperia reveals the names of the murderers. Lorenzo suspects Balthazar's servant of betraying him, and arranges to have him shot by Pedringano, another servant. Pedringano is hanged for the deed, but a letter from him confirms the guilt of Lorenzo and Balthazar. While Bellimperia continues to resist the advances of Balthazar, the distracted Hieronimo seeks justice from the King, but Lorenzo's intervention causes him to be dismissed as a lunatic. When confronted with his son's killers, Hieronimo pretends to be at peace with them and is upbraided by Bellimperia for his cowardice. Hieronimo however arranges for Balthazar and Bellimperia to perform in a tragedy as part of their wedding celebrations. Hieronimo's grieving wife commits suicide. During the play-within-a-play Hieronimo stabs Lorenzo and Bellimperia stabs Balthazar and then kills herself. Hieronimo now reveals the truth to the King, bites off his tongue so that he cannot reveal more, and finally stabs the King's brother and himself. Andrea is satisfied by this bloodbath and prepares to welcome Bellimperia into the underworld.

One of the best-known and most powerful Elizabethan/Jacobean revenge tragedies based on Seneca, this is the only original play definitely by Kyd's hand, although he may have contributed to other contemporary plays. The play is compelling not only in terms of its tight plotting and violent incident, but also in the exploration of the character of Hieronimo, a much more subtle portrayal than the revenge figures found in Seneca. Hugely popular on the stage of the day, it influenced many later writers. In **Hamlet*, for example, we find again the Ghost demanding revenge, the play-within-the-play, and the disturbed mental condition and initially tentative behaviour of the central character – not to mention the high body-count as the curtain falls (five in *The Spanish Tragedy*, four in *Hamlet*).

Speed the Plough

A: Thomas Morton **Pf:** 1800, London **Pb:** 1800 **G:** Com. in 5 acts; prose **S:** A Gothic castle and its environs, Hampshire, late 18th c. **C:** 11m, 4f, extras

Sir Philip Blandford, a widower, having been abroad for 20 years, returns to his Gothic castle to give his only daughter's hand in marriage to the dashing young Bob, son of Sir Abel Handy, who has himself recently married a snobbish country woman with no breeding.

Unfortunately, Bob is in love with a simple country girl Susan Ashfield. At a ploughing competition, Henry, an orphaned young man of elegant manners, wins first prize and meets Sir Philip's daughter Emma, with whom he dances. They fall in love. However, when she introduces Henry to her father, Sir Philip is distressed. He reveals that he lost all his money to a mysterious Morrington, but that an anonymous donor restored his wealth to him when he married. When Morrington gives a bond to Henry to pay off his foster-father's debt to Sir Philip, Sir Philip feels that Morrington is toying with him. He confesses to Bob Handy that 20 years ago he had discovered his brother making love to his fiancée, and stabbed him, his brother subsequently dying from his wounds. His fiancée gave birth to his brother's child, Henry, and then died. Bob and Susan agree to get married, and Sir Abel's wife turns out to be already married, so he is free of the harridan. Sir Abel accidentally sets fire to the castle, and Henry saves Emma from the flames. Morrington appears, and is revealed as Sir Philip's brother who survived his brother's stabbing. The brothers are reconciled, and Henry will marry Emma.

The contrived plot, noble sentiments, the villainous and mysterious figure of Morrington, and the Gothic setting were to provide ingredients for 19th-century melodrama. Some of the delight of the piece is in peripheral elements, like the disastrous inventions of Sir Abel Handy, or the unseen figure of Mrs Grundy, whose pronouncements on local matters made her name legendary.

Speed-the-Plow

A: David Mamet **Pf:** 1988, New York **Pb:** 1988 **G:** Drama in 3 acts **S:** Gould's office and home, Hollywood, 1980s **C:** 2m, 1f

Bobby Gould, just promoted to Head of Production in a big film studio, learns from his friend and junior Charlie Fox that a top director is so interested in one of their scripts set in a prison that he is offering to 'cross the street' and work for their production company. Excited at the prospect and congratulating each other on their mutual loyalty, the two men set up a meeting with the company chief the following day. Fox bets Gould $500 that he cannot date his temporary secretary Karen that evening. Admitting that he is a 'whore' interested only in the money-making potential of a script, Gould gets Karen to read a book about increasing levels of radiation and arranges for her to call at his home – and so has won the bet. That evening, Karen enthuses about the book. When Gould doubts that he can push a film about 'the End of the World', Karen insists that the book's message about feeling frightened is relevant to everyone. She then surprises Gould by offering herself to him. The next morning, Gould is a changed man, who recognizes that until now his life has been a sham. He infuriates Fox by telling him that he's dropping the prison film and making the radiation film instead. However, when Fox gets Karen to admit that she would not have slept with Gould if he had rejected 'her' film, Gould admits: 'I wanted to do Good . . . But I became foolish.' Gould and Fox leave for the meeting to push the prison film.

The title, an old-fashioned rural wish for prosperity, reflects the cynicism of the film industry, which deals in profits not art. Mamet, well acquainted with his subject, continues American theatre's attack on the movies, which dates back at least as far as **Once in a Lifetime*. The Broadway premiere featured Madonna in the role of Karen.

Sphēkes. See WASPS.

Spitzel, Der. See FEAR AND MISERY OF THE THIRD REICH.

Spokesong

AT: *The Common Wheel* **A:** Stewart Parker **Pf:** 1978, New Haven, Connecticut **Pb:** 1979 **G:** Com. in 2 acts; prose and songs **S:** Bicycle shop, Belfast, 1890–1900s, 1914, 1970s **C:** 4m, 2f

After an introductory song, Frank Stock, whose shop is about to be demolished for a new road, appeals before a public inquiry to have cars replaced by bicycles. Daisy (Margaret Bell), a teacher, brings in an old bike for repair. Back in the 1890s, a clergyman complains to Frank's grandfather Francis Stock about the immorality of the bicycle. Francis falls in love with fellow cyclist Kitty Carberry, a woman with very progressive ideas. Thanks to the new tyres of Ulsterman John Boyd Dunlop, Francis wins a major cycle race. 1970s: Frank's younger brother Julian, a journalist, arrives home from England, surprised about the normality of life in Belfast. 1900s: Francis marries Kitty without her father's blessing. Francis joins the British army to fight in the Great War, and Kitty insists on becoming pregnant before he leaves. 1970s: Julian charms Daisy into coming with him to London. Duncan, Daisy's father, a loyalist racketeer, tries to get Frank to make a donation to his 'loyalist' gunmen after a car bomb goes off opposite Frank's shop. Julian, to whom the shop was willed, sells it to Duncan for a new headquarters. Julian is questioned by the army, who insist he leave Belfast at once. Daisy buys the shop, threatening her father with the police if he objects, and Frank fetches out a tandem for them both.

Bicycles, with a Trick Cyclist featuring prominently, offer a splendidly theatrical element to this amusing piece by Northern Irish writer Stewart Parker. They are also a metaphor for good common sense which the political strife in Belfast singularly fails to display. Clearly, bicycles are a healthier, cheaper, more environmentally friendly alternative to the motor car, but few will actually use them. In the same way, Belfast careers towards its own self-destruction both through demolition for roads and through bombs.

Spöksonaten. See GHOST SONATA, THE.

Spook Sonata, The. See GHOST SONATA, THE.

Spring's Awakening (*Frühlings Erwachen*)

AT: *The Awakening of Spring; Spring Awakening* **A:** Frank Wedekind **Pf:** 1906, Berlin **Pb:** 1891 **Tr:** 1909 **G:** Trag. in 3 acts; German prose **S:** Small German town, 1890s **C:** 30m, 7f, extras

Wendla Bergmann is dismayed at having to wear a long dress now she is 14. She has friends who are also troubled by adolescence: Moritz Stiefel, who is desperate to pass his exams, and Melchior Gabor, whose mother is more liberal than most. Melchior offers to explain 'the facts of life' to Moritz, but the latter insists on studying hard. Melchior and Wendla meet in the woods, and their erotic attraction gets out of hand when she begs him to beat her. For Moritz's benefit, Melchior puts into writing the facts of sex. When Wendla asks her mother to explain where babies come from, the mother evades her questions. Melchior has sex with Wendla in a hay loft. Hänschen Rilow masturbates on the toilet. Moritz fails his examinations and, terrified at his parents' reaction, rejects the advances of the uncomplicated Ilse, a prostitute, and then shoots himself. The teachers meet and, spending more time discussing whether or not to open a window, expel Melchior, because they identify his letter about sex as the cause of Moritz's death. Melchior is sent to a reform school, where the boys entertain themselves by seeing who can ejaculate furthest. When Wendla's mother discovers that the unsuspecting Wendla is pregnant, she calls in an abortionist, who brings about Wendla's death. By contrast, Hänschen and another boy are seen enjoying an idyllic homoerotically charged meeting in the countryside. Melchior, having escaped from the reformatory, goes to the graveyard where Moritz and Wendla are buried. Moritz rises from his grave, his head under his arm, and urges Melchior to join him in death. The Man-in-the-Mask intervenes and persuades Melchior to opt for life.

Although it took 15 years for *Spring's Awakening* to reach the stage, when it was offered, with predictable omissions, in a chamber performance by Max Reinhardt, the play became the most frequently performed German play of the 20th century. Its exploration of nascent sexuality and the hypocrisy of adults for the first time opened up in the theatre the taboo subject of sex (and even today it would still be hard to imagine performing the full text on national television without eliciting a public outcry). Moreover, this was the first play, subtitled 'A Children's Tragedy', where contemporary action is seen from the perspective of children. In terms of theatrical development, almost everything prefigures Expressionism: youth in revolt against their repressive elders; the optimistic conclusion in Melchior's decision to prefer life to suicide; the economy of language; the episodic structure; the grotesque caricatures, especially of the absurdly named teachers; and the symbolic figure of the Man-in-the-Mask (played originally by Wedekind himself). Thus Wedekind provided a link in the chain from Büchner to modernist playwriting.

Spy, The. See FEAR AND MISERY OF THE THIRD REICH.

Stablemaster, The (*Il marescalco*)

AT: *The Captain* A: Pietro Aretino Pf: 1527, Mantua Pb: 1533 Tr: 1978 G: *Commedia erudita* in 5 acts; Italian prose S: A square in Mantua, early 16th c. C: 15m, 5f

The town of Mantua is buzzing with news that the Duke is that very evening making his (unnamed) Stablemaster marry a beautiful young bride. Since it rapidly becomes clear that the Stablemaster's sexual proclivities lie in another direction, he resists the order to marry. The Nurse describes marriage as paradise on earth, and the Pedant warns him that he will be punished by God if he has no offspring. Despite further urgings by various courtiers, the Stablemaster remains adamant in his refusal to marry, supported by Ambrogio, an old man who regards marriage as living hell. Only when the Count threatens him with a dagger, does the Stablemaster yield to the Duke's will. When the ceremony is concluded, the Stablemaster discovers that the Duke has given him a handsome pageboy as a bride. The Stablemaster is delighted, everyone enjoys the joke, and they all go off to celebrate the nuptials.

Aretino, author of one tragedy and five comedies, based this play on an actual incident at the Court of Mantua. It is notable as the first overtly gay drama in European theatre. The plot is very simple, focusing solely on the forthcoming marriage, and characters are fairly stereotypical. The pleasure of the piece lies mainly in the passages of monologue and dialogue, which, in the words of the Italian Scholar Richard Andrews, are 'moralistic, satirical, sarcastic, celebratory, or just verbally fanciful'.

Stallerhof

AT: *Farmyard* A: Franz Xaver Kroetz Pf: 1972, Hamburg Pb: 1971 Tr: 1976 G: Drama in 3 acts; German prose S: Farm and fairground, Bavaria, *c.*1970 C: 2m, 2f

Beppi is the mentally retarded teenage daughter of farmer Staller and his wife. She is seen first haltingly reading a postcard from her aunt. Her mother hits her when she gets a word wrong, and when Beppi triumphantly finishes her reading, is ordered to dry the dishes. There is little warmth in the family, and the only friendship Beppi finds is with the hired farm-hand Sepp, a man in his fifties. While Beppi milks a cow and he shovels manure, he tells her a romantic story about a white Captain who 'rescues' an Indian maiden. He takes Beppi to a fair. When she soils her knickers after a ride on the ghost train, he cleans her up and uses the opportunity to have sex with her. When Beppi becomes pregnant and admits who the father is, her father shoots Sepp's dog and sends Sepp away. The parents decide that Beppi must have an abortion. The mother makes preparations and gets Beppi to strip naked. At the last moment, however, the mother relents, the only time she shows compassion towards her daughter. The play ends with Beppi in labour, crying out for her mother and father.

Kroetz wrote a number of ultra-realistic and desolate plays, of which *Stallerhof* is the best known. His first play *Work at Home* (1971), depicting an attempted abortion with a knitting needle, provoked riots in Munich. His recurrent theme is the inability of the working classes, whether urban or rural, to articulate, and this is portrayed in their use of cliché and in long passages of silence.

starkare, Den. See STRONGER, THE.

Statements after an Arrest under the Immorality Act

A: Athol Fugard Pf: 1974, London Pb: 1974
G: Drama in 1 act; prose and free verse
S: Library and other locations, South African town, 1966 C: 2m, 1f

'A Coloured Man' (Errol Philander), a married school principal from the local black township, is lying naked on the floor of the library with 'a White Woman' (Frieda Joubert), a librarian six years older than him. Their love is threatened not only by the fear of being discovered breaking the law forbidding sex between blacks and whites but also by the tensions between them, owing to the suffering of the black citizens especially during a period of drought. A white neighbour reports her suspicions to the authorities, and two police arrive with torches and a camera with flashbulbs. Panicked by being discovered, the Woman gabbles an incoherent explanation, while the Man desperately pretends that he has come with a formal request for water for his family. Lit only by the torches, the Woman describes how they became lovers. Finally, the Man describes in verse how his arrest has dispossessed him of everything: 'there is only the emptiness left'.

Starting from the unadorned simplicity of two naked bodies lying on a blanket, this piece passes through the torchlit nightmare of the police raid to the poetic insights of the ending. As in C. P. Taylor's **Good*, this play demonstrates too how one of the most disturbing features of an oppressive regime is the breakdown in trust between those who are closest.

States of Shock

A: Sam Shepard Pf: 1991, New York Pb: 1992, prose and songs G: Drama in 1 act
S: Restaurant in indeterminate location, early 1990s C: 3m, 2f

A White Man and White Woman, dressed all in white, wait motionless in a restaurant for clam chowder. The Colonel pushing Stubbs in a wheelchair sits at another table and orders coffee and dessert. The Colonel is taking Stubbs out on the anniversary of the death of his son in battle, when Stubbs was wounded and rendered impotent by artillery fire. The Colonel tries to find out exactly how his son died, but Stubbs is evasive (later revealing that the son tried to desert and was accidentally killed by friendly fire). The Colonel toasts 'the enemy', for 'without the enemy we're nothing'. At two points the restaurant becomes a battle scene; the manager dies and the cook is wounded, although the waitress Glory Bee had hoped that they 'were invulnerable to attack'. The White Man refuses his clam chowder, so Glory Bee tips it in his lap. As he cleans himself up, he masturbates to a climax. The Colonel, showing Glory Bee how to carry drinks, breaks into a dance with her, and then plans to run away with her to Mexico. Stubbs staggers to his feet, and ends up embracing Glory Bee, finding himself no longer impotent. Suddenly Stubbs remembers: it was the Colonel who wounded him and killed his own son. Donning a gas mask, Stubbs is just about to decapitate the Colonel with his sword, when he freezes, and the others break into song.

Subtitled 'a vaudeville nightmare', Shepard's angry absurdist piece, reminiscent of early Albee, was written in response to the 1991 'Desert Storm' repulsion of Iraq from Kuwait. However, its analysis of the 'American nightmare' ('This country wasn't founded on spineless, spur-of-the-moment whimsy. The effects are international! UNIVERSAL!') is even more relevant to the 'war against terrorism' and the invasion of Iraq a decade later. John Malkovich played the Colonel at the premiere.

Statue at the Banquet, The. See DON JUAN.

Statue at the Feast, The. See DON JUAN.

Stellvertreter, Der. See REPRESENTATIVE, THE.

Sticks and Stones. See DONNELLYS, THE.

Stone Guest, The. See DON JUAN.

Storm, The. See THUNDERSTORM, THE.

Strange Interlude

A: Eugene O'Neill Pf: 1928, New York Pb: 1928 G: Drama in 9 acts S: New England and New York, *c.*1919–*c.*1943 C: 5m, 3f

Nina Leeds is resentful of her father's scruples that prevented her sleeping with her dashing fiancé Gordon Shaw, who was killed in action in the Great War. Defiantly, she becomes a nurse and has sex with scores of crippled soldiers. Returning home after her father's death, she is wooed by three men: Charles Marsden, a father figure, Dr Edward (Ned) Darrell, a coolly objective scientist, and the ineffectual Sam Evans. Marsden and Darrell both agree that, to save her from further promiscuity, Nina should marry Evans. When Evans's mother warns Nina of insanity in the family, Nina has an abortion and secretly becomes pregnant by Darrell. When she and Darrell find themselves in love, he escapes to Europe, and Evans, proud about 'his' son, grows rich and successful. When Darrell returns to her, she refuses to disillusion Evans and rejoices in the love of her four 'men', her husband, her lover, her substitute father, and her son. On his eleventh birthday, her son Gordon senses that Darrell is a rival to his 'father' Evans, and angrily smashes Darrell's present. Ten years later, Gordon is engaged and wins a rowing race. In the excitement, Evans has a fatal stroke. Gordon and Darrell argue, but Nina keeps his paternity a secret. As Gordon flies off with his fiancée, Nina agrees to end the 'strange interlude' of life married to the faithful old Marsden.

One of the most ambitious of O'Neill's plays, *Strange Interlude* plays for nine hours. Alongside conventional dialogue, it is filled with interior monologues, unheard by the other characters. O'Neill again rehearses his major preoccupation: the search for meaning, which is no longer satisfied by restrictive and conventional religion nor by the cold rationality of science. The answer lies somewhere in the vitality and power of Nina, who stands as a less destructive incarnation of Wedekind's Lulu.

Streetcar Named Desire, A

A: Tennessee Williams Pf: 1947, New York Pb: 1947 G: Drama in 11 scenes S: Kowalskis' apartment and street outside, New Orleans, mid-20th c. C: 6m, 6f

Blanche Dubois, an English teacher, comes to stay with her sister Stella and her husband Stanley Kowalski, of Polish descent, who live in a poor neighbourhood of New Orleans full of the sounds of jazz. To reach the area, Blanche has taken a 'streetcar named Desire'. Fussing about her looks, she tells Stella that she left schoolteaching because of a nervous breakdown. Stanley is very brusque with Blanche, especially when he learns that her family has lost their southern estate through mismanagement. At a poker game that evening, Blanche is attracted to Harold Mitchell ('Mitch') and flirts with him. They start dancing to the radio. Furious at having his poker game interrupted, Stanley flings the radio out of the window and hits Stella when she intervenes. Although Blanche tries to hurry her away, Stanley bellows for her to come back and carries her into their apartment. The next day Blanche is horrified that her sister is happy to stay with the brutal 'sub-human' Stanley.

Watched by Blanche, Stella passionately embraces Stanley. Blanche tells Mitch of her earlier marriage: she found her husband with another man, and shortly afterwards, at a dance, he ran out and shot himself. As music is heard in the background, Mitch proposes to her. Some months later, Stanley has told Mitch what he has learned about Blanche: that this preening, 'virginal lady' is in fact a promiscuous nymphomaniac who lost her teaching post for seducing a pupil. Mitch stays away from her birthday party. As a birthday present, Stanley gives Blanche a bus ticket back to her home town. Stella goes into labour and is taken to hospital. Mitch drunkenly confronts Blanche, and she admits her promiscuous past. Mitch tries to have sex with her, but when she begs him to marry her, he rejects her cruelly. Stanley returns from the hospital and takes Blanche savagely. Some weeks later Stella has arranged for Blanche to be committed; it was either that or believing that Stanley really had raped her. Blanche appears, asking whether her rich admirer has phoned her. As the doctor leads her away, Blanche simpers: 'I have always depended on the kindness of strangers.' Stanley 'voluptuously, soothingly' comforts the sobbing Stella.

A Streetcar Named Desire is, with the possible exception of **Death of a Salesman*, the best-known American play, performed the world over and made into a seminal film, in which Marlon Brando reprised the stage role of Stanley, his last live performance. Apart from the unrestrained way in which sexual passion is depicted, the figure of Blanche Dubois, famously played by Jessica Tandy in the States and by Vivien Leigh in Britain and on film, is utterly compelling: prudish yet licentious, yearning to give love yet obsessed with herself, a virgin with the appetite of a tigress (an embodiment of Williams's own problematic homosexual longings).

Street Scene

AT: *Landscape with Figures* **A:** Elmer Rice **Pf:** 1929, New York **Pb:** 1929 **G:** Drama in 3 acts **S:** The street outside a New York apartment block, 1920s **C:** 28m, 17f, extras

In a rundown area of New York, tenement dwellers come down on to the street to escape the stifling June heat. They are from many different nationalities and with different religious and political affiliations. The main gossip is about Frank and Anna Maurrant, an Irish couple with a young son and a 20-year-old daughter Rose. Mrs Maurrant is having an affair with a married milk-company collector Steve Sankey, and the neighbours fear the consequences if the violent Maurrant finds out. Rose Maurrant is brought home by her office manager Harry Easter, who offers to buy her an apartment away from all this sordidness. But Rose loves her young Jewish neighbour Sam, a law student. The next day Maurrant returns unexpectedly to find his wife with Sankey. He shoots them both and escapes. Sankey dies, and Mrs Maurrant is taken off dying on a stretcher. Maurrant is later arrested and bids Rose a tearful farewell. Rose again refuses Easter's offer to become his mistress, and also declines an offer of marriage from Sam, who is prepared to give up law school. Depending only on herself, she will go and live with her brother in the suburbs.

The importance of *Street Scene*, which won the Pulitzer Prize, does not lie with the rather melodramatic plot but with the detailed cross-section of New York urban life with its parade of colourful characters, a kind of American **Lower Depths*. The major difference is that, while Gorky's characters are crushed by their environment, Rose's optimism suggests that there may be a way out. Kurt Weill wrote an operatic version in 1947, with lyrics by Langston Hughes.

Stretch of the Imagination, A

A: Jack Hibberd **Pf:** 1972, Melbourne **Pb:** 1973 **G:** Monodrama in 1 act **S:** Monk O'Neill's hut and surroundings, Australian outback, 1960s **C:** 1m

Monk O'Neill has rejected society, or been rejected by it, and now lives in complete isolation on One Tree Hill. We follow him through the course of one day (perhaps his last?). He gets up, urinates, carries out his daily chores, eats, and talks non-stop about his life, past and present. He reminisces about climbing Mount Kosciusko with his mate Les Darcy, about visiting Paris, about a love affair that went wrong because of his own macho thoughtlessness, about a snap frost that destroyed his vegetables. A particular source of guilt is that he cut down the tree on One Tree Hill, and he is now attempting to atone by collecting his urine to feed nutrients into the soil. He is aware that he will not be able to continue much longer like this, now that his legs and bladder are failing. Overcoming the terror of his impending demise, he settles down to sleep for the night.

Australian drama tends to deal with the urban environment in which most Australians live, clinging to the coast of their vast continent. Hibberd's play about an eccentric individual living miles from any human society has proved one of the most popular of his plays and has been performed internationally. The authentic setting and language may be a naturalistic portrayal of a not wholly likeable character, but it goes beyond mere naturalism to explore man in relation to his environment and, curiously for a monodrama, in relation to other people.

Strife

A: John Galsworthy **Pf**: 1909, London **Pb**: 1910 **G**: Drama in 3 acts **S**: The Manager's and the Roberts's home in a Welsh village, 1900s **C**: 22m, 7f, 1 boy, extras

At the Trenartha Tin Plate Works a bitter industrial dispute has lasted five months. The founder of the company, the staunch conservative John Anthony, refuses to accede to the demands of the workforce, despite the cessation of output and the resultant decline in share value and despite the human suffering the strike is causing, especially to the families of the workers. Equally uncompromising is the strike leader David Roberts, who even opposes his own union by holding out for the workers' demands. The firm's directors come from London in an attempt reach a settlement, but neither Anthony nor Roberts will give way. When Roberts's wife dies of cold and starvation as a result of the strike, the men turn to Harness, the union negotiator, to effect a compromise deal with the management. One of their conditions is that Anthony must resign. The play ends with the two bitter opponents, Anthony and Roberts, now both broken by events, coming together in mutual recognition.

Although *Strife* is the first significant English play to dramatize an industrial dispute, its treatment of workers' revolt contrasts interestingly with that portrayed in Gerhart Hauptmann's *The * Weavers* a decade and a half previously. Whereas *The Weavers* treats the workers as a collective protagonist, here the focus is very much on the two main individuals, and the resolution of the action lies in their final meeting rather than the victory of moderation in the settlement of the strike.

Stripwell

A: Howard Barker **Pf**: 1975, London **Pb**: 1977 **G**: Pol. com. in 2 acts **S**: Stripwell's home, various locations in London and the Home Counties, and the jungle, 1970s **C**: 5m, 3f

When Graham Stripwell, a judge, sentences Cargill to prison, Cargill swears that he will one day murder Stripwell. Stripwell lives with his wife Dodie and his cantankerous father-in-law Jarrow Houghton, a former Labour politician. He also has a relationship with a young go-go dancer Babs. His son Tim is intending to smuggle drugs into the country hidden inside elephants. When Tim meets Babs, she switches her affections to Tim and refuses to leave with Stripwell as planned. Stripwell informs the police about Tim's drug smuggling. Dodie walks out on him in disgust. Finally, Cargill reappears and shoots Stripwell.

Stripwell is quite different from most of Barker's plays, especially his more recent postmodernist excursions into ambiguity. Barker said that it was 'planned coldly to be a commercially successful play', and he now refuses to list it under his published work. It is an accessible, witty piece, made more enjoyable at its Royal Court premiere by the playing of Michael Hordern in the title role. In appropriating the genre of West End comedy, Barker set out to explore 'the ambiguous state of power, its mediation, the complicity of victims' and so challenged Establishment figures from a Socialist viewpoint. As his wife says, Stripwell is 'The sort of person who ends up running concentration camps'. More integrity is in fact shown by Cargill, the violent criminal. Barker employs a variety of styles: verbal wit, grotesque humour, psychological realism (as in Stripwell's confession of his affair to his wife), direct address to the audience, abrupt theatrical changes (e.g. from courtroom to a dance bar), and shock (e.g. the final murder).

Strolling Gentlemen, The. See WILD OATS.

Strongbox, The (*La Cassaria*)

AT: *The Chest; The Coffer* **A**: Ludovico Ariosto **Pf**: 1508, Ferrara (prose); 1531 (verse) **Pb**: 1509 (prose); 1546 (verse) **Tr**: 1975 **G**: *Commedia erudita* in 5 acts; Italian prose, later verse **S**: A square in the city of Metellino (Mitylene), Lesbos, *c.*2nd c. BC **C**: 14m, 2f

Two young men Erofilo and Caridoro are in love with Eulalia and Corisca, who are virgin slaves of the pimp Lucrano. Erofilo's father Crisobolo has been given a chest of rich cloth for safekeeping, but has left on a journey. Erofilo plots with his servant Volpino that an accomplice, disguised as a merchant, will take the chest to Lucrano to buy the freedom of Eulalia. Erofilo will then report the chest missing, accusing Lucrano of having stolen it. Since Caridoro's father is Captain of Justice, Lucrano will then curry favour with Caridoro by giving him Corisca. Things go wrong when five other servants kidnap Eulalia to save her from the 'merchant', and Crisobolo unexpectedly returns home. Discovering the chest missing, Crisobolo raids Lucrano's home to retrieve it. Soon learning the truth, however, Crisobolo orders Volpino to be punished. Another servant comes to the rescue by convincing Lucrano that he must flee the city and by persuading Crisobolo to pay for his flight. Finally, Erofilo is forgiven, Volpino is freed, and the four young lovers join in celebration.

Best known for his epic poetry, Ariosto wrote five plays, *The Strongbox* being the first. Although it reveals strong elements of Plautus (e.g. *The *Rope*) and Terence (e.g. *The *Girl from Andros*) in its plotting, and is notionally set in the ancient world, Ariosto was the first major European playwright to write in the vernacular instead of Latin. Indeed, much of the perceptive characterization and comic fun derives more from Boccaccio's *Decameron* than from Roman models and reflects the people and interests of his own age. This helped to set the style for the successful and influential 'erudite comedy' of Renaissance Italy.

Stronger, The (*Den starkare*)

A: August Strindberg **Pf**: 1889, Copenhagen **Pb**: 1890 **Tr**: 1912 **G**: Drama in 1 act; Swedish prose **S**: Café, Sweden, 1880s **C**: 3f

Madame X, a married actress, enters a café with Christmas shopping and sees an old acquaintance Amelia (Mademoiselle Y), an unmarried actress. She pities Mlle Y for sitting alone on Christmas Eve and repeats that she should not have broken off her engagement. Mme X shows off the presents she has bought for her children and the slippers that she has embroidered for her husband. When she assures Mlle Y that she did not cause her to be sacked from the theatre, Mlle Y remains silent. Mme X invites her for dinner, but still Amelia says nothing. Gradually, it occurs to Mme X that Amelia has had an affair with her husband, which is why she broke off her engagement and will not come to dinner. She believes that all her husband's likes and dislikes have been determined by Mlle Y: she is like a snake or a stork ready to pounce on her victims. However, Mme X feels triumphant: she is going home to her husband and children.

This tightly wrought psychological mini-drama is based primarily on an affair Strindberg had with an actress in 1882, for which his wife Siri von Essen forgave him. Strindberg allows Mme X to reveal her own insecurities and unhappiness without her antagonist uttering a single word. Although Strindberg seemed to view the wife as 'the stronger', there is some doubt: is it the voluble woman claiming to have a happy marriage, or is it the silent woman who taught Mme X's husband how to love?

Struggle of the Dogs and the Black *(Combat de nègre et de chiens)*

AT: *Come Dog, Come Night; Black Battles with Dogs* **A**: Bernard-Marie Koltès **Pf**: 1982, New York; 1984, Paris **Pb**: 1980 **Tr**: 1989 **G**: Drama in 20 scenes; French prose **S**: Construction site, West African country, *c.*1980 **C**: 3m, 1f

Horn, 60-year-old foreman of a soon-to-be abandoned project to build a large bridge, has just brought out Leona (Leonie), a former chambermaid, from Paris to be with him in Africa. Because he was spat at, Cal, an engineer in his thirties, shot a black worker and dumped his body in a sewer. Alboury, from the neighbouring village, comes in search of his brother's body, which Horn promises to release the following day. When Horn learns of Cal's crime, Horn tries to talk Alboury out of demanding his brother's body, offering bribes and appealing to his better sense. To the background of distant barking dogs and the calling of the guards, Cal asks Leona whether she knows that Horn was castrated by African rebels and then tries to seduce her. Horn resolves to get rid of Alboury, with whom Leona has now fallen in love. Cal tries unsuccessfully to recover the body from the sewer and now plans to shoot Alboury, but is prevented by Horn. Horn tries again to buy off Alboury, but Alboury demands a gun to avenge his brother's murder. When Leona pleads with Alboury to desist and take her as his wife, he spits in her face. Horn drives him away and pleads with Leona to marry him. She responds by cutting tribal markings in her cheeks, and is forced by Horn to leave. As fireworks explode in the sky, Cal, about to kill Alboury, is shot by the black guards.

The intense, poetically expressed action, confined to one night, reflects differing European attitudes to black Africa: the paternalism of Horn; the vicious arrogance of Cal; and the absurd romanticism of Leona, against which is set the quiet dignity of Alboury, who bears the name of a 19th-century tribal king who resisted white colonizers. Cal ends dead, Leona mutilated, and Horn disillusioned and alone.

Submerged. See LOWER DEPTHS, THE

Subscription List, The *(Kanjinchō)*

A: Namiki Gohei III **Pf**: 1840, Japan **Tr**: 1953 **G**: Kabuki play in prose and song **S**: A checkpoint between Kyoto and north-west Japan, *c.*1192 **C**: 10m

Yoritomo has seized power in Japan and has set up checkpoints across his empire in order to capture his younger brother Yoshitsune. Yoshitsune and his retainers, all disguised as mendicant priests, approach the checkpoint manned by the determined Togashi and three soldiers. The warrior-priest Benkei, who serves Yoshitsune, persuades him and his men not to attempt to fight but to let him outsmart Togashi. Benkei first begs Togashi to let the 'priests' through, claiming that they have to collect alms to rebuild a Buddhist temple. Togashi refuses, and so Benkei and his men pretend to prepare for death. Impressed but still suspicious, Togashi demands to see the subscription list of donors to the temple. Benkei reads from a blank scroll so convincingly and with such pious exhortations that Togashi is won over. As he lets the men pass, however, his suspicion is suddenly aroused by the figure of Yoshitsune. In order to persuade Togashi that Yoshitsune is merely a worthless servant, Benkei beats his master. This is a terrible breach of the samurai code and causes Benkei huge remorse, but the subterfuge works, and after a humorous sequence in which Benkei drinks and dances with Togashi and his soldiers, Yoshitsune and his men are free to continue.

Based on a Nō play, *Ataka*, this is one of the most popular kabuki plays, and is still performed today. Benkei is a favourite character in Japan: strong, courageous, resourceful, and loyally devoted to his master. This play offers to the performer opportunities for clever dialogue (Benkei's verbal sparring with Togashi), vigorous if symbolic action (Benkei beating his master), subtle emotion (Benkei's remorse after the beating), and comedy (Benkei's drunken dance).

Suburban Motel (Problem Child; Criminal Genius; Risk Everything)

A: George F. Walker Pf: (1, 3, 6) 1997, New York; (2, 4, 5) no known production Pb: 1997 G: 6 linked 1-act dramas S: Rundown motel on outskirts of Canadian city, 1990s C: (1) 2m, 2f; (3) 3m, 2f; (6) 2m, 2f

(1) *Problem Child.* R. J. Reynolds ('R.J.') and his wife Denise have been staying for a week in a desolate motel room, waiting to hear whether Denise will be able to get their baby daughter back from foster care. The social worker Helen Mackie comes to check on them, in particular to see whether Denise has given up prostitution and drugs, for which she has a conviction. Helen leaves and comes back drunk, having bought a gun. Since her mother reported her to the police, Denise considers murdering her. Helen returns and warns Denise that she may not get her baby. Helen cuts her hand and faints from loss of blood, her head hitting the toilet bowl. Denise and Phillie the alcoholic motel manager bury her body, and he is sent off to kidnap the baby. Phillie loses his nerve, and Helen, who was merely unconscious, crawls out of the mud and gets herself to hospital where she takes time to recover from her head injury. She still hopes to reform Denise, who stays on with R.J. for another six months in the motel room, but Denise is not optimistic: 'things don't work out.... Not for people like us. They just get worse.' (3) *Criminal Genius.* Petty criminals Rolly Moore and his son Stevie have been given the job of torching a restaurant. However, fearing they might hurt somebody, Rolly decides instead to kidnap the female chef and owner. Shirley 'the Pearl' Katakis comes to their motel room, furious at Rolly, because the chef is Amanda Castle, the daughter of the man who had contracted the arson attack on a rival restaurant, so that Amanda would 'come back to her father's loving embrace'. While Phillie demands payment for the room, Amanda and Stevie escape, and Rolly belatedly goes off to burn down the restaurant. Amanda joyously burns down her father's restaurant in retaliation. She so hates her father that she lays plans to kill him. Later that evening, Rolly, Stevie, and Phillie have run away from a gun battle. Shirley and Amanda return, having killed seven of her father's guards, and threaten to shoot the three men for running away. Amanda's father and the remaining guards come to the motel and shoot all five dead. (6) *Risk Everything.* Some time after the events of *Problem Child*, Denise brings her injured mother Carol to their motel room. Although Carol claims that she was beaten up by her occasional lover Ray, Denise realizes that her mother was injured by Steamboat Jeffries for cheating on a deal involving $68,000. However, Murray Lawson has supposedly absconded with the money. Awaiting Steamboat Willie's revenge, Carol consoles herself in bed with Michael, a pornographic film director who was shooting a movie in the neighbouring cabin. Denise is shocked and throws him out. R.J. goes in search of Murray Lawson, encounters Steamboat Willie, and returns with explosives strapped to his body. Michael returns, also wired with explosives for attempting to intervene on Carol's behalf. Denise plans to take R.J. so that they can 'explode all over Steamboat Willie', but are seized by him as they leave the motel. Carol admits that she has the missing money, grudgingly hands it over, and the two men have the explosives removed. Denise cannot believe that her mother would risk everything for the sake of money.

In the transient world of the motel, no-hopers, 'the scum of the earth', fail to fulfil their aspirations, sometimes poignantly (*Problem Child*), sometimes farcically (*Criminal Genius*), sometimes with a mixture of both (*Risk Everything*). In the confines of one shabby room, Canadian playwright George F. Walker creates a world inhabited by extreme but believable characters.

Successful Strategies. See GAME OF LOVE AND CHANCE, THE.

Such Stuff as Dreams Are Made Of. See LIFE IS A DREAM.

Suddenly Last Summer

A: Tennessee Williams Pf: 1958, New York Pb: 1958 G: Drama in 1 act S: Mansion in the

Garden District of New Orleans, 1936 **C:** 2m, 5f

Mrs Venable, a frail and elderly widow, has invited a doctor to help her find out the truth about her son Sebastian's death 'suddenly last summer'. Although Sebastian, a sickly and fastidious poet, usually went on holiday with his mother, that year he travelled to South America with his cousin Catharine. Catharine had been raped by a married stranger after a dance, and, after witnessing Sebastian's death, became completely unhinged and is now confined to a mental institution. Mrs Venable is distressed by 'the obscenities and babblings' that Catharine utters about her precious son's death, but Catharine insists that she is telling the truth. Mrs Venable offers the doctor a large amount of money to lobotomize Catharine to shut her up. First, though, he gives Catharine a truth serum, and she retells the story of Sebastian's death. He had made her go to the beach in a see-through bathing costume in order to procure local young men for his pleasure. Then one day, he was first abused then pursued by starving, naked black children. When Catharine found his body, parts of it had been eaten. Outraged, Mrs Venable insists on the lobotomy, but the doctor wonders if Catharine's story may not be true.

Presented in a double bill with *Something Unspoken* under the general title of *Garden City*, this play went further than Williams's earlier excursions into sexual fantasy and violence, and with Gore Vidal was in 1959 made into an even more lurid film. Sebastian carries the same name as the gay icon St Sebastian, martyred by having his naked body pierced with arrows. Although the play focuses on the narration of a past event, its shocking content and the reactions of a doting and self-deluding mother develop tension in performance.

Suehirogari. See SHOPPING FOR AN UMBRELLA.

Suicide, The (*Samoubiytsa*)

A: Nikolai Erdman **W:** 1928–31 **Pf:** 1969, Malmö, Sweden; 1982, Moscow **Pb:** 1973 **Tr:** 1973 **G:** Com. in 5 acts; Russian prose **S:** A Soviet town, 1920s **C:** 13m, 9f, extras

Semyon Semyonovich Podsekalnikov is a sad individual who is unable to find a job. He is embarrassed at having to send his wife out to work and takes up the tuba as a source of income, but he is as much a failure at this as at everything else. He decides that the only way out is to commit suicide. Alerted by his gossipy neighbour, a number of different groups visit him in order to enlist his suicide as a protest by their faction: intellectuals, women, Marxists, shopkeepers, and clergy. They celebrate his send-off with a banquet, but, with his customary ineptitude, he is too cowardly to commit suicide and just lies down in his coffin in a drunken sleep. Imagining that he is dead, the funeral party carries him to the graveyard, where he suddenly revives, jumps out of the coffin, and declares himself for life.

This product of the early Soviet theatre became internationally famous only towards the end of the 20th century. It was already in rehearsal for both Stanislavsky's Moscow Art Theatre and Meyerhold's theatre, when on Stalin's instructions the Soviet censor banned its performance. Its manuscript circulated for decades in the Soviet underground, where it probably acquired additional satirical barbs against the regime. In fact, the play is still not particularly subversive: Podsekalnikov is hardly an admirable hero, and satirical treatment of the vying factions, with the possible exception of the Marxists, is no frontal assault on the Communist state.

Summerfolk (*Dachniky*)

AT: *Vacationers* **A:** Maxim Gorky **Pf:** 1904, St Petersburg **Pb:** 1904 **Tr:** 1975 **G:** Drama in 4 acts; Russian prose **S:** Bassov's estate, rural Russia, 1900s **C:** 15m, 11f, extras

Bassov, a somewhat unscrupulous lawyer, has invited 12 fellow professionals (lawyers, doctors, engineer, writer, etc.) to stay at his dacha (holiday villa) for the summer. They fill their idleness with aimless pastimes, empty love affairs, and trivial quarrels. Bassov's wife Varvara, disillusioned with her husband, seeks love with the writer Shalimov, but he too has entered a state of gentle despair and can offer her nothing. Ryumin loves Varvara, and when she rejects him, he attempts to commit suicide but succeeds only in wounding himself. The doctor Maria Lvovna is wooed by Varvara's brother Vlas, an anarchic figure, but she insists on devoting herself to her work. Indeed, it is she who rejects the hollowness of their bourgeois lifestyle, seeks contact with the proletariat, and at the end leads four of the party, including Varvara and Vlas, away from the dacha towards a new and purposeful life in the city.

This is in some ways a middle-class version of *The *Lower Depths*, with a group of people living out empty existences. The major difference with both his earlier play and with Chekhov, to which *Summerfolk* clearly owes so much (the disillusioned writer, the failed suicide, the prevailing lethargy and triviality), is that, while Gorky could be forgiving to those stuck in the lower depths, he was angered by the idleness of the well educated. So he provides the figure of the proto-revolutionary Maria Lvovna to show a way forward. Peter Stein's spectacular staging in Berlin in 1974 was invited to the National Theatre in London as its first foreign-language production.

Summer of the Seventeenth Doll

A: Ray Lawler Pf: 1955, Melbourne Pb: 1957; rev. 1978 G: Drama in 3 acts S: Cottage in Carlton, Melbourne, Dec. 1952–Jan. 1953 C: 3m, 4f

Barney Ibbot and Reuben (Roo) Webber are good mates, who work together most of the year as sugar-cane cutters and then spend their summer lay-off period in Melbourne. For 16 summers they have joined up with the same girls Nancy Wells and Olive Leech, bringing them presents which always include a kewpie doll. Nancy has married a steady but boring bookseller, so Olive tries to find Barney a substitute in the form of a sceptical widow Pearl Cunningham. Since Roo left work when his prowess was challenged by a younger cutter, he now has to find a summer job. Barney manages to win over Pearl, but the fun has gone out of the summer break. Olive's mother Emma reminds Roo that he is now too old for 'chasin' wimmen' and 'bein' top dog'. So he decides to stay in his job and asks Olive to marry him and settle down. But, weeping hysterically, she demands to have the 'heaven' of their summers back again. Roo realizes the past is dead, smashes the seventeenth doll, and leaves to go back to cane cutting.

This was the first Australian play to become internationally famous and was made into a film. Its authentic dialogue and courage in addressing contemporary Australian concerns were decisive in establishing a native dramatic tradition. The *Doll Trilogy* also comprises *Kid Stakes* (1975), which showed how in 1935 marriage was out of the question for the foursome, and *Other Times* (1976), showing Barney and Roo returning from active service in the Second World War.

Suppliants (*Hiketides; Supplices*)

AT: (*The*) *Suppliant Women* A: Aeschylus Pf: *c.*463 BC, Athens Tr: 1777 G: Greek drama in verse S: Argos, in the mythical past C: 3m, 2 choruses (f)

The 50 daughters of Danaus have left their Egyptian home to seek asylum in their ancestral Greek city of Argos. They are fleeing from being forced to marry the 50 sons of Aegyptus. King Pelasgus of Argos listens to their pleas, consults with the citizens of Argos, and agrees to offer them refuge. A herald from the angry Aegyptus demands the release of the suppliants, threatening Argos with invasion if they do not comply. Pelasgus stoutly rejects their demands, and the Danaid women are granted a new home in the city of Argos.

Long thought to be the first extant Greek tragedy, *Suppliants* appears to have a primitive, undramatic structure, consisting mainly of exchanges between one actor and the chorus. Since the discovery of a fragment of papyrus in 1952, it is now known to be a work of Aeschylus' maturity. It appears to be the first part of a trilogy, since the traditional myth tells how the Danaids are eventually forced into marriage. However, they take their revenge on the wedding night, slaying all the bridegrooms but one. A fragment of the final part of the trilogy, entitled *Danaids*, reveals that the goddess Aphrodite has power over all things, so that it is possible that the final part consisted of a trial exonerating both the men for their violent rape and the women for their bloody revenge. Seen as part of this imagined whole, *Suppliants* may therefore be considered more as a choral prelude to the main action rather than a complete play in itself.

Suspect Truth (*La verdad sospechosa*)

AT: *The Truth Suspected* **A:** Juan Ruiz de Alarcón y Mendoza **Pf:** 1619, Madrid **Pb:** 1628 **Tr:** 1962 **G:** Drama in 3 acts; Spanish verse **S:** Madrid, Renaissance period **C:** 10m, 3f, extras

Don García is a young gallant, who has returned home to Madrid from his studies. He is clever and personable but is unable to tell the truth. The following day he meets Jacinta and falls in love with her, mistakenly believing her to be her friend Lucrecia. When he meets an old friend Don Juan, who is in love with Jacinta, García cannot stop himself lying and ironically pretends to have developed a liaison with Jacinta. García's father has arranged for his son to marry Jacinta, but García refuses, pretending that he is already married, because he still believes he loves Lucrecia. At Jacinta's request, Lucrecia invites him to come below her window. Jacinta, pretending to be Lucrecia, challenges him about his supposed marriage, and García denies being married and says that he loves only Lucrecia. It is arranged that García shall marry Lucrecia, but when he joyously goes to take his bride, he discovers at last that he has been wooing the wrong woman. Jacinta marries Don Juan, and García is forced to wed Lucrecia.

The 24 or so plays that Alarcón wrote had as a recurrent theme a satirical view of Spanish society, no doubt in good part because he was a Mexican-born outsider with a hunchback and so himself often an object of ridicule. In probably his best play, *Suspect Truth*, we encounter the irony that García is made to suffer the deceptions of those around him, while he is seemingly punished for his fantastic lies. There is no easy comic resolution for him (nor for Lucrecia in getting a husband who loves another); however unfairly, his lies have trapped him. *Suspect Truth* provided the source for Corneille's *The Liar* (1643), in turn the source for Steele's *The Lying Lover* (1703) and for Goldoni's *The Liar* (1750).

Swaggering Soldier, The. See BRAGGART SOLDIER, THE.

Sweeney Agonistes (*Sweeney Agonistes: Fragments of an Aristophanic Melodrama*)

AT: *Wanna Go Home, Baby?* **A:** T. S. Eliot **Pf:** 1933, Poughkeepsie, New York **Pb:** 1931 **G:** Drama in 1 act; free verse **S:** London flat, 1930s **C:** 7m, 2f

Flatmates Dusty and Doris discuss Pereira, who seems to be an unpleasant pimp but at least pays the rent. When they cut cards, they draw the two of spades – a coffin. They have visitors: Sam, a crook, his sidekick Horsfall, and two American friends from the war. Sweeney, a gangster figure, suggests leaving for a cannibal island where there is only 'Birth, and copulation, and death'. Songs about life on the island are sung, and Sweeney tells of the brutal murder of a young woman. Then there is an ominous knock on the door.

This fragment of a verse drama, its title satirically referring to Milton's *Samson Agonistes* (1671), is included in the 1969 *Complete Poems and Plays* not as a play but as an 'Unfinished Poem'. It is an irony that it is the most innovative and potentially the most theatrical of all Eliot's dramatic writing, like a bizarre piece of *film noir* with songs. However, the English stage, unlike the American and Irish, was hesitant to embrace the Expressionistic impulses coming from continental Europe, and Eliot's playwriting led him instead to the somewhat desiccated verse dramas for which he is now better known.

Sweet Bird of Youth

AT: *The Enemy: Time* **A:** Tennessee Williams **Pf:** 1956, Coral Gables, Florida **Pb:** 1959 **G:** Drama in 3 acts **S:** Hotel and its garden, Gulf Coast town, 1950s **C:** 15m, 7f

Chance Wayne, a handsome but dissipated gigolo in his late twenties, has returned to his hometown with a faded movie star Alexandra del Lago, who calls herself Princess

Kosmonopolis. Chance uses her to promote his failing career in the movies; the Princess, dependent on alcohol and drugs, exploits his youth for sexual oblivion. Chance was driven from the town by the local political chief 'Boss' Finlay, whose daughter Heavenly he seduced. On his last visit to her, Chance infected her with venereal disease, and she had to be 'spayed like a dawg'. Finlay now intends to castrate Chance in revenge. When the Princess's latest film about the ravages of age becomes a success, she invites Chance to leave town with her. But Chance, recognizing that his only asset, youth, has now passed, decides to stay and await the punishment laid down for him.

Based on a one-act play, this disturbing essay on the effects of ageing marked the beginning of the decline in quality of Williams's playwriting. It is a very personal statement by Williams, 45 at the time of its premiere as *The Enemy: Time*, and almost implies that castration might ease his homosexual angst. The strongest feature is the portrayal of the faded movie star, performed by Geraldine Page at its New York premiere.

Table Manners. See NORMAN CONQUESTS, THE.

Tage der Commune, Die. See DAYS OF THE COMMUNE.

Take Me Out

A: Richard Greenberg **Pf**: 2002, New York **Pb**: 2003 **G**: Tragicom. in 3 acts; English with some Spanish and Japanese **S**: Baseball clubhouse and other locations, New York, late 20th c. **C**: 12m

Darren Lemming, son of a white father and black mother, superstar of the New York Empire baseball team, announces that he is gay. The Skipper and the most intelligent team member Kippy Sunderstrom are quite accepting of Darren's 'coming out'. Others are less supportive, their response ranging from the nervous to the hostile. Mason Marzac, Darren's business manager and himself a gay, regards baseball as 'a perfect metaphor for hope in a democratic society. . . . Everyone is given exactly the same chance.' As the team struggles to win, a brilliant new pitcher is brought in: Shane Mungitt from Arkansas, who was orphaned as a baby when his father shot his mother then himself. Shane is repelled by Darren's homosexuality, says so on television, and is suspended from the team. Darren finds himself being treated like an oppressed victim and reveals his true secret: that he is tired of baseball. Shane is allowed back into the team. Darren threatens to resign, then embraces the unwilling and angry Shane in the shower. Shane pitches so violently that his ball kills the batter. Kippy learns from Shane about the 'attempted rape' in the shower. Shane is permanently suspended and later goes berserk with a shotgun. The Empires go on to win the World Series, and Darren invites Mason as his escort to the celebratory party.

Against the exciting background of top-class baseball, Greenberg explores issues of race and sexuality in a fast-moving sequence of monologues and dialogues, penetrating the platitudes of conventional confrontations between liberal attitudes and bigotry to engender some sympathy for the 'red-neck' Shane and to reveal the clay feet of the superstar Darren.

Taking Sides

A: Ronald Harwood **Pf**: 1995, Chichester **Pb**: 1995 **G**: Hist. drama in 2 acts **S**: Major Arnold's office, bombed-out German city (Berlin), 1946 **C**: 4m, 2f

US Major Steve Arnold is collecting evidence for the Tribunal of Artists of the Denazification Commission. Specifically, he is looking into the great conductor Wilhelm Furtwängler's relationship with the Nazi regime, aided by a keen young assistant Lieutenant David Wills. Each member of Furtwängler's orchestra insists that he was anti-Hitler, and the wife of a Jewish pianist gives evidence that Furtwängler helped him to escape to Paris. However, Arnold admits that he is not interested in 'justice, evidence, facts', but in 'nailing the bastard'. He aggressively interrogates Furtwängler, who denies any support for the Nazis and merely wished to see that Germany's 'glorious musical tradition . . . was intact when we woke from the nightmare'. Arnold is delighted to discover Nazi files on all prominent German musicians, one of which exposes a second violinist

Helmuth Rode as a former Nazi informer. Rode confirms Arnold's suspicion that Furtwängler collaborated with the Nazis. Furtwängler is interrogated again at length. He defends himself by stressing the importance of keeping culture alive amidst barbarism: 'Human beings are free wherever Wagner and Beethoven are played.' Arnold, who has seen the rotting corpses of Belsen, remains unimpressed, orders Furtwängler to stand trial before the Tribunal, and makes sure that his name is smeared in the American press.

Tom Stoppard once said that part of the pleasure of writing plays is that one can contradict oneself in public. As with Klaus Mann's novel *Mephisto* (1936) about Gustaf Gründgens's relationship with the Nazis, *Taking Sides* debates the position of the artist within an oppressive totalitarian system. Offering no physical action, concentrated in one room, Harwood's play still offers a totally absorbing experience.

Tale of Mystery, A. See COELINA.

Tales from the Vienna Woods (*Geschichten aus dem Wiener Wald*)

A: Ödön von Horváth **Pf:** 1931, Berlin **Pb:** 1931 **Tr:** 1977 **G:** Tragicom. in 3 acts; German prose and songs **S:** Vienna, Vienna Woods, and the Wachau, *c.*1930 **C:** 11m, 11f

Alfred, an impoverished layabout, gambler, and minor aristocrat, has a relationship with 49-year-old Valerie, who owns a newsagent's and tobacconist's in Vienna. In the same street, the butcher Oskar becomes engaged to Marianne, the daughter of the toyshop owner. Alfred has a row with Valerie, breaks with her, and meets Marianne for the first time. Oskar and Marianne celebrate their engagement with a picnic, to which Alfred and Valerie are invited. Valerie begins a relationship with an anti-Semitic German student Erich, while Marianne falls in love with Alfred, and breaks off her engagement with Oskar. A year later, Marianne, Alfred, and their baby live in a rundown flat, and Alfred insists that the child should be given in care to his mother in the country, claiming he cannot find work at a time of high unemployment. He arranges for Marianne to join a troupe of dancers and leaves her. Marianne's father discovers her working as a naked artiste in a nightclub and rejects her. She steals money from a customer and is arrested. Erich leaves Valerie, who renews her friendship with Alfred. Oskar tells Marianne he would marry her, were it not for her child. She returns to her father. When Marianne, her father, Oskar, Alfred, and Valerie go to fetch Marianne's child, they discover it has died. To the sounds of Strauss's *Tales from the Vienna Woods*, Oskar leads Marianne away.

After Brecht, Horváth was the most significant German-language playwright of the inter-war years, and this is his major play. Termed a *Volksstück* ('people's play'), it is written in the comedic tradition of Nestroy, but exploits the genre by introducing irony and setting it against a contemporary political background.

Tamburlaine the Great (Parts 1 and 2)

A: Christopher Marlowe **Pf:** *c.*1587, London **Pb:** 1590 **G:** Trag. in 2 parts, each 5 acts; blank verse **S:** Persia, Damascus, Babylon, and other locations in the Middle East, late 14th c. **C:** 43m, 5f, extras

Part 1. Formerly a Scythian shepherd, Tamburlaine is now a brigand chief who robs travellers. In order to rid his kingdom of this Tartar robber, Mycetes, King of Persia, sends out an army under the leadership of Theridamas. Meanwhile, Cosroe, Mycetes' brother, plots the overthrow of Mycetes. Tamburlaine persuades Theridamas to join forces with him and goes on to defeat first Mycetes, then Cosroe, to become King of Persia himself. Bajazeth, Emperor of Turkey, goes to war against Tamburlaine, but is captured and humiliated by being displayed with his wife in a cage. Eventually the tormented couple dash their brains out on the bars of the cage. Tamburlaine's next battle is with the Soldan of Egypt. Earlier he had captured Zenocrate, the Soldan's daughter, on her way to marry the King of Arabia, and had fallen in love with her. Now he lays siege to Damascus, cruelly kills Zenocrate's fiancé, slaughters innocent virgins, and forces Zenocrate's father to attend the wedding of his daughter to his enemy. *Part 2.* Some time has elapsed since Part 1. Zenocrate, now mother of three sons, dies. Enraged by the loss of the one person he loved, Tamburlaine becomes more merciless than ever: he defeats a mighty army under the leadership of Bajazeth's son Calapine and stabs one of his own sons for cowardice. He forces four captive kings to be harnessed to his chariot, lays waste Babylon, and murders all the inhabitants. In a final act of pride, he defies the Prophet Mahomet and burns the Koran. Overcome by a strange sickness, even as he approaches death, he yearns to conquer more lands.

It is often asserted that, had Shakespeare not lived, Marlowe would be the great tragedian of the English language. Certainly, *Tamburlaine*, based on the historical figure of Timur, the Tartar conqueror (although much of Part 2 is pure invention), represented a major innovation for the English stage. The medieval chronicle play is replaced by historical drama, with its exciting incidents, powerful characters, and strongly worded conflicts couched in sinewy blank verse. One has only to compare this to **Gorboduc* two decades earlier to recognize the massive contribution made by Marlowe.

Taming of the Shrew, The (*The Tamynge of a Shrowe*)

A: William Shakespeare Pf: *c.*1591–4, London Pb: 1594; 1st folio 1623 G: Com. in 5 acts; blank verse and prose S: Padua, and Petruchio's house in the country, Renaissance period C: 13m, 3f, extras

A tinker Christopher Sly is found drunk and, for a joke, is taken to a lord's house, where he is persuaded that he is a nobleman. He is to be entertained by a play, in which Petruchio, in search of a wealthy wife, decides to woo Katharina, a woman of such violent temper that her father despairs of ever finding a husband for her. Once married, Petruchio takes his new wife to his house in the country, where he keeps her in isolation, bullying, teasing, and starving her, until at the end she relents and becomes a subservient wife preaching the value of obeying her husband. Against this is set a sub-plot in which Katharina's younger sister Bianca enters a much more conventional marriage with Lucentio.

Although structured as a play-within-a-play, the Induction with Sly is soon lost sight of, since he plays no further part in the action. Nevertheless, this context does suggest that the events of the play are, like the 'rags to riches' transformation of Sly, the fulfilment of a fantasy. This recognition may help to make the play more acceptable to modern audiences, who now find it hard to treat the play as a merry farce, when witnessing the brutalization of a woman which forces her into abject submission to her husband. Some modern productions have attempted to undercut Katharina's last speech about wifely duty but it is probably best played 'straight', as in Jonathan Miller's BBC television production. The effect of a strong woman reduced to such unquestioning obedience and Petruchio's smug response is quite chilling enough. The play was also successfully adapted as a musical, *Kiss Me, Kate* (1948), with music and lyrics by Cole Porter.

Tango

A: Sławomir Mrożek Pf: 1965, Warsaw Pb: 1964 Tr: 1968 G: Pol. drama in 3 acts; Polish prose S: Stomils' living room, Poland, 1960s C: 4m, 3f

Arthur Stomil returns home from university to discover that his family is living a life of moral anarchy. Unimpressed by the arguments of his father Stomil and his mother Eleanor that this freedom to act on impulse has been won dear, Arthur determines to become a doctor and get married to his cousin Ala in the traditional manner. If his family will not behave properly, then he will force them to. But Arthur's plans founder: he discovers that the servant Eddie has seduced his mother, and Stomil refuses to shoot Eddie when ordered to do so. Ala, who prefers just to sleep with Arthur, agrees to a traditional wedding only because she looks good in white, and his hedonistic grandmother Eugenia would rather die than submit to Arthur's new moral order. Eventually, Eddie, the anti-intellectual proletarian, kills Arthur and with Arthur's uncle Eugene performs a tango, the dance of overt sexuality, over his corpse.

Like Gombrowicz's *The *Wedding*, *Tango* is based on **Hamlet* (and also owes something to **Bacchae*), but here the political allegory is much clearer, and the behaviour of the Hamlet figure much more determined. The grandparents represent the self-indulgent pleasures of the past, his parents the moral confusion after the Second World War, Arthur the attempt to organize Polish society on rational lines, and Eddie, the brutish man of action, who like Stalin (and the future Polish leader Jaruzelski) would take over the state, using force to impose totalitarian ideas. Its exuberant theatricality helped it to become the most widely performed post-war Polish play.

Tartuffe (*Le Tartuffe, ou L'Imposteur*)

A: Molière **Pf:** 1664, Versailles (banned 3-act version); 1667, Paris (5-act version) **Pb:** 1669 **Tr:** 1670 **G:** Com. in 5 acts; French alexandrines **S:** Orgon's home, Paris, 17th c. **C:** 8m, 5f

Orgon and his elderly mother have fallen under the spell of a hypocritical rogue Tartuffe, whose pretended piety is a cover to exploit the gullible Orgon. Despite the protests of his family, Orgon will not acknowledge his obsession with Tartuffe and even promises to marry his daughter Mariane to him, although she is already engaged to Valère, the man she loves. Even when Orgon's son Damis reveals that Tartuffe is trying to seduce his stepmother Elmire, Orgon refuses to believe him and spites the family by making over all his possessions to the monstrous impostor. Only when Orgon conceals himself under a table and can witness for himself how Tartuffe makes lascivious advances to Elmire, does Orgon see Tartuffe for what he is and throws him out of the house. Tartuffe retaliates by insisting on taking possession of his property and also tries to incriminate Orgon with the use of some subversive documents, which Orgon was keeping for a friend. Fortunately, the King, 'whose eyes see into every heart', intervenes, ordering the arrest of Tartuffe, forgiving Orgon and restoring to him his property.

Possibly based on Pietro Aretino's *The Hypocrite* (1527) and probably the best known of Molière's comedies, *Tartuffe* was regarded by Goethe as a model of dramatic structure. Most notable is the fact that the title character does not appear until Act 3. The audience, by observing the obsessive intransigence of Orgon, is already conditioned to question Tartuffe's behaviour, so that, by the time he enters, it can see his hypocrisy for what it is. *Tartuffe,* in a three-act version about which little is now known except that Tartuffe is here a priest, was banned after its first performance at court because it exposed the hypocritical conduct of the clergy. In the longer revised version, Molière is at pains to distinguish between true faith and false piety, and this, coupled with the fulsome praise of the Monarch at the end, allowed the play eventually to be performed. Nevertheless, scenes like the attempted seduction of Elmire and lines like, 'If you see clearly, you're called a freethinker', would have seemed very bold to the audience of the day. While more modern audiences may have little experience of religious hypocrisy, it is easy to relate to the well-meaning gullibility of Orgon, whose obsessive behaviour makes him in fact the central comic figure. Orgon may be cured of his gullibility, but it is only the 'deus ex machina' intervention of the King that saves him and his family.

Taste of Honey, A

A: Shelagh Delaney **Pf:** 1958, London **Pb:** 1959 **G:** Drama in 2 acts **S:** Flat in Salford, 1950s **C:** 3m, 2f

Helen, a peroxide-blonde 'semi-whore', has a tense relationship with her teenage daughter Josephine (Jo). When Helen's boyfriend Peter, a used-car salesman ten years younger than her, proposes to her, she leaves Jo alone in their seedy northern bedsit. Jo consoles herself with a black naval rating, Jimmy, whom she lets stay over Christmas, and becomes pregnant. When Jimmy too abandons her, she finds a job, and some months later meets Geoff, an effeminate art student. Although he is a homosexual, he and Jo develop a close relationship, and he even makes a crib for her expected baby. Misguidedly, he sends for Helen, but she is dragged away by the angry Peter. After Peter goes off with a 'bit of crumpet', Helen reappears while Jo is asleep. She throws out Geoff, the 'pansified little freak'. Jo awakes and begins labour, dismayed at Geoff's absence. Helen promises to stay with her, but, when she learns that the baby will be half black, rushes out for drink.

Written by a 19-year-old working-class northern girl, and premiered by Joan Littlewood, this has been probably the most performed play by a post-war British woman playwright. In the wake of **Look Back in Anger*, it formed part of the new vogue for gritty realist plays, many of which were filmed. Despite the almost melodramatic misery of her existence, Jo's display of good-humoured resourcefulness was an encouragement to post-war British women, and the sympathetic depiction of types at the fringe of society, the black and the homosexual, was ground-breaking.

Tea and Sympathy

A: Robert Anderson **Pf:** 1953, New York **Pb:** 1953 **G:** Drama in 3 acts **S:** Boys' boarding school, New England, 1950s **C:** 9m, 2f

Tom Lee is a sensitive 18-year-old schoolboy, whose manner and whose interest in art make his tough and sporty fellow scholars suspect him of homosexuality. Even Tom's father has his doubts, and his bullying housemaster Bill Reynolds is particularly cruel towards him. Only Bill's wife Laura, unhappy in her marriage and reminded by young Tom of her first husband who was killed in the war, shows any sympathy towards Tom. However, school rules permit her to dispense only 'tea and sympathy'. Tom tries to lose his virginity to a local whore, but the episode ends in fiasco. Now convinced that he is 'queer', Tom tries to kill himself, and is expelled from the school as a consequence. Laura, who accuses Bill of persecuting Tom because of his own repressed homosexuality, decides to leave him and goes to comfort Tom in his room. She assures him of his manhood, and begins gently to seduce him as the curtain falls.

Like William Inge, Robert Anderson wrote plays that contained some of the taboo elements of sexuality so powerfully dissected by Tennessee Williams, but Inge and Anderson rendered the topics more digestible for mainstream audiences by introducing a note of gentleness and by showing the 'villains' to be unambiguously unpleasant. All of which explains the critical success of Williams, and the Broadway success of Anderson.

Teahouse of the August Moon, The

A: John Patrick **Pf:** 1953, New York **Pb:** 1954 **G:** Com. in 3 acts **S:** Okinawa, 1946 **C:** 13m, 5f, 4 children, extras

As part of the democratization programme of the American occupation forces on the island of Okinawa, Colonel Wainwright Purdy III sends the good-natured Captain Fisby to the village of Tobiki, accompanied by the wily interpreter Sakini. Fisby is welcomed by the villagers, who, after centuries of being invaded, are well equipped to deal with awkward outsiders and make Fisby a present of a gifted and charming geisha Lotus Blossom. When Fisby tries to build a schoolhouse, the villagers request a teahouse, arguing that this is their democratic wish and so accords with the new American teachings. Equally, Fisby is induced to encourage the distilling of the local brandy and to get Lotus Blossom to give lessons to the local women in the arts of seduction. Purdy becomes so concerned about reports from Tobiki that he sends a psychiatrist Captain McLean to check on Fisby's mental health. McLean is so impressed with the idyllic village that he decides to base his organic crop experiments there. Purdy himself arrives and orders the destruction of the teahouse and the brandy stills, believing that he has unearthed a Communist collective. Just as his sergeant reports the completion of the demolition, news comes that Tobiki is being hailed as a model of American democratic initiative and that a delegation of generals is coming to view the village. Fortunately, the resourceful villagers have merely hidden everything and the teahouse is quickly reassembled.

In a period when the Japanese were still all too frequently regarded as cruel war criminals and as politically antediluvian, this gentle comedy helped to break down prejudice. Significantly, when the American Colonel discovers a society that operates to the benefit of all, he assumes it must be Communist – a dig at the prevalent McCarthyite hysteria of the early 1950s.

Tempest, A (*Une tempête*)

A: Aimé Césaire Pf: 1969, Hammamet, Tunisia Pb: 1969 Tr: 1985 G: Com. in 3 acts; French prose S: An island, indeterminate period C: 15m, 1f

This 'adaptation for a black theatre' follows the main lines of Shakespeare's plot, but there are significant changes. The translation simplifies and shortens the original. Ariel is a resentful mulatto. Caliban is a rebellious black slave, who has been taught Prospero's language only so that he can understand his orders and who asks to be called X, since Prospero has stolen his identity. In a specially written scene, Ariel and Caliban argue about modes of resistance: Ariel pleads for non-violence; Caliban calls him an Uncle Tom and demands 'Freedom now!' Instead of Ariel appearing as the avenging Fury, he criticizes Prospero for using the courtiers' hunger as a means of punishing them. In the Masque, the figure of Eshu appears, 'a god to his friends, a devil to his enemies', and sings an obscene song. Despite Ariel's warning, Prospero orders the arrest of Caliban and his fellow conspirators. Gonzalo attempts to convert Caliban to Christianity but fails. Caliban delivers an eloquent speech rejecting Prospero's colonialist domination and threatening revenge. Prospero decides that his duty is to remain on the island not to be master but 'the leader of the orchestra' and to counter Caliban's violence with violence. In a final image, Prospero is a futile old man, ruler over a population of one, and fragments of Caliban's song are heard in the distance.

Martiniquan-born Césaire adapts Shakespeare's *The* **Tempest* in order to debate colonial politics, introducing the figure of Eshu, and making Prospero's oppression more obviously racial. The major change in the plot, that Prospero regards it as his duty to remain behind on the island, suggests that, however futile his gesture, whites and blacks will have to develop some form of mutually supportive relationship rather than remain antagonists.

Tempest, The

A: William Shakespeare Pf: *c.*1610–11, London Pb: 1623 G: Com. in 5 acts; blank verse and prose S: Mediterranean island, indeterminate period C: 14m, 1f, extras

Twelve years ago Prospero lost the dukedom of Milan to his scheming brother Antonio, and was put out to sea with his 3-year-old daughter Miranda. They now live on an isolated island, accompanied by two slaves, the spirit Ariel and the brutish Caliban. Using his magic powers, Prospero causes the ship in which Antonio is travelling with the King of Naples and his son to be wrecked on the island. Imagining his father to be drowned, the King's son Ferdinand encounters Prospero and falls in love with Miranda. Prospero orders him to commit menial tasks. The King himself is about to be murdered by the treacherous Antonio, when Ariel intervenes and drives all the courtiers to distraction. Caliban meets with two sailors and together they plot the downfall of Prospero. The courtiers discover a banquet in the forest, but it magically disappears, to be replaced by Ariel as an avenging Fury to remind them of their guilt towards Prospero. Miranda and Ferdinand are entertained by a masque and are reminded to remain chaste. Caliban and his drunken mutineers dress themselves in Prospero's finery but are chased through swamps by dogs. At last, Prospero takes his leave of his magic powers, confronts and forgives the evil courtiers, gives his blessing to the marriage of Miranda and Ferdinand, acknowledges Caliban as his, and gives Ariel his freedom. He then prepares to return in the magically restored ship to resume his rule in Milan.

The Tempest is a fable which appears full of enigmatic meanings. On one level, remembering that this was probably the last play that Shakespeare wrote on his own, it is his farewell to the stage: like Prospero he determines to bury his magic and no longer create magical beings. The play can also be read as a political parable, in which one is only too painfully aware that, once free of the island's magic, the evil forces of power politics will re-establish themselves. There is also a personification of the human psyche in the aggressive and lustful drives of Caliban, the tortured ego of Prospero, and the imaginative creativity represented by the airborne spirit Ariel. In the Restoration, William Davenant and John Dryden collaborated in creating a new version, subtitled *The Enchanted Island* (1667), in which Prospero has two daughters. In more recent times, the ambivalent way in which the island has been seized from its native population by Prospero has suggested readings of the play which emphasize the theme of colonialism, as in Césaire's *A *Tempest*.

Ten Blocks on the Camino Real. See CAMINO REAL.

Tenth Man, The

A: Paddy Chayefsky Pf: 1959, New York Pb: 1960 G: Drama in 3 acts S: Orthodox synagogue, New York, 1950s C: 12m, 1f

On a freezing morning in a poor Orthodox synagogue, eight men have assembled for morning prayers. They are joined by Foreman, who has brought his schizophrenic granddaughter Evelyn, so that the dybbuk that is making her crazy can be exorcized rather than have her committed to a mental institution. However, they cannot proceed, as there are only nine men present, and a tenth is needed to make up the *minyon* or quorum of ten. Speaking through Evelyn, the dybbuk shocks those present by revealing some of their sexual secrets. The Sexton manages to persuade a passer-by to make up the number. He is Arthur Landau, a young clean-cut Jewish lawyer, who also turns out to be a troubled individual: he has been on a three-day drinking binge and is now eager to get to his psychiatrist. After morning prayers, he and Evelyn develop a mutual attraction, but he rebuffs her: 'I simply do not believe anybody loves anyone.' When the Cabalist proceeds to the exorcism, it is Arthur who begins to scream and release his dybbuk. Coming to himself, he has gained 'the ability to love' and promises to care for Evelyn, believing that his love will cure her mental problems. The men begin to dispute whether he found God or only love, and whether indeed there is a difference.

It is easy to be cynical about the optimistic ending of Chayefsky's best play for the stage, since Arthur's conversion to love and caring is so sudden, and Evelyn's problems are so serious. Chayefsky's championing of simple faith and native wisdom over psychiatric medicine is heart-warming but dubious.

testör, A. See GUARDSMAN, THE.

Teufels General, Des. See DEVIL'S GENERAL, THE.

Theatrical Illusion, The (*L'Illusion comique*)

AT: *The Illusion* A: Pierre Corneille Pf: 1635–6, Paris Pb: 1639 Tr: 1975 G: Com. in 5 acts; French alexandrines S: Alcandre's grotto, early 17th c. C: 10m, 2f, extras

Pridamant, desperate to discover the whereabouts of his missing son Clindor, seeks help from the magician Alcandre, who conjures scenes of Clindor's adventures. After leaving home, he became the servant of the braggart soldier Matamore, who is wooing the beautiful young Isabelle. Adraste also pays court to Isabelle, but she secretly returns Clindor's love. To rid himself of his rival, Adraste and a group of brigands attack Clindor, who manages to fight them off, killing Adraste in the set-to. Although it was in self-defence, the slaying of a bourgeois by a seeming servant is a serious matter, and Clindor finds himself confined to a miserable prison. Fortunately, Isabelle's maidservant Lyse, who is attracted to young Clindor, bribes the jailer to free him. Clindor and Isabelle run away, marry, and become prosperous. When Clindor has an affair with the wife of his benefactor Prince Florilame, he is ambushed and killed. Pridamant is overwhelmed at seeing his son's death, but grief gives way to anger when he discovers that Clindor and the other characters are merely actors in a tragedy, a calling unfit for his son. However, Alcandre persuades Pridamant of the value of theatre and of the illusions it creates.

This is the most accomplished French comedy before Molière and was written before the unities of time and place exerted their stranglehold over French drama. In its indulgent depiction of melodramatic incident, Corneille involves the audience, like Pridamant, in a charming illusion, and by playing with levels of appearance and reality, argues that the theatre provides worthwhile moral entertainment.

There Is Nothing Bad Which Could Not Turn into Something Worse. See MADMAN AND THE NUN, THE.

Thérèse Raquin

AT: *Guilty* A: Émile Zola Pf: 1867, Paris Pb: 1863 Tr: 1956 G: Trag. in 4 acts; French prose S: The Raquins' room, Paris, 1860s C: 4m, 3f

Laurent, who is painting the portrait of his friend Camille, seems to dislike Camille's wife Thérèse, but, when alone together, they rush into each other's arms. All three plan a boating trip together, during which Laurent and Thérèse drown the weakling Camille. A year later, Camille's mother, believing that Laurent had bravely tried to save her precious son, urges him to marry the 'mourning' widow Thérèse. With a show of reluctance, they agree to 'do their duty'. When at last their happiness seems assured, they find that on their wedding night their guilt has completely drained their relationship of love. Madame Raquin overhears Laurent's confession to murder, and the shock causes a stroke which leaves her paralysed. Regaining the use of one hand, she begins to write a note denouncing the pair, but stops, recognizing that they will be punished more by suffering slowly and privately from their guilt than if she were to hand them over to the law. Deaf to their pleas for pity, she watches as they poison themselves.

Based on his 1867 novel *Thérèse Raquin*, this play stands as one of the few lastingly successful adaptations from prose fiction in the history of drama. While the end is undeniably melodramatic, Zola's detailed 'autopsy' (his own term) of a disintegrating relationship is truthful and brilliantly compelling. Although attracting much hostility in its day for its sordid theme, it may now be recognized, with Ostrovksy's **Thunderstorm*, as a seminal work of stage naturalism.

Thesmophoriazusae. See WOMEN AT THE THESMOPHORIA.

Thesmophoriazusai. See *WOMEN AT THE THESMOPHORIA.*

They Knew What They Wanted

A: Sidney Howard Pf: 1924, New York Pb: 1925 G: Com. in 3 acts S: Tony's living room, Napa Valley vineyard, California, 1920s C: 9m, 4f

Tony is a prosperous Italian-born winegrower in need of a wife. He has fallen in love with Amy, a San Francisco waitress, and wooed her by letter. Concerned that he is too old and unattractive, he has sent her a photo of Joe, his handsome young assistant. So when Amy arrives at the house, she mistakenly unburdens her longing for security to Joe. Tony is brought in injured from a car crash, and she is disappointed in her bridegroom and furious at his deception. But she decides to stay. At the wedding that evening, Tony gradually wins Amy over with his love and kindness. Resolving to be a good wife, she prepares to nurse him back to health by remaining all night at his bedside. Joe, who is devoted to Tony, has also come to keep a vigil. As Tony slumbers in a drugged sleep, Joe and Amy, after some initial reproaches by her, embrace passionately. Three months later Amy learns that she is carrying Joe's baby. She and Joe have not been alone together since the wedding night, and both regret the passion of the moment. Tony, at first abandoned to a jealous rage, soon relents, asking Amy and Joe to stay, and saying that he will bring up the baby as his own. Joe goes back on the road again, leaving the happy couple to their future.

Pulitzer Prizewinner and hugely successful in its day, this play reworks the theme of illicit passion and mistaken identity of **Francesca da*

Rimini in a realistic American setting and with a happy ending. Although there is some discussion of prohibition and capitalism, the play offers little social commentary but instead a pleasing portrayal of unspectacular individuals who win through to happiness by generosity of spirit.

Thing Happens, The. See BACK TO METHUSELAH.

Threepenny Opera, The (*Die Dreigroschenoper*)

A: Bertolt Brecht (with Elisabeth Hauptmann) **Pf:** 1928, Berlin **Pb:** 1929 **Tr:** 1949 **G:** Musical drama in 3 acts; German prose with songs **S:** Soho, London, late 19th c. **C:** 7m, 4f, many extras

Peachum runs a very prosperous business, sending out suitably costumed beggars on to the streets of London, but fears that his daughter Polly has eloped with the notorious robber Macheath, 'Mack the Knife'. Macheath and Polly celebrate their wedding in a stable amongst stolen presents, and welcome as a guest 'Tiger' Brown, the Police Chief, who is a close friend and former army comrade of Macheath's. When Polly admits to her parents that she has married Macheath, they resolve to denounce him to the authorities. Forced to flee, Macheath places Polly in charge of his gang, but only gets as far as his regular brothel, where he is entertained by the whores. To 'Tiger' Brown's embarrassment and dismay, Macheath is arrested, and is visited in prison by Brown's daughter Lucy. Polly arrives, and the two women fight over whom Macheath really loves and is married to. When Lucy helps Macheath to escape, Peachum warns Brown that if he does not recapture Macheath, he will disrupt the Queen's impending coronation by sending all his disgusting beggars out on to the London streets. When Macheath is irresistibly drawn back to his whore, Jenny betrays him to the police. Peachum persuades Brown that he will have to hang Macheath. In his death cell, Macheath fails to raise enough cash to buy his way out, while Polly and Lucy, now reconciled, hold a vigil. As he stands on the scaffold, a mounted messenger brings the Queen's pardon, and Macheath, given a knighthood, a pension, and a country house, is reprieved in a joyous 'Happy End'.

Brecht's rewriting, with his collaborator Elisabeth Hauptmann, of Gay's **Beggar's Opera*, the plot of which (apart from the introduction of 'Tiger' Brown) he followed fairly closely, is Brecht's most popular work – and therein lies a problem in terms of its political comment. While the piece is intended to show that major crime and the capitalist establishment are mutually interdependent, the colourful characters, racy songs (some of them lifted from writers like François Villon and Rudyard Kipling), and, above all, Kurt Weill's unforgettable music, too easily make *The Threepenny Opera* a piece of uncomplicated entertainment. As Edward Bond commented, audiences chew their chocolates in time with the music. The opening *Moritat*, which includes child rape as one of Mack the Knife's crimes, has become a swinging number by Louis Armstrong that we can all sing along with.

Three Sisters (*Tri Sestry*)

AT: *The Three Sisters* **A:** Anton Chekhov **Pf:** 1901, Moscow **Pb:** 1901 **Tr:** 1916 **G:** Drama in 4 acts; Russian prose **S:** The Prozorovs' house and garden, Russian provincial town, 1900 **C:** 9m, 5f, extras

The Prozorovs, Andrey and his three sisters, live out a tedious existence in the provinces, brought there when their late father was posted from Moscow 11 years previously. Andrey is engaged to a boorish and grasping local girl Natasha. The eldest sister Olga is a schoolteacher, still unmarried at the age of 28. The second daughter Masha is unhappily married to a boring schoolmaster, and the youngest Irina is celebrating her twentieth birthday. Guests come to the house, including the new arrival from Moscow Vershinin. Eighteen months later Andrey is married and so bored that he takes up gambling. Vershinin has fallen in love with Masha, but is worried about his neurotic and suicidal wife. Natasha rides out with a former suitor. Two further years pass. A fire is raging in the town. Olga collects clothes for the homeless, Natasha is openly pursuing an affair. Because of his debts, Andrey has had to mortgage the house. Irina considers a proposal from an army lieutenant, Baron Tuzenbach, but only if this will get her to Moscow. A little while later the battery are leaving town, and Irina will marry Tuzenbach and go to Moscow with him. Masha says farewell to Vershinin. News comes that Tuzenbach has been killed in a meaningless duel, and the three sisters resign themselves once more to their hollow existence.

Apart from the muted offstage death of Tuzenbach, very little happens in this play, thus setting a pattern for a 20th-century theatre that is not necessarily based on external action. Instead, the piece saunters through some four years in the lives of the visitors and inhabitants of a Russian provincial town, where the great desire of the three sisters is for escape to Moscow, just as some half a century later two figures imagine that all will be put to right when Godot comes.

Thunderstorm, The (*Groza*)

AT: *The Storm; Thunder* A: Aleksandr Ostrovsky Pf: 1859, Moscow Pb: 1860 Tr: 1927 G: Drama in 5 acts; Russian prose S: Fictitious town of Kalinov on the Volga, Russia, mid-19th c. C: 7m, 5f, extras

Katerina (Katya) is married to Tikhon, a merchant in a small Russian town. Although they did not marry for love, all would be well were it not for the behaviour of Tikhon's mother Kabanova, a tyrannical and mean-spirited old widow. Her constant nagging drives Katya to despair, while Kabanova allows her own daughter Varvara to behave as she likes. When Tikhon has to leave on a business trip, Varvara exploits the opportunity to invite two men to a secret meeting with Katya and herself: Boris, the nephew of a miserable old merchant Dikoy, and one of Dikoy's employees Vanya Kudryash. Having stolen the key from Kabanova, Varya and Katya escape by the garden gate to spend an idyllic time of free and gentle love with the two young men. Tikhon returns unexpectedly, and as a thunderstorm gathers, Katya is forced to confess her infidelity. Her guilt and the reproaches of husband and mother-in-law drive her to drown herself in the Volga. Meanwhile Boris's uncle sends him to Siberia.

Ostrovsky grew up in the merchants' quarter in Moscow, where, as also later as a court official, he was able to observe the domestic dramas of ordinary Russian life. In particular he was fascinated by what is called in Russia the *samodur*, the boorish, tyrannical, and complacent figure, represented here by Kabanova and Dikoy. Because they wield unchallenged power over their unfortunate employees and relatives, they can set tragedy in motion as surely as the royal tyrants of classical drama. The result is a play combining harsh realism with the gentle idyll of the scene between the lovers (hissed at by contemporary audiences for its immorality). Jánaček wrote an operatic version, *Kátia Kabanová*, in 1921.

Thyestes

A: Lucius Annaeus Seneca W: AD 25–65 Tr: 1560 G: Latin trag. in 5 acts; verse S: The palace of Mycenae, in the mythical past C: 8m, 1f, chorus (m)

The ghost of Tantalus is temporarily released from the torments of the underworld to warn his grandsons, Atreus and Thyestes, to abandon their violence towards each other in their struggle over their father's throne. Atreus at present rules in Mycenae but still wishes to be avenged on his brother for all the wrongs he has done him. He deceptively invites Thyestes and his three sons to return from exile and share power with him. Though cautious, Thyestes accepts Atreus' invitation, and they appear to be reconciled. Once in his power, Atreus ritually slaughters Thyestes' three sons, roasts their dismembered bodies, and serves them as a feast to their father. Jubilant at the success of his plan, Atreus reveals to Thyestes that he has murdered his sons, and when Thyestes begs for their bodies to bury them, Atreus tells him that Thyestes has eaten them himself. In despair, Thyestes can hope only that the gods will avenge this terrible crime.

Although a fragment of a *Thyestes* by Sophocles survives, it is likely that Seneca based his version on the *Thyestes* of L. Varius

Rufus (29 BC). Seneca's play represents Latin tragedy at its most violent and melodramatic. There is no subtlety of characterization, no surprising twist in the plot, no moral dilemma explored. Atreus is committed to his plan of revenge without any psychological build-up to his evil plan, and most of the play is devoted to a powerfully poetic recital of the atrocity and its aftermath. Even Tantalus' exhortation to abandon the cycle of revenge is obscured by the violent narration, and one can have little faith that the gods, invoked by Thyestes, will intervene to right this terrible wrong. *Thyestes*, translated by Jasper Heywood in 1560, influenced the many bloody revenge tragedies of Elizabethan and Jacobean drama and provided the source for the scene in Shakespeare's **Titus Andronicus* in which children are baked in a pie for their parent to eat. Caryl Churchill wrote a version of *Thyestes* in 1994.

Ticket-of-Leave Man, The

A: Tom Taylor Pf: 1863, London Pb: 1863 G: Melodrama in 4 acts S: Tea Gardens, May's room, an office, an inn, a street, and a churchyard, London, late 1850s to early 1860s C: 9m, 3f, extras

Robert Brierly, a young Lancashire lad, is tasting the pleasures of London for the first time. He falls easy prey to a pair of criminals, Melter Moss and James Dalton. Dalton lends him money in the form of a forged note. When Brierly changes this for gold sovereigns, he is arrested and imprisoned for four years.

A young girl May, to whom he had shown kindness, waits patiently for his release from jail as a 'ticket-of-leave man', a form of parole. When Brierly discovers that his forged note caused the ruin of May's loquacious landlady Mrs Willoughby, he secretly repays the money. Brierly and May arrange to marry, and he gets a job as messenger in a brokerage firm. When his employer learns that he is a 'jailbird', he is dismissed. Brierly tries to find any kind of employment, but even navvies will not let him work with them. Moss and Dalton imagine that he will now be forced to assist them to rob the firm he was sacked from. Brierly pretends to agree, but betrays them to the police. In a dramatic ending the criminals are apprehended, and the wounded Brierly has his honour restored.

While the action has some spectacularly melodramatic moments, like Brierly's dismissal on the day of his wedding, the police detective's sudden removal of his disguise, and the exciting fight in the churchyard, the play also has a serious underlying theme. This play, based on a French original, shows how a former prisoner (and conveniently Brierly is totally innocent) has virtually no hope of rejoining society and may be forced back into crime.

Till Damaskus. See TO DAMASCUS.

Time of Your Life, The

A: William Saroyan Pf: 1939, New York Pb: 1939 G: Drama in 5 acts S: San Francisco waterfront bar, Oct. 1939 C: 18m, 9f

The regulars in Nick's Pacific Street Saloon are drinking, talking, and playing the pinball machine and jukebox. Joe sits and drinks, because without alcohol life would be just 'Minutes on the clock, *not time of living*'. Kitty Duval, a pretty prostitute, enters, and Joe's slow-witted friend Tom instantly adores her. Joe gives Tom $5, so that he can go with Kitty to her room. The arrival of the villainous vice-squad chief Blick spoils the easygoing atmosphere. The proprietor Nick throws him out, and hires a comedian as a dancer and a black boy Wesley as a pianist. Tom reappears to tell Joe that Kitty is weeping about her past, and Joe goes to console her. Giving her some toys, he urges Tom to love and protect her. As the day moves into evening, more customers appear. Joe finds Tom a job as a truck driver and urges him and Kitty to marry and start a new life. Blick reappears, forces the unwilling Kitty to perform a striptease, and beats up Wesley and an old trapper called Kit Carson, when they protest about his treatment of Kitty. Joe tries and fails to shoot Blick, but Carson kills Blick in the street and begins to reminisce about the time he shot a man in San Francisco.

This is the best of Saroyan's 45 plays and a winner of the Pulitzer Prize, which he rejected. With obvious echoes of *The *Lower Depths* and anticipating *The *Iceman Cometh*, Saroyan's play is randomly constructed, with the Tom–Kitty relationship forming the only progression in the plot (Blick's removal is almost incidental to it and possibly has not even happened). While the naturalistic setting and dialogue are in the tradition of American realist theatre, musical underscoring and the abandonment of sustained narrative look forward to new theatre forms.

Timon of Athens (*The Life of Timon of Athens*)

A: William Shakespeare **Pf:** *c.*1607, London? **Pb:** 1623 **G:** Trag. in 5 acts; blank verse and prose **S:** Athens and nearby woods, 5th c. BC **C:** 30m, 2f, extras

Timon, an Athenian nobleman, is excessively generous with his wealth. Despite warnings from his servant Flavius that he will soon be bankrupt, Timon is confident that he will be able to call on his beneficiaries should the need arise. When his coffers are empty, he seeks money from his 'friends', but they all refuse help. The senators even condemn him to death for his extravagance. Timon invites all his former flatterers to a banquet, where he serves them lukewarm water, curses them, and drives them from his house. Fulminating against mankind, he withdraws to the woods, where he lives off berries and roots. When he discovers gold, he merely uses it to corrupt the Athenians further and to reward his loyal Flavius. Still embittered, Timon refuses to help the Athenians against the general Alcibiades, who takes Athens and avenges Timon's wrongs. Meanwhile Timon has gone off to die, and is buried in a grave bearing a curse on humankind.

There is much that is untypical for Shakespeare in this play: an embittered central figure with little heroic stature, a failure fully to integrate the Alcibiades sub-plot, irregular versification, and several loose ends. This has given rise to thinking that *Timon of Athens* was written with a collaborator (possibly Thomas Middleton), or that it remained unfinished and was never performed in his lifetime. The play may however be recognized as a product of a dark period in Shakespeare's maturity before he turned to his four late romances, which all end in reconciliation. In Alcibiades' willingness to confine his revenge to those who wronged Timon, one can detect the generosity of spirit that was to become evident in *The *Tempest*. Peter Brook opened the Paris base of his Centre for Theatrical Research with a successful production of the play in 1974.

Tiny Alice

A: Edward Albee **Pf:** 1964, New York **Pb:** 1965 **G:** Drama in 3 acts **S:** Cardinal's garden, and library and sitting room in Miss Alice's castle, 1960s **C:** 4m, 1f

A Lawyer brings a Cardinal a proposal from Miss Alice, the richest woman in the world, that she donate $2 billion to the Catholic Church with the proviso that the lay brother Julian come to her castle to finalize the deal. Julian enters Miss Alice's strange castle, one of whose extraordinary features is a large model of the castle in the library which exactly reflects events in the 'real' castle. Brother Julian, who had already endured a loss of faith resulting in being committed to an asylum, finds himself attracted to Alice. Once again, he enters a crisis of faith, as his love for Alice and the need to secure her donation conflict with his vow of celibacy. He marries Alice, but her servants, the Lawyer and the Butler, reveal that he has married merely a fleshly surrogate of the 'Tiny Alice' living in the model. Julian is unable to accept the truth of the situation, and the Lawyer shoots him. The Cardinal leaves with a briefcase full of money, while Julian dies backed against the model as though crucified. As he finally expires, saying that he accepts Alice's will, her shadow plunges the stage into darkness.

After the popular success of **Who's Afraid of Virginia Woolf*, Albee flouted all expectations by creating a piece that he conceded might not be understood in 'a single viewing'. On one level, the play explores the struggles of a man of faith with sexual attraction and financial expediency. On another, the play 'is an examination of how much false illusion we need to get through life'.

Discovering Miss Alice to be a mere illusion of a Platonic reality represented by the model, Julian is asked to face the truth and live without religion, and accept that death will envelop him in total darkness.

'Tis Folly to be Wise. See WOE FROM WIT.

'Tis Pity She's a Whore

A: John Ford **Pf:** *c.*1629–33, London **Pb:** 1633 **G:** Trag. in 5 acts; blank verse and prose **S:** Parma, Italy, Renaissance period **C:** 11m, 4f, extras

Annabella, a beautiful lady of Parma, has three suitors: Grimaldi, a Roman; Soranzo, a wealthy nobleman from Parma, who is also pursuing Hippolita, a married woman at court; and a simpleton Bergetto. But no one compares with her brother Giovanni, who has already confessed to his tutor that he has an incestuous infatuation for his sister. Giovanni begs Annabella to kill him to expiate his sin, but she admits to her own love for him, and they embrace. Although Hippolita declares that her husband has died on a sea voyage, Soranzo rejects her, and so she plots revenge. Grimaldi too wishes to dispose of his rival, Soranzo, but in the dark mistakenly kills poor Bergetto. At the ensuing wedding of Annabella and Soranzo there is a masque led by a lady in white, who reveals herself as Hippolita. As she dies from drinking a poisoned cup given by Soranzo's loyal servant, she curses the marriage. Discovering that Annabella is pregnant and learning from her servant that her brother Giovanni is the father, Soranzo plans his revenge on the incestuous couple at a public banquet. Forewarned, Giovanni saves Annabella's honour by stabbing her to death, enters the banquet with her heart on his dagger, fights with Soranzo, and kills him. Giovanni is slain by Soranzo's followers, and Giovanni's father dies of grief.

Ford offers here a compassionate view of two young lovers, who discover a pure and beautiful love amidst the treachery and deceit of the Italian court. This, the best of Ford's plays and arguably the last significant classical tragedy in the English language, goes beyond the usual elements of revenge drama to introduce a truly tragic recognition, that, however honourable Giovanni's and Annabella's feelings for each other, their love is doomed. Ford is not excusing incest nor lost in a macabre fascination for it; instead, as the title implies, he feels keenly the terrible pity of it all and the sense of waste of two young and admirable individuals. The theme of incest was too delicate for audiences until the 20th century, when it has been performed as frequently as *The *Duchess of Malfi* and *The *Changeling*.

Titus Andronicus (*The most lamentable Romaine Tragedie of Titus Andronicus*)

A: William Shakespeare **Pf:** *c.*1592–4, London **Pb:** 1594 **G:** Trag. in 5 acts; blank verse and prose **S:** Ancient Rome **C:** 18m, 2f, extras

Returning triumphant from the wars against the Goths, Titus Andronicus orders his son slain in battle to be buried. He also commands that the eldest son of Tamora, the captive Queen of the Goths, should be sacrificed. Despite having been nominated emperor by popular assent, he steps down in favour of Saturninus, the older son of the late emperor, and even offers him the hand of his daughter Lavinia, although she is betrothed to Saturninus' brother Bassianus. Lavinia escapes with her lover, assisted by her brothers, and Titus kills one of them. Bassianus marries Lavinia, and Saturninus marries Tamora, who vows to have vengeance on all the Andronici. Another captive Aaron the Moor, who is Tamora's secret lover, is resolved to destroy all the Romans. Tamora's sons murder Bassianus, and rape Lavinia, cutting out her tongue and severing her hands. Titus is persuaded to sacrifice his hand to ransom his two sons, whose heads are then sent to him. Maddened with rage, Titus sends out his son Lucius to raise an army to march on Rome, murders Tamora's sons, and offers them to her baked in a pie. At the banquet Titus kills first Lavinia, and then Tamora, Saturninus murders Titus, and Lucius kills Saturninus. Lucius, the new emperor, then orders the death of Aaron, who had tried to escape.

Written in the tradition of the Senecan revenge tragedy, the crudely sensational action of *Titus Andronicus* consigned it after early popularity to relative obscurity, many critics doubting whether it was indeed written by Shakespeare. At least since Peter Brook's 1955 production, however, with Laurence Olivier as Titus, the play has enjoyed many revivals, and its qualities have been recognized, most notably its powerful language and sophisticated structure. Its extreme cruelty is now well understood by a society aware of the atrocities of the last 100 years and by an audience with a taste for the grotesque.

To Damascus (Parts 1, 2, and 3) (*Till Damaskus*)

AT: *The Road to Damascus* **A:** August Strindberg **W:** 1898–1904 **Pf:** (1) 1900, Stockholm; (2) 1924, Gothenburg; (3) 1922, Gothenburg **Pb:** (1 and 2) 1900; (3) 1904 **Tr:** 1913 **G:** (1) Drama in 5 acts; (2 and 3) Dramas in 4 acts; Swedish prose **S:** Various locations in an indeterminate country, 1890s **C:** (1) 12m, 5f, extras; (2) 8m, 9f, 3 children, extras; (3) 14m, 8f, extras

Part 1. The Stranger (or The Unknown – *den Okände*) stands at a street corner, undecided about his future direction. He accosts a passing Lady and begs her to stay with him. Although he is expecting mail, he refuses to go to the post office for fear of what a letter might contain. He persuades the Lady to leave her husband, a Doctor, whom they then visit. The Doctor gives his consent to their elopement, and the Stranger and the Lady go to a hotel, where their dreams of freedom are shattered by their feelings of guilt. Penniless, they walk the roads until they come to the Lady's parental home. Her pious Mother forces her daughter to read the Stranger's book. Having 'eaten of the tree of knowledge', the horrified Lady drives the Stranger away. Three months later, he is recuperating at an asylum in a convent, having been found delirious on the mountain clutching a cross. The Confessor curses him, and the Stranger retraces his steps. He returns to the Mother, who tells him that he is on the road to Damascus and that he [like Saul] must seek forgiveness. He finds the Lady, and goes with her to the Doctor, who refuses to forgive him. Back at the street corner, the Stranger collects his mail, which contains money. This will allow them to return to the mountains, but first the Lady induces him to go with her to church. *Part 2.* The Stranger and the Lady are living together unhappily. She is pregnant and makes his life miserable by intercepting his mail and preventing his scientific work. The Doctor, now very resentful about their elopement, reappears to add to their unhappiness. When the Lady goes into labour, her Mother tortures the Stranger by telling him that it is not his child. His experiments at making gold are nevertheless successful, and he is invited to a lavish banquet to hail the great scientist. However, the banquet transforms itself into a nightmarish occasion, and the Stranger is exposed as a charlatan who cannot pay the bill. At the Lady's bedside, he wonders whether he merely dreamed of the banquet. When a daughter is born, he abandons the Lady, fearful lest he should become too attached to the little girl. He is persuaded to return to them by an alter ego, the Beggar, whom he had encountered in Part 1. The Confessor persuades him to accompany him back to a monastery. *Part 3.* The Stranger is led by the Confessor up long mountain paths, where they encounter fellow pilgrims, including his daughter from his first marriage Sylvia. He then meets the Lady, who is in mourning for the death of their baby Mitzi. His way takes him past sulphur springs and Venus-worshippers, where he meets the Tempter and Maja, the old nurse of his first child. The Lady has become beautiful in her suffering, and she reveals herself as the Stranger's mother, ready to console him. They marry again and enjoy brief happiness. But the Stranger continues his search. Reaching the monastery, the Prior urges him to learn to forgive himself and to abandon questioning. Instead, the Stranger gives himself up to a symbolic death, and the Confessor prays that he may enjoy eternal rest.

Considered by some to be Strindberg's greatest work, *To Damascus* is certainly a major achievement: a dream-like blending of Strindberg's own life, powerfully theatrical scenes, and a relentless searching after enlightenment, informed by the philosophy of

Swedenborg. It had a decisive influence on modernist drama, offering a model of the *Stationendrama* (drama of stations), a common feature of German Expressionist plays, in which a central character passes through a series of stations, usually in the quest for redemption. On his journey he encounters unnamed figures, many of whom are manifestations of aspects of his own personality or the same character reappearing in a different guise. Most disturbingly, the Lady, who contains the redemptive features of the 'eternal womanly' celebrated in Goethe's **Faust*, can, especially in Part 2, be transformed into an evil persecutor.

Toller

A: Tankred Dorst **Pf:** 1968, Stuttgart **Pb:** 1968 **Tr:** No pub. trans. **G:** Hist. drama in 30 scenes; German prose **S:** Various locations in Munich, 1919, and USA, 1939 **C:** 28 actors, playing over 50 roles

In the political vacuum following the defeat of Germany in the First World War, the revolutionary poet Erich Mühsam proclaims the establishment of a Councils' Republic in Bavaria on 6 April 1919. The Central Council comprises a motley collection of intellectuals, workers, and peasants, and appoint as its chairman Ernst Toller, a young Jewish playwright and poet. Eugen Leviné, a Russian Communist, opposes the romantic and non-violent aspirations of the Council (characterized by an extract from Toller's **Masses and Men*) and wants to place it under the control of the Communist Party. Because most of the leading Council members are Jewish, they face anti-Semitic ridicule. On 13 April, Mühsam is arrested by government forces, and Leviné takes over the Council, insisting to the reluctant Toller on the use of force. In 1939 Toller is seen reading his memoirs to an audience of American ladies. Back in 1919, as the Communists proceed with arrests and shootings, government forces prepare to march on Munich. As the Council faces defeat, Leviné prepares to escape to Switzerland. Members of the Central Council are arrested, and Toller goes into hiding with an aristocratic friend. Toller is brought to trial on 16 July, and while he delivers an impassioned speech in defence of the revolution, workers are led away to be shot. Toller, the harmless poet, is merely sentenced to five years' imprisonment.

In 1968, the year of student revolts across Europe, Dorst's play explored the role of the intellectual in a revolutionary context and confronted the sombre recognition that successful revolutions had to be achieved and maintained by force and not through the unrealistic idealism of a writer like the Expressionist Toller. The intricacies of the political situation are represented by a sequence of skilfully composed scenes covering the whole spectrum of those involved, from government to workers, making this one of the most significant post-Brechtian political plays of European theatre.

Tom Thumb (*The Tragedy of Tragedies, or the Life and Death of Tom Thumb the Great*)

A: Henry Fielding **Pf:** 1730, London **Pb:** in expanded version, 1731 **G:** Burlesque in 3 acts; blank verse and a little prose **S:** King Arthur's court and a plain nearby, indeterminate period **C:** 11m, 5f, extras

King Arthur and his drunken wife Dollallolla await the return of the tiny Tom Thumb, who has slain a band of invading giants. The King is in love with the captured giantess Glumdalca, while the Queen secretly yearns for Tom Thumb. As a reward for his victory Tom requests the hand of the King's daughter Huncamunca. This is granted, to the dismay of both the Queen and of Tom's rival at court, the evil Lord Grizzle. At first enchanted by Tom, then equally rapidly won over by Grizzle, Huncamunca finally marries Tom. When the disappointed Grizzle appears with a marriage licence, Huncamunca offers to marry both men. Angrily rejecting this proposal, Grizzle leads a rebellion against the King. In the ensuing battle Grizzle kills Glumdalca, but Tom wins the day by slaying Grizzle. Leading a victory parade, Tom is swallowed by a cow. Distraught at the news, the courtiers murder each other, until only the King is left. He commits suicide.

Shaw regarded Fielding as the best dramatist since Shakespeare, and *Tom Thumb* was his most successful burlesque. Written at the age of 23 as a short afterpiece, it was published the following year in a longer version with extensive mock erudite annotations. While the satire of the bombast and improbable events of contemporary tragedy have lost their resonance today, the ludicrous language and parade of lively grotesques (even the lovely Huncamunca has a 'Brandy Nose') can still be a source of theatrical fun, in a way similar to that of Jarry's youthful farce **King Ubu*.

Tongue-Lashing. See OFFENDING THE AUDIENCE.

Tonight We Improvise (*Questa sera si recita a soggetto*)

A: Luigi Pirandello **Pf**: 1930, Königsberg **Pb**: 1930 **Tr**: 1932 **G**: Drama in 3 acts; Italian prose **S**: A theatre and a Sicilian town, 1920s **C**: 9m, 3f

Noises are heard backstage, and suddenly the director Doctor Hinkfuss appears in the auditorium. With interruptions from the audience, he announces the adaptation of a short story by Pirandello. After philosophizing on the permanence of art compared with the flux of reality, he introduces the Sicilian setting and characters. The leading lady Signora Ignazia, mother to four pretty daughters, scandalizes the locals by throwing wild parties, to which airmen are invited. Her long-suffering husband consoles himself with a lugubrious singer. The leading man playing one of the airmen, Rico Verri, declares that he will improvise tonight, speaking words that spring spontaneously from the character he is to play. After the family and escorts have pushed their way into the audience to watch a film, Hinkfuss offers the spectators the choice between watching actors continuing the play in the foyer or observing the scene changes on stage. At another party the father insists that he cannot die according to the script, whereupon he drops dead. By now the actors are totally identified with their characters and dismiss the restricting influence of Hinkfuss. The leading lady is now made up to represent her eldest daughter, who gets married to Verri. Violently jealous, Verri drives her to her death as she sings from *Il trovatore*. Hinkfuss reappears and congratulates everyone on their performances, due largely, he claims, to his direction.

This is a remarkable example of postmodernist deconstruction, some half a century before this phrase became current. Sometimes unhappily verbose, the play is nevertheless an extraordinary exploration of the relationship between art and reality and of the nature of the theatrical process, including action offstage and the original idea of actors watching a film, now a cliché of contemporary performance.

Too Clever by Half. See WOE FROM WIT.

Top Girls

A: Caryl Churchill **Pf**: 1982; London **Pb**: 1982; rev. 1984 **G**: Pol. drama in 2 acts **S**: Restaurant and employment agency office, London, and Joyce's home, rural England, early 1980s **C**: 16f

Marlene celebrates her promotion to manager of the Top Girls Employment Agency by inviting to a meal a curious selection of female guests drawn from history and legend. The Victorian explorer Isabella Bird, the 9th-century Pope Joan, and the belligerent peasant woman Dull Gret from Brueghel's painting are distinguished for fulfilling normally male roles; the 13th-century Japanese courtesan Lady Nijo and the legendary Patient Griselda, who tolerated unbelievable cruelty from her husband, represent suffering but resilient women. Marlene interviews a candidate for a dead-end secretarial job. Two teenage girls, Angie and Kit, discuss sex and the threat of nuclear war. Angie plans to leave her mother Joyce to visit her aunt in London. She duly arrives at Marlene's office, where her aunt is surprised to see her but allows her to stay. Mrs Kidd, wife of Howard, one of Marlene's employees, comes to complain about Marlene's promotion over his head: 'What's it going to do for him working for a woman?' Howard has a heart attack, and Marlene tells her clever, well-educated assistants that Angie is 'not going to make it'. A year earlier, Marlene visits her sister Joyce. It turns out that Marlene is Angie's real mother, and that, with some resentment, Joyce has brought her up, so that Marlene could have a successful career.

After its curiously surreal first scene, *Top Girls* becomes a wholly naturalistic piece about the new type of achieving woman, embodied and promoted by Margaret Thatcher. With an honesty that upset radical feminists, Churchill showed how characters like Marlene could become even more ruthless than men ('I believe in the individual. Look at me'); only Joyce's semi-articulate socialism can provide an answer to Angie's final word: 'Frightening.'

Torch Song Trilogy (The International Stud; Fugue in a Nursery; Widows and Children First!)

A: Harvey Fierstein **Pf:** (1) 1978, (2 and 3) 1979, New York; (as trilogy) 1982, New York **Pb:** 1981 **G:** 3 dramas in 1 act **S:** (1) Gay bar, Arnold's apartment, and Ed's hotel room, New York, *c.*1973; (2) Arnold's apartment and gay bar, New York, and Ed's farmhouse near Montreal, *c.*1974; (3) Arnold's apartment and park bench, *c.*1979 **C:** (1) 2m, 1f; (2) 3m, 1f; (3) 3m, 1f

(1) *The International Stud.* Arnold Beckoff is a 24-year-old Jewish drag queen at the International Stud. He is already disillusioned with life, aware that, as gay culture becomes accepted, his days as a performer may be numbered. Longing for an 'international stud', a sophisticated older man, he meets Ed Reiss, a rich Canadian teacher and landowner in his thirties, and they begin dating. However, Ed is bisexual, and Arnold becomes very jealous when Ed begins an affair with Laurel, a lively 35-year-old. Reluctantly, but prompted by his despair over Ed, Arnold has anonymous sex in the back room at the International Stud. After five months' separation, Ed comes looking for Arnold. Arnold is angry, they fight, declare their love, and Arnold decides to risk seeing him again. (2) *Fugue in a Nursery.* A year later, Laurel, who is now living with Ed, invites Arnold and his handsome new boyfriend Alan (18) to spend the weekend at Ed's farm. Arnold still has strong feelings for Ed but is excited by Alan; Ed is annoyed that Arnold has brought Alan; Laurel proves remarkably tolerant, apparently attracted by bisexual and gay men. Ed and Arnold spend the afternoon together, and Laurel gets closer to Alan. Arnold confesses that he is in love with a man he meets regularly in the back room of the International Stud. While Ed seduces Alan, Arnold warns Laurel that she is merely 'living proof of [Ed's] normality'. Arnold and Alan leave early, and Laurel walks out, perhaps never to return. Soon after, Arnold and Alan decide to settle down together, and Ed and Laurel resolve to get married. (3) *Widows and Children First!* Five years later, Alan has died in a homophobic attack, Arnold has adopted 15-year-old David, and Ed, who has separated from Laurel, comes to stay with Arnold. Arnold's mother, an archetypal Jewish mother, comes to visit him. David returns from school, and Ma imagines he must be Arnold's latest lover. She is even more horrified to discover that he is his son. Arnold seeks a reconciliation with his mother, since they are both 'widows'. However, she insists on leaving; but Ed decides to stay, and David dedicates a record on a phone-in radio show to his adoptive father.

One of the most acclaimed gay plays of the 20th century, *Torch Song Trilogy* explores with great sensitivity and honesty the tense but profound relationship between Arnold and Ed (a torch song was a popular song of the 1930s expressing unrequited love, and the action, especially in *The International Stud,* is frequently interrupted with sad song). Going well beyond the camp bitchiness of Crowley's **Boys in the Band*, Fierstein explores pain and joy which proceed from emotions that are universally recognizable and not confined to homosexual relationships.

Tot, kto poluchaet poshchechiny. See HE WHO GETS SLAPPED.

Tou E Was Wronged. See INJUSTICE TO DOU E.

Tou O Was Wronged. See INJUSTICE TO DOU E.

Tour Guide, The (*Die Fremdenführerin*)

AT: *The Tourist Guide* A: Botho Strauss **Pf:** 1986, Berlin **Pb:** 1986 **Tr:** 1987 **G:** Drama in 2 acts; German prose **S:** Olympia stadium, holiday bungalow, and mountain cabin, Greece, 1980s **C:** 2m, 1f, extras

Kristina, working as a tourist guide in Olympia, meets Martin, a German teacher of about 45. Kristina spends the night with Martin, even though she loves a young archaeologist Vassily, who is an alcoholic. Later she brings her drunken lover to Martin's house, and he accuses her of being totally dependent on this wastrel. Martin sleeps with her again and wants to be hers, but is dismayed to find Vassily in his house and throws him out. Kristina sleeps on the grass outside Martin's house, but only after some days does he let her in again. Kristina asks Martin for 1,000 Deutschmarks to send Vassily back to Germany for his health. Vassily's sister comes to take him away. Martin wants Kristina to come to Germany with him, but she remains elusive. Vassily drinks himself to death, and Martin and Kristina go to live in a primitive mountain cabin. Kristina's grieving, the silence and isolation of the cabin, and the oppressiveness of their relationship begin to take their toll. Martin becomes severely dehydrated. Kristina has to beat off a Pan figure, who appears at the window. Kristina leaves and returns, saying that she has found someone else to love. Martin is left alone, reading about Pan, who 'held in his hands reeds instead of a nymph's body', reeds that he then fashioned into pan pipes.

In lyrical language and hauntingly evocative scenes, Strauss traces the doomed affair between a teacher in a mid-life crisis and a young woman, who is 'the *woman*, something that will never cease, as everything else, to be the opposite' of Martin. She guides him into dangerous areas of experience, and although she abandons him, he, like Strauss, can make music from the reeds he is left clutching.

Towneley Cycle of Mystery Plays, The

AT: *The Wakefield Cycle* **A:** Anon ('The Wakefield Master') **Pf:** Late 15th–16th c., probably West Yorkshire **Pb:** 1897 **G:** Cycle of 32 mystery plays; Middle English (Yorkshire dialect) verse **S:** Heaven and earth, from the Creation to the Last Judgement **C:** approx. 50m, 5f, many extras

The one incomplete manuscript comprises 32 scenes. Closely following the sequence of scenes in *The *York Cycle of Mystery Plays*, *The Towneley Cycle* however omits scenes devoted to Adam and Eve in the Garden of Eden and their banishment, crossing the Red Sea, the trials before Herod and Pilate, and the beatification of the Virgin Mary. The main addition is *The Second Shepherds' Play* (*Alia Eorundem* or *Secunda Pastorum*).

Towneley refers to the family which owned the manuscript and is now preferred to the *Wakefield* title, since links to that city are somewhat tenuous. In some scenes like *Herod the Great*, which deals with the massacre of the Innocents, and in *The Shepherds' Plays*, the second of which introduces a character from folklore, Mak the Sheep-stealer from the South, the hand of a skilful dramatist can be detected. The so-called Wakefield Master was arguably the greatest English playwright before Shakespeare. He wrote vigorously, creating recognizable contemporary characters: the raging tyrant, like the contemporary Earl of Suffolk, and simple and humorously drawn shepherds, like many of those in the audience; for it was money from West Yorkshire wool that probably financed the staging of this cycle. Unlike the **Chester* and **York Cycles, it is possible that this cycle, like The *N-Town Plays, was staged on fixed platforms rather than on pageant wagons. The cycle was successfully revived in Wakefield in 1980.*

Toy Cart, The. See LITTLE CLAY CART, THE.

Trachiniae. See WOMEN OF TRACHIS.

Tragedy of an Elderly Gentleman, The. See BACK TO METHUSELAH.

Tragedy of Jane Shore, The. See JANE SHORE.

Tragedy of Tragedies, The See TOM THUMB.

Tragedy Rehearsed, A. See CRITIC, THE.

Traitors

A: Stephen Sewell **Pf:** 1979, Melbourne **Pb:** 1983 **G:** Drama in 3 acts, prologue, and epilogue **S:** Leningrad and Moscow, 1927, and a village south of Moscow, 1941 C: 3m, 5f, extras

In the Prologue in 1941, Anna, a Trotskyist, and her cousin Ekaterina discuss the German advance on Moscow and the hanging of Russian traitors, i.e. Nazi sympathizers. In 1926 in Leningrad, Anna is hoping to join forces with the supporters of Zinoviev to oppose Stalin, even though she is discomfited by the Zinovievist Rubin's chauvinistic attitude to women. At the station, Anna encounters Giorgi Krasin, a secret policeman pretending to be an animal trainer. They travel together to Moscow and have sex on the train. Rubin is arrested. At Cheka (Secret Police) headquarters in Moscow, Krasin complains to his superior officer Kolya Lebeshev that the killing of the anarchist Oppositionist Makarov in London was an arbitrarily brutal act. But Lebeshev argues that 'you have to prod [Russia] with burning irons before it'll do what's good for it'. Lebeshev no longer trusts Krasin and has him followed. Anna teams up with Nadezdah, an old Bolshevik, who believe his 'duty is to the Revolution, not the Party'. Rubin is forced to confess after being interrogated and brutalized by Krasin, and Stalin and Bukharin begin to eliminate the Oppositionists. In desperation, the Oppositionists hold a street demonstration and are fired on. Krasin warns Anna to flee then shoots himself. In the Epilogue set in 1941, Anna and Ekaterina prepare to fight against the Germans.

Sewell's play, the first of his to enjoy a professional production and to be transferred to London, deftly blends political debate over the need to use force to 'defend the Revolution' with personal questions of love and betrayal. Although somewhat predictable, the play is a refreshing departure in that it goes beyond Australian issues.

Translations

A: Brian Friel **Pf:** 1980, Derry, Northern Ireland **Pb:** 1981 **G:** Hist. drama in 3 acts **S:** Hedge-school in a barn, County Donegal, Ireland, 1833 **C:** 7m, 3f

In the fictional village of Baile Beag (Ballybeg), Hugh, a 60-year-old who is fond of his drink, runs the 'hedge-school' with the help of his lame son Manus. A new 'National School' is being built, and Hugh has applied for the post of teacher there. The other innovation in the area is the arrival of British soldiers ('Redcoats'), who are engaged in an ordnance survey of the country. Manus opens up the school, since his father has not yet staggered back from a local christening. Manus tries to get the seemingly dumb Sarah to speak; teaches Maire, Bridget, and Doalty, all in their twenties; and exchanges Greek and Latin tags with 60-year-old Jimmy Jack Cassie, who is fluent in both languages. Eventually, it becomes clear that they are all speaking Irish, for this is the Gaeltacht, an Irish-speaking community. There is talk of missing Redcoats' horses, of the risk of potato blight, and of the fact that only English will be spoken in the new National School. Hugh eventually arrives, but is soon surprised by the return after six years of a younger son Owen, now the wealthy owner of several shops in Dublin. Owen acts as interpreter for the English soldiers, diplomatically translating Captain Lancey's colonialist undertaking to make it sound as though the map-making will benefit the locals. Owen and Lancey's subordinate Lieutenant Yolland translate Irish place names into Anglicized versions for the map. Yolland develops an affection and respect for the place and its language. Manus is offered the post of teacher on a little offshore island, hoping that this might induce Maire to come with him, but Yolland and Maire, despite difficulties of communication, fall in love with each other. The next day Yolland has gone missing, a probable victim of Irish rebels, and Manus decides to go away, although Owen warns him that this will make him a prime suspect. The army threatens to raze the area and evict everyone, if Yolland is not found. The army camp goes up in flames. Hugh learns that he is not to be made the teacher of the new school, but Maire, now mentally unbalanced, wants him to teach her English.

Friel became Ireland's leading playwright, and this is probably his finest play, in which he discovers a sophisticated metaphor for British colonialism in Ireland, with well-meaning but disastrous 'translation' of its subtle language and remarkably sophisticated culture into alien forms – an impoverishment for the rulers as well as for the natives. This was the first production of the Field Day Theatre Company, which set out to give a voice to the local community of Londonderry or Derry (itself a city with two names, each representing one side of the sectarian divide). At a time when languages are dying out, and with it community identity and dignity, at the rate of one every two weeks, Friel's play seems particularly relevant.

Travesties

A: Tom Stoppard **Pf**: 1974, London **Pb**: 1975 G: Com. in 2 acts S: Zurich, 1918 and *c.*1960 C: 5m, 3f

During the First World War a number of major figures gather in the safe haven of a library in Zurich: James Joyce has come from Paris and is dictating *Ulysses* to his secretary; Romanian-born Tristan Tzara paves the way for Dadaism by cutting up a poem and randomly drawing words from a hat; and Lenin discusses revolution in Russian with his wife Nadya. Amongst discussions on the nature and function of art, the action centres on Joyce's forthcoming production of *The *Importance of Being Earnest*, in which Joyce plays Lady Bracknell, and Tzara Jack Worthing. Having been cast in the major role of Algernon Moncrieff, Henry Carr, a minor British consular official, reminiscing in old age, imagines that he was at the centre of historical events, even relegating the Consul himself to the role of his manservant. Scenes from Wilde's play are enacted, passages from *Ulysses* get muddled with Lenin's work on imperialism, and Carr sues Joyce for the return of money spent on his costume. Despite attempts by the British to detain him, Lenin leaves for Russia, where he will play a decisive part in the October Revolution. Carr marries the librarian, fortuitously named Cecily.

Just as Stoppard had spectacularly revisited **Hamlet* in **Rosencrantz and Guildenstern Are Dead*, he here turned to another classic of the English-language theatre, using Wildean dialogue and situations to bring together very diverse characters to debate the function of art and to contemplate historical events and the role played by chance in their outcome. Significantly, Lenin plays no role in Joyce's production, and his tedious presence, which cuts across the sparkle of otherwise witty dialogue, invites the audience to view his aspirations negatively.

Trelawny of the 'Wells'

A: Arthur Wing Pinero **Pf**: 1898, London **Pb**: 1899 G: Com. in 4 acts S: London, 1860s C: 11m, 7f, extras

Rose Trelawny is taking her leave of the company of the Wells Theatre. She is engaged to be married to Arthur Gower, and his family intend that, before the union is finally agreed, she should give up her career and stay with them in Cavendish Square. One month later, and Rose is utterly bored by the Gowers and their friends. Letting her theatrical friends into the house, they drink and are having noisy fun, when they are confronted by Arthur. Rose admits that she can never marry him or attune to his way of life. Returning to the stage, she is no longer able to act the empty roles of contemporary plays. Encouraging one of the company Tom Wrench to produce one of his own plays entitled *Life*, fellow actress Avonia Bunn and she even get Arthur's grandfather Sir William to help back the production. Watched by Sir William, the rehearsal of the play begins – with Arthur cast as the leading man. Rose and Arthur will be able to marry after all.

The character of Tom Wrench is a tribute to Pinero's predecessor T. W. Robertson, whose plays injected new realism into the theatre of the 1860s. At the same time, Pinero offers a corrective to the somewhat unrealistic aspirations of **Caste* by recognizing that Rose's transference to high society cannot be accomplished as easily as Esther's in the earlier play. On the other hand, the comic solution of Arthur dropping to Rose's social level and joining her milieu is ultimately as impractical within the Victorian class system as that depicted by Robertson. No matter; the lively depiction of theatrical life, drawn from Pinero's own experience, makes for an entertaining and still popular drama.

Trial of Dedan Kimathi, The

A: Ngugi wa Thiong'o and Micere Githae Mugo **Pf:** 1975, Nairobi **Pb:** 1976 **G:** Pol. drama in 3 acts; English and Swahili prose and free verse **S:** Courtroom, cell, street, Nairobi, street in Nyeri, guerrilla camp in the forest, 1956 **C:** 24m, 3f, extras

Dedan Kimathi is on trial for possessing a firearm. Waitina, a white police officer, and his soldiers terrorize the natives, searching them and demanding their passbooks, and arresting innocent villagers in case they support the Mau Mau terrorists. The soldiers hope that when Kimathi is hanged, the fight for independence will stop. Kimathi challenges the validity of a court set up by colonialist oppressors to administer their own laws. When the Judge adjourns the trial, an armed white settler rages at the blacks in the courtroom. The Judge visits Kimathi in his cell. He is Shaw Henderson, charged by the British to negotiate with Kimathi. He offers to spare Kimathi's life if Kimathi will plead guilty and help him root out the terrorists. Kimathi refuses. He is then visited by bankers who promise prosperity for Kenya if he will end the armed struggle, and is further tempted by a black business executive, a politician, and a priest. When these appeals fail, Henderson strikes Kimathi and orders him to be whipped. In flashback, we see Kimathi generously forgiving collaborators, but they betray him, leading to his arrest. Kimathi is sentenced to death, but two young Kenyans produce a gun and lead a final triumphant chorus.

This play is an honestly one-sided view of Kenya's struggle for independence: only the gun-toting white settler has lines that offer an alternative perspective; all the others are anonymous figures uttering bland clichés. It is a fluent propagandistic piece of theatre, whose call for freedom resonates well beyond the struggle for Kenyan independence.

Trickster, The. See PSEUDOLUS.

Trickster of Seville, The (*El Burlador de Sevilla y convidado de piedra)*

AT: *The Rogue/The Playboy/The Joker/The Deceiver of Seville* **A:** Tirso de Molina **Pf:** 1625, Naples **Pb:** 1630 **Tr:** 1923 **G:** Drama in 3 acts; Spanish verse **S:** Naples, Tarragona, Seville, and Dos Hermanas, 14th c. **C:** 14m, 6f, extras

At the Court of Naples Don Juan seduces the Duchess Isabella by pretending to be her fiancé. He manages to escape only thanks to the help of his uncle, the Spanish ambassador. On his voyage to Spain, his ship is wrecked and he is saved by a fishermaiden, whom he promptly seduces. Once back at the Court of Seville, he is ordered by the king to marry Isabella in order to restore her honour. Her desperate fiancé is compensated with the hand of Donna Anna. She is not best pleased, since she loves another, the Marquese de la Mota. Once again pretending to be her lover, Don Juan succeeds in gaining access to Donna Anna. However, Anna recognizes him in time and calls for help. Her father arrives and is killed by Don Juan in a sword fight. The unfortunate Marquese is arrested for the crime, while Don Juan occupies himself by seducing the peasant girl Aminta on her wedding day. Don Juan now invites the statue of Anna's father to a banquet. The statue appears and challenges Don Juan to come with him into his tomb. Finally, Don Juan's servant describes to all the victims of his lechery how in the tomb he began to experience the torments awaiting him in hell and was dragged off to his death. The King is now able to pair off the ill-treated lovers.

Molina's work is now best known as the original on which Mozart's *Don Giovanni* (1787) was ultimately based and has also been adapted by playwrights as diverse as Molière (1665), Grabbe (1829), Pushkin (1836), Alexandre Dumas (1836), Zorrilla (1844), Shaw (1903), E. Rostand (1921), Horváth (1937), Tennessee Williams (1953), and Max Frisch (1953). However, Molina's play deserves attention not just as source material, but in its own right as a piece distinguished by an absorbing plot and bold characterization. While Molina confronts an audience with a moral tale in which the protagonist is given his just deserts for his immoral behaviour, it is impossible not to enjoy the skill with which Don Juan exploits each situation to achieve his goal. In the moral ambiguities of the story lie not only the pleasure of this play but also the longevity of the theme.

Trick to Catch the Old One, A

A: Thomas Middleton Pf: *c.*1604–6, London Pb: 1608 G: Com. in 5 acts; prose and blank verse S: Leicestershire and London, early 17th c. C: 29m, 3f, extras

Through riotous living, Theodorus Witgood has lost all his money, some of it to his miserly old uncle Pecunius Lucre. Witgood hatches a plan to bring his Courtesan to London, pretending that she is a rich widow Jane Medler. He is convinced that his uncle, smelling money, will help him win his 'widow's' hand, and indeed Lucre offers his support. When news of Jane Medler's arrival spreads, she becomes a sought-after prize, wooed even by Lucre's business rival Walkadine Hoard. Witgood advises Widow Medler to marry Hoard, who thinks that her protestations of poverty are made to hide her wealth. They marry secretly, but Lucre, imagining he can still win Widow Medler for his nephew, restores all Witgood's money to him. Meanwhile Witgood serves a writ on the new Mistress Hoard, claiming breach of promise. Hoard agrees to pay Witgood's debts, if he will drop all claims on his new wife's wealth. Financially buoyant once more, Witgood is now free to marry his true love Mistress Joyce. Witgood and the Courtesan/Widow finally confess to their plot, which Hoard accepts with good grace, and all retire to celebrate the double wedding.

T.S. Eliot described Middleton as the greatest realist in Jacobean comedy, and it is certainly the case that his settings have greater authenticity than those of Ben Jonson. Moreover, while still delighting in the cunning stratagems of Jonsonian tricksters, we can see that a greater social dimension and awareness of class are replacing Jonson's focus on humours, thus forming a bridge between Elizabethan and Restoration comedy.

Trifles

A: Susan Glaspell Pf: 1916, Provincetown, Mass. Pb: 1920 G: Drama in 1 act S: Kitchen of a rundown Midwest farmhouse, *c.*1916 C: 3m, 2f

A farmer has been discovered strangled, and the sheriff and his men are investigating the case. The sheriff's wife Mrs Peters and a female neighbour Mrs Hale go through the household trifles in the kitchen and note the untidy room, uneven stitching in a quilt, a dead canary carefully laid in 'a pretty box', etc. They piece together enough evidence to convict the farmer's widow of the murder. However, in reconstructing the crime, the two women reflect on the life of abuse that the farmer's wife had to endure and agree that the poor woman was pushed beyond reasonable limits. Feeling guilty that they did nothing to help her, they agree to conceal the evidence, while the sheriff and his men vindicate their deception by dismissing their efforts as 'worrying over trifles'.

Co-founder of the Provincetown Players in 1915, Glaspell, who acted the role of Mrs Hale at the premiere, is at last receiving the recognition which is her due. *Trifles* is her most popular play, providing small casts with a piece that is well constructed and full of suspense. It also contains a progressive message about the failure of men to understand the significance of the domestic environment for women.

Trip to New York, A. See LION OF THE WEST, THE.

Trip to Washington, A. See LION OF THE WEST, THE.

Tri Sestry. See THREE SISTERS.

Troades. See TROJAN WOMEN.

Troilus and Cressida (*The Historie of Troylus and Cresseida*)

A: William Shakespeare Pf: *c.*1602–3, London Pb: 1609, 1623 G: Drama in 5 acts; blank verse and prose S: Troy and nearby plains, during the Trojan War C: 24m, 4f, extras

Troilus, a Trojan prince, is in love with Cressida, the daughter of the priest Calchas. So it is an easy task for her uncle the old Pandarus to bring them together. Meanwhile, in the opposing Greek camp the generals discuss how to end the war. Ulysses points to their lack of unity: above all, Achilles is to blame for refusing to fight. The Trojans propose a single combat to decide the war. Hector will represent the Trojans, and, on Ulysses' advice, Ajax will be the Greek champion. This decision infuriates Achilles, who intends to prove his valour again. Although Troilus and Cressida swear eternal love, she is taken by her father to the Greek camp, where she proves unfaithful, falling into the arms of the Greek general Diomedes. The single combat between Hector and Ajax is soon resolved: reminded of their blood ties, they abandon the fight. Despite the warnings of Cassandra and of his wife Andromache, Hector is treacherously waylaid by Achilles and brutally killed. The Greek leader Agamemnon now looks forward to an early end to the war, while the vengeful Troilus is determined to continue fighting.

Shakespeare's one venture into material dramatized by the Greek tragedians, based on the Homeric account of the Trojan War, is a curious piece. It has tragic elements, but no resolution; the title suggests that the focus is on the ill-fated love of Troilus and Cressida, but the events of the war are far more than a backdrop, dwarfing their personal problems. Shakespeare's cynical attitude to war, which seemed to earlier ages an unsuitable accompaniment to the stature of the Greek heroes, is now, in our unheroic age, much more acceptable, and the play is now quite frequently revived.

Trojan Women (*Troades*)

A: Euripides AT: *The Women of Troy* Pf: 415 BC, Athens Tr: 1780 G: Greek trag. in verse S: Outside the walls of Troy, just after its fall C: 3m, 5f, extras, chorus (f)

In the Prologue, Athene and the sea god Poseidon agree that they will subject the Greeks to violent storms and hardship on their journey home to Greece. After ten long years of the Trojan War, the Greeks are finally victorious and are disposing of the captive women of Troy. Their cruel orders are announced by a herald: the young prophetess Cassandra will become Agamemnon's slave-girl. Andromache, widow of the Trojan hero Hector, will have to go with Neoptolemus. The former queen of Troy Hecabe is to be enslaved to Odysseus. Cassandra prophesies how the Greeks will suffer, how Agamemnon will be killed, and how Odysseus will also have to endure hardship. Worse than the humiliation to which Andromache is to be subjected, news now comes that her little son Astyanax will have to be killed. When Menelaus arrives, Hecabe pleads with him to take revenge on his errant wife Helen for causing the war. Helen defends herself, and Menelaus weakens, claiming that she will be punished in Sparta after their return. The mangled body of little Astyanax is brought on, and, against the background of the flames destroying Troy, the mourning women are led away.

As in Aeschylus' **Persians*, Euripides takes the bold step of focusing on the suffering of those defeated at the hands of the Greeks. It may seem unjust that in the Prologue the gods determine that the Greeks shall have to suffer, but in the course of the play the inhuman behaviour of the victorious Greek army shows that they deserve everything that the gods have preordained. Euripides was also warning his contemporary Athenians: the previous year they had dealt brutally with the citizens of Melos, massacring all its adult men and enslaving its women and children. Here, in a series of powerfully dramatic episodes, the group of desolate, powerless women gain in moral stature what they cannot achieve in actual power. Because its theme of the sufferings caused by war has resonated down the centuries, *Trojan Women* is, together with **Medea*, one of the most frequently performed of Euripides' plays and has reappeared in later versions, notably by Seneca (1st c. AD) and by Franz Werfel (1916), in which Hecabe must endure the ultimate loss of freedom by being restrained from committing suicide in the flames of Troy. In 1965 Sartre adapted Euripides' play as a comment on France's colonial war in Algeria.

Trommeln in der Nacht. See DRUMS IN THE NIGHT.

True West

A: Sam Shepard Pf: 1980, San Francisco Pb: 1981 G: Drama in 2 acts S: Kitchen and alcove, southern Californian suburban home, 1970s C: 3m, 1f

Austin is a moderately successful screenwriter in his early thirties, who is living in his mother's house, while she is on holiday. He is surprised by the arrival of his older brother Lee, a drifter and petty criminal. Austin meets the Hollywood producer Saul Kimmer, who expresses interest in Austin's story. Lee arrives back with a stolen television set, invites Saul to a game of golf, and suggests that he might supply him with a real-life, 'true west' story. Lee gets Austin to type his story of the rivalry between two cowboys. The game of golf is a success, and Lee manages to sell his story to Saul, who now asks Austin to work on his brother's script. Angry at being ousted by his brother, Austin goes out and steals toasters, while Lee tries to write the story himself. Austin relents and agrees to script Lee's story if Lee will promise to take him to the desert with him. In a drunken bout, Lee smashes up his mother's kitchen and Austin's typewriter. Their mother arrives back unexpectedly to discover the mess they have made. Lee decides he has had enough and prepares to leave, but Austin insists that Lee must finish his story. Lee punches Austin, and Austin almost strangles Lee. Mom leaves, disgusted at their violence. Austin releases the inert Lee, but just as Austin is about to leave, Lee blocks his path. Blackout.

This is one of the less overtly theatrical pieces by Shepard, depicting in realistic dialogue the hostility but mutual dependence of the two brothers. In some ways they reflect the conflict within Shepard himself between the carefree amoral drifter and the sensitive writer: 'I just wanted to give a taste of what it feels like to be double-sided.'

Truth Suspected, The. See SUSPECT TRUTH.

Tsvishn Tsvey Veltn: De Dibuk. See DYBBUK, THE.

Tueur sans gages. See KILLER, THE.

Turandot

A: Carlo Gozzi Pf: 1762, Venice Pb: 1772 G: Fairy tale in 5 acts; Italian prose and some verse S: Peking and environs, indeterminate period C: 9m, 3f, extras

The beautiful but selfish Turandot, Princess of China, sets her suitors three riddles. She will marry any man who solves them; if he fails, he is beheaded and his head impaled on the city gates. Young Prince Calaf falls in love with Turandot, and, despite many warnings, undergoes her tests. He succeeds in solving all three riddles, but the furious Turandot treacherously denies him her hand. Calaf offers her a second chance: if she can guess his name and origin, he will withdraw. Adelma, a slave at the court, recognizes Calaf, and, frustrated in her own love for him, betrays his secret to Turandot. When Turandot solves Calaf's riddle, he decides to take his own life rather than live without Turandot. Holding him from suicide, she relents, and her happy father gives him Turandot's hand in marriage and all the lands of the empire. Adelma is rewarded with her freedom and the restoration of her kingdom.

In his *fiabe* (fables) Gozzi combined fairy-tale magic with elements of the *commedia dell'arte*, producing a popular and effective theatrical style. Beneath the beguiling exoticism there are moreover serious issues: Turandot's seemingly cruel behaviour proceeds at least in part from a desire to maintain her independence as a woman, and Adelma betrays Calaf out of desperation not malice. Operatic versions of *Turandot* were composed by Busoni (1918) and Puccini (1926).

Turista, La

A: Sam Shepard Pf: 1967, New York Pb: 1968 G: Com. in 2 acts S: A Mexican and an American hotel room, 1960s C: 6m, 1f

Kent and his wife Salem are American tourists, confined to bed in their hotel room in Mexico because of severe sunburn and an attack of 'la turista', i.e. diarrhoea. A native Boy comes to their room and refuses money to go away. Kent goes to the toilet and re-emerges very pale, wearing a cowboy hat and gun belt, and acknowledges that the USA is so 'clean and pure and immaculate' that its citizens are becoming 'lily-livered weaklings'. Discovering the Boy in his bed, Kent drops in a faint. Salem phones for a doctor and then has to rush to the toilet herself. A Witch-Doctor and his Son appear and conduct a ritual over Kent's body, which involves the sacrifice of two chickens. The Boy says that it is too late, since both Kent and Salem are dead, and refuses to leave with Salem to the States, because he is going to meet his father. The scene is transformed into a hotel room in the States. A Doctor (played by the same actor as the Witch-Doctor), who is dressed in Civil War costume, examines Kent. The Doctor diagnoses sleepy sickness and prescribes benzedrine, so that the couple can continue their journey to Mexico. The Doctor's Son wonders whether they should not go to Canada, where a corpse would be 'less noticeable'. Kent begins to transform into Frankenstein's monster. Doc shoots him but fails to stop Kent, who finally escapes by swinging off on a rope.

This wildly theatrical piece was Shepard's first full-length play and established his reputation as a new force in the American theatre. The sudden leaps of the plot, the reversal of time between the two acts, and the extravagant characters are all exploited to satirize the American way of life: the stereotypical American couple, named after cigarette brands, who are already dead, but for Kent apotheosis is achieved by becoming a monster created by science.

Tutor, The (*Der Hofmeister, oder Vorteile der Privaterziehung*)

AT: *The Advantages of Private Education* A: Jakob Michael Reinhold Lenz **Pf**: 1778, Hamburg **Pb**: 1774 **G**: Com. in 5 acts; German prose **S**: Insterburg, Heidelbrunn, Halle, Leipzig, and Königsberg in Germany, 18th c. **C**: 14m, 9f

Läuffer becomes tutor to the children of Major von Berg, whose daughter Gustchen is in love with her cousin Fritz. When Fritz is sent away to university, Gustchen gives herself to Läuffer and becomes pregnant by him. She leaves her parents and hides in the home of an old lady, where she gives birth to her child. Läuffer also runs away and assumes a false identity as a schoolteacher. He is discovered by Major von Berg, who shoots at him, wounding him in the arm. Consumed with guilt, Läuffer castrates himself. Gustchen tries to drown herself, but is providentially saved by the arrival of her father. All ends happily. Fritz, who has also endured serious problems, even being imprisoned for helping a friend, will marry Gustchen, and Läuffer is fortunate in finding a peasant girl who is willing to marry him despite his emasculation.

Based on a historical incident, *The Tutor* is one of the major plays of the *Sturm und Drang* ('Storm and Stress'). Within the framework of a conventional comedy, even including a resolution through the discovery of the parentage of one of the minor characters, Lenz addresses serious contemporary issues – in this case the dangers of ignoring the romantic and erotic impulses of the young. Lenz's play is innovative in many respects: the realism of the language and situations emphasize its social concern (seen also in his next best-known play, *The Soldiers*, pub. 1776), the structure is episodic (under the influence of Shakespeare), and the 'comedy' ventures into areas of the grotesque, as in the self-castration by Läuffer. Brecht adapted the play in 1950.

Tutto casa, letto e chiesa. See FEMALE PARTS.

TV. See AMERICA HURRAH.

Twelfth Night (*Twelfe Night, Or what you will*)

AT: *What You Will* A: William Shakespeare **Pf**: *c*.1601–2, London **Pb**: 1623 **G**: Com. in 5 acts; blank verse and prose **S**: Illyria, Renaissance period **C**: 11m, 3f, extras

Orsino, Duke of Illyria, is in love with Olivia, who is mourning for her brother. Shipwrecked on the shore of Illyria, Viola believes that her identical twin brother has been drowned. She disguises herself as a boy Cesario, and finds employment with Orsino. Olivia's steward Malvolio, a puritanical guardian of decorum in his mistress's household, finds himself obliged to reprimand her drunken cousin Sir Toby Belch and his friend Sir Andrew Aguecheek, who fancies himself as Olivia's suitor. The two knights plan to take revenge on Malvolio: they leave a letter for him to find, which purports to reveal that Olivia loves him and wishes to see him in cross-gartered yellow stockings. Meanwhile, Viola, as Cesario, is sent by Orsino to woo Olivia on his behalf. S/he performs this task so well that Olivia falls in love with Cesario, while Viola has by now fallen in love with Orsino. Malvolio approaches Olivia in his absurd attire and, since it is assumed that he must be mad, is locked away. Viola's brother Sebastian, who has survived the shipwreck, is set upon by the jealous Aguecheek, who takes him for his sister. Olivia intervenes and takes the only too willing Sebastian to the altar. When Orsino discovers that his Cesario is a woman, he offers his hand in marriage. Malvolio, now freed, threatens vengeance on them all.

Shakespeare here exploits traditional theatrical devices, like the confusions arising from identical twins, used in *The *Brothers Menaechmus* and *The *Deceived*, and also employs elements of folk myth to produce a very sophisticated comedy, arguably his finest. The (albeit biologically impossible) identical twin sister and brother emerge from the sea to end both Orsino's desolate loving and Olivia's obsessive mourning, just as at Twelfth Night with its joyful celebrations, there is promise of an end to the deprivations of winter. Twelfth Night was also traditionally the day of topsy-turveydom, when servants were waited on by their masters. Here the steward Malvolio dreams of becoming Olivia's husband, just as Viola/Cesario longs to wed Orsino. That these aspirations are merely the stuff of comedy is seen when the happy end is undercut by the clown Feste's song: 'the rain it raineth every day'. It is all too likely that Malvolio the Puritan will have the last word (and indeed the Puritans would order the closing of all the English theatres in 1642).

Twin Brothers, The. See BROTHERS MENAECHMUS, THE.

Twin Menaechmi, The. See BROTHERS MENAECHMUS, THE.

Twins, The. See BROTHERS, MENAECHMUS, THE.

Twisting of Another Rope, The. See QUARE FELLOW, THE.

Two Daughters of Mr Sawa, The (*Sawa-shi no futari musume*)

A: Kishida Kunio Pf: 1935, Tokyo Pb: 1955 Tr: 1995 G: Drama in 3 acts; Japanese prose S: Sawa's living room and a boarding house, Tokyo, late 1920s C: 3m, 3f, 1 child (f)

Sawa Kazuhisa is a 55-year-old widower, a former vice-consul who has travelled the world and had a chequered career, which included a spell in the Foreign Legion. He now lives in the suburbs of Tokyo with his two daughters in their twenties, Etsuko, a cheerful, traditionally minded teacher, and Aiko, her younger sister, a rather sullen rebel, who works for a record company. A visiting friend Kamiya Nitake suggests that Aiko should marry a young Frenchman of his acquaintance, but Sawa is hesitant about her marrying a foreigner. Sawa tells his daughters that he is now sleeping with their maid Raku. Several days later, Sawa is visted by Tadokoro Rashiki, a sailor who was a close friend of Sawa's son who died at sea. Tadokoro is unhappy that Aiko pretends she cannot remember him. Sawa imagines that Aiko made some sort of promise to Tadokoro; in fact they had sex together on an outing. Aiko's refusal to see him sends Tadokoro angry from the house. She confesses the truth, and, despite the forgiving attitude of her father, decides she must leave the family home. Two years later, Aiko has married the Frenchman, Sawa lives in a rundown boarding house, and Etsuko is having an affair with two teachers at once, and has been asked to leave by her principal. When Etsuko seeks Aiko's advice, her sister laughs at her, feeling that they are now even. They part, never to speak again, and leave Sawa alone in his grubby room.

Kishida was the major pre-war Japanese playwright, and this is his finest play. It gently observes the decline of traditional family relationships in Japan and offers a close-up observation of human behaviour without moralizing. As the Japanese critic Saeki Ryuko says: 'Everything that happens just happens; the conflict is unclear; ... all that we have here is the present.'

Two Gentlemen of Verona, The

A: William Shakespeare **W:** 1587–9 **Pf:** *c.*1592–8, London **Pb:** 1623 **G:** Romantic com. in 5 acts; blank verse and prose **S:** Duke's palace, Milan; houses and streets in Verona, forest, Renaissance period **C:** 10m, 3f, extras

The noble Valentine falls in love with Silvia, daughter of the Duke of Milan, while the fickle and treacherous Proteus loves Julia. When Proteus arrives in Milan, he too falls in love with Silvia, and in order to get rid of his rival, Proteus betrays to the Duke Valentine's plan to elope with Silvia. The Duke banishes Valentine, who goes off to lead a band of outlaws in the forest. Julia disguises herself as a boy and becomes Proteus' page at the Court of Milan. When the Duke tries to force Silvia into marriage with Thurio, she flees to the forest and is captured by the outlaws. She is saved by Proteus, who takes advantage of the situation: he is on the point of raping her, when Valentine appears just in time. Overcome by Proteus' penitence, Valentine yields Silvia to him. This prompts the 'pageboy' Julia to swoon and reveal herself. Proteus is so impressed by her devotion that he falls in love with her afresh. Thurio renounces Silvia, the Duke forgives Valentine, and the outlaws are pardoned.

Almost certainly Shakespeare's first comedy, *The Two Gentlemen* depends on a convoluted plot, a fairy-tale setting and a fantastical ending, in which all but the foolish Thurio achieve happiness. The romantic yearnings of the lovers are balanced by the broad comedy of the servants Speed and Launce, who performs a famous monologue with his dog Crab. Julia's disguise as a pageboy to the man she loves anticipates the situation of Viola in **Twelfth Night*, just as Silvia's flight from the court to the forest adumbrates Rosalind's escape to the Forest of Arden in **As You Like It* and may owe something to her namesake in Tasso's **Aminta*.

Two into One

A: Ray Cooney **Pf:** 1981, Leicester **Pb:** 1985 **G:** Farce in 2 acts **S:** London hotel, 1980s **C:** 5m, 5f, extras

Richard Willey MP, a handsome man in his forties, 'number two at the Home Office', has come up to London from his country home with his wife Pamela to stay at the Westminster Hotel in order to attend a parliamentary debate about pornography. Richard gets his private secretary George Pigden to book him another suite so that he can spend the afternoon with Jennifer Bristow, one of Margaret Thatcher's secretaries. Through a series of accidents and misunderstandings, Richard is booked into the suite next to his own, and Pamela thinks that George is trying to seduce her, while all attempts by George to sort out the mess complicate matters further. George pretends to be homosexual to conceal the compromising situation Richard finds him in. Eventually, Richard and Pamela encounter each other half-naked and pretend to be delighted. Richard sends Jennifer and George away, but Jennifer's husband Edward unexpectedly turns up at the hotel. Jennifer gets wedged in a trolley while trying to hide, and everyone assumes that Edward is George's suicidal boyfriend. At last Pamela guesses the truth about Richard's intended affair, but cannot accuse him without divulging her own secret.

Cooney, the master craftsman of English farce, uses multiple sets and ingenious plotting to create a very funny piece, in which, typically for anodyne West End entertainment, no one actually gets anywhere near committing a sexual act, and comments about politics, pornography, and sexual orientation are designed to provoke easy laughter rather than insight.

Two Noble Kinsmen, The

A: William Shakespeare and John Fletcher **Pf:** *c.*1613, London **Pb:** 1634 **G:** Romance in

5 acts; blank verse and prose S: Athens, Thebes, and their environs, in the mythical past C: 26m, 12f, extras

Suppliants beg Theseus, King of Athens, to wage war on Creon, King of Thebes. Theseus defeats Creon's army and captures his two nephews Palamon and Arcite. In their Athenian prison they remain blithe and devoted to each other until they spy Princess Emilia, Theseus' sister-in-law, whereupon each claims her for himself. Arcite is released from prison, disguises himself, and is employed as Emilia's attendant. Meanwhile the Jailer's Daughter has fallen in love with Palamon and enables him to escape. Meeting by the woods, the two kinsmen eat and drink together and then begin a duel to the death. Interrupted by Theseus' arrival, the two rivals are commanded to fight a tournament before the assembled court. Arcite is victorious but is thrown from his horse on his way to Emilia. With his dying breath he bequeaths Emilia to Palamon, just in time to prevent Palamon's execution.

This second collaboration by Shakespeare and Fletcher (alongside – probably – **Henry VIII*) fits Fletcher's definition of a tragicomedy: 'it wants deaths, which is enough to make it no tragedy, yet brings some near it, which is enough to make it no comedy'. True, Arcite dies, but through an accident, not through the ill will of his devoted relative, and his demise is the only possibility of providing a comedic outcome, and of fulfilling the promises made by the deities to whom the kinsmen and Emilia pray. It is impossible to disentangle which scenes were written by Shakespeare, but it is now generally accepted that several passages are by him. The recognition that the self-sacrifice of the feisty Jailer's Daughter reflects more nobility of spirit than that shown by the kinsmen, points strongly to the younger writer, Fletcher. The play was adapted by William Davenant as *The Rivals* (1664).

U

Ubu Rex. See KING UBU.

Ubu Roi. See KING UBU.

Uncle Tom's Cabin

AT: *Life among the Lowly* A: George L. Aiken Pf: 1852, Troy, NY Pb: 1868? G: Drama in 6 acts S: Various locations in rural America and New Orleans, mid-19th c. C: 20m, 7f, 1 child (m)

George Harris, a black slave, decides that he will seek freedom by escaping to Canada. When his wife Eliza learns that she and her young son are to be sold, they too plan to run away, even though it means crossing an icy river and leaving behind the lovable Uncle Tom. Uncle Tom is bought by a plantation owner St Clare, whose daughter Eva Tom had saved. Eva is brought up with a little black girl called Topsy, who, knowing nothing of her background, thinks she just 'growed'. St Clare is a benevolent master, who welcomes the reunited George and Eliza, and promises to free his slaves. However, his heavy drinking, which Uncle Tom gently warns him about, leads St Clare into trouble. He is stabbed to death by the ruthless Simon Legree, before St Clare has signed the papers giving Tom and the others their freedom. Predictably, Legree is a cruel master, but is shot dead while resisting arrest for St Clare's murder. Little Eva dies and is carried to heaven on the back of a milk-white dove.

Aiken's was the most popular of the many adaptations of Harriet Beecher Stowe's novel and is reputed to be the first play to be performed on its own on Broadway. Its success endured well into the following century. In 1879 there were 49 touring versions of *Uncle Tom's Cabin*, and still 12 in 1927. Although now a byword for a patronizing and sentimental white attitude towards the suffering of African-Americans, the play at the time contributed strongly to the abolitionist cause. It also gave to the language the phrase 'to grow like Topsy'.

Uncle Vanya (*Dyadya Vanya*)

AT: *Uncle Vania; August* A: Anton Chekhov Pf: 1897, Russian provinces; Moscow, 1899 Pb: 1897 Tr: 1912 G: Drama in 4 acts; Russian prose S: Serebryakov's estate, rural Russia, 1890s C: 5m, 4f

Ivan Voinitsky (Uncle Vanya), with the help of Sonya, his niece, manages the estate of his brother-in-law Aleksandr Serebryakov, who is a celebrated retired professor of art. Serebryakov arrives with his young new wife Yelena. Soon Vanya, who is disillusioned about Serebryakov's achievements, falls in love with Yelena, as does Mikhail Astrov, an idealistic doctor. Yelena rebuffs Vanya's advances, and Sonya tries to make Astrov understand that she loves him. She asks Yelena to sound out Astrov's feelings about her, and Astrov imagines that Yelena is attracted to him. Serebryakov announces that he intends to sell the estate so that he can live in town. Vanya, frustrated over Serebryakov's ingratitude and selfishness, fires a gun at him but misses. Serebryakov and Yelena leave, and Astrov goes off to his work. Vanya, having contemplated suicide, now settles down to the estate accounts with Sonya. Despite her unhappiness, she remains positive about life.

Uncle Vanya was based on Chekhov's earlier failed play *The Wood Demon* (*Leshy*), premiered in Moscow in 1889, in which the figure of Astrov, then called Khrushchev, is the 'wood demon' committed to ecological concerns. As in the **Three Sisters* very little happens (as Tolstoy commented: 'Where's the drama? The play treads water'). There is no heroic central figure, merely the hard-working, well-intentioned but blundering Vanya, demeaned by the ageing and patronizing label of 'Uncle'. It was this defeatism that inspired Howard Barker to write his own more vigorous and iconoclastic version *(Uncle) Vanya* (1993), and it has been adapted by Mamet (1988), Friel (1998), and Julian Mitchell as *August* (1994).

Underground Lovers, The (*Les Amants du métro*)

A: Jean Tardieu **Pf:** 1952, Paris **Pb:** 1954 **Tr:** 1968 **G:** Com. in 2 scenes; French prose **S:** Paris metro platform and train, *c.*1950 **C:** 1m, 1f, extras

Two lovers come and go amidst passengers on the metro platform, some exchanging platitudes, two students discussing the Hero and Leander legend, foreigners speaking unintelligibly. He and She exchange loving sentiments: 'I am nothing without you.' 'We are.' 'Say: we shall be.' 'We shall be.' Soon after, they begin arguing: 'You're no longer you!' 'Yes I am, I'm me!' 'No you're not!' 'It's you who aren't you!' They eventually have a row, and She runs off in tears. He follows her, calling her by a catalogue of different names. The train arrives, and six passengers board, leaving room only at each end of the line for She and He to stand. While the passengers chant a series of names, He desperately tries to push his way through to She. He gets past each of the passengers by engaging them in turn in nonsensical conversations. She encourages He's efforts by passing a note along the line, although She grows jealous when she sees him chatting for too long to a young film star. He's last obstacle is a man who is haunted by terror. By the time He arrives beside She, She has become as motionless and transfixed as the other passengers. Only when a whistle blows and the train suddenly stops, does She awake from her trance, and the lovers go off happily together.

In this absurdist piece, Tardieu offers an amusing cross-section of Paris society, and traces in almost balletic terms the movements of a love affair, from total devotion to pointless altercation. Then like Leander, He manages to overcome obstacles to reach his beloved. At first, it seems that their love has died, but Tardieu allows a happier ending than the Greek legend.

Under Milk Wood

AT: *Quite Early One Morning* **A:** Dylan Thomas **W:** 1944–53 **Pf:** 1956, Edinburgh **Pb:** 1954; rev. for stage, 1958 **G:** Drama in 2 acts; prose and songs **S:** Small Welsh seaside town, 1930s **C:** 33m, 35f

As the town of Llaregub slumbers, the Narrator introduces the locals: Captain Cat dreams of drowned souls; Mog Edwards the draper, 'mad with love' for the sweetshop-keeper Myfanwy Price, although he only ever writes to her; Mr Waldo, recently widowed, consoling himself with loose-living Polly Garter; the fastidious Mrs Ogmore-Pritchard, twice widowed; Benyon, the butcher, and his schoolteacher daughter Gossamer, in love with rough Sinbad Sailors; Organ Morgan, the organist; Utah Watkins, the farmer up the hill; Willy Nilly, the postman; Attila Rees, the policeman; the nymphomaniac Mae Rose Cottage; Bessie Bighead, slovenly hired help; Ocky Milkman; Dai Bread; Mr Pugh, schoolmaster; 85-year-old Mary Ann Sailors; eccentric Lord Cut-Glass with his collection of clocks; several others, and, of course, the gossiping neighbours. Revd Eli Jenkins greets the new spring day with a song; Mr Pugh, who hates his nagging wife, brings her tea, while plotting to poison her; Mr and Mrs Cherry Owen laugh about his drunken escapades; and everyone goes about their daily business until it is night once more.

Originally written for radio, *Under Milk Wood* has been performed as a stage play with international success. It remains what its subtitle suggests: 'A Play for Voices', with little action, sparse dialogue, and much narration, couched in Thomas's luscious lyricism. It is like a Welsh *Our Town*, without Wilder's insights, but redeemed by beguiling comedy, especially about the sexual goings-on beneath the respectable veneer of Llaregub (which, when spelt backwards, reveals Thomas's amusement at his fellow countrymen).

Underpants, The (*Die Hose*)

AT: *A Pair of Drawers; The Bloomers* A: Carl Sternheim Pf: 1911, Berlin Pb: 1911 Tr: 1927 G: Com. in 4 acts; German prose S: The Maskes' living room, Berlin, *c.*1910 C: 4m, 2f

Theobald Maske, a petty civil servant, is outraged because his wife Luise accidentally dropped her bloomers while watching the Kaiser's procession. The mishap attracts lodgers to their house: Scarron the poet, who idealizes his lust for Luise, and Mandelstam the barber, who is more forthright in declaring his desire. At first Luise is won over by Scarron's wooing, but he disappoints her by rushing off to write a poem about it. By contrast, Mandelstam kisses her impulsively, but injures himself when he faints at the thought of offending her. In a discussion after dinner Maske reveals himself as an opinionated philistine in opposition to Scarron's Nietzschean beliefs. When a neighbour brings Luise a new pair of bloomers, Maske seduces her. After spending the night with a prostitute worshipping her naked form, Scarron leaves, and Theobald lets his room to an old academic. With the additional income from the lodgers the Maskes will now at last be able to afford a child.

This formed the first play in Sternheim's cycle of six satirical plays entitled *Scenes from the Heroic Life of the Middle Classes*. Because its title was too shocking, it was premiered as *Der Riese* (*The Giant*), a reference to the giant-like quality of Theobald, the German common man, pushy, amoral, self-satisfied, and philistine – but successful, as is seen in the family's rise to power in the sequels *The Snob* (1914) and *1913* (1915). Sternheim shares with Expressionism the depiction of larger-than-life characters and idiosyncratic language, but his coolly detached vision, untypical of Expressionism, establishes him as a forerunner of Brecht.

Under the Gaslight

AT: *Life and Love in These Times* A: Augustin Daly Pf: 1867, New York; rev. 1881 Pb: 1867 G: Melodrama in 5 acts S: New York, 1860s C: 16m, 7f, 1 child (m)

The beautiful young Laura Courtland is looking forward to marriage with Captain Ray Trafford, but when he discovers that she was adopted when arrested as a child-pickpocket, he turns from her. In despair, she runs away from home and ends in court, where the villainous Byke claims to be her father. A decent one-armed ex-soldier Snorkey and a repentant Trafford intervene to prevent Byke abducting Laura to New Jersey. In the ensuing fight, Byke throws Laura in the river. She swims to safety and returns to her adoptive home, where she selflessly urges Trafford to marry her cousin Pearl. When Snorkey tries to foil Byke's plan to burgle the Courtlands' home, Byke ties him to a railroad track in the path of an advancing train. Laura breaks out of the shed where Byke has trapped her and frees Snorkey in the nick of time. She returns home and learns that she and Pearl were exchanged as babies, and that Laura is the legitimate Courtland heir. She is now able to marry Trafford.

Daly was better known as a successful theatre manager than playwright, but he wrote some 112 plays, mainly adaptations from English and French originals, of which this was the most popular. The 'sensation' scene, in which Snorkey is tied to railroad tracks, imitated from an English play *The Engineer* (1865), established this as a favourite moment on stage, in silent films, and in numerous cartoons. Behind the melodramatic plot, the play offers the perennial message that nobleness of mind is more important than the accident of birth, and one may recall that Daly himself was brought up by a poor widow, a soldier's daughter.

Up 'n' Under

A: John Godber Pf: 1984, Edinburgh Pb: 1985 G: Com. in 2 acts; prose and some verse S: Yorkshire, 1980s C: 6m, 1f

In a pastiche of the prologue to *Romeo and Juliet* Frank introduces Rugby League, the northern working-class and amateur version of rugby football. Former rugger star Arthur Hoyle bets £3,000 with Reg Welsh that he can train any team in five weeks to beat the reigning champions, the Cobblers. Reg names the Wheatsheaf from near Hull, a team that has never won a match. The Wheatsheaf play a match with only four men and lose heavily. Arthur tries to get the team to train but they prefer their beer. Arthur meets the attractive Hazel, who owns a gym, and suddenly the men become interested in getting fit. When they learn that they are training to win a bet for Arthur, they almost quit, but come back provided they can share any winnings. Reg arranges a bye to the final, and the Wheatsheaf have to square up to the formidable Cobblers, with Hazel now on the team. At the end of an exciting match, The Wheatsheaf are defeated by one point, but they are now inspired to go on and win the next time.

Brecht for one wanted his theatre to be as exciting as sport, while encouraging a critical viewpoint. Plays like McGee's *Foreskin's Lament*, Greenberg's *Take Me Out*, and Godber's *Up 'n' Under* all focus on sporting events, generating involvement in the audience but also celebrating human achievement. Godber, in 1993 the third most produced playwright in Britain, here celebrates rough northern camaraderie, which cuts across gender and class (Phil is a teacher), contrasting with Rugby Union, which is identified with upper-class institutions, professional competitions, and southern complacency.

Useless Precaution, The. See BARBER OF SEVILLE, THE.

Utinaya okhota. See DUCK HUNTING.

V

Vacationers. See SUMMERFOLK.

Valse des toréadors, La. See WALTZ OF THE TOREADORS, THE.

Vendidos, Los

A: Luis Valdez (with El Teatro Campesino) **Pf**: 1967, Los Angeles **Pb**: 1967 **G**: Pol. drama in 1 act; English with some Spanish **S**: Honest Sancho's shop, 1960s **C**: 5m, 1f

Miss Jiménez, a secretary in Governor Reagan's office, comes to Honest Sancho's Used Mexican lot in search of a token Mexican for the State Administration. She is first shown a Farm Worker, very hard-working, economical to run (one plate of beans and tortillas per day), and easy to store in one of Reagan's labour camps. Since the only English he knows is 'Strike!', Jiménez asks to see another model. Sancho proudly displays Johnny Pacucho, a stylish easygoing criminal, self-maintaining on drugs and petty theft, but, although she is allowed to kick him viciously, Jiménez reckons there are enough thieves in the Administration already. She is then shown the glamorous Mexican hero, star of many Hollywood romances, the Revolucionario. However, she is most impressed by the Mexican-American, an educated clean-cut man in a suit. Having bought him for an exorbitant sum, she is alarmed to hear him shout revolutionary slogans in Spanish. The other models all advance on Jiménez, who runs off in terror. The models reveal themselves as actors who divide up the spoils, then put away Sancho, who is the 'best model we got!'

In 1965, in response to a farm workers' strike, Valdez formed El Teatro Campesino ('The Farm workers' Theatre'), which gave a voice to the exploited Chicano workers of California. *Los Vendidos*, one of the short agitprop 'actos' for which the Teatro Campesino became famous, means 'those who are sold' but also 'the sell-outs', represented especially by Miss Jiménez, a Mexican-American collaborating with Reaganite oppression.

Venice Preserved (*Venice Preserv'd*)

AT: *A Plot Discovered* **A**: Thomas Otway **Pf**: 1682, London **Pb**: 1682 **G**: Trag. in 5 acts; blank verse and prose **S**: Venice, 1618 **C**: 19m, 2f, extras

Jaffier has a grudge against Priuli, a Venetian senator. Jaffier, after saving the life of Priuli's daughter Belvidera, has secretly married her, but Priuli refuses to offer him financial support. Jaffier's friend Pierre, who also has a personal grudge, persuades Jaffier to join a conspiracy against the Senate. When Jaffier learns that the conspirators intend to slaughter all the senators and their families, he hurries with Belvidera to the Senate, where he betrays his fellow conspirators on condition that their lives are spared. Pierre, learning that it was his friend who betrayed them, strikes Jaffier in the face. Reneging on their promise of an amnesty, the senators prepare to torture and execute the conspirators. Jaffier spares Pierre from being broken on the wheel by stabbing him and then stabs himself. Belvidera, now insane, sees their ghosts and dies.

Often accounted the best tragedy of the Restoration, *Venice Preserved* combines a powerful theme like that of Jacobean tragedy with the order and decorum of Restoration dramaturgy. It dares to explore the grotesquely comic, as in a scene where an elderly senator plays at being a dog with his young mistress (probably a satirical jibe at the Whig leader, the Earl of Shaftesbury). While never actually showing extreme violence, the torturer's wheel and the scaffold appear on stage. Although containing clear contemporary references to the 'Popish Plot' of 1678, the analysis of a conspiracy, especially the portrayal of honourable people caught up in a murderous plan by extremists, still has resonance today. Edward Gordon Craig prepared set designs for Hofmannsthal's translation of 1905.

Venticinque monologhi per una donna. See FEMALE PARTS.

verdad sospechosa, La. See SUSPECT TRUTH.

Verfolgung und Ermordung Jean-Paul Marats, dargestellt durch die Schauspielgruppe des Hospizes zu Charenton unter Anleitung des Herrn de Sade, Die. See MARAT/SADE.

Verge, The

A: Susan Glaspell Pf: 1921, New York Pb: 1922
G: Drama in 3 acts S: A greenhouse and a 'twisted tower', USA, 1920s C: 5m, 4f

Claire Archer is a plant scientist, attempting to cultivate an entirely new species in her experimental greenhouse. Similarly, in her relations with her husband Harry, her friend Dick, and her lover Tom Edgeworthy, she is hoping to go beyond conventional gender relationships to 'achieve integrity in otherness'. She dismisses her daughter Elizabeth, who seems entirely happy to conform to the conventional role of woman. Although it appears to 'go outside what it was', her newly developed 'Edge Vine' proves infertile, so Claire uproots it. Despite the scepticism of the men, she persists with her experiments and succeeds in producing a new plant capable of reproduction, 'The Breath of Life'. Her lover Tom seems to begin to understand her quest, but she finds his love oppressive, and fearing that she may succumb to conventional feminine quiescence, strangles him in a last embrace.

Significantly, a male writer in 1972 described this as being a play about a woman 'on the verge of insanity'. A post-feminist era may recognize that it is about a woman, in however extreme a manner, on the verge of transforming conventional biological patterns. Glaspell presents this challenging figure in a symbolic setting, using Expressionistic lighting and sound. It stands as Glaspell's most provocative and interesting play and as a powerful piece of early feminist writing.

Verre d'eau, Le. See GLASS OF WATER, THE.

Vespae. See WASPS.

Vicious Circle. See NO EXIT.

Victor (*Victor ou Les Enfants au pouvoir*)

AT: *Children Take Over* A: Roger Vitrac
Pf: 1928, Paris Pb: 1946 Tr: None known
G: Drama in 3 acts; French prose S: The Paumelles' apartment, Paris, 1909 C: 5m, 7f

Victor Paumelle is a precocious, obnoxious boy of 5 foot 9 celebrating his ninth birthday. He makes indecent proposals to the maid and blames her for breaking an expensive vase that he deliberately smashed. His 6-year-old friend Esther tells him that his father Charles and her mother Thérèse are having an affair. When the parents arrive, Victor says that Esther broke the vase, and her mother strikes her. Eventually, all the guests assemble for the birthday party, including a general and Esther's unhinged father, who recites entries from the encyclopedia and bursts into tears. The children embarrass their parents by acting out their parents' affair. Suddenly, Ida, a beautiful lady, arrives, claiming to be a friend of Victor's mother but insisting that she is not the woman she knows. Esther runs from the 'dirty woman', followed by the adults, but Victor remains and kisses Ida. She leaves quickly when he demands that she fart for him. Esther is brought back dishevelled and bleeding, but Victor reassures her that he has killed Ida. When Victor goes to bed, his father reads out items from the newspaper, then wood-planes and files his bed. No one is able to sleep, and Esther arrives, wanting to be with Victor. Thérèse discovers that her husband has hanged himself, and Victor complains of feeling unwell. The Doctor cannot save him, and Victor dies. In despair, his parents shoot themselves, and the maid comments: 'What a drama!'

Together with Artaud, who directed the premiere of *Victor*, Vitrac was expelled from André Breton's Surrealist inner circle for proposing to stage avant-garde theatre commercially. *Victor* and Apollinaire's **Breasts of Tiresias* are the two most important Surrealist plays of the period. *Victor's* language, clearly influencing Ionesco, ranges from lyrical (often juxtaposing ideas in characteristically Surrealist manner) to newspaper clippings to the obscene, and much of its action derives from the adult world observed through the eyes of grotesquely precocious children.

vida es sueño, La. See LIFE IS A DREAM.

View from the Bridge, A

A: Arthur Miller **Pf**: 1955; New York **Pb**: 1955; rev. 1957 **G**: Trag. in 2 acts, verse and prose
S: Street and house front of tenement building, Brooklyn, 1950s. **C**: 10m, 3f, extras

Eddie Carbone, a 40-year-old longshoreman, lives with his wife Beatrice and his pretty orphaned niece Catherine in an apartment overlooked by Brooklyn Bridge. As Catherine grows up and takes a job, Eddie becomes unnaturally edgy about her. Two young cousins of Beatrice come from Italy as illegal immigrants ('submarines') to live in the apartment: Marco is serious-minded, intent on finding a job so that he can send regular remittances to his family in Sicily; Rodolpho is good-looking and light-headed. Catherine is attracted to Rodolpho, and Eddie, jealously implying that Rodolpho is homosexual, warns Catherine that he wants to marry her only to obtain an American passport. When Eddie discovers Rodolpho emerging from Catherine's bedroom, he orders him out of the house. Catherine says she will leave with him, so Eddie, breaching the Italian code of honour, calls the Immigration Bureau and has the 'submarines' arrested. Marco spits at Eddie and denounces him. When Marco is allowed out on bail to attend the wedding of Rodolpho to Catherine, Eddie, now shunned by his neighbours, threatens him with a knife. They fight, and Eddie is killed. The lawyer Alfieri, who has commented on the action throughout, cannot help admiring Eddie's passion: 'he allowed himself to be wholly known ... And yet, it is better to settle for half.'

Originally written as a one-act play, much of it in verse, this represents Miller's attempt to recapture something of the power of Greek tragedy in a modern setting. Like Willy Loman, Eddie deludes himself, but, as the chorus-figure Alfieri says, Eddie's total if misguided commitment to his incestuous fascination with his niece raises him above 'all my sensible clients'.

Vildanden. See WILD DUCK, THE.

Vinegar Tom

A: Caryl Churchill **Pf**: 1976, Hull **Pb**: 1978
G: Hist. drama in 21 scenes; prose with songs
S: An English village, 17th c. **C**: 7m, 7f

In a small rural community, Alice, a loose woman, lives with her eccentric old mother Joan Noakes, whose main company is her cat Vinegar Tom. An upright couple, Jack and Margery, make plans for their farm but are dismayed when their cattle get sick. Because Margery was cursed by Joan when she refused her some yeast, and Jack was rejected by Alice when he tried to seduce her, the two accuse Joan and Alice of being witches. Betty, the daughter of the local gentry, is bled by the doctor to cure her, because she refuses to get married. Ellen, the cunning woman, gives Alice a potion to win her lover and provides Susan, another villager, with a draught to rid her of an unwanted baby. Jack is now alarmed because he has become impotent, and demands his penis back from Alice. Henry Packer, the witchfinder, comes with his assistant Goody, and they arrest Joan and Alice, and prick them to find where the devil has made them insensitive to pain. Susan is examined for marks of the devil, and Ellen is condemned for being a cunning woman. Joan and Ellen are hanged, and Alice and Susan await their fate. In a final scene, the authors of *The Hammer of Witches* do a music-hall act citing their work about the evil that women induce in men.

Written with and for the Monstrous Regiment Theatre Group, *Vinegar Tom* goes beyond Miller's *The *Crucible* by showing how the persecution of witchcraft was a suppression of ancient wisdom and traditional medicine, as practised by the gentle Ellen, and is related to contemporary debasement of women: 'Evil women | Is that what you want? | Is that what you want to see?'

Virtue in Danger. See RELAPSE, THE.

Vishnevy sad. See CHERRY ORCHARD, THE.

Visit, The (*Der Besuch der alten Dame*)
A: Friedrich Dürrenmatt Pf: 1956, Zurich Pb: 1956 Tr: 1958 G: Drama in 3 acts; German prose S: Imaginary Swiss town of Güllen, 1950s C: 29m, 8f, extras

Güllen has become such a backwater that express trains no longer stop there, but on this occasion the townspeople are at the station to welcome the return of a local girl Claire Zachanassian. She has become the richest woman in the world and, after an air crash, is put together entirely with artificial body parts. The Gülleners are hoping for a sizeable donation to help their economic problems, but she is willing to give money on only one condition. Many years previously she became pregnant by Alfred Ill (sometimes translated as Anton Schill), now a prosperous shopowner and mayor-elect of Güllen. He got two witnesses to lie on his behalf, and they are now Claire's castrated companions. Claire had to leave Güllen in disgrace, and her child died. She will hand over $1 billion if the townspeople murder Ill on her behalf. At first, they all reject this preposterous proposal. However, Ill notices that more and more people are buying goods on credit, notably yellow shoes, certain of soon becoming wealthy. When even his own family have acquired new outfits, Ill resigns himself to his fate. Facing death serenely, he goes to a town meeting, where there is unanimous acceptance of Claire's offer. Surrounded by his executioners, Ill drops to the ground. The Mayor proclaims: 'He died of joy,' and the happy Gülleners, now assured of future prosperity, process with Claire and Ill's coffin to the station.

This was for some years the most frequently performed post-war German-language play. Using forcefully grotesque images and sparse dialogue, Dürrenmatt not only reflected on Switzerland's ambiguous relationship with Nazi Germany and on the wealth it acquired through the war, but also addresses the universal theme of people's willingness to compromise and deceive themselves while doing so.

Visitor from Forest Hills. See PLAZA SUITE.

Visitor from Hollywood. See PLAZA SUITE.

Visitor from Mamaroneck. See PLAZA SUITE.

Vlast tmy. See POWER OF DARKNESS, THE.

Voix humaine, La. See HUMAN VOICE, THE.

Volksbefragung. See FEAR AND MISERY OF THE THIRD REICH.

Volpone
AT: *The Fox* A: Ben Jonson Pf: 1606, London Pb: 1607 G: Com. in 5 acts; blank verse and prose S: Venice, Renaissance period C: 22m, 2f, extras

Volpone (the fox), a rich magnifico of Venice, has no relatives to be his heirs. Encouraged by his devious parasite Mosca (the fly), several people call on Volpone, bringing gifts and flattery in the hope that they will inherit his fortune. Amongst these are: Voltore (the vulture), a lawyer; Corbaccio (the crow), an old miser; Corvino (the raven), a merchant; and Lady Would-Be, an ambitious English visitor. When Volpone discovers the beauty of Corvino's wife Celia, he determines to win this prize too. Mosca tells Corvino that unless a beautiful young woman can be found to sleep with him, Volpone will die – without leaving a will. Corvino agrees that his wife should be brought to Volpone. She refuses all his advances, however, and he is suddenly surprised by Corbaccio's son, Bonario, who denounces Volpone. Mosca ingeniously turns the tables on Bonario, who is taken before the senate. Here Volpone's cunning pleading succeeds in convincing the senate that Bonario and Celia are lovers and that Bonario had designs on his father's life. Volpone now pretends to be dead, making Mosca his heir, and encourages Mosca to taunt the disappointed flatterers by flaunting his wealth, unaware that Mosca will exploit the situation to claim the wealth as his own. Incensed by this turn of events, Voltore, Corbaccio, and Corvino denounce Mosca before the senate. When the truth is revealed, all the malefactors are punished, Bonario is compensated with his father's estates, and Celia is sent back to her father with an increased dowry.

Typically for Jonson, greedy tricksters overreach themselves and get their comeuppance. But, amongst the satire of mercenary acquisitiveness and lust, the audience cannot but help enjoy the ingenuity and fun of Volpone's plotting and Mosca's quick-wittedness. In this respect, there is something of the sympathy won by Shakespeare's Richard III or Iago – until they all go too far and alienate the audience, who then welcome their downfall. This is the morality play at its most subtle.

Von morgens bis mitternachts. See FROM MORNING TO MIDNIGHT.

Vor Sonnenaufgang. See BEFORE DAWN.

Vortex, The

A: Noël Coward **Pf:** 1924, London **Pb:** 1925
G: Drama in 3 acts **S:** London and a country house, 1920s **C:** 6m, 4f

Florence Lancaster is a rich socialite, who spends her time with meretricious acquaintances and, tolerated by her amiable husband David, with her lover Tom Veryan, an athletic young man. She struggles to pretend to herself that she is still young and adored by everyone. Her effete, drug-addicted son Nicky returns from Paris with his fiancée Bunty Mainwaring, who turns out to be the former mistress of Tom. At a party at the Lancasters' country home, Bunty and Tom fall in love again, and she breaks off her engagement with Nicky. When Florence discovers Bunty and Tom kissing, she throws a scene and makes a fool of herself. Nicky is forced to re-examine his wasted life and confronts his mother: 'We swirl about in a vortex of beastliness. This is a chance – don't you see – to realize the truth – our only chance.'

Coward was the most popular British playwright of the inter-war years, and this was his first major success and the first of his plays to be performed in New York. Although the decadent behaviour of the characters, emphasized by Coward's own stylish performance as Nicky, shocked early audiences, the piece is in fact a latter-day morality play.

Votes for Women

A: Elizabeth Robins **Pf:** 1907, London
Pb: 1909 **G:** Pol. drama in 3 acts
S: Wynnstay House, Hertfordshire, Trafalgar Square, and Eaton Square, London, 1900s
C: 7m, 7f, extras

Lord John Wynnstay has invited politicians of various persuasions, together with their wives, to come and stay. His wife and some of her friends, and a mysterious single woman Miss Vida Levering, are involved in charities for homeless women and, despite the sneering attitude of the men, are sympathetic to the suffrage movement. It is revealed that Miss Levering, a 'fallen woman', had ten years previously been persuaded to have an abortion and is therefore strongly committed to the cause of women. Lord John's niece Jean (or Beatrice) Dunbarton is sufficiently interested to travel to London to attend a suffragette meeting, and persuades her fiancé Geoffrey Stonor, a Unionist MP, to drive her there. At a noisy meeting in Trafalgar Square, the women's case is put forward by several speakers, ending with a spirited speech by Miss Levering. To Stonor's disquiet, Jean joins the suffragettes. That evening Jean confronts Stonor: she has realized that it was he who deserted Miss Levering. She is prepared to sacrifice her own happiness by demanding that he should marry Miss Levering. However, Vida Levering is no longer seeking marriage; instead, she persuades Stonor to commit himself to supporting women in their agitation for votes.

American-born Elizabeth Robins was best known as an actress, who did much to champion the new drama of Ibsen on the London stage. The original playbill unashamedly described the piece as 'A Dramatic Tract', and while it makes a well-argued case for women's suffrage, the play has also well-drawn characters, impressively avoiding crude depictions of the men. The realistic stage directions too suggest someone familiar with performance practice.

Voysey Inheritance, The

A: Harley Granville Barker. Pf: 1905, London
Pb: 1909; rev. 1938 G: Drama in 5 acts
S: Solicitor's offices, Lincoln's Inn, London, and the Voyseys' home, Chislehurst, 1900s
C: 10m, 8f

Edward Voysey is an honest hard-working young man, who is a partner in his father's highly respected firm of solicitors in Lincoln's Inn. He discovers with dismay that his supposedly upright father has been using his clients' money to speculate with, succeeding only in running up thousands of pounds of debts. Only by paying out dividends and interest when they are due has Mr Voysey Senior avoided detection. When Mr Voysey suddenly dies, Edward calls his extended family together to apprise them of the state of their 'inheritance'. He argues that they must put the matter in the hands of the law, but his family, alarmed at the prospect of a scandal, urges him to reconsider. Courageously, he agrees that the firm will continue as normal, while he works hard to claw back the debts. This bold determination and his loyalty to the family so impress his girlfriend Alice Maitland that she agrees to marry him.

Although there is a conventional comic ending with the promise of marriage, the main focus of the play is on business ethics, specifically the choice between an uncompromisingly honest public declaration of wrongdoing, which would benefit no one, and the more pragmatic but suspect course of staying silent, which at least stands a chance of preserving the good name of the family firm and of restoring the embezzled money. While it may seem that Granville Barker favours the latter course in order to arrive at his happy ending, the choice clearly remains problematic. What makes the play still absorbing on the stage today is the wide range of realistically drawn characters.

Vultures, The. See CROWS, THE.

Vyrozuměni. See MEMORANDUM, THE.

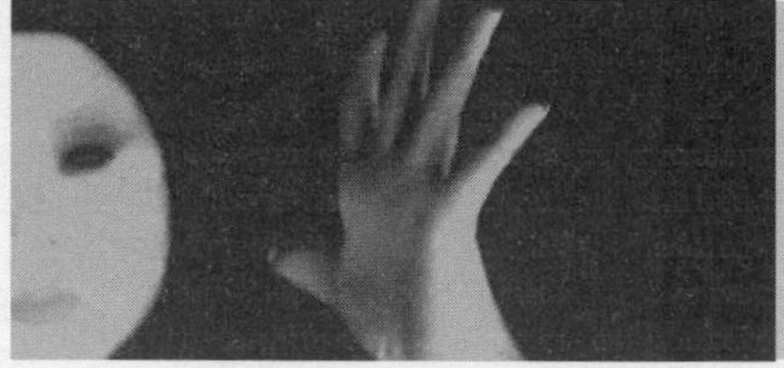

W

Waber, De. See WEAVERS, THE.

Waiting for Godot (*En attendant Godot*)

A: Samuel Beckett Pf: 1953, Paris Pb: 1952
Tr: 1956 G: Drama in 2 acts; French prose
S: Country road, indeterminate modern period
C: 4m, 1 child (m)

On a bleak country road beside a tree, two shabbily dressed men, Estragon (Gogo) and Vladimir (Didi), await the arrival of Godot, following instructions they have received. They pass the time by discussing how they spent the night (Gogo was beaten up as usual), variants in the Gospel description of the Crucifixion, and whether to hang themselves on the tree. They review the instructions about meeting Godot and agree that it is the right place. A loud cry heralds the arrival of Pozzo, an arrogant gentleman leading his servant Lucky with a rope round his neck. Lucky is carrying heavy bags for Pozzo, which he sets down only when ordered to do so. Pozzo eats a picnic, and Gogo and Didi enjoy his cast-off chicken bones. Didi asks that Lucky entertain them, and Lucky is ordered to do a strange silent dance. He then is commanded to think, and, mute until now, suddenly pours forth an incoherent tirade, which is stopped only when Gogo and Didi wrestle him to the ground. Eventually Pozzo leaves, and the two men are pleased that it helped to pass the time, but then agree that 'it would have passed anyway'. A Boy arrives with a message: Mr Godot will not be coming today, 'but surely tomorrow'. The men settle for the night and continue their wait, but neither leaves. The next day, the tree has grown some leaves. Uncertain that they are at the same spot as before, they discover Lucky's hat, and a hat-swapping routine follows. They play at being Pozzo and Lucky, and abuse each other, ending with the final insult: 'Critic!' They are rejoined by Pozzo and Lucky, but Pozzo is now blind and enfeebled, and Lucky is dumb. When they fall, Didi and Gogo try to help them but collapse too. Eventually Pozzo, who does not remember meeting them the day before, moves off again. Gogo wants to leave too, but they must wait for Godot. The Boy, who denies being the same one as yesterday, brings a message: Mr Godot won't come this evening, but tomorrow 'without fail'. In desperation, the men try to hang themselves with Gogo's belt, but he succeeds only in dropping his trousers. They agree to leave, but do not move.

Never in the history of the theatre did a writer's first performed play have such a far-reaching influence. After its controversial premiere in Paris, hailed by Anouilh as '*The Thoughts* of Pascal performed by clowns', the play was translated into every major language in the world and played to enraged and bewildered audiences everywhere. The drama, in which 'nothing happened—twice' (Vivien Mercer) was not particularly innovative because of its lack of action and open-ended structure, nor because of its theme of promised salvation that never comes (already explored in O'Neill's *The *Iceman Cometh* and Ionesco's *The *Chairs*). What made *Waiting for Godot* the supreme modern classic is its blend of humour and tragic insight, its uncompromising minimalism, its perfect structure, and its dazzling poetic prose.

Waiting for Lefty

A: Clifford Odets **Pf**: 1935, New York **Pb**: 1935 **G**: Pol. drama in 7 scenes **S**: Union meeting, New York, 1935 **C**: 14m, 3f

Harry Fatt, leader of the New York taxi drivers' union, urges his members to accept the low pay on offer and to resist calls for a strike. The drivers, planted in the audience, call for Lefty Costello, their militant spokesman, but he is delayed. While they wait, Joe Mitchell, a member of the strike committee, suggests that the drivers enact scenes from their own lives, showing why a strike is inevitable: (1) Joe's wife Edna, who has just seen their furniture repossessed, threatens to leave him if he doesn't have the courage to strike. (2) A former laboratory assistant shows how he refused to work secretly on producing poison gas and punched his industrialist boss in the face. (3) A cab driver cannot afford to marry his girlfriend, while her brother earns good money learning to kill for the navy. (4) Someone intervenes to support Fatt and is exposed by his own brother as a company spy. (5) A Young Actor discusses *The Communist Manifesto*, declaring: 'The Militant will inherit the earth.' (6) A hospital doctor is replaced by an incompetent senator's nephew, because the former is a Jew. The patient dies, and the intern becomes a cab driver, vowing to fight for a better society. (7) A worker insists that they no longer wait for Lefty but strike at once. News comes that Lefty has been murdered by company gunmen, and the meeting erupts in calls for a strike.

Written to express the discontent of workers in the Depression, Odets here created the first notable piece of American agitprop theatre, a form that had been popular with revolutionary groups in Germany and Russia in the 1920s and early 1930s and was to see a revival in the 1970s and 1980s. In vain does one look for subtle characterization or complex debate. The point is to offer stark alternatives – here between acquiescence in an unjust capitalist system and a socialist alternative. Scene 5 was later omitted. The use of 'plants' in the audience inviting spectators to participate actively in the performance anticipates the Forum Theatre of Augusto Boal.

Waiting for the Parade

A: John Murrell **Pf**: 1977, Calgary, Alberta **Pb**: 1980 **G**: Drama in 24 scenes **S**: Janet's home, Calgary, Second World War **C**: 5f

Five women come together at Janet's home to prepare bandages for the Canadian armed forces in the Second World War. Their existence is determined by the men in their lives, which is revealed in dialogue, monologue, song, and dance. Janet, the bossy organizer, is a strong, reliable individual, totally supportive of her husband. Margaret is a widow, previously devoted to her husband and now to her children. Marta, like the biblical Martha, is a passive figure, a dutiful daughter, while Eve, like her Garden of Eden namesake, is the easily manipulated innocent. Catherine, the most outrageous of the group, is a loose woman but genuinely kind. Despite the absence of their menfolk, they maintain the roles assigned to them by their patriarchal society.

Despite the fact that the play is based on interviews, there remains the inevitable problem of 'ventriloquism': how can a male playwright know how women communicate when on their own? Murrell suggests that these women are so conditioned by the men in their lives that they have lost the positive qualities of female togetherness, reflected in the fact that they never address each other by name. The play is both an indictment of male attitudes to women and an exhortation to women to break free of these constrictions.

Wakefield Cycle, The. See TOWNELEY CYCLE OF MYSTERY PLAYS, THE.

Waking Up. See FEMALE PARTS.

Waltz of the Toreadors, The (*La Valse des toréadors*)

A: Jean Anouilh **Pf**: 1952, Paris **Pb**: 1952 **Tr**: 1956 **G**: Com. in 5 acts; French prose **S**: France, *c.*1910 **C**: 4m, 7f

General Saint-Pé is constantly interrupted as he dictates his memoirs: his insanely jealous bedridden wife demands to know what woman he is thinking of; his ugly daughters want new dresses; his wife's doctor considers her paralysis hysterical. Only the visit of Ghislaine is a welcome distraction. They have loved each other chastely for 17 years, ever since they danced the 'Waltz of the Toreadors' together. When Ghislaine discovers love letters which the General's wife has written to the doctor, the General believes he can now consummate his love. The General confronts the doctor over the affair with his wife, but the doctor points out that the letters were never sent, and urges the General to abandon his wife and marry Ghislaine. His wife overhears this and runs away. When the General goes after her, Ghislaine, convinced that she is no longer loved, throws herself out of a window and lands on the young secretary rocking in his hammock. The secretary falls in love with her, and, encouraged by the disillusioned General, goes to her. Meanwhile the wife admits that she has faked her illness to hold on to the General and taunts him with her past affairs. The secretary, who turns out to be the General's illegitimate son, is going to marry Ghislaine. The General's daughters, who both loved the secretary, run off, leaving a suicide note. As his wife shouts jealous admonitions, the General takes the new serving maid for a walk in the moonlight.

In this bitter-sweet comedy, Anouilh explores an unusual area of romantic love: the older man, a serial womanizer, who is unable to commit himself to a real relationship. Despite a lifelong pursuit of love, he watches impotently as the object of his longing is taken off by his son, leaving him with the burnt-out embers of his marriage.

Wanna Go Home, Baby? See SWEENEY AGONISTES.

Wariat i zakonnica. See MADMAN AND THE NUN, THE.

Wasps (*Sphēkes; Vespae*)

A: Aristophanes Pf: 422 BC, Athens Tr: 1819 G: Greek com. in verse S: Before the house of Philocleon in Athens, the present C: 7m, 1f, extras, chorus (m)

In order to avoid the possibility of corruption, the law courts of Athens enlist the services of a jury of 500 men. Philocleon (= 'lover of Cleon') has become so flattered by the power that this has granted him that he has become addicted to jury service. His son Bdelycleon (= 'hater of Cleon') has imprisoned him in his own house to try to cure him of his judging obsession. The chorus of fellow jurors, the Wasps, arrive to take Philocleon to court. His son intervenes to point out how miserably they are paid for their services and that the state is swallowing up the profits from the trials. The Wasps are convinced, but Philocleon is not. To keep his father happy, Bdelycleon arranges for a dog to be put on trial for having stolen some cheese. Although Philocleon is determined as ever to find the defendant guilty, he is horrified to discover that he has acquitted the dog. His son consoles him by promising to take him out on social occasions. Philocleon goes to a party, where he gets drunk, insults everyone, and makes off home with the flute girl who was entertaining them. The play ends with Philocleon leading the chorus in a merry dance.

Yet again Aristophanes launches a satirical attack on an Athenian society that has been corrupted by the prolonged war with Sparta, by now in its ninth year. He also continues his mockery of the hated demagogue Cleon, who was to die in battle later that year. Of more interest to a modern audience is the satire at the expense of the law, the first example in European drama of one of the favourite targets of comic playwrights. From Shakespeare's Justice Shallow to Howard Barker's Stripwell, the corrupt or incompetent lawyer has been a favourite butt of satirical comedy. Aristophanes' surreal treatment of the topic, especially in the trial of the dog, can be very effective in performance.

Waters of Immortality. See AT THE HAWK'S WELL.

Way of the World, The

A: William Congreve Pf: 1700, London Pb: 1700 G: Com. in 5 acts; prose S: London, 1700 C: 6m, 6f, extras

Fainall and Mirabell are rivals, not only at the card table, but also in financial matters. Mirabell is in love with Mrs Millamant, but has incurred the displeasure of her aunt Lady

Wishfort, because he insincerely paid court to her only to distract from his love for her niece. Fainall, though married to Lady Wishfort's daughter, is in love with Mrs Marwood. Lady Wishfort wants Millamant to marry her nephew Sir Wilfull Witwoud, to keep her fortune in the family. Fainall, in league with Marwood, is hoping that Mirabell will marry Millamant, so that Lady Wishfort disinherits her, and Fainall will gain the fortune through his wife. After more comic fun with a disguised servant pretending to be a suitor for Lady Wishfort's hand, Fainall now threatens to expose his wife as Mirabell's former mistress, unless Lady Wishfort disinherits Millamant. Finally, Fainall's scheming is exposed, and a deed is found protecting his wife's estates from his greed. Millamant and Mirabell will now marry.

The convoluted plot of this play reveals that good nature, wit, and indeed a successful outcome may all go hand in hand. In this regard Congreve's humour is more gentle than the satirically corrective humour of Wycherley and Etherege. Indeed, in his dedication Congreve writes that many comic figures of the Restoration 'instead of moving our mirth . . . ought very often to excite our compassion'. One of the delights of the play is the witty repartee between Mirabell and Millamant, reminiscent of Beatrice and Benedick in Shakespeare's **Much Ado about Nothing*. One such scene, where the two protagonists plan their life together, is very progressive in the way the future wife demands a large measure of independence. *The Way of the World*, although now one of the most popular Restoration comedies, was unsuccessful at the time, and Congreve, having been attacked throughout his brief career, wrote little more for the stage after the age of 30.

Wealth (*Ploutus; Plutus*)

A: Aristophanes **Pf:** 388 BC, Athens **Tr:** 1659 **G:** Greek com. in verse **S:** A street in Athens, 4th c. BC **C:** 9m, 3f, extras, chorus (m)

Chremylus has been to the oracle in Delphi to find out whether it makes sense to remain poor but honest, and the god Apollo tells him to follow the first person he encounters on leaving the oracle. He dutifully follows a blind beggar, who turns out to be the god of Wealth. Chremylus persuades Wealth to have his sight restored. Now Poverty appears, arguing that it is she who benefits humankind by making people more productive. She is sent on her way, but she says that she will return one day. After Wealth has been cured, Chremylus becomes hugely rich and soon receives a stream of visitors wanting to share in his riches. One of these is Hermes, bringing threats from Zeus. However, Hermes is so hungry that he agrees to take a job in Chremylus' household. The final visitor is the priest of Zeus, who is persuaded that the new god is Wealth.

Wealth is the last of Aristophanes' extant plays and reflects the transition from the Old Comedy, in which the chorus was a central feature, to the New Comedy of Menander and the Romans, where the humour derives from primarily social situations and comic types. The role of the slave Carion is also much more prominent than in earlier pieces, and this too was to become a characteristic feature of much European comedy. The moral nature of the play made it popular in the 16th and 17th centuries.

Weapons of Happiness

A: Howard Brenton **Pf:** 1976, London **Pb:** 1976 **G:** Pol. drama in 2 acts **S:** Street, factory, waste-ground, Planetarium, and drain, London, and farm in Wales, 1976; interrogation room, Prague, 1951; Moscow, 1947; Ruzyn Prison, Czechoslovakia, 1952 **C:** 25m, 3f, extras

Josef Frank has come to London from Czechoslovakia and now works in a crisp[potato chip]-making factory. He witnesses his boss Ralph Makepeace being mugged by three young people wearing balaclavas (in fact his own employees, resentful that he will not allow them to become unionized). During the police investigation, Frank, a former Czech government minister, has a flashback to his 1951 interrogation by the Communist security police. In 1947, Frank and a senior minister, Victor [*sic*] Clementis, successfully negotiate with Stalin over a trade deal. The English factory workers tell Bob

Hicks from the union that Makepeace intends to close the works, but Hicks merely urges caution. Janice, a politically well-informed factory worker, seduces Frank in the London Planetarium. The workers occupy the factory, which is anyway on the verge of bankruptcy. Frank relives the false confessions of Clementis and himself at the Prague Treason Trials and witnesses Clementis being hanged. The rebellious workers escape through a drain and arrive at a farm in Wales, abandoned by the farmer because he could no longer survive there. Frank dies of a heart attack.

Set against Britain in decline, with the crisp-factory under threat of closure and a farmer who could no longer make ends meet, different political responses are proposed: the idealistic revolt of the young, devoid of serious strategy and soon to fizzle out; hard-line Communism, with its lies and brutality, represented by the disillusioned Josef Frank (in fact hanged with Vladimir Clementis in 1952); the gradual reformism of Hicks, the Trade Unionist; and the despairing resignation of the Establishment, represented by Makepeace.

Weavers, The (*Die Weber, De Waber*)

A: Gerhart Hauptmann **Pf**: 1893, Berlin; 1st public perf. 1894 **Pb**: 1892 **Tr**: 1899 **G**: Drama in 5 acts; German prose, also version in Silesian dialect **S**: Silesia, 1844 **C**: 26m, 11f, 3 children, extras

The rich employer Dreissiger pays miserable amounts to the starving weavers who bring him the cloth they have woven at home. Although he promises more employment to the unhappy workers, this is in fact a move to lower their rates of pay. One of the weavers, who has not eaten meat for two years, cooks his dog and eats it, but cannot keep the meal down. Moritz Jäger, a soldier, urges the weavers to rebel and begins to sing the defiant 'Weavers' Song'. As the tension mounts, the Dreissigers dine well at home, entertaining the complacent Pastor and angrily dismissing the concerns of the young tutor Weinhold. Jäger is arrested as one of the leaders of the mob, but he answers all questions defiantly. The mob attack the police, free Jäger, and beat the Pastor. The Dreissigers escape just before the weavers burst into their home, smashing everything they find. The army are called in to quell the riot, and while the pious old Hilse sits weaving, he is shot by a stray bullet.

Although set in the 1840s, *The Weavers* became a focus for contemporary revolutionary sentiment in the repressive regime of the Kaiser. It was licensed for public performance only on the grounds that the ticket prices would be too high for working-class audiences to be affected by the events of the play. Dramaturgically, its interest lies in the way that the tragedy focuses not on an individual but on a whole community, thus marking a change from classical historical tragedy to the wider perspective of documentary drama.

Weber, Die. See WEAVERS, THE.

We Can't Pay? We Won't Pay! See CAN'T PAY? WON'T PAY!

Wedding, The (*Wesele*)

A: Stanisław Wyspiański **Pf**: 1901, Cracow **Pb**: 1901 **Tr**: 1904 **G**: Drama in 3 acts; Polish verse, 4-stress rhymed lines **S**: Living room of farmhouse near Cracow, Poland, 1900 **C**: 23m, 12f

A noisy wedding celebration takes place in the neighbouring hall, as characters come and go in the living room where the buffet has been set out. We meet the Groom, a writer from Cracow, and Jadwiga, his pretty, simple peasant Bride. They have married in the home of the Groom's brother, a painter, who after also marrying a peasant girl is now a prosperous farmer. Politics are discussed, flirtations take place, and the Priest instructs the young couple. Intellectuals and peasants are united in their desire to return to an independent Poland, free of foreign rule. At midnight, the Straw-man enters, and Phantoms appear: a 16th-century court jester, who wittily interrogates the Journalist; the Poet encounters a heroic medieval Knight about whom he has written; Jakub Szela, leader of the 1846 peasant uprising, appears; finally, they are joined by Vernyhora, the legendary 18th-century Ukrainian bard, who foretold the destruction and resurrection of Poland. Vernyhora gives the Host a battle-horn to rally the peasants for an uprising. However, the horn gets lost, and, instead of rebelling, the wedding guests lay aside their scythes and swords and dance puppet-like to the soothing music played by the Straw-man.

This is a classic of the Polish theatre, frequently performed in the national repertoire. Its call for intellectuals and peasants to unite in the fight for freedom was relevant to nationalist sentiments during the period of Polish partition from 1795 to 1918 when Cracow was under Austrian rule, and has been appropriated by Polish patriots since. Its symbolist use of mythical figures and apparitions provides opportunities for great theatricality.

Wedding, The (*Ślub*)

AT: *The Marriage; The Wedding Ceremony* **A:** Witold Gombrowicz **Pf:** 1964, Paris; 1976, Wroclaw **Pb:** 1950 **Tr:** 1969 **G:** Drama in 3 acts; Polish prose **S:** France, Second World War **C:** 6m, 2f, extras

Henryk, a Polish soldier fighting in France during the Second World War, dreams of returning to his homeland. Arriving at an inn, he finds that his parents are the innkeepers and that his fiancée Maria is also there but avoiding him. A Drunk and his companions abuse Henryk's father and calls Maria a whore. Suddenly, Henryk's Father declares that he is King; the inn becomes a palace, and the Drunk the Royal Ambassador. The Ambassador encourages Henryk to seize power by overthrowing the King. Since he cannot bring himself to believe in the reality of what is happening, Henryk removes his Father from the throne by touching him. When he comes to marry Maria, however, the Drunk behaves as though she is already wed to his comrade-in-arms Władzio. With Henryk now in charge, he encourages Władzio to commit suicide, so that Maria's honour is restored. When the Drunk declares that Henryk is a cuckold, Władzio's corpse is revealed. Although Henryk protests his innocence, he has himself imprisoned and sentenced to death.

The Wedding appears to be a political allegory, and although it deals with topics like the abuse of power, clearly relevant to Poland under Communism, the play's focus is not on national politics. Rather, it is a poetic drama, like **Hamlet* seen through the eyes of Genet, a nightmarish world where the rules of logic no longer apply and a word once uttered can determine the course of all future action.

Wedding Band

A: Alice Childress **Pf:** 1966, Ann Arbor **Pb:** 1974 **G:** Drama in 2 acts **S:** Black homes, South Carolina, 1918 **C:** 3m, 6f, 2 children (f)

Julia Augustine, a black woman, has just moved into the middle house in a block of three surrounding a backyard. For ten years, contrary to racial laws she has been the lover of Herman, a white man who runs a bakery shop, and wears his 'wedding band' hidden on a chain round her neck. Both would like to acknowledge their relationship openly, but this would be possible only if they can move to New York City. However, Herman feels a responsibility to his mother and sister Annabelle, especially as he is trying to pay off a debt to his mother which financed his bakery. While secretly visiting Julia, Herman falls seriously ill with influenza, and her landlady, horrified at having a white man in a black neighbourhood, orders her to 'Get him out of my yard.' Herman's mother and Annabelle arrive to take him home, provoking a clash of cultures between the intolerant whites and the resentful blacks, one of whom Mattie has a husband whom she hardly sees because he is forced to work away from home. Herman's mother tells of her unhappy marriage to a drunkard and of her seven babies, only two of whom survived. Annabelle begs Herman to abandon Julia and to marry his mother's choice of bride, so that Annabelle is free to marry the man she loves. Finally, while Herman and Julia steadfastly cling to their doomed love, he dies.

Subtitled 'A Love/Hate Story in Black and White', this early and untypical play by Childress provoked controversy because of its representation of a sexual relationship between blacks and whites, an American version of a

*Romeo and Juliet love which cannot survive amidst intolerance and rejection by both racial groups. In Childress's generous and therefore much criticized portrayal, working-class whites like Herman are seen to be victims too.

Wedding Ceremony, The. See WEDDING, THE (Gombrowicz).

Weihnachtseinkäufe. See ANATOL.

Weir, The

A: Conor McPherson **Pf**: 1997, London **Pb**: 1997 **G**: Drama in 1 act **S**: Bar in north-west Ireland, 1990s **C**: 4m, 1f

Brendan Byrne, a bar-owner in his thirties, is serving Jack Mullen, a garage mechanic (fifties) and his friend Jim Curran (forties), occasional handyman. The talk is of the weather, betting, and especially of a new arrival in the area: a woman from Dublin, Valerie (thirties), who is renting an old house from Finbar Mack (late forties), a local hotelier. Finbar has been showing Valerie around and they now come into the bar. They talk about the weir built to generate electricity in 1951, and Jack tells of the fairy road upon which Valerie's house was supposedly built. Many years ago, and again when the weir was built, knocking was heard on the door and windows, supposedly by angry fairies. Finbar then tells of a neighbour who saw a ghost of a woman she knew who died that same evening. Jim caps this with a story about the ghost of a paedophile who asked to be buried in the grave of a young girl. The other three men find Jim's story in poor taste. Valerie then tells how her daughter drowned but that she heard her voice on the telephone. She hints that she was treated for a nervous breakdown and separated from her husband. Meeting with these men may be a renewal for all of them.

McPherson offers an accurate and undramatic image of contemporary rural life in Ireland. Just as a weir interrupts the flow of the river but cannot actually halt its progress, so this group of men repeat their banter and their stories and maintain their companionship in the steady flow of rural living. It is a sympathetic and optimistic view.

Wesele. See WEDDING, THE (Wyspiański).

Western Dock. See QUAY WEST.

West Indian, The

A: Richard Cumberland **Pf**: 1771, London **Pb**: 1771 **G**: Romantic com. in 5 acts; prose **S**: London, 1770s **C**: 9m, 6f, extras

Belcour, son of the merchant Stockwell by a secret marriage, has made his fortune in the West Indies. His father intends to test his son before acknowledging him. Belcour befriends the impoverished Captain Dudley and gives him money. Dudley's son Charles is in love with his cousin Charlotte Rusport, but cannot marry her because he is without means. Belcour has fallen in love with Charles's sister Louisa, and believing her to be 'an attainable wanton', proposes that she become his mistress. Charles is so infuriated by this proposal that he challenges Belcour to a duel. When Belcour learns who Louisa is, he apologizes to Charles, and the two men are reconciled. Through the intervention of an Irish Major O'Flaherty, a will is produced that bestows a fortune on Charles. Belcour is revealed as Stockwell's son, and he and Charles are now free to wed their loves and become brothers.

The genre of 'sentimental' or 'lachrymose' comedy, derived from plays like Steele's *The *Conscious Lovers*, reflected the new emphasis on the moral usefulness of theatre, and became immensely popular, especially with the rising bourgeoisie across Europe (cf. *drames* in France, *weinerliche Lustspiele* in Germany). In Oliver Goldsmith's words, 'the virtues of private life are exhibited, rather than their vices exposed; and the distresses, rather than the faults of mankind make our interest in the piece'. Belcour is a rough diamond, not unlike Fielding's Tom Jones, whose larger-than-life generosity of spirit is both naive and heart-warming. Thanks to 'Providence', potential misfortune is averted, and he is justly rewarded for his good nature.

We Won't Pay? We Won't Pay! See CAN'T PAY? WON'T PAY!

What Price Glory?

A: Maxwell Anderson and Laurence Stallings Pf: 1924, New York Pb: 1926 G: Drama in 3 acts S: Farmhouse and cellar near the battlefront in France, 1918 C: 26m, 1f

In a French farmhouse converted into the headquarters of a detachment of US Marines, Captain Flagg is preparing to go on leave in Paris. His friend and rival First Sergeant Quirt, who is placed in charge of the men, consoles Charmaine, the local innkeeper's daughter, over Flagg's departure. A week later Flagg returns, having been imprisoned for assaulting a military policeman. Charmaine's father insists that Flagg should marry his daughter, but a call to battle intervenes. In a cellar at the battlefront, news of the terrible slaughter arrives and casualties are carried in. One officer, describing the dreadful suffering of a German sniper, asks: 'What price glory now?' Quirt is slightly wounded and Flagg captures a German officer, so both are allowed to withdraw from the front. Later, at Charmaine's inn, the men agree to gamble to decide who shall have her. The one who loses will get a gun and a head start, while the other remains behind to have Charmaine and to continue fighting in the war. Quirt loses and gets away. Orders come to resume battle, and Flagg reluctantly obeys. Quirt, who has been hiding upstairs, cannot resist the call to arms, kisses Charmaine goodbye, and rushes out after his friend.

This, together with **Journey's End* and *The *Silver Tassie*, stands as one of the best known and most powerful plays about the First World War. Its grim humour and its combination of rough male camaraderie with gentle compassion, made it an instant hit on Broadway and led to its being filmed several times. Its unflinching depiction of conditions at the battlefront (largely the work of Stallings) contributed to the development of stage realism, so successfully exploited by Eugene O'Neill and later American playwrights.

What the Butler Saw

A: Joe Orton Pf: 1969, London Pb: 1969 G: Farce in 2 acts S: Room in a private clinic, 1960s C: 4m, 2f

Dr Prentice, a psychiatrist interviewing Geraldine Barclay, an attractive young orphan, for the post of secretary, requires her to get undressed for a full examination. As she lies naked behind a screen, Prentice's wife enters. With her is Nicholas Beckett, a pageboy who seduced her the previous evening in her hotel. He now demands payment for pornographic photographs taken of their lovemaking. When he goes, Mrs Prentice alleges that Nick raped her and stole her dress. She leaves with Geraldine's dress. Dr Rank, a government inspector, discovers the naked Geraldine, and Prentice pretends that she is a patient with delusions. As she is confined to the ward, a search is instituted for the 'genuine' Geraldine. Nick returns the photographs provided that Prentice gives him a job as secretary. When the arrival of a policeman is announced, both Nick and Prentice panic. Prentice gets Nick to put on his wife's dress and wig and to pretend to be Geraldine. Meanwhile, Geraldine staggers in from the ward and dresses herself in Nick's pageboy uniform. Sergeant Match arrests them both, and Rank declares them insane. In order to escape, Nick gets Prentice to drug the Sergeant and give Nick his uniform. Eventually the stage is filled with semi-naked figures dashing around frantically and being shot at by Mrs Prentice. Finally, it turns out that Geraldine and Nick are the long-lost twin offspring of the Prentices.

Premiered posthumously, two years after Orton had been hammered to death by his homosexual lover, no play, however shocking, could match his own dramatic demise. Often accounted his best play, *What the Butler Saw* (the name taken from suggestive slot-machines on British piers) is a remarkable cross between Oscar Wilde and vulgar seaside postcards. The bitter undertone of Orton's earlier plays is replaced here with exuberantly chaotic fun, reflecting the insight that 'You can't be a rationalist in an irrational world. It isn't rational.'

What You Will. See TWELFTH NIGHT.

When We Dead Awaken (*Når vi døde vågner*)

A: Henrik Ibsen Pf: 1900, Stuttgart Pb: 1899 Tr: 1907 G: Drama in 3 acts; Norwegian prose S: A seaside resort and near a mountain sanatorium, 1890s C: 3m, 3f, extras

Professor Arnold Rubek, an elderly sculptor unhappily married to the childlike Maja, is staying at a spa hotel, visited by a bear-hunting landowner Ulfheim and a strange lady attended by a nun. Maja develops an attraction for Ulfheim, and Rubek is only too happy to let her accompany Ulfheim to the mountains, especially when he discovers the identity of the lady. She is Irene, who inspired his greatest sculpture, 'The Day of Resurrection', which they called 'their child'. Rubek callously abandoned her once his work was complete, and she suffered a breakdown, inwardly dying. Rubek admits that he added a figure to his sculpture 'a man weighed down with guilt', for, as Irene says, he was not a man, just an artist. She concludes: 'When we dead awaken, we see that we have never lived.' Rubek and Irene follow Maja and Ulfheim up the mountain, but, while the latter return to the comfort of Ulfheim's castle, the former continue ecstatically towards the summit and are killed by an avalanche.

This last play by Ibsen, attacked by several critics, was praised by Shaw and James Joyce for its brutally honest self-assessment of the artist and for its symbolic elements. Ibsen looks back at his artistic career, admits to compromise, and mourns the fact that he has not engaged with life with the same healthy vigour as Maja and Ulfheim. He opts for the ethereal transfiguration on the mountain top with the statuesque Irene, but, as with Brand and Solness, this leads only to his own destruction.

Where Ignorance Is Bliss. See GUARDSMAN, THE.

Whistle in the Dark, A

A: Tom Murphy Pf: 1961, London Pb: 1970; rev. 1989 G: Trag. in 3 acts S: Living room of house in Coventry, *c.*1960 C: 7m, 1f

Michael Carney is a 35-year-old Irishman working in Coventry and living with his English wife Betty and his three wild younger brothers Harry, Iggy, and Hugo. Their father ('Dada') and youngest brother Des are coming for a week's holiday. Michael hopes that Des will return to Mayo with his father and not get drawn into his brothers' violent way of life, especially as they are squaring up for a fight with the Mulryans. Dad sneers at Michael: 'Any man can't fight isn't worth his salt.' The following night, word comes that the Mulryans are ready to fight the Carneys, and the brothers leave. Michael admits to Betty that his brothers saved him recently in a racial attack and that he had run away. Betty urges him to join their fight now. Dad spends the night in the pub, but pretends to have been detained by muggers when his sons return victorious, but without Michael. Eventually Michael comes home drunk to find his family celebrating. The despairing Betty asks them all to leave and is hit by Michael for her pains. She packs and leaves, while Dad and the others urge Des to fight Michael. At first Michael hardly defends himself then hits Des with a bottle, killing him.

This powerful early play by arguably Ireland's greatest contemporary dramatist depicted the male violence and mindless arrogance of a group of thugs, dangerously reinforcing English stereotypes about the Irish. However, the Carney brothers are representatives of any deprived class (indeed Pinter, influenced by Murphy's play, portrayed similar family relationships in *The *Homecoming*). Rather than being a social document, *A Whistle in the Dark* has all the force of a tragedy: Michael the protagonist commits fratricide not through wickedness but because of the almost impossible pressure he is subjected to.

White Devil, The (*The White Divel*)

AT: *The Tragedy of Paulo Giordano Ursini, Duke of Brachiano, with the Life and Death of Vittoria Corombona, the Famous Venetian Courtesan* A: John Webster Pf: *c.*1612, London Pb: 1612 G: Trag. in 5 acts; blank verse and prose S: Rome and Padua, 1580–5 C: 25m, 5f, extras

On a visit to the home of Camillo and Vittoria Corombona, the Duke of Brachiano (or Bracciano) falls in love with Vittoria. Vittoria plants the idea in Brachiano's head of murdering her old husband and Brachiano's wife Isabella. Isabella comes to Rome seeking reconciliation with her husband, but is rejected by him. Engaging the help of Vittoria's unscrupulous brother Flamineo, Brachiano carries out the plan to kill Isabella and Camillo. Vittoria is arrested and tried as an accomplice to her husband's murder and is condemned to imprisonment. Isabella's brother, Francisco, Duke of Florence, plots revenge on Brachiano by writing a love letter to Vittoria, making sure that the letter falls into Brachiano's hands. The violently jealous Brachiano helps Vittoria to escape from prison and marries her, leading to his excommunication. Prompted by Francisco and believing he has the blessing of the Pope, Lodovico, who is an admirer of Vittoria, poisons and strangles Brachiano in front of Vittoria. Flamineo, who has already stabbed to death his own brother Francisco, now demands the life of Vittoria. Her screams summon Lodovico, whose followers kill both Flamineo and Vittoria. Brachiano's virtuous son arrives, promising to bring the surviving malefactors to justice.

Based on a true story, Webster's play with its seven deaths onstage confirmed the Jacobean English view of Catholic Italy as a place of intrigue, lechery, and extreme violence. (Significantly, Lodovico and his followers disguise themselves as monks.) Structurally a revenge tragedy, it differs from most in that the revengers are themselves contaminated with evil. While piling up the macabre horrors, Webster explores the fascinating moral ambiguity of Vittoria. It is the energy of the action and the power of its language that lifts the play from sheer melodrama to something greater.

White Guard, The. See DAYS OF THE TURBINS, THE.

Whiteheaded Boy, The

A: Lennox Robinson **Pf**: 1916, Dublin **Pb**: 1920 **G**: Com. in 3 acts **S**: Irish village, *c*.1915 **C**: 6m, 5f

Denis Geoghegan is notionally studying medicine in Dublin, but spends his time having fun. It is therefore no surprise when he learns at home that he has once again failed his examinations. His long-suffering and indulgent parents decide reluctantly that he should go to Canada to seek his fortune there. Denis, unwilling to be cast out from the comfort of life in Ireland, retaliates by breaking off his engagement with Delia Duffy. She responds by serving a writ for breach of promise. Denis is saved by the resourceful Aunt Ellen, who schemes cleverly to save the family embarrassment: she agrees to marry Delia's widower father and makes over her shop to Denis, inviting Delia to manage it. Having being secured a comfortable existence once more, the ambition-less 'whiteheaded boy' Denis can relax back into domestic life with his loving family.

This was Robinson's best and most successful play, the careful crafting of which acted as a model to a whole generation of Abbey playwrights. The title character, reminiscent of Fonvizin's *The *Minor*, was intended by Robinson to reflect the idleness and complacency of many of his fellow Irishmen, allowing their nation to become a European backwater. Only the memorable Aunt Ellen possesses the drive and resourcefulness, Robinson implies, truly to fulfil Ireland's dream of independence.

Who's Afraid of Virginia Woolf

AT: *The Exorcism* **A**: Edward Albee **Pf**: 1962, New York **Pb**: 1962 **G**: Drama in 3 acts **S**: Living room on the campus of a small New England College, *c*.1960 **C**: 2m, 2f

George, a 46-year-old college professor of History, and his buxom 52-year-old wife Martha return home late from a party given by the College President, Martha's father. As usual they are bickering, and George is angry that Martha has invited a young couple back for drinks. They arrive: 28-year-old Nick, a handsome new staff member in Biology and his mousey 26-year-old wife Honey. George and Martha now use their guests as an audience for their verbal duels. George complains about being married to the President's daughter and attacks Nick for being a biologist and 'rearranging ... genes, so that everyone will be like everyone else'. Despite being warned not to mention their son, Martha tells Honey that it is his 21st birthday the next day. Martha changes into a more provocative dress and begins to flirt with Nick. Honey goes off to be sick. Nick confesses to George that he married Honey because of her money and a phantom pregnancy. When Honey and Martha return, Martha and Nick dance sensuously. Martha then reveals that her father had stopped George publishing a novel about a boy who murdered his parents, which George claimed to be a true story. George is so furious at Martha's betrayal that he tries to strangle her, but is pulled off by Nick. George suggests that having played 'Humiliate the Host' they should now play 'Get the Guests'. He proceeds to reveal the story of how Nick and Honey got married. Honey goes off to be sick again, while Martha reproaches George for his cruelty. Martha then begins to seduce Nick, while George feigns indifference by reading a book. Martha and Nick retire to the kitchen, and Honey returns, half aware that Martha and Nick are having sex. When Martha and Nick reappear, it is clear that he has been too drunk to 'perform'. George comes to the front door, like the Mexican Woman in *A *Streetcar Named Desire*, bringing 'flowers for the dead'. Urged by George, Martha begins to tell about their son, how he grew up strong and healthy. George recites the funeral service in Latin, and then announces that their son has just been killed in a car accident. Martha is distraught that George has decided to have him killed. Nick understands that they were unable to conceive children, and leaves with Honey. George and Martha, now exhausted and tender, go to bed.

This was Albee's first full-length play and his greatest success, performed internationally and made into a film with Elizabeth Taylor and Richard Burton. Its dialogue sparkles, and stage time corresponds to real time. On one level it is a Strindbergian analysis of a marriage that depends on its violently hostile games to survive; it also represents the failure of the American dream (George and Martha share the names of Washington and his wife, and George is History, while young Nick is a biologist, one of the 'ants' that will take over the world); the three acts, entitled 'Fun and Games', 'Walpurgisnacht', and 'Exorcism' (the original title of the play), also suggest an exploration of evil that can be exorcized only though the sacrifice of their child.

Who Is Sylvia? See GOAT, THE.

Wide Open Cage, The

A: James K. Baxter **Pf:** 1959, Wellington, New Zealand **Pb:** 1959 **G:** Trag. in 3 acts **S:** Skully's two-room shack, rural New Zealand, 1950s **C:** 3m, 3f

Jack Skully, an old seaman in his fifties living off his pension, has just spent the night with Norah Vane, a Maori prostitute in her twenties. Now with his friend Father Tom O'Shea, he rejects the priest's faith, calling God the prison governor of the cage they live in. He is visited by his solicitous landlady Ma Bailey, then by Ted, a bored and sexually frustrated teenager, and finally by Eila, a pretty 17-year-old, from whom Skully steals a kiss. Father Tom warns Skully about his drunken friend Ben Hogan, recently released from prison. Ted brings news that Skully has had a big win on the horses, and Ted and Eila become mutually attracted. Norah arrives with Hogan, who is so drunk that, after a tussle with Skully, he ends up unconscious on the floor. Skully asks Norah to marry him, but she knows they will end up caged in a boring marriage. They go to bed together. Two evenings later, Skully, Hogan, and Norah are still celebrating the win. Hogan's drunken singing prompts Ma Bailey to give Skully his notice, and he has to calm her. Ted offers Norah £5 for sex, which she angrily rejects. Father Tom hears Norah's confession that she once murdered her baby, and they then leave together. Incited by an old Maori skull, Hogan murders Skully and steals his money. Father Tom administers the last rites.

A poet of some standing, Baxter wrote some of the first major plays of the nascent post-war New Zealand theatre. *The Wide Open Cage* contains fine language and a sympathetic portrayal of a Maori, but its awkward construction, thinly drawn characters, gratuitous introduction of the supernatural, and melodramatic ending mean that outside its national context, it has little to offer.

Widowing of Mrs Holroyd, The

A: D. H. Lawrence **W**: 1911–14 **Pf**: 1920, Altrincham **Pb**: 1914 **G**: Drama in 3 acts **S**: The Holroyds' kitchen, mining village near Nottingham (Eastwood ?), early 20th c. **C**: 4m, 4f, 2 children, 2 extras

Lizzie Holroyd's children tell her that Holroyd is at the local pub dancing with women from Nottingham. She would like to console herself with Blackmore, the colliery electrician, but their mutual affection remains unspoken. Later that evening Holroyd comes home tipsy with two of the women, who are alarmed by a rat running across the kitchen. Holroyd follows them back to the pub. Disgusted with him and her miserable existence, his wife tells him never to come back. That night Blackmore helps the now drunk Holroyd back to his home. Holroyd suspects Blackmore's motives and picks a fight with him. Blackmore knocks him flying on to the stone floor and begs Lizzie to come with him to Spain. Holroyd revives and staggers up to bed. Lizzie agrees to come to Blackmore with her children on the following Saturday. The next evening Blackmore comes in search of Holroyd, who has not returned from the mine. News comes that he has died in a pit fall. His body is brought in, and Mrs Holroyd is consumed with guilt, since she and Blackmore had wished his death. She and Holroyd's mother begin to wash his body.

Influenced by Synge's **Riders to the Sea*, this play is perhaps the best known of Lawrence's plays, which did not enjoy a full professional production until 1968 with a production at the Royal Court in London. By then its depiction of working-class life seemed at last in tune with the 'kitchen-sink' drama of the 1960s.

Widows and Children First! See TORCH SONG TRILOGY.

Wild Duck, The (*Vildanden*)

A: Henrik Ibsen **Pf**: 1885, Bergen **Pb**: 1884 **Tr**: 1890 **G**: Drama in 5 acts; Norwegian prose **S**: Werle's and Ekdal's homes, Norway, 1880s **C**: 12m, 3f, extras

Hjalmar Ekdal has a small photographic studio, bought for him by the rich merchant Werle, whose housekeeper Gina Hjalmar has married. An old friend, Werle's son Gregers, returns home and soon suspects that his father was involved in the crime that ruined Hjalmar's family and that Gina had been his father's mistress. Gregers resolves to tell Hjalmar the truth about his situation, so that Hjalmar, an indolent character who claims to be working on a spurious invention but prefers to hunt rabbits in a little wood he has created in the loft, will no longer live a lie. When Hjalmar hears the truth, however, far from embarking on a new relationship of trust with Gina, he rejects her and his devoted 14-year-old daughter Hedvig, whom he now suspects to be Werle's child. Too lazy to be decisive, Hjalmar does not actually leave home. Gregers urges Hedvig to sacrifice a pet duck to show her love for her father, but instead she shoots herself.

Frequently concerned to attack the 'life-lie' on which so many lives are built, Ibsen here with unflinching honesty, considers what may happen to those not able to confront the truth. Gregers is an unrepentant idealist, and therefore highly dangerous, a less mythical version of Brand. The extraordinary loft with its simulated woodland and wild life, though justified in terms of realist theatre, points forwards to a more symbolic treatment of the stage towards which Ibsen was tending in his later years.

Wild Oats

AT: *The Strolling Gentlemen* **A**: John O'Keeffe **Pf**: 1791, London **Pb**: 1791 **G**: Com. in 5 acts; prose **S**: Hampshire, late 18th c. **C**: 19m, 3f, extras

Sir George Thunder is a retired naval captain, who many years previously entered into a 'sham marriage' with Amelia Banks, in order to seduce her and then abandon her. In fact, unbeknown to him, the marriage was genuine, and Amelia gave birth to a son. By chance Sir George arrives at the country home of his niece Lady Amaranth Thunder. A member of Sir George's party is a strolling player Jack Rover, who falls in love with Amaranth. It turns out that the abandoned wife Amelia lives nearby. There is a tender reconciliation between her and her errant husband Sir George, and it is discovered that Jack Rover is in fact her long-lost son Charles. Jack/Charles, now Sir George's heir, is free to marry the lovely Amaranth.

Like Goldsmith and Sheridan, O'Keeffe was one of the long line of supposedly English playwrights who came from Ireland. Characteristically, as we see in fellow countrymen Wilde and Shaw, there is a great facility for dialogue. Here the lines of the play contain country dialect and Quaker forms of address and are peppered with quotations (mainly by the actor Rover) from plays, especially Shakespeare. This colourful speech, coupled with the intricate, if predictable, comic plot, makes *Wild Oats* a neglected masterpiece, which was successfully revived by the RSC in 1976.

William Tell (*Wilhelm Tell*)

A: Friedrich Schiller **Pf:** 1804, Weimar **Pb:** 1804 **Tr:** 1825 **G:** Drama in 5 acts; German blank verse **S:** Various locations on the Lake of Lucerne, Switzerland, 1307–8 **C:** 41m, 7f, extras

An idyllic picture of Swiss rural life is shattered by the violence of Austrian forces, thwarted by William Tell in their attempt to seize a fleeing Swiss assassin. The tyranny of the Austrians even requires that everyone must bow down before the Governor's hat set on a pole in the local marketplace. Representatives from three cantons swear to join together as a 'free nation of brothers' and to repel the Austrians from their land. Tell refuses to bow before the hat, and is forced by the evil Governor Gessler to shoot an apple from his son's head. Despite succeeding, Tell is arrested by Gessler but manages to get free during a storm. Tell then kills Gessler with his crossbow, and lends the final spark to the uprising. Castles are attacked, and the Austrians driven from the land. The jubilant Swiss fighters gather to honour their hero Tell. The Holy Roman Emperor has been murdered by his nephew, who now comes to seek support from Tell. Tell rejects him, denouncing 'Parricida's' selfish act, and sets him on the path to Rome to seek absolution.

Based on an early 18th-century Swiss chronicle, Schiller wrote *William Tell* at Goethe's prompting. In it he skilfully combines the personal story of the superhero Tell with the wider political struggle for freedom. It is notable that Tell, despite effectively committing murder, remains unsullied by political events by remaining aloof from the popular struggle for liberation ('The strong man is strongest alone'). Those in the mainstream of political events, who kill and burn, cannot achieve such serenity. Popular as a folk play, it has also served as a call for freedom, as in the first production at the Berlin State Theatre in the new Weimar Republic (1919). Rossini's operatic version dates from 1829.

Winners. See LOVERS.

Winslow Boy, The

A: Terence Rattigan **Pf:** 1946, London **Pb:** 1946 **G:** Drama in 4 acts **S:** Living room of the Winslows' home, London, 1912–14 **C:** 7m, 4f

Fourteen-year-old Cadet Ronnie Winslow is expelled from the Royal Naval College for stealing a five-shilling postal order. Convinced of his innocence, his father Arthur Winslow engages an excellent if apparently unlikeable expert lawyer Sir Robert Morton to prove his son's innocence. The case drags on, draining Arthur's health and money and forcing him to take his older son out of Oxford when he can no longer afford the fees. To the dismay of his wife, and despite becoming a laughing stock to many, Arthur persists, pursuing the affair as far as the House of Commons. His daughter Kate, a suffragette and trade unionist, supports her father, even though it leads to her losing her fiancé. Eventually, Morton wins the case and Ronnie's innocence is proved. Kate discovers that the seemingly supercilious Morton had turned down appointment to the office of Lord Chief Justice so that he could be free to see that 'Right be done'.

Based on the actual case of George Archer-Shee's expulsion from the Royal Naval College for petty theft, this was Rattigan's first major success with a serious drama (his comedy *French Without Tears* had broken box-office records in 1936), and it has since become a modern classic. With characteristically skilful craftsmanship, Rattigan portrays a man with an almost Ibsenite obsession, who rejects the easy way out and defies authority in order to prove the innocence of his son. That, by this stage, the family has suffered greatly and his son seems almost indifferent to the outcome, makes the piece more complex than the simple morality play it might otherwise have become.

Winter's Tale, The

A: William Shakespeare **Pf:** 1611, London **Pb:** 1623 **G:** Romance in 5 acts; blank verse and prose **S:** Sicilia and Bohemia, indeterminate period **C:** 16m, 6f, extras

King Leontes of Sicilia begs his old friend Polixenes, King of Bohemia, to prolong his visit, but it is only the entreaties of Leontes's wife Hermione that persuades Polixenes to remain. This induces in Leontes an insane jealousy and he orders the death of Polixenes, who however escapes back to Bohemia. Hermione is cast into prison, where she bears a second child, a daughter, and is reported to have died. Their little son Mamillius dies of grief, and on Leontes's orders, their daughter is abandoned on the 'coast of Bohemia'. She is found by a shepherd, who brings up the child as Perdita. As a young woman Perdita falls in love with Florizel, the son of Polixenes, who disapproves of his son marrying a common shepherdess. So the young couple flee to Sicilia, where the grieving Leontes discovers that Perdita is his lost child. Leontes then visits the 'statue' of his maligned wife, which miraculously comes to life. Polixenes now gives his blessing to his son's marriage, and all ends happily.

Based on a prose romance of 1588 by Robert Greene, *The Winter's Tale* is, after *The *Tempest*, the most successful of Shakespeare's four romances. Unlike his other study of jealousy, **Othello*, this play shows Leontes's violent emotion as utterly unreasonable and unmotivated. Although – like **Pericles* – *The Winter's Tale* involves a great leap of time dividing the action into two halves, this does not jar in performance, and the fact that time heals all and restores a proper perspective is the essential theme of the play. The hope of spring replaces the cold chill of winter.

Wit. See W;T.

Witch of Edmonton, The

A: Thomas Dekker, John Ford, and William Rowley **Pf:** 1621, London **Pb:** 1658 **G:** Trag. in 5 acts; prose and blank verse **S:** Edmonton and environs, Tyburn, London, 1621 **C:** 12m, 6f, extras

Frank Thorney marries his fellow servant Winnifride, unaware that she is already their master's lover. Because his father will disapprove of his marriage, Thorney keeps it secret. Soon, however, his father obliges him to marry Susan, daughter of a rich yeoman. In the vicinity lives Mother Sawyer, who, accused of being a witch, resolves to summon a spirit. A devil duly appears as a black dog, which she sends out on missions of mischief against her neighbours. Unable to continue the pretence of his second marriage, Thorney plans to flee the country with Winnifride. When Susan insists on accompanying him, Mother Sawyer's dog induces him to kill Susan and tie himself to a tree, pretending to have been attacked by robbers. Thorney is haunted by Susan's ghost, and the murder weapon is found in his pocket. Despite a spirited defence, Mother Sawyer is taken to Tyburn to be executed for witchcraft, together with Thorney, who confesses his guilt.

This play is theatre at its most topical, dealing with the execution in 1621 for witchcraft of Elizabeth Sawyer within months of the event. Indeed, this remarkably sympathetic treatment of a woman driven to witchcraft by slander rather than by evil would have been sufficient to sustain the action. However, it is loosely linked to a conventional story of enforced marriage and its unhappy consequences. At a time when more women were being acquitted of witchcraft, Mother Sawyer's defence is very persuasive. She argues that many supposedly reputable self-seeking and vain women sooner deserve to be called witches rather than a 'poor, deformed, and ignorant' creature like herself.

Woe from Wit (*Gore ot uma*)

AT: *Intelligence Comes to Grief; The Misfortune of Being Clever; Wit Works Woe; 'Tis Folly to be Wise; Chatsky; Too Clever by Half; The Misery of Having a Mind* **A:** Aleksandr Griboedov **Pf:** 1825, St Petersburg; complete version 1831, Kiev **Pb:** 1825; complete censored edn. 1833; uncensored edn. 1875 **Tr:** 1902 **G:** Com. in 4 acts; Russian verse **S:** Famusov's home, Moscow, 1824 **C:** 12m, 13f, extras

Aleksandr Chatsky has grown up in the home of a Moscow official Paul Famusov, and is in love with Paul's daughter Sophie, a rather shallow creature. Famusov, a greedy and ambitious bureaucrat, is hoping to find a rich son-in-law. Deciding to seek a wider education than is possible in the midst of Moscow hypocrisy and arrogance, Chatsky travels off for three years. Returning with his head full of new ideas, he is dismayed to discover that his beloved Sophie is infatuated with Molchalin, her father's obnoxious secretary, who while wooing Sophie is, like Famusov himself, trying to have an affair with the maid Liza. Frustrated in love and dismayed at the boorishness of Moscow society, Chatsky denounces both officials and nobility. Supported by Sophie, who wishes to be rid of him, these respond in the only way they know how by declaring Chatsky insane. Disillusioned, Chatsky leaves Moscow, while Molchalin will have some explaining to do with regard to Liza.

Although *The *Government Inspector* is much better known outside Russia, this comedy, from which most Russians can quote one or two lines, is a much fiercer satire of Russian officialdom than Gogol's play. Moreover, Gogol focused on the corruption of small town officials, an unproblematic source of humour for St Petersburg audiences, whereas Griboedov directed his elegant barbs much closer to home. Small wonder then that the premiere of the full text did not take place until two years after Griboedov's death and that it took half a century for an uncensored version of the play to be published.

Woman Alone, A. See FEMALE PARTS.

Woman from Samos, The (*Samia*)

AT: *The Girl from Samos; The Samian Woman* **A:** Menander **Pf:** *c.*315–309 BC, Athens **Tr:** 1929 (more complete text, 1972) **G:** Fragmentary Greek com. in verse **S:** A street in Athens, the present **C:** 5m, 3f, extras

Demeas, a prosperous Athenian, lives with his adopted son Moschion, and with Chrysis, 'the woman from Samos'. Although she is freeborn, Chrysis as a Samian is not allowed according to Athenian law to become Demeas' wife. Moschion has fallen in love with the daughter of their neighbour, who is, however, too poor to provide a dowry for his daughter. Demeas has been away for several months, during which time Chrysis has given birth to their child, which has not survived. The neighbour's daughter has also had a child by Moschion, and, in order to keep this a secret from their parents, gets Chrysis to bring up their baby. On his return, Demeas overhears the old nurse saying that Moschion is the father of the baby Chrysis is rearing. Overcome by jealous rage, he turns Chrysis and the baby out of the house, until Moschion protests his innocence and reveals the truth. On discovering that the baby is his daughter's, the neighbour now flies into a rage, threatening to kill the child. Demeas reveals that Moschion is the father, and reiterates his approval of the marriage of the two young people. Recognizing that he could hardly make a better or more profitable match, the neighbour relents, and the play ends with general forgiveness and wedding festivities.

The Woman from Samos and The **Bad-Tempered Man* are the only almost complete surviving pieces of Menander and the New Comedy. Here both comedy and moral lessons derive from the way in which Demeas and his neighbour in turn fly into unjustified rages, based on misunderstanding the situation. Like the trials of young lovers in the search for happiness, the irascibility of the old was to become a standard feature of classic comedy. However, here it is forgivable that they should both be misled by the evidence, and the potentially tragic consequences of these genuine misunderstandings give Menander's comedy a serious edge.

Woman Killed with Kindness, A (*A Woman Kilde with Kindnesse*)

A: Thomas Heywood Pf: 1603, London Pb: 1607 G: Trag. in 5 acts; blank verse and prose S: A country estate in England, early 17th c. C: 17m, 3f, extras

Master Frankford, who has just married, plays host to two gentlemen Sir Francis and Sir Charles. They quarrel, and come to blows, ending in the arrest of Charles for killing Francis's servants. Frankford's friend Wendoll brings the news and is invited to stay. He falls in love with Mistress Frankford, who finally yields. Sir Francis, still resolved on revenge, relents when he falls in love with Charles's sister Susan. Meanwhile, Frankford has learned of his wife's adultery and catches the two lovers in bed together. Wendoll escapes, and Mistress Frankford pleads for mercy. Frankford agrees to punish her gently by sending her to live alone in a nearby manor. Charles cynically resolves to deliver Susan to Francis. Her reluctance is overcome by Francis's gentle love, and they marry. Mistress Frankford, full of guilt, wastes away and is visited by Frankford just in time for a deathbed reconciliation.

Heywood wrote over 200 plays, of which this is accounted the best of those that survive, a fraction of the total. Continuing the genre of domestic tragedy first significantly established with **Arden of Faversham*, but here without any violence except for the killing of the servants. Heywood presents a carefully structured piece, which reveals that plain country gentlefolk – as opposed to kings and princes – can experience deep-felt emotion. It is true that the ending now strikes us as melodramatic rather than tragic, and the desperate remorse of Mistress Frankford which leads to her death now appears an exaggerated reaction to her husband's supposedly 'kind' treatment. Much of the interest of the play now lies in its details of Elizabethan country life. Jacques Copeau opened his Vieux-Colombier theatre with it in 1913.

Woman of No Importance, A

A: Oscar Wilde Pf: 1893, London Pb: 1894 G: Drama in 4 acts S: English country house and Mrs Arbuthnot's house, 1890s C: 8m, 7f

At his imposing house of Hunstanton Chase the charming bachelor Lord Illingworth is entertaining several guests, among whom are an outspoken young American heiress Hester Worsley and her fiancé Gerald Arbuthnot. Gerald is hoping to become Illingworth's secretary, but his mother attempts to dissuade him. She reveals to Illingworth that Gerald is his son, the product of a liaison which Illingworth broke off, because he considered her 'a woman of no importance'. When Illingworth molests Hester, Gerald is so incensed against him that he is prepared to kill him. This forces Mrs Arbuthnot to reveal the secret of his parentage. Gerald demands that Illingworth marry his mother, but, encouraged by Hester, she refuses, preferring instead to live with the young couple and dismissing Illingworth as 'a man of no importance'.

When attacked by critics for including too little action in **Lady Windermere's Fan*, Wilde responded by gleefully writing this play, in whose first act, 'There is absolutely no action at all.' Equally successful with audiences, Wilde transformed the Victorian interest in the 'fallen woman' into a witty and elegant piece, in which the abused Mrs Arbuthnot triumphs morally over the elegant but empty Lord Illingworth.

Women at the Thesmophoria (*Thesmophoriazusai; Thesmophoriazusae*)

AT: *The Poet and the Women; Women Celebrating/Keeping the Thesmophoria; Ladies' Day* A: Aristophanes Pf: 411 BC, Athens Tr: 1853 G: Greek com. in verse S: A street, and before the temple of Demeter Thesmophorus in Athens, *c.*410 BC C: 7m, 4f, extras, chorus (f)

Euripides tells an elderly relative Mnesilochus that he is worried that the women of Athens will use their private festival, the

Thesmophoria, to plot Euripides' death for revealing their secrets in his plays. He begs the beautiful young poet Agathon to disguise himself as a woman to spy on the worshippers. When Agathon refuses, Mnesilochus offers to go instead, and there is much comic business as he is shaved and suitably dressed. At the festival, Euripides is denounced, but Mnesilochus defends him stoutly. Cleisthenes, an effeminate man trusted by the women, interrupts to warn them that a disguised man is violating the sacred festival. Those present are examined, and Mnesilochus is soon exposed. Learning of the old man's arrest, Euripides arrives, pretending to be Menelaus, come to free his Helen from Egypt (see HELEN). When this fails, he appears as Perseus liberating Andromeda. Still unsuccessful, Euripides undertakes never to malign women again, distracts the barbarian guard with a dancing girl, and escapes with the ill-treated Mnesilochus.

**Lysistrata* was to be Aristophanes' last attempt to persuade the Athenians to give up their suicidal war against Sparta. Just before this, in 411, he turned to a gentle parody of his great contemporary Euripides. Euripides was by then 74, and it is entirely possible that he was in the audience of the Dionysia when it was first performed. Even though some of the allusions are now obscure (especially since Euripides' Andromeda play, performed the previous year, no longer survives), there is still a lot of fun to be gained from the elements of disguise and the outwitting of the stupid guard. It is notable for offering the first cross-dress role in European drama, with the additionally amusing twist that all the 'women' of the play would, as in the Elizabethan theatre, have been performed by men anyway.

Women Beware Women

A: Thomas Middleton Pf: *c.*1625–7, London Pb: 1653 G: Trag. in 5 acts; blank verse and prose S: Florence, Italy, Renaissance period C: 11m, 4f, extras

Leantio, a factor, has married Bianca, a beautiful Venetian lady, against the wishes of her parents. A lady at court Isabella, threatened with marriage to a rich numbskull, at first refuses. But when she and her uncle Hippolito fall in love, she consents to the marriage to provide cover for their incestuous relationship. The Duke of Florence, who lusts after Bianca, succeeds in seducing her. Once allied with the Duke, Bianca becomes vain and arrogant and hardly greets her husband Leantio when he returns home after an absence. The Duke sends for Bianca to attend his banquet, and Leantio realizes that he is being cuckolded. However, Leantio finds some consolation when the Duke promotes him and when Livia, Isabella's aunt, falls in love with him. The Duke informs Livia's brother Hippolito that Livia is consorting with a servant, and Hippolito kills Leantio in a sword fight. The Duke is now free to marry Bianca. At the wedding a masque is performed, during which Isabella, Livia, Hippolito, the Duke, and Bianca all die. The Duke's virtuous brother the Cardinal lives on to reflect on the price that has to be paid for lust.

Unlike the majority of Jacobean tragedies depicting the dire consequences of love and greed, the women in this play are not the passive victims of evil, but active participants in their own downfall. Bianca gives in easily to the attraction of power and ambition offered by the Duke, Isabella marries her comical young bridegroom to further her own incestuous desires, and the widow Livia uses her freedom to win the man she lusts after. It is hardly a flattering portrayal of women, but at least the play treats them as forces to be reckoned with.

Women Celebrating the Thesmophoria. See WOMEN AT THE THESMOPHORIA.

Women in Assembly (*Ekklēsiazousai; Ecclesiazusae*)

AT: *Women Holding an Assembly; Women in Parliament; Women in Power; The Parliament of Women; The Assemblywomen* A: Aristophanes Pf: *c.*392 BC, Athens Tr: 1833 G: Greek com. in verse S: A street in Athens, *c.*390 BC C: 9m, 8f, extras, chorus (f)

The women of Athens, under the leadership of Praxagora, have agreed to take over the Assembly. They disguise themselves as men and arrive at the Assembly at dawn to vote in a number of radical measures: all power in Athens shall be transferred from men to women, and all property shall be held communally. There is also to be complete sexual liberation, with men and women free to have intercourse, and children regarding all men as their fathers. In order to protect the old and ugly, however, these will have priority in choosing their lovers. This last rule persuades Praxagora's ageing husband that there is some merit in the new legislation. While two men debate whether they really need to give up their property, everyone is summoned to a banquet by the 'general' (Praxagora in disguise). A young girl, now free to consummate her love with her boyfriend, has to yield him first to one old woman and then to an even older, uglier one. The play ends with a choral song, as everyone goes off for the communal dinner.

It is tempting to regard *Women in Assembly* as both a proto-communist play and as an early manifesto of feminism. It was however understood by Athenians that each citizen had to be prepared to sacrifice individual wealth for the good of the *polis*, and Plato, who established his Academy at about the time this play was performed, recommended in his *Republic* that the ruling class of his ideal state should not own any private property. Moreover, as with **Lysistrata*, the possibility that women might take control is not so much a political programme as a good joke. Despite these reservations, however, the play now seems remarkably ahead of its time in its portrayal of an ideal state run by women. Given the ineptitude of male-dominated rule, Aristophanes implies, even women would make a better job of governing.

Women Keeping the Thesmophoria. See WOMEN AT THE THESMOPHORIA.

Women of Trachis (*Trachiniae*)

A: Sophocles **Pf:** *c.*425 BC, Athens? **Tr:** 1729 **G:** Greek trag. in verse **S:** Before the house of Heracles at Trachis, in the mythical past **C:** 5m, 2f, extras, chorus (f)

Deianira, wife of Heracles, is anxiously awaiting the return of her husband, who has been away for months, completing the labours that he is obliged to fulfil. She is particularly distressed, because she has received an oracle that Heracles will now either die or that he will at last be able to rest from his labours. She is just sending out her son to look for Heracles, when news arrives that he is alive and well and is following the band of captives, who now arrive in Trachis. One of those captured is a beautiful young princess, and Deianira, anxious that she has lost Heracles' affections, steeps his shirt in what she believes is a love potion. This potion was given to her by the dying Nessus, a centaur whom Heracles had shot with his arrow, and is in fact a deadly poison. Deianira's son returns and reveals that Heracles is dying a terrible death, because of the poisoned shirt she sent him. Overcome by guilt, Deianira takes her own life. Heracles is brought in, is persuaded of Deianira's innocence, and prepares to mount his own funeral pyre.

Sophocles returns here to the terrible recognition that tragedy can be brought about by carelessness rather than wickedness. The paradox is that Deianira's love drives her to bring about the very act that destroys the object of her love; she is innocent, but she also should have known better than to have believed the wounded Nessus, who was hardly likely to wish Heracles well. We also note again the ambiguity of oracles, for here Heracles' death is not an alternative to rest from his labours but the very means by which he will indeed find rest. Despite the interest of the perennial theme of jealousy, the play has inspired only a few adaptations, including a rather uninspired version by Ezra Pound in 1954.

Women of Troy, The. See TROJAN WOMEN.

Wonder! A Woman Keeps a Secret, The

A: Susannah Centlivre **Pf:** 1714, London **Pb:** 1714 **G:** Com. in 5 acts; prose **S:** Lisbon, 1714 **C:** 10m, 4f, extras

The War of Spanish Succession has just ended. Don Lopez, a Grandee of Portugal, has two children. His son Don Felix is in hiding, since he has wounded a rival in a duel. His daughter Isabella is confined to the house awaiting enforced marriage to an elderly but rich suitor.

In desperation Isabella leaps from her window and is carried by a passer-by, Colonel Briton, to the home of Violante, the beloved of Felix. Violante promises to conceal Isabella in her home. Felix visits Violante, but is disturbed to find Colonel Briton at the window, pleading entry to the woman he has fallen in love with. Violante, faithful to her promise, cannot reveal Isabella's whereabouts, and so Felix storms off in a jealous rage. Don Lopez calls in the police to search for Isabella and unwittingly reveals the presence of his son. A bribe is paid to save Felix from arrest. Felix and Violante are reconciled, and after further misunderstandings and narrow escapes, Felix is married to Violante, Colonel Briton to Isabella. Despite everything, Violante has managed to keep her friend's secret, so proving 'That man has no advantage but the name.'

Centlivre was immensely popular throughout the 18th and 19th centuries – second only to Shakespeare. *The Wonder!* was performed at least 250 times by 1800, often with David Garrick in the role of Don Felix, a part he chose again for his farewell performance. Centlivre's achievement was to write tightly constructed pieces with clever sources of misunderstandings, a range of parts of essentially decent characters, and witty, sometimes even bawdy, dialogue. Her portrayal of the resourcefulness and ingenuity of women, reflected in the ironical title, should encourage revivals of her plays in today's theatre.

Words upon the Window-Pane, The

A: W. B. Yeats **Pf**: 1930, Dublin **Pb**: 1934 **G**: Drama in 1 act **S**: Lodging house, Dublin, 1930s **C**: 4m, 3f

The Dublin Spiritualists' Association is about to hold a seance in rooms once visited by Stella, the name Jonathan Swift gave to his beloved Esther Johnson. One of the windows has part of a poem by Stella scratched in the glass. After some debate between the various attendees at the seance, amongst whom are a clergyman, a gambler, and a Cambridge student writing a thesis on Swift, the medium Mrs Henderson begins. A spirit Lulu is driven away by an ugly old man, who turns out to be Swift, to whom Vanessa (Hester Vanhomrigh) makes a declaration of love. Swift refuses to be responsible for a child coming into the world, wishing to leave only his intellect to posterity. Quoting Stella's poem, Swift then tells of his love for her. The Cambridge student John Corbet is suitably impressed by Mrs Henderson's performance, but she denies all knowledge of Swift. Left on her own, Swift speaks through her once more: 'Perish the day on which I was born!'

This is the only play by Yeats with a realistic contemporary setting. Dramatic tension is developed by allowing a comic introduction to precede the disturbingly mysterious seance (Yeats was himself a spiritualist) and its horrible vision of the elderly and insane Swift. Here Yeats also expounds his belief that the great Irish statesmen of the early 18th century represented a golden age of enlightened government, to be destroyed by the advent of democracy.

Workhouse Donkey, The

A: John Arden **Pf**: 1963, Chichester **Pb**: 1964 **G**: Drama in 3 acts; prose, with some verse and songs **S**: West Yorkshire industrial town, early 1960s **C**: 31m, 14f, extras

In a northern town, the Labour Mayor Alderman Boocock and the ex-Mayor Alderman Charlie Butterthwaite ('the workhouse donkey', born in the workhouse and stubborn as a donkey) welcome the new Chief Constable Colonel Feng. While Feng is enjoying dinner with the Conservative Councillors, the Labour Councillors are arrested for drinking after hours. The unscrupulous Doctor Blomax conspires with the disreputable police Superintendent Wiper to induce Butterthwaite to believe that Feng is in the pocket of the Conservatives. Butterthwaite retaliates by visiting the seedy Copacabana Club, owned by the head of the Tories Sir Harold Sweetman, and by making allegations of immorality against it, forcing its closure. In order to pay the gambling debts he owes Blomax, Butterthwaite steals from the Town Hall. With Blomax's help, Butterthwaite makes it look like a burglary, causing the police more embarrassment: 'Corruption they can live with, but incompetence—ho ho!' The police, however, are unconvinced by Butterthwaite's story and suspect him of the theft. The Labour Councillors are so angry that they demand Feng's resignation. When Sweetman reopens the Copacabana Club as a smart art gallery, Butterthwaite organizes local working-class people to storm the gallery. Butterthwaite and his demonstrators are arrested, and Feng, defeated by the anarchy of northern politics, resigns.

Arguably the most Brechtian of British plays with its larger-than-life characters, vibrant theatricality, and easy shift into verse and song, *The Workhouse Donkey* possesses, in Arden's words, 'the old essential attributes of Dionysus: noise, disorder, drunkenness, lasciviousness, nudity, generosity, corruption, fertility, and ease'. There are no rights and wrongs: the workhouse donkey is a scoundrel, everyone is corrupt (even Feng is swayed by his feelings for Blomax's daughter), politics are a mess, and English morality absurd (the Club is closed, 'because of who saw what of what girl below the waist').

World We Live In, The. See INSECT COMEDY, THE.

World Well Lost, The. See ALL FOR LOVE.

Would-Be Gentleman, The (*Le Bourgeois Gentilhomme*)

AT: *The Citizen Turned Gentleman; The Merchant Gentleman; The Prodigious Snob; The Self-Made Gentleman; The Middle-Class Gentleman; The Proper Gent; The Bourgeois Gentleman* **A:** Molière **Pf:** 1670, Château de Chambord **Pb:** 1670 **Tr:** 1672 **G:** Com.-ballet in 5 acts; French alexandrines **S:** M. Jourdain's home, Paris, *c.* 1670 **C:** 10m, 4f, extras

M. Jourdain is a vain middle-class individual, who imagines that he can use his wealth to raise himself to the status of the gentry. He has preposterously uncomfortable and hideous clothes tailored and insists on instruction in music, dance, fencing, and philosophy, without having a real interest in any of them. From the Philosopher, Jourdain is delighted to learn that he has been speaking prose all his life without knowing it. Jourdain hopes to initiate an affair with Countess Dorimène, supposedly assisted by an unscrupulous nobleman Dorante, who borrows money from Jourdain and is intent on winning Dorimène for himself. Jourdain's daughter Lucile is in love with Cléonte, who asks Jourdain for Lucile's hand in marriage. However, Jourdain is determined that Lucile shall marry only a 'gentleman'. While Jourdain entertains his aristocratic guests Dorimène and Dorante, the arrival of the son of the Grand Turk is announced (in fact, Cléonte in disguise). This 'royal visitor' has fallen in love with Lucile and wishes to confer the title of 'Mamamouchi' on Jourdain. In a ballet, Jourdain is duly crowned with a colossal turban, and he willingly gives his daughter to Cléonte. Meanwhile Dorimène, impressed by Dorante's apparent generosity, consents to marry him.

The genre of the comedy-ballet (this was Moliére's tenth and best, with music by Lully) provided spectacle, song, and dance, as well as comedy (what would now be termed a multi-media performance). Molière's laughter at a merchant trying to become a gentleman does not derive from snobbery, for Jourdain's attempts to better himself are not in themselves reprehensible. What is ludicrous is that he imagines he can use his wealth to buy culture, philosophy, and illicit aristocratic sex, while blocking the happiness of the young lovers. Unlike most of Molière's comedies, the play ends before he is forced to recognize the truth.

Would-Be Invalid, The. See HYPOCHONDRIAC, THE.

Woyzeck

A: Georg Büchner **W:** 1836–7 **Pf:** 1913, Munich **Pb:** 1875 **Tr:** 1927 **G:** Fragmentary trag.; German prose **S:** A small town in Germany, early 18th c. **C:** 10m, 3f, extras

Johann Woyzeck is a simple-minded soldier, who earns some extra cash by doing odd jobs, cutting sticks and shaving the Captain, and by acting as a guinea pig for scientific experiments for the obsessive Doctor. He needs the extra money to support his common-law wife Marie and their child. He takes her to the fair, where she meets the glamorous Drum Major, who seduces her. Taunted by the Captain, and haunted by voices in his head, Woyzeck is driven to desperation. When he sees Marie dancing with the Drum Major, he is on the verge of breaking down. After being beaten by the Drum Major, Woyzeck buys a knife, takes Marie into the woods, and stabs her to death. Returning to the tavern, he dances wildly and is questioned about the blood on his hand. He tries to hide the knife in the waters of a pond. A character comments on the quality of the murder.

It is one of the tragedies of world drama that one of the greatest playwrights, acknowledged by writers as diverse as Artaud and Brecht to be the father of modern theatre, died at the age of 23, leaving only **Danton's Death*, a comedy *Leonce and Lena*, and this unfinished masterpiece. *Woyzeck* is remarkable in many respects. Its episodic structure formed a model for the fragmentary, kaleidoscopic depiction of reality beloved of modernist theatre. Its terse, highly charged poetic language showed how effective minimal dialogue can be. Above all, focusing a tragedy on a simple working-class figure opened up the possibility, especially for naturalist drama later in the century, of showing that ordinary people could be something more than comic characters. The play lay for decades as a neglected fragment, and even its title was initially misread as *Wozzeck* (as in Alban Berg's opera of 1925). It is uncertain how Büchner intended to order the scenes and to end the play, whether with Woyzeck's suicide (as in the opera) or with his trial (as in the historical case on which the play is based). What is clear is that Büchner's sympathies are with the simple-minded downtrodden Woyzeck, compared with the complacent, unimaginative, and unnamed figures of authority. Because of its fragmentary nature, *Woyzeck* has attracted many adventurous theatrical treatments, for example, by Robert Wilson (2002).

W;t

AT: *Wit* **A:** Margaret Edson **Pf:** 1995, Costa Mesa, California **Pb:** 1993 **G:** Drama without act or scene divisions **S:** US hospital, 1990s **C:** 4m, 2f, extras

In dialogue scenes, monologues, and flashbacks, we follow the experiences of Vivian Bearing, a 50-year-old professor of 17th-century poetry, from the diagnosis of advanced ovarian cancer to her death about a year later. Professor Kelekian recommends the full force of chemotherapy for eight months, so that Vivian can make a 'significant contribution to research'. As her hair drops out, she becomes nauseous, and her immune system is eradicated, it becomes clear that her 'treatment imperils [her] health'. The endless waiting is almost unbearable: 'If I were writing this scene, it would last a full 15 minutes. I would lie here, and you would sit there.' Her main consolation is the poetry of John Donne, and she recalls in flashback how her tutor Evelyn Ashford pointed out that, contrary to the punctuation in most editions, Donne's famous line contains a comma, not a semicolon: 'And death shall be no more, death, thou shalt die,' i.e. only a breath separates this life from the life beyond. This is not merely 17th-century 'wit' but 'truth'. Suffering the humiliation of pelvic examinations and being prodded by medical students, Vivian confronts the uncaring attitude of Jason Posner, a young researcher, as the cancer takes hold. Now aware that she was herself not kind enough, she finds human warmth in a nurse, and asks not to be resuscitated when her heart stops. The final indignity occurs when her instructions are initially ignored and she is handled like a lump of meat in Jason's panicky attempt to keep his research object alive.

Edson studied Literature before working in the research unit of a cancer hospital, and this Pulitzer Prizewinning play brilliantly combines and confronts these two areas of human enquiry. The illness is the main character of the play, and Vivian, Kelekian, Jason, the nurse, and Evelyn Ashford, all respond to it differently, with the women significantly showing more human warmth, even if, in Vivian's case, somewhat belatedly: 'I have been found out.'

y

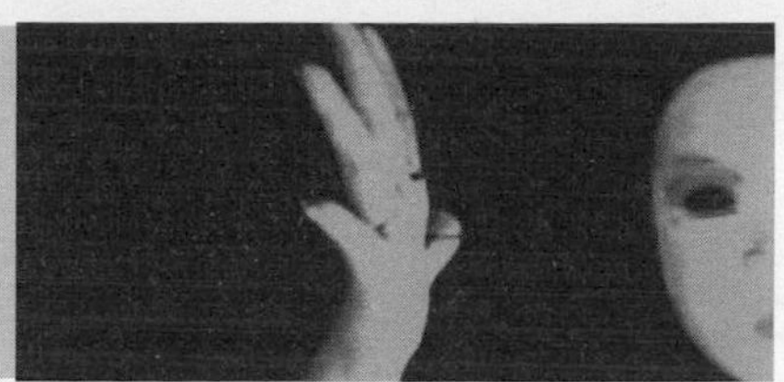

Yerma

A: Federico García Lorca **Pf**: 1934, Madrid **Pb**: 1937 **Tr**: 1947 **G**: Trag. in 3 acts, Spanish prose and verse **S**: Village in Andalusia, Spain, early 20th c. **C**: 6m, 17f, 1 child

Yerma is desperate to have a child, but her husband Juan, though he loves her, will not make her pregnant, preferring instead to work hard on the farm. An old neighbour woman tells Yerma that she will never conceive unless she enjoys sex, and for that she needs the right man. Yerma finds herself strongly attracted to a shepherd, but Juan forces her to remain at home and arranges for his sisters to watch over her. Yerma becomes even more estranged from her husband. Juan buys out the shepherd, who takes his leave from Yerma. Despite her yearnings, Yerma's code of honour will not allow her to take him as a lover. At night, she escapes from the house to visit a sorceress. As she prays in the cemetery for a child, Juan arrives, furious at the public humiliation her absence has caused. She begs him to give her a child, but he rejects her. She participates in a fertility rite in the mountains, but, again because of her honour, refuses the possibility of becoming pregnant by another man. Juan, who has been spying on her, reveals that he has never wanted children. In anger and despair, Yerma strangles him, thereby destroying her hope of ever having a child.

This was the second of García Lorca's 'rural tragedies', here focusing on the plight of one individual, that of Yerma, whose name means barren. Her desperation to be pregnant is intensified by all the images of fertility of the soil which surround her.

York Cycle of Mystery Plays, The (48 parts)

A: Anon ('The York Realist') **Pf**: Late 14th–15th c., York **Pb**: 1915 (part), 1957 (all) **G**: Cycle of 48 mystery plays; Middle English verse **S**: Heaven and earth, from the Fall of Lucifer to the Last Judgement **C**: approx. 60m, 6f, many extras

The cycle stretches from the Creation to the end of time. Based on the evidence of one almost complete extant manuscript, the cycle probably comprised: (1) *The Fall of Lucifer* (the creation of evil); (2) *The Creation* (the beginning of the physical universe); (3) *God Creates Adam and Eve* (the creation of humankind); (4) *Adam and Eve in the Garden of Eden* (the idyll before 'the Fall of Man'); (5) *Man's Disobedience and Fall* (humankind's separation from God); (6) *Adam and Eve Driven from Eden* (their banishment into a world of suffering and death); (7) *Cain and Abel* (the first murder); (8) *Building of the Ark*; (9) *Noah and the Flood* (a pious man is saved from God's anger); (10) *Abraham's Sacrifice* (a model of obedience to God); (11) *The Israelites in Egypt, The Ten Plagues, and the Passage of the Red Sea* (the trials of God's chosen people); (12) *Annunciation and the Visit of Elizabeth to Mary*; (13) *Joseph's Trouble about Mary*; (14) *Journey to Bethlehem: Birth of Jesus*; (15) *The Angels and the Shepherds*; (16) *Coming of the Three Kings to Herod*; (17) *Coming of the Three Kings, the Adoration*; (18) *Flight into Egypt*; (19) *Massacre of the Innocents*; (20) *Christ with the Doctors in the Temple* (the events surrounding the birth and childhood of the Saviour); (21) *Baptism of Jesus*; (22) *Temptation of Jesus*; (23) *The Transfiguration*;

(24) *Woman Taken in Adultery, Raising of Lazarus* (major events in Christ's life, including the miracle of bringing Lazarus back from the dead); (25) *Entry into Jerusalem*; (26) *Conspiracy to Take Jesus*; (27) *The Last Supper*; (28) *The Agony and Betrayal*; (29) *Peter Denies Jesus, Jesus Examined by Caiaphas*; (30) *Dream of Pilate's Wife, Jesus Before Pilate*; (31) *Trial Before Herod*; (32) *Second Accusation before Pilate, Remorse of Judas, Purchase of Field of Blood*; (33) *Second Trial Continued, Judgement on Jesus*; (34) *Christ Led Up to Calvary*; (35) *The Crucifixion of Christ*; (36) *The Mortification of Christ* (events surrounding the trials and death of Christ on the Cross); (37) *Harrowing of Hell* (Christ saves the good from hell and leads them into paradise); (38) *Resurrection, Fright of the Jews*; (39) *Jesus appears to Mary Magdalen after the Resurrection*; (40) *Travellers to Emmaus* (Christ rises from the dead); (41) *Purification of Mary* (Mary presents Christ in the temple – usually placed, as in *The *Chester Cycle*, before Scene 20); (42) *Incredulity of Thomas* ('doubting Thomas' is convinced that Christ lives again); (43) *The Ascension* (Christ is taken up into heaven); (44) *Descent of the Holy Spirit* (the third element of the Holy Trinity descends to help humankind); (45) *The Death of Mary*; (46) *Appearance of Our Lady to Thomas*; (47) *Assumption and Coronation of the Virgin* (Christ's mother dies and rises to heaven to intercede for humankind); (48) *The Judgement Day* (the final reckoning).

The York Cycle is the most extensive and probably best known of the surviving mystery cycles and may claim to be one of the longest running plays in theatre history (from the mid-14th century to 1580, when it was suppressed because of its Catholic content). The long cycle would have been presented over the course of a whole day (Corpus Christi) by amateur performers, members of different city guilds. Each guild played a different scene, often suited to their trade (e.g. shipwrights: *Building of the Ark*; bakers: *The Last Supper*), performing their scene at different points in the city on pageant wagons. The content of the drama is taken from the Bible and from Christian myth, especially the Catholic elevation of the Virgin Mary, together with robust and often comic elements taken from everyday medieval life. It is notable how here, as in all the mystery cycles, the one week of the Passion of Christ (his suffering leading up to and during his crucifixion) is allotted a quarter of the scenes. This concentration on the Crucifixion gave rise to the popular Passion play of central Europe, as in Oberammergau. *The York Cycle* has been successfully revived in York since 1951, in Leeds, and by the National Theatre in a vigorous version by Tony Harrison in the mid-1980s and in 2002.

York Realist, The

A: Peter Gill **Pf:** 2001, Salford **Pb:** 2001
G: Drama in 4 scenes **S:** Living room of farm labourer's cottage outside York, early 1960s
C: 4m, 3f

George, a farm labourer, lives with his elderly Mother in a tied cottage. He is visited by his friend John, who has come to the theatre in York for a week and drives out to see him. Curiously, John seems not to see Mother when she comes downstairs, and soon leaves. We then shift back in time. Mother goes out to chapel with Doreen, a woman who fancies George and got him a part in the mystery plays to be staged in York. John, the assistant director of the plays, calls to ask why George has been missing rehearsals. The two men are mutually attracted, and when they return from wandering over the farm, with John thrilled at the countryside sights and smells, George invites John to share his bed with him. A month later, George's family and Doreen return from seeing the mystery plays, excited by the experience, especially seeing George playing a convincingly sadistic crucifier. George asks John to stay on in Yorkshire, and John suggests that George come with him to London to embark on an acting career, but George will not leave his Mother. A few months later, Mother has died. Suddenly, we revert to the first scene: John pleads again with George to join him in London, but George refuses. John leaves, and Doreen comes to fuss over George.

In a series of scenes, with convincingly naturalistic dialogue yet with surprising time-shifts and the surreal if brief appearance of Mother after death, Gill sensitively portrays the growth and decline of a homosexual relationship, which founders on the 'Yorkshire realism' of George – an irony since George and John met working on the **York Cycle of Mystery Plays*, ascribed to 'the York realist'.

Yorkshire Tragedy, A

A: Anon. (Middleton or Shakespeare?)
Pf: *c.*1605–7, London **Pb:** 1608 **G:** Trag. in 10 scenes; blank verse and prose **S:** Calverley Hall, Yorkshire, and its environs, 1605 **C:** 14m, 2f, extras

The first scene appears to be a flashback: the prospective Husband is a dissolute gambler, who, unknown to his loyal and virtuous bride, has lost all his money, even using his younger brother as a guarantor. Moreover, he has already been secretly married to another woman. Once married to his present long-suffering Wife, he abuses her and demands that she should sell her dowry to finance his loose living. He ignores the pleas of his friends and is wounded in a duel, when one defends the Wife's honour. The Wife finds him a place at court, but the Husband haughtily rejects the offer. Only when his brother is arrested for debt, does the Husband pause to consider his slide into evil. But awareness of his guilt just makes him mad: he murders two of his sons, wounds his Wife, and sets out to kill his third son. He is captured, expresses his remorse to his Wife, and is led off to prison.

Based on a true story of a Walter Calverley, who murdered his own children and was executed in York in 1605, this play was originally attributed to Shakespeare, but is more likely to have been written by Middleton. The unsubtle characterization of the brutal Husband and of the unbelievably patient Wife, together with the less than sparkling dialogue make it unlikely that Shakespeare had anything to do with it other than possibly to cut it to its present fragmentary length. Performed by a strong actor, the central figure can develop a fierce passion, which can be effective in the theatre. The piece stands in a line from **Arden of Faversham* to the domestic tragedies of the 17th century and eventually to Victorian melodramas.

Young Hopeful, The. See MINOR, THE.

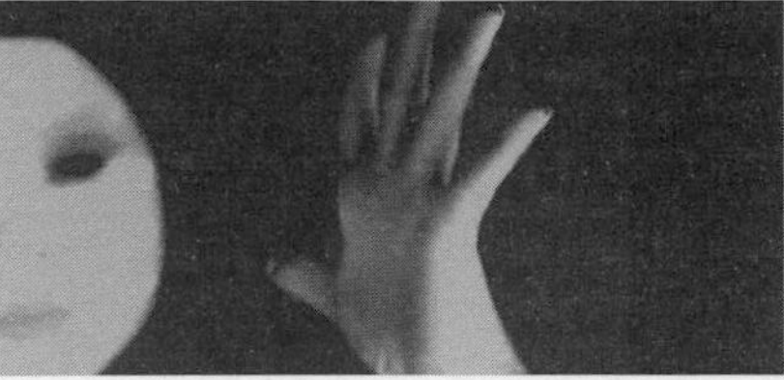

Z

Zaïre

AT: *Zara* A: Voltaire Pf: 1732, Paris Pb: 1733 Tr: 1736 G: Trag. in 5 acts; French alexandrines S: Jerusalem, 13th c. C: 7 m, 2 f, extras

Zaïre is a slave-girl in the palace of the enlightened sultan Orosmane, who has fallen in love with her and, contrary to Muslim custom, wishes to make her his sole wife. Orosmane has captured many French knights engaged in the seventh crusade of Louis IX. Nérestan, a young knight, comes with ransom money to free some of the captives, and Zaïre pleads that their old commander Lusignan should be included. It transpires that Lusignan is the father of Nérestan and of his long-lost daughter Zaïre. Lusignan, who is dying, begs Zaïre to reconvert to Christianity. So, while affirming her love for Orosmane, she asks him to defer their wedding without being able to explain why. Orosmane suspects that she has fallen in love with Nérestan, and, when he finds a letter inviting Zaïre to a secret meeting (so that she may be baptized), he intercepts her and murders her in a fit of jealous rage. When he learns the truth, he releases all the French prisoners, hands over Zaïre's body to Nérestan, and stabs himself.

Possessing neither the quality of language nor the psychological insights of Racine, Voltaire's plays are now seldom performed. But *Zaïre*, which has obvious parallels with **Othello* (although the handkerchief is replaced by a satin cushion), has a number of points of interest. In his attempt to revitalize neo-classical tragedy in France, Voltaire, no doubt influenced by his love of English drama, provided a much greater sense of history than the mythical settings of his predecessors. As a man of the Enlightenment he also cast the Muslim Orosmane in a very favourable light.

zerbrochene Krug, Der. See BROKEN JUG, THE.

Ze života hmyzů. See INSECT COMEDY, THE.

Zoo Story, The

A: Edward Albee Pf: 1959, Berlin; 1960, New York Pb: 1960 G: Drama in 1 act S: Central Park, New York, *c.*1958 C: 2m

Peter, a publisher in his early forties, is sitting on a park bench reading a book as he does every Sunday afternoon. Jerry, a scruffy individual in his late thirties, enters and strikes up a conversation with Peter, announcing that he has come from the zoo and that Peter will 'see it on TV tonight'. He probes Peter's life and establishes that Peter has a settled bourgeois existence, married with two daughters, owner of parakeets and cats. By contrast, Jerry has no family and lives in a tiny room in a brownstone rooming house. His 'fat, ugly, mean, stupid' landlady lusts after him, and her dog always tries to bite him. So Jerry insists on telling Peter at length 'The Story of Jerry and the Dog'. After failing to win over the dog with kindness, he tries to poison the dog. The hideous creature recovers, but no longer attacks Jerry. Feeling somehow threatened by Jerry's crazy story, Peter now does not want to hear the 'zoo story'. Jerry starts to shove Peter off his bench, telling him to sit elsewhere. When Peter indignantly refuses, Jerry begins to fight with him. Jerry throws Peter a knife, and while Peter holds it defensively, Jerry rushes on to its blade and kills himself. As he dies, he finishes the zoo story: that at the zoo he

decided to walk until he found someone like Peter. He urges Peter to go home to his parakeets and dies, uttering:
'Oh ... my ... God.'

Albee's first play launched his reputation as a significant new playwright. Although often described as absurdist, the action is entirely plausible as a piece of realistic theatre. There are wider issues though: Peter is the quintessential settled middle-aged American, who is jolted out of his uneventful and complacent life by the maverick Jerry. Beyond this, it is possible to see Jerry (=Jesus?) as spirituality being betrayed and martyred by Peter's lack of caring.

Index of Characters

Notes: One to four main characters are normally given for each play, plus occasionally a significant minor character.

Initial 'The', 'A', and 'An' of play titles are omitted. If no play title is given, it indicates that the name of the character is the title of the play or the main element in it. An asterisk in the play title indicates that the play has an entry in this Guide; play titles which are not asterisked, or where the playwright's name is followed by date of performance or publication (whichever is earlier), do not have entries in this volume but are listed for comparison. Plays are listed chronologically within each entry and in their common English form.

Characters are listed under the name which is used in the play text: thus Tom Allworth appears under 'Allworth', while Cyrano de Bergerac appears under 'Cyrano'. In the commonly sexist practice of the theatre, most male names in classical plays are surnames, while most female names are first names.

In foreign-language plays the spelling of the original name is kept, unless it is well known in English in another form (e.g. Maria Stuart becomes Mary Stuart).

Index of Characters

Adela: García Lorca, **House of Bernarda Alba*
Adele Eloise Parker: Elder, **Ceremonies in Dark Old Men*
Adelheid von Walldorf: Goethe, **Götz von Berlichingen*
Adelma: Gozzi, **Turandot*
Adhémar de Gratignan: Sardou, **Let's Get a Divorce!*
Admetus: Euripides, **Alcestis*. *See also* ALCESTIS
Adriana: Shakespeare, **Comedy of Errors*
Adrian West: Minghella, **Made in Bangkok*
Advocate, The (The Lawyer): Strindberg, **Dream Play*
Aegisthus: Aeschylus, **Oresteia*; Sophocles, **Electra;* Alfieri, *Orestes* (1776); Hofmannsthal, *Electra* (1903); Giraudoux, *Electra* (1937); Sartre, **Flies*; G. Hauptmann, *Iphigeneia in Aulis* (1943), *Electra* (1947)
Aeschinus: Terence, **Brothers*
Aeschylus: Aristophanes, **Frogs*
Agamemnon: Aeschylus, **Oresteia*; Euripides, Sophocles, **Ajax*; Euripides, **Hecuba, *Iphigenia at Aulis*; Seneca, *Agamemnon, Trojan Women* (1st c. AD); Shakespeare, **Troilus and Cressida*; Racine, *Iphigeneia at Aulis* (1674); Alfieri (1783); Claudel (1896); G. Hauptmann, *Iphigeneia in Aulis* (1943), *Agamemnon's Death* (1947); Jeffers, *Tower beyond Tragedy* (1950); Hensen (1953); Obey (1955); Berkoff (1971)
Agatha: Eliot, **Family Reunion*
Agatha Posket: Pinero, **Magistrate*
Agave: Euripides, **Bacchae*. *See also* DIONYSUS (BACCHUS)
Agitators: Brecht, **Measures Taken*
Agnes: (from Norway) Ibsen, **Brand*; (Indra's daughter) *see* INDRA'S DAUGHTER; (American housewife) Albee, **Delicate Balance*
Agnès: Molière, **School for Wives*
Agrippina: Racine, **Britannicus*
Aguecheek, Sir Andrew: Shakespeare, **Twelfth Night*
Aiko: Kishida, **Two Daughters of Mr Sawa*
Aimwell: Farquhar, **Beaux' Stratagem*
Ajax: Sophocles, **Ajax;* Shakespeare, **Troilus and Cressida;* Wyspiański (1913); Giraudoux, *Trojan War Will Not Take Place* (1935); Fassbinder (1968); Bond, *Woman* (1978)
Aksyusha (Axinya): Ostrovsky, **Forest*
Akulina: L. Tolstoy, **Power of Darkness*
Alan: Crowley, **Boys in the Band*
Alan Jeffcote: Houghton, **Hindle Wakes*
Alan Strang: Shaffer, **Equus*
Albie Sachs: Edgar, **Jail Diary of Albie Sachs*
Alboury: Koltès, **Struggle of the Dogs and the Black*
Alcandre: P. Corneille, **Theatrical Illusion*
Alceste: Molière, **Misanthrope*
Alcestis: Euripides, **Alcestis;* Hardy (1624); Quinault (1674); La Grange-Chancel (1703); Alfieri (1831); Hofmannsthal (1909); Kesten, *Admetus* (1928); H. von Heiseler (1929); Hensen (1953); Wilder (1955); Usigli (1963); T. Hughes (1999)
Alcibiades: Shakespeare, **Timon of Athens*; Quinault (1658); Otway (1675); Cumberland (1771); Kaiser (1920)
Alcmena: Euripides, *Children of Heracles* (*c.* 430 BC); Plautus, **Amphitryon*; Michael, *Excursion with Ladies* (1944). *See also* AMPHITRYON
Alec Kooning: Eveling, **Dear Janet Rosenberg, Dear Mr Kooning*
Aleksei: Vishnevsky, **Optimistic Tragedy*
Aleksei Turbin: Bulgakov, **Days of the Turbins*
Alençon Duc d' (Monsieur): Chapman, **Bussy D'Ambois, Revenge of Bussy D'Ambois* (1610)
Alexandra del Lago: *see* PRINCESS KOSMONOPOLIS
Alfie: Naughton, **Alfie*
Alfred von Zentner, Baron: Horváth, **Tales from the Vienna Woods*
Algernon Moncrieff: Wilde, **Importance of Being Earnest*; Stoppard, **Travesties*
Alice: (Swedish) Strindberg, **Dance of Death;* (Englishman) Brenton, **Magnificence;* (Englishwoman) Churchill, **Blue Heart*
Alice, Miss: Albee, **Tiny Alice*
Alice Ayres (Jane Jones): Marber, **Closer*
Alice (Childie) McNaught: Marcus, **Killing of Sister George*
Alice Maitland: H. G. Barker, **Voysey Inheritance*
Alice Noakes: Churchill, **Vinegar Tom*
Alice Park: Hare, **Plenty*

Levene, Shelly: Mamet, **Glengarry Glen Ross*
Levering, Miss Vida: Robins, **Votes for Women*
Leviné, Eugen: Dorst, **Toller*
Levison, Sir Francis: Mrs Wood, **East Lynne*
Levy, Abraham (Abie): A. Nichols, **Abie's Irish Rose*
Lidio: Bibbiena, **Follies of Calandro*
Li'l Bit: Vogel, **How I Learned to Drive*
Liliom: Molnár, **Liliom*
Lilith: G. B. Shaw, **Back to Methuselah (Part 5)*
Lincoln, Abraham: Drinkwater (1918); A. Thomas *Copperhead* (1918); Sherwood (1938); Conkle, *Prologue to Glory* (1938); Parks, **America Play*
Linda Loman: Miller, **Death of a Salesman*
Lindsay, Sir David: Arden, **Armstrong's Last Goodnight*
Link, Mr: Mercer, **After Haggerty*
Lionel Carteret: H. A. Jones, **Mrs Dane's Defence*
Littlewit, John: Jonson, **Bartholomew Fair*
Liu, Party Secretary: Hare, **Fanshen*
Livia: Middleton, **Women Beware Women*
Lizzie Boles, *née* Flynn: Woods, **At the Black Pig's Dyke*
Lizzie Borden: Pollock, **Blood Relations*
Lloyd Dallas: Frayn, **Noises Off*
Loam, Earl of: Barrie, **Admirable Crichton*
Lola Delaney: Inge, **Come Back, Little Sheba*
Long: O'Neill, **Hairy Ape*
Loomis, Herald: A. Wilson, **Joe Turner's Come and Gone*
Lopakhin, Yermolay Alexeevich: Chekhov, **Cherry Orchard*
Loreleen Marthraun: O'Casey, **Cock-a-Doodle Dandy*
Lorenzo: Kyd, **Spanish Tragedy*
Lorenzo de' Medici (Lorenzaccio): Musset, **Lorenzaccio*; Mann, *Fiorenza* (1904); Benelli, *Mask of Brutus* (1908)
Loth, Alfred: G. Hauptmann, **Before Dawn*
Lotus Blossom: Patrick, **Teahouse of the August Moon*
Louis VI: Anouilh, **Becket*
Louis XIII: Whiting, **Devils*
Louis XIV: Bulgakov, **Cabal of Hypocrites*
Louisa Rusport: Cumberland, **West Indian*
Louis Ironson: Kushner, **Angels in America*
Løvborg, Ejlert: Ibsen, **Hedda Gabler*
Loveit: Etherege, **Man of Mode*
Loveless: Vanbrugh, **Relapse*
Lovell, Lord: Massinger, **New Way to Pay Old Debts*
Lovewell: Garrick and Colman the Elder, **Clandestine Marriage*
Lucia d'Alavadorez, Donna: B. Thomas, **Charley's Aunt*
Lucienne Homénides de Histangua: Feydeau, **Flea in Her Ear*
Lucifer: *see* DEVIL, THE
Lucile: Anouilh, **Rehearsal*
Lucille Cadeau: Ayckbourn, **House and Garden*
Lucky: Beckett, **Waiting for Godot*; Bulatović, *Godot Has Come* (1966)
Lucky Eric: Godber, **Bouncers*
Lucre, Pecunius: Middleton, **Trick to Catch the Old One*
Lucrece: Medwall, **Fulgens and Lucrece*
Lucretia Cenci: Shelley, **Cenci*
Lucy: Parks, **America Play*
Lucy Brown: Brecht, **Threepenny Opera*
Lucy Lockit: Gay, **Beggar's Opera*
Luigi: Fo, **Can't Pay? Won't Pay!*
Luise Maske: Sternheim, **Underpants*
Luka: Gorky, **Lower Depths*
Luke Marks: Hazlewood, **Lady Audley's Secret*
Lula: Baraka, **Dutchman*
Lulu: (German seductress) Wedekind, **Lulu Plays*; Barnes (1970); Nowra (1981); (English actress) Ravenhill, **Shopping and Fucking*
Lumpkin, Tony: Goldsmith, **She Stoops to Conquer*; O'Keeffe (1778)
Lumumba, Patrice: Kennedy, **Funnyhouse of a Negro*; Césaire, *Season in the Congo* (1966); O'Brien, *Murderous Angels* (1968)
Lussurioso: Middleton, **Revenger's Tragedy*
Luther, Martin: G. Moore and Lopez (1879); Strindberg, *Nightingale in Wittenberg* (1904); Sorge, *Christ's Victory* (1922); Johst, *Prophets* (1923); Osborne, **Luther*; Forte (1971)
Luther Gascoigne: Lawrence, **Daughter-in-Law*
Luton, Edward: Maugham, **Circle*

Index of Playwrights

Page numbers in bold type indicate entries on plays by the playwright. Other numbers indicate shorter references.

Index of playwrights

Index of playwrights